FINANCIAL MANGEMENT WITH NEW APPROACH

SUVENDU NARAYAN ROY

Financial Analyst and Consultant,
Former Director/Head of Academics in B-Schools
Faculty Member of Financial Management

Himalaya Publishing House

MUMBAI • NEW DELHI • NAGPUR • BENGALURU • HYDERABAD • CHENNAI • PUNE
LUCKNOW • AHMEDABAD • ERNAKULAM • BHUBANESWAR • INDORE • KOLKATA • GUWAHATI

First Edition : 2013

Published by : Mrs. Meena Pandey for **Himalaya Publishing House Pvt. Ltd.,**
"Ramdoot", Dr. Bhalerao Marg, Girgaon, **Mumbai - 400 004.**
Phone: 022-23860170/23863863, Fax: 022-23877178
E-mail: himpub@vsnl.com; Website: www.himpub.com

Branch Offices :

New Delhi : "Pooja Apartments", 4-B, Murari Lal Street, Ansari Road, Darya Ganj, New Delhi - 110 002. Phone: 011-23270392, 23278631; Fax: 011-23256286

Nagpur : Kundanlal Chandak Industrial Estate, Ghat Road, Nagpur - 440 018. Phone: 0712-2738731, 3296733; Telefax: 0712-2721216

Bengaluru : No. 16/1 (Old 12/1), 1st Floor, Next to Hotel Highlands, Madhava Nagar, Race Course Road, Bengaluru - 560 001. Phone: 080-22286611, 22385461, 4113 8821, 22281541

Hyderabad : No. 3-4-184, Lingampally, Besides Raghavendra Swamy Matham, Kachiguda, Hyderabad - 500 027. Phone: 040-27560041, 27550139

Chennai : 8/2 Madley 2nd street, T. Nagar, Chennai - 600 017. Mobile: 09320490962

Pune : First Floor, "Laksha" Apartment, No. 527, Mehunpura, Shaniwarpeth (Near Prabhat Theatre), Pune - 411 030. Phone: 020-24496323/24496333; Mobile: 09370579333

Lucknow : House No 731, Shekhupura Colony, Near B.D. Convent School, Aliganj, Lucknow - 226 022. Mobile: 09307501549

Ahmedabad : 114, "SHAIL", 1st Floor, Opp. Madhu Sudan House, C.G. Road, Navrang Pura, Ahmedabad - 380 009. Phone: 079-26560126; Mobile: 09377088847

Ernakulam : 39/104 A, Lakshmi Apartment, Karikkamuri Cross Rd., Ernakulam, Cochin - 622011, Kerala. Phone: 0484-2378012, 2378016; Mobile: 09387122121

Bhubaneswar : 5 Station Square, Bhubaneswar - 751 001 (Odisha). Phone: 0674-2532129, Mobile: 09338746007

Indore : Kesardeep Avenue Extension, 73, Narayan Bagh, Flat No. 302, IIIrd Floor, Near Humpty Dumpty School, Indore - 452 007 (M.P.). Mobile: 09303399304

Kolkata : 108/4, Beliaghata Main Road, Near ID Hospital, Opp. SBI Bank, Kolkata - 700 010, Phone: 033-32449649, Mobile: 7439040301

Guwahati : House No. 15, Behind Pragjyotish College, Near Sharma Printing Press, P.O. Bharalumukh, Guwahati - 781009, (Assam). Mobile: 09883055590, 08486355289, 7439040301

DTP by : Elite-Art, New Delhi

Printed at : M/S Sri Sai Art Printer Hyderabad. On behalf of HPH

PREFACE

I have immense pleasure in publishing this book for the Finance students which is a simple and lucid presentation, explanation and analysis of financial planning, policies and functions. The structure of the content of my book is as follows:

Part I : General Chapters (Chapters 1 to 15) – with solved exercises and problems

Part II : Financial Analysis (Chapters 16 to 21) – with solved exercises and problems

Part III : Introduction of Special Addition: Some Emerging Areas of Finance (Chapters 22 to 35)

Part IV : Exercises on Emerging Concepts (Chapters A to D)

Part V : Case Studies

Part VI : Appendix A to F – with analysis, models and guidelines

This book has been designed to equip the students pursuing study in Financial Management paper, with corporate exposure and need-based practical knowledge. That is why we have kept special issues entitled 'Part III: Some Emerging Areas of Finance', 'Part IV: Exercises on Emerging Concepts (Chapters A to D)', along with Case Studies, analysis (both Financial and Technical) and examples. This will help not only the students of this area but also the newly-joined corporate people who are working in the related areas.

This book will enable the students of M.Com, CFA., ICAI, ICWAI and last but not the least, the MBA even BBA students of different B-Schools and Universities across our country and of many more. The theories and concepts have been simplified and lot of illustrations have been backed up which will be absolutely need-based and also student-worthy.

In this book, besides presenting the general financial management in details we have also focused on how financial managers are using derivative products such as options, futures, swaps and forwards to eliminate financial risk. Besides showing financial analysis by using management accounting and statistical techniques, discussions also have taken place in the area of technical analysis along with economic analysis of Derivative market so that we can offer the updated knowledge for that area which is either continuing or upcoming and perhaps the most important for the students to work in there in near future.

Unlimited is my own indebtedness to my respected parents, beloved wife and rest of the family for getting continuous inspiration to accept this challenge. Unlimited is my gratitude to Himalaya Publishing House Pvt. Ltd. who have given me the approval to write this book under their banner. I also express my sincere gratitude to my colleagues, students who have continuously inspired me to prepare this book.

Extreme care has been taken while writing and editing this book. Still then, if there is any mistake or error, I will be grateful to those readers, who shall draw attention of those mistakes to us. We also earnestly solicit suggestions and constructive criticisms from academic colleagues, students and other persons for improving the quality of this book in the next edition.

—Author

CONTENTS

1 Introduction of Financial Management

1.1 DEFINITION: TRADITIONAL APPROACH, MODERN APPROACH, DIFFERENCE

Financial management is concerned with the managerial decisions regarding investment, acquisition of asset, procurement and use of funds in meeting financial needs, overall objectives of the concerned organization.

Traditionally, until about the middle of 20th century, it was generally considered a branch of knowledge with focus on the procurement and administering of funds. This function was necessary for the events of expansion, promotion, formation, merger, acquisition, restructuring, legal and institutional framework. The traditional approach focused financial management from the investor's point of view., *i.e.*, arranging the funds from the right sources at the right time and administering the funds to meet the financial needs of the organisation and fulfill the obligations of investors. The term 'Corporate Finance' was used in place of present term 'Financial Management'.

The modern approach transformed the field of study from traditional narrow approach to the most analytical nature at the beginning of 1950s. In traditional approach there was no concern regarding allocation of funds. The modern approach focused financial Management as an integral part of general management which emphasized managerial decisions and efforts concerned with procurement of capital funds at least cost and its effective utilization and allocation of funds with view to maximize shareholder's wealth. The ultimate focus is now "*Employment of fund at least cost in the form of long-term and short-term assets in profitable projects to generate profit as much as possible and concerning decision regarding distribution of profit as dividend (Dividend Decision) to maximize wealth*".

Therefore, we may define financial management as the managerial activity concerning with the planning and controlling of the economic resources, namely capital funds.

5 E's are involved in Financial Management namely:

- Emphasizing financial needs.
- Employment of fund.
- Effective utilization and allocation of fund.
- Ensuring firm's liquidity.
- Ensuring wealth maximization.

1.2 IMPORTANCE OF FINANCIAL MANAGEMENT, CONCEPT OF FINANCE

By the term 'Finance', we generally refer 'Business Finance' which is the 'Master Key' providing access to sources required for running the business activities as per the Financial need of the concerned business. It concerns with the procurement of funds and its conservation in meeting needs. Efficiency management of business enterprises is closely linked with the efficient management of finance. Without efficient utilization of finance it is not possible for any organization to utilize its potential for growth and expansion.

Sound Financial Management is essential in all types of organization where funds are involved because it essentially optimizes the output from given input of funds. Reduction of capital employed *vis-a-vis* improvement of return on investment is possible if sound financial management techniques are used.

Financial Management is very much important in the following three aspects:

Carrying Successful Business Operation

Sound financial planning is essential at each stage of business to provide adequate capital to meet the requirements of fixed and working capital. Without adequate and planned capital, no business enterprise can carry its operations successfully.

Minimizing Risk and Maximizing Return

Financial Management seeks courses of action that can take the challenge for facing the necessary risk and avoid unnecessary risk while maximizing returns. To ensure maximum returns, inflow and outflow of funds should be monitored to assure that they are safeguarded and properly utilized. The Financial Management can design such a financial reporting system so that progress is accurately reported to management at a regular interval and any deviations from plans are clearly identified.

Helping in Financial Decision-Making

Financial Management provides scientific analysis of financial facts and figures so that proper financial decisions can be taken. There are likely to include strategic investment decisions such as investing in new facilities on the acquisition of another company, strategic financing decisions, the decision to raise additional long-term loan etc.

The actions taken by the Financial Management of a business enterprise influence the size, profitability, growth, risk and survival of the firm. Hence those will affect the overall value of the firm.

1.3 SCOPE AND FUNCTIONS OF FINANCIAL MANAGEMENT

Scope

Financial Management is concerned with making financial policies which are devised to fit production, marketing and HR decisions. For example, recruitment, training and promotion of employees is a responsibility of HR department but it requires payment of salaries, other benefits and thus, involves finance. The Finance Department will procure the funds and allocate those accordingly. Similarly sales promotion, advertisement, brand development require fund which is also procured by the Finance Department Therefore, Financial Management has scopes to implement the financial decisions on the other departments. The scopes of Financial Management lie in the following functional areas of an organization:

1. Forecasting cash inflows, outflow and future profits.
2. Procuring Funds.
3. Managing Funds (both long-term and short-term).
4. Pricing.
5. Cost Control.
6. Measuring Cost of Control.
7. Fixed Asset Management.
8. Working Capital Management.
9. Distribution of Profit among Shareholders.
10. Mergers and Acquisitions.
11. Corporate Taxation.
12. Determining Optimum Capital Structure.
13. Ratio analysis, Fund Flow Analysis, CVP Analysis.
14. Project Planning, Evaluation and its Control.
15. Maintaining healthy solvency and liquidity position.
16. Risk Management.
17. Forex Management.
18. Treasury Operations.
19. Budgeting and Budgetary Control.

20. Financial Structuring.
21. Maintaining Share Prices etc.

The common thread running through all the decisions taken by the various managers is money and there is hardly any manager working in any organization to whom money does not matter.

The Finance Manager should be involved in all financial matters of the organization since all activities have financial implications. The R&D Manager has to justify the money spent on research by coming up with new products and processes which would help to reduce costs and increase revenue. The Materials Manager should be aware that inventory of different items in stores is nothing but money in the shape of inventory.

Functions

The functions of Financial Management can be broadly clarified into two parts as follows:

Part I: Routine Finance Functions like custody of cash and bank accounts, borrowing, payment, collection of receivablee etc. have to be done at regular intervals which are clerical in nature and are incidental to the effective handling of the managerial finance functions.

Part II: There are decision-making oriented financial functions which require managerial ability to carry them out. There are four important managerial finance functions:

(a) Investment Decisions: This is concerned with the allocation of capital funds and committing funds to long-term assets which would yield benefits in future. Because of uncertain future, it is very difficult task to measure the profitability of new investments and investment proposals are to be evaluated in terms of both expected return and risk. Hence investment decisions are based on risk and uncertainty. Investment decision also involves the question of recommitting funds when an existing asset becomes obsolete and less productive.

Two critical issues to be considered in these decisions are:

1. Evaluation of expected profitability of the new investments.
2. Rate of retune required on the project.

The rate of return required by the investor is normally known by hurdle rate or cut-off rate or opportunity cost of capital. The whole exercise is called 'Capital Budgeting'.

(b) Financing Decision: This decision involves in determining where, when and how to acquire fund to meet the investment needs and besides that, determining the best financing mix on capital structure of the firm. The financing mix refers to the combination of debt and equity. The ideal combination ensures the maximum market value of shares and also procurement of fund at least cost. The use of debt capital may increase the return of equity but always increases risk. The finance manager has to ensure maximum market value per share with minimum risk and hence he has to strike a proper balance between risk and return. An optimal capital structures is one which also gives least cost structure, ensures the ability of the firm to manage risk.

(c) Dividend Decision: The most important matters of dividend decision are:

Whether the firm should distribute all profits, or retain them, or distribute a portion and retain the balance, how much cash dividend should be paid etc. The finance manager has to determine the dividend policy in terms of wealth maximization and hence objective to determine the optimum dividend-payout ratio which may be 0% or 100% or may be between 0% to 100%. The optimum payout ratio reflects the optimum dividend policy which maximizes the market value of shares. The finance manager should also consider the stability in dividend rate and bonus dividend.

(d) Liquidity Decision: To achieve the healthy liquidity position the finance manager should also manage current assets because investment of funds in current assets reduces the profitability of the firm. On the other hand, the finance manager should also look after the current financial needs to maintain optimum productions. He must see that proper balance is maintained between the profitability and liquidity. He should estimate firms need for current assets and make sure that funds would be made available when needed.

1.4 GOALS/OBJECTIVES OF FINANCIAL MANAGEMENT, PROFIT MAXIMIZATION -*Vs*- WEALTH MAXIMIZATION

The results of good performance are reflected in the profits the firm earns. Hence the finance manager should make an effort to maximize profit as much as possible. Moreover a Financial Management in a corporate has to ensure good share price where form the owners or shareholders would realize much more than what they had invested. This increase in shareholder's wealth as much as possible should be another objective which leads to maximization of the value of the firm and is reflected in Earnings Per Share (EPS) and the market price of its shares.

Profit Maximization

It simply means maximizing the rupee income of the firm through either maximizing output for a given amount of inputs or minimizing the use of inputs and also cost for producing a given output. The whole process requires efficient and effective utilization of resources. It is argued that under conditions of competitive markets where prices reflect true values, profits maximization objective leads to an efficient allocation of resources and hence ensures maximum operational efficiency. Under profit maximization principle price system is the key factor if the firms can produce desired goods and services for the society. Goods and services in great demand reflect higher prices which results higher profit. The interaction between demand of consumers and supply of producers along with competition firm determines the price and affects the allocation of resources. Profit maximization objective provides as a yard - stick to judge the economic performance, leads to efficient and optimum allocation of resources and ensure maximum welfare in the form of maximum dividend, higher wages, timely payments etc.

But Profit Maximization objective suffers from so many limitations. In the face of imperfect modern markets, it can not be the sole objective. The modern business environment reflects corporate or joint stock company which is financed by shareholders, lenders and others. The other stakeholders of the company are suppliers, customers, employees, society, tax authorities etc. In the changed organization and business structure the sole ownership-manager concept had been replaced by stakeholders-professional management concept and profit maximization objective, being not relevant in all cases, not realistic in all kinds of business environments, has to be reconciled with different mismatching objectives of all the stakeholders connected with the business. The other limitations of Profit Maximization are as follows:

1. The term 'profit' is ambiguous. It is not clear whether it refers short-term on long-term profit, profit before or after tax, total profit or profit per unit or profit per capital employed or profit /share, total operating profit or profit available for shareholders. Therefore profit maximization objective is vague.
2. It ignores 'time value of money',, *i.e.*, timing of future profits from investment. It should have taken consideration of present value of expected future profits.
3. It ignores risks and uncertainties existing in business environment which reduces profit.
4. A project may give a higher amount of profits from investment in compare to other profitable projects, but if profit from that project is expected to flow say, 3 years later, second best proposal may be preferred where estimated profit is slightly lower but flow of returns is more quickly. But the profit maximization objective does not recognize this fact.
5. It is argued that profit maximization behaviour may tend to produce wasteful goods and services from the society's point of view.
6. It is also argued that profit maximization objective encourages concentration of money, wealth and monopoly power and hence it leads to inequality of income and wealth.

Value Maximization

Value Maximization is the extension of profit maximization. Professor Ezra Solomon suggested the adoption of wealth the maximization objective which removes all the shortcomings of profit maximization objective which is also called value maximization.

Value is reflected by present and prospective future earnings per share, the timing and risk of the earnings, the dividend policy of the firm and many other factors influencing the market price per share. Value maximization means maximizing the net present value of a course of action. Net Present Value (NPV) is the difference between present value of expected future cash inflows and the capital outlay.

In the context of value or wealth maximization the finance manager has to take the three important decisions namely – Investment Decision, Financing Decision and Dividend Decision. Wealth maximization criterion always considers the time value of money and risk involved in earning expected future profits. When the profit is maximized with minimum risk and dividend policy is sound, market value of the share will be maximized. It indicates how well the performance of the financial management is on behalf of the shareholders. The course of action with expected positive NPV should be desirable and preferred to other courses of action to maximize the value of the firm. Wealth-maximization principle also takes care of employees, management, lenders, customers etc. and ultimately of the society.

1.5 EXTERNAL FINANCIAL ENVIRONMENT

A finance manager has to work under that external environment where there are some important aspects:

Form of Business Organization

(i) Sole proprietorship, *i.e.*, organization owned by a single person named proprietor.

(ii) Partnership, *i.e.*, organization owned by two or more than two persons.

(iii) Company which is registered under the Companies Act, 1956 as per Sec. 3(1)(i) of the Act under any of the following two forms.

- Private Limited Company, *i.e.*, a company, by its articles, restricts the right to transfer its shares and to issue the shares to the public.
- Public Limited Company, *i.e.*, a company which issues shares and debentures to the public.

Financial System

A financial system is a composition of the following sub-systems and facilitates public savings to go into the hands of seekers of funds mainly business firms and government through financial intermediaries and markets.

1. Financial Institutions
2. Financial Markets
3. Regulations and Laws
4. Practices and Procedures
5. Fund Manager, Analysts
6. Financial Transactions
7. Claims and Liabilities

Regulatory Framework

1. RBI norms
2. Industrial Policy Statements
3. FEMA Act *w.e.f.* June 1, 2000
4. Companies Act, 1956
5. SEBI

6. Regulation of Foreign Investment etc.
7. IDRA, 1951

Corporate investment and financing decisions are limited by the above mentioned regulatory frame works.

Others

1. Monetary and Credit Policy
2. Fiscal and Tax Policy etc.

1.6 INTERFACE WITH OTHER FUNCTIONAL AREAS (FINANCIAL MANAGEMENT AND OTHER DISCIPLINES – INTER-RELATIONSHIP)

HR–Finance Interface

An organization has to pay competitive and attractive salary package to their potential employees for retaining them.Though it is costly, but it improves organizational capital and productivity. The better the quality human resource, the higher the value of human capital and consequently the higher the productivity.

It HR Departments' objective is to enhance the productivity, the Finance Department should allow that competitive salary packages.

Production and Operations-finance Interface

Decisions on facilities layout, plant and process layout, technological upgradation for modernization, inventory control, make or buy etc. are all the decisions of production and operations management decisions. But the concerned manager has to evaluate the financial implications before arriving at those decisions and the sufficient finance needs to be provided by the Finance Department.

Marketing – Finance Interface

Many marketing decisions like new product development, selection of channels of distribution, advertisement policy, competitive remuneration packages of the employees of marketing department, pricing extension of credit to the customers for increasing the sales revenues, allowing discount and rebate to the customers, sales promotional campaigns etc. have financial implications. The concerned Marketing Manager should have a clear understanding of the impact of those decisions on profits of the company. Implementation of all decisions required budget which, in turn, requires the clearance from Finance Department because funds are locked in and those have opportunity cost of capital.

Today, quantitative techniques of analysis are used in the process of financial decision making. Finance Managers often determine the feasibility of certain project proposals and financing decisions and hence they are to make interface with financial accounting to know the firm's cash flow position. Moreover they must be concerned with two areas of Economics namely micro-economics and macro-economics.

1.7 ORGANIZATION OF FINANCE FUNCTION

Board of Directors

↓

Chief Finance Officer (CFO)

↓

TREASURER	CONTROLLER
1. Managing working capital	Accounting
2. Obtaining finance	Auditing
3. Investments in real assets	Budgeting
4. Credit and collection	Finance planning
5. Investor relations	Profit planning
6. Payment of cash	Taxation
	Invesment decisions etc.

The most important function of the treasurer is to manage the funds while the main function of the controller is to manage and control the assets. CFO (may be VP – Finance or other) reports to Board of Directors. Under that level, the Finance Manager and executives perform the treasurer and controller functions.

1.8 AGENCY PROBLEM

Agency problem

An agency problem occurs when the interests of stockholders, the board of directors and/or the management of the company are not perfectly aligned or when these entities conflict. In publicly-held companies, there are a variety of individuals with an interest in the performance of the company. The managers and executives who run the company on a day-to-day basis, the shareholders who own stock, and the board of directors who oversee the company's business development all may have different aims or ideas of how the business can be run. Since each of these entities has a vested interest in the corporation, an agency problem occurs when there is conflict among them.

Conflict arises when people (the agents) entrusted to look after the interest of their (the principals) use the authority or power (given to them, directly or indirectly, by the principals) for their own benefit instead. It is a pervasive problem and exists in practically every organization whether a business, church, club, or government. Organizations try to solve it by instituting measures such as tough screening processes, incentives for good behaviour and punishments for bad behaviour, watchdog bodies, and so on but no organization can remedy it 100 per cent because the costs of doing so sooner or later outweigh the worth of the results. It is also called principal-agent problem or principal-agency problem .

A situation in which agents of an organization (*e.g.* the management) use their authority for their own benefit rather than that of the principals (*e.g.* the shareholders). The agency problem also refers to simple disagreement between agents and principals. For example, a publicly-traded company's board of directors may disagree with shareholders on how to best invest the company's assets. It especially applies when the board wishes to invest in securities that would favor board members' outside interests.

Agency Problem is not new in the Indian context, though it is less talked of here than the other more developed markets. In the past, companies like Reliance Power and Vedanta Resources have witnessed this while issuing their IPO and restructuring respectively. The latest glaring example of this anomaly is the Ramalinga Raju and Satyam Computer Services' board-approval to buy majority stake in Maytas Infra Ltd. and Maytas Properties. It is no coincidence that Maytas is Satyam spelt backwards. Infact, Raju's family members are the promoters and board-members in both Maytas Infra and Maytas Properties.

At the background of the problem is the Indian infrastructure sector that has seen a massive erosion of wealth and reputation in the last few months. Unitech, at less than 8% of its January' 08 valuation, is a live example of the crunch this industry faces today.The story of the other companies in this sector is more or less the same. The haunting prospect of a possible liquidity crunch is forcing infrastructure firms to look for ways and means to finance their business commitment and projects.

SUMMARY

Financial management is concerned with the managerial decisions regarding investment, acquisition of asset, procurement and use of funds in meeting financial needs, overall objectives of the concerned organization The traditional approach focused Financial Management from the investor's point of view., *i.e.*, arranging the funds from the right sources at the right time and administering the funds to meet the financial needs of the organisatiion and fulfill the obligations of investors.The modern approach focused Financial Management as an integral part of general management which emphasized managerial decisions and efforts concerned with procurement of capital funds at least cost and its effective utilization and allocation of funds with view to maximize shareholder's wealth.

The functions of financial management can be broadly clarified into two parts as follows:

Part I: Routine finance functions like custody of cash and bank accounts, borrowing, payment, collection of receivable etc. have to be done at regular intervals which are clerical in nature and are incidental to the effective handling of the managerial finance functions.

Part II: There are decision-making oriented financial functions which require managerial ability to carry them out. There are four important managerial finance functions:

Investment Decision
Financing Decisions
Dividend Decisions
Liquidity Decisions

The results of good performance are reflected in the profits the firm earns. Hence the finance manager should make an effort to maximize profit as much as possible. Moreover a financial management in a corporate has to ensure good share price where form the owners or shareholders would realize much more than what they had invested. This increase in shareholder's wealth as much as possible should be another objective which leads to maximization of the value of the firm and is reflected in Earnings per share (EPS) and the market price of its shares.

An agency problem occurs when the interests of stockholders, the board of directors and/or the management of the company are not perfectly aligned or when these entities conflict. In publicly-held companies, there are a variety of individuals with an interest in the performance of the company. The managers and executives who run the company on a day-to-day basis, the shareholders who own stock, and the board of directors who oversee the company's business development all may have different aims or ideas of how the business can be run. Since each of these entities has a vested interest in the corporation, an agency problem occurs when there is conflict among them.

EXERCISE

Short Questions

1. Define Finance?
2. What is Financial Management?
3. Write at least two limitations of profit maximization objective.
4. What is Company?
5. What are the forms of business organization?

Moderate and Broad Questions

1. What are the natures and scope of financial management?
2. What are the functions of financial management? Explain all of them.
3. 'Wealth Management objective is the more superior one in compare to profit maximization objective'. Critically examine the statement.
4. Explain the goals of financial management.
5. Examine the relationship of financial management with other functional areas of a firm.
6. Briefly explain how does a firm arrive at an optimal capital structure?
7. Differentiate the functions of a Treasurer and a controller of Finance.
8. Explain the financial environment under which a Finance Manger has to operate.

❑❑❑

2 Time Value of Money

2.1 CONCEPT, DEFINITIONS, REASONS OF TIME VALUE

'The value of money received today is more than its value received at a later time'

A rupee today has more value than a rupee power after a year. Therefore, rational investors would prefer current receipts to future receipts. There lies the importance of the concept 'Time Value of Money' which is the value of a unit of money changing at different time intervals.

Time Value of Money is also called as 'time preference for money' because due to risks and uncertainty in future as individuals have subjective preference for present or current receipts for current consumptions. Here we assume that value of money remains same irrespective of different time intervals.

For example:

It someone receives ₹ 15 lakhs today, will its value be same after two years.

Answer is No because ₹ 15 lakhs received today has higher purchasing power than ₹ 15 lakhs received after two years.

Now the question is how do we build the time value of money into the future cash inflows of a project?

Here lies the concept of future value. We might invest ₹ 15 lakhs if we are confirmed that we will be paid more than ₹ 15 lakhs after two years and the difference is interest.

Why money should has Time Value? (*i.e.* different values over a period of time)

1. Money can be invested to earn real time. For example, if cost of production (including cost of raw materials consumption, direct labours, direct expenses and cost of different overhead expenditures) is 10 lakhs and value of finished goods is worth ₹ 11 lakhs, we can say that the investment of ₹ 10 lakhs, has earned a rate of return of 10% after selling the finished goods.
2. Amount of ₹ 10 lakhs receiving today has more value than amount of ₹ 10 lakhs received after six months or two years in an inflationary period because ₹ 10 lakhs received today has a higher purchasing power.
3. Rational investors prefer current consumptions and receipts to future consumptions and receipts since there are risks and uncertainty in future.

Determinants of rate of interest causing Time Value

1. Risk free rate of return
2. Expected inflation rate
3. Risk premium

The above three determinants collectively determine the nominal rate of interest which is also called opportunity cost of capital.

2.2 METHODS OF CALCULATION OF TIME VALUE OF MONEY COMPOUNDING AND DISCOUNTING FUTURE VALUE AND PRESENT VALUE

(A) Compound Techniques:

The future values of all cash inflows of the end of the time horizon at a particular compound interest rate are found under this technique, *i.e.*, compounding is the technique of applying the concept of compound interest to find out the future values of all cash inflows.

Future Value: Compound Value:

The amount of money which an investor expects to receive after a certain period of time which will contain both investment or principal and return on investment in the form of compound interest is called Future Value or Compound Value.

For example, Future Value of ₹ 1000 at the end of three years @ 8% p.a. is as follows:

Amount at the end of the year 1 = 1000 (1+.08) = 1080

Amount at the end of the year 2 = 1080 (1+.08) = 1166.4

Amount at the end of the year 3 = 1166.4 (1+.08) = 1259.712

Alternatively: $1000\ (1+.08)^3 = 100 \times 1.259712$

$= 1259.712$

So ₹ 1259.71 is the F.V. at the end of 3 years.

A1 : Future Value of a single flow/lump-sum

Calculation of Future Value of a single flow or one time lump-sum investment is as follows:

$FV_n = PV\ (1+k)^n$

Where, FV_n = Future Value of the initial flow in n years hence

PV = Initial cash flow

= Present amount of investment at k rate of compound interest

k = Annual rate of compound interest [No. of compounding p.a. = 1]

n = Life of investment

$(1+k)^n$ = F.V. interest factor (FVIF) of a lump-sum of ₹ 1 and it always has a value greater than 1 for positive k, indicating that FVIF increases.

Illustration 1

It Mr. A has ₹ 10,000 to be invested, how much does it grow in four years, if the fixed deposit scheme of a commercial bank offers the following interest rates :

Period of deposit	*Rate per annum*
46 days to 179 days	7.5%
180 days to 364 days	8%
365 days to and above	8.5%

Solution

$FV_n = PV\ (1+k)^n$

$= 10{,}000\ (1+.085)^4$

= ₹ 13,858.00

Note: Computation by this formula can also be solved by using interest rates as per 'Future Value Interest Factor' table or FVIF table, if we are to calculate F.V. at a full value rate of compound interest say 8% or 9% or 12%.

Say: If the question is – What is the Future Value of ₹ 500 to be invested @ 10% p.a. at the end of four years, we can calculate this by using FVIF table as follows:

$FVn = PV(1+k)^n$

Where, PV = ₹ 500

$(1+k)^n$ = Future Value Interest Factor of a lump sum of ₹ 1 at the end of 4 years at 10% p.a.

= 1.464 (as per FVIF table)

FV_n = 500 × 1.464

= ₹ 732

Alternatively,

$FV_n = PV\ (1+k)^n$

$= 500(1+10)^4$

= 500 × 1.464

= ₹ 732.00

If No. of compounding is more than 1 per year (Multi compounding Period), how to Calculate Future Value:

Interest can be compounded more than once in a year. For example, if someone has deposited ₹ 5000.00 in a commercial bank which offers 10% interest p.a. compounded half – yearly, it means that interest is paid after every 6 months and calculated as follow :

		₹
	PV(Present value)	5,000.00
Add:	Compound Interest @ 10% p.a.	
	For first 6 months	
	[5,000 × 10/100 × 6/12] =	250
	F.V. after first 6 months.	5,250.00
Add:	Compound interest @ 10% p.a.	
	For 2nd 6 months	
	[5250 × 10/100 × 6/12] =	262.50
	F.V. after 1 year	5512.50

But the problem is if we are asked to calculate F.V. at the end of minimum 3 to 4 years or above, the above process of calculation is time consuming. Therefore, we apply the following generalized formula to calculate F.V. where no. of compounding is more than one time.

$$FV_n = PV(1+k/m)^{m \times n}$$

Where, m = no. of times compounding per years.

It compounding is done semi-annually

Or half-yearly,

$$FV_n = PV(1+k/2)^{2 \times n} \qquad [i.e.\ m=2]$$

It compounding is done quarterly

$$FV_n = PV(1+k/4)^{4 \times n} \qquad [i.e.\ m=4]$$

It compounding is done monthly

$$FV_n = PV(1+k/12)^{12 \times n} \qquad [i.e.\ m=12]$$

Illustration 2

What will be the compound or future value of ₹ 1,30,000 after 4 years if 8% p.a. interest is compounded

At (i) half yearly
(ii) quarterly.

Solution

If interest is compounded half yearly

$$FV = PV(1+k/2)^{2 \times n}$$
$$=130000\ (1+.08/2)^{2 \times 4}$$
$$=130000\ (1+.04)^{8}$$
$$=130000 \times 1.36857$$
$$= ₹\ 177914$$

If interest is compounded quarterly

$$FV = PV(1+k/4)^{4 \times n}$$
$$= 130000(1+.08/4)^{4 \times 4}$$
$$=130000(1+.02)^{16}$$
$$= 130000 \times 1.37278$$
$$= ₹\ 178461$$

Effective *-vs-* nominal rate of interest

The rate of compound interest given to us is the nominal rate of interest p.a. (for instance, from illustration 2, nominal rate of interest p.a. is 8%). If number of compounding is more than 1 per year, say semi-annually or quarterly or monthly, the rate of compound interest p.a. under annual compounding that produces the same effect as that produced by the nominal rate of interest (8%) under semi-annual or half-yearly or monthly.

The relation between effective and nominal rate of interest is as follows:

$$r = (1+k/m)^{m} - 1$$

Where, r = Effective rate of interest p.a. under annual compounding

k = Nominal rate of interest under multi compounding period

m = No. of times compounding per year.

Illustration 3

Calculate the effective rate of interest if the nominal rate of interest is 8% and interest is compounded

(i) Half yearly
(ii) Quarterly

Solution

(i) $r = (1+k/m)^m - 1$

$= (1+0.08/2)^2 - 1$

$= (1+.04)^2 - 1$

$= 1.0816 - 1$

$= 0.0816$

$= 8.16\%$ p.a.

∴ 8% interest, compounded half yearly

= 8.16% p.a. interest, compounded annually

(ii) $r = (1+k/m)^m - 1$

$= (1+0.08/4)^4 - 1$

$= (1+0.02)^4 - 1$

$= 1.0824 - 1$

$= 0.0824$

$= 8.24\%$ p.a.

∴ 8% interest, compounded quarterly

= 8.24% p.a. interest, compounded annually.

Comment: More will be the No. of compounding; more will be the effective rate of interest.

Doubling Period

How long amount of investment will take to be doubled for a given rate of interest?

Rule of 72: 72/Interest rate = doubling period

For example, if the given rate of interest is 9%, the doubling period

= 72/9 = 8 years

Rule of 69: The more accurate way to calculate doubling period is 'rule of 69' which is as follows:

0.35 + 69/interest rate

For example, if the given rate of interest is 9%, the doubling period

= 0.35 + 69/9

= 0.35 + 7.67

= 8.02 years

A2 : Future Value of series of cash flows or multiple flows

Calculation of future value of uneven cash flows.

Illustration 4

It Mr. X interest ₹ 5000, ₹ 10000, ₹ 15000, ₹ 17000 and ₹ 20000 at the end of each year for 5 years, how much will these flows accumulate to at the end of year 5 at a rate of interest of 6% p.a.

Solution

Table : Future Value

End of years	Amount Invested [PV] ₹	No. of years compounded (n)	FVIF $=(1+k)^n$	FV ₹
1	5000	4	1.2625	6312
2	10000	3	1.1910	11910
3	15000	2	1.1236	16854
4	17000	1	1.0600	18020
5	20000	0	1.0000	20000
Amount (FV) at the end of 5 years				**73096**

F.V. = ₹ 73096

$k = 6\% = 0.06$

$(1+.06)^4 = 1.2625$

$(1+.06)^3 = 1.1910$

$(1+.06)^2 = 1.1236$

$(1+.06)^1 = 1.0600$

$(1+.06)^0 = 1.0000$

Illustration 5

If Mr. Y invest ₹ 1000 at the beginning of 1st year, ₹ 2000 at the end of the 2nd year, ₹ 3000 at the end of the 3rd year, what will be the amount of money he will have at the end of 4 years, if invest being 10% compound half-yearly?

Solution

Table : Future Value

End of Years/Beginning of Years	Amount Invested ₹	No. of Years compounded(n)	FVIF $= \left(1+\frac{k}{m}\right)^{m\times n}$	F.V. ₹
1	1000	4	$\left(1+\frac{.10}{2}\right)^{2\times 4}$ =1.4774	1477
2	2000	2	$\left(1+\frac{.10}{2}\right)^{2\times 2}$ =1.2155	2431
3	3000	1	$\left(1+\frac{.10}{2}\right)^{2\times 1}$ =1.1025	3307
		Amount at the end of 4 years		**7215**
		Future Value = ₹ 7215		

A3 : Future Value of an Annuity

Periodic inflows or outflows of equal on even amounts are called annuity. For example, if someone has subscribed to the pension plan of LIC to pay ₹ 50000 annually for 15 years this stream of fixed outflow in called "Annuity".

Calculation of Future Value of an Annuity can be done in a tabular form or by applying the following formula:

$$FVA_n = A\left[\frac{(1+k)^n - 1}{k}\right]$$

$$= A \times FVIFA$$

Where,

FVA_n = Future Value of an Annuity at the end of n years

k = Rate of interest

A = Amount of annuity to be deposited or invested at the end of every year for a years.

FVIFA = Future Value Interest factor for Annuity representing the accumulation of ₹ 1 invested at the end of every year for n years at k rate of interest.

$$= \frac{(1+k)^n - 1}{k}$$

Illustration 6

Mr. Deposits ₹ 1000 at the end of every year for 5 years into his account, interest being 5% compounded annually what will be the accumulated amount at the end of 5 years.

Solution

$$FVA_n = A \times FVIFA$$

Table : FVIFA (Taking 3 decimals)

End of Years	No of years compounded	FVIF = $(1+k)^n$
1	4	$(1+.05)^4 = 1.216$
2	3	$(1+.05)^3 = 1.158$
3	2	$(1+.05)^2 = 1.102$
4	1	$(1+.05)^1 = 1.05$
5	0	$(1+.05)^0 = 1$
	FVIFA	5.526

$$\begin{aligned} \mathbf{FVA_n} &= A \times FVIFA \\ &= 1000 \times 5.526 \\ &= ₹\ 5526 \end{aligned}$$

Alternatively, using FVIFA Table,

$$\begin{aligned} \mathbf{FVA_n} &= A \times FVIFA\ (5\%, 5) \\ &= 1000 \times 5.526 = ₹\ 5526 \end{aligned}$$

Alternatively,

$$\begin{aligned} \mathbf{FVA_n} &= \frac{A\left[(1+k)^n - 1\right]}{k} \\ &= 1000\ [(1+.05)^5 - 1/.05] \\ &= 1000\ [1.2763 - 1/.05] \\ &= 1000 \times .2763/.05 \\ &= 1000 \times 5.526 \\ &= ₹\ 5526 \end{aligned}$$

Illustration 7

Under the recurring deposit scheme of a bank, a fixed sum is deposited every month. The rate of interest is 8% p.a. and is compounded at quarterly intervals. What will be the maturity value of a monthly installment of ₹ 100 after 8 months?

Solution

Effective rate of interest p.a.

$$\begin{aligned} &= \left(1 + \frac{0.08}{4}\right)^4 - 1 \\ &= (1+.02)^4 - 1 \\ &= 1.0824 - 1 \end{aligned}$$

$= .0824$
$= r$

Effective rate of interest p.m. = $k = \dfrac{.0824}{12} = 0.00686$

$$FVA_n = A\left[\frac{(1+k)^n - 1}{k}\right]$$

$$= 100 \times \left[\frac{(1+.00686)^8 - 1}{.00686}\right]$$

$$= 100 \times \frac{1.05621 - 1}{.00686}$$

$$= 100 \times \frac{.05621}{.00686}$$

$$= 100 \times 8.1938$$

$$= ₹\ 819.38$$

Note: (a) It the payments are made at the beginning of every year, then

$FVA_n = A\ (1+k)\ FVIFA_{k,\,n}$
$= \text{annuity due}$

(b) $$A = FVA_n \left[\frac{k}{(1+k)^n - 1}\right]$$

$= FVA_n$ X Sinking Fund Factor

Sinking Fund Factor is the reciprocal of FVIFA.

(B) Discounting Techniques:

Discounting is the process of determining present value of a future lump-sum payment or a series of future even or uneven payments. It is exactly opposite of that of compounding technique.

Present Value (PV)

The present value of a future payment or a series of future payments is the amount of the current or present worth that is equivalent to the investor. The basis of present value is that opportunity cost exists for money lying idle that means interest can be earned on that money. This opportunity cost is called 'discounting rate'or 'interest rate' or 'cost of fund'.

B1: Present Value of a single flow or future lump-sum payment

$$FV_n = PV(1+k)^n$$

Or $$PV = \frac{FV_n}{(1+k)^n}$$

where, present value interest factor (PVIF) = $\frac{1}{(1+k)^n}$

Ilustration 8

What will be the issue price of the cash certificates issued by the Post Office having a value of ₹ 9000 after 2 years, given an interest rate of 8% p.a. ?

Also calculate the issue price it rate of interest is compounded quarterly.

Solution

$$\text{Issue price, } PV = \frac{FV_n}{(1+k)^n}$$

$$= \frac{9000}{(1+.08)^2}$$

$$= \frac{9000}{1.1664}$$

$$= ₹\ 7716$$

If interest rate is compounded quarterly then,

$$FV_n = PV\left(1+\frac{k}{m}\right)^{m\times n}$$

$$= PV\left(1+\frac{k}{4}\right)^{4\times n}$$

$$= PV\left(1+\frac{k}{4}\right)^{4\times 2}$$

$$= PV\left(1+\frac{.08}{4}\right)^{8}$$

$$= PV(1+.02)^8$$

$$\text{Or, } PV = \frac{FV_n}{(1+.02)^8}$$

$$= \frac{9000}{1.1716}$$

$$= ₹\ 7681$$

B2 Present Value of a series of cash flows/uneven multiple flows.

Illustration 9

Given the cost of fund is 10%, a project involves an initial investment of 80 lakhs and future cash inflow, will be received over next 3 years.

Year	*Cash inflow (Profits after tax)*
1	30 lakhs
2	35 lakhs
3	40 lakhs

What will be the present value of the future cash inflows?

Solution

Year	**Cash flow (₹ in lakh)**	**PVIF at 10%**	**Present Value (₹ in lakh)**
1	2	3	4 = (2 × 3)
1	30	$\frac{1}{1+.10} = 0.909$	27.27
2	35	$\frac{0.909}{1+.10} = 0.826$	28.91
3	40	$\frac{0.826}{1+.10} = 0.751$	30.04
Present Value			₹ 86.22 lakhs

B3 Present Value of an Annuity (even inflows)

$$PVA_n = A \times \frac{(1+k)^n - 1}{k(1+k)^n}$$

$$= A \times PVIFA$$

Where, $$PVIFA = \frac{(1+k)^n - 1}{k(1+k)^n}$$

Representing the present value of a regular annuity of ₹ 1 for the given value of k and n. Calculation of PVA_n can also be done through tabular method.

Illustration 10

If Mr. X expects ₹ 1000 to be received annually for 3 years, calculate the present value of future even inflows if discounting factor is 10%.

Solution

Table : PVIFA

Year	PVIF at 10%
1	$\frac{1}{1+.10} = 0.909$
2	$\frac{0.909}{1+.10} = 0.826$
3	$\frac{0.826}{1+.10} = 0.751$
PVIFA	**= 2.486**

$$PVA_n = A \times PVIFA$$
$$= 1000 \times 2.486$$
$$= ₹\ 2486$$

Alternatively: By using PVIFA table

$$PVA_n = A \times PVIFA$$
$$= 1000 \times 2.486$$
$$= ₹\ 2486$$

Alternatively:

$$PVA_n = A \times \frac{(1+k)^n - 1}{k(1+k)^n}$$

$$= 1000 \times \frac{(1+.10)^3 - 1}{.10(1+.10)^3}$$

$$= 1000 \times \frac{1.331 - 1}{.10 \times 1.331}$$

$$= 1000 \times \frac{0.331}{0.1331}$$

$$= 1000 \times 2.486$$

$$= ₹\ 2486$$

Present Value of a perpetual Annuity

An annuity for an infinite time period is perpetuity. A person may get continuous and fixed return yeai after year. The present value of perpetuity is calculated as $PV = \frac{A}{k}$

For example:

Mr. Baidyanathan, the CMD of a management institution wants to institute a scholarship of ₹ 2500 to a outstanding student every year. What is the present value of investment which would yield ₹ 2500 in perpetuity, discounted at 8%?

Solution

$$P = \frac{A}{k}$$

$$= \frac{2500}{8\%}$$

$$= ₹\ 31250$$

Illustration 11

<u>**Re:** Annuity (A) and Capital Recovery Factor</u>

A loan of ₹ 500000 is to be repaid in 15 equal annual installments. What is the amount of each installment or annuity of the loan if the loan carries a rate of 9% p.a.?

Solution

$$PVA_n = A \times PVIFA_{15,9\%}$$

Or $$A = \frac{PVA_n}{PVIFA_{15,9\%}} = \frac{500000}{8.061} \text{ (by using PVIFA table)}$$

$$= ₹\ 62028$$

Alternatively:

Using 'Capital Recovery Factor'

$$PVA_n = A \times \frac{(1+k)^n - 1}{k(1+k)^n}$$

Or $$A = PVA_n \frac{k(1+k)^n}{(1+k)^n - 1}$$

Or $$A = 500000 \frac{.09(1+.09)^{15}}{(1+.09)^{15}-1}$$

$$= 500000 \frac{.09 \times 3.6425}{3.6425-1}$$

$$= 500000 \frac{0.32782}{2.6425}$$

$$= 500000 \times 0.124056$$

= ₹ 62028

Here Capital Recovery factor is the reciprocal of the present value annuity factor (PVIFA)

$$= \frac{k(1+k)^n}{(1+k)^n-1}$$

$$= 0.124056$$

Ilustration 12

The annuity deposit scheme of UBI provides for fixed monthly income. The amount of initial deposit to receive that monthly installment of ₹ 500 for 24 months is to be made. The rate of interest, being compounded quarterly is 10% p.a. what is the amount of initial deposit?

Solution

Firstly, the effective rate of interest p.a. is being calculated as:

$$\frac{(1+0.10)^4-1}{4}$$

$$= (1+.025)^4 - 1$$

$$= 1.1038 - 1$$

= .1038 or 10.38%

Now, effective rate of interest p.m.

$$= \frac{.1038}{12}$$

$$= 0.00865$$

The initial deposit can be calculated as:

$$PVA_n = A \times \frac{(1+k)^n - 1}{k(1+k)^n}$$

$$= 500 \times \frac{(1+.00865)^{24} - 1}{.00865(1+.00865)^{24}}$$

$$= 500 \times \frac{.22962}{.010636}$$

$$= 500 \times 21.5889$$

$$= ₹\ 10795$$

Present Value of a Growing Annuity Here we will calculate the present value of cash inflows growing at a constant rate with the help of following formula:

(with an adjustment in the discount rate for growth)

$$PVA_n = \frac{A}{1+g} \frac{1-(1+k)^{-n}}{k}$$

$$= \frac{A}{1+g} \times \frac{1-\frac{1}{(1+k)^n}}{k}$$

$$= \frac{A}{1+g} \frac{(1+k)^n - 1}{(1+k)^n . k}$$

$$= \frac{A}{1+g} \frac{(1-k)^n - 1}{k(1+k)^n}$$

$$= \frac{A}{1+g} \text{PVIFA } (k, n)$$

k = required rate of return adjusted of growth

$$= \frac{i-g}{1+g}$$

Where, g = growth rate of cash inflows

And i = discounting rate/required rate of return,

A = Cash inflow in the 1st year.

Illustration 13

What is the present value of the expected series of cash inflow in the form of dividend streams which is expected to grow after one year at ₹ 55 at 10% p.a. for 10 years and then ceases. Given that required rate of return is 15.5%.

Solution

$$PVA_n = \frac{A}{1+g}\ \frac{(1+k)^n - 1}{(1+k)^n . k}$$

$$= \frac{55}{1+.10}\ \frac{(1+k)^n - 1}{(1+k)^n . k}$$

$$= 50\ \frac{(1+k)^n - 1}{k(1+k)^n}$$

$$k = \frac{i-g}{1+g}$$

$$= \frac{0.155-0.10}{1+1.10}$$

$$= \frac{0.055}{1.10}$$

$$= 0.05 \quad \text{or} \quad 5\%$$

So,

$$PVA_n = 50\ \frac{(1+0.5)^{10} - 1}{.05(1+.05)^{10}}$$

$$= 50\ \frac{1.628894 - 1}{.05 \times 1.628894}$$

$$= 50\ \frac{.628894}{0.0814447}$$

$$= 50 \times 7.7217$$

$$= 50 \times 7.722$$

$$= ₹\ 386.1$$

Alternatively,

Using the PVIFA Table,

$$PVA_n = \frac{A}{1+g}\ PVIFA_{(k,\ n)}$$

$$= \frac{55}{1+.10}\quad PVIFA_{(5\%,\ 10)}$$

$= 50 \times 7.722$ (from PVIFA table)

$=$ ₹ 386.10

Problem

Re: Rate of Return by interpolation and F.V.

1. Under the annuity plan of ICICI prudential, if the amount issued is ₹ 15000, the concerned person will get the maturity value of basic sum of ₹ 15000 alongwith bonus which does not vary with the term of annuity plan. The person aged 18, enters the plan. The term is 15 years and annual premium is ₹ 250. What is the required rate of return the person will get?
2. It the person could have attained at the age of 45 and entered the same policy, with same term where premium is to be paid ₹ 300. What will be rate of return?
3. Calculate the Future Value in both cases.

Solution

Maturity value = Premium adjusted with return $\times$ $FVIFA_{k,\,n}$

Or $MV = P(1+k)\ FVIFA_{k,\,n}$

Where, P = Annual Premium

k = Rate of Return

n = Term of Policy (years)

On the other hand,

Minimum Maturity Value = Basic Sum + Bonus

= 15000 + Bonus, which does not vary and hence can be overlooked

= ₹ 15000

1. $P(1+k)\ FVIFA = 15000$

Or, $250\ (1+k).\ FVIFA_{k,15} = 15000$

Or, $(1+k).\ FVIFA_{k,15} = \dfrac{15000}{250} = 60$

From FVIFA table, we get

[Applying 16% rate, 15 years]

$(1+.16)\ FVIFA_{16\%,\,15}$

$= 1.16 \times 51.66$

$= 59.9256$

and [Applying 17% rate, 15 years]

$$(1+.17)\ FVIFA_{17\%,15}$$
$$= 1.17 \times 56.11 = 65.6487$$

So, we can arrange this:

16%	→ ←	59.9256
17%		65.6487

By interpolation,

$$k = 16\% + (17\% - 16\%) \times \frac{60 - 59.9256}{65.6487 - 59.9256}$$
$$= 16\% + 1 \times \frac{0.0744}{5.7231}\%$$
$$= 16\% + 0.01299\%$$
$$= 16\% + 0.013\%$$
$$= 16.013\%$$

2. $300(1+k)\ FVIFA_{k,15} = 15000$

Or, $(1+k)\ FVIFA_{k,15} = 50$

From FVIFA table, we get [Applying 14% rate, 15 years]

$$(1+.14) \times 43.842$$
$$= 49.9798, \textit{ i.e. almost } 50$$

So, $k = 14\%$ (approximate)

This required rate of return is comparatively lower since the 45 years old person's policy plan has greater risk coverage in spite of payment of higher premium.

3. FVA_n (18 years of age)

$$= A \times \frac{\left[(1+k)^n - 1\right]}{k}$$
$$= 250\ \frac{\left[(1+0.16013)^{15} - 1\right]}{.16013}$$
$$= 250\ \frac{\left[(1.16013)^{15} - 1\right]}{.16013}$$
$$= 250 \times \frac{9.28111 - 1}{.16013}$$

$$= 250 \times \frac{8.28111}{.16013}$$

$$= 250 \times 51.714$$

$$= ₹\ 12928.50$$

FVA_n (45 years of age)

$$= A \times \frac{\left[(1+k)^n - 1\right]}{k}$$

$$= 300 \times \frac{\left[(1+0.14)^{15} - 1\right]}{0.14}$$

$$= 300 \times \frac{7.1393 - 1}{0.14}$$

$$= 300 \times \frac{6.13793 - 1}{0.14}$$

$$= 300 \times 43.842$$

$$= ₹\ 13152.60$$

SUMMARY

A rupee today has more value than a rupee power aft4r a year. Therefore, rational investors would prefer current receipts to future receipts. There lies the importance of the concept 'Time Value of Money' which is the value of a unit of money changing at different time intervals.

Time value of money is also called as 'time preference for money' because due to risks and uncertainty in future as individuals have subjective preference for present or current receipts for current consumptions. We assume that value of money remains same irrespective of different time intervals.

The future values of all cash inflows of the end of the time horizon at a particular compound interest rate are found under compounding technique, *i.e.*, compounding is the technique of applying the concept of compound interest to find out the future values of all cash inflows. The amount of money which an investor expects to receive after a certain period of time which will contain both investment or principal and return on investment in the form of compound interest is called Future Value or Compound Value.

Discounting is the process of determining present value of a future lump-sum payment or a series of future even or uneven payments. It is exactly opposite of that of compounding technique. The present value of a future payment or a series of future payments is the amount of the current or present worth that is equivalent to the investor. The basis of present value is that opportunity cost exists for money lying idle that means interest can be earned on that money. This opportunity cost is called 'discounting rate' or 'interest rate' or 'cost of fund'.

EXERCISE

Short Questions

1. What is 'Time Value of Money'?
2. What are the methods by which time value of money can be calculated?
3. What are the determinants of required rate of return?
4. What is Future Value?
5. What is Present Value?
6. What is Compounding Technique?
7. What is Discounting Technique?
8. What is Capital Recovery Factor?
9. What is Sinking Fund Factor?
10. Write 'rule of 72' and 'Rule of 69'.

Moderate and Broad Questions

1. Why money should have time value?
2. Explain compounding and Discounting techniques and also the difference between two?

Problems

1. It an employee of a company deposits ₹ 20000 into his Provident Fund account at the end of each year for 25 years. What is the amount he will accumulate in his Provident Fund at the end of 25 years if the rate of interest given by PF authorities is 8.5% ?
   [**Hints:** 200000 $\text{FVIFA}_{8.5\%, 25}$]
2. Under a Banks Cash Multiplies Scheme deposits can be made for periods ranging 6 months to 12 years. Every half – year interest is added to the principal. The rate of interest is 8% for investment less than 36 months and 9% for period, for than 36 and above months. What will be the amount of ₹ 50000 of investment after 6 years?

   Hints: $50000 \times \left(\frac{1+0.09}{2}\right)^{2\times 6}$
3. Given the time value of money as 9% as the discounting factor, what is the present value of the following future cash inflows that will be received over next 5 years:

Year	inflows (₹)
1	10000
2	12000
3	17000
4	18000

4. The annuity deposit scheme of SBI provides for fixed monthly income. After the first month of deposit, the depositor receives monthly installments. What is the value of monthly annuity if an initial deposit of ₹ 3000 is made for an annuity period of 60 months and the rate of interest is 10% p.a., being compounded at quarterly intervals?

5. Someone has ₹ 50000 to invest. What will be the compound value if the interest rate is 6.5% p.a., being compounded quarterly and the term of the investment is 9 years?
6. You are planning to buy a flat of 700 sq.feet of ₹ 980000. You will be required to pay monthly installment of ₹ 10500 for 15 years. What compound rate of interest will you be paying?
7. The cash certificate of ICICI Bank is a term deposit scheme under reinvestment plan. Interest is reinvested at quarterly rests. Given an interest rate of 8% p.a., having a value of ₹ 1000 of certificate after 2 years. What is the issue price of the certificate?
8. The annuity deposit scheme of a commercial bank provides for monthly fixed income where the rate of interest is 10.5% p.a. compounded, half yearly and initial deposit of ₹ 10000 has been made for an annuity period of 24 months. What is the value of the monthly annuity?
9. In a Rozgar Yojana, the amount of compound interest is compounded at half yearly interest. What is the amount of initial deposit to receive a monthly installment of ₹ 2000 for 2 years at 12% interest p.a.?
10. If Mr. Aditya borrows a 5 years loan of ₹ 15 lakh at 9% interest p.a. from his employer to buy a 2-storied house, what will be the value of annual installment, if his employer requires 15 equal end-of-year repayments? Also prepare loan Amortization schedule for 1st 4 years term.

[Hints:

$$PVA_n = A \times PVIFA_{15.9\%}$$

$$A = \frac{PVA_n}{PVIFA_{15.9\%}}$$

$$= \frac{1500000}{8.061}$$

$$= ₹\ 186081$$

Loan Amortization Schedule

End of year	Payment	Interest	Principal repayment	Outstanding balance
0				
1	186081	135000	51081	1448919
2	186081	130403	55678	1393241
/	/	/	/	/
/	/	/	/	/
/	/	/	/	/

Outstand balance:

15 lakhs – 51081 = 1448919

1448919 – 55678 = 1393241

Interest :

15 lakhs × 9% = 135000

1448919 × 9% = 130403]

❑❑❑

3 Risk and Return

3.1 CONCEPT OF RISK AND RETURN, TYPES OF FUTURE RETURNS

Risk measures the variability or dispersion of future returns, *i.e.,* risk implies either actual return is higher than expected one or lower than expected one. This is because we cannot predict accurately about the future cash inflows due to inability to anticipate the occurrence of the possible future events with certainty. It happens due to uncertain economic conditions. The greater the variability on dispersion of future possible returns, the more riskier the project.

For example, if a company launches a new product with higher technological up gradation and is confident to get the potential customers it can forecast the future cash inflow. But the problem is either the demand of the product is would be very high due to economic growth or would be higher low due to economic slowdown and other reasons. Risk would be arised out of those uncertain economic conditions under which that company has to operate its activities. The other factors which may affect forecasts of future cash inflow are taxation, interest rates, industry specific factors, change in management etc.

The variability can be best measured by standard deviation or coefficient of variation.

Types of Risks/Sources of Risk

The riskiness of each investment can be divided into two components.

A. Market Related Risk or Non-diversiable Risk

Market related risk cannot be avoidable and eliminated by diversification. The alternative name is systematic risk which is related to the general economy or the stock market. The following some important risks are market related risks:

(i) Interest rate Risk: This risk mainly affects adversely the lenders *e.g.* debenture holders or bondholders. It is the variability in the return of a security due to changes in the level of interest rates.

(ii) Inflation Risk: Interest rates go up with inflation rate. Rise in inflation rate causes reduction of purchasing power which in turn, affects adversely the ability of the investors to buy the securities at their choice.

(iii) Market on beta Risk: Firms cannot diversity these unavoidable factors like changes in political environment, economic depression, fluctuations in the securities market etc. Market risk is the most important risk of having direct influence on stock prices.

(iv) Financial Risk: It is the risk of using debt capital in the capital structure of a firm. The higher the debt financing, the greater the financial risk of the concerned firm. But the company has to us debt capital to a certain extent for controlling the ownership, increasing market price per share etc. So, financial risk is unavoidable.

(v) Competition Risk: The actions and strategies of the competitors, in most cases, are unanticipated which has an adverse effect on the expected future cash inflows, from a project. The competitor's competitiveness are absolutely unanticipated and unavoidable.

(vi) International Risk: This type of risk may arise due to rupee-dollar crisis, rupee gaining and dollar weakening, governments delay in taking decision on pricing of exported essential commodities, impact of crisis of US economy, an increase in international oil prices , unanticipated and sudden increase in the raw material in international market etc.

B. Diversifiable on Specific Risk

The alternative name of this risk is unsystematic risk which stems from factors which are specific to a firm as follows:

1. Managerial deficiencies, low profitability
2. Company strike low productivity
3. Plant breakdown
4. Death of a key employee, turnover of them
5. Development of a new process/concept/idea
6. Commodity risk arising from the effect of price changes on production and distribution
7. Legal risk, *e.g.,* imposition of service tax
8. Changes in EXIM policy of Government of India

Unsystematic risk is avoidable. The business and firm specific factors are mostly random. In case of building portfolio of securities, we can include sufficient number of securities in the portfolio so that the risk of poor portfolio of a company can be offset against strong portfolio of another company in terms of productivity, brand etc.

Return

There is no authentic definition of return. It, basically, is the form of reward to the investors whose objective is to maximize it from his investments, subject to various constraints, particularly risk.

But what should be the exact reward? Is it return on investment, or return on assets? Is it return on capital employed or return on equity? Is it profit after tax on before tax, operating profit only or net profit? Actually, use of any specific definition depends upon the objective for which the return is being measured. Say from equity shareholders point of view return implies to return from equity. Again from the point of view of operating efficiency, return implies to 'operating profit on sales'.

Types of Return

There are two broad categories of return:

(A) Returns on the basis of investor's observation and anticipation –

1. Realized Return: It is historical return generated by an investment which is ex-post or after the fact-return that was earned or could have been earned.

For example, an investor earns ₹ 3 per share as dividend and also ₹ 5 per share as capital gain. If his average investment is ₹ 40 per share then the return on the stock will be

$\frac{3+5}{40} = \frac{8}{40}$ or 20% which is the historical or realized return.

2. Expected Return: It is anticipated return from an asset or financial instrument which investors expect over some future period, against uncertainty or risk.

The expected return or ex-ante return from investment is the weighted average of the expected returns, weighted by the proportion on chance of total funds invested in each.

For example:

Types of Securities	Investment (₹ in lakhs)	Proportion	Return (%)	Weighted Average (%)
A	25	0.25	20	5
B	50	0.50	10	5
C	25	0.25	15	3.75
	100	1.00		13.75

(B) Return based on time horizon –

I. Single Period Returns: When return is calculated for the single period only say, one day, one week, one month or one year.

II. Multi Period Returns: When return is calculated for more than a single period say annual return over a span of three years.

3.2 RELATIONSHIP BETWEEN RISK AND RETURN

An investor generally selects a portfolio that helps to bring a balance between the risk involved and the expected returns from the portfolio. An aggressive investor undertakes high risk and expects high return. But an average investor expects maximum return but with minimum risk. There might be two options in front of them if there is more than 1 portfolio.

Option 1: When 2 or more portfolio have identical risks, an investor will select that portfolio which has the highest expected return.

Option 2: If all portfolios have identical expected return an investor selects that portfolio which has the lowest risk.

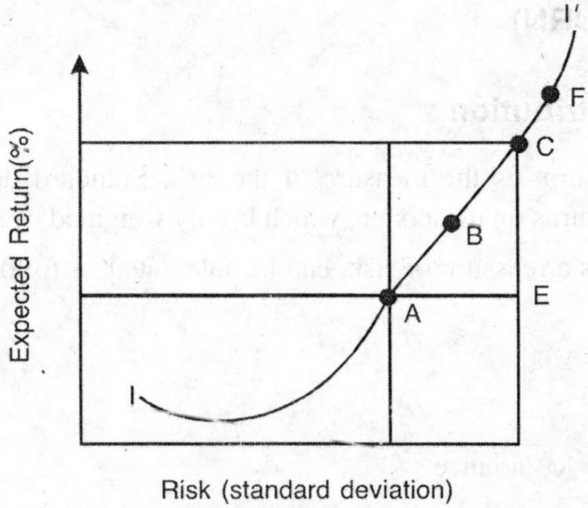

Indifference Curve (of an investor)

The curve II′ is an investor's indifference curve, *i.e.,* he has no preference between portfolios which lie on the curve since each of them has same level of utility which is to be expected. All portfolios (A, B, C, F) are good and better in compare to portfolio E. Portfolio E offers a lower expected return in compare to portfolios B, C and F and also it has higher risk in compare to portfolios A and B. Portfolio C is most preferred since it has comparatively higher expected return in compare to portfolios A, B and E.

Though F has the highest expected return but its risk is also highest in compare to all other portfolios. We can conclude that portfolio C is the balanced portfolio between risk and expected return, though an aggressive investor wants to hold that portfolio of securities that will give him highest expected return at highest risk (portfolio F). Lowest risk portfolio (A) usually gives lowest expected return. High risk portfolio (F) might yield highest return but due to highest risk, there is greater possibility of getting bleak picture.

Relationship between Risk and Return

Intensity of Risk	Name of Portfolio	Expected Return	Nature of Investor
Lowest	A	Lowest	Risk avoider
Highest	F	Highest	Aggressive
Below Highest	C	High	Rational

We also refer CAPM model in our coming section in this chapter to show the relationship between risk and return.

3.3 RISK MEASUREMENT AND ITS REDUCTION (ALSO MEASUREMENT OF EXPECTED RETURN)

Using Probability Distribution

The variability of returns is the measure of the risk. Standard deviation (σ) is the best measure of variability of returns on dispersion, which is duly weighted by probability of outcomes.

Standard deviation, as a reassure of risk, can be calculated as follows:

$$\text{Variance} = \sum_{i=1}^{n} P_i (x_i - \dot{x})^2$$

$$\text{Standard deviation} = \sqrt{\text{Variance}}$$

$$\sqrt{\sum_{i=1}^{n} P_i (x_i - \overline{x})\, 2}$$

Where, $\overline{x}$ = expected value of rate of return

x_i = rate of return from an investment 'i'

P_i = probability associated with the ith possible outcome

x = number of outcomes

The higher the value of standard deviation, higher is the risk and *vice versa*

$\overline{x}$ = Expected value of rate of return

$$= E(R) = \sum_{i=1}^{n} R_i P_i = \text{Weighted Average of returns.}$$

Illustration 1

Rate of Return from investments (%)	Probability of outcomes
6	0.20
10	0.30
12	0.20
8	0.30
	1.0

We are to find out the standard deviation and expected rate of return

Solution

Table 1. $\overline{x}$ = Expected value of Rate of Return

Returns (R_i)%	Probability [weight] (P_i)	R_i P_i = Expected value (%)
6	0.20	1.20
10	0.30	3.00
12	0.20	2.40
8	0.30	2.40
Total	$Ep_i = 1.00$	$\Sigma R_i P_i = 9 = \overline{x}$

Therefore expected rate of return = 9%

i.e., $\overline{x}$ = 9%

Table 2. Standard Deviation

Possible Outcomes	x_i(%)	$\overline{x}$ (%)	$(x_i - \overline{x})^2$	P_i	$P_i (x_i - \overline{x})^2$
1	6	9	$(6\text{-}9)^2 = 9$	0.20	1.80
2	10	9	$(10\text{-}9)^2 = 1$	0.30	.30
3	12	9	$(12\text{-}9)^2 = 9$	0.20	1.80
4	8	9	$(8\text{-}9)^2 = 1$	0.30	.30
Total	—	—	—	$\Sigma P_i = 1.00$	$\Sigma P_i (Xi - \overline{X})^2 = 4.20$

$$\text{.So, Variance} = \sum_{i=1}^{n} P_i (x_i - \overline{x})^2 = 4.20$$

$$\text{Standard Deviation} = \sqrt{\text{Variance}}$$

$$= \sqrt{420}$$

$$= 2.0493\%$$

In case of two – assets portfolio:

Further, we are considering proportion of investment to the total investment of the two-assets portfolio.

Illustration 2

Investment in Company A's share	= 15 lakhs
Investment in Company B's share	= 30 lakhs
Total investment employed	= 45 lakhs

Now, If we could have calculated expected return on Company A's share (say 8%) and expected return on company B's share (say 12%), what will be the expected rate of return on the portfolio?

The expected rate of return of the portfolio:

$$E(R_p) = E(R_A)\,W_A + E(R_B)W_B$$

Where, $E(R_p)$ = Expected rate of return on the portfolio

$E(R_A)$ = Expected rate of return (%) on company A's share

$E(R_B)$ = Expected rate of return (%) on company B's share

W_A = Proportion of investment in Company A's share = $\frac{15 \text{ lakhs}}{45 \text{ lakhs}} = \frac{1}{3}$

W_B = Proportion of investment in Company B's share = $\frac{30 \text{ lakhs}}{45 \text{ lakhs}} = \frac{2}{3}$

So, expected rate of return on the portfolio = $E(R_P)$

$$= 8 \times \frac{1}{3} + 12 \times \frac{2}{3}$$

$$= \frac{8}{3} + \frac{24}{3} = \frac{32}{3} = 10.67\%$$

Standard deviation, as a measure of risk from two-assets portfolio

$$\sigma_P = \sqrt{W_A^2\,\sigma_A^2 + W_B^2\,\sigma_B^2 + 2\,W_A\,W_B\,\sigma_{A,B}}$$

$$= \sqrt{W_A^2\,\sigma_A^2 + W_B^2\,\sigma_B^2 + 2\,W_A\,W_B\,r_{A.B}\cdot\sigma_A\cdot\sigma_B}$$

Correlation Coefficient, $r_{AB} = \frac{\text{COV (A.B)}}{\sigma_A\,,\,\sigma_B} = \frac{\sigma_{A,B}}{\sigma_A\,.\,\sigma_B}$

where, $\sigma_{A,B}$ = COV between returns on A and B = $COV_{(A,B)}$

r_{AB} = correlation coefficient between returns from asset A and asset B

σ_A = Standard deviation of returns from A

σ_B = Standard deviation of returns from B

Hence, $COV_{(A,B)} = r_{AB} \cdot \sigma_A \cdot \sigma_B = \sigma_{A,B}$

Risk Reduction and Diversification: *Special Note*

The portfolio risk on 2-assets portfolio may be lower than the risk of individual investments due to diversification. It the returns are positively correlated (r = 1), risk cannot be reduced through the process of diversification. Diversification helps to reduce risk even upto 0 level if returns are perfectly negatively correlated (r = –1).

Absence of correlation (r = 0) means that both assets on securities A and B are independent. In that case, COV (A, B) will also be 0 since

$$\nabla_{AB} = COV_{(A,B)} = 0 \times \nabla_A \cdot \nabla_B \; [r_{AB} = 0]$$

$COV_{(A,B)}$ = deviations of returns from asset A and asset B from their expected returns weighted by probability of outcomes.

$$= \Sigma p_i \{R_A - E(R_A)\} \{R_B - E(R_B)\}$$

R_A = return from Asset A

R_B = return from Asset B

Therefore, risk will be reduced when r = 0, in compare to 0 < r > 1.

The thing which is mainly observed that is positive correlation coefficient (r < + 1) indicating the tendency of two returns to move in the same direction. When the market witnesses booms condition, both asset A and asset B would register a rise in prices and when the market witnesses recession, both securities would show decline in price due to this positive correlation.

Portfolio risk can be reduced by combining investments with negative correlation. The next preference should be where correlation is not significant.

Illustration 3

We are holding a portfolio with 60% in A and 40% in B. We are to evaluate the impact on the gains from diversification, for the following values of $r_{(AB)}$:

$r_{AB} = -1$

$r_{AB} = .5$

$r_{AB} = +1$

Considering 2 securities A and B :

$E(R_A)$ = Expected return on Security A = 10%

$E(R_B)$ = Expected return on Security B = 16%

σ_A = σ of security A = 5%

σ_B = σ of security B = 6%

Solution

Expected portfolio return

$= E(R_p) = E(R_A)\ W_A + E(R_B)\ W_B$

$= 10 \times 0.6 + 16 \text{ X } 0.4$

$= 6 + 6.4$

$= 12.4\%$

Variance of return on portfolio depends on both variability of the security returns but also on correlation coefficients.

Hence,

$$\sigma_P = \sqrt{W_A^{\ 2}\ \sigma_A^{\ 2} + W_B^{\ 2}\ \sigma_B^{\ 2} + 2 W_A W_B \cdot r_{AB} \cdot \sigma_A \cdot \sigma_B}$$

Where, $W_A = 60\% = .60,\ W_B = .40$

It $r_{AB} = -1$, (Returns are negatively correlated)

than $\sigma_P = \sqrt{(.60)^2 \times (.05)^2 + (.40)^2 \times (.06)^2 + 2 \times .60 \times .40 \times (-1) \times .05 \times .06}$

$= \sqrt{.0009 + .000576 - 0.00144}$

$= \sqrt{0.000036} = .006 = 0.6\%$

It $r_{AB} = +1$ (Returns are positively correlated and two securities A,B move in perfect tandem with each other)

than $\sigma_P = \sqrt{(.60)^2 (.05)^2 + (.40)^2 .(.06)^2 + 2 \times .60 \times .40 \times (+1) \times .05 \times .06}$

$= \sqrt{.0009 + .000576 + 0.00144}$

$= \sqrt{.002916}$

$= 0.054$

$= 5.4\%$

It $r_{AB} = 0.5$

than $\sigma_P = \sqrt{(.06)^2 \times (.05)^2 + (.40)^2 \times (.06)^2 + 2 \times .60 \times .60 \times (.5) \times .05 \times .06}$

$= \sqrt{.0009 + .000576 + .00072}$

$= \sqrt{.002196}$

$= 0.0468$

$= 4.68\%$

Standard deviation of portfolio return (σ_P) will be 5.4% when, the correlation coefficient (r) between returns on A and returns on B is +1. So long as A and B have, $r_{AB} < +1$, σ_P will be less than 5.4%. For instance, when $r_{AB} = 0.5$, $\sigma_P = 4.68\%$. This implies that there has been l little amount of gain from diversification. If $r_{AB} = -1$, σ_P will be 0.6%, then the gain from diversification is significant due to reduction of risk significantly.

Special Note: Risk of diversification and number of stocks

The amount of risk reduction achieved by diversification will be good up to a level of first specific number of stocks in the portfolio. As the number increases beyond this point the diversifying effect of each additional stock diminishes.

3.4 MEASUREMENT OF RATE OF RETURN OF A STOCK

Rate of return of a stock on security is the income in the form of cash inflow which in turn, is the difference in price of that security between the beginning and the end of the holding period.

Rate of return of an individual stock, K

$$= \frac{D + (P_n - P_o)}{P_o}$$

Where, D = Income or cash inflows during the holding period in the form of dividend or interest

P_n = Price of the stock at the end of holding period

P_o = Purchase price or price at the beginning of the holding period

K = rate of return (%)

Illustration 4

Mr. X purchased a share of a multinational company. The purchase price was ₹ 1560 as on September 26, 2009 and sales price was ₹ 1700 on November 5, 2009. During the holding period, he received dividend of ₹ 25 for the year. What is the rate of return from that security?

Solution

$$K = \frac{D + (P_n - P_o)}{P_o}$$

$$= \frac{25 + (1700 - 1560)}{1560}$$

$$= \frac{25 + 140}{1560}$$

$$= .10576$$

$$= 10.58\%$$

Illustration 5

Calculate expected return of market portfolio from the following particular where the portfolio consists of 3 securities:

Securities	Market Price	
	At the beginning ₹	End of 2009 ₹
A Equity share	100	90
A, 14% Debenture (convertible)	1000	1250
A, 8% Flexi Bond	1000	1100

The investor has got dividend on his shareholding ₹ 20.

Solution

Securities	Dividend & Interest (D)	Market Price at the beginning(P_O)	Market Price at the end (P_n)	P_n–P_o
Equity shares	20	100	90	(10)
Debenture	140	1000	1250	250
Flexi Bond	80	1000	1100	100
Total	240	2100	2440	340

So, Expected return on the market portfolio (at the end of 2009), $E(R_m)$

$$= \frac{\text{Total Dividend \& Interest + Capital Gain (Loss)}}{\text{Market price at the beginning}}$$

$$= \frac{240 + (2440 - 2100)}{2100}$$

$$= \frac{240 + 340}{2100}$$

$$= \frac{580}{2100}$$

$$= 0.2762$$

$$= 27.62\%$$

3.5 MEASUREMENT OF NON-DIVERSIFIABLE OR MARKET RISK / RISK OF STOCKS IN A PORTFOLIO (IN CASE OF MORE THAN ONE STOCK)

The real risk of a security is systematic risk which cannot be diversified. Beta (β_j) measures the systematic risk. Higher the riskiness of a security, the higher the beta and *vice versa*.The standard deviation of a portfolio is certainly a good and best measure of variability of returns on dispersion but to the extent that if addition of a security to the portfolio increases the standard deviation of the portfolio, the stock adds risk to that portfolio. But that added risk depends not only on standard deviation of that stock but also on that risk which cannot be diversified.

Therefore, in case of diversified investor, the risk of a stock in the portfolio is that portion of total risk which is systematic on market risk or non-diversifiable. If an investor holds only one security, risk cannot be diversified and then, the risk is the standard deviation. The beta of a portfolio is nothing but the weighted average of the betas of the securities that comprise the portfolio, the weights being the proportion of investments in the respective securities.

For example,

Security	Portfolio proportion (W)	Beta factor of security (β)	Weighted Beta factor (β) × W
I	0.25	1.05	.2625
II	0.40	1.10	.44
III	0.35	1.15	.4025
	1.00		1.105

∴ The beta of the above portfolio comprising of the 3 securities = 1.105

The beta factor (β) for a particular security or beta coefficient of a security is the ratio of that securities covariance of return on a share (A) with the market returns as a whole to the variance of market returns (M).

$$\therefore \quad \beta = \frac{COV_{(A,M)}}{\sigma_M^2}$$

Which is slope of the following linear regression equation developed by William sharp , and measures the responsiveness of the portfolio to the general market by measuring the relative risk of individual risk against the risk of market portfolio.

$$\therefore \quad \beta = \frac{\text{Non-diversifiable risk of portofolio j}}{\text{Risk of market portfolio}}$$

Linear Regression equation : $A = \alpha + \beta M + C$

$\propto = \overline{A} - \beta\,\overline{M}$ = intercept of the line indicating the return of portfolio when the market return is zero.

C = unexpected return not identified by the model.

A = return on a company's share with the market as a whole (dependent variable)

M = return on market portfolio (independent variable)

Now, β = slope of above regression equation

$$= \frac{COV_{(A,M)}}{\sigma_M^2} = \frac{COV_{(A,M)}}{Var_{(M)}}$$

$$= \frac{\sigma_A \cdot \sigma_M \cdot r_{(A,M)}}{\sigma_M^2}$$

$$\left[\because r_{(A,M)} = \frac{COV_{(A,M)}}{\sigma_A \cdot \sigma_M}\right]$$

$$= \frac{\sigma_A \cdot r_{(A,M)}}{\sigma_M}$$

Where, $r_{(A,M)}$ = coefficient of correlation of returns, between A and M.

σ_A = S.d. of returns from share A

σ_M = S.d. of market rate of returns

If $\beta = 1$, the risk is an average risk

If $\beta > 1$, the risk is above-average risk

If $\beta < 1$, the risk is below-average risk or, risk of the asset is lower than market risk.

Alternatively,

$$\beta = \frac{COV_{(A, M)}}{Var_{(M)}}$$

$$= \frac{\Sigma P\left(A-\overline{A}\right)\left(M-\overline{M}\right)}{\Sigma P\left(M-\overline{M}\right)^2}$$

3.6 CAPITAL ASSET PRICING MODEL (CAPM)

CAPM is based on the principal that the required rate of return of a security equals to risk-free rate of return along with risk premium. The required rate of return is expected by the investors who are in firm belief that firm will earn this return on its equity. Therefore, it can be taken as cost of equity capital of the firm.

CAPM was developed in connection with portfolio management in the U.S.A. by William Sharp, John Linter and John Mossin. It is one of the portfolio theories which told that expected return from a portfolio comprises both reward for waiting and reward for risk.

Hence, CAPM is represented mathematically by: $A_j = R_F + \beta_j (M - R_F)$

= Risk free rate + risk premium.

Where,

B = Beta coefficient showing non-diversifiable risk of the asset relative to the market risk.

A_j = Required rate of return on security 'j' or expected rate of return on security 'j'

R_F = Risk-free rate of return

β_j = beta coefficient of security j

M = return on market portfolio

$\beta_j\ (M - R_F)$ = Risk premium

CAPM is based on the following assumptions:

(i) The capital market is efficient and hence, is in equilibrium.

(ii) Investors decide to invest on the basis of single-time horizon, *i.e.*, the next immediate time period.

(iii) Investors are risk-averse. The greater the expected risk of a portfolio, the higher expectation of the investors for compensating the excess risk.

(iv) All investors have the same expectations about the risk and return.

(v) Transaction costs are ignored and taxes do not affect the choice of buying assets.

(vi) Expected rate of return is equal to the required rate of return, for a given level of market risk.

About Beta:

Already discussed in para 3.5

About Risk Premium: (Capital Market Line)

The size of risk premium will increase as the risk of the market portfolio increases. It can be shown by Capital Market Line (CML).

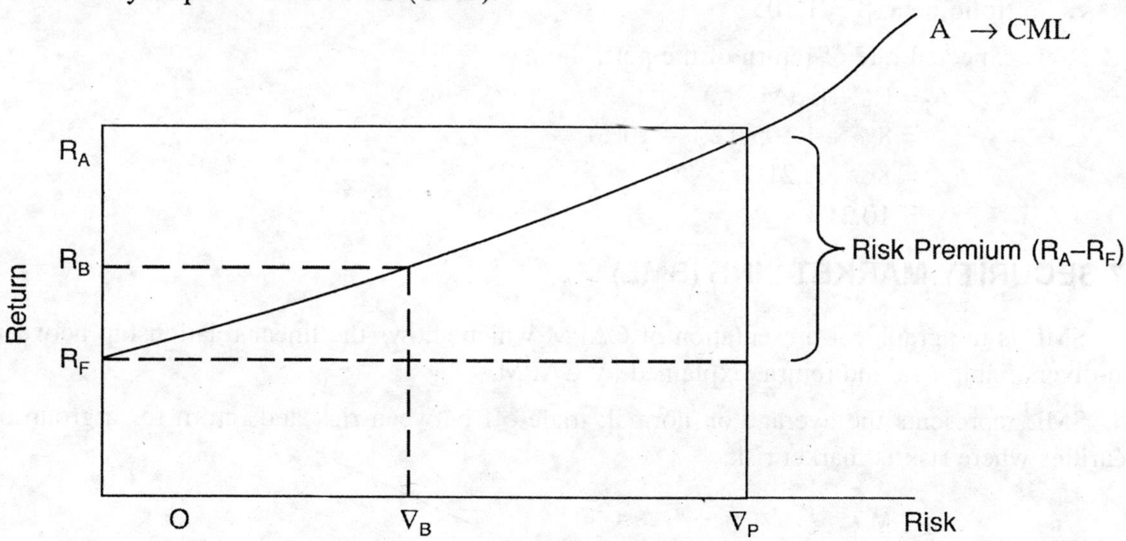

R_A = Return from a portfolio (efficient portfolio)

R_B = Return from inefficient portfolio B

R_F = Risk free return

Graphical Presentation of CAPM (SML)

See Para 3.7

Illustration 6

A portfolio consists of following three securities:

Security	Proportion of portfolio	Beta factor
I	0.25	1.05
II	0.40	1.10
III	0.35	1.15
	100	

If risk-free rate of return is 8% and the average market return is 12% what is the expected rate of return of the portfolio?

Solution

Working: Portfolio beta (β_j)

Security	(W)	β	β × W
I	0.25	1.05	.2625
II	0.40	1.10	.44
III	0.35	1.15	.4025
	100		1.105

∴ Portfolio beta, $\beta_j = 1.105$

Now, expected rate of return of the portfolio,

$$A_j = R_F + \beta_j\,(M - R_F)$$
$$= 8\% + 1.105(12\% - 10\%)$$
$$= 8\% + 2.21\%$$
$$= 10.21\%$$

3.7 SECURITY MARKET LINE (SML)

SML is the graphical presentation of CAPM which shows the linear relationship between non-diversifiable risk and return, explained by CAPM.

SML represents the average on normal, trade-off between risk and return for a group of securities where risk is market risk.

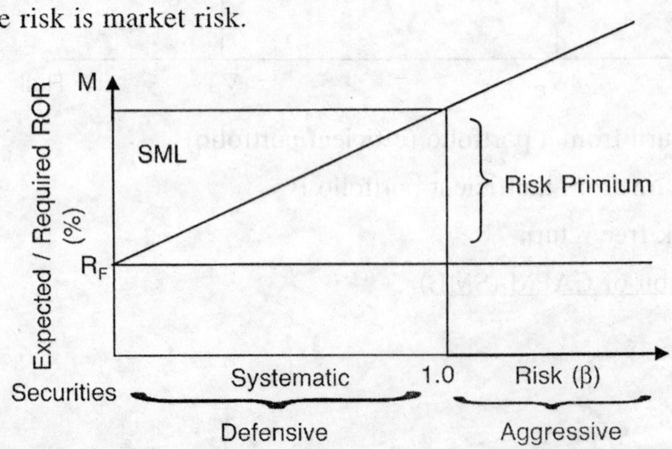

SML intersects the vertical axis at R_F and M–R_F is the slope of SML. Above R_F, the expected /required ROR (%) is proportional to the systematic on non-diversifiable risk (β). As per CAPM assumptions, expected ROR of a security and market risk should lie on the SML. SML helps to determine expected ROR of a security if β is known.

An Ex-post SML

SML can be written as –

Normal Return: $N\left(\bar{r}_j\right) = r_o + r_j\beta$

When, r_o = intercept of SML (ex-post)

r_j = slope of the SML

$$\propto_j = \bar{r}_j - N\left(\bar{r}_j\right) = \bar{r}_j - (r_o + r_j\beta)$$

In the ex-post SML, average historical rates of return (ex-post or after the fact-return) for securities are plotted against their market risks (β).

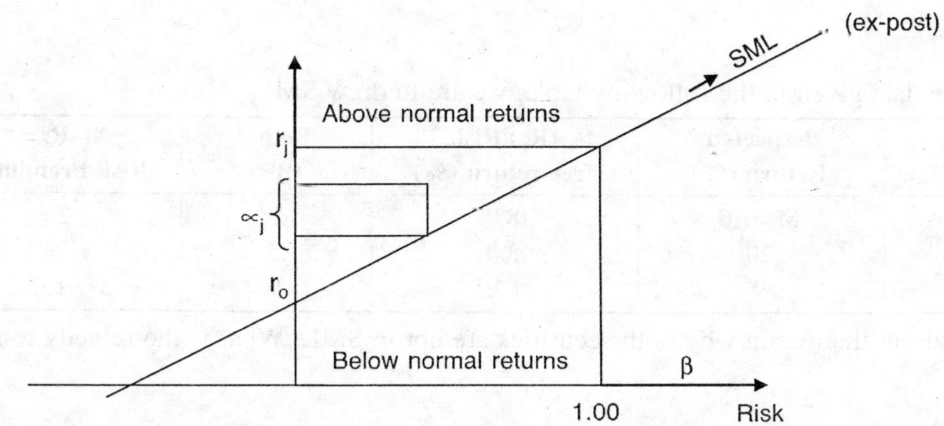

The securities plotted above the ex-post SML, generate above normal returns for their market risk (β), and *vice versa*.

An ex-ante SML

SML can be written as –

Normal expected return or required return :

$$A_j = R_F + \beta_j (M - R_F)$$

Where, R_F = Risk-free interest rate

$M - R_F$ = slope of SML

= Risk premium

$$\beta = E(R_j) - [R_F + \beta_j (M - R_F)]$$

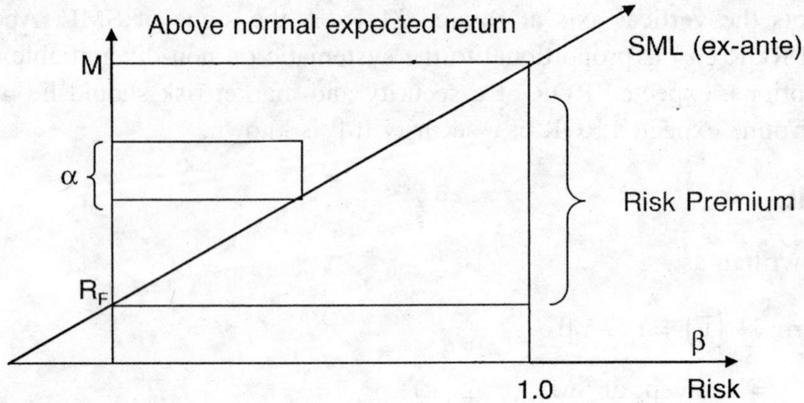

In the ex-ante SML, average expected rates of return (ex-ante) for securities are plotted against their market risks (β).

The securities plotted above the ex-ante SML, generate above normal expected return for their market risk (β) and *vice versa*.

Illustration 7

From the data given in the following table, we are to draw SML

	Expected Return (%)	(R_F) Risk free return (%)	Beta (β)	$M–R_f$ = Risk Premium
Market	M = 10	8.0	1.0	2
Security A	20	8.0	1.2	?
Security B	9	8.0	1.9	?

Also find out the reason why both securities are not in SML. What is the remedy to reach equilibrium?

Solution

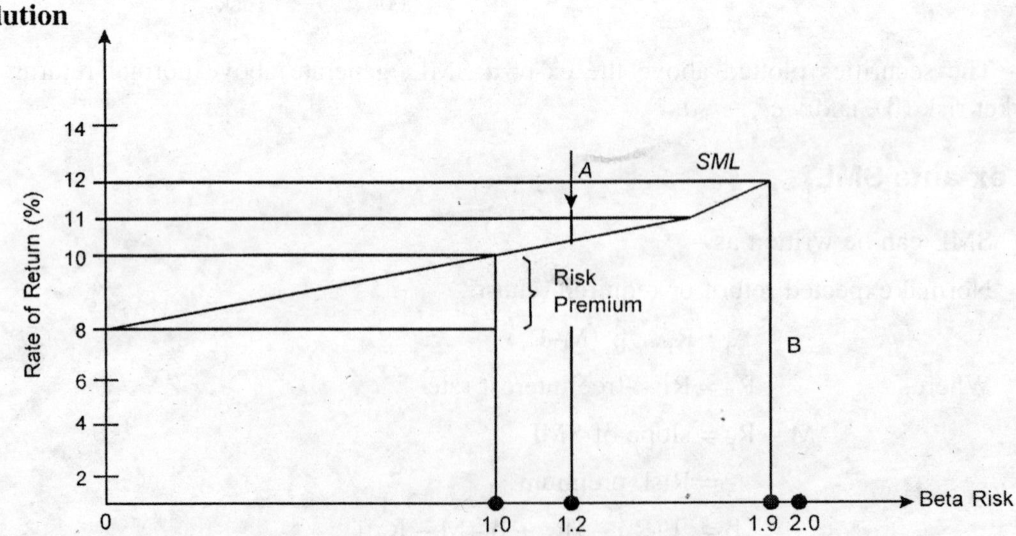

Both securities should have been on the SML but are not. The expected rate of return of A is 20%. But at a beta of 1.2, using SML, the required rate of return need be only around 11%. This tells us that security A is undervalued or prices took low.

On the other hand, security B with a beta of around 1.9, has expected rate of return is 9%. But using SML, the required rate of return need be around 12%. Hence, the security B is overvalued or overpriced and therefore, unattractive.

Securities A and B should move toward their equilibrium – expected rate of return must be equal to required rate of return.

Expected return [see para 3.4]

$$\text{On the SML} = \frac{D+(P_n - P_o)}{P_o}$$

To reach equilibrium, both securities A and B has to go for price adjustment.

In case of Security A, the denominator of the formula (P_o) has to be increased so that expected return of A has to be brought down equal to required rate of return and be plotted on SML.

On the other hand, in case of Security B the denominator (P_o) has to be reduced so that expected return of B has to be brought up equal to required rate of return and be plotted on SML.

SUMMARY

Risk measures the variability or dispersion of future returns, *i.e.*, risk implies either actual nature is higher than expected one or lower than compacted one. This is because we cannot predict accurately about the future cash inflows due to inability to anticipate the occurrence of the possible future events with certainty. There is no authentic definition of return. It, basically, is the form of reward to the investors whose objective is to maximize it from his investments, subject to various constraints, particularly risk. An investor generally selects a portfolio that helps to bring a balance between the risk involved and the expected returns from the portfolio. An aggressive investor undertakes high risk and expects high return. But an average investor expects maximum return but with minimum risk.

The variability of returns is the measure of the risk. Standard deviation (σ) is the best measure of variability of returns on dispersion, which is duly weighted by probability of outcomes. The portfolio risk on 2-assets portfolio may be lower than the risk of individual investments due to diversification. It the returns are positively correlated (r = 1), risk cannot be reduced through the process of diversification. Diversification helps to reduce risk even up to 0 level if returns are perfectly negatively correlated (r = –1).

CAPM is based on the principal that the required rate of retirn of a security equals to risk-free rate of return along with risk premium. The required rate of return is expected by the investors who are in firm belief that firm will earn this return on its equity. Therefore, it can be taken as cost of equity capital of the firm. Beta (β_j) measures the systematic risk. Higher the riskiness of a security, the higher the beta and *vice versa*.The standard deviation of a portfolio is certainly a good and best measure of variability of returns on dispersion but to the extent that if addition of a security to the portfolio increases the standard deviation of the portfolio, the stock adds risk to that portfolio.

EXERCISE

Short Questions

1. Define 'Risk'.
2. What are the most common measures of riskiness of security?
3. What is 'Unsystematic risk'?
4. What is 'Systematic Risk'?
5. What are the types of Return?
6. What is Security Market Line?

Moderate and Broad Questions

1. How do you measure expected return and risk of individual securities?
2. How does diversification reduce risk?
3. What is CML? How would you select 'efficient' and 'inefficient' portfolio through CML?
4. What is a market portfolio? How would you measure expected return of market portfolio?
5. What is SML? Explain it in relation to risk and return.
6. What does portfolio beta (β) indicate? How do you measure it?
7. Explain CAPM model along with its assumptions.
8. What does 'beta' in CAPM represent?. How would you measure bate factor of a security?
9. How do you measure the expected rate of return and risk in case of two-assets portfolio?
10. Which is the best measure of risk in case of a diversified investor and shy?

Problems

1. Given below are the returns with probabilities of occurrence of shares of a public limited company:

Probability	Returns (%)
0.15	5
0.25	8
0.20	10
0.30	12
0.10	4

   (a) What is expected value of return?

   (b) How would you measure the risk and what is its value?

2. A security has a beta coefficient of 1.2, its required rate of return on the market is 15% p.a. and its risk free interest rate is 8% p.a. What is the required rate of return?

3. Ift a 12.5%, ₹ 1000, bond was purchased for ₹ 1200 and the price of the bond rises to ₹ 1400 by the end of the current financial year. What is the rate of return of this bond?
4. The beta coefficient of ABC Ltd. Is 1.6. The company has been maintaining 8% rate of growth in dividends and earnings. The last dividend paid was ₹ 6 per share. Return on govt. securities is 9% and return on market portfolio is 12%. The current market price of ABC Ltd. ₹ 30.

   (a) What will be the equilibrium price/share of ABC Ltd.?

   (b) Would you advise purchasing the share?

[Hints:

(a) $$E\ (R) = ke = \frac{D}{P} + g$$

$$E\ (R) = 9\% + (12\text{-}9) \times 1.6\%$$

Now, $$E\ (R) = \frac{D}{P} + g$$

Or, $$E\ (R) = \frac{6 \times 1.08}{P} + .08]$$

(b) It current market price of ₹ 30 is below P on equilibrium price, it is advisable to purchase share

5. Risk-free return $(R_F) = 10\%$.

σ_f (no risk) = 0

Expected return from risky

Portfolio (A) = 20%

$\sigma_A = 15\%$

If an investor decide to invest 40% in R_F oriented security and 60% in risky portfolio A, what will be the expected rate of return and risk from the portfolio?

[Hints:

Expected rate of return = (10% × .40) + (20% × .60)

Expected risk = (0 × .40) + (15% × .60)]

6.

Companies	Mean $(\overline{X})$ %	Standard deviation (σ)
A Ltd.	0.75	8.75
B Ltd.	0.82	7.03

Coefficient of correlation = 0.37

(a) Calculate covariance between the stocks of A Ltd. and B Ltd.

[Hints:

$$r_{AB} = \frac{COV(A, B)}{\nabla_A \cdot \nabla_B}$$

Or, $$Cov_{(A,B)} = r_{AB} .\ \sigma_A \cdot \sigma_B$$

$$= 0.37 \times 8.75 \times 7.03]$$

(b) Calculate variance and standard deviation of the above portfolio comprising stocks of A Ltd. and B Ltd., subject to the following information's:

Proportion of investment in A Ltd., stock = $\frac{2}{3}$

Proportion of investment in B Ltd., stock = $\frac{1}{3}$

Also calculate portfolio mean return

[Hints:

Portfolio mean return

$$= 0.86\% \times \frac{2}{3} + 0.82\% \times \frac{1}{3}$$

Portfolio variance

$$= W_A^{\ 2} \ \sigma_A^{\ 2} \times W_B^{\ 2} \ \sigma_B^{\ 2} + 2W_A . W_B . r_{AB} . (\sigma_A . \sigma_B)$$

$$= \frac{2^2}{3^2} \times (8.75)^2 + \frac{1^2}{3^2} \times (7.03)^2 + 2. \frac{2}{3} \times \frac{1}{3} \times .37 \times 8.75 \times 7.03$$

Portfolio S.d. $= \sqrt{\text{portfolio variance}}$]

❑ ❑ ❑

4 Valuation of Securities

4.1 CONCEPT OF VALUATION, INTRINSIC VALUE AND OTHER VALUES

Valuation is the process of determination of the worth of an asset. Valuation of securities refers to the determination of the worth of financial assets.

Value of a financial asset depends on the cash inflow which is expected during the life of that asset. The cash inflows are either series of dividends or interest receivable. A security can be valued as the present value of those future cash streams, which is alternatively called as 'intrinsic value'. In this process the cash flows are discounted with the required rate of return which is linked with risk.

Mathematically, it can be represented as follows:

$$V_0 = \frac{C_1}{(1+i)^1} + \frac{C_2}{(1+i)^2} + \frac{C_3}{(1+i)^3} + \ldots\ldots\ldots\ldots + \frac{C_n}{(1+i)^n} = \sum_{t=1}^{n} \frac{C_n}{(1+i)^n}$$

Where, V_0 = Present Value / intrinsic value of the asset at time (t) is zero.

C_n = Expected cash flow at the end of period 'n'

i = Required rate of return or discount rate or required rate of interest

n = Expected life of an asset.

Alternatively,

V_0 = annual cash flow × PVIFA (i%, n years)

Different concepts of value:

Book Value: It refers to the value of the historical cost of the asset or cost of acquisition minus amortized value.

$$\text{Book value / share} = \frac{\text{Networth}}{\text{No. of shares outstanding}}$$

Where Net worth = Book value of assets – book value of liabilities

Market Value: It refers to current price at which a financial asset or a security is bought or sold in the financial market, or in other words, in the price at which a security is traded.

Face Value: It refers to the par value or value at which shares are issued or value stated on the face of the bond. 'Below face value' refers to discount and 'above face value' refers to premium.

Redemption Value: It is the amount which a redeemable preference share holder or redeemable debenture gets on maturity either at par or at a premium – or at a discount. In other words, it refers to 'maturity value' of a redeemable preference share or bond after a certain period of time.

Liquidation Value: It is the minimum amount a company can realize from sale of financial assets after that company terminates business.

Illustration 1

Calculate the value of a financial asset if the annual cash inflow is ₹ 3000 per year for the next four years and the discount rate is 18%.

Solution

Year	*PVIF @ 18%*
1	$\frac{1}{1+0.18} = 0.84745$
2	$\frac{0.84745}{1+0.18} = 0.71818$
3	$\frac{0.71818}{1+0.18} = 0.60863$
4	$\frac{0.60863}{1+0.18} = 0.51578$
	PVIFA = 2.69004

The value of the assets (Intrinsic value)

$= A \times PVIFA$

$=$ Annual cash inflow $\times$ PVIFA

$= 3000 \times 2.69004$

$=$ ₹ 8070.12

Alternatively: By using PVIFA table

$V_0 =$ Annual Cash inflow $\times$ PVIFA (18%, 4 years)

$= 3000 \times 2.69004$

$=$ ₹ 8070.12

4.2 VALUATION OF IRREDEEMABLE, REDEEMABLE BONDS, ZERO COUPON BONDS, BOND-YIELD MEASURES — CONCEPT OF CURRENT YIELD AND YTM

A bond or debenture is a negotiable promissory note of long–term debt issued by a borrower. The rate of interest is fixed and known to investors.

A. Present Value of a Redeemable Bond or Debenture: (has a definite maturity period)

$V_0 =$ Present Value of interest + present value of principal at the end of maturity period.

$$= \frac{I_1}{(1+K_d)^1} + \frac{I_2}{(1+K_d)^2} + \dots\dots\dots \frac{I_n + M}{(1+K_d)^n}$$

When, $V_0 =$ Present value of the bond or debenture

$I =$ Annual interest payment

$M =$ Maturity Value of the bond or debenture

$K_d =$ cost of bond/debenture or the capitalization rate or the discount rate

Alternatively, [Using PVIFA and PVIF tables]

$V_0 = I \times$ PVIFA (K_d%, n years) + $M \times$ PVIF (K_d%, nth year)

Illustration 2

A 8% infrastructural bond of ₹ 1000, issued by a company, will mature in four years. The capitalization rate is 6%. Calculate the present value of the bond or what is the price he would be willing to pay now to purchase the bond?

Solution

Year	*PVIF @ 18%*
1	$\frac{1}{1+0.06} = 0.94339$
2	$\frac{0.94339}{1+0.06} = 0.88999$
3	$\frac{0.88999}{1+0.06} = 0.83961$
4	$\frac{0.83961}{1+0.06} = 0.79209$
	PVIFA = 3.46508 = 3.465

Present Value, V_0

$= I \times$ PVIFA (6%, 4 years) + M $\times$ PVIFA (6%, 4th year)

= (80 × 3.465) + (1000 ´0.792)

= 277.2 + 792

= ₹ 1069.2

The investor is willing to pay maximum ₹ 1069.2 for the bond today.

Alternatively,

$$V_0 = \frac{I_1}{(1+K_d)^1} + \frac{I_2}{(1+K_d)^2} + \frac{I_3}{(1+K_d)^3} + \frac{I_4 + M}{(1+K_d)^4}$$

$$= \frac{80}{(1+.06)^1} + \frac{80}{(1+.06)^2} + \frac{80}{(1+.06)^3} + \frac{80+1000}{(1+.06)^4}$$

= 80 × 0.943 + 80 × 0.890 + 80 × 0.840 + 1080 × 0.792

= 75.44 + 71.20 + 67.20 + 855.36

= ₹ 1069.20

- **Bond/Debenture values with semi-annual interest:**

$$V_0 = \sum_{t=1}^{2n} \frac{I/2}{\left(1+\frac{k_d}{2}\right)^t} + \frac{M}{\left(1+\frac{k_d}{2}\right)^{2n}}$$

$$= \frac{I}{2}\left(\text{PVIFA}_{\frac{K_d}{2},\ 2n}\right) + M\left(\text{PVIF}_{\frac{K_d}{2},\ 2nth}\right)$$

Where, V_0 = Present value of the bond or debenture

I/2 = Semi-annual interest payment

M = Maturity value

$K_d/2$ = required rate of return for the half-year period.

2n = maturity period expressed in half-yearly periods

Illustration 3

A debentures of ₹ 5000 value caries a coupon rate of 10% and a maturity period of four years. If the required rate of return is 14% and interest is payable semi-annually, calculate the present value of the debenture.

$$\text{Present Value, } V_0 = \sum_{t=1}^{2\times4} \frac{500/2}{\left(1+\frac{0.14}{2}\right)^t} + \frac{5000}{\left(1+\frac{0.14}{2}\right)^{2\times4}}$$

$$= \sum_{t=1}^{8} \frac{250}{(1+0.07)^t} + \frac{5000}{(1+0.07)^8}$$

$$= \frac{500}{2}\ (PVIFA_{7\%,\,8}) + 5000(PVIF_{7\%,\,8th})$$

$$= 250 \times 5.971 + 5000 \times 0.582$$

= ₹ 1492.75 +2910

= ₹ 4402.75

B. Present Value of an Irredeemable or Perpetual Bond or Debenture:

(Has no specified maturity period)

$$V_0 = \frac{I}{K_d}$$

Where, I = annual interest payment

K_d = capitalization rate or discount rate

V_0 = present value of the irredeemable bond or debenture

Illustration 4

There is one 9%, ₹ 1000 irredeemable debenture issued by a public limited company. The capitalization rate is 6%. What is the present value of the debenture?

Solution

$$V_0 = \frac{I}{K_d} = \frac{9\% \times 1000}{0.06} = \frac{90}{0.06}$$

= ₹ 1500

4.3. ZERO COUPON BONDS: (DEEP DISCOUNT BONDS)

Features:

1. Long-term bonds (maturity: 25-30 years)
2. They have no coupon rate (no interest to be paid)
3. There bonds are issued at a discount to their face value
4. Face value is the amount payable to the holders on maturity
5. Effective interest earned by the investors
   = Amount payable after maturity – Discounted issue price

Illustration 5

A company issued zero coupon bond of the face value of ₹ 500000 payable after 20 years at an issue price of ₹ 100000. What is the effective interest and interest rate earned by an investor from this bond?

Solution

$$\text{Effective interest} = 500000 - 100000$$
$$= ₹\ 400000$$
$$A = P\,(1 + r)^n$$
Or, $$500000 = 100000\,(1 + r)^{20}$$
Or, $$5 = (1 + r)^{20}$$
Or, $$1 + r = 5^{1/20}$$
Or, $$r = 5^{1/20} - 1 = 1.083798387 - 1 = .0838 = 8.38\%$$

Bond Yield Measures:

A. Current Yield: It is rate of return on a bond if it is purchased at its current market price and the coupon interest is received.

$$\text{Current yield} = \frac{\text{Coupon interest}}{\text{Current market price}}$$

Illustration 6

An investor buys a bond at a current market price of ₹ 900, whose face value is ₹ 1000, maturity period of three years with a coupon interest rate of 9%. Calculate the current field (CY) or rate of return earned on that bond?

Solution

$$\text{Interest payable} = \text{Rate of interest } (\%) \times \text{Face Value}$$
$$= 9\% \times 1000$$
$$= ₹\ 90$$
$$CY = \frac{\text{Coupon interest}}{\text{Current market price}}$$
$$= \frac{90}{900} = 10\%$$

B. Yield to Maturity (YTM): YTM is the rate of return on a bond if it is held till maturity. It is ROR earned if it is purchased at its current market price and coupon interest is received but investors hold the bond till maturity. YTM is the discount rate equaling the present value of cash flows to the market price that means YTM determines the market value of the bond.

Illustration 7

A bond has a face value of ₹ 10000 with a maturity period of 10 years. Its current market price is ₹ 9500. The interest rate offered by the company is 10%. What will be the rate of return on the bond if it is held till its maturity?

Solution

$$V_0 = P_0 = I \times PVIFA\ (k_{d\%,\ n\ years}) + F \times PVIF\ (k_{d\%,\ nth\ year})$$

$$L.H.S = 1000 \times PVIFA\ (k_{d\%,\ 10\ years}) + 10000\ PVIF\ (k_{d\%,\ 10th\ year})$$

$$R.H.S. = 9500$$

To find out the value of k_d, Trial and Error method is to be followed. We are to start with a value of k_d. It L.H.S. < R.H.S. we are to take then lesser value of discount rate.

However, if k_d lies between 2 discount rates with an attempt of equaling L.H.S. to R.H.S., we are to interpolate to find out k_d.

Alternatively,

Since the above method is a very tedious procedure and it takes a lot of time, the following formula can be used to get a rough idea about k_d

$$YTM = \frac{I + \dfrac{F - P}{n}}{\dfrac{F - P}{2}}$$

Where,

I = Annual Interest Payment

F = Face value of the bond

P = Current market price of the bond

N = Number of years to maturity

$$YTM = \frac{1000 + \dfrac{10000-9500}{10}}{\dfrac{10000 + 9500}{2}}$$

$$= \frac{1000 + 50}{9750}$$

$$= \frac{1050}{9750}$$

$$= 10.7692\%$$

4.4 VALUATION OF IRREDEEMABLE, REDEEMABLE PREFERENCE SHARES

A. Present Value of a Redeemable Preference Share : (has a definite maturity period)

V_0 = Present Value of Dividend Payment + Present Value of Preference Share at the end of maturity period

$$= \frac{D_1}{(1+K_p)^1} + \frac{D_2}{(1+K_p)^2} + \ldots\ldots + \frac{D_n + M}{(1+K_p)^n}$$

Where, V_0 = Present Value of the preference share

D = Annual Dividend Payment

M = Maturity Value of the preference share.

K_p = Capitalization/discount rate.

Alternatively, $V_0 = D \times \text{PVIFA}\ (K_{d\%,\ n\ years}) + M \times \text{PVIF}\ (K_{d\%,\ nth\ year})$

Illustration 8

A company has issued 6% redeemable preference shares of ₹ 100 each. The discount rate is 5%. The shares are redeemable after 5 years. Calculate the present value of a preference share.

Solution

Year	*PVIF @ 5%*
1	$\frac{1}{1+0.05} = 0.952$
2	$\frac{0.952}{1+0.05} = 0.907$
3	$\frac{0.907}{1+0.05} = 0.864$
4	$\frac{0.864}{1+0.05} = 0.823$
5	$\frac{0.823}{1+0.05} = 0.784$
	PVIFA = 4.330

The value of the redeemable preference share, V_0

$= D \times \text{PVIFA}_{(5\%,\ 5years)} + M \times \text{PVIF}_{(5\%,\ 5th\ year)}$

$= 6 \times 4.330 + 100 \times 0.784$

$= 25.98 + 78.40 =$ ₹ 104.38

Alternatively,

$$V_0 = \frac{D_1}{(1+K_p)^1} + \frac{D_2}{(1+K_p)^2} + \frac{D_3}{(1+K_p)^3} + \frac{D_4}{(1+K_p)^4} + \frac{D_5 + M}{(1+K_p)^5}$$

$$= \frac{6}{(1+0.5)^1} + \frac{6}{(1+.05)^2} + \frac{6}{(1+.05)^3} + \frac{6}{(1+.05)^4} + \frac{6+100}{(1+.05)^5}$$

$$= 6 \times 0.952 + 6 \times 0.907 + 6 \times 0.864 + 6 \times 0.823 + 106 \times 0.784$$

$$= 5.712 + 5.442 + 5.184 + 4.938 + 83.104$$

$$= ₹\ 104.38$$

B. Valuation of an Irredeemable or Perpetual Preference Share (has no specified maturity period)

$$V_0 = \frac{D}{K_p}$$

Where, D = annual dividend payment
K_p = capitalization/discount rate
V_0 = present value of the irredeemable preference share

Illustration 9

A company issued 9% irredeemable preference shares of ₹ 100 each. The capitalization rate is 8%. What is the present value of the preference share?

Solution

$$V_0 = \frac{D}{K_P} = \frac{9}{0.08}$$

$$= ₹\ 112.5$$

4.5 VALUATION OF EQUITY SHARES

Valuation of Equity shares is based two approaches:

A. Dividend Capitalization Approach

According to this approach, the value of an equity share is equivalent to the present value of future dividends plus the present value of the price expected to be realized on its re-sale.

Assumption:

1. Dividends are paid annually
2. The dividend is received after the expiry of a year of purchase of equity share.

Single Period Valuation Model:

$$P_0 = \frac{D_1}{(1+k_e)} + \frac{P_1}{(1+k_e)}$$

When, P_0 = Current price of the equity share.

D_1 = Dividend per share expected at the end of 1st year.

P_1 = Expected market price of the share at the end of 1st year.

K_e = the required rate of return or capitalization rate.

Illustration 10

An equity share of ₹ 10 is expected to earn an annual dividend of ₹ 2 and the share will be sold for ₹ 18 after a year. The required rate of return is 12%. Calculate the value of the equity share.

Solution

$$P_0 = \frac{D_1}{(1+K_e)} + \frac{P_1}{(1+K_e)}$$

$$= \frac{2}{1+0.12} + \frac{18}{1+0.12}$$

$$= ₹\ 17.86$$

Multi-period Valuation Model

Case (i): *When the dividend rate is constant*

$$P_0 = \frac{D_e}{K_e}$$

Where, P_0 = Current value of an equity share

D_e = Expected annual dividend per equity share

K_e = The required rate of return or capitalization rate.

Illustration 11

A Company is currently paying a dividend of ₹ 25 per share. It is expected that the company will pay the same rate in future. Calculate the present value of the share if the required rate of return is 10%.

Solution

$$P_0 = \frac{D_e}{K_e} = \frac{25}{0.10} = ₹\ 250$$

***Case (ii)**: When there is a constant growth in dividends.*

$$P_0 = \frac{D_1}{K_e - g}$$

Where, D_1 = Dividend at the end of the year.

K_e = Capitalization rate

g = Growth rate in dividends

Illustration 12

Prajna Ltd. is expected to pay a dividend of ₹ 4 per equity share. The dividend is expected to grow at 8%. The current capitalization rate is 12%. Find the value of the Equity share.

Solution

$$P_0 = \frac{D_1}{K_e - g}$$

$$= \frac{4}{0.12 - 0.08} = ₹\ 100$$

***Case (iii)**: When there is a variable growth in dividends*

Illustration 13

A company is expected to pay a dividend of ₹ 10 per share after a year. Its dividends are then expected to grow at 10% for next three years and then at the rate of 7% indefinitely. Find out the present value of its share, if the capitalization rate is 12%.

Solution

Step (i): *Present value of dividends*

Years	*Dividends*	*P.V. Factor @ 12%*	*Present Value*
1	10	0.893	8.93
2 (10 + 10%)	11	0.797	8.767
3 (11 + 10%)	12.1	0.712	8.615
4 (12.1 + 10%)	13.31	0.636	8.465
5 (13.31 + 7%)	14.24	0.567	8.07
			42.847

Step (ii) : The dividend for the 6th year is likely to be:

$$14.24 + 14.24 \times \frac{7}{100}$$

$$= 14.24 + 0\ .9968$$

$$= 15.2368$$

Applying the formula for valuation of shares under constant growth in dividend, for finding out present value at the end of year 5, *i.e.*

$$P_5 = \frac{D_6}{K_e - gn}$$

Where, P_5 = Present value of share at the end of year 5

D_6 = Expected Dividend for the 6th year.

gn = Normal growth in dividends.

K_e = Capitalization rate.

On substituting,

$$P_5 = \frac{15.2368}{0.12 - 0.07}$$

$$= \frac{15.2368}{0.05}$$

$$= ₹\ 304.736$$

Step (iii): Present value of shares

$$= 304.736 \times 0.567$$

$$= 172.785$$

Step (iv): Value of share = Present value of the share + Present value of dividends

$$= 172.785 + 42.847 = 215.632$$

B. Earning Capitalization Approach

Under the following two cases, the value of an equity share can be determined by capitalizing the expected earnings.

(*i*) When the earnings of the firm are stable

(*ii*) When there is no growth but simply there is only expansion situation.

$$P_0 = \frac{E_1}{K_e}$$

Where, E_1 = Expected earnings per share

K_e = Capitalization rate.

P_0 = Current value of an equity share.

Illustration 14

Calculate the price of an equity share when the earnings of the firm are stable, EPS = ₹ 20, Capitalization rate = 10%, and Retained Earnings = Nil.

Solution

$$P_0 = \frac{E_1}{K_e}$$

$$= \frac{20}{.10} = ₹\ 200$$

SUMMARY

Valuation is the process of determination of the worth of an asset. Valuation of securities refers to the determination of the worth of financial assets.

Value of a financial asset depends on the cash inflow which is expected during the life of that asset. The cash inflows are either series of dividends or interest receivable. A security can be valued as the present value of those future cash streams, which is alternatively called as 'intrinsic value'. There are different concepts of value. Book value refers to the value of the historical cost of the asset or cost of acquisition minus amortized value. Market value refers to current price at which a financial asset or a security is bought or sold in the financial market, or in other words, in the price at which a security is traded. Face value refers to the par value or value at which shares are issued or value stated on the face of the bond. Redemption value is the amount which a redeemable preference share holder or redeemable debenture gets on maturity either at par or at a premium – or at a discount. Liquidation Value is the minimum amount a company can realize from sale of financial assets after that company terminates business.

Current yield is rate of return on a bond if it is purchased at it's current market price and the coupon interest is received. YTM is the rate of return on a bond if it is held till maturity. It is ROR earned if it is purchased at its current market price and coupon interest is received but investors hold the bond till maturity. YTM is the discount rate equaling the present value of cash flows to the market price that means YTM determines the market value of the bond.

EXERCISE

Short Questions

1. What is called 'valuation'?
2. What is 'intrinsic value'?
3. What is the difference between book value and market value?
4. What is bond?
5. What is liquidation value?
6. What is current yield?
7. What is redemption value?

Moderate and Broad Questions:

1. Explain the meaning and importance of valuation concept. How does valuation concept help in decision making?

2. Explain the two approaches of valuation of equity shares.
3. What are the features of Zero Coupon bond? How to calculate the effective interest? Explain it by an example.
4. How will you value redeemable preference shares?

Problems:

1. XYZ bank pays 12% and compounds interest quarterly. If ₹ 1000 are deposited initially, how much shall it grow at the end of 5 years.

   [**Ans.** 1806]
2. A debenture of ₹ 1000 carries a coupon rate of 14%. It is to mature after 5 years. The required rate of return is 13%. Calculate the value of the debenture.

   [**Ans.** ₹ 1035.40]
3. Mr. X holds an equity share giving him an annual dividend of ₹ 20. He expects to sell the share of ₹ 180 at the end of a year. Calculate the value of the share if the required rate of return is 12%.

   [**Ans.** 178.57]
4. A Company has a share capital of ₹ 50,00,000. The company has the policy of retaining 60% of its earnings. Calculate the growth rate in dividends if the company earns 10% on its capital employed.
5. XYZ Ltd. Is expected to pay a dividend at ₹ 40 per share? Dividends are expected to grow perpetually at 10%. Calculate the market value of the share if capitalization rate is 15%.

   [**Ans.** ₹ 800]
6. ABC Ltd. is expected to pay a dividend of ₹ 4 per share after a year. Its dividends are then expected to grow at 15% for next 5 years and then at the rate of 8% indefinitely. Find the present value of its share, if the capitalization rate is 12%.

   [**Ans.** 133.13]

❑❑❑

5 Introduction to Indian Financial System

5.1 INTRODUCTION TO INDIAN FINANCIAL SYSTEM

Financial System and its Importance

A financial system functions as an intermediary and facilitates the flow of funds from the areas of surplus to the areas of deficit. It may be defined as a set of institutions, instruments and markets which fosters savings and channels them to their most efficient use.

The system consists of the following sub-systems:

- Various Financial Institutions
- Financial Instruments
- Markets
- Users of savings (government, public and private sector entities)
- Regulations and laws
- Practices
- Money Managers
- Analysts
- Transactions
- Claim and liabilities
- Intermediaries

Economic activity and growth are greatly facilitated by the existence of a financial system developed in terms of the efficiency of the market in mobilizing savings and allocating them among competing users. Market efficiency would be reflected in wide dissemination of information, reduction of transaction costs, volume of credit and allocation of capital to the most productive uses which can be ensured by an effective financial system.

Since the liberalization of the economy in 1992-93 and the initiation of reform measures, the financial system is getting market-oriented. Economic reform aimed freeing the financial system from government interference along with improvement of financial viability and institutional strengthening. The RBI issued several measures aimed at encouraging disciplined NBFCs.

5.2 FUNCTIONS OF FINANCIAL SYSTEM

When the savings flows decline the growth of investment and living standard begins to fall. Similarly when the savings flows increase the growth of investment and living standard begins to improve. Savings of suppliers of funds (mainly households) find their way into the hand of those in production through the financial system.

Liquidity Function

The value of money is mostly eroded by inflation. Therefore, the investors always like to invest in financial instruments like, stock, bond, debentures etc. The financial market helps the investors to liquidate the investments that is conversion of the claims into money.

Payment Function

In India, the cheque system of payment is widely practiced, The credit card system is existing in urban area only to pay for consumption expenditure. Through these payments system adopted by the financial system, the cost and time of tram actions are reduced.

Risk Function

Financial System helps investor to protect themselves against life, health and income risks. There are life, health accidental, fire, property insurance policies. The financial markets provide immense opportunities for the investor to hedge himself against or reduce the possible risks.

Growth Function

Financial markets within the financial system have made possible the exchange of current income for future income and transformation of savings into investments, so the production and income grow.

5.3 INDIAN FINANCIAL MARKET – MONEY MARKET AND CAPITAL MARKET

Indian financial market was highly segmented until the initiation of reforms in 1992-93.

After reforms, broad linkage among the money market, government securities market and foreign exchange market has been established. The financial system consists of the capital market and money market.

Capital Market

Corporates need long term funds with tenure of 365 days or more for the purpose of meeting capital expenditure like acquiring technology, machinery, undertaking capacity expansion, strategic acquisition of other companies etc. Capital Market is important for the economic development of the country.

The capital market provides the fund resources needed by medium and large-scale industries by channeling long-term funds (with more than 1 year maturity). *The capital market consists of primary and secondary markets.*

Primary market deals with the issue of new instruments by the corporate sector such as equity shares, preference shares and debentures. The issue includes the following:

(a) Issue of bonds and shares as a part of disinvestment of government holdings;

(b) New issues by non-government companies, banks and financial institutions;

(c) New issue of shares and bonds through private placement markets; etc.

Secondary market is the one which provides liquidly and marketability to those long term instruments earlier created by the primary market. The secondary market consists of 23 stock exchanges including the NSE (National Stock Exchange), the OTCEI (Over-the-Counter Exchange of India) and ISEIL (International Stock Exchange of India Ltd.)

Relationship between Primary and Secondary Market

The primary market creates long-term instruments through which corporate entities borrow from the capital market. But the secondary market is the one which provides liquidity and marketability to these instruments. There is a very close interaction between primary and secondary market. It the secondary market is active and mobile it enables the corporate entities to enter the new issue market depends upon the activities of the primary market because it is only when corporate sectors or business sectors enter into the market and raise funds through the capital market that more financial instruments are available in the secondary market for the purpose of improved activities in this market. Small investors and highly net-worth individual invest in the primary market if secondary marketly provides liquidity of the financial instruments or securities.

Primary Market

Primary market deals with the issues of securities like shares, bonds and debentures from where the corporate entities raise capital to meet the financial requirements of their projects. Public buys securities directly from the issuing company. The important guidelines relating to the primary market concern the following

(a) Registration of merchant bankers

(b) Issue of securities, registering venture capital funds. (SEBI Regulation).

(c) Mergers and Amalgamations.

Companies sell their new stocks or bonds for the first time to the public in this market. It is otherwise called as Initial Public Offering (IPO).

SEBI

A. SEBI – Introduction

Public issues of the companies were controlled by the Capital Issue Control act, 1947. Pricing of the issues were determined by the Controller of Capital Issues. The objective was to prevent the diversion of investible resources to non-essential projects. The above Act was repealed on May 29, 1992 and CCI was abolished as the practice of government control over capital issues as well as overpricing of issues has lost its relevance in the changed circumstances. The SEBI Act, 1992 was established and as a consequence, the issue of capital and pricing of issue by corporate entities had become free of prior approval. The objective of the SEBI Act, 1992 was to ensure proper disclosure and investor protection through issuing certain guidelines. The Govt. of India empowered SEBI (The Securities and Exchange Bond of India) as the role authority for regulating the issuance and transfer of shares of listed companies. The regulations issued by the SEBI may be grouped under primary and secondary markets. Mutual Funds are also regulated by SEBI.

B. SEBI – Guidelines (A few)

The guidelines broadly cover the requirements as to the first issue by new companies and existing private/closely held companies and also further issues of capital by the companies by way of shares, debentures and bonds. The guideline applies to all the issues of capital.

SEBI has issued guidelines of the following matters:

Book building

Public issues

Rights issues

Bonus issues

Debentures issues

Take over of companies

Underwriting

Private placement

Pricing of issues

Venture capital etc.

- Companies are allowed to issue capital provided the issues are in conformity with the published guidelines relating to disclosure and other matters relating to investors protection.
- Subscription list for public issues should be kept open for three working days and it should be mentioned in the prospectus. But in the case of rights issue, it should not be kept open for more than 60 days.

- Companies are required to convert their partly paid-up shares into fully paid-up or forfeit the same, before making a public/rights issue.
- No prior approval of SEBI is required by the companies for raising capital through public issues, rights, in the capital market, subject to the fulfillment of certain criteria.
- The quantum of rights or public issue should not exceed the amount specified in the prospectus or letter of offer. No retention of oversubscription is permitted.
- In case of issue at premium, the amount payment on application, allotment and calls by each applicant shall not be less than ₹ 5000, irrespective of the size of the premium.
- In case of public issue at par, the minimum number of shares for which the application is to be made should be fixed at 200 shares of the face value of ₹ 10 each.
- In case of fully convertible debentures (FCD), SEBI restricts the conversion period to 36 months, except the conversion is made optional with call and put options.
- Credit rating is required for all kinds of debentures.
- In case of non-convertible dentures, a Debenture Redemption Reserve (DRR) has to be created.

C. Major Players in the Primary Market

Merchant Bankers

Mutual Funds

Financial Institution

Foreign Institutional Investors (FIIs)

Individual Investors

D. Function of SEBI

The SEBI was constituted by the govt. in April 1988, with a objective to regulate and promote securities market, as a supervision body to ensure the following :

- Protection of the investors and safeguard their rights and interest
- Steady flow of savings into the market
- Control of horde of malpractices on the part of the companies, stock brokers, merchant bankers, investment consultants involved in new issues.
- Promoting fair dealings by the issuers

E. Power of SEBI

- Power to make or amend bye laws of Stock Exchange or to direct recognized stock exchanges to make rules;
- Licensing of dealers in securities in certain areas;

- Power to compel a public company to list its share in any Stock Exchange;
- Power to regulate depositories, custodians, debenture trustees and trust deeds, FIIs, insider trading, merchant bankers, mutual funds, portfolio managers, stock brokers etc.
- Power to appoint any person to make inquiries into the affairs of the Stock Exchange;
- Power to call for direct enquiries or periodical returns from Stock Exchanges, subject to the fulfillment of certain criteria;
- Powers to supersede the governing body on to suspend business of any recognized Stock Exchange;
- Powers to ask every Stock Exchange to furnish a copy of the annual report containing particulars that may be prescribed;
- Power to call upon the Stock Exchange or any member of the exchange to furnish relevant information.

F. Types of Issue of Shares and Debentures

- Public issue – Raising of funds directly from the public
- Rights issue – Raising additional funds from existing shareholders by offering on pro-rata basis through a 'letter of offer'.
- Bonus issue – issuing bonus shares in lieu of cash div. to existing shareholders for distributing profits, in the ratio of existing shares held
- Private placement – sale of shares or debentures directly by a public or private. Limited Co., to a limited no. of sophisticated investor's like UTI, LIC, UIC, SFC. The merchant bankers, credit rating agencies, financial advisors are the intermediates.
- Brought-out doals – equity shares are offered to a — sponsor/mechant banker who, in turn, buys and off loads the shares to the public at a later date or disinvest in favour of the public at an appropriate time.

Secondary Market

The secondary market is that segment of capital market where the outstanding securities are traded. From the investor's point of view, the secondary market imparts liquidity to the long-term securities held by them by providing an auction market for these securities. The secondary market operates through the medium of Stock Exchanges which regulate the trading activities in this market and ensure a measure of safety and fair dealing to the investors. The salient and striking feature of the secondary market is that the investors trade among themselves. It does not include issuing companies and investors trade previously-traded securities.

A. Type of Secondary Market

(a) ***Auction Market*** **–** All individuals and institutions assemble to trade securities at one area and announce the prices at which they are willing to purchase or buy. The NYSE is the best example of an Auction a Market which is the largest Stock Exchange in the world.

(b) Dealer Market – Individuals on companies will specialize in specific securities and buy or sell according to the demand of the market. Over-the-counter markets as a grouped under dealer markets as the demand and supply for particular stocks is not enough to meet the requirements of different investors. Most bonds are traded in dealer market and NASDAQ is an example for dealer market.

B. Effect of Liberalization of the Financial System

In the area of secondary markets, measures to control volatility and transparency in dealings have been taken by adoption of the followings:

- Dematerializing the shares by setting up depositories and trading in derivatice securities
- On line trading which is screen- based (In OTCEI, NSE)
- Rolling and uniform settlement
- Initiating regulatory measures to protect integrity of markets

C. Major Players in the Secondary Market

- The stock brokers who are members of the Stock Exchanges
- Individual Investors
- Mutual Funds
- Financial Institutions
- Foreign Institutional Investors (FII)

D. Stock Exchanges

The first Indian Stock Exchange established at Mumbai in 1875. The Stock Exchange is an auction market in shares and other securities. A bull is the buyer and a bear is the seller in the market. Stock Exchanges regulate the trading activities and ensure a measure of safety and fair dealing to the investors.

Trading System: Earlier Trading on all Stock Exchanges, was being carried out by "public outcry" 'in the trading ring which was an out-dated and in efficient system, resulted lack of transparency in trade. The first exchange to introduce screen based trading in India was the Over the Counter Exchange of India (OTCEI). After the commence of the activities of National Stock Exchange (NSE), the screen based trading received a big boost since trading terminals were set up all over the country for getting nationwide access to investors and terminals were networked through satellite links. The trading system in now fully automated enabling market participants to login orders, execute deals. The competition from NSE forced the regional Stock Exchanges including BSE to switch over to screen based trading.

E. Types of Trading

- Order driven – NSE Trading system is order driven.
- Quote driven – OTCEI system is quote driven.
- Mixed – BSE online trading (BOLT) is a mixture of both quote system and order driven system.

All orders are captured and matched with each other to execute the transaction under order driven system. On the other hand, dealer gives two way quotes and the order logged in its matched against the best quote given by the market maker.

F. Depositors

Earlier there was problem in physical storage and transfer as the securities were held in the form of certificates. The transaction costs were also higher due to physical movement of paper and the incidence of stamp duty. NSDL (National Securities Depository Ltd) was the first depository in India which holds the securities in electronic form on behalf of the investor. Further it also handles collection of dividends, credit for bonus, exercising of warrants, etc. on behalf of the investor.

Money Markets

Money Market deals with short-term fund requirement. The funds are available for the period of a single day to one year. The instruments in the money market are of short-term nature and highly liquid. The market where short time finance is borrowed and lent is called money market. Money market performs the following functions:

(i) It provides on equilibrating mechanism to balance demand for and supply of short-term funds to meet daily expenses like purchase, wage payment etc.

(ii) It provides a focal point for the RBI for its invention in the markets for the purpose of influencing liquidity and interest rates in the economy.

(iii) It provides access to providers and users of short-term funds to fulfill their borrowing and investment requirements.

A. Major Constituent of Money Market:

RBI: (Reserve Bank of India) – Its function in Money Market –

The most important constituent of money market is RBI who ensures that liquidity and short-term interest rates are maintained at levels required for achieving objectives of monetary policy. The development and regulation of money markets in the Indian Financial System is an important function of RBI.

RBI introduced new instruments reducing dependence of participants on uncollateralized exposure, facilitate price discovery in the short-end and upgrades the payment system infrastructure.

For the past few years, the RBI has been trying to develop a proper short-term rupee yield curve with deep liquidity in the money markets.

RBI's strategically efforts broadly aimed at the following development of Indian Money Market:

(i) Development of the payment system infrastructure with the introduction of the Negotiated Dealing System (NDS) and formation of the Clearing Corporation of India Ltd. (CCIL) and the implementation of Real time Gross Settlement (RTGS) system in March 2004

(ii) Development of call/notice money market with a view to augmenting short-term liquidity

(iii) Stability in the short-term interest rates within a certain range through Market Stabilization Scheme (MSS) Launched in April 2004 and Open Market Operations (OMO)

(iv) Transferring the call/notice markets into a pure inter-bank market with participation of banks and primary dealers.

(v) Measures to make various other money market instruments, *e.g.,* CDs, CPs freely accessible to non-bank participants.

(vi) Introducing repose operations foreign exchange purchase, enhancing government securities, refinancing to stabilize call rate.

B. Money Market Instruments

Money-market instrument is a document issued by the debtor or creditor of short-term nature (less than 1 year) the claim on which is early transferable.

(i) Govt. and quasi-government securities.
- Treasury Bills (T-Bills)
- Government Dated Securities/Gilt-Edges Securities

(ii) Banking Sector Securities
- Call and Notice Money Market
- Certificate of Deposit (CDs)
- Participation Certificates

(iii) Private Sector Securities
- Bills of Exchange (commercial) and trade bills/factorization bills)
- MMMF (Money Market Mutual Fond)
- Corporate Bonds/Debentures
- Commercial Paper (CPs)
- Inter-Corporate Deposits/Investments

C. Money Market Players

Players	Role
1. RBI	Regulatory
2. Government	Borrower/Issuer
3. Banks (Commercial and co-operative)	Borrowers/lenders
4. Dealers	Intermediaries
5. Insurance Companies	Lenders
6. Corporates	Issuers/lenders
7. FIIs	Investors
8. Mutual funds	Investors
9. Discount and Acceptance Houses	Market Makers
10. Other small players	Investors/Borrowers
11. Financial Institutions (FIs)	Investors/Borowers

Central Government is a borrower in the money market through the issue of T-Bills. The T-Bills are issued through the RBI. The PSU can issue commercial paper in order to obtain its working capital finance. Being cash surplus entities, both general and life insurance companies are usual leaders in the money market, though they invest more in capital market instruments. Mutual Funds offer verities of schemes for the different objectives of the public, *e.g.*, MMMF or Liquid Schemes – Schedule Commercial Banks are very big borrowers and lenders in the money market. They borrow and lend in call money market, short and notice market, repo and reverse repo market. Corporates borrow by issuing commercial papers which are nothing but short-term promissory notes which can be issued after obtaining the necessary credit ratio. They are the lenders to the lanks which they buy CDs issued by the banks.

.4 FINANCIAL INSTITUTIONS

The financial institutions are divided in two categories. The first type refers to the regulatory titutions and the second type refers to the intermediaries.

The regulators are assigned with the job of governing all the divisions of the Indian ncial system. These regulatory institutions are responsible for maintaining the transparency the national interest in the operations of the institutions under their supervision.

The regulatory bodies of the financial institutions in India are as follows:

- Reserve Bank of India (RBI)
- Securities and Exchange Board of India (SEBI)
- Central Board of Direct Taxes (CBDT)
- Central Board of Excise and Customs

part from the Regulatory bodies, there are the Intermediaries that include the banking and nking financial institutions. Some of the specialized financial institutions in India are as f

(a) Unit Trust of India (UTI)

(b) Securities Trading Corporation of India Ltd. (STCI)

(c) Industrial Development Bank of India (IDBI)

(d) Industrial Reconstruction Bank of India (IRBI), now (Industrial Investment Bank of India)

(e) Export-Import Bank of India (EXIM Bank)

(f) Small Industries Development Bank of India (SIDBI)

(g) National Bank for Agriculture and Rural Development (NABARD)

(h) Life Insurance Corporation of India (LIC)

(i) General Insurance Corporation of India (GIC)

(j) Shipping Credit and Investment Company of India Ltd. (SCICI)

(k) Housing and Urban Development Corporation Ltd. (HUDCO)

(l) National Housing Bank (NHB)

The banking institutions of India play a major role in the economy of the country. The banking institutions are the providers of depository and transaction services. These activities are the major sources of creating money. The banking institutions are the major sources of providing loans and other credit facilities to the clients.

Apart from the banking financial institutions, there are a number of specialized financial institutions in India that have been incorporated for a definite purpose. These institutions include the insurance companies, the housing finance companies, mutual funds, merchant banks, credit reporting and debt collection companies and many more.

Apart from these, there are several other financial institutions that are existing in the country. These are the stock brokers and sub-brokers, portfolio managers, investment advisors, underwriters, foreign institutional investors and many more.

5.5 COMMERCIAL BANKS IN INDIA

Commercial Banks in India are broadly categorized into Scheduled Commercial Banks and Unscheduled Commercial Banks. The Scheduled Commercial Banks have been listed under the Second Schedule of the Reserve Bank of India Act, 1934. The selection measure for listing a bank under the Second Schedule was provided in Section 42 (60) of the Reserve Bank of India Act, 1934.

Activities of Commercial Banks:

The modern Commercial Banks in India cater to the financial needs of different sectors. The main functions of the commercial banks comprise.

(a) transfer of funds

(b) acceptance of deposits

(c) offering those deposits as loans for the establishment of industries

(d) purchase of houses, equipments, capital investment purposes etc.

(e) The banks are allowed to act as trustees. On account of the knowledge of the financial market of India the financial companies are attracted towards them to act as trustees to take the responsibility of the security for the financial instrument like a debenture.

(f) The Indian Government presently hires the commercial banks for various purposes like tax collection and refunds, payment of pensions etc.

Some Lists of Commercial Banks in India

SBI & Associates:

1. State Bank of India
2. State Bank of Bikaner and Jaipur
3. State Bank of Hyderabad
4. State Bank of Indore
5. State Bank of Mysore
6. State Bank of Patiala
7. State Bank of Travancore

Nationalized Banks:

1. Allahabad Bank
2. Andhra Bank
3. Bank of Baroda
4. Bank of India
5. Bank of Maharashtra
6. Canara Bank
7. Central Bank of India
8. Corporation Bank etc.

Foreign Banks:

1. ABN Amro Bank
2. Abu Dhabi Commercial Bank
3. American Express Banking Corporation
4. Antwerp Diamond Bank
5. AB Bank
6. Bank International Indonesia
7. Bank of America etc.

Other Scheduled Commercial Banks:

1. Axis Bank
2. Bank of Rajasthan
3. Catholic Syrian Bank
4. City Union Bank
5. Development Credit Bank
6. Dhanalakshmi Bank
7. Federal Bank
8. HDFC Bank
9. ICICI Bank
10. Indusind Bank
11. ING Vysya Bank
12. Jammu & Kashmir Bank etc.

5.6 FINANCIAL SECTOR REFORMS IN INDIA

Financial sector reforms are at the centre stage of the economic liberalization that was initiated in India in mid 1991. This is partly because the economic reform process itself took place amidst two serious crises involving the financial sector:

(a) the balance of payments crisis that threatened the international credibility of the country and pushed it to the brink of default;

(b) the grave threat of insolvency confronting the banking system which had for years concealed its problems with the help of defective accounting policies. Moreover, many of the deeper rooted problems of the Indian economy in the early nineties were also strongly related to the financial sector;

(c) the problem of financial repression in the sense of McKinnon-Shaw (McKinnon, 1973; Shaw, 1973) induced by administered interest rates pegged at unrealistically low levels;

(d) large scale pre-emption of resources from the banking system by the government to finance its fiscal deficit;

(e) excessive structural and micro regulation that inhibited financial innovation and increased transaction costs;

(f) relatively inadequate level of prudential regulation in the financial sector;

(g) poorly developed debt and money markets; and

(h) outdated (often primitive) technological and institutional structures that made the capital markets and the rest of the financial system highly inefficient.

The following sections review the progress of financial sectors in some key areas:

Exchange Control and Convertibility

One of the early successes of the reforms was the speed with which exceptional financing was mobilized from multilateral and bilateral sources to avert what at one stage looked like a imminent default on the country's external obligations. Subsequently, devaluation, trade reforms and the opening up of the economy to capital inflows helped to strengthen the balance of payments position.

The significant reforms in this area were:

(a) Exchange controls on current account transactions were progressively relaxed culminating in current account convertibility.

(b) Foreign Institutional Investors were allowed to invest in Indian equities subject to restrictions on maximum holdings in individual companies. Restrictions remain on investment in debt, but these too have been progressively relaxed.

(c) Indian companies were allowed to raise equity in international markets subject to various restrictions.

(d) Indian companies were allowed to borrow in international markets subject to a minimum maturity, a ceiling on the maximum interest rate, and annual caps on aggregate external commercial borrowings by all entities put together.

(e) Indian mutual funds were allowed to invest a small portion of their assets abroad.

(f) Indian companies were given access to long dated forward contracts and to cross currency options.

Banking and Credit Policy

At the beginning of the reform process, the banking system probably had a negative net worth when all financial assets and liabilities were restated at fair market values (Varma 1992). This unhappy state of affairs had been brought about partly by imprudent lending and partly by adverse interest rate movements. At the peak of this crisis, the balance sheets of the banks, however, painted a very different rosy picture. Accounting policies not only allowed the banks to avoid making provisions for bad loans, but also permitted them to recognize as income the overdue interest on these loans. The severity of the problem was thus hidden from the general public. The threat of insolvency that loomed large in the early 1990s was, by and large, corrected by the government extending financial support of over ₹ 100 billion to the public sector banks.

The banks have also used a large part of their operating profits in recent years to make provisions for non-performing assets (NPAs). Capital adequacy has been further shored up by revaluation of real estate and by raising money from the capital markets in the form of equity and subordinated debt. With the possible exception of two or three weak banks, the public sector banks have now put the threat of insolvency behind them.

The major reforms relating to the banking system were:

(a) Capital base of the banks were strengthened by recapitalization, public equity issues and subordinated debt.

(b) Prudential norms were introduced and progressively tightened for income recognition, classification of assets, provisioning of bad debts, marking to market of investments.

(c) Pre-emption of bank resources by the government was reduced sharply.

(d) New private sector banks were licensed and branch licensing restrictions were relaxed. At the same time, several operational reforms were introduced in the realm of credit policy.

(e) Detailed regulations relating to Maximum Permissible Bank Finance were abolished.

(f) Consortium regulations were relaxed substantially.

(g) Credit delivery was shifted away from cash credit to loan method.

The government supports to the banking system of ₹ 100 billion amounts to only about 1.5% of GDP. By comparison, governments in developed countries like the United States have expended 3-4% of GDP to pull their banking systems out of crisis (International Monetary Fund, 1993) and governments in developing countries like Chile and Philippines have expended far more. However, it would be incorrect to jump to the conclusion that the banking system has been nursed back to health painlessly and at low cost. The working results of the banks for 1995-96 which showed a marked deterioration in the profitability of the banking system was a stark reminder that banks still have to make large provisions to clean up their balance sheets completely. Though bank profitability improved substantially in 1996-97, it will be several more years before the unhealthy legacy of the past (when directed credit forced banks to lend to uncreditworthy borrowers) is wiped out completely by tighter provisioning. It is pertinent to note that independent estimates of the percentage of bank loans which could be problematic are far higher than the reported figures on non-performing assets worked out on the basis of the central bank's accounting standards. For example, a recent report estimates potential (worst case) problem loans in the Indian banking sector at 35-60% of total bank credit pessimism, but the lower end of the range is perhaps a realistic assessment of the potential problem loans in the Indian banking system. The even more daunting question is whether the banks' lending practices have improved sufficiently to ensure that fresh lending (in the deregulated era) does not generate excessive non-performing assets (NPAs). That should be the true test of the success of the banking reforms. There are really two questions here. First, whether the banks now possess sufficient managerial autonomy to resist the kind of political pressure that led to excessive NPAs in the past through lending to borrowers known to be poor credit risks. Second, whether the banks' ability to appraise credit risk and take prompt corrective action in the case of problem accounts has improved sufficiently. It is difficult to give an affirmative answer to either of these questions.

Turning to financial institutions, economic reforms deprived them of their access to cheap funding via the statutory pre-emptions from the banking system. They have been forced to raise resources at market rates of interest. Concomitantly, the subsidized rates at which they used to lend to industry have given to market driven rates that reflect the institutions' cost of funds as well as an appropriate credit spread. In the process, institutions have been exposed to competition from the banks who are able to mobilize deposits at lower cost because of their large retail branch network. Responding to these changes, financial institutions have attempted to restructure their businesses and move towards the universal banking model prevalent in continental Europe. It is too early to judge the success of these attempts.

Interest rate deregulation and financial repression

Perhaps the single most important element of the financial sector reforms has been the deregulation of interest rates.

(a) Interest rates were freed on corporate bonds, most bank lending, and bank deposits above one year maturity.

(b) Introduction of auctions coupled with reduced pre-emption led to more market determined interest rates for government securities.

(c) Administered interest rates are now confined mainly to short-term bank deposits, priority sector lending, and deposits of non-banking financial companies. For all practical purposes, financial repression is a thing of the past. Even on short-term retail bank deposits which are still regulated, the ceiling rate is well above the historic average rate of inflation. Moreover, quite often the ceiling has not been a binding constraint in the sense that actual interest rates have often been below the regulatory ceiling.

Similarly, the prices of most other financial assets are also now determined by the more or less free play of market forces. Consequently, financial markets are increasingly able to perform the important function of allocating resources efficiently to the most productive sectors of the economy. This must count as one of the most enduring and decisive successes of the financial reforms.

Capital Market's Reform

The major reform in the capital market was the abolition of capital issues control and the introduction of free pricing of equity issues in 1992. Simultaneously the Securities and Exchange Board of India (SEBI) was set up as the apex regulator of the Indian capital markets. In the last five years, SEBI has framed regulations on a number of matters relating to capital markets. Some of the measures taken in the primary market include:

(a) Entry norms for capital issues were tightened.

(b) Disclosure requirements were improved.

(c) Regulations were framed and code of conduct laid down for merchant bankers, underwriters, mutual funds, bankers to the issue and other intermediaries. In relation to the secondary market too, several changes were introduced:

(d) Capital adequacy and prudential regulations were introduced for brokers, sub-brokers and other intermediaries.

(e) Dematerialization of scrips was initiated with the creation of a legislative framework and the setting up of the first depository.

(f) On-line trading was introduced at all stock exchanges. Margining system was rigorously enforced.

(g) Settlement period was reduced to one week; carry forward trading was banned and then reintroduced in restricted form; and tentative moves were made towards a rolling settlement system.

In the area of corporate governance:

(a) Regulations were framed for insider trading

(b) Regulatory framework for take-overs was revamped

SEBI has been going through a protracted learning phase since its inception. The apparent urgency of immediate short term problems in the capital market has often seemed to distract SEBI from the more critical task of formulating and implementing a strategic vision for the development and regulation of the capital markets. In quantitative terms, the growth of the Indian capital markets since the advent of reforms has been very impressive. The market capitalization of the Bombay Stock Exchange (which represents about 90% of the total market capitalization of the country) has quadrupted from ₹ 1.1 trillion at the end of 1990-91 to ₹ 4.3 trillion at the end of 1996-97. As a percentage of GDP, market capitalization has been more erratic, but on the whole this ratio has also been rising. Total trading volume at the Bombay Stock Exchange and the National Stock Exchange (which together account for well over half of the total stock market trading in the country) has risen more than ten-fold from ₹ 0.4 trillion in 1990-91 to ₹ 4.1 trillion in 1996-97. The stock market index has shown a significant increase during the period despite several ups and downs, but the increase is much less impressive in dollar terms because of the substantial depreciation of the Indian rupee It may also be seen from the chart that after reached its peak in 1994-95, the stock market index has been languishing at lower levels apart from a brief burst of euphoria that followed an investor friendly budget in 1997. For the primary equity market too, 1994-95 was the best year with total equity issues (public, rights and private placement) of ₹ 355 billion.

Thereafter, the primary market collapsed rapidly. Equity issues in 1996-97 fell to one-third of 1994-95 levels and the decline appears to be continuing in 1997-98 as well. More importantly, most of the equity issues in recent months have been by the public sector and by banks. Equity issues by private manufacturing companies are very few.

Structural Deregulation

In its midterm review of the reform process (Ministry of Finance, 1993a), the government stated: "Our overall strategy for broader financial sector reform is to make a wide choice of instruments accessible to the public and to producers. This requires a regulatory framework which gives reasonable protection to investors without smothering the market with regulations. ... It requires the breaking up of monopolies and promotion of competition in the provision of services to the public. ... It requires the development of new markets such as security markets for public debt instruments and options, futures and forward markets for financial instruments and commodities."

Unfortunately, this is one area where actual progress has lagged far behind stated intent. It is true that some steps have been taken to increase competition between financial intermediaries both within and across categories. Banks and financial institutions have been allowed to enter each other's territories. Fields like mutual funds, leasing, merchant banking have been thrown open to the banks and their subsidiaries. The private sector has been allowed into fields like banking and mutual funds. Nevertheless, major structural barriers remain:

All major banks and financial institutions continue to be government owned and government managed :

(a) The entire mechanism of directed credit and selective credit controls built up over the years is still in place, and is being strengthened in certain areas.

(b) Financial intermediaries have often been compelled to set up separate arms' length subsidiaries while entering various segments of the financial services industry. This has prevented them from benefiting from economies of scope.

(c) Competition has also been hindered by the undiminished power of cartels like the Indian Banks Association (IBA). In fact, these cartels have been accorded the tacit support of the regulators. Similarly, the Securities and Exchange Board of India (SEBI) has been reluctant to permit aggressive competition among the different stock exchanges. These half hearted attempts at promoting competition raise fears about the extent to which our regulators have succumbed to regulatory capture by the organizations that they are supposed to regulate.

(d) Insurance continues to be a public sector monopoly. As a result, financial products which combine the features of life insurance with those of equity related instruments have not developed. The range of insurance products (life and non-life) available in the country is also limited.

(e) The regulators have not yet moved to create a full fledged options and futures market.

(f) On the technological front, progress has been slow in important areas. The payment system continues to be primitive despite the central bank's attempts to create an Electronic Fund Transfer System (EFTS). Archaic elements of the telecom regulations have prevented the financial services industry from benefiting from the confluence of communications and computing technologies.

Monetary Policy and Debt Market's Reform

In the early nineties, the Indian debt market was best described as a dead market. Financial repression and over-regulation were responsible for this situation. Reforms have eliminated financial repression and created the pre-conditions for the development of an active debt market:

(a) The government reduced its pre-emption of bank funds and moved to market determined interest rates on its borrowings. Simultaneously, substantial deregulation of interest rates took place as described earlier.

(b) Automatic monetization of the government's deficit by the central bank was limited and then eliminated by abolishing the system of *ad hoc* treasury bills. Several operational measures were also taken to develop the debt market, especially the market for government securities:

(c) Withdrawal of tax deduction at source on interest from government securities and provision of tax benefits to individuals investing in them

(d) Introduction of indexed bonds where the principal repayment would be indexed to the inflation rate.

(e) Setting up of a system of primary dealers and satellite dealers for trading in government securities

(f) Permission to banks to retail government securities

(g) Opening up of the Indian debt market including government securities was made to Foreign Institutional Investors. Meanwhile a spate of well subscribed retail debt issues in 1996 and 1997 shattered the myth that the Indian retail investor has no appetite for debt. While only ₹ 6 billion was raised through public debt issues in 1994 and ₹ 11 billion in 1995, the amounts raised in 1996 was ₹ 56 billion. Debt accounted for more than half of the total amount raised through public issues in 1996 compared to less than 10% two years earlier. In 1997, public issues of debt fell to ₹ 29 billion, but with the collapse of the primary market for equity, the share of debt in all public issues increased to 57%. Meanwhile, private placement of debt (which is a much bigger market than public issues) has grown very rapidly. Private placement of debt jumped from ₹ 100 billion in 1995-96 to ₹ 181 billion in 1996-97; in the first half of 1997-98, it grew again by over 50% with ₹ 136 billion mobilized in these six months alone1. India is perhaps closer to the development of a vibrant debt market than ever before, but several problems remain:

(h) The central bank has repeatedly demonstrated its willingness to resort to micro-regulation and use market distorting instruments of monetary and exchange rate policy rather than open market operations and interventions For example, as late as 1996, the central bank was relying on moral suasion and direct subscriptions to government securities (devolvements) to complete the government's borrowing programme. The RBI's response to the pressure on the rupee in late 1997 and early 1998 also reveal an undiminished penchant for micro-regulation.

(i) Some of the vibrancy of debt markets in 1996 and 1997 was due to the depressed conditions in the equity markets.

(j) Little progress has been made on the major legal reforms needed in areas like bankruptcy, foreclosure laws, and stamp duties.

All figures in this paragraph are from the Prime database on the primary market in India.

Corporate Law

Two successive governments have introduced legislation for comprehensive overhaul of the corporate law in India, but neither of them lasted long enough to get the proposals enacted into law. Some administrative simplifications have been carried out in areas like managerial remuneration and inter-corporate investments, but the major reforms in corporate governance and disclosure await a new government.

Impact on Corporate Sector

Corporate Governance

In the mid nineties, corporate governance became an important area of concern for regulators, industrialists and investors alike. Indian industry considered the matter important enough for them to propose model corporate governance code (Bajaj, 1997). However, the major pressure for better corporate governance came from the capital markets. Capital markets have always had the potential to exercise discipline over promoters and management alike, but it was the structural changes created by economic reform that effectively unleashed this power. Minority investors can bring the discipline of capital markets to bear on companies by voting with their wallets. They can vote with their wallets in the primary market by refusing to subscribe to any fresh issues by the company. They can also sell their shares in the secondary market thereby depressing the share price. Financial sector reforms set in motion several key forces that made these forces far more potent than in the past:

Deregulation: Economic reforms have not only increased growth prospects, but they have also made markets more competitive. This means that in order to survive companies will need to invest continuously on a large scale. The most powerful impact of voting with the wallet is on companies with large growth opportunities that have a constant need to approach the capital market for additional funds.

Disintermediation: Meanwhile, financial sector reforms have made it imperative for firms to rely on capital markets to a greater degree for their needs of additional capital. As long as firms relied on directed credit, what mattered was the ability to manipulate bureaucratic and political processes; the capital markets, however, demand performance.

Globalization: Globalization of our financial markets has exposed issuers, investors and intermediaries to the higher standards of disclosure and corporate governance that prevail in more developed capital markets.

Institutionalization: Simultaneously, the increasing institutionalization of the capital markets has tremendously enhanced the disciplining power of the market. Large institutions (both domestic and foreign), in a sense, act as the gatekeepers to the capital market. When they vote with their wallets and their pens, they have an even more profound effect on the ability of the companies to tap the capital markets. Indian companies that opened their doors to foreign investors have seen this power of the minority shareholder in very stark terms. International investors can perhaps be fooled for the first time about as easily as any other intelligent investor, but the next time around, the company finds that its ability to tap the international markets with an offering of Global Depository Receipts (GDRs) or other instrument has practically vanished. In the mid-90s, company after company in India has woken up in this manner to the power that minority shareholders enjoy when they also double up as gatekeepers to the capital market.

Tax reforms: Tax reforms coupled with deregulation and competition have tilted the balance away from black money transactions. It is not often realized that when a company makes profits in black money, it is cheating not only the government, but also the minority shareholders. Black money profits do not enter the books of account of the company at all, but usually go into the pockets of the promoters. The past few years have witnessed a silent revolution in Indian corporate governance where managements have woken up to the disciplining power of capital markets. In response to this power, the more progressive companies are voluntarily accepting tougher accounting standards and more stringent disclosure norms than are mandated by law. They are also adopting more healthy governance practices. Nevertheless, it is still true that the state of corporate governance in India remains pathetic. It is this more than anything else that lies behind the prolonged slump in the primary market today.

Risk Management

In the days when interest rate were fixed by the government and remained stable for long periods of time, interest rate risk was a relatively minor problem. The deregulation of interest rates as a part of financial sector reform has changed all that and made interest rates highly volatile. For example, the rate of interest on short-term commercial paper was about 12-13% at the end of 1994, rose to about 17% by the end of 1995, peaked at about 20% in April 1996, dropped back to about 13% by the end of 1996, continued to fall through 1997 reaching about 8% in November 1997 before climbing back to double digits by the end of the year. Companies which borrow short-term to fund their new projects may face difficulties if interest rates go up sharply. It may turn out that at the higher cost of finance, the project is not viable at all. Worse, companies may find it difficult to refinance their borrowings at any price in times when money is tight. Many companies which borrowed in the Inter Corporate Deposit (ICD) market in 1994 to finance acquisitions and expansions faced this difficulty in 1995 and 1996 when the ICD market dried up. Large scale defaults (euphemistically described as rollovers) took place during this time. On the other hand, companies which issue long term bonds may start regretting the decision when they find interest rates coming down. In the last few years, companies have tried to protect themselves from this risk by introducing a call provision in their bonds by which they can redeem the bonds prematurely under certain conditions. Of course, such call options make the bonds more expensive (in terms of a higher coupon rate) or more difficult to sell.

Companies have also tried to make the bonds more attractive to investors by giving them a put option to seek premature redemption of the bonds. This may make the bond easier to sell, but it exposes the issuing company to interest rate risk. If interest rates rise, many investors will exercise the put option, and the company will have to borrow from elsewhere at high cost to meet the redemption requirements. Put and call options do make a big difference to the pricing of some of these bonds (Varma 1996a) making the design of these instruments quite complex.

In the next few years, many of these companies would also be faced with the decision of the optimal exercise of the call options on the callable bonds that they have issued in recent years. In the post reform era, corporates have also been faced with high volatility in foreign exchange rates. The rupee-dollar rate has on several occasions moved up or down by several percentage points in a single day as compared to the gradual, predictable changes of the eighties. Indian companies have found to their dismay that foreign currency borrowings which looked very cheap because of a low coupon rate of interest can suddenly become very expensive if the rupee depreciates against the currency in which the bond is denominated. Foreign currency convertible bonds issued by many Indian companies in 1993 and 1994 illustrate the devastating effects of volatility in interest rates, foreign exchange rates and stock prices. At the time of issue, the bonds carried a low coupon rate (often only 2 or 3% in US dollars), and were convertible into stock at prices which were at a modest premium (5 to 10%) over the then prevailing stock price. Issuers thought of them as deferred equity and found the instruments very attractive because they allowed equity to be priced at a premium to the market prices and offered the benefit of a low coupon till the conversion date. As it turned out, stock prices fell during 1995 and 1996, and investors chose not to convert the bonds. Issuers then realized that they would have to redeem the bonds in dollars, and that the depreciation of the rupee has increased their effective borrowing cost substantially. To make worse, investors exercised put options wherever they had them, and companies had to raise money in the domestic markets to pay off the foreign bondholders. In some cases, this happened at a time when Indian monetary policy was extremely tight and interest rates were very high. In this case, volatility in three different markets combined to make things difficult for the companies concerned.

Capital Structure

At the beginning of the reform process, the Indian corporate sector found itself significantly over-levered. This was because of several reasons:

(i) Subsidized institutional finance was so attractive that it made sense for companies to avail of as much of it as they could get away with. This usually meant the maximum debt-equity ratios laid down by the government for various industries.

(ii) In a protected economy, operating (business) risks were lower and companies could therefore afford to take more risks on the financing side.

(iii) Most of the debt was institutional and could usually be rescheduled at little cost. The reforms changed all of this. The corporate sector was exposed to international competition and subsidized finance gave way to a regime of high real interest rates. One of the first tasks for the Indian companies was substantial deleveraging. Fortunately, a booming equity market and the appetite of foreign institutional investors for Indian paper helped companies to accomplish this to a great extent in 1993 and 1994. The downturn in the stock market that has followed since then has stopped this process from going any further and has probably left many companies still excessively levered. According to the figures compiled by the Centre for Monitoring the Indian Economy, the average debt-equity ratio of private sector manufacturing companies in India fell from 1.72 in 1990-91 to 1.05 in 1996-97, and more than half of this reduction took place in one single year - 1994-95. Over the longer term, economic reforms have also been reshaping the control dimension of the leverage decision. Corporate control is an important consideration in the choice of debt or equity in the capital structure. An equity issue clearly involves loss of control, and as discussed under the section on corporate governance, reforms have increased the power of the minority shareholders. Equally, a debt issue also can have control implications in the form of debt covenants, rating discipline and cash flow discipline. Reforms have impacted these too, but more slowly:

(iv) *Bond covenants:* Internationally bond covenants are quite restrictive specially for companies whose credit worthiness is less than top class. These covenants may restrict the investment and dividend policies of the company, may mandate sinking funds, may include cross-default clauses and may contain me-too clauses which restrict the future borrowing ability of the company. Bond covenants have typically been quite lax in India. Moreover bond (and debenture) trustees have been generally very lax in the performance of their duties.

(v) *Rating discipline:* The most dramatic example of the power of rating discipline was demonstrated in 1996 when in the face of a constitutional deadlock between the US President and the Congress over the approval of the budget, the rating agencies threatened to downgrade US government securities to default grade. It was shown that even the most powerful borrower in the world can be subjected to rating discipline; it is believed that the raters' threat played a role in the speedy resolution of the constitutional deadlock. Rating discipline is gradually asserting itself in India. The last couple of years have seen a series of rating downgrades as corporate balance sheets deteriorated in an environment of tight money. Rating agencies are becoming more stringent in their rating standards and are paying greater attention to key financial parameters like the interest coverage ratio (Raghunathan and Varma, 1997). Already some companies are beginning to informally sound out their rating agencies before taking major financial decisions to ensure that their rating is not adversely affected. This is standard practice in many other countries of the world where credit rating is well developed.

(vi) *Cash flow discipline:* Equity has no fixed service costs and year to year fluctuations in income are not very serious so long as overall enough is earned to provide a decent return to the shareholders. Debt on the other hand has a fixed repayment schedule and interest obligation. A company that is unable to generate enough cash flow to meet this debt service requirement faces insolvency or painful restructuring of liabilities. Again,

Indian companies have not experienced much of this discipline in the past because much of their debt was owed to banks and institutions who have historically been willing to reschedule loans quite generously. Institutions may be less willing to do so in future. More importantly, rescheduling is not an easy option when the debt is raised in the market from the public. Bonds are typically rescheduled only as part of a bankruptcy proceeding or a BIFR restructuring. As the next phase of economic reforms targets bankruptcy related laws, cash flow discipline can be expected to become far more stringent.

5.7 IRDA

The Insurance Regulatory and Development Authority (IRDA) is a national agency of the Government of India, based in Hyderabad. It was formed by an act of Indian Parliament known as IRDA Act, 1999, which was amended in 2002 to incorporate some emerging requirements. Mission of IRDA as stated in the act is "to protect the interests of the policyholders, to regulate, promote and ensure orderly growth of the insurance industry and for matters connected therewith or incidental thereto."

In 2010, the Government of India ruled that the Unit Linked Insurance Plans (ULIPs) will be governed by IRDA, and not the market regulator Securities and Exchange Board of India.

The law of India has following expectations from IRDA:

1. To protect the interest of and secure fair treatment to policyholders.
2. To bring about speedy and orderly growth of the insurance industry (including annuity and superannuation payments), for the benefit of the common man, and to provide long term funds for accelerating growth of the economy.
3. To set, promote, monitor and enforce high standards of integrity, financial soundness, fair dealing and competence of those it regulates.
4. To ensure that insurance customers receive precise, clear and correct information about products and services and make them aware of their responsibilities and duties in this regard.
5. To ensure speedy settlement of genuine claims, to prevent insurance frauds and other malpractices and put in place effective grievance redressal machinery.
6. To promote fairness, transparency and orderly conduct in financial markets dealing with insurance and build a reliable management information system to enforce high standards of financial soundness amongst market players.
7. To take action where such standards are inadequate or ineffectively enforced.
8. To bring about optimum amount of self-regulation in day to day working of the industry consistent with the requirements of prudential regulation.

Duties, Powers and Functions of IRDA

Section 14 of IRDA Act, 1999 lays down the duties, powers and functions of IRDA:

(a) Subject to the provisions of this Act and any other law for the time being in force, the Authority shall have the duty to regulate, promote and ensure orderly growth of the insurance business and re-insurance business.

(b) Without prejudice to the generality of the provisions contained in sub-section (1), the powers and functions of the Authority shall include:

1. issue to the applicant a certificate of registration, renew, modify, withdraw, suspend or cancel such registration;
2. protection of the interests of the policy holders in matters concerning assigning of policy, nomination by policy holders, insurable interest, settlement of insurance claim, surrender value of policy and other terms and conditions of contracts of insurance;
3. specifying requisite qualifications, code of conduct and practical training for intermediary or insurance intermediaries and agents;
4. specifying the code of conduct for surveyors and loss assessors;
5. promoting efficiency in the conduct of insurance business;
6. promoting and regulating professional organizations connected with the insurance and re-insurance business;
7. levying fees and other charges for carrying out the purposes of this Act;
8. calling for information from, undertaking inspection of, conducting enquiries and investigations including audit of the insurers, intermediaries, insurance intermediaries and other organizations connected with the insurance business;
9. control and regulation of the rates, advantages, terms and conditions that may be offered by insurers in respect of general insurance business not so controlled and regulated by the Tariff Advisory Committee under Section 64U of the Insurance Act, 1938 (4 of 1938);
10. specifying the form and manner in which books of account shall be maintained and statement of accounts shall be rendered by insurers and other insurance intermediaries;
11. regulating investment of funds by insurance companies;
12. regulating maintenance of margin of solvency;
13. adjudication of disputes between insurers and intermediaries or insurance intermediaries;
14. supervising the functioning of the Tariff Advisory Committee;
15. specifying the percentage of premium income of the insurer to finance schemes for promoting and regulating professional organizations referred to in Clause (f);

16. specifying the percentage of life insurance business and general insurance business to be undertaken by the insurer in the rural or social sector; and
17. exercising such other powers as may be prescribed from time to time, IRDA consists of a Chairman and some permanent as well as part time members. The regulations, however, are enacted under the guidance of a statutory advisory committee.

5.8 FINANCIAL INSTRUMENTS IN INDIA

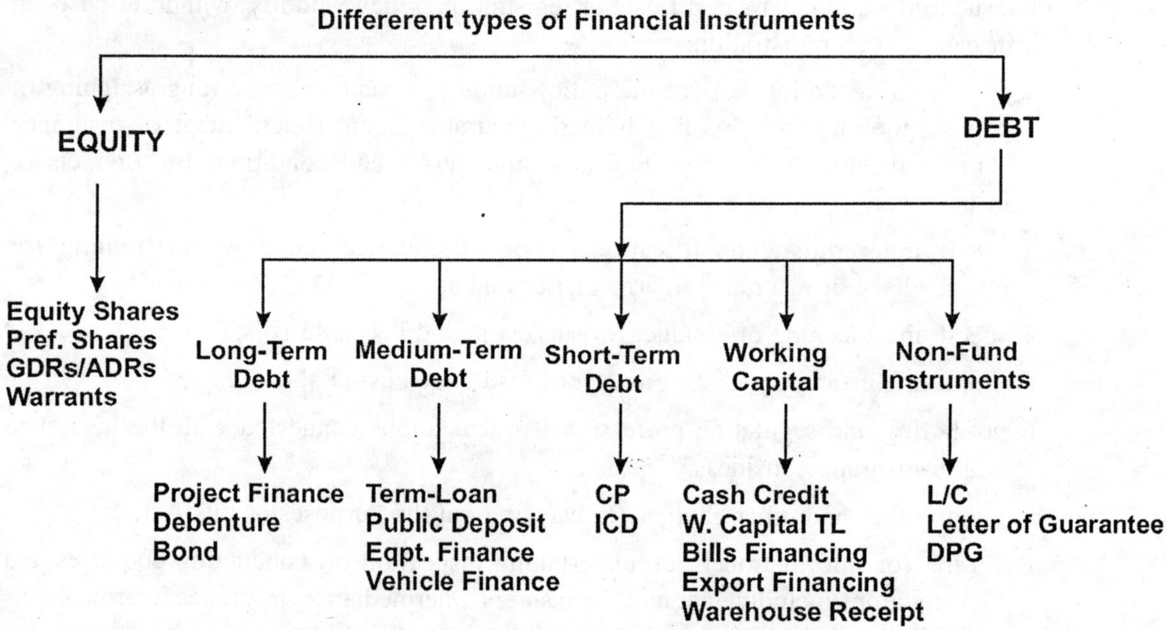

A Money market instruments:

1. Call/Notice Money
2. Treasury Bills
3. Term Money
4. Certificate of Deposit
5. Commercial Papers

1. Call/Notice-Money Market: Call/Notice money is the money borrowed or lent on demand for a very short period. When money is borrowed or lent for a day, it is known as Call (Overnight) Money. Intervening holidays and/or Sunday are excluded for this purpose. Thus money, borrowed on a day and repaid on the next working day, (irrespective of the number of intervening holidays) is : Call Money and quote; When money is borrowed or lent for more than a day and up to 14 days, it is and quote; Notice Money and quote;. No collateral security is required to cover these transactions.

2. Inter-Bank Term Money: Inter-bank market for deposits of maturity beyond 14 days is referred to as the term money market. The entry restrictions are the same as those for Call/ Notice Money except that, as per existing regulations, the specified entities are not allowed to lend beyond 14 days.

3. Treasury Bills: Treasury Bills are short-term (up to one year) borrowing instruments of the union government. It is an IOU of the Government. It is a promise by the Government to pay a stated sum after expiry of the stated period from the date of issue (14/91/182/364 days, *i.e.*, less than one year). They are issued at a discount to the face value, and on maturity the face value is paid to the holder. The rate of discount and the corresponding issue price are determined at each auction.

4. Certificate of Deposits: Certificates of Deposit (CDs) is a negotiable money market instrument and issued in dematerialised form or as a Usance Promissory Note, for funds deposited at a bank or other eligible financial institution for a specified time period. Guidelines for issue of CDs are presently governed by various directives issued by the Reserve Bank of India, as amended from time to time.

CDs can be issued by (i) scheduled commercial banks excluding Regional Rural Banks (RRBs) and Local Area Banks (LABs); and (ii) select all-India Financial Institutions that have been permitted by RBI to raise short-term resources within the umbrella limit fixed by RBI.

Banks have the freedom to issue CDs depending on their requirements. An FI may issue CDs within the overall umbrella limit fixed by RBI, *i.e.,* issue of CD together with other instruments *viz.,* term money, term deposits, commercial papers and inter-corporate deposits should not exceed 100 per cent of its net owned funds, as per the latest audited balance sheet.

5. Commercial Paper: CP is a note in evidence of the debt obligation of the issuer. On issuing commercial paper the debt obligation is transformed into an instrument. CP is thus an unsecured promissory note privately placed with investors at a discount rate to face value determined by market forces. CP is freely negotiable by endorsement and delivery.

A company shall be eligible to issue CP provided — (a) the tangible net worth of the company, as per the latest audited balance sheet, is not less than ₹ 4 crore; (b) the working capital (fund-based) limit of the company from the banking system is not less than ₹ 4 crore and (c) the borrowal account of the company is classified as a Standard Asset by the financing bank's. The minimum maturity period of CP is 7 days. The minimum credit rating shall be P-2 of CRISIL or such equivalent rating by other agencies.

B. Capital Market Instruments: The capital market generally consists of the following long-term period, *i.e.,* more than one year period, financial instruments; In the equity segment Equity shares, preference shares, convertible preference shares, non-convertible preference shares etc and in the debt segment debentures, zero coupon bonds, deep discount bonds etc.

C. Hybrid Instruments: Hybrid instruments have both the features of equity and debenture. This kind of instruments is called as hybrid instruments. Examples are convertible debentures, warrants etc.

SUMMARY

A financial system functions as an intermediary and facilitates the flow of funds from the areas of surplus to the areas of deficit. It may be defined as a set of institutions, instruments and markets which fosters savings and channels them to their most efficient use. The capital market provides the fund resources needed by medium and large-scale industries by channeling long-term funds (with more than 1 year maturity).*The capital market consists of primary and secondary markets.* Primary market deals with the issue of new instruments by the corporate sector such as equity shares, preference shares and debentures. Secondary market is the one which provides liquidly and marketability to those long term instruments earlier created by the primary market. The secondary market consists of 23 stock exchanges including the NSE (National Stock Exchange), the OTCEI (Over-the-Counter Exchange), of India and ISEIL (International Stock Exchange of India Ltd.). Public issues of the companies were controlled by the Capital Issue Control act, 1947. Pricing of the issues were determined by the Controller of Capital Issues. The objective was to present the diversion of investible resources to non-essential projects. The above Act was repealed on May 27, 1992 and CCI was abolished as the practice of government control over capital issues as well as overpricing of issues has lost its relevance in the changed circumstances. The SEBI Act, 1992 was established and as a consequence, the issue of capital and pricing of issue by corporate entities had become free of prior approval. The objective of the SEBI Act, 1992 was to ensure proper disclosure and investor protection through issuing certain guidelines.

The stock exchange is an auction market in shares and other securities. A bull is the buyer and a bear is the seller in the market. Stock Exchanges regulate the trading activities and ensure a measure of safety and fair dealing to the investors. Earlier Trading on all stock exchanges, was being carried out by "public outcry" in the trading ring which was an out-dated and in efficient system, resulted lack of transparency in trade. The first exchange to introduce screen bused trading in India was the Over the Counter Exchange of India (OTCEI). After the commence of the activities of National Stock Exchange (NSE), the screen based trading received a big boost since trading terminals were set up all over the country for getting nationwide access to investors and terminals were networked through satellite links.

The most important constituent of money market is RBI who ensures that liquidity and short-term interest rates are maintained at levels required for achieving objectives of monitory policy. The development and regulation of money markets in the Indian Financial system is an important function of RBI. RBI introduced new instruments reducing dependence of participants on uncollateralized exposure facile rate price discovery in the short-end and upgrades the payment system infrastructure. For the past few years, the RBI has been trying to develop a proper short-term rupee yield curve with deep liquidity in the money markets.

The banking institutions of India play a major role in the economy of the country. The banking institutions are the providers of depository and transaction services. These activities are the major sources of creating money. The banking institutions are the major sources of providing loans and other credit facilities to the clients. Apart from the banking financial institutions, there are a number of specialized financial institutions in India that have been incorporated for a definite purpose. These institutions include the insurance companies, the housing finance companies, mutual funds, merchant banks, credit reporting and debt collection companies and many more. Apart from these, there are several other financial institutions that are existing in the country. These are the stock brokers and sub-brokers, portfolio managers, investment advisors, underwriters, foreign institutional investors and many more.

EXERCISE

Short Questions

1. What is 'Financial System'?
2. What are the subsystems of 'Indian financial system'?
3. What is Primary Market?
4. What is Secondary Market?
5. What are the differences between Money Market and Capital Market?
6. What is Stock Exchange?
7. What was the first depository in India holding the securities in electronic from?
8. None one of the major constituents of Money Market?
9. Mention at least 2 investors and borrowers in the money market?
10. Who the issuer of T – Bills and Government-dated securities on behalf of the Central Government?
11. Who is the first exchange to introduce screen based trading in India?
12. What are the types of issue of shares in the primary market?
13. Give one example of Auction Market?
14. None at least 3 major Players of the Primary Market?
15. What is a Money market instrument? Gove at least 2 examples.

Moderate and Broad Questions

1. What are the Financial Sector Reforms in India? Explain.
2. Explain the role and functions of 2 major Financial Institutions.
3. Explain the importance of IRDA in the Indian Financial System.
4. What is the role of RBI in Indian Money Market? Explain its powers and functions.
5. Who are the money market players and explain their roles?
6. Explain the trading system in the stock market.
7. What are the types of Secondary Market? Explain each ofthem with one example.
8. What are the functions of financial system?
9. What is the impact of liberalization of Indian economy over Indian financial system? What is the impact of liberalization of the financial system over secondary market?

❑❑❑

6 Long-term Sources of Financing and Venture Capital

6.1 CONCEPT OF LONG-TERM SOURCE OF FINANCING

Long-term financing is a form of financing that is provided for a period of more than a year. Long-term financing services are provided to those business entities that face a shortage of capital.

It is different from short-term financing. Short-term financing is normally used to provide money that has to be paid back within a year.

Long-term sources of finance are those that are needed over a longer period of time– generally over a year. The reasons for needing long-term finance are generally different to those relating to short-term finance. Examples of long-term financing include a 30 year mortgage or a 10 year Treasury note. Equity is another form of long-term financing, such as when a company issues stock to raise capital for a new project.

The kind of long-term financing that is provided to a particular company depends on its type. For example, the long-term financing that is provided to a solo proprietorship is different from the long-term financing that a partnership would receive.

Uses of Long-term Financing

Long-term financing is used in separate ways by different types of business entities.

The business entities that are not corporations are only supposed to use long-term financing for the purposes of debt. However, the corporations can use long-term financing for both debt and equity purposes.

6.2 IMPORTANCE OF LONG-TERM FINANCING

Business firms need finance for two purposes:

(a) To fund the long-term decisions
(b) To meet the working capital requirement

The long-term decision of a firm involves setting up of the firm. Expansion, diversification, modernization and other similar capital expenditure decisions. All these decisions involve huge investment, the benefits of which will be seen only in the long-term and these decisions are also irreversible in nature. By nature of these projects, long-term sources of funds become the best suited means of financing. One of the most important considerations for an investment and financing decision will be proper asset-liability-management. Companies will have to face a severe asset-liability mismatch if the long-term requirements are funded by the short-term sources of funds. Such a mismatch will lead to an interest rate risk thereby enhancing the interest burden of the firm and a liquidity risk with the short-term funds being held up in long-term projects.

Purpose of long-term finance

(a) To Finance fixed assets
(b) To finance the permanent part of working capital
(c) Expansion of Companies
(d) Increasing Facilities
(e) Construction Projects on a big Scale
(f) Provides Capital for funding the Operations. This helps in adjusting the cash flow.

6.3 FACTORS DETERMINING LONG-TERM FINANCIAL REQUIREMENTS

The amount required to meet the long-term capital needs of a company depends upon many factors. These are:

(a) Nature of business:

The nature and character of a business determines the amount of fixed capital. A manufacturing company requires land, building, machines etc. So it has to invest a large amount of capital for a long period. But a trading concern dealing in, say, washing machines will require a smaller amount of long-term fund because it does not have to buy building or machines.

(b) Nature of goods produced:

If a business is engaged in manufacturing small and simple articles it will require a smaller amount of fixed capital as compared to one manufacturing heavy machines or heavy consumer items like cars, refrigerators etc. which will require more fixed capital.

(c) Technology used:

In heavy industries like steel the fixed capital investment is larger than in the case of a business producing plastic jars using simple technology or producing goods using labour intensive technique.

6.4 SOURCES OF LONG-TERM FINANCING

(a) Shares:

These are issued to the general public. The holders of shares are the owners of the business. These may be of two types: (i) Equity and (ii) Preference.

(b) Debentures:

These are also issued to the general public in the form of secured loans. The holders of debentures are the creditors of the company.

(c) Public deposits:

General public also like to deposit their savings with a popular and well established company which can pay interest periodically and pay-back the deposit when due.

(d) Retained earnings:

The company may not distribute the whole of its profits among its shareholders. It may retain a part of the profits and utilize it as capital.

(e) Term loans from banks:

Many industrial development banks, cooperative banks and commercial banks grant medium-term loans for a period of three to five years.

(f) Loan from financial institutions:

There are many specialized financial institutions established by the Central and State governments which give long-term loans at reasonable rate of interest.

A. EQUITY SHARE CAPITAL

Equity share capital is also referred to as ordinary shares and in Indian context it is defined by Section 85(2) of the Companies Act 1956. They are the real risk-takers and care-takers of the company and they enjoy the right of voting.

Equity capital represents investments that financial market participants make in a company. Buyers of equity capital are also known as shareholders or stockholders. After investing in a company, they receive voting rights and can attend annual shareholders' meetings. Equally important, equity holders receive periodic dividends and make profits when share prices rise in financial markets. Shareholders invest in two types of stock—common and preferred. Common stockholders are traditional, regular equity buyers. Preferred stockholders have the same benefits as common shareholders but preferred dividends take precedence. In other words, preferred shareholders receive dividends before common stockholders.

In accounting and finance, equity is the residual claim or interest of the most junior class of investors in assets, after all liabilities are paid. If valuations placed on assets do not exceed liabilities, negative equity exists. In an accounting context, Shareholders' equity (or stockholders' equity, shareholders' funds, shareholders' capital or similar terms) represents the remaining interest in assets of a company, spread among individual shareholders of common or preferred stock.

Accounts listed under ownership equity include (example):

(a) Share capital (common stock)

(b) Preferred stock

(c) Capital surplus

(d) Retained earnings

(e) Treasury stock

(f) Stock options

(g) Reserve

Advantages of Equity Shares

The advantages of equity shares can be discussed from the point of view of company and investors.

(a) Advantages to Company:

(i) It is permanent long-term source of finance.

(ii) There is no repayment liability.

(iii) It does not create any obligation to pay finance.

(iv) This capital can be issued without creating any charges over assets of the company.

(v) Issue of equity share capital increases the credit worthiness of the company.

(b) Advantages to Investors:

(i) Equity share provides more income (residual income).

(ii) Equity shares gives right to participate in the control and management of the company.

(iii) Capital appreciation (if share price increased when compared to purchase price).

Disadvantages of Equity Shares

The disadvantages of equity shares can be discussed from the point of view of company and investors.

(a) Disadvantages to Company:

(i) High cost source of fund.

(ii) Involves high flotation costs.

(iii) Issue of additional shares dilutes control.

(iv) No tax advantage (dividends are not tax deductable).

(v) It make capital structure rigid.

(b) Disadvantages to Investors:

(i) No guarantee, and regularity in receipt of dividend.

(ii) No guarantee in receipt of principle amount of investment.

(iii) Loss of capital due to fluctuations in share prices.

B. PREFERENCE SHARE CAPITAL

Capital stock which provides a specific dividend that is paid before any dividends are paid to common stock holders, and which takes precedence over common stock in the event of liquidation, is called preference share capital. Like common stock, preference shares represent partial ownership in a company, although preferred stock shareholders do not enjoy any of the voting rights of common stockholders or equity shareholders. Also unlike common stock, preference shares pay a fixed dividend that does not fluctuate, although the company does not have to pay this dividend if it lacks the financial ability to do so. The main benefit to owning preference shares are that the investor has a greater claim on the company's assets than common stockholders. Preferred shareholders always receive their dividends first and, in the event the company goes bankrupt, preferred shareholders are paid off before common stockholders. In general, there are four different types of preferred stock: cumulative preferred, non-cumulative, participating, and convertible.

According to financial theory, preference capital is one type of financing.

Preference capital carries preference to the shareholders at the time of winding up of company and dividend payment. The preference capital is also referred to as the capital contributed by the preference shareholders. The preference shareholders receive dividends in the fixed rate but they do not enjoy voting rights.

The concept of preference capital financing is believed to be the hybrid of two financing forms that are — debentures financing and equity financing. Like equity financing, in the preference capital financing also the preference dividends are paid depending on the distributable profit and the preference dividends are not obligatory payments. Like equity dividends, the preference dividends are also not tax-deductible.

The various features of preference capital are:

1. Dividends Cumulating.
2. Call ability.
3. Convertibility.
4. Redeemability.
5. Participation in surplus profits and assets.
6. Voting rights.

The advantages of preference capital are:

1. Preference capitals are usually considered as a part of the net worth.
2. There is no legal obligation for the company to pay the preference dividends.
3. Usually preference shares do not carry voting rights.
4. Financial distress due to obligation of redemption is not high in preference capital because the periodic sinking fund payments are not needed.
5. No assets need to be pledged favouring the preference shareholders.

The disadvantages of preference capital are:

1. The preference capitals can be very expensive financing source while compared with debt financing.
2. The preference shareholders enjoy prior claims on the earnings and assets of the company.
3. Skipping dividend payment may affect the image of the company adversely.
4. The preference shareholders may gain voting rights if the company skips dividends for a period of time.

Types of Preference Shares

1. Cumulative or Non-cumulative: A non-cumulative or simple preference shares gives right to fixed percentage dividend of profit of each year. In case no dividend thereon is declared in any year because of absence of profit, the holders of preference shares get nothing nor can they claim unpaid dividend in the subsequent year or years in respect of that year. Cumulative preference shares however give the right to the preference shareholders to demand the unpaid dividend in any year during the subsequent year or years when the profits are available for distribution. In this case dividends which are not paid in any year are accumulated and are paid out when the profits are available.

2. Redeemable and Non-Redeemable: Redeemable Preference shares are preference shares which have to be repaid by the company after the term of which for which the preference shares have been issued. Irredeemable Preference shares means preference shares need not repaid by the company except on winding up of the company. However, under the Indian Companies Act, a company cannot issue irredeemable preference shares. In fact, a company limited by shares cannot issue preference shares which are redeemable after more than 10 years from the date of issue. In other words the maximum tenure of preference shares is 10 years. If a company is unable to redeem any preference shares within the specified period, it may, with consent of the Company Law Board, issue further redeemable preference shares equal to redeem the old preference shares including dividend thereon. A company can issue the preference shares which from the very beginning are redeemable on a fixed date or after certain period of time not exceeding ten years provided it comprises of following conditions —

1. It must be authorized by the articles of association to make such an issue.
2. The shares will be only redeemable if they are fully paid up.
3. The shares may be redeemed out of profits of the company which otherwise would be available for dividends or out of proceeds of new issue of shares made for the purpose of redeem shares.
4. If there is premium payable on redemption it must have provided out of profits or out of shares premium account before the shares are redeemed.
5. When shares are redeemed out of profits a sum equal to nominal amount of shares redeemed is to be transferred out of profits to the capital redemption reserve account. This amount should then be utilized for the purpose of redemption of redeemable preference shares. This reserve can be used to issue of fully paid bonus shares to the members of the company.

3. Participating Preference Share or non-participating preference shares: Participating Preference shares are entitled to a preferential dividend at a fixed rate with the right to participate further in the profits either along with or after payment of certain rate of dividend on equity shares. A non-participating share is one which does not such right to participate in the profits of the company after the dividend and capital have been paid to the preference shareholders

Advantages of Preference Shares

The advantages of preference shares can be studied under two heads, these are companies and investors:

(a) Advantages to Company

- There is no legal obligation to pay preference dividend.
- There is no share in control of the company through participation in voting.
- They provide flexibility in capital structure by issue of redeemable preference shares.
- It enhances credit worthiness, because preference share capital is generally treated as a part of net worth.
- Preference shares provide long-term capital for the company.
- Mortgageable assets are conserved, due to the issue of preference share capital without pledging assets.

(b) Advantages to Investors

- Stable rate of preference dividend.
- Prior claim on assets.
- Less risk when compared to equity shareholders.

Disadvantages of Preference Shares

The disadvantages of preference shares can be studied under two heads, they are companies and investors:

(a) Disadvantages to Company

- Tax disadvantage, because preference dividend is not a tax deductible, which makes preference shares capital as costly source of finance.
- Adverse effect on credit worthiness, if the company avoids payment of dividend.
- Permanent burden of payment of dividends, if the preference shares are cumulative in nature.

(b) Disadvantages to Investors

- Limited return, as preference shareholders do not have voting rights, their return depends on managerial decisions, which is arbitrary, and shareholders cannot force management to pay more dividends.
- The rate of preference dividend is generally less than the rate of dividend on equity shares.
- The market prices of preference shares fluctuates more when compares to debentures.

C. DEBENTURE CAPITAL

A debenture or a bond is an acknowledgement of a debt. In India distinction in made between debenture and bonds.

In law, a debenture is a document that either creates a debt or acknowledges it. In corporate finance, the term is used for a medium to long-term debt instrument used by large companies to borrow money. In some countries the term is used interchangeably with bond, loan stock or note.

Debentures are generally freely transferable by the debenture holder. Debenture holders have no voting rights and the interest paid to them is a charge against profit in the company's financial statements.

Security in Different Jurisdictions:

In the United States, debenture refers specifically to an unsecured corporate bond, *i.e.*, a bond that does not have a certain line of income or piece of property or equipment to guarantee repayment of principal upon the bond's maturity. Where security is provided for loan stocks or bonds in the US, they are termed 'mortgage bonds'. However, in the United Kingdom a debenture is usually secured.

In Asia, if repayment is secured by a charge over land, the loan document is called a mortgage; where repayment is secured by a charge against other assets of the company, the document is called a debenture; and where no security is involved, the document is called a note or 'unsecured deposit note'.

Features of a Debenture

1. Trustee: When a debenture issue is sold to the investing public, a trustee is appointed through a deed. The trustee is usually a bank or an insurance company or a reputable firm of attorneys. Entrusted with the role of protecting the interest of debenture holders, the trustee is responsible to ensure that the borrowing firm fulfils its contractual obligations.

2. Security: Debentures are typically secured by a charge on the immovable properties, both present and future, of the company by way of an equitable mortgage, which is effected by deposit of the title deeds relating to mortgaged assets in favour of the trustees. Debentures not protected by any security are called unsecured or naked debentures.

3. Redemption: Debentures are generally redeemable-perpetual debentures are very rare. The redemption takes place in a pre specified manner. Typically, it occurs between the 5th year and the 9th year. Companies are now required to create a debenture redemption reserve to facilitate timely redemption. A major requirement is that the company should create a Debenture Redemption Reserve equivalent to 50 per cent of the amount of debenture issue before debenture redemption commences.

4. Interest: The interest payment on debentures is a fixed obligation, irrespective of the financial situation of the issuing firm. Typically payable semi-annually, it is a tax-deductible expense.

Right Debentures for Working Capital Public limited companies can issue "rights" debentures to their share-holders with the object of augmenting the long-term resources of the company for working capital requirements. The key guidelines applicable to such debentures are as follows:

The amount of the debenture issue should not exceed (a) 20 per cent of the gross current assets, loans and advances minus the long-term funds presently available for financing working capital, or (b) 20 per cent of the paid-up share capital, including preference capital and free reserves, whichever is the lower of the two:

- The debt: equity ratio, including the proposed debenture issue, should not exceed 1:1.
- The debentures shall first be offered to the existing Indian resident shareholders of the company on a pro rata basis.

Types of Debentures

There are two types of debentures:

1. ***Convertible debentures***, which are convertible bonds or bonds that can be converted into equity shares of the issuing company after a predetermined period of time. "Convertibility" is a feature that corporations may add to the bonds they issue to make them more attractive to buyers. In other words, it is a special feature that a corporate bond may carry. As a result of the advantage a buyer gets from the ability to convert; convertible bonds typically have lower interest rates than non-convertible corporate bonds.

2. ***Non-convertible debentures***, which are simply regular debentures, cannot be converted into equity shares of the liable company. They are debentures without the convertibility feature attached to them. As a result, they usually carry higher interest rates than their convertible counterparts.

Others

1. **Simple naked or unsecured debentures:** These debentures are not given any security on assets. They have no priority as compared to other creditors.

2. **Secured or mortgage debentures:** These debentures are given a security on assets of the debentures company. In case of default in the payment of interest or principle amount, debenture holders can sell the assets in order to satisfy their claims.

3. **Bearer debentures:** These debentures are easily transferable. They are just like negotiable instruments. The debenture is handed over to the purchaser without any registration deed.

4. **Registered debentures:** As compared to bearer debenture which is transferred by mere delivery, registered debenture require a procedure to be followed for the transfer.

5. **Redeemable debenture:** These debentures are to be redeemed on the expiry of ascertain period. The interest on the debenture is paid periodically but the principle amount is returned after a fixed period.

6. **Irredeemable debentures:** Such debentures are not redeemable during the life time of the company. These are payable either on the winding up of the company or at the time of any default on the part of the company.

Advantages

1. Control of company is not surrendered to debenture holders because they do not have any voting rights.

2. Trading on equity is possible as debenture holders get a lower rate of return than the earnings of the company.

3. Interest on debenture is an allowable expenditure under Income Tax Act, hence incidence of tax on the company is decreased.

4. Debenture can be redeemed when company has surplus funds.

Disadvantages

1. Cost of raising capital through debentures is high due to high stamps duty.

2. Common people cannot buy debenture as they are of high denominations.

3. They are not meant for companies earning greater than the rate of interest which they are paying on the debentures.

D. OTHER LONG-TERM SOURCES OF FINANCE

1. Lease Financing

A lease is an agreement allowing one party to use another's property, plant, or equipment for a stated period of time in exchange for consideration. Leases have become more prevalent as businesses and consumers look for alternatives to finance the acquisition of fixed assets. A lease agreement involves at least two parties, a lessor (such as a bank), who owns the property, and a lessee, who uses the property. The lessor, essentially a creditor in the transaction, is repaid from a combination of lease or rental payments, tax benefits, and proceeds from the sale or re-lease of the property at the end of the lease term.

For bank lessors, leasing is another competitive product that can satisfy the needs of bank customers; leases may be safer than other bank products because the transactions are secured; and leases are generally more profitable than commercial loans because of advantages inherent in their structure, such as tax benefits. Leasing is a way for lessees (customers) to conserve capital because, in effect, they obtain 100 per cent financing. Depending on the structure of the lease, the risks of ownership (such as the possibility that the product will become obsolete) can be transferred to the lessor. Tax benefits could also be transferred to a lessor, resulting in lower lease payments to the lessee. ***Operating leases*** are off-balance-sheet, which may improve certain of the lessee's key financial ratios. A special type of transaction, the ***sale-leaseback***, allows the owner of a piece of property (usually real estate) to raise funds while retaining use of the property. In such a transaction (actually two separate transactions), the owner of the property sells the property and immediately leases it back. There is no physical transfer of the property. From a safety and soundness perspective, leases that result from sale-leaseback transactions should be reviewed in essentially the same manner as other leases. Long-term, non-cancellable lease contracts are known as ***financial leases***. The essential point of financial lease agreement is that it contains a condition whereby the lessor agrees to transfer the title for the asset at the end of the lease period at a nominal cost. At lease it must give an option to the lessee to purchase the asset he has used at the expiry of the lease. Under this lease the lessor recovers 90% of the fair value of the asset as lease rentals and the lease period is 75% of the economic life of the asset. The lease agreement is irrevocable. Practically all the risks incidental to the asset ownership and all the benefits arising there from are transferred to the lessee who bears the cost of maintenance, insurance and repairs. Only title deeds remain with the lessor. ***Financial lease is also known as 'capital lease'***. In India, financial leases are very popular with high-cost and high technology equipment.

An operating lease stands in contrast to the financial lease in almost all aspects. This lease agreement gives to the lessee only a limited right to use the asset. The lessor is responsible for the upkeep and maintenance of the asset. The lessee is not given any uplift to purchase the asset at the end of the lease period. Normally the lease is for a short period and even otherwise is revocable at a short notice. Mines, Computers hardware, trucks and automobiles are found suitable for operating lease because the rate of obsolescence is very high in this kind of assets.

Types of Lease:

Leases are classified into following:

Finance Lease and Operating Lease: Finance lease, also known as Full Payout Lease, is a type of lease wherein the lessor transfers substantially all the risks and rewards related to the asset to the lessee. Generally, the ownership is transferred to the lessee at the end of the economic life of the asset. Lease term is spread over the major part of the asset life. Here, lessor is only a financier. *Example of a finance lease is big industrial equipment.*

On the contrary, in operating lease, risk and rewards are not transferred completely to the lessee. The term of lease is very small compared to finance lease. The lessor depends on many different lessees for recovering his cost. Ownership along with its risks and rewards lies with the lessor. Here, lessor is not only acting as a financier but he also provides additional services required in the course of using the asset or equipment. *Example of an operating lease is music system leased on rent with the respective technicians.*

Sale And Lease Back and Direct Lease: In the arrangement of sale and lease back, the lessee sells his asset or equipment to the lessor (financier) with an advanced agreement of leasing back to the lessee for a fixed lease rental per period. It is exercised by the entrepreneur when he wants to free his money, invested in the equipment or asset, to utilize it at whatsoever place for any reason.

On the other hand, direct lease is a simple lease where the asset is either owned by the lessor or he acquires it. In the former case, the lessor and equipment supplier are one and the same person and this case is called 'bipartite lease'. In bipartite lease, there are two parties. Whereas, in the latter case, there are three different parties *viz.* equipment supplier, lessor, and lessee and it is called tripartite lease. Here, equipment supplier and lessor are two different parties.

Single Investor Lease and Leveraged Lease: In single investor lease, there are two parties — lessor and lessee. The lessor arranges the money to finance the asset or equipment by way of equity or debt. The lender is entitled to recover money from the lessor only and not from the lessee in case of default by lessor. Lessee is entitled to pay the lease rentals only to the lessor.

Leveraged lease, on the other hand, has three parties - lessor, lessee and the financier or lendor. Equity is arranged by the lessor and debt is financed by the lender or financier. Here, there is a direct connection of the lender with the lessee and in case of default by the lessor; the lender is also entitled to receive money from lessee. Such transactions are generally routed through a trustee.

Domestic and International Lease: When all the parties of the lease agreement reside in the same country, it is called domestic lease.

International lease are of two types – Import Lease and Cross Border Lease. When lessor and lessee reside in same country and equipment supplier stays in different country, the lease arrangement is called import lease. When the lessor and lessee are residing in two different countries and no matter where the equipment supplier stays, the lease is called cross border lease.

2. Government Grant

Some firms might be eligible to get funds from the government. This could be the local authority, the national government or the European Union. These grants are often linked to incentives to firms to set up in areas that are in need of economic development.

One famous example of how a business project can be developed using European Union funding was the Eden Project. The EU was not the only source of finance to help set up the project but was an important partner in helping to realize this important tourist destination for a deprived part of Cornwall.

3. Bank Loans

As with short term finance, banks are an important source of longer term finance. Banks may lend sums over long periods of time – possibly up to 25 years or even more in some cases. The loans have a rate of interest attached to them. This can vary according to the way in which the Bank sets interest rates. For businesses, using bank loans might be relatively easy but the cost of servicing the loan (paying the money and interest back) can be high. If interest rates rise then it can add to a business's costs and this has to be taken into account in the planning stage before the loan is taken out.

4. Term Loan of Financial Institutions

Term Loans constitute one of the major sources of debt finance for a long term project. Term Loans are generally repayable in more than one year but less than ten years. These term loan are offered by the All India Financial Institutions *viz,* IDBI, ICICI, etc., and by the State Level Financial Institutions. The salient features of the term loan are the interest paid, Security offered and the restrictive covenants.

The major advantage of this source of finance is its post-tax cost, which is lower than the equity/preference capital and there will be no dilution of control.

5. Mortgage

A mortgage is a loan specifically for the purchase of property. Some businesses might buy property through a mortgage. In many cases, mortgages are used as a security for a loan. This tends to occur with smaller businesses. A sole trader, for example, running a florists shop might want to move to larger premises. They find a new shop with a price of ₹ 200,00,000. To raise this sort of money, the bank will want some sort of security – a guarantee that if the borrower cannot pay the money back the bank will be able to get their money back somehow.

The borrower can use their own property as security for the loan – it is often called taking out a second mortgage. If the business does not work out and the borrower could not pay the bank the loan then the bank has the right to take the home of the borrower and sell it to recover their money. Using a mortgage in this way is a very popular way of raising finance for small businesses but as you can see carries with it a big risk.

6. Owner's Capital

Some people are in a fortunate position of having some money which they can use to help set up their business. The money may be the result of savings, money left to them by a relative in a will or money received as the result of a redundancy payment. This has the advantage that it does not carry with it any interest. It might not, however, be a large enough sum to finance the business fully but will be one of the contributions to the overall finance of the business.

7. Retained Profit

This is a source of finance that would only be available to a business that was already in existence. Profits from a business can be used by the owners for their own personal use or can be used to put back into the business. This is often called 'ploughing back the profits'.

The owners of a business will have to decide what the best option for their particular business is. In the early stages of business growth, it may be necessary to put back a lot of the profits into the business. This finance can be used to buy new equipment and machinery as well as more stock or raw materials and hopefully make the business more efficient and profitable in the future.

8. Selling Assets

As firms grow they build up assets. These assets could be in the form of property, machinery, equipment, other companies or even logos. In some cases it may be appropriate for a business to sell off some of these assets to finance other projects.

6.5 VENTURE CAPITAL

Venture Capital is a form of "risk capital". In other words, capital that is invested in a project (in this case – a business) where there is a substantial element of risk relating to the future creation of profits and cash flows. Risk capital is invested as shares (equity) rather than as a loan and the investor requires a higher "rate of return" to compensate him for his risk.

What is Venture Capital?

Venture capital provides long-term, committed share capital, to help unquoted companies grow and succeed. If an entrepreneur is looking to start-up, expand, buy-into a business, buy-out a business in which he works, turnaround or revitalize a company, venture capital could help do this. Obtaining venture capital is substantially different from raising debt or a loan from a lender. Lenders have a legal right to interest on a loan and repayment of the capital, irrespective of the success or failure of a business. Venture capital is invested in exchange for an equity stake in the business. As a shareholder, the venture capitalist's return is dependent on the growth and profitability of the business. This return is generally earned when the venture capitalist "exits" by selling its shareholding when the business is sold to another owner.

Venture capital in the UK originated in the late 18th century, when entrepreneurs found wealthy individuals to back their projects on an ad hoc basis. This informal method of financing became an industry in the late 1970s and early 1980s when a number of venture capital firms were founded. There are now over 100 active venture capital firms in the UK, which provide several billion pounds each year to unquoted companies mostly located in the UK.

What kinds of Businesses are Attractive to Venture Capitalists?

Venture capitalist prefers to invest in "entrepreneurial businesses". This does not necessarily mean small or new businesses. Rather, it is more about the investment's aspirations and potential for growth, rather than by current size. Such businesses are aiming to grow rapidly to a significant size. As a rule of thumb, unless a business can offer the prospect of significant turnover growth within five years, it is unlikely to be of interest to a venture capital firm. Venture capital investors are only interested in companies with high growth prospects, which are managed by experienced and ambitious teams who are capable of turning their business plan into reality.

For how long do Venture Capitalists Invest in a Business?

Venture capital firms usually look to retain their investment for between three and seven years or more. The term of the investment is often linked to the growth profile of the business. Investments in more mature businesses, where the business performance can be improved quicker and easier, are often sold sooner than investments in early-stage or technology companies where it takes time to develop the business model.

Where do Venture Capital firms obtain their money?

Just as management teams compete for finance, so do venture capital firms. They raise their funds from several sources. To obtain their funds, venture capital firms have to demonstrate a good track record and the prospect of producing returns greater than can be achieved through fixed interest or quoted equity investments. Most UK venture capital firms raise their funds for investment from external sources, mainly institutional investors, such as pension funds and insurance companies.

Venture capital firms' investment preferences may be affected by the source of their funds. Many funds raised from external sources are structured as Limited Partnerships and usually have a fixed life of 10 years. Within this period the funds invest the money committed to them and by the end of the 10 years they will have had to return the investors' original money, plus any additional returns made. This generally requires the investments to be sold, or to be in the form of quoted shares, before the end of the fund.

Venture Capital Trusts (VCT's) are quoted vehicles that aim to encourage investment in smaller unlisted (unquoted and AIM quoted companies) UK companies by offering private investors tax incentives in return for a five-year investment commitment. The first were launched in autumn 1995 and are mainly managed by UK venture capital firms. If funds are obtained from a VCT, there may be some restrictions regarding the company's future development within the first few years.

What is Involved in the Investment Process?

The investment process, from reviewing the business plan to actually investing in a proposition, can take a venture capitalist anything from one month to one year but typically it takes between 3 and 6 months. There are always exceptions to the rule and deals can be done in extremely short time frames. Much depends on the quality of information provided and made available.

The key stage of the investment process is the initial evaluation of a business plan. Most approaches to venture capitalists are rejected at this stage. In considering the business plan, the venture capitalist will consider several principal aspects:

- Is the product or service commercially viable?
- Does the company have potential for sustained growth?
- Does management have the ability to exploit this potential and control the company through the growth phases?
- Does the possible reward justify the risk?
- Does the potential financial return on the investment meet their investment criteria?

In structuring its investment, the venture capitalist may use one or more of the following types of share capital:

Ordinary/Equity Shares

These are equity shares that are entitled to all income and capital after the rights of all other classes of capital and creditors have been satisfied. Ordinary shares have votes. In a venture capital deal these are the shares typically held by the management and family shareholders rather than the venture capital firm.

Preferred Ordinary Shares

These are equity shares with special rights. For example, they may be entitled to a fixed dividend or share of the profits. Preferred ordinary shares have votes.

Preference Shares

These are non-equity shares. They rank ahead of all classes of ordinary shares for both income and capital. Their income rights are defined and they are usually entitled to a fixed dividend (*e.g.* 10% fixed). The shares may be redeemable on fixed dates or they may be irredeemable. Sometimes they may be redeemable at a fixed premium (*e.g.* at 120% of cost). They may be convertible into a class of ordinary shares.

Loan capital

Venture capital loans typically are entitled to interest and are usually, though not necessarily repayable. Loans may be secured on the company's assets or may be unsecured. A secured loan will rank ahead of unsecured loans and certain other creditors of the company. A loan may be convertible into equity shares. Alternatively, it may have a warrant attached which gives the loan holder the option to subscribe for new equity shares on terms fixed in the warrant. They typically carry a higher rate of interest than bank term loans and rank behind the bank for payment of interest and repayment of capital.

Venture capital investments are often accompanied by additional financing at the point of investment. This is nearly always the case where the business in which the investment is being made is relatively mature or well-established. In this case, it is appropriate for a business to have a financing structure that includes both equity and debt.

Other forms of finance provided in addition to venture capitalist equity include:

— Clearing banks – principally provide overdrafts and short to medium-term loans at fixed or, more usually, variable rates of interest.

— Merchant banks – organize the provision of medium to longer-term loans, usually for larger amounts than clearing banks. Later they can play an important role in the process of "going public" by advising on the terms and price of public issues and by arranging underwriting when necessary.

— Finance houses – provide various forms of installment credit, ranging from hire purchase to leasing; often asset based and usually for a fixed term and at fixed interest rates.

Factoring companies – provide finance by buying trade debts at a discount, either on a recourse basis (you retain the credit risk on the debts) or on a non-recourse basis (the factoring company takes over the credit risk).

Making the Investment – Due Diligence

To support an initial positive assessment of your business proposition, the venture capitalist will want to assess the technical and financial feasibility in detail.

External consultants are often used to assess market prospects and the technical feasibility of the proposition, unless the venture capital firm has the appropriately qualified people in-house. Chartered accountants are often called on to do much of the due diligence, such as to report on the financial projections and other financial aspects of the plan. These reports often follow a detailed study, or a one or two day overview may be all that is required by the venture capital firm. They will assess and review the following points concerning the company and its management:

— Management information systems

— Forecasting techniques and accuracy of past forecasting

— Assumptions on which financial assumptions are based

— The latest available management accounts, including the company's cash/debtor positions

— Bank facilities and leasing agreements

— Pensions funding

— Employee contracts, etc.

The due diligence review aims to support or contradict the venture capital firm's own initial impressions of the business plan formed during the initial stage. References may also be taken up on the company (*e.g.* with suppliers, customers, and bankers).

6.6 VENTURE CAPITAL FINANCING

Venture capital financing is a type of financing by venture capital: the type of private equity capital is provided as seed funding to early-stage, high-potential, growth companies and more often after the seed funding round as growth funding round (also referred as series A round) in the interest of generating a return through an eventual realization event such as an IPO or trade sale of the company.

Overview

To start a new start-up company or to bring a new product to the market, the venture may need to attract financial funding. There are several categories of financing possibilities. If it is a small venture, then perhaps the venture can rely on family funding, loans from friends, personal bank loans or crowd funding.

For more ambitious projects, some companies need more than what mentioned above, some ventures have access to rare funding resources that is called Angel investors. These are private investors who are using their own capital to finance a ventures' need. Apart from these investors, there are also venture capitalist firms) who are specialized in financing new ventures against a lucrative return.

When a venture approaches the last one, the venture is going to do more than negotiating about the financial terms. Apart from the financial resources these firms are offering; the VC-firm also provides potential expertise the venture is lacking, such as legal or marketing knowledge. This is also known as Smart Money.

Venture Capital Financing Process

As written in the previous paragraph, there are several ways to attract funding. However in general, the venture capital financing process can be distinguished into five stages:

— The Seed stage

— The Start-up stage

— The Second stage

— The Third stage

— The Bridge/Pre-public stage

The Seed Stage

This is where the seed funding takes place. It is considered as the setup stage where a person or a venture approaches an angel investor or an investor in a VC-firm for funding for their idea/product. During this stage, the person or venture has to convince the investor why the idea/product is worth to invest in. The investor will investigate into the technical and the economical feasibility (Feasibility Study) of the idea. In some cases, there is some sort of prototype of the idea/product that is not fully developed or tested.

If the idea is not feasible at this stage, and the investor does not see any potential in the idea/product, the investor will not consider financing the idea. However if the idea/product is not directly feasible, but part of the idea is worth for more investigation, the investor may invest some time and money in it for further investigation.

At this stage, the risk of losing the investment is tremendously high, because there are so many uncertain factors. From research, we know that the risk of losing the investment for the VC-firm is around the 66.2% and the causation of major risk by stage of development is 72%.

The Start-up Stage

If the idea/product/process is qualified for further investigation and/or investment, the process will go to the second stage; this is also called the start-up stage. At this point many exciting things happen. A business plan is presented by the attendant of the venture to the VC-firm. A management team is being formed to run the venture. If the company has a board of directors, a person from the VC-firms will take seats at the board of directors.

While the organization is being set up, the idea/product gets its form. The prototype is being developed and fully tested. In some cases, clients are being attracted for initial sales. The management-team establishes a feasible production line to produce the product. The VC-firm monitors the feasibility of the product and the capability of the management-team from the Board of Directors.

To prove that the assumptions of the investors are correct about the investment, the VC-firm wants to see result of market research to see whether the market size is big enough, if there are enough consumers to buy their product. They also want to create a realistic forecast of the investment needed to push the venture into the next stage. If at this stage, the VC-firm is not satisfied about the progress or result from market research, the VC-firm may stop their funding and the venture will have to search for another investor(s). When the cause relies on handling of the management in charge, they will recommend replacing (parts of) the management team.

Now the venture has attracted an investor, the venture need to satisfy the investor for further investment. To do that, the venture needs to provide the investor a clear business plan how to realize their idea and how the venture is planning to earn back the investment that is put into the venture, of course with a lucrative return.

Together with the market researchers, provided by the investor, the venture has to determine how big the market is in their region. They have to find out who are the potential clients and if the market is big enough to realize the idea. From market research, the venture comes to know that there are enough potential clients for their portal site. But there are no providers of lunches yet. To convince these providers, the venture decided to do interviews with providers and try to convince them to join. With this knowledge, the venture can finish their business plan and determine a pretty good forecast of the revenue, the cost of developing and maintaining the site and the profit the venture will earn in the following five years. After reading the business plan and consulting the person who monitors the venture activities, the investor decides that the idea is worth for further development.

The Second Stage

At this stage, we presume that the idea has been transformed into a product and is being produced and sold. This is the first encounter with the rest of the market, the competitors. The venture is trying to squeeze between the rest and it tries to get some market share from the competitors. This is one of the main goals at this stage. Another important point is the cost. The venture is trying to minimize their losses in order to reach the break-even.

The management-team has to handle very decisively. The VC-firm monitors the management capability of the team. This consists of how the management-team manages the development process of the product and how they react to competition.

If at this stage the management-team is proven their capability of standing hold against the competition, the VC-firm will probably give a go for the next stage. However, if the management team lacks in managing the company or does not succeed in competing with the competitors, the VC-firm may suggest for restructuring of the management team and extend the stage by redoing the stage again. In case the venture is doing tremendously badly whether it is caused by the management team or from competition, the venture will cut the funding.

Example: The portal site needs to be developed. (If possible, the development should be taken place in house. If not, the venture needs to find a reliable designer to develop the site.) Developing the site in house is not possible; the venture does not have this knowledge in house. The venture decides to consult this with the investor. After a few meetings, the investor decides to provide the venture a small team of web-designers. The investor also has given the venture a deadline when the portal should be operational. The deadline is in three months. In the meantime, the venture needs to produce a client-portfolio, who will provide their menu at the launch of the portal site. The venture also needs to come to an agreement how these providers are being promoted at the portal site and against what price. After three months; the investor requests the status of development. Unfortunately for the venture, the development did not go as planned. The venture did not make the deadline. According to the one who is monitoring the activities, this is caused by the lack of decisiveness by the venture and the lack of skills of the designers.

The investor decides to cut back their financial investment after a long meeting. The venture is given another three months to come up with an operational portal site. Three designers are being replaced by a new designer and a consultant is attracted to support the executives' decisions. If the venture does not make this deadline in time, they have to find another investor.

Luckily for the venture, with the come of the new designer and the consultant, the venture succeeds in making the deadline. They even have two weeks left before the second deadline ends.

The Third Stage

This stage is seen as the expansion/maturity phase of the previous stage. The venture tries to expand the market share they gained in the previous stage. This can be done by selling more amount of the product and having a good marketing campaign. Also, the venture will have to see whether it is possible to cut down their production cost or restructure the internal process. This can become more visible by doing a SWOT analysis. It is used to figure out the strength, weakness, opportunity and the threat the venture is facing and how to deal with it.

Except that the venture is expanding, the venture also starts investigate in follow-up products and services. In some cases, the venture also investigates how to expand the life-cycle of the existing product/service.

At this stage the VC-firm monitors the objectives already mentioned in the second stage and also the new objective mentioned at this stage. The VC-firm will evaluate if the management-team has made the expected reduction cost. They also want to know how the venture competes against the competitors. The new developed follow-up product will be evaluated to see if there is any potential.

Example: Finally the portal site is operational. The portal is getting more orders from the working class everyday. To keep this going, the venture needs to promote their portal site. The venture decides to advertise by distributing flyers at each office in their region to attract new clients. In the meanwhile, a small team is being assembled for sales, which will be responsible for getting new lunchrooms/bakeries, any eating-places in other cities/region to join the portal site. This way the venture also works on expanding their market.

Because of the delay at the previous stage, the venture did not fulfill the expected target. From a new forecast, requested by the investor, the venture expects to fulfill the target in the next quarter or the next half year. This is caused by external issues the venture does not have control of it. The venture has already suggested to stabilize the existing market the venture already owns and to decrease the promotion by 20% of what the venture is spending at the moment. This is approved by the investor.

The Bridge/Pre-public Stage

In general this stage is the last stage of the venture capital financing process. The main goal of this stage is to achieve an exit vehicle for the investors and for the venture to go public. At this stage the venture achieves a certain amount of the market share. This gives the venture some opportunities like for example:

— Hostile take over;

— Merger with other companies;

— Keeping away new competitors from approaching the market;

— Eliminate competitors.

Internally, the venture has to reposition the product and see where the product is positioned and if it is possible to attract new market segmentation. This is also the phase to introduce the follow-up product/services to attract new clients and markets.

As we already mentioned, this is the final stage of the process. But most of the time, there will be an additional continuation stage involved between the third stage and the Bridge/pre-public stage. However there are limited circumstances known where investors made a very successful initial market impact might be able to move from the third stage directly to the exit stage. Most of the time the venture fails to achieves some of the important benchmarks the VC-firms aimed.

Example: Now the site is running smoothly, the venture is thinking about taking over the competitors' website happen.nl. The site is promoting restaurants and is also doing business in online ordering food. This proposal is being protested by the investor, because it may cost a lot of the ventures' capital. The investor suggests a merge instead.

To settle down their differences, the venture requested an external party to investigate into the case. The result of the investigation was a take-over. After reading the investigation, the investor agrees to it and happen.nl is being taken over by the venture. With the take-over of a competitor, the venture has expanded its' services.

Seeing the ventures' result, the investor comes to the conclusion that the venture still have not reach the target that was expected, but seeing how the business is progressing, the investor decides to extend its' investment for another year.

Venture Capital Companies in India

These are venture capital companies in India.

— Accel Partners India

— Artheon Ventures

— Artiman Ventures

— Blue Run Ventures

— Cannan Partners

— DFJ India

— Epiphany Ventures

— Helion Venture Partners

— IFCI Venture Capital Funds

— India Innovation Investors

— Intel Capital

— Inventus (India) Advisory Company

— JAFCO Asia

— Lightspeed Venture Partners

— Netz Capital

— Nexus India Capital

— Norwest Venture Partners

— Ojas Venture Partners

— Reliance Venture

— SAIF Partners

— Trident Capital

— Venture East

— Apax Partners

Stages of Venture Capital Financing in India

In India, the venture capital recognizes different stages of financing, namely:

Early stage financing – This is the first stage financing when the firm is undertaking production and need additional funds for selling its products. It involves seed/initial finance for supporting a concept or idea of an entrepreneur. The capital is provided for product development, R&D and initial marketing.

Expansion financing – This is the second stage financing for working capital and expansion of a business. It involves development financing so as to facilitate the public issue.

Acquisition/buyout financing – This later stage involves:

Acquisition financing in order to acquire another firm for further growth.

Management buyout financing so as to enable the operating groups/investors for acquiring an existing product line or business, and

Turnaround financing in order to revitalize and revive the sick enterprises.

Types of Venture Capital Fund in India

In India, the venture capital funds (VCFs) can be categorized into the following groups:-

1. Those promoted by the Central Government Controlled Development Finance Institutions, for example:

   ICICI Venture Funds Ltd.

   IFCI Venture Capital Funds Limited (IVCF)

   SIDBI Venture Capital Limited (SVCL)

2. Those promoted by State Government Controlled Development Finance Institutions, for example:

   Gujarat Venture Finance Limited (GVFL)

   Kerala Venture Capital Fund Pvt. Ltd.

   Punjab Infotech Venture Fund

   Hyderabad Information Technology Venture Enterprises Limited (HITVEL)

3. Those promoted by public banks, for example:

   Canbank Venture Capital Fund

   SBI Capital Markets Limited

4. Those promoted by private sector companies, for example:

   IL&FS Trust Company Limited

   Infinity Venture India Fund

5. Those established as an overseas venture capital fund, for example:

   Walden International Investment Group

   SEAF India Investment & Growth Fund

   BTS India Private Equity Fund Limited

All these venture capital funds are governed by the Securities and Exchange Board of India (SEBI). SEBI is the nodal agency for registration and regulation of both domestic and overseas venture capital funds. Accordingly, it has made the following regulations, namely, Securities and Exchange Board of India (Venture Capital Funds) Regulations 1996 and Securities and Exchange Board of India (Foreign Venture Capital Investors) Regulations 2000. These regulations provide broad guidelines and procedures for establishment of venture capital funds both within India and outside it; their management structure and set up; as well as size and investment criteria's of the funds.

SUMMARY

Long-term sources of finance are those that are needed over a longer period of time – generally over a year. The reasons for needing long-term finance are generally different to those relating to short-term finance. The kind of long-term financing that is provided to a particular company depends on its type. For example, the long-term financing that is provided to a solo proprietorship is different from the long-term financing that a partnership would receive. Long-term financing is used in separate ways by different types of business entities. The business entities that are not corporations are only supposed to use long term financing for the purposes of debt. However, the corporations can use long term financing for both debt and equity purposes.

The long-term decision of a firm involves setting up of the firm. Expansion, diversification, modernization and other similar capital expenditure decisions. All these decisions involve huge investment, the benefits of which will be seen only in the long-term and these decisions are also irreversible in nature. By nature of these projects, long-term sources of funds become the best suited means of financing. One of the most important considerations for an investment and financing decision will be proper asset-liability-management. Companies will have to face a severe asset-liability mismatch if the long-term requirements are funded by the short-term sources of funds.

Buyers of equity capital are also known as shareholders or stockholders. After investing in a company, they receive voting rights and can attend annual shareholders' meetings. In accounting and finance, equity is the residual claim or interest of the most junior class of investors in assets, after all liabilities are paid. Capital stock which provides a specific dividend that is paid before any dividends are paid to common stock holders, and which takes precedence over common stock in the event of liquidation, is called preference share capital. Like common stock, preference shares represent partial ownership in a company, although preferred stock shareholders do not enjoy any of the voting rights of common stockholders or equity shareholders. In law, a debenture is a document that either creates a debt or acknowledges it. In corporate finance, the term is used for a medium – to long-term debt instrument used by large companies to borrow money. In some countries the term is used interchangeably with bond, loan stock or note.

Debentures are generally freely transferable by the debenture holder. Debenture holders have no voting rights and the interest paid to them is a charge against profit in the company's financial statements.

A lease is an agreement allowing one party to use another's property, plant, or equipment for a stated period of time in exchange for consideration. Leases have become more prevalent as businesses and consumers look for alternatives to finance the acquisition of fixed assets. A lease agreement involves at least two parties) a lessor (such as a bank), who owns the property, and a lessee, who uses the property.

Venture capital provides long-term, committed share capital, to help unquoted companies grow and succeed. If an entrepreneur is looking to start-up, expand, buy-into a business, buy-out a business in which he works, turnaround or revitalize a company, venture capital could help do this. Obtaining venture capital is substantially different from raising debt or a loan from a lender.

Venture capital financing is a type of financing by venture capital: the type of private equity capital is provided as seed funding to early-stage, high-potential, growth companies and more often after the seed funding round as growth funding round (also referred as series A round) in the interest of generating a return through an eventual realization event such as an IPO or trade sale of the company.

EXERCISE

A. Fill in the blanks with appropriate words given within brackets against each sentence:

1. Long-term finance is required for ____________ (Fixed Assets/Current Assets).
2. Long-term sources of finance are also required for____________ of working capital (whole/ permanent part).
3. Investments in machines require _________ (Short-term finance/long-term finance).
4. Fixed capital requirement is more in __________ business (manufacturing/trading).

B. Name the long-term source of finance in the following cases:

1. A part of profits of the company that is used as capital.
2. Savings of the public invested in companies for safety and interest earning.
3. Available to a company as ownership capital.
4. Long-term loans from the public.

C. Objective Type Questions:

1. Write the meaning and purpose of long-term finance.
2. Identify the various sources of long-term finance.
3. Define equity shares and preference shares.
4. Distinguish between equity shares and preference shares.
5. Define debenture.
6. What in venture capital?
7. Write one difference between financial lease and operating lease.
8. What is 'Due Diligence'?
9. What is 'retained profit'?
10. What is meant by 'lease'?

D. Other Questions

1. Explain the advantages and disadvantages of equity shares from the point of view of (a) shareholders and (b) management.
2. Enumerate the types of preference shares alongwith its advantages & disadvantages.
3. Enumerate the types of debentures.
4. Explain the merits and demerits of debentures as a source of long-term finance.
5. Compare the relative advantages of issuing equity shares and debentures.
6. Explain the benefits and limitations of 'retained earnings as a source of finance'.
7. Explain the merits and demerits of Public Deposits.
8. Outline the rules and regulations about inviting and accepting public deposits by companies.
9. Discuss the merits and demerits of long-term borrowing from Commercial banks.

❑❑❑

7 COST OF CAPITAL

7.1 CONCEPT OF COST OF CAPITAL

'Cost of capital' is, in fact, the price which becomes payable since use of capital involves the period of 'time' for which the owner actually is deprived of its possession.

Price is payable by a firm is received by the suppliers for holding back their capital in production process of the different categories of financial capital and hence, price as 'cost of capital' is synonymous with the 'cost of finance'.

'Cost of finance' includes the following important costs:

- Payment of dividend;
- Payment of interest.

Cost of capital may be defined 'as overall cost of capital' of a firm which comprises the costs of the difference sources of financing from which capital is raised by a firm. Overall cost of capital is the 'weighted average cost of capital' from different sources.

Example: ABC Ltd. has a total capital base of 600 lakhs in the ratio of 3:2 debt-equity. If the after tax costs of debt and equity are 8% and 10% respectively, the cost of capital to the company will be equal to weighted average cost, calculated as follows:

Sources of finance	Amount ₹ (lakhs)	Weight (proportion)	After –tax cost (%)	Weighted average cost
(1)	(2)	(3)	(4)	(5) = (3) × (4)
Debt	360	3/5	8	24/5
Equity	240	2/5	10	20/5
Total	600	1	—	44/5

Thus, weighted average cost of capital is 44/5 = 8.8%

The cost of capital to a company is the minimum rate of return that it must earn on its investments in order to satisfy the various categories of investors who have made investments in the form of shares, debentures or term loans.

Components of Cost of Capital:

Return at zero risk level: Rate of return expected from the zero – risk project undertaken by the firm.

Business risk premium: Additional return expected from the business investment carrying the feature of business risk resulting variability in operating profit. Higher the risk, higher will be the risk premium that is higher will be the expectation of additional return.

Financial Risk Premium: Additional return expected from the investment in fixed income securities like debt, preference capital carrying the feature of financial risk. Higher the financial risk, higher will be the expected rate of return by the investors.

Significance of Cost of Capital (Reasons for Determining Cost of Capital)

Investment Decisions (Investment Decisions are taken after considering NPV of the project or comparing return with cost of capital or profitability index and in all cases, cost of capital is used to discount the cash flows).

Financing Decisions (while taking financing decision, the ultimate aim is always to obtain the cheapest combinations of different sources of finance/cheapest source of finance, in an effort to reduce overall cost of capital/specific cost of capital)

Dividend Decision (Cost of capital helps to determine whether the earnings of the company should be retained or distributed among the shareholder.)

Performance Appraisal of the Management (Actual cost of capital is compared with the standard cost of capital).

Others

- Leasing
- Hire purchase
- Working Capital Management

7.2 COMPUTATIOIN OF SPECIFIC COST OF CAPITAL

A. Cost of Debenture (K_d)

The cost of a debenture is the discount rate which equates the net proceeds from issue of debentures to the expected cash out flows in the form of interest and principal repayments.

I. Cost of Redeemable Debentures

$$K_d = \frac{I(1-t)+\dfrac{F-P}{n}}{\dfrac{F+P}{2}}$$

The interest payment (I) is multiplied by the factor (1 – t) because interest on debt is a tax-deductible expenses and post-tax costs are considered.

I = Annual Interest payment per debenture
F = Redemption price per debenture
P = Net amount realized per debenture
t = Corporate Tax rate
n = Maturity Period

Problem 1

A company issued convertible debentures for ₹ 1000 lakhs. Each debenture has a face value of ₹ 100 and carries a rate of interest of 12 per cent. The company realized ₹ 97 per debenture. The interest is payable annually. What is the cost of debenture to the company ?

(a) When the debenture is redeemable at par after 5 years?

(b) When the debenture is redeemable at a premium of 5% after 5 years?

The corporate tax rate is 30%

Solution

(a) Given, I = 12% × Face Value = ₹ 12
F = ₹ 100
n = 5 years
t = 0.3
p = ₹ 97

$$\therefore\ k_d = \frac{12(1-0.30)-\dfrac{100-97}{5}}{\dfrac{100+97}{2}} = \frac{9}{98.5} = 0.09137 = 9.137\% = 9.14\%$$

(b) F= 100 + 5% = ₹ 105

$$\therefore\ k_d = \frac{12(1-0.30)+\dfrac{105-97}{5}}{\dfrac{105+97}{2}}$$

$$= \frac{8.4+1.6}{101}$$

$$= \frac{10}{101} = 0.0991$$
$$= 9.91\%$$

II. Cost of Irremediable Debentures (perpetual)

K_d = Rate of Interest (1 – t)
= I (1 – t)

Where, t = corporate tax rate
I = rate of interest

B. Cost of Preference Capital (K_p):

I. Cost of Redeemable Preference Shares

The cost of a redeemable preference share is defined as that discount rate which equates the proceeds from preference capital issue to the payments associated with the same *i.e.* dividend payment and principal payments, which can be—

$$K_p = \sum_{t=1}^{n} \frac{D}{(1+K_p)^t} + \frac{F}{(1+K_p)^n}$$

Where, D = Dividend per share payable annually

F = Redemption price

n = Maturity period

Approximate Formula:

$$K_p = \frac{D + \frac{F-P}{n}}{\frac{F+P}{2}}$$

Where, P = net amount realized per share.

Unlike interest payment on debt, dividend payable on preference capital is not tax deductible. Therefore no adjustment is required for taxes while calculating K_p.

Problem 2

A public limited company made an issue of 10000 preference shares under the following terms:

- Each preference share has a face value of ₹ 100
- Rate of preference dividend is 10% payable annually
- The preference share is redeemable after 10 years at par
- Net amount realized per share is ₹ 95.

What is the cost of the preference capital?

Solution

Given, $D = 10\% \times ₹\ 100 = ₹\ 10$

$F = ₹\ 100$

$P = ₹\ 95$

$n = 10$ years

$$K_p = \frac{10 + \frac{100-95}{10}}{\frac{100+95}{2}} = \frac{10+0.5}{97.5}$$

$= 10.77\%$

$= 0.1077$

II. Cost of Irredeemable (perpetual) Preference Share

The cost of preference capital which has no specific maturity date is given by the following equation:

$$K_p = \frac{D}{P_0(1-f)}$$

OR, $$= \frac{D}{NP}$$

When, NP = Net proceeds from the issue

D = Dividend out flow each share.

P_0 = Price at which the share is issued

f = Foliation cost (cost of issue).

C. Cost of Equity Capital (K_e)

Cost of equity is the minimum rate of return expected by the share holders. Even if there is no compulsory payment to equity shareholders, they invest their money in the company with an expectation of earning some return, which is at least to their opportunity cost.

Several approaches are adopted for estimating this rate of return which are as follows:

I. Bond yields plus risk premium approach: The required rate of return of equity share capital is higher than that of bonds, as Equity shareholders are taking more risk than the bondholders.

$\therefore K_e$ = yield on the bonds + risk premium.

II. Realized yield approach: The past returns on a security are taken as a proxy for the return required in the future by the investors.

The realized return over a n – year period is calculated as:

$$(W_1 \times W_2 \times \text{- - - -}\ W_n)^{1/n} - 1.$$

Where, $W_t = \dfrac{D_t + P_t}{P_{t-1}}$ and t = 1, 2, ..., n

D_t = Dividend per share for year t payable at the end of year t

P_t = Price per share of the end of year t

Problem 3

Year	1	2	3
D P S (₹)	1.50	2.00	1.50
Price per share at the end of the year	12.00	11.00	12.00

What is the realized yield if the price per share at the beginning of the year 1 is ₹ 10?

Solution

Year	1	2	3
Wealth ratio	1.35	1.08	1.23

$$W_1 = \frac{D_1 + P_1}{P_{1-1}} = \frac{D_1 + P_1}{P_0} = \frac{1.50 + 12.00}{10} = 1.35$$

$$W_2 = \frac{D_2 + P_2}{P_{2-1}} = \frac{D_2 + P_2}{P_1} = \frac{2 + 11.00}{12} = 1.08$$

$$W_3 = \frac{D_3 + P_3}{P_{3-1}} = \frac{D_3 + P_3}{P_2} = \frac{1.50 + 12.00}{11} = 1.23$$

Realized yield $= (W_1 \times W_2 \times W_3)^{1/3} - 1$

$= (1.35 \times 1.08 \times 1.23)^{1/3} - 1$

$= 0.2149$

$= 21.5\%$

III. CAPM Approach

According to this approach, the cost of equity is shown by using the following equation:

$$A_j = R_F + B_J\ (M - R_F)$$

Where, β = Beta coefficient showing non-diversitiable risk of the asset relative to the market risk.

A_j = Required rate of return on security j

B_j = Beta coefficient on security j

R_F = Risk-free rate of return

M = Return on market portfolio

$\beta_J(M- R_F)$ = Risk premium

After we compute Aj, we take it as cost of equity capital (K_e) because it is the rate that the investors expect the firm to earn on its equity.

Problem 4

If the rate of IDBI Flexible bond is 8% and the expected return for the market is 16% and beta is 0.6 for a given equity share, what is the cost of equity capital:

Solution

$$K_e = 8 + 0.6\,(16 - 8)$$
$$= 8 + 4.8$$
$$= 12.8\%$$

Note: Return on bond is a risk-free return

IV. Earnings Price Ratio Approach:

This approach assumes that the shareholders capitalize a stream of earnings by the capitalization rate. The earnings price ratio is calculated by dividing earnings per share by the average price per share. Thus, cost o equity, (K_e) is measured by:

$$K_e = \frac{E_1}{P}$$

Where, E_1 = Earnings per share for the next year.

P = Current market price of the share.

Problem 5

The share capital of a company comprises of 5,00,000 shares of ₹ 10 each fully paid. The current market price of the share is ₹ 25. Earnings available to equity shareholders amount to ₹ 30,00,000 at the end of a period. Calculate the cost of equity capital, using earnings price ratio?

Solution

$$(E_1)\text{ Earnings per share} = \frac{\text{Earnings available to Equity Shareholders}}{\text{No of shares issued}}$$

$$= \frac{30,00,000}{5,00,000} = ₹\ 6$$

(P) Current market price per share = ₹ 25

$$\text{Cost of equity capital } (k_e) = \frac{E_1}{P} = ₹\ \frac{6}{25} \times 100$$

$$= 24\ \%$$

V. Dividends Price Approach:

In this approach the investor arrives at the market price of an equity share by capitalizing the set of expected dividend payments.

$$K_e = \frac{D_1}{P}$$

Where, D_1 = Dividend per share expected at the end of a period.

P = Current market price.

VI. Dividend Price Plus Growth Approach (Dividend Growth Model)

Under this mode, cost of equity is the dividend yield plus the expected dividend growth rate. Symbolically,

$$K_e = \frac{D_1}{P} + g$$

Where, D_1 = Dividend per share at the end of a period

P = Current market price, and

g = Growth rate in dividends.

This model shows a market value approach to determine the cost of equity capital. The market price of an ordinary share equals the cash flow of expected future incomes. Assumption of this model is that incomes will grow at a constant compound rate.

Problem 6

Current market price of an equity share of a company is ₹ 100, the expected dividend at the end of the year is ₹ 12. Calculate the cost of equity, in case the dividends are expected to grow at 6%.

Solution

$$K_e = \frac{D_1}{P} + g$$

$$= \frac{12}{100} + 0.06$$

$$= 0.12 + 0.06$$

$$= 0.18 \text{ or } 18\%$$

VII. Earnings Growth Model

$$K_e = \frac{E_1}{P} + g$$

Where, E = Earnings per share at the end of a period
P = Current market price and
g = Growth rate in earnings.

Earnings model is preferable to the dividend model because the growth of dividends would be extremely difficult because of many variables, such as tax rates, general economic conditions, earnings, shareholder's reaction etc.

The market price per share (P) will be adjusted by (1 – f) where f stands for rate of floatation costs, *e.g.*, brokerage, underwriting commission etc. Because of floating costs, the full market value per share cannot usually be realized; the net amount per share would be issue price less floating cost per share, thus, the cost of new equity will be as follows:

$$K_e = \frac{E_1}{P(1-f)} + g$$

Problem 7

A Public Limited Company has decided to issue new equity shares of ₹ 10 each to raise additional capital of ₹ 2, 50,00,000. The cost of floatation is expected to be 4%. The earnings per share would be ₹ 12.50 and growth rate in earnings would be 6% respectively. It the current market price per share is ₹ 80, find out the cost of new equity.

Solution

$$K_e = \frac{E_1}{P(1-f)} + g$$

$$= \frac{12.50}{80(1-.04)} + 0.06$$

$$= \frac{12.50}{76.8} + 0.06$$

$$= 0.1627 + 0.06$$

$$= 0.2227$$

$$= 22.27\%$$

D. Cost of Retained Earnings (K_r)

Retained Earnings may be treated at per with equity shares capital. In other words, the cost of retained earnings may be measured in exactly the same way as equity share capital.

$$\therefore \quad K_r = K_e$$

The retained earnings are assumed as the investment of existing shareholders in the firm itself. The cost of retained earnings is always less than the cost of new issue of common stock due to absence of floating costs.

E. Cost of Term Loans (K_t)

The cost of Term Loans will be equal to the interest rate multiplied by (1 – Tax rate) or (1 – t). The interest rate to be used here will be interest rate applicable to the new term Loan.

$$K_t = I(1 - t)$$

Where, I = Rate of interest

t = Corporate tax rate

7.3. AFTER-TAX WEIGHTED AVERAGE COST OF CAPITAL

After-weighted or overall cost of capital is more appropriate due to the following reasons:

(a) There is no difference between after-tax cost of equity and before-tax cost of equity and also between after-tax cost of preference capital and before-tax cost of preference capital. But difference lies between after-tax cost of debt and before-tax cost of debt. While combining all their specific costs of capital into an overall or weighted average cost of capital, it is desirable that after-tax basis is adopted in order to bring in uniformity among the various components of cost of capital.

(b) Cost of capital is taken as cut-off rate or the discounting rate and used for making investment decisions. Since dividend (equity and pref.) is paid only out after-tax profits, cost of capital should be computed on after-tax basis.

7.4. IS EQUITY CAPITAL FREE OF COST?

Equity shareholders purchase the share with the expectation of dividends and capital gains. Though a company is not legally bound to pay dividends, payment of dividends enhances the market value of shares and therefore, equity capital cannot be taken as 'free of cost'.

7.5. COMPUTATION OF WEIGHTED AVERAGE / OVERALL COST OF CAPITAL (WAAC)

Computation of overall cost of capital involves the following steps:

Step 1: Calculation of each specific source of fund, *e.g.*, cost of equity capital.

Step 2: Determining the weights associated with each source of finance.

Step 3: multiplying the cost of each source by the appropriate weights

Step 4: WAAC = $W_e \times K_e + W_p \times K_p + W_d \times K_d + W_r \times K_r + W_t \times K_t$

Problem 8

A limited company has the following capital structure:

	₹ in lakhs
Equity share capital (₹ 10 / share)	200
14% Preference share Capital (₹ 100 /share)	100
Retained Earnings	200
12% Debentures (₹ 100 each)	450
10% Term Loan from IDBI Bank	50
Total	1000

The market price per equity share is ₹ 25. The company is expected to declare a dividend per share of ₹ 2 per share and there will be a growth of 10% in the dividends for the next 5 years. The preference shares are redeemable at a premium of ₹ 5 per share (5%) after 6 years and are currently traded at ₹ 95 in the market. Redemption of debentures will take place after 7 years at par and their current market price is ₹ 90 per unit. The corporate tax rate ₹ 40%. Calculate the WACC.

Solution

Step 1:

$$K_e = \frac{D_1}{P} + g$$

$$= \frac{2}{25} + 0.10$$

$$= 0.08 + 0.10$$

$$= 0.18 = 18\%$$

$$K_P = \frac{D + \frac{F - P}{n}}{\frac{F + P}{2}}$$

$$= \frac{14 + \frac{105 - 95}{6}}{\frac{105 + 95}{2}} = \frac{15.6667}{100}$$

$$= 0.1566667 = 15.67\%$$

$$K_r = K_e = 18\%$$

$$K_d = \frac{I(1 - t) + \frac{F - P}{n}}{\frac{F + P}{2}}$$

$$= \frac{12\,(1-0.4) + \dfrac{100-90}{7}}{\dfrac{100+90}{2}}$$

$$= \frac{8.62857}{95}$$

$$= 0.0908 = 9.08\%$$

$$K_t = I\,(1-t)$$

$$= 0.10(1-0.4) = 0.06 = 6\%$$

Step 2:

$$W_e = \frac{200}{1000} = 0.20$$

$$W_p = \frac{100}{1000} = 0.10$$

$$W_r = \frac{200}{1000} = 0.20$$

$$W_d = \frac{450}{1000} = 0.45$$

$$W_t = \frac{50}{1000} = 0.05$$

$$\text{Total} = 1.00$$

Step 3:

$$W_e \times K_e = 0.20 \times 0.18 = 0.036$$

$$W_p \times K_p = 0.10 \times 0.1567 = 0.0157$$

$$W_r \times K_r = 0.20 \times 0.18 = 0.036$$

$$W_d \times K_d = 0.45 \times .0908 = 0.0409$$

$$W_t \times K_t = 0.05 \times 0.06 = 0.003$$

Step 4:

$$WACC = W_eK_e + W_pK_p + W_rK_r + W_dK_d + W_tK_t$$

$$= 0.036 + 0.0157 + 0.036 + 0.0409 + 0.063$$

$$= 0.1316$$

$$= 13.16\%$$

Alternatively

Table: Calculation of WACC

Sources	Total ₹ in lakhs	Weights	After-tax cost of capital	Weighted cost
Equity Capital	200	$\frac{200}{1000} = 0.20$	0.18	0.0360
14% Pref. Capital	100	$\frac{100}{1000} = 0.10$	0.1567	0.0157
Retained Earnings	200	$\frac{200}{1000} = 0.20$	0.18	0.0360
12% Debentures	450	$\frac{450}{1000} = 0.45$	0.0908	0.0409
10% Term Loan	50	$\frac{50}{1000} = 0.05$	0.06	0.003
Total	1000	1	—	0.1316

WACC = 0.1316 = 13.16%

Problem 9

ABC Ltd. has assets of 30 lakhs which have been financed with ₹ 18 lakhs of term loan, ₹ 10 lakhs of equity shares and a general reserve of ₹ 2 lakhs. The firms' total profits after interest and taxes for the year ended 31st March, 2010 were ₹ 1,80,000. It pays 10% interest on borrowed funds and is in the 30% tax brocket. It has 18,000 equity shares of ₹ 100 each selling at a market price of ₹ 200 per share. What is the weighted average cost of capital?

Solution

Working

(i) $K_e = \frac{E_1}{P} = \frac{10}{200}$

$= 0.05$ or 5%

E_1 = Earnings / share = $\frac{₹\ 1,80,000}{18,000}$ = ₹ 10

(ii) $K_r = K_e = 5\%$ or 0.05

(iii) $K_d = I\ (1 - t)$

$= 0.10\ (1 - 0.30) = 0.07 = 7\%$

Sources	Total ₹ in lakhs	Weights	After-tax cost	Weighted cost
Equity Capital	10	$\frac{10}{30} = 0.333$	0.05	0.01665
Reserves	2	$\frac{2}{30} = 0.067$	0.05	0.00335
Debts.	18	$\frac{18}{30} = 0.600$	0.07	0.04200
Total	30	1	-----	0.062

WACC = 0.062 = 6.20%

Problem 10

The share of ABC Ltd. is quoted in the market at ₹ 40 currently. The company pays a dividend of ₹ 2 per share and the investors expect a growth rate of 10% per year.

(i) Compute the company's equity cost of capital.

(ii) If the anticipated growth rate is 11% p.a., calculated the indicated market price per share.

(iii) If the company's cost of capital is 9% and the anticipated growth rate is 6% p.a., calculate the indicated market price, if the dividend of ₹ 2 per share is to be maintained.

Solution

(i) $K_e = \frac{E_1}{P} + g = \frac{₹\,2}{₹\,40} + 10\% = 5\% + 10\% = 15\%$

(ii) $K_e = \frac{E_1}{P} + g$

Or $\frac{E_1}{P} = K_e - g$

Or $\frac{E_1}{P} = 15\% - 11\% = 4\%$ or, $P = \frac{E_1}{4\%}$

Or $P = \frac{2}{4\%} = \frac{2}{0.04} = ₹\,50$

(iii) $P = \frac{E_1}{K_e - g} = \frac{2}{9\% - 6\%} = \frac{2}{3\%} = \frac{2}{0.03} = ₹\,66.67$

Problem 11

A Company is to expand its business and accordingly if desires to increase assets by 60% by the end of the year 2010-2011. The existing capital structure of the company is given as under:

9% Debentures (Par value ₹ 1,000/debenture)	10,00,000
9.5% Preference Share Capital (Par value ₹ 100/share)	3,00,000
Equity share capital (Par value ₹ 100/share)	12,00,000
Total	25,00,000

New debentures can be sold at par at 10% interest rate. Preference shares will have a 14% dividend rate and can be sold at par. Equity shares can be sold to net ₹ 95 per share. The shareholder's required rate of return is 8% which is expected to grow at the rate of 5%. Retained earnings for the year are estimated to be ₹ 5,00,000. You are required to determine the following:

(i) What is the required amount of new capital expenditure?

(ii) What should be the optimal structure of new financing?

(iii) Calculate the cost of individual capital components. Assume average shareholder's marginal tax rate is 30% and corporate tax rate is 40%.

(iv) Calculate the weighted average cost of capital of the new financing to be made by the company.

Solution

(i) The company desires to expand its assets by 60%. The present level of capital is ₹ 25,00,000 which will increase to ₹ (25,00,000 + 60% of 25,00,000) or to ₹ 40,00,000. Hence, the required amount of new capital expenditure will be 60% of 25,00,000 or ₹ (40,00,000 – 25,00,000) or ₹ 15,00,000.

(ii) Existing pattern of capital structure:

Sources	Total ₹	Proportion
9% Debenture	10,00,000	40% = .40
9.5 % Preference share capital	3,00,000	12 % = .12
Equity share capital	12,00,000	48 % = .42

Ratio of the proportion = 40:12:48 = 10:3:12

Since retained earnings available for the expansion purpose are expected to be ₹ 5,00,000; the rest ₹ 10,00,000 will have to be raised by external sources in the above ratio of the proportion.

The proposed capital structure of new financing of ₹ 15,00,000

Sources	Proportion		Total ₹
Retained Earnings	33.33%	5,00,000/15,00,000	5,00,000
Balance ₹ 10,00,000			
will have to be raised by: (10 : 3 : 12)			
10% Debenture	26.67%	4,00,000/15,00,000	4,00,000
14% Preference share capital	8%	1,20,000/15,00,000	1,20,000
Equity share capital	32%	4,80,000/15,00,000	4,80,000
Total	100% = 1		15,00,000

(iii) Cost of debenture (irredeemable), K_d:

$$K_d = \text{Rate of Interest } (1 - t)$$
$$= 1(1 - t)$$
$$= 10\% \ (1 - .40)$$
$$= 10\% \times .60$$
$$= 6\%$$

Cost of preference share (irredeemable), K_p:

$$= \frac{D}{NP} = \frac{14\% \times 100}{100} = \frac{14}{100} = 14\%$$

When, NP = Net proceeds from the issue

Cost of Equity share, K_e:

$$= \frac{D_1}{P} + g = \frac{8}{95} + 0.05 = 0.1342 = 13.42\%$$

When, D_1 = Dividend per share after 1 year.

= 8% × ₹ 100 = ₹ 8

P = Current market price = ₹ 95/share.

g = growth rate in dividends = 5% = 0.5

Cost of retained earnings = $K_r = K_e$ = 13.42%

(iv) Weighted average cost of capital of new financing

Sourcesof capital	Total ₹ in lakhs	Weights	After-tax cost of capital	Weighted cost
10% Debentures	4,00,000	.2667	.06	.0160
14% Preference share capital	1,20,000	.08	.14	.0112
Equity share capital	4,80,000	.32	.1342	0.0429
Retained Earnings	5,00,000	.3333	.1342	0.0447
Total	**15,00,000**	**1.00**		**0.1148**

Weighted Average Cost of Capital of new financing = 11.48%

Example 12

The following is the capital structure of ABC Ltd.

Sources of capital	Amount ₹	Weight %	Before-tax cost (%)
Equity share capital (10,000 shares of ₹ 100 each)	10,00,000	40	13
9% Preference share capital (2500 shares of ₹ 100 each)	2,50,000	10	9
10% Term Loan (debt)	7,50,000	30	10
Retained Earnings (Reserve)	5,00,000	20	13

(i) Calculate the weighted average cost of capital of the company. Corporate tax rate is 35%.

(ii) Assuming in the above exercise, that the company can raise additional loan or debt at 12% for ₹ 5,00,000 to finance an expansion. Calculate the revised weighted average cost of capital.

Solution

(i) Table: Calculation of Weighted Average Cost of Capital

Sourcesof capital	Amount ₹	Weights	After-tax cost of capital	Weighted cost
Equity share capital	10,00,000	.40	.13	0.052
9% Preference share capital	2,50,000	.10	.09	0.009
10% Term Loan	7,50,000	.30	.10(1-.35)= .065	0.0195
Retained Earnings	5,00,000	.20	.13	0.026
Total	**25,00,000**	**1**		**0.1065**

Weighted Average cost of Capital = 10.65%

(ii) Table: Calculation of Revised Weighted Average Cost of Capital

Sources of capital	Total ₹ in lakhs	Weights	After-tax cost	Weighted cost of capital
Equity share capital	10,00,000	.3333	.13	0.0433
9% Preference share capital	2,50,000	0.0833	.09	0.0075
10% Term Loan	7,50,000	0.25	.065	0.01625
12% Term Loan (Addl)	5,00,000	0.1667	.12(1-.35)= .078	0.0130
Retained Earnings	5,00,000	0.1667	.13	0.0216
Total	**30,00,000**	**100%=1**		**0.1016**

Revised weighted Average Cost of Capital = 10.16%

SUMMARY

'Cost of capital' is, in fact, the price which becomes payable since use of capital involves the period of 'time' for which the owner actually is deprived of its possession.

Price is payable by a firm is received by the suppliers for holding back their capital in production process of the different categories of financial capital and hence, price as 'cost of capital' is synonymous with the 'cost of finance'.

'Cost of finance' includes the following important costs:

- Payment of dividend;
- Payment of interest.

Cost of capital may be defined 'as overall cost of capital' of a firm which comprises the costs of the difference sources of financing from which capital is raised by a firm. Overall cost of capital is the 'weighted average cost of capital' from different sources.

Return at zero risk level: Rate of return expected from the zero-risk project undertaken by the firm.

Business risk premium: Additional return expected from the business investment carrying the feature of business risk resulting variability in operating profit. Higher the risk, higher will be the risk premium that is higher will be the expectation of additional return.

Financial risk Premium: Additional return expected from the investment in fixed income securities like debt, preference capital carrying the feature of financial risk. Higher the financial risk, higher will be the expected rate of return by the investors.

EXERCISE

Short Questions

1. What is 'cost of capital'?
2. Is cost of equity zero?
3. Name at least three financial decisions where cost of capital is used.
4. What is the difference between earning price ratio approach and Earning Growth Model to determine cost of capital?
5. What is meant by perpetual preference capital?
6. Which one is tax deductible expenditure among interest payment on debt and dividend payable on equity and preference capital both?
7. What is 'cost of equity'?
8. What is the difference between specific and combined or overall cost of capital?
9. What is 'Business Risk Premium'?

Broad and Moderate Questions

1. Explain the different concepts of cost of capital and also significance of cost of capital.
2. Explain the components of cost of capital.
3. Explain the concept of "cost of capital" as a device for establishing cut-off point of capital investment proposal.

4. What do you mean by preference shares? How do you calculate the cost of preference capital and debenture capital?
5. Describe all approaches which have adopted for estimating cost of equity?
6. Explain CAPM used in computing cost of capital.

Problems

1. Bharat chemicals has the following capital structure:

Equity share capital (₹ 10 per share)	₹	4,00,000
13% Term Loan from ICICI bank	₹	1,50,000
9% Preference shares (₹ 100 per share)		
Currently traded at ₹ 95 with 6 years maturity period	₹	1,00,000
Total	₹	6,50,000

The company is expected to declare a dividend of ₹ 5 next year and the growth rate of dividends is expected to be 8%. Equity shares are currently traded at ₹ 27 in the market. Assume tax rate of 30%. What is WACC?

2. A company has three divisions – A, B and C. Each division has a capital structure with debt, preference shares and equity shares in the ratio of 3:4:3 respectively. The company is planning to raise debt, preference shares and equity for all the 3 divisions together. Further, it is planning to take a bank loan (a) 12% interest. The preference shares have a face value of ₹ 100, dividend @ 12%, 6 years maturity and currently prices at ₹ 88. Calculate the cost of preference shares and debt if taxes rate applicable is 40%

3. Excel Industries Ltd. has assets of ₹ 16,00,00,000 which has been financed with ₹ 7,20,00,000 of 12% debenture, ₹ 7,00,00,000 of equity share capital and a general reserve of ₹ 1,80,00,000. The firms' EBIT for the year ended 31.03.2009 was ₹ 2,25,00,000. The corporate tax rate is 35%. The company has 7,00,000 equity shares of ₹ 100 each selling at a market price of ₹ 150 each share. What is the weighted average cost of capital?

4. From the following details ascertain the 'specific cost' of each source of capital:

   (i) The equity share capital of a public limited company consists of 1 crore rupees divided into 10 lakhs equity shares of ₹ 10 each. Currently these shares are quoted in the market at ₹ 20 each. The company has paid a dividend of ₹ 2.50 per share and the investors market expects growth in dividend at the rate of 5% p.m. What is the cost of equity capital to the firm?

   (ii) A company has raised ₹ 95,00,000 by the issue of 1,00,000, 10% debentures of ₹ 100 each at a discount of 5%, repayable or redeemable at par after 10 years. If the rate of company's tax is 40%. What is the cost of debt capital to the firm?

   (iii) A company has collected ₹ 47,50,000 by the issue of 50,000, 12% redeemable preference shares of ₹ 100 each at a discount of 5%. The floatation cost for the purpose had been ₹ 2,375. What is the cost of preference capital to the firm?

5. Given below is the summary of the Balance sheet of a company as at 31st March, 2005:

Assets	₹
A. Fixed assets	5,00,000
B. Investments	1,25,000

		₹	
C. Working capital:			
Current assets		3,25,000	
Less: Current liabilities:			
Short-term loan	2,00,000		
Trade creditor	50,000	2,50,000	75,000
			7,00,000

Liabilities:	
A. Equity share capital (40000 shares of ₹ 10 each)	4,00,000
B. Reserve & surplus	1,30,000
C. 10% Debentures (Redeemable at par in 31st March 2009, Face value = ₹ 100 per debenture)	1,70,000
	7,00,000

You are required to calculate the company's weighted average cost of capital using balance sheet valuations. The following additional information are also available:

(a) 10% Debentures were issued at par.

(b) All interest payments are up-to-date and equity dividend is currently 14%.

(c) Short-term loan carries at 20% p.a.

(d) The shares and debentures of the company are all quoted on the Stock Exchange and current market prices are as follows:

Equity shares:	₹ 15 each
10% Debentures:	₹ 97 each

(e) The corporate tax rate is 35%.

❑❑❑

8 Working Capital Management

8.1 INTRODUCTION

Working capital is the life blood and nerve centre of a business. Just as circulation of blood is essential in the human body for maintaining life, working capital is very essential to maintain the smooth running of a business. No business can run successfully without an adequate amount of working capital. Working capital refers to that part of firm's capital which is required for financing short term or current assets such as cash, marketable securities, debtors, and inventories. In other words working capital is the amount of funds necessary to cover the cost of operating the enterprise.

Working capital means the funds (*i.e.,* capital) available and used for day to day operations (*i.e.,* working) of an enterprise. It consists broadly of that portion of assets of a business which are used in or related to its current operations. It refers to funds which are used during an accounting period to generate a current income of a type which is consistent with major purpose of a firm existence.

Objectives of working capital

Every business needs some amount of working capital. It is needed for following purposes

- For the purchase of raw materials, components and spares.
- To pay wages and salaries.
- To incur day-to-day expenses and overhead costs such as fuel, power, and office expenses etc.
- To provide credit facilities to customers etc.

8.2 CONCEPTS OF WORKING CAPITAL

A. Balance Sheet Concept

1. Gross Working Capital

Total or gross working capital is that working capital which is used for all the current assets. Total value of current assets will equal to gross working capital.

2. Net Working Capital

Net working capital is the excess of current assets over current liabilities.

Net Working Capital = Total Current Assets – Total Current Liabilities

This amount shows that if we deduct total current liabilities from total current assets, then balance amount can be used for repayment of long term debts at any time.

B. Operating Cycle Concept

Working capital is also known as revolving capital and a circular path of conversion/ reconversion takes place. This revolution of cycle is called as the operating cycle. Let us consider an example to better understand operating cycle. A person starts a business with an initial investment. With credit extended by expense creditors, he starts production process. Goods of varying levels of finish results, and thus called as work-in-progress. Once complete processing is done, it is called as finished goods. Until these goods are sold, they remain in stock. Sales may be for cash and/or credit basis. The business person needs to wait a little to realize cash from credit customers. The realized cash is used to pay creditors. But he needs to maintain cash balance for day-to-day operations as well as for meeting sudden spurt in payment obligations accompanied by sluggish cash collections from debtors. Thus a revolution or cycle from cash to raw materials to Work-in-Progress, to finished goods, to debtors, and back to cash takes place. This revolution is called as operating cycle.

Thus, we can say that the term operating cycle, otherwise called as cash cycle refers to the length of time necessary to complete the following cycle of events:

1. Conversion of cash into inventory
2. Conversion of inventory into debtors
3. Conversion of debtors into cash

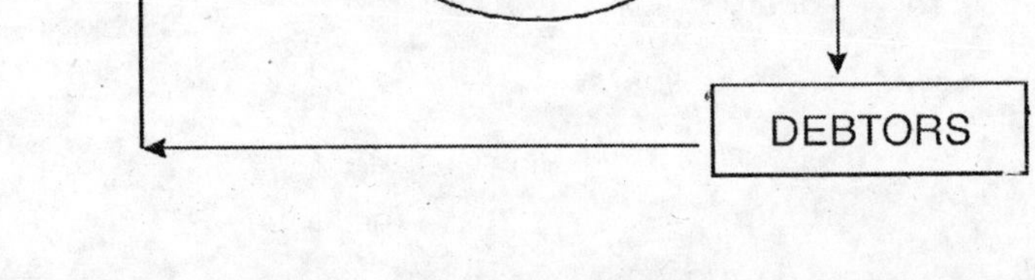

Stage 1: Cash to Inventory – In this stage, cash first gets converted into raw materials, then work-in-progress and then finished goods in a typical manufacturing concern. As regards non-manufacturing concerns, when the goods are purchased, cash gets converted into inventory.

Stage 2: Inventory to Debtors – The inventory thus produced or purchased, gets converted into debtors or receivables upon credit sales.

Stage 3: The debtors or accounts receivables get in turn converted back into cash when they make payment.

Length of Operating Cycle: When raw materials remain in store pending issue for production for a less duration, when raw materials gets converted into WIP in a short duration, when finished goods remain in warehouse pending for sales for a short duration only, and when cash realizations out of sales are made quickly and finally when payment to creditors is made slowly, the operating cycle would be smaller and consequently the working capital will also be reasonable. Thus shorter duration of operating cycle indicates an efficient working capital management.

8.3 TYPES OF WORKING CAPITAL

There are two kinds of working capital.

1. Permanent Working Capital: Permanent working capital refers to the minimum amount of all current assets that is required at all times to ensure a minimum level of uninterrupted business operations. Some minimum amount of raw materials, work-in-progress, bank balance, finished goods etc., a business has to carry all the time irrespective of the level of manufacturing or marketing operations. This level of working capital is referred to as core working capital or core current assets. But the level of core current assets is not a constant sum at all the times. For a growing business the permanent working capital will be rising, for a declining business it will be decreasing and for a stable business it will almost remain the same with few variations. So, permanent working capital is perennially needed one though not fixed in volume. This part of the working capital being a permanent investment needs to be financed through long-term funds.

2. Temporary Working Capital: The temporary or varying working capital varies with the volume of operations. It fluctuates with the scale of operations. This is the additional working capital required from time to time over and above the permanent or fixed working capital. During seasons, more production/sales take place resulting in larger working capital needs. The reverse is true during off-seasons. As seasons vary, temporary working capital requirement moves up and down. Temporary working capital can be financed through short term funds like current liabilities. When the level of temporary working capital moves up, the business might use short-term funds and when the level for temporary working capital recedes, the business may retire its short-term loans.

Both permanent and temporary working capitals are necessary to facilitate the sales and production process through operating cycle.

8.4 WORKING CAPITAL MANAGEMENT

In working capital management, we analyze following three points:

What is the need for working capital?

After study the nature of production, we can estimate the need for working capital. If company produces products at large scale and continues producing goods, then company needs high amount of working capital.

What is optimum level of working capital in business?

Have you achieved the optimum level of working capital which has invested in current assets? Because high amount of working capital will decrease the return on investment and low amount of working capital will increase the risk of business. So, it is very important decision to get optimum level of working capital where both profitability and risk will be balanced. For achieving optimum level of working capital, finance manager should also study the factors which affect the requirement of working capital and different elements of current assets. If he will manage cash, debtor and inventory, then working capital will automatically optimize.

What are main working capital policies of businesses?

Policies are the guidelines which are helpful to direct business. Finance manager can also make working capital policies.

Liquidity Policy: Under this policy, finance manager will increase the amount of liquidity for reducing the risk of business. If business has high volume of cash and bank balance, then business can easily pays his dues at maturity. But finance manger should not forget that the excess cash will not produce any earning and return on investment will decrease. So liquidity policy should be optimized.

Profitability Policy: Under this policy, finance manger will keep low amount of cash in business and try to invest maximum amount of cash and bank balance. It will sure that profit of business will increase due to increasing of investment in proper way but risk of business will also increase because liquidity of business will decrease and it can create bankruptcy position of business. So, profitability policy should make after seeing liquidity policy and after this both policies will helpful for proper management of working capital.

Significance of Working Capital Management

The management of working capital is important for several reasons. For one thing, the current assets of a typical manufacturing firm account for half of its total assets. For a distribution company, they account for even more. Working capital requires continuous day to day supervision. Working capital has the effect on company's risk, return and share prices, There is an inevitable relationship between sales growth and the level of current assets. The target sales level can be achieved only if supported by adequate working capital. Inefficient working capital management may lead to insolvency of the firm if it is not in a position to meet its liabilities and commitments.

8.5. FACTORS DETERMINING WORKING CAPITAL REQUIREMENT

A firm should have neither low nor high working capital. Low working capital involves more risk and more returns, high working capital involves less risk and less returns. Risk here refers to technical insolvency while returns refer to increased profits/earnings. The amount of working capital is determined by a wide variety of factors.

1. Nature of business
2. Seasonality of operations
3. Production cycle
4. Production policy
5. Credit policy
6. Market conditions
7. Conditions of supply

Nature of Business: The working capital requirement of a firm depends on the nature of the business. For example, a firm is involved in sale of services rather than manufacturing or a firm is allowing only cash sales. In the first instance, no investment is required in either raw materials or WIP or finished goods, while in the second instance there exists no receivables as there is immediate realization of cash. Hence the requirement of working capital will be lower.

Seasonality of Operations: If the product of the firm has a seasonal demand like refrigerators, the firms need high working capital in the periods of summer, as the demand for the refrigerators is more and the firm needs low working capital in the periods of winter, as the demand for the product is low.

Production Cycle: The term production cycle refers to the time involved in the manufacture of goods. It covers the time span between the procurement of the raw materials and the completion of the manufacturing process leading to the production of goods. As funds are necessarily tied up during the production cycle, the production cycle has a bearing on the quantum of working capital. The longer the time span of production cycle, the larger will be the funds tied up and therefore the larger the working capital needed and *vice versa*.

Production Policy: The quantum of working capital is also determined by production policy. The production policy of the firm determines the amount of working capital requirement. If the firm has production policy to carry production at a steady level to meet the peak demand, this will result in a large accumulation of finished goods (inventories) during the off-seasons and the abrupt sale during the peak season. The progressive accumulation of finished goods will naturally require an increasing amount of working capital. If the firm has production policy to produce only when there is a demand then the firm needs low working capital during the slack season and high working capital during the peak season.

Credit Policy: The level of the working capital is also determined by the credit policy, as the firm's credit policy determines the amount of receivables. If the firm has a liberal credit policy, then the firm needs high working capital and the firm needs low working capital if the company's credit policy does not allow it to extend credit to the buyers.

Market Conditions: The working capital requirements are also determined by the market conditions. In case of the high degree of competition prevailing in the market the firm has to maintain larger inventories as customers are not inclined to wait for the product. This needs higher working capital requirements. If there is good demand for the product and the competition is weak, a firm can manage with smaller inventory of finished goods, as customers can wait for the product if it is not available in the market. Thus, a firm can manage with low inventory and will need low working capital requirements.

Conditions of Supply: The availability of raw materials and spares also determine the level of working capital. If there is ready availability of raw materials and spares, a firm can maintain minimum inventory and need less working capital. If the supply of raw materials is unpredictable, then the firm has to acquire stocks as and when they are available for ensuring continuous production. Thus, the firm needs to maintain larger inventory average and needs larger requirement of working capital.

8.6. LIQUIDITY PROFITABLE TANGLE

When return on capital employed (Fixed Assets + Working Capital) is used as the measure of profitability, the following ratio shows the relation between profitability and liquidity, *e.g.*:

Profitability

OR

$$\text{(Return on Capital Employed)} = \frac{\text{Operating Profit before Interest and Tax}}{\text{Net Fixed Assets + Working Capital}}$$

$$= \frac{\text{Operating Profit before Interest and Tax}}{\text{Capital Employed}}$$

Other things remaining constant, with more and more economy in the use of working capital for attaining the same volume of sales in a firm, the overall profitability increases. However we cannot be optimistic in this regard since profitability depends on other so many factors e.g. pricing policy, cost structure etc. Thus, it is usually assumed that there is a always a negative relationship between liquidity and profitability.

Management of current assets leads to trade off between 'Profitability and Liquidity':

Since the total amount of financial resources is limited and there resources can be put to alternative uses, the larger the amount of investment in current assets, the smaller will be the amount available for investment in other profitable avenues at hand with the company. A conservative attitude in respect of investment in current assets leaves less amount for other investments than an aggressive approach does. Further since, since current assets will be more for a given level of sales forecast under the conservative approach, the turnover of current assets (calculated as the ratio of net sales to current assets) will be less than what they would be under the aggressive approach. This being so, even if we assume the same level of sales revenues, operating profit before interest and tax and net fixed assets, the company following a conservative policy will have a lower percentage of operating profitability than what they would be under the aggressive approach.

From the following illustration, we will show that an aggressive approach results in greater profitability but lower liquidity while a conservative approach results in lower profitability but higher liquidly.

Sl. No.	Particulars	Conservative Policy	Aggressive Policy
1.	Net Sates	₹ 10 crores	₹ 10 crores
2.	Operating Profit before Interest & Tax	₹ 1 crore	₹ 1 crore
3.	Net (operating) Fixed Assets	₹ 2 crores	₹ 2 crores
4.	Current Assets	₹ 1.6 crore	₹ 1 crore
5.	Total Operating Assets = 3 + 4	₹ 3.6 crores	₹ 3 crores
6.	Net Operating Profit Margin = $\frac{2}{1}$	1/10 = 10% = .10	1/10 = 10% = .10
7.	Turnover of Net Operating Fixed Assets = 1/3	10/2 = 5 times	10/2 = 5 times
8.	Turnover of Current Assets = 1/4	10/1.6 = 6.25 times	10/1 = 10 times
9.	Turnover of Total Operating Assets = 1/5	10/3.6 = 2.78 times	10/3 = 3.33 times
10.	Rate of Return on Total Operating Assets = 6 × 9	27.8%	33.3%
11.	Ratio of Current Assets to Net Operating Fixed Assets = 4/3 (Degree of liquidity)	1.6/2 = 0.80 OR 80% (higher liquidity)	1/2 = 0.5 or 50% (lower liquidity)
12.	Current Liabilities (Current Ratio = 2:1)	₹ 0.8 crore	₹ 0.5 crore
13.	Working Capital = 4-12	₹ 0.8 crore	₹ 0.5 crore
14.	Capital Employed = Net Fixed Asset + Working Capital = 3 + 13	₹ 2 + 0.8 = ₹ 2.8 crores	₹ 2 + 0.5 = ₹ 2.5 crores
15.	Return on Capital Employed = 2/14	1/2.8 × 100% = 0.3571 = 35.71	1/2.5 × 100% = 0.4 = 40%
16.	Status	Lower Profitability	(Higher Profitability)

Note: The firm is maintaining 2:1 current ratio. If level of current liabilities is same under both conservative and aggressive approach say 0.8 crore then more higher profitability will be seen under aggressive approach in compare to earlier level of current liability (0.5 crore).

The above result can be resolved to a certain extent by the management by following a moderate policy which is neither highly conservative nor highly aggressive where some liquidity and profitability have to be scarified so that the resultant figures of liquidity and profitability are reasonably satisfactory to the company. If the management decides to follow a moderate approach which leads to an investment of ₹ (1.6 + 1)/2 =1.3 crores in current assets, the following result will be seen where profitability is higher in compare to profitability under conservative approach but is lower in compare to profitability under aggressive approach.

[Profitability = return on capital employed]

Sl. No.	Particulars (Sales, Operating Profit and Fixed Assets are same)	Moderate Approach
1.	Current Assets	₹ 1.3 crores
2.	Current liabilities = $\frac{1}{2}$ × Current Assets	₹ 0.65 crores
3.	Net operating Fixed Asset,	₹ 2 crores
4.	Total Operating Fixed Assets = 1+3	₹ 3.3 crores
5.	Net Operating Profit Margin (as earlier)	10%
6.	Turnover of Total Operating Assets	10 crores/3.3
	$= \frac{\text{Net Sales}}{\text{Total Operating Assets}}$	= 3.0303 times
7.	Rate of Return on Total Operating Assets = 5 × 6	30.03%
8.	Working Capital = 1 – 2	₹ 0.65 crore
9.	Capital Employed 3 + 8	₹ 2.65 crores
10.	Return on Capital Employed	= 1/2.65 crores = .3773
	$= \frac{\text{Operating Profit Before Interest and Tax}}{\text{Capital Employed}}$	= 37.73%
11.	Degree of liquidity = $\frac{\text{Current Asset}}{\text{Net op. Fixed Asset}}$	1.3/2 = 0.65 = 65%

Under degree of liquidity of 65%, we can bring a proper balance between liquidity where level of investment in current assets is maintained at 1.3 crores.

8.7 STRATEGIES / APPROACHES OF FINANCING OF CURRENT ASSETS

Both long-term and short-term sources can be used by a firm for financing its fixed & current assets. The proportion of short-term and long-term sources for financing current assets will depend upon a number of factors like flexibility, risk, cost, demand and supply position in the money market, preference and so ok. In practice, any of the following strategies on approaches can be adopted for financing of current assets.

A. Hedging Policy: (Matching Policy)

Under this approach, fixed assets and Hard core or permanent current assets are financed out of long-term sources (Equity and Debt.) and fluctuating or temporary current assets are financed out of short-term sources of finance. The justification of this policy is that since the purpose of financing is to invest in an asset, the liability should be liquidated when the life of the asset expires. Use of long-term sources for financing short-term assets will be costly as the funds will remain idle after the expiry of asset's lifes. Similarly, financing long-term assets with short-term sources is inconvenient and costly as they are to be renewed on a continuous basis up to the lifes of the assets concerned. When the level of permanent current assets increases long-term finance also increases. Temporary current assets are financed entirely by short-term sources.

B. Conservative Policy

Under this approach, Fixed Assets, Hard-core permanent current assets and part of fluctuating current assets are financed out of long-term sources (Equity and Debt) and part of fluctuating current assets are financed out of short-term sources of finance. The justification of this policy is that a firm wants to be safe by resorting to more and more long-term financing and it meets its peak requirements only from short-term sources. The larger the percentage of funds obtained from long-term sources, the more conservative is a firm's financing policy and *vice versa*.

C. Aggressive Policy

Under this approach, Fixed Assets, part of hard core current assets are financed out of long-term sources (Equity and Debt) and Fluctuating current assests along with other part of hard core current assets are financed out of short-term sources of funds. The firm may rely more on short-term sources than on long-term sources to finance its current assets. The larges the percentage of funds obtained from short-term sources for financing current assets of a firm, the more aggressive is the financing policy and *vice versa*.

D. Highly Aggressive Policy

Under this approach,, major part of fixed assets are financed out of long-term sources (Equity and Debt) and entire current assets (hard-core + fluctuating) and even a minor part of fixed assets are financed out of short-term sources of finance.

There is almost no justification behind adopting this police due to the following reasons:

- Policy is highly riskily as short-term sources will have to be renewed on a continuous basis not only for financing current assets but also for a part of fixed assets.
- It this policy is followed, net current assets will be negative.

Hard-core current assets represent the minimum amount of investment in different components of working capital that a firm is required to make to continue with its operation at a given volume of activity. Investment is current assets like WIP, finished goods, spares, debtors, cash, is as permanent as that in fixed assets.

8.8 CRITERIA FOR EVALUATION OF WORKING CAPITAL MANAGEMENT

Working Capital, in one hand, is the difference between 'current assets' and 'current liabilities, which is needed to meet the current obligations of a company as and when they become due. On the other hand, working capital is looked upon as the amount held in different forms of current assets to provide adequate support to the smooth functioning of the normal business operations of a company with the objective of deciding on the trade-off between liquidity and profitability.

The following criteria may be adopted for evaluating the working capital management of a company:

Over Trading

Firm should have avoided disproportionally high turnovers of assets which is indicative of less amount of cash invested in current assets which can creat problems of liquidity at the time of making payments for current obligations.

Liquidity

The efficiency of working capital management can be regarded as the ability of a company to have adequate liquidity in the current assets so that current obligations can be meet without creating embarrassment of 'technical insolvency'. The criterion of liquidity can be quantitatively assessed by means of the ratios.

For examples,

- Current Ratio $= \dfrac{\text{Current Assets}}{\text{Current Liabilities}}$

- Quick Ratio $= \dfrac{\text{Liquid Assets}}{\text{Current Liabilities} - \text{Income received in advance}}$

$$= \frac{\text{Current Assets} - \text{Stock}}{\text{Current Liabilities} - \text{Incomes received in advance}}$$

Inventory Turnover

Too high level of inventory and too low level of inventory both are not conducing to the financial health of a company. Too high level of inventory creates the problem of liquidity and too low level of inventory can affect profitability. The ideal level of inventory ensures a proper balance between liquidity and profitability.

Availability of Cash

Companies keep some minimum cash balance. But we should remember that the larger the proportion of cash and bank balances in the current assets, the liquidity position improves but at the cost of sacrificing profitability.

Under Trading

The firms should avoid such a situation when the volume of sales is much lower than the amount assets of employed. Besides that they also should avoid the Lower turnover of working capital which arises from that situation when funds of the company is locked up in current assets.

Credit Obtained for Suppliers

Working capital management should provide adequate facility to the purchase department so that they can obtain better terms for order of suppliers. Timely Payment of suppliers should be there to bring the confidence in the minds of the suppliers. This can be qualified by the average payment period.

Credit Extended to Customers

Largest is the extension of the credit period to customers to whom goods are sold on credit, higher is the amount of credit sales which results higher amount of cash locked up in the form of debtors and higher incidence of bad debt losses. Therefore, reasonable credit should be provided to customers. This can be qualified in the form of turnover of receivables on average collection period.

8.9. WORKING CAPITAL RATIOS

Working Capital Ratios for evaluating working capital management

Current Ratio : $\frac{\text{Current Assets}}{\text{Current Liabilities}}$

Quick Ratio : $\frac{\text{Current Asset} - \text{Stock}}{\text{Current Liabilities} - \text{Income received in advance}}$

Turnover of Cash : $\frac{\text{Sales}}{\text{Cash}}$

Average Collection : $\frac{365}{\text{Debtors Turnover Ratio}} = \frac{365}{\frac{\text{Net Credit Sales}}{\text{Average Debtors}}}$ days

Or

$\frac{12}{\frac{\text{Net Credit Sales}}{\text{Average Debtors}}}$ months

Inventory Turnover Ratio : $\frac{\text{Cost of Goods Sold}}{\text{Average Stock}}$

Cash to Current Assets : $\frac{\text{Cash}}{\text{Current Assets}}$

Working Capital turnover : $\frac{\text{Sales}}{\text{Working Capital}}$

Importance of the above ratios

Higher the working capital turnover, the better it is for the company since higher will be rate of return on net operating capital employed. The higher the inventory turnover, the better it is from the point of view of efficiency in working capital management. Average collection period can be compared with the credit period. A high ratio of cash to current assets reflects better liquidity position of a company. The higher the current ratio, the higher is the ability of a company to meet its current liabilities. Quick ratio is supposed to provide a better measure of the liquidity position of a company in meeting its current liabilities in compare to current ratio. Higher the turnover of cash, better it is from the company's point of view though it can also indicate that the cash balance is less, for a given level of sales.

8.10 CALCULATION OF OPERATING CYCLE

Normal business operations of a manufacturing and trading company start with cash, go through the successive segments of the cycle *viz.*, raw material storage period, conversion period, finished goods storage period and average collection period before getting back cash along with profit. The cycle is called 'operating cycle'. The total duration of all the segments mentioned above is known as gross operating cycle period.

Raw Material Storage Period	xxx
Conversion Period	xxx
Finished goods storage period	xxx
Average Collection Period	xxx
Gross Operating cycle Period	xxx

When the average payment period of the company to its suppliers is deducted from the gross operating cycle period, the resultant period is called net operating cycle period or simply 'operating cycle' period.

Gross Operating Cycle Period	xxx
Less: Average Payment Period	xxx
(Net) Operating Cycle Period	xxx

The step by step calculation of the different segments of operating cycle is presented below:

A. Raw Material Storage Period (say in months)

1. Average stock of Raw Materials, components etc.

$$= \frac{\text{Opening stock} + \text{Closing stock}}{2}$$

2. Average consumption (say monthly) of raw materials

$$= \frac{\text{Annual consumption}}{12}$$

3. Raw Material storage period (months) $= \frac{1}{2}$

B. Conversion Period (say in months)

1. Average WIP $= \frac{\text{Opening WIP} + \text{Closing WIP}}{2}$

2. Average cost (say monthly) of

$$\text{Production} = \frac{\text{Annual Cost of Production}}{12}$$

3. Conversion Period (months) $= \frac{1}{2}$

C. Finished Goods Storage Period (say in months)

1. Average stock of finished goods

$$= \frac{\text{Opening stock} + \text{Closing stock}}{2}$$

2. Average cost of sales (months)

$$= \frac{\text{Annual cost of sales}}{12}$$

3. Finished Goods Storage Period (months) $= \frac{1}{2}$

D. Average Collection Period (say in months)

1. Average balance of Sunday Debtors

$$= \frac{\text{Opening Debtors} + \text{Closing Debtors}}{2}$$

2. Average Credit Sales (monthly)

$$= \frac{\text{Annual Credit Sales}}{12}$$

3. Average Collection Period (months) = $\frac{1}{2}$

E. Average Payment Period (say in months)

1. Average balance of Sunday Creditors

$$= \frac{\text{Opening Creditors + Closing Creditors}}{2}$$

2. Average credit purchase (monthly)

$$= \frac{\text{Annual credit purchase}}{12}$$

3. Average payment Period (months)

$$= \frac{1}{2}$$

Notes:

Statement: cost of production/sales

	₹	₹
Opening Raw Materials	xxx	
Add: Raw materials Purchased	xxx	
Less: Closing Raw Materials	(xxx)	
Cost of Raw Materials Consumed		xxx
• Productive Wages		xxx
• Direct Expenses		xxx
PRIME COST		xxx
Add: Opening WIP		xxx
Less: Closing WIP		(xxx)
Add: Manufacturing Expenses or Works Overheads or Production overheads (power, fuel, etc.)		xxx
Add: Depreciation of factory assets		xxx
WORKS COST OF PRODUCTION		xxx
Add: Opening finished goods		xxx
Less: Closing finished goods		(xxx)
		xxx
Add: Selling & distribution overheads		xxx
Add: Office/administrative Overheads including Depreciation on office assests		xxx

Add: Financial costs	xxx
Add: Excise duty	xxx
Annual Cost of Sales/or Operating Expenses	xxx

8.11. ESTIMATION OF WORKING CAPITAL

Estimation of Current Assets

Estimation of Raw Materials Inventory

Estimation of WIP (work-in-progress)

Estimation of Finished Goods

Estimation of Receivables (Both Debtors and Bills Receivables)

Bases on the firm's attitude towards risk, assess to borrowing sources, nature of Business firms decide on the policy of maintaining the minimum cash balance.

Estimation of Current Liabilities

Estimation of Trade Creditors

Estimation of outstanding wages, overhead

PROBLEMS

1. A Proforma cost sheet of a company provides the following data:

	₹ per unit
Raw Material	20
Direct Labour	30
Overheads	30
Total Cost	80
Profit	20
Selling price	100

The following additional information is available:

(a) Average raw material in stock = One month
(b) Average materials in process = Half-a month
(c) Average finished goods in stock = One month
(d) Credit allowed by suppliers = One month
(e) Credit allowed to debtors = Two months
(f) Time lag in payment of wages = Half-a month
(g) Time lag in payment of overheads = One month
(h) One – fourth of sales on cash basis
(i) Cash balance expected to be maintained in ₹ 1,00,000.

You are required to prepare a statement having the working capital required to finance a level of activity of 60,000 units of output in the year. You may assume that production is curried on evenly throughout the year and wages and overheads occur similarly. Assume 360 days in a year.

Solution

$$\text{Unit per month} = \frac{60000}{12} = 5000 \text{ units}$$

Statement showing working capital requirement

Particulars	Calculations (units p.m. × no. of months) × Rate	Amount ₹
A. Current Assets		
Raw Materials	(5000 × 1) × 20	100000
WIP	(5000 × ½) × (20 +15 + 15)	125000
Finished Good	(5000 × 1) × 80	400000
Debtors	(5000 × 2) × 100	1000000
Cash Balance	Given	100000
	Total Current Assets (A)	*17,25,000*
B. Current Liabilities		
Creditors	(5000 × 1) × 20	100000
Outstanding wages	(5000 × ½) × 30	75000
Outstanding Overheads	(500 × 1) × 30	150000
	Total Current Liabilities (B)	*325000*
C. Working Capital = A-B	**Total = A – B**	**1400000**

2. A company has submitted the following informations :

The following annual figures relate to ABC Ltd.	₹
Sales (at 2 months credit)	36,00,000
Materials Consumed (Supplier extend two months credit	9,00,000
Wages paid (monthly in arrears)	7,20,000
Cash manufacturing expenses paid	9,60,000
Total administrative expenses paid (are paid one month in arrear)	2,40,000
Sales promotion expenses, paid	1,20,000
Manufacturing expenses outstanding	80,000

The company sells its product on gross profit of 25% counting depreciates as part of the cost of production. It keeps one months' stock each of raw materials and finished goods and a cash balance of ₹ 1,00,000. Assume a 20% safety margin calculate the working capital requirements of the company on cash cost basis. Ignore work in process.

Solution

(a) Calculation of total manufacturing expenses

Particulars	₹
Sales	36,00,000
Less: gross profit (25% × 3600000)	90,00,00
Cost of Goods Sold or total manufacturing cost	27,00,000
Less: Materials : 9,00,000.00	
Wages : 7,20,000.00	(16,20,000)
Total manufacturing expenses	10,80,000
Cash manufacturing expenses	9,60,000

(b) Depreciation:

Total Manufacturing expenses – Cash manufacturing expenses
= 10,80,000 – 9,60,000
= ₹ 1,20,000

(c) Total Cash Cost

	₹
Total Manufacturing Cost	27,00,000
Less: Depreciation	120,000
Cash Manufacturing Cost	25,80,000
Add: Total Administrative expenses	2,40,000
Sales promotion expenses	1,20,000
Cash Cost of Sales/Total Cash Cost	29,40,000

Statement of Working Capital

Particular	Calculation	Amount ₹
A. Current Assets		
Raw material	$\frac{9,00,000}{12} \times 1$	75,000
Finished Good	$\frac{25,80,000}{12} \times 1$	2,15,000
Debtors	$\frac{36,00,000}{12} \times 1$	6,00,000
Cash balance	Given	1,00,000
	Total of Current Assets (A)	**9,90,000**
B. Current Liabilities		
Creditors	$\frac{9,00,000}{12} \times 2$	1,50,000

	Outstanding wages	$\frac{7,20,000}{12} \times 1$	60,000
	Outstanding manufacturing expenses	Given	80,000
	Outstanding administration expenses	$\frac{2,40,000}{12} \times 1$	20,000
		Total of Current Liabilities (B)	**3,10,000**
C.	Working Capital	Total (A) – Total (B)	6,80,000
D.	20% safety margin	20% × 6,80,000	1,36,000
E.	Working capital required	Total (C) + Total (D)	8,16,000

3. A Company is operating at 60% capacity producing 24000 units per annum, at the following cost-price structure:

	₹ per unit
Raw Materials	5
Wages	3
Overheads: Variable	2
Fixed	1
Profit	2
Selling Price	13

On December 2009, the current assets and liabilities were as follows:

	₹
Raw materials 4000 units, at cost	20,000
Work in process 1000 units, at cost	8,000
Finished Goods 3000 units, at cost	33,000
Sunday debtors	78,000
Creditor for goods	30,000
Liability for wages	3,000
Liability for expenses	6,000

In view of increased demand for the product, it has been decided that from 1st April, 2009 the unit should operate at 90% capacity. You are required to ascertain the additional working capital as would be necessary in view of additional production. The prices of materials, rate of wages and expenses and selling price per unit will not be changed. The period of credit allowed to customers, credit allowed by suppliers and also time lag in payment of wages and expenses shall remain the same as before.

Solution

Working: (a) Units p.m. (at 60% capacity) = $\frac{24,000}{12}$ = 2000 units p.m.

(b) Working Capital Requirement at 60% Capacity

Particulars	Rates/unit Col. 1	Amount Col. 2	Units p.m. Col. 3	Block period (months)
A. Current Assets				Col. 4 = $\frac{\text{Col. 2}}{\text{Col 1.Col 3}}$
Raw Materials	5	20,000	2,000	2
Work-in-process	8	8,000	2,000	½
Finished Goods	11	33,000	2,000	1.5
Sunday Liabilities	13	78,000	2,000	3
		1,39,000		
B. Current Liabilities				
Creditor	5	30,000	2,000	3
Outsanding wages	3	3,000	2,000	½
Outstanding expenses	3	6,000	2,000	1
		39,000		
C. Working Capital = A – B		**100000**		

Statement Showing Working Capital Requirement (at 90% Capacity)

Particulars	Units p.m. Col. 1	Rate/unit Col. 2	Block period Col. 3	Amount ₹ Col. 4 = Col. × 1 × Col. 2 × Col. 3
A. Current Assets				
Raw Material	$2000 \times \frac{90}{60}$ = 3,000	5	2	30,000
Work-in-process	3,000	8	1/2	12,000
Finished	3,000	10.667	1.5	48,002
Debtors	3,000	13	3	1,17,000
				2,07,002
B. Current Liabilities				
Creditors	3,000	5	3	45,000
Outstanding wages	3,000	3	1/2	4,500
Outstanding expenses	3,000	2.667	1	8,001
				57,501
C. Working Capital = A – B				**1,49,501**

Additional Working Capital = 1,49,501 – 1,00,000 = ₹ 49,501

Note (a) Revised Cost-price Structure

	₹/Unit (At 90% capacity)
Raw Material	5
Wages	3
Prime Cost	8
Overheads:	
Variable	2
Fixed $\left(1 \times \frac{60}{90}\right)$	0.667
	10.667
Profit (bal.)	2.333
Selling price	13.000 (unchanged)

(b) WIP is valued at prime cost, Finished goods is valued at total cost.

4. A firm has applied for working capital finance to a commercial bank. You are requested by the bank to prepare an estimate of the working capital requirements of the firm. You may add 10% to your estimated figure to account for exigencies. The following is the firms' projected profit & loss account:

	₹
Sales	19,85,000
Cost of Goods sold	14,85,000
Gross Profit	**5,00,000**
Less:	
(a) Administrative expenses	(1,00,000)
(b) Selling expenses	(1,30,000)
Profit before tax	**2,70,000**
Tax provision	90,000
Profit after tax	**1,80,000**

Cost of Goods Sold:	₹
Materials used	8,00,000
Wages and other manufacturing expenses	6,50,000
Depreciation	2,00,000
Cost of Production	**16,50,000**
Less: Stock of finished goods (10% product not yet sale)	1,65,000
Cost of Goods Sold	**14,85,000**

The figure given above relate only to the goods that have been finished and not to work in progress, goods equal to 15% of the years' production (in terms of physical units) are in progress on an average requiring full material but only 30% of labours. The firm has a policy of keeping two months consumption of material in stock. All expenses are paid one month in arrears. Suppliers of material grant one and half months credit; sales are 20% cash while remaining sold on two months credit 30% of the income tax has to be paid in advance in quarterly installments.

Solution

Statement showing estimation of the working capital requirements of the firm.

Particulars of Current Assets and Current Liabilities	Amount ₹	Amount ₹
A. Investment in inventories:		
1. Raw Materials		
$\frac{8,00,000}{12} \times 2$	1,33,333	
2. Work-in-Progress = (8,00,000 + 30% of 6,50,000) × 15% = 9,95,000 × 15%	1,49,250	
3. Finished Goods: (10% of 16,50,000 – 10% of depreciation of ₹ 2,00,000) = 1,65,000 – 20,000	1,45,000	
B. Investment in Debtors :		
$\frac{\text{Credit Sales}}{12} \times 2$		
$= \frac{80\% \text{ of Sales}}{12} \times 2$		
$= \frac{80\% \times 19,85,000}{6}$	2,64,667	
C. Current Assets (A + B)	6,92,250	6,92,250
D. Current Liabilities:		
1. Creditors:		
$\frac{8,00,000}{12} \times \frac{3}{2}$		
$= \frac{8,00,000}{24} \times 3$	1,00,000	
2. Deferred wages & other manufacturing, administration and selling expenses		
$\frac{6,50,000 + 1,00,000 + 1,30,000}{12} \times 1$	73,333	
E. Total Current Liabilities		1,73,333
F. Net Working Capital = C – E		5,18,917
G. Safety margin @ 10% for emergency		51,892
H. Working Capital Required = F + G		5,70,809

Notes:

(1) Debtors can be valued alternatively at cost of sales or total cost as follows:

Cost of Sales = Cost of Goods Sold – Depreciation + Administrative Expenses.

= 14,85,000 – 2,00,000 + 1,00,000 + 1,30,000 = ₹ 1515000

$$\text{Debtors} = \frac{80\% \text{ of Cost of Sales}}{12} \times 2 = \frac{80\% \times 15,15,000}{12} \times 2$$

$$= \frac{12,12,000}{12} \times 2$$

$$= ₹\ 2,02,000$$

(2) Depreciation is a non-cash item, hence it has been ignored in calculation at of cost of sales and finished stocks.

(3) Profit, payment of income tax out of profit, advance payment of taxes have been ignored in calculation.

(4) Finished goods are valued at cost of production.

6. An engineering firm is considering its working capital requirement for 2009-2010. Calculate the following for each of the financial policies mentioned below:

(a) Rate of return (on total assets or on shareholders' equity, on the basis of information)

(b) Not working capital position;

(c) Current ratio; and

(d) Current assets to fixed asset ratio.

Also evaluate the return-risk trade offer of those policies.

(i) The company is examining the following alternative working capital policies:

Working Capital Policy	Investment in current asset (₹ in crore)	Estimated Sales (₹ in crore)	EBIT (₹ in crore)
Conservative	3.00	10.00	1.20
Moderate	2.50	9.00	1.15
Aggressive	1.60	7.50	1.05

Estimate fixed assets and current liabilities for the 2009-2010 are respectively ₹ 1.60 crores and 1.40 crores. Sales and earnings before interest and taxes (EBIT) depend on current assets of particularly inventories and Sunday Debtors.

(ii) The company after examining working capital policies now is examining the use of long-term and short-term borrowing for financing its assets. The company will use ₹ 2.30 crores of equity. The corporate tax rate is 40%. The company is considering the following:

Financing Policy	Short-term debt (₹ in crore)	Long-term debt (₹ in crore)
Conservative	0.61	1.04
Moderate	1.00	0.65
Aggressive	1.50	0.15

The average effective interest rate on short-term debt is 10% while on long-term debt it is 15%. We are assuming that the company has chosen the moderate working capital policy (that is investment of 2.50 crores in current assets) after examining working capital policies.

Solution (i)

(₹ in crores)

Working Capital Policy	Conservative	Moderate	Aggressive
A Current assets (CA)	3.00	2.50	1.60
B Fixed Assets (FA)	1.60	1.60	1.60
C Total Assets = A + B	4.60	4.10	3.20
D Current liabilities	1.40	1.40	1.40
E Forecasted sales	10.00	9.00	7.50
F Expected EBIT	1.20	1.15	1.05
(a) Rate of Return = $\frac{F}{C}$	$\frac{1.20}{4.60} = 26.08\%$	$\frac{1.15}{4.10} = 28.05\%$	$\frac{1.05}{3.20} = 32.81\%$
(b) Net Working Capital = A–D	1.60	1.10	0.20
(c) Current Ratio = $\frac{A}{D}$	$\frac{3.00}{1.40} = 2.14$	$\frac{2.50}{1.40} = 1.78$	$\frac{1.60}{1.40} = 1.14$
(d) $\frac{CA}{FA} = \frac{A}{B}$	$\frac{3}{1.60} = 1.875$	$\frac{2.5}{1.6} = 1.5625$	$\frac{1.6}{1.6} = 1.00$

Risk-Return Trade off: expected return, in thr form of rate of return on total assets are minimum under conservative policy and highest under agressive policy. Similarly on the other hand, risk in the form of net working position & current ratio is minimum under conservative policy and highest under aggresive policy. It implies that if firm wants to increase its profitability, it has to bear more risk of being unable to meet its financial obligation.

Working Capital Policy	Conservative	Moderate	Aggressive
A Current Assets (CA)	2.50	2.50	2.50
B Fixed Assets (FA)	1.60	1.60	1.60
C Total Assets = A + B	4.10	4.10	4.10
D Current Liabilities	1.40	1.40	1.40
E Short-term debt	0.61	1.00	1.50
F Long-term debt	1.04	0.65	0.15
G Equity Capital	2.30	2.30	2.30
H Total Capital = D+E+F+G	5.35	5.35	5.35
I Forecasted Sales	9.00	9.00	9.00
J Expected GBIT	1.15	1.15	1.15
K Interest = STD	0.06	0.10	0.15
LTD	0.16	0.10	0.02
L Profit before Tax = J – K	0.93	0.95	0.98
M Taxes	0.37	0.38	0.39
N Profits after Tax = L – M	0.56	0.57	0.59

(a) Return on Equity = $\frac{N}{G}$	24.35%	24.78%	25.65%
(b) Not working Capital = A – (D + E)	0.49	0.10	(0.40)
(c) Current Ratio = $\frac{A}{D+E}$	$\frac{2.50}{2.01} = 1.24$	$\frac{2.50}{2.40} = 1.04$	$\frac{2.50}{2.90} = 0.86$
(d) $\frac{CA}{FA} = \frac{A}{B}$	$\frac{3}{1.60} = 1.56$	$\frac{2.50}{1.60} = 1.56$	$\frac{2.50}{1.60} = 1.56$

Risk-Return trade off: expected return and risk are minimum under the conservative policy and highest under the aggressive policy. It implies that if the company wants more return, if has to be ready to bear more risk of using short-term debt (financing policy)

Re: Calculation of operating cycle

7. Mr. A.C. Majumder is responsible Finance Manager of a company. The data given below are estimates relating to the year ending 31st March, 2010.

		₹ in crores
(i)	**Opening balances:**	
	Raw Material	400
	Work-in-progress	100
	Finished goods	450
	Sunday Debtors	500
	Sunday Creditors	400
(ii)	**Closing balances:**	
	Raw Material	410
	Work-in-progress	110
	Finished goods	600
	Sunday Debtors	800
	Sunday Creditors	350
(iii)	Purchase of Raw Materials	1,800
(iv)	Manufacturing Expenses like power, fuel, salary of supervisor	1,250
(v)	Selling, administration and Financing Costs	500
(vi)	Sales	5,000

Calculate: (i) operating cycle period, (ii) cash working capital, assume 360 days in the year.

Solution

Working :

Statement : Cost of production / Sales	*₹ in crores*
Opening Raw materials	400
Add: Raw Materials Purchased	1,800

	2,200
Less: Closing Raw Materials	410
Cost of Raw Materials consumed	1,790
Productive Wages	NIL
Direct Expenses	NIL
PRIME COST	1,790
Add: Opening WIP	100
	1,890
Less: Closing WIP	110
	1,780
Add: Manufacturing Expenses	1,250
WORKS COST OF PRODUCTIOIN	3,030
Add: Opening Finished goods	450
	3,480
Less: Closing finished goods	600
	2,880
Add: Selling, administration and Financial Costs	500
Annual Cost of Sales/Operating Expenses	3,380

(i) Statement: Operating cycle Period

Particulars	Days
Raw Material Storage Period	
$= \dfrac{\text{Average Raw Material}}{\text{Average Consumption(daily)}} = \dfrac{\frac{400+410}{2}}{\frac{1790}{360}} = \dfrac{405}{4.9722}$	82
Conversion Period	
$= \dfrac{\text{Average WIP}}{\text{Average Cost of Production (daily)}} = \dfrac{\frac{100+110}{2}}{\frac{3030}{360}} = \dfrac{105}{8.4167}$	13
Finished Goods Storage Period	
$= \dfrac{\text{Average Finished Goods}}{\text{Average Cost of Sales (daily)}} = \dfrac{\frac{450+600}{2}}{\frac{3380}{360}} = \dfrac{525}{9.3889}$	56

Average Collection Period	
$= \dfrac{\text{Average Sundry Debtors}}{\text{Average Credit Sales (daily)}} = \dfrac{\frac{500+800}{2}}{\frac{5000}{360}} = \dfrac{650}{13.8889}$	47
Gross Operating Cycle Period	198
Less: Average Payment Period	
$= \dfrac{\frac{400+350}{2}}{\frac{1800}{360}} = \dfrac{375}{5}$	75
(Net) Operating cycle period	123

(ii) Cash working capital

$$= \frac{\text{Operating Expenses}}{\text{No. of operating cycles}} = \frac{3380}{360/123} = 1155 \text{ crores}$$

8.12 REGULATION OF BANK FINANCE OF WORKING CAPITAL

Traditionally, bank finance is an important source of financing the current assets of companies. The banking sector provides the funds so long as there is adequate security for the funds lent. The security-oriented approach followed by the banking sector has resulted in over-financing large and, to some extent, medium scale companies who could provide adequate security. As a result, those companies could utilize the money for piling up stocks with a view to derive holding period gains as the rate of inflation was high and for the diversion of bank finance, which is basically meant to meet the short-term credit needs, for acquiring fixed assets.

In the wake of nationalization of major banks in 1969, the banking sector had been called upon to act as catalyst in the overall development of different sections of society. The development potential approach had to be adopted by the banking sector in place of security-oriented approach. Consequently, the demand on bank finance had gone up considerably. This had resulted in focusing attention on the weakness of the system followed by the banks earlier.

First, the cash credit/overdraft system followed by the banks had been tilted to favor borrowers rather than the banks. Once the cash credit limit is decided, then the quantum of funds to be utilized is decided by the needs of the borrower and not on the availability of funds lying with the bank at that point in time. As a result, credit planning by the banks had become extremely difficult.

Secondly, the banks are called upon o provide financial assistance to weaker sections of the society who may not be in a position to provide security.

Thirdly, large and medium borrowers abused bank finance to acquire stock much more than warranted by the production programs and to divert funds for other uses unrelated to working capital.

It is against this backdrop, that the Reserve Bank of India had appointed some special study groups for streamlining the practices followed by banks so that the weaknesses of the existing practices are removed and a better sense of direction provided to the banking sector. We shall confine ourselves to the recommendation of Tandon Committee.

WCM: Summary of Recommendations of the Tandon Committee

The Reserve Bank of India (RBI) constituted in July 1974 a study group to finance guidelines for the follow-up of bank credit programs under the chairmanship of P.L.Tandon. The report submitted by the committee in August, 1975 is popularly referred to as the Tandon Committee Report. The terms of reference for the committee were:

- To suggest guidelines for commercial banks to follow up and supervise credit to ensure proper end-use of funds and to keep a watch on the safety of that may be obtained by banks periodically from such borrowers and by the Reserve Bank of India from the lending banks.
- To make recommendations for obtaining periodical forecasts from borrowers of (a) business/production plans and (b) credit needs.
- To make suggestions for prescribing inventory norms for different industries both in the private and public sectors and indicate the broad criteria for deviating from these norms.
- To suggest criteria regarding satisfactory capital structure and sound financial basis in relation to borrowings.
- To make recommendations regarding sources for financing the minimum working capital requirements.
- To make recommendations as to whether the existing pattern of financing working capital requirements by cash credit/overdraft system etc., requires to be modified, and if so, to suggest suitable modifications, and
- To make recommendations on any other related matter as the group may consider germane to the subject of enquiry or any other allied matter which may be specifically referred to it by the Reserve Bank of India.

The study group reviewed the existing practices, obtained views from different associations of industries, chambers of commerce and executives and came up with a comprehensive set of recommendations.

Norms for Inventory and Receivables

The committee has come out with a set of norms that represent the maximum levels for holding inventory and receivables in each of 15 major industries, covering about 50 percent of industrial advances of banks. As norms cannot be rigid, deviations from norms can be permitted under extenuating circumstances such as bunched receipt of raw materials including imports, power-cuts, strikes, transport bottlenecks etc., for usually short periods. Once normalcy is restored, the norms should become applicable. The norms should be applied to all industrial borrowers with aggregate limits from the banking system in excess of ₹ 10 lakhs and extended to smaller borrowers progressively.

Approach to Lending

- As a lender, the bank should only supplement the borrower's resources in carrying a reasonable level of current assets in relation to his production requirements.
- *The difference between total current assets and current liabilities other than bank borrowing is termed as working capital gap.* The bank should finance a part of the working capital gap and the balance should be financed through long-term sources comprising equity and long-term borrowings.
- Three alternative methods have been suggested for calculating the maximum permissible bank borrowing. These methods will progressively reduce the maximum permissible bank borrowing. These three methods are explained by means of a numerical illustration which indicates the projected financial position as at the end of the next year.

Illustration

The financial position of Simplex Co. Ltd. has been projected for the forthcoming year as summarized below:

Current Liabilities	(₹ in lakhs)	Current Assets	(₹ in lakhs)
Accounts Payable	150	Raw Materials	250
Other Current Liabilities	50	Work-in- Progress	50
	200	Finished Goods	150
Bank borrowings (including bills discounted with banks)	360	Receivables (including bills discounted with banks)	90
		Other Current Assets	20
	560		560

Core Current Assets = 140 lakhs.

Under Method I, the bank will finance at the most 75 per cent of the working capital gap, *i.e.*, maximum permissible bank finance = 0.75 (Current Assets – Current Liabilities). This method will ensure a minimum current ratio of unity.

Under Method II, the borrower will finance 25 per cent of total current assets (140) through long-term sources. The bank will finance at the most 220 of the working capital gap (360 – 140). *i.e.*, maximum permissible bank finance = (0.75 × Current Assets) – Current Liabilities. This method will ensure a current ratio of 1.33.

Under Method III, there will be further reduction in bank borrowings which will ensure a still higher current ratio. The amount of excess borrowing calculated as the difference between the amount of bank borrowing and the maximum permissible bank borrowing to which the borrower is eligible will be converted into a term loan, that is to be repaid over a suitable period, depending upon the cash generating capacity and ability to raise additional equity etc., *i.e.*, maximum permissible bank finance = 0.75 (Current Assets – Core Current Assets) – Current Liabilities.

Method I

Total Current Assets:	560
Less: Current Liabilities other than Bank Borrowings	200
Working Capital Gap	360
25% of above from long-term sources	90
Maximum Permissible Bank Borrowings (75% of 360)	270
Excess Borrowing:	90
Current Ratio = $\frac{560}{470} = \frac{560}{200+270}$	1.19

Method II

Total Current Assets:	560
25% of above from long-term sources	140
75% of Current Assets	420
Less: Current Liabilities other than Bank Borrowings	200
	220
Working Capital Gap = 560 – 200	360
Maximum Permissible Bank Borrowings	220
Excess Borrowing:	140
Current Ratio = $\frac{560}{420} = \frac{560}{200+220}$	1.33

Method III

Total Current Assets:	560
Less: 'Core' Current Assets (illustrative figure) from Long-term sources	140
Real Current Assets	420
25% of above long-term sources	105
	315
Less: Current liabilities other than Bank Borrowings	200
	115
Working Capital Gap: 560 – 200	360
Maximum Permissible Bank Borrowings = 0.75 (560 – 140) – 120 =	115
Excess Borrowing:	245
Current Ratio: = $\frac{560}{315} = \frac{560}{200+115}$	1.7777

EXERCISE

Short Questions

1. What is meant by 'working capital'?
2. What is the difference bettween gross working capital and net working capital?
3. What is 'Positive Working Capital'?
4. What is 'Negative Working Capital'?
5. What is 'Operating Cycle'?
6. How one can determine gross operating cycle period and net operating cycle period?
7. What is Current Ratio?
8. What is Liquid Ratio?

Broad and Moderate Questions

1. Explain 'Liquidity – Profitability Tangle'.
2. Explain the concepts of working capital.
3. What are the factors determining working capital requirement?
4. Explain – 'An aggressive approach results greater profitability but lower liquidity while a conservative approach results in lower profitability but higher liquidity'.
5. Explain the approaches of financing of current assets.
6. What are the criteria's for evaluation of working capital management?
7. Stated all working capital ratios and also importance of each of the ratio.
8. How do you calculate operating cycle period?

Problems

1. A proforma cost sheet of a company provides the following data:

Cost (per unit)	₹
Raw materials	52.0
Direct labour	19.5
Overheads	39.0
Total cost (per unit)	110.5
Profit	19.5
Selling price	130.0

The following is the additional information available:

Average raw materials in stock: One month; average materials in process = half a month; credit allowed by suppliers: three months; credit allowed to debtors: two months; Time lag in payment of wages: one and a half weeks; overheads: one month. One month. One-third of sales are on cash basis. Cash balance is expected to be ₹ 1,40,000.

You are required to prepare a statement showing the working capital needed to finance a level of activity of 72,000 units of output. You may assume that the production is carried on evenly throughout the year and wages and overheads accrue similarly.

2. A firm has applied for working capital finance to a commercial bank. You are requested by the bank to prepare an estimate of the working capital requirements of the firm. You may add 10% to your estimated figure to account for exigencies. The following is the firms projected profit and loss account:

	₹
1. Sales	22,47,000
2. Cost of Goods Sold	16,37,100
3. Gross profit (1 – 2)	6,09,900
4. Administrative expenses	1,49,800
5. Selling expenses	1,39,100
6. Profit before tax [3 – (4 + 5)]	3,21,000
7. Tax provision	1,07,000
8. Profit after tax (6 – 7)	2,14,000

The cost of goods sold is calculated as follows:

	₹
Materials used	8,98,800
Wages and other mfg. expenses	6,68,750
Depreciation	2,51,450
Less; stock of finished goods	18,19,000
(10% product not yet sold)	1,81,900
Cost of Goods Sold	16,37,100

The figures given above relate only to the goods that have been finished and not to WIP, goods equal to 15% of the year's production (in terms of physical units) are in progress on an average requiring full material but only 40% of other expenses. The firm has a policy of keeping two months consumption of materials in stock.

All expenses are paid one month in arrears. Suppliers of material grant one and a half months credit-sales are 20% cash which remaining sold on two months credit. 40% of the income tax has to be paid in advance in quarterly installments

3. Calculate operating cycle period and cash working capital from the following date (Assume 360 days in a year).

Sl. No.	Particulars	Amount ₹ (in lakhs)
1.	**Opening Balance**	
	(a) Raw Materials stores and spares etc.	3,500
	(b) WIP	55
	(c) Finished Goods	650
	(d) Accounts Receivable	750
	(e) Accounts Payable	2,500
2.	**Closing Balance**	
	(a) Raw Materials	4,090
	(b) WIP	73
	(c) Finished goods	1,035

	(d) Accounts Receivable	1,200
	(e) Accounts Payable	3,085
3.	Purchase of Raw Materials, stores	10,670
4.	Manufacturing expenses	1,140
5.	Depreciation	250
6.	Customs and Excise duties	35,025
7.	Selling, administration and Financial expenses	4,555
8.	Sales	56,200

4. Your company is operating at 60% capacity, producing 30000 units p.a., at the following cost-price structure:

	₹ per unit
Raw Materials	5
Wages	4
Overheads: Variable	3
Fixed	2
Profit	1
Price	15

On 31st December, 2010, the current assets and liabilities were as follows:

		₹
Raw Materials 4000 units at cost	:	20,000
WIP 1000 units, at cost	:	8,000
Finished goods 3000 units, at cost	:	33,000
Sunday Debtors	:	78,000
Creditor for goods	:	30,000
Liability for wages	:	3,000
Liability for expenses	:	6,000

In view of increased demand, it is proposed to double production by working an extra sift. It is expected that a 10% discount will be available from suppliers of raw materials in views of increased volume of business. There will be no change in selling price, credit period allowed to customers, credit period availed from suppliers, log in payment in wages and expenses, and other periods. Calculate additional working capital requirements.

❑❑❑

9 Cash and Liquidity Management

9.1 DEFINITIONS OF CASH

- Money in the form of bills or coins; "there is a desperate shortage of hard cash"
- Prompt payment for goods or services in currency or by cheque.
- Exchange for cash; "I cashed the check as soon as it arrived in the mail"

Cash refers to money in the physical form of currency, such as banknotes and coins.

Cash is an asset to the business and is usually considered to be one of the current assets. The other current assets are stocks and debtors. Under the heading 'cash' on the balance sheet may be included a number of items of varying liquidity. A small amount may actually be cash held as petty cash, but the majority is likely to be held in various bank accounts. However, since money in current accounts rarely earns interest, if a business has a surplus of cash it may invest it in various ways. As with the debtors, the amount of cash required will vary according to the line of business the firm is in. Retail firms may have higher levels of liquid cash than businesses that operate mostly on a credit basis and therefore rarely handle notes and coins.

The importance of cash

To make a profit, most businesses have to produce and deliver goods or services to their customers before being paid. Unfortunately, no matter how profitable the contract, if you don't have enough money to pay your staff and suppliers before receiving payment from your customers, you'll be unable to deliver your side of the bargain or receive any profit.

To trade effectively and be able to grow your business, you need to build up cash balances by ensuring that the timing of cash movements puts you in a positive cash flow situation overall.

But bear in mind that having a lot of cash in your bank does not necessarily make good business sense. If you do not need to use it immediately, put spare cash into an account where it will earn a higher rate of interest, or use it as capital for short-term investments.

9.2 CASH FLOW MANAGEMENT : THE BASICS

Cash flow is the measure of your ability to pay your bills on a regular basis. It depends on the **timing** and **amounts** of money flowing into and out of the business each week and month. Good cash flow means that the pattern of income and spending in a business allows it to have cash available to pay bills on time.

Your available cash includes:

- coins and notes
- money in current accounts and short-term deposits
- any unused bank overdraft facility
- foreign currency and deposits that can be quickly converted to your currency

It does not include:

- long-term deposits (if these cannot be withdrawn)
- money owed by customers
- stock

Difference between cash and profit

It is important not to confuse cash balances with profit. Profit is the difference between the total amount your business earns and all of its costs, usually assessed over a year or other trading period. You may be able to forecast a good profit for the year, yet still face times when you are strapped for cash.

Elements of a cash flow forecast

The cash flow forecast identifies the sources and amounts of cash coming into your business and the destinations and amounts of cash going out over a given period. There are normally two columns listing forecast and actual amounts respectively. Cash flow forecasting enables you to predict peaks and troughs in your cash balance. It helps you to plan borrowing and tells you how much surplus cash you're likely to have at a given time. Many banks require forecasts before considering a loan.

The forecast is usually done for a year or quarter in advance and divided into weeks or months. In extremely difficult cash flow situations a daily cash flow forecast might be helpful. It is best to pick periods during which most of your fixed costs - such as salaries - go out. The forecast lists:

- receipts
- payments
- excess of receipts over payments - with negative figures shown in brackets
- opening bank balance
- closing bank balance

Cash management in action

The following **simple example** shows how a small, profitable business can run into unforeseen cash flow problems when it takes on a new large order.

XYZ manufacturer is a small but profitable gift designer and supplier with three full-time staff (including the two owners). It outsources production, but supplies the raw materials itself to save on costs. It then finishes and packages the final product on site.

XYZ does not have any loans or overdrafts. It has a long-term customer base of small gift shops and visitor centres. XYZ suddenly wins a large order to supply bespoke wall plaques for a chain of stores. The contract promises to double its turnover. The team takes on an additional employee and works flat out to meet the deadlines. It doesn't notice an impending **cash flow crisis** resulting from a fall in repeat orders from existing customers combined with a jump in raw material costs. To make matters worse; the new client keeps changing its mind about designs. A misunderstanding means the first run of goods is rejected, causing a delay in payment and increased production costs. XYZ orders additional materials to make-up the shortfall in the run.

By the time the order is complete, XYZ is running an expensive overdraft. Profit margins have been squeezed to the limit and it has lost several of its existing customers. A downturn in the fortunes of the retail chain means that it doesn't place any further orders. After a lot of hard work, XYZ finds itself back where it was five years earlier. Tighter cash flow management would have highlighted the fall in repeat orders and rise in raw material costs. XYZ would also have benefited from a client contract that included:

- milestone payments and penalty provisions for changes such as those to designs - *e.g.*, increased fees
- sharing the cost of additional materials with the new client or getting the client to pay for them
- Managing incomes and expenditures

Effective cash flow management is as critical to business survival as providing services or products. Below are some of the key methods to help reduce the time gap between expenditure and receipt of income.

Customer management

- Define a **credit policy** that clearly sets out your standard **payment terms**.
- Issue invoices promptly and regularly chase outstanding payments. Use an **aged debtor** list to keep track of invoices that are overdue and monitor your performance in getting paid.
- Consider exercising your right to charge **penalty interest** for late payment.
- Consider offering **discounts** for prompt payment.

- Negotiate **deposits** or **staged payments** for large contracts. It's in your customers' interests that you don't go out of business trying to meet their demands.
- Consider using a third party to buy your invoices in return for a percentage of the total.

Supplier management

Ask for **extended credit** terms. Giving your suppliers incentives such as large or regular orders may help, but make sure you have a market for the orders you're placing. Alternatively, consider **reducing stock levels** and using **just-in-time** systems.

Taxation

You may be liable for several different taxes including income tax, VAT, stamp duty. It is important to keep good records to help you calculate your liability and complete your returns accurately.

A cash flow forecast can be an invaluable business tool if it is used effectively. Bear in mind that it is dynamic – you will need to change and adjust it frequently depending on business activity, payment patterns and supplier demands.

It's helpful to set up a regular **review** of the forecast, changing the figures in light of your sales, purchases and staff costs. Legislation, interest rates and tax changes will also impact on the forecast.

Having a regular review of your cash flow forecast will enable you to:

- see when problems are likely to occur and sort them out in advance
- identify any potential cash shortfalls and take appropriate action
- ensure you have sufficient cash flow before you take on any major financial commitment

You could, for example, separate cash flow for **business operations** from **funding** cash flow. This gives a clearer picture of the actual performance of your business and is a format that many accountants prefer.

9.3 CASH FLOW FROM OPERATIONS, CASH MANAGEMENT

Includes inflows such as:

- cash sales
- receipts from credit sales in earlier periods
- interest on savings etc.

Includes outflows such as:

- payments to suppliers, cash purchases
- hire purchase and lease payments
- expenses – rent, rates, insurance, utilities, telephone, etc.
- wages

- taxes and National Insurance contributions
- interest on loans and bank charges etc.

Funding cash flows

Includes inflows such as:

- loans from banks
- increase in share capital

Includes outflows such as:

- dividends paid
- loans repaid

Cash Management

Cash management involves the efficient collection, disbursement and temporary investment of cash. The treasurer's department of a company is responsible for the company's cash management system. A cash budget tell us how much cash we are likely to have, when we are likely to have it and for how long. Thus it serves as the foundation for cash forecasting.

- Is the maintaining of liquidity of a firm to minimize the risk of insolvency? (An insolvent company is one where it is unable to meet its maturing liabilities on time because it has inadequate liquidity to meet its debt obligation)
- Cash Management is also about the proper balancing of keeping cash without letting it idling around.
- Remember that profit is not equating to cash flow.

A highly profitable company might collapse if without adequate cash flow due to the tying-up of company's funds with the accounts receivable and worsen by the needs to make regular payments like wages, rent and utilities, taxes.

9.4 OBJECTIVE OF CASH MANAGEMENT

1. To make Payment According to Payment Schedule : Firm needs cash to meet its routine expenses including wages, salary, taxes etc.

Following are main advantages of adequate cash

1. To prevent firm from being insolvent.
2. The relation of firm with bank does not deteriorate.
3. Contingencies can be met easily.
4. It helps firm to maintain good relation's with suppliers.

2. To minimize Cash Balance: The second objective of cash management is to minimize cash balance. Excessive amount of cash balance helps in quicker payments, but excessive cash may remain unused and reduces profitability of business. Contrarily, when cash available with firm is less, firm is unable to pay its liabilities in time. Therefore optimum level of cash should be maintained.

9.5 MOTIVES/REASONS OF HOLDING CASH

(a) Transaction motive,

(b) Precautionary motive, and

(c) Speculative motive.

(a) The Transaction motive:

- Maintaining cash for the purpose of meeting cash needs arising in the ordinary course of doing business.
- Includes regular payments like wages, utilities, acquisition of fixed assets and inventories.
- The amount of cash needed for transaction requirements depends on the nature of business and varies from industry to industry.

(b) The Precautionary motive:

- Either holding in cash or marketable securities that can be liquidated easily
- To maintain a safety cushion or buffer to meet unexpected cash needs. The more predictable the inflows and outflows of cash for a person / company the less cash that needs to be held for precautionary needs.

(c) The Speculative motive:

- Holding cash for potential profit making situation like purchasing raw materials in bulk in anticipation of a fall in price.
- To take advantage of temporary opportunities such as a sudden decline in the price of a raw material or sudden window of opportunity for buying an asset or making an investment.

9.6 EFFICIENT CASH MANAGEMENT – A CASE EXAMPLE

Efficient cash management processes are pre-requisites to execute payments, collect receivables and manage liquidity. Managing the channels of collections, payments and accounting information efficiently becomes imperative with growth in business transaction volumes. This includes enabling greater connectivity to internal corporate systems, expanding the scope of cash management services to include "full-cycle" processes (i.e., from purchase order to reconciliation) via ecommerce, or cash management services targeted at the needs of specific customer segments. Cost optimization and value-add services are customer demands that necessitate the creation of a mechanism to service the various customer groups.

Banks are increasingly becoming innovative and anticipating the needs of corporate towards standardization, ERP integration, reconciliation, real-time reporting, providing an end-to-end view of cash management value chain besides offering the ability to reach and be reached by their own customers. The mounting pressure from competitors forces the Banks to look for an

Information Technology vendor who can offer better solutions and services in Cash Management and Internet Banking.

Case example: HCL's service offering

As an established market leader in multi-service delivery engagements, HCL's integrated services in Operations Support, Software services and Infrastructure Management services provide customers the benefits of dealing with a single service provider, significantly increasing linkage and reducing governance and management overheads thus resulting in a customer satisfaction on the delivery, product and service fronts.

Keeping in view clients special needs, HCL has set up Cash Management as one of its key sub-verticals. HCL's offerings include various facets of Cash Management in the area of:

- Application design, development
- Onsite-offshore model for providing application management services
- Legacy application modernization
- SOA framework based solution for end-to-end testing
- Application re-engineering
- System Integration services
- Business Process Outsourcing
- Consulting services to select a suitable platform / product
- Infrastructure Management.

9.7 CASH BUDGETING, CASH BUDGET

Cash budgeting is nothing but of short-term forecasting of cash through the preparation of cash budget. Cash Budget is the estimate of closing cash balance at the end of a month, week etc. with the following purposes:

- Estimating cash requirements,
- Planning short-term financing,
- Scheduling payments in connection with capital expenditure projects,
- Planning purchase of materials,
- Developing credit policies, and
- Checking the accuracy of long-term forecasts of cash.

CASH BUDGET PREPARATION

I. Methods of short-term cash forecasting

Receipts and Payment Method : The principal method of short-term cash forecasting is the receipts and payments method. Sometimes the adjusted net income method is used though this method is employed mainly for long-term cash forecasting. The cash budget prepared under receipts and payment method shows the timing and magnitude of expected cash receipts and payment over the forecast period. It includes all expected cash receipts and payments irrespective of how they are classified in accounting. The items of cash receipts and cash payments and the bases for estimating them are shown in following exhibit 1.

Exhibit 1: Cash Budget (Summary Cash Forecast)

Particulars	May, 2010	June, 2010	July, 2010	August, 2010
A. Opening Cash balance	xxx	xxx	xxx	xxx
B. Cash Receipts / In flows: • Cash Sales • Collection From Debtors • Sale of Asset • Loan taken • Cash incomes • Issue of shares /Debentures				
Total (B)	xxx	xxx	xxx	xxx
C. Total Cash Receipt = **A + B**	xxx	xxxx	xxx	xxx
D. Cash Payments / Out flows: • Cash purchase • Payment to creditors • Purchase of assets • Loan Payment • Cash expense • Redemption of prof share/debenture				
Total (D)	xxx	xxx	xxx	xxx
E. Closing Cash balance = **C-D**	xxx	xxx	xxx	xxx
F Minimum Cash balance required (fixed)	xxx	xxx	xxx	xxx
G Surplus or deficit i.r.t. the minimum cash balance required = **E – F** [If positive – surplus. If negative – deficit]	xxx	xxx	xxx	xxx
H. Short-term Loan / Bank Overdraft i.r.t. deficit	xxx	xxx	xxx	xxx

II. Long-term cash forecasting: The dividing line between short-term cash forecasts and long-term cash forecasts in usually one year. Long-term cash forecasts are generally prepared for a period ranging from 2 to 5 years and served to provide a broad picture of a firm's financing needs and availability of investable surplus in future. Such forecasts are helpful in planning capital investments outlays and long-term financing.

Adjusted net income method: The method that is generally used for the purpose is the adjusted net income method which, resembling the funds flow statements, seeks to estimate the firms need for cash at some future date and indicate whether this need can be met from internal sources or not. A format for forecasting cash or preparation of cash budget under the Adjusted Net Income Method is shown in following exhibits 2.

Exhibit 2: Cash Budget (Summary Cash Forecast)

Particulars	2010	2011	2012
A. Sources			
• Net income after taxes			
• Non-cash charges (Depreciation, amortization etc.)			
• Increase & borrowings			
• Sale of shares, debentures			
• Miscellaneous			
Total (A)	xxx	xxx	xxx
B. Uses			
• Capital expenditures			
• Increase in CAs			
• Repayment of borrowings			
• Interest/Dividend payment			
• Miscellaneous –wages, taxes, office expenses etc.			
Total (B)	xxx	xxx	xxx
Surplus/Deficit	xxx	xxx	xxx
Opening Cash Balance	xxx	xxx	xxx
Closing Cash Balance	xxx	xxx	xxx

9.8 CASH REPORT, TREASURY REPORT (REPORTS FOR CONTROL)

The periodical, *e.g.*, daily or monthly cast reports can be prepared when cash inflows and outflows are more or less stable due to very small fluctuations in collection and payment patters. If there are wide fluctuations in collection and payment of cash and hence, high uncertainty in cash flows, then cash position should be monitored at a short and regular intervals, say weekly or sometimes on daily basis and cash budget, prepared earlier, should be revised for the subsequent period based on the variance between the actual and budgeted figures and the reasons thereof.

The cash report provides information on the cash position on a daily basis. But since it does not provide the informations regarding positions of Accounts Receivable, Accounts payable and makeable securities of a company, a daily treasury report has to be preferred, besides preparation of a daily cash report since, the treasury report indicates the opening and closing net treasury positions.

A. Daily Cash Report

1. Opening Cash Balance	xxx
2. Cash Receipts:	
• Cash sales	
• Collection from Debtor	

- Sate of Assets (in cash)
- Issue of shares, debentures
- Loan taken
- Cash incomes (others) xxx

3. Cash payments:
   - Cash purchases
   - Payment to creditors
   - Purchase of Assets (in cash)
   - Redemption of Pref. shares and debentures
   - Loan payment
   - Cash expenses (other) – dividends, taxes, wages etc. xxx
4. Net Cash flow (2-3) xxx
5. Closing Cash Balance (1 + 4) xxx

B. Daily Treasury Report

	Today	This month to date
1. Cash		
(a) Opening balance		
(b) Receipts		
(c) Payments		
(d) Closing Balance (a + b – c)		
2. Marketable Securities		
(a) Opening Balance		
(b) Purchases		
(c) Sales		
(d) Closing Balance (a + b – c)		
3. Accounts Receivable		
(a) Opening balance		
(b) Bills raised		
(c) Cash Receipts		
(d) Closing Balance (a + b – c)		
4. Accounts payable		
(a) Opening Balance		
(b) Bills Received		
(c) Cash payment		
(d) Closing Balance (a + b – c)		

5. **Opening Net Treasury Position**
(1a + 2a + 3a – 4a)

6. **Closing Net Treasury Position**
(1d + 2d + 3d – 4d)

C. Monthly Cash Report : Monthly cash report shows the cash position on a monthly basis and provides a comparative picture of actual with budgeted figures along with variances between actual and budget. The following is the format of a monthly Cash Report.

Cash Report for the Month of ...., 2011

	Current Month			Year to Date		
	Actual	**Budget**	**Variance**	**Actual**	**Budget**	**Variance**
Cash Receipts						
Cash Sales Collection from debtors Loan taken Issue of shares, debentures Sales of Assets, Other cash incomes						
Total						
Cash Payments						
Cash purchase Payment to Suppliers Loan Repayment Redemption of pref. shares, debentures Purchase of Asset, Other cash expenses .... manufacturing, administration & selling expenses, taxes etc.						
Total						

9.9. SYNCHRONIZING CASH INFLOWS AND OUTFLOWS (Matching of the timings of inflows and outflows)

A firm can hold its transactions balances to a minimum by arranging that cash inflows coincide with the timings of cash outflows or *vice versa*. Matching of the timings of inflows and outflows will involve the following:

(a) Slowing down cash payments or cash disbursement to the suppliers of materials and stores.

(b) Speeding up cash collections

(c) Combining (a) and (b)

(a) Deferring disbursement

If may be difficult to defer payments of wages, salaries etc. Hence our focus would be deferring or slowing down cash payments to the suppliers of materials and stores, which may include the following:

(i) Stretching the period of credit granted : This process may be good till it does not affect the credit reputation of the firm. In absence of cash discount offer from the supplier, company, the customer company can take the opportunity to stretch the period of credit granted. When cash discounts are available, the amount of loss of discounts should be compared with the benefits that may accrue if the said funds are otherwise diverted instead of liquidating the payables.

(ii) Using Float : Slowing down cash payments, with or without stretching credit period, taking advantage of float accomplishes the same objective by keeping cash on hand for longer periods.

The term 'disbursement delay' refers to the periods that affect cash as it moves through the process of disbursement. Keeping the cash on hand for longer periods, which slows down cash payments, depends on the following factors:

- If the purchases and payment of suppliers are centralized at the head office if can take more time for processing the cheques to be issued to the suppliers
- If the cheques are sent by post, it will take a few days' time more to reach the customer.

(b) Speeding up Collection

To speed up collection, companies may use the following ways:

(i) Introduction of cash discounts for the suppliers to get early payment from them;

(ii) Reducing collection time delay and playing the cash float;

(iii) Lock Box system;

(iv) Concentration Banking.

Reducing Collection Time Delay

The term collection delay refers to the period that affect cash as it moves through the different stages of the collection process stored below:

Billing time delay: It is the time between the sale and the mailing of the invoice or bill. This is to be reduced as far as possible. Accurate billing and billing in time should be the two important things in this regard.

Post office time delay: It is the time taken by the post office, messenger service us other means of delivery, to deliver the cheques sent by the customers to the companies. This is to be reduced as far as possible by setting up multiple collection centers at important places which will collect cheques and deposit in local banks for collection. This will reduce the post office float or mailing float.

Cheque processing time delay: It is the time between the receipt of cheques by the collection centers on companies and depositing them into bank. This is to be reduced it cheques collected are not kept in a drawer and deposited into bank on the same day.

Bank time delay: In India, local cheques take 2 to 3 days for collection whereas outstation cheques may take 10 to 15 days. To reduce this time float the decentralized collection system may be suggested. It will be financially justified if all outstation cheques can be converted into 'iocal cheques' through decentralization.

Cash float: (Playing the Cash Float)

The cash balance shown by a firm on its book is called the book or ledger balance whereas the balance shown in its bank account is called the available or collected balance. The difference between the available balance and the ledger balance is referred to as 'Cash Float'. There are three kinds of cash floats as follows:-

Cash Collection Float: The amount of cheques deposited by a company in the bank awaiting clearance is called 'cash collection float'.

Cash Disbursement Float: The amount of cheques issued by the company awaiting payment by the bank is called 'cash disbursement/payment float'.

Net cash float: It is the difference between 'cash payment float' and 'cash collection float'. Where this float is positive, the balance in the books of the company in less than that in the bank's book; where this float is negative the book balance of the company is more than that in the bank's book. Where a company has a 'positive net cash float', it may issue cheques to the extent that the amount shown in the bank's book is higher than the amount shown in the company's book. The company is then said to have been playing the cash float.

Illustration: The opening credit balance of a company with the bank is ₹ 50,00,000. We assume that it deposits cheques daily to the amount of ₹ 1,50,00,000 and it takes 3 days for realization. We also assume that the company issues cheques daily to the amount of ₹ 1,50,00,000 and it takes 4 days for actual payment. The opening balance in the company's book as also in the bank's books will remain the same at ₹ 50,00,000. The closing balance in the books of the company and in the books of the bank are presented as follows.

Closing Balance

Days	Book of the Company	Book of the Bank
1	₹ 50,00,000	₹ 50,00,000
2	Do	Do
3	Do	Do
4	Do	₹ 2,00,00,000 (increased due to encashment of 1st day's cheque)
5	Do	₹ 2,00,00,000 increased due to encashment of 2nd day's cheque and decreased due to payment of the cheque issued on the first day [₹ 2,00,00,000 + 1,50,00,000 – 1,50,00,000]

Closing balance from 5th day onwards will remain at ₹ 2,00,00,000 in the books of the bank which reflects a stable cash balance. The closing balance in the company's' book will remain at ₹ 50,00,000. The company will continue to enjoy a net float of ₹ 1,50,00,000 (2,00,00,000 – 50,00,000) and can issue cheques amount to even ₹ 1,20,00,000 or ₹ 1,30,00,000, or ₹ 1,40,00,000. But we are to remember that there are certain inherent risks involved. When the clearing system operates much faster than anticipated, the cheques issued may come for payment earlier than anticipated. In order to minimize the risks associated with playing the cash float, a company can take the following precautionary measures.

- A minimum amount of cash can always be maintained with the bank.
- Preferably having an overdraft arrangement with the bank to avoid financial embarrassment.

To speed up collection, other system like Lock box system and Concentration Banking may be followed which are not widely used in India yet. But these systems are also useful for expeditious decentralized collection by reducing mail and clearing delays.

Lock box system

Under this system, customers are advised to mail their payments to special post office box called lock box which is attended to by local collecting banks, instead of sending them to corporate headquarters. The local bank collects the cheques from the boxes once or more a day, deposits the cheques directly into the local bank account of the company and furnishes details to them. After the cheques are realized, surplus funds from the local banks are transferred (through usually by wire) to the Central account or accounts of the firm.

The lock box system has the certain following advantages as it provides the following:

(a) Cuts down the mailing time delay

(b) Eliminates the cheque processing time delay

(c) Shortens the availability delay as cheques are typically drawn on local banks.

Is it financially worthwhile to have a lock box? The answer is if the interest saving exceeds the cost of the lock box, it is advantageous to set up the lock box. It can be understood from the following illustration:

(a) Average number of daily payments	60
(b) Average size of payment	5,000
(c) Saving in mailing and processing time	2 days
(d) Annual rental for the lock box	2,000
(e) Bank charges for operating the lock box	48,000
(f) Interest rate	12%

The lock box will increase your company's collected balance by:

60 × ₹ 5,000 × 2 = ₹ 6,00,000

The annual benefit in the form of interest saving on account of this is:

₹ 6,00,000 × 0.12 = ₹ 72,000

The annual cost of the lock box is:

₹ 2,000 (rental) + ₹ 48,000 (bank charged)

= ₹ 50,000

Since the interest saving exceeds the cost of the lock box, it is advantageous to set up the bock box.

Concentration Banking

A concentration bank is one which the firm has a major account-usually a disbursement account. Under the system of concentration banking, the company asks its customers in a particular area to send payment to a local branch office. The cheques received by the local branch office are deposited into local bank. Surplus funds from local banks are then transferred from the local bank accounts to a major on concentration account at one of the company's principal banks. The main advantages of the system are as follows:

(a) It reduces mailing time delay significantly.

(b) It reduces average bank time delay.

Concentration banking can be combined with lock box arrangement to ensure that the funds are pooled centrally as early as possible.

9.10 INVESTMENT OF SURPLUS CASH – ITS MANAGEMENT

Surplus funds can be invested in a variety of short-term instruments like fixed Deposits with Bank, Treasury Bills, Mutual Fund Schemes, Commercial paper, Certificates of Deposits, Inter-corporate Deposit and Bills Discounting. Managing the investment of surplus cash is a very important responsibility of the Finance Manager. He should consider the following:

A. Determining the amount of surplus cash

Step I: Minimum cash balance required by the organization has to be accounted (safety level of cash)

During Normal Period, safety level of cash = Desired days of cash × Average daily cash outflows

During Peak Period, safety level of cash = Desired days of cash × Average of highest daily cash outflows

Step II : Comparing Safety level of Cash with actual Cash Balance, we are to find out whether the firm has cash surplus or cash deficiency. It Actual Cash balance > Safety level of cash, surplus cash exists.

Problem 1

The finance manager desires sufficient cash to cover cash payment for a week (7 days) during normal period and for 5 days during the peak periods. The firms' average daily cash outflows for a week during the normal periods are ₹ 25,000 and for 5 busiest days during the peak period are ₹ 50,000. Actual cash balance for normal period is ₹ 1,30,000 and for peak period is ₹ 3,00,000. Find out surplus cash in both cases.

Solution

	Normal Period	Peak Period
(a) Desired days of cash	7	5
(b) Average daily outflows (₹)	25,000	50,000
(c) Actual cash balance ₹	1,30,000	3,00,000
(d) Safety level of cash ₹ = a × b	1,75,000	2,50,000
(e) Surplus Cash ₹ = c – d	(45,000)	50,000
	= Deficiency	

B. Determining the channels of Investment

The above mentioned surplus cash may be either of a temporary or a permanent nature. The Finance Manager has to determine the period of investment for that surplus cash whether it will be the period of maximum six months on the period ranging from six months to a year. Then he should have considered the investment portfolio. It may be useful to divide a firm's short-term investment portfolio into following three segments (not necessarily equal)

Ready cash segment: It refers to that part of investment portfolio which means that cash resources should be augmented to meet unforeseen disbursement. Such cash, therefore, should be invested in securities which can be immediately sold without much loss. Investments in this segment must necessarily be highly liquid in nature which is more important than yield.

Controllable cash segment: It refers to that part of investment portfolio which means that cash resources should be augmented to meet the needs of future knowable outflows like taxes, dividend, interest repayment, and repayment of loans. Such cash, should, therefore be invested in securities whose maturities, coincide with the date of payment.

Free cash segment: It refers to that part of investment portfolio which means that neither to augment unforeseen current cash needs not to meet any future knowable outflows. Such cash therefore, be invested in securities with relatively larger maturities and more favorable yield without much concern of liquidity.

For evaluating the investment instruments, the Finance Manager should take into consideration the following factor:

(a) *Security:* This can be ensured by investing in securities whose price remain more or less stable and where a minimum return is guaranteed.

(b) *Liquidity:* This can be ensured by investing in securities which are short-term including short-term FDs with bank.

(c) *Yield:* This can be ensured by investing in securities which are Treasury Bills, Commercial Papers which do not pay interest but they are sold at a discount and redeemed at face value. The yield of an instrument is the return earned from it by way of interest, dividend and capital appreciation which can be achieved through aggressive investment policies.

(d) *Maturity:* Maturity refers to the life of instrument. While some instruments (like Treasury Bills) have fixed original maturity, others (like certificates of deposit) can have tailor-made maturity. Generally, the longer the maturity the greater the yield.

9.11 INVESTMENT OPTIONS (TYPES OF MARKETABLE SECURITIES)

Fixed Deposits with Banks: Purchasing the fixed-deposit certificates from the banks is very safe short-term investment. The firm regularly gets the interest and gets back its original investment at maturity.

Treasury Bills: Treasury bill is a money market instrument issued by the central bank on behalf of the govt. to borrow for the govt's short-term financial needs. It is regarded as a Bill of Exchange as it is issued at a discount to its face value. Eligible participants to invest are the banks, insurance companies like LIC, GIC, NABARD, UTI, FII, Corporates etc.

Mutual Fund Schemes: A variety of schemes are offered by mutual funds for different categories of investors where a pool of money is collected from them and invested according to their financial needs and objectives. The schemes may be broadly classified as follows:

- Equity schemes
- Balance scheme (equity and debt)
- Debt scheme

Commercial Paper: Commercial Paper is a short-term unsecured promising note issued by well established corporates with the requisite credit rating to raise working capital. The investors or buyers of CPs are Joint Stock Companies, Public sector companies and Corporations, Banks etc. The net worth of the issuing company should not be less than 4 crores. The working capital limit of the company should also be not less than ₹ 4 crores.

Certificates of Deposit (CD): CD is a negotiable certificate issued by a bank on the receipt of a large deposit and payable to bearer. It is a short-term security where the investors are generally Joint Stock Companies, High Net worth Individuals, Institutions etc. The face value of the CD is its maturity value. It is issued at a discount to the face value. On receiving the deposit, the banks issue the negotiable receipt which can be transferred or sold in the secondary market.

Interoperate Deposits: It is a deposit made by one company with another, normally for a period of up to 6 months. Such deposits are usually of three types:

(1) Call deposits – The lender has to wait for at least three days.

(2) Three month deposits – These deposits are taken by borrowers' to tide over a short-term cash inadequacy.

(3) Six month deposits – such deposits are usually made with first class borrowers.

Commercial Bill: Commercial Bill is a bill of exchange arising out a genuine trade transaction. It is a single instrument may be either clean or documentary. A bill of exchange generally has three parties. A trader or a manufactures writes up a document whereby he orders his credit customer to pay the amount mentioned to the supplier on credit basis. A company may also deploy its surplus funds to discount or purchase the bills the way a bank does.

Problem 2

Prepare a Cash Budget of M/s Panduranga Sheet Metals Ltd. for the six months ending 30th June, 2010 from the following information. It has an opening cash balance of ₹ 6,00,000 on 1st January, 2010.

Month	Sales	Purchases	Wages	Production Overheads	Selling Overheads
January	600000	240000	100000	60000	50000
February	700000	270000	110000	63000	55000
March	820000	320000	100000	64000	62000
April	850000	350000	105000	66000	65000
May	960000	388000	110000	64000	72000
June	1100000	416000	125000	65000	75000

The company has a policy of selling its goods 50% on cash basis and the rest on credit terms. Debtors are given a month's time period to pay their dues. Purchases are to be paid off two months from the date of purchase. The company has a time lag in the payment of wages of ½ a month and the overheads are paid after a month. The company is also planning to invest in a machine which will be useful for packing purposes, the cost being ₹ 4,50,000, payable it 3 equal installments starting bi-monthly from April. It also expects to make a loan application to a bank for ₹ 5,00,000 and the loan will be granted in the month of July. The company has to pay advance income tax of ₹ 2,00,000 in the month of April. Salesmen are eligible for a commission of 4% on total sales affected by them and this is payable one month after the date of sales.

Solution

Cash budget (Jan – June, 2010)

Particulars	Jan	Feb	March	April	May	June
A. Opening Cash Balance	600000	850000	1261000	1530000	1483700	1796200
B. Cash Receipts:						
Cash Sales	300000	350000	410000	425000	480000	550000
Collection from Debtors		300000	350000	410000	425000	480000
Total (B)	300000	650000	760000	835000	905000	1030000
C. Total Cash Available (A + B)	900000	1500000	2021000	2365000	2388700	2826200
D. Cash Payments:						
Materials			240000	270000	320000	350000

	Wages	50000	105000	105000	102500	107500	117500
	Production O/Hs		60000	63000	64000	66000	64000
	Selling Overheads		50000	55000	62000	65000	72000
	Sales commission		24000	28000	32800	34000	38400
	Purchase of machine				150000		150000
	Payment of advance IT				200000		
	Total (D)	50000	239000	491000	881300	592500	791900
E	Closing Cash balance (C+D)	**850000**	**1261000**	**1530000**	**1483700**	**1796200**	**2034300**

Note: Wages

Jan	Feb	March	April	May	June
100000	110000	100000	105000	110000	125000
50000	55000 (Feb)	50000 (Mar)	52500 (Apr)	55000 (May)	62500 (June)
	50000 (Jan)	55000 (Feb)	50000 (Mar)	52500 (Apr)	55000 (May)
50000	105000	105000	102500	107500	117500

Problem 3

A manufacturing company has prepared a budget for the year ended 31st December, 2009. Using the following date, prepare a cash budget for each of months of February, March and April 2009.

Estimated variable cost per unit :	₹
Direct Materials	3
Direct Wages	4
Production overhead	2
Total	9

Fixed overheads are estimated at ₹ 48,000 p.a. These are expected to be incurred in equal amounts each month during the budget period. Estimated sales at ₹ 11 per unit for the first 5 months are given below:

Month	**Unit**
January	6200
February	6800
March	5400
April	6000
May	6000

10% of sales will be made on cash; balance will be made on one month's credit. The following further information is available:

1. Finished Goods stock: 75% of each month's invoiced sales units to be produced in the month of sale and 25% of each month's invoiced sales units to be produced in the previous month.

2. Stock, direct materials: 50% of direct material, required for each months' production to be purchased in the previous month.

3. Terms of Payments:

(a) Direct Materials: to be paid for in the month following the month of purchase.

(b) Direct wages: 50% in the month used and the balance in the following month.

(c) Expenses: 1 month's lag.

4. Estimated Cash balances as on Ist February 2009: ₹ 5,000

Solution

(a) Cash sales and collection from debtors

	Jan	Feb	March	April	May
Sales (units)	6200	6800	5400	6000	6000
Sales value @ ₹ 11	68200	74800	59400	66000	66000
Collection (₹):					
Cash (10%)	6820	7480	5940	6600	6600
Credit Collection (90% of previous Month's sales)		61380	67320	53460	59400

(b) Production (units), purchase (units) Purchase value, wages, and expenses:

	Dec	Jan	Feb	March	April	May
(a) Production (units)						
–75% in the current month	–	4650	5100	4050	4500	4500
– 25% in the previous month	1550	1700	1350	1500	1500	–
Total (units)		**6350**	**6450**	**5550**	**6000**	
(b) Purchase (units)	775	3175	3225	2775	3000	–
– 50% in the current month						
– 50% in the previous month	3175	3225	2775	3000	–	–
	3950	**6400**	**6000**	**5775**		
(c) Purchase of Direct Material @ ₹ 3	11850	19200	18000	17325	–	–
Payment to creditors	–	11850	19200	18000	17325	–
(d) Wages @ ₹ 4 p.u. of Production		25400	25800	22200	24000	–
Payment of wages:						
50% in the month	–	12700	12900	11100	12000	–
50% in the next month	–	–	12700	12900	11100	12000
		–	25600	24000	23100	–
(e) Expense Variable @ ₹ 2	–	12700	12900	11100	12000	–
Fixed	4000	4000	4000	4000	4000	4000
	–	16700	16900	15100	16000	–
Payment of expenses		–	16700	16900	15100	16000

Cash Budget Year : 2009

	February	March	April
A. Opening Cash Balance	5000	12360	26720
B. Cash Receipt:			
Cash Sales	7480	5940	6600
Collection	61380	67320	53460
	68860	**73260**	**60060**
C. Total Cash Available (A + B)	**73860**	**85620**	**86780**
D. Payments:			
Payments to creditors	19200	18000	17325
Wages	25600	24000	23100
Expenses	16700	16900	15100
Total (D)	**61500**	**58900**	**55525**
E. Closing Balance = C – D	12360	26720	31255

9.12 DETERMINING THE CASH NEEDS – MODELS FOR DETERMINING OPTIMAL CASH

One of the prime responsibilities of a Finance Manager is to maintain an appropriate balance between cash and marketable securities. The amount of cash balance will depend on risk-return trade-off. A firm with less cash balances has a weak liquidity position but may be earning profits by investing its surplus cash and on the other hand it loses on the profits by holding too much cash. A balance has to be maintained between these aspects at all times. So how much is optimum cash? This section explains the models for determining the appropriate balance. Two important models ate studied here – Baumol model and Miller-Orr model.

A. Baumol Model

The Baumol model helps in determining the minimum cost amount of cash that a manager can obtain by converting securities into cash. It is an approach to establish a firm's optimum cash balance under certainty. As such, firms attempt to minimize the sum of the cost of holding cash and the cost of converting marketable securities to cash. The Baumol model is based on the following assumptions:

- The firm is able to forecast its cash requirement in an accurate way.
- The firm's pay-outs are uniform over a period of time.
- The opportunity cost of holding cash is known and does not change with time.
- The firm will incur the same transaction cost for all conversions of securities into cash.

A company will sell securities and realizes cash and this cash is used to make payments. As the cash balance comes down and reaches a point, the Finance Manager replenishes its cash balance by selling marketable securities available with it and this pattern continues. Cash balances are refilled and brought back to normal levels by the acts of sale of securities. The average cash balance is C/2. The firm buys securities as and when they have above normal cash balances. This pattern is explained below:

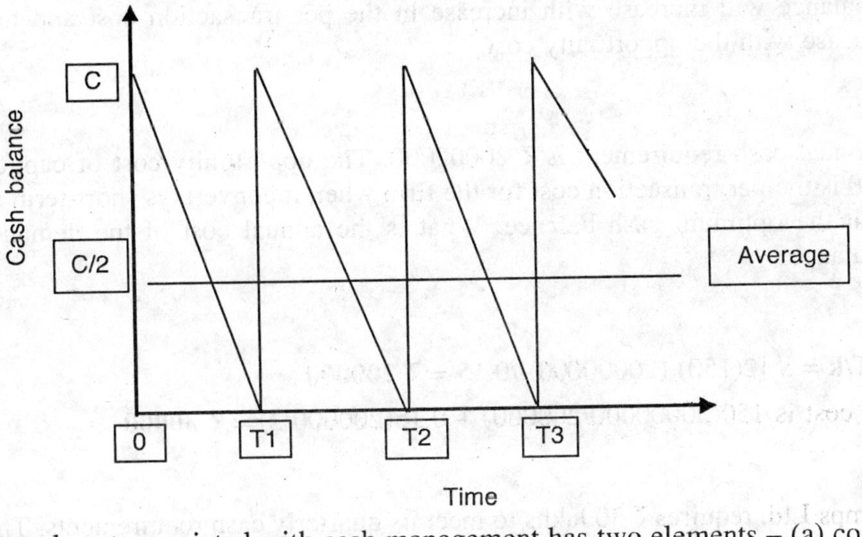

The total cost associated with cash management has two elements – (a) cost of conversion of marketable securities into cash and (b) the opportunity cost.

The firm incurs a holding cost for keeping cash balance which is the opportunity cost. Opportunity cost is the benefit foregone on the next best alternative for the current action. Holding cost is K(C/2).

The firm also incurs a transaction cost whenever it converts its marketable securities into cash. Total number of transactions during the year will be the total funds requirement, T, divided by the cash balance, C, *i.e.* T/C. if per transaction cost is C, then the total transaction cost is C(T/C).

The total annual cost of the demand for cash is K(C*/2) + C(T/C*).

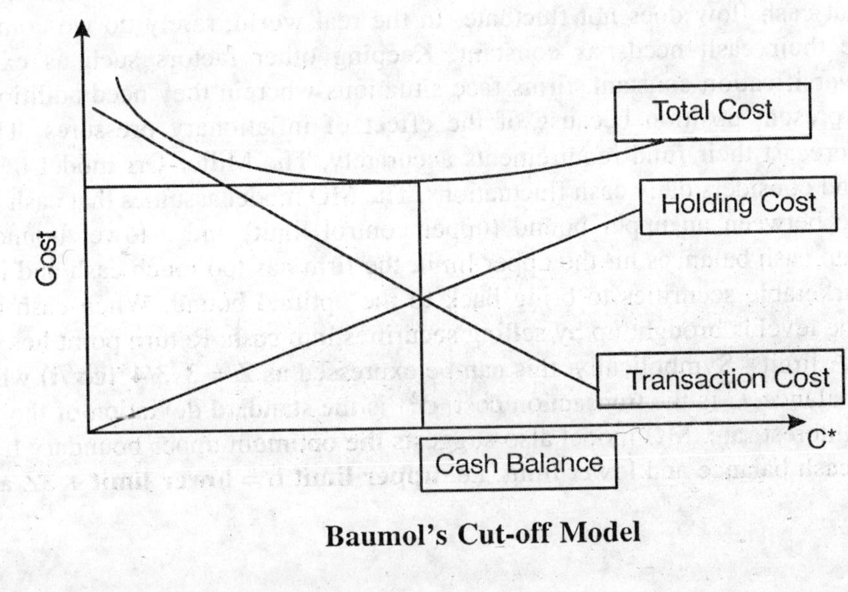

Baumol's Cut-off Model

The optimum cash balance C^* is obtained when the total cost is minimum which is expressed as $C^* = \sqrt{2c\ T/k}$ where C^* is the optimum cash balance, C is the cost per transaction, T is the total cash needed during the year and k is the opportunity cost of holding cash balance. The optimum cash balance will increase with increase in the per transaction cost and total funds required and decease with the opportunity cost.

Example

A firm's annual cash requirement is ₹ 20000000. The opportunity cost of capital is 15% per annum. ₹ 150 is the per transaction cost for the firm when it converts is short-term securities to cash. Find out the optimum cash balance. What is the annual cost of the demand for the optimum cash balance?

Solution

$C^* = \sqrt{2c\ T/k} = \sqrt{[2(150)\ (20000000)]/0.15}$ = **₹ 200000**

The annual cost is 150(20000000/200000) + 0.15(200000/2) = **₹ 30000**

Example

Mysore Lamps Ltd. requires ₹ 30 lakhs to meet its quarterly cash requirements. The annual return on its marketable securities which are of the tune of ₹ 30 lakhs is 20%. The conversion of the securities into cash necessitates a fixed cost of ₹ 3000 per transaction. Compute the optimum conversion amount.

Solution

$C^* = \sqrt{2cT/k} = \sqrt{[2*3000*3000000]/\ 0.05}$ @ = ₹ 600000

5% or 0.05 is 20% /4 as 20% is annual return and fund requirement is done on a quarterly basis.

B. Miller-Orr model

Miller-Orr came out with another model due to the limitation of the Baumol model. Baumol model assumes that cash flow does not fluctuate. In the real world, rarely do we come across firms which have their cash needs as constant. Keeping other factors such as expansion, modernization, diversification constant, firms face situations wherein they need additional cash to maintain their present position because of the effect of inflationary pressures. The firms therefore cannot forecast their fund requirements accurately. The Miller-Orr model overcomes this shortcoming and considers daily cash fluctuations. The MO model assumes that cash balances randomly fluctuate between an upper bound (upper control limit) and a lower bound (lower control limit). When cash balances hit the upper limit, the firm has too much cash and it is time to buy enough marketable securities to bring back to the optimal bound. When cash balances touch zero level, the level is brought up by selling securities into cash. Return point lies between the upper and lower limits. Symbolically, this can be expressed as $\mathbf{Z = 3\sqrt{3/4*(c\sigma^2/i)}}$ where Z is the optimal c ash balance, C is the transaction cost, σ^2 is the standard deviation of the net cash flows and I is the interest rate. MO model also suggests the optimum upper boundary b as three times the optimal cash balance and lower limit, i.e. **upper limit b = lower limit + 3Z** an

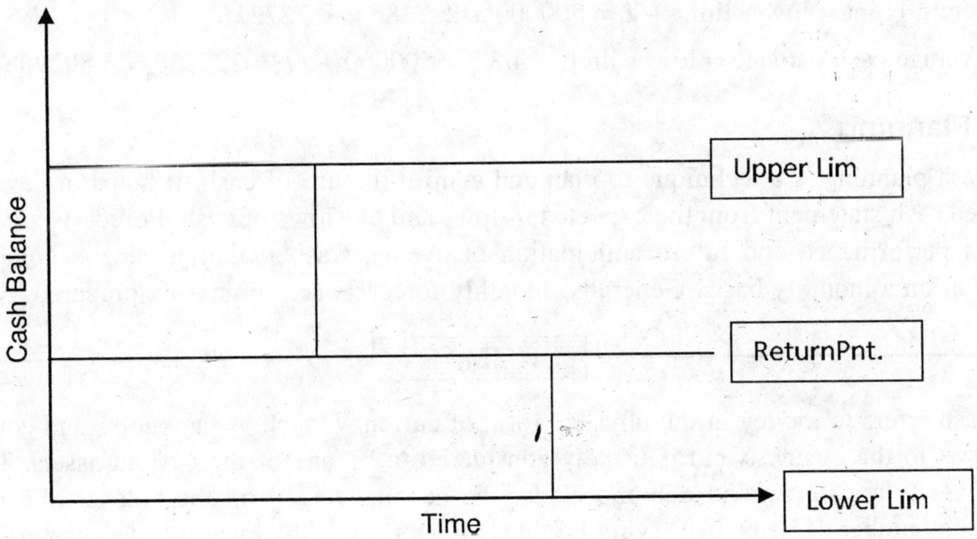

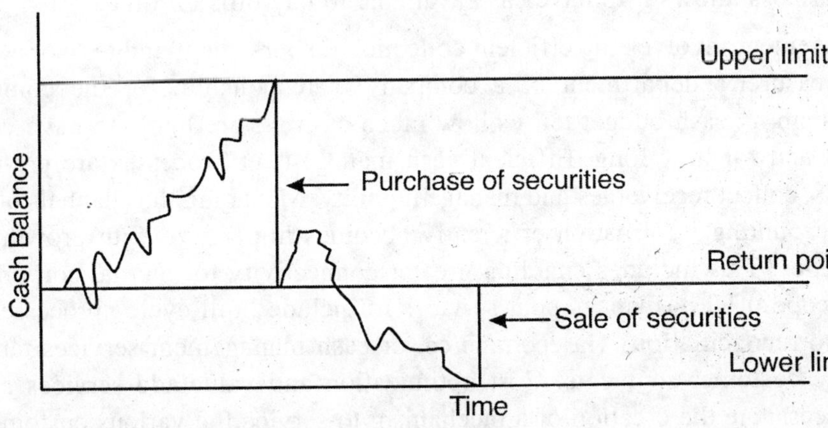

Example

Mehta industries have a policy of maintaining ₹ 500000 minimum cash balance. The standard deviation of the company's daily cash flows is ₹ 200000. The interest rate is 14%. The company has to spend ₹ 150 per transaction. Calculate the upper and lower limits and the return point as per MO model.

Solution

$Z = 3\sqrt{3/4 * (cs^2/i)}$

$3\sqrt{3/4 * (150 * 200000^2) / 0.14/365} = ₹\ 227226$

The upper control limit = lower limit 3Z = 500000 + 3*227226 = ₹ **1181678**

Return point = lower limit + Z = 500000 + 227286 = ₹ **727226**

Average cash balance = lower limit + 4/3Z = 500000 + 4/3* 227226 = ₹ **802968**

Cash Planning

Cash planning is a technique to plan and control the use of cash. It helps in developing a projected cash statement from the expected inflows and outflows of cash. Forecasts are based on the past performance and future anticipation of events. Cash planning can be done a daily, weekly or on a monthly basis. Generally, monthly forecasts are commonly prepared by firms.

SUMMARY

Cash refers to money in the physical form of currency, such as banknotes and coins. Cash is an asset to the business and is usually considered to be one of the current assets. The other current assets are stocks and debtors. Under the heading 'cash' on the balance sheet may be included a number of items of varying liquidity. Cash flow is the measure of your ability to pay your bills on a regular basis. It depends on the timing and amounts of money flowing into and out of the business each week and month. Good cash flow means that the pattern of income and spending in a business allows it to have cash available to pay bills on time.

Cash management involves the efficient collection disbursement and temporary investment of cash. The treasurer's department of a company is responsible for the company's cash management system. A cash budget tell us how much cash we are likely to have, when we are likely to have it and for how long. Efficient cash management processes are pre-requisites to execute payments, collect receivables and manage liquidity. Managing the channels of collections, payments and accounting information efficiently becomes imperative with growth in business transaction volumes. This includes enabling greater connectivity to internal corporate systems, expanding the scope of cash management services to include "full-cycle" processes (*i.e.*, from purchase order to reconciliation) via ecommerce, or cash management services targeted at the needs of specific customer segments. Cost optimization and value-add services are customer demands that necessitate the creation of a mechanism to service the various customer groups.

The periodical, *e.g.*, daily or monthly cast reports can be prepared when cash inflows and outflows are more or less stable due to very small fluctuations in collection and payment patters. If there are wide fluctuations in collection and payment of cash and high uncertainly in cash flows, then cash position should be monitored at a short and regular intervals, say weekly or sometimes on daily basis and cash budget, prepared earlier, should be revised for the subsequent period based on the variance between the actual and budgeted figures and the reasons thereof. The cash report provides information on the cash position on a daily basis. But since if does not provide the information's regarding positions it does not provide the information's regarding positions of Accounts Receivable

One of the prime responsibilities of a Finance Manager is to maintain an appropriate balance between cash and marketable securities. The amount of cash balance will depend on risk-return trade-off. A firm with less cash balances has a weak liquidity position but may be earning profits by investing its surplus cash and on the other hand it loses on the profits by holding too much cash. A balance has to be maintained between these aspects at all times.

A firm can hold its transactions balances to a minimum by arranging that cash inflow coincide with the timing of cash outflow or *vice versa.* Matching of the timings of inflows and outflows will involve the following:

(a) Slowing down cash payments or cash disbursement to the suppliers of materials and stores;

(b) Speeding up cash collections;

(c) Combining (a) and (b).

EXERCISE

Short Questions

1. What is 'Cash budgeting'?
2. What is 'Cash budget'?
3. What is 'cash Report'?
4. What is 'Treasury Report'?
5. What is meant by the term 'Disbursement delay'?
6. What do you mean by 'Cash Float'?
7. What is 'Concentration Banking'?
8. In which three segments firm's short-term investment portfolio can be divided?
9. What is 'Commercial Paper'?
10. What is 'Treasury Bill'?
11. What is 'Commercial Bill'?

Moderate and Broad Questions

1. Explain the principal motives for holding cash?
2. What is cash management? How it can become effective?
3. Explain Cash Management Models.
4. What are the criteria's for evaluating investment instruments?
5. Explain each of the investment options.
6. How do you defer disbursement? What are the techniques?
7. What are the techniques of speeding up collections?
8. What are the methods, of cash forecasting?
9. How the amount of surplus cash can be determined?
10. How do you prepare the portfolio of firm's short-term investment of surplus cash?
11. Discus various cash reports used for control purpose.
12. Explain the importance of 'Cash float' in cash management?
13. What are models for determining optimal cash?

PROBLEMS

1. Visionary Ltd. a newly started company wishes to prepare cash budget from January. Prepare a cash budget for the first 4 months from the following information's:

Months	Total Sales ₹	Materials ₹	Wages ₹	Production Overheads ₹	Administrative Selling & Distribution O/Hs
January	40000	40000	8000	6400	1600
February	44000	28000	8800	6600	1800
March	56000	28000	9200	6800	1800
April	72000	44000	9200	7000	2000
May	60000	40000	8000	6400	1800
June	80000	50000	10000	7200	2400

Cash balance on 1st January was ₹ 20000. A new machinery is to be installed at ₹ 40000 on credit, to be repaid by 4 equal installments in February, March, April and May. Sales commission @ 5% on total sales is to be paid within a month following actual sales. ₹ 20000 being the amount of 2nd call may be received in March. Share premium amounting to ₹ 4000 is also obtainable with the 2nd call.

Period of credit allowed by suppliers – 2 months

Period of credit allowed to customers – 1 month

Delay in payment of overheads – 1 month

Delay in payment of wages – ½ month.

Assume cash sales to be 50% of total sales.

2. A limited company is formed to take over a running business. It has been decided to raise ₹ 55 lakhs by issuing equity shares and the balance of capital required in the first 6 months is to be financed by ICICI against an issue of ₹ 5 lakhs, 8% debenture (interest payable annually) in its favour.

Initial outlay consists of:

	₹
Freehold Premises	25 lakhs
Plant and Machinery	10 lakhs.
Stock	6 lakhs.
Vehicles and other items	5 lakhs.

Payments, an above item are to be made in the month of incorporation. Sales during the 1st 6 months ending on June 30 are estimated as under:

January	₹ 14 lakhs.
February	₹ 15 lakhs.
March	₹ 18.50 lakhs.
April	₹ 25 lakhs.
May	₹ 26.50 lakhs.
June	₹ 28 lakhs.

Log in payment:

Debtors 2 months

Creditor 1 month

Others information

(a) Preliminary expenses = ₹ 50,000 (payable in February)

(b) General expenses = ₹ 50,000 (per month, at the end of each month)

(c) Monthly wages and salaries (payable on the 1st day of the next month)

- ₹ 80,000 for the first 3 months
- ₹ 95,000 thereafter.

(d) Gross profit rate is expected to be 20% on sales

(e) The shares and debentures are to be issued on 1st January.

(f) The stock level throughout is to be same as the outlay.

Prepare a cash budget and a projected Trading and Profit & Loss Account for the Six months ended June 30 and the projected Balance Sheet as at that date.

Hints:

Co. Ltd's Cash Budget
for the six months ending on June 30, 2010 (in lakhs of rupees)

Particulars	January	February	March	April	May	June	Total
A. Opening Balance	—	13.50	1.30	2.80	2.50	0.50	—
B. Receipts:							
Shares	55.00	–	–	–	–	–	55.00
8% Debenture	5.00	–	–	–	–	–	5.00
Sales	–	–	14.00	15.00	18.50	25.00	72.50
C. Total receipts (A+B)	60.00	13.50	15.30	17.80	21.00	25.50	132.50
D. Payments:							
• Freehold Premises	25.00	–	–	–	–	–	25.00
• Plant & Machinery	10.00	–	–	–	–	–	10.00
• Vehicles	5.00	–	–	–	–	–	5.00
• Preliminary Expenses	–	0.50	–	–	–	–	0.50
• Wages	-	0.80	0.80	0.80	0.95	0.95	4.30
• General expenses	0.50	0.50	0.50	0.50	0.50	0.50	3.00
• Purchases	6.00	10.40	11.20	14.00	19.05	20.25	80.90
TOTAL	***46.50***	***12.20***	***12.50***	***15.30***	***20.50***	***21.70***	***128.70***
E. Closing Balance	**13.50**	**1.30**	**2.80**	**2.50**	**0.50**	**3.80**	**2.80**

Projected Trading and Profile & Loss Account
for the six months ending on June, 30th 2010

Dr. *Cr.*

Particulars	₹ In lakhs	Particulars	₹ In lakhs
To Purchase (Balancing figure)	102.35	By Sales (14 + 15 + 18.50 + 25 + 26.50 + 28)	127
To Wages (3 × 0.8 + 3 × 0.95)	5.25	By Closing Stock	6
To Gross Profit c/d — 20% on sales	25.40		
	133.00		133.00
To Expenses	3.00		
To Deb.Interest (6th month)	0.20		
To Net Profit	22.20	By Gross Profit b/d	25.40
	25.40		**25.40**

Note: Purchase and Payment for purchase

Gross Profit = 20% on Sale

Cost of Goods sold = 80% on sale

Purchase = Cost of goods sold-wages

= 80% of sales-wages

(₹ in lakhs)

Particulars	January	February	March	April	May	June	Total
Sales	14	15	18.50	25	26.50	28	127
Cost of goods sold – 80% of sales	11.20	12	14.80	20	21.20	22.40	
Less: Wages	.80	.80	.80	.95	.95	.95	
Purchase	10.40	11.20	14.00	19.05	20.25	21.45	
Payment after 1 month	6	10.40	11.20	14.00	19.05	20.25	80.90

Projected Balance sheet
As on June, 30th 2010 …………

Liability	₹ In lakhs	Assets	₹ In lakhs
Authorized share Capital	?	**Fixed Assets:**	
Subscribed and Paid up		• **Freehold premises**	25.00
Equity share Capital	55.00	• Plant & Machinery	10.00
Reserves & surpluses		• Vehicles etc.	500
Profit & Loss account	22.20		

Secured Loan		**Investments**	NIL
8% Debenture	5.00	**Current Assets, Loans and Advances**	
Unsecured Loan	NIL		
Current Liabilities & Provision		Stock-in-trade	6.00
		Bank	3.80
Interest due	0.20	Debtor (26.50 + 28)	54.50
Wages outstanding	0.95	**Fictitious Assets**	NIL
Trade Creditor	21.45	**Misc. Expenditures:**	
		Prel. Expenses	0.50
	104.80		**104.80**

3. A manufacturing company has been experiencing difficulties in its operations due to various reasons. It has, however, planned its operations for the year ended 30th June, 2010. From the following relevant particulars prepare cash budget for each of the months of July, August, September and October, 2010.

Estimated variable production cost p.a. :

	₹
Direct materials	4.00
Direct wages	3.00
Production overhead	2.00
	9.00

Fixed overhead, estimated to be ₹ 50000 is expected to be incurred in equal amounts each month during the budget period. Estimated sales for the first 5 months are:

Months	**Units**	**Sales Value**
July	Nil	Nil
August	6250	62500
September	6800	68000
October	5900	59000
November	6200	62000

Other Informations:

(i) Finished Goods stock: 70% each months invoice sales units to be produced in the month of sales and 30% in the previous month.

(ii) Raw Material Stock: 50% of direct material required for each month's production to be purchased in the previous month.

(iii) Terms of payment:

(a) *Direct Material:* To be paid for in the month following the month of purchase .

(b) *Direct wages:* To be paid 60% the month used and 40% in the following month.

(c) *Expenses:* To be paid within the month due.

There is an expected bank overdraft of ₹ 25,000 in the month of September 2010.

❑❑❑

10 Debtors Management

10.1 DEFINITION OF DEBTORS, DEBTOR'S MANAGEMENT

Debtors are receivables representing as 'debts owed to the organization by customers to whom goods or services are sold on credit'. Business firms generally sell goods on credit to facilitate sales from those customers. Debtor's Management considers receivables as one of the significant portion of the total assets and ultimately manages receivable with the objective of increasing total sales *vis-a-vis* ensuring total profits along with the objective of meeting increasing competition by offering better credit facilities than those offered by its competitors. But extension of credit to customers involves costs and risk. Management should weigh benefits for taking risk against risk.

10.2 OBJECTIVE OF DEBTOR'S MANAGEMENT

The objective is to increase sales for increasing profits until returns that the business firms get from funding or investment of receivables is less than the cost that the company has to incur in order to fund their receivables or cost of capital. Other objective is to meet increasing competition and for this the business firms may have to grant better credit facilities than those offered by it's competitors. Thus by adopting its credit term of trade, the firms avoid loss of sales from customers who would buy elsewhere if they did not receive the expected credit.

10.3 VARIABLES OF CREDIT POLICY

There are three credit policy variables which the financial management must consider in establishing an optimum credit policy. These are the major controllable decision variables which are as follows:

I. Credit Standards

Credit standards are the criteria which a firm follows in selecting customers for the purpose of credit extension. The firms may maintain any of the three credit standards as follows:

(a) *Tight credit standards:* The firms may sell mostly on cash basis and credit sales facility may be extended to those few customers only who are most reliable and financially sound. The benefits are no bad-debt losses or less cost of credit administration. The disadvantage of tight credit standard is that the firms may loose potential customers who are opting credit sales facilities from the firm.

(b) *Liberal credit standards:* The firms may sell mostly on credit basis to customers. In that case the firms may have larger sales but will have to carry large debtors or receivables, along with the risk of higher bad debt losses, and higher cost of credit administration.

(c) *Moderate credit standards:* The firms may sell 50% on cash and 50% on credit basis to bring the balance between additional benefits from additional sales and additional default risks along with additional cost of credit administration.

The bases for setting credit standards are – Credit Terms and Collection Policy.

2. Credit Terms

Credit terms include the stipulations under which the business firms sell to customers on credit which are as follows:

(a) *Credit Period:* The credit period refers to the length of time allowed to customers to pay for their purchases. If a firm allows say, 30 days of credit where no discount is given to induce early payment, it's credit term are stated as "net 30".

(b) *Cash Discount:* Business firms offer cash discount facilities to customers to induce early payment. If a firm allows say, "1/30, net 45" means that a discount of 1% is offered if the payment is made by 30th day, otherwise, the full payment is due by 45th day where no cash discount is available.

3. Collection Policy

With a view to collect receivables within stated time period and ultimately to release funds which are locked up in receivables for a longer period than they should have been under the credit terms and also to minimize bad debt losses, the business firms adopt effective collection policy. It is needed since all customers do not pay the firm's bills in time. The entire collection programmes should aim at accelerating collections from 'slow-payers customers', reducing bad-debt losses and costs of collections of receivables. The collection program must consist of the following:

(a) Despatch of reminder letter to customers whose due date is coming,

(b) Despatch of official letter to 'slow-payers customers' whose dues still remain uncollected after the stipulated time period, following by telephone, telegram or personal visit.

(c) Taking of legal action, after examining the financial condition, if the payment is still not made by those customers to whom earlier official letters have been dispatched.

(d) If the financial condition of the customer is weak and same as like insolvency, either keeping patient for the time being or sending letter to that customer to accept reduced payment due as per settlement of account,

(e) Finding out the temporarily 'slow-payers' due to the present economic conditions so that firms are not giving to be strict to them.

The optimum collection policy aims at maximizing the profitability by bringing a trade-off between strict collection efforts and liberal collection efforts- so that firms do not loose the permanent customers, *vis-à-vis*, receivables could not increase and profitability could not reduce. The incremental financial benefits, in the form of cost of funds released by a reduction in the level of receivables and the reduction of bad debt losses, have to be compared with the incremental cost associated with the additional collection expenses and a new policy is warranted only if incremental net benefit is positive.

10.4 COSTS AND LOSSES ASSOCIATED WITH MAINTAINING RECEIVABLES

Capital Costs: Selling goods on credit has consequences of blocking the firm's resources in receivables where additional funds are arranged to meet firm's own obligation of monthly as well as daily recurring expenditures either out of profits or from outside. In both cases, the firm incurs a cost. In the former case there is the opportunity cost of the income the firm could have earned had the same been invested in some other profitable avenue. In the latter case of obtaining funds from outside, the firm has to pay interest on the loan taken. Therefore, sanctioning credit to customers on sale of goods on credit has a capital cost.

Administration Costs: When a firm sells goods on credit it has to incur two types of administration cost viz. Credit investigation and supervision costs. Before granting credit to any customer, the firm has to investigate the credit rating of the customer. Moreover, additional expenses on staff for administering process of collection of receivables from the customers are incurred.

Delinquency Cost: These are the costs of sending remainders and costs of legal charges when the customers fail to pay the amount due on credit sales on the expiry of credit period.

Bad-debts Losses/Default Costs: It arises when the firms are unable to realize or recover the amount due from its customers to whom goods have been sold on credit.

10.5 EFFECT OF RELAXING THE CREDIT STANDARDS ON PROFIT

Change in profit = [Incremental contribution – Bad Debts on new sales] (1–t) – cost of incremental investment in receivables

i.e., $\Delta P = [\Delta S(1 - V) - \Delta S\, b_n] (1 - t) - [k\, \Delta I]$

where, ΔP = change in profit on new sales

ΔS = increase in sales

b_n = bad debt loss ratio on new sales

$\Delta S\ b_n$ = increase in bad debt

Losses = $\Delta S \times b_n$

T = corporate – tax rate

V = ratio of variable costs to sales

1 – V = Ratio of contribution to sales

k = after – tax cost of capital (%)

ΔI = increase in investment of receivables.

$= \frac{\text{Increase in Sales}}{\text{360 days}} \times$ Avg. collection period (days) × Variable cost to sales ratio.

$= \frac{\Delta S}{360} \times$ Avg. collection period XV

Problem 1

Examines the effect of relaxing the credit policy on the profitability from the following details of an organization:

The current sales is ₹ 10 crores. The organization is considering relaxation of its credit policy. Such relaxation may have effect on sales by ₹ 1 crore 50 lakhs on which bad debt losses would be 10%. The contribution margin ratio for the organization is 20%. Average collection period is 40 days. After-tax cost of funds is 10%. Tax rate applicable to the firm is 30%. Assume 360 days in a year.

Solution

$$\Delta P = [\Delta S\ (1 - V) - \Delta S\ b_n\ ]\ (1 - t) - [\ k\ \Delta I]$$

$$= \left[15000000\ (1 - .80) - 15000000 \times \frac{10}{100}\right]\ (1 - .30) - \left[\frac{10}{100} \times \left(\frac{15000000}{360} \times 40 \times .80\right)\right]$$

$$= [3000000 - 1500000] \times .70 - \left[\frac{10}{100} \times 1333333\right]$$

$$= 10,50,000 - 133333$$

$$= 9,16,667$$

10.6. EFFECT ON CASH DISCOUNT ON PROFIT.

Change in profit = [Incremental contribution – increase in discount cost] (1– t)

+ Opportunity cost savings in receivables investment

+ Decrease in collection expenditure

+ Reduction of bad debt

i.e., $\Delta P = [\Delta S\ (1 - V) - \Delta DIS]\ (1 - t) + [k\ \Delta I] + \Delta C + \Delta BD$

Where, $\Delta 1$ = Savings in receivables investments

ΔDIS = increase in discount cost

= discount cost after liberalization of discount terms – discount cost before liberalization of discount terms.

Problem 2

Present credit terms of a company are '1/10 net 30'. Its sales are ₹ 10 croers and average collection period is 20 days. Variable cost to sales ratio is 80% and cost of capital is 10%. The proportion of sales on which customers currently take discount is 50%. The company is considering relaxing its discount terms to '2/10 net 30'. Such a relaxation is expected to increase sales by ₹ 1 crore and to reduce average collection period to 14 days and to increase discount sales to 80%. Tax rate is 30%. Examine the effect of relaxing the discount policy on profits of the organization. Assume 360 days in a year.

Solution

$\Delta P = \Delta S\ (1 - V) - DIS]\ (1 - t) + [k \times \Delta I] + \Delta C + \Delta BD$ {ΔBD = Reduction in bad debt}

$= [10000000\ (1 - .80) - 1260000]\ (1 - .30) + [\frac{10}{100} \times 1355556] + NIL + NIL$

[ΔC = Decrease in collection expenditure = NIL]

$= [2000000 - 1260000] \times .70 + 135556$

$= 518000 + 135556$

= ₹ 6,53,556

Notes (a) Increase in discount cost (Δ DIS)

Discount cost before liberalization of discount terms

= % of discount sales × Existing Sales × discount rate

$= \frac{50}{100} \times 100000000 \times \frac{1}{100}$

= ₹ 5,00,000

Discount cost after liberalization of discount terms

= expected % of discount sales × Expected Sales after increase × New expected discount rate

$= \frac{80}{100} \times 110000000 \times \frac{2}{100}$

= ₹ 17,60,000

∴ ΔDIS = increase in discount cost

= ₹ 17,60,000 – 500000

= ₹ 12,60,000

(b) Savings in receivables investments (ΔI)

ΔI = Savings in receivable investments

$$= \frac{S_o}{360}(ACP_o - ACP_n) - V\frac{\Delta S}{360}ACP_n$$

Where, S_o = Sales before liberalizing the discount terms = 100000000

ACP_o = Average collection period before liberalizing the discount terms = 20 days

ACP_n = Average collection period after liberalizing the discount terms = 14 days

$$\therefore \quad \Delta I = \frac{100000000}{360}(20-14) - \frac{80}{100} \times \frac{10000000}{360} \times 14$$

$$= \frac{100000000}{60} - 311111$$

$$= 1666667 - 311111 = ₹\ 13{,}55{,}556$$

10.7 EFFECT OF CHANGING THE CREDIT PERIOD ON PROFITS (INCREASING THE CREDIT PERIOD)

Effect of changing the credit period on profits (Increasing the credit period):

Change in profit = [Incremental contribution – bad debts on new issues] (1 – t) – Cost of incremental investment in receivables.

Or $\Delta P = [\Delta S(1 - V) - \Delta Sb_n](1 - t) - [k \times \Delta I]$

$$\Delta I = \frac{S_0}{360}(ACP_n - ACP_o) - V\frac{\Delta S}{360}ACP_n = \text{increase in investment in receivables}$$

Problem 3

An organization currently provides 30 days credit to its customers. It's current sales is ₹ 50 million. The firm's cost of capital is 10% and the ratio of variable costs to sales is 85%. The organization is considering extending it's credit period to 60 days. Such an extension is likely to push sales up by ₹ 5 million. The bad debt proportion on additional sales would be 8%. The tax rate is 40%. Examine the effect of lengthening the credit period on profit. Should the company go for a policy change or not?

Solution

$$\Delta P = [\Delta S(1 - V) - \Delta SB_n](1 - t) - [k \times \Delta I]$$

$$= \left[5000000(1 - .85) - 5000000 \times \frac{8}{100}\right](1 - .40) - \left[\frac{10}{100} \times \Delta I\right]$$

$$= [750000 - 400000] \times 0.60 - [0.10 \times \Delta I]$$

$$\therefore \quad \Delta I = \frac{50000000}{360}(60 - 30) + \frac{85}{100} \times \frac{5000000}{360} \times 60$$

$= 4166667 + 708333$

$= ₹\ 48,75,000$

$\therefore \quad \Delta P = [\ 750000 - 400000]\ X\ 0.60 - [\ 0.10\ X\ 4875000]$

$= 210000 - 487500$

$= - 277500$

Since the impact of increasing the credit period on profits of the firm is negative, the proposed change in credit period is not desirable.

10.8 EFFECT OF CHANGING COLLECTION PROGRAMMES ON PROFIT

Change in profit = [Incremental contribution – increase in bad debt loss] (1-t) – cost of increase in investment in receivables

Or, $\Delta P = [\Delta S\ (1 - V) - \Delta BD]\ (1 - t) - k \times \Delta I - \Delta C$

Where, ΔC = Increase in collection expenses.

ΔBD = increase in bad debt loss

$$\Delta I = \frac{S_o}{360}\ (ACP_n - ACP_o) + \frac{\Delta S}{360}\ .\ ACP_n\ .\ V$$

$\Delta BD = b_n\ (S_o + \Delta S) - b_o\ S_o$ where, b_n = new bad debt ratio.

Problem 4

A company is considering relaxing its collection effort. Its present sales are ₹ 30 million, 'Average collection Period = 30 days. Variable cost to sales ratio = 80%, cost of capital is 10%. The bad debt ratio is 5%. The relaxation in collection effort is expected to increase sales by ₹ 10 million, increase average collection period to 45 days and the bad debts ratio to 6%. Tax rate is 35%.'

Examine the effect of change in collection effort on profits. Assume 360 days in a year. Should the company relax the collection effort to increase sales?

Solution

$\Delta P = [\Delta S(1 - V) - \Delta BD]\ (1 - t) - k \times \Delta I - \Delta C$

$= [10000000\ (1 - .80) - 900000]\ (1 - .35) - [.10 \times 2250000] - NIL$

$= [2000000 - 900000]\ (1 - .35) - [.10 \times 2250000]$

$= [1100000 \times .65] - [.10 \times 2250000]$

$= 715000 - 225000$

$= ₹\ 4,90,000$

Note: $\Delta BD = b_n\ (S_o + \Delta S) - b_o\ S_o$

$= 6\%\ (30000000 + 10000000) - 5\% \times 30000000$

$= 24,00,000 - 15,00,000$

$= ₹\ 9,00,000$

$$\Delta I = \frac{30000000}{360} \times (45 - 30) + \frac{10000000}{360} \times 45 \times .80$$

$$= 12{,}50{,}000 + 10{,}00{,}000 = ₹\ 2250000$$

Since the change will lead to increase in profit, it is desirable to refer the collection programme of the firm.

10.9 CREDIT GRANTING DECISIONS

Once the credit worthiness of a customer is assessed, the next query must be whether the credit or facilities of receivables should be offered. There are two situations in these occasions.

Situation 1

If there is no possibility of a repeat order

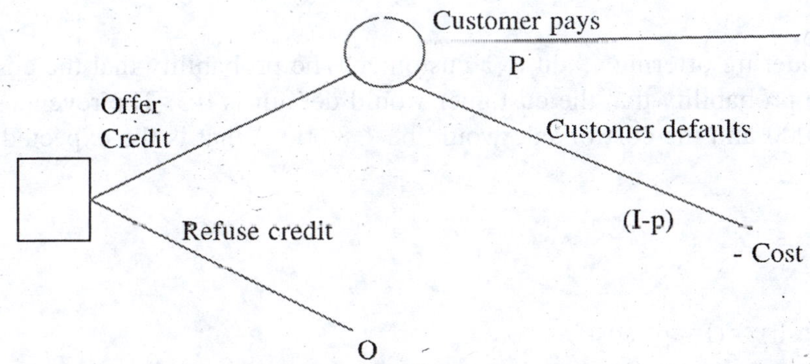

A Decision Tree for Credit Granting Decision

P is probability that the customer pays his dues, (I – p) is the probability that the customer defaults, Rev is the revenue from sales. Cost is the cost of goods sold. The expected profit for the action 'offer credit' is

p (Rev – Cost) – Cost (I – p)

The expected profits for the action 'refuse credit' is 0. This is because, if the expected profit of the course of action 'offer credit' is positive it is desirable to extend / offer credit; otherwise to refuse credit.

Situation 2

When there is a possibility of a repeat order.

The repeat order would be accepted only if the customer does not default on the first order.

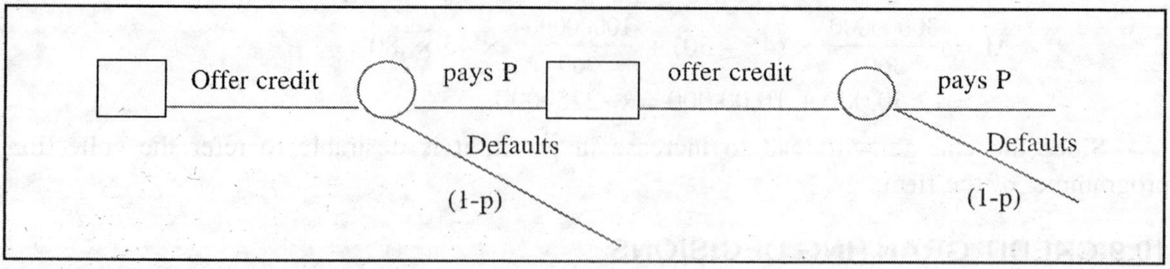

A Decision Tree for Credit Granting Decision

P is probability that the customer pays his dues, (I – ρ) is the probability that the customer defaults. One the customer pays for the first order, the probability that he would default on the second order is less than the probability of his defaulting on the first order.

Expected profit of offering credit = Expected profit on initial order + (probability of payment and repeat order × Expected profit on repeat order).

Problem 5

A company is considering offering credit to a customer. The probability that the customer would pay is 0.7 and the probability that the customer would default is 0.3. The revenues from the sale would be ₹ 12,000 and the cost of sale would be ₹ 8,000. What is the expected profit from offering credit?

Solution:

Expected profit

= ρ(Rev – Cash) – (I – p) cost

= 0.7 (12,000 – 8,000) – (1 – 0.7) 8,000

= 0.7 × 4,000 – 0.3 × 8,000

= 2,800 – 2,400

= ₹ 400

Problem 6

A company is considering extending credit to a customer who is expected to place a repeat order. The probability of default on the first order is 0.1 and the probability of default on the second order decreases to 0.05. The revenues from the sale would be 1200 and the cost of sale would be ₹ 800. What is the expected profit of extending credit?

Solution:

Expected profit of offering credit to a customer who is expected to place a repeat order = Expected profit on initial order + (probability of payment and repeat order × Expected profit on repeat order).

$$= [\, p_1 \text{ (Rev – Cost)} - (1 - p_1) \text{ Cost}] + [p_1 \times \{p_2 \text{ (Rev – Cost)} - (1 - p_2) \text{ Cost}\}]$$

When p_1 = prob. of payment of first order = 1 – 0.1 = 0.9, 1 – p_1 = 0.1

P_2 = prob of payment of second order = 1 – 0.05 = 0.95, 1 – p_2 = 0.05

∴ Expected profit

= [0.9(1200 – 800) – 0.1(800)] + 0.9 [0.95 (1200 – 800) – 0.05 × (800)]

= [360 – 80] + 0.9 [0.95 × 400 – 40]

= 280 + 0.9 [380 – 40]

= 280 + 0.9 × 340

= 280 + 306

= ₹ 586

10.10. PROCESS OF CREDIT EVALUATION

Before granting credit to a customer, a firm seeks information of the creditn worthiness of that customer.

How to judge the creditworthiness of an applicant?

5 C's, have to be considered – character, capital, capacity, collateral and conditions. Character refers to the willingness of the customer to honour his obligations. Capacity refers to the ability of the customer to pay on time. Collateral represents the security offered by the time in the form of mortgages. Capital is the financial reserves of the customer. Conditions reflect general economic conditions that affect the customer.

Credit evaluation of the prospective customer involves obtaining information from which the financial capacity as also the paying habits can be evaluated. Company's annual reports provide considerable & relevant information's in the form of balance sheets and profit and loss accounts besides detailed notes and the auditors reports over the past 3 or 4 years. The financial strengths and weaknesses can be judged by the following important ratios:

A. Liquidity Ratios (short-term solvency)

- Current Ratio
- Liquidity Ratio
- Cash Position Ratio
- Stock Turnover Ratio
- Debtors Turnover Ratio and Average Collection Period
- Creditors Turnover Ratio and Average Payment Period.

B. Capital Structure /Leverage Ratios

- Debt Equity Ratio
- Debt Service Coverage Ratio
- Interest Coverage Ratio
- Fixed Assets to Net Worth

C. Profitability Ratios

- Return on Equity
- Operating Profit Ratio
- Net Profit Ratio

Experience of the firm while dealing with customer:

If the organization or firm has previous experience of dealing with the customers, it can judge the customer's credit worthiness by his/her promptness in payments in the past.

Bank References

The reference of the customer's bank may be taken into consideration while judging the creditworthiness of that customer. This task may be done through the banker of the organization who in a better position to obtain information from the customer's bank instead of approaching directly to the customer's bank for information.

Framing numerical credit index: The credit index is simply a weighted sum of facts which has a bearing on creditworthiness. For example, any Commercial bank offering house building loan may determine the numerical credit index of its applicants as follow:

Credit Index = W_1 Incomes Level (as per last 3 years' Tax Returns)
+ W_2 (Securities)
+ W_3 (Guaranter)
+ W_4 (No. of earners in the family)

Preparing Credit Evaluation Report

Format of the Report

Item Head	For Company	Standard	Remarks
A. Liquidity Ratios:			
Current Ratio			
Quick Ratio			
....			
....			
B. Profitability Ratios:			
Net Profit Ratio			
....			
....			
C. Leverage:			
Debt-Equity			
....			
....			

Paying habit	:	
Integrity & Honesty	:	
Risk class	:	Say, customer with negligible risk of default.

Construction of a Credit Rating Index (based on a 5-point rating scale)

Factor	Factor weight	Rating 5	4	3	2	1	Factor Score
Past payment	0.35		√				1.40
Net profit margin	0.15		√				.60
Current ratio	0.20			√			.60
Debt-equity ratio	0.10		√				.40
ROE	0.20		√				1.00
			Rating Index				4.00

10.11 CONTROL OF ACCOUNTS RECEIVABLES/DEBTORS, MONITORING OF RECEIVABLES

A. Traditional Methods:

I. Days Sales Outstanding: The average number of day's sales outstanding at any time, say end of the month or end of the quarter, is obtained by following the formula which is not very different from the usual formula for average collection period:-

$$\text{Day's Sales outstanding (DSO) at a given time, } t = \frac{\text{Accounts receivables at time } t}{\text{Average daily sales}}$$

According to this method, accounts receivable are deemed to be in control if the Day's Sales outstanding is equal to or less-than a certain norm. If the value of Day's sales outstanding exceeds the specified norm linked to the credit period, then the collection policy has to be strengthened as the collections are slow.

To illustrate the calculation of this measure, we are considering the monthly sales and month-end account receivable for a product line of an organization as shown in the following table:

Table 10.1
Sales and Receivables Data [₹ In crores]

Month Year 2010-2011	Sales	Receivable
April 10	20	45
May	20.5	48
June	24	50
July	16.8	35.6
August	15	28
September	18	32
October	22	40
November	22	42.8
December	22.5	42.8
January 11	23	43
February 11	24.5	52
March 11	26	54

If the Day's Sales Outstanding is calculated at the end of each quarter, we get the following picture:

Quarter	Calculation of DSO	Day's Sales Outstanding (DSO)
First (April'10-June'10)	$\frac{50}{(20 + 20.5 + 24) \div 91}$	71 days
Second (July'10 – Sept'10	$\frac{32}{(16.8 + 15 + 18) \div 92}$	60 days
Third (Oct'10 – Dec'10)	$\frac{42.8}{(22 + 22 + 22.5) \div 92}$	60 days
Fourth (Jan'11 – March'11)	$\frac{54}{(23 + 24.5 + 26) \div 90}$	66 days

Looking at the Day's Sales Outstanding (DSO), we observe that it decreased significantly over the year, suggesting that collections have been improved a lot during the Fourth Quarter of 2010-2011 financial years.

II. Ageing Schedule: The ageing schedule depicts the age-wise distribution of accounts receivable at a given point of time, *i.e.*, classifies outstanding accounts receivables at a given point of time into different age brackets. An illustration of Ageing Schedule (AS) at the end of various-quarters is shown in the following table:

Table 10.2
Outstanding Accounts Receivable (% of Receivables)

Age Group (in days)	1st Quarter	2nd Quarter	3rd Quarter	4th Quarter
0-30	35	40	45	48
30-60	32	30	28	25
61-90	22	24	26	24
> 90	12	10	5	6

The actual AS of the organization is compared with some standard AS at periodic intervals (say quarterly intervals) to identify changes in the payment behavior of customers or in broader sense, to determine whether account receivables are in control or not.

When the percentage of receivables belonging to higher age groups is above a stipulated norm, action has to be initiated before they run into bad debts. If the organization's credit terms are say 'net 45 days' then control needs to be exercised in the form of follow-up measures in respect of the bottom 22% accounts.

Limitations of the Traditional Methods: Traditionally, the above mentioned two methods have been suggested for monitoring and controlling accounts receivable; DSO and AG. But both the methods are based on an aggregation of Sales and receivables. Moreover these both methods are influenced by the sales patterns as well as payment behaviors of the customers.

Average collection period and the ageing schedule, both cannot show the same against different pattern of sales-increasing, decreasing or constant.

B. Collection matrix Approach:

To overcome the short comings of the traditional methods and in order to study accurately the changes in the payment behavior of customers, it is helpful to look at the pattern of collections associated with credit sales. The following table shows an illustrative collection matrix. For example, the collection of dues from credit sales during the month of April, 2010 is as follows:

15% in April, 2010 (the month of sales)
40% in May, 2010 (the first following month)
35% in June, 2010 (the second following month)
10% in July, 2010 (the third following month)

From the collection pattern, one can judge whether the collection is getting improved, stable or deteriorating. A secondary benefit of such an analysis is that it provides a historical record of collection percentages that could be useful in projecting monthly receipts for each budgeting period.

Table 10.3
Collection Matrix

Percentage of Receivable collected during the	April' 2010 Sales	May Sales	June Sales	July Sales	Aug Sales	Sept Sales
Month of Sales	15	18	20	16	14	18
First following month	40	35	38	36	33	28
Second following month	35	40	22	23	26	25
Third following month	10	7	20	19	23	23
Fourth following month	–	–	–	6	4	6

10.12 CREDIT MANAGEMENT IN INDIA

In practice, very few Indian Companies have a stated and systematic credit management. Most of the companies in India are still far away from attempting articulation and formalisation of their credit policies. They are stating credit policy in general language – 'to maximize sales growth consistent with an acceptable degree of risk'. But the credit policy needs to be articulated in explicit terms and revised periodically in the light of internal and external changes. Very few Indian companies have well-defined systems for monitoring and controlling accounts receivables. They do not have still a well-defined collection programme.

Problem 7

The credit term of an organization is '1/10 net 30'. Its sales are ₹ 400 lakhs, its average collection period is 25 days, its contribution margin is 15% and its cost of capital is also 20%. The proportion on sales on which customers currently take discount is 40%. The finance manager made a proposal of changing its discount terms to '2/10 net 30'. An expectation is there to increase the sales by ₹ 100 lakhs, reducing the average collection period to 20 days and increasing the proportion of discount sales to 60%. The change in the cash discount policy is expected to generate two additional benefits viz. –

(*i*) The percentage of bad debt losses on total sales will come down from 6% to 4%;

(*ii*) The collection expenditure would be reducing by ₹ 30,000.

Advise the company as to the desirability of relaxing the discount terms. You may assume a 360 day year.

Solution

Change in profit = [incremental contribution – Increase in discount cost] (1-t) – opportunity cost savings in receivable investment + reduction in collection expenditure + decrease in bad debt

Or $\Delta P = [\Delta S\ (1 - V) - \Delta DIS]\ (1 - t) + [\ k\ \Delta I\ ] + \Delta c + \Delta BD$

$$= [100 \text{ lakhs } (1 - .85) - 4{,}40{,}000]\,(1 - \text{NIL}) + \left[\frac{20}{100} \times 83{,}000\right] + 30{,}000 + 5{,}00{,}000$$

$= (15 \text{ lakhs} - 4{,}40{,}000) + 16{,}600 + 5{,}30{,}000$

$= 10{,}60{,}000 + 16{,}600 + 5{,}30{,}000$

= ₹ 16,06,600

Notes (a) Increase in discount cost (ΔDIS)

Discount cost before liberalization of discount terms

= % of discount Sales × Existing Sales × discount rate

$$= 40\% \times 400 \times \frac{1}{100} \text{ lakhs}$$

$$= \frac{40}{100} \times 400 \times \frac{1}{100} \text{ lakhs}$$

= 1.6 lakhs = ₹ 1,60,000

Discount cost after liberalization of discount terms

$$= \frac{60}{100} \times (400 + 100) \times \frac{2}{100} \text{ lakhs} = \frac{60}{100} \times 500 \times \frac{2}{100} \text{ lakhs}$$

= 6 lakhs = ₹ 6,00,000

ΔDIS = increase in decrease cost

= 6 lakhs – 1.6 lakhs

= 4.4 lakhs

= ₹ 4,40,000

(b) Saving in receivable investments

ΔI = Savings in receivable investments

$$= \frac{S_o}{360}(ACP_o - ACP_n) - V.\frac{\Delta S}{360} ACP_n$$

Where, S_o = Sales before liberalization of discount terms = 400 lakhs

ACP_o = Average collection period before liberalizing the discount terms = 25 days.

ACP_n = Average collection period after liberalizing the discount terms = 20 days

ΔS = increase in sales = 100 lakhs

∴ Ratio of V = Ratio of Variable Costs to Sales = 85% [since contribution margin = 15%]

$$\therefore \quad \Delta I = \frac{400}{360}(25\text{-}20) - \frac{85}{100} \times \frac{100}{360} \times 20 = 5.55 - 4.72 = 0.83 \text{ lakhs} = ₹\ 83{,}000$$

C. Decrease in bad debt-losses

Bad Debt, before liberalization of discount terms

= % of bad debt loss × Existing Sales

= 5% × 400 lakhs

= 20 lakhs

Bad Debts after liberalization of discount terms

= 3% × (400 + 100) lakhs

= 3% × 500 lakhs

= 15 lakhs.

Reduction of bad debts = ΔBD = 20 – 15 = 5 lakhs = ₹ 5,00,000.

Problem 8

A trader, whose current sales are in the region of ₹ 6 lakhs per annum and an average collection period of 30 days, wants to implement a more liberal policy to increase sales.

Credit policy	Increase in collection period	Increase in Sales	Present default anticipated
A	10 days	₹ 30000	1.5%
B	20 days	₹ 48000	2%
C	30 days	₹ 75000	3%
D	45 days	₹ 90000	4%

The selling price p.u. is ₹ 3. Average cost per unit is ₹ 2.25 and variable cost p.u. is ₹ 2. The current bad debt loss is 1%. Required return on additional investment is 20%. Assume a 360 day year.

Which of the above policies would you recommend for adoption?

Solution:

Giving b_n = bad debt ratio on new sales, V= Ratio of variable cost of sales = $\frac{2}{3}$ or 66.67%.

Table: Evaluation of Credit Policies

Particulars	Credit policy				
	Existing	**A**	**B**	**C**	**D**
Average collection period = Credit Period (days)	30	40	50	60	75
b_n = bad debt loss ratio	–	1.5%	2%	3%	4%
ΔS = increase in sales (₹)	–	30000	48000	75000	90000
Sales (₹)	600000	630000	648000	675000	690000
Investment in Receivables = (Sales ÷ 360) × Avg. Collection period × V	$\frac{600000}{360} \times 30 \times \frac{2}{3}$ = 33333	$\frac{630000}{360} \times 40 \times \frac{2}{3}$ = 46667	$\frac{648000}{360} \times 50 \times \frac{2}{3}$ = 60000	$\frac{675000}{360} \times 60 \times \frac{2}{3}$ = 75000	$\frac{690000}{360} \times 75 \times \frac{2}{3}$ = 95833
ΔI = Increase in investment of receivables	–	= 13334	= 26667	= 41667	= 62500
K × ΔI = cost of incremental investment in receivable = 20% × ΔI	–	= 2667	= 5333	= 8333	=12500
Bad Debts	6000= (600000 × 1%)	9450 = (630000 ×1.5%)	12960= (648000 ×2%)	20250= (675000 ×3%)	27600= (690000 ×4%)
$\Delta S \times b_n$ = Addl bad debt	–	3450	6960	14250	21600
Incremental Contribution= ΔS (1 – V)	–	$30000 \times (1 - \frac{2}{3})$ = 10000	$48000 \times (1 - \frac{2}{3})$ = 16000	$75000 \times (1 - \frac{2}{3})$ = 25000	$90000 \times (1 - \frac{2}{3})$ = 30000

Particular	Credit policy				
	Existing	A	B	C	D
Additional profit = [ΔS (1 – V) ΔSb_n] – (k × Δ1)	–	10000 – 3450 –2667 = 3883	16000 – 6960 –5333 =3707	25000 –14250 –8333 =2417	30000 –21600 –12500 =(4100)

Policy A will result in maximum additional profit among policy B and policy C. Policy D should be rejected outrightly since it will reduce existing profit by ₹ 4,100.

SUMMARY

Debtors are receivables representing as 'debts owed to the organization by customers to whom goods or services are sold on credit'. The purpose of receivable can be under stood from the basic objectives which are as follows:

- To increase total sales; because when a company sells goods or services on credit, it will be in position to sell more goods than if it insists on immediately cash payment.
- To increase profits, because this results in an increase in sales not only in volume, but also because companies charge a higher margin of profit on credit sales as compared to cash sales.
- To meet increasing competition; and for this the company may have to grant better credit facilities than those offered by its competitors.

There are three credit policy variables which a finance manager must consider in establishing an optimum credit policy. These are the major controllable decision variables in debtors management which are as follows:

- Credit standards,
- Credit terms,
- Collection Policy.

The costs and losses associated with maintain receivables are as follows:

- Capital costs,
- Administration Costs,
- Delinquency costs,
- Bad Debt losses.

While making credit granting decisions a firm seeks information of the credit worthiness of that customer. In judging the creditworthiness of an applicant's 5 basic factors – 5 c' s – character, capacity, capital, collateral and conditions have to be considered.

Credit evaluation of the prospective customer involves obtaining information from which the financial capacity as also the paying habits can be evaluated. The annual reports of a company provide considerable informations in the form of balance sheets and profit and loss accounts. When the financial statements are obtained, the financial strengths and weaknesses can be judged by the application of ratio analysis. Some of the important ratios are as follows:

- Current ratio
- Quick ratio
- Average collection period
- Average payment period
- Return on Equity
- Capital structure ratios etc.

Accounts receivables constitute the third most important asset category for business firms after plant & equipment and inventories. Traditionally two methods have been commonly suggested for monitoring accounts receivable: DSO and ageing schedule.

EXERCISE

Short Questions

1. What is meant by the term 'debtors'?
2. What is the basic objective of receivable management?
3. What are the 3 credit policy variables?
4. What are the costs and losses associated with maintaining receivables?
5. What are 5 basic factors which are considered in judging the credit worthiness of a customer while making credit granting decisions?
6. Name 3 ratios for evaluating credit.
7. What are the traditional methods of monitoring and controlling receivables?
8. What is meant by 'credit period'?
9. What is meant by 'collection program'?
10. What is 'DSO' ?

Moderate and Broad Questions

1. Explain the various costs of maintaining debtors in an organization.
2. As a credit manager, what steps would you take to grant credit to prospective customers?
3. A new customer has approached you for credit. Discuss in detail how you can judge his credit-worthiness before finally granting his credit.
4. Explain 'collection matrix' approach.
5. Explain the methods of controlling of accounts receivable in brief.
6. Discuss the process of credit evaluation.
7. How do the 'decision tree approach help in making credit granting decisions? Explain with a numerical example the all 2 situations in brief.
8. Explain all 3 credit standards.
9. How do business firms can formulate the effective collection programs?

PROBLEMS

1. A company presently gives credit terms of "net 30 days". It has ₹ 50 million in credit sales and its average collection period is 40 days. To stimulate sales, the company may give credit term "net 60 days". If it instigates these terms, sales are expected to increase by 10%. After the change the average collection period is expected to be 68 days with no difference in payment habits between old and new customers. Variable cost is ₹ 0.80 for every ₹ 1.00 of sales, and the company's after tax required rate of return on investment in receivables is 20%. Should the company extend its credit period? (Assume a 360 day year).

2. A company's existing sales is ₹ 150 lakhs. It is currently extending a credit period of 'net 30 days' to its customers. The company's contribution to sales ratio is 25% and the cost of funds is 20%. The company is planning to increase its sales by ₹ 15 lakhs to be achieved by means of lengthening the existing period to 'net 45 days'. The bad debt losses on additional sales are expected to be 5%. Should the company go in for a policy change or not?

3. The current sales of a company are ₹ 100 million. The company has classified its customers into 4 credit categories. Customers in category 1 have the highest credit rating and customers in category 4 have the lowest credit rating. The company presently extends unlimited credit to customers in categories 1 and 2, limited credit to customers in category 3, and no credit to customers in category 4. As a result of this credit policy the company is foregoing sales to the extent of ₹ 10 million to customers in category 3 and ₹ 10 million to customers in category 4. The firm is considering the adoption of a more liberal credit policy under which customers in category 3 would be extended unlimited credit and customers in category 4 would be extended limited credit. Such relaxation would increase the sales by ₹ 15 million on which bad debt loss would be 10%. The contribution margin ratio is 20%. The average collection period is 40 days and the post-tax cost of funds is 10%. The tax rate for the company is 40%.

   Examine the effect of relaxing the credit policy on profit.

   Hints: $\Delta P = [\Delta S\ (1 - V) - \Delta S b_n\ ]\ (1 - t) - [k\Delta I]$

   Or

   $$\Delta P = [15000000\ (1 - 0.80) - 15000000 \times 10\%](1\text{-}0.4) - [0.10 \times \frac{15000000}{360} \times 40 \times 0.80]$$

   $= ₹\ 7{,}66{,}667$

4. The present sales of a company are ₹ 100 lakhs; the average collection period is 60 days. The bad debt losses are 6% of sales and collection expenses are ₹ 1 lakh. The company's cost of funds is 15%. It is contemplating to increase the collection effort through special programs to reduce the amount of receivables and the incidence of bad debt losses. Two separate collection programs called A and B are under consideration. Program A is likely to reduce the average collection period to 45 days, decrease bad debt losses to 40% of sales and involve collection expenses of ₹ 3 lakhs. Program B is envisaged to reduce the average collection period to 30 days, decrease bad debt losses to 3% sales and involve collection expenses of ₹ 5 lakhs. On the assumption that sales are not likely to get affected, should the company go in for any of the programs under consideration?

   Hints: $\Delta P = \Delta S(1 - V) - \Delta BD - k\ \Delta I - \Delta C$

Where, $\Delta I = \frac{S_o}{360} (ACP_n - ACP_o) + \frac{\Delta S}{360} \times ACP_n \times V$

$\Delta BD = b_n (S_o + \Delta S) - b_o S_o$

Program A: ΔBD = 0.04 (108 + NIL) – 0.06 × 108

$= 0.04 \times 108 - 0.06 \times 108$

$= -$ ₹ 2.16 lakhs

$\Delta I = \frac{108}{360} (45 - 60) + \frac{NIL}{360} \times ACP_N \times V$

$= \frac{108}{360} \times (-15)$

$= -$ ₹ 4.5 lakhs

$\Delta C = 3 - 1 =$ ₹ 2 lakhs

$\Delta P = \Delta S (1 - V) - \Delta BD - k\Delta I - \Delta C = 0 (1 - V) - (-2.16) - 0.15 (-4.5) - 2$

$= 0 + 2.16 + .675 - 2$

$= 2.835 - 2$

$= .835$ lakhs

$=$ ₹ 83,500

Program B:

$\Delta BD = 0.03(108 + NIL) - 0.06 \times 108$

$= 0.03 \times 108 - 0.06 \times 108$

$= 3.24 - 6.48$

$= -$ ₹ 3.24 lakhs

$\Delta I = \frac{108}{360} (30 - 60) + \frac{NIL}{360} \times ACP_n \times V$

$= \frac{108}{360} \times -30 = -$ ₹ 9 lakhs

$\Delta C = 5 - 1 =$ ₹ 4 lakhs

$\Delta P = \Delta S (1 - V) - \Delta BD - K\Delta I - \Delta C$

$= 0 (1 - V) - (-3.24) - 0.15 (-9) - 4$

$= 0 + 3.24 + 1.35 - 4$

$= 4.59 - 4 = .59$ lakhs $=$ ₹ 59,000

5. A company whose current sales is in the order of ₹ 10 lakhs per annum and an average collection period of 30 days wants to pursue a more liberal policy to push up sales. A study by a management consultant firm reveals the following information:

Credit Policy	Increase in collection period	Increase in Sales ₹	Anticipated default rate %
A	15 days	40000	1.5%
B	20 days	50000	2.0%
C	30 days	80000	3.5%
D	40 days	100000	4.0%

The selling price p.u. of the product sold by the company is ₹ 6. Average cost p.u. is ₹ 4 and variable costs p.u. are ₹ 3. The current bad debt loss is 1%. Required return on additional investment is 25%. Assuming 360 days a year which of the above 4 policies would you recommend for the company for adoption.

❑❑❑

11 Inventory Management

11.1 DEFINITION OF INVENTORY

Inventory can be broadly defined as the stock of tangibles goods, commodities or other economic resources that are: (1) held for sale in the ordinary course of any business, (2) in the process of production for such sale or (3) to be currently consumed in the production of goods or services. Inventory for example, may include raw materials waiting to be used in producing goods (raw material inventory), semi-finished goods or goods in process temporarily stored during the production process (work-in-process inventory), finished goods awaiting shipment from the factory, wholesaler or retailer (finished-goods inventory). The nature of inventory is largely dependent upon the type of operation carried on.

11.2 TYPES OF INVENTORY

The term inventory may be divided into two classes:

A: Direct Inventories: Direct Inventories include those terms which play a direct role in the manufacture and become an integral part of finished goods. Direct inventories may be classified into 4 groups.

(a) Raw materials and Supplies ('consumable', *i.e.*, to be currently consumed in the production of goods or services to be available for sale);

(b) Work-in-progress ('convertible' *i.e.*, in the process of production for sale);

(c) Finished goods ('saleable' *i.e.*, to be held for sale in the ordinary course of business);

(d) Spares and Parts

B: Indirect Inventories: Indirect inventories include those items which are necessary for manufacturing but do not become component of the finished production such as lubricants, grease oil, petrol, office materials, maintenance material, etc.

11.3 INVENTORY DECISIONS

There are two basic inventory decisions inventory managers must make as they attempt to accomplish the functions of inventory just reviewed. These two decisions are made for every item in inventory while controlling them which are as follows:

- How much of an item to order at one time when the inventory of that item is to be replenished.
- When to order the inventory of that item.

Types of Decision	Departments Responsible
• Raw Materials polices	Purchasing and Production Departments
• Work-in-progress inventory policies	Production Department
• Finished goods inventory policy	Production and Marketing Departments
• Regarding Inventory Control	Finance Department

The Finance manager has to ensure that monitoring and controlling inventories are executed in a scientific manner for attaining the goal of wealth maximization.

11.4 INVENTORY MANAGEMENT ITS OBJECTIVES

Inventory management involves the control of tangible goods or services being produced for the purposes of sale in the normal course of the company's operations. Both excess and shortage of inventory affects the firm's profitability. Inventory management brings the balance between excess and shortage inventories. Inventories are the most significant part of current assets of most of the organizations in India. Since they constitute an important element of total current assets held by an organization, the need to manage inventories efficiently and effectively for ensuring optimal investment in inventory cannot be ignored. Inventory management ensures optimization in investment of inventories. The major objectives of inventory management are:

(a) Maximum satisfaction to customer

(b) Minimum investment in inventory

(c) JIT Manufacturing [JIT → Just in time]

(d) Ensuring the timely delivery of the order under strict cost control.

(e) Minimizing the total costs – direct and indirect – that are associated with holding inventories.

Generally large amounts remain invested in inventories. But there should be optimum level of investment for any asset whether it is a plant, cash or inventories. Again, inadequate inventories will disrupt production and lose sales. All these call for an effective inventory management programme.

A good inventory management brings the balance between the following two conflicting demands.

Viz.-

- To maintain a large quantity of inventories for smooth operations and efficient customer service, and
- To maintain only a minimum possible inventory because of inventory holding costs and the opportunity cost of funds invested in inventory.

There are two basic questions relating to inventory management: what should be the size of the order? At what level should the order be placed?

11.5 INVENTORY CONTROL AND ITS OBJECTIVES

Inventory control may be defined as the function of directing the movement of goods through the entire manufacturing cycle from the requisitioning of raw materials to the inventory of finished goods in orderly manner to meet the objectives of maximum customer service with minimum investment and efficient (low-cost) plant operation.

Inventory control is a highly significant function not only because inventories constitute substantial portion of total current assets of an organization but also because it has to satisfy the following objectives:

(a) To minimize the financial investment in inventories – Since the capital required to carry inventories costs money and holding assets in the form of inventories, it results in decreased liquidity.

(b) To ensure that the value of material concerned is minimum – There should be proper control over materials from the time orders are placed with supplies till the materials have been effectively utilized in production.

(c) To provide a safeguard for variations in raw material delivery time or lead time – The safety stock would have to be maintained to account for the inherent variability of lead times of the raw material supply.

(d) To allow flexibility in production scheduling – The maintenance of higher levels of finished goods inventory relieves the pressure on production system and gives them scheduling flexibility that can substantially reduce unit production costs. This further improves customer services.

(e) To reduce surplus stock – Inventory control offers an opportunity to critically examine the causes of excessive stocking and take appropriate measures to bring down stock to a reasonable level and thus reduce investment in inventory and at the same time avoid obsolescence losses.

11.6 NEED FOR INVENTORIES

Organizations carry inventories for a number of the following reasons: (Reasons for holding inventories)

- Smooth production by reducing risk of production stoppages,
- Ensuring prompt delivery to customers,

- Availability of quantity discounts by buying raw materials inventory in large volumes,
- Avoiding uncertain lead time (*i.e.*, the time required to procure fresh supplies of inventory) by maintaining higher level of inventories,
- Reducing ordering costs and time.

11.7 MOTIVES FOR HOLDING INVENTORIES

The motives for holding inventories are:

- **Transaction motive** – for making available inventories to facilitate smooth production and sales.
- **Precautionary motive** – for guarding against the risk of unexpected changes in demand and supply.
- **Speculative motive** – for making benefit out of the changes in prices organizations increase or decrease the inventory levels.

11.8 COSTS ASSOCIATED WITH INVENTORIES

Materials Costs: Costs of purchasing the goods and related cost such as transportation and handling costs associated with it. [Annual Demand (A) × Cost p.u.]

Ordering Costs: The expenses incurred to place orders with suppliers and replenish the inventory of raw material are called ordering costs. They include cost of the following :

(a) Requisitioning
(b) Purchase ordering or set-up
(c) Receiving, inspecting the raw materials

[Total No. of orders p.a. × Cost per order

$$= \frac{\text{Annual Demand of Raw Material}}{\text{Quantity ordered/order}} \times \text{Cost/order} = \frac{A}{Q} \times 0]$$

Carrying Costs: Costs incurred for maintaining the inventories in ware house are called carrying costs. They include costs of the following:

(a) Interest on capital locked up in inventory
(b) Cost of storage
(c) Insurance
(d) Taxes
(e) Obsolescence
(f) Spoilage
(g) Salaries of warehouse staffs
(h) Expenses on maintenance of warehouse building.

$$[\text{Average stock holdings} \times \text{Carrying cost/unit} = \frac{Q}{2} \times c]$$

11.9 INVENTORY MANAGEMENT TECHNIQUES AND MODELS

To manage the inventories efficiently, an organization should use a systems approach in inventory management. A systems approach considers all factors affecting the inventories in a single model which is an inventory model.

An inventory model is concerned with two decisions: how much to order at one time and when to order so as to minimize total cost? For taking these two decisions in respect of quantity and time, many inventory models have been developed.

A. system for effective inventory management involves namely Economic order Quantity (EOQ), Reorder point and Stock level.

A. Economic order Quantity (EOQ) : Order quantity (how much to order)

EOQ refers to the optimal order size that minimizes the total cost associated with inventory management.

I. MODEL 1: EOQ model with Uniform Demand. EOQ model answers the following key questions of inventory management.

- What should be the quantity ordered for each replenishment of stock?
- How many orders are to be placed in a year to ensure effective inventory management?

EOQ is based on the following assumption:

- Constant or uniform demand – The demand or usage is even throughout the period.
- Demand or usage is known – The demand rate is deterministic, *i.e.*, known with certainty.
- Immediate replenishment – Inventories can be replenished immediately as the stock level reaches exactly equal to zero. Consequently there is no shortage of inventory.
- Constant unit price – Quantity discounts are not allowed, *i.e.*, purchase price or cost per unit is constant.
- Constant ordering Cost – Cost per order (O) is constant whatever be the size of the order.
- Constant Carrying Cost – The cost of carrying is a fixed percentage of the average value of inventory.
- Lead-time is known – Lead time, *i.e.*, the time between placing the order and receipts of the order is known and fixed and is equal to or greater than zero.

(a) Graphical Presentation: EOQ is taken at that level where the cost of carrying approximately equals to cost of ordering. At this point total cost is also minimum.

The EOQ function is illustrated in following figure:

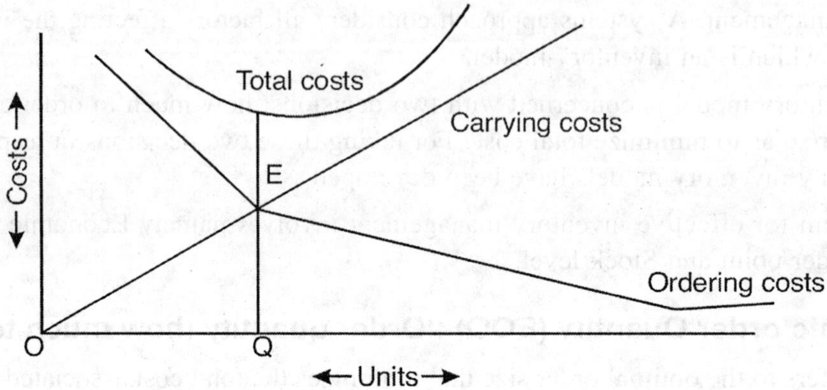

In the above figure the ordering costs, carrying costs and total costs (*i.e.*, the sum of the two types of costs) are plotted. While carrying costs tend to vary directly with the size of the order, ordering costs vary inversely with the size of the order. The total costs line declines first when fixed costs of ordering are spread over more units. Subsequently, it begins to rise when the decrease in average ordering costs is more than offset by the additional carrying costs. Thus, point 'Q' represents the optimum order size per order which minimizes the total costs of inventory management. The total cost curve reaches its minimum at the point of intersection (E) between the ordering costs curve and the carrying costs line. The value it Q corresponding to it will be the EOQ.

(b) 1. EOQ formula: Algebraic Approach (without quantity discount offer of supplier)

The order quantity Q becomes EOQ when the total ordering costs at Q is equal to the total carrying costs.

i.e., ordering costs = carrying costs

Or $$\frac{A}{Q} . O = \frac{Q}{2} . C$$

Or $$\frac{A . O}{C} = \frac{Q^2}{C}$$

Or $$\frac{Q^2}{2} = \frac{A . O}{C}$$ Or $$Q^2 = \frac{2.A.O}{C}$$

Or $$Q = \sqrt{\frac{2.A.O}{C}} \text{ units} = \text{EOQ}$$

To distinguish EOQ from other order quantities, we can say

$$\text{EOQ} = Q^* = \sqrt{\frac{2.A.O}{PC}}$$

Where, A = Annual Requirements of raw materials

O = Ordering cost/order

PC = Carrying cost/unit = Unit purchase price × inventory carrying cost%

(b) 2. Modified EOQ formula to include varying units prices: EOQ Model with quantity discounts. Bulk purchase discount is offered when the size of the order is at least equal to some minimum quantity specified by the supplier. To determine the optimum order size when quantity discounts are available, the following procedure may be used.

- We are to determine order quantity using the standard EOQ formula assuming no quantity discount. Call it Q*.
- If Q* enables the firm to get quantity discount then it represents the optimal order size.
- If Q* is less than the minimum order size required for quantity discount (call it Q^1) compute the change in profit as a result of increasing the order quantity from Q* to Q^1 as follows:-

Net incremental benefit (change in profit)

$$= A \times D + \left(\frac{A}{Q^*} - \frac{A}{Q^1}\right) \times O - \left(\frac{Q^1\,(P-D)\,C}{2} - \frac{Q^*\,.\,PC}{2}\right)$$

Where, A = Annual usage / demand
D = Discount p.u. when quantity discount is available
Q* = EOQ assuming no quantity discount.
Q^1 = Minimum order size required for quantity discount
O = Fixed cost of placing an order
P = Purchase price p.u. without discount
C = Inventory carrying cost expressed as a percentage.

$$\text{Total increment benefit} = A \times D + \left(\frac{A}{Q^*} - \frac{A}{Q^1}\right) \times O$$

$$\text{Total incremental carrying cost} = \left(\frac{Q^1\,(P-D)\,C}{2} - \frac{Q^*\,.\,PC}{2}\right)$$

- If the net incremental benefits are positive, then the optimal order quantity (EOQ) becomes Q^1 otherwise Q* will continue to remain valid even in a situation of bulk purchase discount.

(c) Finding Economic Order Quantity – Tabular Method Approach. A simple approach for solving the EOQ is by trial and error method. The approach of this method can be summarized as follows:

(i) Select a number of possible lot (order) size to purchase.

(ii) Determine the total costs for each lot size chosen.

(iii) Select the ordering quantity that minimizes the total cost. This method can be used to determine EOQ at both without discount and with discount offer of suppliers.

II. MODEL 2: Production Inventory Model. We shall now consider when the firm may receive its inventory over a period of time. Such cases require a different model, one that does not require the instantaneous receipt assumption. This model is applicable when inventory continuously flows or builds up over a period of time after an order has been placed or when units are produced and sold at a constant rate. Further, it is assumed that the production rate is greater than the demand rate otherwise there will be no inventory buildup and stock outs will cccur.

Now to build up model, we define the following additional parameters:

P = production rate per period

A = demand rate or usage rate per period

All other models are the same as for the original EOQ models.

t = length of the production in period = $\frac{Q}{P}$ [Since, Q = P × t = Set-up or order quantity/ Set-up]

$$\text{Economic Order Quantity } Q^* = \frac{2 \,.\, A \,.\, O}{DC\left\{1 - \left(\frac{A}{P}\right)\right\}}$$

Where, O = Set up cost/set up (like ordering cost/order)

DC = Stock holding cost per unit per period (like carrying cost/unit)

= Direct costs p.u. × % at of stock holding cost

Q* = Optimal set up quantity/set up (like ordering quantity/order)

Proof: Set-up cost per period = No of set ups × set-up cost/set up

$$= \frac{\text{Demand rate per period}}{\text{Optimal set up quantity/set up}} \times \text{set up cost/set up}$$

$$= \frac{A}{Q} \times O$$

Inventory holding cost per period

= Average inventory level × inventory holding cost p.u. per period

$$= \left[\frac{1}{2}\,(\text{maximum inventory level})\right] \times DC$$

$$= \left[\frac{1}{2}\,(\text{Total produced during the production run} - \text{total used during the production run})\right] \times DC$$

$$= \left[\frac{1}{2}\,(Pt - At)\right] \times DC$$

$$= \left[\frac{1}{2}\left(P.\frac{Q}{P} - A.\frac{Q}{P}\right)\right] \times DC$$

$$= \left[\frac{1}{2}\left(Q - \frac{AQ}{P}\right)\right] \times DC$$

$$= \left[\frac{1}{2} \times Q\left(1 - \frac{A}{P}\right)\right] \times DC$$

$$= \frac{Q}{2}\left[\left(1 - \frac{A}{P}\right)\right] \times DC$$

Here, again, the algebraic approach can be used. Because setup costs are decreasing and carrying costs are increasing as production quantity increases and a minimal total cost occurs when those two costs are equal.

Setting the set up costs equal to inventory holding costs, *i.e.*,

$$\frac{A}{Q} \times O = \frac{Q}{2}\left[\left(1 - \frac{A}{P}\right)\right] \times DC \qquad \text{Or,} \qquad Q^2 = \frac{2 . A . O}{DC\left\{1 - \left(\frac{A}{P}\right)\right\}}$$

$$\text{Or,} \quad Q^* = \sqrt{\frac{2 . A . O}{DC\left\{1 - \left(\frac{A}{P}\right)\right\}}} = \text{optimal set up quantity (Q is referred as Q*)}$$

Total cost, TC(Q*) = Direct cost + total ordering cost per period + Total Inventory holding cost per period

$$= A \times \text{Direct cost.unit} + \frac{A}{Q} \times O + \left[\frac{Q^*}{2}\left(1 - \frac{A}{P}\right) \times DC\right]$$

$$\text{Optimal number of productions runs (Set-ups)} = N = \frac{A}{Q^*}$$

Problem 1. Re: EOQ without discount offer.

The annual demand for a product of a firm is 52000 units at ₹ 10 per unit. The firm can purchase if at ₹ 6.1538 p.u. assuming carrying cost at 20 percent of inventory value and fixed cost per order is ₹ 2,000. Determine

(i) Economic Order quantity
(ii) No of order p.a
(iii) Time between 2 conclusive orders
(iv) Total cost of inventory

Solution: Given

A = annual requirements of raw materials = 52000 units

O = ordering cost/order = ₹ 2,000/order

PC = Carrying cost/unit

= unit purchase price × inventory carrying cost %

= 20% × 6.1538

= ₹ 1.23076

(i) EOQ, $Q^* = \sqrt{\frac{2 . A . O}{PC}} = \sqrt{\frac{2 \times 52000 \times 2000}{1.23076}}$ = 13000 units/order(appro.)

(ii) No of orders p.a. $= \frac{A}{Q^*} = \frac{52000}{13000}$ = 4 orders

(iii) Time between 2 consecutive orders

$$= \frac{\text{No. of Months p.a.}}{\text{No. of orders p.a.}} = \frac{\text{12 months}}{\text{4 orders p.a.}} = \text{3 months}$$

Or, $\frac{\text{360 days p.a.}}{4}$ = 90 days (assuming 360 days/year)

(iv) Total cost of inventory

= Materials cost + Ordering Cost + Carrying Costs

$$= (A \times \text{Cost p.u.}) + \left(\frac{A}{Q} \times O\right) + \left(\frac{Q}{2} \times C\right)$$

$$= (52{,}000 \times 6) + (4 \times 2000) + \left(\frac{13{,}000}{2} \times 1.23076\right)$$

= 312000 + 800 + 8000 = ₹ 328000.

Problem 2. Re: EOQ calculation without discount offer – Tabular Method

Taking reference to the illustration 1, the annual demand for a product of a firm is 52000 units. Ordering cost per order is ₹ 2,000. Unit purchase price is ₹ 6.1538 per unit. Assuming carrying cost at 20% of inventory value, determine EOQ using tabular Method.

A = 52000 units, O = ₹ 2000 / order			Table: Table Cost Of Inventory			
No. of orders p.a.= $\frac{A}{Q}$	(Assumed) 1	2	3	4	5	6
Ordering quantities (Q) [units/order]	$\frac{A}{1}$ = 52000	$\frac{A}{2}$ = 26000	$\frac{A}{3}$ = 17333	$\frac{A}{4}$ = 13000	$\frac{A}{4}$ = 10400	$\frac{A}{6}$ = 8667
A. Ordering Cost = $\frac{A}{Q} \times O$	₹ 1 × 2000 = 2000	₹ 2 × 2000 = 4000	₹ 3 × 2000 = 6000	₹ 4 × 2000 = 8000	₹ 5 × 2000 = 10000	₹ 6 × 2000 = 12000
B. Carrying Cost = $\frac{Q}{2} \times C$	$\frac{52000}{2} \times$ 1.23076 = 32000	$\frac{26000}{2} \times$ 1.23076 = 16000	$\frac{17333}{2} \times$ 1.23076 = 10667	$\frac{13000}{2} \times$ 1.23076 = 8000	$\frac{10400}{2} \times$ 1.23076 = 6400	$\frac{8667}{2} \times$ 1:23076 = 5333
C. Material Cost = A × Cost p.u.	52000 × 6.1538 = 320000	320000	320000	320000	320000	320000
Total Cost of inventory	354000	340000	336667	336000	336400	337333

Carrying cost and ordering cost equal to each other when ordering quantity is 13000 units. At this level total costs are also minimum therefore EOQ = 13000 units.

Total Cost of Inventory = Ordering Cost (A) + Carrying Cost (B) + Material Cost (C)

Problem 3:

Re: EOQ determination against discount offer – *comparison of EOQ with discount offer (also applying alternatively, the modified EOQ model)*

XYZ factory buys and uses a component for production at ₹ 10 per piece. Annual requirement is 2000 units. Carrying cost of inventory is 10% p.a. and ordering cost is ₹ 40 per order. The purchase manager argues that as the ordering cost in very high, it is advantageous to place a single order for the entire annual requirement. He also says that if we order 2000 at a time, we can get a 3% discount from the supplier. Evaluate the proposal and make your recommendation.

Solution

Economic Order Quantity (Without discount offer)

$$= \sqrt{\frac{2 \times A \times O}{PC}} = \sqrt{\frac{2 \times 2000 \times 40}{10\% \text{ of } 10}}$$ when, A = 2000 units

$$= \sqrt{\frac{2 \times 2000 \times 40}{1}} = 400 \text{ units / order.}$$ O = ₹ 40 / order

C = 10% of 10 = ₹ 1

Table: Evaluation of Purchase manager's proposal - calculation of total cost under EOQ and suppliers discount offer stated by purchase manager. [after discount, carrying cost = 10% of 9.97, as cost = 10 – 3% = 9.70 p.u.]

Ordering Quantities (Q) A = 2000 units, O = ₹ 40/order	**EOQ = 400 units**	**As per proposal = 2000 units**
	₹	₹
A. Ordering Cost $\left(\frac{A}{Q} \times O\right)$	$\frac{2000}{400} \times 40 = 200$	$\frac{2000}{2000} \times 40 = 40$
B. Carrying Cost $\left(\frac{Q}{2} \times C\right)$ $= \left[\frac{400}{2} \times 1\right], \left[\frac{2000}{2} \times (1 - 3\%)\right]$	200	970
C. Materials Cost = [A × Cost p.u.] = [2000 × 10], [2000 × 9.70]	20000	19400
Total Cost of inventory	20400	20410

The argument of the purchase manager to place a single order for the entire annual requirement in view of the above computation is not justified. We are considering 400 units as EOQ ultimately since it is showing lower cost of inventory and a saving of ₹ 10.

Alternatively: **Applying Modified EOQ model**

(a) We are determining, Economic Order Quantity without discount offer;
Using the standard EOQ formula, assuming no discount

$$Q^* (EOQ) = \sqrt{\frac{2 \times A \times O}{PC}} = \sqrt{\frac{2 \times 2000 \times 4}{10\% \text{ of } 10}} = 400 \text{ units / order}$$

(b) Minimum order size for quantity discount of 3% = Q^1 = 2000 units / order

Hence, $Q^* < Q^1$

Net incremental benefit after considering discount offer or change in profit as a result of increasing the order quantity from Q* to Q^1 as follows:

$$= \text{total incremental benefit} - \text{total incremental carrying cost}$$

$$= A \times D + \left(\frac{A}{Q^*} - \frac{A}{Q^1}\right) \times O - \left(\frac{Q^1\,(P-D)\,C}{2} - \frac{Q^*\,.\,PC}{2}\right)$$

When D = Discount p.u. when quantity discount is available = 3% × ₹ 10 = ₹ 0.30

P = purchase price p.u. without discount = ₹ 10

A = Annual usage/demand = 2000 units

Q* = 400 units

Q^1 = 2000 units

O = ordering cost/order = ₹ 40

C = inventory carrying cost expressed as a percentage = 10% p.a. = .10

PC = 10% × 10 = ₹ 1

∴ Change in profit

$$= 2000 \times .30 + \left(\frac{2000}{400} - \frac{2000}{2000}\right) \times 40 - \left(\frac{2000\,(10-.30)\,.10}{2} - \frac{400 \times 1}{2}\right)$$

$$= 600 + (5-1) \times 40 - \left(\frac{2000 \times 9.70 \times 1.10}{2} - \frac{400 \times 1}{2}\right)$$

$$= 6000 + 160 - [970 - 200]$$

$$= 760 - 770$$

$$= -\ ₹\ 10$$

Since, the net incremental benefit or change in profit is negative, the optimal order quantity is Q*, *i.e.*, 400 units (EOQ).

Re: Finding EOQ with discount offer – Tabular method (Trial and Error)

Problem 4

A firm is able to obtain quantity discounts on orders of material as follows:

Price per ton ₹	Tons
6.00	Less than 250
5.90	250 and less than 800
5.80	800 and less than 2000
5.70	2000 and less than 4000
5.60	4000 and over

The annual demand for the materials is 4000 tons. Stock holding costs are 20% of material cost per annum. The delivery cost per order ₹ 6.00. You are required to calculate the best quantity to order (EOQ):

Solution

A = 4000 tons
O = ₹ 6/order
C = 20% of cost p.u.

Table: Total Cost of Inventory

Ordering quantities (θ) [units/order]	200	250	800	2000	2500
No. of orders $= \frac{A}{Q}$	$\frac{4000}{200} = 20$	$\frac{4000}{250} = 16$	$\frac{4000}{800} = 5$	$\frac{4000}{2000} = 2$	$\frac{4000}{2500} = 1.6 = 2$
A. Ordering Cost $= \frac{A}{\theta} \times O$	₹ 120	₹ 96	₹ 30	₹ 12	₹ 12
B. Carrying Cost $= \frac{Q}{2} \times C$	$\frac{200}{2} \times$ (6 × 20%) = 120	$\frac{250}{2} \times$ (5.9 × 20%) = 147.5	$\frac{800}{2} \times$ (5.80 × 20%) = 464	$\frac{2000}{2} \times$ (5.70 × 20%) = 1140	$\frac{2500}{2} \times$ (5.60 × 20%) = 1400
C. Material Cost = A × cost p.u.	4000 × 6 = 24000	4000 × 5.9 = 23600	4000 × 5.8 = 23200	4000 × 5.7 = 22800	4000 × 5.6 = 22400
Total cost of inventory	24240	23843.5	23694	23952	23812

At order quantity of 800 units, the total cost of inventory is minimum, hence EOQ = 800 units.

Re: Optimal set up quantity – applying production inventory model (production rate > demand rate)

Problem 5

A contractor has to supply 10000 paper cones per day to a Textile unit. He finds that, when he starts a production run he can produce 25000 paper cones per day. The cost of holding a paper cone in stock for one year is ₹ .02 which is 25% of Direct Cost and the set up cost of a production run is ₹ 18. Calculate optimal set up quantity (EOQ). Also calculate the total inventory cost per day on the basis of optimal policy and optimal number of set ups.

Solution

Holding, Cost = DC = Stock holding cost per paper cone per unit

$$= \frac{₹\ 0.02 \text{ per paper cone per year}}{365 \text{ days}}$$

= ₹ 0.00055 per cone per day

Direct cost = ₹ 0.00055 × 4 = .0022

Set up cost/production run = O = ₹ 18

Production rate (25000) per day > Demand rate (10000) per day.

A = Demand/supply rate per day

= 10000 paper cones per day

P = production rate per day = 25000 paper cones per day.

Optimal set up quantity (EOQ), Q*

$$= \sqrt{\frac{2. A. O.}{DC\left\{1-\left(\frac{A}{P}\right)\right\}}} = \sqrt{\frac{2 \times 10000 \times 18}{0.00055\left\{1-\left(\frac{10000}{25000}\right)\right\}}} = 105000 \text{ Cones}$$

$$\text{Optimal no. of set up per day} = \frac{A}{Q^*} = \frac{10000}{105000} = 0.0952$$

Optimal number of set ups per year

$$= \frac{A \times 365}{Q^*} = \frac{10000 \times 365}{105000} = 34.76$$

Total inventory cost per day on the basis of optimal policy,

TC(Q*) = Direct cost + Total Ordering cost per day + Total Inventory Holding cost per day

$$= 10000 \times 0.0022 + \frac{A}{Q^*} \times O + \left[\frac{Q^*}{2}\left(1-\frac{A}{P}\right) \times DC\right]$$

$$= 22 + \frac{10000}{105000} \times 18 + \left[\frac{105000}{2}\left(1-\frac{10000}{25000}\right) \times 0.00055\right]$$

$$= 22 + 1.7143 + [52500 \times 0.6 \times 0.00055]$$

$$= 22 + 1.7143 + 17.325 = ₹\ 41.0393$$

Problem 6

A company uses 100000 units of a particular item per year. Each item costs ₹ 2. The production engineering department estimates set up cost at ₹ 25 and the accounting department estimates the holding cost as 12.5% of the value of the inventory per day. Replenishment rate is uniform 500 units per day. Assuming 250 working days (per replenishment purpose), calculate

- Optimal set up quantity
- Total inventory cost on the basis of optimal policy and
- Optimal number of set ups.

Solution

(a) Total Cost

$$= A \times \text{Direct cost/unit} + \left(\frac{A}{Q} \times O\right) + \left[\left(\frac{Q}{2}\right)\left(1 - \frac{A}{P}\right) \times DC\right]$$

$$= (100000 \times 2) + \left(\frac{100000}{Q} \times 25\right) + \left[\frac{Q}{2}\left(1 - \frac{100000}{125000}\right) \times 0.25\right]$$

[Since $DC = 2 \times \frac{125}{1000}$ = ₹ 0.25 per year]

Or $TC(Q) = 200000 + \frac{2500000}{Q} + \frac{Q}{40}$

Differentiating w.r.t. θ we get $\frac{dTC(Q)}{d\theta} = \frac{-2500000}{Q^2} + \frac{1}{40}$

Equating it equal to Zero and solving for θ, we obtain

$$\frac{-2500000}{Q^2} = -\frac{1}{40}$$

or, Q = 10000 units.

At θ = 10000 units, $\frac{d^2 TC(\theta)}{d\theta^2} = \frac{50000000}{Q^3} > 0$ ∴ TC (θ) is minimum when run size is 10000 units

(b) Accordingly, TC (10000) = 200000 + 250 + 250 = ₹ 200500

(c) Optimum no. of Set ups. $= \frac{A}{Q} = \frac{100000}{10000}$ = 10 Set ups.

11.10 ORDER POINT PROBLEM (WHEN TO ORDER) – REORDER LEVEL

Apart from knowing the EOQ, another important point to be decided is the re-order point, *i.e.*, when to place the order for replenishment of inventories. It is also called re-order level which may be defined as that level of inventory when fresh order should be placed with the suppliers for procuring additional inventory equal to the EOQ. The re-order level would be established at a point such that the stock in hand would be sufficient to meet the demand during the lead time and sometime also to meet the unexpected increase in demand.

Reorder level = Lead time consumption + Minimum/Buffer/Safety Stock

Alternatively Reorder level = maximum usage × maximum lead time

Assumptions:

(i) constant daily usage of inventory

(ii) fixed lead time

Illustration: From the following particulars, calculate the reorder level:

- Annual demand: 52000 units
- Lead time : 2 weeks
- Sales will be made evenly over the period
- Safety stock = 1000 units

[Lead time is the time between ordering a replenishment of an item and actually receiving the item into inventory]

Solution

Re-order level = Lead time consumption + Safety stock

= {Average weakly usage × lead time (weeks)} + Safety stock

$$= \left(\frac{52000}{52} \times 2\right) + 1000 = (1000 \times 2) + 1000 = 2000 + 1000 = 3000 \text{ units}$$

11.11 LEVELS OF INVENTONY MAINTAINANCE

- **Maximum Level:** This is the level beyond which inventory cannot be maintained. The main objective is to avoid over-stocking. This level is:

  Reorder level + Re-order Quantity – (Minimum consumption × Minimum re-order period)

- **Minimum Level:** This is the level below which the inventory cannot be maintained.

  Minimum Level = Reorder level – (Normal consumption × Normal re-order period)

- **Average Level:** $\frac{1}{2}$ (Maximum Level + Minimum Level)

- **Reorder level** is the point fixed between maximum and minimum stock levels at which time it is essential to initiate purchase requisition for purchased items and manufacturing requisition for manufactured items in the factory for fresh supplies of the material. (Maximum Usage × Maximum Lead time)

11.12 SAFETY STOCK: (BUFFER OR MINIMUM OR RESERVE) – WITH OPTIMAL LEVEL OF SAFETY STOCK

Safety stock may be defined as the minimum additional inventory to serve as a safety margin to meet an unanticipated increase in usage resulting from various uncontrollable factors.

In real-life situations, firms operate under conditions of uncertainty relative both to demand as well as procurement time. Total actual demand and actual procurement time may vary from time to time. In order to minimize the effect of uncertainty in demand and/or lead time, a firm maintains safety stock.

Say, if an even sales rate of 250 units per week is assumed and Reorder level is placed is at 3000 units level, with 8 weeks as the lead time, even if we assume a maximum conceivable sales rate of twice the normal figure during the last 4 weeks, the firm will not face the problem of stock-outs since, there is a—

Safety stock = Reorder level – lead time consumption

= 3000 – (250 × 8)

= 1000 units

If no safety stock is provided, stock-outs would arise whatever be the purchased quantity with which one may start. Stock outs are not only costly but highly embrassing in that they attract adverse attention which leads to inflation of requirements.

The optimum level of safety stock is the result of trade-off between stock-out costs and carrying costs which are conflicting with each other. If safety stake is inadequately low, the inventory costs would-be low but stock-out costs would be very high and *vice-versa*.

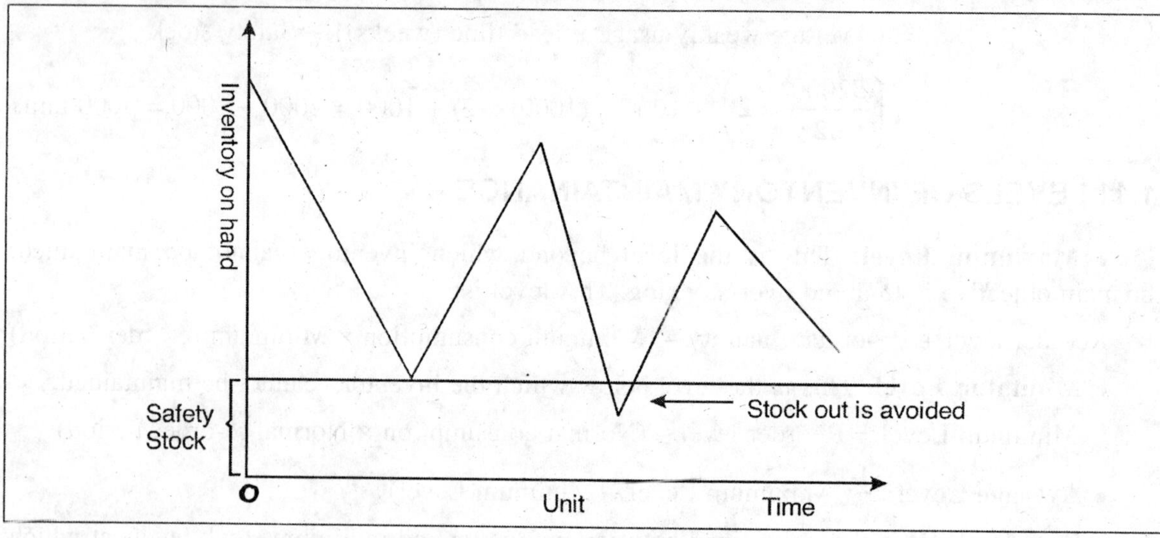

Safety stock = (maximum lead time – average lead time) × average usage p.u. of time.

= (Maximum lead time × Average usage p.u. of time) – (Average lead time × average usage p.u. of time)

= Reorder level – Lead time consumption.

11.13. SELECTIVE CREDIT CONTROL TECHNIQUES

A. The Classification Problem: ABC Analysis (Proportional Value Analysis)

The classification of items of materials is made on the basis of annual consumption value of inventories.

ABC Analysis contemplates to classify all the inventory items in number of categories generally in 3 categories based on their values. Items of high value but small in number are classified as 'A' items which would be under strict control. 'C' items represent relatively small value items and would be under normal control. 'B' items represent moderate value and moderate size and would attract reasonable attention of the management. Accordingly, a table may be constructed:

Table 1 : A, B and C items

Inventory items	% of total items	% of total value	Nature of Inventory control
A	(5 – 10)%	70%	Strict
B	(10 – 20)%	20%	Reasonable
C	70%	10%	Normal

Extra care will be taken in the determination of minimum, maximum, reorder level, etc. of the 'A' items. 'A' items may be purchased a number of items during the year. 'C' items may be purchased only once in a year, only a bin card may be maintained for these items.

Objective: The objective of ABC analysis is to develop policy guidelines for selective control. Such a policy can be designed in a variety of ways. In general, 'A' items merit a tightly controlled inventory system with constant attention (perpetual inventory system, say), 'B' items moderately through reasonable inventory system (say, routine inventory system) with periodic attention and 'C' items to subject to lose control with casual attention.

Diagram

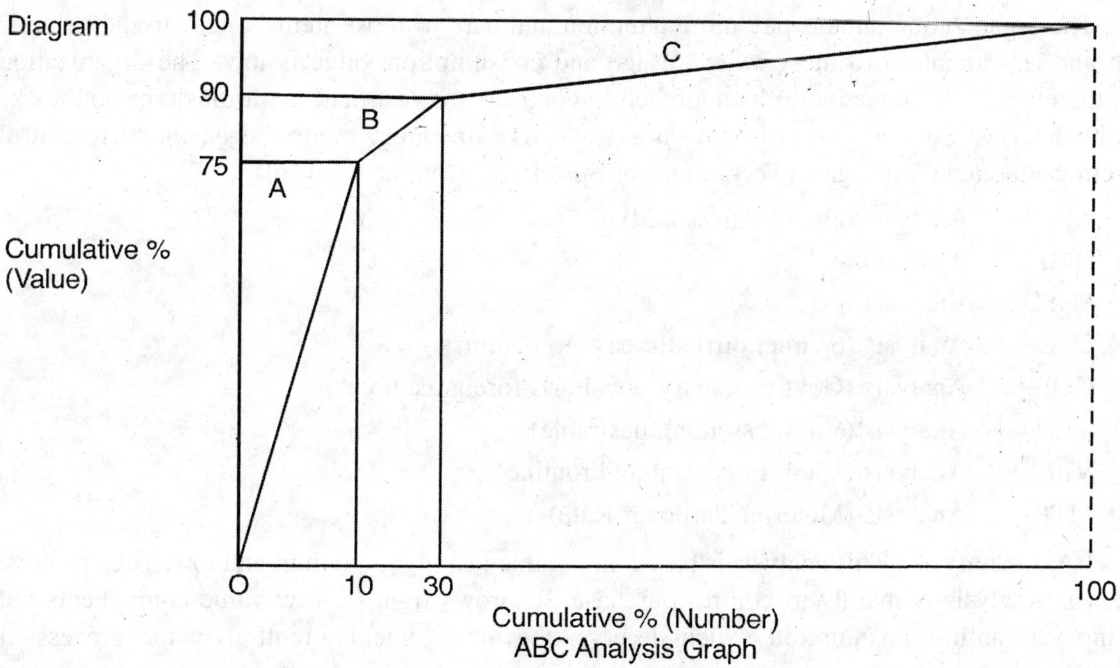

ABC Analysis Graph

Table: Features of ABC Analysis along with policy guidelines

Nature	A items (high Value)	B items (Moderate Value)	C items (Low Value)
1. Extent on control	Strict control	Moderate control	Normal control
2. Safety stock coverage	Low safety stocks	Medium safety stocks	Large safety stocks
3. Value analysis	Rigorous	Moderate	Minimum
4. Purchasing	Centralized	Both centralized and decentralized	Decentralized
5. Follow up and expediting	Maximum	Periodic	As per requirement or in exceptional cases
6. Level of management	Senior management	Middle management	Stores Supervisor
7. Ordering	Frequently	Less frequent ordering	Bulk ordering (Say, once in 6 months)
8. Control Reports	Weekly	Monthly	Quarterly
9. Control over surplus and obsolete items	Fortnightly or monthly	Quarterly	Annual Review

B. Selective Inventory Control (Other Scientific Inventory Management Techniques)

• Selective Inventory Control: Meaning and Techniques

The organization should pay more attention and care to those items whose usage value is high and less attention to those whose usage and consumption value is low. The organization has, therefore, to be selective in its approach to control its investment in various types of stocks and inventories. Such a system is known as 'selective inventory control' system, such control system can be done through: (Techniques of Selective Inventory Control)

ABC Analysis (already discussed)
HML Analysis
FNSD Analysis
SDE Analysis (Scarce, difficult, easy to obtain)
GOLF Analysis (Govt., ordinary, local and foreign sources)
VED Analysis (Vital, essential, desirable)
VIR Analysis (Vital, important and routine)
MTR Analysis (Material Turnover Rate)

HML Analysis : This analysis is based on volume *i.e.*, high, medium and low. The objective of HML Analysis is mainly to control purchase. It throws light on low value components but having substantial consumption which deserve due management attention in the process of inventory control.

FNSD Analysis : It divides the items into 4 categories in the descending order of their usage rate.

'F' ❒ Fast moving items

'N' ❒ Normal moving items

'S' ❒ Slow moving items

'D' ❒ Dead Stock

'F' items are consumed in a short span of time. 'N' items are exhausted over a period of a year or so. 'S' indicates existing stock of which would last for two years or more at the current rate of usage but it is still expected to be used up. For 'D' items, no further demand can be foreseen. Stock of 'F' items must be observed constantly and replenishment orders be placed in time to avoid stock-out situations. 'S' items must be reviewed very carefully before any replacement orders are placed. 'D' items should be put for alternative uses; otherwise, it must be disposed of.

Problem 7

Re: Reorder level, EOQ

A company uses annually 48000 units of raw material costing ₹ 1.20 p.u. Placing each order costs ₹ 45 and inventory carrying costs are 15% p.a. of the average inventory values.

(a) Find EOQ

(b) If lead time is 12 days and safety stock is 500 units find Re-order level and all other levels. (assume Company operates for 300 days a year)

Solution

(a) $EO\theta = \sqrt{\frac{2.\ A.\ O.}{PC}} = \sqrt{\frac{2 \times 45 \times 48000}{15\% \times 1.20}} = 4899$ units.

(b) Reorder Level

$$= \text{Normal lead time consumption} + \text{Safety Stock} = \left(\frac{48000}{300} \times 12\right) + 500$$

$= 1920 + 500 = 2420$ units.

Maximum Level = EOθ + Safety Stock = 4899 + 500 = 5399 units.

Minimum Level = Safety Stock = 500 units.

$$\text{Average Level} = \frac{EO\theta}{2} + 500 \text{ (Safety Stock)} = \frac{4899}{2} + 500 = \frac{5899}{2} = 2949 \text{ units.}$$

Or, ½ (5399 + 500) = ½ × 5899 = 2949 units

SUMMARY

Inventory can be broadly defined as the stock of tangibles goods, commodities or other economic resources that are— (1) held for sale in the ordinary course of any business, (2) in the process of production for such for sale or (3) to be currently consumed in the production of goods or services.

There are two basic inventory decisions inventory managers must make as they attempt to accomplish the functions of inventory just reviewed. These two decisions are made for every item in inventory while controlling them which are as follows:

- How much of an item to order at one time when the inventory of that item is to be replenished.
- When to order the inventory of that item.

Inventory management brings the balance between excess and shortage inventories. Inventories are the most significant part of current assets of most of the organizations in India. Since they constitute an important element of total current assets held by an organization, the need to manage inventories efficiently and effectively for ensuring optimal investment in inventory cannot be ignored. Inventory management ensures optimization in investment of inventories. The major objectives of inventory management are:

(a) Maximum satisfaction to customer

(b) Minimum investment in inventory

(c) JIT Manufacturing [JIT → Just in time]

(d) Ensuring the timely delivery of the order under strict cost control.

(e) Minimizing the total costs – direct and indirect – that are associated with holding inventories.

Inventory control may be defined as the function of directing the movement of goods through the entire manufacturing cycle from the requisitioning of raw materials to the inventory of finished goods in orderly manner to meet the objectives of maximum customer service with minimum investment and efficient (low-cost) plant operation.

The motives for holding inventories are:-

- **Transaction motive:** for making available inventories to facilitate smooth production and sales.
- **Precautionary motive:** for guarding against the risk of unexpected changes in demand and supply.
- **Speculative motive:** for making benefit out of the changes in prices organizations increase or decrease the inventory levels.

A system for effective inventory management involves namely Economic order Quantity (EOQ), Reorder point and Stock level.

EOQ refers to the optimal order size that minimizes the total cost associated with inventory management. EOQ model answers the following key questions of inventory management.

- What should be the quantity ordered for each replenishment of stock?
- How many orders are to be placed in a year to ensure effective inventory management?

Apart from knowing the EOQ, another import point to be decided is the re-order point, *i.e.*, when to place the order for replenishment of inventories. It is also called re-order level which may be defined as that level of inventory when fresh order should be placed with the suppliers for procuring additional inventory equal to the EOQ. The re-order level would be established at a point such that the stock in hand would be sufficient to meet the demand during the lead time and sometime also to meet the unexpected increase in demand. Safety stock may be defined as the minimum additional inventory to serve as a safety margin to meet an unanticipated increase in usage resulting from various incontrollable factors.

The organization should pay more attention and care to those items whose usage value is high and less attention to those whose usage and consumption value is low. The organization has, therefore, to be selective in its approach to control its investment in various types of stocks and inventories. Such a system is known as 'selective inventory control' system, such control system can be done through: (Techniques of Selective Inventory Control).

ABC	Analysis
HML	Analysis
FNSD	Analysis
SDE	Analysis
GOLF	Analysis
VED	Analysis
VIR	Analysis
MTR	Analysis

EXERCISE

Short Questions

1. What is 'Inventory'?
2. Why inventory is needed?
3. What is 'Inventory Management'?
4. What is 'Inventory Control'?
5. What is 'Selective Inventory Control'?
6. What is 'EOQ'?
7. What is 'Safety Stock'?
8. What is 'Re-order Level'?
9. What is 'Maximum Level'?
10. What is 'Minimum Level'?
11. What is 'Average Level'?

Broad and Moderate Questions

1. Explain the types of inventory?
2. What are the inventory decisions to be taken to accomplish the functions of inventory?
3. Explain the term 'Inventory Management' along with its objectives and functions of an effective inventory management.
4. Explain the term 'Inventory Control' along with its objectives.

5. Explain briefly the needs and motives for holding inventories.
6. State the costs associated with inventories and explain each of them.
7. Illustrate Inventory Management Techniques and models with assumptions and graphical presentations if any.
8. Illustrate selective inventory control techniques including ABC Analysis.
9. Explain 'Re-order Level'. How safety stock can be determined?

PROBLEMS

1. The annual demand for a product of a firm is 52000 units at ₹ 20 per unit. The firm can purchase if at ₹ 12 p.u. assuming carrying cost at 25 per cent of inventory value and fixed cost per order is ₹ 2000. Determine

(i) Economic Order quantity
(ii) No of order p.a.
(iii) Time between two conclusive order
(iv) Total cost of inventory

2. A company uses annually 24000 units of raw material costing ₹ 2.40 p.u. Placing each order costs ₹ 25 and inventory carrying costs are 20% p.a. of the average inventory values.

(c) Find EOQ

(d) If lead time is 10 days and safety stock is 1000 units find Re-order level and all other levels. (assume Company operates for 300 days a year)

3. From the following particulars calculate the reorder level:

- Annual demand: 104000 units
- Lead time : 4 weeks
- Sales will be made evenly over the period
- Safety stock = 2000 units

4. A company uses 200000 units of a particular item per year. Each item costs ₹ 4. The production engineering department estimates set up cost at ₹ 40 and the accounting department estimates the holding cost as 17.5% of the value of the inventory per day. Replenishment rate is uniform 1000 units per day. Assuming 250 working days (per replenishment purpose), calculate-

- Optimal set up quantity
- Total inventory cost on the basis of optimal policy and
- Optimal number of set ups.

5. A contractor has to supply 40000 paper cones per day to a Textile unit. He finds that, when he starts a production run he can produce 100000 paper cones per day. The cost of holding a paper cone in stock for one year is ₹ .04 which is 25% of Direct Cost and the set up cost of a production run is ₹ 18. Calculate optimal set up quantity (EOQ). Also calculate the total inventory cost per day on the basis of optimal policy and optimal number of set ups.

6. XYZ factory buys and uses a component for production at ₹ 10 per piece. Annual requirement is 8000 units. Carrying cost of inventory is 20% p.a. and ordering cost is ₹ 80 per order. The purchase manager argues that as the ordering cost in very high, it is advantageous to place a single order for the entire annual requirement. He also says that if we order 2000 at a time, we can get a 4% discount from the supplier. Evaluate the proposal and make your recommendation.

7. A firm is able to obtain quantity discounts on orders of material as follows:

Price per ton ₹	Tons
6.00	Less than 500
5.90	500 and less than 1000
5.80	1000 and less than 2000
5.70	2000 and less than 4000
5.60	4000 and over

The annual demand for the materials is 16000 tons. Stock holding costs are 20% of material cost per annum. The delivery cost per order ₹ 6.00. You are required to calculate the best quantity to order (EOQ).

8. The following information is available in respect of a material of ABC Co. Ltd:

Record quantity	:	12000 units
Lead (Delivery) time	:	4 to 8 weeks
Maximum Consumption	:	4000 units per week
Normal Consumption	:	3000 units per week
Minimum Consumption	:	1550 units per week

Ascertain:

(a) Re-order Level
(b) Minimum Stock Level
(c) Maximum Stock Level
(d) Average Stock Level

Hints:

(a) Re-order Level = Maximum consumption × Maximum Delivery Period

= $4000 \times 8 = 32000$ units

(b) Minimum Stock Level = Re-order Level – (Normal Consumption × Normal Delivery Period)

= $32000 - (3000 \times 6)$

= 14000 units

(c) Maximum Stock Level = Re-order Level – (Minimum Delivery Period × Minimum Rate of Consumption) + Re-ordering Quantity

= $32000 - (4 \times 1550) + 12000$

= 37,800 units

(d) Average Stock Level

$$= \frac{1}{2}(\text{Maximum Stock Level} + \text{Minimum Stock Level})$$

$$= \frac{1}{2}(37800 + 14000)$$

= 25900 units

9. The past experiences, disclosed by the analysis of rolevant accounting records of a firm regarding stock-outs is given below:

Stock-out (No. of units)	No. of items	% of time the firm has been out of stock
800	1	1
600	2	2
400	3	3
200	4	4
100	8	8
0	82	82
	100	100

The above mentioned information reveals that cost of 100 times, the firm faced shortage of 800 units once, shortage of 600 units twice, shortage of 400 units 3 times and so on. As many as 82 times, there was no stock out or shortage of even one unit. Estimated stock-out costs are ₹ 50 per unit and carrying costs are ₹ 5 per unit.

Determine the optimum level of safety stock.

❑❑❑

12 Capital Budgeting

12.1 CAPITAL EXPENDITURE DECISIONS OR CAPITAL BUDGETING DECISIONS, IMPORTANCES, LIMITATIONS

Capital budgeting is the process of financial planning of capital expenditures which involve current outlays in the long-term assets but are likely to produce benefits over a period of time longer than one year. These benefits may be either increase in revenue on reduction in cost.

Capital expenditure planning includes the following:

- Addition of fixed assets;
- Launching of new product or new service;
- Disposition of fixed assets;
- Penetrating into new geographical area;
- Modification of fixed assets;
- Replacement of fixed assets;
- Increase of present operating level on expansion;
- Profitability of a firm;
- Competitive position of the company;
- Company's future cost structure;

Importances:

Capital budgeting or capital expenditure decisions occupy a very important plane in corporate finance for the following reasons:

(a) Capital expenditure decisions have its effect over a long time span, invariably affect the company's future cost structure, and influence the risk complexion of the company. The most crucial variable is the sales.

(b) These decisions involve huge amount of capital outlay. Majority of the companies have scarce capital resources.

(c) Capital expenditure decisions, once taken, are almost irreversible. There are not easily reversible without much financial loss to the company because there may be no market for second-hand fixed assets, *e.g.*, plant and machineries, equipment's and their conversion to other uses may not be financially viable.

(d) Capital budgeting decisions determine the future destiny of the company. A proper investment decision can yield substantial returns.

(e) These decisions are the most difficult to make when the company is faced with various potentially viable investment opportunities.

Capital budgeting or investment decisions or capital expenditure decisions may be defined as the company's decision to invest its current funds most efficiently in long-term assets in anticipations of an expected flow of benefits over a series of years. There decisions are of considerable significance as the future success and growth of the firm depends heavily on them.

Limitations:

While capital expenditure decisions are extremely important, managers find it extremely difficult to analyze the pros and cons and arrive at a decision because:

(a) The benefits from investments are received in some future period. The future is uncertain and full of risks. For example, a decision to acquire a plant which is going to last for about 4 to 5 years requires a 4-5 years forecast. A failure to forecast correctly will lead to serious errors which can be corrected only at considerable costs. The future revenue involves estimating the size of the market for a product.

(b) Measuring costs and benefits of an investment proposal whether it be for mini-steel plant on a small office is difficult because all costs and benefits cannot be expressed in tangible terms.

(c) The benefits of capital expenditure are expected to occur for a number of years in the future which is highly uncertain.

(d) Time value of money is very much relevant in evaluating the investment proposals. The costs and benefits occur at different points of time. For a proper analysis of the viability of the investment proposal, all these have to be brought to a common time-frame.

12.2 ELEMENT OF RISK AND COMPLEXITIES INVOLVED IN CAPITAL BUDGETING DECISIONS

Capital budgeting decisions involve huge investment of funds in the long-term assets in anticipation of cash flows in future. An organization may spend large sums of money on, say, expansion of its production facilities based on its sales forecast. We can take an example of

Metal Box Ltd. In this affair they had done the same. During these periods, huge investments in R&D in packaging industry brought about new packaging facilities totally replacing metal as an important component of packing boxes. At the end of the expansion Metal Box Ltd. became sick company from the position it enjoyed earlier prior to the execution of expansion as a blue-chip. Employees lost their jobs. If affected adversely the cash flow position of its employees.

Therefore, the following risks are involved in capital budgeting decisions:

- Fast changing of technology making of the products obsolete;
- Difference in anticipation and original picture of sales forecast or cash inflows in future;
- Uncertainly in Business environment;
- Difference in anticipation and actual figure of return on investment (ROI);
- Fear of increased in cost of the investment etc.

Forecasting the future cash flows demands the necessity to make certain assumptions about the behaviour of costs and revenues in future. Fast changing environment makes the technology considered for implementation many times obsolete. For example, the arrival of mobile revolution totally made the pager technology obsolete. The firm's which invested in pagers faced the problem of pagers losing its relevance as a means of communication.

Estimation of future cash flows of capital budgeting decisions is really complex and difficult commitment of funds on long-term basis along with the associated problem of irrevocability of decisions and difficulty in estimating cash flows makes capital expenditure decisions complex in future.

12.3 PHASES OF CAPITAL BUDGETING DECISIONS

Phase 1

***Identification of investment opportunities/proposals*:**

A firm is in a position to identify investment proposal only when it is responsive to the ideas for capital projects emerging from various levels of the organization. The proposal may be adding now products to the company's product line, expansion of capacity to meet the emerging market demand for company's product or new technology based processes of manufacture that will reduce the cost of production.

For example, a sales manager may come with a proposal to produce a new product as per the requirements of company's consumers. Marketing manager, based on the sales manager's proposal may conduct a market survey to determine the expected demand for the new product under consideration. Once he is convinced of the market potential for proposed new product, the proposal goes to the production dept. and the production dept. examines the same with all aspects of production process. Then the proposal goes to the cost department to translate the entire gamut of the proposal into costs and revenues in terms of incremental cash flows both outflow and inflows. The cost benefit analysis is done which includes all incremental costs and benefits that the firm will incur and derive on commercialization of the proposal under consideration.

In the above connection, the following points deserve to be considered:

A. Sources of potential investment proposals/opportunities

Market Characteristics: Analyzing the demand and supply conditions of the market for the company's product could be a fertile source of potential investment proposals.

Reports and Information's: Various reports submitted coupled with the information's obtained through market surveys and consumer's perception of company's product could be source of potential investment proposals to redefine the company's products in terms of consumer's expectation.

Research and Development: Companies which invest in R&D constantly get exposure to the benefit of adopting the new technology quite relevant to keep the firm competitive in the most dynamic business environment. Reports emerging from R&D department could be a potential source of investment proposal.

Social and Economic Trends: Economic growth of the country and the emerging middle class endowed with purchasing power could generate new business opportunities to existing firms.

Public Awareness: Public awareness of their rights compels many firms to intimate projects from environmental protection angle.

Product Profiles of Various Industries: A study of the end products (including by products) of the various industries can throw up new project ideas. An analysis of the inputs required for the various industries can also help in the identification of new projects.

Consumption Patterns in Foreign Countries: An analysis of the consumption patterns on abroad can provide clues for launching new projects. To give an example, Brook Bond and Food Specialities promoted projects for manufacturing grumbled coffee in India after recognizing a shift in the consumption pattern abroad from powdered instant coffee to granulated office.

Revival of Sick Units: A sick unit presents a potential investment opportunity to an entrepreneur who has the capability of turning it around. For example, Gujarat Narmada auto took over Girnar Scooters as a part of it diversification strategy and successfully revitalized the unit.

B. Appraisal of the investment proposals – (Aspects of project appraisal)

Commercial Viability: a proposal should be commercially viable. The following aspects are examined to ascertain the commercial viability of any investment proposal:

- Market for the products
- Availability of raw materials
- Sources of raw materials
- Elements influencing of the location of a plant.

Infrastructural Viability: A proposal should be infrastructural viable. The following aspects are examined to ascertain the infrastructural viability of any investment proposal:-

- Roads
- Communications facilities
- Financial Services such as banking
- Public transport service.

Market Appraisal: In appraisal of market of new product, the following details are compiled and analyzed:

- Consumption trends
- Levels of imports and exports
- Competitions
- Availability of substitutes
- Purchasing power of consumers
- Regulations stipulated by government on pricing the proposed products or services
- Production constraints.

Technical Appraisal: This appraisal is done to ensure that following technical aspects of the implementation of the project are considered:

- Selection of process know how
- Determination of plant capacity
- Selection of plant and equipment
- Scale of operation
- Plant design and layout
- General layout and material flow

Economic Appraisal (Social Cost benefit analysis): This appraisal examines the project from the social point of view. It is also known as SCBA.

It examines:

- The impact of the project on the environment
- The impact of the project on the income distribution in the society
- The impact of the project on fulfillment of certain social objective like generation of employment, attainment of self-sufficiency etc.
- Will it materially alter the level of savings and investment in the society?

Financial Appraisal: This appraisal assesses the risk and returns at various stages of project exception. Besides, it examines whether the risk adjusted return exceeds the cost of financing the project:

- Cost of the project
- Cost of capital
- Means of financing
- Expected profitability

- Expected incremental cash flows
- Breakeven point
- Risk dimensions
- Tax benefits etc.

The financial appraisal of a project can be viewed as a two-step procedure:

Step 1: Defining the stream of cash inflows and outflows

Step 2: Appraising the cash flow stream to determine whether the project is financially viable or not. A number of criteria have been evolved for evaluating the financial desirability of a project.

A. Non-Discounting Criteria:

(i) Payback period (PBP)
(ii) Accounting rate of return (ARR)

B. Discounting Criteria:

(i) Net present value (NPV)
(ii) Internal Rate of Return (IRR)
(iii) Modified Internal Rate of Return (MIRR)
(iv) Profitability Index (PZ)
(v) Discounted payback period.

Phase 2

Preparing the statements of costs and benefits of investment proposal;

Phase 3

Estimating and comparing the net present value of the investment proposals that have been approved by the management on the basis of screening criteria;

Phase 4

Examining the government policies and regulatory guidelines to be observed for execution of each investment proposal screened and fondly approved based on the criteria stipulated by the management;

Phase 5

Budgeting for capital expenditure for obtaining financial approval by the management;

Phase 6

Post completion audit.

12.4 ESTIMATION OF CASH FLOW

A. Computation of cash flows with the assumptions (i) the firm is an entirely equity-financed firm (ii) No taxes:

We can obtain the following definition of cash flows as follows:

Cash Flow = (Revenue – Expenses – Depreciation) + Depreciation – Capital Expenditure
= profit + Depreciation – Capital Expenditure

In the absence of taxes, depreciation is worthless since it has no impact on cash flows. The measurement of profit excludes capital expenditures and includes some non-cash/terms such as depreciation. Revenue expenditures are entirely charged to profits.

B. Computation of cash flows under incremental approach – (tax exists and employment of debt):

All additional cash flows that are directly attributable to the investment project should be considered. A cash flow stream is a series of cash receipts and payments over the life of investments. The estimation of amounts of cash flows resulting from the investment must be made on incremental basis.

Incremental cash flows:

The incremental cash flows will be determined by comparing cash flows resulting with and without the introduction of the new project or product.

Components of cash flows

(i) Initial Investment – initial investment or cash outlay is to be determined after considering any post tax inflows, if any. Say, in replacement decisions i.r.o. of an old machinery, initial cash outlay = net cash out flow = Total cash required for investment in new machinery – after tax cash inflow on disposal of old machinery. .

Incremental cash outflow in construction project decisions: Initial cash outlay = Cash required for investment of project development (Factory building, land and site development) + Miscellaneous capital expenditure (expenditure on electrification, water supply etc.) + preliminary expenses (legal and promotional expenses, brokerage, commission) + additional net working capital

(ii) Operating Cash Inflows – operating cash inflows are estimated for the entire economic life of investment on project. Operating cash inflows constitute a stream of inflows and outflows over the life of the project.

Operating Cash inflows	= Revenues – Expenses – Tax
Tax	= Tax rate × profit
	= Tax rate × (Revenue – Expenses – Depreciation)

∴ Operating Cash

Inflows = Net Cash flow (NCF)

= Revenues – Expenses – Tax Rate (Revenue – Expenses – Depreciation)

= REV – EXP – T(REV – EXP – DEP)

= (REV – EXP) – T(REV – EXP) + T(DEP)

= (REV – EXP) (1 – T) + T(DEP)

= EBDIT (1 – T) + T(DEP)

= EBDIT (1 – T) + Depreciation Tax shield

When EBDIT = Earnings before depreciation, interest and taxes; T = tax rate

Alternative definition of net cash flows:

NCF = (REV – EXP – DEP) – TAX + DEP

= EBIT – TAX + DEP

= EBIT – T(EBIT) + DEP

= EBIT (1 – T) + DEP

Changes in working capital and some reinvestment of cash flows should be taken into consideration while computing NCF from the profit & loss account as follow:

NCF = EBDIT (1 – T) + Depreciation Tax Shield – Net Working Capital – Additional Capital Expenditures

Or Alternatively

EBIT (1 – T) + DEP – Net working capital – Cash outflows for additional capital expenditure (CAPEX)

Any savings in cost on installation of new machinery in the place of the old machinery will have to be accounted to after-tax basis.

In case of implementation of a new proposal on project incremental cash inflows and incremental cash outflows attributable to operating activities are considered. Here net cash flows are stated on incremental basis in investment analysis which is as follows: (after considering operating cash inflows and initial investments)

$$\Delta NCF = \Delta EBIT (1 - T) + \Delta DEP - \Delta NWC - \Delta CAPEX$$

(iii) Terminal Cash Inflows – Salvage value is the most common example of terminal cash inflows which may be defined as the market price of an investment at the time of its sale. At the end of the economic life of the project, the operating assets installed now will be disposed of which is normally known as salvage value of equipment's. The cash proceeds from the sale of the asset is treated as cash inflow in the terminal (last) year.

Besides salvage value, terminal cash inflows may include the release of net working capital. Sometimes removal costs may have to be incurred to replace an existing asset. Salvage value should be computed after adjusting their costs. After considering initial investment, operating cash inflows and terminal cash inflows, incremental cash flow can be calculated as follows:

$$\Delta \text{ NCF} = \text{incremental cash flows}$$
$$= \Delta \text{ EBIT } (1 - t) + \Delta \text{ DEP} - \Delta \text{ NWC} - \Delta \text{ CAPEX} + \text{salvage value}$$

Problem 1

A company is planning to replace its existing machinery. The new machine will cost ₹ 3,20,000 and have a life of 5 years. The new machine will yield annual cash revenue of ₹ 500000 and incur annual cash operating expenses of ₹ 2,60,000. The estimated salvage of the new machine at the end of economic life is ₹ 16,000. The existing machine if used for the next 5 years is expected to generate annual cash revenue of ₹ 4,00,000 and to involve annual cash expenses of ₹ 2,80,000. The existing machine has a book value of ₹ 80,000 and can be sold for ₹ 40,000. If this machine is sold after 5 years, the salvage value of the existing machine will be negligible. The company pays tax at 30%. The depreciation is written off at 25% on WDV basis.

Compute the incremental cash flows of replacement decision.

Solution

Working (a) Depreciation of New machine:

	₹
Book value	80,000
Add: cost of new machine	3,20,000
	4,00,000
Less: Sale proceeds of old machine	40,000
	3,60,000
Depreciation for 1st year @ 25%	90,000
	2,70,000
Depreciation for 2st year @ 25%	67,500
	2,02,500
Depreciation for 3st year @ 25%	50,625
	1,51,875
Depreciation for 4st year @ 25%	37,968
	1,13,907
Depreciation for 5st year @ 25%	28,476
Book value after 5 years	85,431

(b) Incremental Depreciation (Δ DEP)

Year	Depreciation (New machine)	Depreciation (Old machine) ₹	ΔDEP Incremental Depreciation
1	90,000	80,000 × 25% = 20000	70,000
2	67,500	60,000 × 25% = 15000	52,500
3	50,625	11,250	39,375
4	37,968	8,438	29,530
5	28,476	6,328	22,148

C. Net cash outlay, Annual cash flows from operations

	₹
Initial Investment	
Gross investment for the new machine	3,20,000
Less: Cash received from the sale of existing machine	40,000
Net Cash outlay	2,80,000
Incremental cash flows from revenue = (500000 – 400000)	1,00,000
Incremental decrease in expenditure (280000 – 260000)	20,000

We will apply the following formula to calculate Δ NCF or Incremental cash flows as follows:

$$\Delta \text{ NCF} = \Delta \text{ EBIT } (1 - T) + \Delta \text{ DEP} - \Delta \text{ NWC} - \Delta \text{ CAPEX} + \text{Salvage Value}$$

$$\text{EBIT} = \text{REV} - \text{EXP} - \text{DEP}$$

$$\Delta \text{ EBIT} = \Delta \text{ REV} - \Delta \text{ EXP} - \Delta \text{ DEP}$$

= Increase in revenue – increase in expenses – increase in depreciation.

Since, in this problem there is an incremental decrease in expenditure.

Δ EBIT = Increase in revenue + decrease in expenses – increase in depreciation

$$= \Delta \text{ REV} + \Delta \text{ EXP} - \Delta \text{ DEP}$$

Δ CAPEX = Incremental cash outflows for additional capital expenditure

Table : Statement of Incremental Cash Flow

Particulars	Year 0	1st	2nd	3rd	4th	5th
Net Cash outlay = Δ CAPEX	(280000)					
1. Δ REV = increase in revenue	–	100000	100000	100000	100000	100000
2. Δ EXP = Decrease in expenses	–	20000	20000	20000	20000	20000
3. Δ DEP = Increase in Depreciation	–	(70000)	(52500)	(39375)	(29530)	(22148)
4. Δ EBIT = 1 + 2 – 3	–	50000	67500	80625	90470	97852
5. Δ EBIT (1 – T) = Δ EBIT(1 – .30) = Δ EBIT X .70	–	35000	47250	56438	63329	68496
6. Salvage Value	–	–	–	–	–	16000
7. Incremental cash flow = Δ NCF = Δ EBIT (1–T)+ Δ DEP – Δ CAPEX + Salvage Value = 5+3 – Δ CAPEX + 6	(280000)	35000 + 70000 – NIL + NIL = 105000	47250+ 52500 – NIL + NIL = 99750	56438 + 39375 – NIL + NIL = 95813	63329+ 29530 – NIL + NIL = 92859	68496+ 22148 – NIL + 16000 = 106644

12.5 APPRAISAL CRITERIA

A. Payback Period Method:

Definition: Payback period is defined as the length of time required to recover the initial cash outlay. In other words, payback period refers to the period within which capital investment of a project is recovered out of cash inflows.

Example 1: The following details are available in respect of the cash flows of the two projects X and Y

Year	Project X ₹	Project Y ₹
0	(8,00,000)	(9,00,000)
1	4,00,000	2,00,000
2	2,50,000	4,00,000
3	50,000	3,00,000
4	1,00,000	3,00,000
5	2,50,000	50,000

Compute payback period for X and Y, also state which project would be accepted.

Solution

Year	Project A		Project B	
	Cash flows	Cumulative cash flows	Cash flows	Cumulative cash flows
₹	₹		₹	₹
1	4,00,000	4,00,000	2,00,000	2,00,000
2	2,50,000	6,50,000	4,00,000	6,00,000
3	50,000	7,00,000	3,00,000	9,00,000
4	1,00,000	8,00,000	3,00,000	12,00,000
5	2,50,000	10,50,000	50,000	12,50,000

From the cumulative cash flows column:

Project A recovers the initial cash outlay of ₹ 8,00,000 at the end of the 4th year.

Project B recovers the initial cash outlay of ₹ 9,00,000 at the end of the 3rd year.

Payback period:

Payback period of project A is 4 years

Payback period of project B is 3 years

Therefore, project B should be selected.

Evaluation of payback period method

Merits:

1. Simple calculation and interpretation.
2. It is the best method for evaluation of projects with very high uncertainly since emphasis is on recovery of initial investment.
3. 'Payback period' method emphasizes liquidity. Hence this method is preferred for those firms who are with shortage of funds.
4. It is inexpensive to use.
5. It uses cash flows information.

Demerits:

1. It does not measure the profitability.
2. It does not consider risk.
3. It ignores the time value of money.
4. It ignores cash flows occurring after the payback period.
5. Project selected on the basis of payback criterion may be in conflict with the wealth maximization goal of the firm.
6. There is no proper way to determine the standard payback.

Acceptance Rule

It there is one project → Accept the project if PBP < standard payback, Reject if PBP > standard payback

If there is two or more than two mutually exclusive projects → Accept that project having lower PBP. *From the earlier example, we may accept project B since its PBP is 3 years, i.e., shorter in compare to PBP of project A.*

Discounted Payback Period

Discounted payback period for a project will be always higher than simple payback period because the calculation of discounted payback period is based on discounted cash flows. One of the serious short comings of the payback period it that it does not discount the cash flows for calculating the payback period. We can discount cash flows and then calculate the payback. The discounted payback period is the number of periods taken in recovering the investment outlay on the present value basis. The discounted payback considers time value of money but still fails to consider the cash flows occurring after the payback period.

Example 2: (Considering the figures of project A from the earlier example one of simple payback period).

The additional information: Opportunity cost is 10%. Calculate discounted payback Period.

Solution.

Table: Discounted Payback Period

Year	Cash flows of project A	PV factor at 10%	P.V. of cash flows	Cumulative positive cash flows
0	(800000)	1	(800000)	—
1	400000	0.9091	363640	363640
2	250000	0.8264	206600	570240
3	50000	0.7513	37565	607805
4	100000	0.6830	68300	676105
Discounted PBP	—	—	—	800000
5	250000	0.6209	155225	831330

Discounted payback period: (applying interpolation)

$$= 4 + \frac{800000 - 676105}{831330 - 676105} = 4 + \frac{123895}{155225} = 4.798 = 4.8 \text{ years}$$

B. Accounting Rate of Return: (ARR)

Definition:

The accounting rate of return (ARR), also known as the return on investment (ROI), uses accounting information, as revealed by financial statements, to measure the profitability of an investment.

The accounting rate of return is the ratio of the average after tax profit divided by the average investment as follows:

$$ARR = \frac{\text{Average after tax profit}}{\text{Average investment}} \times 100$$

$$= \frac{\text{Average net operating profit after tax}}{\text{Average investment}} \times 100$$

$$= \frac{\text{Average EBIT } (1 - T)}{\frac{I_0 + I_n}{2}} \times 100$$

Where, I_0 = book value of investment in the beginning

I_n = book value of investment at the end of n number of years

Acceptance Rule:

Accept the project whose ARR > minimum rate established by management.

Reject the project whose ARR < minimum rate established by management.

This method would rank a project as number one if it has highest ARR and lowest rank would be assigned to the project with lowest ARR.

Example 1. The following particularly refer to two projects:-

	A	B
Cost	50000	75000
Estimated life	5 years	5 years
Salvaged Value	₹ 4500	₹ 5000
Estimated Profit after Tax		
1	₹ 4,500	₹ 12,500
2	₹ 5,000	₹ 10,000
3	₹ 8,750	₹ 3,000
4	₹ 9,000	₹ 7,500
5	₹ 10,000	₹ 6,250

Calculate ARR of both projects and after your comments.

Solution

Table: ARR

Estimated profit after Tax:	Project A ₹	Project B ₹
1	4500	12500
2	5000	10000
3	8750	3000
4	9000	7500
5	10000	6250
Total	37250	39250
(a) Average after tax profit = $\frac{\text{Total}}{5}$	7450	7850
(b) Average investment	$\frac{50000 + 4500}{2} = 27250$	$\frac{75000 + 5000}{2} = 40000$
(c) ARR = a/b × 100	₹ $\frac{7450}{27250} \times 100$ = 27.3394%	₹ $\frac{7850}{40000} \times 100$ = 19.625%

Since project A is showing higher ARR, project A should be accepted.

Evaluation of ARR

Merits :

1. Simplicity – ARR method is simple to understand and use.

2. Accounting data – ARR can be readily calculated from the accounting data; unlike in the NPV and IRR methods no adjustments are required to arrive at cash flows of the project.

3. Accounting profitability – ARR rule incorporates the entire stream of incomes in calculating the project's profitability.

Demerits:

1. Cash flows ignored – ARR method uses accounting profits, not cash flows, in appraising the projects. Accounting profits are based on arbitrary assumptions and choices and also include non-cash items. It is, therefore, inappropriate to rely on them for measuring the acceptability of the investment projects.

2. Time value ignored – The averaging of income ignores the time value of money. In fact this procedure gives more weightage to the distant projects.

3. Arbitrary cut-off – The firm employing the ARR rule uses an arbitrary cut-off yardstick. Generally, the yardstick is the firm's current return on its assets (book-value). Because of this the growth companies, earning very high rates on their existing assets, may reject profitable projects, (*i.e.*, with positive NPVs) and the less profitable companies may accept bad project, (*i.e.*, with negative NPVs)

ARR method continues to be used as a performance evaluation and control measure in practice. But its use as investment criteria is certainly desirable. It may lead to unprofitable allocation of capital.

DISCOUNTED CASH FLOW METHODS

Discounted cash flow method is an improvement over the traditional techniques which are time adjusted technique. DCF methods recognize to give weightage to the timing of return which involves:

1. Estimation of cash inflows and outflows of a project over the life of the project
2. Discounting the cash flows by an appropriate interest on discount factor.

DCF methods are of following types:

1. Net Present Value (NPU),
2. Internal Rate of Return (IRR),
3. Modified Internal Rate of Return (MIRR),
4. Profitability Index, and
5. Discounted Payback period.

C. Net Present Value: (NPV)

Definition

The net present value (NPV) method is a process of calculating the net present value of the project's cash flows, using the opportunity cost of capital as the discount rate, and finding out the net present value by subtracting the initial investment from the present value of cash flows. Net present value represents the net increase in the firm's wealth and hence NPV method is consistent with wealth maximization principle.

$$NPV = \sum_{t=1}^{n} \frac{C_t}{(1+r)^t} - Co = \left[\frac{C_1}{(1+r)^1} + \frac{C_2}{(1+r)^2} + \ldots\ldots\ldots + \frac{C_n}{(1+r)^n} \right] - C_o$$

Or NPV = Total of discounted cash inflows or total Present value of all cash inflow – Present value of cash outlay.

NPV method recognizes the time value of money. It correctly admits that cash flows occurring at different time periods differ in value. Therefore, there is the need to find out the present value of all cash flows.

Steps Involved in NPV method:

Step 1: Forecasting the cash inflows and outflows of the project on projects to be taken up for execution.

Step 2: Decision making on discount factor or % of opportunity cost of capital on interest factor.

Step 3: Computation of present value of cash inflows and outflows using the discount factor

Step 4: Calculation of NPV: P.V. of cash inflows – P.V. of cash outflows

Acceptance Rule: Accept the investment project, if its NPV is positive, *i.e.*, NPV > 0.

Reject the investment project, if it NPV < 0, *i.e.*, NPV is negative

Project may be accepted if NPV = 0 (after considering other factors)

In case of two or more than two mutually exclusive projects, accept the project having highest positive NPV.

Evaluation of NPV method

NPV method is the most superior investment criteria as it is always consistent with the wealth maximization principle since net present value represents the net increase in the firm's wealth. This method is preferred, except under capital rationing.

Though both NPV and IRR methods are consistent with the wealth maximization objective and both they give same results regarding acceptance criteria in case of conventional independent projects. But under varying cost of capital conditions, IRR method yields multiple rate of return for non-conventional projects. Moreover, in case of two or more mutually exclusive projects, the use of NPV rule is more recommended since it satisfies the value – additively principle, *i.e.*, NPV's of two or more of these projects can be added.

Merits:

1. If considers time value of money
2. If considers cash flows occurring over the entire life of the project
3. It is consistent with the goal of maximizing the net wealth of the company.
4. If satiation the value – additively principle, *i.e.*, NPVs of two or more projects are added.
5. Since cost of capital of the firm is the hurdle rate, NPV ensures that the project generates profits from the investment made for it.

Demerits:

1. It requires computation of the opportunity cost of capital which reflects practical difficulties;
2. There are practical problems associated with the evaluation of projects with fund's constraint.

3. It requires estimation of cash flows, both inflows and outflows, which is difficult as it involves dealing with the effect of elements of uncertainties on operating activities of the firm and also it is tedious task.
4. NPV expresses the absolute positive or negative present value of net cash flows. Therefore, if fails to capture the scale of investment.

Example 1:

Assume that a project costs ₹ 5000 now and is expected to generate year – end cash inflows of ₹ 2000, ₹ 2250, ₹ 1900, ₹ 1800 and ₹ 1500 in years through 5. The opportunity cost is assumed to be 10%. Calculate the Net Present Value of the project and state whether the project should be accepted or not?

Solution:

Table Calculation of NPV

Year	Cash in flows ₹	PVIF PV factor @ 10%	P.V. of Cash flows ₹
1	2000	0.9091	1818
2	2250	0.8264	1860
3	1900	0.7513	1428
4	1800	0.6830	1229
5	1500	0.6209	931
Sum of the P.V. of cash inflows =			7266
Less: P.V. of cash outflow =			5000
Net present value =			2266

The project generates a positive NPV of ₹ 2266. Therefore, project should be accepted

Example 2:

The Following the details about cash inflow and outlay of 2 projects.

	Project X ₹	Project Y ₹
Cost of the investment at the beginning of year 1	25000	50000
Expected cash inflows: at the end of Year:		
1	10000	20000
2	8000	15000
3	9000	16000
4	6000	10000
5	7000	15000

The cost of capital is 12%. Calculate NPV of the above mentioned project and state which project should be accepted.

Table: Calculation of NPV of project X and project Y

Year	PV factors at 12%	Project Y Cash inflows ₹	PV of cash flows ₹	Project Y Cash inflows ₹	PV of cash flows ₹
1	0.8928	10000	8928	20000	17856
2	0.7972	8000	6378	15000	11958
3	0.7118	9000	6406	16000	11389
4	0.6355	6000	3813	10000	6355
5	0.5674	7000	3972	15000	8511
Sum of P.V. of cash inflows			29497		56069
Less: P.V. of cash outlay.			25000		50000
Net present Value			4497		6069

Both projects are showing positive NPV. However, since project Y is generative highest positive NPV, it should be accepted.

D. Internal Rate of Return: (IRR)

Definitions

The internal rate of return is that rate of interest at which the net present value of a project is equal to zero or in other words, it is that rate which equates the present value of the cash inflows to the present value of the cash outflows. Under IRR method, the rate of discounting or firm's cost of capital which makes NPV zero, has to be found out.

$$NPV = \sum_{t=1}^{n} \frac{C_t}{(1+r)^t} - Co = 0$$

To illustrate this concept we will take the help of the following illustration.

Illustration

A project requires an initial outlay of ₹ 50000. It is expected to generate the following cash inflows:

Year	Cash inflows (₹)
1	25000
2	25000
3	15000
4	20000

What is the IRR of the project?

Solution

To determine the IRR, we have to compute the NPV of the project for different rates of interest until we find that rate of interest at which the NPV of the project is equal to zero or sufficiently close to zero. To reduce the number of iterations involved in this trial and error process, we can use the following short-cut procedure.

Step I: Compute the average annual net cash flow based on the given future net cash flows:

Year	Cash inflows (₹)
1	25000
2	25000
3	15000
4	20000
Total	**85000**

$$\text{Average} = \frac{85000}{4} = ₹\ 21250$$

Step II: Divide the initial outlay by the average annual cash flow.

i.e. $\frac{50000}{21250} = 2.3529 = 2.35$ (approx.)

Step III: From the PVIFA table for 4 years, the annuity factor very near to 2.35 is higher than 25%, *i.e.*, the first initial rate of interest starts from 25% for making trial and error.

Table: First trial rate = 25%

Year	Cash in flows ₹	PV factor at 25%	P.V. of Cash flows ₹
1	25000	0.800	20000
2	25000	0.640	16000
3	15000	0.512	7680
4	20000	0.410	8200
Sum of P.V. of cash inflows			51880

Since the initial investment of ₹ 50000 is less than the computed value at 25% of ₹ 51880 the next trial rate is 26%.

Year	Cash in flows ₹	PV factor at 26%	P.V. of Cash flows
1	25000	0.7937	19843
2	25000	0.6299	15747
3	15000	0.4999	7499
4	20000	0.3968	7936
Sum of P.V. of cash inflows			51025

Since the initial investment of ₹ 50000 is less than the computed value at 26% of ₹ 51025 the next trial rate is 27%.

Table : 3rd trial rate = 27%

Year	Cash in flows ₹	PV factor at 27%	P.V. of Cash flows ₹
1	25000	0.7874	19685
2	25000	0.6200	15500
3	15000	0.4882	7323
4	20000	0.3844	7688
Sum of P.V. of cash inflows			50196

Still the initial investment of ₹ 50000 is less than the computed value at 27% of ₹ 50196, the next trial rate is 28%.

Table: 4th trial rate = 28%

Year	Cash in flows ₹	PV factor at 28%	P.V. of Cash flows ₹
1	25000	0.7813	19532
2	25000	0.6104	15260
3	15000	0.4768	7152
4	20000	0.3725	7450
Sum of P.V. of cash inflows			49394

Since the sum of PV of cash inflows or computed value at 28% of ₹ 49394 is less than the initial investment of ₹ 50000, we are to stop trial and error approach.

Trial Rate	**P.V. or cash inflows**
27%	50196
IRR →	← 50000
28%	49394

By interpolation,

$$\text{IRR} = 27 + \left[(28-27) \times \frac{50196-50000}{50196-49394}\right]$$

$$= 27 + \frac{196}{802}$$

$$= 27 + .2444 \quad = 27.2444\% = 27.24\%$$

Why IRR is popular (Merits)

1. It takes into account the time value of money and generally consistent with wealth maximization principle.
2. Like ARR, it makes sense to businessmen who prefer to think in terms of rate of return on capital employed. IRR calculates the rate of return of the project, taking into account the cash flows over the entire life of the project.

3. IRR gives a rate of return that reflects the profitability of the project.
4. IRR can be compared with the firm's cost of capital.
5. To calculate IRR, there is no need to calculate and employ cost of capital for discounting because the project is evaluated at the rate of return guaranteed by the project.

Demerit:

1. The IRR method requires estimates of cash flows which is a tedious task.
2. It does not hold the value additively principle, *i.e.*, IRRs of two or more projects do not add.
3. The IRR criterion can be misleading when the decision maker has to choose between mutually exclusive projects that differ significantly in terms of outlays.
4. At times, IRR yields multiple rates of return for non-conventional projects.

IRR Vs NPV

Both IRR and NPV methods account for the time value of money and are generally consistent with the wealth maximization objective.

(a) IRR is uniquely defined only for a project whose cash flow pattern is characterized by cash outflows followed by cash inflows. These projects are simple investments. But if the cash flow stream has one or more cash outflows interspersed with cash inflows, there can be multiple internal rates of return. In that case, NPV is much more superior method.

(b) IRR criterion can be misleading when the decision maker has to choose between mutually exclusive projects that differ significantly in terms of outlays. In that case, NPV method is much reliable since we select that project which is generating highest positive NPV.

(c) The projects having substantial outlay especially in the medium and large scale sectors should be evaluated in terms of IRR. Financial institutions insist the concerned organizations that those projects must show the computation of IRR in the Detailed Project Report.

(d) For non-conventional projects, IRR yield multiple rates of return and fails to work under varying cost of capital conditions. As this is not a unique benchmark to compare IRR with cost of capital, the simple, straight forward alternative is to use the NPV rule.

(e) NPV satisfies the value – additive principle, *i.e.*, NPVs of two or more projects are added IRR does not hold this principle. Therefore, NPV aims letter in maximizing the wealth in compare to IRR.

In general, NPV method may be preferred in case of mutually exclusive projects, non-conventional projects except under capital rationing. On the other hand, in other cases, IRR still the best criterion to day to appraise project financially. Both the NPV and IRR methods yield the same accept or reject rule in case of independent conventional investments. The NPV method is superior if the opportunity cost of capital varies since NPV method can easily discount each cash flow by the relevant opportunity cost of capital while IRR method yields a single discount rate.

E. Modified Internal Rate of Return (MIRR):

The modified internal rate of return is the compound average annual rate that is calculated with a reinvestment rate different than the project's IRR.

MIRR is a distinct improvement over the IRR and is a better indicator of relative profitability of the projects.

MIRR is defined as:

PV of costs = PV of terminal value

$$\text{Or PV of costs} = \frac{\text{Terminal value}}{(1 + \text{MIRR})^n} \quad \text{Or PVC} = \frac{\text{TV}}{(1 + \text{MIRR})^n}$$

The procedure for calculating MIRR as follows:

Step 1: Calculate the present value of the costs (PVC) associated with the project, using cost of capital (r) as the discount rate:

$$\text{PVC} = \sum_{t=0}^{n} \frac{\text{Cash outflow}_t}{(1 + r)^t}$$

Step 2: Calculate the terminal value (TV) of the cash inflows expected from the project:

$$\text{TV} = \sum_{t=0}^{n} \text{cash inflow}_t \, (1 + r)^{n-t}$$

To calculate TV, FVIF is based on cost of capital.

Step 3: Obtain MIRR by solving the following equation:

$$\text{PVC} = \frac{\text{TV}}{(1 + \text{MIRR})^n}$$

Acceptance Rule :

Accept the project if MIRR > firm's cost of capital

Reject the project if MIRR < firm's cost of capital

Illustration

An company is evaluating a project that has the following cash flow stream associated with it:

Year	0	1	2	3	4	5
Cash flow (₹ In thousands)	–1200	–849	300	600	900	1000

The cost of capital is 20 per cent. Calculate MIRR.

Solution

Step 1:

Present value of the costs (PVC) associated with the project–

Year	Costs (outflows) ₹ In thousands	PVIF @ 20 %	P.V. of cost ₹ In thousands
0	1200	1	1200
1	849	$\frac{1}{(1+.20)} = 0.8333$	707.47
	P.V. of costs (PVC) =		1907.47

Step 2:

Terminal Value (TV) of the cash inflows expected from the project –

Year	Costs inflow In thousands ₹	FVIF @ 20 %	T.V. of cash inflows In thousands ₹
2	300	$(1+.20)^3 = 1.728$	518.40
3	600	$(1+.20)^2 = 1.44$	864
4	900	$(1+.20)^1 = 1.20$	1080
5	1000	$(1+.20)^0 = 1$	1000
		T.V. of cash inflows =	3462.40

Step 3:

The MIRR is obtained as follows:

$$PVC = \frac{TV}{(1+MIRR)^5}$$

Or. $$1907.47 = \frac{3462.40}{(1+MIRR)^5}$$

Or $$(1+MIRR)^5 = \frac{3462.40}{1907.47} = 1.8152$$

Or, $1 + \text{MIRR} = (1.8152)^{1/5}$

Or, $\text{MIRR} = (1.8152)^{1/5} - 1 = 1.12665 - 1 = .12665 = 12.665\%$

Merits: (Superiority of MIRR over IRR)

(a) MIRR is superior to the regular IRR in two ways:

First, MIRR assumes that project cash flows are reinvested at the cost of capital whereas the regular IRR assumed that project cash flows are reinvested at the project's own IRR. Since reinvestment at cost capital is more realistic than reinvestment at IRR, MIRR reflects better the true profitability of a project.

Second, the problem of multiple rates does not exist with MISS.

(b) MIRR is a distinct improvement over the regular IRR.

Demerit:

For choosing among mutually exclusive projects of different size of capital outlay, NPV is a better alternative in compare to in measuring MIRR, the contribution of each project to the value of the firm.

F. Profitability Index (PI) / BCR

Profitability index is known as benefit cost ratio (BCR) which is defined as the present value of cash inflows divided by the present value of cash outflows.

$$\text{PI (BCR)} = \frac{\text{P.V. of cash inflows}}{\text{P.V. of cash outflow}}$$

$$\text{Or} = \frac{\text{P.V. of cash inflows}}{\text{Initial cash outlay}}$$

NBCR = BCR – 1; where NBCR = Net benefit cost ratio.

Acceptance Rule

Accept the project it PI > 1, *i.e.,* NBCR and NPV = Positive

Reject the project if PI < 1, *i.e.,* NBCR and NPV = Negative

If PI = 1, management may accept the project since P.V. of cash inflows will be equal to the sum of P.V. of cash outflows.

i.e., NPV = 0. It neither adds nor reduces the existing wealth of the company.

Merits:

1. If takes into account the time value of money.

2. Under capital rationing, PI is the best appraisal criteria to examine whether the project is financially desirable or not if the projects are divisible apart from investment.

3. It is consistent with the principle of maximization of shareholder's wealth.
4. It measures the relative profitability.

Demits:

1. Estimation of cash flows and discount rate cannot be done accurately with certainty.

2. A conflict may arise between NPV and PI, if a choice between mutually exclusive projects has to be made.

3. PI role of selecting projects under capital rationing may not yield good result because of project indivisibility

Illustration

Let us consider a project which is being evaluated by a firm that has a cost of capital of 10%.

Initial investment = ₹ 50000

Cash inflow/Benefits:	₹
Year 1	12500
Year 2	20000
Year 3	22000
Year 4	26000

Calculate PI and offer your comment.

Also calculate Net Cost benefit ratio.

Solution

Table: Calculation of PI.

Year	Costs inflow ₹	PVIF @ 10%	P.V. of cash inflows ₹
1	12500	0.9091	11364
2	20000	0.8264	16528
3	22000	0.7513	16529
4	26000	0.6830	17758
P.V. of Cash inflows (benefits)			62179

$$\text{PI or BCR} = \frac{62179}{50000} = 1.24358 > 1$$

$$\text{NBCR} = \text{BCR} - 1 = 1.24358 - 1 = .24358$$

Since PI > 1 or NBCR is positive, project may be accepted.

12.6 CAPITAL RATIONING

When a firm impose constraints on the total size of its capital budget or total available fund for capital expenditure it is known or capital rationing.

The constraints which lead to a decision to keep capital expenditures within a ceiling, within a specified period of time, such as a year, may arise due to market conditions on may be entirely self-imposed. Under capital rationing the objective is to select the combination of investment proposals that provide the highest net present values, subject to the budget constraint for the period. This may be understood by the following illustration, where projects will be ranked under the PI method, in descending order of profitability.

Illustration

Total capital budget for the year 2010-2011 in an organization has been estimated at ₹ 30 crores. The mutually exclusive investment proposals along with profitability index are given:

Project	M	N	O	P	Q	R	S
Investment (₹ in crores)	3.95	5.25	5.0	8.5	3.75	7.5	3.75
PI	0.98	1.16	1.13	1.25	1.03	1.10	1.18

Which of the projects should be accepted?

Solution

Project	PI	Rank	Initial outlay (₹ In crores)
P	1.25	1	8.5
S	1.18	2	3.75
N	1.16	3	5.25
O	1.13	4	5.0
R	1.10	5	7.5 30
Q	1.03		3.75

The first projects, named P, S, N, O and R, which will completely utilize the available fund, will be selected at the optimum mix. Project M has not been included since its PI is less than 1.

TYPES OF CAPITAL RATIONING

(A) External Rationing: where a firm is constrained for following external reasons

- Deficiency in market information's, inability of the firm to procure capital due to lack of investor's confidence, high cost of issue, viability and instability of market etc.

(B) Internal Rationing: where a firm is constrained for following internal reasons

- Financial control, conservative policy imposed on divisional heads etc.

Profitability Index as the basis of Capital Rationing:

It has been stated earlier that NPV method is better than IRR in case of two or more mutually exclusive projects. Between NPV and PI, the difference is that the former attempts to maximize the value of the firm in absolute term while the latter, attempts the same in relative term. In general, PI is the best method.

Ranking of different investment proposal is generally done through NPV, PI or IRR. If the objective is to maximize NPV per rupee of capital, projects should be ranked on the basis PI. But if projects have other constraints besides having financial constraints, *i.e.*, constraints on the total size of its capital budget or if the projects are not divisible apart from capital investment, PI is not the best appraisal criteria to examine whether the project is financially desirable or not.

Steps of Capital Rationing

Step I: Ranking of different investment proposals through NPV, PI or IRR

[If the objective is to maximize NPV per rupee of capital, projects should be ranked on the basis of PI.]

[If the objective is to achieve maximum NPV, subject to many constraints, linear programming approach is used.]

[PI rule for selecting project, may yield sub-optimal result if there is project indivisibility]

Step II: Selection of the most profitable investment proposal

12.7. (A) COST OF CAPITAL: ITS ROLE IN CAPITAL EXPENDITURE DECISIONS

Cost of capital is usually taken to be the out-off rate for determining whether investment opportunities should be rejected or accepted. In calculation of discounted cash flows in case of appraisal methods of NPV, PI, IRR, MIRR, discounted pay-back period, cost of capital is needed.

In case of ROI: Expected rate return to be compared with required rate of return. In case of NPV, PI & Discounted Payback, discounting rate should be the cost of capital rate.

In case of IRR: IRR should not be the lower than cost of capital.

Cost of capital, for decision making in capital investment matters, is used as the cut-off rate or the discounting rate for determining profitability or otherwise of proposed projects.

(B) HOW A FIRM'S COST OF CAPITAL SHOULD BE USED

If the opportunity cost of capital is lower than the weighted average cost, than the latter should be used.

There are two situations which will show how cost of capital be used:

Situation 1:

Where there are shortages of investment opportunities as compared to total funds available:

Both weighted and specific cost of capital can be used. But the most common approach is to take weighted average of capital due to the following justified reasons:

- Most investment proposals are financed from combination of various sources like share capital, debt capital, retained earning etc, not solely from one source.
- Cost of capital rate as a cut-off or standard rate, provides a basis for comparison among projects. If specific costs are taken for different projects as the costs of financing, true comparison is not possible.

Situation 2:

When fund is the key or limiting factor as compared to available investment opportunities:

The most common approach is to take opportunity cost of capital which may be the minimum acceptable rate of return. It is the earnings rate foregone by using funds for one purpose instead of another.

It is needless to mention that dividend is paid only out of after-tax profits. Hence, it is appropriate that cost of capital is computed on after tax profits. Further, for discounting cash flows cost of capital is used. Since net cash flows are ascertained after deducting tax liability, if is better to measure overall cost of capital or weighted average cost of capital on after-tax basis.

Problem 2

An organization can make either of two investments at the beginning of 2011. Assuming a required rate of return of 10% p.a., evaluate the investment proposals under— (i) Return an investment; (ii) Discounted payback period; (iii) Net present Value; (iv) Profitability Index; (v) Internal Rate of Return.

The forecast particulars are given below:

	Proposal A	Proposal B
Cost of Investment (₹)	20000	28000
Life (years)	4	5
Scrap Value	NIL	Nil
Net Income (after depreciation and tax):		
	₹	₹
End of 2011	500	NIL
2012	2000	3400
2013	3500	3400
2014	2500	3400
2015	–	3400

It is estimated that each of the alternative projects will require an additional working capital of ₹ 2000 which will be required back on full after the expiry of each project life. Depreciation is provided under straight line method.

Solution

(i) Using return on Investment: ARR

	Proposal A	Proposal B
• Cost of investment	20000	28000
• Working Capital Requirement	2000	2000
• Book value of investment in the beginning (Initial Investment)	22000	30000
• Book value of investment at the end of project life = Recovery of working capital + Scrap Value	2000 + Nil = 2000	2000 + Nil = 2000
(A) Average investment	$\frac{22000 + 2000}{2}$ = 12000	$\frac{30000 + 2000}{2}$ = 16000
Estimated after tax profit:		
2011	500	Nil
2012	2000	3400
2013	3500	3400
2014	2500	3400
2015	–	3400
(B) Average after tax profit:	$\frac{8500}{4}$ = 2125	$\frac{13600}{5}$ = 2720
(C) Accounting Rate of Return (ARR)	$\frac{2125}{12000} \times 100$	$\frac{2720}{16000} \times 100$
$= \frac{B}{A} \times 100$	= 17.71%	= 17 %
(D) Rank (Evaluation)	1	2

Table: Calculation of NPV

Year End off	PVIF @ 10%	Proposal A NCF ₹	P.V. of NCF ₹	Cum Positive cash flow	Proposal B NCF ₹	P.V.of NCF ₹	Cum Positive cash flow
2011	0.9091	5500	5000	5000	5600	5091	5091
2012	0.8264	7000	5785	10785	9000	7438	12529
2013	0.7513	8500	6386	17171	9000	6762	19291
2014	0.6830	9500	6488	23659	9000	6147	25438
2015	0.6209	–	–	–	11000	6830	32268
Total P.V. of NCF			23659			32268	
Less: P.V. of cash outlay			22000			30000	
NPV			1659		NPV	2268	

Notes:

Calculation of NCF (Net Cash flow):

We have to ascertain net cash flow in each year of the project life of each project by adding depreciation to net profit after depreciation and tax.

Year	Proposal A Net profit after tax	Depreciation ₹	NCF ₹	Proposal B Net profit after tax (₹)	Depreciation ₹	NCF ₹
2011	500	5000	5500	NIL	5600	5600
2012	2000	5000	7000	3400	5600	9000
2013	3500	5000	8500	3400	5600	9000
2014	2500	5000	7500 }	3400	5600	9000
2015	–	–	+2000 }	3400	5600	9000 } 2000 }.
	8500			13600		

Under Straight Line Method

$$\text{Depreciation} = \frac{\text{Cost of investment} - \text{Scrap Value}}{\text{Life}}$$

Depreciation p.a. under proposal A: $\frac{20000 - \text{NIL}}{4} = ₹\ 5000$

Depreciation p.a. under proposal B: $\frac{28000 - \text{NIL}}{5} = ₹\ 5600$

(ii) Discounted payback period

(a) Proposal A: 2013 (3rd) 17171

→ ← 22000

2014 (4th) 23659

$$\text{Discount Payback period} = 3 + \left[(4-3) \times \frac{22000 - NIL}{23659 - 17171}\right]$$

$$= 3 + \frac{4829}{6488}$$

$= 3 + .7442 = 3.7442$ year $= 3$years $(.7442 \times 12)$ months

$= 3$ years 8.91 months (approx.)

(b) Proposal B: 2014 (4th) 25438

→ ← 30000

2015 (5th) 32268

$$\text{Discount Payback period} = 4 + \left[(5-4) \times \frac{30000 - 25438}{32268 - 25438}\right]$$

$$= 4 + \frac{4562}{6830} = 4.6679$$

$= 4$ years $(.6679 \times 12)$months $= 4$ years 8.01 months (approx.)

Evaluation: proposal A is more profitable than proposal B due to its shorter payback period

(iii) Net Present Value (NPV) – from Table

Proposal A: NPV = ₹ 1659

Proposal B: NPV = ₹ 2268

Evaluation: proposal B is more attractive than proposal A due to its higher NPV.

(iv) Profitability Index (PI)

$$\text{Proposal A: } \frac{\text{P.V. of cash inflows}}{\text{Initial casy outlays}} = \frac{23659}{22000} = 1.0754$$

$$\text{Proposal B: } \frac{\text{P.V. of cash inflows}}{\text{Initial casy outlays}} = \frac{32268}{30000} = 1.0756$$

Evaluation: Both the proposals appear to be equally profitable, still Project B may be accepted.

(v) IRR (internal rate of return) :

Table : Calculation of IRR of Project A

Year	NCF ₹	1st Trial Rate @ 11% (₹)		2nd Trial Rate @ 13% (₹)		3rd Trial Rate @ 14% (₹)	
		PVIF	PV of NCF	PVIF	PV of NCF	PVIF	PV of NCF
2011	5500	0.9009	4955	0.8849	4867	.8772	4825
2012	7000	0.8116	5681	0.7831	5482	.7695	5386
2013	8500	0.7312	6215	0.6930	5890	.6750	5737
2014	9500	0.6587	6257	0.6133	5826	.5921	5625
			23108		22065		21573

Note : Since company's required rate of return is 10% p.a., we select 11% as the 1st trial rate.

13% ₹ 22065

IRR → ← 22000

14% ₹ 21573

By interpolation,

$$\text{IRR of Project A} = 13 + \left[(14-13)\times\frac{22065-22000}{22065-21573}\right]$$

$$= 13 + \frac{65}{492} = 13 + .1321 = 13.1321\%$$

Table : Calculation of IRR of Project B

Year	NCF ₹	1st Trial Rate @ 11% (₹)		2nd Trial Rate @ 13% (₹)		3rd Trial Rate @ 12% (₹)	
		PVIF	PV of NCF	PVIF	PV of NCF	PVIF	PV of NCF
2011	5600	0.9009	5045	0.8849	4955	.8928	5000
2012	9000	0.8116	7304	0.7831	7048	.7972	7175
2013	9000	0.7312	6581	0.6930	6237	.7118	6406
2014	9000	0.6587	5928	0.6133	5520	.6355	5719
2015	11000	0.5934	6527	0.5427	5970	.5674	6241
			31385		29730		30541

Note: After selecting 13% Trial Rate, it is clear that trial rate @12% will come as 2nd Trial Rate, since IRR will be between 12% and 13%.

₹ 12% ₹ 30541

IRR → ← 30000

13% ₹ 29730

By interpolation,

$$\text{IRR of Project B} = 12 + \left[(13-12)\times\frac{30541-30000}{30541-29730}\right]$$

$$= 12.67\%$$

Evaluation : Proposal A yields a rate of return of 13.13% as against 12.67% by proposal B. therefore, proposal A is more profitable then proposal A.

Problem 3

A company is engaged in evaluating an investment project which requires an initial cash of ₹ 300000 on a machine. The economic life of the machine is 10 years and its salvage value ₹ 36000. The project would require current assets of ₹ 64000. An additional investment of ₹ 60000 would also be necessary at the end of 4 years to improve the efficiency at the machine. This would be written off completely over the last 6 years. The machine is expected to yield annual cash flow before Tax ₹ 120000. The company follows the straight line method of depreciation. Income tax rate is assumed to be 30%. Calculate NPV if the minimum required rate of return is 20%. Should the proposal be accepted? Also calculate ARR.

Solution:

Workings:

(A) Computation of Net cash inflows:

– For calculation of NPV

Year Col 1	Profits before tax and depr Col 2	Depreciation Col 3	Profit before tax Col 4 = Col 2 – Col 3	Tax @ 30% Col 5	Profit after tax Col 6 = Col 4 – Col 5	Net cash cash flow Col 7= Col 6 + Col 3
	₹	₹	₹	₹	₹	₹
1	120000	26400	93600	28080	65520	91920
2	120000	26400	93600	28080	65520	91920
3	120000	26400	93600	28080	65520	91920
4	120000	26400	93600	28080	65520	91920
5	120000	10000+26400	83600	25080	58520	94920
6	120000	36400	83600	25080	58520	94920
7	120000	36400	83600	25080	58520	94920
8	120000	36400	83600	25080	58520	94920
9	120000	36400	83600	25080	58520	94920
10	120000	36400	83600	25080	58520	94920
Total Return	1200000	–	–	–	613200	–

Note:

$$\frac{\text{Depreciation}}{\text{(Before Additional Investment)}} \text{ p.a.} = \frac{\text{Cost of investment} - \text{salvage value}}{\text{life of the machine}}$$

$$= \frac{300000 - 36000}{10} = \frac{264000}{10} = ₹\ 26400$$

From year 1 to year 4; Depreciation p.a. = ₹ 26400

From year 5 to year 10: Depreciation p.a. = ₹ 26400 + $\frac{60000}{6}$ = ₹ 36400

(After additional expenditure completely written off over the last 6 years)

Table: Calculation of NPV

Year	NCF (Net cash inflow)	P.V. factor @ 20% ₹	P.V. of NCF ₹
1	91920	0.8333	76597
2	91920	0.6944	63829
3	91920	0.5787	53194
4	91920	0.4822	44324
5	94920	0.4018	38139
6	94920	0.3348	31779
7	94920	0.2791	26492
8	94920	0.2325	22069
9	94920	0.1938	18395
10	94920	0.1615	15329
	64000 – recovery	0.1615	10336
	36000	0.1615	5814
Total P.V. of NCF			406297
Less: P.V. of cash outflow:		₹	
– Cost of equipment		300000	
– Current Asset		64000	
– Cash outlay at the end of 4th year (60000 × .4822)		28932	
		392932	392932
Net Present Value			13365

Since NPV is positive the project can be accepted.

(B) Calculation of ARR

$$\text{ARR} = \frac{\text{Average Return (or Average After tax Profit)}}{\text{Average Investment}} \times 100$$

(a) Average Return $= \dfrac{\text{Total After Tax Profit)}}{\text{Life of the project}}$

$= \dfrac{613200}{10}$ (from table)

$=$ ₹ 61320

(b) Average Investment $= \dfrac{(300000 + 64000) + 36000}{2}$

$= \dfrac{400000}{2}$

$=$ ₹ 200000

(c) ARR $= \dfrac{61320}{200000} \times 100$

$= 30.66\ \%$

Problem 4

A company is considering the possibility of manufacturing a particular component which at present is being bought from outside. The manufacture of the component would require an investment of ₹ 750000 in a new machine besides an additional investment of ₹ 50000 in working capital. The life of the machine would be 10 years with a salvage value of ₹ 50000. The estimated savings before tax would be ₹ 180000 p.a. The income tax rate is 50%. The company's required rate of return is 10%. Depreciation is considered on straight line system. Should the company make this investment? Ignore impact at income tax for the system of depreciation followed.

Solution:

Workings:

(a) Net cash inflow:

	₹
Savings before tax	180000
Less: Tax @ 50 % (50% × 180000)	90000
Savings after tax	90000
Add: Depreciation $\frac{(750000 - 50000)}{10}$	70000
Annual cash inflows	160000

(b) PVIFA

Year	**PVIF @ 10%**
1	0.9091
2	0.8264
3	0.7513
4	0.6830
5	0.6209
6	0.5645
7	0.5131
8	0.4665
9	0.4241
10	0.3855
PVIFA =	6.1444

Table: Calculation of NPV

Particulars of inflow	PV factor @ 10%	Present Value of inflows
(A) Annual cash inflow (FV × PVIFA) (160000 × 6.1444)	PVIFA = 6.1444	983104
(B) Salvage Value = (50000 × .3855)	$PVIF_{(10,10\%)}$ = 0.3855	19275
(C) Working capital–recovery = (50000 × .3855)	$PVIF_{(10,10\%)}$ = 0.3855	19275
Present Value		1021654
Less : P.V. of Cash Outflow (750000+50000)		800000
NPV =		221654

The company should accept the investment proposal.

Problem 5

A company is considering the purchase of new leather cutting machine to replace an existing machine that has a book value of ₹ 3000 and can be sold for ₹ 1500. The estimated salvage value of the old machine in 4 years would be zero and it is depreciated on a straight-line basis. The new machine will reduce costs (before tax) by ₹ 7000 per year, *i.e.*, ₹ 7000 cash savings over the old machine. The new machine has a 4-year life, costs ₹ 14000 and can be sold for an expected amount of ₹ 2000 at the end of 4th year. Assuming straight-line depreciation and a 40% tax rate, define the cash flows associated with the investment. Assume that the straight line method of depreciation is used for tax purposes.

Solution:

Table: Cash flows Associated with Replacement Decision

Year	Particulars of inflows	0	1	2	3	4
1	Net investment in new Machine	(12500)				
2	Savings in costs		7000	7000	7000	7000
3	Incremental depreciation		2250	2250	2250	2250
4	Pre-tax profits = (2) – (3)		4750	4750	4750	4750
5	Taxes @ 40% on pre-tax profits		1900	1900	1900	1900
6	After-Tax profits = (4) – (5)		2850	2850	2850	2850
7	Initial flow	(12500)				
8	Operating flow = (6) + (3)		5100	5100	5100	5100
9	Terminal flow					2000
10.	Net cash flow = (7) + (8) + (9)	(12500)	5100	5100	5100	5100

Working Notes: Computation of depreciation:

Existing leather – cutting machine : ₹ $\frac{3000}{4}$ = ₹ 750 p.a.

New Leather – cutting machine : ₹ $\frac{12000}{4}$ = ₹ 3000 p.a.

Incremental depreciation = ₹ 2250 p.a.

SUMMARY

Capital expenditure decisions occupy important place in corporate finance. Capital investment proposals involve current outlay of funds in the expectation of a stream of cash inflow in future. The huge sums involved and the irreversible and long-term nature of the decisions make them very important. Investment decisions begin with identification of the investment opportunities, followed by preliminary screening, feasibility study, implementation and performance review.

Several appraisal criteria's are used for evaluating the financial viability of a project. Some are non-discounting criteria's such as payback period and Accounting rate of Return, some are discounting criteria's are such as NPV, IRR, MIRR, Discounted payback period and PI.

The major traditional techniques are payback period and accounting rate of return. DCF techniques consider the 'time value of money' and hence overcome the limitation of Non-DCF techniques. The most popular method for large project is IRR. For two or more mutually exclusive projects, NPV is the best method. Where there is capital rationing, PI is the best method, when the projects are not divisible apart from capital investment.

The payback period of an investment enables the finance manager to calculate the number of years required to recover the initial capital outlay. The accounting rate of return is the ratio of average profit after tax to average book value of the investment. Like payback period, this criterion also ignores the time value of money. The net present value is the present value of the project's net cash flow less the initial outflow. A project is acceptable only when its NPV is greater than or equal to zero. The profitability index is the alternative name of benefit-cost ratio which measures the present value of a rupee of outflow and is a very useful in ranking projects in order of the efficient usage of capital. If a project's BCR is greater than or equal to 1, the project can be accepted. The internal rate of return is the discount rate that equates the present value of net cash flows of the project with the initial cash outlay. Any project is acceptable if IRR is greater than or equal to the required rate of return, usually the company's cost of capital.

QUESTIONS

A. Short Questions:

1. What is meant by 'capital expenditure decisions'?
2. Name the methods to be used to evaluate the alternative projects.
3. What is 'return on investment'?
4. What is 'payback period'?
5. What is cost of capital?
6. What is capital rationing?
7. What is 'profitability index'?
8. What is 'modified internal rate of return'?
9. What is 'internal rate of return'?
10. What is meant by 'discounted cash flow methods'?
11. What is salvage value?
12. What is operating cash flows?

B. Moderate and Broad Questions:

1. What are the importances of capital budgeting?
2. What are limitations of capital expenditure decisions?
3. Explain risk and cômplexities involved in capital budgeting decisions.
4. Explain the phases in capital budgeting decision.
5. What are the aspects of appraisals of project or investment proposals? Explain all of them.
6. Explain those criteria which have been evolved for evaluating the financial desirability of a project.
7. Discuss the sources of potential investment opportunities.
8. Explain the methods under non-discounting criteria with their advantages and disadvantages which are used to evaluate the financial viability of a project.
9. Explain all methods under discounting criteria in brief, with their advantages and disadvantages which are used to evaluate the financial viability of a project.
10. How cash flows can be estimated?
11. Compare NPV with IRR. Also discuss why IRR is also popular like NPV.
12. Explain 'profitability Index as thĕ basis of capital Rationing.
13. Discuss the steps of capital rationing.
14. Discuss the role of cost of capital in capital expenditure decisions.
15. How a firm's cost of capital should be used in capital expenditure decision?

PROBLEMS

1. A company is considering the purchase of a new machine. Two alternative machines- X and Y – are available for the purpose. From the following information, prepare a statement showing the justification of using the best machine with the help of incremental cash flow approach:

	Machine A	Machine B
Estimated life (Years)	5	6
Cost of machine (₹)	80000	150000
Estimated additional costs (₹):	500	750
Maintenance (per month)	400	500
Indirect material (p.a.)	2000	3000
Supervision (per quarter)	3000	4500
Estimated savings in scrap (p.a.)	8000	12000
Estimated savings in direct wages p.a.:	42000	68000
Employees not required	10	15
Wages per employee (₹)	7200	7200

2. A firm is considering to installing either of the two machines which are mutually exclusive. The details of their purchase price and operating cost are given below:

	Year	Machine X ₹	Machine Y ₹
Purchase cost	0	10000	8000
Operating cash inflows :	1	2000	2500
	2	2000	2500
	3	2000	2500
	4	2500	3800
	5	2500	3800
	6	2500	3800
	7	3000	
	8	3000	
	9	3000	
	10	3000	

Machine X will recover salvage value of ₹ 1500 in the year 10 while Machine Y will recover ₹ 1000 in the 6th year. Determine what machine is cheaper at 10% cost of capital, assuming that both the machines operate at the same efficiency, present value of ₹ 1 at 10% discounting factor is given below:

Year	1	2	3	4	5	6	7	8	9	10
PV Factor	.91	.83	.75	.68	.62	.56	.51	.47	.42	.39

3. An enterprise can make either of two investments at the beginning of 2000. Assuming a required rate of return of 10% p.a., evaluate the investment proposals under

(a) ARR (Return on Investment)

(b) Payback Period

(c) Discounted Payback Period

(d) NPV

(e) Profitability index

(f) IRR

The forecast particular are given below:

	Proposal A	Proposal B
Cost of investments (₹)	20000	28000
Life (years)	5	5
Scrap Value (₹)	2000	2800
Profit (after depreciation and tax)		
	₹	₹
End of 2000	1000	1500
2001	2000	3900
2002	3600	4100
2003	2900	4300
2004	1700	4200

It is estimated that each of the alternative projects will require an additional working capital of ₹ 2000 which will be received back in full after the expiry of each project life. Depreciation is provided under straight line method. Also offer your comments.

4. (a) Consider the following three investments:

Cash flows (₹)

Projects	C_0	C_1	C_2
X	– 2500	0	+ 3350
Y	– 2500	+ 1540	+ 1540
Z	– 2500	+ 2875	+ 0

The discount rate is 12%. Compute NPV, IRR and the rate of return for each project.

(b) A firm has the following information about a project:

	C_1	C_2	C_3
Cash revenue	16000	14000	12000
Cash expenses	8000	7000	6000
Gross profit	8000	7000	6000
Depreciation	4000	4000	4000
Net profit	4000	3000	2000

The initial investment of the project is estimated as ₹ 12000.

(i) Calculate the project's accounting rate of return.

(ii) If it is found that the initial investment will be ₹ 9000 and cash expenses will be more by ₹ 1000 each year, what will be the project's ARR. Also, calculate the project NPV of at the cost of capital is 9%.

5. The initial invetment outlay for a project comists of ₹ 10 crores for plant and machinery and ₹ 4 crores for working capital. Other informations are as follows:

Sales	: 1 lakh units of output p.a. for years 1 to 6 (Selling price = ₹ 120 p.u.)
Variable Cost	: ₹ 60 p.u.
Fixed Overheads	: ₹ 1.5 crores p.a. for years 1 to 6 (excluding depreciation)
Rate of Depreciation	: 25% on WDV method (on plant and machinery)
Salvage Value	: Equal to the WDV at the end of 6 years
Tax rate	: 30%
Expected life	: 6 years
Post-tax cut off rate	: 10%

Indicate the financial viability of the project by calculating the NPV and IRR.

❑❑❑

13 Leverage

13.1 CONCEPT AND NATURE AT LEVERAGE (TYPES OF LEVERAGE)

Leverage is the influence of power to achieve something. In business terminology 'Leverage' describes the ability of a firm to use fixed cost assets or debt and preference capital funds to magnify the return to shareholders. The higher the degree of leverage, the higher is the risk. But at the same time, it increases the possibility of higher rate of return to the shareholders. Ultimately 'Leverage' is the influence of an independent financial variable on a dependent variable, *e.g.*, impact of sales on profit.

Risk: The time risk implies the degree of uncertainty the firm has to face in meeting fixed-payment obligations, *i.e.*, operating fixed costs and cost of debt capital. Therefore there are two types of risks as follows:

- **Operating Risk:** This risk essentially refers to the use of fixed cost assets which reflects the variability in earnings (EBIT) due to this risk.
- **Financial Risk:** This risk essentially refers to the use of debt capital in the capital structure of the firm which reflects the variability in rate of return to equity or EPS (Earning per share).

Nature of Leverage: There are two types of leverage used in business terminology as follows:

(a) Operating leverage: It arises out of fixed operating costs. It may be defined as the ability of a firm to use fixed cost assets or fixed operating costs to magnity effects of changes in sales on its operating profit (EBIT)

$$\therefore \quad \text{Degree of operating leverage (DOL)} = \frac{\%\ \text{change in EBIT}}{\%\ \text{change in sales volume}} > \text{I}$$

The value of DOL must be greater than 1. If DOL is equal to 1, then there is no operating leverage due to absence of fixed operating costs and per cent change in EBIT is equal to % change in sales.

OL results or DOL > 1 when fluctuations in sales an accompanied by disproportionate fluctuations in EBIT.

b. Financial Leverage: It arises due to presence of fixed financial charges, *e.g.*, dividend on preference shares, interest on bond/debenture/Loan. It may be defined as the ability of a firm to use debt and preference capital to magnify effects of changes in EBIT on EPS or rate of return to equity.

$$\therefore \quad \text{Degree of Financial Leverage (DFL)} = \frac{\%\ \text{change in EPS}}{\%\ \text{change in EBIT}} > 1$$

The value of DFL must be greater than 1. If DFL is equal to 1, then there is no financial leverage due to absence of debt capital and hence due to absence of fixed financial changes per cent change in EPS is equal to per cent change in EBIT.

F L results or DFL > I when fluctuations in EBIT are accompanied by disproportionate fluctuations in EPS.

- **Combine Leverage:** The combined effect of operating and financial leverage provides a risk profile or the total risk of the firm. It may be shown by Degree of Combined Leverage (DCL) which can be calculated as follows:

$$\text{DCL} = \text{DOL} \times \text{DFL}$$

13.2 IMPACT ON PROFIT AND EPS

(I) Operating Leverage: Example (Effect on profit / EBIT)

(A) With absence of fixed costs

Illustration:

Unit selling price:	₹ 10
Unit variable cost:	₹ 5
Total Fixed Cost p.a.:	NIL
Present activity:	2000 units
Change in activity: (±) 50%	

Calculate DOL or impact on operating profit (EBIT) due to proposed change in sales.

Solution:

Particulars	Present	Proposed changes in sold units	
Capacity (units)	2000	3000(+50%)	1000(–50%)
1. Sales @ ₹ 10	₹ 20000	30000	10000
2. Variable cost @ ₹ 5	10000	15000	5000
3. Contribution = 1 – 2	10000	15000	5000
4. TFC	NIL	NIL	NIL
5. Profit/EBIT = 3 – 4	10000	15000	5000
6. % change in profit/ EBIT	–	$\frac{15000 - 10000}{100000} \times 100\%$	$\frac{5000 - 10000}{100000} \times 100\%$
$= \frac{\text{Change in Profit}}{\text{Original Profit}} \times 100$		= (+) 50%	= (–) 50%
7. DOL		$1 = \left(\frac{+50\%}{+50\%}\right)$	$1 = \left(\frac{-50\%}{-50\%}\right)$

Note: $\text{DOL} = \frac{\%\text{ change in EBIT}}{\%\text{ change in sales (units)}}$

There is no OL due to absence of fixed cost since DOL = 1. It leads to proportionate change in EBIT or profit due to a given change in sales. So no fixed costs, no operating leverage (OL). A change in 50% of sales leads to an impact on profit by an equivalent change of 50% in profit (EBIT).

(B) With presence of fixed costs

Illustration:

Unit selling price: ₹ 10

Unit variable cost: ₹ 5

Total Fixed Cost p.a. : 5000

Present activity: 2000 units

Change in activity: (±) 50%

Calculate DOL or impact on operating profit (EBIT) due to proposed change in sales.

Solution

Particulars	Present	Proposed changes in sold units	
		(+) 50%	(–) 50%
Capacity (units)	2000	3000	1000
	₹	₹	₹
1. Sales @ ₹ 10	20000	30000	10000
2. Variable cost @ ₹ 5	10000	15000	5000
3. Contribution = 1 – 2	10000	15000	5000
4. TFC	5000	5000	5000
5. Profit/EBIT = 3 – 4	5000	10000	NIL
6. % change in profit/EBIT	–	$\frac{10000 - 5000}{5000} \times 100\%$	$\frac{\text{NIL} - 5000}{5000} \times 100\%$
$= \frac{\text{Change in profit}}{\text{Original profit}} \times 100$		= (+) 100%	= (–) 100%
7. DOL	–	$\frac{(+)\ 100\%}{(+)\ 50\%} = 2$	$\frac{(-)\ 100\%}{(-)\ 50\%} = 2$

The above illustration shows impact on profit due to an increase in sales volume.

Operating leverage is now existing since there is presence of fixed costs (TFC).

A given change in sales (50%) is accompanied by a more than proportionate change in EBIT (100%) or by a disproportionate change in EBIT due to a given change in sales. Thus operating leverage largely depends on the extent of fixed costs of the firm. Operating leverage, may, therefore, be defined as the ability of the firm to use fixed operating costs to magnify the effects of change in sales on its operating profit or profit before interest and taxes (EBIT).

(II) Financial leverage: Example (Effect on EPS)

(A) With absence of debt capital

Illustration

Present Financing: Equity (₹ 10 per share) = ₹ 100000

Present Earnings before interest and Taxes = ₹ 10000

Corporate Tax = 40%

Calculate DFL or impact on Earnings per share (EPS) due to change in EBIT where change in EBIT = +50%, due to increase in sales.

Solution

Particulars	Present EBIT ₹	Change in EBIT (+) 50% ₹
1. EBIT	10000	15000
2. Interest (1)	NIL	NIL
3. EBT = 1– 2	10000	15000
4. Tax @ 40% on EBT	4000	6000
5. PAT = 3 – 4	6000	9000
6. No of Equity Shares	10000 shares	10000 shares
7. EPS = $\frac{5}{6}$	$\frac{₹\ 6000}{10000}$ = ₹ 0.60/ share	$\frac{₹\ 9000}{10000}$ = ₹ 0.90/ share
8. % change in EPS $= \frac{\text{Change in EPS}}{\text{Original EPS}} \times 100$	–	$\frac{.90 - .60}{.60} \times 100\% = +50\%$
9. DFL		$\frac{+50\%}{+50\%} = 1$

Note: $\text{DFL} = \frac{\%\ \text{change in EPS}}{\%\ \text{change in EBIT}}$

There is no FL due to absence of debt capital and hence absence of interest payment since DFL =1. It leads to proportionate change in EPS due to a given change in EBIT. So no debt capital (*i.e.*, no interest payment) no financial leverage (FL). A change in 50% of EBIT leads to an impact on EPS by an equivalent change of 50% in EPS.

(B) With Presence of Debt Capital

Illustration

Present Financing:

Equity (₹ 10 per share)	= ₹ 50000
8% Debenture (₹ 100 per debenture)	= ₹ 50000
	₹ 100000

Present EBIT = ₹ 10000

Corporate Tax = 40%

Calculate DFL or impact on EPS due to change in EBIT where change in EBIT = + 50%; due to increase in sales.

Solution

Particulars	Present EBIT ₹	Change in EBIT + 50% ₹
1. EBIT	10000	15000
2. Interest (1) = 8% × 50000	4000	4000
3. EBT = 1 – 2	6000	11000
4. Tax @ 40% on EBT	2400	4400
5. PAT = 3 – 4	3600	6600
6. No of Equity shares	5000	5000
7. EPS = $\frac{5}{6}$	$\frac{₹ 3600}{5000} = ₹ 0.72$	$\frac{₹ 6600}{5000} = ₹ 1.32$
8. % changes in EPS	–	$\frac{1.32 - 0.72}{.72} = +83\%$
9. DFL	–	$\frac{+83\%}{+50\%} \times 100 = 1.6667$

The above illustration shows impact on EPS due to an increase in EBIT. A given change in EBIT (50%) is accompanied by a more than proportionate change in EPS (83%) or by a disproportionate change in EPS due to a given change in EBIT. Thus financial leverage largely depends on the extent of debt capital of the firm. Financial leverage, may, therefore, be defined as the ability of the firm to use debt capital to magnify the effects of change in EBIT on EPS

13.3 INTERPRETATION OF FINANCIAL LEVERAGE AND OPERATING LEVERAGE (THEIR COMPARISON) DIFFERENCES BETWEEN THEM.

Operating Leverage (OL)	Financial Leaverage (FL)
1. It arises due to the presence of fixed operating costs in the firm's income flows/ EBIT	1. It arises due to presence of Fixed Financial charges; Dividend on preference share, interest on debt like bonds, debentures or other loans in the capital structure.
2. Operating Leverage refers to the ability of a firm to use fixed cost assets or fixed operating costs to magnify effects of changes in sales on its EBIT.	2. Financial Leverage refers to the ability of a firm to use debt capital in the capital structure of project to magnify effects of changes in EBIT on EPS or the return to equity. The way to improve EPS or return to equity is to use debt capital, even without increasing EBIT. This is known as 'Trading on Equity', the alternative name of Financial Leverage.
3. Operating leverage affects a firm's EBIT	3. Financial Leverage affects a firm' EPS.

4. **Measure** of OL:

$$DOL = \frac{Q(S-V)}{Q(S-V)-F} = \frac{\text{Contribution}}{\text{EBIT}}$$

Alternatively, DOL

$$= \frac{\%\text{ Change in EBIT}}{\%\text{ change in units sold}}$$

When, Q = units sold
V = Variable cost/unit
S = Sales price/unit
F = Total Fixed Cost

5. If DOL > I, OL exists, *i.e.*, there is fixed operating costs. If DOL = 1, there is no OL, *i.e.*, there is no fixed operating cost, there is no operating leverage.
6. Higher the DOL, higher is the operating risks. (business risk)
7. Higher operating risks can be taken when levels of EBIT/incomes are rising.

4. **Measure** of FL:

$$DFL = \frac{\text{EBIT}}{\text{EBIT} - I - \frac{D_p}{1-T}}$$

$$\text{Alternatively, DFL} = \frac{\%\text{ change in EPS}}{\%\text{ change in EBIT}}$$

When EBIT = Earnings before interest & Taxes
I = Interest on debt capital
D_p = Preference Dividend
T = Corporate Tax Rate

5. If DFL > I, FL exists, *i.e.*, there is financial charge. If DFL = 1, there is no financial charge, there is no financial leverage.
6. Higher the DFL, higher is the financial risks.
7. Higher financial risks can be taken when level of EPS and PAT are rising.

13.4 COMBINED LEVERAGE

Degree of Combined / Total Leverage (DCL or DTL) measures the total risk of the company as it is a combined measure of both operating and financial risk. It measures the variability of EPS. DCL may be defined as the percentage change in EPS due to the percentage change in sales. Since Operating Leverage affects a firm's EBIT and Financial Leverage affects that firm's EPS, Combined leverage affects both EBIT and EPS. It examines the impact of change in the output upon the EPS of the company

$$DCL = DOL \times DFL$$

$$= \frac{Q(S-V)}{Q(S-V)-F} \times \frac{\text{EBIT}}{\text{EBIT} - I - \frac{D_p}{1-T}}$$

$$= \frac{Q(S-V)}{\text{EBIT}} \times \frac{\text{EBIT}}{\text{EBIT} - I - \frac{D_p}{1-T}}$$

$$= \frac{Q\,(S - V)}{EBIT - I - \dfrac{D_p}{1 - T}} = \frac{Q\,(S - V)}{Q\,(S - V) - F - I - \dfrac{D_p}{1 - T}}$$

$$\text{Alternatively DCL} = \frac{\%\text{ change in EPS}}{\%\text{ change in EBIT}} \times \frac{\%\text{ change in EBIT}}{\%\text{ change in units sold/sales}}$$

$$= \frac{\%\text{ change in EPS}}{\%\text{ change in units sold/sales}}$$

Problem 1

Calculate DFL, DOL and DTL from the following information's:

Quantity produced	=	₹ 5000 units
Variable Cost per unit	=	₹ 200
Selling price per unit	=	₹ 500
No. of Equity shares	=	500000
Total Fixed Cost	=	₹ 900000
Interest	=	₹ 75000
Preference Dividend	=	₹ 50000
Corporate Tax	=	50%
Equity Earnings	=	₹ 163500

Solution:

Given, Q = 5000 units

V = ₹ 200

S = ₹ 500

N = 500000

F = ₹ 900000

I = ₹ 75000

D_P = ₹ 50000

T = 50%

EBIT = Q(S – V) – F = 5000 (500 – 200) – 900000

= ₹ 600000

$$\therefore \quad DFL = \frac{600000}{600000 - 75000 - \dfrac{50000}{1 - 0.50}}$$

$$= \frac{600000}{525000 - \dfrac{50000}{.50}}$$

$$= \frac{600000}{525000 - 100000} = \frac{600000}{425000} = 1.4117647$$

$$DOL = \frac{\text{Contribution}}{\text{EBIT}} = \frac{Q(S-V)}{Q(S-V)-F}$$

$$= \frac{5000(500-200)}{5000(500-200)-900000} = \frac{1500000}{600000} = 2.5$$

$$DTL / DCL = \frac{Q(S-V)}{Q(S-V)-F-I-\frac{D_p}{1-T}}$$

$$= \frac{500(500-200)}{5000(500-200)-900000-75000-\frac{50000}{1-0.50}}$$

$$= \frac{1500000}{425000} = 3.5294$$

Alternatively, DTL/DCL = DOL × DFL = 2.5 × 1.4117647 = 3.5294

13.5 EBIT – EPS ANALYSIS

This analysis is very useful to examine the effect of financial leverage on the behavior of EPS (a) under alternative financial plans and (b) with varying levels of EBIT. The alternative that will give the highest value of EPS (that is the maximum return to the equity) should be selected at the most profitable financing plan or most profitable level of EBIT, as they may be. In our search for an appropriate capital structure, we need to understand how sensitive is earnings per share (EPS) to changes in earnings before interest and tax (EBIT). In general, the relationship between EBIT and EPS is as follows:

$$EPS = \frac{(EBIT - 1)\ (1 - t) - Dp}{n}$$

To illustrate the relationship between EBIT and EPS under alternative financing plans and with varying levels of EBIT, let us consider the following problem in respect of a limited company.

Problem 2

- Existing Capital Structure of a Limited Co. : 1 million Equity Shares of ₹ 10 each = ₹ 10 million
- Tax rate : 50 per cent

The company has planned to raise additional capital of ₹ 10 million for financing an expansion project. In this context, it is evaluating two alternative financing plans:

(i) Issue of equity shares (1 million equity shares of ₹ 10 per share), and

(ii) Issue of debentures carrying 14% interest.

What will be the EPS under the two alternative financing plans for two levels of EBIT, say ₹ 4 million and ₹ 2 million?

Solution:

We will apply the following relationship between EBIT and EPS:

$$EPS = \frac{(EBIT - 1)\ (1 - t) - D_p}{n}$$

Where, EPS = Earnings per share

EBIT = Earnings before interest and taxes

I = Interest burden

t = co. tax rate

n = no. of equity shares

D_P = preference Dividend

Under Alternative Financing Plans: (EPS calculation)

(A) Equity Financing:

(1) At EBIT level of ₹ 2000000

$$EPS = \frac{(2000000 - NIL)\ (1 - .50) - NIL}{1000000 + 1000000}$$

$$= \frac{1000000}{2000000} = ₹\ 0.50 \text{ per share}$$

$$DFL = \frac{EBIT}{EBIT - 1} = \frac{EBIT}{EBIT} = 1 \text{ (since I = NIL)}$$

(2) At EBIT level of ₹ 4000000

$$EPS = \frac{(4000000 - NIL)\ (1 - .50) - NIL}{1000000 + 1000000} = \frac{2000000}{2000000} = ₹\ 1.00 \text{ per share}$$

$$DFL = \frac{EBIT}{EBIT - 1} = \frac{EBIT}{EBIT} = 1 \text{ (since I = NIL)}$$

(B) Debt – financing:

(1) At EBIT level of ₹ 2000000

$$\text{EPS} = \frac{(2000000 - 1400000)(1 - .50) - \text{NIL}}{1000000} = \frac{600000\,(1 - .50)}{2000000} = ₹\ 0.30 \text{ per share}$$

$$\text{DFL} = \frac{\text{EBIT}}{\text{EBIT} - 1} = \frac{2000000}{2000000 - 1400000} = \frac{2000000}{600000} = 3.33 > \text{I}$$

(2) At EBIT level of ₹ 4000000

$$\text{EPS} = \frac{(4000000 - 1400000)(1 - .50) - \text{NIL}}{1000000} = \frac{2600000\,(1 - .50)}{1000000} = ₹\ 1.30 \text{ per share}$$

$$\text{DFL} = \frac{\text{EBIT}}{\text{EBIT} - 1} = \frac{4000000}{4000000 - 1400000} = \frac{4000000}{2600000} = 1.5385 > 1$$

$$= ₹\ 1.30 \text{ per share}$$

The solution shows that the value of EPS is maximum (₹ 1.30 per share) under debt-financing million. So this financing plan is recommended. Its financial leverage is 1.5585 which is greater than 1 due to present of financial charge. Since financing charge is 14% of the debt capital, it looks very heavy at EBIT level ₹ 2000000. Similarly ROE means earnings after tax and dividend in relation to equity share capital.

Thus,
$$\text{ROE} = \frac{(\text{EBIT} - 1)(1 - t) - D_p}{S} \times 100$$

Where S = Equity share capital, ROE = Return on Equity.

Table: Calculation of ROE (Return on Equity) expressed in percentage (%)

Financing Plans	EBIT = ₹ 2000000		EBIT = ₹ 4000000	
	EPS ₹ /Share	**ROE %**	**EPS ₹ /Share**	**ROE %**
Equity	0.50	5	1.00	10
Debt.	0.30	3	1.30	13

$$\text{ROE:} \quad 5\% = \frac{(2000000 - \text{NIL})(1 - .50) - \text{NIL}}{20000000} \times 100$$

$$10\% = \frac{(4000000 - \text{NIL})(1 - .50) - \text{NIL}}{20000000} \times 100$$

$$3\% = \frac{(2000000 - 1400000)(1 - .50) - \text{NIL}}{10000000} \times 100$$

$$= \frac{300000\ (1 - .50) - \text{NIL}}{10000000} \times 100$$

$$13\% = \frac{(4000000 - 1400000)\ (1 - .50) - \text{NIL}}{10000000} \times 100$$

$$= \frac{1300000}{10000000} \times 100$$

It appears when EBIT is expected at ₹ 4000000 under debt-financing. EPS and ROE (Return on Equity) is maximum. Since, financial leverage is existing there is no conflict between financial leverage and EBIT-EPS analysis. Management should also consider variations in EPS under varying levels of EBIT under each financing plan.

Financial Plans	Equity Financing EPS (₹)	Debt financing EPS (₹)
EBIT: ₹ 2000000	.50	.30
EBIT: ₹ 4000000	1.00	1.30
Mean π (₹)	$\frac{.50 + 1.00}{2} = .75$	$\frac{.30 + 1.30}{2} = .80$
Standard deviation (V) ₹	= .25	= .50
Coefficient of Variation		
$= \frac{V}{\pi} \times 100$	$\frac{.25}{.75} \times 100$	$\frac{.50}{.80} \times 100$
	= 33.33%	= 62.5 %

Note: Calculation of S.D. (V) : 1.00 – 0.75 = 0.25, 1.30 – .80 = .50

Equity Financing		Debt Financing	
X	X^2	X	X^2
0.5	0.25	.30	0.09
1.00	1.00	1.30	1.69
Ex = 1.50	Ex^2 = 1.25	Ex = 1.60	Ex^2 = 1.78

$$\text{S.D. (Equity Financing)} = \sqrt{\frac{Ex^2}{n} - \left(\frac{Ex}{n}\right)^2} = \sqrt{\frac{1.25}{2} - \left(\frac{1.50}{2}\right)^2}$$

$$= \sqrt{.625 - .5625} = .25$$

$$\text{S.D. (Debt. Financing)} = \sqrt{\frac{Ex^2}{n} - \left(\frac{Ex}{n}\right)^2} = \sqrt{\frac{1.78}{2} - \left(\frac{1.60}{2}\right)^2}$$

$$= \sqrt{0.89 - 0.64}$$

$$= \sqrt{0.25} = 0.50$$

The variability of EPS as measured by co-efficiencies of variations is shown under each financing plan for varying levels of EBIT. The variability in EPS is highest in case of Debt financing. It may be concluded that with increasing EBIT, shareholders will gain most in case of debt financing at EBIT level of ₹ 4000000 (highest EPS = ₹ 1.30), but at the same time, they would be subjected to a high degree of risk. This is due to relatively high degree of financial leverage in this case.

13.6 INDIFFERENCE POINT-BREAK-EVEN EBIT LEVEL

Indifference point is that point at which alter-tax cost of acquisition of outside fund is equal to the rate of return from the investment. The break-even or indifference point between two alternative methods of financing can be determined by a formula. The firm wants to know the level of EBIT at which EPS would be the same under all plans under all equity and debt-equity.

To find out the break-even level of EBIT, we may set the EPS formula of two plans. At indifference point one is indifferent as to the alternative financing plans.

Step I:

The EPS formula under all equity plans is:

$$EPS = \frac{(1-T)\ EBIT}{N_1}$$

When, T = Corporate Tax Rate

N_I = no. of equity shares under all equity plan

The EPS formula under debt-equity plan is:

$$EPS = \frac{(1-T)\ (EBIT-1)}{N_2}$$

When, I = Interest on debt capital

N_2 = No. of equity shores under debt-equity plan.

Step II:

Then, we use the following equation to calculate indifference point:

$$EPS = \frac{(1-T)\ EBIT}{N_1} = \frac{(1-T)\ (EBIT-1)}{N_2}$$

Problem 3:

	Alternative Financial Plans	
	All equity	Debt – Equity
	₹	₹
Equity Share Capital (₹ 100 each)	400000	200000
10% Debt Capital	NIL	200000
	400000	400000

Corporate Tax = 50%

Find out the level of EBIT level at which EPS would be the same under all-equity and under debt-equity plans or find out Break-even EBIT Level or find out indifference point ..

Solution:

EPS under all-equity plan is as follows:

$$EPS = \frac{(1-T)\ EBIT}{N_1}$$

Or, $$EPS = \frac{(1-.50)\ EBIT}{4000}$$

Or, $$EPS = \frac{.50\ EBIT}{4000}$$

EPS under debt-equity plan is as follows:

$$EPS = \frac{(EBIT - I)\ (1-T)}{N_2}$$

Or $$EPS = \frac{(EBIT - 20000)\ (1-.50)}{2000}$$

$$EPS = \frac{.50\ (EBIT - 20000)}{2000}$$

Now, we use the following equations to calculate indifference point:

$$\frac{.50\ EBIT}{4000} = \frac{.50\ (EBIT - 20000)}{2000}$$

Or, $$\frac{EBIT}{4000} = \frac{EBIT - 20000}{2000}$$

Or, $$\frac{EBIT}{2} = EBIT - 20000$$

Or, EBIT = 2 EBIT – 40000

Or EBIT = ₹ 40000

We can verify whether EPS is the same under all-equity plan and under debt-equity plan at the EBIT Level of ₹ 40000.

EPS:

$$\text{All Equity Plan} = \frac{.50 \times \text{EBIT}}{4000} = \frac{.50 \times 40000}{4000} = ₹\ 5$$

$$\text{Debt- Equity Plan} = \frac{.50\ (\text{EBIT} - 20000)}{2000} = \frac{.50\ (40000 - 20000)}{2000} = \frac{.50 \times 20000}{2000} = ₹\ 5$$

Computation of indifference point under other plans:

(A) Indifference point between equity-debt and equity-debt – preference plans

$$\text{EPS under equity-debt plan} = \frac{(\text{EBIT} - \text{I})\ (1 - \text{T})}{\text{N}_1}$$

$$\text{EPS under equity-debt-preference plan} = \frac{(\text{EBIT} - \text{I})\ (1 - \text{T}) - \text{D}_\text{p}}{\text{N}_1}$$

Then we use the following equation to calculate indifference point:

$$= \frac{(\text{EBIT} - \text{I})\ (1 - \text{T})}{\text{N}_1} = \frac{(\text{EBIT} - \text{I})\ (1 - \text{T}) - \text{D}_\text{p}}{\text{N}_2}$$ [D_P = Preference Dividend]

(B) Indifference point between equity-preference and debt-preference plans.

$$\text{EPS under equity-preference plan} = \frac{\text{EBIT}\ (1 - \text{T}) - \text{D}_\text{p}}{\text{N}_1}$$

$$\text{EPS under debt-preference plan} = \frac{(\text{EBIT} - \text{I})\ (1 - \text{T}) - \text{D}_\text{p}}{\text{N}_2}$$

Then we use the following equation to calculate indifference point:

$$= \frac{(\text{EBIT} - \text{I})\ (1 - \text{T}) - \text{D}_\text{p}}{\text{N}_2} = \frac{\text{EBIT}\ (1 - \text{T}) - \text{D}_\text{p}}{\text{N}_1}$$

Thus, depending upon the components of each alternative mix of financing, the EPS formula may be suitably revised. In other words, what we need is an expression for EPS under each plan.

13.7 GRAPHICAL PRESENTATION OF EBIT-EPS ANALYSIS; AND POINT OF INDIFFERENCE/INDIFFERENCE POINT

We can draw a graph of EBIT – EPS analysis from the figures of following illustration where from indifference point can be better examined.

Illustration:

	Alternative Financial Plans	
	All-equity	Debt-equity
	₹	₹
Equity share Capital	(₹ 100 each) 400000	200000
10% Debt Capital	NIL	200000
	400000	400000

Corporate Tax = 40%

EBIT Levels = ₹ 20000 and ₹ 60000

Solution:

Calculation of EPS under alternative financing plans at varying EBIT Levels:

(a) *EPS under all-equity plan is*

$$EPS = \frac{EBIT\,(1-T)}{N_1} \qquad [T = \text{Corporate Tax Rate}]$$

At EBIT Level of ₹ 20000:

$$EPS = \frac{20000\,(1-.40)}{4000} = \frac{20000 \times .60}{4000} = ₹\ 3.00$$

At EBIT Level of ₹ 60000:

$$EPS = \frac{60000\,(1-.40)}{4000} = \frac{60000}{4000} \times .60 = ₹\ 9.00$$

(b) *EPS under debt-equity plan is*

$$EPS = \frac{(EBIT - I)\,(1-T)}{N_2} \qquad [\,I = \text{Interest on debt capital}\,]$$

At EBIT Level of ₹ 20000:

$$EPS = \frac{(20000 - 20000)\,(1-.40)}{2000} = 0$$

At EBIT Level of ₹ 60000 :

$$EPS = \frac{(60000 - 20000)(1 - .40)}{2000} = \frac{40000 \times .60}{2000} = ₹\ 12$$

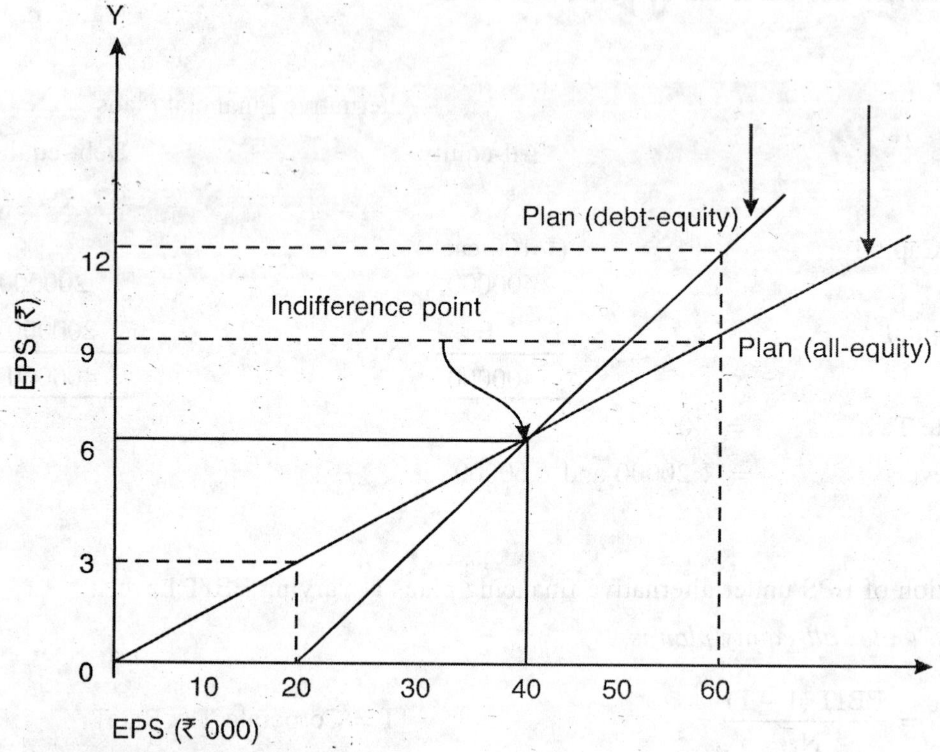

Indifference point calculation:

$$\frac{EBIT\ (1 - T)}{N_1} = \frac{(EBIT - 1)\ (1 - T)}{N_2}$$

$$\text{Or, } \frac{EBIT\ (1 - 0.4)}{4000} = \frac{EBIT - 20000\ (1 - 0.4)}{2000}$$

$$\text{Or, } \frac{EBIT}{4000} = \frac{EBIT - 20000}{2000}$$

$$\text{Or, } \frac{EBIT}{2} = EBIT - 20000$$

Or, EBIT = 2 EBIT – 40000

Or, EBIT = ₹ 40000

We can verify whether EPS is the same under all-equity plan and under debt-equity plan at the EBIT level of ₹ 40000.

$$\text{EPS: All Equity Plan} = \frac{(\text{EBIT} - \text{I})(1 - \text{T})}{N_2} = \frac{40000\,(1 - .40)}{4000} = ₹\ 6$$

$$\text{Debt-Equity Plan} = \frac{(\text{EBIT} - \text{I})(1 - \text{T})}{N_2} = \frac{(40000 - 20000)(1 - .40)}{2000}$$

$$= \frac{20000 \times .60}{2000} = ₹\ 6$$

The X-axis in the graph is used to represent EBIT and the Y-axis to represent EPS. In each of the financing plans, we have to find out EPS value corresponding to zero, that is, the starting point of the financing plan.

All equity plan starts from origin become. EPS would be zero if EBIT is zero. Then we plot EPS value of ₹ 3.00 corresponding to EBIT of ₹ 20000 and ₹ 9.00 corresponding to EBIT of ₹ 60000. Similarly, for debt, equity plan, EPS value is corresponding to EBIT level of ₹ 20000. Therefore, the starting point on origin of debt-equity plan is of EBIT level of ₹ 20000. Then the EPS value of ₹ 12 corresponding to EBIT level of ₹ 60000 is plotted.

The point at which the two lines (All-equity and debt-equity plan) interects, is the indifference point. If we draw a perpendicular to X-axis, we get EBIT ₹ 40000 required for break-even point. Another perpendicular to Y-axis shows the EPS (₹ 6) at the indifference point of EBIT ₹ 40000.

Interpretation:

At ₹ 40000 EBIT level, when EPS is ₹ 6, the firm will be indifference as to the alternative financing plans.

Below indifference point, all equity plans has a distinct advantage over the debt-financing (debt-equity plan) since at any level of EBIT below ₹ 40000, the EPS value under all-equity plan is higher than the EPS value under debt-equity plan. On the other hand, the position changes after the indifference point, where debt-financing under debt-equity plan will be more advantages.

Problem 4

(a) Find the financial leverage from the following data:

Net worth	₹ 28000000
Debt / Equity	2/1
Interest Rate	10%
EBIT (Operating profit)	₹ 15000000

(b) Calculate DOL, DFL and DCL and interpret the results:

Firms	X	Y	Z
Output (units)	60000	15000	100000
Fixed Costs (₹)	7000	14000	1500
Variable cost/unit (₹)	0.20	1.50	0.02
Interest on debt capital (₹)	4000	8000	NIL
Selling price p.u. (₹)	0.60	5.00	0.10

Solution:

(a) $\frac{\text{Debt}}{\text{Equity}} = \frac{2}{1}$ or Debt $= \text{Equity} \times \frac{2}{1}$

$$= \text{Net worth} \times \frac{2}{1}$$

$$= 28000000 \times \frac{2}{1}$$

$$= ₹\ 56000000$$

$$\text{DFL} = \frac{\text{EBIT}}{\text{EBIT} - 1 - \frac{D_p}{1-T}}$$

$$= \frac{15000000}{15000000 - 5600000 - \frac{\text{NIL}}{1-T}} \quad [1 = 10\% \times \text{Debt} = 10\% \times 56000000]$$

$$= \frac{15000000}{9400000} = 1.5957$$

(b) Table: Statement showing leverages

Particular	Firms X	Firms Y	Firms Z
Output (Units)	60000	15000	10000
	₹	₹	₹
Selling price p.u.	0.60	5.00	0.10
Less: Variable Cost p.u.	0.20	1.50	0.02
Contribution p.u.	0.40	3.50	0.08
Total Contribution	24000	52500	8000
Less: Fixed Costs	7000	14000	1500
EBIT or Operating Profit	17000	38500	6500
Less; Interest (1)	4000	8000	NIL
EBIT	13000	30500	6500

Degree of Operating leverage $= \frac{\text{Contribution}}{\text{EBIT}}$	$\frac{24000}{17000}$ = 1.41	$\frac{52500}{38500}$ = 1.36	$\frac{8000}{6500}$ = 1.23
– Degree of Financial Leverage $= \frac{\text{EBIT}}{\text{EBIT}-\text{I}} = \frac{\text{EBIT}}{\text{EBIT}}$	$\frac{17000}{13000}$ = 1.31	$\frac{38500}{30500}$ = 1.26	$\frac{6500}{6500}$ 1.00
– Degree of Combined Leverage = DOL × DFL	1.85	1.71	1.23

High DOL along with high DFL will constitute risky situation. Low DOL along with no – DFL will constitute a cautious approach of management from which it is difficult to maximize the return to the shareholders. Therefore both situations 1st situation shown by firm X and 2nd situation shown by firm Z both should be avoided.

Firm Y is maintaining a position where DOL > DFL and DFL is much lower in compare to DOL. So this situation constitutes a balanced risk. But the limitation is that aggressive debt policy cannot be taken to maximize the return of the equity. So this situation is not the ideal situation.

In all the three firms, DFL < DOL. It is desirable that a firm has low DOL and a high DFL. Viewed from this angle, none of firm X, Y and Z can claim to have adopted an ideal combination of leverage. Among 3 firm, firm Y is showing a little bit good situation with its moderate DCL.

SUMMARY

Leverage describes the ability of a firm to use fixed cost assets or funds to magnify the return to the shareholders. In other words, it implies that, other things remaining constant, a relatively small change in sales results in a large change in income (profit before interest and tax). It may be mentioned that leverage may occur in varying degrees. The higher the degree of leverage, the higher is the risk. Operating leverage arises out of fixed operating costs and financial leverage arises out of fixed financial charges. Operating leverage indicates the degree of operating risk whereas, financial leverage, indicates the degree of financial risk of the firm. Operating risk represents the variability in earnings before interest and taxes (EBIT) due to the risks inherent in the operations of the firm. Variability in EBIT may be due to variability in sales. Financial risk essentially refers to the use of debt capital in the capital structure of the firm.

EBIT – EPS analysis is very useful to examine the effect of financial and (b) with varying levels of EBIT. EBIT-EPS analysis shows the effect of financial leverage on EPS. In planning capital structure, the indifference point is that point at which the after-tax cost of acquisition of outside fund (preference and debt) is equal to the rate of return from the investment. The indifference point is always at the EBIT level at which EPS, on return to equity, are the same regardless of the debt-equity combination.

The total risk involved in a firm can be determined by combining the operating and financial leverages. The Degree of Combined Leverage (DCL) reflects the overall risk of the firm. The utility of DCL lies in the fact that it signifies the effect that changes in sales will have on EPS on EBT, as the case may be. Low operating leverage along with high degree of financial leverage provides a better situation for maximizing return with minimum possible risk. Since the operating leverage is low, full advantage of debt-financing can be taken.

QUESTIONS

A. Short Questions:

1. What is Operating Risk?
2. What is Financial Risk?
3. What is Indifference Point?
4. What is Degree of Operating Leverage?
5. What is Degree of Financial Leverage?
6. What is Degree of Combined Leverage?
7. What is meant by the term 'Leverage'?

B. Broad and Moderate Question:

1. State the meaning of the term 'leverage' and explain various types of leverage used in business terminology
2. Compare and differentiate DFL with DOL.
3. Explain the measures of OL and FL with examples.
4. "Financial Leverage is the firms' ability to use fixed financial charges to magnify the effects of changes in EBIT on the firm's earnings per share" – Do yu agree? Illustrate your answer with an example.
5. Explain EBIT-EPS analysis with an example.
6. Explain 'Indifference point' with an example.
7. Show graph on EBIT-EPS analysis along with indifference point with the help of an example.

PROBLEMS

1. Calculate DFL, DOL and DTL from the following information's:

	₹
Equity Earnings	= 1500000
Quantity produced	= 15000 units
Variable Cost per unit	= 200
Selling price per unit	= 500
No of Equity shares	= 600000
Total Fixed Cost	= 900000
Interest	= 100000
Preference Dividend	= 600000
Corporate Tax	= 40 %

2. Existing Capital Structure of a Limited Co. : 4 million Equity Share of ₹ 10 each

   Tax rate : 40 per cent

   The company has planned to raise additional capital of ₹ 20 million for financing an expansion project. In this context, it is evaluating two alternative financing plans:

   (i) Issne of equity shares (2 million equity shares of ₹ 10 per share), and

   (ii) Issue of debentures carrying 14% interest.

   What will be the EPS under the two alternative financing plans for two levels of EBIT, say ₹ 8 million and ₹ 4 million?

3. Alternative Financial Plans

	All-equity ₹	Debt-equity ₹
Equity Share Capital (₹ 100 each)	8000000	3000000
10 % Debt Capital	NIL	5000000
	8000000	8000000

   Corporate Tax = 45%

   Find out the level of EBIT level at which EPS would be the same under all-equity and under debt-equity plans or find out Break-even EBIT Level or find out indifference point

4. (a) Find the financial leverage from the following data:

Net worth	₹ 56000000
Debt/Equity	2.5/1
Interest Rate	12.5%
EBIT (Operating profit)	₹ 40000000

   (b) Calculate DOL, DFL and DCL and interpret the results:

Firms	X	Y	Z
Output (units)	65000	14000	120000
Fixed Costs (₹)	7000	14000	1500
Variable cost/unit (₹)	0.25	1.57	0.034
Interest on debt capital (₹)	4000	8000	NIL
Selling price p.u. (₹)	0.65	5.07	0.134

5. XYZ LTd. has sales of ₹ 85,00,000, variable cost of ₹ 48,00,000 and fixed cost of ₹ 600,000. The present capital structure of XYZ is given below:

Equity	₹ 65,00,000
Debt (12%)	₹ 55,00,000
Capital Fmployed	₹ 1,20,00,000

(i) What is the ROI of XYZ Ltd?

(ii) Does the company have favourable financial leverage?

(iii) If the industry average of asset turnover is 2, does it have a high or low asset leverage?

(iv) What are the leverages of XYZ?

(v) If sales drop to ₹ 60,00,000, what will be the new EBIT?

(vi) At what level of sales, the EBIT will be zero?

Hints: (i) ROI $= \dfrac{\text{EBT}}{\text{Capital Employed}} = \dfrac{\text{EBIT} - \text{I}}{\text{Capital Employed}} = \dfrac{24{,}40{,}000}{1{,}20{,}00{,}000}$

$$= \frac{(\text{Contribution} - \text{Fixed Cost}) - 12\% \times 5500000}{\text{Debt} + \text{Equity}} = 20.33\%$$

(ii) Since ROI (20.33%) is higher that interest payable on debt (12%), the company have a favourable financial leverage.

(iii) Capital Employed = Total assets = ₹ 1,20,00,000

Net Sales = ₹ 8500000, Turn over ratio $= \dfrac{8500000}{12000000} = 0.7083.$

The industry average is 2 against Co's ratio of 0.7083. Hence Co. has very low asset leverage.

(iv) Operating Leverage $= \dfrac{\text{Contribution}}{\text{EBIT}} = \dfrac{8500000 - 4800000}{(8500000 - 4800000) - 600000}$

$$= \frac{3700000}{3100000} = 1.1935$$

Financial Leverage $= \dfrac{\text{EBIT}}{\text{EBIT} - \text{I}} = \dfrac{3100000}{3100000 - 660000}$

$$= \frac{3100000}{2440000} = 1.2705$$

Combined Leverage $= \dfrac{3700000}{2440000} = 1.5164$

(v) If sales drop to ₹ 60,00,000 from ₹ 85,00,000 the fall is by $\dfrac{8500000 - 6000000}{8500000} \times 100$ or 29.41%.

Hence EBIT will drop by:

% fall in sales × Operating leverage = 29.41% × 1.1935 = 35.10%

∴ New EBIT will be : Old EBIT × (1 – 35.10%)

= 3100000 × (1 – 35.10%)

(vi) EBT to become zero means, 100% reduction in EBT. Since the combined leverage is 1.5164, sales have to drop by $\frac{100}{1.5164}$ or by 65.95%.

Hence new sales will be : ₹ 8500000 × (1 – 65.95%)

❑ ❑ ❑

14 Capital Structure Theories and Planning

14.1 CONCEPT OF CAPITAL

There are two possible approaches to the concept of capital.

(a) **Fund Capital:** Capital is the sum total of the funds employed for running the business operations which may also be treated as financial capital.

(b) **Asset capital:** Capital is amount invested in fixed assets and current assets. In both cases, the assets may be comprising either tangibles or intangibles including fictitious assets.

As per fund concept, capital refers to both long-term and short-term capital comprising all the items of liability side of a balance sheet. As per asset concept, capital comprises all the items of the asset side.

14.2 CONCEPT OF CAPITAL STRUCTURE, ITS IMPORTANCE

The capital structure of a company refers to the mix of long-term finances used by the firm. It is the financing plan of the company.

The primary objectives behind forming a capital structure are maximizing the value of the firm *vis-a-vis* of the equity shares on company's market price per share or minimizing the cost of capital of various sources of long term funds. The strategy behind forming a sound capital structure would be the best or ideal mix of debt and equity. The decision involving forming sound capital structure is investment decision. Value of firm is dependent on expected EBIT and required rate of return.

The capital structure decision is a significant managerial decision which influences the risk and return of the investors. The company will have to plan its capital structure at the time of promoting itself and also subsequently whenever it has to raise additional funds for various new projects. Whenever the company needs to raise finance, it involves a capital structure decision because it has to decide the amount of finance to be raised as well as the source from which is to be raised.

14.3 PROCESS OF CAPITAL STRUCTURE DECISIONS (DIAGRAMMATIC REPRESENTATION)

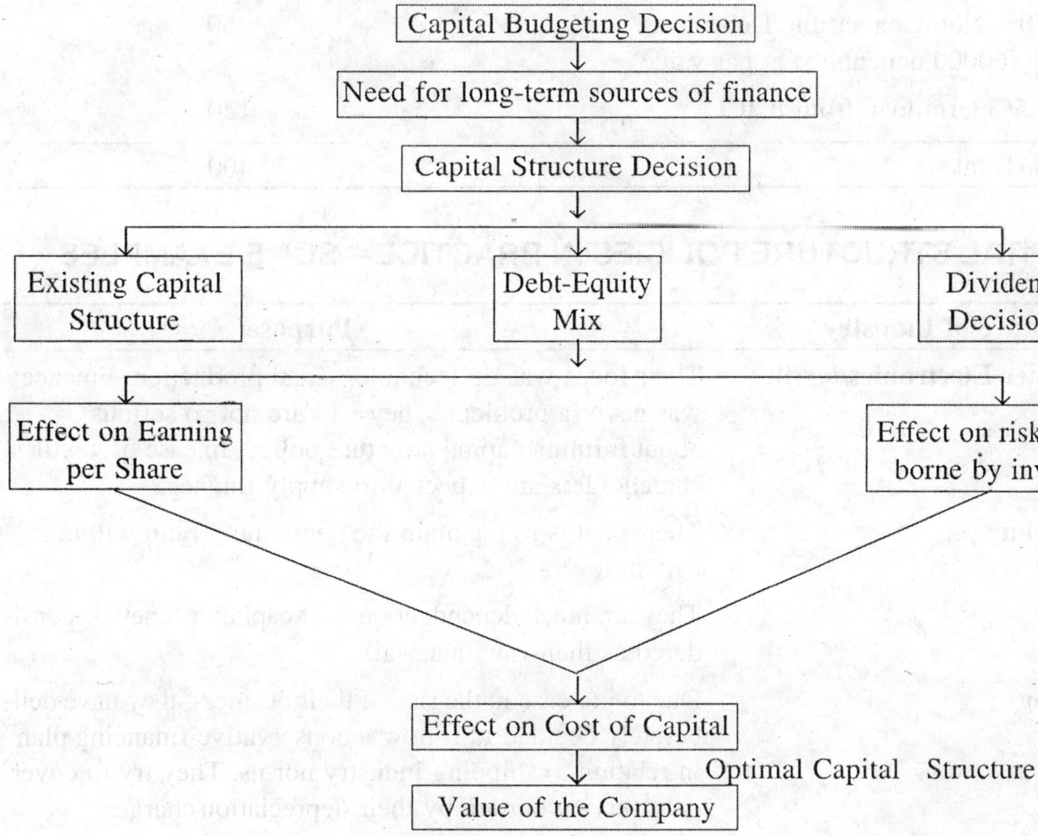

14.4 EXAMPLE OF A CAPITAL STRUCTURE

A public limited company has the following capital structure:

Sources of long-term funds	₹ in crores
(i) Equity Share Capital (10 crores shares at par value)	100
(ii) 11% Preference Share Capital (20 lakh shares at par value)	20
(iii) Retained earnings	100
(iv) 10% Non-Convertible Debenture (60000 debentures at par value)	60
(v) 12.5% term loan from ICICI	120
Total	400

14.5 CAPITAL STRUCTURE POLICIES IN PRACTICE – SOME EXAMPLES

Nature of Industry	Purpose
1. Consumer Electronics/textiles	Their focus was on technology and production. Finance was never a problem. They still are not so serious about forming capital structure policy. In case of textiles, shareholders are expected to supply finance.
2. Aluminum	Their goal is to maintain the debt-equity ratio within a certain level.
3. Leasing	They are much dependent on debt capital. Money is considered as their raw material.
4. Shipping	Due to increase in the risk of their business, they have deliberately decided to follow a conservative financing plan in relation to shipping industry norms. They try to cover debt service burden by their depreciation charges.
5. Truck	The capital structure of the company is carefully planned for optimum financial leverage, while the following corporate objectives for a stable funding pattern are retained: (1) All fixed assets to be funded only by long-term funds, *i.e.,* equity + long-term borrowings. (2) At least 50% of working capital; to be funded only by long-term fund, *i.e.,* equity + long-term borrowings. (3) Total debt to equity ratio not to exceed to 1:1

6. Pharmaceuticals	Earlier, they had a very conservative capital structure. They are now levering themselves, and have set a debt-equity norm of 1.7: 1. This will give them some margin, given the governmental norm of 2:1.

Still many firms in India, have not been able to define their capital structure policy with definitiveness seem to be as follows:

(a) Lack of Long Experience with debt – The experience of the above mentioned firms with debt finance is apparently not sufficiently long to provide a sound basis for delineating their capital structure policies definitively.

(b) Widening of the Instruments of Financing – The range of the instruments of financing has widened over the years. Convertible debentures which were relatively unknown in past years, have assumed great significance in recent years. Likewise, leasing and the purchase are becoming important.

(c) Changing complexion of business risk – The pace of change in the Indian industry has quickened with the introduction of new products and services, adoption of modern techniques, intensification of competition, and shifts in consumer tastes and preferences. These developments are naturally altering the complexion of business risk. In such a situation, it becomes somewhat difficult to articulate capital structure policies because the degree of financial risk a firm can assume depends considerably on the level of its business risk.

Public limited companies are not using as much debt as expected from them (the usual expectation being 2:1 in favour of debt and equity). As against the declaring policy of 1:1 debt – equity ratio, madc by Govt. of India in June 1961, the public enterprises are very close to the declared policy keeping in view the profitability of them.

14.6 GUIDELINES FOR CAPITAL STRUCTURE PLANNING

Planning capital structure means selecting a desired debt-equity combination in advance. The initial capital structure is determined at the time the firm is promoted. So this structure should be designed very carefully. While planning the capital structure, the interest of the equity shareholders is given due weightage. This is done by setting the firm's objective to maximize, in the long-term, the market price of equity shares.

Ultimately, planning a capital structure depends upon the particular need of a firm. A finance manager, while planning the capital structure, he has to consider a number of factors mentioned below. No individual factor is completely satisfactory in itself, rather taken factors collectively; they provide that finance manager with sufficient information for making a rational decision.

Factors for capital structure planning:

(i) Tax advantage of Debt – Debt financing gives rise to tax shelters which enhances the value of the firm lowering cost of debt capital. This is evident from the following cost of debt capital:

$K_d = r(1 - t)$

Where, K_d = cost of debt capital (after tax)

t = corporate tax rate

r = rate of interest= before tax cost of debt-capital.

Example

The interest rate of debenture, with a face value of ₹100 is 9%.

Corporate tax rate is 40%. What will be the after-tax cost of debt capital?

Solution

After-tax cost of debt, $K_d = r(1 - t)$

= 9% (1 – 40%)

= 9% (1 – 0.40)

= 5.4% tax

5.4% is the after-tax cost of debt capital showing lower cost of debt burden after getting tax advantage.

(ii) Finance Leverage: See Chapter 13

(iii) Operating Leverage: See Chapter 13

(iv) EBIT-EPS Analysis: See Chapter 13

(v) Cost of Capital: See Chapter 7

(vi) Cash Flow Analysis: See Chapter 18

(vii) Flexibility: A company should not exploit its debt capacity fully. By doing so, it losses, flexibility which can erode shareholder's value. Flexibility implies that the firm maintains reserve borrowing power to enable it to raise debt capital to respond to unforeseen changes in government policies, recessionary conditions in market place, disruption in supplies, decline in production caused by power shortage or labour unrest, intensification in competition, and, perhaps most importantly, emergence of profitable investment opportunities. The firm must maintain some unused debt capacity as an insurance against adverse future developments. Flexibility is a powerful defense against financial distress and its consequences which may include bankruptcy. Flexibility on financial slack is more valuable to a firm with abundant growth opportunities.

(viii) Reasonable Total Risk Exposure: Generally, the affairs of the firm are, or should be, managed in such a way that the total risk borne by equity shareholders, which consists of operating risk plus financial risk, is not unduly high. If the firm has a low business risk profile, it can assume a high degree of financial risk, otherwise not. Financial risk represents the risk emanating from financial leverage.

14.7 FEATURES OF AN OPTIMAL CAPITAL STRUCTURE

An optimal capital structure should have the following features:

(i) **Profitability** – The Company should make maximum use of leverage at a minimum cost.

(ii) **Flexibility** – The capital structure should be flexible to be able to meet the changing conditions. The company should be able to raise funds whenever the need arises and also retire debts whenever it becomes too cost to continue with that particular source.

(iii) **Control** – The capital structure should involve minimum dilution of control of the company.

(iv) **Solvency** – The excessive interest payment on debt threatens the solvency of the company. Now the Indian companies are launching public issues with the sole purposes of reducing debt.

14.8 THEORIES OF CAPITAL STRUCTURE

The key question with which we are concerned is whether a firm can affect its total valuation (debt–plus equity) and its cost of capital by changing its financial mix. That is, what happens to the total valuation of the firm and to its cost of capital when the ratio of debt to total capital or degree of leverage is varied? First of all, one should know whether there is any relationship between the financial leverage and firm valuation. To understand this many approaches have been propounded, some say that these exists a relationship between the two, and some state that there is no relation.

Assumptions:

(a) There are only two long-term sources of fund-debt and equity;

(b) There is no corporate tax;

(c) Company's dividend payout ratio is 100%, *i.e.,* company pays off the entire earnings to its equity shareholders;

(d) Total assets of the company do not change since, the firm does not invest further in its assets;

(e) EBIT or operating profits are not expected to grow, *i.e.,* payment of dividend is not expected to grow;

(f) All the investors are assumed to have same expectations about the future profits;

(g) The company can change its capital structure or degree of leverage either by issuing shares to retire debt or by raising more debt to redeem the shares;

(h) The company's business risk is taken as constant over time and is independent of the capital structure and financial risk of the company;

(i) The company has infinite life.

Terms and Symbols:

(i) Cost of equity capital (K_e) = $\frac{D_1}{P_0} + g$

Where, D_1 = Dividend to the paid after 1 year

P_0 = Current market price

g = expected growth rate

Since, g = 0, due to the 5th assumption mentioned above $K_e = \frac{D_1}{P}$

Since, payout ratio = 100% as per 3rd assumption mentioned above,

$D_1 = E_1$ = Earnings per share after 1 year.

$$\therefore \quad K_e = \frac{E_1}{P_0} = \frac{E_1 \times N}{P_0 \times N} \text{ (N= no. of equity shares)}$$

$$\text{Or,} \quad K_e = \frac{NI}{S}$$

EBT = NI = Net income available to equity shareholders = EBIT – I

S = Total Market Value of equity share

(ii) M.V of Equity Share Capital: (S)

$$K_e = \frac{NI}{S}$$

$$\text{Or,} \quad S = \frac{NI}{K_e}$$

• Cost of debt capital (K_d) = $\frac{\text{Total Interest Payment}}{\text{Total M.V. of debts}} = \frac{I}{B}$

• M.V of debt capital: (B)

$$k_d = \frac{1}{B}$$

$$\text{Or,} \quad B = \frac{1}{K.d}$$

• Overall cost of capital (K_0) : or Weighted average cost of capital (WACC)

Source	M.V.	Proportion	Cost of Capital	Weighted Cost of Capital (K_0)
Debt	B	$\frac{B}{V}$	K_d	$K_d.\frac{B}{V}$
Equity	S	$\frac{S}{V}$	K_e	$K_e.\frac{S}{V}$
Total	V = B + S			$K_0 = K_d.\frac{B}{V} + K_e.\frac{S}{V}$

$$(\text{WACC}),\ K_0 = K_d.\frac{B}{V} + K_e.\frac{S}{V} \quad [\text{V= total market value of the firm}]$$

$$= \frac{B.K_d}{V} + \frac{S.K_e}{V}$$

$$= \frac{\text{Total Interest Payment}}{V} + \frac{\text{Net Income available to equity share holders}}{V}$$

$$= \frac{1}{V} + \frac{NI}{V}$$

$$= \frac{I + NI}{V} = \frac{NOI}{V} \quad [\text{Net Operating Income, NOI = I + NI = EBIT, no taxes}]$$

$$= \frac{EBIT}{V}$$

$$\therefore K_0 = \frac{EBIT}{V}$$

or $$V = \frac{EBIT}{K_0}$$

There are a number of theories that explain the relationship between cost of capital, capital structure and value of the firm. They are:

A. Net Income Approach (NI Approach)

This approach has been suggested by David Durand. According to this approach, the company is able to increase its total valuation (V), and lower its cost of capital (K_0), as it increases the degree of leverage $\left(\frac{B}{S}\right)$ and capital structure decision is relevant to valuation of the company.

As the ratio of debt to equity $\left(\frac{B}{S}\right)$ increases, the WACC declines and Market Value of firm (V) increases due to use of debt on increase of debt. Reduction in the cost of capital (K_0) with more and more use of debt capital and increase in the value of the firm will be possible when –

(a) $K_d < K_e$ and K_d remain constant.

(b) The firm's risk perception does not change with the increase in degree of leverage.

Assumptions:

So NI approach makes the above two points as assumptions and also another assumptions as follows:

(a) The use of debt capital does not change the risk perceptions of investors and therefore, cost of debt (K_d) and cost of equity (K_e) also remains same irrespective of the degree of leverage.

(b) Cost of debt is less than cost of equity, *i.e.*, $K_d < K_e$.

(c) The corporate tax does not exist.

The following graphical representation of net income approach may help us to understand the letter:

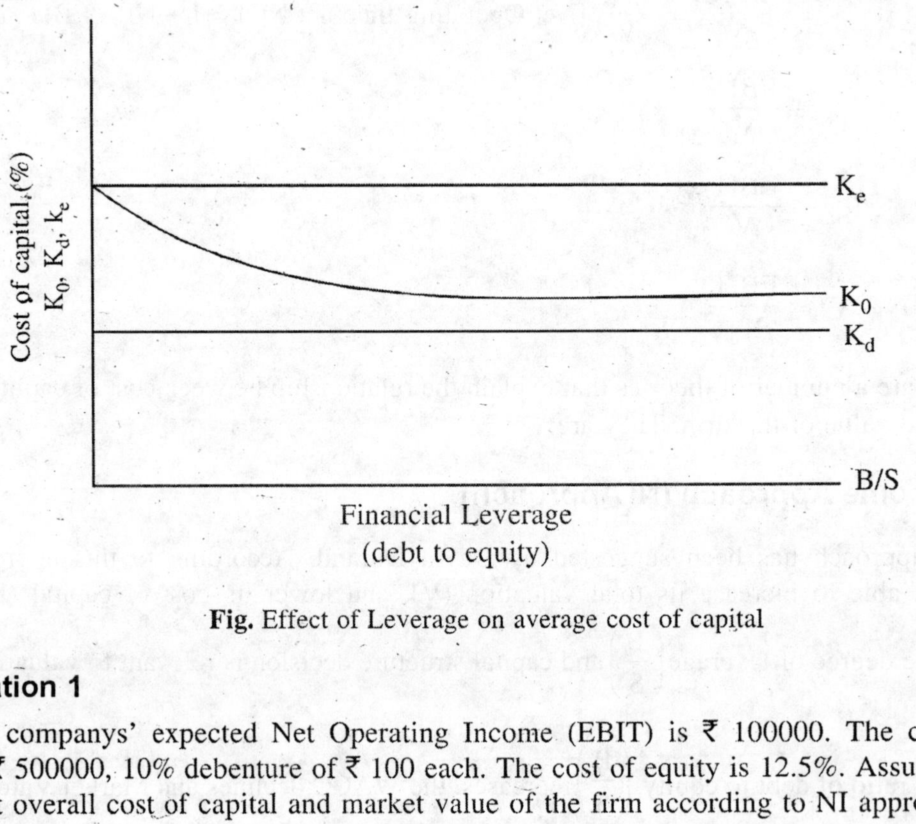

Fig. Effect of Leverage on average cost of capital

Illustration 1

A companys' expected Net Operating Income (EBIT) is ₹ 100000. The company has issued ₹ 500000, 10% debenture of ₹ 100 each. The cost of equity is 12.5%. Assume no taxes; find out overall cost of capital and market value of the firm according to NI approach under 2 conditions:

Condition 1: when debt capital (M.V of debt) is ₹ 500000.

Condition 2: when debt capital (M.V of debt) is ₹ 600000.

Solution

Particular	Condition 1	Condition 2
EBIT (₹) [NOI]	100000	100000
Less: Interest (I) @ 10%	50000	60000
Earnings available to equity shareholder (NI)	50000	40000
Cost of equity capital (K_e)	12.5%	12.5%
(a) B = M.V of debt (₹)	500000	600000 (increases)
(b) S = M.V of equity (₹)		
$= \frac{NI}{K_e}$	$\frac{50000}{12.5\%}$	$\frac{40000}{12.5\%}$
	= 400000	= 320000
(c) V = B + S (₹)	900000	920000 (increases)
(d) Overall cost of capital (K_0)		
$= \frac{EBIT}{V}$	$\frac{100000}{900000}$	$\frac{100000}{920000}$
	= 11.1%	= 10.87% (decreases)
Alternatively,		
WACC (K_0)	$\frac{B}{B+S}.K_d + \frac{S}{B+S}K_e$	$\frac{B}{B+S}.K_d + \frac{S}{B+S}K_e$
	$\frac{500000}{900000} \times 10.0\%$	$= \frac{600000}{920000} \times 10.0\%$
	$+ \frac{400000}{900000} \times 12.5\%$	$+ \frac{320000}{920000} \times 12.5\%$
	= 11.1%	= 10.87%
Degree of Financial Leverage (β/S)	$\frac{500000}{400000}$	$\frac{600000}{320000}$
	= 1.25	= 1.875 (increases)

Problem 1

Given below are two firms – firm A and firm B, which are identical in all respects except the degree of leverage employed by them. The cost of equity is 15%. Assume no taxes. What is the weighted average cost of capital of both the firms from the following informations available:

(a) Expected EBIT = ₹ 100000

(b) Firm B has a debt capital : 10% Debenture @ ₹ 100 each = ₹ 250000

(c) Firm A has no debt capital.

Solution:

Particular	Firm A	Firm B
EBIT (₹) [NOI]	100000	100000
Less: Interest (I) (₹)	Nil	25000
NI (₹)	100000	75000
K_e (Cost of Equity Capital)	15%	15%
(a) B = M.V. of debt	Nil	250000
(b) S = M.V. of equity = $\frac{NI}{K_e}$ (₹)	$\frac{100000}{15\%}$ = 666667	$\frac{75000}{15\%}$ = 500000
(c) V = B + S (₹)	666667	750000
(d) Overall/Weighted Cost of Capital, $K_0 = \frac{EBIT}{V}$	$\frac{100000}{666667}$ = 14.9999% = 15%	$\frac{100000}{750000}$ = 13.3333%
Alternatively		
WACC (K_e)	$\frac{B}{B+S}.K_d + \frac{S}{B+S}K_e$	$\frac{B}{B+S}.K_d + \frac{S}{B+S}K_e$
	$= \frac{0}{666667} \times 10\% + \frac{666667}{666667} \times 15\%$ = 15%	$= \frac{250000}{750000} \times 10\% + \frac{500000}{750000} \times 15\%$ = 13.3333%

B. Net Operating Income Approach: (NOI Approach)

This theory has again be propounded by David Durand. This is just opposite to the NI approach. According to NOI approach, the capital structure decision is irrelevant, to the total valuation of the company. In other words, total valuation of the company is unaffected by its capital structure. This approach is purely definitional, *i.e.,* no behavioral or economic meaning is attached to them.

In broader sense, the MV of the firm will not lead to any change due to change in leverage or capital structure.

$$MV = \frac{NOI/EBIT}{K_o}$$

Where, V = B + S

$= \text{Value of debt} + \text{Value of Equity}$

$K_0 = \text{WACC or overall cost of capital or overall capitalization rate}$

$= \text{Constant.}$

$$K_0 = \frac{B}{B+S} \cdot K_d + \frac{S}{B+S} \cdot K_e$$

If NOI and K_0 is constant, the M.V.(V) of the firm must remain constant regardless of leverage $\left(\frac{B}{S}\right)$.

Assumption:

(i) The market capitalizes the value of the firm as a whole. Thus the split between debt and equity is not important.

(ii) The value of the firm is obtained by capitalizing NOI by the K_0, which depends on the business risk. If business risk is constant, k_0 is also constant. Therefore, $V = \frac{EBIT}{K_0}$

(iii) The use of debt increases the risk of shareholders. So, K_e increases with the leverage and an increase in the use of debt capital is offset exactly by the increases in the cost of equity, K_e. Thus, the weighted average of K_e and K_d remain unchanged for all degrees of leverage, *i.e.,* K_0 is constant.

(iv) Cost of debt (K_d) remains constant regardless of leverage.

(v) Corporate tax does not exist.

(vi) The value of equity, S is found as a residual by subtracting the value of the debt, B from the constant value of the firm V as follows:

$$S = V - B$$

(vii) Since EBIT and K_0 are constant, V is also constant.

$$K_e = \frac{EBIT - I}{S} = \frac{NI}{S} = \frac{EBT}{S}$$

K_e is not constant.

The following graphical representation of net income approach may help us to understand the better:

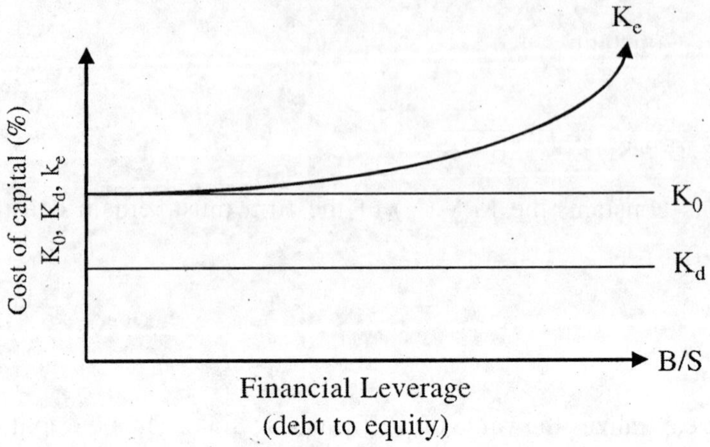

Fig. Effect of leverage on cost of capital

The graph shows that as the firm increases its degree of leverage, it becomes increasingly more risky. So cost of equity (K_e) increases. But use of more cheaper debt capital offset the increases in the cost of equity. K_0 remains constant even though degree of leverage changes.

Illustration 2

Given below are two firms X and Y which are similar, in all respects except the degree of leverage employed:

EBIT = ₹ 100000

K_0 = 12%

K_d = 10%

Interest on Debt (I):

For firm X = ₹ 30000

For firm Y = ₹ 60000

Calculate the Total MV of the equity, leverage and cost of equity capital.

Solution

	Firm X	Firm Y
EBIT (₹) [NOI]	100000	100000
Less: Interest (I) (R)	30000	60000
(Earnings to Equity Shareholder) EBT/NI (₹)	70000	40000
Total MV (V) = $\frac{EBIT}{K_0}$	$\frac{100000}{12\%}$	$\frac{100000}{12\%}$
	(₹) = 833334	= 833334

MV of debt, $B = \frac{K_d}{I}$	$\frac{30000}{10\%}$	$\frac{60000}{10\%}$
	(₹) = 300000	600000
MV of Equity, S = V – B (₹)	533334	233334
Leverage $= \frac{B}{S}$	$\frac{300000}{533334}$	$\frac{600000}{233334}$
	(₹) = 0.5625	= 2.57
Cost of equity capital $K_e = \frac{NI}{S}$ (%)	$\frac{70000}{533334}$	$\frac{40000}{233334}$
	= 13.125%	= 17.143%

Problem 2

Assuming,

Average cost of capital, K_0 = 12%

Cost of debt capital, K_d = 10%

Net Operating Income (or EBIT) = ₹ 15000

Total Capital = ₹ 100000

Calculate the cost of equity, K_e and the value for firm V for the following alternative leverage under NOI approach:

Leverage: 0%, 50% and 100%

Solution

Particulars	Leverage		
	0	0.5	1.0
Capital structure: (₹)			
Debt	Nil	50000	100000
Equity	100000	50000	Nil
Total	100000	100000	100000
EBIT [NOI] (₹)	15000	15000	15000
Less: Interest (I) @ 10% (₹)	Nil	5000	10000
EBT/ NI (₹)	15000	10000	5000
Total MV of the firm			
$V = \frac{EBIT}{K_0}$ (₹)	$\frac{15000}{12\%}$	$\frac{15000}{12\%}$	$\frac{15000}{12\%}$
	= 125000	= 125000	= 125000
MV of debt, $B = \frac{1}{K_d}$ (₹)	----	$\frac{5000}{10\%}$	$\frac{10000}{10\%}$

		= 50000	= 100000
MV of equity S = V - B (₹)	125000	75000	25000
Cost of Equity Capital, $K_e = \frac{NI}{S}$ (₹)	$\frac{15000}{125000}$ = 12%	$\frac{10000}{75000}$ = 13.3%	$\frac{5000}{25000}$ = 20%
K_0	12%	12%	12%
K_d	10%	10%	10%

The value of the firm (V) remains constant at all levels. But cost of equity increases with increase in leverage. In other words, an increase in the use of debt capital is offset by the increase in the cost of equity, K_e. Thus, weighted average cost of capital (K_o) and K_d remains constant for all degrees of leverage.

C. Traditional Approach

The traditional approach is a midway between the net income approach and the net operating income approach, which is known as intermediate approach. As per this approach, the value of the firm can be increased or cost of capital can be reduced by a judicious mix of debt and equity capital. The capital structure that gives the maximum value of the firm and cheapest cost of debt capital is the optimum one.

Propositions:

(i) K_d remains more or less constant up to a certain degree of leverage and thereafter rises at an increasing rate.

(ii) K_e remains more or less constant or rises gradually up to a certain degree of leverage and thereafter rises very sharply.

(iii) K_0, as a consequence of the above behavior of K_e and K_e (a) decreases up to a certain point: (b) remains more or less unchanged for moderate increases in leverage thereafter, and (c) rises beyond a certain point.

Graphical representation: There is a point (P) at which cost of capital (K_0) is minimum.

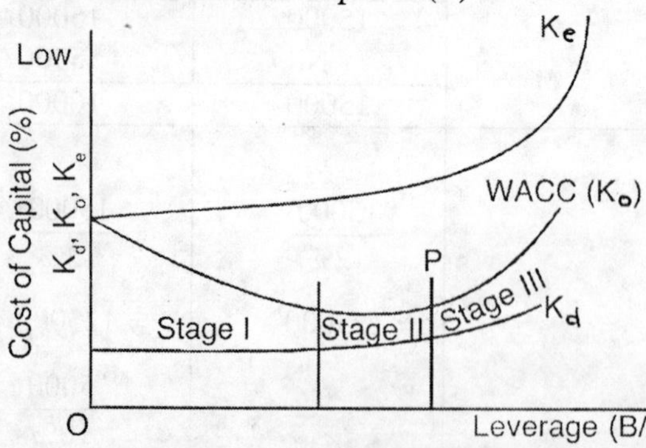

Effect of leverage on cost of capital (Treditional approach)

Problem 3

Total investment	₹ 100000
EBIT	₹ 15000
Cost of Equity:	
Up to ₹ 50000	15%
Beyond that level but up to ₹ 80000	18%
Between ₹ 80001 and ₹ 100000	20%
Cost of debt:	
Up to ₹ 50000	10%
Beyond that level but up to ₹ 80000	13%
Between ₹ 80001 and ₹ 100000	15%

Assuming the following leverage, calculate cost of capital and value of the firm for each level of alternative plans and recommend Debt/ total Capital : 0%, 50% and 100%.

Solution:

Particulars	Leverage		
	0	0.5	1.0
K_d	----	10 %	15%
K_e	20%	15%	----
$K_0 = K_d \times \frac{B}{V} + K_e \times \frac{S}{V}$	20%	12.5%	15%
	$\left(0 \times \frac{0}{100000} + 20 \times \frac{100000}{100000}\right)$	$\left(10 \times \frac{50000}{100000} + 15 \times \frac{50000}{100000}\right)$	$\left(15 \times \frac{100000}{100000}\right)$
EBIT (₹)	15000	15000	15000
Less: Interest (I) [$K_d \times B$] (₹)	NIL	5000	15000
NI/EBT/ Earnings to Equity (₹)	15000	10000	Nil
Value of Debt (B) = $\frac{1}{K_d}$ (₹)	Nil	50000	100000
Value of Equity (S) = $\frac{NI}{K_e}$ (₹)	75000	66667	—
Total MV of the firm: V = B + S (₹)	75000	116667	100000

The above table shows that K_e is lowest (12.5%) and V is the highest (116667), when debt equity combination is 1:1, *i.e.*, ₹ 50000 debt and ₹ 50000 equity in the above case. Therefore, optimum capital structure, in this case, would be ₹ 50000 equity capital and ₹ 50000 debt capital to maximize the value of the firm or to minimize the overall cost of capital.

D. Miller and Modigliani Approach (MM)

MM approach developed a theoretical argument which supports the net operating income approach. Modigliani and Miller have stated that the relationship between leverage and the cost of capital is explained by the net operating income approach in terms of three basic propositions. They argue against the traditional approach by offering behavioral jurisdiction for having the cost of capital, K_0, remain constant through all degrees of leverage. They also argue that, in the absence of corporate tax, the cost of capital and the market value of the firm remain invariant to change in the capital structure or degree of leverage.

Assumption:

(i) The capital markets are perfect. Information is costless and readily available to all informations. There are no transaction costs, and all securities are infinitely divisible.

(ii) Investors are assumed to be rational and behave accordingly, *i.e.*, choose a combination of risk and return that is most advantageous to them.

(iii) The average expected future operating earnings of a firm are subjected by random variables. It is assumed that the expected probability distribution values of all the investors are the same.

(iv) Firms can be grouped into a homogeneous risk classes on the basis of their business risks. All firms falling into one class have the same degree of risk and hence their expected future earnings are capitalized at the same rate.

(v) The dividend payout ratio is 100%.

(vi) There is no corporate tax.

Based on the above assumptions, the MM approach developed two propositions – Proposition I and Proposition II – which are discussed as follows:

Proposition I

The total market value of the firm (V) and its cost of capital (K_0) are independent of its capital structure, *i.e.*, independent of the degree of leverage.

$$V = B + S$$

Or, Total Market Value of the firm = Total MV. of debt + Total MV of equity

Total MV of the firm (V) is established by capitalizing net operating income (NI =EBIT) at a rate appropriate for the firm's risk class:

$$V = \frac{EBIT}{K_o} \quad \text{[EBIT is independent of capital structure]}$$

$$\Rightarrow \quad K_0 = \frac{EBIT}{V}$$

$$\text{Or,} \quad K_0 = K_0 \times \frac{B}{V} + K_e \times \frac{S}{V}$$

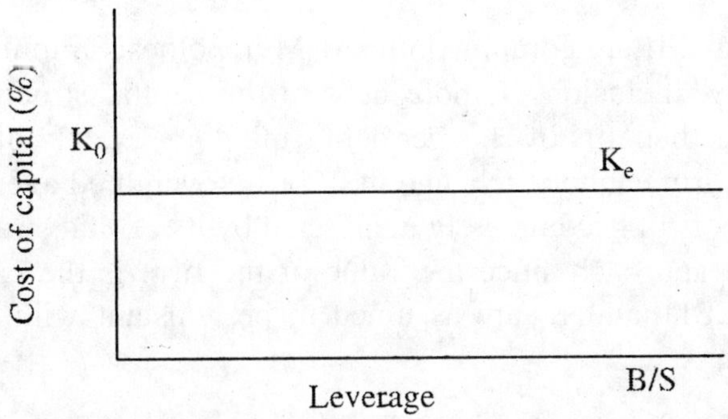

Fig.

Like, NOI approach, the cost of capital K_0 is constant irrespective of changes in the capital structure. The proposition emphasizes the point that K_0 is not affected by financing decisions as both investment and financing decisions are independent.

Proposition II

MM argue that the cost of equity, K_e is equal to a constant average cost of capital, K_0, plus a risk premium that depends on the degree of leverage.

$$K_e = K_0 + \text{Risk Premium}$$

$$\text{Or,} \quad K_e = K_0 + (K_0 - K_d) \times \frac{B}{S}$$

Proposition II implies a linear relationship between K_e and the debt-equity ratio (B/S). K_e increases in a manner to offset exactly the use of cheaper debt capital. In other words, as the firm's use of debt increases, its cost of equity also increases.

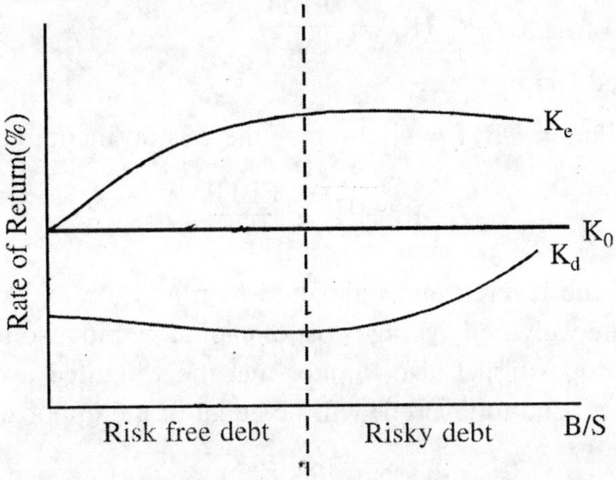

Fig. Implications of MMs Proposition II

The figure assumes that for low levels of debt, the firms' debt is considered risk-free. This implies that K_d is independent of D/E and hence K_e increases likely with D/E. as the debt of the firm crosses a threshold limit, the risk of default increases and K_d increases.

Interpretation of M-M Hypothesis

When proposition I and II are combined, the M-M hypothesis implies that although debt is less expensive than equity, inclusion of more debt in the capital structure of a firm will not increase it's value since the benefits of cheaper debt capital are exactly offset by the increase in the cost of equity. Thus a firm cannot exchange its V or it's weighted average cost of capital, K_0 by leverage. The value of a firm is completely unaffected by its capital structure. MM's approach is a net operating income approach since the value of the firm is the capitalized value of net operating income. Both EBIT and K_0 are assumed to be constant with regard to the level of financial leverage.

Proposition I and Arbitrage Process

Arbitrage is the process of buying of lower price in one market and selling it another market at a higher price bringing about equilibrium.

For a levered firm: The expected net operating income is sum of the income of shareholders and the income of debt-holders.

Income of shareholders = EBIT – I = NI
Income of debt holders = I
Total Net Operating Income = (EBIT – I) + I = EBIT

$$\text{Value of the levered firm} = B + S = V_L = \frac{NOI}{K_L = K_0}$$

$$\text{Expected rate of return of the levered firm} = \frac{\text{Net Operating Income (EBIT)}}{V_L}$$

(Average expected return)

$$\text{Or, } K_L (K_0) = \frac{EBIT}{V_L}$$

In case of unlevered firm:

Income of shareholders = EBIT = NOI (since there is no income of debt holder)

$$K_0 = K_u = \frac{EBIT}{V_u}$$

Since the values of the levered and unlevered firm and the expected NOI do not change with financial leverage, the weighted average cost of capital would also not change with financial leverage. Hence MM's proposition I also implies that the weighted average cost of capital for two identical firms (levered and unlevered) will be equal to the opportunity cost of capital:

$$K_L = K_u = K_o$$

Arbitrage Mechanism: (Proof of MM Argument)

The basic argument for Proposition I is that equilibrium is restored in the market by the arbitrage mechanism. The simple logic of Proposition I is that two firms, being levered and unlevered firms, with identical assets cannot command different market values, irrespective of how these assets have been financed. Suppose this was not true and two firms, except for their capital structures, have different market values. In this situation, arbitrage (switching) will take place to enable investors to engage in the personal leverage as against the corporate leverage to restore equilibrium in the market. The switching operation will continue till the market prices of two firms become identical. To prove their argument, MM suggested an arbitrage mechanism. Two firms X (unlevered, *i.e.*, no debt capital) and Y (leverage, having D/E) in the same risk class and same expected NOI or EBIT but with varying financial leverages are considered.

	X Unlevered	Y Levered	Remark
Expected EBIT	0	0	same
Market value of Equity	S_x	S_y	
Market value of debt	—	β_y	
Market value of the firm	S_x	$\beta_y + S_y$	
	$= V_x$	$= V_y$	$V_x < V_y$
Interest rate on debt	—	r	
I = interest	—	$r \times \beta_y$	

Consider the case where in the unlevered firm has a market value which is less than that of the levered firm Y ($V_x < V_y$). Now if an investor holds S_y rupees worth of equity shares (s_y) of firm Y, representing a fraction of the total outstanding market value of equity shares of firm Y ($s_y = \propto S_Y$), the return he gets is:

$P_y = \propto (o - r\ \beta_y)$ .... Eq. (i)

If the same investor sells his shares, *i.e.*, $\propto S_y$ worth of shares of firm Y and borrows $\propto$ by at an interest rate of r percent or his personal account, thus he can purchase $\propto \frac{(S_y + \beta_y)}{S_x}$ of the equity shares of firm X. (for firm X, $V_x = S_x$ since it is an all-equity firm).

After the above transactions, the return obtained by the investor would be:

$$P_x = \propto \frac{(S_y + \beta_y)}{S_x}\ 0 - r \propto \beta y$$

$$= \propto \frac{V_y}{V_x}\ 0 - r \propto \beta y \text{ ....Eq. (ii)}$$

Comparing the above equation (i) and (ii), we find that as long as $V_y > V_x$ we have $P_x > P_y$ which means that the equity shareholders of firm Y will sell their shareholding and acquire shares of firm X by resorting to personal leverage since it is profitable to do so. The difference in the values of the levered firm and the unlevered firm would be abolished by the personal leverage of the investors.

Next is the case which $V_x > V_y$. say $\frac{V_x}{V_y} = \beta > 1$. For instance, if an investor holds equity shares worth S_x of firm X, representing a fraction $\propto_x$ of the total MV of the outstanding shares, S_x , the return he gets is:

$$P_x = \frac{s_x}{S_x} \; 0 = \propto 0$$

If he sells his shareholding worth $\propto V_x$ $(V_x = S_x)$ he can buy a fraction $\propto\beta$ of the equity shares and bonds of firm Y because the MV of the firm X is β times the market value of the firm Y which will therefore make his return equal to:

$$P_y = \propto \beta\, (0 - r\, B_Y) + \propto \beta\, (r\, B_y) = \propto\beta 0$$

Without any change in the level of risk borne by him ....Eq.(iii)

Caring equation (ii) and (iii), we find as long as $V_x > V_y$ $(\beta > 1)$, we have $P_y > P_x$ which means that equity shareholders of firm X will sell their shareholding and buy a portfolio consisting of shares and bonds of firm Y since it is profitable to do so. In this process, V_x will get depressed and V_y will rise till the equality between V_x and V_y is established.

Illustration of Arbitrage Process

Firm X and Y are identical firms in every respect except financial structure. There are no corporate taxes and capital markets are assumed to be perfect. Their relevant particulars are as follows:

	Firm X Unlevered	Firm Y Levered
Equity Capital (₹ 100 per Share)	₹ 800000	₹ 200000
12% Bond	NIL	₹ 600000
Total Capital	₹ 800000	₹ 800000
Net operating Income (EBIT)	₹ 200000	₹ 200000
Equity Capitalization rate (K_e)	15%	16%

According to the traditional position, firm Y may have a higher total value and lower average cost of capital than Firm X. the valuation of two firms is given below:

	Firm X	Firm Y
EBIT (₹) = NOI	₹ 200000	₹ 200000
Less: interest (I) @ 12%	----	₹ 72000
NI = EBT = Earnings	₹ 200000	₹ 128000
K_e = Equity Capitalization rate	0.15	0.16
$S = \frac{NI}{K_e}$	₹ 1333333	₹ 800000

	Firm X	Firm Y
$B = \frac{I}{K_d} = \frac{72000}{12\%}$	----	₹ 600000
$V = MV$	₹ 1333333	₹ 1400000
Cost of Capital $= \frac{EBIT}{V} = K_0$	$\frac{200000}{1333333}$ = 15%	$\frac{200000}{1400000}$ = 14.29%
Leverage $= \frac{B}{V}$		$\frac{600000}{1400000}$ = 0.42857 = 42.86%

Thus, the value of the levered firm Y exceeds that of the unlevered Firm X, and MM argue that this situation cannot continue as arbitrage will drive the total values of the two firms together.

Say, Mr. Narayan is a rational investor and owned 10% shares worth ₹ 80000 (market value) in Firm Y. According to MM, one can increase his/her total returns without increasing financial risk by:

(a) Selling the shares in Firm Y for ₹ 80000:

(b) Borrowing an amount equal to 10% of firm Y's debt (₹ 600000 × 10% = ₹ 60000) at 12%; and

(c) Buying 10% of X's shares for ₹ 133333(10% of 1333333)

Now, the investor has received ₹ 140000 from sale of shares (₹ 80000) plus borrowing (₹ 60000) and spend ₹ 133333 on firm X's shares, so he has an uncommitted fund of ₹ 6667 (*i.e.*, 140000 – 133333). Now considering the income position of the investor:

Particulars	₹	₹
Old income: 16% of Y's ₹ 80000		12800
New income: 15% of X's ₹ 133333	20000	
Less: 12% of ₹ 60000	7200	12800

Thus his income from investment is exactly the same as before, but he has left ₹ 6667 left over for investment elsewhere, so his total return will rise. But the risk is the same as before he has simply substituted personal or "home-made" leverage for corporate leverage.

According to MM, the action of a number of investors undertaking similar arbitrage transactions will tend to drive up the price of the firm X's shares, and lower its K_e, drive down the price of firm Y, and increases it's K_e. The arbitrage process will continue until there is no further opportunity for reducing ones' investment outlay and achieving the same rupee return. At this equilibrium, the total value of the two firms must be same. As a result, their average cost of capital, K_o also must be same.

The important thing is the purchase of rational investors in the market who are willing to submit personal leverage for corporate leverage.

Criticism of the MM hypothesis

The leverage irrelevance theorem of MM is valid if the perfect market assumptions underlying their analysis are satisfied. The real world, however, is characterized by various imperfections:

(i) Firms are liable to pay taxes on their income. In addition, investors who receive returns from their investment in firms are subjected to taxes at a personal level.

(ii) Agency cost exists because of the conflict of interest between managers and shareholders and between shareholders and creditors.

(iii) Personal leverage and corporate leverage are not perfect substitutes.

(iv) Bankruptcy costs can be quite high.

(v) Manager seems to have a preference for a certain sequence of financing.

Problem 4

The following are costs and values of XYZ Ltd. (unlevered) and ABC Ltd. (levered) according to Traditional Approach.

	XYZ Ltd.	ABC Ltd.
(i) NOI = EBIT (₹)	20000	20000
(ii) $I = K_d \times B$, Interest on Debt (₹) @ 12%	—	7200
(iii) NI = Earnings available to equity shareholder	20000	12800
(iv) K_e = Equity Capitalization rate	15%	16%
(v) $\frac{NI}{K_e}$ = S = Market Value of Equity (₹)	133334	80000
(vi) $\frac{I}{K_d}$ = B = Market Value of debt (₹)	—	60000 $\left(\frac{7200}{12\%}\right)$
(vii) V = Total MV of the firm (B+S)	133334	140000
(viii) K_0 = Average Cost of Capital (%)		
$= K_d \times \frac{B}{V} + K_e \times \frac{S}{V}$		
$= \left[12 \times \frac{0}{133334} + 15 \times \frac{133334}{133334}\right]$	15%	
$= \left[12 \times \frac{60000}{140000} + 16 \times \frac{80000}{140000}\right]$		14.3%
Debt/Total Capital	0%	$\frac{60000}{140000} \times 100 = 42.86\%$
Debt/Equity	0%	$\frac{60000}{80000} = 0.75$

Compare the equilibrium value for XYZ Ltd. and ABC Ltd., using the MM hypothesis assuming that —

(i) There are no taxes; and

(ii) The equilibrium value of cost of capital (K_0) is 14.5%

Solution:

Particulars	XYZ Ltd.	ABC Ltd.
NOI = EBIT (₹)	20000	20000
I = Interest on Debt (₹)	----	7200
NI = Earnings available to Equity Shareholder (₹)	20000	12800
K_0 = Cost of Capital	0.145	0.145
V = Value of the firm = $\frac{EBIT}{K_o}$	$\frac{20000}{0.145}$	$\frac{20000}{0.145}$
	= 137931	= 137931
B = Market Value of debt (₹)	----	60000
S = Market value of debt = V – B (₹)	137931	77931
K_e = Cost of equity = $\frac{NI}{S}$ (%)	$\frac{20000}{137931} \times 100$	$\frac{12800}{77931} \times 100$
	= 14.5%	= 16.43%

14.9 TAXATION AND CAPITAL STRUCTURE – IMPLICATIONS OF CORPORATE AND PERSONAL TAX FOR THE CAPITAL STRUCTURE, VALUE OF THE FIRM

A. Corporate taxes – (MM Model with corporate tax effect) When taxes are applicable to corporate income, debt financing is advantageous. The value of a firm, when corporate taxation is considered is as follows:

$$V = \frac{O(1-t)}{r} + tB$$

Where, V = value of the firm. (levered firm) = V_L

O = operating income

t = corporate tax rate,

B = market value of Debt

r = capitalization rate applicable to the unlevered firm.

In other words, $V_L = V_u + tB$

Or, V_L = value of the unlevered firm + present value of tax shield arising out of financial leverage or gain from leverage.

Or, $$V_L = \frac{O(1-t)}{r} + tB \qquad \text{... Eq(i)}$$

The combined income of levered firm (debt holders and shareholders) is higher than the unlevered firm by the following amount:

Interest on Debt × tax rate

The value of levered firm is higher than the unlevered firm by the following amount; which is present value tax shield arising out of financial leverage:

$$tB$$

= corporate tax rate × Market Value of Debt.

From the equation (i) it is evident that greater the financial leverage (Debt Capital), greater the value of the levered firm, other things being equal. This implies that the optimal strategy of a firm should be to maximize the degree of leverage in its capital structure.

Equation (i) shows the Modigliani and Miller position after taxing account only corporate taxes.

B. Corporate Taxes and Personal Taxes

When personal taxes are considered, along with corporate taxes, the gain in value per rupee of debt is equal to:

$$\left[1 - \frac{(1-t)(1-t_{pe})}{(1-t_{pd})}\right]$$

Where, t = corporate tax rate

t_{pe} = personal tax rate on equity income

t_{pd} = personal tax rate on debt income.

Value of levered firm

= Value of unlevered firm + gain from leverage

Or, $V_L = V_u$ + gain from leverage

Or, $$V_L = V_u + B\left[1 - \frac{(1-t)(1-t_{pe})}{(1-t_{pd})}\right] \qquad \text{...Eq. (ii)}$$

Where, B = Face value of risk free debt .

From the above equation, we get the following:

When	The value of the firm is
$t_{pe} = t_{pd}$	$V_L = V_u + tB$
$t_{pe} < t_{pd}$	$V_L < V_u + tB$
but $(1 - t_{pd}) > (1 - t)(1 - t_{pe})$	but $V_L > V_u$
$(1 - t_{pd}) = (1 - t)(1 - t_{pe})$	$V_L = V_u$
$(1 - t_{pd}) < (1 - t)(1 - t_{pe})$	$V_L < V_u$

Thus, the effect of financial leverage on levered firms' value depends on corporate tax rate, personal tax rate on equity income, and personal tax rate on debt income.

Effect of financial leverage on levered firm's value with corporate and personal taxes:-

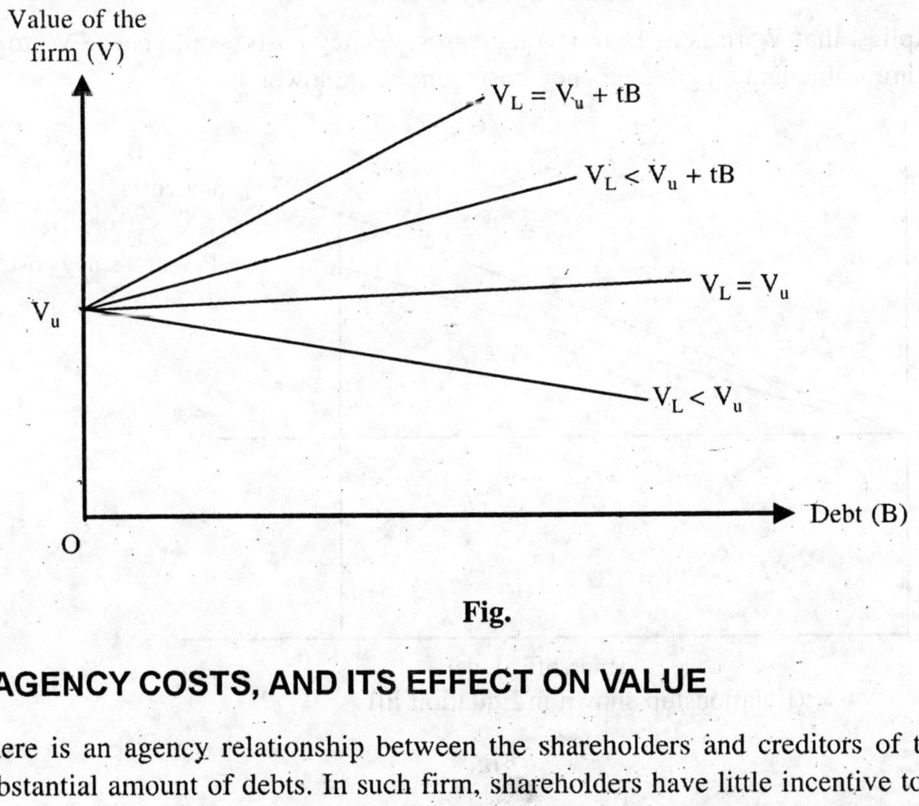

Fig.

14.10 AGENCY COSTS, AND ITS EFFECT ON VALUE

There is an agency relationship between the shareholders and creditors of the firm that have substantial amount of debts. In such firm, shareholders have little incentive to limit losses in the event of a bankruptcy. Hence, managers acting in the interest of shareholders tend to invest in highly risky and volatile projects that increase the wealth of shareholders at the expenses of creditors. So, creditors face the problem of moral hazard when they lend to a firm that has a large outstanding debt in relation to the value of its assets. Because shareholders may exploit creditors in these and other ways, creditors seek protection in the form of various restrictive covenants which may hamper the operational flexibility of the firm. In addition, the firm has to be monitored to ensure that the covenants are also being adhered to and the costs of monitoring are almost invariably passed on to shareholders in the form of higher debt costs. The loss in efficiency on account of restrictions on operational freedom plus the cost of monitoring represent agency costs associated with debt.

Effect of Agency Costs on Value:

$$V_L = V_u + tB$$

If the MM model with tax effect is considered.

Now, considering the agency costs, value of a levered firm may be expressed as,

$V_L = V_u$ + Tax advantage of debt

– Present value of agency costs

Or, $V_L = Vu + tB$ – present value of agency costs ...Eq(iii)

This implies, that V_L rises as Debt (B) increases, agency costs would cause V_L to decline. When assets are stable and tangible, agency costs tend to be lower.

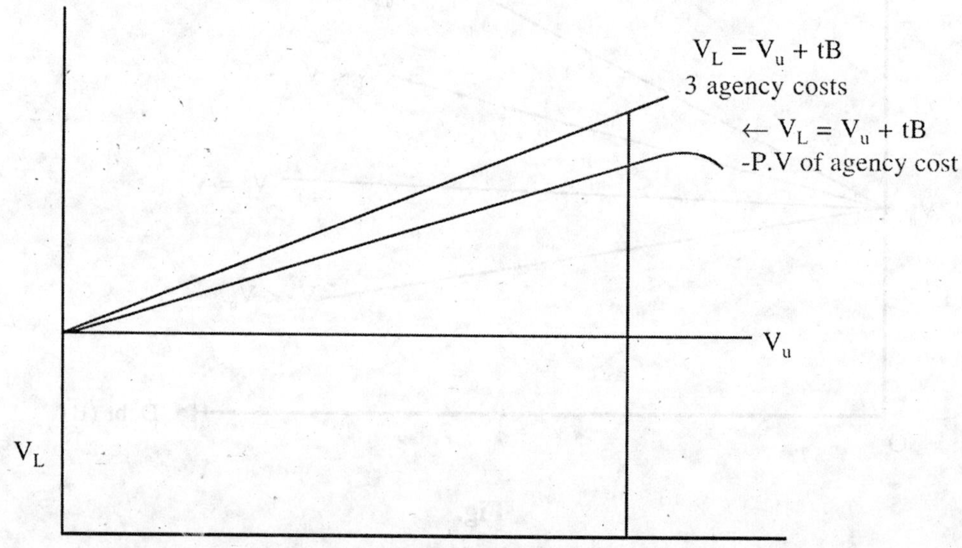

Trade off Model
(Relationship shown in Equation iii)

Fig.

SUMMARY

According to NI approach, overall cost of capital continuously decreases as and when debt goes up in the capital structure. Optimal capital structure exists when the firm borrows maximum. NOI approach believes that capital structure is not relevant. K_0 is dependent business risk which is assumed to be constant. Traditional approach states that K_0 decreases with leverage in the beginning, reaches its maximum point and further increases. Miller and Modigliani approach also believes that capital structure is not relevant. The MM view differs from the traditional view. The theory states that, assuming perfect markets without taxes and transaction costs, a firm's market value and the cost of capital do not change as the capital structure changes. This is because the value of the firm depends on it's net operating income and the risk of its assets (business risk) rather than the way in which the assets have been financed. MM's approach is a NOI approach as the value of the firm is the capitalized value of NOI.

A levered firm uses both equity and debt for financing its assets. On the other hand, an unlevered firm finances its assets only through equity. A firms' overall cost of capital is the weighted average cost of capital of all the firms' securities.

MM's proposition I basically assumes that two firms which belong to the same industry and face similar competitive and business conditions, have the same NOI. The basic argument for Proposition I is that equilibrium is restored in the market by arbitrage mechanism. Arbitrage is the process of buying a security at lower price in one market and selling it another market at a higher price bringing about equilibrium. This is a balancing act.

The unrealistic assumption of MM hypothesis is that, they assume no existence of taxes. Wher orporate taxes are assumed, the market value of the levered firm will be equal to the market value of an all-equity or unlevered firm (V_u) plus the present value of interest tax shield (TB); $V_L = V_u + TB$; when taxes are applicable to corporate income, debt financing is advantageous.

EXERCISE

A. Short Questions

1. What are 'agency costs'?
2. What is the difference between a levered firm and unlevered firm?
3. What is the relation between level of debt and probability of financial distress?
4. What is the value of a firm, when corporate taxation is considered?
5. How do you express the beta of the firms' equity?

   $$\left[\textbf{Hints: } \beta_E = \beta_A + \frac{B}{E}(\beta_A - \beta_B)\right]$$

6. What is the MM's second proposition?
7. What is 'arbitrage'?
8. Why are shareholders indifferent to increased leverage when it enhances expected returns?

   [**Hints:** The reason is that an increase in risk which in turn raises the shareholder's required rate of return]
9. Under which approach of capital structure theory, the overall capitalization rate remains constant for all levels of financial leverage, K_d remains constant and K_e increases linearly with financial leverage?

   [**Hints:** NOI approach]

B. Moderate and Broad Questions

1. What is the relationship between leverage and cost of capital as per the net income approach?
2. Discuss the relationship between leverage and cost of capial as per the net operating income approach.
3. What simplifying assumptions are commonly made to study the relationship between capital structure and firm value?
4. Briefly explains the capital structure policies in practice in India with some examples.
5. State NI and NOI approaches. What are the differences between these two?
6. State the propositions of Traditional approach. Show the point with graphical representation when cost of capital (K_o) is minimum under this approach.
7. Explain Miller and Modigliani Approach. Interpret it. Also state its criticisms.
8. Explain 'Arbitrage' mechanism and illustrate arbitrage process with an example.
9. Explain the process of determining value of a firm when there is also personal taxation.
10. What is the effect of agency costs on value of the firm?

Problems

1. The following data are available in respect of two firms. What is the average cost of capital?

	Firm A	Firm B
NOI	₹ 500000	₹ 500000
Interest on debt	Nil	₹ 50000
Equity earnings	₹ 500000	₹ 450000
Cost of equity capital	15%	15%
Cost of debt	Nil	10%
MV of equity shares	₹ 2000000	₹ 1400000
MV of debt	Nil	₹ 400000
Total value	₹ 2000000	₹ 1800000

2. The market value of debt and equity are 10 crore and ₹ 20 crore respectively and their respective costs are 12% and 14%. The overall cost of capital is 13.33%. Assuming the company has a 100% dividend payout ratio and there are no taxes, calculate the net operating income of the firm.
3. A companys' expected EBIT is ₹ 200000. The company has issued ₹ 1000000, 10% debenture of ₹ 100 each. The cost of equity is 12%. Assume no taxes, find out overall cost of capital and market value of the firm according to NI approach under two conditions:

   Condition 1: when debt capital (MV of debt) is ₹ 1000000.

   Condition 2: when debt capital (MV of debt) is ₹ 1200000.
4. Given below are 2 firms X and Y which are similar in all aspects except the degree of leverage employed according to the NOI approach.

	Firm X	Firm Y
EBIT	₹ 10000	₹ 10000
K_o	18%	18%
$V = \dfrac{EBIT}{K_o}$	₹ 55555	₹ 55555

Interest on debt (I)	₹ 1000	₹ 2000
Cost of capital (K_d)	11%	11%

Calculate the following:

(a) Market value of debt (B)
(b) Market value of equity (S)
(c) Leverage (B/S)
(d) Equity Capitalization rates (K_e) for both the firms.

5. The following are the costs and values for the firms A and B according to the traditional approach:

	Firm A ₹	Firm B ₹
Total Value of the firm (V)	₹ 50000	₹ 60000
Market value of debt (B)	0	₹ 30000
Market value of equity (S)	₹ 50000	₹ 30000
Expected Net Operating Income (NOI)	₹ 5000	₹ 5000
Interest (I) = $K_d \times B$	0	₹ 1800
Net income (NI) = NOI – I	₹ 5000	₹ 3200
Cost of Equity, $K_e = \frac{NI}{S}$	10%	10.70%
K_o, Average Cost of Capital	10%	8.33%

Compute the equilibrium value for Firm A and B in accordance with MM hypothesis. Assume that –

(i) taxes do not exist and
(ii) the equilibrium value of K_o is 9.09%

6. X Ltd. and Y Ltd. belongs to the same risk class – these companies are identical in all respects except A Ltd. has no debt in its capital structure where as B Ltd. employs debt in its capital structure. The relevant financial particulars of the two companies are given below:

	A Ltd.	B Ltd.
NOI/ EBIT	₹ 1000000	₹ 1000000
Interest on debt (I)	----	₹ 300000
Equity earnings (NI) = EBIT – I	₹ 1000000	₹ 700000
K_d = Debt Capitalization rate	----	10%
K_e = Equity Capitalization rate	14%	18%
Market value of debt (B)	----	₹ 3000000
Market value of equity (S)	₹ 7142857	₹ 3888888
Total market value (V)= B + S	₹ 7142857	₹ 6888888
Average cost of capital (K_o)	14%	14.52%

Mr. S.K. Route owns ₹ 100000 worth of A Ltd's equity. What arbitrage will be the resort to?

[Hints: As a rational investor, S.K. Route would do well as:

1. Sell his equity holding of ₹ 100000 in A Ltd.
2. Buy 1.452% of equity as well as debt of B Ltd.(This is what A Ltd. can buy with ₹ 1000000)

3. If he does so he sacrifices an income of ₹ 14000 (the income from ₹ 100000 investment in the equity of A Ltd.) but gains an amount of ₹ 14520 (₹ 4356 from debt and ₹ 10164 from equity of B Ltd.)

7. Consider the following information for MN Ltd:

4. EBIT = ₹ 250 million
5. Corporate tax rate = 35%
- Market (as well as book value) = ₹ 400 million
- Capitalization rate applicable to a debt-free firm in the risk class to which MN Ltd. belongs.

What will be the value of MN Ltd. according to the MM approach?

❑❑❑

15 Dividend Policy

15.1 CONCEPT

The dividend policy of a firm determines what proportion of earnings is to be paid to shareholders by way of dividends and what proportion is ploughed back in the firm for reinvestment purpose. Dividends are distributed profits which are distributed among the shareholders as per declaration in annual general meeting. There are basically about two options which a firm has while utilizing its profit after tax. The first option of declaring dividends (either in cash or kind) out of profits after tax, will lead to maximization of the share holders wealth. The second option suits those forms which need funds to finance their long-term projects. However, such projects should have enough growth potential and sufficient profitability.

15.2 IMPACT OF DIVIDEND POLICY (IMPORTANCE)

The dividend policies of the firms have impact on the returns to the shareholders either by the way of dividend receipts or capital gains.

The dividend policy of the firm gains importance especially due to unambiguous relationship that exists between the dividend policy and the equity returns. In other words, investors' expectation can be fulfilled by the dividend decisions.

Dividend policy divides the retention ratio and pay-out ratio (dividend as a per cent of profits), which causes to bring the expected returns to the shareholders.

15.3 MODELS IN WHICH INVESTMENT AND DIVIDEND DECISIONS ARE RELATED: (MODELS TO MAXIMIZE THE MARKET VALUE OF EQUITY SHARES)

Since the principle objective of corporate financial management is to maximize the market value of equity share, the key question of interest is as follows:

"What is the relationship between dividend policy and market price of equity shares?"

The following models discuss this relationship with a objective to maximize the market value of equity shares.

(a) Traditional Position.
(b) Walter Model.
(c) Gordon Model.
(d) Miller Modigliani Position.
(e) Rational Expectancy Model.

(a) Traditional Position

According to the traditional approach to the dividend policy, expounded by Graham and Dott, the stock market places considerably more weight on dividends than on retain earnings.

This approach lays a clear emphasize on the relationship between the dividends and the stock market. The stock value responses positively to hire dividend and negatively when there are low dividends. This view is expressed quantitatively in the following valuation model as follows:

$P = m (D+E/3)$, where, P = Market Price per share,
D = Dividend per share,
E = Earning per share,
m = Multiplier

Limitations: A firm's share price may rise even in case of a low pay-out ratio if its earnings are increasing. It does not necessarily mean that market price per share increases only with increase in the dividend payment or high dividend pay-out ratio.

Moreover, for a firm having a high dividend pay-out ratio with a slow growth rate, there will be a negative impact on the market price of share because of lower earning.

In addition, there may be a few investors of the company who would prefer the dividend to the uncertain capital gains and a few others who would prefer lower taxed capital gains. But it has not been properly explained in the traditional approach.

(b) Walter Model: (Dividend Relevance Model)

Similar to the traditional approach, the dividend policy given by James E. Walter also considers that dividends are relevant and they do affect the share price. In this model he studied the following relationship between the internal rate of return (r) and the cost of capital of the firm ($k = k_e$), to give a dividend policy that maximizes the wealth of the shareholders, *i.e.*, market price per share (P).

$r > K_e$ (Growth Firms): When $r > K_e$, the market price per share increases as the dividend pay-out ratio decreases. The optimal pay-out ratio for a growth firm is nil, where market price per share (P) is maximum. For a growth firm, the earning can be retained as much as possible to re-invest those earnings in the profitable projects.

$r < K_e$ (Declining Firms): When $r < K_e$, the market price per share increases as the dividend pay-out ratio increases. The optimal pay-out ratio for a declining firm is 100%, where market price per share (P) is maximum.

$r = K_e$ (Normal Firms): When $r = K_e$, the market price per share (P), does not vary with the changes in dividend pay-out ratio. Optimal pay-out ratio for a normal firm is irrelevant. In other words, dividend pay-out ratio and hence dividend payment has no effects to the market price of equity share.

Assumptions :

(i) Retained earning is the only source of finance available to the firm with no outside debtor or additional equity used. The firm is an all-equity financed firm.

(ii) r & K_e are assumed to be constant and thus additional investment made by the firm will not change its risk and return profile.

(iii) For a given value of the firm, the dividend per share and the earning per share remain constant.

(iv) Firm has an infinite life.

Based on the above assumptions, Walter put forward the following formula for the valuation of the market price per equity shares as follows:

$$P = \frac{D + \frac{r(E-D)}{K}}{K}$$

When,
P = Market Price per share,
D = Dividend per Share,
= D/P ratio × EPS (E)
r = Internal rate of Return,
K = Cost of Capital,
E = Earning per share,
(E-D) = Retained Earning per share.

Limitations : Most of the limitations arise due to the assumptions made.

The first assumption of exclusive financing by retained earnings make the model suitable only for all-equity firms.

Secondly, assumption of constant return on investments (r) is not true for firms making high investments.

Finally Walter's model on dividend policy ignores the business risk of the firm which has a direct impact on the value of the firms. Thus k cannot be assumed to be constant.

Problem 1

Cost of Capital (k) = 10%. Assumed rate of return on investment (r) :- (i) 15%; (ii) 10% & (iii) 8% respectively. Earning per share (E) = ₹ 10.

Assuming that dividend pay-out ratios are zero, 50%, 75% and 100%, examine the effect of different dividend policies for 3 alternative levels of r.

Solution

Given $k = k_e$ = 10%; E = ₹ 10; $P = \dfrac{D + \dfrac{r(E-D)}{K}}{K}$

(i) r = 15% (when r > k)

(a) D/P ratio = 0 [D = D/P ratio × E = 0% × 10 = 0]

$$P = \frac{0 + \frac{0.15\,(10-0)}{0.10}}{0.10} = \frac{1.5}{0.01} = ₹\ 150$$

(b) D/P ratio = 50% [D = D/P ratio × E = 50% × 10 = ₹ 5]

$$P = \frac{5 + \frac{0.15\,(10-5)}{0.10}}{0.10} = \frac{12.5}{0.10} = ₹\ 125$$

(c) D/P ratio = 75% [D = D/P ratio × E = 75% × 10 = ₹ 7.5]

$$P = \frac{7.5 + \frac{0.15\,(10-7.5)}{0.10}}{0.10} = \frac{11.25}{0.10} = ₹\ 112.50$$

(d) D/P ratio = 100% [D = D/P ratio × E = 100% × 10 = ₹ 10]

$$P = \frac{10 + \frac{0.15\,(10-10)}{0.10}}{0.10} = \frac{10}{0.10} = ₹\ 100$$

(ii) r = 10% (when r = k)

(a) D/P ratio = 0 [D = D/P ratio × E = 0% × 10 = 0]

$$P = \frac{0 + \frac{0.10\,(10-0)}{0.10}}{0.10} = ₹\ 100$$

(b) D/P ratio = 50% [D = D/P ratio × E = 50% × 10 = ₹ 5]

$$P = \frac{5 + \dfrac{0.10\,(10-5)}{0.10}}{0.10} = ₹\ 100$$

(c) D/P ratio = 75% [D = D/P ratio × E = 75% × 10 = ₹ 7.5]

$$P = \frac{7.5 + \dfrac{0.10\,(10-7.5)}{0.10}}{0.10} = ₹\ 100$$

(d) D/P ratio = 100% [D = D/P ratio × E = 100% × 10 = ₹ 10]

$$P = \frac{10 + \dfrac{0.10\,(10-10)}{0.10}}{0.10} = ₹\ 100$$

(iii) r = 8% (when r < k)

(a) D/P ratio = 0 [D = D/P ratio × E = 0% × 10 = 0]

$$P = \frac{0 + \dfrac{0.08\,(10-0)}{0.10}}{0.10} = ₹\ 80$$

(b) D/P ratio = 50% [D = D/P ratio × E = 50% × 10 = ₹ 5]

$$P = \frac{5 + \dfrac{0.08\,(10-5)}{0.10}}{0.10} = ₹\ 90$$

(c) D/P ratio = 75% [D = D/P ratio × E = 75% × 10 = ₹ 7.5]

$$P = \frac{7.5 + \dfrac{0.08\,(10-7.5)}{0.10}}{0.10} = ₹\ 95$$

(d) D/P ratio = 100% [D = D/P ratio × E = 100% × 10 = ₹ 10]

$$P = \frac{10 + \dfrac{0.08\,(10-10)}{0.10}}{0.10} = ₹\ 100$$

Criticism of Walter's Model

(a) It is assumed that all the investments are financed by the firm through retained earnings. Thus it ignores the benefits of optimum capital structure by assuming financing by retained earning only.

(b) Walter states that P would be highest if no dividend are declared where $r > K_e$. Similarly P would be maximum if dividend pay-out ratio is 100% where $r < K_e$. Both of these situations are abnormal and impracticable.

(c) It is assumed in this model that r would remain constant. This stands against real world situation as r generally declines when more and more investment proposals are taken up by the firm.

(d) In practice, the assumption that cost of capital K remains constant, may not hold good because if the risk complication of the firm changes, cost of capital also changes.

(e) Walter's model ignores the effects of risk on the value of firm.

(f) Walter ignores the fact that the market prices of share are dependent on many factors, and the present value of the future expected dividend is only one of them.

(c) Gordon's Model: (Dividend Relevance Model)

Yet another model that has given importance to the dividend policy of the firm is the Gordon Model. Myron Gordon used the dividend capitalization approach to a study the effect of the firm's dividend policy on the stock price. Gordon also contends that dividends are relevant and that dividend policy affects the value of the firm. Gordon's model is based on the following assumptions:

Assumptions:

(i) It is assumed that all investment, are financed by the firm through retained earnings. Thus it ignores benefits of optimum capital structure by assuming financing by retained earning.

(ii) Gordon states that P would be highest if no dividend are declared where $r > k$. Similarly P would be maximum if dividend pay-out ratio is 100% where $r < k$, both of these situations are abnormal and impractical.

(iii) The retention ratio remains constant and hence the growth rate also is constant ($g = br$).

(iv) $k > br$, *i.e.*, cost of equity capital is greater than the growth rate.

(v) Corporate tax does not exist.

Gordon's model assumes that the investors are rational and risk averse. They prefer certain returns to uncertain returns and thus put a premium to the certain returns and discount the uncertain returns. Thus investors would prefer current dividends and avoid risk.

In his model, Gordon studies the following relationship between the internal rate of return (r) and the cost of capital of the firm (k), to give a dividend policy that maximizes the wealth of the shareholders that is market price per share (P).

$r > k_e$ (Growth Firms): When $r > k_e$, the market price per share increases as the dividend pay-out ratio decreases. The optimal pay-out ratio for a growth firm is nil, where market price per share (P) is maximum. For a growth firm, the earning can be retained as much as possible to re-invest those earnings in the profitable projects.

$r < k_e$ (Declining Firms): When $r < k_e$, the market price per share increases as the dividend pay-out ratio increases. The optimal pay-out ratio for a declining firm is 100%, where market price per share (P) is maximum.

$r = k_e$ (Normal Firms): When $r = k_e$, the market price per share (P), does not vary with the changes in dividend pay-out ratio. Optimal pay-out ratio for a normal firm is irrelevant. In other words, dividend pay-out ratio and hence dividend payment has no effects to the market price of equity share.

A simplified version of Gordon's Model is expressed as follows:-

$$P = \frac{E(1-b)}{k-br}$$

Where,
P = Market price per equity share,
E = Earnings per share,
b = retention ratio, *i.e.*, percentage of earnings retained,
(1-b) = Dividend pay-out ratio,
br = g = growth rate in r,
r = rate of return on investment.

Problem 2

If $k_e = 11\%$ and E = ₹ 15, calculate the stock value of Swan Ltd. (i) r = 12%; (ii) r = 11%; (iii) r = 10% for the various levels of D/P ratios.

D/P ratio (1-b)	Retention ratio (b)
(a) 10%	90%
(b) 20%	80%
(c) 30%	70%
(d) 40%	60%
(e) 50%	50%

Solution

(i) $r > k_e$ ($r = 12\%$, $k_e = 11\%$)

(a) D/P ratio = 10%; b = 90%; g = br = 0.90 × 0.12 = 0.108

$$P = \frac{E\,(1-b)}{K_e - br} = \frac{15\,(1-0.9)}{0.11-0.108} = ₹\,750$$

(b) D/P ratio = 20%; b = 80%; g = br = 0.80 × 0.12 = 0.096

$$P = \frac{15\,(1-0.8)}{0.11-0.096} = ₹\,214.28$$

(c) D/P ratio = 30%; b = 70%; g = br = 0.70 × 0.12 = 0.084

$$P = \frac{15(1-0.7)}{0.11-0.084} = ₹\ 173.08$$

(d) D/P ratio = 40%; b = 60%; g = br = 0.60 × 0.12 = 0.072

$$P = \frac{15\ (1-0.6)}{0.11-0.072} = ₹\ 158$$

(e) D/P ratio = 50%; b = 50%; g = br = 0.50 × 0.12 = 0.06

$$P = \frac{15\ (1-0.5)}{0.11-0.06} = ₹\ 150$$

(ii) $r = k_e$ ($r = 11\%$, $k_e = 11\%$)

(a) D/P ratio = 10%; b = 90%; g = br = 0.90 × 0.11 = 0.099

$$P = \frac{E\ (1-b)}{K_e - br} = \frac{15\ (1-0.9)}{0.11-0.099} = ₹\ 136.36$$

(b) D/P ratio = 20%; b = 80%; g = br = 0.80 × 0.11 = 0.088

$$P = \frac{15\ (1-0.8)}{0.11-0.088} = ₹\ 136.36$$

(c) D/P ratio = 30%; b = 70%; g = br = 0.70 × 0.11 = 0.077

$$P = \frac{15\ (1-0.7)}{0.11-0.077} = ₹\ 136.36$$

(d) D/P ratio = 40%; b = 60%; g = br = 0.60 × 0.11 = 0.066

$$P = \frac{15\ (1-0.6)}{0.11-0.066} = ₹\ 136.36$$

(e) D/P ratio = 50%; b = 50%; g = br = 0.50 × 0.11 = 0.055

$$P = \frac{15\ (1-0.5)}{0.11-0.055} = ₹\ 136.36$$

(iii) $r < k_e$ ($r = 10\%$, $k_e = 11\%$)

(a) D/P ratio = 10%; b = 90%; g = br = 0.90 × 0.10 = 0.09

$$P = \frac{E\ (1-b)}{K_e - br} = \frac{15\ (1-0.9)}{0.11-0.09} = ₹\ 75$$

(b) D/P ratio = 20%; b = 80%; g = br = 0.80 × 0.10 = 0.08

$$P = \frac{15\ (1-0.8)}{0.11-0.08} = ₹\ 100$$

(c) D/P ratio = 30%; b = 70%; g = br = 0.70 × 0.10 = 0.07

$$P = \frac{15\ (1-0.7)}{0.11-0.07} = ₹\ 112.50$$

(d) D/P ratio = 40%; b = 60%; g = br = 0.60 × 0.10 = 0.06

$$P = \frac{15\ (1-0.6)}{0.11-0.06} = ₹\ 120$$

(e) D/P ratio = 50%; b = 50%; g = br = 0.50 × 0.10 = 0.05

$$P = \frac{15\ (1-0.5)}{0.11-0.05} = ₹\ 125$$

The above illustration explains the relevance of dividends as given by the Gordon's model. In the given three situations the firm's share value is positively correlated with the pay-out ratio when $r < k_e$ and decreases with an increase in the pay-out ratio, when $r > K_e$. Thus firms with a rate of return greater than the cost of capital should have a higher retention ratio and those firms which have a rate of return less than the cost of capital should have a lower retention ratio. The dividend policy of firms which have a rate of return equal to the cost of capital will, however, not have any impact on its share value.

Limitations: Some of the assumptions of this model are identical with those made in Walter's model. When r = k, dividend policy has no relevance to the value of the share, when r < k the firm should distribute all earnings as dividend, when r > k, the firm should retain earnings so long as the value of b does not exceed k/r. For any value of b exceeding k/r but less than 1, (k – br) becomes negative thus giving negative value for P. These absurd values are obtained because of some of the unrealistic assumptions of the model, such as k and r are constant.

(d) Miller and Modigliani Model: (Dividend Irrelevance Theory)

The MM hypothesis seeks to explain that a firm's dividend policy is irrelevant and has no effect on the share prices of the firm. This model advocates that it is the investment policy through which the firm can increase its share value and hence this should be given more importance.

Assumptions

(i) ***Existence of perfect capital markets:*** All interior are rational and have access to all information free of cost. There is no floatation or transaction costs, securities are infinitely divisible and no single investor is large enough to influence the share value.

(ii) ***No taxes:*** There are no taxes, or there is no tax differential between capital gains and dividends, or between dividends and retained earnings.

(iii) ***Constant investment policy:*** The investment policy of the firm does not change. The implication is that there is no change in the business risk position and the rate of return.

(iv) ***No risk:*** There is certainty about future investments, dividend, and profits of the firm. This assumption was, however, dropped out of the model.

Based on the above assumptions, MM hypothesis have explained the irrelevance of dividend as the crux of the arbitrage argument. *The arbitrage process refers to setting off or balancing two transactions which are entered into simultaneously. The two transactions are paying out dividends and raising external funds to finance additional investment programmes.* If the firm pays out dividend, it will have to raise capital by selling new shares for financing activities. The arbitrage process will neutralize the increase in share value (due to dividends) with the issue of new shares. This make the investor indifferent to dividend earnings and capital gains as the share value is more dependent on the future earnings of the firm than on its current dividend policy.

Symbolically, the model is given as:

Step I:

$$P_0 = \frac{1}{(1+K_e)}(D_1 + P_1) = \frac{D_1}{1+K_e} + \frac{P_1}{1+K_e}$$

i.e., Market Price per share in the beginning = P.V. of Dividends paid + P.V. of market price at the end of period

Where, P_0 = Current Market Price per share,

P_1 = Market Price at the end of the period 1,

D_1 = Dividends to be paid at the end of the period 1,

K_e = Cost of Equity Capital.

Step II: Assuming that there is no external financing, the value of the firm is as follows:

$$nP_0 = \frac{1}{(1+K_e)} \times n(D_1 + P_1) = \frac{1}{1+K_e} \times (nD_1 + nP_1)$$

[When, n = Number of shares outstanding]

Step III: If the firm's internal sources of financing its investment opportunities fall short of funds required, new shares (n_1) are issued at the end of year 1 at price P_1. The capitalized value of the dividends to be received during the period plus the value of the number of shares outstanding is less than the value of new shares.

$$nP_0 = \frac{1}{(1+K_e)} \times \{nD_1 + (n + n_1)P_1 - n_1P_1\}$$

Firms will have to raise additional capital to fund their investment requirements after utilizing their retained earnings, that is,

$$n_1P_1 = I - (E - nD_1)$$

Or, $n_1P_1 = I - E + nD_1$

Where, I = Total investment required,

nD_1 = total dividends paid,

E = earnings during the period,

$(E - nD_1)$ = retained earnings.

Step IV: The value of share is thus:-

$$nP_0 = \frac{1}{(1+K_e)} \times \{nD_1 + (n+n_1)P_1 - n_1P_1\}$$

$$= \frac{1}{(1+K_e)} \times \{nD_1 + (n+n_1)P_1 - (I - E + nD_1)\}$$

$$= \frac{1}{(1+K_e)} \times \{nD_1 + (n+n_1)P_1 - I + E - nD_1)\}$$

or, $$nP_0 = \frac{(n+n_1)P_1 - I + E}{(1+K_e)}$$

Dividend does not figure in the equation to calculate share price.

Thus, according to the MM model, the market value of the share is not affected by the dividend policy and this is explicitly shown in above equation.

Critical Analysis of the Assumptions

The MM approach to the irrelevance of dividends has been based on a few assumptions which need to be evaluated critically especially since a perfect market and absence of floatation costs and transaction costs are situations which do not happen in reality. Few assumptions have been critically viewed below:

Tax Effect: This assumption cannot be true, since in the real world the tax rate for he dividend income is higher than the tax rate applicable to the capital gains.

Floatation Costs: The proceeds which the firm gets from the issue of securities will be net off the issue expenses. The total issue expenses which include the underwriting expenses, brokerage, and other marketing costs will be around 10-15% of the total issue (in India). With the costs of mobilizing capital from the primary market being high, these costs cannot be ignored.

Transaction Costs: This is an unrealistic assumption, since investors do have to incur certain transaction costs like the brokerage expenses while they dispose off their shares. Thus, if the investors are to equate the capital gains to the dividend income, they should sell off the shares at a higher price. In addition to this, the inconvenience and the uncertainty involved in the share price movements make the investors prefer current income by way of dividends to plough back profits.

Marketing Conditions: Sometimes the market conditions do effect the investment decisions of the firm. For instance, through a firm has profitable investment opportunities, the bad market condition may not allow it to mobilize the funds. In such cases, the firms will have to depend on the retained earnings and have a low dividend pay-out ratio. In still other cases, there may be certain sub-standard investment opportunities in which the firm will invest just because there is an easy access to funds from the market.

Underpricing of Shares: If the company has to raise funds from the market, it will have to sell the shares to the new shareholders at a price that is less than the prevailing market price. Thus, with the shares being underpriced the firm will have to sell more shares to replace the dividend amount.

These criticisms and the preference for current income, uncertain market conditions, presence of transaction and floatation costs, under pricing etc. highlight the shortcomings of the Miller and Modigliani's dividend irrelevance policy. Thus, the dividend policy of a company does have an effect on its share value.

Problem 3

The capitalization rate of XYZ Ltd. is 14%. The company has outstanding shares to the extent of 20000 shares selling at the rate of ₹ 100 each. Anticipating a net income of ₹ 355000 for the current financial year, the company has planned to declare a dividend of ₹ 4 per share. The company also has a new project, the investment requirement for which is ₹ 605000. Show that under the MM model, the dividend payment does not affect the value of the firm.

Solution:

(i) the value of the firm, when dividends are paid:

Step I:

$$P_0 = \frac{1}{(1+K_e)}(D_1 + P_1) = \frac{D_1}{1+K_e} + \frac{P_1}{1+K_e}$$

Or, $$100 = \frac{1}{1.14}(4+P_1) \quad \text{or, } P_1 = ₹\ 110$$

Step II: Amount to be raised by the issue of new share:

$$n_1P_1 = I - (E - nD_1) = 605000 - (355000 - 80000) = ₹\ 330000\ [nD_1 = 20000 \times 4]$$

Step III: Number of additional shares to be issued

$$n_1 = \frac{330000}{110} = 3000$$

Step IV: The value of the firm is as follows:

$$nP_0 = \frac{1}{(1+K_e)} \times \{nD_1 + (n+n_1)P_1 - n_1P_1\}$$

$$= \frac{1}{(1+K_e)} \times \{nD_1 + (n+n_1)P_1 - (I - E + nD_1)\}$$

$$= \frac{1}{(1+K_e)} \times \{nD_1 + (n+n_1)P_1 - I + E - nD_1\}$$

or, $$nP_0 = \frac{(n+n_1)P_1 - I + E}{(1+K_e)}$$

$$= \frac{(20000+3000)110 - (605000-355000)}{1.14}$$

$$= ₹\ 2000000$$

(ii) Value of the firm when dividends are not paid:

Step I: $$P_0 = \frac{1}{(1+K_e)}(D_1 + P_1) = \frac{D_1}{1+K_e} + \frac{P_1}{1+K_e}$$

Or, $$100 = \frac{1}{1.14}(0+P_1) \quad \text{or, } P_1 = ₹\ 114$$

Step II: Amount to be raised by the issue of new share:

$$n_1P_1 = I - (E - nD_1) = 605000 - (355000-0) = ₹\ 250000 \ [nD_1 = 20000 \times 0]$$

Step III: Number of additional shares to be issued

$$n_1 = \frac{250000}{114}$$

Step IV: The value of the firm is as follows:

$$nP_0 = \frac{1}{(1+K_e)} \times \{nD_1 + (n+n_1)P_1 - n_1P_1)\}$$

$$= \frac{1}{(1+K_e)} \times \{nD_1 + (n+n_1)P_1 - (I - E + nD_1)\}$$

$$= \frac{1}{(1+K_e)} \times \{nD_1 + (n+n_1)P_1 - I + E - nD_1)\}$$

or, $$nP_0 = \frac{(n+n_1)P_1 - I + E}{(1+K_e)}$$

$$= \frac{(20000 + \frac{250000}{114})\ 114 - (605000 - 355000}{1.14}$$

$$= ₹\ 2000000$$

Thus, according to the MM model, the market value of the share is not affected by the dividend policy since the value of the firm, in both the cases remains the same.

(e) Rational Expectations Model

According to the rational expectations model, there would be no impact of the dividend declaration on the market price of the share as long as it is at the expected rate. However, it may show some adjustments in case the dividends declared are higher or lower than the expected level. For instance, when a firm declares dividends higher than what was expected, it would result in an upward movement of the share price as there would be expectations of higher earnings and similarly low dividends would be taken as a fall in future earnings. Thus the rational expectations model suggests that alterations in the market price will not be necessary where the dividends meet the expectations and only in case of unexpected dividends will there be a change in the market prices as stated above.

15.4 STABILITY OF DIVIDENDS: (INDICATORS)

Stability of dividends is the consistency in the stream of dividend payments. It is the payment of certain amount of minimum dividend to the shareholders. The steadiness is a sign of good health of the firm and may take any of the following forms:

(a) Constant dividend per share,

(b) Constant D/P ratio and

(c) Constant dividend per share plus extra dividend.

(a) Constant dividend per share: As per this norm of dividend policy, a firm pays a fixed amount of dividend per share, year after year. For example, a firm may have a policy of paying 30% dividend on its paid-up capital of ₹ 10 per share. It implies that ₹ 3.00 is paid out every year irrespective of its earnings. Generally a firm following such a policy will continue payments even if it incurs loss. In such years, when there is loss, the amount accumulated in the dividend equalization reserve is utilized.

(b) Constant D/P ratio: With this type of D/P policy (D/P = Dividends payment ratio), the firm pays a constant percentage of net earnings to the shareholders. For example, if a public limited company fixes its D/P ratio as 20% of its earnings, it implies that shareholders get 20% of earnings as dividend year after year.

(c) Constant dividend per share plus extra dividend: Under this policy, a firm usually pays a fixed dividend ordinarily and in years of good profits, additional or extra dividend is paid over and above the regular dividend. The stability of dividends is desirable because of the following advantages:

- Builds confidence amongst investors and remove uncertainty in their minds;
- Investors desire for current income;
- Information about firm's profitability;
- Institution investors (LIC, GIC, MF) requirements;

- Raises additional finance;
- Stability in market price of shares.

15.5 FORMS OF DIVIDENDS

Cash Dividends: The investors, especially the old and retired investors depend on this forms of payment for want of current income.

Scrip Dividends: In this form of dividends, equity shareholders are issued transferable promissory notes with shorter maturity periods which may or may not have interest bearing. This form is adopted if the firm has earned profits and it will take some time to convert the assets into cash. Payment of dividend in this form is done only if the firm is suffering from weak liquidity position.

Bond dividends: Bond dividends carry longer maturity period and bear interest, whereas scrip dividends carry shorter maturity period and may or may not carry interest.

Stock dividend (Bonus Shares): Stock dividend or bonus shares is India, is the distribution of additional shares to the shareholders at no additional cost. This has the effect of increasing the number of outstanding shares of the firm. The reserves and surplus (retained earnings) are capitalized to give effect to bonus issue. The investors are allotted shares in proportion to their present shareholding.

15.6 STOCK SPLIT

A stock split is a method to increase the number of outstanding shares by proportionately reducing the face value of a share. A stock split affects only the per value and does not have effect on the total amount outstanding in share capital. The reasons for splitting shares are:

(i) To make shares attractive to investors by reducing the market price of a share;

(ii) Expectations of higher future profits to be communicated by management to investors by splitting shares;

(iii) Higher dividends to shareholders with stock split.

SUMMARY

Dividend Policy: The dividend policy of a firm determines what proportion of earnings is to be paid to shareholders by way of dividends and what proportion is ploughed back in the firm for reinvestment purpose. Dividends are distributed profits which are distributed among the shareholders as per declaration in annual general meeting. There are basically about two options which a firm has while utilizing its profit after tax. The first option of declaring dividends (either in cash or kind) out of profits after tax, will lead to maximization of the share holders wealth. The second option suits those forms which need funds to finance their long-term projects. However, such projects should have enough growth potential and sufficient profitability.

Traditional Position: According to the traditional approach to the dividend policy, expounded by Graham and Dott, the stock market places considerably more weight on dividends than on retain earnings.

Walter Model: Similar to the traditional approach, the dividend policy given by James E. Walter also considers that dividends are relevant and they do affect the share price. In this model he studied the following relationship between the internal rate of return (r) and the cost of capital of the firm (K), to give a dividend policy that maximizes the wealth of the shareholders, *i.e.*, market price per share (P).

Gordon's Model: Yet another model that has given importance to the dividend policy of the firm is the Gordon Model. Myron Gordon used the dividend capitalization approach to a study the effect of the firm's dividend policy on the stock price. Gordon also contends that dividends are relevant and that dividend policy affects the value of the firm.

Miller and Modigliani Model: The MM hypothesis seeks to explain that a firm's dividend policy is irrelevant and has no effect on the share prices of the firm. This model advocates that it is the investment policy through which the firm can increase its share value and hence this should be given more importance.

Stability of Dividends: Stability of dividends is the consistency in the stream of dividend payments. It is the payment of certain amount of minimum dividend to the shareholders.

Stock Split: A stock split is a method to increase the number of outstanding shares by proportionately reducing the face value of a share. A stock split affects only the per value and does not have effect on the total amount outstanding in share capital.

EXERCISE

Short Questions

1. What is "Dividend"?
2. What is dividend pay-out ratio (D/P)?
3. What is meant by "Stock Split"?
4. What is the difference between scrip and bond dividends?
5. Which model of maximizing the market value of equity shares is called "Dividend Irrelevance Theory"?
6. What is "Bonus or Stock Dividends"?

Moderated and Broad Questions

1. Write a short note on the different types of dividend.
2. What is "Dividend Policy"? Explain its importance.
3. Compare between Walter and Gordon's model.
4. Why Walter and Gordon's model are called "Dividend Relevance Model"? Why MM hypothesis is called "Dividend Irrelevance Model"? Explain MM model.
5. What is "Stock Split"? What are its advantages?
6. Explain each of the indication of "Stability of Dividends".

PROBLEMS

1. The following information is available about a public limited company: -

Equity Capitalization	12%
EPS	₹ 20
Dividend Pay-out ratio	30%
ROI	10%

What is the price of the share as per Walter and Gordon's model?

2. Considering the following information, what is the price of the share as per Gordon's model?

Net Sales	₹ 120 lakhs.
Net Profit Margin	12.5%
Outstanding preference share	₹ 50 lakhs @ 12% dividend
No. of Equity shares	250000
Cost of Equity shares	12%
Retention ratio	40%
ROI	16%

3. The following information relates to XYZ Ltd. Show the effect of the dividend policy on the market price of its shares using the Walter's model – taking the D/P ratio as zero, 25%, 50%, 75% and 100%. [K_e = 11% ; EPS = ₹ 10 ; ROI = r = 15%, 11% & 8%]

4. Given K_e as 11%, EPS = ₹ 10, calculate the market value of a share using Gordon's model for (a) r = 12% ; (b) r = 11% and (c) r = 10% for various levels of D/P ratios given under:

	D/P ratio (1 – b)	**Retention ratio (b)**
A	5%	95%
B	25%	75%
C	30%	70%
D	45%	55%
E	60%	40%

5. A company has a capitalization rate of 10%. It currently has outstanding shares worth 50000, selling currently at ₹ 100 each. The firm expects to have a net income of ₹ 2000000 for the current financial year and it is contemplating to pay a dividend of ₹ 5 per share. The company also requires ₹ 1200000 to fund its investment requirements. Show that under MM model, the dividend payment does not affect the value of the firm.

❑❑❑

16 Financial Statement Analysis

16.1 ACCOUNTING RATIO

The term **"accounting ratios"** is used to describe significant relationship between figures shown on a balance sheet, in a profit and loss account, in a budgetary control system or in any other part of accounting organization. ***Accounting ratios*** thus shows the relationship between accounting data.

Ratios can be found out by dividing one number by another number. Ratios show how one number is related to another. It may be expressed in the form of co-efficient, percentage, proportion, or rate. For example the current assets and current liabilities of a business on a particular date are ₹ 200000 and ₹ 100000 respectively. The ratio of current assets and current liabilities could be expressed as 2 (*i.e.* 200000/100000) or 200 per cent or it can be expressed as 2:1, *i.e.*, the current assets are two times the current liabilities. Ratio sometimes is expressed in the form of rate. For instance, the ratio between two numerical facts, usually cover a period of time, *e.g.*, stock turnover is three times a year.

16.2 RATIO ANALYSIS, ITS ADVANTAGES AND LIMITATIONS

Ratio analysis is an important and age-old technique of financial analysis. It is a tool used by individuals to conduct a quantitative analysis of information in a company's financial statements. Ratios are calculated from current year numbers and are then compared to previous years, other companies, the industry, or even the economy to judge the performance of the company. Ratio analysis is predominately used by proponents of fundamental analysis.

The following are some of the advantages/benefits of ratio analysis:

1. Simplifies financial statements: It simplifies the comprehension of financial statements. Ratios tell the whole story of changes in the financial condition of the business.

2. Facilitates inter-firm comparison: It provides data for inter-firm comparison. Ratios highlight the factors associated with successful and unsuccessful firm. They also reveal strong firms and weak firms, overvalued and undervalued firms.

3. Helps in planning: It helps in planning and forecasting. Ratios can assist management, in its basic functions of forecasting. planning, co-ordination, control and communications.

4. Makes inter-firm comparison possible: Ratios analysis also makes possible comparison of the performance of different divisions of the firm. The ratios are helpful in deciding about their efficiency or otherwise in the past and likely performance in the future.

5. Help in investment decisions: It helps in investment decisions in the case of investors and lending decisions in the case of bankers etc.

Limitations of Ratios Analysis

The ratios analysis is one of the most powerful tools of financial management. Though ratios are simple to calculate and easy to understand, they suffer from serious limitations.

1. Limitations of financial statements: Ratios are based only on the information which has been recorded in the financial statements. Financial statements themselves are subject to several limitations. Thus ratios derived, there from, are also subject to those limitations. For example, non-financial changes though important for the business are not relevant by the financial statements. Financial statements are affected to a very great extent by accounting conventions and concepts. Personal judgment plays a great part in determining the figures for financial statements.

2. Comparative study required: Ratios are useful in judging the efficiency of the business only when they are compared with past results of the business. However, such a comparison only provide glimpse of the past performance and forecasts for future may not prove correct since several other factors like market conditions, management policies, etc. may affect the future operations.

3. Ratios alone are not adequate: Ratios are only indicators; they cannot be taken as final regarding good or bad financial position of the business. Other things have also to be seen.

4. Problems of price level changes: A change in price level can affect the validity of ratios calculated for different time periods. In such a case the ratio analysis may not clearly indicate the trend in solvency and profitability of the company. The financial statements, therefore, should be adjusted keeping in view the price level changes if a meaningful comparison is to be made through accounting ratios.

5. Lack of adequate standard: No fixed standard can be laid down for ideal ratios. There are no well accepted standards or rule of thumb for all ratios which can be accepted as norm. It renders interpretation of the ratios difficult.

6. Limited use of single ratios: A single ratio, usually, does not convey much of a sense. To make a better interpretation, a number of ratios have to be calculated which is likely to confuse the analyst than help him in making any good decision.

7. Personal bias: Ratios are only means of financial analysis and not an end in itself. Ratios have to be interpreted and different people may interpret the same ratio in different way.

8. Incomparable: Not only industries differ in their nature, but also the firms of the similar business widely differ in their size and accounting procedures etc. It makes comparison of ratios difficult and misleading.

16.3 IMPORTANCES OF RATIO ANALYSIS

Ratio analysis is an important tool for analyzing the company's financial performance. The following are the important advantages of the accounting ratios.

1. Analyzing Financial Statements: Ratio analysis is an important technique of financial statement analysis. Accounting ratios are useful for understanding the financial position of the company. Different users such as investors, management, bankers and creditors use the ratio to analyze the financial situation of the company for their decision-making purpose.

2. Judging Efficiency: Accounting ratios are important for judging the company's efficiency in terms of its operations and management. They help to judge how well the company has been able to utilize its assets and earn profits.

3. Locating Weakness: Accounting ratios can also be used in locating weakness of the company's operations even though its overall performance may be quite good. Management can then pay attention to the weakness and take remedial measures to overcome them.

4. Formulating Plans: Although accounting ratios are used to analyze the company's past financial performance, they can also be used to establish future trends of its financial performance. As a result, they help formulate the company's future plans.

5. Comparing Performance: It is essential for a company to know how well it is performing over the years and as compared to the other firms of the similar nature. Besides, it is also important to know how well its different divisions are performing among themselves in different years. Ratio analysis facilitates such comparison.

16.4 CLASSIFICATION OF RATIOS

Ratios may be classified in a number of ways to suit any particular purpose. Different kinds of ratios are selected for different types of situations. Mostly, the purpose for which the ratios are used and the kind of data available determine the nature of analysis. The various accounting ratios can be classified as follows:

Classification of Accounting Ratios/Financial Ratios

(A) Traditional Classification or Statement Ratios	(B) Functional Classification or Classification According to Purpose	(C) Significance Ratios or Ratios According to Importance
• Profit and loss account ratios or revenue income statement ratios • Balance sheet ratios or position statement ratios • Composite/mixed ratios or inter statement ratios	• Profitability ratios • Liquidity ratios • Activity ratios • Leverage ratios or long term solvency ratios	• Primary ratios • Secondary ratios

I. Classification By Purpose/Function

1. Profitability ratios:

- Gross profit ratio
- Net profit ratio
- Operating cost to sales ratio
- Operating profit ratio
- Expense ratio
- Return on Proprietor's Fund
- Return on equity
- Return on capital employed (ROCE) ratio
- Dividend yield ratio
- Dividend payout ratio
- Earnings Per Share Ratio
- Price earning ratio
- P/V ratio
- Earning power

2. Solvency (Stability)

Short-term (liquidity) ratios:

- Current ratio
- Liquid /Acid test/ Quick ratio
- Cash position ratio

- Stock ratio/stock turnover ratio
- Debtor's turnover ratio/ velocity
- Creditor's turnover ratio/velocity

Long-term (solvency) ratios:

- Proprietary ratio
- Debt-equity ratio
- Leverage ratio
- Interest coverage ratio
- Debt service coverage ratio

3. Activity (Performance) ratios:

- Capital turnover ratio
- Debtors/receivables turnover ratio, average collection period
- Stock ratio/stock turnover ratio
- Creditors/payable turnover ratio, Average payment period
- Working capital turnover ratio
- Fixed assets turnover ratio
- Total assets turnover ratio

4. Leverage ratios or capital structure ratios:

- Debt equity ratio
- Proprietary or equity ratio
- Gearing ratio
- Gear ratio
- Ratio of fixed assets to net worth
- Debt-asset ratio
- Interest coverage or debt service ratio
- Over and under capitalization

5. Investment/Earning ratio:

- Dividend cover for equity share
- Dividend yield ratio
- Dividend payout ratio

- Earnings per share ratio
- Price earnings ratio

II. Classification By Financial Statements

1. Balance Sheet ratios:

- Current ratio
- Liquidity ratio
- Cash position ratio
- Debt-equity ratio
- Debt-assets ratio
- Capital gearing ratio etc.

2. Profit & Loss Account ratios (operating ratios):

- Gross profit ratio
- Net profit ratio
- Operating cost to sales ratio
- Operating profit ratio
- Expenses ratio etc.

3. Inter-statement ratios (Composite/Mixed ratios):

- Return on capital employed
- Return on shareholder's fund
- Turnover of working capital
- Debtor's turnover ratio
- Creditor's turnover ratio
- Stock turnover ratio etc.

III. Classification By Users

1. Ratios for management:

- Operating ratio
- Debtor's turnover
- Stock turnover ratio
- Operating profit ratio
- Expense ratio
- Solvency ratios

- Return on capital
- Return on assets etc.

2. Ratios for Creditors:

- Current ratio
- Liquid /Acid test / Quick ratio
- Solvency ratios
- Creditor's turnover ratio/velocity
- Fixed assets ratio etc.

3. Ratios for Shareholders:

- Dividend cover for equity share
- Dividend yield ratio
- Dividend payout ratio
- Earnings Per Share Ratio
- Price Earnings ratio
- Return on Equity

16.5 DETAILS OF DIFFERENT RATIOS - EXPLANATIONS AND RORMULAS

	Formulas of ratio	Definition and significance
1. Current ratio	$\frac{\text{Current Assets}}{\text{Current Liabilities}}$ Current Assets include: • Cash in hand • Cash at bank • Sundry Debtors • Bills Receivable • Prepaid Expenses • Money at call & short notice • Stock • Sundry supplies • Other amounts receivables within a year Current Liabilities include: • Bank Overdraft • Sundry Creditors • Bills Payables	It measures short-term solvency, *i.e.*, the ability of a firm to meet short-term obligations. As a measure of short-term financial liquidity, it indicates the rupees of current assets available for each rupee of current liability. The higher the current ratio, the larger the amount of rupees of current assets available for each rupee of current liability, the more the firm's ability to meet current obligations and the greater the safety of funds of short-term creditors. In a sound business, a current ratio of 2 : 1 is considered as an ideal ratio. The reason is that all current assets do not have the same liquidity or all current assets can not be immediately converted into cash. Even if the ratio is favourable the firm may be in financial trouble because of more stock, work-in-progress etc, which are not easily converted into cash. Therefore, the current ratio is not a conclusive index of the real liquidity of a firm.

Name of ratios	Formulas of ratio	Definition and significance
	• Outstanding Expenses • Interest due on payable • Reserve for unbilled expenses • Interest payable on long-term loan • Other amounts payables within a year	
2. Liquid (Acid Test) ratio or Quick ratio or Near Money ratio	$\frac{\text{Quick or Liquid Assets}}{\text{Quick Liabilities}}$ OR $\frac{\text{Current Assets} - (\text{Stock} + \text{Prepaid expenses})}{\text{Current Liabilities} - \text{Bank Overdraft} - \text{Incomes received in advance}}$	It measures short-term solvency or short-term financial liquidity more accurately in compare to current ratio. As a measure of short-term liquidity, it indicates the rupee of quick assets which are readily converted into cash, for each rupee of quick liability which are required to be paid off in the immediate future. The higher the ratio, the larger the amount of rupees of quick assets available for each rupee of quick liability, the more the firm's ability to meet quick obligations, and the greater the safety of funds of short-term creditors. Generally speaking, the ratio of 1:1 is considered satisfactory as a firm can meet all quick liabilities. If the ratio is less than 1:1, the financial position shall be deemed to be unsound. The quick ratio provides a better check on the liquidity of a firm in compare to current ratio.
3. Working Capital ratio	$\frac{\text{Working Capital}}{\text{Net Assets}}$ Net Assets = Fixed Assets + Current Assets + Investments – Current Liabilities	It is a measure of company's liquidity position. At the same time, it measures the firm's potential reservoir of funds. One firm having a larger working capital ratio, has the greater ability to meet it's current obligations.
4. Cash position ratio (Absolute liquidity Ratio)	$\frac{\text{Cash marketable securities}}{\text{Current Liabilities}}$ OR $\frac{\text{Current Assets} - (\text{Stock} + \text{Debtors})}{\text{Current Liabilities}}$	It is a variation of quick ratio. When liquidity is restricted in terms of cash and cash equivalents, this ratio should be calculated. Generally 0.75:1 ratio is recommended to ensure liquidity. More then this ratio indicates better position of cash on hand to meet all current obligations.

Name of ratios	Formulas of ratio	Definition and significance
5. Proprietary Ratio	$\frac{\text{Shareholder's Fund}}{\text{Total Assets/Resources}}$ OR	It shows the long-term credit strength of the company by showing the long-term solvency. It is very important to creditors too since it helps them to find out the proportion of shareholder's funds in the total assets including the amount of risk to creditors.
Further analyzed to:	$\frac{\text{Equity Share Capital + Preference Share Capital + Reserves \& Surpluses}}{\text{Total Assets including goodwill}}$	Generally 1:3 ratio is recommended to ensure long-term or future solvency of the business. But the ratio below 1: 2 may be risky for the creditors since they may have to loose heavily in the event of company's liquidation on account of heavy losses. Higher ratio indicates lesser dependence on external sources.
(a) Fixed Assets to Proprietor's Fund	$\frac{\text{Fixed Assets}}{\text{Proprietor's Funds or Internal Equities}}$ Internal Equities = Preference Share Capital + (Equity Share Capital + Reserves & Surpluses) – Fictitious Assets = Proprietor's Funds.	This ratio shows the percentage of owners' funds invested in fixed assets. The higher the ratio, higher is the use of creditor's obligations towards acquisition of a part of fixed assets.
(b) Current Assets to Proprietor's Fund	$\frac{\text{Current Assets}}{\text{Proprietor's Funds}}$	This ratio shows the percentage of owner's funds invested in current assets.
6. Debt/Equity Ratio	$\frac{\text{External Equities}}{\text{Internal Equities}}$ $= \frac{\text{Total Outside Liabilities}}{\text{Proprietor's Funds or Shareholder's Funds}}$	It measures the relation between debt and equity in the capital Structure of a firm. This ratio is determined to ascertain soundness of the long term financial policies of the company. It shows the extent to which debt financing has been used in the business. In India, many financial institutions prescribe a norm of 2:1 ratio. In case of capital-intensive industries, 4:1 ratio is an acceptable norm and 6:1 in case of shipping units.The higher the ratio, the higher is the possibility of increasing the rate of return to the equity so long as the cost of debt is lower than the rate of return from the

Name of ratios	Formulas of ratio	Definition and significance
	External Equities = Total Debts = Total Outside Liabilities = Long-term Debt/ Loan + Short-term Debts / Current Liabilities (as they are not cost free). Long-term Debt = Term Loan + Debentures + Redeemable Preference Share Capital. *Internal Equities = Preference Share Capital + (Equity Share Capital + Reserves & Surpluses) - Fictitious Assets = **Proprietor's Funds = Shareholder's Funds*** ***As a long-term financial ratio, Debt/ Equity ratio may be calculated as follows:*** $\frac{\text{Total long term debts}}{\text{Proprietor's Funds or Shareholder's Funds or Internal Equities}}$	investment. But higher the ratio, higher is the risk of shareholders which is measured by the variability in the earnings per share. Therefore, a very high ratio is unfavourable from the firm's point of view. A low ratio is favourable from the point of view of creditors since a higher proportion of equity provides a margin of safety for them. Therefore, from the above discussion, we may conclude that not a very low ratio neither a very high ratio is preferable.
7. Capital Gearing Ratio or Capitalization Ratio or Leverage Ratio	$\frac{\text{Fixed Interest Bearing Fund}}{\text{Equity Share Capital}}$ Fixed Interest bearing funds = Debentures/Bonds + Term Loan + Preference Share Capital (Assumed) ***Possible variation of this ratio is Gear Ratio which is as follows:*** $\frac{\text{Total debts + Pref. Share Capital}}{\text{Equity}}$ Equity = Equity Share Capital + Reserves + Surpluses	It is the relation between fixed income bearing capital and variable income bearing capital. This ratio may be considered from the point of view of long-term solvency and profitability. This ratio is mainly used to analyze the firm's capital structure and is important to both the company and prospective investors. • If Equity Capital > Loan Capital : Low Gear = Overcapitalization • If Equity Capital < Loan Capital : High Gear = Undercapitalization. From the solvency point of view, a high equity base (low geared) may be more welcoming due to lower risk of liquidating long-term debt. But from the profitability point of view, return to equity shareholders in the form of EPS will be higher in case of low equity base or high debt (high geared) based firm.

Name of ratios	Formulas of ratio	Definition and significance
8. Stock or Inventory Turnover Ratio	$\dfrac{\text{Cost of Goods Sold}}{\text{Average Inventory}}$ Cost of Goods Sold = Sales – Gross Profit. Average Inventory = $\dfrac{\text{Opening Stock + Closing Stock}}{2}$	This ratio reveals the number of times finished stock is turned over during a given accounting period. It is alternatively known as Stock Velocity. It measures how quickly inventory is sold which is a test of efficient inventory management. The higher the ratio, the shorter is the average time between investment in stock and the sales transaction. The lower the ratio, the higher is the bad buying with higher accumulation of obsolete stock.
9. Debtor's Turnover Ratio	$\dfrac{\text{Total Credit Sales}}{\text{Average Debtors}}$ Average Debtors = $\dfrac{\text{Opening Debtors + Closing Debtors}}{2}$ **Average Collection Period (days)** $= \dfrac{365}{\text{Debtors Turnover}}$ days Or, **Average Collection Period (months)** $= \dfrac{12}{\text{Debtors Turnover}}$ months	This ratio shows how many days or month's credit is outstanding in the value of amounts owing by debtors. It gives a measurement of the efficiency of the credit collection policies of the firm or liquidity of the receivables. The average collection period measures the quality of debtors since it indicates the rapidity or slowness of their collectibles. The higher the turnover ratio, the shorter is the average collection period indicating better trade credit management and better liquidityof receivables that is better prompt payment on the parts of debtors.
10. Creditor's Turnover Ratio	$\dfrac{\text{Total Credit Purchase}}{\text{Average Creditors}}$ Average Creditors = $\dfrac{\text{Opening Creditors + Closing Creditors}}{2}$ Average Payment Period (days) $= \dfrac{365}{\text{Creditors Turnover}}$ days OR, Average Payment Period (months) $= \dfrac{12}{\text{Creditors Turnover}}$ months	This ratio shows how many days or month's payment to suppliers or creditors is outstanding in the value of amounts owing by creditors. The higher the turnover ratio, the lower is the average payment period indicating better payable management and better payments of creditors or suppliers.

Name of ratios	Formulas of ratio	Definition and significance
11. Fixed Assets Turnover	$\frac{\text{Net Sales}}{\text{Average Net Fixed Assets}}$ Average net fixed assets = $\frac{\text{Opening net fixed assets + Closing net fixed assets}}{2}$ Net fixed assets = Total Fixed Assets – Depreciation on assets	This ratio is supposed to measure the efficiency with which fixed assets are employed. A high ratio indicates a high degree of efficiency in asset utilization. Similarly a low ratio reflects inefficient use of assets.
12. Capital Turnover Ratio	$\frac{\text{Net Sales}}{\text{Capital Employed}}$ Capital Employed = Net Fixed Assets + Working Capital (= Current assets – Current Liabilities) OR Net Worth + Long-term Liabilities – Misc. expenditures – non-operating assets. Net Worth = Proprietor's Equity	It indicates the extent to which capital employed contributes towards sales. A high ratio will signify that there has been efficient utilization of the capital employed by the firm. Similarly a low ratio will signify that there has not been efficient utilization of the capital employed.
13. Working Capital Turnover	$\frac{\text{Net Sales}}{\text{Working Capital}}$ Working Capital = Current assets – Current Liabilities	If a low capital turnover ratio exists, we require further analysis into working capital turnover that is whether working capital has been put to use properly to contribute/improve sales. A high ratio signifies the efficient use of working capital to contribute/improve sales.But if the ratio is low, we may call further analysis into : a. stock turnover b. debtor's turnover and c. creditor's turnover
14. Fixed Assets to Net Worth	$\frac{\text{Fixed assets}}{\text{Net Worth or Proprietor's Equity}}$	This ratio indicates the extent to which fixed assets are being financed by equity interests. Higher the ratio, higher the fixed assets are financed by long-term debt capital. If the ratio is less than 100% it may mean the non-existency of any long-term fixed interest bearing finance in the firm or long-term debt capital.

Name of ratios	Formulas of ratio	Definition and significance
15. Return on Capital Employed (ROCE) OR Return on Net Assets (RONA)	$\frac{\text{Profit}}{\text{Capital Employed/Net Assets}}$ Capital Employed = Net Fixed Assets + Working Capital (= Current assets – Current Liabilities) Profit refers to 'Net Profit after Tax' from shareholder's point of view and 'Trading Profit before Interest and Tax' from the management point of view. The ratio can be further elaborated as follows: $= \frac{\text{Profit}}{\text{Net Sales}} \times \frac{\text{Net Sales}}{\text{Capital Employed}}$ = Profitability × Capital Turnover Ratio $= \frac{\text{Sales}}{\text{Net Assets}} \times \frac{\text{EBT}}{\text{Sales}} \times \frac{\text{EBIT}}{\text{EBT}}$ = Capital Turnover × Gross Profit Margin × Operating Leverage From the point of view of Equity Shareholders only : ROCE = Return on Equity $= \frac{\text{Earning available to equity shareholders (Refer 22)}}{\text{Equity}}$ Equity = Paid-up Equity share capital + Reserves and Surpluses	This ratio reveals the overall efficiency or otherwise with which the firm is operated. The higher the ratio, the higher is the profitability and may be also with higher capital turnover *i.e.*, higher efficient utilization of capital employed by firm towards improvement of sales at minimum proportionate rate. **This ratio is also called the return on net worth.** *The return on equity, being another form of ROCE, reflects the productivity of the ownership capital employed by the firm.*
16. Return on Assets (for shareholders) OR Return on investment (ROI)	$\frac{\text{Net Profit after Tax}}{\text{Average Total Assets}}$ (known as Return n Investment) Or Return on Assets **DU PONT ANALYSIS** Return on Assets = Net Profit Margin × Total Assets Turnover Ratio	This ratio reveals the efficiency of utilization of fixed and current assets towards increasing earnings power of shareholders. The higher the ratio, the higher the efficiency in utilization of assets for profit earnings.

Name of ratios	Formulas of ratio	Definition and significance
	$= \frac{\text{Net Profit}}{\text{Net Sales}} \times \frac{\text{Net Sales}}{\text{Avg. Total Assets}}$ $= \frac{\text{Net Profit (before int. \& tax)}}{\text{Average Total Assets}}$	
17. Earning Power	**(a) Earning power (for firms)** $= \frac{\text{Net Profit (before Int. \& Tax)}}{\text{Average Total Assets}}$ $= \frac{\text{EBIT}}{\text{Average Total Assets}}$ **(b) RONA/ROCE:** It measures firm's operating performance. It also indicates net earning power of shareholders. **(c) Equity Growth:** Return on Equity(ROE) × Retention Ratio $= \text{ROE} \times \frac{\text{Retained Earning}}{\text{Profit after Tax}}$	Earning power measures operating profitability and hence business performance. Broadly speaking, the earning power measures the operating business performance which is not effected by interest charges and tax payments. The higher the ratio, better is the operating profitability. This ratio is best suited for inter-firm comparison.
18. Asset Turnover Ratio Or Turnover of Total Assets	$\frac{\text{Net Sales}}{\text{Average Total Assets}}$	This ratio measures how efficiently assets are employed on an overall basis. It is important that sales be compared to the asset base. If a firm can not produce a satisfactory turnover and if it affects profit adversely, it might be misusing its assets. This ratio highlights the amount of assets that the firm used to generate its total sales. The ability to generate a large volume of sales on a small asset base is an important part of the firm's profitability picture. The higher the ratio, higher is the reduction of financing costs and expenses for maintenance and upkeep and ultimately better is the utilization of assets resulting increase of eventual profit to its owners.

Name of ratios	Formulas of ratio	Definition and significance
19. Gross Profit Ratio	$= \frac{\text{Gross Profit}}{\text{Sales} - \text{Excise Duty}} \times 100$ Gross Profit = Sales – Cost of goods sold. Cost of goods sold = Opening Stock + Manufacturing/ Production costs + direct trading costs – Closing Stock Net Sales = Sales – Excise Duty	This ratio shows the gross profit margin after meeting manufacturing costs and direct trading costs. It should preferably be found out for each product separately. This ratio measures the efficiency of production/trading as well as pricing. The higher the gross profit ratio, higher is the efficiency of the production/trading operations apart from costing point of view and also higher is the efficiency to earn the trading profit.
20. Net Profit Ratio (NP Ratio)	**There are 2 possible NP ratios:** (a) $\frac{\text{Net Profit after tax}}{\text{Net Sales}} \times 100$ (b) $\frac{\text{Operating Net Profit}}{\text{Net Sales}} \times 100$ **= Operating Profit Ratio** Operating net profit = Gross Profit – Operating Expenses *(before adjusting non-operating incomes like interest on investment, profit on sale of assets, dividend and non-operating expenses/ losses like loss on sale of assets, provision for claim for damage etc.)* Operating Expenses = Administrative/ Office Expenses + Selling and Distribution Expenses + Depreciation.	This ratio shows the earnings left for equity and preference shareholders as a percentage of net sales. It measures the overall efficiency of business operations and tax management. This ratio indicates what portion of sales is left after all costs; charges and expenses have been deducted. The higher the ratio, higher is the control of costs and/or promotion of sales and ultimately the efficiency of operating the firm.
21. Operating Profit Ratio	**See 20 (b)**	**Same as written in 20**
22. Return on Equity (ROE) [Another form of ROCE from the point of view of equity shareholders]	$\frac{\text{Earning (available to equity shareholders)}}{\text{Equity}}$ Equity = Paid-up Equity Share Capital + Reserves and Surpluse Earning available to equity share-holders = Profit after Tax – Reserve – Preference Dividend **DU PONT ANALYSIS** $\text{ROE} = \frac{\text{Earning}}{\text{Equity}}$	The ROE is an important profit indicator to shareholders of firms.The higher the ratio, the higher is the profitability of equity funds invested in the business or in other words, higher productivity of capital employed in the firm.

Name of ratios	Formulas of ratio	Definition and significance
	$= ROA \times \frac{\text{Total Assets}}{\text{Equity}}$ $= \left(\frac{\text{Net Profit}}{\text{Net Sales}} \times \frac{\text{Net Sales}}{\text{Avg. Total Assets}}\right)$ $\times \frac{\text{Total Assets}}{\text{Equity}}$ = (Net Profit Margin × Total Assets Turnover Ratio) × $\frac{1}{1 - \text{Debt Asset Ratio}}$ While debt Asset Ratio = $\frac{\text{Total Debts}}{\text{Total Asset}}$	
23. Operating Cost to Sales Ratio OR Operating Ratio OR Operating Cost Ratio	$\frac{\text{Operating Costs}}{\text{Net Sales}}$ $= \frac{\text{Costs of goods sold + Other operating Exps.}}{\text{Net Sales}} \times 100$ Other operating expenses = Admin/Office Expenses + Selling and Distribution Expenses + Depreciation. Operating Cost Ratio can be divided into following 2 ratios as follows : (*i*) Cost of goods sold ratio $= \frac{\text{Costs of goods sold}}{\text{Net Sales}} \times 100$ (ii) Other operating Expenses ratio $= \frac{\text{Other operating Exps.}}{\text{Net Sales}} \times 100$	The ratio shows that percentage of net sales is eaten by operating costs. Of the balance (Net Sales – Operating Costs) part is covered by non-operating expenses and the remaining portion is profit. Higher the ratio, lower the profit portion will be and lower will be the profitability.
24. Interest Coverage Ratio	'Net profit before interest and tax' has been considered since it represents the amount available to cover interest.	It shows the ability of the firm to meet its due interest payment. Higher the ratio, higher is the solvency; moreover higher is the satisfaction of the

Name of ratios	Formulas of ratio	Definition and significance
	$\frac{\text{Net Profit before Interest and Taxes (EBIT)}}{\text{Interest}}$	lenders since this position is more desirable to cover up interest expenses even under worst situation.
25. Debt-Asset Ratio	$\frac{\text{Total Debt}}{\text{Total Assets}}$ $= \frac{\text{Long-term Debt+Short-term Debt Current Liabilities}}{\text{Total Assets as indicated in the Balance Sheet}}$	This ratio measures the extent to which borrowed funds support the firm's assets. Higher debt-asset ratio implies that higher % of the total assets are financed with debt sources. From creditor's point of view, a low ratio is desirable. From firm's point of view higher ratio is desirable, since firms with stable earnings may go for higher proportion of debt to finance total assets than those with relatively less stable earnings.
26. Debt-Service Coverage Ratio	$\frac{\text{PAT + Depreciation + Interest on term loan + other non-cash charges}}{\text{Interest on long-term loan + Term loan installment}}$ $= \frac{\text{Profit after tax before depreciation, Interest and other non-cash charges}}{\text{Total obligations}}$	This ratio reflects the ability of the business firms to make interest payment along with loan installment. The term lending financial institutions are mainly using this ratio to ascertain debt servicing capacity of the firm. The higher the ratio, higher is the debt servicing capacity of the firm. A ratio of 2 or more is a good ratio.
27. P/V Ratio	$\frac{\text{Contribution / unit}}{\text{Sales / unit}}$ OR $\frac{\text{Total Contribution}}{\text{Total Sales}}$ OR $\frac{\text{Change in Profit (loss)}}{\text{Change in Sales}}$ Contribution/unit = Sales Price/unit- Variable Cost/unit	This ratio is a ratio of contribution to sales. Higher the ratio, higher is either the selling price or lower is variable cost or both, causing enhancement of profitability.
28. Dividend Payout Ratio	$\frac{\text{Dividend per Share}}{\text{Earning per Share}}$	This ratio reflects what percentage of total earnings is distributed as dividend among the shareholders.

Name of ratios	Formulas of ratio	Definition and significance
		Higher the payout ratio, higher may be the market price per share, but it will affect the future earning which is the internal source of financing.Lower the payout ratio, higher is the retention for future investment to take care of growth factor, but it may affect the market price per share.
29. Earnings per Equity Share	$\frac{\text{Earnings available for Equity share holders}}{\text{Number of Equity Shares}}$ Earnings available for Equity share holders = PAT – Reserves – Preference Dividend	This ratio is the concern of equity shareholders. It is an indicator of profitability on investment from their point of view.The higher the ratio, the more profitable is the financial plan and vice versa.
30. Dividend Yield	$\frac{\text{Dividend per Share}}{\text{Market Price per Shares}}$ **If it is yield ratio, then yield =** $\frac{\text{Dividend per share + Price Changes}}{\text{Initial Price per Share}}$ **Dividend coverage ratio:** (i) Preference = $\frac{\text{PAT – Reserve}}{\text{Dividend payable to Preference shareholders}}$ (ii) Equity = $\frac{\text{PAT – Reserve-Pref. Dividend}}{\text{Dividend payable to Equity shareholders}}$	This ratio gives current return on investment of shareholders. Dividend yield measures the real rate of return to the shareholders. The higher the yield, the more profitable is the investment due to higher current return on investment.
31. Return on Proprietor's Fund	$\frac{\text{Earning after Int. \& Tax}}{\text{Proprietor's Funds}} \times 100$ ***Proprietor's Funds** =Preference Share Capital + (Equity Share Capital + Reserves & Surpluses) - Fictitious Assets*	It is the ratio reflecting the profitability in relation to investment of shareholder's capital and claim. Higher the ratio, higher is the satisfaction level of equity and preference shareholders apart from return on investment.
32. Price-Earnings Ratio(Price-earnings multiple)	$\frac{\text{Market Price per Share}}{\text{Earnings per Share}}$	This ratio is important to investors of secondary market since it reflects how earnings affect the market price per share. This ratio is also important to the financial analysts for market evaluation of a share. Higher the ratio, higher is valuation of stock.

16.6 COMMON SIZE FINANCIAL STATEMENTS/COMMON-SIZE ANALYSIS

A useful and convenient way of standardizing financial statements is to express each item on the Profit & Loss Account on a percentage of sales and each item on the Balance Sheet as a percentage of total assets. The resulting financial statements are called common size statements which are very well suited to intercompany comparison.

Example:

Exhibit – 1

Common Size Financial Statement

Part A: Profit & Loss Account

Particulars	2008-09 ₹ in crores	2009-10 ₹ in crores	Common Size (%) 2008-09 (%)	2009-10 (%)
A. Net Sales	100	120	100	100
B. Cost of goods Sold	80	90	80	75
C. Gross profit = A – B	20	30	20	25
D. PBIT	15	12	15	10
E. Interest	5	4	5	3.34
F. PBT = D – E	10	8	10	6.66
G. Tax @ 40% of PBT	4	3.2	4	2.66
H. PAT = F – G	6	4.8	6	4.00

Part B: Balance Sheet (No Sub-groups) ₹ in Crores

Particulars	₹ in crores	₹ in crores	Common size (%)	
	2008-09	2009-10	2008-09	2009-10
• Shareholders Fund, (Equity)	40	50	57	55
• Loan funds	30	40	43	45
Total	**70**	**90**	**100**	**100**
• Fixed Assets	45	49	64	54
• Investments	8	8	12	9
• Net Current assets or working capital	17	33	24	37
Total	**70**	**90**	**100**	**100**

The common size analysis can be carried out further and extended to an examination of what proportion of a subgroup, rather than the total, an item is, In assessing the liquidity of current assets, it is better to know what proportion of current assets is invested in inventories.

16.7 DU PONT ANALYSIS

It provides an insight into the 2 determinants of return on assets – net profit margin and total asset turnover ratio. The Du Pont Company of the US pioneered this system of financial analysis which considers important inter-relationship based on informations found in financial statements. Many firms adopted it through a Du Pont Chart. **A format of that chart is shown below with the help of the figures taken from Exhibit 1:**

Du Pont Chart:

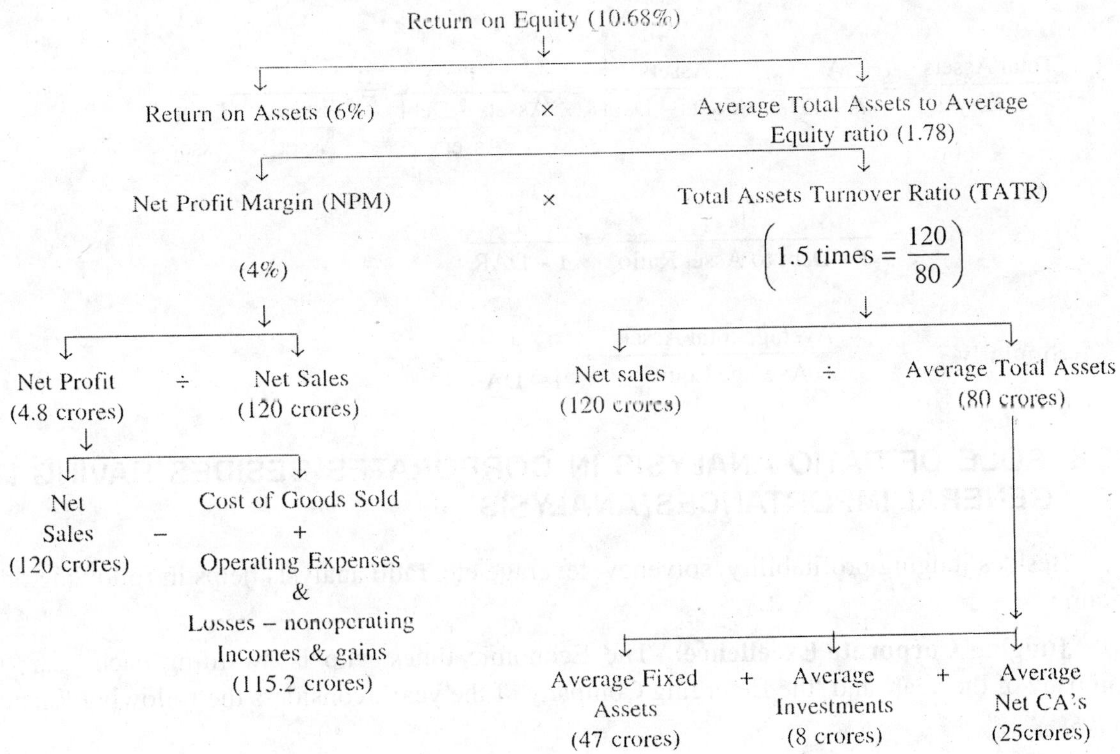

Average Total Assets to Average Total Equity

$$= \frac{\text{Average Total Assets}}{\text{Average Total Equity}} = \frac{\frac{70+90}{2}}{\frac{40+50}{2}} = \frac{80}{45} = 1.78$$

Return on Assets **(ROA)** = Net Profit Margin **(NPM)** × Total Assets Turnover Ratio

$$\textbf{(TATR)} = \frac{\text{Net Profit}}{\text{Net Sales}} \times \frac{\text{Net Sales}}{\text{Average Total Assets}}$$

Such decomposition helps in understanding how the return on total assets is influenced by the Net profit margin and total assets turnover ratio. The basic Du Pont analysis may be extended (evident from format of Du Pont chart) to explore the determinants of the return on equity (ROE).

$$ROE = NPM \times TATR \times \frac{1}{1 - DAR}$$

$$= \frac{\text{Net Profit}}{\text{Net Sales}} \times \frac{\text{Net Sales}}{\text{Average Net Assets}} \times \frac{\text{Average Total Assets}}{\text{Average Equity}}$$

$$\frac{\text{Total Assets}}{\text{Equity}} = \frac{A}{A - D} = \frac{\text{Assets}}{\text{Assets} - \text{Debt}} = \frac{1}{\frac{\text{Assets} - \text{Debt}}{\text{Asset}}} = \frac{1}{\frac{\text{Assets}}{\text{Asset}} - \frac{\text{Debt}}{\text{Asset}}}$$

$$= \frac{1}{1 - \text{Debt to Asset Ratio}} = \frac{1}{1 - DAR}$$

Similarly, $$\frac{\text{Average total Assets}}{\text{Average Equity}} = \frac{1}{1 - DAR}$$

16.8 ROLE OF RATIO ANALYSIS IN CORPORATES BESIDES HAVING ITS GENERAL IMPORTANCES/ANALYSIS

Besides judging profitability, solvency, leverage etc. ratio analysis helps in following other affairs:

Judging Corporate Excellence: The Economic times who is awarding each year 'the company of the year' and 'the Emerging Company of the year', considers the following financial ratios:

→ Return on Capital Employed

→ EPS

→ Price – earnings ratio

→ Net profit Margin

→ Return on Equity

→ Debt Equity Ratio

→ Working Capital Turnover

→ Dividend coverage

→ Return on Assets

Judging Creditworthiness: For assessing creditworthiness of a potential customer, a number of adhoc scoring models employing several financial variables and ratios have been used.

Format of a Credit Scoring Model

Character Average past Payment	On time	Up to 30 days Late	Up to 60 days Late	Points
Capacity				
• Net Profit Margin	0 – 5%	6 – 10%	> 10%	
• Quick Ratio	< 0.75	0.75 – 1.25	> 1.25	
• Cash flow	Low	Average	High	
Capital				
• Current ratio	< 1	1 – 1.15	> 1.5	
• Debt-equity ratio	< 1	1 -2	> 2	
• Interest Earned	< 2 X	2 X -3X	> 3X	
Collateral				
• Net worth	Low	Average	High	
• Market Value to net worth	Low	Average	High	

Valuing Equity Shares: We can use 4 financial indicators to value equity shares as follows:

- Price- earnings multiple
- Pay-out ratio
- Variability in earning
- Growth rate in earnings

Guessing the ratings of the bonds: Following financial ratios are used to guess the rating of the bonds as per suggestion of empirical research :

- Debt Equity ratio
- Interest coverage ratio
- Return on assets

Estimating Market Risk of a Company's Stock: The market risk is measured by *beta.* If debt equity ratio is high, other things being equal, *equity beta* is also high.

Capital Structure Analysis: How does the capital structure of the firm affect the cost of capital and the return to shareholders? Following ratios are used:

- Net worth to total Assets
- Fixed Assets to Net worth

Investment Analysis: The shareholders, take over bidders, management are interested to know how the market prices for a share reflect a firm's performance. Following ratios are used:

- Dividend Yield
- Earnings per Equity Share
- Price Earnings Ratio

16.9 COMPARATIVE ANALYSIS

The comparison of financial statements is accomplished by taking the individual items of different financial statements and reviewing the changes occurred from year-to-year and over the years.

- Comparison among many players in the same industry (cross-sectional analysis)
- Comparison over a period of time (time series analysis)

Different types of comparative analysis

A. Cross-Sectional analysis (inter - Firm analysis)

B. Time series analysis

(a) year-to-year change (Trend Analysis)

(b) Index analysis

A. Cross-sectional analysis (Inter-Firm analysis)

It refers to the analysis of the financial performance of all firms in an industry and their comparison at a given point of time with their immediate competitors or with the industry average.

The following table gives the cross-sectional analysis of an industry A with competitor industries B and C where Industry B have better liquidity as per all liquidity ratios. Though industry B has lower debt-equity and debt-asset ratio, it has low coverage because of low EBIT. Apart from profitability ratios, industry A is the best performer.

TABLE 1

Ratios	Formulas	Industry A	Industry B	Industry C
(A) LIQUIDITY				
• Current Ratio	$\frac{CA}{CL}$	2.27	2.61	2.45
• Liquid ratio	$\frac{\text{CL} - \text{Inventory}}{\text{CL}}$	1.04	1.18	1.26
• Absolute liquidity Ratio	$\frac{\text{CA} - \text{Inventory} - \text{Debtors}}{\text{CL}}$	0.73	0.87	0.81
(B) ACTIVITY/ PERFORMANCE				
Inventory turnover	$\frac{\text{COGS}}{\text{Avg. Inventory}}$	4.23	2.83	3.21

• Debtors turnover	$\frac{\text{Total Credit Sales}}{\text{Avg. Debtors}}$	3.17	2.53	2.73
(C) LEVERAGE				
• Debt-Equity Ratio	$\frac{\text{Total Debt}}{\text{Shareholder's fund}}$	1.33	0.79	1.89
• Debt-Asset Ratio	$\frac{\text{Total Debt}}{\text{Total Assets as per Balance Sheet}}$	0.46	0.41	0.59
• Interest coverage	$\frac{\text{EBIT}}{\text{Interest}}$	2.19	1.61	1.71
(D) PROFITABILITY				
• Gross profit margin	$\frac{\text{Gross profit}}{\text{Net Sales}}$	23%	10.24%	13.7%
• Net profit margin	$\frac{\text{Net profit after Tax}}{\text{Net Sales}}$	5.94%	5.33%	5.47%

B. (a) Time – series analysis (Trend analysis)

Time series or trend analysis reflects the direction of changes over a period of years which is particularly applicable to the items of profit & loss account. A comparison of financial statements over 2 to 3 years can be undertaken by computing the year-to-year change in absolute amounts and in terms of percentage changes. Longer-term comparisons are best explained by means of index number trend series (**Index Analysis**).

Example: Assumed trends from 3 year's financial Statements of some important financial variables in the financial analysis (Say, trend of Activity, profitability and leverage ratios)

TABLE 2

Financial year	2009-2010	2008-2009	2007-2008	Remarks
A. Activity Ratios				The gross margin of the firm is improving. The declining stock turnover confirms that stock is getting heavier. The firm is showing efficiency in collecting the out-standing amounts from customers. The company is generating a sale of ₹ 1.84 for a capital employed of
• Stock Turnover	1.63	2.08	2.12	
• Debtors turnover	18	8	9	
• Day's Sales in receivable (360 days)	20	45	40	
• Capital turnover ratio	1.84	1.66	1.58	
• Fixed Assets turnover	3.70 times	3.61 times	3.95 times	
B. Profitability Ratios				
• Return on capital Employed	49.43%	45.49%	41.36%	

• Operating ratio	27.3%	26.2%	24.5%	Re. 1. This has improved over the years. Debt-equity ratio has declined over a period of time and interest coverage ratio also increased which are positive signs.
• Gross profit ratio	30.9%	29.8%	29.6%	
• Net profit ratio	6.7%	5.8%	9.6%	
C. Leverage Ratios				
• Debt to Equity	1.30	1.17	1.92	
• Interest Coverage	3.19	2.73	1.78	

(b) Index analysis

Longer-term trend comparison of financial statements (say, more than 3 years) is best way understood by means of index number trend series because in this case, year-to-year method of comparison may become too cumbersome.

Here, we select a base year which has an index number of 100.

EXHIBIT 2
Balance Sheet of ABC Industries Ltd. for the year 2006-2007 to 2009-2010

(₹ in crores)

	2009-2010	2008-2009	2007-2008	2006-2007
Sources of Funds				
(A) Total shareholders fund	83.01	71.15	46.68	28.08
(B) Total Debt	74.32	60.59	70.96	64.93
(C) Total Liabilities (A+B)	157.33	131.74	117.64	93.01
Application of Funds				
(D) Net Block	58.03	53.87	46.44	35.01
(E) Capital WIP	6.88	5.51	4.77	3.76
(F) Investments	6.63	3.03	2.89	2.89
(G) Current Assets				
Loans & Advances:				
• Inventories	46.30	40.48	34.57	35.53
• Debtors	49.85	37.30	37.75	30.53
• Cash and Bank bal.	1.85	1.62	1.10	1.62
• Loans and advances	23.10	14.88	11.16	10.23
(H) *Less;* Current Liabilities and provisions:				
• Current Liabilities	32.36	21.53	19.17	24.63
• Provisions	4.24	3.42	2.17	1.93
(I) Net current Assets (G – H)	84.50	69.33	63.54	51.35
(J) Misc. Expenses - not w/o	1.29	0.00	0.00	0.00
(K) Total Assets = D + E + F + I + J	157.33	131.74	117.64	93.01

Table from Exhibit 2

(Index number trend series of ABC Industries Ltd. over last 4 years starting from 2006-07 to 2009-10 given in this table reflects the over-all picture of change at a time) we select a base year 2006-2007 which has an index number of 100.

	2006-2007	2007-2008	2008-2009	2009-2010
Sources of Funds				
(A) Total shareholders fund	100	166.23	253.38	295.61
(B) Total Debt	100	109.28	93.31	114.46
(C) Total Liabilities (A + B)	100	126.48	141.64	169.15
Application of Funds				
(D) Net Block	100	132.65	153.87	165.75
(E) Capital WIP	100	126.86	146.54	182.97
(F) Investments	100	100	104.84	229.41
(G) Current Assets, Loans & Advances:				
• Inventories	100	97.29	113.93	130.31
• Debtors	100	123.65	122.17	163.28
• Cash and Bank bal.	100	67.90	100	114.19
• Loans and advances	100	109.09	145.45	225.81
(H) *Less;* Current Liabilities and provisions:				
• Current Liabilities	100	77.83	87.41	131.38
• Provisions	100	112.43	177.20	219.69
(I) Net current Assets (G-H)	100	123.74	135.01	164.55
(J) Total Assets	100	126.48	141.64	169.15

SOLVED PROBLEMS

1. Following are the financial statements of an organization for the year 2009-2010

Balance Sheet as on 31st March, 2010

Liabilities	₹	Assets	₹
Owner's Equity :		**Fixed Assets :**	
14.3% Preference Share Capital	50000	Building less Depr.	350000
Equity Share Capital	300000	Plant & Machinery less Depr.	200000
General Reserve	400000	Furniture less Depr.	100000
Retained Earnings for 2009-2010	50000	Patents	50000
Debt :		**Investment :**	
6% Debenture	100000	Govt. Securities	200000
12.5% Loan (long-term)	80000		
8% Bonds	140000		
Current Liabilities :		**Current Assets :**	
Creditors	30000	Sundry Debtors	45000
Bills Payable	20000	Bills Receivable	30000
Bank Overdraft	20000	Stock-in-trade	80000
Outstanding Expenses	10000	Prepaid Expenses	5000
Proposed Dividends	50000	Cash in hand	120000
		Cash at Bank	70000
	1,25,0000		1,25,0000

Profit and Loss Statement for the year ended 31st March, 2010

	Particulars	₹
	Sales	1300000
Less :	Cost of Goods sold	800000
	Gross Profit	500000
Less:	Administration, Selling & Warehouse Expenses and Depreciation	350000
	Net Profit / EBIT	150000
Less:	Interest (6000 + 10000 + 11200)	27200
	Profit before Tax (PBT)	122800
Less:	Tax	40650
	Profit after Tax	82150
Less:	Dividend (Preference Div. + Equity Div.)	32150
	Retained Earnings	50000

Compute the following ratios:

- Current Ratio
- Acid Test Ratio
- Absolute Liquidity Ratio
- Return on Proprietor's Fund

- Return on Capital Employed
- Debt-Equity Ratio
- Fixed Assets to Proprietor's Fund
- Current Assets to Proprietor's Fund
- Operating Ratio
- Gross Profit Ratio
- Net Profit Ratio
- Capital Gearing Ratio

Solution:

(a) Current Ratio: $\frac{\text{Current Assets}}{\text{Current Liabilities}}$

$$= \frac{\text{Debtors + B/R + Stock + Prepaid Expenses + Cash in hand + Cash at Bank}}{\text{Creditors + B/P + B/O + Outstanding Expenses + Proposed Dividend}}$$

$$= \frac{45000 + 30000 + 80000 + 5000 + 120000 + 70000}{30000 + 20000 + 20000 + 10000 + 50000}$$

$$= \frac{350000}{130000} = 2.6923 = 2.6923 : 1$$

(b) Acid Test Ratio: $\frac{\text{Liquid Assets}}{\text{Quick Liabilities}}$

$$= \frac{\text{Current Assets} - (\text{Stock + Prepaid Expenses})}{\text{Current Liabilities} - \text{Bank Overdraft}}$$

$$= \frac{350000 - (80000 + 5000)}{130000 - 20000}$$

$$= \frac{265000}{110000} = 2.4091 = 2.4091{:}1$$

(c) Absolute Liquidity Ratio: (Cash Position Ratio)

$$\frac{\text{Cash Marketable Securities}}{\text{Current Liabilities}}$$

$$= \frac{\text{Current Assets} - (\text{Stock + Debtors})}{\text{Current Liabilities}}$$

$$= \frac{350000 - (80000 + 45000)}{130000}$$

$$= \frac{225000}{130000} = 1.7307 = 1.7307:1$$

(d) Return on Proprietor's Fund :

$$= \frac{\text{Net Profit}}{\text{Shareholder's / Proprietor's Fund}}$$

$$= \frac{\text{Net Profit after interest and tax}}{\text{Equity Share Capital + Preference Share Capital + General Res. + Retained Earnings}}$$

$$= \frac{150000}{300000 + 50000 + 400000 + 500000} \times 100$$

$$= \frac{150000}{800000} \times 100$$

$$= 18.75\%$$

(e) ROCE or Return on Net Assets: From Management point of view

$$= \frac{\text{Net Profit before interest and tax (EBIT)}}{\text{Capital Employed or Net Assets}}$$

$$= \frac{150000}{\text{Owner's Equity + Debt (Alternatively FA + CA – CL)}}$$

$$= \frac{150000}{(300000 + 50000 + 400000 + 50000) + (100000 + 80000 + 140000)} \times 100$$

$$= \frac{150000}{1120000} \times 100$$

$$= 13.39\%$$

ROCE or Return on Net Assets: From Equity and Preference Shareholder's point of view

$$\frac{\text{PAT (Profit after tax)}}{\text{Capital Employed or Net Assets}}$$

$$= \frac{82150}{1120000} \times 100 = 7.33\%$$

ROCE: From Equity Shareholder's point of view only

$$\frac{\text{Earning available to equity shareholders}}{\text{Equity}}$$

$$= \frac{\text{PAT – Preference Dividend (assumed dec.)}}{\text{Equity Share Capital + General Res. + Retained Earning for 2009-2010}}$$

$$= \frac{82150 - (14.3\% \times 50000)}{300000 + 400000 + 50000}$$

$$= \frac{82150 - 7150}{750000} \times 100$$

$$= \frac{75000}{750000} \times 100 = 10\%$$

(f) Debt-Equity: $\frac{\text{Debt}}{\text{Equity}}$

$$= \frac{\text{External Equities}}{\text{Internal Equities}}$$

$$= \frac{\text{Total Outside Liabilities}}{\text{Proprietor's or Shareholder's Funds}}$$

$$= \frac{\text{Debentures + Long-term loans + Bonds + Redeemable Preference Share Capital}}{\text{Preference Share Capital + Equity Share Capital + Reserves + Retained Earnings}}$$

$$= \frac{100000 + 80000 + 140000 + \text{Nil (assume irredeemable)}}{50000 + 300000 + 400000 + 50000}$$

$$= \frac{320000}{800000} = 0.40 = \frac{40}{100} = \frac{2}{5}$$

% of Debt $= \frac{2}{7} \times 100 = 28.57\%$

% of Debt $= \frac{5}{7} \times 100 = 71.43\%$

(g) Fixed Assets to Proprietor's Fund (Fixed Assets to Net Tangible worth ratio)

$$\frac{\text{Fixed Assets}}{\text{Proprietor's Fund}}$$

$$= \frac{\text{Fixed Assets}}{\text{Internal Equities or Shareholder's Fund}}$$

$$= \frac{350000 + 200000 + 100000 + 50000}{800000}$$

$$= \frac{700000}{800000}$$

$$= \frac{7}{8} = 0.875 = 0.875:1$$

(h) Current Assets to Proprietor's Fund

$$\frac{\text{Current Assets}}{\text{Proprietor's Fund}}$$

$$= \frac{45000 + 30000 + 80000 + 5000 + 120000 + 70000}{800000}$$

$$= \frac{350000}{800000} \times 100 = 0.4375 = 0.4375:1$$

(i) Operating Ratio: $\frac{\text{Cost of Goods Sold + Operating Expenses}}{\text{Sales}} \times 100$

$$= \frac{800000 + 350000}{1300000}$$

$$= \frac{1150000}{1300000} \times 100$$

$$= 88.46\%$$

(j) Gross Profit Ratio: $\frac{\text{Gross Profit}}{\text{Sales}} \times 100 = \frac{500000}{1300000} \times 100 = 38.46\%$

(k) Net Profit Ratio: $\frac{\text{Net Profit after tax (PAT)}}{\text{Sales}} \times 100 = \frac{82150}{1300000} \times 100$

$$= 6.3192\%$$

(l) Capital Gearing Ratio: $\frac{\text{Fixed Interest bearing funds}}{\text{Equity Share Capital}}$

$$= \frac{\text{Debentures + Long-term Loan + Bond + Preference Share Capital}}{\text{Equity Share Capital}}$$

$$= \frac{100000 + 80000 + 140000 + 50000}{300000}$$

$$= \frac{370000}{300000} = 1.2333 = 1.2333:1$$

2. Extracts from the figures of a Balance Sheet of an organization are given below:

Financial Years	2008-2009 ₹	2009-2010 ₹
Assets		
Stock	20000	40000
Debtors	60000	60000
Prepaid Expenses	4000	
Cash at Bank	40000	30000
Liabilities		
Sundry Creditors	50000	60000
Bills Payable	30000	24000
Bank Overdraft		10000

Sales amounted to ₹ 700000 in 2008-09 and ₹ 600000 in 2009-10. Compute the solvency position of the organization and comment.

Solution

Solvency Ratios	Calculation	2008-2009	2009-2010
Short-term (Liquidity)			
• Current Ratio	$\frac{\text{Current Assets}}{\text{Current Liabilities}}$	$\frac{124000}{80000} = 1.55:1$	$\frac{130000}{94000} = 1.38:1$
• Liquid Ratio	$\frac{\text{CAs – Stock – Prepaid expenses}}{\text{CLs – Bank O/D}}$	$\frac{124000 - 20000 - 4000}{80000 - \text{NIL}}$ = 1.25:1	$\frac{130000 - 40000 - \text{NIL}}{94000 - 10000}$ = 1.07:1
• Stock Turnover Ratio	$\frac{\text{Net Sales}}{\text{Average Inventory}}$	$\frac{700000}{20000} = 35$	$\frac{600000}{30000} = 20$
• Debtors Turnover Ratio	$\frac{\text{Net Sales}}{\text{Average Debtors}}$	$\frac{700000}{60000} = 11.67$	$\frac{600000}{60000} = 10$

Notes:

(a) In absence of 'Cost of Goods Sold', we have considered 'Net Sales' while calculating Stock Turnover Ratio. We can also calculate 'cash position' OR 'Absolute liquidity' ratio to judge absolute liquidity position. The ratio is as follows :

$$\frac{\text{Current Assets – (Stock + Debtors)}}{\text{Current Liabilities}}$$

In 2008-2009 : Cash Position Ratio $= \dfrac{124000 - (20000 + 60000)}{80000}$

$= \dfrac{44000}{80000} = .55$

$= 0.55 : 1$

In 2009-2010 : Cash Position Ratio $= \dfrac{130000 - (40000 + 60000)}{94000}$

$= 0.3191$

$= 0.3191 : 1$

Both ratios are below the role of thumb *i.e.*, 0.75 : 1.

(b) Current Assets(CAs) and Current Liabilities(CLs) :

	2008-2009	**2009-2010**
Assets		
Stock	20000	40000
Debtors	60000	60000
Prepaid Expenses	4000	–
Cash at Bank	40000	30000
	124000	130000
Liabilities		
Sundry Creditors	50000	60000
Bills Payable	30000	24000
Bank Overdraft	–	10000
	80000	94000

(c) Assumed all sales are made in credit.

Comments: The liquidity position is not sound. The current ratio for the year 2009-2010 does not appear to be good enough as it is below the rule of thumb, *i.e.,* 2:1. In the year 2009-2010, the position has further been deteriorated to 1.38:1. The ratio shows a definite weakening in the solvency position of the company. As regards the liquid ratio, it is satisfactory in the year 2008-2009, and not alarming in the year 2009-2010.. However, the fall in the cash balance and appearance of the bank overdraft in the year 2009-2010 shows a definite deterioration in the financial position. Moreover, because of factors concerning sales, stock and debtors, the liquid ratio is likely deteriorated soon. As regards inventory turnover ratio, it indicates an alarming deterioration in the year 2009-2010. Also, the comparison of debtor's turnover ratios of the two years indicates little bit worsening of the company's liquid position. Lower turnover of stock and debtors in 2009-2010 reflects lower cash realization.

3. From the ratios and other data set forth below for the Auto accessories Ltd. indicate your interpretation of the company's financial condition:

	Year 3 2009-2010	Year 2 2008-2009	Year 1 2007-2008
Current ratio	3.02	2.78	2.65
Acid-test ratio	.99	1.10	1.55
Working capital turnover (times)	3.25	3.00	2.75
Receivable turnover (times)	7.2	8.41	9.83
Collection period (days)	50	43	37
Inventory to working capital (%)	110	100	95
Inventory turnover (times)	5.41	6.01	6.11
Earnings per equity share (₹)	2.5	4.05	5.10
Net income to net worth (%)	7	8.5	11.07
Operating exps. to net sales (%)	25	23	22
Sales increase during the year (%)	23	16	10
Cost of goods sold to net sales (%)	73	71	70
Dividend per share (₹)	3	3	3
Fixed assets to net worth (%)	22.7	18.0	16.4
Net profit on net sales (%)	2.0	5.09	7.03

Solution:

The interpretation of the financial condition of Auto Accessories Ltd. as revealed by the ratios and other data yields the following inferences:

(i) Declining profitability is evident from the following:

(a) Decrease in gross profit ratio from 30 per cent in year 1 to 27 per cent in year 3, (b) Decrease in net profit ratio from 7.03 per cent in year 1 to 2 per cent in year 3, and (c) Decrease in rate of return on net worth from 11.1 per cent in year 1 to 7 per cent in year 3. This is in spite of increase in sales from 10 per cent in year 1 to 23 per cent in year 3.

In interpreting the profitability of the company, another relevant factor is the expenses ratios. The ratio of cost of goods sold to net sales has gone up from 70 per cent to 73 per cent during the period. Likewise, there has been an increase in operating expenses ratio from 22 per cent to 25 per cent. The high inventories as reflected in lower inventory turnover ratio of 5.41 in year 3 as compared to 6.11 in year I have also adversely affected the profit margin.

As a consequence, the EPS has declined by more than 50 per cent during year 1-3 from ₹ 5.1 in year 1 to ₹ 2.5 in year 3.

(ii) The emerging liquidity position of the company appears to be highly satisfactory. The current ratio has increased from 2.65 in year 1 to 3.02 in year 3. Though, the acid-test ratio has declined from 1.55 1 to 0.99 it meets the standard. The company is unlikely to encounter any serious difficulty in paying the short-term obligations as and when they become due for payment.

However, the management should realize that the policy relating to collection of debt is not sound as reflected in the declining trend of receivables turnover from 9.83 in year 1 to 7.2 in year 3. In other words, the average debt collection period has increased from 37 days to 50 days. Either there is carelessness in: (i) Collecting the payments from debtors or (ii) Extending credit sales to customers leading to an increase in bad debts and thereby, an increase in the expenses ratio. Further, the inventory holding period requires investigation as the consistent increase in the current ratio and the consistent decrease in the acid-test ratio result from large accumulation of inventories. The excessive investments in current assets seem to be affecting the rate of return.

The investment in fixed assets appears excessive as shown by a consistent increase in the ratio of fixed assets to net worth. However, the overinvestment in fixed assets is not as clear as the overinvestment in working capital.

The stable dividend policy of the company is commendable and is likely to have a salutary effect on the market price of its shares.

In conclusion, the firm's financial position has not become so bad that it cannot be cured. What is required is a thorough probe into overinvestment in working capital, particularly inventories and fixed assets.

4. You have been supplied data for the Supreme Plastic Company Ltd. and its industry averages:

(i) Determine the indicated ratios for the Supreme Plastic Company.

(ii) Indicate the company's strengths and weaknesses as shown by your analysis.

Balance Sheet as at March 31, 2010

Liabilities	Amount ₹	Assets	Amount ₹
Equity share capital	1200000	Net fixed assets	605000
10% debentures	230000	Cash	220000
Sundry creditors	165000		
Bills payable	220000	Sundry debtors	275000
Other current liabilities	110000	Stock	825000
	1925000		1925000

Statement of profit for the year Ending March 31, 2010 current Year

Year	₹	₹
Sales		2750000
Less cost of goods sold:		
Materials	1045000	
Wages	660000	
Factory overheads	324500	2029500
Gross profit		720500
Less: selling and distribution expenses		(275000)
Less: administrative and general expenses		(307000)
Earnings before interest and taxes		138500
Less: interest		(23000)
Earnings before taxes		115500
Less income taxes (0.35)		40425
Net profit		75075

The company has no retained profit and reserve.

Ratio	Industry Average	Supreme Plastic
Current assets/current liabilities	2.4	
Sales/debtors	8.0	
Sales/stock	9.8	
Sales/total assets	2.0	
Net profit/sales (per cent)	3.3	
Net profit/total assets (per cent)	6.6	
Net profit/net worth (per cent)	12.7	
Total debt/total assets (per cent)	63.5	

Solution:

(i) Determination of Ratios:

Ratios	Computation ₹	Indicated Result	Industry Average
(a) $\frac{\text{Current assets}}{\text{Current liabilities}}$	$\frac{1320000}{495000}$	2.7	2.4
(b) $\frac{\text{Sales}}{\text{Debtors}}$	$\frac{2750000}{275000}$	10.0	8.0
(c) $\frac{\text{Sales}}{\text{Stock}}$	$\frac{2750000}{825000}$	3.3	9.8
(d) $\frac{\text{Sales}}{\text{Total Assets}}$	$\frac{2750000}{1925000}$	1.43	2.0

(e) $\frac{\text{Net profit}}{\text{Sales}}$ (%)	$\frac{75075}{2750000}$	2.73	3.3
(f) $\frac{\text{Net profit}}{\text{Total assets}}$ (%)	$\frac{75075}{1925000}$	3.9	6.6
(g) $\frac{\text{Net profit}}{\text{Equity share capital}}$ (%)	$\frac{75075}{1200000}$	6.25	12.7
(h) $\frac{\text{Total debt}}{\text{Total assets}}$ (%)	$\frac{725000}{1925000}$	37.7	63.5

(ii) The level of stock maintained by the Supreme Plastics is alarmingly high in that it is a almost three times the industry average. The other turnover ratios are in conformity with that of the industry. In fact, current ratios and debtor's turnover reelecting debt collection period of the company are better than those of the industry.

The greatest weakness of the company is the high level of inventories. It has caused a steep decline in the total assets turnover. The cost of carrying stocks is likely to adversely affect the profit margin. As a result of its low turnover and profit margin, the company's rate of return on net worth is less than one-half of the industry. The rate of return on equity capital of the company is also low because the company is using relatively less debt, that is, 37.7 per cent as against the industry figure of 63.5 per cent.

Problem 5

From the following particulars, you are required to prepare Statement of proprietary Fund:

(i) Gross profit ratio = 20% of sales.
(ii) Stock turnover ratio = 6
(iii) Avg. collection period = 4 months
(iv) Creditor's payment period = 3 months
(v) Fixed Assets Turnover ratio = 4
(vi) Capital turnover ratio = 3
(vii) Gross profit is ₹ 60000
(viii) Reserves & Surplus is ₹ 20000
(ix) Closing stock was ₹ 5000 higher than the opening stock.

Solution:

$$\text{G.P. ratio} = \frac{\text{Gross Profit}}{\text{Net Sales}} \times 100$$

Or, $$20 = \frac{60000}{\text{Net Sales}} \times 100$$

Or, $$\text{Net Sales} = \frac{60000}{20} \times 100 = ₹\ 300000$$

Cost of goods sold = Net Sales – Gross profit

= 300000 – 60000 = ₹ 240000

Now: $$\text{Inventory Turnover Ratio} = \frac{\text{Cost of Good Sold}}{\text{Average Stock}}$$

Or, $$6 = \frac{240000}{\text{Average Stock}}$$

Or, Average Stock = ₹ 40000

Again $$\text{Average Stock} = \frac{\text{Op. Stock} + \text{Cl. Stock}}{2}$$

Or, $$40000 = \frac{\text{Op. Stock} + (5000 + \text{Op. Stock})}{2}$$

Or, 80000 = 2 × Op. Stock + 5000

Or, 75000 = 2 × Op. Stock

Or, Op. Stock = ₹ 37500

So, Closing Stock = ₹ 42500 = ₹ (37500 + 5000)

$$\text{Fixed Assets Turnover Ratio} = \frac{\text{Net Sales}}{\text{(Net) Fixed Assets}}$$

Or, $$4 = \frac{300000}{\text{Fixed Assets}}$$ or, Fixed Assets = ₹ 75000

Capital Turnover Ratio = 3

Or, $$\frac{\text{Net Sales}}{\text{Capital Employed}} = 3$$

Or, $$\frac{300000}{\text{Capital Employed}} = 3$$

Or, Capital Employed = ₹ 100000

Debtors Collection Period = 4 months

Or, $$\frac{12}{\text{Debtors Turnover}} = 4$$

Or, $$\frac{12}{\frac{\text{Sales (credit)}}{\text{Closing Debtor}}} = 4$$

Or, $$\text{Debtors (Closing)} = \frac{4 \times 300000}{12} = ₹\ 100000$$

Creditors Payment Period= 3 months

Or, $\frac{12}{\text{Creditors Turnover}} = 3$

Or, $\frac{12}{\frac{\text{Credit Purchase}}{\text{Closing Creditors}}} = 3$

Or, Creditors (closing) = $3 \times \frac{\text{Purchase}}{12}$

Cost of Goods Sold = ₹ 240000

Or, Op stock + Purchase – CI. Stock = ₹ 240000

Or, Purchase = ₹ 240000 + CI. Stock – Op Stock

= ₹ 240000 + 42500 – 37500

= ₹ 245000

∴ Creditors = $3 \times \frac{245000}{12}$ = ₹ 61250

Cash balance /Bank O/D

= Total Liabilities – Total assets

= (Capital employed + Creditors) – (CI. Stock + Debtors + Fixed Assets)

= (₹ 100000 + 61250) – (₹ 42500 + 100000 + 75000)

= ₹ 161250 – 217500 = ₹ (56250)

= ₹ 56250 (Bank Overdraft)

Statement of Proprietary Fund

	₹	₹	₹
Fixed Assets			75000
Working Capital:			
Closing Stock:		42500	
Debtors		100000	
		142500	
Less:			
Creditors	61250		
Bank O/D	56250	117500	25000
Proprietary Fund			100000
Represented by:			
Share Capital			80000
Reserves & Surplus			20000
			100000

16.10 VALUE ADDED (OR ADDED VALUE) RATIO – MEASUREMENT OF OVERALL PRODUCTIVITY

Value added is the difference between the sales and bought in goods and services. Broadly speaking, it is the wealth that a firm creates by its own efforts. The value added performance of an organization is a good measure of the overall productivity of that organization. This performance can be measured from the following ratios:

Value added/ Fixed Assets

Value added/ Current Assets

Value added/ Per Employee

Value added/ per ₹ of direct waged and others.

Statement of Added Value for the year to .... (with assumed figures)

		₹ In lakhs
Sales		65
Less: Bought in goods and services		40
Added Value		25
Applied as follow:		
• To employed (wages, pensions and other benefits)		15.50
• To suppliers of capital		
— Dividend	1.8	
— Interest on loans	.75	2.55
• To pay Govt. taxation		.80
• To provide for maintenance and expression of assets		
— Depreciation		1.50
— Retained Profits		4.65
Added Value		25

SUMMARY

A financial ratio is a relationship between two financial variables which helps to ascertain financial status and positions of a firm.

The principal tool of financial statement analysis is financial ratio analysis which essentially involves a study of ratios between various items or group of items in financial statements.

Financial ratios may be divided into 6 broad types: Liquidity ratios, Solvency ratios, Profitability or Efficiency ratios, Activity ratios, Investment ratios, and Capital structure or coverage rations. Liquidity refers to the ability of the firm to meet its obligations in the short-run, usually one year etc. The liquidity ratios are current ratio, acid-test ratio, working capital ratio, cash position ratio, etc.

Solvency is the debt paying ability of the firm over a long period of time. The solvency ratios are Proprietary ratio, Debt Equity ratio, Leverage ratio, Interest coverage ratio, Debt service coverage ratio.

Profitability ratios are calculated to measure the operating efficiency of the company. Besides management of the company, creditors and owners are also interested in the profitability of the firm. Generally two major types of profitability ratios are calculated:

(i) Profitability in relation to sales

- Gross profit Margin – P/V Ratio
- Net profit Margin
- Operating cost Ratio

(ii) Profitability in relation to investment

- Return on Equity
- Return on Assets
- Return on Capital Employed
- Return on proprietor's fund
- Earning power.

Activity ratios reflect the firm's efficiency in utilizing its assets in generating sales, and are calculated by establishing relationships between sales and assets. The activity ratios are Capital Turnover, Creditor's Turnover, Debtor's turnover, Stock Turnover, Working Capital Turnover.

Leverage ratios measure the proportion of debt (outsiders) capital in financing the firm's assets and also in compare to equity capital. The leverage ratios are Gearing ratio, Debt Equity ratio, Deb-Asset ratio, Proprietary ratio, Interest Coverage ratio etc.

Du Pont analysis divides a particular ratio into components and studies the effect of each and every component on the ratio.

There are three types of users to whom financial statement analysis could be very useful. They are short-term lenders, long-term lenders and finally stockholders. There are three analyses we use.

- Ratio Analysis
- Comparative Analysis
- Du Pont Analysis

The Du Pont Analysis is a useful tool of financial analysis which provides an insight into the two determinants of return on assets – net profit margin and total assets turnover ratio. In common size analysis the items of balance sheet are stated as % of total assets and the items in the profit & loss account are expressed as % of total sales.

EXERCISE

Short Questions

1. Define Ratio
2. What is meant by the term 'Ratio Analysis'?
3. Write the names of 'operating ratios'?

4. What is Du Pont analysis?
5. What are Common Size Financial Statements?
6. What is Dividend yield?
7. What is the difference between 'activity Ratios' and 'leverage Ratios'?
8. Write the names of Financial Statement analysises.
9. What is solvency?
10. What is 'Proprietor's Fund'?
11. What is the difference between 'External Equities' and 'Internal Equities'?
12. What is the difference between 'Over capitalization and 'Undercapitalization?

Moderate and Broad Questions

1. Clarify the accounting ratios.
2. Explain the difference between current ratio and acid test ratio? Show one example each.
3. Explain Du Pont chart with an example.
4. What are the advantages and limitations of ratio analysis?
5. What are the roles of ratio analysis in corporates? Explain the importance of ratio analysis in this regard.
6. What is comparative analysis? Explain each type of comparative analysis with an example?

PROBLEMS

1. (a) A company sells goods as well as credit. The following particulars are extracted from their books of account for the current-year-end.

	₹
Total gross Sales	500000
Cash Sales	100000
Sales Returns	35000
Total debtors at the end	45000
Bills Receivable	10000
Provision for doubtful debts at the end of the year	5000

Calculate the average collection period

[**Hints:** Net Credit Sales = Gross Sales – Cash Sales – Sales return

= Credit Sales – Sales return

= ₹ 365000

$$\text{Debtors turnover} = \frac{\text{Net Credit Sales}}{\text{Debtor} + \text{B/R}}$$

$$\text{Average Collection Period} = \frac{365}{\text{Debtors Turnover}} \text{ days}$$]

(b) The Capital of XYZ Ltd. is as follows:

10% Debenture, ₹ 100 each	₹ 15,00,000
9.5% Preference Share Capital, ₹ 10 each	₹ 10,00,000
Equity Share Capital, ₹ 100 each	₹ 25,00,000
	₹ 50,00,000

Additional Informations

(EBIT) Earnings before tax and interest = ₹ 800000, tax rate is 30%, depreciation is ₹ 50000, Equity dividend has been paid @ 10%, market price of equity share is ₹ 50. You are required to calculate the following:

(i) Dividend Yield on the equity share

(ii) Cover for the preference and equity dividends

(iii) Earnings per share

(iv) Price-earnings ratio.

Hints:

$$\text{[Dividend Yield} = \frac{\text{Dividend per share}}{\text{Market price per share}}$$

Dividend Coverage Ratio

- Preference

$$= \frac{\text{EBIT – Interest – Tax rate (EBIT – Interest)}}{\text{Dividend payable to preference share holders}}$$

$$= \frac{\text{PAT OR Profit after Tax}}{\text{Dividend payable to Pref. Shareholders}}$$

- Equity

$$= \frac{\text{EBIT – Interest – Tax rate (EBIT – Interest) – Preference Dividend}}{\text{Dividend payable to equity share holders}}$$

$$= \frac{\text{PAT – Pref. Dividend}}{\text{Dividend payable to Equity Shareholders}}$$

$$= \frac{\text{Earnings available to equity share holders}}{\text{Dividend payable to equity share holders}}$$

Earnings per Equity share

$$= \frac{\text{Earning available to equity share holders}}{\text{No. equity share holders}}$$

Price – earnings ratio

$$= \frac{\text{Market price share holders}}{\text{Earnings per share}}$$

2. The following are the summarized Profit & Loss Account of a company for the year ending 31st March, 2011 and the Balance Sheet as on that date-

Dr. **Profit & Loss Account** **Cr.**

For the year ended 31st March, 2011

Particulars	₹	Particulars		₹
To Opening Stock	99500	By Sales		
To Purchases	545250	Cash	170000	
To Trade Expenses & Wages	14250	Credit	680000	**850000**
To Gross profit c/d	340000	By Closing Stock		149000
	999000			**999000**
To Administration Expenses	150000	By Gross profit b/d		340000
To Finance Expenses	15000	By Non – Operating Incomes –		
To Selling & Dist. Expenses	30000	Interest on loan		3000
To Non-operating Expenses		Dividend on shares		6000
– Net loss on sale				
of fixed Assets	4000			
To Net profit	150000			
	349000			**349000**

Balance Sheet

As at 31.03.2011

Liabilities	₹	Assets	₹
Issued Capital:		**Fixed Assets :**	
2000 Equity Shares of		Land and Buildings	150000
₹ 100 each	200000	Plant and Machinery	80000
Reserves & Surplus:			
Reserves	90000		
Profit & Loss (App.)		**Current Assets :**	
Account	60000		
		Stock-in-trade	149000
Current Liabilities:		Sundry Debtors	41000
Creditors	90000	Bills Receivable	30000
Bills payable	40000	Cash and bank balance	30000
	480000		480000

From the above Statement, you are required to calculate the following ratios:

(i) Current Ratio
(ii) Liquid Ratio
(iii) Stock Turnover Ratio
(iv) Debtor's Turnover Ratio
(v) Creditor's Turnover Ratio
(vi) Sales to working Capital
(vii) Sales to Fixed Assets or Turnover of Fixed Assets
(viii) Sales to Capital Employed
(ix) Operating Ratio
(x) Return on total Resources
(xi) Turnover of Total Assets

[Hints.

(iii) Stock Turnover Ratio $= \dfrac{\text{Cost of goods sold}}{\text{Avg. Inventory}} = \dfrac{\text{Sales – gross profit}}{\dfrac{\text{Op. Stock \& cl. stock}}{2}}$

(vii) Turnover of Fixed Assets $= \dfrac{\text{Net Sales}}{\text{Fixed Assets}} = \dfrac{850000}{150000 + 80000}$

(viii) Sales to Capital Empl. $= \dfrac{\text{Sales}}{\text{Capital Empl.}} = \dfrac{850000}{\text{Sh. Cap + Res. \& Surpl.}}$

(ix) Operating Ratio $= \dfrac{\text{Cost of Goods Sold + Other operating expenses}}{\text{Net Sales}}$

$= \dfrac{\text{(Sales – G.P.) + (Adm. exps. + Finance exps. + Selling \& Dist. Expenses)}}{\text{Net Sales (850000)}}$

(x) Return on Total Resource $= \dfrac{\text{Net profit}}{\text{Total Assets}} \times 100 = \dfrac{150000}{480000} \times 100$

(xi) Turnover of Total Assets $= \dfrac{\text{Net Sales}}{\text{Total Assets}} = \dfrac{850000}{480000}$

3. From the following figures relating to the accounts of ABC Ltd. comment upon the present state and trend in respect of Profitability, Solvency and Capitalization of the company:

Statement of Profit & Loss

		2009 – 2010		2010 – 2011	
		₹	₹	₹	₹
	Sales		1400000		1800000
Less:	Cost of Goods Sold:				
	Opening Stock	280000		350000	
Add:	Purchase	1000000		1150000	
		1280000		1500000	
Less:	Closing Stock	(400000)	880000	(420000)	1080000
	Gross Profit		520000		720000
Less:	Operating expenses	300000		320000	
	Depreciation	75000	375000	155000	475000
Earning before Int. & Tax (EBIT)			145000		245000
Less:	Interest on O/D		15000		40000
			130000		205000
Less:	Interest on Loan		15000		50000
	Profit before Tax (PBT)		115000		155000
Less:	Tax @ 30%		34500		46500
PAT (Profit after Tax)			80500		108500
Less:	Proposed Dividend		37500		50000
Transfer to Reserve			43000		58500

Balance Sheet

	2009 – 2010		2010 – 2011	
	₹	₹	₹	₹
A. FIXED ASSETS: Net Block		600000		900000
B. WORKING CAPITAL: (a) – (b)				
Current Assets :				
Receivable	350000		510000	
Cash at bank	100000		160500	
Quick Asset	450000		670500	
Stock-in-trade	185000		307000	
Total (a)	635000		977500	
Current Liab. :				
Payables	–		165000	
Provision for Taxation	120000		–	
Proposed Dividend	37500		50000	
Bank Overdraft	150000		400000	
Total (b)	307500		615000	
Working Capital = Total (a) – Total (b)		327500		362500
Total = A + B		**927500**		**1262500**
Represented by:				
Share Capital		600000		600000
Reserve & Surplus		207500		262500
12.5% Loan		120000		400000
Total Capital Employed		**927500**		**1262500**

[Hints: Profitability: Gross profit Ratio $= \frac{\text{G.P.}}{\text{Sales}} \times 100$

Return on Capital employed $= \frac{\text{EBIT}}{\text{Capital Employed}} \times 100$

Solvency : Current Ratio
Liquid Ratio

Capitalization : Debt Equity Ratio
Capital Gearing Ratio
Fixed Assets Ratio]

4. From the following details, prepare the Balance Sheet of XYZ Ltd.

Stock Velocity/Turnover	6
Capital Turnover Ratio	2
Fixed Assets Turnover Ratio	4
Gross Profit	20%

Debt Collection Period 2 months

Creditors Payment Period 73 days

The gross profit was ₹ 60000. Closing Stock was ₹ 5000 in excess of the opening stock.

[Hints: Gross Profit Ratio = $\frac{\text{GP}}{\text{Sales}} \times 100$

Sales = ₹ 300000

Cost of goods sold = Sales – Cost of good sold = ₹ 240000

Stock Turnover Ratio = $\frac{\text{Cost of goods sold}}{\text{Average Stock}}$

Average Stock = ₹ 40000 (= 240000 ÷ 6)

Closing Stock – Opening Stock = ₹ 5000; Closing Stock = ₹ 42500

Capital Turnover = $\frac{\text{Sales}}{\text{Capital Employed}}$

Capital Employed = ₹ 150000 (= 300000 ÷ 2)

Fixed Assets Turnover Ratio = $\frac{\text{Sales}}{\text{Fixed Assets}}$

Fixed Assets = ₹ 75000 (= 300000 ÷ 4)

Debt Collection Period = $\frac{12}{\text{Debtor's Turnover}}$ months

Or, Debtor's Turnover = $\frac{12}{\text{Debt Collection Period}} = \frac{12}{2} = 6$

Or, $\frac{\text{Credit Sales}}{\text{Debtors}} = 6$

Or, Debtors = $\frac{\text{Credit Sales}}{6} = \frac{₹\ 300000}{6}$ = ₹ 50000

Creditor's Payment Period = $\frac{365}{\text{Creditor's Turnover}}$ days

or, Creditors Turnover = $\frac{365}{\text{Creditor's Payment}} = \frac{365}{73}$

Or, $\frac{\text{Credit Purchase}}{\text{Creditors}} = 5$

Cost of goods sold = Op. Stock + Purchase (*assumed all credit*) – Closing Stock

Or, 240000 = 37500 + Credit Purchase – 42500

Or, Credit Purchase = ₹ 245000

So, Creditors = $\frac{245000}{5}$ = ₹ 49000

Balance Sheet

Liabilities	₹	Assets	₹
Capital Employed	150000	Fixed Assets	75000
Creditors	49000	Debtors	50000
		Closing Stock	42500
		Cash (balancing Figure)	31500
	199000		199900

5. You, as a Credit Manager, of the ICICI Bank Ltd. have been approached by two companies for a loan of ₹ 100000 for 6 months, with no collateral offered. Since the bank has reached its quota for loan of this type, only one of these requests can be granted. The relevant information supplied to you by the two companies are presented below: (₹ in lakhs)

	Company A	Company B
Assets:		
Cash at bank	170	300
Accounts Receivable	274	424
Stock-in-trade	900	1350
Total current Assets	1344	2074
Other Assets	1000	1020
Total Assets	2344	3094
Liabilities & Capital:		
Equity Share Capital	800	1200
Retained Earnings	244	254
Long term Loans	800	1000
Current liabilities	500	640
Total	2344	3094
Other informations:		
Sales	2400	1700
Rate of gross profit on Sales	0.30	0.40

6. A firm has owner's equity of ₹ 100 crores. The ratios for the firm are:

Short-term debt to Total debt	0.42
Total debt to owner's equity	0.58
Fixed Assets to owner's equity	0.55
Total Assets turnover	3 times
Inventory Turnover	10 times

Complete the following Balance Sheet from the information given above:

Liabilities	₹	Assets		₹
Short-term debt (CL)	......	Fixed Assets		......
Long-term debt (CL)	......	Current Assets :		
Total debt	......	Cash	......	
Owner's Equity	......	Stock	......	......
Total Capital & liabilities.	......	Total Assets		......

7. You are presented with the following figures presented from the Balance Sheet of Reality Cares Ltd.

(₹ in thousands)

Assets :	**2008-09 Year 1 ₹**	**2009-10 Year 2 ₹**	**2010-11 Year 3 ₹**
Debtors	2500	4000	5000
Stock-in-trade	6000	6850	7550
Plant & Machinery	1150	1500	1500
Building	650	650	650
	10300	13000	14700

Liabilities :	**2008-09 ₹**	**2009-10 ₹**	**2010-11 ₹**
Bank Overdraft	1500	2800	3000
Creditors	2000	3200	4500
Profit & Loss A/c	800	1000	1200
Equity Share Capital – paid up capital (₹ 10 per share; ₹ 7.50 paid)	6000	6000	6000
	10300	13000	14700

The opening stock at the beginning of 2008-2009 was ₹ 4000. You are requested to show in respect of each year the following ratios and make comment on the changes in the profitability, liquidity and financial position of the company :

(*i*) Current Ratio

(*ii*) Debtor's Turnover Ratio

(*iii*) Creditor's Turnover Ratio

(*iv*) Stock Turnover Ratio

❑❑❑

17 Analysis of Budget

17.1 DEFINITION OF BUDGET, FEATURES AND ADVANTAGES

A budget is a financial document used to project future income and expenses. The budgeting process may be carried out by individuals or by companies to estimate whether the person/ company can continue to operate with its projected income and expenses.

A budget is a plan cxpressed in quantitative, usually monetary term, covering a specific period of time, usually one year. In other words a budget is a systematic plan for the utilization of manpower and material resources.

In a business organization, a budget represents an estimate of future costs and revenues. Budgets may be divided into two basic classes: Capital Budgets and Operating Budgets.

Capital budgets are directed towards proposed expenditures for new projects and often require special financing. The operating budgets are directed towards achieving short-term operational goals of the organization, for instance, production or profit goals in a business firm. Operating budgets may be sub-divided into various departmental of functional budgets.

The main Characteristics of a Budget are

1. It is prepared in advance and is derived from the long-term strategy of the organization.
2. It relates to future period for which objectives or goals have already been laid down.

It is expressed in quantitative form, physical or monetary units, or both.

Different types of budgets are prepared for different purposes *e.g.* Sales Budget, Production Budget, Administrative Expense Budget, Raw-material Budget etc. All these sectional budgets are afterwards integrated into a master budget, which represents an overall plan of thc organization.

Advantages of Budgets

A budget helps us in the following ways:

1. It brings about efficiency and improvement in the working of the organization.
2. It is a way of communicating the plans to various units of the organization. By establishing the divisional, departmental, sectional budgets, exact responsibilities are assigned. It thus minimizes the possibilities of buck passing if the budget figures are not met.
3. It is a way of motivating managers to achieve the goals set for the units.
4. It serves as a benchmark for controlling on-going operations.
5. It helps in developing a team spirit where participation in budgeting is encouraged.
6. It helps in reducing wastage and losses by revealing them in time for corrective action.
7. It serves as a basis for evaluating the performance of managers.
8. It serves as a means of educating the managers.

17.2 DEFINITION OF BUDGETING, OBJECTIVES

Budgeting in a business sense is the planned allocation of available funds to each department within a company. Budgeting allows executives to control overspending in less productive areas and put more company assets into areas which generate significant income or good public relations. Budgeting is usually handled during meetings with accountants, financial experts and representatives from each department affected by the budgeting.

In a personal financing sense, budgeting can mean estimating monthly living expenses based on previous bills and wages. If your monthly income is a steady ₹ 7000, for example, you can subtract all of your known monthly bills from that figure even before they arrive. Some bills can be estimated and subtracted from the original income figure. The remaining balance after fixed expenses now becomes your household budget. Instead of assigning amounts for sundries such as groceries, entertainment, gas and clothing, budgeting allows you to use percentages instead.

The key to successful budgeting is both flexibility and inflexibility. Certain expenses are fixed, so payment of those bills should be an inflexible element. Nothing is more important than paying those particular bills in full. In business, departments need to know the absolute ceiling on spending. Budgeting works best when very few exceptions are made to the upper limits. The idea of fiscal responsibility is to form a workable budget and stick to it as best as possible.

The Objectives of Budgeting are

1. To encourage self study in all aspects of a Company's operations.

2. To get all members of management to "put their heads" to the basic question of how the business should be run, to make them of a coordinated team operating towards clearly defined objectives.

Advantages of Budgets

A budget helps us in the following ways:

1. It brings about efficiency and improvement in the working of the organization.
2. It is a way of communicating the plans to various units of the organization. By establishing the divisional, departmental, sectional budgets, exact responsibilities are assigned. It thus minimizes the possibilities of buck passing if the budget figures are not met.
3. It is a way of motivating managers to achieve the goals set for the units.
4. It serves as a benchmark for controlling on-going operations.
5. It helps in developing a team spirit where participation in budgeting is encouraged.
6. It helps in reducing wastage and losses by revealing them in time for corrective action.
7. It serves as a basis for evaluating the performance of managers.
8. It serves as a means of educating the managers.

17.2 DEFINITION OF BUDGETING, OBJECTIVES

Budgeting in a business sense is the planned allocation of available funds to each department within a company. Budgeting allows executives to control overspending in less productive areas and put more company assets into areas which generate significant income or good public relations. Budgeting is usually handled during meetings with accountants, financial experts and representatives from each department affected by the budgeting.

In a personal financing sense, budgeting can mean estimating monthly living expenses based on previous bills and wages. If your monthly income is a steady ₹ 7000, for example, you can subtract all of your known monthly bills from that figure even before they arrive. Some bills can be estimated and subtracted from the original income figure. The remaining balance after fixed expenses now becomes your household budget. Instead of assigning amounts for sundries such as groceries, entertainment, gas and clothing, budgeting allows you to use percentages instead.

The key to successful budgeting is both flexibility and inflexibility. Certain expenses are fixed, so payment of those bills should be an inflexible element. Nothing is more important than paying those particular bills in full. In business, departments need to know the absolute ceiling on spending. Budgeting works best when very few exceptions are made to the upper limits. The idea of fiscal responsibility is to form a workable budget and stick to it as best as possible.

The Objectives of Budgeting are

1. To encourage self study in all aspects of a Company's operations.

2. To get all members of management to "put their heads" to the basic question of how the business should be run, to make them of a coordinated team operating towards clearly defined objectives.

2. **Defining Responsibilities:** Laying down the responsibilities of each individual so that everyone knows what is expected of him and how he will be judged.

3. **Basis for Performance Evaluation:** Providing basis for the comparison of actual performance with the predetermined targets and investigation of deviation, if any, of actual performance and expenses from the budgeted figures. It helps to take timely corrective measures.

4. **Optimum use of Resources:** Ensuring the best use of all available resources to maximize profit or production, subject to the limiting factors.

5. **Coordination:** Coordinating the various activities of the business and centralizing control, but also making a facility for the Management to decentralize responsibility and delegate authority.

6. **Planned action:** Engendering a spirit of careful forethought, assessment of what is possible and an attempt at it. It leads to dynamism without recklessness. It also helps to draw up long range plans with a fair measure of accuracy.

7. **Basis for policy:** Providing a basis for revision of current and future policies.

Steps: The process of budgetary control involves the following steps:

(a) Defining and specifying the objectives to be achieved by the business.

(b) Preparing business plans in order to ensure that the desired objectives are accomplished.

(c) Translating the plans into budgets, and relating the responsibilities of individual executives and managers to particular sections of the budget.

(d) Continuous comparison of actual results with the budget, and the calculation of differences between the budgeted and actual performance.

(e) Investigating major differences in order to establish the causes.

(f) Presentation of the information to management in a suitable form, relating the variances to individual responsibility.

(g) Corrective action by the management in order to avoid a repetition of any wastage or over-expenditure. Alternatively, where it is not possible to achieve the budgeted targets due to change in circumstances, the revision of the budget.

17.4 ADVANTAGES AND LIMITATIONS OF THE BUDGETARY CONTROL SYSTEM

Advantages of Budgetary Control:

The advantages of a budgetary control system are as follows:

1. It defines the objectives of the organization as a whole, and within this overall framework, it defines the results which each department should achieve.
2. It reveals the extent by which actual results have exceeded or fallen short of the budget.
3. It indicates, with variances or other measures of performance, the reasons why actual results differ from those budgeted, and establishes the magnitude of the adverse trends.

4. As a result of reporting on actual performance along with variances and other performance measures, it provides a basis for guiding executive action to correct adverse trends.
5. It provides a basis for the revision of the current budget or for the preparation of future budgets.
6. It provides a system whereby the resources of the organization are used in the most have been co-ordinated.
7. It indicates the efficiency with which the various activities of the organization have been co-ordinated.
8. It provides some centralizing control where activities and responsibilities are decentralized.
9. Where the activities of an organization are subject to seasonal variations, it provides a means of stabilizing the organization's activities.
10. It establishes a basis for internal audit by means of regular examination of departmental results.
11. It enables standard costs to be used.
12. It provides a basis for measuring productive efficiency with a view to paying a bonus to employees.

Limitations of the Budgetary Control System

1. **Estimates:** Budgets may or may not be true, as they are based on estimates. The assumptions about future events may or may not actually happen.

2. **Rigidity:** Budgets are considered as rigid document. Too much emphasis on budgets may affect day today operations and ignores the dynamic state of organizational functioning.

3. **False Sense of Security:** Mere budgeting cannot lead to profitability. Budgets cannot be executed automatically. It may create a false sense of security that everything has been taken care in the budgets.

4. **Lack of coordination:** Staff cooperation is usually not available during Budgetary Control exercise.

5. **Time and Cost:** The introduction and implementation of the system may be expensive.

17.5 DIFFERENCE BETWEEN BUDGET, BUDGETING AND BUDGETARY CONTROL

The difference between budget, budgeting and budgetary control may be stated thus budgets are the individual objectives of a department etc., whereas budgeting may be said to be the act of setting budgets. Budgetary control embraces all and includes the science of planning the budgets themselves and utilization of such budgets as an overall management tool for the business planning and control. Thus, the term budgetary control is wider in meaning and it includes both budget and budgeting.

17.6 CASH BUDGET

A cash budget is a tool for budgeting and controlling cash which is prepared in advance and is based on plan for future cash inflows and outflows of cash. Ultimately it focuses on expected closing cash balance at the end of each week, fort night, month or quarter. The closing cash balance can be determined after subtracting future cash outflows from total cash inflows (Opening Balance + Cash Receipt).

A specimen of cash budget under this method is given below:

Cash Budget for the period from January to June, 2003

	January	February	March	April	May	June
	₹	₹	₹	₹	₹	₹
A. Opening Balance	....	....	....	....	....	....
B. Receipts:						
Cash Sales	....	....	....	....	....	....
Collection from Debtors	....	....	....	....	....	....
Sale of Assets	....	....	....	....	....	....
Other Receipts	....	....	....	....	....	....
Total (B)	....	....	....	....	....	....
C. Total Cash inflow = A + B	....	....	....	....	....	....
D. Payments:						
Cash Purchases	....	....	....	....	....	....
Payment to Creditors	....	....	....	....	....	....
Wages	....	....	....	....	....	....
Overheads	....	....	....	....	....	....
Purchase of Assets	....	....	....	....	....	....
Taxes	....	....	....	....	....	....
Others	....	....	....	....	....	....
Total (D)	....	....	....	....	....	....
E. Closing Balance = C – D	....	....	....	....	....	....

17.7 DISTINCTION BETWEEN CASH BUDGET AND CASH FLOW STATEMENT

The following are the important points of distinction between a cash budget and a cash flow statement:

1. A cash budget is futuristic in approach. It is prepared in advance and is based on future plan of action. A cash flow statement is based on past data.

2. A cash budget relates to objectives to be achieved and is a plan for future inflows and outflows of cash. A cash flow statement is a post mortem analysis of actual inflows and outflows of cash.

3. The period of cash budget is usually short (may be a week, fortnight, month or quarter). A cash budget may be prepared covering a long period also (say, a year) but divided into short sub-budget periods (say, a month or quarter). The time span to be covered by a cash budget will vary from one firm to another, depending on the nature of its businesses and the degree of accuracy with which estimates can be made. A cash flow statement covers a relatively longer period, usually an accounting year, and it is not divided into sub-periods.

4. A cash budget requires previous data only for the purpose of judicious forecasting. A cash flow statement is prepared from accounting data at the beginning and end of an accounting year.

5. A cash budget is a tool for budgeting and controlling cash. A cash flow statement is an analysis of the working of the concern for the past accounting year.

6. A cash budget usually serves the purposes of management only. A cash flow statement may serve the purposes of management as well as external parties.

17.8 MEANING OF ZERO-BASE BUDGETING

The technique of zero-base budgeting suggests that an organization should not only make decision about the proposed new programmes but it should also, from time to time, review the appropriateness of the existing programmes. Such review should particularly be done of such responsibility centers' where there is relatively high proportion of discretionary costs.

Zero-base budgeting (or review), as the term suggests, examines a programme or function or responsibility from 'scratch'. The reviewer proceeds on the assumption that nothing is to be allowed. The manager proposing the activity has, therefore, to prove that the activity is essential and the various amounts asked for are reasonable taking into account the volume of activity. Nothing is allowed simply because it was being done or allowed in the past. Thus, it means writing on a clean slate.

In order to understand the correct concept of zero base budgeting it will be useful here to go through the definitions given by eminent management experts.

"An operating planning and budgeting process which requires each manager to justify his entire budget requests in detail from scratch (hence zero-basis). Each manager states why he should spend any money at all. This approach requires that all activities be identified as decision packages which would be evaluated by systematic analysis ranked in order of importance."

"ZBB is a technique which complements and links the existing planning, budgeting and review processes. It identifies alternative and efficient methods of utilizing limited resources in effective attainment of selected benefits. It is a flexible management approach which provides a credible rationale for re-allocating resources by focusing on the systematic review and justification of the funding and performance levels of current programmes or activities."

"ZBB is a management tool which provides a systematic method for evaluating all operations and programmes, current or new, allows for budget reductions and expansions in a rational manner and allows re-allocation of sources from low to high priority programmes"

On the basis of the above definitions, it can be concluded that ZBB is a technique whereby each programme, whether new or existing, must be justified in its entirely, each time a new budget is formulated. It involves:

(i) Dealing with practically all elements of managers' budget requests.

(ii) Critical examination of ongoing activities as closely as the proposed activities:

(iii) Providing each manager a range of choices in setting priorities in respect of different activities and allocating resources.

Advantages of Zero-base Budgeting

Zero-base budgeting offers the following advantages:

1. It provides the organization with a systematic way to evaluate different operations and programmes undertaken by the management. It enables management to allocate resources according to priority of the programmes.
2. It ensures that every programme undertaken by the managers is essential for organization and is being performed in the best possible way.
3. It enables the management to approve departmental budgets on the basis of cost-benefit analysis. No arbitrary cuts or increases in budget estimates are made.
4. It helps in identifying areas of wasteful expenditure and if desired it can also be used for suggesting alternative courses of action.
5. It links budgets with the corporate objectives. Nothing will simply be allowed only because it was being done in the past if it does not help in achieving goals of the enterprise.
6. It can be used for introduction and implementation of the system of management by objectives. Thus, it cannot only be used for fulfillment of the objectives of traditional budgeting but it can also be used for a variety of other purposes.

Limitation of Zero-base Budgeting

The limitations of zero-base budgeting are largely due to the following types of problems:

(i) **Implementation problems:** Successful implementation of Zero-base Budgeting requires wholehearted support from the top management. Such co-operation is generally lacking because of fear and problems in the minds of top management regarding the implementation of the Zero-base Budgeting technique.

Zero-base Budgeting also requires that the concerned managers should not be frequently transferred. In case frequent transfers are made, considerable time will be lost in training and developing new manager resulting in waste of time as well as resources.

(ii) **Decision packages formulation problems:** Considerable problems are faced while formulating decision packages. One of such problems is the fixation of minimum level of effort. The managers would never like to fix the minimum level of effort below the current level. They may like to fix it at a higher level than the current levels. Similarly, it is difficult to identify meaningful work measures for the purposes of evaluation.

(iii) **Ranking decision packages:** Ranking of the decision packages is also full of problems are: (a) who will do the ranking? (b) What methods or procedures would be followed to review and rank the procedures? (c) To what level within each organization the decision packages will be ranked?

It is usually found that managers strive to keep continuing their "pet projects" for the reasons best known to them. Ranking also becomes difficult on account of involvement of a large number of decision packages, particularly in a multi-product manufacturing organization.

(iv) **Cost problems:** Zero-base budgeting involves time as well as cost. It needs properly trained management personnel to do the required job.

Worked-Out Problems

Re: Material Purchase

Problem 1

The sales director of a manufacturing company reports that next year he expects to sell 54,000 units of a certain product.

The product manager consults the store-keeper and casts his figure as follows:

Two kinds of raw materials, A and B are required for manufacturing the product. Each unit of the product requires two units of A and three units of B. The estimated opening balances at the commencement of the next year are:

Finished product 10,000 units, A 12,000 units, B 15,000 units.

The desirable closing balances at the end of the next year are:

Finished product 14,000 units, A 13,000 units, B 16,000 units.

Draw up a quantitative chart showing the materials purchases budget for the next year.

Solution

Materials Purchases Budget for the year

	Material A Units	Material B Units
Materials required:		
A (58,000 × 2)	1,16,000	
B (58,000 × 3)		1,74,000
Closing Stock	13,000	16,000
	1,29,000	1,90,000
Opening Stock	(12,000)	(15,000)
Budgeted Purchases (in units)	1,17,000	1,75,000

Working:

Budgeted production for the year:

	Units
Sales	54,000
Closing Stock	14,000
	68,000
Opening Stock	(10,000)
Budgeted production (in units)	58,000

Re: Sales Budget

Problem 2

M/s Kritika Manufacturing Company manufactures three products A, B and C and sells them through cities Mumbai, Delhi and Chennai. Sales Budget for the current year based on the estimates of the sales division manager were:

Product	Bengaluru	Delhi	Chennai
A	5,000 units @ ₹ 5	10,000 units @ ₹ 5	12,000 units @ ₹ 5
B	10,000 @ ₹ 10	5,000 units @ ₹ 10	9,000 units @ ₹ 10
C	15,000 units @ ₹ 15	12,000 units @ ₹ 15	5,000 units @ ₹ 15

Actual sales for the current year ending 31st Dec., 08 are as follows:

Product	Bengaluru	Delhi	Chennai
A	20,000 units @ ₹ 5	12,000 units @ ₹ 5	12,000 units @ ₹ 5
B	12,000 units @ ₹ 10	5,000 units @ ₹ 10	18,000 units @ ₹ 10
C	14,000 units @ ₹ 15	12,000 units @ ₹ 15	3,000 units @ ₹ 15

A market research conducted by the management revealed that product A has found favour among customers but is underpriced, it is expected that if price is increased by ₹ 1.00, its sales will not be affected. The price of the product B is to be reduced by ₹ 1 as it is overpriced. Product C is rightly priced, extensive advertisement is required to push up the above sales. On the basis of the above information, it is estimated that there will be an increase in sales over current budget:

Bengaluru – 10%	Delhi – 10%	Chennai – 5%
Bengaluru – 5%	Delhi – 5%	Chennai – 10%
Bengaluru – 5%	Delhi – 10%	Chennai – 15%

With the help of the intensive advertisement campaign, the following additional sales are expected:

Bengaluru – 200 units	Delhi – 100 units	Chennai – 200 units
Bengaluru – 50 units	Delhi – 50 units	Chennai – 100 units
Bengaluru – 100 units	Delhi – 120 units	Chennai – 250 units

Prepare a Sales budget 5 incorporating the above adjustments.

Solution

Sales Budget of Kritika Manufacturing Company for the year ended 31st Dec., 08

Division		(Prepaid)	Budget for the future period		Budget for the current period			Actual sales for the current period		
		Qty.	*Price* ₹	*Amount* ₹	*Qty.*	*Price* ₹	*Amount* ₹	*Qty.*	*Price* ₹	*Amount* ₹
Bangalore	A	16,600	6	99,600	15,000	5	75,000	20,000	5	100000
	B	10,550	9	94,950	10,000	10	1, 00,000	12,000	10	120000
	C	15,850	15	2,37,750	15,000	15	75,000	14,000	15	210000
		43,000		4,32,000	40,000		2,50,000	46,000		430000
Delhi	A	11,100	6	66,600	10,000	5	50,000	12,000	5	60,000
	B	5,300	9	47,700	5,000	10	50,000	5,000	10	50,000
	C	13,320	15	1,99,800	12,000	15	1,80,000	12,000	15	1,80,000
		29,720		3,14,100	27,000		2,80,000	29,000		2,90,000
Chennai	A	12,800	6	76,800	12,000	5	60,000	12,000	5	60,000
	B	6,700	9	60,300	6,000	10	60,000	8,000	10	80,000
	C	6,000	15	90,000	5,000	15	75,000	3,000	15	45,000
		25,500		2,27,100	23,000		1,95,000	23,000		1,85,000
Total		98,220		9,73,500	90,000		7,25,000	98,000		9,05,000

Re: Production Budget

Problem 3

Prepare a production Budget for three months ended March 31, 2010 for a factory producing three products, on the basis of the following information:

Type of Product	Estimated Stock on Jan. 1, 2010 (units)	Estimated Sales (units) During Jan. – March 2010	Desired Closing Stock On March 31, 2010 (units)
A	5,000	25,000	5,000
B	5,000	28,000	5,000
C	5,000	22,000	3,000

Solution:

Production Budget for Three Months to March 31, 2010

	Units	*Units*
Product A: Estimated Sales	25,000	
Add: Desired Closing Stock	5,000	
Less: Estimated Opening Stock	(5,000)	25,000
Product B: Estimated Sales	28,000	
Add: Desired Closing Stock	5,000	
Less: Estimated Opening Stock	(5,000)	28,000
Product C: Estimated	22,000	
Add: Desired Closing Stock	3,000	
Less: Estimated Opening Stock	(5,000)	20,000
Total Units to be produced		73,000 units

Re: Cash Budget

Problem 4

Sales :

	₹
May	60,000
June	70,000
July	80,000
August	100,000

All sales are on credit. Records show that 60 per cent of the customers pay during the month of the sale, 20 per cent pay the month after the sale, and the remaining 15 per cent pay the second month after the sale. 5 per cent are uncollectable.

Prepare a cash collections budget for July and August.

Solution

July Cash Collections (₹)

July sales = 80,000 * .6 = 48,000

June sales = 70,000 * .2 = 14,000

May sales = 60,000 * .15 = 9,000

Total Cash Collection In July = 71,000

August Cash Collections (₹)

August sales = 100,000 * .6 = 60,000

July sales = 80,000 * .2 = 16,000

June sales = 70,000 * .15 = 10,500

Total Cash Collections in August = 86,500

Problem 5

Prepare a cash Budget of m/s Panduranga Sheet Metals Ltd. for the 6 months ending 30th June, 2010 , from the following information. It has an opening cash balance of ₹ 600000 on 1st January, 2010.

Month	Sales	Purchases	Wages	Production Overheads	Selling Overheads
January	600000	240000	100000	60000	50000
February	700000	270000	110000	63000	55000
March	820000	320000	100000	64000	62000
April	850000	350000	105000	66000	65000
May	960000	388000	110000	64000	72000
June	1100000	416000	125000	65000	75000

The company has a policy of selling its goods 50% on cash basis and the rest on credit terms. Debtors are given a month's time period to pay their dues. Purchases are to be paid off two months from the date of purchase. The company has a time lag in the payment of wages of ½ a month and the overheads are paid after a month. The company is also planning to invest in a machine which will be useful for packing purposes, the cost being ₹ 450000, payable it three equal installments starting bi-monthly from April. It also expects to make a loan application to a bank for ₹ 500000 and the loan will be granted in the month of July. The company has to pay advance income tax of ₹ 200000 in the month of April. Salesmen are eligible for a commission of 4% on total sales affected by them and this is payable one month after the date of sales.

Solution

Cash budget (Jan-June, 2010)

Particulars	January	February	March	April	May	June
(A) Opening Cash Balance	600000	850000	1261000	1530000	1483700	1796200
(B) Cash Receipts:						
Cash Sales	300000	350000	410000	425000	480000	550000
Collection from Debtors		300000	350000	410000	425000	480000
Total (B)	300000	650000	760000	835000	905000	1030000
(C) Total Cash Av. (A+B)	900000	1500000	2021000	2365000	2388700	2826200
(D) Cash Payments:						
Materials			240000	270000	320000	350000
Wages	50000	105000	105000	102500	107500	117500
Production O/Hs		60000	63000	64000	66000	64000
Selling Overheads		50000	55000	62000	65000	72000
Sales commission		24000	28000	32800	34000	38400
Purchase of machine				150000		150000
Payment of advance IT				200000		
Total (D)	50000	239000	491000	881300	592500	791900
E Closing Cash Balance (C–D)	**850000**	**1261000**	**1530000**	**1483700**	**1796200**	**2034300**

Note: Wages

January	February	March	April	May	June
100000	110000	100000	105000	110000	125000
50000	55000 (Feb)	50000 (Mar)	52500 (Apr)	55000 (May)	62500 (June)
	50000 (Jan)	55000 (Feb)	50000 (Mar)	52500 (Apr)	55000 (May)
50000	105000	105000	102500	107500	117500

Problem 6

Prepare a Cash Budget for the three months ending 30th June, 2010 from the information given below:

(a)

Monthly	*Sales* ₹	*Materials* ₹	*Wages* ₹	*Overheads* ₹
February	14,000	9,600	3,000	1,700
March	15,000	9,000	3,000	1,900
April	16,000	9,200	3,200	2,000
May	17,000	10,000	3,600	2,200
June	18,000	10,400	4,000	2,300

(b) Credit terms are: Sales/Debtor-10% sales are on cash, 50% of the credit sales are collected next month and the balance in the following month.

Creditors	– Materials	2 month
(Time Lag)	– Wages	¼ month
	– Overheads	½ month

(c) Cash and Bank balance on 1st April, 2010 is expected to be ₹ 16,000.

(d) Other relevant information is:

(i) Plant and Machinery will be installed in February 2010 at a cost of ₹ 96,000. The monthly installments of ₹ 2,000 is payable from April onwards.

(ii) Dividend @ 5% on Preference share capital of ₹ 1, 00,000 will be paid on 1st June, 2010.

(iii) Advance to be received for sale of vehicles ₹ 9,000 in June.

(iv) Dividends from investments amounting to ₹ 1,000 are expected to receive in June.

(v) Income tax (advance) to be paid in June is ₹ 2,000.

Solution:

Cash Budget
April-June 2010

Particulars		*April (₹)*	*May (₹)*	*June (₹)*	*Total (₹)*
Opening balance		16,000	13,950	13,000	42,950
Add : **Extimated Cash Receipts :**					
Sales		14,650	15,650	16,650	46,950
Dividend		–	–	1,000	1,000
Advance against vehicle		–	–	9,000	9,000
Total	**(A)**	**30,650**	**29,600**	**39,650**	**99,900**
Estimated Cash Payments :					
Creditor*		9,600	9,000	9,200	27,800
Wages*		3,150	3,500	3,900	10,550
Overheads*		1,950	2,100	2,250	63.00
Capital Expenditure		2,000	2,000	2,000	6,000
Dividend on Preference Shares		–	–	5,000	5,000
Income Tax Advance		–	–	2,000	2,000
Total	**(B)**	**16,700**	**16,600**	**24,350**	**57,650**
Closing balance	**(A) – (B)**	**13,950**	**13,000**	**15,300**	**42,250**

Working Notes.

Collection from Sales/Debtors

Month	Calculation	April (₹)	May (₹)	June (₹)
February	(14,000 – 10% of 14,000) × 50%)	6,300		
March	(15,000 – 10% of 15,000) × 50%)	6,750	6,750	
April	10% of 16,000	1,600		
	(16,000 – 10% of 16,000) × 50%		7,200	7,200
May	10% of 17,000		1,700	
	(17,000 – 10% of 17,000) × 50%	–	–	7,650
June	10% of 18,000	–	–	1,800
		14,650	15,650	16,650

Please note that Payment for creditors, wages and overhead have also been computed on the same pattern.

Overheads 50% of previous month + 50% of current month

Wages 75% of current month + 25% of previous month, for example,

April –75% of ₹ 3,200 (₹ 2,400) + 25% of ₹ 3,000 (750) = ₹ 3,150

17.9 BUDGET ON THE BASIS OF CAPACITY

Fixed Budget

A budget which is prepared on the basis of standard or fixed level of activity is known as fixed budget. It is based on the assumption that there will no changes in the budgeted level of activity. According to **CIMA, London**, "*a fixed budget is a budget which is designed to remain unchanged irrespective of the level of activity actually attained.*" The utility of the budget becomes doubtful when the level of activity actually attained does not conform, to the budgeted level of activity. This budget is more suitable for only a small period of time when the actual level of output is not expected to differ much from the budgeted level of output. Fixed budget is practically of less use and has limited application and ineffective as a tool for cost control because it does not make any distinction between fixed, variable and semi-variable costs.

Flexible Budget

According to **CIMA, London**, "a *budget designed to change in accordance with the level of activity actually attained.*" It is one which is prepared in such a manner as to facilitate determination of budgeted cost for any level of activity. It is also known as 'Variable Budget' or 'Sliding Scale Budget'. It recognizes the behavior of costs and classifies them into variables, fixed and semi-variable costs. Fixed cost remains fixed irrespective of volume of output. Variable cost changes with the level of output. Semi variable costs are partly fixed and partly variable in nature. Therefore, this budget is designed to change in relation to the level of activity actually attained.

Difference between Fixed and Flexible Budget

Sl No.	Basis	Fixed	Variable
1.	Definition	It is known as rigid or inflexible budget.	It is not rigid.
2.	Level of Activity	It operates on one level of activity and under one set of conditions. It assumes that there will be no change in the prevailing conditions, which is unrealistic.	It consists of various budgets for different level of activity.
3.	Analysis of Variance	All costs like F. Costs; V.C. and S.V.C. are related to only one level of activity, so analysis does not give useful information.	Here, analysis of information provides useful information as each cost is analyzed as to its behaviour.
4.	Cost ascertain and price fixation	If the budgeted and actual activity levels differ significantly, than the aspects like Cost Statement and price fixation do not reveal a correct picture.	It provides a meaningful basis of comparison of the actual performance with the budgeted targets.
5.	Basis of comparison	Comparison of actual performance with budgeted target will be meaningless especially where there is difference between the two activity levels.	It provides a meaningful basis of comparison of the actual performance with the budgeted targets.

Problem 7

XYZ Ltd. manufactures a single product for which market demand exists for additional quantity. Present sales of ₹ 60,000 per month are at 60% capacity of the plant.

The following data are available:

(i) Selling Price	₹ 25 per unit
(ii) Variable cost	₹ 13 per unit
(iii) Semi-variable cost	₹ 6,000 fixed + 50 paisa per unit
(iv) Fixed cost	₹ 20,000 at present level estimated to be ₹ 24,000 at 80% capacity

You are required to prepare the following statements:

1. The operating profit at 60%, 70% and 80% levels at current selling price, and
2. The operating profit at proposed selling price at the above levels.

Solution

Statement showing Operating Profit at Current as well as at Proposed Selling Prices

Capacity utilization	**60%**	**70%**	**80%**
Production/Sales Volume (units)	6,000 Units	7,000 Units	8,000 Units
A. Sales at present S.P. (₹ 25 per unit)	₹ 1,50,000	₹ 1,75,000	₹ 2,00,000
B. Costs :			
Variable @ ₹ 3 per unit	78,000	91,000	1,04,000
Semi-Variable Cost :			
Variable portion @ ₹ 0.50 per unit	3,000	3,500	4,000
Fixed portion	6,000	6,000	6,000
Fixed cost	20,000	20,000	24,000
Total Cost	1,07,000	1,20,500	1,38,000
Profit at existing S.P. (A – B)	43,000	54,500	62,000

Problem 8

Prepairing flexible budget at different capacity levels. The following data are available in a manufacturing company for yearly period.

	₹ (in lakhs)
Fixed Expenses	
Wages and salaries	19.5
Rent, rates and taxes	16.6
Depreciation	17.4
Sunday administrative expenses	16.5
Semi-Variable Expenses : (at 50% of capacity)	
Maintenance and repairs	3.5
Indirect labour	7.9
Sales department salaries etc.	3.8
Sunday adminisatrative expenses	2.8
Variable Expenses : (at 50% of capacity)	
Materials	21.7
Labour	20.4
Other expenses	7.9
	138.0

Assume that the fixed expenses remain constant for all levels of production. Semi-variable expenses remain constant between 45% and 65% of capacity, increasing by 10% between 65% and 80% capacity and by 20% between 80% and 100% capacity.

Sales at various levels are :	*₹ (Lakhs)*
50% Capacity	200
60% Capacity	220
75% Capacity	250
90% Capacity	280
100% Capacity	300

Prepair flexible budget for the year and forecash the profit at 60%, 75%, 90% and 100% of capacity.

Solution:

Flexible budget for the year ending

(₹ in lakhs)

Capacity utilisation	50%	60%	75%	90%	100%
1. Sales	200	220	250	280	300
2. Total Costs :					
Variable costs:					
Material	21.70	26.04	32.55	39.06	43.40
Labour	20.40	24.48	30.60	36.72	40.80
Other expenses	7.90	9.48	11.85	14.22	15.80
Semi-Variable costs:					
Maintenance and repairs	3.50	3.50	3.85	4.20	4.20
Indirect labour	7.90	7.90	8.69	9.48	9.48
Sales dept. salaries	3.80	3.80	4.18	4.56	4.56
S. Admn. expenses	2.80	2.80	3.08	3.36	3.36
Fixed costs:					
Wages and Salaries	19.50	19.50	19.50	19.50	19.50
Rent, rates and taxes	16.60	16.60	16.60	16.60	16.60
Depreciation	17.40	17.40	17.40	17.40	17.40
S. Admn. expenses	16.50	16.50	16.50	16.50	16.50
Total Costs	138.00	148.00	164.80	181.60	191.60
Profit (1-2)	62.00	72.00	85.20	98.40	108.40

Problem 9

The monthly budgets for manufacturing overhead of a concern for two levels of activity were as follows:

Capacity	80%	100%
Budgeted Production (Unit)	1600	2000

	₹	₹
Wages	3,200	4,000
Consumable stores	2,400	3,000
Maintenance	2,100	2,500
Power and fuel	2,600	3,000
Depreciation	4,000	4,000
Insurance	1,000	1,000
	15,300	17,500

You are required to:

(i) Indicate which of items are fixed, variable and semi variable;

(ii) Prepare a budget for 90% capacity; and

(iii) Find the total cost, both fixed and variable, per unit of output at 80%, 90% and 100% capacity.

Solution:

(i) Fixed :

Depreciation – Since it remains constant at both the given levels.

Insurance – Same as above

Variable :

Wages – Because it is ₹ 2 per unit at both the given levels.

Consumable Stores – Because it is ₹ 1.50 per unit at both the given levels.

Semi-Variable

Maintenance – Since it is neither fixed nor the quantum of increase is proportionate to the increase in volume.

Power and Fuel – Same as above

(ii) Cost of Production Budget for 90% Capacity Level

Particulars	Amount (₹)
Budgeted Production (90% Capacity)	1800 units
Wages @ ₹ 2 per unit	3,600
Consumable stores @ ₹ 1.5 per unit	2,700
Maintenance (Working Note) [1800 + 500]	2,300
Power and Fuel (do) [1800 + 1000]	2,800
Depreciation (fixed in nature)	4,000
Insurance (fixed in nature)	1,000
Total Cost	16,400

(iii) Variable Cost Per Unit = ₹ 5.50
= Wages (₹ 2.00) + Consumable Stores (₹ 1.50) + Maintenance (₹ 1.00) + Power and Fuel (₹ 1.00) = ₹ 5.50

Total Fixed Cost

Depreciation (₹ 4,000) + Insurance (₹ 1,000) + Maintenance (₹ 500) + Power and Fuel (₹ 1,000) = 6,500

Total Cost Per Unit

Particulars	80% capacity	90% capacity	100% capacity
Production (Units)	1600	1800	2,000
Variable cost	₹ 5.50	₹ 5.50	₹ 5.50
Fixed Cost (₹ 6,500 ÷ Production)	₹ 4.0625	₹ 3.61	3.25
Total Cost	9.5625	9.11	8.75

Working Notes :

Maintenance : Variable Portion= $\frac{\text{Change in overhead}}{\text{Change in activity}}$ = ₹ 400 ÷ 400 = ₹ 1 per unit

Fixed Portion = ₹ 2,100 – (1,600 units × ₹ 1) = ₹ 500

At 90% Capacity level, TC = (1,800 units × ₹ 1) + ₹ 500 = ₹ 2,300

Power and Fuel :

Variable Portion = ₹ 400 ÷ 400 = ₹ 1 per units.

Fixed Portion = ₹ 2,600 – (1,600 units × ₹ 1) = ₹ 1,000

At 90% capacity level, TC = (1,800 unit × ₹ 1) + ₹ 1,000 = ₹ 2,800

Problem 10

The expenses for the budgeted production of 10,000 units in a factory are furtnished below:

	Per Unit (₹)
Materials	70.0
Labour	25.0
Variable overhead	20.0
Fixed overhead (₹ 1,00,000)	10.0
Variable Expenses (Direct)	5.0
Selling Expenses (10% fixed)	13.0
Distribution Expenses (20% fixed)	7.0
Administration Expenses (₹ 50,000)	5.0
Total Cost Per Unit	155.0

Prepare a budget for production of (a) 8,000 units, (b) 6,000 units, and (c) indicate cost per unit at both the levels. Assume that the administration expenses are fixed for all levels of production. *(MBA, AIMA)*

Solution:

Flexible Budget

Particulars	10,000 Units		8,000 Units		6,000 Units	
	Per unit (₹)	Amount (₹)	Per Unit (₹)	Amount (₹)	Per Unit (₹)	Amount (₹)
Production cost :						
Material	70.0	7,00,000	70.0	5,60,000	70.0	4,20,000
Labour	25.0	2,50,000	25.0	2,00,000	25.0	1,50,000
Overhead	20.0	2,00,000	20.0	1,60,000	20.0	1,20,000
Direct Variable Expenses	5.0	50,000	5.0	40,000	5.0	30,000
Fixed Overhead (₹ 1,00,000)	10.0	1,00,000	12.5	1,00,000	16.67	1,00,000
Selling Expenses :						
Fixed	1.3	13,000	1.625	13,000	2.167	13,000
Variable	11.7	1,17,000	11.70	93,600	11.70	70,260
Distribution Expenses :						
Fixed	1.4	14,000	1.750	14,000	2.33	14,000
Variable	5.6	56,000	5.60	44,800	5.60	33,600
Administration Expenses	5.0	50,00	6.25	50,000	8.33	50,000
Total Cost	155.0	15,50,000	159.43	12,75,400	166.8	10,00,800

17.10 MASTER BUDGET

The master budget is the consolidated summary of all functional budgets. It normally comprises of budgeted profit and loss and budgeted balance sheet. The master budget generally contains details regarding sales, cost of production, cash balance and other account balance (e.g., debtors, fixed assets, bills receivable, creditors, etc.). The important components of master budget are :

(a) Operating Budget

(b) Cash Budget

(c) Capital Expenditure Budget

(d) Projected Financial Position Budget

Steps in the preparation of Master Budget:

The following steps are usually involved in the preparation of a master budget –

(i) Preparation of functional budgets like Sales Budget, Production Budget, Cost of Production Budget etc. by incorporating the expected in the budget period;

(ii) Preparation of Cash Budget (as the next step to i);

(iii) Use of the informations for preparing the Projected Income Statement / Profit or Loss Account for the budget period;

(iv) Preparation of Projected Balance sheet as on the date of budget period on the basis of last year's Balance Sheet and information collected by taking step (i) to step (ii).

Main components of Company's Master Budget:

The main components of company's master budget are as follows :

(a) Projected Profit and Loss Account.

(b) Projected Balance Sheet.

SUMMARY

A budget is a financial document used to project future income and expenses. The budgeting process may be carried out by individuals or by companies to estimate whether the Person/ company can continue to operate with its projected income and expenses. A budget is a plan expressed in quantitative, usually monetary term, covering a specific period of time, usually one year. In other words a budget is a systematic plan for the utilization of manpower and material resources. In a business organization, a budget represents an estimate of future costs and revenues. Budgets may be divided into two basic classes: Capital Budgets and Operating Budgets. Capital budgets are directed towards proposed expenditures for new projects and often require special financing. The operating budgets are directed towards achieving short-term operational goals of the organization, for instance, production or profit goals in a business firm. Operating budgets may be sub-divided into various departmental of functional budgets.

Budgeting in a business sense is the planned allocation of available funds to each department within a company. Budgeting allows executives to control overspending in less productive areas and put more company assets into areas which generate significant income or good public relations. Budgeting is usually handled during meetings with accountants, financial experts and representatives from each department affected by the budgeting.

The key to successful budgeting is both flexibility and inflexibility. Certain expenses are fixed, so payment of those bills should be an inflexible element. Nothing is more important than paying those particular bills in full. In business, departments need to know the absolute ceiling on spending. Budgeting works best when very few exceptions are made to the upper limits. The idea of fiscal responsibility is to form a workable budget and stick to it as best as possible.

Budgetary Control is defined as "the establishment of budgets, relating the responsibilities of executives to the requirements of a policy, and the continuous comparison of actual with budgeted results either to secure by individual action the objective of that policy or to provide a base for its revision. Budgetary control is the methodical control of an organization's operations through establishment of standards and targets regarding income and expenditure, and a continuous monitoring and adjustment of performance against them.

The difference between budget, budgeting and budgetary control may be stated thus : Budgets are the individual objectives of a department etc., whereas budgeting may be said to be the act of setting budgets. Budgetary control embraces all and includes the science of planning the budgets themselves and utilization of such budgets as an overall management tool for the business planning and control. Thus, the term budgetary control is wider in meaning and it includes both budget and budgeting.

A cash budget is a tool for budgeting and controlling cash which is prepared in advance and is based on plan for future cash inflows and outflows of cash. Ultimately it focuses on expected closing cash balance at the end of each week, fort night, month or quarter. The closing cash balance can be determined after subtracting future cash outflows from total cash inflows (Opening Balance + Cash Receipt).

Zero-base budgeting (or review), as the term suggests, examines a programme or function or responsibility from 'scratch'. The reviewer proceeds on the assumption that nothing is to be allowed. The manager proposing the activity has, therefore, to prove that the activity is essential and the various amounts asked for are reasonable taking into account the volume of activity. Nothing is allowed simply because it was being done or allowed in the past. Thus, it means writing on a clean slate.

A budget which is prepared on the basis of standard or fixed level of activity is known as **fixed budget.** It is based on the assumption that there will no changes in the budgeted level of activity. This budget is more suitable for only a small period of time when the actual level of output is not expected to differ much from the budgeted level of output. Fixed budget is practically of less use and has limited application and ineffective as a tool for cost control because it does not make any distinction between fixed, variable and semi-variable costs.

Flexible Budget is a *budget designed to change in accordance with the level of activity actually attained.*" It is one which is prepared in such a manner as to facilitate determination of budgeted cost for any level of activity. It is also known as 'Variable Budget' or 'Sliding Scale Budget'. It recognizes the behaviour of costs and classifies them into variables, fixed and semi-variable costs. Fixed cost remains fixed irrespective of volume of output. Variable cost changes with the level of output. Semi variable costs are partly fixed and partly variable in nature. Therefore, this budget is designed to change in relation to the level of activity actually attained.

EXERCISES

Short Questions

1. What is budget?
2. What is budgeting?
3. What is budgetary control?
4. What is Cash Budget?
5. What is Fixed Budget?
6. What is Flexible Budget?
7. What is the main difference between fixed and flexible budget?
8. What is Zero Based Budgeting?
9. What is Master Budget?

Moderate and Broad Questions

1. Explain the main characteristics of a budget.
2. What are the Features, Objectives and steps of budgetary control?
3. Explain the advantages and limitations of Zero Based Budgeting.
4. What are the distinctions between Cash Budget and Cash Flow Statement?
5. Explain the differences between Fixed and Flexible Budget.
6. What are the steps in preparation of Master Budget?

PROBLEMS

Problem 1

The monthly budgets for manufacturing overhead of a concern for two levels of activity were as follows:

Capacity	*60%*	*100%*
Budgeted Production (Unit)	1200	2000
	₹	₹
Wages	2,400	4,000
Consumable stores	1,800	3,000
Maintenance	2,100	2,500
Power and fuel	2,600	3,000
Depreciation	4,000	4,000
Insurance	1,000	1,000

You are required to:

(i) Indicate which of items are fixed, variable and semi variable;

(ii) Prepare a budget for 80% capacity.

Problem 2

Prepare a cash Budget for the three months ending 30th June, 2010 from the information given below:

(e) Monthly	Sales	Materials	Wages	Overheads
	₹	₹	₹	₹
February	24,000	10,600	4,000	700
March	22,000	10,000	5,000	2,900
April	24,000	10,200	4,200	3,000
May	27,000	10,000	6,600	1,200
June	28,000	10,400	4,000	2,300

(f) Credit terms are: Sales/Debtor-20% sales are on cash, 60% of the credit sales are collected next month and the balance in the following month:

Creditors (Time Lag)	— Materials	2 month
	— Wages	¼ month
	— Overheads	½ month

(g) Cash and Bank balance on 1st April, 2010 is expected to be ₹ 19,000.

(h) Other relevant information is:

(i) Plant and Machinery will be installed in February 2010 at a cost of ₹ 1,06,000. The monthly installments of ₹ 2,000 is payable from April onwards.

(ii) Dividend @ 6% on Preference share capital of ₹ 1, 00,000 will be paid on 1st June, 2010.

(iii) Advance to be received for sale of vehicles ₹ 10,000 in June.

(iv) Dividends from investments amounting to ₹ 3,000 are expected to receive in June.

(v) Income tax (advance) to be paid in June is ₹ 4,000.

Problem 3

Vikrant Manufacturing Company requires you to calculate and present the master budget for the next year from the following information:

Sales:	
Product A	₹ 5,00,000
Product B	₹ 6,00,000
Direct material cost	50% of sales
Direct wages	25 workers @ ₹ 200 per unit
Factory Overheads :	
Indirect labour :	
Works manager	₹ 600 per month
Quality Inspector	₹ 500 per month
Stores and spares	2% on sales
Depreciation on machinery	₹ 15,000
Heat and Power	₹ 20,000
Repairs and maintenance	10% on direct wages

Administration, selling and distribution expenses ₹ 50,000 per year.

Hints:

Master Budget of Vikrant Manufacturing Company

for the period ending on...

Particulars	₹	₹	₹
Sales (as per sales budget)			
Product A			5,00,000
Product B			6,00,000
Total			11,00,000
Less : Costof Production (as per Cost of Production Budget)			
Direct Materials (50% of sales)		5,50,000	
Direct Wages (25 × 200 × 12 months)		60,000	
Prime Cost		6,10,000	
Factory Overhead :			
Variable :			
Stores and Spares (2% of sales)	22,000		
Heat and Power	20,000		
Repairs and Maintenance	6,000	48,000	

Fixed :			
Works Manager's Salary	7,200		
Quality Inspector's Salary	6,000		
Depreciation on Machinery	15,000	28,200	
Works Cost			(6,86,200)
Gross Profit			4,13,800
Less : Administration, Selling and Distribution Overheads			(50,000)
Net Profit			3,63,800

Problem 4

Ayush Ltd. decided to take over a running business. It had decided to raise ₹ 60 lakhs by issuing equity shares, and the balance of capital required in the first six months is to be financed by a financing institution against an issue of ₹ 20 lakhs 10% debentures (interest payable annually) in its favour.

Initial quantity consists of :

Freehold Premises	₹ 30 lakhs
Plant and Machinery	₹ 15 lakhs
Building	₹ 10 lakhs
Furniture	₹ 2 lakhs

Payments on above items are to be made in the month of incorporation. Sales during the first six months ending on June 30 are estimated as under :

January	₹ 15 Lakhs	April	₹ 25 Lakhs
February	₹ 20 Lakhs	May	₹ 30 Lakhs
March	₹ 20 Lakhs	June	₹ 28 Lakhs

Log in Payment :

Debtors	2 months
Creditors	1 months

Other Information :

(a) Preliminary Expenses: ₹ 1,20,000 (Payable in February).

(b) General Expenses : ₹ 20,000 per month (at end of each month).

(c) Monthly wages and salaries (payable on the 1st day of the next month) :
₹ 60,000 for the first three months
₹ 70,000 there after

(d) Gross profit rate is expected to be 30% on sales.

(e) The shares and debentures are issued on 1st January, thereafter calls on equity share received in the month of April for ₹ 15,20,000.

(f) The stock level throughout is to be the same as the outlay.

Prepare a Cash Budget, and a Projected Trading and Profit and Loss account for the six months ending, June 30 and the Projected Balance Sheet as on that date.

Hints :

AYUSH LIMITED

Cash Budget for the six month ending on 30 June,

(in lakhs of rupees)

Receipts/Payments	Jan	Feb	March	April	May	June	Total
Opening Cash		22.8	10.90	11.7	32.7	35.0	113.1
Receipts :							
Shares	60.00	-	-	15.2			75.2
10% Debentures	20.00	-	-				20.0
Sales	-	-	15.0	20.0	20.0	25.0	80.0
Total Receipts (A)	80.0	22.8	25.90	46.9	52.7	60.0	288.3
Payments :							
Fixed Assets :							
Freehold Premises	30.0	-	-			-	30.0
Plant and Machinery	15	-	-			-	15.0
Furniture	2.0	-	-			2.0	
Building	10.0	0	0			-	10.0
Preliminary Expenses	-	12	-				1.2
Wages	-	0.60	0.60	0.60	0.70	0.70	3.20
General Expenses	0.20	0.20	0.20	0.20	0.20	0.20	1.20
Purchases	-	9.9	13.40	13.40	16.8	20.30	73.80
Total Payment (B)	57.2	11.90	14.2	14.2	17.7	21.2	136.40
Closing balance (A) – (B)	22.8	10.90	11.7	32.7	35.0	38.8	151.90
Total	80.0	22.8	25.90	46.9	52.70	60.0	288.3

Ayush Limited

Projected Trading, Profit and Loss Account

for six months ending on June 30,

(in lakhs of rupees)

Particulars	Amount (₹)	Particulars	Amount (₹)
To Purchases	92.7	By Sales	138.0
To Wages and Salaries	3.90	By Closing Stock	-
To Gross Profit	41.4		
	138.0		138.0
To expenses	1.20	By Gross Profit b/d	41.40
To interest on debentures (6 months)	1.00		
To Net Profit			
(Subject to depreciation)	39.2		
	41.40		41.40

Balance Sheet as on June 30,

Liabilities	Amount (₹)	Assets	Amount (₹)
Equity Share Capital	75.20	Freehold Premises	30.0
Profit and Loss Account	39.2	Plant and Machinery	10.52
10% Debentures	20.0	Building	10.0
Interest due	1.00	Furniture	2.0
Wages and Salaries Outstanding	0.70	Stock	-
		Bank	38.8
		Debtors	58.0
Trade Creditors	18.90	Preliminary Expenses	1.2
	155.0		155.0

(i) Purchases : G.P. Ratio is 30% of sales. Therefore, purchase will be equivalent to 70% of sales less wages.

Month	Sales	Wages	Gross Profit (30% of Sales)	Purchases (B/figure)
January	15	0.60	4.5	9.9
February	20	0.60	6.0	13.4
March	20	0.60	6.0	13.4
April	25	0.70	7.5	16.8
May	30	0.70	9.0	20.3
June	28	0.70	8.4	18.9

❑❑❑

18 Cash Flow Analysis

18.1 CONCEPT, OBJECTIVE, CASH INFLOWS, CASH OUTFLOWS

Concept: Cash Flow Statement analyzes the movement of funds in terms of cash *i.e.* cash transactions where in cash moved in and out of the organization. The movement of cash into the organization is called cash inflows. The movement of cash out of the organization is called cash outflows. A cash flow statement shows changes in the financial position on cash basis.

Objective: It is prepared to study the impact of various transactions on the cash position of the firm. It may be defined as, a summary of receipts and disbursements during the period, reconciling the opening balance of cash with the closing balance of cash with the help of informations gathered from Balance Sheet and Profit and Loss Account. It explains reasons for changes in the cash position of the firm. Cash Flow Statement is prepared to know the changes in cash position from one period to another with analysis showing total changes, transaction wise changes, sources and application of the cash *i.e.* the manner in which cash has been utilized during the year. A business must view its cash position and the availability of the cash for taking important decisions in the near future.

18.2 DIFFERENCE BETWEEN CASH FLOW STATEMENT AND FUND FLOW STATEMENT

Points of difference	Cash Flow Statement (CFS)	Fund Flow Statement (FFS)
(a) Concept of fund	Follows narrower concept of fund *viz.* cash, one of the constituents of working capital.	Follows broader concept of fund *viz.* working capital which includes all CA's including cash and CL's
(b) Basis of Accounting	Cash basis of Accounting which includes all cash receipts and cash payments.	Accrual basis of Accounting which includes all movements of working capital.

(c) Planning Horizon	Useful for Short-term financial planning to meet short term obligations.	Useful for intermediate and long-term financial planning to meet the requirement of funds according to current level of business operations.
(d) Schedule of changes in fund	No separate schedule in prepared to show changes in fund or cash	Separate schedule is prepared to show changes in fund on working capital and with changes in the constituents of working capital.
(e) Level requirement	As per the revised AS-3, the preparation of cash flow statement according to the requirements laid down in the standard is mandatory.	The preparation of Fund Flow Statement is no longer a compulsory requirement for the companies.

18.3 ADVANTAGES, LIMITATIONS OF CASH FLOW STATEMENT, IMPORTANCE OF CFS AS PER LEGAL REQUIREMENT

Advantages

A cash flow statement is a useful tool for short term financial planning to meet short-term obligations, such as payment of short-term interest on debentures, dividend on shares etc. It is used to provide information about the cash inflows and cash outflows which is necessary for taking decisions regarding the important cash requirements.

It provides the following advantages:

(a) **Short-term planning:** It is helpful in short-term planning by indicating the important sources and immediate cash requirements in the future.

(b) **Liquidity position:** It helps management for knowing the magnitude, direction and causes of variation in the liquidity position of the business enterprise.

(c) **Cash Management:** It is an important tool for the management of cash. The management can determine the requirements of funds for repayment of interest on loans, payment of dividend etc.

(d) **For Management:** It helps management in terms of followings:

(i) Generating idea as to the nature of estimated cash transactions during the period and their impact on cash balance

(ii) Assessment of firm's ability to generate cash from operating, financing and investing activities.

(iii) Making short-term investment decisions in case of expected surplus of cash.

(iv) Highlighting the amount that is to be arranged from appropriate sources for making expected commitment of the firm.

(v) Providing information (by a projected cash flow statement) regarding the amount and period of investment for making both investment and financing decisions.

(e) **For users:** A cash flow statement brings immense benefits for the users of published accounts and other financial statements. For example, for determining the liquidity position, prospective creditors will find this statement extremely useful. A prospective investor should also consult this statement is determining not only for the profitability but also for ensuring that his investment would get regular return (cash dividend) in future. Banks do insist on, among other things, projected cash flow statement while considering applications from firms for term-loans or cash credit.

Limitations

(a) Cash Flow Statement includes only those transactions which are related to cash. It does not indicate the true liquidity position as many important transaction relating to the changes of financial position which are non-cash nature, are ignored.

(b) The management can manipulate the cash flow statement by postponing purchase and other payments.

Importance (as per legal requirements): Clause 32 of listing agreement was amended by SEBI which laid down that all the listed companies are required to supply a copy of CFS to each shareholder as a part of Annual Report.

18.4 PREPARATION OF CASH FLOW STATEMENT

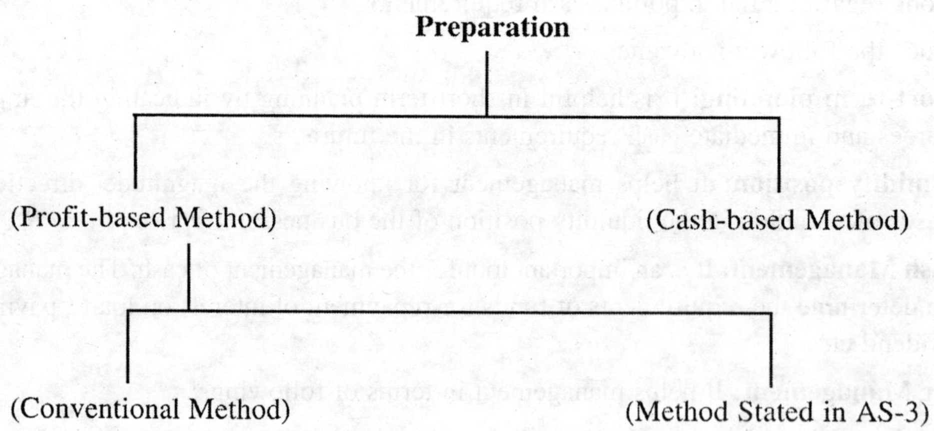

18.5 A PROFIT-BASED METHOD

(I) Conventional Method
Proforma of Cash Flow Statement
T- Form or an Account Form

Sources of cash inflow	Amount	Applications of cash outflow	Amount
Opening Cash and Bank		Outflow of Cash	–
Balance	–	Purchase of Investment	–
Inflow of Cash	–	Purchase of Fixed Asset	–
Cash from Operation	–	Payment of Dividend	–
Issue of Shares	–	Payment of Tax, Drawings	–
Issue of Debenture	–	Repayment of long-term loan	–
Sale of Fixed Assets	–	Repayment of Pref. Share	–
Long-term loan raised	–	Redemption of Debenture	–
Sale of Investment	–	Cash lost from Operation	–
Non-trading receipt *i.e.*		Buy back of equity Share	–
Dividend received	–	Payment of Interest	–
Rent received etc.	–	Closing Cash and Bank Balance	–
Further capital introduced	–		

Statement of cash from operation

Trading Profit /Loss as per adjusted Profit & Loss A/C	–	(+/–)
Add: Decrease in Current Assets (*i.e.* Stock, Debtors, B.R. etc.)	–	
Add: Increase in Current Liabilities	–	–
Less: Increase in Current Assets (*i.e.* S.C., B.P. out exp. Etc.)	–	–
Less: Decrease in Current liabilities	–	–
Cash from Operation		–

Alternative Method
Proforma of Cash Flow Statement
(Vertical form)

Particulars	Amount ₹	Amount ₹
Opening Cash and Bank Balance		–
Add: **Inflow of cash**	–	
Cash from Operation	–	
Issue of shares	–	
Issue of Debentures	–	
Sale of Fixed Assets	–	
Long-term Loan raise	–	
Sale of Investment	–	

Non-trading receipts, *i.e.*, Dividend received	–	–
Rent Received	–	–
		–
Less: **Outflow of Cash**	–	
Purchase of Investment	–	
Purchase of fixed Asset	–	
Payment of Dividend	–	
Payment of tax	–	
Repayment of Long-term Loan	–	
Redemption of Pref. Shares	–	
Redemption of Debentures	–	
Cash lost in operation	–	
Buy-back of equity shares	–	
Payment of Interest	–	–
Closing Cash and Bank Balance		–

(II) Method Stated in AS-3

Accounting Standard 3 (AS-3): As per amendment of AS-3, made by ICAI:

Cash Flow Statement (Direct Method) Revised AS-3

Particulars	Amount ₹	Amount ₹	Amount ₹
A. Cash Flow from Operating Activities:			
Cash receipts from customer			
Less: Cash paid to supplier/employees			
Less: Cash paid for operating expenses			
Add: (i) Decrease in CA's (excluding Debtors)			
(ii) Increase in CL's			
Less: (i) Decrease in CL's			
(ii) Increase in CA's (excluding Debtors)			
+/- Loss/Profit on sale of fixed assets			
Cash from Operation			
Less: Income Tax Paid			
Cash Flow before extraordinary items			
Add: Extraordinary receipts			
Net Cash Flow from Operating Activities			
B. Cash Flow from Investing Activities			
Sales of fixed asset			
Less: Purchased of fixed assets			
Sale of investment			
Less: Purchase of investment			
Less: Loan to Subsidiaries			
Add: Interest collected			
Dividend collected			
Net Cash Flow from Investing Activities			

C. Cash flow From Financing Activities			
(i) Issue of equity shares			
(ii) Issue of preference shares			
(iii) Issue of debentures			
Long-term borrowing			
(Including premium wherever applicable)			
Less: (a) Redemption of Preference shares			
(b) Redemption of debentures			
Buy-back of equity shares			
Repayment of long-term borrowing dividend paid			
Interest paid (Including premium wherever applicable)			
Net Cash Flow from Financing Activities			
D. Net Increase or Net Decrease			
In Cash and Cash Equivalents (A+B+C)			
Add: Cash and Cash equivalent at the opening of the period			
Cash and Cash equivalent at the closing of the period			

Cash Flow Statement
(Indirect Method) Revised AS-3

Particulars	Amount ₹	Amount ₹	Amount ₹
(1) Cash flow from operating activities			
Operating profit			
(Before adjustment of working capital changes)			
(as per note)			
Add : Increase in Current Liabilities			
Add : Decrease in Current Assets			
Less : Decrease in Current Liabilities			
Less : Increase in Current Assets			
Cash Generated from operation			
Less : Income Taxes paid			
Cash Flow before extra ordinary items			
Add : Extra ordinary receipts *e.g.* earthquake disaster settlement.			
Net cash from operation activities			
(2) Cash Flow from investing activities:			
(As mentioned in the direct method)			
(3) Cash Flow from financing activities:			
(As mentioned in the direct method)			
Net Increase /Decrease in Cash and Cash equivalents			
Add: Cash and Cash equivalent as on opening date			
Cash and Cash equivalent in the Closing date			

Statement of cash from operation

Particulars	Amount ₹	Amount ₹
Closing Capital	****	
Less: Opening Capital	****	
		****
Add: Drawings		****
		****
Less: Further capital		****
Add: Depreciation	****	****
Abnormal loss	****	
Decrease in Current Assets	****	
Increase in Current Liabilities	****	****
		****
Less: Abnormal profit	****	
Increase Current Assets	****	
Decrease Current Liabilities	****	****
Cash from operation		****
Note: Operating Profit (before adjustment of working capital changes):		
Net Profit before taxation and extraordinary item Given or, (increase in P&L: closing–opening balance balance, considering revaluation of stocks)		****
Add: Increase in General Reserve	****	
Depreciation	****	
Provision for tax-current year	****	
Foreign exchange loss	****	
Provision on redemption of debenture-Written off	****	
Loss on sale of fixed assets/investment	****	
Proposed dividend for current year	****	
Preliminary exp. written off	****	
Interest/Dividend paid	****	****
		****
Less: Profit on sale of fixed assets/ investment	****	
Interest income	****	
Dividend income	****	
	****	****
Operating Profit (before adjustment of working capital changes)		****

18.6 CLASSIFICATIONS OF EACH FLOWS AS PER MODEL PRESCRIBED BY AS-3 (IAS-7)

A. Cash Flows from Operating Activities

Operating activities are the revenue producing activities of the business enterprise. It includes those transactions and other events that enter into the determination of net profit or net loss.

Example of cash flows from operating activities:

(i) Cash receipts from sale of goods/services, royalties, fees, commissions and other revenues.

(ii) Cash payment to supplier for goods/services to and on behalf of employees, refund of income-tax unless they are specifically identified with financing and investing activities.

(iii) Cash receipts and payments in terms of following:

(a) Of an insurance enterprise for premiums and claims, annuities and other policy benefits.

(b) Relating to future contracts, forward contracts, option contracts and swap contracts when the contracts are held for dealing on trading purpose.

B. Cash Flows from Investing Activities

Cash flows from investment activities are related to capital expenditure, inter-corporate investments and acquisitions. Investing activities are related to transactions and events that involve the purchases and sales of long term productive assets not held for sale and other investments.

Examples of cash flows from investment activities:

(i) Cash payments to acquire

(a) Property, tangible and intangible fixed assets, self-constructed fixed assets,

(b) Shares, warrants, debt instruments of other companies.

(ii) Cash receipts from disposal of

(a) Fixed assets(both tangibles and intangibles)

(b) Share, warrants or debt instruments of other companies

(iii) Cash payments for others/Cash receipts for others

(a) Related to capitalized research and development cost costs – only for cash payment

(b) Interests in joint venture – both for cash payment and cash receipts

(c) Future contracts, forwards, option contracts and swap contracts except when the contracts are held for dealing or trading purposes – both for cash payment and cash receipts

(d) Third parties in the form of cash advances and loans (other than advances/loans of a financial company) – only for cash payment

(e) Third parties in the form of repayment of cash advances and loans made to them (other than advances/loans of a financial Co. – only for cash receipts).

C. Cash Flows from Financing Activities

Financing activities are those which are related to owners' capital and borrowed funds. It relates to change in capital structure of the enterprise.

Examples of cash flows from financing activities:

(i) Cash proceeds from issuing shares, debentures, loans, notes, bonds and other short term or long term borrowers.

(ii) Cash repayment of amounts borrowed.

(iii) Cash payment of interest and dividend.

18.7 SPECIAL ITEMS: (TREATMENT OF CASH FLOWS OF CERTAIN SPECIAL ITEMS AS PER REVISED AS-3)

1. Foreign currency cash flows: While calculating the cash flows from operating activities, exchange rate gains should be deducted from the net profit, while the exchange rate losses should be added to the net profit. This unrealized gains or losses (which are not cash flows) should be reported in cash flow statement in order to reconcile cash and cash equivalents at the beginning and the end of the period.

2. Extra ordinary items : The cash flows arising from extra ordinary items such as bad debts recovered, winning of a suit should be disclosed separately as resulting from operating, investing or financing activities in the cash flow statement.

3. Income Tax: The cash flows arising from taxes on income should be disclosed separately and classified as cash flows from operating activities unless specifically identifiable with financing or investing activities.

4. Interest and Dividends: In case of financial enterprise, dividend or interest paid or received should be classified as cash flows from operating activities. In case of other enterprises interest paid should be classified as cash flows from financing activities, dividend paid should be classified as cash from financing activities. Collectively interest and dividend paid should be classified as cash flows from investing activities.

Example

You are given below the profit and loss account of ABC Ltd. for the year ended March 31, 2010. The company is engaged in the manufacture of plastic cans.

	₹
Sales	10,00,000
Operating expenses (excluding depreciation)	(5,00,000)
Depreciation	(1,20,000)
Net profit before tax	3,80,000
Extra ordinary income- Gain on speculation	50,000
	4,30,000
Provision for taxes @ 30%	1,29,000
Net Profit after tax	3,01,000

Additional Informations :

(1) Included in operating expenses is loss on sale of machinery ₹ 30,000.

(2) Actual taxes paid in respect of 2009-10 ₹ 50,000.

(3) The balances relating to current items taken from the balance sheets of 2008-2009 and 2009-10 are given below:

	2008-09 ₹	2009-10 ₹
Current Asset		
Trade Debtors	1,00,000	80,000
Inventory	75,000	50,000
Current Liabilities:		
Trade Creditors	1,00,000	1,05,000

Required: Cash Flow from operation by (1) Direct Method and (2) Indirect Method.

Solution:

Cash Flow from Operation — Direct Method

Particulars	₹	₹
Cash receipts from customers:		
Credit sales	10,00,000	
Add: Trade Debtors:		
Opening	1,00,000	
	11,00,000	
Less: Trade Debtors:		
Closing	80,000	
		10,20,000
Less: Cash paid to Supplier/employees		Nil
Less: Cash paid for operating expenses (excluding depreciation)		(5,00,000)
		5,20,000
Add: (i) Decrease in Inventory	25,000	
(ii) Increase in Trade Creditors	5,000	30,000
		5,50,000
Add: Loss on sale of machinery		30,000
Cash from operation		5,80,000
Less: Income Tax paid		50,000
Cash flow before extra ordinary items		5,30,000
Add: Extra ordinary receipts		
-gain on speculation		50,000
Cash flow from Operating Activities or from operation		5,80,000

Cash Flow from Operation — Indirect Method

Particulars	₹	₹
Operating profit (before adjustment of working capital changes) See Note		5,30,000
Add: Decrease in Inventory	25,000	
Increase in Trade Creditors	5,000	
Decrease in trade debtors	20,000	50,000
Cash from operation		5,80,000
Less: Income Tax paid		50,000
Cash flow before extra ordinary items		53,000
Add: Extra ordinary receipts -gain on speculation		5,000
Cash flow from Operating Activities or from operations		5,80,000

Note: Operating Profit (before adjustment of working capital charges)

		₹
Net Profit before taxation and extraordinary items-given		3,80,000
Add: Depreciation	1,20,000	
Loss on sale of machinery	30,000	1,50,000
Operating Profit (before adjustment of working capital changes)		5,30,000

Problem 1

The Balance Sheet of XYZ Ltd. as on March 31, 2009 and 2010 are given below:

Balance Sheet XYZ Ltd.

Liabilities	31.03.09	31.03.10	Assets	31.03.09	31.03.10
Equity Share Capital	6,00,000	8,00,000	Fixed Assets	16,00,000	19,00,000
Capital Reserve	----	20,000	Less: Depreciation	(4,60,000)	(5,80,000)
General Reserve	3,40,000	4,00,000		11,40,000	13,20,000
Profit & Loss A/c	1,20,000	1,50,000	Investment	2,00,000	1,60,000
Debentures	4,00,000	2,80,000	Current Assets	5,60,000	6,60,000
Current Liabilities	2,40,000	2,60,000	Preliminary Expenses	40,000	20,000
Proposed Dividend	60,000	72,000			
Provision for Tax	1,80,000	1,70,000			
Unpaid Dividend	----	8,000			
	19,40,000	21,60,000		19,40,000	21,60,000

Additional Information

During the year 2009-2010, the company

(1) Sold one machine for ₹ 50000, the cost of which was ₹ 100000 and the depreciation provided on it was ₹ 40000.

(2) Charged ₹ 180000 as depreciation.

(3) Sold some investments at a profit of ₹ 20000, which was credited to Capital Reserve.

(4) Redeemed 30% of Debenture @ ₹ 105

(5) Stock has been valued at cost, where as previously the practice was to value stock at cost less 10%. The stock according to books on 31.03.2009 was ₹ 138000. The stock on 31.12.2005 was correctly valued at ₹ 150000.

(6) Fixed Asset has been written off as costing ₹ 28000 on which depreciation amounting to ₹ 20000 has been provided.

Prepare the cash flow statement for the year 31.3.2010 using AS-3 format.

Solution:

Cash Flow Statement for the year ending 31.3.2010

(As per AS-3, Indirect Method)

	Particulars	₹	₹
A.	**Cash Flow from Operating Activities:** (cash from operations)		
	Operating profit (before adjustment of working capital change)		5,44,000
	Add: Increase in Current Liabilities		20,000
			5,64,000
	Less: Increase in Current Assets [6,60,000 – (5,60,000 + 12,000)], being opening balance of current assets = 5,60,000 + 12,000 = 5,72,000;		(88,000)
	Cash from Operation		4,76,000
	Less: Income Taxes paid during the year.		(1,80,000)
	Cash flows from Operating Activities or from operations		2,96,000
B.	**Cash Flows from Investment Activities:**		
	Purchase of Fixed Assets [1,80,000 + 50,000 + 10,000 + 8,000 + 13,20,000 – 11,40,000]	(4,28,000)	
	Sale of Investment [(2,00,000 – 1,60,000) + 20,000]	60,000	
	Sale of Fixed Asset	50,000	
			(3,18,000)
C.	**Cash Flows from Financial Activities:**		
	Issue of Share Capital (8,00,000 – 6,00,000)	2,00,000	
	Redemption of Debenture [1,20,000 + 5%]	(1,26,000)	
	Dividend paid (60,000 – 8,000)	(52,000)	22,000
	Increase/Decrease in Cash and Cash equivalents		Nil

Note: Operating Profit (before adjustment of working capital changes)
Net profit before taxation and extraordinary items- increase in P&L A/c :

		₹	
Opening balance of P&L A/c		1,20,000	
Add:	Undervaluation of stock (1,50,000 – 1,38,000)	12,000	
		1,32,000	
Closing balance of P&L A/c		1,50,000	18,000
Add:	Increase in General Reserve	60,000	
	Depreciation	1,80,000	
	Provision for tax for current year	1,70,000	
	Loss on sale of machine (60,000 – 50,000)	10,000	
	Provision for redemption of Debenture	6,000	
	Proposed dividend for current year	72,000	
	Loss on sale of fixed assets (280,00 – 20,000)	8,000	
	Preliminary expenses (40,000 – 20,000)	20,000	
		5,26,000	5,26,000
	Operating Profit (before adjustment of working capital changes)		5,44,000

Problem 2

From the following information prepare Cash Flow Statement for the year ended 31.3.2010 using conventional method.

Balance Sheet as at 31.3.09 and 31.3.10

Liabilities	**31.03.09 (₹000)**	**31.03.10 (₹000)**	**Assets**	**31.03.09 (₹000)**	**31.03.10 (₹000)**
Share Capital	200.0	250.0	Land & Building	200.0	190.0
General Reserve	50.0	60.0	Plant & Machinery	150.0	169.0
Profit & Loss A/c	30.5	30.6	Stock	100.0	74.0
Bank Loan	70.0	–	Sundry Debtors	80.0	64.2
Sundry Creditors	150.0	135.2	Cash	0.5	0.6
Provision for Taxation	30.0	35.2	Bank	–	8.0
			Good will	–	5.0
	530.5	510.8		530.5	510.8

Additional Informations:

(a) Dividend ₹ 23,000 was paid.

(b) The following assets of another company were purchased for a consideration of ₹ 50,000 paid for in shares; stock ₹ 20,000, Machinery ₹ 25,000.

(c) Further machinery was purchased ₹ 25,000 during the year.

(d) Net Profit for the year was ₹ 66,000

(e) Depreciation written off on Building ₹ 10,000, Machinery ₹ 14,000.

(f) Income Tax paid during the year ₹ 28,000.

Solution:

Cash Flow Statement for the year ended 31st March, 2010

Sources	Amount ₹	Application	Amount ₹
Opening Cash & Bank Balance	500	Dividend Paid	23,000
Cash from operation	1,37,100	Purchase of Machinery	25,000
Sale of Plant & Machinery	17,000	Payment of Tax	28,000
		Bank Loan Paid	70,000
		Closing Cash & Bank Balance [600 + 8,000]	8,600
	1, 54,600		1, 54,600

Working Notes:

Statement of cash from operation for the year ended 31.3.2010

Particulars	Amount ₹	Amount ₹
Trading Profit as per Profit & Loss A/c		90,100
Add: Stock Decrease [1,00,000 + 20,000 -74,000]	46,000	
Debtors Decrease [80,000 – 64200]	15,800	61,800
		1, 51,900
Less: Creditors Decrease [1,50,000 – 1,35,200]		14,800
Cash Adjusted from operations		1, 37,100

Dr. **Adjusted Profit & Loss A/c** *Cr.*

Particulars	Amount ₹	Particulars	Amount ₹
To Dividend A/c	23,000	By Balance b/d	30,500
To Depreciation on			
Machinery A/c	14,000	By Trading Profit (B. fig.)	90,100
Building A/c	10,000		
To Provision for Tax A/c	33,000		
To General Reserve A/c	10,000		
To Balance c/d	30,600		
	1,20,600		1,20,600

Dr. **Land & Building A/c** *Cr.*

Particulars	Amount ₹	Particulars	Amount ₹
To Balance b/d	2,00,000	By Depreciation A/c	10,000
		By Balance c/d	1,90,000
	2,00,000		2,00,000

Dr. **Machinery A/c** Cr.

Particulars	Amount ₹	Particulars	Amount ₹
To Balance b/d	1,50,000	By Depreciation A/c	14,000
To Vendor Co. A/c (sh cap)	25,000	By Bank A/c (sale-B. fig.)	17,000
To Bank A/c (Purchase)	25,000	By Balance c/d	1,69,000
	2,00,000		2,00,000

Dr. **Vendor Co. A/c** Cr.

Particulars	Amount ₹	Particulars	Amount ₹
To Share Capital A/c	50,000	By Stock A/c	20,000
		By Machinery A/c	25,000
		By Goodwill A/c	5,000
	50,000		50,000

Dr. **Provision for Tax A/c** Cr.

Particulars	Amount ₹	Particulars	Amount ₹
To Bank A/c	28,000	By Balance b/d	30,000
By Balance c/d	35,000	By Profit & Loss A/c (B. fig.)	33,000
	63,000		63,000

Dr. **Goodwill A/c** Cr.

Particulars	Amount ₹	Particulars	Amount ₹
To Vendor Co. A/c (Purchase by issue of Share)	5,000	By Balance c/d	5,000
	5,000		5,000

Dr. **Share Capital A/c** Cr.

Particulars	Amount ₹	Particulars	Amount ₹
To Balance c/d	2,50,000	By Balance b/d	2,00,000
		By Vendor Co. A/c	50,000
	2,50,000		2,50,000

Dr. **General Reserve A/c** Cr.

Particulars	Amount ₹	Particulars	Amount ₹
To Balance c/d	60,000	By Balance b/d	50,000
		By Profit & Loss A/c	10,000
	60,000		60,000

Dr. **Bank Loan A/c** Cr.

Particulars	Amount ₹	Particulars	Amount ₹
To Bank A/c	70,000	By Balance b/d	70,000
To Balance c/d	Nil		
	70,000		70,000

Problem 3

From the following particulars prepare a Cash Flow Statement of Sundry Ltd. for the year ended 31 st December, 2010.

Profit & Loss A/c for the year ended 31st December, 2010

Particulars	₹	Particulars	₹
To Opening Stock	5,500	By Sales	2,16,000
To Purchase	80,500	By Closing Stock	20,000
To Wages	16,000	By Loss on Stock	5,000
To Gross Profit	1,39,000		
	2,41,000		2,41,000
To Expenses	10,000	By Gross Profits	1,39,000
To Insurance Claim	1,000	By Other Income	6,000
To Loss on sale of plant	5,000		
To Deferred Expenses	5,000		
To Depreciation	12,000		
To Bad Debt	1,000		
To Income Tax	10,000		
To Net Profit	1,01,000		
	1,45,000		1,45,000
To Dividend	8,000	By Balance b/d	30,000
To Reserve	23,000	By Net Profit	1, 01,000
To Balance c/d	1, 00,000		
	1,31,000		1, 31,000

Balance Sheet

Liabilities	2009 ₹	2010 ₹	Assets	2009 ₹	2010 ₹
Share Capital	80,000	90,000	Fixed Assets	60,000	1,80,000
Profit & Loss A/c	30,000	1,00,000	Investment	68,500	30,000
Reserve A/c	50,000	73,000	Stock in Trade	5,500	20,000
Creditors	30,000	20,000	Debtors	50,000	55,000
Liability for Expenses	8,000	10,000	Cash & Bank	3,500	1,500
Advance Income	5,000	3,000	Deferred Expenses	10,500	5,500
			Prepaid Expenses	5,000	4,000
	2,03,000	2,96,000		2,03,000	2,96,000

Solution:

In the Books of Sundry Ltd.
Cash flow Statement for the year ended 31.12.2010

Sources of Cash	Amount ₹	Applications of Cash	Amount ₹
Opening Cash & Bank Balance	3,500	Purchase of Fixed Assets	1,37,000
Cash from operation	1,00,500	Payment of dividend	8,000
Issue of Shares (90,000 – 80,000)	10,000	Payment of Income Tax	10,000
Insurance claim received	4,000	Closing Cash & Bank	
Sale of investments	38,500	Balance	1,500
	1,56,500		1,56,500

Working Notes:

Dr. **Fixed Asset A/c** Cr.

Sources	Amount ₹	Applications	Amount ₹
To Balance b/d	60,000	By Depreciation A/c	12,000
To Bank A/c	1,37,000	By Loss On Sale of Plant	
(Purchase)- B.fig.		(P/L A/c)	5,000
		By Balance c/d	1,80,000
	1,97,000		1,97,000

Dr. **Investment A/c** Cr.

Particulars	Amount ₹	Particulars	Amount ₹
To Balance c/d	68,500	By Bank A/c (Sale of Investment)	38,500
		By Balance c/d	30,000
	68,500		68,500

Dr. **Equity Share Capital A/c** Cr.

Particulars	Amount ₹	Particulars	Amount ₹
To Balance c/d	90,000	By Balance b/d	80,000
		By Bank A/c (Issue of Shares)	10,000
	90,000		90,000

Dr. **Debtors A/c** Cr.

Particulars	Amount ₹	Particulars	Amount ₹
To Balance b/d	50,000	By Bad Debt A/c	1,000
To Sales A/c (Assumed as credit)	2,16,000	By Bank A/c (Collection- B.Fig)	2,10,000
		By Balance c/d	55,000
	2,66,000		2,66,000

Dr. **Creditors A/c** Cr.

Particulars	Amount ₹	Particulars	Amount ₹
To Bank A/c (Payment - B. fig)	90,500	By Balance b/d	30,000
To Balance c/d	20,000	By Purchases A/c (Assumed as credit)	80,500
	1,10,500		1,10,5000

Dr. **Expenses A/c** Cr.

Particulars	Amount ₹	Particulars	Amount ₹
To Balance c/d	5,000	By Outstanding Expenses b/d	8,000
To Bank A/c	7,000	By Profit & Loss A/c	10,000
To outstanding Expenses c/d	10,000	By Balance c/d	4,000
	22,000		22,000

Dr. **Income A/c** Cr.

Particulars	Amount ₹	Particulars	Amount ₹
To Profit &Loss A/c	6,000	By Balance b/d	5,000
To Balance c/d	3,000	By Bank A/c	4,000
	9,000		9,000

Dr. **Loss on Stock A/c** Cr.

Particulars	Amount ₹	Particulars	Amount ₹
To Trading A/c	5,000	By Profit & Loss A/c	1,000
		By Cash A/c	4,000
	5,000		5,000

Statement of Cash from Operation for the year ended 31.12.2005

Particulars	₹	₹
Cash collection from Debtors	2,10,000	
Other Income received	4,000	
		2,14,000
Less: Outflow of Cash:		
Payment to creditors	90,500	
Wages	16,000	
Expense Paid	7,000	1,13,500
		1,00,500

Note: Assuming that the disposal value of plant is Zero.

Problem 4

From the following Balance Sheet of Mani Ltd. make out a Cash Flow Statement:

Assets	2009 ₹	2010 ₹	Liabilities	2009 ₹	2010 ₹
Equity Share Capital	3,00,000	4,00,000	Goodwill	1,00,000	80,000
8% Redeemable			Land & Building	2,00,000	1,70,000
Preference share Capital	1,50,000	1,00,000	Plant	80,000	2,00,000
Capital Reserve	----	20,000	Investment	20,000	30,000
General Reserve	40,000	50,000	Sundry Debtors	1,40,000	1,70,000
P&L A/c	30,000	48,000	Stock	77,000	1,09,000
Proposed Dividend	42,000	50,000	B/R	20,000	30,000
Sundry Creditors	25,000	47,000	Cash in hand	15,000	10,000
Bills Payable	20,000	16,000	Cash at Bank	10,000	8,000
Liability for Expenses	30,000	36,000	Preliminary		
Provision for Taxation	40,000	50,000	Expenses	15,000	10,000
	6,77,000	8,17,000		6,77,000	8,17,000

Notes:

(i) A piece of land had been sold out in 2010 and the profit on sale had been credited to Capital Reserve.

(ii) A machine has been sold for ₹ 10,000. The written down value of the machine was ₹ 12,000. Depreciation of ₹ 10,000 is charged on plant account in 2010.

(iii) The investments are Trade Investment ₹ 3,000 by way of dividend is received including ₹ 1,000 from pre-acquisition profit which has been credited to Investment Account.

(iv) An interim dividend of ₹ 20,000 has been paid in 2010.

(v) Proposed dividend for 2009 was paid in 2010.

Solution:

Cash Flow Statement
for the year ended 31.12.2010

Sources	₹	Uses	₹
Opening Cash and Bank Balance on 31.12.09 (₹ 15,000 + ₹ 10,000)	25,000	Purchase of Plant	1,42,000
		Purchase of Investment	11,000
		Redemption of Pref. Shares	50,000
Issue of Shares	1,00,000	Interim Dividend paid	20,000
Sale of Land	50,000	Proposed Dividend of 2009 paid	42,000
Sale of Plant and Machinery	10,000	Payment of Liability for Expenses	30,000
Increase in Creditors	22,000		
(₹ 47,000 – ₹ 25,000)		Decrease in Bills Payable	4,000
Income from Dividend	3,000	Increase in Debtors	30,000
Cash from Operations	1,79,000	Increase in Stock	32,000
		Increase in B/R	10,000
		Cash and Bank Balance on 31.12.2010	18,000
	3,89,000		3,89,000

Working Notes:

Plant A/c

Dr. Particulars	Amount ₹	Particulars	Cr. Amount ₹
To Balance b/d	80,000	By Profit & Loss A/c (Depreciation)	10,000
To Bank A/c (Purchase – Balancing figure)	1,42,000	By Profit & Loss A/c (Loss on Sale)	2,000
		By Bank A/c (Sale)	10,000
		By Balance c/d	2,00,000
	2,22,000		2,22,000

Land and Building A/c

Dr. Particulars	Amount ₹	Particulars	Cr. Amount ₹
To Bank A/c	2,00,000	By Bank(Balancing figure)	50,000
To Capital Reserve (Profit on Sale)	20,000	By Balance c/d	1,70,000
	2,20,000		2,20,000

Investment A/c

Dr. Particulars	Amount ₹	Particulars	Cr. Amount ₹
To balance b/d	20,000	By Dividend	1,000
To Bank A/c(purchases)	11,000	By Balance c/d	30,000
	31,000		31,000

Adjusted Profit & Loss A/c

Dr. Cr.

Particulars	Amount ₹	Particulars	Amount ₹
To Plant A/c (Depreciation)	10,000	By Balance b/d	30,000
To General Reserve	10,000	By Dividend	
To Goodwill	20,000	(₹ 3,000 – ₹ 1,000)	2,000
To Preliminary expenses	5,000	By Trading Profit	
To Plant A/c (loss on sale)	2,000	(cash from operations)	1,79,000
To Interim Dividend	20,000		
To Proposed Dividend	50,000		
To Provision for Taxation	10,000		
To Outstanding Liability for Expenses	36,000		
To Balance c/d	48,000		
	2,11,000		2,11,000

Problem 5

The following were the Balance Sheets of Sakshi Goel limited as on March 31, 2009 and 2010.

Liabilities	2008-2009 ₹	2009-2010 ₹	Assets	2008-2009 ₹	2009-2010 ₹
Equity Share Capital	2,00,000	2,50,000	Freehold Property at cost	2,10,000	2,30,000
Profit & Loss	38,500	70,000	Plant & Machinery		
Securities Premium	25,000	45,000	at cost	1,30,000	1,61,000
8.5% Debentures	60,000	30,000	Fixtures & Fittings		
Bank Overdraft	15,000	----	at cost	34,000	29,000
Creditors	35,000	52,000	Stock	38,000	51,000
Proposed Dividend	10,000	15,000	Debtors	45,000	50,000
Depreciation:			Bank Balance	----	16,000
Plant	61,000	58,000	Premium on		
Fixtures	13,000	19,000	redeemed		
			Debentures	----	2,000
	4,57,000	5,39,000		4,57,000	5,39,000

The following additional informations are relevant:

(i) There had been no disposal of freehold property in the year.

(ii) A machine which had cost ₹ 10,000 and in respect of which ₹ 8000 depreciation had been provided, was sold for ₹ 3000 and fixtures which had cost ₹ 5,000 in respect of which depreciation of ₹ 2000 had been provided, were sold for ₹ 1000. The profits and losses on these transactions had been dealt with through the Profit and Loss account.

(iii) The actual premium paid on redemption of the debentures was ₹ 3000 out of which ₹ 1000 had been written off to the profit and loss account.

(iv) No interim dividend has been paid.

(v) Shares have been issued at premium.

You are required to prepare Cash Flow Statement as per Revised AS-3.

Solution:

Cash Flow Statement
for the year ended 31.3.2010

Particulars	Amount ₹	Amount ₹
A. Cash Flow from Operating Activities		
Operating Profit (before adjustment of working capital changes)		62,000
Add: Increase in Current Liabilities		
— Sundry Creditors (52,000 – 35,000)		17,000
		79,000
Less: Increase in Current Assets		
— Stock (51,000 – 38,000)		(13,000)
— Debtors (50,000 – 45,000)		(5,000)
Cash Flows from Operating Activities or from operations		61,000
B. Cash Flow from Investing Activities		
Purchase of Plant and Machinery	(41,000)	
Purchase of freehold property (2,30,000 – 2,10,000)	(20,000)	
Sale of plant and fixtures (3,000 + 1,000)	4,000	
		(57,000)
C. Cash Flows from Financing Activities		
Issue of share capital (including premium on share capital)	70,000	
Redemption on debentures at premium (30,000 + 3,000)	(33,000)	
Dividend paid	(10,000)	
		27,000
Net increase in cash and cash equivalents = A+B+C		31,000
(+) Cash and Cash equivalents at the beginning of the year.		(15,000)
Cash and cash equivalent at he close of the year		16,000

Notes:

1. Opening Profit (before adjustment of working capital changes)

	₹
Net profit before taxation and extraordinary item	
— Increase in Profit & Loss A/c (70,000 – 38,000)	32,000
Add: Depreciation – Plant and Machinery	5,000
Fixtures	8,000
Proposed Dividend for current year	15,000
Premium on redemption of debenture	1,000
Loss on sale of fixtures {3000- (10000-8000)}	2000
	63000

Less: Profit on sale of machine {3000 - (10000-8000)}	(1000)
Operating Profit (before adjustment of working capital change)	62000

2.

Dr. **Plant and Machinery A/c** Cr.

Particulars	**Amount ₹**	**Particulars**	**Amount ₹**
To Balance b/d	130000	By Machine tools disposal A/c	10000
To Cash A/c – purchase of plant (balancing figure)	41000	By Balance c/d	161000
	171000		171000

Problem 6

A Company finds on 1.1.2010 that it is short of funds with which to implement its programme of expansion. On 1.1.09 it had a Credit balance of ₹ 1,80,000. From the following information, Prepare a Statement for Board of Directors to show how the Overdraft of ₹ 68,750 as at 31.12.09 has arisen.

Figures as per Balance Sheet as at 31st December of each year are as follow:

	2008 (₹)	**2009 (₹)**
Fixed Assets	7,50,000	11,20,000
Stock and Stores	1,90,000	3,30,000
Bank Balance	(Cr.) 1,80,000	(O/D) 68,750
Debtors	3,80,000	3,35,000
Trade Creditors	2,70,000	3,50,000
Share Capital @ ₹ 10/share	2,50,000	3,00,000
Bills Receivable	87,500	95,000

The Profit for the Year ended 31.12.2009 before charging depreciation and income tax was ₹ 2,40,000. The 5,000 share were issued on 1.1.09 at a Premium of ₹ 5 per Share. ₹ 1,37,500 were paid in March 2009 by way of income tax. Dividend was paid as follows:

2008(final) on the Capital on 31.12.08 at 10% less tax at 25% and 2009 (interim) at 5% free of tax.

Solution:

(i) Final Dividend ₹ 2,50,000 × 10 ÷ 100 = ₹ 25,000. Net Payment ₹ 25,000 – Tax 25% = ₹ 18,750.

(ii) Interim Dividend ₹ 3,00,000 × 5% = 15,000.

(iii) ₹ 15,000 × 25 ÷ 75 = ₹ 5000 is payable to the Govt. on account of tax.

(iv) Assumed that the amount of tax paid, *i.e.,* ₹ 1,37,500 includes ₹ 11,250 (6,250 + 5,000) in respect of final and interim dividend.

(v) Assumed that fixed assets appeared **At Cost.**

(vi) It is evident that the profit for the year 2009 ₹ 2,40,000 is before charging Final and Interim Dividend.

Cash Flow Statement
for the year ended 31.12.09

Particulars	Amount ₹	Particulars	Amount ₹
Bank Balance on 1.1.09	1,80,000	Cash outflows:	
Cash inflows:		Purchase of Fixed Assets	3,70,000
Issue of Share Capital including		Increase in Stock	1,40,000
Premium of ₹ 5 per Share	75,000	Increase in Bills Receivable	7,500
Increase in Creditors	80,000	Payment of Dividend	
Decrease in Debtors	45,000	for 2008 (final)	18,750
Operating Profit	2,40,000	2009 (interim)	15,000
Bank overdraft on 31.12.2009	68,750	Payment of income tax	1,37,500
	6,88,750		6,88,750

18.7B. CASH BASED METHOD OF 'CASH FLOW STATEMENT' PREPARATION

Step (i):

Dr. **Debtors A/c** Cr.

To balance b/d	xxxx	By Cash/Bank A/c	
To Sales – credit sales	xxx	– collection from debtors	xxx
		By Discount Allowed A/c	xxx
		By bad Debt A/c	xxx
		By return Inward A/c	xxx
		By Balance c/d	xxx

Step (ii):

Dr. **Cretors A/c** Cr.

To Cash /Bank A/c - Cash paid to creditors	xxx	By Balance B/d	xxx
		By Purchase – credit purchase	xxx
To Discount Received A/c	xxx		
To Return Outward A/c	xxx		
To balance C/d	xxx		

Step (iii):

Dr.	Expenses A/c		Cr.
To Balance b/d – opening prepaid exp.	xxx	By Balance B/d – opening o/s exp.	xxx
To Cash/ bank A/c- amt. paid	xxx	By Profit & Loss A/c(total exp.)	xxx
To balance C/d – closing o/s exps.	xxx	By Balance B/d – closing prepaid exp.	xxx

Step (iv):

Statement of Cash from Operation

Cash collection from Debtors (as per step i)	xxx
Add: Cash Sales	xxx
Less: Cash paid to creditors (as per step ii)	(xxx)
Add: Cash purchases	xxx
Less: Cash outflow for expenses (as per step iii)	(xxx)
Cash generated from operation	xxx

Step (v):

Next as per conventional method or, as per format of AS-3 we prepare cash flow statement.

SUMMARY

Cash Flow Statement analyzes the movement of funds in terms of cash, *i.e.,* cash transactions where in cash moved in and out of the organization. The movement of cash into the organization is called cash inflows. The movement of cash out of the organization is called cash outflows. A cash flow statement shows changes in the financial position on cash basis.

A cash flow statement is a useful tool for short term financial planning to meet short-term obligations, such as payment of short-term interest on debentures, dividend on shares etc. It is used to provide information about the cash inflows and cash flows which is necessary for taking decisions regarding the important cash requirements.

As per the revised AS-3, the preparation of cash flow statement according to the requirements laid down in the standard is mandatory.

Cash Flow Statement helps management in terms of following :

(i) Generating idea as to the nature of estimated cash transactions during the period and their impact on cash balance

(ii) Assessment of firm's ability to generate cash from operating, financing and investing activities.

(iii) Making short-term investment decisions in case of expected surplus of cash.

(iv) Highlighting the amount that is to be arranged from appropriate sources for making expected commitment of the firm.

(v) Providing information (by a projected cash flow statement) regarding the amount and period of investment for making both investment and financing decisions.

EXERCISE

A. Short Questions

1. What is Cash Flow Statement?
2. What is the basis of Accounting under 'Cash Flow Statement'?
3. What is meant by 'Operating Activities'?
4. What is meant by 'Cash Flow from Investing Activities'?
5. What is meant by 'Financing Activities'?

B. Moderate and Broad Questions

1. Distinguish between cash flow and funds flow statement?
2. Explain the limitation of cash flow statements. What is its utility?
3. Write down the important provisions related to preparation of cash flow statement stipulated by AS-3.
4. Explain the formats provided by AS-3 for classification of cash flows.
5. Explain the preparation of cash flows statement on the basis of 'Cash based Method'.

Problem 1

1. A Company furnished you the following Balance Sheets for the year ended 31st March, 2009 and 2010. You are required to prepare a Cash Flow Statement for the year ended 31st March, 2010.

Liabilities	2008-2009 ₹	2009-2010 ₹	Assets	2008-2009 ₹	2009-2010 ₹
Equity Share Capital	10,000	10,000	Goodwill	1,200	1,200
General Reserve	1,400	1,800	Land	4,000	3,600
Profit &Loss A/c	1,600	1,300	Building	3,700	3,600
Sundry Creditors	800	540	Investments	1,000	1,100
Outstanding Expenses	120	80	Inventories	3,000	2,340
			Receivables	2,000	2,220
Prov. for Taxation	1,600	1,800	Bank Balance	600	1,520
Prov. for Bad Debts	40	60			
	15,560	15,580		15,560	15,580

Following additional information has also been supplied to you:

(i) A piece of land has been sold for ₹ 400.

(ii) Depreciation amounting to ₹ 700 has been charged on building.

(iii) Provision for taxation has been made for ₹ 1,900 during the year.

Problem 2

From the information provided, you are required to prepare cash flow statement:

Liabilities	2009 ₹	2010 ₹	Assets	2009 ₹	2010 ₹
Issued Share Capital	2,00,000	3,00,000	Freehold Property (at cost)	2,20,000	2,60,000
Share Premium	30,000	70,000			
Profit & Loss A/c	56,000	1,40,000	Plant & Machinery (at cost)	2,40,000	3,02,000
Debenture	1,40,000	60,000			
Bank Overdraft	28,000	–	Furniture (at cost)	48,000	58,000
Creditors	68,000	96,000	Stock	74,000	1,02,000
Proposed Dividend	30,000	40,000	Debtors	86,000	88,000
Depreciation;			Bank Balance	–	32,000
Plant	90,000	1,08,000	Redemption of Debenture	–	2,000
Furniture	26,000	30,000			
	6,68,000	8,44,000		6,68,000	8,44,000

Additional Information:

(a) There has been no disposal of freehold property during the year.

(b) A machine which had cost ₹ 16,000 and in respect of which ₹ 12,000 depreciation had been provided was sold for ₹ 6,000 and furniture which had cost ₹ 10,000 in respect of which depreciation of ₹ 4,000 had been provided was sold for Rs.2000. the profits and losses on share transaction had been dealt with through the Profit & Loss A/c.

(c) The actual premium in redemption of debenture was ₹ 4,000 of which ₹ 2,000 had been written off to the Profit & Loss A/c.

(d) No interim dividend had been paid.

Problem 3

From the following information, prepare a Cash Flow Statement for the year ended 31st December, 2010:

Balance Sheet (₹ 000)

Liabilities	2009	2010	Assets	2009	2010
Issue and Paid up Capital	1,575.00	1,575.00	Long-term Assets(Net)	1,125.00	2,047.50
Profit & Loss A/c	157.50	225.00	Closing Stock	337.50	900.00
Mortgage Loan	—	900.00	Repayment (relating to Administrative Expenses)	45.00	90.00
Tax unpaid (Accrued)	22.50	67.50			
Trade Creditors	315.00	877.50			
			Sundry Debtors	112.50	450.00
			Cash	450.00	157.50
	2,070.00	3,645.00		2,070.00	3,645.00

Statement of Profit & Loss for the year ended 31st Dec., 2010 (₹ 000)

Sales		2,250.00
Opening Stock (1.1.2010)	337.50	
Add: Purchase	2,205.00	
Less: Closing Stock (31st Dec., 2010)	(900.00)	1,642.50
Gross Profit		607.50
Less: Administrative expenses	247.50	
Depreciation	180.00	
Taxes (provision)	90.00	517.50
Net Profit		90.00
Less: payment of dividend		22.50
		67.50
Add: Profit & Loss A/c (31.12.99)		157.50
Balance on 31.12.2010		225.00

On 15th January 2010, a new building was purchased for ₹ 11,02,500. For making the payment of the building, the company paid a deposit of 2,02,500 and obtained a mortgage loan of ₹ 9,00,000 for the balance of purchase price of the building.

❑❑❑

19 Risk Analysis in Capital Budgeting

19.1 INTRODUCTION: RISK, FACTORS OF RISK, EFFECT

Where there is uncertainty in obtaining expected RO1/rate of return we may say that risk exists.

The effect of risks can be stated as follows:

(i) Risk Influences the required rate of return of the investors. Generally the projects that generate high returns are risky.

(ii) Risk is associated with the variability of future return. The greater the variability of the expected returns, the riskier the project.

(iii) Risk arises out of uncertain conditions under which a firm has to operate its activities.

(iv) Risk exists due to inability of the companies to make perfect forecasts of cash flows.

Risk in capital budgeting decisions is the variability that is highly to occur in future between the estimated and the actual returns.

Factors

(i) Business environment Factors → the business is affected by change in monetary policies, interest rates, lending policies of RB1, taxation, political situations.

(ii) Industry Specific Factors → these factors influence the demand for the products of the industry to which the firm belongs.

(iii) Company Specific Factors → the factors are change in management, wage negotiations, strikes or lockout which affect cost and revenue positions of the company.

19.2 SOURCES OF RISK

(i) Project Specific Risk: (Something quite specific to the projects)

(a) Stand-alone risk which is variability of expected returns or discount rates;

(b) Portfolio risk which is the degree of change in risk when new project is added to the existing portfolio of a project;

(c) Beta risk that is market risk of a project which normally cannot be diversified.

(ii) Competition Risk: It refers to the unanticipated actions of a firm's competitors. For this reason, actual cash flows from a project will be less than that of the forecasted cash flows.

(iii) Industry-Specific Risk:

(a) Technological Risk (example, From two stroke auto to LPG Gas Auto);

(b) Commodity Risk (arising from the effect of price change on goods produced and marketed);

(c) Legal Risk (Arising from change in lows and regulations applicable to the industrys, changes in Import-Export policy of the Government of India).

(iv) International Risk: (Example rupee-dollar cruising affected the software and BPOs earlier).

(a) Risk of processing raw materials from international markets;

(b) Fluctuations in Exchange rate;

(c) Change in international polities.

(v) Market Risk: (cannot be diversified in the normal course of business)

(a) Inflation;

(b) Rise in inflation rates;

(c) Changing economic condition.

19.3 METHODS OF RECOGNIZING RISK ASSOCIATED WITH A PROJECT ON CAPITAL BUDGETING PROPOSAL

Conventional techniques/methods of incorporating risk under uncertainty.

A. Pay back period:

The eldest and commonly used method of recognizing risk is pay back period. If prefers projects of short-term payback to that long-term payback. The emphasis of the liquidity of the firm is through recovery of capital investment as soon as possible.

Detailed discussion took place in Chapter 12:
Capital Budgeting, Sec 12.5 → Appraisal criteria.

The usual risk in business is more concerned with the forecast of cash flows. It is the downside risk of lower cash flows arising from lower sales and higher costs of operation that matters in formulating standards of pay back. Since pay back period ignores time value of money, we can prefer discounted pay back period which considers time value of money.

The pay back method considers only time related risks and ignores all other risks of the project under consideration.

B. Risk Adjusted Discount Rate

It there is risk, a normal discount rate cannot be applicable. High Risky project may be accepted if there is a possibility to yield high return. Therefore to motivate companies or individuals to take up riskily project, particular those, who by nature are risk – averse and tries to avoid risk, expected return from the project shall have to be adequate.

Uncertainty of returns of the projects leads to risk, hence lead, to risk premium which needs to be incorporated in discount rate in the evaluation of risky project proposals.

So, risk adjusted Discount Rate (Applying CAPM)
= Risk free rate + Risk premium

Where Risk premium = expected additional return as compensation for the investors taking additional risks associated with the project.

We can not use NPV while evaluating a project if it uses risk adjusted discount rate. NPV using risk free rate is greater than NPV using risk – adjusted discount rate. If a firm is to use the IRR, then the project would be accepted when IRR is greater than the risk – adjusted discount rate. Otherwise by using risk-adjusted discount rate, if NPV is positive, the project can be accepted.

Problem 1

A project cost ₹ 5,000. It is expected to generate cash inflows as under;

Year	Cash inflows ₹
1	2,000
2	2,250
3	1,900
4	1,800
5	1,500

Risk free rate of interest is 10%. Risk premium is 10%.

(a) Compute NPV using risk free rate

(b) Compute NPV using risk-adjusted discount rate.

Solution:

(a) Table : Calculation of NPV using risk-free ratio

Year	Cash inflows ₹	PVIF- PV factor @ 10%	P.V. of Cash inflows ₹
1	2,000	0.9091	1,818
2	2,250	0.8264	1,860
3	1,900	0.7513	1,428
4	1,800	0.6830	1,229
5	1,500	0.6209	931
Total P.V. of cash inflows			7,266
Less; P.V. of cash out flows			5,000
NPV			2,266

(b) Table: Calculate of NPV using Risk Adjusted Discount Rate

Year	Cash Inflows ₹	PVIF - PV factor @ 20%	P.V. of cash inflows ₹
1	2,000	0.8333	1,667
2	2,250	0.6944	1,562
3	1,900	0.5787	1,099
4	1,800	0.4822	868
5	1,500	0.4018	603
Total P.V. of cash inflows			5,799
Less: P.V. of cash our flows			5,000
NPV			799

The project would be acceptable when no allowance is made for risk (*i.e.*, at risk free rate) and also when risk premium is added to the risk free rate.

Evaluation of Risk-adjusted discount rate

Advantages

1. It is Simple and easy.
2. Risk premium takes care of the risk element in future cash flows.
3. It satisfies the businessmen who are risk – averse

Limitations

1. Cash flows are not adopted to incorporate the risk adjustment for net cash inflows.

2. The assumption that investors are risk-averse may not be true in respect of certain investors who are willing to take risks.
3. There are no proper or authentic bases of arriving at the risk premium.

C. Certainly Equivalent

Under this method, the risky, uncertain, unexpected future cash flows are converted into cash flows with certainty. Here we multiply uncertain future cash flows by the certainly-equivalent coefficient to convert uncertain cash flows into certain cash flows.

$$\text{Certainly Equivalent} \quad \infty = \frac{\text{Certain Cash Flow}}{\text{Expected/Risky Cash Flow}}$$

(Risk – adjustment factor)

Certainty Equivalent coefficient is between 0 and 1. If risk is high, a lower coefficient is used. If risk is low, a higher coefficient is used.

This method is much more superior method than 'Risk-adjusted discount rate' method.

Problem 2

The cost of a project is ₹ 40,000, it is expected to generate cash inflows as follows:

Year	Cash inflows	Certainly Equivalent
1	₹ 30,000	0.8
2	₹ 25,000	0.6
3	₹ 15,000	0.4

Risk-free discount rate is 10%. Compute NPV and evaluate the project.

Solution:

Year	Uncertain Cash inflows ₹	Certainty Equivalent ₹	Certain Flows ₹	PVIF @ 10% ₹	PV of certain cash inflows
Col 1	Col 2	Col 3	Col 4 = Col 2 X Col3	Col 5	Col 6 = Col 4 X Col 5
1	30,000	0.8	24000	0.9091	21,818
2	25,000	0.6	15000	0.8264	12,396
3	15,000	0.4	6000	0.7513	4,508
P.V. of certain cash inflow					38,722
Less: initial cash outlay					40,000
NPV					(1,278)

Since project has negative NPV, it has to be rejected.

1. **Acceptance Criteria:** Accept the project if NPV is positive.

   If IRR is used, Accept the project if IRR > Specified minimum risk free rate. Otherwise rejects.

2. **Evaluation of Certainty Equivalent:**

Advantages:

1. This method is considered to be the radically superior to the risk-adjusted discount rate.
2. CE approach recognizes risk by certainty equivalent facilitating the conversion of riskily cash inflows into certain cash inflows.

Disadvantages:

1. When forecasts pass through many layers of management, original forecasts may become highly conservative.
2. There are chances of being inconsistent in the procedure employed from one project to another.

D. Sensitivity Analysis

This technique is currently used by many firms to ascertain a project's risk characteristics. Sensitivity analysis refers to analyzing the change in the project's NPV or IRR on account of a given change one of the variables like sales, cost of sales, investment, tax rates etc. In other words, sensitivity analysis measures the sensitivity of NPV or IRR of a project i.r.t. a change in one of the above mentioned variables. This process highlights the most sensitive factors and a range of returns can be related to the risk attached by management. Here Forecasts are made under different economic conditions viz pessimistic, expected and optimistic.

Problem 3

A company has 2 mutually exclusive projects.

	Project A ₹	**Project B** ₹
Initial Outlay	1,00,000	80,000
Life	4 years	4 years
Company's cost of capital	10%	10%
Annual cash inflows:		
Pessimistic	30,000	20,000
Expected	40,000	50,000
Optimistic	50,000	30,000

What is the NPV of the project? Which project should management consider? Which project is risky?

Solution:

Table: NPV of Project A
[Capital outlay: ₹ 1,00,000]

Economic Environment	Project cash inflow ₹	PVIFA at 10%, 4 years	P.V. of Cash inflows ₹	NPV ₹
Pessimistic	30,000	3.1698	95,094	(4,906)
Expected	40,000	3.1698	1,26,792	26,792
Optimistic	50,000	3.1698	1,58,490	58,490

Table: NPV of Project B
[Capital outlay : ₹ 80000]

Economic Environment	Project cash inflow ₹	PVIFA at 10%, 4 years	P.V. of Cash inflows ₹	NPV ₹
Pessimistic	20,000	3.1698	63,396	(16,604)
Expected	50,000	3.1698	1,58,490	78,490
Optimistic	30,000	3.1698	95,094	15,094

Note: PVIFA

Year	PVIF @ 10%
1	0.9091
2	0.8264
3	0.7513
4	0.6830
PVIFA	3.1698

Decision

Under pessimistic: No project should be accepted as all have negative NPV.

Under Expected: Project B should be accepted since its NPV is higher.

Under Optimistic: Project A should be accepted since its NPV is higher.

Difference in NPV range (*i.e.,* optimistic and Pessimistic NPV):-

For Project A = 58490 – (– 4906) = 58490 + 4906 = ₹ 63,396

For project B = 15094 – (– 16604) = ₹ 31,698

Project A is risky compared to Project B because the NPV range is of larger difference in compare to Project B.

Evaluation of Sensitivity Analysis:

Advantages:

1. Sensitivity analysis shows where resources can be most effectively utilized,
2. In conjunction with probability distribution it provides a powerful management tool.
3. it can be used in conjunction with risk profiles.

Disadvantages:

1. The main problem in sensitivity analysis is deciding the amount by which each factor should be altered, very careful assessments must be made of the maximum likely alteration in each factor.

E. Probability Distribution Approach

Here the chances of assurance, expressed in the form of probabilities, are incorporated. (Total probability = 1). After assigning probabilities to future cash inflows, expected NPV is computed.

The aim of probability distribution approach is to provide some assessment of the range of possible outcomes and thus provides additional information for the decision-maker. Using the information and relying on expected value criteria, a relatively simple decision rule may be formulated that is the higher the expected value, the more profitable is the project and *vice-versa*.

Problem 4

A company has identified a project where initial cost of investment is ₹ 20,000. The following distribution of cash flow, for the economic life of the project of two years where discount rate is 10% is given below:

Economic	Year 1		Year 2	
Condition	Cash inflow	Probability	Cash inflow	Probability
	₹		₹	
Upward price	15,000	0.40	20,000	0.40
Moderate price	8,000	0.50	10,000	0.40
Downward price	2,500	0.10	3,000	0.20
		1.00		1.00

Calculate NPV and standard deviation of NPV

Solution:

(a) **Table: Calculation of NPV**

Year	Expected cash inflows ₹	PVIF @ 10%	P.V. if Cash inflows
1	(15,000 × .40) + (8,000 × .50) + (2,500 × .10) = 10,250	0.9091	9,318
2	(20,000 × .40) + (10,000 × .40) + (3,000 × .20) = 12,600	0.8264	10,413
P.V. of expected cash inflows			19,731
Less: P.V. of expected outlay			20,000
Expected NPV			(269)

This project should not be accepted due to its negative NPV.

(b) Standard Deviation for 1st year:

Cash inflow C (₹)	Expected Value E (₹)	$(C - E)^2$ (₹)	Probability	(C – E) 2 × Prob. (₹)
15,000	10,250	$(4750)^2$	0.40	9025000
8,000	10,250	$(-2250)^2$	0.50	2531250
2,500	10,250	$(-7750)^2$	0.10	6006250
			Total =	17562500
			S.D. = $\sqrt{\text{Total}}$ =	$\sqrt{17562500}$
				= 4190.7637

Standard Deviation for 2nd year:

Cash inflow C (₹)	Expected Value E (₹)	$(C - E)^2$	Probability (₹)	$(C - E)^2$ × Prob.
20,000	12,600	$(7400)^2$	0.40	21904000
10,000	12,600	$(-2600)^2$	0.40	2704000
3,000	12,600	$(-9600)^2$	0.20	18432000
			Total =	43040000
			S.D. = $\sqrt{\text{Total}}$ =	$\sqrt{43040000}$
				= 6560.4878

S.D. of NPV (if there is no relationship between cash flows from 1st year to 2nd year)

$$= \sqrt{\left(\frac{\text{S.D. of 1}^{\text{st}} \text{ year}}{(1 + \text{discount rate})^1}\right)^2 + \left(\frac{\text{S.D. of 2}^{\text{nd}} \text{ year}}{(1 + \text{discount rate})^2}\right)^2}$$

$$= \sqrt{\left(\frac{4190.7637}{(1+.10)^1}\right)^2 + \left(\frac{6560.4878}{(1+.10)^2}\right)^2}$$

$$= \sqrt{\frac{17562500}{1.21} + \frac{43040000}{1.4641}}$$

$$= \sqrt{14514463 + 29396899}$$

$$= \sqrt{43911362}$$

$$= 6626.5649$$

S.D. of NPV (if cash flow of 1st and 2nd year is perfectly correlated)

$$= \frac{\text{S.D. of 1}^{\text{st}}\text{ year}}{(1+\text{discount rate})^1} + \frac{\text{S.D. of 2}^{\text{nd}}\text{ year}}{(1+\text{discount rate})^2}$$

$$= \frac{4190.7637}{(1+.10)^1} + \frac{6560.4878}{(1+.10)^2}$$

$$= \frac{4190.7637}{1.10} + \frac{6560.4878}{1.21}$$

$$= 3810 + 5422 = 9232$$

Note: The S.D. of NPV when cash flows are perfectly correlated will be higher than that under the solution of independent cash flows.

F. Decision Tree Approach

Investment decisions sometimes involve a complex under locking of decisions and outcomes in which later decisions depend on the outcomes of earlier decisions. Decision Tree deals with such problems. The decision-tree approach to the evaluation of risk and uncertainty rests on the impact of all probabilistic estimates of potential outcomes. In other words, when using decision – tree analysis every potential event is weighted in probabilistic terms and that is the basis for evaluation.

The decision tree is an analytical technique used especially is sequential decisions, where various decision points are studied in relation to subsequent points. A decision tree is a pictorial presentation of a 'tree form' indicating the magnitude, probability and inter-relationship of all possible outcomes and is of immense importance in cases when the cash flows cannot be easily clarified as either independent or perfectly correlated and the correlation is of moderate order.

Illustration

Assuming a firm is expecting a substantial increase in demand for one of its products in the near future. Three alternative courses of action are available to meet this demand viz- (i) increasing shift work in its existing plant (ii) extending the existing plant and (iii) building a new plant. The firm is not sure of the actual increase in demand and thus cannot, with certainty, relate the correct capacity decision to the expected rise in demand. Output will increase with each choice along with cost. The potential increase in demand is estimated as follows:

Action	Increase in production (units) p.a.
Shift work	20000
Extension of plant	30000
New plant Building	60000

The market division has estimated the following increases in demand and their associated probabilities:

Increase in demand	Units p.a.	Probability of occurrence
Low	20000	0.3
Medium	50000	0.6
High	80000	1.0
		1.0

Action	Increase in Demand	Net present value (NPV) (₹)
Shift work	Low	5,000
	Medium	10,000
	High	15,000
Extension	Low	10,000
	Medium	20,000
	High	30,000
New Building	Low	(10,000)
	Medium	30,000
	High	50,000

The information regarding expected value (EV) or mean in terms of possible outcomes of each decision can be presented in the form of a decision tree as follows:

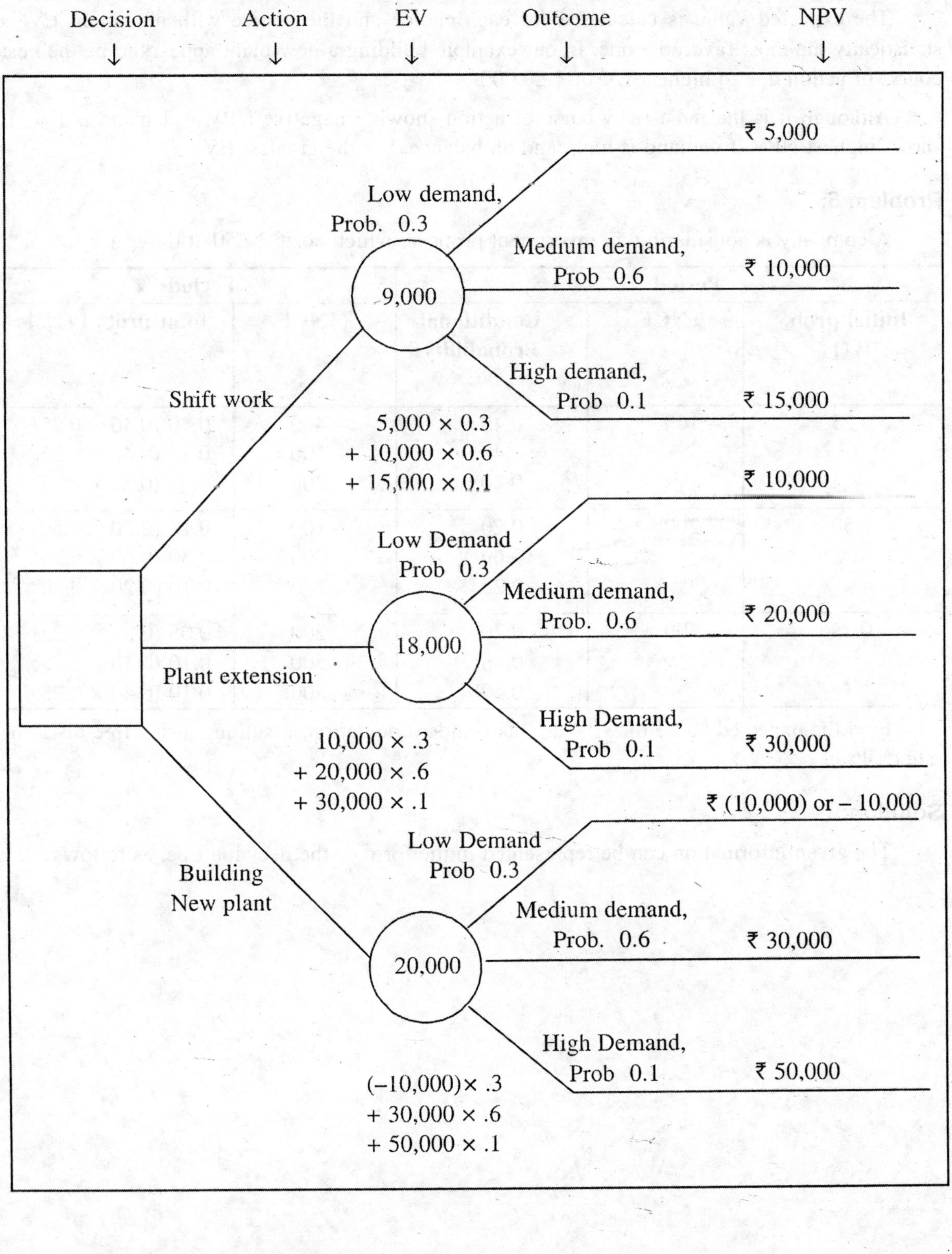

Decision
Action
EV
Outcome
NPV
Shift work
Low demand,
Prob. 0.3
₹ 5,000
Medium demand,
Prob 0.6
₹ 10,000
9,000
High demand,
Prob 0.1
₹ 15,000
5,000 × 0.3
+ 10,000 × 0.6
+ 15,000 × 0.1
Plant extension
Low Demand
Prob 0.3
₹ 10,000
Medium demand,
Prob. 0.6
₹ 20,000
18,000
High Demand,
Prob 0.1
₹ 30,000
10,000 × .3
+ 20,000 × .6
+ 30,000 × .1
Building
New plant
Low Demand
Prob 0.3
₹ (10,000) or – 10,000
Medium demand,
Prob. 0.6
₹ 30,000
20,000
High Demand,
Prob 0.1
₹ 50,000
(–10,000)× .3
+ 30,000 × .6
+ 50,000 × .1

The expected value is calculated for each choice and the choice with maximum EV is statistically the most favorable one. In our example building a new plant appears to be the best course of action due to highest EV of ₹ 20,000.

Although it is the most risky curse of action showing negative NPV it demand is low, it shows highest NPV if demand is high, and on balance, has the greatest EV

Problem 5:

A company is considering an investment proposal which costs ₹ 250 at time t = o

Period 1			Period 2	
Initial prob. P (1)	**NCF** ₹	**Conditional Probability**	**NCF** ₹	**Joint prob. P(1,2)**
0.25	– 100	0.40	– 400	0.10 (0.40 × 0.25)
		0.40	– 100	0.10 (0.40 × 0.25)
		0.20	200	0.05 (0.20 × 0.25)
0.50	200	0.20	– 100	0.10 (0.20 × 0.50)
		0.60	200	0.30 (0.60 × 0.50)
		0.20	500	0.10 (0.20 × 0.50
0.25	500	0.20	200	0.05 (0.20 × 0.25)
		0.40	500	0.10 (0.40 × 0.25)
		0.40	800	0.10 (0.40 × 0.25)

Find the expected value of NPV and its standard deviation, assuming a risk free discount rate of 4%.

Solution:

The given information can be represented in the form of the decision tree, as follows:

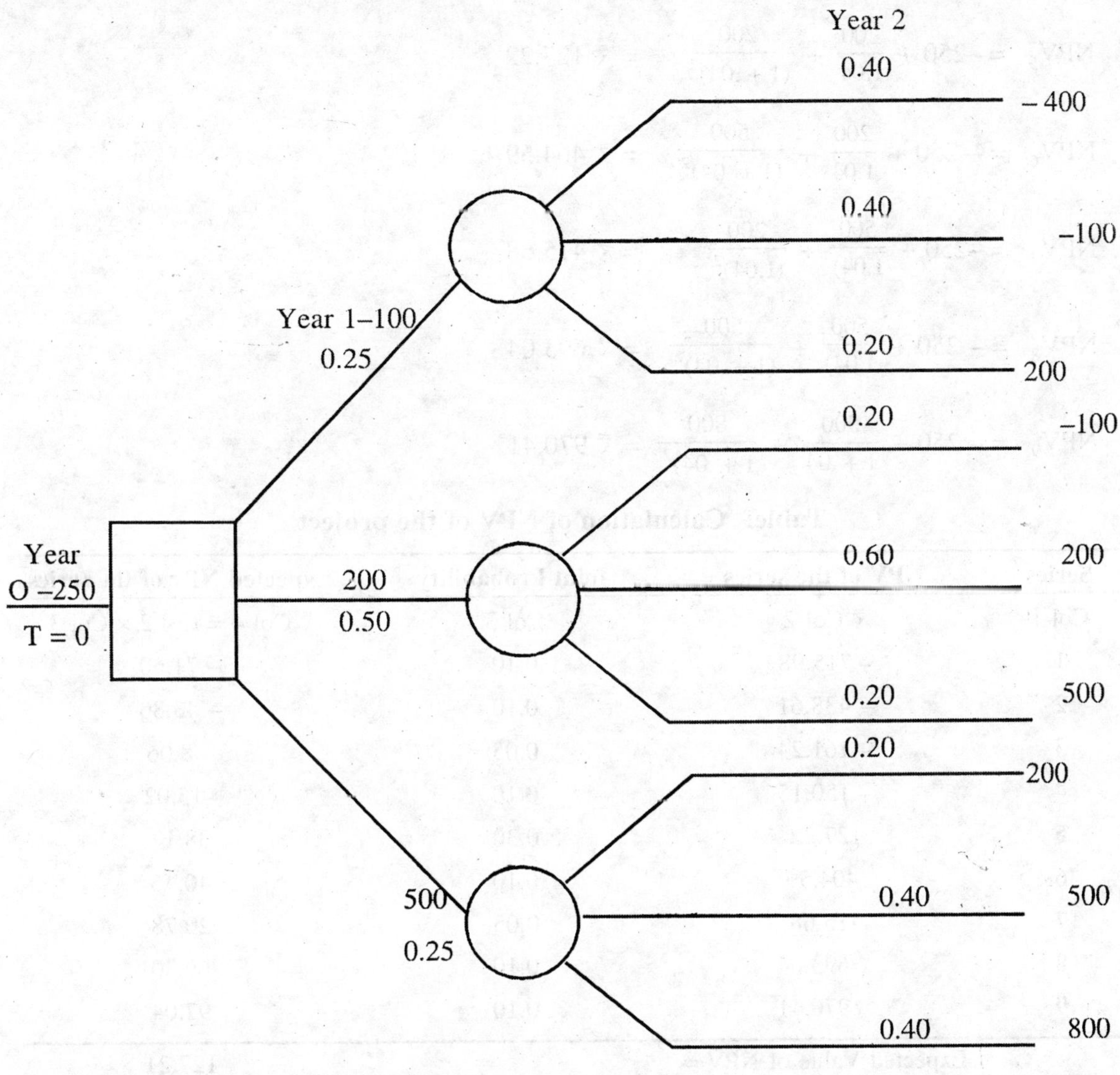

In this problem there are 9 possible series of NCF (net cash flows).

$$NPV_1 = -250 - \frac{100}{1.04} - \frac{400}{(1.04)^2} = -₹\ 715.98$$

$$NPV_2 = -250 - \frac{100}{1.04} - \frac{100}{(1.04)^2} = -₹\ 438.61$$

$$NPV_3 = -250 - \frac{100}{1.04} + \frac{200}{(1.04)^2} = -₹\ 161.24$$

$$NPV_4 = -250 + \frac{200}{1.04} - \frac{100}{(1.04)^2} = -₹\ 150.15$$

$$NPV_5 = -250 + \frac{200}{1.04} + \frac{200}{(1+.04)^2} = ₹\ 127.22$$

$$NPV_6 = -\ 250 + \frac{200}{1.04} + \frac{500}{(1+.04)^2} = ₹\ 404.59$$

$$NPV_7 = -250 + \frac{500}{1.04)} + \frac{200}{(1.04)^2} = ₹\ 415.68$$

$$NPV_8 = -\ 250 + \frac{500}{1.04)} + \frac{500}{(1+.04)^2} = ₹\ 693.04$$

$$NPV_9 = -\ 250 + \frac{500}{1+.04} + \frac{800}{1+.04)^2} = ₹\ 970.41$$

Table: Calculation of NPV of the project

Series	NPV of the series	Joint Probability	Expected NPv of the series
Col 1	₹ Col 2	Col 3	₹ Col 4 = Col 2 × Col 3
1	– 715.98	0.10	– 71.60
2	– 438.61	0.10	– 43.86
3	– 161.24	0.05	– 8.06
4	– 150.15	0.10	–15.02
5	127.22	0.30	38.17
6	404.59	0.10	40.46
7	415.68	0.05	20.78
8	693.04	0.10	69.30
9	970.41	0.10	97.04
	Expected Value of NPV =		127.21

The S. D. of the NPV's:

$$S.D. = \sqrt{\Sigma\ (C-E)^2 \times \text{Joint Probability}}$$

Table: S.D. of the NPV

Net Cash flow Series of NPV C (₹)	Expected NPV NPV E	$(C-E)^2$ (₹)	Joint Prob.	$(C-E)^2$ × joint Prob. ₹
– 715.98	127.21	710969.37	0.10	71096.94
– 438.61	127.21	320152.27	0.10	32015.23
– 161.24	127.21	83203.40	0.05	4160.17
– 150.15	127.21	76928.57	0.10	7692.86
127.22	127.21	0.0001 = 0	0.30	0
404.59	127.21	76939.64	0.10	7693.96
415.68	127.21	83214.94	0.05	4160.75
693.04	127.21	320163.59	0.10	32016.36
970.41	127.21	710986.24	0.10	71098.62
	$\Sigma (C-E)^2$ × joint prob. =			229934.89

$$S.D. = \sqrt{\Sigma (C-E)^2 \times \text{Joint Probability}} - \sqrt{229934.89} = 479.515$$

SUMMARY

Where there is uncertainly in obtaining expected ROI/rate of return we may say that risk exists. The factors of risk are Business Environmental Factors, Industry Specific Factors, and Company Specific Factors. There are project specific risk, competition risk, industry Specific Risk, International Risk and Market Risk. The methods of incorporating risk under uncertainty are payback period, risk adjusted Discount Rate, Certainty Equivalent, Sensitivity Analysis, probability Distribution approach. Payback periods prefer projects of short-term paybacks to that of long-term paybacks. The basis of 'risk Adjusted Discount Rate' approach is that there should be adequate reward in the form of return to firms which decide to execute risky business projects. Risk premium needs to be incorporated in discount rate in the evaluation of risky project proposals. Therefore, the discount rate for appraisal of projects has two components-risk-free rate and risk premium. Under the method of certainty equivalent, the unexpected future cash flows are converted into cash flows with certainty. The certainty equivalent co-efficient is also known as the risk-adjustment factor. Sensitivity analysis is a technique that shows the change in NPV given a change in one of the variables that determine cash flows of a project. It measures the sensitivity of NPV of a project in respect to a change in one of the input variables of NPV. Under probability distribution approach, the chances of occurrences of various economic environments are expressed in the form of probability. After assigning probabilities to future cash flows expected net present value is computed. A decision tree presents graphically the relationship between a present decision and future events, future decisions and the consequences of such decisions. The decision of taking up an investment project is broken into different stages. At each stage the proposal is examined to decide whether to go ahead or not. This multi-stage approach can be handled effectively with the help of decision trees under 'Decision-free approach'. Complex projects involve huge capital outlay and hence risky. There is the need to define and evaluate scientifically the complex managerial problems arising out of the sequence of interrelated decisions with consequential outcomes of high risk. It is effectively answered by decision tree approach. Moreover structuring a complex project decision with many sequential investment decisions demands effective project risk management. This is possible only with the help of an analytical tool like decision tree approach. This approach is able to eliminate unprofitable outcomes and helps in arriving at optimum decision stages in time sequence.

EXERCISE

A. Short Questions

1. Define risk.
2. What are the factors of risk?
3. What is Beta risk?
4. What is portfolio risk?
5. What is competition risk?
6. State the names of industry-specific risk.
7. What are the methods of incorporating risk under uncertainty?
8. What are the components of Risk Adjusted Discount Rate?
9. What is certainty equivalent?
10. What is sensitivity Analysis?
11. What is a decision tree?

B. Broad and Moderate Questions

1. Examine the type and sources of risk in capital budgeting?
2. Examine the features of Decision – tree Approach.
3. What are the advantages of Decision – tree approach?
4. How do you evaluate 'risk-adjusted discount rate'?
5. What is the acceptance criteria of a project under certainty equivalent method ? What are the and disadvantages of this method?
6. What are the advantages and limitations of payback period?

C. Problems

1. R & D section of a company has developed an electric moped. The firm is ready for pilot production and test marketing. This will cost ₹ 20 million and take 6 months. Management believes that there is a 70% chance that the pilot production and test marketing will be successful. If it is successful the company can build a plant costing ₹ 200 million. The plant will generate annual cash inflow of ₹ 50 million for 20 years if the demand is high or an annual cash flow of ₹ 20 million if the demand is low. High demand has a probability of 0.8 and the low demand has a probability of 0.2 Cost of capital is 12%. Suggest the optimal course of action using decision tree analysis.
2. Calculate the Expected NPV and S.D. of NPV from the following details in respect of a project which requires an initial cost of ₹ 5,00,000.

Year	Economic conditions	Cash flows (₹)	Probability
1	High growth	2,00,000	0.3
	Average Growth	1,60,000	0.5
	No Growth	45,000	0.2
2	High growth	3,20,000	0.3
	Average Growth	2,00,000	0.5
	No Growth	55,000	0.2
3	High growth	4,00,000	0.2
	Average Growth	2,50,000	0.6
	No Growth	35,000	0.2

3. A company has two mutually exclusive projects under consideration viz. project A and project B.

Each project requires an initial cash outlay of ₹ 300000 and has an effective life of 10 years. The company's cost of capital is 10%. The following forecast of cash flows is made by the management.

Economic Environment	Project A Annual cash inflows	Project B Annual cash inflows
Pessimistic	₹ 60,000	₹ 20,000
Expected	75,000	80,000
Optimistic	1,00,000	1,10,000

What is the NPV of the project?

Which project should the management consider?

❑❑❑

20 CVP Analysis and Marginal Costing

20.1 TECHNIQUES OF ASCERTAINING THE COST OF A PRODUCT ON SERVICE – ABSORPTION COSTING AND MARGINAL COSTING

Absorption and marginal Costing are the two techniques of ascertaining the cost of a product on service using the different elements of cost.

Absorption Costing: It is known as 'Traditional' or 'conventional' or 'Full Cost method'. According to this method, the cost of a product is determined after taking into account both fixed and variable cost. Fixed costs are period costs which do not very with changes with the volume of production and sales. Variables costs are those operating expenses or a group of operational expenses which vary directly and in proportion to level of activity *viz;* sales or production. Examples are cost of raw materials consumed, productivity wages, power, etc.

Under this method, both variable and fixed costs are charged to products processes or operations .Net profit is arrived at by deducting administration, selling and distribution from gross profit. Inventory is valued at factory cost which includes production overheads – both fixed and variable.

This technique is useful if:

(i) The enterprise is producing only one product;

(ii) There is no closing or opening inventory;

(iii) The rate of recovery of overheads is based on the normal capacity instead of actual level of activity;

(iv) The management is more concerned with overall profit margin on the products.

Marginal Costing

Marginal costing is a technique which considers only the marginal costs while computing the cost of a product on service, as the cost of production, leaving out fixed or period costs to be absorbed from the marginal contribution. CIMA defines marginal costing as "the ascertainment of marginal costs and effect of changes in volume or output on the company's profit by segregating total costs into variable and fixed costs".

Under this technique, the contribution is computed first. Then the fixed costs are deducted from the contribution to get the profit figure. Following is the marginal costing equation:

SALES – VARIABLE COSTS = CONTRIBUTION = FIXED COST + PROFIT

OR, S – V = C = F + P

20.2 MARGINAL COST (ALSO KNOWN AS VARIABLE COST)

Marginal Cost in the increase on decrease in total cost arising due to small changes in output or change in one unit of production, as follows:

$$\text{Marginal Cost (MC)} = \frac{dTC}{d\theta} = \frac{\Delta TC}{\Delta \theta}$$

(i) Economists view marginal costs as the cost of producing one additional unit of output as follows:

TABLE: Marginal cost

Unit	Total Cost of Production (TC)	MC
1	17	17
2	32	15
3	45	13
4	56	11
5	60	4

(ii) Accountants view marginal costs as the increase in production cost due to the increase in variable costs only arising from one unit change in output. Thus for them, marginal costs and variable costs are synonymous terms.

Thus Marginal Costs = Total Variable costs

= Direct material + Direct Wages + Variable Overheads

Illustration

Variable cost = ₹ 20 p.u.

Total Fixed Cost for a specified period = ₹ 5,000

Present Output = 200 units

If output is increased by one unit what will be the marginal cost?

Solution

Marginal Cost = Increase in Variable Cost
= (201 × 20) – (200 × 20)
= 4,020 – 4,000 = ₹ 20

20.3 MARGINAL COSTING VS ABSORPTION COSTING

Absorption costing is based on the recovery of total product cost while under marginal costing, variable costs are charged to the production. The differences between them are as follows:

(i) Charging to Overheads: Under Absorption Costing both variable and fixed costs are charged to products processes or operations. Under marginal Costing, only variable costs are charged to products, process or operation.

(ii) Recovery of Overheads: Under Absorption costing both variable and fixed costs are charged to production. Fixed overheads are apportioned on the basis of some suitable basis, e.g., on the basis of output direct materials consumed, etc. thus, there is always a problem of over on under recovery of overheads.

(iii) Valuation Closing Stock: Under Absorption costing, stock of work-in-progress and finished goods are valued on the basis of works cost and cost of production respectively inclusive of fixed costs. Thus, the closing stock is overvalued as compared to marginal costing. Under marginal costing, only variable costs are considered for the valuation of inventory as compared to absorption costing.

(iv) Decision Making: Under absorption costing, managerial decisions are based on profit, *i.e.*, excess of sales value over total costs. Under marginal costing managerial decisions are based on the contribution, *i.e.*, the excess of sales values over variable costs.

20.4 INCOME DETERMINATION UNDER ABSORPTION AND MARGINAL COSTING

TABLE: Income Statement: under absorption costing

Particulars	₹	₹
1. Sales Revenue (Units Sold × Selling price)		xxx
2. Total costs of manufacturing for goods sold		
(i) Direct material cost	xxx	
(ii) Direct wages	xxx	
(iii) Direct expenses	xxx	
Prime Cost	xxx	
Add: Manufacturing Overhead (both fixed & variable)	xxx	
Cost of Goods Manufacturing	xxx	

Add: Opening Stock of inventory	xxx	
Less: Closing Stock of inventory	(xxx)	
Cost of Goods Sold	xxx	xxx
3. Gross Profit (1-2)		xxx
4. **Non-Production Overheads:** (both fixed & variable)		
(i) Selling & Distribution Cost	xxx	
(ii) Administrative Cost	xxx	
	xxx	xxx
5. Profit before Taxes (3-4)		xxx
6. Taxes		(xxx)
7. Profit after taxes (PAT) (5-6)		xxx

Income Statement - Marginal Costing

	Particulars	₹	₹
1.	**Sales Revenue (Units Sold X Selling price)**		xxx
2.	**Variable Cost of Sales:**		
	Direct Material	xxx	
	Direct Labour	xxx	
	Direct Expenses	xxx	
	Prime Cost	xxx	
	Add: Variable Factory/Production Overheads	xxx	
	Variable Cost of Goods Manufactored	xxx	
	Add: Opening Stock of inventory	xxx	
		xxx	
	Less: Closing Stock of inventory	(xxx)	
	Variable cost of goods sold	xxx	
	Add: Variable administrative costs	xxx	
	Add: Variable Selling and distribution costs	xxx	
	Variable cost of Goods sold	xxx	xxx
3.	Contribution (1-2)		xxx
4.	**Total fixed Overheads:**		
	Fixed Production Overheads	xxx	
	Fixed Selling & Distribution Overheads	xxx	
	Fixed Administrative Overheads	xxx	xxx
5.	Profit before Tax = (3-4)		xxx
6.	Taxes		(xxx)
7.	Profit after Tax (5-6)		xxx

Problem 1:

ABC Ltd. is manufacturing 2 products A and B. The cost of their manufacture is as follows:

	A	B
Direct material p.u.	₹ 5	₹ 4
Direct Wages p.u.	₹ 3	₹ 2
Sales price	₹ 20	₹ 20
Goods produced	2000 units	1000 units
Goods sold	1800 units	900 units

The total factory overheads are ₹ 12,000 out of which ₹ 6,000 are fixed and rest are variable. It was decided to apportion these costs over different products in the ratio of output. Prepare a statement showing cost and profit of each product according to Absorption Costing and Marginal Costing. Selling and Distribution Overheads (all fixed) amounted to ₹ 9,000 are to be apportioned in the ratio of 1:1. Offer your comments.

Solution:

Statement of Profit under Absorption Costing Method

	Particular	Product A ₹	Product B ₹
1.	Sales (1800 × 20), (900 × 20)	36,000	18,000
2.	**Total Costs of manufacturing:**		
	Direct Material (2000 × 5), (1000 × 4)	10,000	4,000
	Direct wages (2000 × 3), (1000 × 2)	6,000	2,000
	Factory Overheads:		
Add:	Variable $(6000 \times \frac{2}{3})$, $(6000 \times \frac{1}{3})$	4,000	2,000
	Fixed $(6000 \times \frac{2}{3})$, $(6000 \times \frac{1}{3})$	4,000	2,000
	Cost of Goods Manufactured	24,000	10,000
Less:	Closing stock of inventory (200 × 12), (100 × 10)	(2,400)	(1,000)
	Manufacturing Costs of Goods Sold	21,600	9,000
3.	Gross profit = (1-2)	14,400	9,000
4.	Non-production Overheads: Selling & Distribution Overheads	4,500	4,500
5.	Profit before taxes (3-4)	9,900	4,500

Note:

(1) Cost of Goods manufactured p.u.:

Product A – $\frac{24,000}{2,000}$ = ₹ 12/units

Product B – $\frac{10,000}{1,000}$ = ₹ 10/units

(2) Selling & Distribution Overheads:

Product A – 9,000 × $\frac{1}{2}$ = ₹ 4,500

Product B – 9,000 × $\frac{1}{2}$ = ₹ 4,500

(3) **Closing stock:** [Unsold Units × Cost goods manufactured p.u.]

Product A – 200 × 12 = ₹ 2,400
Product B – 100 × 10 = ₹ 1,000

Statement of profit under Marginal Costing Method

	Particulars	Product A ₹	Product B ₹
1.	Sales : (1,800 × 20), (900 × 20)	36,000	18,000
2.	**Variable cost of sales:**		
	Direct Material (2,000 × 5), (1,000 × 4)	10,000	4,000
	Direct wages (2,000 × 3), (1,000 × 2)	6,000	2,000
	Add: Variable Factory overheads.	4,000	2,000
	Less: Closing stock	(2,000)	(800)
	Variable Cost of Goods sold	18,000	7,200
	Add: Variable adm. selling & dist. Exp.	NIL	NIL
	Overheads		
	Variable cost of sales		
		18,000	72,000
3.	Contribution (1-2)	18,000	10,800
4.	Total Fixed Overheads:		
	Fixed Factory/Production overheads	4,000	2,000
		4,500	4,500
	Fixed selling & dist. Overheads	8,500	6,500
5.	Profits before Taxes (3-4)	9,500	4,300

Note:

(1) Variable cost of goods manufactured p.u.

Product A – $\frac{20,000}{2,000}$ = ₹ 10/units

Product B – $\frac{8,000}{1,000}$ = ₹ 8/ units

(2) Closing stock:

[Unsold Units × variable cost of goods manufactured p.u.]

Product A – 200 × 10 = ₹ 2,000

Product B – 100 × 8 = ₹ 800

Comments:

Profit under absorption costing:

Product A –	₹ 9,900
Product B –	₹ 4,500
	₹ 14,400

Profit under absorption costing:

Product A –	₹ 9,500
Product B –	₹ 4,300
	₹ 13,800

Difference in profit: ₹ 600 (14,400 – 13,800)

Reason: difference in the value of closing stock by 600 as follows:

Product A: closing stock difference = (2,400 – 2,000) =	400
Product B: closing stock difference = (1,000 – 800) =	200
	₹ 600

20.5 ADVANTAGES AND DISADVANTAGES OF MARGINAL COSTING

Advantages

(i) Marginal Costing makes for a more systematic and meaningful presentation of cost data based on the logic of treating the fixed expenses separately as period cost and not product cost.

(ii) Forecasting profit or loss under varying activity-levels and under varying alternatives is facilitated.

(iii) Profit planning both short-term and long-term, is almost impossible without the use of marginal costing.

(iv) Pricing decisions, especially under competitive conditions, are also made easier with the use of this technique.

(v) Inventory valuation based on marginal cost prevents shifting of one year's fixed expenses to another as is done under total costing approach.

(vi) Many and varied decision-making problems in business can be tackled successfully with the use of marginal costing data.

Disadvantages

(i) Marginal costing is essentially *a short-term concept* and therefore, long-term decisions based on this concept may be at time erroneous.

(ii) In real life business situation, *segregation of costs into fixed and variable may not be easy. Any broad approximations in this area would lead to inaccurate marginal cost data and hence wrong decisions at times.*

(iii) Inventory valuation based on marginal cost creates problems due to the fact that *conventional accounting and audit practices are based on total cost-valuation of inventory.* Any changeover from the age-old convention will not only be resisted but brings in some practical problems in accounting and audit, particularly in the first year of such changeover.

(iv) It is alleged by some experts that under marginal costing technique, fixed costs get ignored or are underplayed. *At times situations arise when, during pricing against bulla tenders of big made-to-order jobs, adequate consideration is not given to the existence of fixed costs or to the fact that a part of such fixed costs has to be recovered through the proposed price.* This is not a limitation of marginal costing technique itself but its improper application in practical situations.

20.6 BREAK-EVEN CONCEPTS, BREAK-EVEN CHART, BREAK-EVEN ANALYSIS (CVP ANALYSIS)

Break-even point refers to 'no-profit-no loss' under following situations:

(a) Total Sales = total cost

(b) Total Contribution = total fixed Cost (F)

We know, C – F = P

At Break-even points C – F = O or C = F

At Break-even point, the total contribution earned is equal to what would be necessary to meet only the total Fixed cost (F) of the business under marginal costing technique.

The Break-even point may be worked out by following manner:

(a) Break-even Units:

(No of units sold to achieve 'no profit no loss' situation)

At Break-even point, total contribution (C) = Total fixed Cost (F)

Or Units × contribution /unit = Total fixed Cost

Or, $\text{Units} = \dfrac{\text{Total fixed Cost (TFC)}}{\text{Contribution/unit}}$

$\therefore$ $\text{Breakeven Units} = \dfrac{\text{TFC}}{\text{Contribution/unit}}$

(b) Breakeven Sales

(Amount of Sales to achieve 'no profit no loss' situation)

Breakeven Sales = break-even units × Selling price per unit

$$= \frac{\text{TFC}}{\text{Contribution/unit}} \times \text{S.P. per unit} = \frac{\text{TFC}}{\dfrac{\text{Contribution/unit}}{\text{S.P./unit}}}$$

$\therefore$ $\text{Break-even Sales} = \dfrac{\text{TFC}}{\text{P/V Ratio}}$ OR BE units × SP p.u.

Where, P/V Ratio = C/S ratio (contribution to Sales ratio)

$$= 1 - \frac{\text{Variable cost}}{\text{Sales}} = 1 - \text{Variable cost to sales ratio}$$

$$= \frac{\text{Contribution}}{\text{Sales}} \text{ OR } \frac{\text{Contribution/unit}}{\text{SP/unit}}$$

Or $\dfrac{\text{Change in profit}}{\text{Change in Sales}}$

(I) Break-even Analysis (CVP Analysis)

Break-even analysis indicates at which level costs and revenue are in equilibrium. To speak broadly, break-even analysis means an analytical technique that can be used to determine the probable profit at any level on production or sale. It is basically an extension of marginal costing. Break-even analysis may be performed both graphically as well as algebraically; it establishes and explains the relationship among costs (fixed and variable cost) of production, profit and sales value. Hence, this analysis is also termed 'Cost-Volume-profit' (CVP) analysis. Ultimately CVP analysis means any analysis to study the effect or impact on cost and profit of changes in volume and *vice versa*.

Break-even chart : When the break-even analysis is performed graphically, it is known as a break-even chart. It is a graphical representation of marginal costing. It has been defined as a chart which shows the profitability on otherwise of an undertaking at various levels of activity and indicates the point at which 'neither profit nor loss' is made.

There are various methods of drawing a break-even chart to show C/S ratio, margin of safety, break-even point, profit etc. The most popular and simple chart is given below:

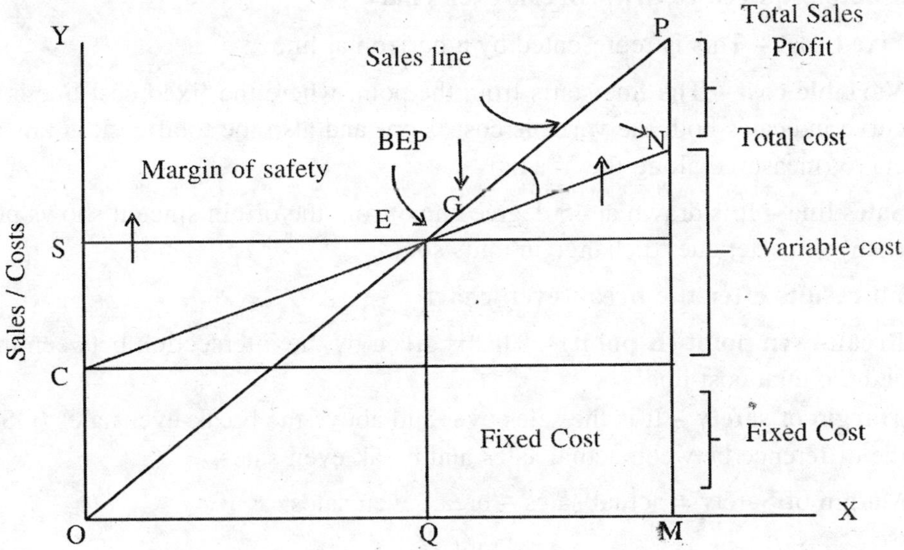

Output (production = Sales), Units (Breakeven chart)

OP = Sales line

CN = Variable cost Line (Also total Cost Line)

E = Break-even point

OQ = Break-even Point (in units) or break-even units

OS = Break-even Sales.

G = Angle of incidence indicating c/s Ratio or profibility created by intersection of sales line and Variable (total) cost line. This angle is an indicator of profit earning capacity over the break-even point.

P/V ratio (C/S Ratio) – it expresses the relation between contribution and sales and makes the change in the percentage of contribution in relation to changes in the volume of sales. It is one of the most important ratios for studying the profitability of operation of a business and it is another method to determine the cost volume profit relationship. This ratio is also known as marginal Income Ratio on contribution Ratio or profit volume (P/V) Ratio.

In Break-even chart, it is the trigonometrically measure of the angle of incidence created by the intersection of sales line and total cost line.

$$\text{P/V Ratio} = \frac{\text{Contribution}}{\text{Sales}} \times 100$$

$$\text{Or } \frac{\text{Contribution p.u.}}{\text{Sales price p.u.}} \times 100$$

$$\text{Or } \frac{\text{Change in profit}}{\text{Change in Sales}} \times 100$$

Or 1 – variable cost to sales ratio.

Input date required to draw break-even chart

(i) **Fixed cost –** This is represented by a horizontal line

(ii) **Variable cost –** The line starts from the point where the fixed cost line is drawn. The curve indicates both the variable cost 'slop' and also the total cost, at any point of the curve (measured along the Y-axis)

(iii) **Sales line –** It is drawn at 45 degree angle from the origin since it shows proportionate change in sale, due to change in units sold.

Output results after the break-even chart

(i) **Break-even point (E point) –** This is given by the intersection between the sales line and the total cost line

(ii) **Margin of safety –** It is the sales over and above the break-even sales (OS) level. It is the difference between actual sales and break even sales.

Margin of Safety = actual sales – break-even sales

$$\text{Or } \frac{\text{Profit}}{\text{P/V Ratio}}$$

(iii) **P/V ratio –** This is the trigonometrically measure of the angle of incidence created by the intersection of sales line and total cost line.

(iv) **The absolute profit –** This is measured along the Y-axis as the difference between the two points, the actual sales point and the point where total cost line ends.

(II) CPV Analysis – (from the break-even charts)

On an analysis of the break-even chart, the following facts would be clear:

Change	Impact/effect
(i) If fixed cost:	BE units – increase
(a) Increases	P/V ratio – same margin of Safety – decreases, Profit – decreases
(b) decreases	The reverse of above (in each case)
(ii) If variable cost:	
(a) Increases	BE units – increase, P/V ratio – decreases margin of Safety – decreases, Profit – decreases
(b) decreases	The reverse of above (in each case)
(iii) If sale price:	
(a) Increases	BE units – decreases, P/V ratio – increases, margin of Safety – increases, Profit – increases
(b) decreases	The reverse of above (in each case)
(iv) If the sale units:	
(a) Increases	Margin of safety and profit increase (others, no change)
(b) decreases	Margin of safety and profit decrease (others, no change)

(III) Break-even Analysis – in a Multi-product situation

Let us take a simple illustration to show how the break-even sales for the business as a whole can be worked out in a multiproduct situation.

Illustration

			Sales (₹ in crores)			Contribution (₹ In crores)		
Product	**Units (crore)**	**p/v Ratio**	**Product Wise**	**SP p.u.**	**Cumulative**	**Product Wise**	**Contrib p.u.**	**Cumulative**
X	4	35%	20	5	20	7	1.75	7
Y	5	36%	25	5	45	9	1.80	16
Z	5	20%	25	5	70	5	1.0	21
Total	14	Total Fixed Cost of the business = ₹ 12 crores.						

Analysis

(a) Composite p/v ratio $= \frac{21}{70} = 30\%$

(b) Break-even Sales $= \frac{\text{TFC}}{\text{Composite p/v Ratio}} = \frac{\text{12 crores}}{30\%} = \text{40 crores.}$

Following a similar approach, BE units also can be worked out by using the following format.

$$\text{BE units} = \frac{\text{TFC}}{\text{Weighted average contribution p.u.}}$$

$$\text{Weighted average contribution p.u.} = \frac{\text{Total contribution p.u.}}{\text{Total Units}} = \frac{21}{14} = ₹\ 1.50 \text{ p.u.}$$

$$\text{Accordingly, B.E. units} = \frac{\text{12 crores}}{₹\ 1.50 \text{ p.u.}} = \text{8 crores units}$$

[Check: BE sales = BE units × SP p.u. = 8 crores units × ₹ 5 p.u. = ₹ 40 crores]

The concept of composite P/V ratio is based on a given sales mix. Thus, if the sales mix changes, as it does happen in reality, the composite P/V ratio will change and consequently the break-even sales to will change.

20.7 ASSUMPTION, ADVANTAGES AND LIMITATIONS OF BREAK-EVEN ANALYSIS/CVP ANALYSIS

Assumptions

The following assumptions usually underline break-even analysis:

(a) Costs may be segregated into fixed and variable costs.

(b) Cost revenue volume relationship is linear.

(c) Selling prices remain unchanged.

(d) Prices of cost factors, *i.e.*, raw materials, wages, rent etc., remain unchanged

(e) Operating efficiency of human, machine, technical resources and productivity are to remain unchanged, product mix and sales mix will be constant in case of multiproduct analysis.

(f) Inventory is maintained at an uniform level.

(g) There is no improvement or deterioration in cost control.

(h) Profits are function of output.

Advantages/User

Break-even analysis helps management in a number of ways. Some advantages of Break-even Analysis are listed below:

(i) **Product planning:** It refers to adding a new product line to the existing product line or dropping an existing product from a product line in the light of its estimated revenue and cost.

(ii) **Activity planning:** It refers to expansion or reduction of capacity.

(iii) **Profit planning:** CVP analysis provides the most important managerial tool for profit planning. Profit can be forecasted fairly and correctly by taking into account the projected level of output, optimum product combination, estimated revenue and total cost of productions.

(iv) **Decisional:** The following decisions can be taken by applying break-even analysis:

(a) make or buy decision;

(b) Accepting an order or not;

(c) Selling prices of the product/products;

(d) Price policies;

(e) whether accept a certain business at a specified price;

(f) whether increase the sales of a particular product or not;

(g) whether explore intensively in one or more territory or not;

(v) **Cost control:** CVP analysis enables to achieve control over costs by setting up flexible budgets which indicates costs at different levels of output. Since fixed cost is segregated from variable cost, the budgeted cost for each level of output can be ascertained which helps the management in instituting control over costs.

Limitations

(i) When CVP analysis is based on accounting data, as it usually happens, it may suffer from various limitations of such data, *e.g.*, neglect of inputted cost, arbitrary depreciation estimates and inappropriate allocation of overhead costs.

(ii) Costs and prices are subject to constant change from unit to unit as also from period to period.

(iii) The assumption of linear relationship among cost, volume and revenue is realistic only over narrow ranges of output.

(iv) CVP/Break-even analysis is not an effective tool for long-range use and its use should be restricted to the short-run only.

(v) Costs in a particular period need not be caused entirely by output in that period

(vi) Profits are caused not only by change in output but also by other factors like, technological changes, improved management and so on.

20.8 SIGNIFICANCE OF P/V RATIO, ADVANTAGES/USES, IT'S IMPROVEMENT

The real significance of P/V ratio lies in its use for appraising profitability of different operations, product lines, sales area, method of sales, classes of customers, etc.

A higher P/V ratio reflects greater profitability and lower ratio indicates lesser profitability. The P/V ratio is used for determination of break-even point, level of output or sales to earn desired amount of profit, calculation of variable cost and profit for any volume of sales.

Importance and uses of P/V Ratio

(i) Most useful guide to the profitability of the business

(ii) Key to many problems in decision making viz sales area, product line etc. giving larger contribution to profits

(iii) Can indicate the extent to which the volume of sales should be achieved to maintain the same amount of profit.

(iv) Helps to determine the most profitable product mix which gives the maximum possible profits with the limited amount of resources available.

(v) Helps to determine break-even point.

20.9 SUMMARY OF FORMULAS

(a) Contribution = Sales – Variable Cost OR Total Fixed Cost + Profit
or, Sales × P/V Ratio

(b) P/V Ratio = 1 – variable cost to sales ratio

Or, $\frac{\text{Contribution p.u.}}{\text{Sales price p.u.}} \times 100$ Or, $\frac{\text{Total contribution}}{\text{Total Sales}} \times 100$

Or, $\frac{\text{Change in profit}}{\text{Change in Sales}} \times 100$

(c) Variable Cost = Sales – Contribution

Or, Sales × Variable cost to sales Ratio

Or Sales (1 – P/V Ratio)

(d) Break-even point:

$$\text{Break-even Units} = \frac{\text{TFC}}{\text{Contribution/unit}}$$

$$\text{Break-even Sales} = \frac{\text{TFC}}{\text{P/V Ratio}}$$ or Break-even Units × Sales price per unit

(e) Margin of Safety: Actual Sales – break-even Sales

$$\text{Or, } \frac{\text{Profit}}{\text{P/V Ratio}}$$

(f) Profit = Contribution – Total Fixed Cost

Or, (Sales × P/V ratio) – Total Fixed Cost

Or, (Sales – variable cost) – Total Fixed cost, *i.e.*, Contribution – Total Fixed Cost

(g) Variable cost to sales ratio

= (1 – P/V ratio)

$$\text{Or } \frac{\text{Variable cost}}{\text{Sales}} \times 100$$

Fixed Cost = Break-even sales × P/V Ratio

(h) Sales of earn profit:

$$\text{Unit to be sold} = \frac{\text{TFC + desired profit}}{\text{Contribution p.u.}}$$

$$\text{Sales (₹)} = \frac{\text{TFC + desired profit}}{\text{P/V ratio}}$$

Or, units to be sold to earn desired profit × sales price p.u.

(i) Profit from a given amount of sales : (Given Sales × P/V ratio) – Total Fixed Cost

20.10 PROBLEMS AND SOLUTIONS – SHORT QUESTIONS

Problem 1

Find the contribution and profit earned : Selling price per unit ₹ 25. Variable cost per unit ₹ 20. Fixed Cost ₹ 3,05,000. Output 80,000 units.

Solution:

Total Contribution = Total Sales – Total Variable cost. = 80000 × 25 – 80000 × 20 = 20,00,000 – 16,00,000 = ₹ 4,00,000 or, Total Contribution = Contribution p.u. × No. of units

= (Sales price p.u. – variable cost p.u.) × No. of units

= (₹ 25 – ₹ 20) × 80,000 = ₹ 4,00,000

Profit = Contribution – Fixed Cost or 4,00,000 – 3,05,000 = ₹ 95,000

Problem 2

Calculate the profit earned: Fixed cost ₹ 5,00,000. Variable cost ₹ 10 per unit. Selling price ₹ 15 per unit. Output 150,000 units

Solution:

C = S – V = F + P [C = Contribution, V = Variable Cost, S = Sales, F = Fixed Cost]

or, C = (1,50,000 × 15) – (1,50,000 × 10) = Fixed Cost (₹ 5,00,000) + Profit

or, Profit = 22,50,000 – 15,00,000 – 5,00,000 = ₹ 2,50,000

Problem 3

Find the fixed costs: Sales ₹ 2,00,000. Variable Cost ₹ 40,000. Profit ₹ 30,000

Solution:

C = S – V = F + P [V = Variable Cost]

or, 2,00,000 – 40,000 = Fixed Cost + 30,000

or, Fixed Cost = 2,00,000 – 40,000 – 30,000 = ₹ 1,30,000

Problem 4

Calculate the Variable Cost: Sales ₹ 1,50,000. Profit ₹ 40,000. Fixed cost ₹ 30,000. Find the amount of variable cost.

Solution:

C = S – V = F + P [V = Variable Cost]

or, 1,50,000 – V = 30,000 + 40,000

or, V = 1,50,000 – 30,000 – 40,000 = ₹ 80,000

Problem 5

Calculate P/V Ratio: Marginal cost ₹ 24, 000. Sales ₹ 60, 000

Solution:

Contribution = Sales – Marginal Cost = 60,000 – 24,000 = 36,000

P/V Ratio = Contribution/Sales × 100 = 36,000/60,000 × 100 = 60%

Problem 6

The sales turn over and profits during two periods are as under:

	Period 1	Period 2
Sales	₹ 20,000	₹ 30,000
Profit	₹ 2,000	₹ 4,000

Calculate the P/V Ratio and Fixed cost.

Solution:

P/V Ratio = Change in Profit / Change in Sales × 100

= 4,000 – 2,000 / 30,000 – 20,000 × 100

= 2,000/10,000 × 100 = 20%

Fixed Cost under period 1 = Sales of period 1 × P/V ratio – Profit of period 1

= 20,000 × 20% – 2,000 = ₹ 2,000

Fixed Cost under period 2 = Sales of period 2 × P/V ratio – Profit of period 2

= 30,000 × 20% – 4,000 = ₹ 2,000

Therefore Fixed Cost = ₹ 2,000

Problem 7

Calculate: P/V Ratio

	Total Sales	Total Costs
Year ending 31st December 2009	₹ 22,23,000	₹ 19,83,600
Year ending 31st December 2010	24,51,000	21,43,200

Solution:

Profit for the year 2009 = Total Sales – Total Costs = 22,23,000 – 19,83,600

= ₹ 2,39,400

Profit for the year 2010 = Total Sales – Total Costs = 24,51,000 – 21,43,200

= ₹ 3,07,800

P/V Ratio = Change in profit/change in sales × 100

= 307800 – 239400/2451000 – 2223000 × 100

= 68400/228000 = 30%

Problem 8

Calculate the selling price if marginal cost is ₹ 2,400 and P/V Ratio is 20%.

Solution:

P/V Ratio = 20%, therefore the variable cost to sales ratio is 100 – 20 = 80%

Variable or Marginal cost given is ₹ 2,400: Therefore, Selling price is 24,000/80% = ₹ 30,000.

Problem 9

Calculate break-even point : Fixed costs ₹ 80,000. Variable cost per unit ₹ 4. Sales ₹ 2,00,000. The number of units involved coincides with expected volume of output. Each unit sells at ₹ 20.

Solution:

BEP in units: Fixed expenses / contribution per unit

Contribution = S – V or ₹ 20 – ₹ 4 or ₹ 16 p.u.

BEP in units = ₹ 80,000 / ₹ 16 or 5,000 units.

Problem 10

Calculate the Break-even point: Sales ₹ 2, 00,000. Fixed expenses ₹ 50, 000. Variable expenses ₹ 1,00,000.

Solution:

Since no information about the number of units produced and costs per unit is given, only Break-even point in value OR Break-even Sales can be ascertained.

$$\text{Break Even Sales} = \frac{\text{TFC}}{\text{P/V Ratio}}$$

$$= \frac{50000}{\dfrac{200000 - 100000}{200000} \times 100}$$

$$= \frac{50000}{50\%} = ₹\ 100000$$

Problem 11

Calculate P/V Ratio and break-even point: Sales ₹ 5,00,000. Fixed Costs ₹ 1,00,000. Profit ₹ 1,50,000.

Solution:

P/V Ratio = Contribution / Sales × 100

Contribution = Fixed Costs + Profit = ₹ 1,00,000 + ₹ 1,50,000 = ₹ 2,50,000

P/V Ratio = 2,50,000 / 5,00,000 = 50%

BEP in ₹ = Fixed Costs / P/V Ratio = 1,00,000 / 50 % = ₹ 2,00,000.

Problem 12

Find BEP : Variable cost per unit ₹ 12. Selling price per unit ₹ 20. Fixed expenses ₹ 60,000. What will be the selling price per unit if the BEP is brought down to 6000 units?

Solution:

BEP in units: FC / Contribution p.u., Contribution p.u. = 20 – 12 = 8

BEP in units = 60000 ÷ 8 = 7,500 units

BEP = 7,500 units × ₹ 20 = ₹ 1,50,000 = BEP (Sales).

Selling price if BEP is 6000 units: FC / CPU or FC / (SP – VP) per unit or 60,000 / (x – 12)

[Let selling price be ₹ x]

OR, 6,000 = 60,000 / x – 12 or 6000 (x – 12) = 60,000 or x = ₹ 22, *i.e.*, New S.P.p.u. = ₹ 22

Problem 13

(1) Calculate P/V Ratio (2) Profit when sales are ₹ 20, 000 (3) New BEP if selling price is reduced by 20%. Given fixed expenses ₹ 4,000 and Break-even point ₹ 10,000. Variable cost remains constant even after change in selling price.

Solution:

BEP sales = FC / P/V Ratio

Cross multiplying, P/V Ratio = FC / BEP Sales or 4,000 / 10,000 × 100 or 40%.

P/V Ratio × Sales = 40% × 20,000 = Contribution = ₹ 8,000 (When sales = ₹ 20,000)

C = F + P or 8,000 = 4,000 + P or Profit = ₹ 4,000.

<u>New BEP is SP is reduced by 20%:</u>

Let the original SP be ₹ x.

Therefore, at 20% reduction, the Revised SP would become x – 20% of x.

Hence the revised SP would be x – 0.2x or 0.8x

New contribution is S – V or x – (60% of x) = C or 0.8x – 0.6x = 0.2x.

Hence, New P/V Ratio = 0.2x ÷ 0.8x = 25% = .25

BEP in value = 4,000 / 0.25 or ₹ 16,000

MODERATE AND BROAD PROBLEMS AND SOLUTIONS

Problem 1

The cost per unit of the three products A, B and C of a concern is as follows:

	A	B	C
	₹	₹	₹
Direct Materials	10	8	9
Direct Labor	6	7	6
Variable Expenses	4	5	3
Fixed Expenses	3	3	2
Total	23	23	20
Profit	9	7	6
Selling Price	32	30	26
Number of Units produced	10,000	5,000	8,000

Production arrangements are such that if one product is given up, the production of the others can be raised by 50%. The directors propose that C should be given up because the contribution in that case is lowest. Do you agree?

Solution:

Fixed expenses under the present arrangement are:

				₹
Product A	–	10,000 units @ ₹ 3 per unit	=	30,000
Product B	–	5,000 units @ ₹ 3 per unit	=	15,000
Product C	–	8,000 units @ ₹ 2 per unit	=	16,000
		Total Fixed Cost		61,000

Fixed expenses will remain same even though production arrangement may be changed.

Contribution per unit = Selling Price - Marginal Cost

	A ₹	B ₹	C ₹
Selling Price	**32**	**30**	**26**
Variable Costs:			
Direct Materials	10	8	9
Direct Cost	6	7	6
Variable Expenses	4	5	3
Total - Variable Cost	**20**	**20**	**18**
Contribution per cost	**12**	**10**	**8**

There can be three production arrangements as follows:

Case 1:

If product A is given up, the production of B and C will be increased by 50%.

	B	C	Total
Existing output	5,000	8,000	
To be increased by 50% of existing output	2,500	4,000	
Increased Output	7,500	12,000	
	₹	₹	₹
Contribution per unit	10	8	
Contribution in value	75,000	96,000	171,000
Less: Fixed Expenses			61,000
Total Profit			110,000

Case 2

If product B is given up, the production of A and C will be increased by 50%.

	A	C	Total
Existing output	10,000	8,000	
To be increased by 50% of existing output	5,000	4,000	
Increased Output	15,000	12,000	
	₹	₹	₹
Contribution per unit	12	8	
Contribution in value	180,000	96,000	276,000
Less: Fixed Expenses			61,000
Total Profit			215,000

Case 3

If product C is given up, the production of A and B will be increased by 50%.

	A	**B**	**Total**
Existing output	10,000	5,000	
To be increased by 50% of existing output	5,000	2,500	
Increased Output	15,000	7,500	
	₹	₹	₹
Contribution per unit	12	10	
Contribution in value	180,000	75,000	255,000
Less: Fixed Expenses			61,000
Total Profit			194,000

From the above analysis it is clear that the profit is the maximum when product B is given up. Therefore, we do not agree with the directors that C should be given up and recommend that product B should be given up in order to have the maximum profit.

Problem 2

X Ltd. is a recently formed company manufacturing vehicles. Its cost structure is such that sale of every ₹ 2,000, it spends ₹ 1400. In 2009, when the total sales revenue was ₹ 10,00,000, it sustained loss of ₹ 2,00,000.

You are required to compute the break-even point. If the minimum net profit to be earned is ₹ 2,00,000 in order to justify the survival, what must be sales revenue?

Solution:

(i) Break-even Point

PV Ratio = 600/2,000 = 30% = 0.30

Sales – VC = Contribution p.u. = 2,000 – 1,400 = ₹ 600

Fixed Cost = Contribution – Net profit = Sales × P/V Ratio – Net Profit

= [(10,00,000) × 30%] – (–2,00,000)

= 5,00,000

BEP = TFC/P/V Ratio = 5,00,000/0.30 = ₹ 16,66,667

(ii) Sales required

$$= \frac{\text{TFC + Desired Profit}}{\text{P/V ratio}}$$

$$= \frac{500000 + 200000}{30\%}$$

= (7,00,000/0.30)

= 23,33,334

OR

Sales required = BEP + Margin of Safety

$$\text{Margin of Safety} = \frac{\text{Profit}}{\text{P/V ratio}} = \frac{200000}{30\%} = 6{,}66{,}667$$

Sales Required = 16,66,667 + 6,66,667 = ₹ 23,33,334

Problem 3

From the following particulars, you are required to calculate:

(i) P/V Ratio

(ii) BEP for sales;

(iii) Margin of Safety;

(iv) Profit when sales are ₹ 2,00,000

(v) Sales required to earn a profit of ₹ 40,000

Year	Sales	Profit
I	₹ 2,40,000	₹ 18,000
II	₹ 2,80,000	₹ 26,000

You may make plausible assumptions. Also evaluate the effect on II year's profit of

(a) 20% decrease in sales quantity.

(b) 20% decrease in sales quantity accompanied by 10% increase in sales price and reduction of ₹ 3,500 in fixed costs.

Solution:

(i) P/V Ratio:

In year 2, additional Net Profit which means additional contribution = ₹ 8,000

Additional sales = 40,000

P/V Ratio = Change in Profit/Change in Sales × 100

= 8000/40000 × 100 = 20% = 0.20

(ii) BEP: Fixed cost = Contribution – Net Profit = (Sales × P/V Ratio) – Net Profit

= (2,40,000 × 20%) – 18,000 = 48,000 – 18000 = ₹ 30, 000

BEP Sales = FC/PV Ratio = 30,000/0.20 = ₹ 1,50,000

(iii) Margin of Safety: Sales – BEP Sales

Year 1: 2,40,000 – 1,50,000 = ₹ 90,000

Year 2: 2,80,000 – 1,50,000 = ₹ 1, 30,000

(iv) Net Profit: Contribution – Total Fixed Cost (TFC)

(Sales × PV Ratio) – Fixed Cost = (2,00,000 × 20%) – 30,000 = 10,000

OR

Sales of 2,00,000 – BEP of 1,50,000 = Margin of Safety of ₹ 50,000

$$\text{Margin of Safety} = \frac{\text{Profit}}{\text{P/V ratio}}$$

or, profit = Margin of Safety × P/V ratio = ₹ 50000 × 20% = ₹ 10000

(v) Sales Required:

$$\text{Sales (₹)} = \frac{\text{TFC + Desired Profit}}{\text{P/V ratio}} = \frac{30000 + 40000}{20\%} = ₹\ 350000$$

Effect on II Year's Profit

(a) 20% decrease in Sale Qty: Reduction in Contribution and in net profit = 20% × (2,80,000 × 20%) = 20% × 56,000 or, Reduction in Contribution and in net profit = ₹ 11,200

(b)

Sales (2,80,000 × 80%) × 110% =		2,46,400
Less: Variable Cost (2,80,000 × 80%) × 80% =		1,79,200
Contribution		67,200
Less: Total Fixed Cost	30000 – 3500 =	(26,500)
Net Profit		40,700
(–) Given Net Profit		26,000
Increase in NP		14,700

OR

(b) Revenue Sales (2,80,000 × 80%) × 110% = ₹ 2,46,400

P/V Ratio (old) = 20%

$$\text{P/V Ratio (new)} = \frac{110-80}{110} = 30/110 = \frac{3}{11} \text{ OR } \frac{3}{11} \times 100 = 27.27\%$$

(1) Reduction in Contribution [See (a)] = ₹ 11,200, due to 20% decrease in sales quantity.

(2) Increase in Sales Price (2,80,000 × 80% × 10%) = ₹ 22,400

(3) Reduction in Fixed Cost = ₹ 3500

Increase in NP = ₹ 22400 – 11200 + 3500 = ₹ 14,700

SUMMARY

Marginal Costing and Absorption costing are the techniques which used for the purpose of product costing, inventory planning and other important managerial decisions. Absorption costing is a technique where all costs are charged to manufactured products, processes or operations. Marginal Costing is a technique which considers only the marginal costs while computing the cost of product. Under marginal costing for the determination of profit, the contribution is computed first. The total fixed costs are deducted from the total contribution to get the profit figure.

CVP analysis is popularly known as 'Break-even Analysis'. The narrower interpretation of break-even analysis is the determination of the level of activity at which the firm achieves break-even, *i.e.*, the point of no profit and no loss, when the total cost equals to the total sales.

P/V ratio establishes the relationship between the contribution and sales. Therefore, this ratio may also be called as 'contribution to Sales Ratio'. A higher P/V ratio indicates greater profitability and *vice versa*. Break-even point is the level of sales at which there shall neither be profit nor loss. It is point where contribution is equal to the fixed cost. If the sales volume is increased beyond the break-even sales, the profit shall be earned by the business. It sales volume is decreased beyond the break-even sales; the loss shall be suffered by the business. In multi-product firms, a composite break-even point is computed for which a composite P/V ratio is to be calculated. Cost Break-even point refers to a situation when the costs of operating of two alternative plants are equal. Cash Break-even point is the point where cash realizations on account of sales will be equal to immediate cash liabilities. Margin of safety is the sales over and above break-even sales. When the break-even analysis is performed graphically, it is known as a break-even chart which indicates break-even point and profitability at various levels.

QUESTIONS

A. Short questions

1. What is a marginal cost?
2. Is there any difference between marginal cost and variable cost?
3. What is P/V ratio?

4. What is break-even point?
5. What is break-even chart?
6. What is the difference between cost break-even point and cash break-even point?
7. What do you mean by 'Margin of Safety'?

B. Broad and Moderate Questions

1. What are the differences between absorption costing and marginal castings?
2. How do you determine profit under both Absorption Costing and Marginal Costing?
3. What are the advantages and disadvantage of marginal costing?
4. Explain CVP Analysis.
5. Explain Break-even chart with a diagram.
6. What are the assumptions, advantages and limitations of break-even analysis?
7. What is the significance of P/V Ratio?

PROBLEM

Objective type problems

1. A factory is manufacturing sewing machines. The variable cost of each machine is ₹ 200 and each machine is sold for ₹ 250. Fixed costs are ₹ 12,000. Calculate the BEP for Output.
2. Calculate break-even point and margin of safety. Fixed cost ₹ 1,60,000. Variable cost per unit ₹ 12 and Selling price per unit ₹ 18. Also compute the margin of safety if the company is earning a profit of ₹ 36,000.
3. Calculate the break-even point and turnover required to earn a profit of ₹ 3,600. Fixed overheads ₹ 1,80,000. Variable cost per unit ₹ Selling price ₹ 20. If the company is earning a profit of ₹ 36,000, express the margin of safety available to it.
4. Given variable cost ₹ 6,00,000. Fixed cost ₹ 3,00,000. Net profit ₹ 1,00,000. Sales ₹ 10,00,000. Find (a) P/V Ratio (b) BEP (c) Profit when sales amounted ₹ 12,00,000 (d) sales required to earn a profit of ₹ 2,00,000.
5. Given: Fixed costs ₹ 4,000. Break-even sales ₹ 20,000. Profit ₹ 1,000. Selling price per unit ₹ 20. Calculate (a) sales and marginal cost of sales (b) new break-even point if selling price is reduced by 10 %.
6. Find the margin of safety if profit is ₹ 20,000 and MCSR or P/V Ratio is 40 %.
7. Calculate Break-even sales and margin of safety. Given Sales ₹ 10,00,000. Fixed costs ₹ 3,00,000 and Profit ₹ 2,00,000.
8. Given Sales ₹ 20,000. Total Costs ₹ 16,000 and Variable Costs ₹ 12,000. Compute Break-even sales, Margin of safety and sales to earn a profit of ₹ 4,000.

Subjective Problems

1. A company has supplied you the following information i.r.o. one of its products.

(i) Total Fixed Cost	₹ 18,000
(ii) Variable Cost	₹ 30,000

(iii) Total Sales	₹ 60,000
(iv) Units Sold	₹ 20,000

Calculate:

(a) Contribution p.u.;
(b) Breakeven Point;
(c) Margin of safety;
(d) Profit;
(e) Volume of sales to earn profit of ₹ 24,000

2. The following information's are given

(i) Total fixed Cost = ₹ 1,20,000
(ii) Variable cost p.u. = ₹ 3
(iii) Selling price p.u. = ₹ 7
(iv) Output = 50000 units

Determine the profit for each of the following situations:
(a) With the data above
(b) With a 10% increase in output and sales
(c) With a 10% increase in fixed costs
(d) With a 10% increase in variable costs
(e) With a 10% increase in selling price

3. (a) Calculate P/V ratio and fixed cost from the following information's:

	Sales	Profit
First year	₹ 50,00,000	₹ 12,00,000
Second year	₹ 60,00,000	₹ 15,00,000

(i) Calculate the amount of profit or loss where sales are ₹ 40,00,000.

(ii) The amount of sales required to cash a profit of ₹ 30,00,000.

(b) From the following data draw a simple break-even chart to show the break-even point:

	₹
Selling price p.u.	20
Variable Cost p.u.	10
Total fixed cost	20,000
Present production and sale:	4000 units.

If sales are 20% above the break-even point, calculate the amount of net profit.

4. A firm proposes to introduce a product in the market. There is sufficient demand for the product. The sales manager estimates that it is possible to sell 5000 units. It is the policy of the firm to maintain 30% P/v ratio. Given the following costs, you are required to ascertain the selling price that the firm should quote:

	Per unit ₹
Direct material	100

Direct Labour	30
Variable Overhead	10
	140

Hints: $\frac{140}{100\% - 30\%}$

(b) The directors of XYZ Ltd. proposed to reduce the selling price of product X by 10%. By doing so, they anticipate that sales volume may be increased and that present profit may be maintained. On the following information advise management as to the proposal:

	₹
Selling price	10
Variable cost	6
Total fixed Cost	20,000

Present production and sales: 8000 units.

5. XYZ Ltd. is manufacturing two products A and B. the cost of their manufacture is as follows:

	A	B
Direct Wages p.u.	₹ 6	₹ 5
Sales price	₹ 40	₹ 38
Goods produced	2000 units	1000 units
Goods sold	1800 units	900 units

The total factory overheads are ₹ 22,000 out of which ₹ 13,000 are fixed and rest are variable. It was decided to apportion these costs over different products in the ratio of output. Prepare a statement showing cost and profit of each product according to Absorption Costing and Marginal Costing. Selling and Distribution Overheads (all fixed) amounted to ₹ 11,000 are to be apportioned in the ratio of 1:1. Offer your comments.

❑❑❑

21 Variance Analysis and Standard Costing

21.1 MEANING OF STANDARD COST

In simple words, standard costs are scientifically 'predetermined costs' assuming a given level of efficiency. These are created by management and the success of standard costing depends upon the accuracy with which standards are set for each element of cost.

Brown and Howard have defined standard cost as '*a predetermined cost which determines what each product or service should cost under given circumstances*'. **Blocker and Weltmer** said that standard cost as, "*a pre-determined cost based upon engineering specifications and representing highly efficient production for quantity standards and forecasts of future market trends for price standards, with fixed amount expressed in rupees for materials, labour and overheads for an estimated quantity of production.*"

According to **CIMA, London**, "standard cost is the predetermined cost based on technical estimates for material, labour and overheads for a selected period of time and for a prescribed set of working conditions."

From the above definitions, it can be understood that standard costs are the model or target costs which can be achieved under standard operating conditions. Standard costs are comprised of two parts, a quantity and a cost.

21.2 MEANING OF STANDARD COSTING, STEPS

According to **CIMA, London,** standard costing is, "*the preparation and use of standard cost, their comparison with actual costs, and the analysis of variance as to their causes and points incidence.*" Ultimately, standard costing is the preparation of standard costs and their comparison with actual costs and the analysis of variances to their causes and points of incidence.

Brown and Howard opined that standard costing as "*a technique of cost accounting which compares the standard cost of each product or service with actual cost to determine the efficiency of the operation, so that any remedial action may be taken immediately.*"

A careful analysis of the above definitions reveal that the important steps followed in standard costing are summarized as below:

1. Determination of standard costs for each elements of cost.
2. Collection of information about various elements of actual costs.
3. Comparison of actual costs with the standard costs to find out the variance. Variance is the difference between standard cost and actual cost. Variances are unfavourable when actual costs are more than the standard cost, favourable variances occur when actual costs are less than the standard costs. Variances may be controllable or non-controllable.
4. Identification of reasons for variance between actual costs and standard costs through variance analysis.
5. Suggesting and taking appropriate action on the basis of nature of variances.

The technique of standard costing can be used for all industries and activities. However, the use of standard costing is more effective in industries which have standardized repetitive nature of operations (for example, process industry).

21.3 ESSENTIALS OF EFFECTIVE SYSTEM OF STANDARD COSTING

The successful implementation of cost control plan under standard costing depends upon certain essential or pre-requisites which are as follows:

(i) Planable technical process of operation.

(ii) Setting standards to give cost of operation rather than products so that variances may be traced to their source without laborious investigation.

(iii) Ensuring full support and co-operation of every member of the management team while controlling costs.

(iv) Setting up standards properly so as to have confidence in the fairness of standards both by management and operating personnel.

(v) Necessity of adequate accounting system in the business (this necessity lies since historical accounting datas form the basis of future of standard costs).

(vi) Preparation of reports constantly to keep management at all levels informed of progress relative to standards, a periodical comparison of the actual costs with the standard costs, variances so as to get instructions from superiors for correction of the differences or deviations communicated to them.

21.4 STANDARD COSTING AND BUDGETARY CONTROL – THEIR COMPARISON

Budgeting control and standard costing techniques though different, have a common objective of managerial control and planning. That is, in both the systems, predetermined targets are set,

TABLE

Sr. No.	Nature of Difference	Budgetary Control	Standard Costing
1	Scope	Budgetary control can be applied to a part of business. Budgets are generally laid down for all activities of the enterprise that is, production, sales, cash, research and development, etc. Therefore, it has a wider scope and is more extensive in nature.	Standard costing cannot be operated in parts. Standard costing is primarily related to one function, *i.e.*, production. It is related with setting standards for various elements of costs and sales. Hence, it has narrow scope and is more intensive in nature.
2	Limit of Expenses	Budgets set up maximum ceiling of expenses above which actual expenditure should not normally exceed.	Standard costing set the minimum targets which are to be attained by actual performance under specified operating conditions.
3	Projection	Budgets are projection of financial accounts because financial accounting deals with overall efficiency of the business such as sales, production, purchases, etc.	Standard costs are projection of cost accounts. It is so because cost accounting is related with ascertaining and control of costs of individual products and process.
4	Inter dependency	Budgetary control system can be operated without standard costing system.	Standard costing system cannot exist without the system of budgetary control.
5	Variances	Under budgetary control system, variances are generally not analyzed in detail but are revealed in total.	Under standard costing system, variances are generally analyzed in detail.
6	Standardization of operations	Budgetary control system does not normally require standardization of operations.	Standard costing system is based on scientific standards and thus requires standardization of operations.
7	Expressions	Budgets are expressed in terms of money and/or quantities.	Standards are for a unit of production or a hour of production.
8	Ledger posting	Budget figures are not entering in any accounting ledger.	Standard costs are entered in cost ledger.

actual performance is compared with the standards and necessary corrective measures are initiated to achieve optimum level of efficiency. Both the systems are complementary to each other. But they are not interdependent. Budgetary control can be operated without the system of standard costing but standard costing cannot function without the system of budgetary control. Therefore, both the systems are used simultaneously to reap the most fruitful benefits. However, both the systems are different and the most important points of distinction between the two are summarized in the above table.

21.5 ADVANTAGES OF STANDARD COSTING

The important advantages of standard costing are summarized as below:

(i) Evaluation of Actual Performance: Standard costing provides a benchmark for different elements of cost against which actual costs are compared. The extent, nature and cause of variances are analyzed. The study of variances enables the management to analyze the impact of controllable and uncontrollable variances on the efficiencies of the business and the necessary remedial measure on time.

(ii) Control over Costs and Elimination of Wastages: Standard costing is an effective tool for exercising control over costs as the variances are regularly ascertained and analyzed. Under this system, proper control of man, materials, and machines eliminates avoidable wastage and losses and make everyone in the organization cost conscious.

(iii) Fixation of Prices and Formulation of Production Policies: Standard costing provides a basis for fixation of prices. Actual costs cannot be a sound basis for fixation of prices as it varies from time to time. It is an indispensable tool to the management for determination of pricing policies, planning for profit levels, inventory planning, preparing quotations and planning of production under alternative methods of production, etc.

(iv) Management by Exception: Standard costing makes it possible to follow the principle of 'Management by Exception' because it is possible to identify those Cost centres or the elements of cost in which the actual are not in line with the set standards. The management can direct its effort and time for control of adverse variances only.

(v) Effective Delegation of Authority and Responsibility: Under standard costing system with a view to facilitate better control, different cost centres can be set up. The identification of cost centres helps in clear demarcation of responsibilities. In case of adverse variance, it becomes possible to fix accountability on a particular department of centre.

(vi) Incentive for Employees: The use of appropriate standards has a desirable effect on the workers. If standards have been properly set up, it is possible to evolve proper incentive scheme for the employees. It motivates workers to perform better and achieve standards. Employees may be rewarded with monetary benefits on achievement of standards. Many incentives like cash bonus, individuals group bonus, prizes, can be awarded for keeping the costs in line with the standards.

(vii) Helpful for Forecasting: Standard costing can be used for formulation of budgets in the future by knowing and analyzing deviations between actual costs and standard costs. Standard costs increase the capacity of the enterprise for forecasting under changing condition in the future.

(viii) Economical and Efficient Production: Under Standard Costing System, all the operation are carefully and analyzed and inefficiencies are disclosed. Standards are fixed for all elements of cost and constant efforts are made to keep the costs in line with the standards, it results in economical and efficient production.

21.6 LIMITATIONS OF STANDARD COSTING

Standard costing is an indispensable tool for management control. The important limitations are discuss as follows:

(i) Difficulty in Setting Standards: It is difficult to set realistic standards. Standards are fixed on technical estimates under assumed operating conditions which may deviate from actual operating conditions.

(ii) Frequent Revisions Required: Standards are set at a point of time under assumed operating conditions which may change. The frequent changes in prices and then conditions requires a frequent review and revision of standards, which if not done, standards tend to become rigid and ineffective as a measure of performance and cost control.

(iii) Not-Suitable for Small Firms: In small firms, the system of standard costing may not be justified on the basis of cost benefits analysis. The operation of standard costing requires a high degree of technical efficiency and is a costly exercise.

(iv) Problems in Variance Analysis: Standard costing system in incomplete without variance analysis. However, it is very difficult to classify the variances into controllable and non controllable elements. The heads of centres can be held accountable only for controllable variances and not for uncontrollable variances.

(v) Non-Suitable for Non-Standardized Products: Standard costing system cannot be used in those concerns where non standard products are produced. In case of job order industries, where the production is undertaken according to the specifications of customers may not find the system of standard costing suitable.

21.7 VARIANCE ANALYSIS

Variance analysis is the process of analyzing variances by sub-dividing the total variance in such a way that management can assign responsibility for off-standard performance. The standard costing is incomplete without variances analysis. Variance is the difference between actual and standard. In relation to cost, variance refers to the difference between actual cost and standard cost in relation to each element of cost, *viz;* direct material, direct labour and factory overhead. If the actual cost is less than the standard cost, it is called favourable variance. However, if the actual cost is more than the standard cost, it will be an unfavourable variance. In case of sales, things are different. If the actual sales are more than the budgeted sales, the variance will be favourable variance and if *vice-versa* is the case, the variance will be unfavourable. Standard costing through variance analyses attempts at elimination of unproductive cost and control over cost for reduction of overall cost and achieving maximum efficiency.

All variances are summarized below:

Cost Variances

A. Direct Material Cost Variance

Material Cost Variance (Total)

(i) Material Price Variance

(ii) Material Quantity or Usage variance

(a) Material Mix Variance

(b) Material Yield Variance or Material Sub Usage Variance

B. Labour Cost Variances (Total)

(i) Labour Rate Variance

(ii) Labour Efficiency Variance

(a) Labour Gang Variance or Max Variance

(b) Labour Yield Variance or Sub Efficiency Variance

(iii) Idle Time Variance

C. Overhead Cost Variance (Total)

1. Variance Overhead Cost Variance
2. Fixed Overhead Cost Variance

Variance Overhead Cost Variance

1. Variance Overhead Expenditure Variance
2. Variable Overhead Efficiency Variance

Fixed Overhead Cost Variance (Tatal)

1. Fixed Overhead Cost Variance (total)

(i) Fixed Overhead Expenditure Variance

(ii) Fixed Overhead Volume Variance

(a) Fixed Overhead Efficiency Variance

(b) Fixed Overhead Capacity Variance

(c) Fixed Overhead Calendar Variance

D. Sales Variance (Total)

1. Sales Value Variance

(i) Sales Price Variance

(ii) Sales Volume Variance

(a) Sales Mix Variance

(b) Sales Quantity Variance.

In variance analysis, responsibilities allocated to different managerial persons and that is why it is also known as 'responsibility accounting'.

21.8 COMPUTATION OF COST VARIANCES

The computation of cost variance refers to finding difference between actual cost and standard cost. Standard cost always refers to the standard cost of actual output. Therefore, one needs to ascertain the standard cost of actual output in respect of each element of cost, viz., materials, labour, and overheads. The calculations of variances are discussed as below:

A.1. Direct Material Cost Variance

It is the difference between the standard cost of direct materials specified for the output achieved and the actual cost of direct materials used.

Material Cost Variance
↓
Material Usage Variance | Material Price Variance
↓
Material Mix Variance | Material Yield Variance (Sub-usage)

2. Material Price Variance

"It is that portion of the material cost variance which is due to the difference between the standard price specified and the actual price paid."

Material Price Variance = Actual Quantity (Standard Price per unit – Actual Price per unit)

The possible causes of such variances are :

(1) Fluctuations in the market price of materials.

(2) Purchase of quality of materials other than specified; due to its non-availability.

(3) Purchase of an uneconomic quantity thereby loosing the facility of trade discount.

(4) Payment of excess or less transport costs.

3. Material Usage (or Quantity) Variance

It is the difference between the standard quantity specified and the actual quantity used.

Material Usage Variance = Standard Unit Price (Standard Quantity – Actual Quantity)

The possible causes of such variance are:

(1) Using sub standard quantity of materials.

(2) Losses due to scrap, spoilage or inefficiency of worker.

(3) Improper setting of standards.

(4) Wrong material mix.

(5) Losses due to careless handling of materials or pilferage.

(6) Variation in product design specifications.

(7) Defective tools and equipments which leads to wastage of materials.

4. Material Mix Variance

It is that portion of direct material usage variance which is due to the difference between the standard and the actual composition of a mixture.

Material Mix Variance = Standard Price (Std. Qty. of Mix – Actual Qty. of Mix)

If the mix is revised, the mix variance is calculated as follows:

Material Mix Variance = Standard Price (Revised Std. Qty. – Actual Qty. of Mix)

Where, Revised Std. Quantity

$$= \frac{\text{Total Weight of Actual Mix}}{\text{Total Weight of Std. Mix}} \times \text{Std. Qty.}$$

5. Material Yield Variance

It is the part of usage variance which is due to the difference in standard output specified and the actual output obtained.

Material Yield Variance

= Standard cost per unit × (Actual Yield – Standard yield for actual input)

Where, Standard Cost per unit

$$= \frac{\text{Total Std. Cost of Inputs}}{\text{Std. outputs in Units}}$$

A high yield indicates favourable variance and *vice versa.*

Problem 1

Find out the Material Variances from the given data:

	Std. Qty Kg.	Standard Price ₹	Value ₹	Act. Qty kg	Actual Price ₹	Value ₹
Material A	80	5	400	100	4.80	480
Material B	220	4	880	200	4.50	900
	300		1,280	300		1,380

Solution:

(a) *Material Cost Variance:*

= (Standard Quantity × Standard Price) – (Actual Quantity × Actual Price)

= ₹ 1,280 – ₹ 1,380 = ₹ 100 (Adv.)

(b) *Material Price Variance:*

= (Standard Price – Actual Price) × Actual Quantity.

Material A: = (₹ 5 – ₹ 4.80) × 100 = 20 (Fav.)

Material B: = (₹ 4 – ₹ 4.50) × 200 = 100 (Adv.)

₹ 80 (Adv.)

(c) *Material Usage Variance:*

= (Standard Quantity – Actual Quantity) × Std. Price.

Material A: = (80 – 100) × 5 = ₹ 100 (Adv.)

Material B: = (220 – 200) × 4 = ₹ 80 (Fav.)

₹ 20 (Adv.)

(d) *Material Mix Variance:*

= (Standard Cost of Standard Mix) – (Standard Cost of Actual Mix)

= ₹ 1,280 – (100 × 5 + 200 × 4)

= ₹ 1,280 – (500 + 800)

= ₹ 1,280 – ₹ 1300 = ₹ 20 (Adv.)

Note: As the total quantities are same Material Usage Variance is Equal to Material Mix Variance, so there is no Material Sub usage or yield Variance in the problem.

Problem 2

Find out Material Variances from the given information:

	Std. Qty Kgs.	Standard Price ₹	Value ₹	Act. Qty. Kgs.	Actual Price ₹	Value ₹
Material A	100	5	500	100	4	400
Material B	40	2	80	50	3	150
Material C	80	4	320	90	5	450
	220		900	240		1,000

[Std. kgs = 220, Act. kgs = 240]

Solution:

(a) *Material Cost Variance:*

= (Standard Quantity × Standard Price) – (Actual Quantity × Actual Price)

= ₹ 900 – ₹ 1,000 = ₹ 100 (Adv.)

(b) *Material Price Variance:*

= (Standard Price – Actual Price) × Actual Quantity

Material A = (₹ 5 – ₹ 4) × 100 = ₹100 (F)

Material B = (₹ 2 – ₹ 3) × 50 = ₹ 50 (A)

Material C = (₹ 4 – ₹ 5) × 90 = ₹ 90 (A)

= ₹ 40 (A)

(c) *Material Usage Variance:*

Standard Price (Standard Quantity – Actual Quantity)

Material A = 5(100 – 100)	=	Nil
Material B = 2(40 – 50)	=	20 (A)
Material C = 4(80 – 90)	=	40 (A)
		₹ 60 (A)

(d) *Material Mix Variance:* It will arise since there is a difference between standard and actual composition of mixture).

Standard Price (Std. Proportion of Std. Qty. – Actual Qty.)

Standard Proportion of Std. Qty :

Material A = $100 \times \frac{240}{220}$ = 109 kgs.

Material B = $40 \times \frac{240}{220}$ = 43.63 kgs.

Material C = $80 \times \frac{240}{220}$ = 87.27 kgs.

Mix Variance:

Material A: 5(109 – 100) = ₹ 45 (F)

Material B: 2(43.63 – 50) = ₹ 12.74 (A)

Material C: 4(87.27 – 90) = ₹ 10.92 (A)

₹ 21.34 (F) = 21 (F)

Material Yield Variance = SP p.u. (AY – SY) = $\frac{900}{220}$ × (240 – 220) = 81(A)

Problem 3

Find out the material variances from the given data:

Materials	Standard			Actual		
	Kgs.	Rate	Amt.	Kgs.	Rate	Amt.
		₹	₹		₹	₹
A	50	6	300	60	5	300
B	100	5	500	120	4	480
Total	150		800	180		780

[Std. kgs = 150, Act. kgs = 180]

Solution:

(a) *Material Cost Variance:*

(Standard Price × Standard Quantity) – (Actual Price × Actual Quantity)

= 800 – 780 = ₹ 20 (F)

(b) *Material Price Variance:*

(Standard Price – Actual Price) × Actual Quantity.

A = (6 – 5) × 60 = 60 (F)

B = (5 – 4) × 120 = 120 (F)

₹ 180 (F)

(c) *Material Usage Variance:*

(Standard Quantity – Actual Quantity) × Standard Price

A = (50 – 60) × 6 = 60 (A)

B = (100 – 120) × 5 = 100 (A)

₹ 160 (A)

(d) *Material Mix Variance:*

There is no Mix Variance as both the standard quantities and actual quantities are in the same ratio.

(e) *Material Sub-usage Variance:*

(Total Standard Quantity – Total Actual Quantity) × Total standard rate.

$$(150 - 180) \times \frac{800}{150} = 160(A)$$

Verification

Material Price Variance + Material Usage Variance = Material Cost Variance.

= 180 (Fav.) + 160 (Adv.) = 20 (F)

Problem 4

The standard mix for each batch of 250 units of Product A is:

Material A: 15 Kgs. at ₹ 10	= ₹ 150
Material B: 10 Kgs. at ₹ 8	= ₹ 80
25 Kgs.	₹ 230

During April, 10 batches were completed with actual consumption as follows:

Material A: 160 Kgs. at ₹ 8	= ₹ 1,280
Material B: 120 Kgs. at ₹ 10	= ₹ 1,200
280 Kgs.	₹ 2,480

Actual output was 2400 Units. Calculate

(a) Material Price Variance (b) Material Usage Variance (c) Material Mix Variance.

Solution

(a) *Price Variance:*

= Actual Quantity × (Standard price – Actual Price)

Material A = 160(10 - 8) = ₹ 320 (Fav.)

Material B = 120(8 - 10) = ₹ 240 (Adv.)

Total Price Variance = ₹ 80 (Fav.)

(b) *Material Usage:*

= Standard Price × (Standard Quantity – Actual Quantity)

Material A = 10(150 - 160) = ₹ 100 (Adv.)

Material B = 8(100 - 120) = ₹ 160 (Adv.)

Total Usage Variance = ₹ 260 (Adv.)

(c) *Material mix Variance:*

= Standard Price × (Revised Standard Qty. – Actual Quantity)

Revised Standard Quantity

$$= \frac{\text{Total Weight of Actual Mix}}{\text{Total Weight of Standard Mix}} \times \text{Standard Quantity}$$

$$\text{Material A} = \frac{280}{250} \times 150 = 168 \text{ Kgs.}$$

$$\text{Material B} = \frac{280}{250} \times 100 = 112 \text{ Kgs.}$$

Material Mix Variance =

Material A = (168 – 160) × 10 = ₹ 80 (Fav.)

Material B = (112 – 120) × 8 = ₹ 64 (Adv.)

Material Mix Variance = ₹ 16 (Fav.)

B. Labour Variances

1. Labour Cost Variance: ***"It is difference between standard direct wages specified for the achieved and the actual direct wages paid."***

Labour Cost Variance = Standard Direct Wages – Actual Direct Wages.

= (Std. time for actual production × Std. Rate) – (Actual time × Actual Rate)

Labour Cost Variance

- Labour Rate Variance
- Labour Efficiency Variance
    - Labour Mix Variance
    - Labour Yield Variance
    - Idle time Variance

2. Labour Rate Variance: It is the difference between the standard rate of pay specified and the actual rate paid.

Labour Rate Variances = Actual Time (Std. Wage Rate – Actual Wages Rate)

Causes of such Variances are:

(i) Engagement of higher or lower rated worker than that specified.

(ii) Changes in the rate of wages or incentive system.

(iii) Changes in the methods of payment, *i.e.,* piece rate basis instead of time rate basis and *vice versa.*

(iv) Overtime wages paid in excess of that specified.

(v) New workers being paid for which there was no provision in the standard.

3. Labour Efficiency Variance: It is the difference between the standard labour hours specified for the activity achieved and the actual hours expended.

Labour Efficiency Variance = Std. Wage Rate (Std. Time – Actual Time)

The causes of such variances are:

1. Ineffective supervision.
2. Non-co-operative attitude of workers.
3. Inappropriate training programme.

4. High labour turnover.
5. Bad working conditions.
6. Power failure or machine breakdown.
7. Delays due to waiting for instructions or materials.
8. Improper standards set.
9. Faulty planning and scheduling.

4. Idle Time Variance: It is the variation caused by abnormal idle time on account of failure of power supply, machine breakdown.

Idle Time Variance = Idle Hours × Std. Rate Per hour.

5. Labour Mix Variance: It is the variance due to the difference in standard composition of labour and the actual composition of labour.

Mix variance = Std. Cost of Std. Mix – Std. Cost of Actual Mix.

6. Labour Yield Variance: This is due to the difference in the standard output specified and the actual output obtained.

Yield Variance = Std. Labour Cost per Unit × (Actual Output – Std. Output)

If actual output is more than the standard, it is a favourable variance and *vice versa.*

Problem 5

From the given information, calculate :

(a) Labour Cost Variance.
(b) Labour Rate Variance.
(c) Labour Efficiency Variance.
(d) Idle time Variance.

(i) Standard Hours	=	3000
(ii) Actual Hours	=	4000
(iii) Standard Rate	=	₹ 3 per hour
(iv) Actual Rate	=	₹ 2.50 per hour
(v) Idle time on account of Machinery breakdown	=	400 hours

Solution:

(a) Labour Cost Variance:

= Standard Cost – Actual Cost

= (Standard Hours × Std. Rate) – (Actual Hours × Actual Rate)

= (3000 × 3) – (4000 × 2.50)

= 9,000 – 10,000 = ₹ 1,000 (Adv.)

(*b*) *Labour Rate Variance*

= Actual Hours × (Std. Rate – Actual Rate)

= 4,000 (3 – 2.50) = ₹ 2,000 (F)

(*c*) *Labour Efficiency Variance:*

= Std. Rate (Std. Time – Actual Time)

= 3 (3,000 – 3,600) = ₹ 1,800 (Adv.)

Actual Time

= Actual Hours – Idle Time.

= 4,000 – 400 = 3,600 hours.

(*d*) *Idle Time Variance;*

= Idle Time × Std. Rate

= 400 × 3 = ₹ 1200 (Adv.)

Verification

Labour Cost Variance = 1000 (Adv.)

= Labour Rate Variance + Efficiency Variance + Idle Time Variance.

= 2000 (Fav.) + 1800 (Adv.) + 1200 (Adv.)

Problem 6

From the following information, calculate

(i) Labour Cost Variance

(ii) Labour Rate Variance.

(iii) Labour Efficiency Variance.

(iv) Labour Mix Variance.

Standard	₹	**Actual**	₹
Workmen A – 20 Hrs. @ ₹ 3/-	60	Workman A – 30 Hrs. @ ₹ 4/-	120
Workman B – 20 Hrs. @ ₹ 7/-	140	Workman B – 30 Hrs. @ ₹ 6/-	180
40 Hrs.	200	60 Hrs.	300

Solution:

(*1*) *Labour Cost Variance*

= (Standard Hrs. × Standard Rate) – (Actual Hrs. × Actual Rate)

= (20 × 3 + 20 × 7) – (30 × 4 + 30 × 6) = 200 – 300

= ₹ 100(Adv.)

(*2*) *Labour Rate × Variance*

= (Standard Rate – Actual Rate) × Actual Hrs.

A : (₹ 3 – ₹ 4) × 30 Hrs. = ₹ 30 (Adv.)

B : (₹ 7 – ₹ 6) × 30 Hrs. = ₹ 30 (Fav.)

Total Variance = Nil

(3) Labour Efficiency Variance:

= (Standard Hrs. – Actual Hrs.) × Std. Rate

A: (20 Hrs. – 30 Hrs.) × ₹ 3 = ₹ 30.00 (Adv.)

B: (20 Hrs. – 30 Hrs.) × ₹ 7 = ₹ 70.00 (Adv.)

Total Variance = ₹ 100.00 (Adv.)

(4) Labour Mix Variance:

= Std. Rate (Std. Proportion × Actual Hrs.)

Std. Proportion:

$$A - 20 \text{ Hrs.} \times \frac{60}{40} = 30 \text{ Hrs.}$$

$$B - 20 \text{ Hrs.} \times \frac{60}{40} = 30 \text{ Hrs.}$$

Mix Variance:

A: 3(30 Hrs. – 30 Hrs.) = Nil

B: 7(30 Hrs. – 30 Hrs.) = Nil

Variance = Nil

C. Overhead Variance

Overhead cost variance is defined as "the difference between the standard cost of overhead absorbed in the actual output achieved and the actual overhead cost." These variances are of two broad categories:

(1) Fixed Overhead Variances (2) Variable Overhead Variances.

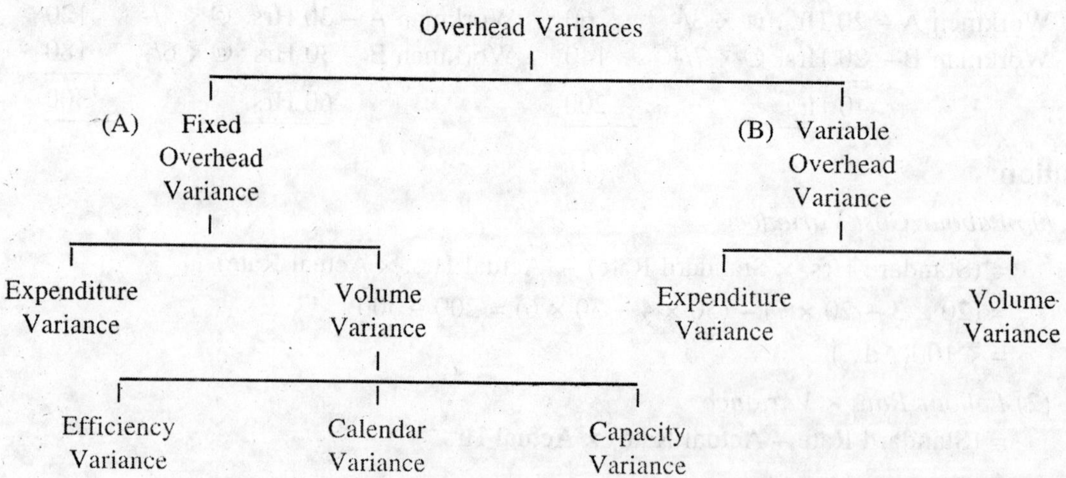

A. (1) Fixed Overhead Cost Variance: Fixed overhead Variance is the difference between fixed overhead recovered and the actual fixed overhead cost incurred.

Fixed Overhead Cost Variance

= (Actual Output × Std. Fixed Overhead Rate) – Actual Overheads

$$\text{Std. Fixed Overhead Rate} = \frac{\text{Budgeted Fixed Overhead}}{\text{Budgeted Output (Units)}}$$

This variance arises because of two reasons:

(1) The difference in the standard fixed overhead allowed and actual overhead incurred and /or

(2) Change in the volume of output.

Accordingly, this variance is divided into-

(a) Expenditure Variance

(b) Volume Variance.

(2) Fixed Overhead Expenditure Variance: It is the difference between actual fixed overhead expenditure and the budgeted expenditure.

Expenditure Variance = Budgeted Fixed Overheads — Actual Fixed Overheads = (Budgeted Qty. × Std. Rate) – Actual Fixed Overheads

Excess of actual overhead cost leads to an adverse variance and *vice versa.*

The causes of such variances are:

(1) Rise in price

(2) Change in production methods

(3) Lack of control over expenditure

(4) Inefficiency or non-availability of specified service.

(3) Volume Variance: It is the difference between the overhead recorded at standard rate on the actual output attained and the overhead on budgeted volume of output.

Volume Variance = Std. Fixed Overhead Rate × (Actual Quantity – Budgeted Quantity)

If the actual output is more than the budgeted output, it leads to favourable variance and *vice-versa.*

Causes:

(1) Inefficiency of workers.

(2) Under utilization of production capacity.

(3) Ineffective supervision.

(4) Decline in sales.

(5) Breakdown of machinery.

(4) Overhead Efficiency Variance : It is the portion of volume variance which is due to the difference between the budgeted efficiency (in standard units) and the actual efficiency achieved.

Efficiency Variance = Std. Overhead Rate × (Actual Qty – Std. Qty)

If the actual output is more than the standard quantity of output, it leads to favourable variance and *vice-versa.*

Causes:

(1) Ineffective supervision
(2) Non-co-operative attitude of workers
(3) High labour
(4) Bad working conditions
(5) Power failure
(6) Improper standards set
(7) Faulty planning and scheduling.

(5) Capacity Variance: It is a part of volume variance which arises due to over or under utilization of plant and machinery. It may be caused by reasons of idle time, strike and lockout, failure of power, machine breakdown.

It the standard overheads are more than the budgeted overheads the variance is favourable and *vice versa.*

(6) Calendar Variance: It is a part of capacity variance. "It arises on account of the difference between the number of working days in the budget period and the number of working days is the period to which the budget is applied."

Calendar Variance (in Hrs.) = Standard Rate per Hour (Possible Hrs. – Budgeted Hrs)

Or

Calendar Variance (in units) = Std. Rate per unit (Possible Units – Budgeted Units)

$$\text{Possible Units} = \frac{\text{Possible Hours}}{\text{Std. Hours per unit}}$$

B. Variable Overhead Variances

(i) Variable Overhead Variance: This represents the difference between standard variable overheads allowed for actual output and the actual overhead.

Variable Overhead Variance = Std. Variable overhead of actual production – Actual Variable Overheads.

(ii) Variable Expenditure Variance: This is the difference between the standard overhead allowed for the actual time worked and the actual overhead incurred.

Variable Expenditure Variance = (Actual Time × Std. Variable Overhead Rate) – Actual Variable Overheads.

(iii) Variance Overhead Efficiency Variance: This is the difference between standard variable overhead allowance of actual production and the standard variable overhead of Actual Time.

Variable Overhead Efficiency Variance

= Std. Overhead rate × (Actual Time – Std. Time for Actual Production)

= Std. Variable overhead of Actual Production – Std. Variable Overhead Actual Time.

Problem 7

From the given information, calculate the overheads variances:

	Budgeted	Actual
Fixed overheads	₹ 20,000	₹ 25,000
Hours	10,000	12,500
Output (in units)	1,000	1,200

Solution:

(a) *Expenditure Variance:*

= Budgeted Fixed Overheads – Actual Fixed Overheads

= 20,000 – 25,000 = ₹ 5,000 (Adv.)

(b) *Volume Variance:*

$$\text{Standard Rate} = \frac{\text{Budgeted Overheads}}{\text{Budgeted Output}}$$

$$= \frac{₹\ 20{,}000}{1{,}000} = ₹\ 20 \text{ per unit}$$

Volume Variance = Standard Rate × (Actual Quantity – Budgeted Qty.)

= 20 (1,200 – 1,000) = ₹ 4,000 (Fav.)

(c) *Efficiency Variance:*

Standard Quantity of Output

$$= \frac{\text{Budgeted Outputs}}{\text{Budgeted Hours}} \times \text{Actual Hours}$$

$$= \frac{1{,}000}{10{,}000} \times 12500 = 1250 \text{ Units}$$

Efficiency Variance

= Standard Rate × (Actual Quantity – Std. Qty.)

= 20 (1,200 – 1,250) = ₹ 1,000 (Adv.)

(d) *Capacity Variance*

= Standard Rate (Actual Quantity – Std. Qty.)

= 20 (1,250 – 1,000) = ₹ 5,000(Fav.)

(e) *Fixed Overhead Cost Variance:*

= Fixed Overhead Recovered – Actual overhead

= (Standard Rate × Actual output) – Actual overhead

= (₹ 20 × 1,200) – ₹ 25,000

= ₹ 24,000 – ₹ 25,000 = ₹ 1,000 (Adv.)

Verification

Efficiency Variance + Capacity Variance = Volume Variance

Or, ₹ 1,000 (Adv.) + ₹ 5,000 (Fav.) = ₹ 4,000 (Fav.)

Volume Variances + Expenditure Variance = Fixed Overhead Variance.

₹ 4,000 (Fav.) + ₹ 5,000 (Adv.) = ₹ 1,000 (Adv.)

Problem 8

From the following information, compute (a) Price and (b) Usage variances:

Std.	Quantity (Kilos)	Standard Price Unit	Total	Act. Quantity (Kilos)	Actual Unit Price	Total
Material A	10	₹ 2.00	₹ 20	5	₹ 3.00	₹ 15
Material B	20	3.00	60	10	6.00	60
Material C	20	6.00	120	15	5.00	75
Total	50	4.00	200	30	5.00	150

Solution:

(a) Material price variance = Actual Quantity × (Standard Price – Actual Price)

Material A = 5(2 – 3) = ₹ 5(A)
Material B = 10(3 – 6) = ₹ 30(A)
Material C = 15(6 – 5) = ₹ 15(F)
= ₹ 20(A)

(b) Material usage variance = Standard price × (Standard quantity – Actual quantity)

Material A = 2(10 – 5) = ₹ 10(F)
Material B = 3(20 – 10) = ₹ 30(F)
Material C = 6(20 – 15) = ₹ 30(F)
₹ 70(F)

Note : Material Mix Variance = Standard Price × (Revised standard quantity – Actual quantity)

$$\text{Revised Std. quantity} = \frac{\text{Total Weight of actual mix}}{\text{Total Weight of standard mix}} \times \text{Standard Quantity}$$

Problem 9

The standard cost of a certain chemical mixture is:

35% Material A at ₹ 25 per kg.
65% Material B at ₹ 36 per kg.

A standard loss of 5% is expected in production

During a period there is used:

125 kg. of Material A at ₹ 27 per kg. and
275 kg. of Material B at ₹ 34 per kg.

The actual output was 365 kg.

Calculate:

(a) Material cost variance (b) Material Price Variance (c) Material Mix Variance (d) Material yield Variance

Solution:

Materials	Std. Kgs.	Standard rate	Amount ₹	Actual Kgs.	Actual Rate	Amount ₹
A	140	25	3500	125	27	3375
B	260	36	9360	275	34	9350
	400		12860	400		12725

Standard output = 400 – 20 = 380 kg.

Actual output = 365 kg.

Standard cost per kg. = 12860/380 = ₹ 33.84

The various variances can now be calculated as follows:

(a) **Material Cost Variance** = (Actual cost – Standard cost for actual output)
= 12725 – 365 × 33.84 = 12725 – 12352 = ₹ 373(Adv.)

(b) **Material Price Variance** = Actual quantity × (AP – SP)

A = 125 × (27 – 25) = 250(A)
B = 275 × (34 – 36) = 550(F)
= 300(F)

(c) **Material Mix Variance** = Standard Price (AQ – Revised standard quantity)

A = 25 × (125 – 140) = 375 (F)
B = 30 × (275 – 260) = 540 (A)
= 165 (A)

(d) **Material Yield Variance** = Standard cost × (Actual output for actual mix – Standard output)

$= 33.84 \times (365 - 380)$

$= ₹\ 508\ (A)$

Working Notes:

(i) Standard quantity for actual mix

Material A: $400 \times 35/100 = 140$ kg.

Material B: $400 \times 65/100 = 260$ kg.

(ii) Since Standard mix and Actual mix are the same, the revised standard quantity and Standard quantity will also be the same.

Problem 10

Swandu Ltd. manufactures a single product, the standard mix of which is:

Material A 60% at ₹ 20 per kg.

Material B 40% at ₹ 10 per kg.

Normal loss in production is 20% of input. Due to shortage of Material A, the standard mix was changed.

Actual results for March 1989 were:

Material A 105 kg. at ₹ 20 per kg.	
Material B 95 kg. at ₹ 9 per kg.	
Input	200 kg.
Loss	35 kg.
Output	165 kg.

Calculate:

(i) Material price variance
(ii) Material Usage Variance
(iii) Material Mix Variance
(iv) Material Yield Variance

Solution:

Workings:

(i) Standard quantity for actual production :

$$\text{Material A} = \frac{60 \times 165}{80} = 495/4 \text{ kg.}$$

$$\text{Material B} = \frac{40 \times 165}{80} = 165/2 \text{ kg.}$$

(ii) Calculation of revised standard quantity:

Material A = $200 \times \frac{3}{5} = 120$ kg.

Material B = $200 \times \frac{2}{5} = 80$ kg.

(iii) Calculation of Standard quantity:

Material A = $\frac{120 \times 165}{160} = 495/4$

Material B = $\frac{80 \times 165}{160} = 165/2$

(iv) Calculation of standard cost per unit of output:

Material A	=	60 × 20 =	₹ 1200
Material B	=	$\frac{40 \times 10}{100}$ –	₹ 400
			₹ 1600
Less: Loss 20%	=	20	—
Cost	=	80 =	1600
Cost per unit		=	$\frac{1600}{80}$ = ₹ 20

Calculation of variances:

(1) **Material Price Variance** = (AP – SP) × AQ

Material A = (₹ 20 – 20) × 105 = Nil

Material B = (Rs 9 – 10) × 95 = ₹ 95 (F)

Total = ₹ 95 (F)

(2) **Material Usage Variance** = (AQ – SQ) × SP

Material A = $105 - \frac{495}{4} \times$ ₹ 20 = ₹ 375 (F)

Material B = $95 - \frac{165}{2} \times$ ₹ 10 = ₹ 125 (A)

Total = ₹ 250 (F)

(3) **Material Mix Variance** = (AQ – RSQ) × SP

Material A = (105 – 120) × ₹ 20= ₹ 300(F)

Material B = (95 – 80) × ₹ 10 = ₹ 150(A)

Total = ₹ 150(F)

(4) **Material Yield Variance** = (AO – SO) × Std. cost per unit output

= (165 – 160) × ₹ 20 = ₹ 100(F)

D. Sales Variance

Total Sales variance = Budgeted Sales – Actual Sales = BS – AS
It is divided into 2 pats:

(a) Sales Price Variance = AQ(SR – AR)
(b) Sales Volume Variance = SR(BQ – AQ)

Sales Volume Variance:

(a) Sales Mix Variance = Revised Standard Sales – Standard Sales
(b) Sales Quantity Variance = Budgeted Sales – Revised Standard Sales
= BS – RSS

Problem 11

Calculate all sales variances and total sales variance from the following information:

Product	Budgeted Sales			Actual Sales		
	Units	Std. Rate p.u (₹)	Total	Units	Rate p.u	Total
A	5000	5	25000	6000	6	36000
B	4000	6	24000	5000	5	25000
C	3000	7	21000	4000	8	32000
Total	12000		70000	15000		93000

Solution:

(a) Total Sales Variance = BS – AS = 70,000 – 93,000 = 23,000 (F)

(b) Sales Price Variance = AR(SR – AR)

A = 6000 (5 – 6) = 6,000 (F)
B = 5000 (6 – 5) = 5,000 (A)
C = 4000 (7 – 8) = 4,000 (F)
₹ 5,000 (F)

(c) Sales Volume Variance: SR(BQ – AQ)

A = 5(5000 – 6000) = 5,000 (F)
B = 6(4000 – 5000) = 6,000 (F)
C = 7(3000 – 4000) = 7,000 (F)
₹ 18,000 (F)

Standard Sales:

Product	AQ	SR	SS (Standard Sales)
A	6,000	5	30,000
B	5,000	6	30,000
C	4,000	7	28,000
	15,000		₹ 88,000 = SS

$$\text{Standard Price p.u of standard mix} = \frac{BS}{BQ} = \frac{70{,}000}{12{,}000} = \frac{70}{12}$$

Revised standard sales (RSS) = AO × standard price p.u of standard mix

$$= 15{,}000 \times \frac{70}{12} = ₹\ 87{,}500$$

(d) Sales Mix Variance = RSS – SS = 87,500 – 88,000 = ₹ 500(F)

(e) Sales Quantity Variance = BS – RSS = 70,000 – 87,500 = ₹ 17,500(F)

Verification

Total Sales Variance = SPV + SVV or, 23,000(F) = 5,000(F) + 18,000(F)

Sales Volume Variance = SMV + SQV or, 18,000(F) = 500(F) + 17,500(F).

Problem 12

The following data is available in connection with the fixed overheads of a factory:

Budgeted Fixed overheads for March	₹ 1,00,000
Budgeted output for March	50000 Units
Standard time for 1 unit	5 Hours
Actual Hours Worked	255000
Actual fixed overheads for the month	₹ 1,10,000
Units produced during the month	52000

Calculate Fixed Overhead Variances for the month.

Solution:

(1) Overhead cost variance

= Standard Overhead Cost – Actual Overhead Cost
= ₹ (52,000 × 2) – ₹ 1,10,000
= ₹ 6,000 (Adv.)

Note : Standard Cost per unit

$$= \frac{\text{Budgeted Fixed Overheads}}{\text{Budgeted Output}}$$

$$= \frac{₹\ 1{,}00{,}000}{50{,}000 \text{ Units}} = ₹\ 2 \text{ per unit}$$

Standard Overhead Cost

= Actual Output × Std. Cost per unit
= 52,000 × ₹ 2 per unit
= ₹ 1,04,000

(2) Overhead Expenditure Variance

= Budgeted Cost – Actual Cost

= ₹ 1,00,000 – ₹ 1,10,000

= ₹ 10,000 (Adv.)

(3) Overhead Volume Variance

= Std. Rate (Actual Qty – Budgeted Qty.)

= ₹ 2 (52,000 – 50,000)

= ₹ 4,000 (Fav.)

(4) Overhead Efficiency Variance

= Std. Rate (Actual Qty – Std. Qty.)

= ₹ 2 (52,000 – 51,000)

= ₹ 2,000 (Fav.)

Note : Standard Quantity

= Actual Hrs. × Std. Qty per hour

= 2,55,000 × 1/5 = 51,000 Units.

(5) Overhead Capacity Variance

= Std. Rate (Std. Qty – Budgeted Qty)

= ₹ 2 (51,000 – 50,000)

= ₹ 2,000(Fav.)

Verification

Overhead Cost Variance
₹ 6,000 (Adv.)

- Overhead Expenditure Variance ₹ 10,000 (Adv.)
- Overhead Volume Variance ₹ 4,000 (Fav.)
    - Overhead Efficiency Variance ₹ 2,000 (Fav.)
    - Overhead Capacity Variance ₹ 2,000 (Fav.)

Problem 13

The following are extracted from the books of a company :

	Budget	Actual
Output (in units)	6,000	6,500
Hours	3,000	3,300
Overhead Cost-Fixed	1,200	1,250
Variable	₹ 6,000	₹ 6,650
Number of days	25	27

Compute and analyse the overhead variances.

Solution:

1. Overhead Cost Variance

= Recovered overheads – Actual overheads

= (Actual Output × Budgeted overhead) – (Actual output × Actual Rate)

= (6500 × 1.20) – 7900

= 7800 – 7900 = ₹ 100 (Adv.)

(a) Variable Overhead Variance

Cost variance = Recovered overhead – Actual Overheads

= (6,500 × Re. 1) – (6,650)

= ₹ 150 (Adv.)

(b) Fixed Overhead Cost Variance

= Recovered Overheads – Actual Overheads

= (.20 × 6,500) – (1250)

= 1,350 – 1,250

= ₹ 50 (Fav.)

Verification

Overhead Cost Variance

= Fixed Overhead Cost variance + Variable overhead Cost variance

= ₹ 150 (Adv.) + ₹ 50 (Fav.)

= ₹ 100 (Adv.)

2. Fixed Overhead variance can be classified into :

(a) **Fixed Expenditure Variance**

= Budgeted Overheads – Actual Overheads.

= ₹ 1,200 – ₹ 1,250

= ₹ 50 (Adv.)

(b) **Fixed Overhead Volume Variance**

= Recovered Overheads – Budgeted Overheads.

= ₹ 1,300 – ₹ 1,200

= ₹ 100 (Fav.)

Verification

Fixed Overhead Cost Variance

= Expenditure Variance + Volume Variance

= ₹ 50 (Adv.) + ₹ 100 (Fav.)

= ₹ 50 (Fav.)

(3) Fixed Overhead Volume Variance can be classified into

(a) Efficiency Variance

= (Std. rate per unit × Actual output) – (Std. rate per unit × Std. output for actual time)

= (.30 × 6,500) – (.20 × 6,480)

= ₹ 1,300 – ₹ 1,296

= ₹ 4(Fav.)

(b) Capacity Variance

= Standard overhead – Budgeted overhead

= 1.296 – 1.200

= ₹ 96 (Fav.)

Verification

Fixed overhead volume variance = Efficiency variance + Capacity Variance

= ₹ 4(fav) ₹ 96 (Fav.)

= ₹ 100 (Fav.)

4. Capacity Variance can be classified into :

(a) Calendar Variance

= Possible overheads – Buidgeted Overhead

= ₹ 1,296 – ₹ 1,200

= ₹ 96(Fav.)

Where possible overheads

= Possible days × Std. rate per day

= 27 × ₹ 48 = ₹ 1,296

(b) Revised Capacity Variance

= Standard Overheads – Possible Overheads

= ₹ 1,296 – ₹ 1,296

= Nil

Verification

Capacity Variance = Calendar Variance + Rvd. Capacity Variance

= 96(Fav.) + 0 = ₹ 96 (Fav)

SUMMARY

Standard cost are scientifically 'predetermined costs' assuming a given level of efficiency. They are created by management. There are the model target costs which can be achieved under standard operating conditions. Standard costing is the preparation of standard costs and their comparison with actual cost and the analysis of variances to their causes and points of incidence. The technique of standard costing can be used for all industries and activities. However, the use of standard costing is more effective in industries which have standardized repetitive nature of operations, for example, process industries.

Budgeting control and standard costing technique though different, have a common objective of managerial control and planning. Budgetary control can be operated without the system of standard costing but standard costing cannot function without the system of budgetary control. Standard costing uses standard cost which are based on scientific estimates of various elements of costs. Under budgetary control, budgets are generally based on incremental approach. Budgets set up maximum ceiling of expenses above which actual expenditure should not normally exceed. Standard costing set the minimum targets which are to be attained by actual performance under specified operating conditions.

Variance analysis is the process of analyzing variances, which sub-divides the total variances into different elements of cost *i.e.* material, labour and overheads for the purpose of management control. The reasons for such variances are ascertained, so that remedial measures can be taken by the management. This enables the management to identify the responsibility for adverse variance to executives.

The success of standard costing system depends upon the accuracy with which standards have been set to make it more relative. The responsibility of setting standards is therefore entrusted to a committee which comprises the production Manager, Purchase Manager, Personal Manager, Production Engineer, Cost Accountant etc.

In standard costing, output or an amount of work can be expressed in terms of 'standard hour'. It is defined by I.C.W.A. London as a "a hypothetical hour which represents the amount of work which should be performed in one hour under which should be performed in one hour under standard conditions." It is useful in ascertaining overhead variances.

EXERCISE

Short Questions

1. What is 'standard cost'?
2. What is 'standard costing'?
3. What is 'budgetary control'?
4. What is 'variance'?
5. What is "variance analysis'?
6. What is direct material cost variance?
7. What is difference between material price variance and material usage variance?
8. What is the difference between "material mix variance and 'material yield variance'?"
9. What is 'labour cost variance'?
10. What is the difference between 'labour rate variance' and 'labour efficiency variance'?
11. What is 'idle time variance'?
12. What is 'overhead variance'?
13. What is the difference between standard cost and budgeted cost?

Moderate and Broad Questions

1. Explain the difference between 'standard costing' and 'budgetary control'.
2. Illustrate the advantages and limitations of standard costing system.
3. Explain 'Variance Analysis'. Classify the cost variances.
4. State all classifications of 'Fixed Overhead' and 'Variable Overhead' variances.
5. Explain all overhead and sales variances.
6. Explain all material and labour variances.

PROBLEMS

1. Find out the Material Variances from the given data:

	Standard			Actual		
	Qty	**Price**	**Value**	**Qty**	**Price**	**Value**
	Kg.	**₹**	**₹**	**Kg.**	**₹**	**₹**
Material A	200	4	800	180	4.50	810
Material B	100	5	500	120	4.80	576
	300		1300	1300	300	1386

2. Find out the material variances from the given data:

	Standard			Actual		
	Qty	**Price**	**Value**	**Qty**	**Price**	**Value**
	Kg.	**₹**	**₹**	**Kg.**	**₹**	**₹**
Material X	80	4	320	90	5	450
Material Y	40	5	200	50	4	200
Material Z	100	2	200	110	3	330
	220		720	250		980

3. The standard mix for each batch of 250 units of product A is:

Material M	15 Kgs.	at ₹ 15 = ₹ 225
Material N	10 Kgs.	at ₹ 10 = ₹ 100
	25 Kgs.	₹ 325

During September, 10 batches were completed with actual consumption as follows:

Material M	155 kgs. at ₹ 14	= ₹ 2,170
Material N	110 kgs. at ₹ 11	= ₹ 1,210
	265 kgs.	₹ 3,380

Actual output was 2400 units. Calculate

(a) Material Price Variance

(b) Material Usage Variance

(c) Material Mix Variance

4. From the following information, calculate
   (a) Labour Cost Variance
   (b) Labour Rate Variance
   (c) Labour Efficiency Variance
   (d) Labour Mix Variance

Standard :		₹	Actual :		₹
Workman X	30 hours @ ₹ 4 =	120	Workman X	45 hours @ ₹ 5 =	225
Workman Y	35 hours @ ₹ 6 =	210	Workman Y	40 hours @ ₹ 5 =	200
	65 hours	330		85 hours	425

5. From the following information calculate labour variances:

   Actual hours = 8000
   Standard hours = 6400
   Actual rate = ₹ 2.50/hour.
   Standard Rate = ₹ 3/hour.

   Idle time on account of machine breakdown = 320 hours.

6. From the given information, calculate the overhead variance:

	Budgeted	Actual
Hours	10,000	12,500
Output (in units)	2,000	2,500
Fixed overheads	₹ 50,000	₹ 60,000

7. The details regarding composition and the weekly wage rates of labour force engaged on a job scheduled to be completed to 35 weeks are as follows:

	Standard		Actual	
Category of worker	No. of labourers	Weekly Rate (₹)	No. of labourers	Weekly Rate (₹)
Skilled	75	60	70	70
Semi-skilled	45	40	30	50
Unskilled	60	30	80	20

   The work is actually completed in 40 weeks. Calculate the various labour variances.

8. The following figures are extracted from the books of a limited company:

	Budget	Actual
Output (in units)	6,000	6,600
Hours	3,000	3,300
Overhead cost –		
Fixed (₹)	1,200	1,250
Variable (₹)	6,000	6,650
No. of days	25	27

   Compute and analyze the overhead variances.

9. ABC Ltd. manufactures a single product, the standard mix of which is :

   Material A : 60% at ₹ 10 per kg.

   Material B : 40% at ₹ 20 per kg.

Normal loss in production is 10% of input. Due to shortage of material A, the standard mix was changed. Actual results for March, 2010 were:

Material A : 105 kg. at ₹ 9 per kg.

Material B : 95 kg. at ₹ 18 per kg.

Input : 200 kg.

Loss : 25 kg.

Output : 175 kg.

Calculate

(i) Material price variance
(ii) Material usage variance
(iii) Material mix variance
(iv) Material yield variance.

10. A cost accountant of a company was given the following information:

	Standard	Actual
Production	5000 units	4000 units
Working days	25	30
Fixed overhead (₹)	40,000	38,000
Variable overhead (₹)	12,000	12,000

He is required to calculate the following overhead variances:

(a) Variable Overhead Variance
(b) Fixed Overhead Variances
  (i) Expenditure variance
  (ii) Volume variance
  (iii) Efficiency variance
  (iv) Calendar variance.

❑❑❑

22 Merchant Banking

22.1 INTRODUCTION — MERCHANT BANK

Merchant bank is a financial institution that specializes in providing various financial services such as hire purchase or installment buying, international trade financing, acceptance of exchange bills, long term loans, and so on. It provides advice on portfolio management. Merchant banks act as an intermediary between issuer and purchase of securities.

Dictionary meaning of 'merchant bank' refers to an organization that underwrites corporate securities and advices such clients on issues like corporate merger etc. involved in the ownership of commercial ventures. The organization may be a bank, corporate body firm or proprietary concern.

22.2 MERCHANT BANKERS

Merchant bankers manage the new issue of companies. They give services in designing the capital structure of a company and also hire issue houses and advertising agencies for pre and post publicity of the issue.

The merchant bankers have pre and post issue obligation. In case of pre issue the merchant bankers have to make arrangements for filling the prospectus and relevant documents with SEBI and in case of post issue they have to make arrangements for getting the shares allotted and despatched within specified period to the applicants.

Merchant bankers (category I), are mandated by SEBI to manage public issues (as lead managers). Issue management activity has a big fall out on the integrity of the market. It affects investor's interest and hence transparency has to be ensured.

SEBI (Merchant Bankers) Rules 1992 states : "A merchant banker has been defined as any person who is engaged in the business of issue management either by making arrangements regarding selling, buying or subscribing to securities or acting as management consultant, adviser or rendering corporate advisory services relation to issue management.

22.3 MERCHANT BANKING SERVICES

Merchant banking is an essential service provided by financial institutions that help in the growth of corporate sector, which eventually reflects in the overall growth and economic development of the country. Actually, merchant banking includes the entire range of financial services. The services are subject to the inclination and resources of merchant banking outfits — technical and financial.

The diverse services rendered by Merchant Banks are as follows:

(i) Organizing and extending finance for investment in projects;

(ii) Assistance in financial management;

(iii) Acceptance of house business;

(iv) Raising Eurodollar loans;

(v) Issuing of foreign currency bonds;

(vi) Financing export of capital goods;

(vii) Financing of hire purchase transaction;

(viii) Equipment leasing;

(ix) Mergers and take-over;

(x) Valuation of assets;

(xi) Investment managements;

(xii) Promotion of investment trusts etc.

Different merchant banks are specialized in different services. Later merchant bankers have been mandated in making public offers for acquisition of shares or voting rights and assisting listed companies to make letter of offer for buy-back of shares and give due diligence certificate.

22.4 MERCHANT BANKING IN INDIA

Merchant Banking in India started with management of public issues and loan syndication and has been slowly and gradually covering activities like project counselling, portfolio management, investment counselling, mergers and amalgamation of the corporate firms.

The need for merchant banking was felt with the rapid growth in number of issues made and initiated into Indian capital market. The Grindlays Bank then got the license from RBI in 1967. Later in 1970, City Bank set up a merchant banking division. As a commercial activity, merchant banking took shape in India through the management of public issues of capital and loan syndication. During that time the main services offered by the merchant banks to the corporate enterprises involved management of public issues and financial consultancy. State bank of India was the first Indian bank to set up its Merchant Banking Division in 1972. There was a boom for merchant banking organizations in the country in mid-seventies as various financial institutions and commercial banks entered into the field of merchant banking. From 1992, reform measures were introduced in the capital market. The reform measures included conferring of statutory powers on the Securities and Exchange Board of India (SEBI) and the repeal of Capital Issues Control Act. These measures brought about major improvement in the regulatory and functional efficiency of the market. The measures also enabled the merchant bankers to take legal and moral responsibility towards the investing public. It includes public sector, private sector and foreign players. Some of the registered merchant banks in India are Kotak Mahindra Capital, HDFC Bank, ICICI Bank, IDBI Bank, SBI Capital Market Ltd, Can Bank Financial Services Ltd, PNB Capital Services Ltd. and so on.

22.5 ROLE OF MERCHANT BANKING

Merchant banking helps with the following:

- Channelize the financial surplus of the public into productive investment prospects.
- Coordinate the activities of intermediaries to the share issue such as bankers, registrars, underwriters, and brokers.
- Ensure the compliance with the rules and regulations governing the market.

Merchant banking helps industry and trade to raise funds, and the investors to invest their saved money in sound and healthy concerns with confidence, safely and expectation for higher yields. Merchant banks have been procuring impressive support from capital market for the corporate sectors for financing their projects.

Merchant banks have to think and device new instruments of financing industrial projects. It has to assume wide responsibilities of saving sick industrial units and guiding industries to set up in industrially backward areas to eliminate regional inbalances in industrial development of the country.

In the days ahead merchant bankers have very significant role to play tuning their activities to the requirements of the growth pattern of the corporate sector, the industry and the economy as a whole. The nature of merchant banking services is development — oriented and promotional to help the industry and trade to grow and survive. It is always awake to renewing the skills, developing expertising in new areas so as to equip itself with the knowledge and techniques to deal with emerging new problems of corporate business world. Last but not the least , section of the community processing surplus money to invest in corporate securities and other productive investment channels, are getting help from the merchant bankers in these issues.

22.6 ELIGIBILITY OF A MERCHANT BANKER

As per the SEBI guidelines, a category I merchant banker must be a corporate body with a net worth of ₹ 5 crores and has to compulsorily register with the SEBI in the interest of the investors. In order to get the registration with SEBI the merchant banker must meet following requirements:

(a) **Capital adequacy:** The merchant banker has to fulfill the minimum prescribed capital adequacy norms in terms of net worth.

(b) **Infrastructure:** The merchant banker needs to have adequate infrastructure.

(c) **Expertise:** The merchant banker must be professionally competent to undertake merchant banking business.

(d) **Responsibility:** The merchant banker has to make payment of the prescribed fee to SEBI and needs to adhere to the obligations, responsibilities and to the code of conduct prescribed by SEBI.

22.7 REGISTRATION OF MERCHANT BANKERS WITH SEBI

It is mandatory for a merchant banker to register with the SEBI. Without holding a certificate of registration granted by the Securities and Exchange Board of India, no person can act as a merchant banker in India.

1. Only a body corporate other than a non-banking financial company shall be eligible to get registration as merchant banker.

2. The applicant should not carry on any business other than those connected with the Securities market.

3. All applicants for Merchant Bankers should have qualification in Finance, law or Business Management.

4. The applicant should have infrastructure like office space, equipment, manpower etc.

5. The applicant must have at least two employees with prior experience in merchant banking.

6, Any associate company, group company, subsidiary or interconnected company of the applicant should not have been a registered merchant banker

7. The applicant should not have been involved in any securities scam or proved guilt for any offence

8. The applicant should have a minimum net worth of ₹ 5 Crores, for become category 1 of merchant banker.

The various categories for which registration can be obtained are:

1. ***Category I*** – to carry on the activity of issue management and to act as adviser, consultant, manager, underwriter, portfolio manager.

2. ***Category II*** – to act as adviser, consultant, co-manager, underwriter, portfolio manager.

3. ***Category III*** – to act as underwriter, adviser or consultant to an issue

4. ***Category IV*** – to act only as adviser or consultant to an issue

The capital requirement for carrying on activity as merchant banker:

The capital requirement depends upon the category. The minimum net worth requirement for acting as merchant banker is given below:

Category I – ₹ 5 crores

Category II – ₹ 50 lakhs

Category III – ₹ 20 lakhs

Category IV – Nil

Procedure for getting registration

An application should be submitted to SEBI in Form A of the SEBI (Merchant Bankers) Regulations, 1992. SEBI shall consider the application and on being satisfied, issues a certificate of registration in Form B of the SEBI (Merchant Bankers) Regulations, 1992.

Registration fee payable to SEBI

₹ 5 lakhs which should be paid within 15 days of date of receipt of intimation regarding grant of certificate. Validity period of certificate of registration is three years from the date of issue. Three months before the expiry period, an application along with renewal fee of 2.5 lakhs should be submitted to SEBI in Form A of the SEBI (Merchant Bankers) Regulations, 1992. SEBI shall consider the application and on being satisfied renew certificate of registration for a further period of three years

22.8 FUNCTIONS OF MERCHANT BANKING

The following are the main functions of merchant banking:

1. Issue Management: A major function of merchant banking is issue management. The issue can be through offer of sale or private placements, prospectus, and so on. The issue management includes the following functions with respect to issue through prospectus:

(i) To obtain approval for the issue from the SEBI.

(ii) To arrange underwriting for the proposed issue.

(iii) To draft and finalize the prospectus and to obtain clearance from the stock exchange, auditors, underwriters and registrar of companies.

(iv) To select advertising agencies, underwriters, bankers and brokers to the issue and finalize the charges to be paid to the registrar.

(v) To arrange press conferences, and investors and brokers through advertising agency.

(vi) To finalize the terms of issue to make the issue more attractive.

2. Pre-investment studies of investors: The merchant bankers undertake the practicality surveys in selected areas of client's interest. It also includes the studies for foreign organizations which are planning for joint ventures in India. The survey covers the advice on the nature of participation and Government regulations. Pre-investment study covers the study of the project and includes the following aspects:

(i) Developing or reviewing of project profile.
(ii) Preparing project reports after analyzing financial, market and economic feasibility.
(iii) Estimating the cost of the project.
(iv) Studying the procedural aspects of project implementation.
(v) Determining the source of financing and deciding the capital structure.
(vi) Assisting in legal formalities for implementing the project.

3. Corporate counselling: Corporate counselling refers to the activities undertaken to ensure effective running of a corporate enterprise through efficient management of finance. A merchant banker guides the clients on organizational goals, choice of product and market survey, forecasting a product, cost analysis, investment decisions, pricing methods, capital management and expenditure control, market strategy and so on. Corporate counselling is a facility provided by merchant bankers to corporate enterprises free of charge. This is to improve the performance of the enterprise. Merchant bankers also provide services such as building a good image among the investors which help in increasing the market value of investor's equity shares. The following are the areas in which the corporate counselling is provided:

(i) Area of diversification considering the Government's licensing and economic policies.
(ii) Market analysis for growth, present and future demand, and profitability of each product produced by the corporate enterprise. The analysis also helps to determine whether to continue the product or not.

4. Project counselling: Project counselling is a part of corporate counselling which is related to project finance. A merchant banker provides the clients project counselling that involves providing advice on procedural aspects of project implementation, conducting financial study of the project, providing assistance in project profiles, providing assistance in seeking approvals from Government of India for foreign technical and financial collaboration agreements.

5. Loan syndication: A merchant banker helps the clients to get loan for the project. They also help in conducting appraisal and designing capital structure.

6. Portfolio management: Portfolio management refers to making decisions related to investment of cash resources of a corporate enterprise in marketable securities by deciding the type of security to be purchased. A merchant banker helps the clients in making the right choice of investment to obtain optimum investment, undertaking investment in securities conducting critical evaluation of investment portfolio, and so on.

7. Project finance: A merchant banker who undertakes a project scheme also assists in arranging a comprehensive package for the project funding. The process involves the study of the pattern of financing available from merchant banks and financial institutions. The merchant bankers work closely with the client and the technical consultant and submit a complete financial report to the client. They also provide assistance in legal documentation for the finance arranged.

8. Working capital: Merchant bankers assist in arranging finance for working capital particularly for new ventures. For existing firms, the merchant bankers arrange the funds from non-traditional sources such as through issue of debentures, and so on. For example, Central Bank of India (CBI) has started working capital finance as one of the merchant banking service area.

9. Managerial and technical services: Merchant bankers provide services to deal with problems in technical, financial and managerial fields.

22.9 FUNCTION AS FINANCIAL INTERMEDIARIES

Financial intermediation is a process by which capital is mobilized from a large number of investors and is made available to all those who need them, mainly to corporate customers. Merchant banking is a financial intermediary which helps to transfer capital from one who owns it to those who require it.

Merchant banks invest their capital in client companies and provide fee-based services for mergers and acquisition. Many companies approach merchant banks to enhance their financial stability or to meet an essential capital requirement. Due to their knowledge in international finances, merchant banks specialize in dealing with multinational corporations. Merchant banks do not offer regular banking services to the public.

Issue Management: Intermediaries

The primary market intermediaries are the merchant bankers, underwriters to issue and brokers to issues. The merchant bankers are the issue managers who bring the issues to the primary market investors. Issue management is a tedious job and is closely regulated by SEBI. In many countries, the regulators implement a licensing mechanism for issue management.

Issue management is one of the important fee-based services provided by financial institutions. There are few large-scale and specialized issue management agencies in the country. The growth of stock market and opening up of economy has increased the scope of issue management activity. SEBI has laid guidelines as ground rules relating to new issue management activities to protect the investor's interest and for development of market. The guidelines are in addition to the company's law requirements for the issue of capital.

Merchant Bankers as Lead Managers

Merchant banker is the person who arranges or assists in funds from investors through stocks, bonds or shares on behalf of the issuer for corporate establishment or for expansion purpose of the corporate firms. The main merchant banker is the lead manager. The lead manager can have associate merchant banker to the issue. The merchant banker is a channel between the issuer and investors. As per SEBI, merchant banker is anyone who is engaged in business of issue management by making arrangements related to buying, selling or subscribing securities or providing corporate advisory service related to issue management. The importance of merchant bankers as sponsors of capital issues is seen in their major services such as determining the composition of securities types to be issued, draft of prospectus, appointment of registrars, arrangement of underwriters, selection of brokers and advertising agents, and so on. The role of merchant bankers in the process of capital issues is very important. All public issues must be managed by merchant bankers who function as lead managers.

Underwriters

A significant intermediary in issue market is the underwriters to issue of capital who take up securities which are not fully subscribed. Underwriter is a person who agrees to take up shares specified in the underwriting agreement of the public, who fails to subscribe them. SEBI has allowed merchant bankers and registered underwriters to act as underwriters. To act as underwriter, a certificate of registration must be obtained from SEBI. The underwriter makes profit on the difference between the public offering price and the price paid to the issuer; that is called the underwriting spread or price spread. Underwriters are appointed by the issuing companies after consulting with the merchant bankers to the issues.

Bankers to an Issue

The bankers to an issue engage in activities such as acceptance of applications along with the application money from the investors with respect to issues of capital and refund of application money. Bankers to an issue accept applications with the subscriptions offered at their designated branches and forward them to the registrar in agreement with instructions issued to them. They undertake publicity to the issue by distributing publicity material, prospectus and application forms. They are entitled for brokerage on shares allocated against applications bearing their stamps. In case of large issues, sufficient numbers of banks with branches at major centres are appointed. According to SEBI regulations, inspection of bankers to an issue is done by the Reserve Bank on request from SEBI.

Brokers to an Issue

Brokers are mainly concerned about obtaining the subscription to the issue from the prospective investors. The appointment of brokers is not compulsory. Members of established stock exchange are appointed as brokers to an issue. Companies are permitted to appoint any number of brokers. The official brokers together with the managers to the issue coordinate the preliminary distribution of securities and acquire direct subscription from many investors. The stock exchange laws prohibit the members from acting as brokers to the issue. The stock exchange grants permission to the members if the members give their approval and the company conforms to the requirements and undertakes to have its securities listed on a recognized stock exchange. The company appoints the broker to the issue at every centre where stock exchanges are located.

Registrar to an Issue and Share Transfer Agents

Registrar to an issue is an intermediary in primary market. They conduct activities such as maintaining records of applications and money received from investors or money paid to the seller of securities, assisting companies in deciding the basis of allotment of securities in consultation with stock exchanges, finalizing the allotment of securities and dispatching allotment letters, refund orders, and other documents related to issue of capital. Merchant bankers have a panel of registrars who help the issuing company to finalize the terms and conditions of application. Lead managers ensure that the registrar to issue is registered with SEBI and is appointed in all public issues. The registrar to issue is completely responsible for all activities allocated to him for issue management.

The share transfer agents deal with all matters related to transfer of the company's securities. They maintain the records of holders of securities for and on behalf of the companies. The agents undertake various activities ranging from transfer of holdings to dispatch of documents, annual reports, notices, and other related activities. SEBI has laid guidelines regarding the authorization to registrar to issue and share transfer agents. According to the guidelines a fee must be paid to SEBI. The authorization has validity for one year which can be renewed annually.

Debenture Trustees

Debenture trustee is the trustee of debenture stock. A debenture stock is issued as loan security to secure debts of the company. It is necessary to get a certificate of registration from the SEBI to act as a debenture trustee. The debenture trustee holds a secured property on behalf of the issuer of security. The trustee has the right to carry on with the sale of secured property in case of default by the issuer of security, according to the procedure in the Transfer of Property Act. The profits of sales will be applied to redeem the debentures. The appointment of debenture trustee is mandatory. A company appoints debenture trustees when there is a need for executing a trust deed. This occurs when the company wants to issue a prospectus or letter of offer to the public for securing subscription to its debentures. A debenture trustee is an intermediary between the issuer of debentures and the holder of debentures. The main responsibility of the debenture trustee is to safeguard the interest of holders of debentures. This includes creation of security by the company issuing the debenture and to compensate their grievances.

Portfolio Managers

Portfolio manager is a person responsible for investing a mutual, exchange-traded fund asset and also responsible for implementing investment strategy and managing the day-to-day portfolio trading. The portfolio manager is an important factor that needs to be considered regarding fund investing. He undertakes the management and administration of portfolio of securities and funds of clients on their behalf. Portfolio management is the art of making decisions about investments and policy, allocating assets for individuals and balancing risk against performance. Portfolio management can be classified into two types:

1. Discretionary portfolio management: it permits the use of discretion regarding investment and management of the portfolio of the securities and funds. In this type of management the manager independently manages the capital of each client.

2. Non-discretionary portfolio management: in this type of management the manager manages funds according to the directions of the client.

It is mandatory to obtain a certificate from SEBI in order to carry on portfolio management services.

22.10 REGULATORY AUTHORITIES OF MERCHANT BANKING ACTIVITY

Merchant banking activities are regulated by the following regulatory authorities:

(i) Guidelines of SEBI and Ministry of Finance,

(ii) Companies Act,1956,

(iii) Listing Guidelines of Stock Exchanges and

(iv) Securities Contracts (Regulation) Act, 1956.

Merchant banking activities especially those covering issue and understanding of shares and debentures are regulated by the Merchant Bankers Regulation of Securities and SEBI. There are two Stock Exchanges recognized by the Central Government under the Securities Contracts (Regulation) Act, 1956 where nearly 8000 brokers and 35000 sub-brokers are engaged in the capital market activities providing directly the marketing aid in selling the capital issues in the primary market and also assisting in their activities of portfolio management. Besides, there are the Over the Country Exchange of India (OTCEI) and National Stock Exchange (NSE) are functioning. NSE which becomes operational on July 1, 1994 has two computerized screen-based trading system for equity and debt instruments. SEBI has already prescribed a code of conduct for the merchant bankers.

22.11 CASE EXAMPLE OF CANARA BANK'S MERCHANT BANKING SERVICES

Canara Bank is also one of the leading Merchant Bankers in India, offering specialized services to Banks, PSUs, State owned Corporations, Local Statutory bodies and Corporate sector.

They are SEBI registered Category I Merchant Banker to render Issue Management (Public/ Rights/Private Placement Issues), Underwriting, Consultancy and Corporate Advisory Services etc.

They also hold SEBI registration Certificate to act as "Bankers to an Issue" with network of exclusive Capital Market Service Branches and over 100 designated CBS Branches to handle Collecting/Refund/Paying Banker assignments.

They do undertake "project appraisals" with linkage to resource raising plans from Capital Market/Debt Markets and facilitate tie-ups with Banks/Financial Institutions and Potential Investors.

As leading Merchant Bankers in India, they have associated with issues ranging from ₹ 1 crore to ₹ 1,500 crores, involving various types of industries, banks, statutory Bodies etc. and have an edge in handling Private Placement issues – both retail and HNIs.

Spectrum of Services

(i) Equity Issue (Public/Rights) Management

(ii) Debt Issue Management

(iii) Private Placements

(iv) Project Appraisals

(v) Monitoring Agency Assignments

(vi) IPO Funding

(vii) Security Trustee Services

(viii) Agriculture Consultancy Services

(ix) Corporate Advisory Services

(x) Mergers and Acquisitions

(xi) Buy Back Assignments

(xii) Share Valuations

(xiii) Syndication

(xiv) ESOS Certification

Issue Management Services

(i) Project Appraisal

(ii) Capital structuring

(iii) Preparation of offer document

(iv) Tie Ups (placement)

(v) Formalities with SEBI / Stock Exchange / ROC, etc.

(vi) Underwriting

(vii) Promotion /Marketing of Issues

(viii) Collecting Banker / Banker to an issue

(ix) Post Issue Management

(x) Refund Bankers

(xi) Debenture Trusteeship

(xii) Registrar and Transfer Agency (our Subsidiary)

22.12 FUNCTIONS AND SERVICES OF MERCHANT BANKS IN INDIA

Merchant banks in india carry out the following functions and services:

- Corporate Counselling
- Project Counselling
- Pre-investment studies
- Capital Structuring
- Credit Syndication and Project Finance.
- Mergers, Amalgamations and Take overs
- Venture Capital.
- Portfolio Management
- Lease Financing
- Fixed Deposit Banking
- Mutual Funds
- Issue Management and underwritting.
- Project Appraisa

❑ ❑ ❑

23 Financial Risk and Its Management

23.1 INTRODUCTION TO FINANCIAL RISK

Although financial risk has increased significantly in recent years, risk and risk management are not contemporary issues. The result of increasingly global markets is that risk may originate with events thousands of miles away that have nothing to do with the domestic market. Information is available instantaneously, which means that change, and subsequent market reactions, occur very quickly. The economic climate and markets can be affected very quickly by changes in exchange rates, interest rates, and commodity prices. Counterparties can rapidly become problematic. As a result, it is important to ensure that financial risks are identified and managed appropriately. Preparation is a key component of risk management.

23.2 WHAT IS RISK?

Risk provides the basis for opportunity. The terms *risk* and *exposure* have differences in their meaning. Risk refers to the probability of loss, while exposure is the possibility of loss, although they are often used interchangeably. Risk arises as a result of exposure. Exposure to financial markets affects most organizations, either directly or indirectly. When an organization has financial market exposure, there is a possibility of loss but also an opportunity for gain or profit. Financial market exposure may provide strategic or competitive benefits. Risk is the likelihood of losses resulting from events such as changes in market prices. Events with a low probability of occurring, but that may result in a high loss, are particularly troublesome because they are often not anticipated. Put another way, risk is the probable variability of returns. Since it is not always possible or desirable to eliminate risk, understanding it is an important step in determining how to manage it. Identifying exposures and risks forms the basis for an appropriate financial risk management strategy.

23.3 HOW DOES FINANCIAL RISK ARISE?

Financial risk arises through countless transactions of a financial nature, including sales and purchases, investments and loans, and various other business activities. It can arise as a result of legal transactions, new projects, mergers and acquisitions, debt financing, the energy component of costs, or through the activities of management, stakeholders, competitors, foreign governments, or weather. When financial prices change dramatically, it can increase costs, reduce revenues, or otherwise adversely impact the profitability of an organization. Financial fluctuations may make it more difficult to plan and budget, price goods and services, and allocate capital.

23.4 SOURCES OF FINANCIAL RISK

There are three main sources of financial risk:

1. Financial risks arising from an organization's exposure to changes in market prices, such as interest rates, exchange rates, and commodity prices.
2. Financial risks arising from the actions of, and transactions with, other organizations such as vendors, customers, and counterparties in derivatives transactions.
3. Financial risks resulting from internal actions or failures of the organization, particularly people, processes, and systems.

23.5 WHAT IS FINANCIAL RISK MANAGEMENT?

Financial risk management is a process to deal with the uncertainties resulting from financial markets. It involves assessing the financial risks facing an organization and developing management strategies consistent with internal priorities and policies. Addressing financial risks proactively may provide an organization with a competitive advantage. It also ensures that management, operational staff, stakeholders, and the board of directors are in agreement on key issues of risk. Managing financial risk necessitates making organizational decisions about risks that are acceptable versus those that are not. The passive strategy of taking no action is the acceptance of all risks by default. Organizations manage financial risk using a variety of strategies and products. It is important to understand how these products and strategies work to reduce risk within the context of the organization's risk tolerance and objectives. Strategies for risk management often involve derivatives. Derivatives are traded widely among financial institutions and on organized exchanges. The value of derivatives contracts, such as futures, forwards, options, and swaps, is derived from the price of the underlying asset. Derivatives trade on interest rates, exchange rates, commodities, equity and fixed income securities, credit, and even weather. The products and strategies used by market participants to manage financial risk are the same ones used by speculators to increase leverage and risk. Although it can be argued that widespread use of derivatives increases risk, the existence of derivatives enables those who wish to reduce risk to pass it along to those who seek risk and its associated opportunities. The ability to estimate the likelihood of a financial loss is highly desirable. However, standard theories of probability often fail in the analysis of financial markets. Risks usually do not exist in isolation, and the interactions of several exposures may have to be considered in developing an understanding of how financial risk arises. Sometimes, these interactions are difficult to forecast, since they ultimately depend on human behaviour. The process of financial risk management is an ongoing one. Strategies need to be implemented and refined as the market and requirements change. Refinements may reflect changing expectations about market rates, changes to the business environment, or changing international political conditions, for example. In general, the process can be summarized as follows:

(a) Identify and prioritize key financial risks.

(b) Determine an appropriate level of risk tolerance.

(c) Implement risk management strategy in accordance with policy.

(d) Measure, report, monitor, and refine as needed.

23.6 DIVERSIFICATION OF RISK — TO REDUCE / MANAGE FINANCIAL RISK

For many years, the riskiness of an asset was assessed based only on the variability of its returns. In contrast, modern portfolio theory considers not only an asset's riskiness, but also its contribution to the overall riskiness of the portfolio to which it is added. Organizations may have an opportunity to reduce risk as a result of risk diversification. In portfolio management terms, the addition of individual components to a portfolio provides opportunities for diversification, within limits. A diversified portfolio contains assets whose returns are dissimilar, in other words, weakly or negatively correlated with one another. It is useful to think of the exposures of an organization as a portfolio and consider the impact of changes or additions on the potential risk of the total. Diversification is an important tool in managing financial risks. Diversification among counterparties may reduce the risk that unexpected events adversely impact the organization through defaults.

Diversification among investment assets reduces the magnitude of loss if one issuer fails. Diversification of customers, suppliers, and financing sources reduces the possibility that an organization will have its business adversely affected by changes outside management's control. Although the risk of loss still exists, diversification may reduce the opportunity for large adverse outcomes.

The riskiness of each investment opportunity can be divided into two components — the market related risk which cannot be diversified away at all and which is called systematic or non-diversifiable risk and the firm or industry-related risk which can be diversified and is called diversifiable or unsystematic risk.

Thus, Total Risk = Systematic Risk + Unsystematic Risk

Systematic Risk	Unsystematic Risk
↓	↓
(non-diversifiable)	(diversifiable)
↓	↓
unavoidable	avoidable
↓	↓
market related	firm/industry related

Let us first talk about the *unsystematic* risk which is *diversifiable* or *avoidable*. This portion of the risk is regarded as the extent of variability in the security's return on account of *firm-specific* or *industry-specific risk factors e.g.* low productivity, labour trouble, low profitability, turnover of most effective executive (*e.g.* Marketing Manager or the Production Engineer leaving the firm), emergence of a strong competitor, scarcity of raw materials, increase in customs duty, etc. Since the firm specific factors are mostly random, they can be diversified by increasing the number of securities in a portfolio. As for example, if the management of a firm in the portfolio is poor, the management of another firm in the portfolio may be very good; if the productivity in one firm is low, that of another may be high: if one firm suffers due to bad weather while the other gains due to the same condition and so on so that by including sufficient number of securities of different firms in a portfolio such factors may tend to cancel out the effect of each other.

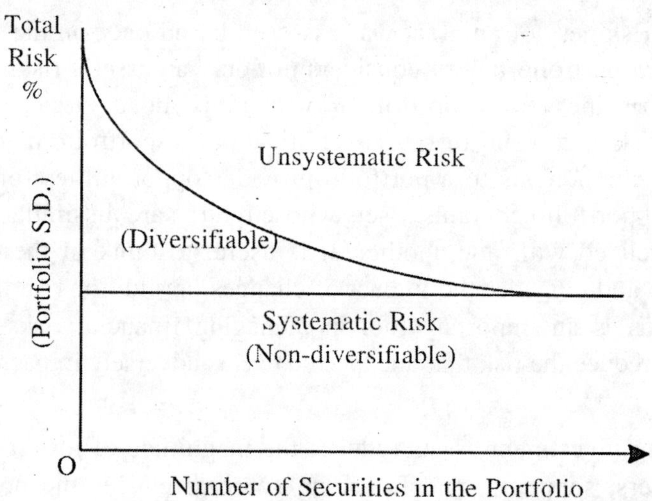

Fig. Total Risk and Diversification

But the other component, the systematic risk, which depends on the market as a whole, cannot be diversified away. They are caused by economic and political factors. These factors affect the entire market in a certain direction. As for example, an increase in the price of crude oil at the international market will certainly affect the domestic market adversely or some favourable changes in the fiscal, financial and monetary policies of Government of India and the Reserve Bank of India may act as a booster to the stock market operations. Thus, risk which is dependent on the economy or market as a whole cannot be reduced by any amount of diversification. That is why; this type of risk is called undiversifiable or unavoidable.

Reducing Risk through Diversification

The principle of diversification requires an investor to invest in more than one share / project so that losses in one may be offset by gains in another. In this way, a prudent investor may avoid too much risk and may hope that the actual returns from his/ her portfolio are much the same as what he/she expected them to be.

Earlier, we have considered individual investments in terms of their risk and return. According to portfolio theory this cannot be done. The *relationship* between the returns from different investments has to be considered to form a portfolio. This relationship can be of three types:

(a) Positive correlation: When there is positive correlation between investments, if one investment does well (or badly) it is very likely that the other will perform likewise. As for example, if you invest in shares of two agro-based companies, whose fortune may depend upon the weather condition, you would expect both the companies to perform badly in dry weather.

(b) Negative correlation: If one investment does badly the other will do very well and *vice versa.* As for example, if you invest in the shares of an ice cream company and also in an umbrella-making company, the weather will affect the performance of these two companies differently.

(c) No correlation: The performance of one investment may be independent of how the other performs. As for example, if you hold shares in a steel company and also in a soap-making company, it is likely that there would be no relationship between the profits and returns from each.

The above relationships can be measured by coefficient of correlation, τ. It can be shown that the value of r lies between ± 1 (perfect correlation). A figure close to +1 indicates high positive correlation, a figure close to -1, a high negative correlation and a figure of 0 indicates absence of correlation. Absence of correlation indicates that the variables are independent of each other.

According to portfolio theory, portfolio risk can be reduced by combining investments with negative correlation. The next preference should be in favour of investments which have no significant correlation.

23.7 RISK MANAGEMENT PROCESS

The process of financial risk management comprises strategies that enable an organization to manage the risks associated with financial markets. Risk management is a dynamic process that should evolve with an organization and its business.

Hedging and Correlation

Hedging is the business of seeking assets or events that offset, or has weak or negative correlation to, an organization's financial exposures. Correlation measures the tendency of two assets to move, or not move, together. This tendency is quantified by a coefficient between –1 and +1. Correlation of +1.0 signifies perfect positive correlation and means that two assets can be expected to move together. Correlation of –1.0 signifies perfect negative correlation, which means that two assets can be expected to move together but in opposite directions. The concept of negative correlation is central to hedging and risk management. Risk management involves pairing a financial exposure with an instrument or strategy that is negatively correlated to the exposure. A long futures contract used to hedge a short underlying exposure employs the concept of negative correlation. If the price of the underlying (short) exposure begins to rise, the value of the (long) futures contract will also increase, offsetting some or all of the losses that occur. The extent of the protection offered by the hedge depends on the degree of negative correlation between the two an organization including treasury, sales, marketing, legal, tax, commodity, and corporate finance.

The risk management process involves both internal and external analysis. The first part of the process involves identifying and prioritizing the financial risks facing an organization and understanding their relevance. It may be necessary to examine the organization and its products, management, customers, suppliers, competitors, pricing, industry trends, balance sheet structure, and position in the industry. It is also necessary to consider stakeholders and their objectives and tolerance for risk. Once a clear understanding of the risks emerges, appropriate strategies can be implemented in conjunction with risk management policy. For example, it might be possible to change where and how business is done, thereby reducing the organization's exposure and risk. Alternatively, existing exposures may be managed with derivatives. Another strategy for managing risk is to accept all risks and the possibility of losses.

There are three broad alternatives for managing risk:

1. Do nothing and actively, or passively by default, accept all risks.
2. Hedge a portion of exposures by determining which exposures can and should be hedged.
3. Hedge all exposures possible.

Measurement and reporting of risks provides decision makers with information to execute decisions and monitor outcomes, both before and after strategies are taken to mitigate them. Since the risk management process is ongoing, reporting and feedback can be used to refine the system by modifying or improving strategies. An active decision-making process is an important component of risk management. Decisions about potential loss and risk reduction provide a forum for discussion of important issues and the varying perspectives of stakeholders.

Factors that Impact Financial Rates and Prices

Financial rates and prices are affected by a number of factors. It is essential to understand the factors that impact markets because those factors, in turn, impact the potential risk of an organization.

Factors that Affect Interest Rates

Interest rates are a key component in many market prices and an important economic barometer. They are comprised of the real rate plus a component for expected inflation, since inflation is reduces the purchasing power of a lender's assets. The greater the term to maturity, the greater is the uncertainty. Interest rates are also reflective of supply and demand for funds and credit risk. Interest rates are particularly important to companies and governments because they are the key ingredient in the cost of capital. Most companies and governments require debt financing for expansion and capital projects. When interest rates increase, the impact can be significant on borrowers. Interest rates also affect prices in other financial markets, so their impact is far-reaching. Other components to the interest rate may include a risk premium to reflect the creditworthiness of a borrower. For example, the threat of political or sovereign risk can cause interest rates to rise, sometimes substantially, as investors demand additional compensation for the increased risk of default.

Factors that influence the level of market interest rates include:

(i) Expected levels of inflation
(ii) General economic conditions
(iii) Monetary policy and the stance of the central bank
(iv) Foreign exchange market activity
(v) Foreign investor demand for debt securities
(vi) Levels of sovereign debt outstanding
(vii) Financial and political stability

Yield Curve

The yield curve is a graphical representation of yields for a range of terms to maturity. For example, a yield curve might illustrate yields for maturity from one day (overnight) to 30-year terms. Typically, the rates are zero coupon government rates. Since current interest rates reflect expectations, the yield curve provides useful information about the market's expectations of future interest rates. Implied interest rates for forward-starting terms can be calculated using the information in the yield curve. For example, using rates for one- and two-year maturities, the expected one-year interest rate beginning in one year's time can be determined. The shape of the yield curve is widely analyzed and monitored by market participants. As a gauge of expectations, it is often considered to be a predictor of future economic activity and may provide signals of a pending change in economic fundamentals. The yield curve normally slopes upward with a positive slope, as lenders/investors demand higher rates from borrowers for longer lending terms. Since the chance of a borrower default increases with term to maturity, lenders demand to be compensated accordingly. Interest rates that make up the yield curve are also affected by the expected rate of inflation. Investors demand at least the expected rate of inflation from borrowers, in addition to lending and risk components. If investors expect future inflation to be higher, they will demand greater premiums for longer terms to compensate for this uncertainty. As a result, the longer the term, the higher is the interest rate (all else being equal), resulting in an upward-sloping yield curve. Occasionally, the demand for short-term funds increases substantially, and short-term interest rates may rise above the level of longer term interest rates. This results in an inversion of the yield curve and a downward slope to its appearance. The high cost of short-term funds detracts from gains that would otherwise be obtained through investment and expansion and make the economy vulnerable to slowdown or recession. Eventually, rising interest rates slow the demand for both short-term and long-term funds. A decline in all rates and a return to a normal curve may occur as a result of the slowdown.

Predicting Change — Yield Curve

Indicators that predict changes in economic activity in advance of a slowdown are extremely useful. The yield curve may be one such forecasting tool. Changes in consensus forecasts and actual short-term interest rates, as well as the index of leading indicators, have been used as warning signs of a change in the direction of the economy. Some studies have found that, historically at least, a good predictor of changes in the economy one year to 18 months forward has been the shape of the yield curve :

(a) Expectations theory suggests forward interest rates are representative of expected future interest rates. As a result, the shape of the yield curve and the term structure of rates are reflective of the market's aggregate expectations.

(b) Liquidity theory suggests that investors will choose longer term maturities if they are provided with additional yield that compensates them for lack of liquidity. As a result, liquidity theory supports that forward interest rates possess a liquidity premium and an interest rate expectation component.

(c) Preferred habitat hypothesis suggests that investors who usually prefer one maturity horizon over another can be convinced to change maturity horizons given an appropriate premium. This suggests that the shape of the yield curve depends on the policies of market participants.

(d) Market segmentation theory suggests that different investors have different investment horizons that arise from the nature of their business or as a result of investment restrictions. These prevent them from dramatically changing maturity dates to take advantage of temporary opportunities in interest rates. Companies that have a long investment time horizon will therefore be less interested in taking advantage of opportunities at the short end of the curve.

23.8 FINANCIAL RISK MANAGEMENT: A SELECTIVE HISTORY

No discussion of financial risk management is complete without a brief look at financial market history. Although this history is by no means complete, it illustrates events and highlights of the past several hundred years.

Early Markets

Financial derivatives and markets are often considered to be modern developments, but in many cases they are not. The earliest trading involved commodities, since they are very important to human existence. Long before industrial development, informal commodities markets operated to facilitate the buying and selling of products. Marketplaces have existed in small villages and larger cities for centuries, allowing farmers to trade their products for other items of value.

These market places are the predecessors of modern exchanges. The later development of formalized futures markets enabled producers and buyers to guarantee a price for sales and purchases. The ability to trade product and guarantee a price was particularly important in markets where products had limited life, or where products were too bulky to transport to market often. Forward contracts were used by Flemish traders at medieval trade fairs as early as the twelfth century, where *letters de faire* were used to specify future delivery. Other reports of contractual agreements date back to Phoenician times. Futures contracts also facilitated trading in prized tulip bulbs in seventeenth-century Amsterdam during the infamous *tulip mania* era. In seventeenth-century Japan, rice was an important commodity. As growers began to trade rice tickets for cash, a secondary market began to flourish. The Dojima rice futures market was established in the commerce center of Osaka in 1688 with 1,300 registered rice traders. Rice dealers could sell futures in advance of a harvest in anticipation of lower prices, or alternatively buy rice futures contracts if it looked as though the harvest might be poor and prices high. Rice tickets represented either warehoused rice or rice that would be harvested in the future. Trading at the Dojima market was accompanied by a slow-burning rope in a box suspended from the roof. The day's trading ended when the rope stopped burning. The day's trading might be cancelled, however, if there were no trading price when the rope stopped burning or if it expired early.

North American Developments

In North America, development of futures markets is also closely tied to agricultural markets, in particular the grain markets of the nineteenth century. Volatility in the price of grain made business challenging for both growers and merchant buyers. The Chicago Board of Trade (CBOT), formed in 1848, was the first organized futures exchange in the United States. Its business was non-standardized grain forward contracts. Without a central clearing organization, however, some participants defaulted on their contracts, leaving others unhedged. In response, the CBOT developed futures contracts with standardized terms and the requirement of a performance bond in 1865. These were the first North American futures contracts. The contracts permitted farmers to fix a price for their grain sales in advance of delivery on a standardized basis. For the better part of a century, North American futures trading revolved around the grain industry, where large-scale production and consumption, combined with expense of transport and storage, made grain an ideal futures market commodity.

23.9 PORTFOLIO THEORY AND PORTFOLIOS

Portfolio theory is based on a simple but fundamental insight investor behaviour. These insights are put into a coherent framework for analysis and decision-making. In investment decisions, an investor — may be an individual or a firm — wants to get answers to the following questions: which shares are to be selected and why? How much to be invested in each type? How to minimize risk? One need to resolve all these and similar issues in order to maximize return and minimize risk.

The portfolio theory is concerned with establishing guidelines for building up a portfolio of stocks and shares, or a portfolio of projects. An individual, or a firm, may be interested in an investment decision. The same theory applies to companies, mutual fund and stock market investors with capital projects to invest in. Each one of them needs to know which shares / projects to select and how much to be invested in each and *how to minimize the risk.* The diversification approach is simply to follow the well-known adage: "do not keep all your eggs in one basket". The theory, therefore, focuses on fundamental insights into a coherent framework for rational analysis and decision-making such that benefits from the decisions can be maximized, or risk minimized.

A portfolio is the combination of different investments that continue an investor's total holding. It may represent an investment in stocks and shares or investments in capital projects. Such investment may be made by an individual, a company, an investment banker or a mutual fund. One of the features of the portfolio theory is that an investor should analyze the portfolio in its entirety and not merely one or two in isolation.

Example

	Investor A		**Investor B**
Shares of UTI Ltd.	20%	Shares of ABC Ltd.	30%
Shares of IDBI	25%	Shares of ICICI	40%
Shares of TISCO	30%	Shares of UTI Ltd,	30%
Share of Hindustan Lever	20%		
Shares of Tata Tea	5%		
Total fund investment	100%	Total fund investment	100%

While A's portfolio comprises shares of five companies, that of B comprises shares of three companies only. In each case, the combination of the shares constitutes the portfolio. If A and B are rational investor, they might have given adequate thought in selecting the type of share for investment as also the amount of money that has been invested in each type, given the total amount of money available for investment.

Risk: An investor generally wants to maximize gains from investments with as minimum risk as possible. Here, risk represents variability of expected return from investments. Risk can be reduced by diversification. That is, an investor who put all his/her money into one type of share risks everything on the fortunes of that investment. A rational approach would be to spread his/her investments into different types such that losses on some may be compensated by gains on others. The risk-return relationship and diversification as a means of reduction of risk have been discussed on chapter 3 — (see para 3.2, 3.3)

Practical Example

Type	Return (R) %	Funds invested (Proportion)	Weighted average of Returns (R × W)
A	20	0.4	8
B	15	0.2	3
C	25	0.4	10
		1.0	Expected Return 21

The risk in an investment, or in a number of investments, is that the actual return is not the same as the expected return — it may be higher or lower than the expected one. Thus, variability of returns is the measure of the risk. Standard deviation is generally regarded as the best measures of variability or dispersion.

Illustration

Year	Share D Expected return %	Share F Expected return %
1	13.0	15
2	6.5	14
3	24.0	17
4	18.5	16
Average return	15.5	15.5

Although the average expected return from both types of investments is the same (15.4%), Share D shows a greater variability of returns and is riskier than Share F. In other words, returns from Share D fluctuate widely from year to year. Variability in returns can be measured as the standard deviation of expected returns. Thus, standard deviation of returns is the measure of the risk. Higher the standard deviation the greater the risk and *vice versa*.

When probabilities of actual returns can be estimated, standard deviation as a measure of risk is computed weighted by the estimated probabilities. The expected value of return here is:

Estimated returns × probabilities of occurrence.

The standard deviation is calculated based on the expected value rather than the average rate of return. The following formulae may be used in computing expected return and risk of individual investments.

$$E(R) = \sum_{i=1}^{n} R_i p_i$$

Where, $E(R)$ = expected value of rate of return

R_i = the return from outcome i

p_i = probability of occurrence of i

n = the number of outcomes.

$$\sigma = \sqrt{\text{Variance}} = \sqrt{\sum_{i=1}^{n}(x_i - \bar{x})^2 p_i}$$

Where, $\bar{x}$ = expected rate of return = E(R)

x_i = rate of return from an investment i

p_i = probability of occurrence i

n = the number of outcomes.

Standard deviation (duly weighted by the probability of outcomes) is the measure of risk. The greater the value of the standard deviation the higher is the risk and *vice versa*. The variance is the square of standard deviation.

Illustration

Return from investment (%)	Probability of occurence	Expected value (%)
10	0.3	3.0
8	0.2	1.6
12	0.3	3.6
14	0.2	2.8
	1.0	$\bar{X}$ = 11.0

Return (X)	$(X - \bar{X})$	$(X - \bar{X})^2$	p	$p(\bar{X} - X)^2$
10	– 1	1	0.3	0.3
8	– 3	9	0.2	1.8
12	+ 1	1	0.3	0.3
14	+3	9	0.2	1.8
			Variance =	4.2

$\therefore$ Standard deviation = $\sqrt{4.2} = 2.05\%$

Thus, expected return from investments is 11% with a standard deviation of 2.05%.

There is a relation between risk and return. Low risk investments usually give low returns. High risk investments might give high returns, but with more possibility of disappointing results. So, how does holding a portfolio of investments affect expected returns and risks? We this important question needs to be assured.

23.10 FINANCIAL DERIVATIVES

Most individual and firms face financial risk due to changes in exchange rates, interest rates and stock market prices. Financial instruments have been developed for the management of such risk. These instruments are known as financial derivatives.

Concepts of Derivatives

The word derivatives indicate that it has no independent value but its value is derived from the value of the cash asset. A cash asset represents an asset that is bought/sold in the market on normal delivery terms. Derivatives are future contracts, *i.e.,* contracts for delivery and payment on a specified future date. **Derivatives are used as risk management tools. The underlying idea of derivatives trading is hedging against risks.**

Hedging Risk

The term hedge means to "secure oneself against loss on speculation by compensating transactions on the other side". Hedging is the equivalent of insurance facility against risk from variation of prices in the market. A world without hedging facility is like a world without insurance with respect to the particular kind of risk. As pointed out earlier, financial derivatives can insulate firms or individuals from different types of risk.

In order to hedge risk, it must first be identified. Once identified, efforts are made to quantify the risk with probabilities and simulations. The idea is to determine what is likely to happen if the underlying situation changes. As for example, if interest rate changes we would like to know what happens to the value of our security or financial position with a change in interest rates.

Once the risk is identified, the idea in hedging is to take a *position opposite to the exposure*. This can be done with futures contracts, with forward contracts, with options or with swaps.

The principles of hedging are the same regardless of the type of hedge undertaken. Suppose we want to hedge an asset the firm owns with an offsetting instrument. That is, the downward price movements in the value of the instrument with which we hedge. Suppose the asset owned by the firm is X and the instrument with which we hedge the risk is Y. The expected change in values of these two instruments can be shown as follows:

$$\text{Value } \overline{X} = a + \delta \text{ (value } \overline{Y})$$

Where, both changes in value are expected, a is constant, δ (delta) reflects the sensitivity of expected changes in X to changes in the value of y. the delta (δ) is known as the *hedge ratio* and tells us the number of units of Y that should be used to hedge the position in X.

Delta (δ) is not constant over time but is ever changing. Consequently, the hedge ratio is to be adjusted over time if risk is to be minimized. This adjustment is known as the *dynamic hedging* and it must be done having regard to the transaction costs. The higher the transaction costs the fewer the adjustment that should be made and *vice versa*. Dynamic hedging requires continuous monitoring with a view to controlling the risk.

However, risk cannot be eliminated altogether as perfect hedges seldom exist. The financial manager must select the best hedging vehicle available to minimize the risk involved.

Most individual and firms face financial risk due to changes in exchange rates, interest rates and stock market prices. Financial instruments have been developed for the management of such risk. These instruments are known as financial derivatives.

❑❑❑

24 Derivative Market and Commodities

PART –1

24.1 WHAT ARE DERIVATIVES?

Derivatives are anything that "derives" its value from another instrument. Options are derivatives of stocks or indexes. Where they trade is the market. In a broader sense a derivative can be defined as something which derives its value from an underlying product being a stock, currency, commodity or anything that carries a market price. The market price of a product is subject to fluctuations due to various factors effecting its demand and supply thereby associating itself to various risk factors. So, derivative is a by-product of the core product which can be used to hedge, speculate and also undertake arbitrage activities.

The word 'derivative' originates from mathematics and refers to a variable, which has been derived from another variable. Derivatives are so called because they have no value of their own. They derive their value from the value of some other asset, which is known as the underlying.

"**Derivatives** are specialized contracts which signify an agreement or an option to buy or sell the underlying asset of the derivate up to a certain time in the future at a prearranged price, the exercise price."

The contract also has a fixed expiry period mostly in the range of 3 to 12 months from the date of commencement of the contract. The value of the contract depends on the expiry period and also on the price of the underlying asset. There are many types of financial instruments that are grouped under the term derivatives, but options/futures and swaps are among the most common. Options or futures are different kinds of contracts where one party agrees to pay a fee to another for the right to buy or sell something to the other.

24.2 COMMON TYPES OF DERIVATIVES

Derivatives are a tool used by investors to manage risk. It is a complex area and one that requires a great deal of study and application to master. In brief, a derivative gets its value from another financial product. There are two primary types of derivative contracts: over-the-counter (OTC) derivatives and exchange-traded derivatives. They differ from each other in the ways they are traded on the market. There are also three major classes of derivatives: some types of warrants, futures and exchange-traded options.

Futures. (Also sometimes called "forwards") are contracts that say an asset block will be sold or bought on an agreed future date

Options. An option gives the contract holder the right to buy or sell on a specified date in the future – but they are under no obligation to take up this "option".

Warrants. A tool used for trading on the stock exchange. They can be held over shares, currency, an index or commodity. Warrants (and options) allow the holder to earn additional income from their shares or to protect value of their existing assets.

Types of warrants

There are also a range of different kinds of warrants commonly in use. They are:

(i) Equity call and put warrants

(ii) Installment warrants

(iii) Endowment warrants

(iv) Low exercise price warrants

Options are traded electronically by brokers on a computerized market called the Derivatives Trading Facility (DTF). Using this system the first order placed is the first order processed and at the end of the day any unexercised orders lapse. Warrants are traded using the ASX share trading system.

24.3 DERIVATIVES MARKET

The **derivatives market** is the financial market for derivatives, financial instruments like futures contracts or options, which are derived from other forms of assets.. The Derivatives Market is meant as the market where exchange of derivatives takes place. Derivatives are one type of securities whose price is derived from the underlying assets. And value of these derivatives is determined by the fluctuations in the underlying assets. These underlying assets are most commonly stocks, bonds, currencies, interest rates, commodities and market indices. As Derivatives are merely contracts between two or more parties, anything like weather data or amount of rain can be used as underlying assets. The Derivatives can be classified as Future Contracts, Forward Contracts, Options, Swaps and Credit Derivatives.

Derivative Market
Derivative (Finance)

(A) Options:	
Terms	Credit spread · Debit spread · Exercise · Expiration · Moneyness · Open interest · Pin risk · Risk-free rate · Strike price · The Greeks · Volatility
Vanilla options	Bond option · Call · Employee stock option · Fixed income · FX · Option styles ·Put warrants
Exotic Option	Asian · Barrier · Binary · Cliquet · Compound option · Forward start option · Interest rate option · Lookback · Mountain range · Rainbow option · Swaption
• Combination	Collar · Fence · Iron butterfly · Iron condor · Straddle · Strangle · Covered call · Protective put · Risk reversal
• Option spreads	Backspread · Bear spread · Bull spread · Butterfly spread · Calendar spread · Diagonal spread · Ratio spread · Vertical spread · Intermarket Spread
• Valuation of options	Binomial · Black · Black–Scholes · Finite difference · Put–call parity · Simulation ·Trinomial
(B) Swaps:	Basic swap · Constant maturity swap · Credit default swap · Currency swap · Equity swap · Forex swap · Inflation swap · Interest rate swap · Total return swap · Variance swap · Volatility swap · Correlation swap · Conditional variance swap
(C) Forwards and futures:	Backwardation · Commodity futures · Contango · Currency future · Financial future · Forward market · Forward price · Forward rate · interest rate future· Margin · Pricing of Forwards · Pricing of Future · Single-stock futures
(D) Other derivatives:	CLN · Contract for difference · CPPI · Credit derivative · ELN · Equity derivative · Foreign exchange derivative · Fund derivative · Inflation derivatives · Interest rate derivative · PRDC · Real estate derivative · Real options
(E) Market issues:	Tax policy · Consumer debt · Corporate debt · Government debt · Late 2000s recession

24.4 TYPES OF DERIVATIVE MARKET

The market can be divided into two, that for **exchange-traded derivatives** and that for **over-the-counter derivatives**. The legal nature of these products is very different as well as the way they are traded, though many market participants are active in both.

Exchange Traded Derivatives are those derivatives which are traded through specialized derivative exchanges whereas Over the Counter Derivatives are those which are privately traded between two parties and involves no exchange or intermediary. Swaps, Options and Forward Contracts are traded in Over the Counter Derivatives Market or OTC market.

The main participants of OTC market are the Investment Banks, Commercial Banks, Govt. Sponsored Enterprises and Hedge Funds. The investment banks market the derivatives through traders to the clients like hedge funds and the rest.

In the Exchange Traded Derivatives Market or Future Market, exchange acts as the main party and by trading of derivatives actually risk is traded between two parties. One party who purchases future contract is said to go "long" and the person who sells the future contract is said to go "short". The holder of the "long" position owns the future contract and earns profit from it if the price of the underlying security goes up in the future. On the contrary, holder of the "short" position is in a profitable position if the price of the underlying security goes down, as he has already sold the future contract. So, when a new future contract is introduced, the total position in the contract is zero as no one is holding that for short or long.

Exchange Traded Derivatives Market or Future Market

Futures exchange

Futures exchanges, such as Euronext liffe and the Chicago Mercantile Exchange, trade in standardized derivative contracts. These are options contracts and futures contracts on a whole range of underlying products. The members of the exchange hold positions in these contracts with the exchange, who acts as central counterparty. When one party goes long (buys a futures contract), another goes short (sells). When a new contract is introduced, the total position in the contract is zero. Therefore, the sum of all the long positions must be equal to the sum of all the short positions. In other words, risk is transferred from one party to another.

Market Size for the Exchange Traded Derivatives

The **equity derivative market size** is about $114.1 trillion. The open interest in the futures and options market grew by 38% while the interest rate futures grew by 42%. Hence the derivative market size for the futures and the options market was $ 49 trillion.

Credit Derivatives

The **credit derivative market size** hiked to $ 4.5 trillion from $ 0.7 trillion in 2001. The increase in the market size for the credit derivatives is also due to the increase in the trading in the **synthetic collateral Debt obligations** and also due to the **electronic trading systems** that have come to exist.

Tracing back to the history of the derivative market, we have seen that the **derivative market size** played a vital role in the regime of commerce and finance over a period of thousand years. In 1750 B.C. in Mesopotamia, the derivative contracts were written on clay tablets.

Futures' trading has taken place in the Japanese market where rice had been used as the warehouse receipts. Forward trading took place in the US through the Chicago Board of trade since 1849. The derivative market size is estimated by the Bank of International Settlements.

Over-the-counter markets

Tailor-made derivatives not traded on a futures exchange are traded on **over-the-counter markets**, also known as the OTC market. These consist of investment banks who have traders who make markets in these derivatives, and clients such as hedge funds, commercial banks, government sponsored enterprises, etc. Products that are always traded over-the-counter are swaps, forward rate agreements, forward contracts, credit derivatives, etc.

Market Size of the Global Over-the-Counter Derivatives

There was a 24% rise in the face value of all the derivative contracts that were traded through the **Over-the-Counter market** and reached a derivative market size of $70,000 billion. This simply reflects the fact that the face value of the derivative contracts has multiplied 30 times the size of the US economy. Since the inception of the decade the **derivative market size** has almost quadrupled. With the increase in the size of the **Over-the-Counter derivative market,** notable increases were recorded for **foreign exchange, interest rate, equity and commodity based derivative.**

The increase in the derivative market size **does not imply** the increase in the risk taking of the investors. Even then, the overshoot in the face value of the derivative contracts shows the pivotal role that these derivative instruments play in the financial market of today.

Global: The UK remains the leading derivatives centers worldwide, with its share of turnover stable at 43% in 2007. The US is the only other major location with 24% of trading. Interest rate instruments remain the key driver of trading, accounting for 88% of UK turnover and 70% of global notional value. Derivatives based on foreign-exchange contracts account for a further 10% of notional value, with credit, equity-linked and commodity contracts also important. Energy, metal and freight derivatives have grown rapidly in recent years. The euro's share of interest rate derivatives turnover worldwide has risen to 39% while the US dollar has fallen to 32%: Pound sterling and yen also increased their market share over the past three years. Trading is becoming more concentrated among the largest banks, while other financial institutions such as hedge funds, mutual funds, insurance companies and smaller banks have become much bigger users of derivatives.

24.5 TYPES OF TRADERS IN A DERIVATIVES MARKET

Hedgers: Hedgers are those who protect themselves from the risk associated with the price of an asset by using derivatives. A person keeps a close watch upon the prices discovered in trading and when the comfortable price is reflected according to his wants, he sells futures contracts. In this way he gets an assured fixed price of his produce.

In general, hedgers use futures for protection against adverse future price movements in the underlying cash commodity. Hedgers are often businesses, or individuals, who at one point or another deal in the underlying cash commodity.

Take an example: A Hedger pay more to the farmer or dealer of a produce if its prices go up. For protection against higher prices of the produce, he hedge the risk exposure by buying enough future contracts of the produce to cover the amount of produce he expects to buy. Since cash and futures prices do tend to move in tandem, the futures position will profit if the price of the produce rise enough to offset cash loss on the produce.

Speculators: Speculators are some what like a middle man. They are never interested in actual owing the commodity. They will just buy from one end and sell it to the other in anticipation of future price movements. They actually bet on the future movement in the price of an asset.

They are the second major group of futures players. These participants include independent floor traders and investors. They handle trades for their personal clients or brokerage firms.

Buying a futures contract in anticipation of price increases is known as 'going long' Selling a futures contract in anticipation of a price decrease is known as 'going short'. Speculative participation in futures trading has increased with the availability of alternative methods of participation.

Speculators have certain advantages over other investments they are as follows:

1. If the trader's judgment is good, he can make more money in the futures market faster because prices tend, on average, to change more quickly than real estate or stock prices.

2. Futures are highly leveraged investments. The trader puts up a small fraction of the value of the underlying contract as margin, yet he can ride on the full value of the contract as it moves up and down. The money he puts up is not a down payment on the underlying contract, but a performance bond. The actual value of the contract is only exchanged on those rare occasions when delivery takes place.

Speculation in the Futures market

Speculation is all about taking position in the futures market without having the underlying. Speculators operate in the market with motive to make money. They take: *Naked positions* – Position in any future contract. *Spread positions* – Opposite positions in two future contracts. This is a conservative speculative strategy.

Speculators bring liquidity to the system, provide insurance to the hedgers and facilitate the price discovery in the market.

Arbitrators: According to dictionary definition, a person who has been officially chosen to make a decision between two people or groups who do not agree is known as Arbitrator. In commodity market Arbitrators are the person who takes the advantage of a discrepancy between prices in two different markets. If he finds future prices of a commodity edging out with the cash price, he will take offsetting positions in both the markets to lock in a profit. Moreover the commodity futures investor is not charged interest on the difference between margin and the full contract value.

Other participants include clearing houses or clearing corporations, brokers, commodity futures trading commission, commodity pool operators, commodity trading advisors, financial institutions and banks, futures exchange, and futures commission merchants.

24.6 UNDERSTANDING DERIVATIVE CONTRACTS

Exotic derivatives

The types of derivative financial instrument which have been described in this section, both exchange traded and over the counter, are commonly and widely used by large companies and financial institutions to hedge risk (or sometimes to speculate). Such products are sometimes referred to as 'vanilla' or 'plain vanilla'.

More innovative and less usual derivative products are often called 'exotic'. The term has no precise meaning. Exotic derivatives have been compared to pornography: both are easier to recognize on sight than to define and the definition of both is dependent on time and place. Interest rate and currency swaps were exotic when they first appeared in the 1980s, but are now standard financial tools. Similarly, proprietary products originally developed by merchant banks or other financial institutions to meet the needs of particular clients may in time diffuse more widely into the market.

The 'exotic' label is commonly applied to the following:

(i) Derivatives with a non-standard subject matter, developed for a particular client or a particular market. For example, a telecommunications company might use a derivative whose underlying subject matter is bandwidth.

(ii) One example is a ladder option: if the price of the underlying asset rises above a certain threshold level, the option holder is guaranteed a minimum payout, even if the price subsequently falls. There may be a number of such steps.

(iii) The investor can therefore lock in the increase in value – although they will pay a hefty premium for the privilege. There are many other types of 'exotic' option.

(iv) The more complex forms of structured product – A structured product is a combination of a loan relationship (or more than one loan relationship) with one or more derivative contracts. A corporate bond with an attached equity warrant is a simple example of a structured note.

(v) Inland Revenue staffs who encounter an unfamiliar type of derivative should ask the company for a non-technical explanation and, if necessary, obtain the contract documentation in order to understand what the company will pay and receive.

24.7 FUTURE OF DERIVATIVES IN INDIA

Derivatives trading began in 1865 when the Chicago Board of Trade (CBOT) listed the first "exchange traded" derivatives contract in the USA. These contracts were called "**futures contracts**". In 1919, the Chicago Butter and Egg Board, a spin-off of CBOT, was reorganized to allow futures trading. Its name was changed to Chicago Mercantile Exchange (CME). The first stock index futures contract was traded at Kansas City Board of Trade. Currently the most popular stock index futures contract in the world is based on the Standard and Poor's 500 Index traded on the CME. In April 1973, the Chicago Board of Options Exchange was set up specifically for the purpose of trading in options. The market for options developed so rapidly that by early 80s the number of shares underlying the option contract sold each day exceeded the daily volume of shares traded on the New York Stock Exchange. And there has been no looking back ever since.

Derivatives in India

Derivatives markets have been in existence in India in some form or other for a long time. In the area of commodities, the Bombay Cotton Trade Association started futures trading in 1875 and, by the early 1900s India had one of the world's largest futures industries. In 1952 the government banned cash settlement and options trading and derivatives trading shifted to informal forwards markets. In recent years, government policy has changed, allowing for an increased role for market-based pricing and less suspicion of derivatives trading. The ban on futures trading of many commodities was lifted starting in the early 2000s, and national electronic commodity exchanges were created.

In the equity markets, a system of trading called "badla" involving some elements of forwards trading had been in existence for decades. However, the system led to a number of undesirable practices and it was prohibited off and on till the Securities and Exchange Board of India (SEBI) banned it for good in 2001. A series of reforms of the stock market between 1993 and 1996 paved the way for the development of exchange-traded equity derivatives markets in India. In 1993, the government created the NSE in collaboration with state-owned financial institutions. NSE improved the efficiency and transparency of the stock markets by offering a fully automated screen-based trading system and real-time price dissemination. In 1995, a prohibition on trading options was lifted. In 1996, the NSE sent a proposal to SEBI for listing exchange-traded derivatives.

The economic liberalization of the early nineties facilitated the introduction of derivatives based on interest rates and foreign exchange. A system of market-determined exchange rates was adopted by India in March 1993. In August 1994, the rupee was made fully convertible on current account. These reforms allowed increased integration between domestic and international markets, and created a need to manage currency risk. The easing of various restrictions on the free movement of interest rates resulted in the need to manage interest rate risk.

The Securities and Exchange Board of India (SEBI) allowed trading in equities-based derivatives on stock exchanges in June 2000. Accordingly **the National Stock Exchange** (NSE) and the Bombay Stock Exchange (BSE) introduced trading in futures on June 9, 2000 and June 12, 2000 respectively. Currently futures and options turnover on the NSE is ₹ 7,000-8,000 crore approximately. In India stock index options were introduced from July 2,2001.

BSE created history on June 9, 2000 by launching the first Exchange traded Index Derivative Contract *i.e.* futures on the capital market benchmark index - the BSE Sensex. The inauguration of trading was done by Prof. J.R. Varma, member of SEBI and Chairman of the committee responsible for formulation of risk containment measures for the Derivatives market. The first historical trade of 5 contracts of June series was done on June 9, 2000 at 9:55:03 a.m. between M/s Kaji and Maulik Securities Pvt. Ltd. and M/s Emkay Share and Stock Brokers Ltd. at the rate of 4755.

In the sequence of product innovation, the exchange commenced trading in Index Options on Sensex on June 1, 2001. Stock options were introduced on 31 stocks on July 9, 2001 and single stock futures were launched on November 9, 2002.

September 13, 2004 marked another milestone in the history of Indian Capital Markets, the day on which the Bombay Stock Exchange launched Weekly Options, a unique product unparallel in derivatives markets, both domestic and international. BSE permitted trading in weekly contracts in options in the shares of four leading companies namely Reliance, Satyam, State Bank of India, and Tisco in addition to the flagship index-Sensex.

24.8 INTRODUCTION OF FUTURES IN INDIA

The first derivative product to be introduced in the Indian securities market is going to be ***"Index Futures"***. In the world, first index futures were traded in U.S. on Kansas City Board of Trade (KCBT) on Value Line Arithmetic Index (VLAI) in 1982.

December 14, 1995	The NSE sought SEBI's permission to trade index futures.
November 18, 1996	The LC Gupta Committee set up to draft a policy framework for index futures.
May 11, 1998	The LC Gupta Committee submitted a report on the policy framework for index futures.
July 7, 1999	Reserve Bank of India gave permission for OTC forward rate agreements and interest rate swaps.
May 24, 2000	SIMEX chose Nifty for trading futures and options on an Indian index.
May 25, 2000	SEBI allowed the NSE and the BSE to trade in index futures.
June 9, 2000	Trading of the BSE Sensex futures commenced on the BSE.
June 12, 2000	Trading of Nifty futures commenced on the NSE.
September 25, 2000	Nifty futures trading commenced on the SGX.

24.9 TYPES OF DERIVATIVE INSTRUMENTS IN INDIA

Derivative instruments are classified as:

Forward Contracts, Futures Contracts, Options, Swaps

Derivatives can also be classified as either forward-based (*e.g.*, futures, forward contracts, and swap contracts), option-based (*e.g.*, call or put option), or combinations of the two. A forward-based contract obligates one party to buy and a counter party to sell an underlying asset, such as foreign currency or a commodity, with equal risk at a future date at an agreed-on price. Option-based contracts (*e.g.*, call options, put options, caps and floors) provide the holder with a right, but not an obligation to buy or sell an underlying financial instrument, foreign currency, or commodity at an agreed-on price during a specified time period or at a specified date.

Forward Contracts: Forward contracts are negotiated between two parties, with no formal regulation or exchange, to purchase (long position) and sell (short position) a specific quantity of a specific quantity of a commodity (*i.e.*, corn and gold), foreign currency, or financial instrument (*i.e.*, bonds and stock) at a specified price (delivery price), with delivery or settlement at a specified future date (maturity date). The price of the underlying asset for immediate delivery is known as the spot price.

Forward contracts may be entered into through an agreement without a cash payment, provided the forward rate is equal to the current market rate. Forward contracts are often used to hedge the entire price changed of a commodity, a foreign currency, or a financial instrument irrespective of a price increase or decrease.

Futures Contracts Futures are standardized contracts traded on a regulated exchange to make or take delivery of a specified quantity of a commodity, a foreign currency, or a financial instrument at a specified price, with delivery or settlement at a specified future date. Futures contracts involve Treasury bonds, agricultural commodities, stock indices, interest-earning assets, and foreign currency.

A futures contract is entered into through an organized exchange, using banks and brokers. These organized exchanges have clearing houses, which may be financial institutions or part of the futures exchange. They interpose themselves between the buyer and the seller, guarantee obligations, and make futures liquid with low credit risk. Although no payment is made upon entering into a futures contract, since the underlying (*i.e.*, interest rate, share price, or commodity price) is at-the-market, subsequent value changes require daily mark-to-marking by cash settlement (*i.e.*, disbursed gains and daily collected losses). Similarly, margin requirements involve deposits from both parties to ensure any financial liabilities.

Futures contracts are used to hedge the entire price change of a commodity, a foreign currency, or a financial instrument since the contract value and underlying price change symmetrically.

Options are rights to buy or sell. For example, the purchaser of an option has the right, but not the obligation, to buy or sell a specified quantity of a particular commodity, a foreign currency, or a financial instrument, at a specified price, during a specified period of time (American option) or on a specified date (European option). An option may be settled by taking delivery of the underlying or by cash settlement, with risk limited to the premium.

The two main types of option contracts are call options and put options. while some others include stock (or equity) options, foreign currency options, options on futures, caps, floors, collars, and swaptions.

American call options provide the holder with the right to acquire an underlying product (*e.g.*, stock) at an exercise or strike price, throughout the option term. The holder pays a premium for the right to benefit from the appreciation in the underlying. American put options provide the holder with the right to sell the underlying product (*e.g.*, stock) at a certain exercise or strike price, throughout the option term. The holder gains as the market price of the underlying (stock price) falls below the exercise price. An interest rate cap is an option that allows a cap purchaser to limit exposure to increasing interest rates on its variable-rate debt instruments. An interest rate floor is an option that allows a floor purchaser to limit exposure to decreasing interest rates on its variable-rate investments.

Generally, option contracts are used to hedge a one-directional movement in the underlying commodity, foreign currency, or financial instrument.

Swaps

A swap is a flexible, private, forward-based contract or agreement, generally between two counter parties to exchange streams of cash flows based on an agreed-on (or notional) principal amount over a specified period of time in the future.

Swaps are usually entered into at-the-money (*i.e.*, with minimal initial cash payments because fair value is zero), through brokers or dealers who take an up-front cash payment or who ad just the rate to bear default risk. The two most prevalent swaps are interest rate swaps and foreign currency swaps, while others include equity swaps, commodity swaps.

Swaptions are options on swaps that provide the holder with the right to enter into a swap at a specified future date at specified terms (stand-alone option in a swap) or to extend or terminate the life of an existing swap (embedded option on a swap).

Swap contracts are used to hedge entire price changes (symmetrically) related to an identified hedged risk, such as interest rate or foreign currency risk, since both counter parties gain or lose equally.

24.10 RISK MANAGEMENT

The main types of risk characteristics associated with derivatives are:

Basis Risk: This is the spot (cash) price of the underlying asset being hedged, less the price of the derivative contract used to hedge the asset.

Credit Risk: Credit risk or default risk evolves from the possibility that one of the parties to a derivative contract will not satisfy its financial obligations under the derivative contract.

Market Risk: This is the potential financial loss due to adverse changes in the fair value of a derivative. Market risk encompasses legal risk, control risk, and accounting risk.

Risk Management Through Futures

Basic objective of introduction of futures is to manage the price risk. Index futures are used to manage the systemic risk, vested in the investment in securities.

Hedge terminology

Long hedge – When you hedge by going long in futures market. Short hedge – When you hedge by going short in futures market. Cross hedge – When a futures contract is not available on an asset, you hedge your position in cash market on this asset by going long or short on the futures for another asset whose prices are closely associated with that of your underlying. Hedge Contract Month – Maturity month of the contract through which hedge is accomplished. Hedge Ratio – Number of future contracts required to hedge the position.

PART – II: COMMODITY

24.11 COMMODITY TREND ANALYSIS – SUPPORT AND RESISTANCE

There are two components to trend, direction and duration. Markets trend in three directions, up, down and sideways. Markets do not move consistently in one direction, but tend to be erratic. Within this erratic behaviour a trend will be present. Trends are characterized by a series of peaks and troughs. An uptrend is a series of rising peaks and troughs, a downtrend shows a series of descending peaks and troughs. A sideways tend is a series of horizontal peaks and troughs, with prices moving within a range, failing to make new highs at the top of the price range and failing to make new lows at the bottom of the price range.

Trend duration is also made up of three time periods; major, intermediate and minor. The major trend will have duration of six to eight months or longer and is best illustrated by weekly and monthly bar charts. Within the major trend significant corrections or reversals of trend will be present; these would be intermediate and minor trends within the major trend. The intermediate trend lasts from three weeks to three months, and the minor trend is anything less, from two to three weeks in duration.

Support and resistance are tools used by technicians to help them identify and follow price trends. Horizontal lines are drawn on the bar chart to indicate areas of support and resistance. The troughs or reaction lows on a price chart are identified as support. Support is an area on the chart where buying pressure overtakes selling pressure and the market reacts higher. Usually support is identified by a previous reaction low or trough on the bar chart. Resistance is an area on the chart where selling pressure overtakes buying pressure and the market reacts lower. A resistance level is identified by a previous price high or peak on the bar chart.

The concepts of support and resistance are critically important tools used by technicians to help them identify and follow trends. Lines are drawn on the chart to indicate areas of price support, price resistance and price trends. In an uptrend, the resistance levels represent pauses in the uptrend which serve to temporarily halt the price advance. In like manner, in a downtrend, support levels will temporarily halt a price decline. Trend lines are drawn above or below the market action depending upon the direction of the move. During an uptrend a line would be drawn from the first significant low to the next, extending across the page from left to right. (Fig. 24.1). If the uptrend is valid you will find the price will move to, or close to, the uptrend line on corrections and then move higher. Each time a trend line is tested and holds, the moresignificant it becomes. Each time a previous support or resistance level is being tested the prevailing trend of the market is critically analyzed by the technician. Failure to exceed a previous resistance peak in an uptrend, or to break a previous support low in a downtrend, provides a warning that the existing trend may be changing. The testing of these support and resistance levels form pictures on the charts that suggest either a trend reversal or simply a pause in the prevailing trend. The basic building blocks on which price patterns are based however are *support and resistance*.

Support and resistance levels reverse roles once they are decisively broken . In other words if the price penetrates a resistance level, then it will generally move upward to the next resistance level, such that the previous resistance level will now become an area of support. The longer the period of time that prices trade in a support or resistance area, the more significant that area becomes. For example, if prices trade sideways for three weeks in a support area before moving higher, that support area would be more significant than if only three days of trading had occurred. The reason for this is that there are now more participants in the market with a vested interest in that support area which will hold prices up.

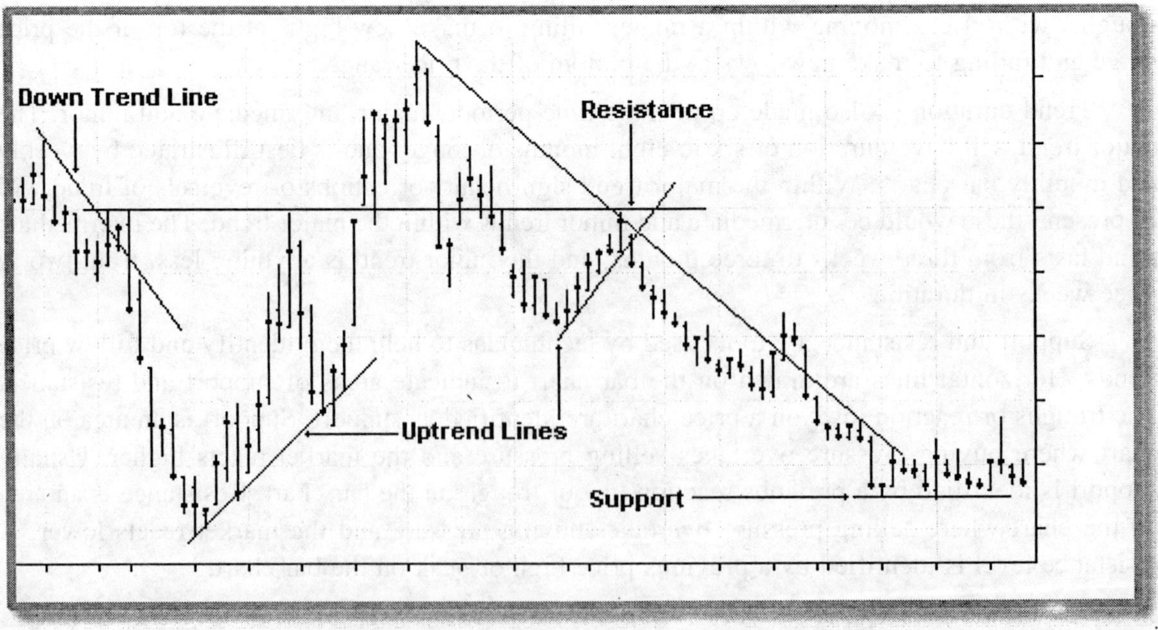

Fig. 24.1. Trendlines, Support and Resistance

Understanding Volume and Open Interest in Commodity Futures

Technicians utilize a three dimensional approach to market analysis which includes a study of price, volume and open interest. Of these three, price is the most important. However, volume and open interest provide important secondary confirmation of the price action on a chart and often provide a lead indication of an impending change of trend. For beginning students of the market these two concepts tend to be somewhat confusing but are very important concepts to understand in-undertaking a thorough analysis of market action.

Volume represents the total amount of trading activity or contracts that have changed hands in a given commodity market for a single trading day. The greater the amount of trading during a market session the higher will be the trading volume. As mentioned earlier, a higher volume bar on the chart means that the trading activity was heavier for that day. Another way to look at this is that the volume represents a measure of intensity or pressure behind a price trend. The greater the volume the more we can expect the existing trend to continue rather than reverse. Technicians believe that volume precedes price, meaning that the loss of upside price pressure in an uptrend or downside pressure in a downtrend will show up in the volume figures before presenting itself as a reversal in trend on the bar chart.

Open Interest is the total number of outstanding contracts that are held by market participants at the end of each day. Where volume measures the pressure or intensity behind a price trend, open interest measures the flow of money into the futures market. For each seller of a futures contract there must be a buyer of that contract. Thus a seller and a buyer combine to create only one contract. Therefore, to determine the total open interest for any given market we need only to know the totals from one side or the other, buyers or sellers, not the sum of both.

Each trade completed on the floor of a futures exchange has an impact upon the level of open interest for that day. For example, if both parties to the trade are initiating a new position (one new buyer and one new seller), open interest will increase by one contract. If both traders are closing an existing or old position (one old buyer and one old seller) open interest will decline by one contract. The third and final possibility is one old trader passing off his position to a new trader (one old buyer sells to one new buyer). In this case the open interest will not change. By monitoring the changes in the open interest figures at the end of each trading day, some conclusions about the day's activity can be drawn. Increasing open interest means that new money is flowing into the marketplace. The result will be that the present trend (up, down or sideways) will continue. Declining open interest means that the market is liquidating and implies that the prevailing price trend is coming to an end. Knowledge of open interest can prove useful toward the end of major market moves. A leveling off of steadily increasing open interest following a sustained price advance is often an early warning of the end to an up trending or bull market.

The relationship between the prevailing price trend, volume, and open interest can be summarized by the following table :

Price	Volume	Open Interest	Interpretation
Rising	Rising	Rising	Market is Strong
Rising	Falling	Falling	Market is Weakening
Falling	Rising	Rising	Market is Weak
Falling	Falling	Falling	Market is Strengthening

It is important to understand that the commodity price chart only records the data. In itself, it has little value. By monitoring the price trend, volume and open interest the technician is better able to gauge the buying or selling pressure behind market moves. This information can be used to confirm a price move or warn that a price move is not to be trusted. This will provide you with valuable information to develop a suitable pricing strategy and an appropriate production-marketing plan for your farming operation.

24.12 CHART PATTERNS AND TECHNICAL ANALYSIS OF COMMODITIES

One of the major premises of technical analysis is that *history repeats itself.* For the technician the recurrence of identifiable patterns and formations that have preceded important movements of the market in the past provide important clues as to the probable direction of price movement in the future. Chart patterns are formations that appear on the charts which provide you with forecasting tools of impending price movement. Some patterns are more reliable than others for price forecasting. **None of the chart patterns are infallible**. They have a high probability of success but are not guaranteed to work all of the time. Technicians must always be on the alert for chart signs that prove their analysis to be incorrect. After trend lines, support and resistance lines have been drawn on a chart, one of the most important and most difficult decisions you will have to make is determining the timing of entering and exiting the market as well as determining when a major top in a rising market or a major bottom in a declining market has occurred.

There are two types of patterns that develop on charts, the *reversal pattern* and the *continuation pattern*. Reversal patterns indicate that an important reversal in trend is taking place. Knowing where certain patterns are most likely to occur within the prevailing trend is one of the key factors in being able to recognize a chart pattern. Some of the most common reversal patterns include; *the head and shoulders top and bottom, double tops and bottoms, triple tops and bottoms, key reversals, island reversals, rounding bottoms and tops, "V" formations or spike bottoms and tops.* There are a few important points to be considered which are common to all of these reversal patterns.

1. The existence of a prior major trend is an important prerequisite for any reversal pattern. If a price pattern has not been preceded by an existing trend, there is nothing to reverse and the pattern would therefore be suspect. Knowing where chart patterns are most likely to occur within a price trend is one of the key factors in identifying price patterns.

2. The first signal of an impending trend reversal is often the breaking of an important trend line. The breaking of a major trend line signals a change in trend, not necessarily a trend reversal. The breaking of an uptrend line might signal the beginning of a sideways trend which may later form either a reversal or continuation pattern.

3. The larger the pattern the greater is the price movement potential. The height of the pattern measures the volatility, the width of the pattern measures the amount of time required to build and complete the pattern. The greater the height of the pattern (the volatility) and the longer it takes to build – the more important the pattern becomes and the greater the potential for the ensuing price move.

4. Topping patterns are usually shorter in duration and more volatile than bottoms. Price swings at major tops are wider and more violent. Tops usually take less time to form than bottoms. For this reason it is usually less risky to identify and trade bottoms than tops however the time spent in establishing a top is generally shorter than the time spent establishing a market bottom. Therefore, a market manager can generally do better by trading the downside of the market rather than the upside of the market. This has important implications for farm managers, due to the fact that the natural tendency is to trade the former rather than the latter.

5. Volume is usually more important on the upside. Volume should generally increase in the direction of the market trend and is an important confirming factor in the completion of all price patterns. The completion of each pattern should be accompanied by a noticeable increase in volume, particularly at market bottoms. Market tops tend to fall on their own weight once a trend reversal is underway. At a market bottom, if the volume pattern does not show a significant increase following the upside breakout, the entire price pattern should be questioned. The second type of chart pattern is the continuation pattern. Continuation patterns suggest that market is only pausing for a while before the prevailing trend will resume. Another difference between reversal and continuation patterns is their time duration. Reversal patterns usually take much longer to form on the chart and represent major changes in trend. Continuation patterns, on the other hand, are usually shorter-term in duration and are often classified as intermediate term chart patterns. Some of the most common continuation patterns include; flags, ascending and descending triangles, symmetrical triangles, pennants, gaps, and rectangles.

COMMODITY SPREADS

Commodity spreads (or straddles) measure the price difference between two different contracts, usually futures contracts. Spreads can also measure the difference between a cash contract and a futures contract (referred to as the basis) or the price difference between two option contracts, or various combinations of the above. For the purpose of this section you will examine spreads from the context of the price difference between two different futures contracts. (See Figure 24.2)

In the grain business the difference between two contract months of the same commodity (*i.e.*, canola) represents the carrying charges or the cost of holding the commodity for a period of time. Carrying charges are determined by the cost of interest and storage when physical commodities are held in store. Grain traders will monitor spread relationships very closely as the relative difference between various contract positions will determine the handling margins or profitability of their involvement in marketing grain. When using spreads, the trader hopes to profit by changes in the spread (difference) between the two contracts. The trader is looking for either a widening or narrowing of the spread relationship over time. Spread trading is considered to be a less risky and often less expensive way in which to participate in the futures market. Margin requirements for spreads are generally lower than outright long or short positions, and whether the price increases or decreases the traders risk is limited to the change in the spread, since both a long and a short position are held at the same time. Since the risk is lower, so will be the potential for profit or loss. Spread trading is more complicated than outright trading and requires a higher degree of sophistication on the part of the trader.

Besides being used for spread trading, tracking the spread relationships between different contracts in the same market or in different markets can provide useful insights into future price direction. The relationships between the nearby and the distant months in the same commodity often tell us about the relative strength or weakness of the market itself. For example; the June 1993 Canola contract traded at a substantial premium to the November, 1993 contract up until May 1993. A perceived shortage of top quality canola following the frost of August 1992 resulted in 1992 canola values gaining on the 1993 contract positions. This relationship continued until it became apparent later in the marketing year that an adequate supply of canola was available to satisfy buyer's needs in addition to farmers' requirements for cash flow prior to seeding a new crop. The spread relationship between the two different marketing years then reversed direction, as buyers and sellers focused their attention on the upcoming 1993/94 canola production prospects.

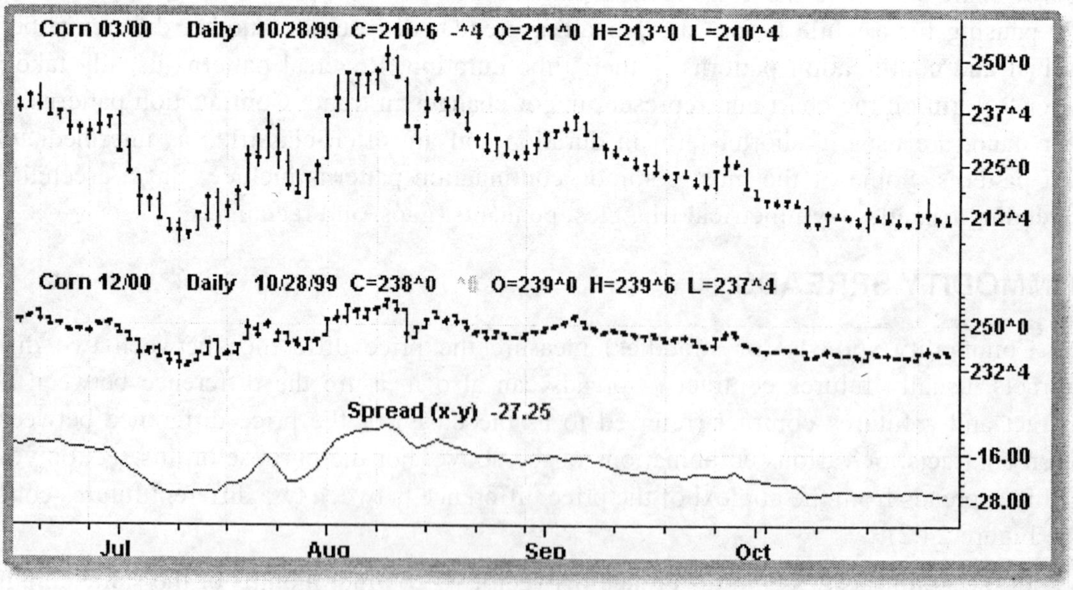

Fig. 24.2. Spread

In situations such as this, caused by perceived tightness of stocks, the nearby months will usually rise faster than the distant months. This is referred to as a bull spread. In order to profit from this relationship you would buy the nearby futures contract and simultaneously sell the more distant contract. Conversely in situations where the near term supplies are in relative over abundance in relation to future supplies, the nearby months will usually fall faster than the distant months. A bearish approach to the market would be undertaken by entering a bear spread.

In order to profit from this relationship you would sell the nearby contract month and buy the distant contract month. By monitoring the relationship between the nearby and the distant months, you often will be provided with a lead indication as to whether the market will trend higher or lower.

TECHNICAL INDICATORS AND COMMODITIES

Technical indicators are additional tools used by the technician in order to develop commodity price forecasts. In this section you will examine a few of the more popular technical indicators used to supplement the basic analytical tools of support, resistance and trend lines. These include; moving averages and oscillators.

The moving average is a trend following indicator which is easy to construct and one of the most widely used mechanical trend following systems used. A moving average, as the name suggests, represents an average of a certain body of data that moves through time. The most common way to calculate the moving average is to work from the last 10 days of closing prices. Each day, the most recent close (days 11) is added to the total and the oldest close (day 1) is subtracted. The new total is then divided by the total number of (days 10) and the resultant average computed.

The purpose of the moving average is to track the progress of a price trend. The moving average is a smoothing device. By averaging the data, a smoother line is produced, making it much easier to view the underlying trend. The decision as to what time period to include (*i.e.* 10 day, 30 day, 40 day) as well as the type of chart (daily, weekly, or monthly) is a subjective one that you will have to make for yourself. If a shorter time period is used (*i.e.*, 10 day moving average), the resultant trend line will exhibit a greater degree of trend variation than a longer term moving average, such that the underlying trend may be more difficult to determine. If a longer term moving average is employed (*i.e.*, 40 day moving average) the time lag between the transformations from an uptrend to a downtrend will be delayed long after the change of price trend is underway. In some markets, it is more advantageous to use a shorter term moving average, and in others, a longer term average proves to be more useful.

Generally the closing price is used to compute the moving average, however opening, high, low and mid point of the trading range values can also be selected. Several types of moving averages can be calculated. Some analysts believe that a heavier weighting should be given to the most recent data and in an attempt to correct this problem, construct other types of moving avenges such as the linearly weighted and exponentially smoothed moving average. The most common application is the simple moving average.

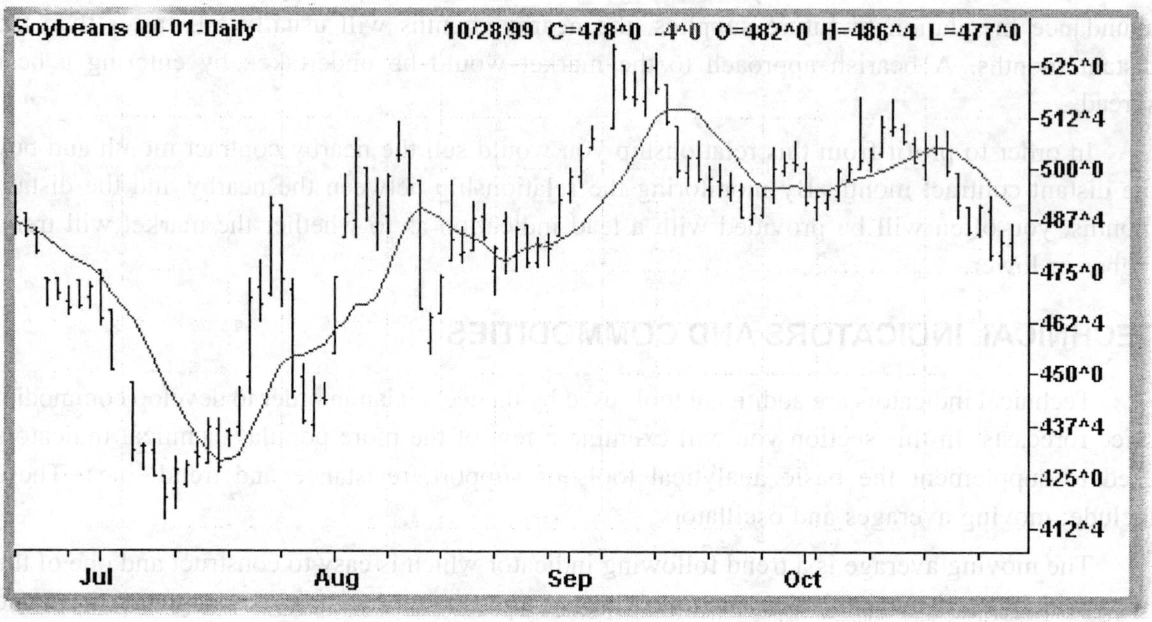

Fig. 24.3. Simple Moving Average

In a simple moving average each day's price receives equal weight. The moving average is plotted on the bar chart on top of the appropriate trading day and along with that day's price action. When the daily closing price moves above the moving avenge a buy signal is generated. When the daily closing price moves below the moving average a sell signal is generated. (See Fig. 24.3).

If a very short term moving average is employed, numerous crossovers will occur such that the trader may be exposed to many false signals and higher commission costs of trading. If a longer term moving average is used the trader may be too slow in responding to a change in trend, forsaking much of the profit potential. A shorter term moving average works best in a sideways trending market, allowing the trader to capture more of the shorter swings. A longer moving avenge works best in trending markets, allowing the trader to stay with the trend and minimizing the chance of getting caught in short term corrections. The correct approach is to use a shorter average during non-trending periods and a longer average during trending periods.

Moving averages are trend following systems which do not have forecasting capabilities. They are used only to help in identifying the underlying trend and as an aid in entering and exiting the market. One of the greatest advantages in using a moving average is that by nature it follows the trend and by selecting a suitable time period, allows profits to run and losses to be cut short. This system works best when markets are trending. During choppy or sideways markets a non trending method such as an oscillator will yield better results.

An oscillator is an extremely useful tool that provides the technical trader with the ability to trade non-trending markets where prices fluctuate in horizontal bands of support and resistance. In this situation, trend following systems such as the moving average do not perform satisfactorily, as many false signals are generated. The oscillator can also be used to provide the technician with an advance warning of short term market extremes, commonly referred to as overbought and oversold conditions. Oscillators provide a warning that a trend is losing momentum before the situation becomes apparent in the price action which is referred to as divergence. As is the case with other types of technical tools there are times when oscillators are more useful than others and they are not infallible.

The concept of momentum is the most basic application of oscillator analysis. Momentum measures the rate of change of prices by continually taking price differences for a fixed time interval. The formula for momentum is:

$$M = C - Cx$$

Where C is today's market close and Cx is the close "x" days prior. To construct a 10 day momentum line, today's closing price is subtracted from the closing price 10 days ago. If the most recent closing price is lower than the closing price 10 days prior, a negative number will be generated. Conversely if today's closing price is higher than the closing price 10 days ago a positive number will be generated. These values are then plotted on the top or bottom of the bar chart with a horizontal zero line in the middle. As with the moving avenge, the number of days chosen to compute the oscillator can vary, with shorter term oscillators (5 day) producing a more sensitive line with more pronounced oscillations. A longer term oscillator (20 days) produces a smoother line in which the oscillator swings are less pronounced.

By plotting price differences over a fixed period of time, the technician is studying rates of change in price trends. If prices are rising and the momentum line is above zero and rising, an accelerating uptrend would be in place. If the momentum line begins to flatten out, the rate of as cent indicates that the uptrend has leveled off and provides the technician with a lead indication that the uptrend may be coming to an end. Because of the nature of its construction, the momentum line will always lead the price action. It will lead the advance or decline of prices by a few days, then will level off while the current price trend is still in effect, before moving in the opposite direction as prices begin to level off. (See Fig. 24.4).

The most widely followed momentum oscillator in technical analysis is Welles Wilder's Relative Strength Index (RSI). The formula for the RSI is as follows:

$$RSI = \frac{100}{1 + RS}$$

Where,

$$Rs = \frac{\text{Average of 14 Day's Up Closes}}{\text{Average of 14 Day's Down Closes}}$$

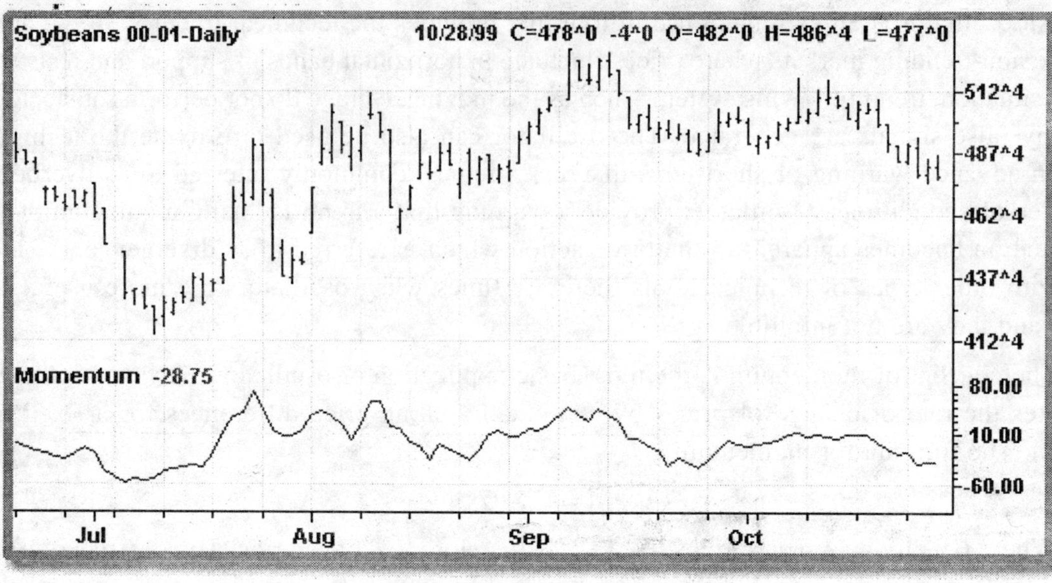

Fig. 24.4. Simple 10-bar Oscillator

The RSI is plotted on a graph with a vertical scale from zero to one hundred, with highlighted horizontal lines drawn at scaled values of 30 and 70. The horizontal axis corresponds to the time line on the bar chart. (See Fig. 24.5).

Interpretation of the RSI is twofold. First the areas on the chart above seventy and below thirty are critical areas for the technician. When the indicator is in the area above 70, the market is said to be overbought. When the indicator is in the area below 30, the market is said to be oversold. These terms refer to a market condition where prices have moved too far too quickly, such that the technician can expect a correction to take place before the market resumes its trend.

One of the most valuable ways to utilize an oscillator is to watch for a divergence. A divergence describes a situation when the trend of the oscillator moves in a different direction from the prevailing price trend. In an uptrend divergence occurs when prices continue to rise, but the oscillator fails to confirm the price move into new highs. This often provides an early warning of a possible price decline and is called bearish or negative divergence. In a downtrend, if the oscillator fails to confirm a new low in the price trend, a positive or bullish divergence exists, which warns of a potential price advance. An important requirement for divergence analysis is that the divergence should take place near the oscillator extremes of 70 and 30 respectively.

Various chart patterns show up on the RSI indicator as well as support and resistance levels. Trend line analysis can then be employed to detect changes in the trend of RSI. The process of updating the RSI on a daily basis is greatly facilitated by accessing technical analysis software programs on a personal computer to perform the calculations and plot the indicator on the bar chart.

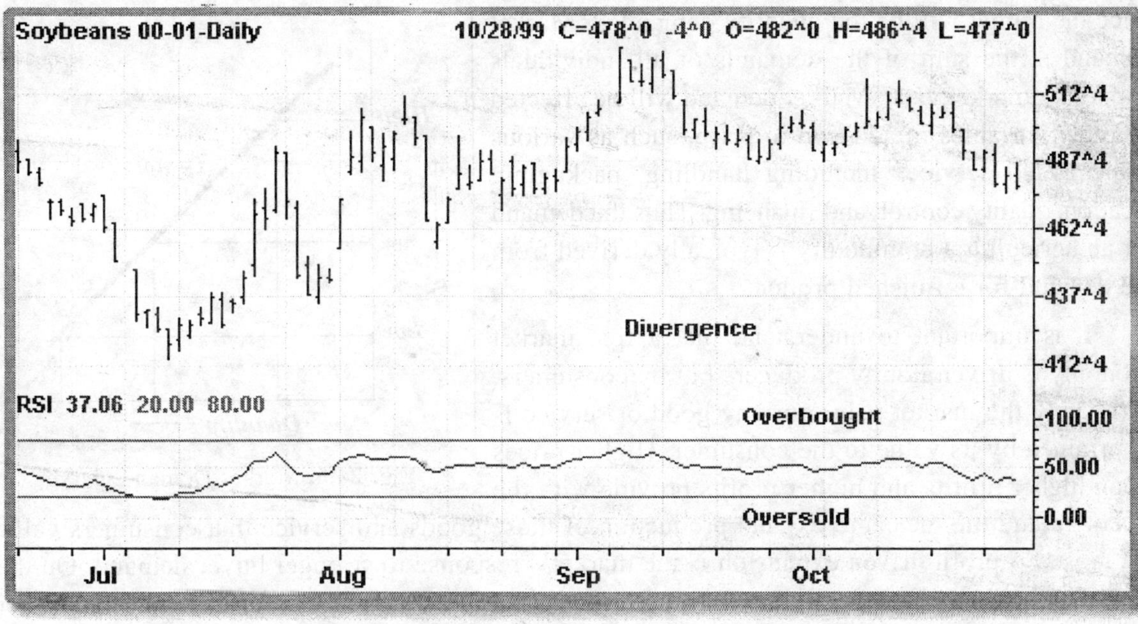

Fig. 24.5. Relative Strength Index (RSI)

24.13 FUNDAMENTAL ANALYSIS OF COMMODITIES

In a market economy, price is determined by the interaction of supply and demand. The study of supply and demand is also known as the study of fundamentals or "fundamental analysis". In this section we will learn how to estimate a market price for commodities using the law of supply and demand as reflected in the "stocks to use ratio". The stocks to use ratio is a closely watched figure in when establishing asking prices for commodities. In order to understand stocks to use, we must understand the economic theory of supply and demand. Supply and demand graphs are useful tools used to illustrate this concept.

Law of Demand and Fundamental Analysis of Commodity Markets

The law of demand and it's application to fundamental analysis of commodities rests upon an understanding of consumer behaviour. The factors which characterize consumer choice and how individual consumer responses are reflected in the market place are key components of this economic theory. Understanding what factors have affected demand in the past will help to develop expectations about demand in the future and the impact on market price.

Demand for a particular product or service represents how much people are willing to purchase at various prices. Thus, demand is a relationship between price and quantity, with all other factors remaining constant. Demand is represented graphically as a downward sloping curve with price on the vertical axis and quantity on the horizontal axis (Figure 24.6).

Generally the relationship between price and quantity is negative. This means that the higher is the price level the lower will be the quantity demanded and, conversely, the lower the price the higher will be the quantity demanded. Market demand is the sum of the demands of all individuals within the marketplace. Market demand will be affected by other variables in addition to price, such as various value added services including handling, packaging, location, quality control, and financing. Thus the demand for an agricultural commodity is typically derived from the demand for a finished product.

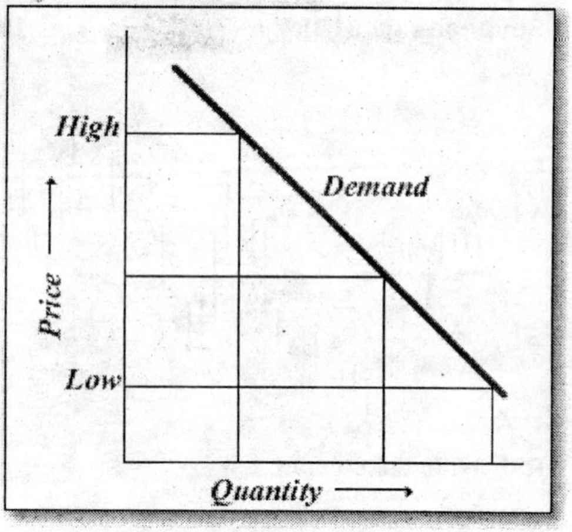

Fig. 24.6. Market Demand Curve

It is important to understand that a free market economy is driven not by producers but by consumers. Ultimately the market value for any good or service is determined by its value to the consumer. Higher prices mean higher profits and higher profits provide with the incentive and the means to expand production of those goods and service that consumers value the most. So profit driven expansion is the market's response to stronger buyer demand. On the other hand, when consumers are unwilling to buy what is offered at the current price, the seller will have to lower the price ultimately resulting in lower profits or losses to you the producer. Losses reduce the producer's incentive to produce things that have weak demand which will ultimately force production cuts as farmers lose more and more money.

This is the discipline of the marketplace. Those who produce things that consumers are willing and able to buy are rewarded. Those who produce things that consumers don't want or can't buy are penalized. Farmers must produce for the markets. They cannot expect to find or create a profitable market for whatever they choose to produce.

LAW OF SUPPLY AND FUNDAMENTAL ANALYSIS OF COMMODITY MARKETS

Supply joins demand as one of the components of fundamental commodity market analysis. Supply characteristics relate to the behaviour of firms in producing and selling a product or service. An understanding of the factors affecting supply in the past will help with the development of supply expectations in the future and the impact upon market price.

The law of supply can be approached from two different contexts. The first is that it represents the sum total of production plus carryover stocks. The other context for supply describes the behaviour of producers. The market or total supply represents the quantities producers are willing to sell over a range of prices for any given time period. At the individual level, one may be willing to produce a given product as long as the market price is equal to or greater than the cost of producing that product. The total supply is the sum of the individual quantities of product that each farmer brings to the market.

Market supply is represented by an upward sloping curve with price on the vertical axis and quantity on the horizontal axis (Figure 24.7).

An increase in price in most instances will result in farmers wanting to increase the quantity of a given product they will bring to the market, therefore the relationship between the price and supply is positive. Market supply will be affected by other variables in addition to the price. Factors that have been identified as important in determining supply behaviour include; the number of firms producing the product, technology, the price of inputs, the price of other commodities which could be produced, and the weather.

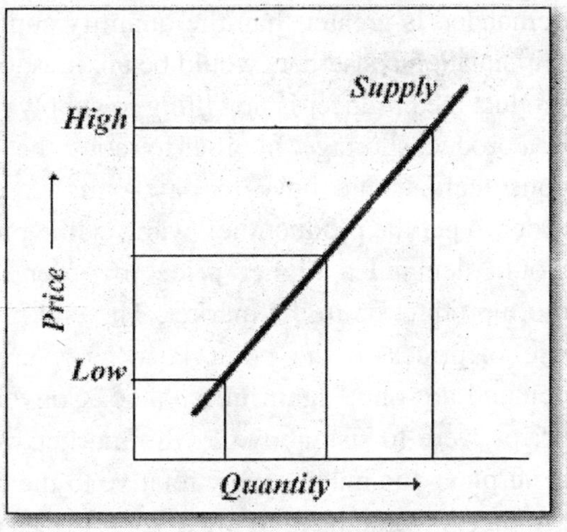

Fig. 24.7. Market Supply Curve

With higher prices the producers of goods and services will receive greater profits. Greater profits will result in the means to expand production increasing the supply. This increased supply will ultimately satisfy the existing demand such that any additional production must be met with new demand in order foı the price increases to be sustained. The firms which handle your grain or livestock products are not free to set prices as they choose. They can raise prices only if consumers are willing and able to pay more. The law of supply, as was the case with demand, illustrates the discipline of the marketplace. The market doesn't care what it costs you to produce something. Lower prices are the market's signal to farmers that they have produced too much of something or that it is something consumers do not want. To be a good marketer, you need to accept the "discipline of the marketplace.' A good marketer learns to produce for the market.

24.14 HOW SUPPLY AND DEMAND DETERMINE COMMODITIES MARKET PRICES

Price is derived by the interaction of supply and demand. The resultant market price is dependant upon both of these fundamental components of a market. An exchange of goods or services will occur whenever buyers and sellers can agree on a price. When an exchange occurs, the agreed upon price is called the "equilibrium price", or a "market clearing price" . This can be graphically illustrated as follows: (Fig. 24.8).

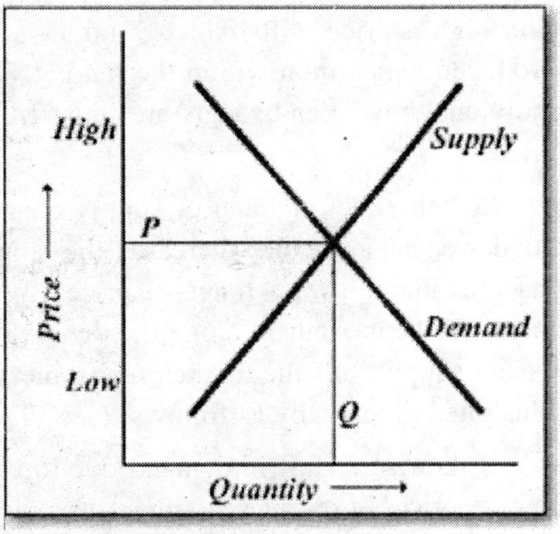

Fig. 24.8. Equilibrium Price

In Figure 24.8, both buyers and sellers are willing to exchange the quantity "Q" at the price "P". At this point supply and demand are in balance or "equilibrium". At any price below P, the quantity demanded is greater than the quantity supplied. In this situation consumers would be anxious to acquire product the producer is unwilling to supply resulting in a product shortage. In order to ration the shortage consumers would have to pay a higher price in order to get the product they want; while producers would demand a higher price in order to bring more product on to the market. The end result is a rise in prices to the point P, where supply and demand are once again in balance. Conversely, if prices were to rise above P, the market would be in surplus - too much supply relative to the demand. Producers would have to lower their prices in order to clear the market of excess supplies. Consumers would be induced by the lower prices to increase their purchases. Prices will fall until supply and demand are again in equilibrium at point P.

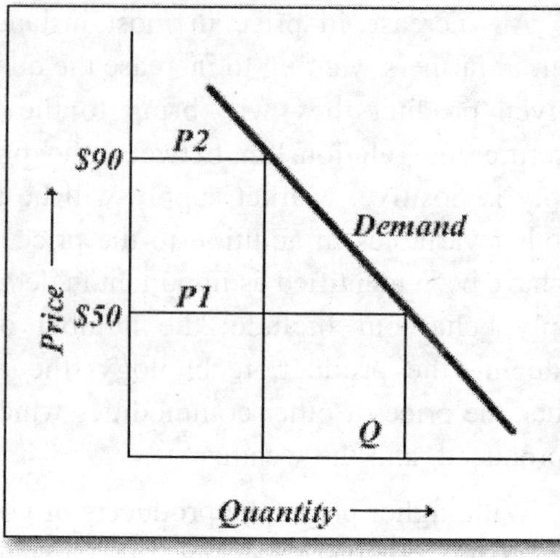

Fig. 24.9. Change in Equilibrium Price

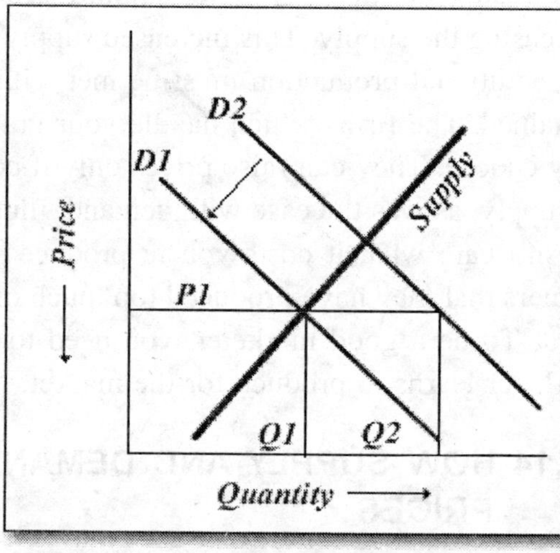

Fig. 24.10. Change in Equilibrium Price

A market price is not a fair price to all participants in the marketplace. It does not guarantee total satisfaction on the part of both buyer and seller or all buyers and all sellers. This will depend on their individual competitive positions within the market. Buyers will attempt to maximize their individual well being within certain competitive constraints. Too low a price will result in excess profits for the buyer attracting competition. Likewise sellers are also considered to be *profit* maximized. Too high a price will likewise attract additional producer competition within the market. Therefore, there will exist different price levels where individual buyers and sellers are satisfied and the sum total will create a market or equilibrium price.

When either demand or supply changes, the equilibrium price will change. For example, good weather normally increases the supply of grains and oilseeds, with more product being made available over a range of prices. With no increase in the quantity of product demanded, there will be movement along the demand curve to a new equilibrium price in order to clear the excess supplies off the market. Consumers will buy more but only at a lower price. This can be illustrated graphically as follows: (see Figure 24.9).

Likewise a shift in demand due to changing consumer preferences will also influence the market price. In recent years there has been a shift in demand on the part of overseas Canadian wheat buyers toward the Canada Prairie Spring varieties, away from the Hard Red Spring varieties. A decline in the preference for Hard Red Spring wheat shifts the demand curve inward, to the left, as illustrated in (Figure 24.10).

With no reduction in supply, the effect on price results from a movement along the supply curve to a lower equilibrium price where supply and demand is once again in balance. In order for prices to increase producers will have to reduce the quantity of hard red spring wheat brought to the market place or find new sources of demand to replace the consumers who withdrew from the marketplace due to changing preferences or a shift in demand.

Changes in supply and demand can be short run or long run in nature. Weather tends to influence market prices generally in the short run. Changes in consumer preferences can have either a short run or long run effect on prices depending upon the goods or services, for example whether they are luxuries or necessities. A luxury good may enjoy a short term shift in demand due to changing styles or snob appeal while necessities tend to have stable or long run demand curves. Another major factor influencing market prices is technology. A major effect of technology in agriculture is to shift out the supply curve rapidly by reducing the costs of production on a per unit basis. At the same time if total demand does not increase sufficiently to absorb the excess goods produced at lower costs, the long run impact of technology on the market place will be to lower prices. The rapidly shifting supply curve coupled with a slower moving demand curve has generally contributed to lower prices for agricultural output when compared to prices for industrial products.

Stocks to Use Ratio

The Stocks to Use Ratio is a convenient measure of supply and demand interrelationships of commodities. The stocks to use ratio indicates the level of carryover stock for any given commodity as a percentage of the total demand or use. The mathematical formula for this relationship is as follows:

$$\frac{\text{Beginning Stock + Total Production – Total Use}}{\text{Total Use}}$$

This can be simplified by consolidating the upper portion of the relationship to:

$$\frac{\text{Carryover}}{\text{Total Use}} \times 100 = \text{Stocks To Use Ratio}$$

Using the long hand formula, beginning stocks represent the previous year's ending or carryover inventories. Total production represents the total grain produced in a given year. Total usage is the sum of all the end uses in which the stock of grain has been consumed. This would include human consumption, export programs, seed, waste, and dockage and feed consumption. By adding carry-over the total production you will obtain the total supply. From the total supply, subtract the total use and the resultant figure will be the year ending carryover stock. The carryover stock divided by the total usage can be expressed as a ratio which when compared with previous years gives the market analyst an indication of the relative supply/demand balance for a particular commodity. This ratio can then be used to indicate whether current and projected stock levels are critical or plentiful. The ratio can also be used to indicate how many days of supply is available to the world marketplace under current usage patterns. (*e.g.*, a 20% stocks to use ratio for wheat indicates that there are 75 days supply of wheat in reserve)

By comparing the current year's stocks to use ratio with years when carryover stocks were below normal as well as years when carryover stocks were above normal, we will be able to develop an estimate as to the direction of the price trend as well as the probable extent of price change whether higher or lower. Some bench mark ratios can be established for various crops by reviewing historical stocks to use data. On a world basis a stocks/use ratio for wheat under 20% has typically led to strong price advances. For corn, the comparable number appears to be under 12%. For soybeans, the critical level is below 10%. It is useful to calculate stocks to use ratios for different crops and compare these projections with historical averages provided by the Canada Grains Council Statistical Handbook, as well as other publications such as the USDA situation and outlook reports, and Specialty Crop Publications. By reviewing past data and estimating the current year's stocks/use ratios on a crop by crop basis, appropriate production/ marketing strategies can be developed.

Example:

Soybeans (Say)

Year	*Beginning Stock*	*Total Production*	*Total Use*	*Carryover Stock*
1983/84	486	2,599	2,965	120
1990/91	749	3,266	3.635	380
10-year Average	623	3,407	3,425	605

Stocks to Use Ratio:

1983/84	$\frac{486 + 2599 - 2965}{2965} = 4\%$	Avg. Cash
Year 1990/91	$\frac{749 + 3266 - 3635}{3635} = 10.4\%$	Avg. Price: ₹ 287
10-year Average	$\frac{623 + 3407 - 3425}{3425} = 17.6\%$	10-year Avg. Price: ₹ 325

24.15 COMMODITIES

1. Aluminium	2. Coppe	3. Crude Oil
4. Gold	5. Goldm	6. Lead
7. Mentha Oil	8. Natural Gas	9. Nickel
10. Silver	11. Silverm	12. Zinc

24.16 COMMODITY TRENDS OF MAJOR COMMODITIES

1. Aluminium Trend and Intraday Levels

(Record Updated for-Oct/12/2010)-CMP-106 The Aluminium is in perfect uptrend. Currently Aluminium is in strong uptrend and the trend is supported with good volume The open interest is not increasing with trend. Cautious point is buying at higher levels seems decreasing. The Aluminium is now trading in overbought level. The Aluminium is now trading in overbought level. The oscillator is showing SELL signal f.or short term Aluminium is in **Hold Long** position.

Aluminium — Short Term Trend :

Currently Aluminium is in **Hold Long** position Aluminium is moving sideways so short term investor better to buy only above 107.25 with stop at 102.6. The oscillator is showing BUY signal.

ALUMINIUM-INTRADAY TREND

Buy is advised above 107 with a stop at 105.2 below 104.7 go for sell

Aluminium Day Trading Levels and Statics

Interday Level of Aluminium			*Probable High*	*Probable Low*
R4	107.7	BULL	109.0	104.0
R3	107	UP BREAKOUT	108.0	105.0
R2	106.7	STOP LEVEL	**HIGH RES**	**LOW SUP**
R1	106.5	SELL	107.0	105.0
PIVOT	106.2		5 DAY HIGH	107.25
S1	105.2	BUY	5 DAY LOW	102.6
S2	105	STOP	AVG VOLUME	36769
S3	104.7	DOWN BREAK OUT	LAST DAY	Strong bear
S4	104	BEAR	HIGH	107.25
TRADING POSITION		**BUY**	LOW	105.6

2. Copper Trend and Intraday Levels

(Record Updated for-Oct/12/2010)-CMP-371 The Copper is in perfect uptrend. Currently Copper is in strong uptrend and the trend is supported with good volume. The open interest is not increasing with trend. Cautious point is buying at higher levels seems decreasing. The Copper is now trading in overbought level. The Copper is now trading in overbought level. The oscillator is showing SELL signal for short term Copper is in **Hold Long** position.

Copper-Short Term Trend

Currently Copper is in **Hold Long** position Copper is in sideways and sellers was at high so for short term better buy above 378.8 or hold with stop at 359.4 The next resistance will be at 373.1 The oscillator is showing BUY signal

Copper-Intraday Trend

Buy is advised only above 378.8 with a stop at 367.4 Below 364.1 go for sell and put stop at 375.5

Copper Day Trading Levels and Statics

Intraday Level of Crudeoil			*Probable High*	*Probable Low*
R4	384.4	BULL	377.0	363.0
R3	378.8	UP BREAKOUT	373.0	367.0
R2	376.8	STOP LEVEL	**HIGH RES**	**LOW SUP**
R1	375.5	SELL	372.0	366.0
PIVOT	366.4		5 DAY HIGH	373.1
S1	367.4	BUY	5 DAY LOW	359.4
S2	366.1	STOP	AVG VOLUME	80498
S3	364.1	DOWN BREAK OUT	LAST DAY	Bull
S4	358.6	BEAR	HIGH	373.1
TRADING POSTION		**BUY**	LOW	370.0

3. Crudeoil Trend and Intraday Levels

(Record Updated for-Oct/12/2010)-CMP-3672 The Crude oil is in perfect uptrend. Currently Crude oil is in strong uptrend and the trend is supported with good volume The open interest is not increasing with trend. Cautious point is buying at higher levels seems decreasing. The oscillator is showing BUY signal for short term. The current position is **BUY.**

Crudeoil-Short Term Trend

Currently Crude oil is in **Hold Short** position Crude oil is in sideways so for short term better buy above 3735.0 with stop at 3583.0 The oscillator is showing SELL signal

Crude oil-intraday Trend

Buy is advised above 3707.4 with a stop at 3650.7 below 3636.7 go for sell

Crudeoil Day Trading Levels and Statics

Intraday level of Crudeoil			*Probable High*	*Probable Low*
R4	3730.7	BULL	3717.0	3629.0
R3	3707.4	UP BREAKOUT	3695.0	3651.0
R2	3698.9	STOP LEVEL	**HIGH RES**	**LOW SUP**
R1	3693.4	SELL	3692.0	3636.0
PIVOT	3679	5 DAY HIGH	3735.0	
S1	3650.7	BUY	5 DAY LOW	3583.0
S2	3645.1	STOP	AVG VOLUME	15334
S3	3636.7	DOWN BREAK OUT	LAST DAY	Bear
S4	3613.5	BEAR	HIGH	3708.0
TRADING POSITION		BUY	LOW	3657.0

4. Gold Trend and Intraday levels

(Record Updated for-Oct/12/2010)-CMP-19669 The Gold is in perfect uptrend. Currently Gold is in strong uptrend and the trend is supported with good volume The open interest is not increasing with trend. In last few days lot of positive accumulation happened in the Gold Cautious point is buying at higher levels seems decreasing. The Gold is now trading in overbought level. The Gold is now trading in overbought level. The oscillator is showing BUY signal for short term. The current position is **BUY.**

Gold Support and Resistance

Support for the Gold is 19280-19208-19119-18937-18640-18614. Immediate resistance for Gold is 19823.

Gold-Introday Trend

Buy is advised only above 19781.6 with a stop at 19593.2 Below 19556.7 go for sell and put stop at 19745.

Gold day Irading Levels and Statics

Intraday level of Crudeoil			*Probable High*	*Probable Low*
R4	19842.4	BULL	19783.0	19402.0
R3	19781.6	UP BREAKOUT	19707.0	19478.0
R2	19759.5	STOP LEVEL	***HIGH RES***	***LOW SUP***
R1	19745	SELL	19589.0	19445.0
PIVOT	19630.7		5 DAY HIGH	19744.0
S1	19593.2	BUY	5 DAY LOW	19317.0
S2	19578.7	STOP	AVG VOLUME	41670
S3	19556.7	DOWN BREAK OUT	LAST DAY	Strong Bull
S4	19496.1	BEAR	HIGH	19678.0
TRADING POSTION		BUY	LOW	19545.0

5. Natural Gas Trend and Intraday Levels

(Record Updated for-Oct/12/2010)-CMP-161 Overall trend of the Natural gas is bearish for medium-long term .Currently Natural gas is in strong downtrend and the trend is supported with good volume. The open interest is not increasing with trend. Noting point is selling at lower levels seems decreasing. The Natural gas is now trading in oversold level. The Natural gas is now trading in oversold level. The oscillator is showing SELL signal for short term Natural gas is in **SELL** position.

Natural Gas-short Term Trend

Currently Natural gas is in **SELL** position. Natural gas is in down trend so buy above 164.0. The sell will again come if below 160.4. The Natural gas is now trading in highly oversold level. The Natural gas is now trading in highly oversold level. The oscillator is showing SELL signal.

Natural Gas-Intraday Trend

Buy is advised above 164 with a stop at 159.9 below 158.8 go for sell

Natural Gas Day Trading Levels and Statics

Intraday Level of Naturalgas			*Probable High*	*Probable Low*
R4	166	BULL	170.0	153.0
R3	164	UP BREAKOUT	166.0	158.0
R2	163.3	STOP LEVEL	**HIGH RES**	**LOW SUP**
R1	162.9	SELL	164.0	161.0
PIVOT	162.3	5 DAY HIGH	173.5	
S1	159.9	BUY	5 DAY LOW	160.4
S2	159.5	STOP	AVG VOLUME	48043
S3	158.8	DOWN BREAK OUT	LAST DAY	Strong bear
S4	156.9	BEAR	HIGH	164.3
TRADING POSITION		**SELL**	LOW	161.2

6. Silver Trend and Intraday Levels

(Record Updated for-Oct/12/2010)-CMP-34894 The Silver is in perfect uptrend. Currently Silver is in strong uptrend and the trend is supported with good volume. The open interest is not increasing with trend. Cautious point is buying at higher levels seems decreasing. The Silver is now trading in highly overbought level. The Silver is now trading in highly overbought level. The oscillator is showing SELL signal for short term. The current position is **BUY.**

Silver–Short-Term Trend

Currently Silver is in **Hold Short** position Silver is in sideways and sellers was at high so for short term better buy above 35187.6 or hold with stop at 33560.0 The next resistance will be at 34980.0 The Silver is now trading in highly overbought level. The Silver is now trading in highly overbought level. The oscillator is showing BUY signal.

Silver–Intraday Trend

Buy is advised only above 35187.6 with a stop at 34712.8. Below 34601.3 go for sell and put stop at 35075.7

Silver Day Trading Levels and Statics

Intraday Level of Naturalgas			*Probable High*	*Probable Low*
R4	35373.3	BULL	35336.0	34059.0
R3	35187.6	UP BREAKOUT	35017.0	34378.0
R2	35120.1	STOP LEVEL	**HIGH RES**	**LOW SUP**
R1	35075.7	SELL	34793.0	34231.0
PIVOT	34816.3		5 DAY HIGH	34980.0
S1	34712.8	BUY	5 DAY LOW	33560.0
S2	34668.5	STOP	AVG VOLUME	2101
S3	34601.3	DOWN BREAKOUT	LAST DAY	Strong Bull
S4	34416.3	BEAR	HIGH	34980.0
TRADING POSITION		**BUY**	LOW	34575.0

7. Zinc Trend and Intraday Levels

(Record Updated for-Oct/12/2010)-CMP-103 The Zinc is in perfect uptrend. Currently Zinc is in strong uptrend and the trend is supported with good volume The open interest is not increasing with trend. The oscillator is showing BUY signal for short-term. The current position is **BUY.**

Zinc-Short Term Trend

Currently Zinc is in **HOLD SHORT** position Zinc is showing some Up momentum So buy above 102.0 with stop at 98.55 The oscillator is showing BUY signal

Zinc-Intraday Trend

Buy is advised only above 104 with a stop at 102.1 below 101.6 go for sell and put stop at 103.5.

Zinc Day Trading Levels and Statics

Intraday Level of Naturalgas			*Probable High*	*Probable Low*
R4	35373.3	BULL	35336.0	34059.0
R4	104.8	BULL	105.0	100.0
R3	104	UP BREAKOUT	104.0	101.0
R2	103.7	STOP LEVEL	**HIGH RES**	**LOW SUP**
R1	103.5	SELL	102.0	100.0
PIVOT	102.6		5 DAY HIGH	103.65
S1	102.1	BUY	5 DAY LOW	98.55
S2	101.9	STOP	AVG VOLUME	113730
S3	101.6	DOWN BREAK OUT	LAST DAY	Bull
S4	100.8	BEAR	HIGH	103.3
TRADING POSITION		**BUY**	LOW	101.55

24.17 CURRENCY DERIVATIVES

Currency derivatives can be described as contracts between the sellers and buyers, whose values are to be derived from the underlying assets, the currency amounts. These are basically risk management tools in forex and money markets used for hedging risks and act as insurance against unforeseen and unpredictable currency and interest rate movements. Any individual or corporate expecting to receive or pay certain amounts in foreign currencies at future date can use these products to opt for a fixed rate – at which the currencies can be exchanged now itself. Risks arising out of borrowings, in foreign currency, due to currency rate and interest rate movements can be contained. If receivables or payments or expenditure are denominated or to be incurred in multiple currencies, derivatives can be used for matching the inflows and outflows.

Today, currency derivatives are available in India as over-the-counter (OTC) instruments from banks. Derivatives available today include forwards, options, swaps and other exotic instruments involving a combination of these instruments and related underlying. Generally, companies are required to demonstrate the underlying exposures to ensure that these instruments are used to hedge risks and not for speculative purposes. These instruments can be used effectively to manage risks and exposures and contain costs.

Is it risk-free?

Market risks can't be avoided, but have to be managed. And currency derivative serve the purpose of financial risk management encompassing various market risks. As in the case of insurance, an upfront premium is payable for buying a derivative.

While there could be some gains, depending on the markets and market movement and the type of derivative selected, losses are contained. Entering into contracts not backed by genuine business cash flows in relevant currencies amounts to speculation and can lead to losses.

What is the difference between forex derivatives and currency derivatives?

There is a thin line dividing the two. Derivatives based on currency exchange rates are forward contracts (or forward rate agreements); options and swaps and are popularly known as forex derivatives. Those are meant to hedge interest rate risks and cash mismatches in different currencies such as currency swaps and options are known as currency derivatives. There are interest rate forward rate agreements and swaps for managing the interest rate movements risk within same currency. On the lines of commodity futures, there are currency and interest rate futures, which are nothing but standardized forward contracts. A committee appointed by the RBI (Reserve Bank of India) has recommended making available the currency futures at authorised dealers.

❑❑❑

25 Portfolio Management

25.1 THE PORTFOLIO

In the IBM view, a portfolio is: One of a number of mechanisms, constructed to actualize significant elements in the Enterprise Business Strategy.

It contains a selected, approved, and continuously evolving, collection of initiatives which are aligned with the organizing element of the Portfolio, and, which contribute to the achievement of goals or goal components identified in the Enterprise Business Strategy.

The basis for constructing a portfolio should reflect the enterprise's particular needs. For example, you might choose to build a portfolio around initiatives for a specific product, business segment, or separate business unit within a multinational organization.

25.2 CONCEPT OF PMS

Portfolio management involves deciding what assets to include in the portfolio, given the goals and risk tolerance of the portfolio owner. Selection involves deciding which assets to acquire/divest, how many to acquire/divest, and when to acquire/divest them. These decisions always involve some sort of performance measurement, most typically the expected return on the portfolio, and the risk associated with this return (*e.g.*, the expected standard deviation of the expected return). However, due to the almost-complete uncertainty of future values, this performance measurement is often done on a casual qualitative basis, rather than a precise quantitative basis (which would give a false sense of precision). Typically the expected return from portfolios of different asset bundles is compared.

Portfolio management in common parlance refers to the selection of securities and their continuous shifting in the portfolio to optimize returns to suit the objectives of an investor. In India, as well as in a number of western countries, portfolio management service has assumed the role of a specialized service now a days and a number of professional merchant bankers compete aggressively to provide the best to high net worth clients, who have little time to manage their investments. The idea is catching on with the boom in the capital market and an increasing number of people are inclined to make profits out of their hard-earned savings. Portfolio management service is one of the merchant banking activities recognized by Securities and Exchange Board of India (SEBI). The service can be rendered either by merchant bankers or portfolio managers or discretionary portfolio manager as define in clause (e) and (f) of Rule 2 of Securities and Exchange Board of India (Portfolio Managers) Rules, 1993 and their functioning are guided by the SEBI.

Portfolio Management Services (PMS) is a sophisticated investment vehicle that offers a range of specialised investment strategies to capitalise on opportunities in the market.

Experienced Fund Managers give you sound investment advice and strategies that help you invest smartly. You get the best fund managers in the industry who craft customised stock portfolios that work wonders. With PMS products distributed by Deutsche Bank you get:

(a) More choice in terms of portfolios to suit individual client needs and risk appetite

(b) Ability to structure products that meet specific investment objectives

(c) Choice of alternate investment products that were traditionally available to the very wealthy.

Professional Management

PMS products distributed by Deutsche Bank combine the benefits of professional money management with the flexibility, control and potential tax advantages of owning individual stocks or other securities. The Portfolio Managers take care of all the administrative aspects of your portfolio with a monthly or semi-annual reporting on the overall status of the portfolio and performance.

Continuous Monitoring

The expert Fund Managers and research team keep a constant watch on your money. The team of experts in these fund houses know exactly how your money is performing through continuous monitoring. You, as a customer are always informed through:

(i) Communications that include relevant information on major market events

(ii) Quarterly or semi-annual performance updates

Hassle Free Operation

As a PMS customer you get hassle-free operations. With total portfolio transparency, in-depth market information for better decision making and direct access to the portfolio management team, PMS brings high service standards.

Portfolio Management is the art and science of making decisions about investment mix and policy, matching investments to objectives, asset allocation for individuals and institutions, and balancing risk against. performance.

Portfolio management is all about strengths, weaknesses, opportunities and threats in the choice of debt vs. equity, domestic vs. international, growth vs. safety, and many other tradeoffs encountered in the attempt to maximize return at a given appetite for risk.

In the case of mutual and exchange-traded funds (ETFs), there are two forms of portfolio management: passive and active. Passive management simply tracks a market index, commonly referred to as indexing or index investing. Active management involves a single manager, co-managers, or a team of managers who attempt to beat the market return by actively managing a fund's portfolio through investment decisions based on research and decisions on individual holdings. Closed-end funds are generally actively managed.

25.3 THE PORTFOLIO STRUCTURE

A portfolio structure identifies and contains a number of portfolios. This structure, like the portfolios within it, should align with significant planning and results boundaries, and with business components. If you have a product-oriented portfolio structure, for example, then you would have a separate portfolio for each major product or product group. Each portfolio would contain all the initiatives that help that particular product or product group contribute to the success of the enterprise business strategy.

25.4 THE PORTFOLIO MANAGER

This is a new role for organizations that embrace a portfolio management approach. A portfolio manager is responsible for continuing oversight of the contents within a portfolio. If you have several portfolios within your portfolio structure, then you will likely need a portfolio manager for each one. The exact range of responsibilities (and authority) will vary from one organization to another, _but the basics are as follows:

(i) One portfolio manager oversees one portfolio.

(ii) The portfolio manager provides day-to-day oversight.

(iii) The portfolio manager periodically reviews the performance of and conformance to expectations for, initiatives within the portfolio.

(iv) The portfolio manager ensures that data is collected and analyzed about each of the initiatives in the portfolio.

(v) The portfolio manager enables periodic decision-making about the future direction of individual initiatives.

25.5 PORTFOLIO REVIEWS AND DECISION-MAKING

As initiatives are executed, the organization should conduct periodic reviews of actual (versus planned) performance and conformance to original expectations.

Typically, organization managers specify the frequency and contents for these periodic reviews, and individual portfolio managers oversee their planning and execution. The reviews should be multi-dimensional, including both tactical elements (*e.g.*, adherence to plan, budget, and resource allocation) and strategic elements (*e.g.*, support for business strategy goals and delivery of expected organizational benefits).

A significant aspect of oversight is setting multiple decision points for each initiative, so that managers can periodically evaluate data and decide whether to continue the work. These "continue/change/discontinue" decisions should be driven by an understanding (developed via the periodic reviews) of a given initiative's continuing value, expected benefits, and strategic contribution. Making these decisions at multiple points in the initiative's lifecycle helps to ensure that managers will continually examine and assess changing internal and external circumstances, needs, and performance.

25.6 GOVERNANCE

Implementing portfolio management practices in an organization is a transformation effort that typically involves developing new capabilities to address new work efforts, defining (and filling) new roles to identify portfolios (collections of work to be done), and delineating boundaries among work efforts and collections.

Implementing portfolio management also requires creating a structure to provide planning, continuing direction, and oversight and control for all portfolios and the initiatives they encompass. That is where the notion of *governance* comes into play. The IBM view of governance is:

"An abstract, collective term that defines and contains a framework for organization, exercise of control and oversight, and decision-making authority, and within which actions and activities are legitimately and properly executed; together with the definition of the functions, the roles, and the responsibilities of those who exercise this oversight and decision-making."

Portfolio management governance involves multiple dimensions, including:

(a) Defining and maintaining an enterprise business strategy.

(b) Defining and maintaining a portfolio structure containing all of the organization's initiatives (programs, projects, etc.).

(c) Reviewing and approving business cases that propose the creation of new initiatives.

(d) Providing oversight, control, and decision-making for all ongoing initiatives.

(e) Ownership of portfolios and their contents.

Each of these dimensions requires an owner — either an individual or a collective — to develop and approve plans, continuously adjust direction, and exercise control through periodic assessment and review of conformance to expectations.

A good governance structure decomposes both the types of work and the authority to plan and oversee work. It defines individual and collective roles, and links them to an authority scheme. Policies that are collectively developed and agreed upon provide a framework for the exercise of governance.

25.7 IMPORTANCE OF PORTFOLIO MANAGEMENT

Stock exchange operations are peculiar in nature and most of the Investors feel insecure in managing their investment on the stock market because it is difficult for an individual to identify companies which have growth prospects for investment. Further due to volatile nature of the markets, it requires constant reshuffling of portfolios to capitalized on the growth opportunities. Even after identifying the growth oriented companies and their securities, the trading practices are also complicated, making it a difficult task for investors to trade in all the exchange and follow-up-on post-trading formalities. That is why professional investment advice through portfolio management service can help the investors to make an intelligent and informed choice between alternative investments opportunities without the worry of loosing their invested money. Hence this is very much important to the stock dealers especially who are new to the market.

25.8 OBJECTIVES OF PORTFOLIO MANAGEMENT

The major objectives of portfolio management are summarized as below:

(i) Keep the security, safety of Principal sum intact both in terms of money as well as its purchasing power.

(ii) Stability of the flow of income so as to facilitate planning more accurately and systematically the re-investment or consumption of income.

(iii) To attain capital growth by re-investing in growth securities or through purchase of growth securities.

(iv) Marketability of the security which is essential for providing flexibility to investment portfolio.

(v) Liquidity *i.e.* nearness to money which is desirable for the investor so as to take advantage of attractive opportunities upcoming in the market.

(vi) Diversification: The basic objective of building a portfolio is to reduce the risk of loss of capital and income by investing in various types of securities and over a wide range of industries.

(vii) Favorable tax status: The effective yield an investor gets from his investment depends on tax to which it is subject. By minimizing the tax burden, yield can be effectively improved.

25.9 BASIC PRINCIPLES OF PORTFOLIO MANAGEMENT

There are two basic principles for effective portfolio management which are given below:

I. Effective investment planning for the investment in securities by considering the following factors:

(a) Fiscal, financial and monetary policies of the Govt. of India and the Reserve Bank of India.

(b) Industrial and economic environment and its impact on industry Prospect in terms of prospective technological changes, competition in the market, capacity utilization with industry and demand prospects etc.

II. Constant review of investment: It requires to review the investment in securities and to continue the selling and purchasing of investment in more profitable manner. For this purpose they have to carry the following analysis:

(a) To assess the quality of the management of the companies in which investment has been made or proposed to be made.

(b) To assess the financial and trend analysis of Company's Balance Sheet and Profit & Loss Accounts to identify the optimum capital structure and better performance for the purpose of withholding the investment from poor companies.

(c) To analysis the security market and its trend in continuous basis to arrive at a conclusion as to whether the securities already in possession should be disinvested and new securities be purchased. If so the timing for investment or dis-investment is also revealed.

25.10 ACTIVITIES IN PORTFOLIO MANAGEMENT, RISK INVOLVED IN THE MARKET

There are three major activities involved in an efficient portfolio management which are as follows:

(a) Identification of objectives of investment protfolio, assets or securities, allocation of investment and also identifying the classes of assets for the purpose of investment.

(b) They have to decide the major weights, proportion of different assets in the portfolio by taking in to consideration the related risk factors.

(c) Finally they select the security within the asset classes as identify.

The above activities are directed to achieve the sole purpose to maximize return and minimize risk in the investment even if there are unlimited risks in the market.

Risks : Let us have a look on the composite risk involve in the market during operation:

I. *Interest rate risk:* This arises due to variability in the interest rates from time-to-time. A changes in the interest rates establishes an inverse relationship in the price of the security *i.e.* price of securities trends to move inversely with change in rate of interest. Long term securities shows greater variability in compare to short term securities by this risk.

II. *Purchasing power risk:* It is also known as inflation risk and the inflation affects the purchasing power adversely. Inflation rates vary over time and changes unexpectedly causing erosion in the value of real return and expected return. Thus purchasing power risk is more in inflationary conditions especially in respect of bond and fixed income securities. It is not desirable to invest in such securities during inflationary situations. Purchasing power risk is however less in flexible income securities like equity shares or common stock where rise in dividend income off-sets increase in the rate of inflation and provides advantage of capital gain.

III. *Business risk:* Business risk arises from sale and purchase of securities affected by business cycles, technological changes etc. Business cycles affect all types of securities viz. there is cheerful movement in boom due to bullish trend in stock price where as bearish trend in depression brings down fall in the prices of all types of securities. Therefore securities bearing flexible income affected more than the fixed rated securities during depression due to decline in their market price.

IV. *Financial Risk:* This arises due to changes in the capital structure of the company. It is also known as leveraged risk and expressed in the terms of debt-equity ratio. Excess of debt over equity in the capital structure of a company indicates that the company is highly geared even if the per capital earnings (EPS) of such company may be more. Because highly dependence on borrowings exposes to the risk of winding up for its inability to honour its commitments towards lenders and creditors. So the investors should be aware of this risk and portfolio manager should also be very careful.

By taking in to accounts of all the above factors, investment decision in portfolio management are taken as following:

I. Investment Decision

By a certain sum of funds, the investment decision are basically depends upon the following factors:

1. Objectives of investment portfolio: This is a crucial point which a Finance Manager must consider. There can be many objectives of making an investment. The manager of a provident fund portfolio has to look for security and may be satisfied with none too high a return, where as an aggressive investment company be willing to take high risk in order to have high capital appreciation.

How the objectives can affect in investment decision can be seen from the fact that the Unit Trust of India has two major schemes : Its "capital units" are meant for those who wish to have a good capital appreciation and a moderate return, where as the ordinary unit are meant to provide a steady return only. The investment manager under both the scheme will invest the money of the Trust in different kinds of shares and securities. So it is obvious that the objectives must be clearly defined before an investment decision is taken.

2. Selection of investment: Having defined the objectives of the investment, the next decision is to decide the kind of investment to be selected. The decision what to buy has to be seen in the context of the following:

(a) There is a wide variety of investments available in market *i.e.* Equity shares, preference share, debentures, convertible bond, Govt. securities and bond, capital units etc. Out of these what types of securities to be purchased.

(b) What should be the proportion of investment in fixed interest dividend securities and variable dividend bearing securities? The fixed one ensures a definite return and thus a lower risk but the return is usually not as higher as that from the variable dividend bearing shares.

(c) If the investment is decided in shares or debentures, then the industries showed a potential in growth should be taken in first line. Industry-wise-analysis is important since various industries are not at the same level from the investment point of view. It is important to recognize that at a particular point of time, a particular industry may have a better growth potential than other industries. For example, there was a time when jute industry was in great favour because of its growth potential and high profitability, the industry is no longer at this point of time as a growth oriented industry.

(d) Once industries with high growth potential have been identified, the next step is to select the particular companies, in whose shares or securities investments are to be made.

To identify the industries, which have a high growth potential the following techniques/ approaches may be taken in to consideration:

(a) Statistical analysis of past performance: A statistical analysis of the immediate past performance of the share price indices of various industries and changes there in related to the general price index of shares of all industries should be made. The Reserve Bank of India index numbers of security prices published every month in its bulletin may be taken to represent the behaviour of share prices of various industries in the last few years. The related changes in the price index of each industry as compare with the changes in the average price index of the shares of all industries would show those industries which are having a higher growth potential in the past few years. It may be noted that a Industry may not remaining a growth Industry for all the time. So we have to make an assessment of the various Industries keeping in view the present potentiality also to finalize the list of Industries in which we will try to spread our investment.

(b) Assessing the intrinsic value of an Industry/Company: After identifying the Industry, we have to assess the various factors which influence the value of a particular share. Those factors generally relate to the strengths and weaknesses of the company under consideration, Characteristics of the industry within which the company fails and the national and international economic scene. The major objective of the analysis is to determine the relative quality and the quantity of the security. It is also to be seen that the security is good at current market prices. This approach is known as intrinsic value approach. Industry analysis can help to assess the nature of demand of a particular product, Cost structure of the industry and other economic and Govt. constraints on the same. An appraisal of the particular industries prospect is essential and the basic profitability of any company depends upon the economic prospect of the industry to which it belongs.

The following factors are important in this regards:

(a) Demand and Supply pattern for the industries products and its growth potential: The management expert identify fives stages in the life of an industry. These are "Introduction, development, rapid growth, maturity and decline". If an industry has already reached the maturity or decline stage, its future demand potential is not likely to be high.

(b) Profitability: It is a vital consideration for the investors as profit is the measures of performance and a source of earning for him. So the cost structure of the industry as related to its sale price is an important consideration. The other point to be considered is the ratio analysis, especially return on investment, gross profit and net profit ratio of the existing companies in the industry.

(c) Particular characteristics of the industry: Each industry has its own characteristics, which must be studied in depth in order to understand their impact on the working of the industry. Because the industry having a fast changing technology become obsolete at a faster rate. Similarly, many industries are characterized by high rate of profits and losses in alternate years. Such fluctuations in earnings must be carefully examined.

(d) Labour management relations in the industry: The state of labour-management relationship in the particular industry also has a great deal of influence on the future profitability of the industry. So it is vital to see that the industry under analysis has been maintaining a cordial relationship between labour and management.

(e) Company Analysis: To select a company for investment a number of qualitative factors have to be seen to visualize the performance of the company in future by analyzing its past performance such as:

1. Size and ranking: In this regard the net capital employed, the net profits, the return on investment and the sales volume of the company under consideration may be compared with similar data of other company in the same industry group to assess the risk associated with the company.

2. Growth record: Three growth indicators may be looked in to, *i.e.*, Price earnings ratio, Percentage growth rate of earnings per annum and percentage growth rate of net block of the company in the past few years should be examined.

3. Financial analysis: By the help of Financial analysis we can understand the financial solvency and liquidity, the efficiency, the profitability and the financial and operating leverage of the company in which the fund are used.

4. Pattern of existing stock holding: This analysis would show the stake of various parties associate with the company. An interesting case in this regard is that of the Punjab National Bank in which the L.I.C. and other financial institutions had substantial holdings. When the bank was nationalized, the residual company proposed a scheme whereby those shareholders, who wish to opt out, could receive a certain amount as compensation in cash. It was only at the instant and bargaining strength of institutional investors that the compensation offered to the shareholders, who wish to opt out of the company, was raised considerably.

5. Marketability of the shares: Mere listing of a share on the stock exchange does not automatically mean that the share can be sold and purchase. There may be inactive shares with no transaction for long period. So we have to examine the speculative interest of such scrip, extent of public holding and the particular stock exchange where it is traded. Fundamental analysis thus is basically an examination of the economics and financial aspects of a company with the aim of estimating future earnings and dividend prospect. So after having analyzed of all the relevant information we have to decide whether we should buy or sell the securities.

II. Timing of Purchases

The timing of dealings in the securities, specially shares is of crucial importance, because after correctly identifying the companies one may lose money if the timing is bad due to wide fluctuation in the price of shares of that companies.

The decision regarding timing of purchases is particularly difficult because of certain psychological factors. It is obvious that if a person wishes to make any gains, he should buy cheap and sell dear, *i.e.,* buy when the share are selling at a low price and sell when they are at a higher price. But in practical it is a difficult task. When the prices are rising in the market, *i.e.,* there is bull phase, everybody joins in buying without any delay because every day the prices touch a new high. Later when the bear face starts, prices tumble down everyday and everybody starts counting the losses. The ordinary investor regretted such situation by thinking why he did not sell his shares in previous day and ultimately sell at a lower price. This kind of investment decision is entirely devoid of any sense of timing.

25.11 VARIOUS THEORIES AND TECHNIQUES TO DEAL WITH THE PORTFOLIO MANAGEMENT

There are various theories and technique to deal with the portfolio management, some of their concept are discuss shortly hereunder:

Dow theory: According to this theory of Charles H. Dow, purchase should be made when bull trend started, *i.e.,* when price of the share are on the rise and sells them when they are on the fall, *i.e.,* at the time when bearish trend started.

Randam walk theory: Basically stock prices can never be predicted because they are not a result of any underlying factors but are mere statistical ups and downs. This hypothesis is known as Randam walk hypothesis. In the Layman's language it may be said that prices on the stock exchange behave exactly the way a drunk would behave while walking in a blind lane, *i.e.* up and down, with an unsteady way going in any direction he likes, bending on the side once and on the other side the second time.

Moving average: It refers to the mean of the closing price which changes constantly and moves ahead in time, there by encompasses the most recent days and deletes the old one.

25.12 TYPES OF PORTFOLIO MANAGEMENT

I. *Investment portfolio management.* In finance, a portfolio is a collection of investments held by an institution or an individual.

Holding a portfolio is a part of an investment and risk-limiting strategy called diversification. By owning several assets, certain types of risk (in particular specific risk) can be reduced. The assets in the portfolio could include bank accounts, stocks, bonds, options, warrants, gold certificates, real estate, futures contracts, production facilities, or any other item that is expected to retain its value. In building up an investment portfolio a financial institution will typically conduct its own investment analysis, while a private individual may make use of the services of a financial advisor or a financial institution which offers portfolio management services.

Over time, other industry sectors have adapted and applied these ideas to other types of "investments," including the following:

II. *Application portfolio management. This refers to the practice of managing an entire group or major subset of software applications within a portfolio. Organizations regard these applications as investments because they require development (or acquisition) costs and incur continuing maintenance costs. Also, organizations must constantly make financial decisions about new and existing software applications, including whether to invest in modifying them, whether to buy additional applications, and when to "sell" — that is, retire — an obsolete software application.*

III. *Product portfolio management. Businesses group major products that they develop and sell into (logical) portfolios, organized by major line-of-business or business segment. Such portfolios require ongoing management decisions about what new products to develop (to diversify investments and investment risk) and what existing products to transform or retire (i.e., spin off or divest).*

IV. *Project or initiative portfolio management. An initiative, in the simplest sense, is a body of work with:*

A specific (and limited) collection of needed results or work products.

A group of people who are responsible for executing the initiative and use resources, such as funding.

A defined beginning and end.

Managers can group a number of initiatives into a portfolio that supports a business segment, product, or product line. These efforts are goal-driven; that is, they support major goals and/or components of the enterprise's business strategy. Managers must continually choose among competing initiatives (i.e., manage the organization's investments), selecting those that best support and enable diverse business goals (i.e., they diversify investment risk). They must also manage their investments by providing continuing oversight and decision-making about which initiatives to undertake, which to continue, and which to reject or discontinue.

25.13 IMPORTANCE OF PORTFOLIO MANAGEMENT IN INDIA

Of course portfolio management definitely means that you are left with more money in your pockets. Efficient portfolio management also reduces overall expenditures by 20% by saving the losses that are otherwise made on loss making investments.

So far in India, most of the middle class earners have been risk-averse and therefore park most of their savings in Fixed Deposits and Other Savings Accounts, though the yield from such investment avenues is very low. However, the recent trend has been such that more people have been attracted towards investment in Mutual Funds and Equities. It is in this light that Portfolio Management Companies have been gaining prominence in India. The trend is only set to go upwards in the years to come, as the Indian middle class becomes more risk friendly.

Indian Case Examples

CASE EXAMPLE: PORTFOLIO MANAGEMENT SERVICES (PMS) IN INDIA INFOLINE

The Portfolio Management Service of India Info line is a product wherein an equity investment portfolio is created to suit the investment objectives of a client. India Info line invests client's resources into stocks from different sectors, depending on his risk-return profile. This service is particularly advisable for investors who cannot afford to give time or don't have that expertise for day-to-day management of their equity portfolio.

It is all about those clients money, being managed by the experts, while we continue with our routine life. Isn't it simple and totally hassle free!

What's more, clients can keep track of their dividends/bonus/rights issues with paperless tracking. So clients know how faster investment is growing. It basically means assigning the right job to the right person".

Salient Features of India Info line PMS:

Expert Team of Research Analysts
Stock Picking done by the Investment Committee
Dedicated Relationship Manager
Technology and Service driven Back-Office

25.14 SOME MODELS OF PORTFOLIO

Some of the financial models used in the process of valuation, stock selection, and management of portfolios include:

A. Three-Factor Model for Portfalio Management

Three-Factor Model for Portfolio Management: Three factor model is a widely followed model for portfolio management. It successfully explains more than 90 per cent of return from markets and products. Three factor model can be used by any type of traders or investors to predict and earn returns on investments.

Three factor model, popularly known as Fama and French three-factor model, is one of the most followed portfolio management models. The model was developed in 1993 by Eugene Fama and Kenneth French; by modifying other very popular investing model Capital Asset Pricing Model (CAPM). Three-factor model is widely followed by investors and fund managers to analyze risk and return associated with instruments/markets and to make highest return for risk taken.

For good understanding of three-factor model, understanding of CAPM, the original model, is necessary. CAPM considers only one factor, the market risk or beta, to determine the risk and return. The formula of CAPM is as follows:

$$A_j = R_F + \beta j \ (M - R_F)$$

Where, A_j is the return, R_F is the return rate of risk-free investments, beta is the risk associated with a security/market, and R_M is the return expected from market. The model says that it is better to invest in instruments/markets whose expected return exceeds required return. CAPM successfully explains around 80% of returns.Three factor model is more evolved than CAPM. In addition to market risk or beta, it considers two more market factors, size or market capitalization and value or book/market ratio of an instrument. The formula of three factor model is as follows:

$$A_j = R_F + \beta_j \times (M - R_F) + \beta_s \times SMB + \beta_v \times HML$$

Where, SMB is 'Small cap Minus Big' (historic excess returns of small cap instruments), HML is 'High value Minus Low' (historic excess returns of value stocks), and β_s and β_v are beta corresponding to small cap and large cap portfolio having values either 0 to 1. For a portfolio having all small cap stocks Bs will be 1 and Bv will be 0 and for a portfolio having all large cap stocks Bs will be 0 and Bv will be 1.

The idea behind the three factor portfolio management model is that, value and small cap stocks often outperform large-cap stocks. Most possible reason for this out performance include (1) higher reward for compensating higher risk taken, (2) early mispricing of equities resulting in later corrections, and (3) small-cap companies often shows higher growth and this is reflected on their stock prices:

The widespread adoption of three factor model by investors is a result of the fact that mutual funds and portfolio managers following three factor model of investment outperformed most others. Investors can also add custom factors to the model to make it more precise and to enhance reward. But investing only in small cap or value stocks can cause problems for investors, especially in periods of high volatility. Investors should diversify their portfolio investments and should be aware of other risk minimizing strategies.

B. Modern Portfolio Theory — a model proposed by Harry Markowitz among others

Modern portfolio theory (MPT) is a theory of investment which attempts to maximize portfolio expected return for a given amount of portfolio risk, or equivalently minimize risk for a given level of expected return, by carefully choosing the proportions of various assets. Although MPT is widely used in practice in the financial industry and several of its creators won a Nobel memorial prize for the theory, in recent years the basic assumptions of MPT have been widely challenged by fields such as behavioral economics.

MPT is a mathematical formulation of the concept of diversification in investing, with the aim of selecting a collection of investment assets that has collectively lower risk than any individual asset. That this is possible can be seen intuitively because different types of assets often change in value in opposite ways. For example, as prices in the stock market tend to move independently from prices in the bond market, a collection of both types of assets can therefore have lower overall risk than either individually. But diversification lowers risk even if assets' returns are not negatively correlated—indeed, even if they are positively correlated.

More technically, MPT models an asset's return as a normally distributed function (or more generally as an elliptically distributed random variable), defines risk as the standard deviation of return, and models a portfolio as a weighted combination of assets so that the return of a portfolio is the weighted combination of the assets' returns. By combining different assets whose returns are not perfectly positively correlated, MPT seeks to reduce the total variance of the portfolio return. MPT also assumes that investors are rational and markets are efficient.

MPT was developed in the 1950s through the early 1970s and was considered an important advance in the mathematical modeling of finance. Since then, many theoretical and practical criticisms have been leveled against it. These include the fact that financial returns do not follow a Gaussian distribution or indeed any symmetric distribution, and that correlations between asset classes are not fixed but can vary depending on external events (especially in crises). Further, there is growing evidence that investors are not rational and markets are not efficient.

C. Capital Assets Pricing Model (CAPM)

CAPM provides a conceptual framework for evaluating any investment decision. It is used to estimate the expected return of any portfolio with the following formula:

See the Chapter of Risk and Return (Chapter 3, para 3.6)

The CAPM model of portfolio management can be used effectively to:

1. Estimate the required rate of return to investors on company's common stock.
2. Evalute risky investment projects involving real Assets.
3. Explain why the use of borrowed fund increases the risk and increases the rate of return.
4. Reduce the risk of the firm by diversifying its project portfolio.

❑❑❑

26 Corporate Restructuring

26.1 CORPORATE RESTRUCTURING

Restructuring is the corporate management term for the act of partially dismantling and reorganizing a company for the purpose of making it more efficient and therefore more profitable. It generally involves selling off portions of the company and making severe staff reductions.

Restructuring is often done as part of a bankruptcy or of a takeover by another firm, particularly a leveraged buyout by a private equity firm. It may also be done by a new CEO hired specifically to make the difficult and controversial decisions required to save or reposition the company.

The "Corporate restructuring" is an umbrella term that includes mergers and consolidations, divestitures and liquidations and various types of battles for corporate control. The essence of corporate restructuring lies in achieving the long run goal of wealth maximization.

26.2 CHARACTERISTICS OF CORPORATE RESTRUCTURING

The selling of portions of the company, such as a division that is no longer profitable or which has distracted management from its core business, can greatly improve the company's balance sheet. Staff reductions are often accomplished partly through the selling or closing of unprofitable portions of the company and partly by consolidating or outsourcing parts of the company that perform redundant functions (such as payroll, human resources, and training) left over from old acquisitions that were never fully integrated into the parent organization. Other characteristics of restructuring can include:

(i) Changes in corporate management (usually with golden parachutes).

(ii) Retention of corporate management sometimes "stay bonus" payments or equity grants.

(iii) Sale of underutilized assets, such as patents or brands.

(iv) Outsourcing of operations such as payroll and technical support to a more efficient third party.

(v) Moving of operations such as manufacturing to lower-cost locations.

(vi) Reorganization of functions such as sales, marketing, and distribution.

(vii) Renegotiation of labour contracts to reduce overhead.

(viii) Refinancing of corporate debt to reduce interest payments.

(ix) A major public relations campaign to reposition the company with consumers.

(x) Forfeiture of all or part of the ownership share by pre restructuring stock holders.

26.3 RATIONALE AND IMPORTANCES OF CORPORATE RESTRUCTURING

Last year, M&A activities were largely restricted to IT and telecom sectors. They have now spread across the economy. As Business world recently reported, this is the fourth wave of corporate deal-making in India.

The first happened in the 1980s, led by corporate raiders such as Swaraj Paul, Manu Chhabria and R.P. Goenka, in the very early days of reforms. In view of the license raj prevailing then, buying a company was one of the best ways to generate growth, for ambitious corporates.

In the early 1990s, in the liberalized economy, Indian business houses began to feel the heat of competition. Conglomerates that had lost focus were forced to sell non-core businesses that could not withstand competitive pressures. The Tatas, for instance, sold TOMCO to Hindustan Lever. Corporate restructuring, largely drove this second wave of M&As.

The third wave started about five years ago, driven by consolidation in key sectors like cement and telecommunications. Companies like Bharti Tele-Ventures and Hutch bought smaller competitors to establish a national presence.

What makes the most recent wave of M&As different from the three previous ones is the involvement of global players. Foreign private equity is coming into Indian companies, like Newbridge's recent investment in Shriram Holdings.

Multinational corporations are also entering India. Swiss cement, Major Holcim's investment in ACC and Oracle's purchase of a 41 per cent stake in i-flex solutions (for $593 million) are good examples.

Meanwhile, Indian companies, sensing attractive opportunities outside the country are also venturing abroad. Tata Steel has bought Singapore-based NatSteel for $486 million. Videocon has bought the colour picture tubes business of Thomson for $290 million.

Such global forays have become a possibility because foreign exchange is no longer a scarce commodity. They have also become a necessity because in globalizing industries, only players with global scale and reach can survive.

At the same time, the difficulties involved in making M&As click must not be underestimated. A paradigm shift is likely in the coming years. Friendly deals could give way to aggressive ones.

In future, we may see hostile bids and leveraged buyouts. Most M&As so far have been cash deals. With the Sensex crossing 9000, stock deals may become more common. As the appetite for deal making increases, the valuation is also bound to go up. In short, exciting times are ahead.

The term corporate restructuring encompasses three distinct, but related, groups of activities; expansions – including mergers and consolidations, tender offers, joint ventures, and acquisitions; contraction – including sell offs, spin offs, equity carve outs, abandonment of assets, and liquidation; and ownership and control – including the market for corporate control, stock repurchases program, exchange offers and going private (whether by leveraged buyout or other means). Mergers and acquisitions (M&A) and corporate restructuring are a big part of the corporate finance world. One plus one makes three: this equation is the special alchemy of a merger or an acquisition. The key principle behind buying a company is to create shareholder value over and above that of the sum of the two companies. Two companies together are more valuable than two separate companies – at least, that's the reasoning behind M&A.

This rationale is particularly alluring to companies when times are tough. Strong companies will act to buy other companies to create a more competitive, cost-efficient company. The companies will come together hoping to gain a greater market share or to achieve greater efficiency. Because of these potential benefits, target companies will often agree to be purchased when they know they cannot survive alone.

26.4 CATEGORIES OF RESTRUCTURING

We will briefly look at each of the three major categories of restructuring in the section which follow as:

1. Expansions: Expansions include mergers, consolidations, acquisitions and various other activities which result in an enlargement of a firm or its scope of operations. There is a lot of ambiguity in the usage of the terms associated with corporate expansions.

A Merger involves a combination of two firms such that only one firm survives. Mergers tend to occur when one firm is significantly larger than the other and the survivor is usually the larger of the two. A Merger can take the form of:

(i) Horizontal merger involves two firms in similar businesses. The combination of two oil companies or two solid waste disposal companies, for example would represent horizontal mergers.

(ii) Vertical mergers involves two firms involve in different stages of production of the same end product or related end product.

(iii) Conglomerate mergers involve two firms in unrelated business activities.

A **consolidation** involves the creation of an altogether new firm owning the assets of both of the first two firms and neither of the first two survives. This form of combination is most common when the two firms are of approximately equal size.

The joint ventures, in which two separate firms pool some of their resources, is another such form that does not ordinarily lead to the dissolution of either firm. Such ventures typically involve only a small portion of the cooperating firm's overall businesses and usually have limited lives.

The term acquisition is another ambiguous term. At the most general, it means an attempt by one firm, called the acquiring firm to gain a majority interest in another firm called the target firm. The effort to gain control may be a prelude to a subsequent merger to establish a parent subsidiary relationship, to break up the target firm and dispose of its assets or to take the target firm private by a small group of investors. There are a number of strategies that can be employed in corporate acquisitions like friendly takeovers, hostile takeovers etc. The specialist have engineered a number of strategies which often have bizarre nicknames such as shark repellents and poison pills terms which accurately convey the genuine hostility involved. In the same vein, the acquiring firm itself is often described as a raider. One such strategy is to empty a target block repurchases with an accompanying standstill agreement. This combination sometimes describes as greenmail.

2. Contractions: Contraction, as the term implies, results in a smaller firm rather than a larger one. If we ignore the abandonment of assets, occasionally a logical course of action, corporate contraction occurs as the result of disposition of assets. The disposition of assets, sometimes called sell-offs, can take either of three board form:

(a) Spin-offs

(b) Divestitures

(c) Carve outs.

Spin-offs and carve outs create new legal entities while divestitures do not.

3. Ownership and Control: The third method is ownership and control. It has been wrested from the current board, the new managemt will often embark on a full or partial liquidating strategy involving the sale of assets. The leveraged buyout preserves the integrity of the firm as legal entity but consolidates ownership in the hands of small groups. In the 1980s, many large publicly traded firms went private and employes a similar strategy called a leveraged buyout or LBO.

Whether a purchase is considered a merger or an acquisition really depends on whether the purchase is friendly or hostile and how it is announced. In other words, the real difference lies in how the purchase is communicated to and received by the target company's board of directors, employees and shareholders.

26.5 RESTRUCTURING METHODS

There are several restructuring methods: doing an outright sell-off, doing an equity carve-out, spinning off a unit to existing shareholders or issuing tracking stock. Each has advantages and disadvantages for companies and investors. All of these deals are quite complex.

Sell-Offs: A sell-off, also known as a divestiture, is the outright sale of a company subsidiary. Normally, sell-offs are done because the subsidiary doesn't fit into the parent company's core strategy. The market may be undervaluing the combined businesses due to a lack of synergy between the parent and subsidiary. As a result, management and the board decide that the subsidiary is better off under different ownership.

Besides getting rid of an unwanted subsidiary, sell-offs also raise cash, which can be used to pay off debt. In the late 1980s and early 1990s, corporate raiders would use debt to finance acquisitions. Then, after making a purchase they would sell-off its subsidiaries to raise cash to service the debt. The raiders' method certainly makes sense if the sum of the parts is greater than the whole. When it isn't, deals are unsuccessful.

Equity Carve-outs: More and more companies are using equity carve-outs to boost shareholder value. A parent firm makes a subsidiary public through an initial public offering (IPO) of shares, amounting to a partial sell-off. A new publicly-listed company is created, but the parent keeps a controlling stake in the newly traded subsidiary.

A carve-out is a strategic avenue a parent firm may take when one of its subsidiaries is growing faster and carrying higher valuations than other businesses owned by the parent. A carve-out generates cash because shares in the subsidiary are sold to the public, but the issue also unlocks the value of the subsidiary unit and enhances the parent's shareholder value.

The new legal entity of a carve-out has a separate board, but in most carve-outs, the parent retains some control. In these cases, some portion of the parent firm's board of directors may be shared. Since the parent has a controlling stake, meaning both firms have common shareholders, the connection between the two will likely be strong.

That said, sometimes companies carve-out a subsidiary not because it's doing well, but because it is a burden. Such an intention won't lead to a successful result, especially if a carved-out subsidiary is too loaded with debt, or had trouble even when it was a part of the parent and is lacking an established track record for growing revenues and profits.

Carve-outs can also create unexpected friction between the parent and subsidiary. Problems can arise as managers of the carved-out company must be accountable to their public shareholders as well as the owners of the parent company. This can create divided loyalties.

Spinoffs: A spinoff occurs when a subsidiary becomes an independent entity. The parent firm distributes shares of the subsidiary to its shareholders through a **stock dividend.** Since this transaction is a dividend distribution, no cash is generated. Thus, spinoffs are unlikely to be used when a firm needs to finance growth or deals. Like the carve-out, the subsidiary becomes a separate legal entity with a distinct management and board.

Like carve-outs, spinoffs are usually about separating a healthy operation. In most cases, spinoffs unlock hidden shareholder value. For the parent company, it sharpens management focus. For the spinoff company, management doesn't have to compete for the parent's attention and capital. Once they are set free, managers can explore new opportunities.

Investors, however, should beware of throw-away subsidiaries the parent created to separate legal liability or to off-load debt. Once spinoff shares are issued to parent company shareholders, some shareholders may be tempted to quickly dump these shares on the market, depressing the share valuation.

Tracking Stock: A tracking stock is a special type of stock issued by a publicly held company to track the value of one segment of that company. The stock allows the different segments of the company to be valued differently by investors. Let's say a slow-growth company trading at a low price-earnings ratio (P/E ratio) happens to have a fast growing business unit. The company might issue a tracking stock so the market can value the new business separately from the old one and at a significantly higher P/E rating. Why would a firm issue a tracking stock rather than spinning-off or carving-out its fast growth business for shareholders? The company retains control over the subsidiary; the two businesses can continue to enjoy synergies and share marketing, administrative support functions, a headquarters and so on. Finally, and most importantly, if the tracking stock climbs in value, the parent company can use the tracking stock it owns to make acquisitions.

Still, shareholders need to remember that tracking stocks are class B, meaning they don't grant shareholders the same voting rights as those of the main stock. Each share of tracking stock may have only a half or a quarter of a vote. In rare cases, holders of tracking stock have no vote at all.

26.6 MERGERS AND ACQUISITIONS: MANY WAYS TO VALUE COMPANIES

Investors in a company that is aiming to take over another one must determine whether the purchase will be beneficial to them. In order to do so, they must ask themselves how much the company being acquired is really worth.

Naturally, both sides of an M&A deal will have different ideas about the worth of a target company: its seller will tend to value the company at as high of a price as possible, while the buyer will try to get the lowest price that he can.

There are, however, many legitimate ways to value companies. The most common method is to look at comparable companies in an industry, but deal makers employ a variety of other methods and tools when assessing a target company. Here are just a few of them:

Comparative Ratios – The following are two examples of the many comparative metrics on which acquiring companies may base their offers:

Price-Earnings Ratio (P/E Ratio) – With the use of this ratio, an acquiring company makes an offer that is a multiple of the earnings of the target company. Looking at the P/E for all the stocks within the same industry group will give the acquiring company good guidance for what the target's P/E multiple should be.

Enterprise-Value-to-Sales Ratio (EV/Sales) – With this ratio, the acquiring company makes an offer as a multiple of the revenues, again, while being aware of the price-to-sales ratio of other companies in the industry.

Replacement Cost – In a few cases, acquisitions are based on the cost of replacing the target company. For simplicity's sake, suppose the value of a company is simply the sum of all its equipment and staffing costs. The acquiring company can literally order the target to sell at that price, or it will create a competitor for the same cost. Naturally, it takes a long time to assemble good management, acquire property and get the right equipment. This method of establishing a price certainly wouldn't make much sense in a service industry where the key assets – people and ideas – are hard to value and develop.

Discounted Cash Flow (DCF) – A key valuation tool in M&A, discounted cash flow analysis determines a company's current value according to its estimated future cash flows. Forecasted free cash flows (operating profit + depreciation + amortization of goodwill – capital expenditures – cash taxes – change in working capital) are discounted to a present value using the company's weighted average costs of capital (WACC). Admittedly, DCF is tricky to get right, but few tools can rival this valuation method.

26.7 DEBT RESTRUCTURING

Debt restructuring is a process that allows a private or public company – or a sovereign entity – facing cash flow problems and financial distress, to reduce and renegotiate its delinquent debts in order to improve or restore liquidity and rehabilitate so that it can continue its operations.

A debt restructuring is usually less expensive and a preferable alternative to bankruptcy. The main costs associated with a business debt restructuring are the time and effort to negotiate with bankers, creditors, vendors and tax authorities. Debt restructurings typically involve a reduction of debt and an extension of payment terms.

26.8 FINANCIAL RESTRUCTURING

Financial Restructuring :

I. Change in Debt Structure
II. Change in Capital Base
III. Change in Group Structure

I. Change in Debt Structure

1. Corporate Debt Restructuring (CDR): Our strong Business relationship with leading banks and financial institutions has helped us in assisting companies to get their debts restructured. Corporate Debt Restructuring (CDR) has evolved as a voluntary and non-statutory arrangement between lenders and borrowers, for timely and orderly restructuring of debts of corporate entities affected by certain internal and external factors.

Timely corrective actions, when the assumptions made at the time the project was conceived and executed do not materialize, will go a long way in preserving the economic value of the project. To the bankers this is a crucial element in credit management. Even for an impaired loan, restoring the health through a structured restructuring exercise is the first step in NPA Management. If this fails, one needs to look for a quick exit option. Legal steps for recovery of dues take time and in the process, the value of assets goes down. For a banker time value of money is critical. Sale of the assets at the best possible price is the ideal way to recycle the funds blocked in NPAs and also clean up the Balance Sheet

2. One time Settlement (OTS): We can assist companies in getting their long outstanding debts through one Times setlement of RBI.

3. Swapping of Debts: We also assist in getting debts swapped through banks and financial institutions. Swapping of debt can be for cost reduction as well as tenure adjustment

II. Change in Capital Base

1. Buy Back Shares: We assist companies in changing their capital base through buy back of shares. Buy back of shares is permitted in many parts of the World. The main reasons for following this route are return of surplus cash to the shareholders, increasing underlying share value, supporting share prices during temporary weakness, and preventing or blocking hostile takeovers. Buy back is also used as a financial strategy by corporates for streamlining their capital structure, swapping equity for debt, as well as for reducing the number of shareholders to reduce the cost for servicing them, etc.

2. Reduction in Capital: This occurs when a borrower makes a lump sum payment towards the capital owed on a mortgage. Also known as a partial redemption, it often has a minimum permitted amount and is a process whereby the issued capital of a company is reduced. There are two circumstances in which this might take place. These are:

(i) Where future operations of the company are expected to be on a reduced scale so that a smaller level of finance will be required; and

(ii) Where it has to be accepted that past revenue losses can never be made good and that they amount to a permanent loss of capital.

III. Change in Group Structure

1. Merger and De-merger within the Group Companies

(i) Merger: A legal action resulting in the unification of two or more legal entities. Such an event can be advantageous because of Economies of Scale and also give a competitive edge by synergies derived from the unification.

(ii) De-merger: The splitting of a company often originally formed as a result of a merger, into two or more separate companies. It gives the existing shareholders shares in both companies.

2. Amalgamation: The combination of two or more commercial companies into one unit.

26.9 CASE EXAMPLES OF CORPORATE RESTRUCTURING IN INDIA

There were various corporate restructurings in India during the last few years. However, we are dealing with successful corporate restructuring of three Indian companies which immensely enhanced the shareholders' market value and strengthened their competitive edge in recent times. These are Reliance Industries Ltd., Larsen and Toubro Ltd., and Siemens Ltd.

For example, the acquisition, merger, and demerger of Reliance Industries Ltd. like their acquisition of IPCL (5) mergers of Reliance Petrochemicals Ltd., and the recent demergers of four entities like Reliance Communication Ventures Ltd., Reliance Energy Ventures Ltd., Reliance Natural Resources Ventures Ltd., and Reliance Capital Ventures Ltd. which spun off from Reliance Industries Ltd. (RIL), and were perhaps the most prominent restructurings in recent times.

Even the recent demerger of the cement division of Larsen and Toubro Ltd. (L&T), named Ultratech Cement Ltd., seems to be one of the L&Ts grand strategies to concentrate more on infrastructure, engineering, energy and turnkey businesses. Other kinds of restructuring through structural changes, to improve sales and profit, or all round optimization of products, processes and systems in Multinational like Siemens Ltd. are worthy examples of successful restructuring in Indian industry.

A. CASE OF RELIANCE INDUSTRIES LIMITED (RIL)

Background

At the age of 16, a young man left his rural Gujarat village for the Arabian Peninsula in 1949. His first job was pumping gas at Yemen. Soon he demonstrated his entrepreneurial spirit and managed to negotiate for people whose insurance claims had been rejected, splitting the settlements he managed to negotiate. He returned to India in 1958 with $3,150 (in those days) and set up a trading company to export spices to Yemen. It was then called Reliance Commercial Corporation. The entrepreneur of this company was Shri Dhirubhai Ambani. By the late 1960s, with 70 employees, Reliance was manufacturing textiles with four wrap-knitting machines. To explore the need of the society, Dhirubhai applied his innovative spirit when most corporate bosses were content to sit behind India's walls of protectionism and rake in profits from obsolete, overpriced goods. For example, to overcome the wholesaler's monopoly of the cloth market, he set up a chain of franchises. Today the Vimal brand of textiles is one the industry's top sellers. At the starting stage, banks often spurned him; hence, he turned to small investors to fund his expansion plans into synthetics and petrochemicals.

Reliance was one of the first Indian companies to go public in 1977. On 27th June 1985, the name of the company was finally changed, from Reliance Textile Industries Ltd. to Reliance Industries Ltd. Then there was no looking back. The company continued to satisfy its shareholders through big bonuses and hefty dividends. When India instituted market reforms in 1991, RIL was perfectly placed; it was lean, with state-of-the-art facilities, and a cadre of capable and competent managers. At this moment RIL was not very concerned about competition from Indian companies. That is why Dhirubhai Ambani once said, "My real competitors are DuPont, Shell and ICI." Hence RIL's next challenge was to meet its international competitors. By the mid 90s, RIL aggressively diversified into telecommunication, power, finance, and transportation.

The Dhirubhai Saga Continued

The RIL Chairman, Dhirubhai Ambani, was listed among "Asia's 50 most powerful people for 1998" by Asia Week Magazine in 1998. In the same year, he was also the first Indian recipient to get the Wharton School Dean's medal (6). In 1999, the Chairman of RIL was again voted as the "Indian Businessman of the Century" by a worldwide multimedia poll conducted between August to October 1999 by Business Baron Magazine.

RIL entered into the telecom segment in the year 2000. The company also submitted open offers to take control of BSES (7) stocks and took over BSES in 2002. It also planned to merge its finance company with another subsidiary Reliance Petrochemicals Ltd. (RPL). In March 2002, RPL merged with RIL. In the same yea, RIL bagged a 25 per cent share of IPCL. On July 6, 2002 the great Reliance patriarch Dhirubhai Ambani passed away.

Mukesh Ambani, elder son of Dhirubhai Ambani, was elected as Chairman of RIL on July 31st 2002. RIL diversified further into the areas of biotech, life sciences, mining, and insurance.

Ambani Empire Split

RIL, one of India's largest private sectors groups, was split in June 2005 due to differences between two successor brothers. The RIL struggle was not only a clash of egos between estranged brothers, but it was also about big money in the area of ₹ 1,000 billion which was not easy to share. Also not easy to understand were the complexities involved in running such an empire with two power centers.

On January 17th, 2006, a unique trading and investment era was over. As per the demerger approved by RIL board in August 2005, both brothers, Mukesh and Anil—headed different businesses and five listed companies emerged as potential investment opportunities for investors by March 2006.

Among the group companies of RIL, Reliance Energy (earlier name was BSES) and Reliance Capital, were already listed at the exchanges. The remaining four companies were listed by the end of March 2006.

The New Structure

The new RIL structure gave Mukesh complete independent control in the business of oil exploration, refining, petrochemicals, and textile businesses through a standalone entity in RIL along with IPCL. His shares also included biotech firm Reliance Life Sciences and Trevira, a company in Europe which manufactures polyester fibers. Anil got control over power, communication, and financial businesses through four companies which came under Anil Dhirubhai Ambani Enterprise (ADAE) as part of the Reliance group.

These four companies were named as Reliance Capital Ventures Ltd. (proposed to be merged with another listed company Reliance Capital Ltd.), Reliance Energy Ventures Ltd. (proposed to be merged with existing company Reliance Energy Ltd.), Reliance Communication Ventures Ltd.(these include both Reliance Infocomm and Reliance Telecom) and Reliance Natural Resources Ltd. (which includes businesses in gas based energy undertakings).

Outcome of Demerger

After the demerger, share prices of the listed five companies (8) were quoted differently at the Bombay Stock Exchange and National Stock Exchange. Prior to the demerger, RIL's share was traded around ₹ 978 per share, but after the demerger the combined demerged share values of five companies came to around ₹ 1,235. This is a gain of almost 26 per cent for every shareholder.

B. CASE OF LARSEN AND TOUBRO LIMITED (L&T)

Background

L&T was established by two Danish engineers H. Holck Larsen and S.K.Toubro in 1942. Within a span of fifty years L&T became one of the most respected companies in India (9). The sales turnover of the company during last seven years rose from ₹ 53.88 billion in the year 1996/1997 to ₹ 115.25 billion in the year 2003/2004 (10). The company is a leading manufacturer and engineer in turnkey projects having diversified activities in electrical and electronics; construction projects; cement manufacturing; medical equipment; shipping; earthmoving equipment; heavy engineering and information technology. From the year 2000, the company was planning to restructure some of its business divisions through demerger and consolidation in order to concentrate more on infrastructure and turnkey businesses.

Reasons for L&T's Demerger

L&T was trying to protect itself from a takeover bid by Grasim Industries Ltd. (GIL) a flagship company of Aditya Birla Group, from the year 2001. GIL was trying to take over control in L&T management by purchasing shares of L&T from the open market. The company first acquired 15 per cent stake in L&T and also made an open offer to L&T shareholders to increase its stake. However, it could not get very good response from the existing L&T shareholders.

In this situation, if L&T's demerger plan of cement division had gone through, GIL's stake in the cement business would have gone down to 3.75 per cent. At this moment, GIL had already spent over Rs 10 billion in acquiring its L&T stake and was not ready to allow the latter's plan to demerge the cement business. GIL accused L&T that through demerger plan, L&T was trying to retain control of the cement division within itself, without focusing the interest of shareholders. According to GIL, under the L&T demerger plan, L&T shareholders would have only 24 per cent stake in the new cement company where individual shareholders would hold very little control in this new entity.

Demerger: The Three Steps

Finally, at the extraordinary general body meeting held on 3rd February 2004, shareholders approved the demerger of L&T's cement division. The name of the demerged entity was made public as Ultra Tech Cem Co Ltd. (UCL). This extraordinary general body meeting witnessed a lot of heat amongst the shareholders. On two main resolutions, two polls were conducted on the scheme of arrangement, involving the reduction of share capital of residual engineering from ₹ 2.48 billion and demerger of L&T cement division.

The face value of L&T share was also reduced from ₹ 10 to ₹ 2, awaiting poll results. L&T wanted 51 per cent of the shareholder's approval who were present in the meeting and voting of 75 per cent of value to go through for demerger. GIL was interested in acquiring the cement division of L&T and was confident that all the above objectives would be comfortably achieved.

The proposed open offer of cement division closed after the listing with the new company. With the demerger of the cement business, L&T needed to restructure the equity capital.

In a three step demerger plan, it was decided that in the first phase L&T would spin off the cement business into a new company, UltraTech Cem Co Ltd. (UCL), where L&T would hold 20 per cent and the balance of 80 per cent would be held by existing shareholders of L&T.

In the second phase, GIL would buy 8.5 per cent of UCL from L&T @ ₹ 342.60 per share and make an open offer to other shareholders of another 30 per cent at the same price. It would take GIL's stake to 51 per cent in UCL, if this offer was fully subscribed, and on the sale of its stake in UCL, L&T would realize ₹ 3.62 billion.

In the third phase, L&T Employee Welfare Foundation would acquire the GILs 15.3 per cent stake in the residual engineering company.

Hence, after the demerger, GIL gave an open offer to UCL shareholders and purchased the shares to cover a 51 per cent hold in UCL. Table-2 below, shows in short the sequence of the demerger process in L&T Ltd. Immediately after the acquisition, GIL finally changed the name from UltraTech CemCo. Ltd. to UltraTech Cement Ltd.

Outcome of L&T Demerger

There were two important issues in this demerger. The first important issue was that to protect the interests of both existing and former employees, L&T Employees Welfare Foundation was given a stake in the company. The second issue was how shareholders at large also could benefit from this demerger. During early 2003, L&T's ten-rupee face value share prior to demerger was hovering around ₹ 350/400 per share. After the demerger, for every 100 shares of L&T, shareholders got 50 shares of L&T of ₹ 2 face value each and 40 shares of UCL with face value of ₹ 10 each.

Around April 2004, the entire demerger process was complete. Although initially there were some corrections in the market, later share prices of both L&T and UCL started rising. Within three years shareholders of erstwhile L&T increased their wealth with a growth more than SENSEX or Nifty. In March 2006, the face value of ₹ 2 a share of L&T was quoted between ₹ 2,375 to ₹ 2,616 (11) per share, while of UCL was quoted between ₹ 562.5 to ₹ 689 12 per share on the Bombay Stock Exchange. This means shareholders' value went up by more than 100 per cent within two years, which was unprecedented in the history of demergers of any company.

C. CASE OF SIEMENS LIMITED

Background

Siemens Engineering and Manufacturing Company of India Limited was incorporated in the year 1956, as a subsidiary of Siemens AG., Germany. The company started manufacturing switchboard products at its Worli Factory, Mumbai. Thereafter, as the business grew, the company expanded its business into other product segments of power generation, power distribution, and medical engineering products.

By the year 1966, the company had four factories in different parts of the country employing more than 2500 people. In 1990, the name of the company was changed to Siemens India Ltd. In the same year, the company was divided into six products divisions and formed into strategic business units. In the year 1991, there was further restructuring of business divisions. Again, in the year 1994, the name of the company was further changed to Siemens Ltd. In the same year, product divisions were further sub-divided to achieve operational efficiency. The number of business divisions was increased to ten. However, to be very precise, from the wide range of the above-mentioned businesses—the major business segments of Siemens Ltd were in power, communication, medical solution, industrial automation, and railway and transport systems.

Despite many changes and repeated divisional restructuring, the company could not get the desired result to counter all-time competition. Then in the year 1996-97 (13) (18 months period), the company made a loss of almost ₹ 1.5 billion for the first time since its inception in the Indian business. This situation compelled the Siemens management to go for intense all-round corporate restructuring. The meaning of this corporate restructuring was to give a new structure to rebuild and rearrange the organization.

Manpower Downsizing

As a first step in July 1997, the company introduced a voluntary retirement scheme (VRS) followed by three such schemes till the year 2001 for all its employees in the factories at Worli, Kalwa and Joka, especially for those who were above 40 years of age or had completed 10 years of services. Those who were interested in VRS were paid a maximum lump sum amount of six hundred thousand rupees as compensation and those who were not interested in the VRS scheme were offered alternative jobs in different functions/locations. However, regular dialogues with the employees helped the management to reduce and adjust employees at the Worli, Joka and Kalwa factories. At the same time, the company faced the new problem of training the remaining employees who were required to do different jobs in new areas and with new skills.

These downsizing processes on four occasions reduced the employee strength by more than 4500 employees. However, the cost of VRS, relocation, and retraining of around 1000 (out of 4600) employees hit hard on the company's financial result. The company during the financial year 1997-98 made a further loss of Rupees 560 million. With the successes of downsizing, the processes of manpower reorganization had been a commanding task in the organization. The employee strength came down to 3896 in the year 01/02 compared to 8322 in 96/97. These downsizing processes revamped the human resource planning in the organization and removed many operational deficiencies.

Financial Restructuring

From the very inception, the company had engaged a renowned auditing firm, M/s Fergusson & Co. Ltd., to carry out its annual financial audits. However, despite good results year after year, the company fell short of working capital every year. Therefore it had to borrow capital from banks and from other investors at a high interest. At the end of every financial year, after paying the interests to the creditors, the company was short of working capital to run the business.

The company, in the year 1997-98, appointed M/s KPMG Ltd. to look after its financial audit. During the process of preliminary findings, it was observed that a large amount of inventory items were in the stocks, both as finished goods as well as raw materials, which were slow moving for a long time and were continuously audited as stocks, year after year. Similarly, there were some customers who did not pay their dues for long periods of time, on some pretext or another, and were shown as outstanding customers. Hence, the KPMG advised the company to write off the old stocks as well as long outstanding payments from customers.

The decision to write off the old stocks and doubtful dues from customers was agreed upon by the company. These measures added further financial loss during 1997-98. However, the company could dispose off some obsolete stocks and recover few pending dues from customers at later dates. The revenue generated was added up as surplus to the organization. This one time action of writing off the old/obsolete stocks and doubtful dues from customers helped the company to stop borrowing from banks and other financial brokers/institutions. The debt/equity ratio of the company in the year 1997-98 was 1.3:1. In the year 2002-03 this figure went down to 1.1 : 1, which showed how financial restructuring helped the organization to overcome the problem of working capital.

Restructuring of Processes and Systems in Different Divisions of Siemens Ltd.

Apart from downsizing the employee strength in some strategic business units and financial restructuring the company, in the year 1997, introduced Time Optimised Processes (TOP). These were similar to the business process re-engineering segments of its business. The processes started optimizing business processes of every function like sales, marketing, manufacturing, service, finance and human resources which were not tuned to productive performance. The uneconomical processes were removed to cut cost and improve the quality of business.

The company went further to look for economic consideration of its capacity utilization in the factories. It was observed that the return on capital investments made in earlier years in different factories was not paying proper dividends as planned during the budget period. Therefore, the company decided to go for outsourcing of products and services in different factories to achieve operational efficiency through a process of cost reduction. At the same time, the company also introduced stringent measures to follow the ISO 9000 quality system along with resurgence and renewal in all its divisions.

Medical Solutions Division (MSD)

The manufacturing of medical products in Siemens India commenced in the year 1957 at the premises of Worli Works, in Mumbai. The process of restructuring started in the Medical solutions division in early 1993 with the objective of manufacturing high-end medical solutions products for Siemens AG to cater to the South East Asian market. In 1994, a new manufacturing site was selected in the state of Goa, which had the cost advantage as sales taxes were exempted for the first five years for the new companies which set up industries there.

At the same time, the central government also exempted corporate taxes for these industries located in Goa for a period of five years. However, this project did not give any economic advantage to the company, as required by its principal in Germany. The company subsequently decided to restructure the local manufacturing in phases over the next three years to counter the increased manufacturing cost at its Worli factory in Mumbai. In the year 1997, the Medical Solutions Division of the company had manpower of 375 people in the factories which included 340 employees at Worli and 35 employees at Goa, including all officers.

In mid 1997, the company decided to procure the low-end products from outside vendors who had the requisite technology and could spare their machines and equipment for manufacturing these products. The idea was formulated to close down the Worli factory. However, the company continued manufacturing the core technology products like oil immersed multi-pulse X-ray generators at its Goa factory. In mid 1997, despite a lot of opposition from the employees at Worli for relocation, the company discussed the issue with workers and staff unions and offered transfers to relocate people in different departments/divisions of the organization.

With the all-round success of VRS, Siemens was able to transfer 140 employees to other locations and remaining took voluntary retirement from the division. With this action of the management, the employee strength in the Worli factory became zero, while at Goa, it was only 35. By the year 1999, the company was running the business of low-end products at one factory at Goa with just 35 people producing the same sales turnover of rupees 250 million which was earlier produced in the year 1996 at Worli with 340 people. With this restructuring, the low-end medical device products of the company became competitive and the company could regain its strength through a higher margin. The sequence of strategic changes in details that took place in the medical solutions division.

Low Voltage Distribution Systems Division (LVDSD)

With the increased demand of power in the country due to industrialization immediately after the Second Five Years Plan, the company expanded the manufacturing of switchboard products. In the year 1960, the company set up a workshop at Hide Road, Kolkata, for manufacturing and repair of power distribution equipment for the eastern region. In the year 1980, with the further demand of energy equipment, this factory was relocated to a new plant at Joka, just a few kilometers away from Kolkata. This division was then considered as a part of switchboard division. In the year 1999, the name of the switchboard division was changed to Energy Division. When the manufacturing facility at Joka was transformed into a sub division, it was named Low Voltage Distribution Systems Division.

However, in the year 2000-01, the low voltage industry was suffering from excessive manufacturing capacity due to the presence of a large number of players and dwindling demands as a result of depressed market conditions. The overall market for Low Voltage Distribution Systems Division remained stagnant and was characterized by intense competition, putting the price under tremendous pressure. As a consequence, the Lower Voltage Distribution business posted a 40 per cent drop in both turnover and order value. In its endeavor to make operations viable, the division proposed to introduce several measures; this included an offer of alternative jobs to its workers at the Siemens Metering, a plant in the neighborhood. This process of implementation made some delays resulting in the unit making even more production losses, thus affecting the result. At the end of the year 2001, the company closed down the Joka factory and adjusted its employees to Siemens Metering Ltd. After the closure of this factory, the division started procuring the low voltage products from the switchboard factory, thus making full-scale utilization of free capacity at its Kalwa factory.

The twin initiatives of closing down the high cost manufacturing operation at Joka and implementing a completely new business process of deploying a lean cost structure whilst maintaining high quality standards supported the division's turnaround. The entire business restructuring was achieved within a time period of less than two years.

As a result of focused market approach, the division achieved an increase in the market share. Customer loyalty and satisfaction was evidently demonstrated as it received several orders. The division developed new products. The concentrated focus on its spares and service business helped it record a four-fold increase in turnover in this line of business over the last three years. To further augment its service network, the division entered into a franchising arrangement with a Kolkata-based company, which utilizes the services of former employees of Joka works. Below gives a short detail of strategic changes in Low Voltage Distribution Systems Division.

Personnel Division

The process of renewal and resurgence was not confined only to factories of a few divisions, but also to the other areas of corporate systems. Being a part of corporate systems, the personnel division handled the human resource functions in the company. During the year 1994, the personnel division for the first time introduced an Enterprise Resource Planning (ERP) system, People-soft, to upkeep the employee data, and created an information highway for its concerned executives and managers. Then in the year 1997-98, the personnel division of Siemens Ltd. achieved a milestone for successful downsizing and implementation of corporate goals and objectives by retraining and relocating people for the emergent needs of the organization.

Apart from downsizing the manpower in other divisions, the personnel division also initiated VRS and relocations of some of its own employees and managers and outsourced some of the human resource processes and activities from outside parties who had much more experience in this field. For example, the company outsourced the entire process of employee benefit schemes like handling of Provident Fund (PF) and gratuity payments to an outside agency, M/s India Life Pension Services, with headquarters at Bangalore. This outside agency maintained all accounts of PF, gratuity and other pension schemes, and advised the personnel division of Siemens to make necessary payments after the retirement or separation of employees. The personnel division also outsourced the processes of salary payment to one of its affiliates, Siemens Information Systems Ltd. (SISL), which developed a software package of such services.

Then in the year 2000, in order to systemize its operations in personnel, the division opted for the ISO 9000 quality system, to regulate all the processes of personnel function and became one of the very few companies in the country holding independent ISO 9000 certification for its personnel function.

In the year 2005, the company introduced a new HR initiative on performance management to be known as EDGE (16). EDGE stands for Employee Dialogue for Growth and Entrepreneurship. EDGE was developed looking at the overall growth and development of employees from a holistic and long-term perspective. In the same year, as per companies shared service initiative, HR processes across all Siemens' entities were now streamlined and aligned with Siemens BPO global processes under one organization.

Outcome of Restructuring

The overall restructuring in Siemens started showing results after a few years of operations resulting in all-round satisfaction of stakeholders. The financial highlights beginning from 1998-99 the unique results of corporate restructuring. The share price of ₹ 10 (face value) which was hovering on the Bombay Stock Exchange (BSE) or National Stock Exchange (NSE) around ₹ 140/150 in 1997 rose to ₹ 5,500/5,600 in March 2006. As per ET 500 (Feb.'06), Siemens ranks one of top ten performing companies in India and a leader among 49 listed multinational company at BSE/NSE. While in the same footing Siemens AG stock price on 30th Sept., 2005 was quoted 64.10 [euro] compared to 41.89 [euro] in Sept. 2001. The five-year summary of Siemens AG.

Initially, restructuring processes followed by Siemens resulted in some amount of uncertainty in the minds of the employees. However, after the positive results of restructuring started pouring in, the cloud of uncertainty cleared. These were the moments when Siemens took care of handling the remaining productive employees.

The company which had losses for the first time since its inception decided to undertake a cleansing operation by downsizing manpower, optimizing all processes, outsourcing products and services and keeping the quality standards ahead of all future actions. These also included maintaining high employee morale at this juncture of productive changes.

Even when there was a need for financial restructuring, the company did not spare much time to take action. Continuous shortage of working capital forced the company to change auditing systems. Initially, this action made incurred losses for the company but it helped the management to reduce heavy interest payments in the long run. Above all, this course of operational restructuring finally helped the organization to go into the black. From the year 2000-01 onwards, the company did make a turnaround and started earning regular profits, resulted from the processes of progressive restructuring which are still continuing in the organization.

Points for Discussion

From the above cases of restructuring, the point may arise that, prior to restructuring; none of these companies were managed properly. They were huge in size; the company management could not select the right strategic options to push their businesses ahead of other priorities. Or, even, the core competency levels had reached to its saturation points when these business units were no longer viable and therefore restructuring was the only option to avoid losses or stagnation. The above arguments may be well suited to L&T Ltd. and Siemens where these companies had enough strength in power, infrastructure, medical equipment and Turnkey projects. L&T had its weaknesses in the cement business and Siemens had its advanced technologies but with huge manpower and multiple operations which were not cost competitive. All these forced the above companies to go for all-round restructuring. L&T took a wise decision and demerged its cement business.

Siemens Ltd. took a cultural shift and made an all round resurgence and renewal in its business through corporate restructuring. Even the parent company Siemens AG., despite having vast sales regions and business areas could not do that well compared to its counterpart in Siemens India Ltd.

All these studies finally reveal how progressive organizational restructuring can be incorporated in an organization. When any company makes losses or is likely to face odds in business, all-round pro-active changes are needed for the survival of that organization. For Siemens, in implementing the processes of manpower downsizing in different divisions, the company started making changes in a progressive manner.

But for RIL, the recent demerger was the outcome of a family feud between two brothers, which lead to the demerger of four strategic business divisions. This was more of a balancing act between two brothers to gain control in their areas of business. However, this demerger has definitely brought some transparency in the working of RIL which one may say was more complex prior to this arrangement.

However, all the above process of restructuring has added shareholders market value and can be construed as successful restructuring from the point of competitive advantage. Such innovative restructuring should always be made in the strategic plans for the survival, growth, and remain competitive in the market.

❑ ❑ ❑

27 Overview of Manager Control System

27.1 CONTROL

Control is the process of comparison and verification that measures current performance which is actual and guided towards expected performance with the objective of ensuring that the things are proceeding as per plan. If things are not proceeding as per plan, it helps in taking corrective measures.

Control is a continuous process of comparison and verification. Following are the basic steps:

(a) Setting performance standard as per plan

(b) Measuring job performance as per standard

(c) Taking corrective action, if required.

Elements of a Control System

There are 4 basic elements of any control system:

(i) A detector → a device that measures what is actually happening in the process being controlled.

(ii) An assessor → a device that determines the significance of what is actually happening by comparing it with some standard of what should happen.

(iii) An effector → a device, called feedback that alters behavior if the assessor indicated the need to do so.

(iv) A communication network → a device that transits information between the detector and the assessor and between the assessor and the effector.

27.2 TYPES OF CONTROL

Controls can be

(i) Physical in nature, *i.e.*, dealing with units of output or any other physical measures – exercised by personal supervision and checking. (may be quantitative on qualitative)

(ii) Financial in nature, *i.e.*, those generally expressed in monetary terms in relation to time and quantity.

Both forms are essential for management. But financial control plays more important role if overall importance of 'Finance' is considered. Financial control deals with the establishment of 'standards' or 'norms' and then making provisions for reporting deviations from the established standards.

The financial control systems are:

(i) Budgetary Control

(ii) Standard Costing

(iii) Financial Ratio Analysis

(iv) Break even analysis

(v) Responsibility Accounting

(vi) Transfer Pricing

(vii) Fund flow Analysis

(viii) Proprietary and Management Audit

(ix) Cash Flow Analysis

27.3 SCOPE OF CONTROL

The scope of control is very wide. It virtually covers all the areas of business, namely, policies, procedures, men, money, machines and equipments, public relations, human relations, research and developments and so on. Control process involves concentration of key areas of business and key result areas on what the success of the business depends.

Control as a process: (steps of control in detail)

Control as a process involves basic steps (discussed in para 27.1). The detailed discussion of these steps is as follows:

(i) Establishing standards: A standard acts as a reference line or basic of comparison of actual performance. Standards should be set precisely and preferably in quantitative terms. Because it is essential to determine how the performance is going to be appraised. Standards should be accurate, precise, acceptable and workable. Standards should be flexible, *i.e.*, capable of being changed when the circumstances require so.

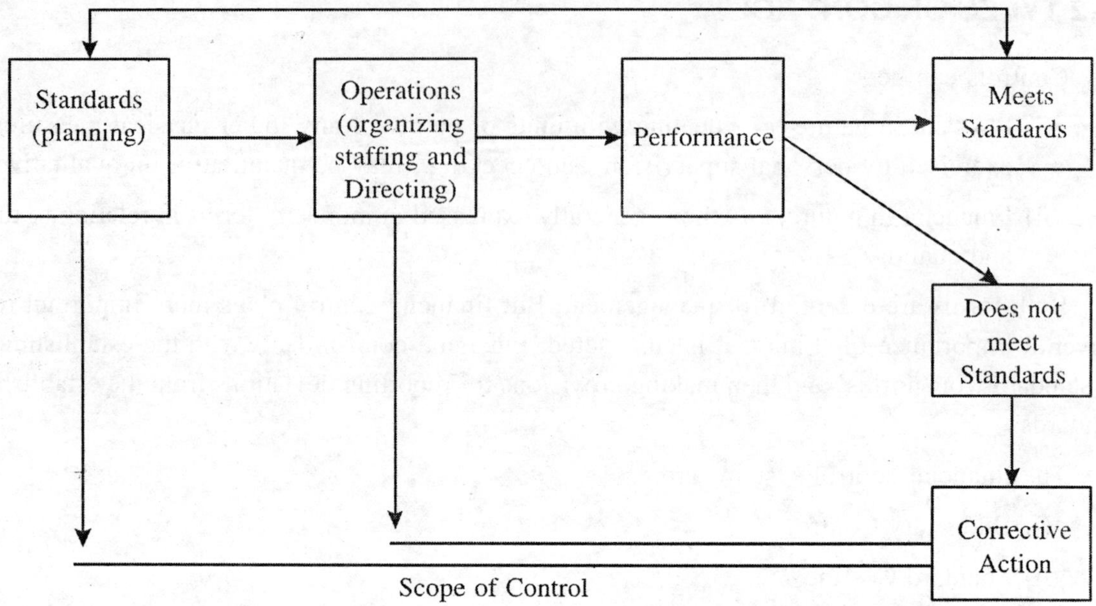

(ii) Appraising performance: This step involves measuring of actual performance of various individuals, groups or units and then comparing it with the standards which have already been set up at the planning stage. The quantitative measurement should be done in cases where standards have been set in quantitative terms. In other cases, performance should be measured in terms of quantitative factors as in case of performance of industrial relations manager.

(iii) Comparison: This is the core of the control process. This phase of control process involves checking to determine whether the actual performance meets the predetermined or planned performance. Manager must constantly seek to answer, "How well are we doing?"

(iv) Taking corrective action: The final step in the control process is taking corrective actions so that deviations may not occur again and the objectives of the organization are achieved. This will involve taking certain decision by the management like preplanning or redrawing of goals or standards, reassignment or clarification of duties. The following are important phases of corrective action:

1. The operative Phase

(a) Prompt investigation of the causes of the deviations.

(b) Decision concerning the required corrective actions.

(c) Prompt directions for correcting the situation in accordance with the decisions.

(d) Close supervision of the corrective actions to ensure that it is taking place according to the instructions and is effective.

2. The Administrative Phase

(a) Further investigation of recurring difficulties to determine the basic factors, either human or physical, that are responsible.

(b) Disciplinary action, either positive or negative, as the situation requires.

(c) Creative planning to prevent a recurrence of the situation.

(d) Recognition of the situation and the introduction of the planned measures.

Often control process is ineffective or fails because the corrective action recommended is not followed through. Specific procedures must be established and the responsibility must be clearly assigned to carry out the corrective action. The responsibility for that corrective action is not over just by making this recommendation. The superior must follow through his recommendation to see whether the individual participates and makes progress in the training programme and to what extent he relates to his actual work situation whatever he has learned in the training programme.

Feedback in Control: Performance information thus measured and channeled back to management is known as Feedback. It tells what kind of job is being done, what variations have occurred, and what kind of temporary measures taken to make adjustments, modifications and so on.

There are two types of feedback controls. One is **self-correcting** and the other is **non-correcting**. The self-correcting or servo-mechanism is one which regulates itself without outside intervention for corrective action to be taken. In steel mills, thermostat systems are used to make sure that heat remains uniform in various production processes.

The non-correcting system requires outside intervention before corrective action can take plane. Statistical quality control is an example of this type. Through statistical sampling, deviations are identified. Quality control charts are used for this purpose.

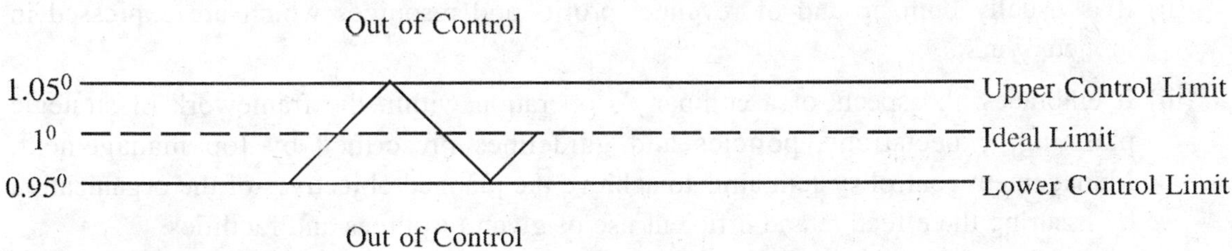

Quality Control Chart

In the above chart, let us say the predetermined standards set for the diameter of pipes as 1 inch. Due to the condition of machines and other factors the acceptable deviations were set at 1.05" (upper limit) and .95" (lower limit). When the diameter of the pipe goes beyond these limits, it is said to be out of control. At this point the process is halted and necessary adjustments are made with outside intervention and the system is brought back into control.

27.4 MANAGEMENT CONTROL

Management control is a systematic management effects to compare performances to predetermined standards, plans, on objectives in order to determine whether performance is in line with those standards and presumably in order to take any remedial action.

In other words, it is the process of evaluating, monitoring and controlling various sub-units so that there is effective and efficient allocation and utilization of resources in achieving the predetermined goals.

Management Control has two Aspects

1. System. The system outlines authority relationships, delegation of authority and responsibility, relationship between various sub-units, parameters for performance evaluation, etc.

2. Process. There are management processes involved in establishing goals and objectives, performance appraisal of responsibility centers ensuing achievement of targets and budgeted estimated performances, follow up of action and remedial action plan etc.

27.5 MANAGEMENT CONTROL SYSTEM, FEATURES AND OBJECTIVES

Management control system refers to a framework or set-up by which the manager can ensure control over the actions of his team members as well as control over the whole operations in an organisation.

Feature

(i) It focuses on programmes (product, produce line R&D Project etc.) and responsibility centers.

(ii) It is usually built around of revenue, profits and resources which are expressed in monetary units.

(iii) It embraces all aspects of a company's operation within the framework of strategic planning, expectations, policies and guidelines prescribed by top management. Management control system aims to achieve the planned objectives of the organization by assuring the effective and efficient use of given resources and facilities.

Objective: The objective of management control system to check whether the actual performance is in line with the expected performance set earlier as per standard on norms. The other objective is certainly to motivate managers to take actions and corrective actions both which are in the best interests of the company on which are in line with the expected performance. The ultimate aim of management control is to develop a process by which manager influence other members of the organization to implement the organizations strategies

27.6 TECHNIQUES OF MANAGEMENT CONTROL SYSTEM

(i) Mathematical Models (Operational control Technique): Operations Research Techniques, *e.g.*, Linear Programming, Integer Programming, Dynamic Programming, Goal Programming.

(ii) Computer Systems: EPP system, MIS, DSS, expert systems.

(iii) Financial Control Techniques: Discussed in para 27.2

(iv) Management Controls in Functional Areas

(a) Production control

(b) Inventory control

(c) Marketing control

(d) Distribution control

(e) Control of personnel and HR Matter

(f) Control of Information systems

27.7 MANAGEMENT CONTROL ACTIVITIES

(a) Planning what the organization should do

(b) Coordinating the activities of several parts of the organization

(c) Communicating and Evaluating information

(d) Deciding what, it any, action should be taken

(e) Influencing people to change their behaviors.

27.8 CONCEPT OF STRATEGY/STRATEGIC PLANNING

A strategy describes the several directions in which an organization plans to move to affair its goals. A firm develops its strategies by matching its core competencies with industry opportunities.

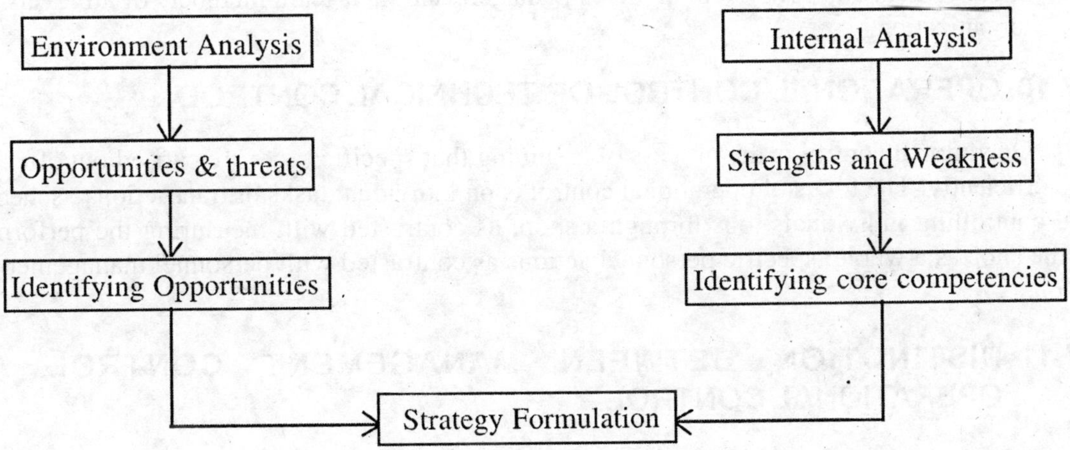

Strategies can be found at two levels:

(a) Strategies for a whole organization

(b) Strategies for business units which the organizations.

Strategies planning is long-term planning and is carried on at the top level of management. It is concerned with deciding the goals of the organization. Strategic planning has become a crucial exercise for the top management of enterprises because of the greater turbulence in environment in which such enterprise operates. Companies with large turnover and operating in diverse fields usually have a corporate planning department which is involved in the process of evaluating the changes in environment and its implication for the enterprise. It is also involved in the evaluation of new opportunities.

27.9 STRATEGY FORMULATION AND ITS DIFFERENCES WITH MANAGEMENT CONTROL

The need for formulation strategies usually arises in response to a perceived threat (*e.g.*, a shift in consumer's tasks and preferences development of new application for existing products etc). Strategies formulation is the process of deciding on the goals of the organization and the strategies for attaining training these goals. In this process, the goals of the organization are usually taken as a given.

Difference between Strategy Formulation and Management Control

(a) Strategy formulation is the process of deciding on new strategies while management control is the process of implementing those strategies.

(b) Strategy formulation is essentially unsystematic where that threats, opportunities and new ideas do not occur at regular intervals. By contrast the management control system involves a series of steps that occur in a predictable sequence according to a more fixed time table and with reliable estimates.

(c) Formulation of strategy involves senior management and other few people. By contrast the management control system involves managers and their team members of all levels in the organization.

27.10 OPERATIONAL CONTROL OR TECHNICAL CONTROL

Operational control is the process of assuming that specific tasks are carried out effectively and efficiently. The focus of operational control is on individual tasks or transactions : scheduling and controlling individuals jobs through a shop, as contrasted with measuring the performance of the shop as a whole; specific personnel actions as contrasted with personnel management; and so on.

27.11 DISTINCTION BETWEEN MANAGEMENT CONTROL AND OPERATIONAL CONTROL

(a) As an example of an activity to which operational control is applicable, consider the inventory area. If the demand for an item, the cost of storing it, its production cost, production time and the loss involved in not filling an order are known then the optimum inventory level and the optimum production or procurement schedule can be calculated. An inventory control system using rules derived form such calculations is an example of operational control.

By contrast, consider the legal department of a company. No device can measure the quality or even the quantity of the legal service that constitutes the output of this department. No formula can show the amount of service the department should render or the optimum amount of costs that should be incurred. The type of control necessary in this situation is management control.

(b) Examples of activities that are susceptible to operational control are automated plants, such as cement plants, oil refineries and power generating stations; the direct production operations of most manufacturing plants; production scheduling; inventory control; the order taking type of selling activity and order processing; premium billing; payroll accounting; cheque handling and similar paperwork activities. Examples of activities for which management control is necessary are the total operation of most manufacturing plants, which includes such judgment inputs as indirect labour, employees benefit and welfare programmes selling (as distinguished from order – taking), and similar marketing activities; most aspects of finance; most aspects of research, development, and design the work of staff units of all types; and, of course, the activities of top management; also safety activities, training and supervision etc.

(c) In management control, psychological considerations are dominant. The management control system at most assists those who take action; it does not directly or by itself results in action without human intervention. By contrast the end product of an inventory control system can be an order such as a decision to replenish a certain inventory item, and this order may be based entirely on calculation from formulas incorporated in the system. In operational control, rational considerations are dominant.

(d) The management control system is ordinarily built around a financial structure whereas operational control data are often nonmonetary. They may be expressed in terms of man-hours, members of items, pounds of waste, and so on. Since each operational control procedure is designed for a limited area of application, it is feasible to use the basis of measurement that is most appropriate for that area.

(e) The most important distinguish between operation control and management control is that many operation control system are sciencetific where management involves the behaviour of managers, it can never reduces to a since.

27.12 DISTINGUISH BETWEEN STRATEGIC PLANNING, MANAGEMENT CONTROL AND OPERATIONAL CONTROL

The strategic planning process is carried on at the top and the involvement of the middle management is small as against management control in which both the top management and middle management are closely involved. While strategic planning relies heavily on external information, management control largely uses data generated within the organization. Operational control uses data generated on specific tasks or activities.

The focus of activity in operational control is on specific tasks, while in management control it is on the whole operation of the organization. While the focus of operational control is on efficiency, management control essentially focuses on organizational effectiveness.

Characteristic	Strategic Planning	Management Control	Operational Control
Level	Top Management	All level top to front line supervision	Supervisory
Scope	Total	Overall, consisting of related subsystem	Operating unit
Time frame	Long range	Short to intermediate (1 to 5 years)	Short periods day-to-day, weekly, monthly
Environment	External, towards developing internal	Internal adjusting to external factors	Internal only
Goals and Objective	Basic objective	Tangible goals within framework of overall objectives	Short term, tangible to operating units of overall objective
Structuring	Relatively unstructured	Fairly highly structured but flexible	Quite rigid pre-establishment

27.13 MANAGEMENT CONTROL PROCESS / CYCLE

In general, it involves informal communication between a manager and others or between a manager and his team members. Informal of communication occurs by means of memorandum meeting, conversation and even by facial expression within a formal planning and control system. This system includes the following:

Step 1 : Strategic Planning

Step 2 : Budget Preparation

Step 3 : Execution

Step 4 : Evaluation of Performance

Strategic Planning is the 1st step in the management Control cycle. Strategies planning is long term planning and is carried on at the top level of management. It is concerned with deciding the goals of the organization. Strategic planning has become a crucial exercise for the top management of enterprises because of the greater turbulence in environment in which such enterprise operates. It is the process of deciding on the major programmes that the organization will undertake to implement its strategies and the allocation of resources to those programmes. Budget preparation comes next to the estimate. A budget is the plan for a specific time period. The estimates are taken for sales, expenses, profit, production and many others. The revenues and expenses are rearranged from programme to responsibility centers. Next comes execution which reflects that during the period of each responsibility the centre managers or departmental heads execute the programme or part of a programme of that centre or department for which they are responsible. They prepare the reports showing in formations both about the execution of programme and responsibility centers, budgeted and actual informations, financial and non financial measures etc. Their reports may be used as a basis of control. The process of evaluation is a comparison between actual and expected performances, which should have been under the circumstances.

27.14 RESPONSIBILITY ACÇOUNTING, RESPONSIBILITY CENTRE

Responsibility accounting collects and reports planned and actual accounting information about the inputs and outputs of responsibility centres, Responsibility accounting represents a method of measuring the performances of various divisions, departments, branch ethics and service centers, product lines, channels of distribution, class of customers and so on.

Features

(i) Input and Output: Inputs are the resources used by an organization which are essentially physical in nature such as quantity of material consumed, hour of labour and so on. When physical resources are expressed in monetary term, they are called cost. Similarly, Output is managed in monetary terms as revenues.

(ii) Tool of Control: It is a tool of cost control and reduction, activities of responsibility centers, divisional performances.

(iii) Planned and Actual: Financial informations contain both historical information about costs / revenues and estimated future cost and revenues dates.

(iv) Responsibility Centers: A **Responsibility center** is sub-unit of organisationthat is headed by a manager who is responsible for its activities and results. An organization sub-unit can be considered a responsibility center if it has a manager; if it has its own objectives guiding its activities; and the manager has control over the resources needed to pursue the objectives. Each manager has responsibilities and operations of each center. For accounting purposes, responsibility centers are classified as cost center, revenue center, profit center, and investment center. A well-designed responsibility accounting system should clearly define *responsibility centers* in order to collect and report revenue and cost information by areas of responsibility.

27.15 TYPES OF RESPONSIBILITY CENTERS

For central purpose responsibility centers are generally categorized into:

(i) Revenue center
(ii) Administrative and Support Center
(iii) R & D Center
(iv) Investment Center
(v) Cost Center
(vi) Profit Center

(i) Revenue Centre : In a revenue center, output in measured in monetary terms, Revenues centers are marketing units. The managers of this responsibility centre are hold accountable for the expenses incurred within this unit but the primary measurement of performance is revenue performance. The goal is to improve market share as per objectives.

Example: Generally the manager heading sales and marketing department is hold responsible for revenue maximization which is his primary accountability. He is also responsible for the related expenses.

(ii) Administrative and support centers: Administrative include senior corporate management and business unit management, along with the managers of supporting staff units. Support centers are units that provide services to other responsibility centers. Typically, managers of administrative department strive for functional excellence. Support centers often charge other responsibility centers for the service they provide.

For example, the MIS dept may charge other responsibility centers for providing computer services.

(iii) Research and Development Centers: In industry, two closely related processes by which new products and new forms of old products are created through technological innovation. The work generally focuses on two types of research, basic and applied. Basic research is directed toward a generalized goal (*e.g.*, genetic research in a pharmaceutical laboratory). Applied research directs the results of basic research toward the needs of a specific industry and results in the development of new or modified products or processes. In addition to carrying out basic and applied research and developing models, R&D staff may evaluate the efficiency and cost of the product. The R&D Manager wants to build the best research which can be acquired even though that may be more expensive than the company can afford.

In many companies, management receives two types of financial reports on R & D activities. The first type compares the latest forecast of total cost with the approved amount for each active project. The second type of financial report consists of a comparison between budgeted expenses and actual expenses in each responsibility center. It's main purpose is to help research and to help manager to anticipate expenses and make sure that expense commitments are being met.

(iv) Investment Centers: It is a responsibility center in which inputs are measured in terms of investment and outputs are measured in terms of revenue and in which assets employed are also measured. The measure of performance in an investment center is based on the relationship between the profits/revenue and the amount of assets employed in generating the profits. The way to relate income to assets is as follows:

$$\frac{\text{Segment profit contribution}}{\text{Segment resources/assets}}$$

$$= \frac{\text{Segment profit contribution}}{\text{Segment sales revenue}} \times \frac{\text{Segment sales revenue}}{\text{Segment assets}}$$

Segment Residual Income = Segment Profit Contribution – (Desired segment ROI × Segment assets/resources)

The investment center approach is an extension of the profit center approach.

(v) Cost Centers: Here, all inputs are measured in monetary terms, The accounting system records only the cost incurred. The performance of the Head of Const Center or Cost Managers is measured on the basis of the cost incurred in his department or division. The analysis of performance is restricted to the consumption of resources in his department/division in producing some given output.

(vi) Profit Centers : Generally the Finance Manager is held accountable for the profit performance. In a profit center, the measure of performance is broader than in a cost or revenue center since, in this center both cost as well as revenue are measured in monetary terms. The financial performance is measured on the basis of profit which is revenue less cost. With reference to responsibility accounting, a profit related performance criterion must be developed to suit the requirements of the divisional performance measurement.

27.16 TRANSFER PRICE

It is a critical aspect of profit center's performance evaluation. It is the price at which divisions of a company transact with each other. Transactions may include the trade of supplies or labor between departments. Transfer prices are used when individual entities of a larger multi-entity firm are treated and measured as separately-run entities.

In managerial accounting, when different divisions of a multi-entity company are in charge of their own profits, they are also responsible for their own "Return on Invested Capital". Therefore, when divisions are required to transact with each other, a transfer price is used to determine costs. Transfer prices tend not to differ much from the price in the market because one of the entities in such a transaction will lose out: they will either be buying for more than the prevailing market price or selling below the market price, and this will affect their performance. Divisional profit is a unique concept, designed to serve specific managerial needs. The selling division which has transferred goods/services is a source of revenue from there inter-divisional exchange of goods/service while, the buying division which is re-acquiring goods/services, is an element of cost. Therefore to calculate the profit of each division, the concept of transfer pricing have a significant bearing.

Types

1. Cost price
2. Cost plus a normal mark-up/ cost plus ROI
3. Incremental cost
4. Market price
5. Two-step price

Transfer pricing is simply the act of pricing of goods and services or intangibles when thesame is given for use or consumption to a related party (*e.g.*, Subsidiary)

There can be either Market-based, *i.e.*, equivalent to what is being charged in the outside market for similar goods or it can be non-market based. Importantly, two-thirds of themanagers say their transfer pricing is non-market based.

There can be internal and external reasons for transfer pricing. Internal includes motivating managers and monitoring performance, *e.g.*, by putting a cost to imported inputs. External would be taxes and tariffs.

Examples of Transfer Pricing

Illustration 1

Your Company fixes the inter-divisional transfer prices for its products on the basis of cost plus a return on investment in the division. The budget for division A for 2004-2005 appears as under:

Investment in Division A:

	₹
Fixed Assets	5,00,000
Current Assets	3,00,000
Debtors	2,00,000
Annual Fixed cost of the Division	2,00,000
Variable cost per Unit of Product	8,00,000
Budgeted volume – 400000 units per year	10
Desired ROI – 28%	

Determine the transfer Price for Division 'A'.

Solution:

		₹
Investment in Division:		
Fixed Assets, Current Assets & Debtors		10,00,000
Desired return on Investment (ROI) 28% on 10,00,000	=	2,80,000
Variable cost 4,00,000 × 10	=	40,00,000
Annual fixed cost of the Divn. A		8,00,000
Total cost:		48,00,000
Add: return in investment		2,80,000
		50,80,000

$$\text{Inter – Divisional transfer price} = \frac{5,00,80,000}{40,00,000} = 12.70 \text{ per unit}$$

Illustration 2

Business Unit A (manufacturer)	Product A
Expected monthly sales to unit B	5000 unit
Variable cost per unit	₹ 5
Monthly fixed cost assigned to product	₹ 25,000
Investment in working capital	12,48,000
Competitive ROI p.c.	10%

Determine the transfer price.

Solution:

One way to transfer product A to Unit B in at a price p.u. is as follows:

	Transfer price of product A
	₹
Variable cost per unit	5
Fixed cost per unit (25000 ÷ 5000)	5
Product per unit	2.08
Total Price per unit	12.08

Note: 10% of monthly investment per unit

$$= \frac{1248000/12 \times .10}{5000}$$

$$= ₹\ 2.08$$

❑ ❑ ❑

28 Mergers and Acquisitions

28.1 MERGERS AND ACQUISITIONS – CONCEPT

An entrepreneur may grow its business either by internal expansion or by external expansion. In the case of internal expansion, a firm grows gradually over time in the normal course of the business, through acquisition of new assets, replacement of the technologically obsolete equipments and the establishment of new lines of products. But in external expansion, a firm acquires a running business and grows overnight through corporate combinations. These combinations are in the form of mergers, acquisitions, amalgamations and takeovers and have now become important features of corporate restructuring. They have been playing an important role in the external growth of a number of leading companies the world over. They have become popular because of the enhanced competition, breaking of trade barriers, free flow of capital across countries and globalization of businesses. In the wake of economic reforms, Indian industries have also started restructuring their operations around their core business activities through acquisition and takeovers because of their increasing exposure to competition both domestically and internationally.

Mergers and acquisitions are strategic decisions taken for maximization of a company's growth by enhancing its production and marketing operations. They are being used in a wide array of fields such as information technology, telecommunications, and business process outsourcing as well as in traditional businesses in order to gain strength, expand the customer base, cut competition or enter into a new market or product segment.

Mergers or Amalgamations

A merger is a combination of two or more businesses into one business. Laws in India use the term 'amalgamation' for merger. The Income Tax Act, 1961 [Section 2(1A)] defines amalgamation as the merger of one or more companies with another or the merger of two or more companies to form a new company, in such a way that all assets and liabilities of the amalgamating companies become assets and liabilities of the amalgamated company and shareholders not less than nine-tenths in value of the shares in the amalgamating company or companies become shareholders of the amalgamated company.

Thus, mergers or amalgamations may take two forms:

1. **Merger Through Absorption:** An absorption is a combination of two or more companies into an 'existing company'. All companies except one lose their identity in such a merger. For example, absorption of Tata Fertilisers Ltd (TFL) by Tata Chemicals Ltd. (TCL). TCL, an acquiring company (a buyer), survived after merger while TFL, an acquired company (a seller), ceased to exist. TFL transferred its assets, liabilities and shares to TCL.
2. **Merger Through Consolidation:** A consolidation is a combination of two or more companies into a 'new company'. In this form of merger, all companies are legally dissolved and a new entity is created. Here, the acquired company transfers its assets, liabilities and shares to the acquiring company for cash or exchange of shares. For example, merger of Hindustan Computers Ltd. Hindustan Instruments Ltd, Indian Software Company Ltd and Indian Reprographics Ltd. into an entirely new company called HCL Ltd.

A fundamental characteristic of merger (either through absorption or consolidation) is that the acquiring company (existing or new) takes over the ownership of other companies and combines their operations with its own operations.

Besides, there are three major types of mergers:

1. **Horizontal merger:** is a combination of two or more firms in the same area of business. For example, combining of two book publishers or two luggage manufacturing companies to gain dominant market share.
2. **Vertical merger:** is a combination of two or more firms involved in different stages of production or distribution of the same product. For example, joining of a TV manufacturing (assembling) company and a TV marketing company or joining of a spinning company and a weaving company. Vertical merger may take the form of forward or backward merger. When a company combines with the supplier of material, it is called backward merger and when it combines with the customer, it is known as forward merger.
3. **Conglomerate merger:** is a combination of firms engaged in unrelated lines of business activity. For example, merging of different businesses like manufacturing of cement products, fertilizer products, electronic products, insurance investment and advertising agencies. L&T and Voltas Ltd are examples of such mergers.

Acquisitions and Takeovers

An acquisition may be defined as an act of acquiring effective control by one company over assets or management of another company without any combination of companies. Thus, in an acquisition two or more companies may remain independent, separate legal entities, but there may be a change in control of the companies. When an acquisition is 'forced' or 'unwilling', it is called a takeover. In an unwilling acquisition, the management of 'target' company would oppose a move of being taken over. But, when managements of acquiring and target companies mutually and willingly agree for the takeover, it is called acquisition or friendly takeover.

Under the Monopolies and Restrictive Practices Act, takeover meant acquisition of not less than 25 per cent of the voting power in a company. While in the Companies Act (Section 372), a company's investment in the shares of another company in excess of 10 per cent of the subscribed capital can result in takeovers. An acquisition or takeover does not necessarily entail full legal control. A company can also have effective control over another company by holding a minority ownership.

28.2 ADVANTAGES OF MERGERS AND ACQUISITIONS

The most common motives and advantages of mergers and acquisitions are:

(a) Accelerating a company's growth, particularly when its internal growth is constrained due to paucity of resources. Internal growth requires that a company should develop its operating facilities- manufacturing, research, marketing, etc. But, lack or inadequacy of resources and time needed for internal development may constrain a company's pace of growth. Hence, a company can acquire production facilities as well as other resources from outside through mergers and acquisitions. Specially, for entering in new products/ markets, the company may lack technical skills and may require special marketing skills and a wide distribution network to access different segments of markets. The company can acquire existing company or companies with requisite infrastructure and skills and grow quickly.

(b) Enhancing profitability because a combination of two or more companies may result in more than average profitability due to cost reduction and efficient utilization of resources. This may happen because of:

  (i) **Economies of scale:** arise when increase in the volume of production leads to a reduction in the cost of production per unit. This is because, with merger, fixed costs are distributed over a large volume of production causing the unit cost of production to decline. Economies of scale may also arise from other indivisibilities such as production facilities, management functions and management resources and systems. This is because a given function, facility or resource is utilized for a large scale of operations by the combined firm.

  (ii) **Operating economies:** arise because, a combination of two or more firms may result in cost reduction due to operating economies. In other words, a combined firm may avoid or reduce over-lapping functions and consolidate its management functions such as manufacturing, marketing, R&D and thus reduce operating costs. For example, a combined firm may eliminate duplicate channels of distribution, or crate a centralized training center, or introduce an integrated planning and control system.

(iii) **Synergy:** implies a situation where the combined firm is more valuable than the sum of the individual combining firms. It refers to benefits other than those related to economies of scale. Operating economies are one form of synergy benefits. But apart from operating economies, synergy may also arise from enhanced managerial capabilities, creativity, innovativeness, R&D and market coverage capacity due to the complementarity of resources and skills and a widened horizon of opportunities.

(c) Diversifying the risks of the company, particularly when it acquires those businesses whose income streams are not correlated. Diversification implies growth through the combination of firms in unrelated businesses. It results in reduction of total risks through substantial reduction of cyclicality of operations. The combination of management and other systems strengthen the capacity of the combined firm to withstand the severity of the unforeseen economic factors which could otherwise endanger the survival of the individual companies.

A merger may result in financial synergy and benefits for the firm in many ways:

(i) By eliminating financial constraints

(ii) By enhancing debt capacity. This is because a merger of two companies can bring stability of cash flows which in turn reduces the risk of insolvency and enhances the capacity of the new entity to service a larger amount of debt

(iii) By lowering the financial costs. This is because due to financial stability, the merged firm is able to borrow at a lower rate of interest.

(d) Limiting the severity of competition by increasing the company's market power. A merger can increase the market share of the merged firm. This improves the profitability of the firm due to economies of scale. The bargaining power of the firm *vis-à-vis* labour, suppliers and buyers is also enhanced. The merged firm can exploit technological breakthroughs against obsolescence and price wars.

The principal **benefits from mergers and acquisitions** can be listed as increased value generation, increase in cost efficiency and increase in market share. Benefits of Mergers and Acquisitions are the main reasons for which the companies enter into these deals. Mergers and Acquisitions may generate tax gains, can increase revenue and can reduce the cost of capital.

Mergers and Acquisitions are also beneficial

(i) When a firm wants to enter a new market

(ii) When a firm wants to introduce new products through research and development

(iii) When a forms wants achieve administrative benefits

(iv) To increased market share

(v) To lower cost of operation and/or production

(vi) To gain higher competitiveness

(vii) For industry know how and positioning

(viii) For Financial leveraging

(ix) To improve profitability and EPS

An increase in market share is one of the plausible **benefits of mergers and acquisitions**. In case a financially strong company acquires a relatively distressed one, the resultant organization can experience a substantial increase in market share. The new firm is usually more cost-efficient and competitive as compared to its financially weak parent organization.

It can be noted that mergers and acquisitions prove to be useful in the following situations: Firstly, when a business firm wishes to make its presence felt in a new market. Secondly, when a business organization wants to avail some administrative benefits. Thirdly, when a business firm is in the process of introduction of new products. New products are developed by the R&D wing of a company.

28.3 PROCEDURE FOR EVALUATING THE DECISION FOR MERGERS AND ACQUISITIONS

The three important steps involved in the analysis of mergers and acquisitions are:

1. Planning: Planning of acquisition will require the analysis of industry-specific and firm-specific information. The acquiring firm should review its objective of acquisition in the context of its strengths and weaknesses and corporate goals. It will need industry data on market growth, nature of competition, ease of entry, capital and labour intensity, degree of regulation, etc. This will help in indicating the product-market strategies that are appropriate for the company. It will also help the firm in identifying the business units that should be dropped or added. On the other hand, the target firm will need information about quality of management, market share and size, capital structure, profitability, production and marketing capabilities, etc.

2. Search and Screening: Search focuses on how and where to look for suitable candidates for acquisition. Screening process short-lists a few candidates from many available and obtains detailed information about each of them.

3. Financial Evaluation: Financial evaluation of a merger is needed to determine the earnings and cash flows, areas of risk, the maximum price payable to the target company and the best way to finance the merger. In a competitive market situation, the current market value is the correct and fair value of the share of the target firm. The target firm will not accept any offer below the current market value of its share. The target firm may, in fact, expect the offer price to be more than the current market value of its share since it may expect that merger benefits will accrue to the acquiring firm.

A merger is said to be at a premium when the offer price is higher than the target firm's pre-merger market value. The acquiring firm may have to pay premium as an incentive to target firm's shareholders to induce them to sell their shares so that it (acquiring firm) is able to obtain the control of the target firm.

28.4 REGULATIONS FOR MERGERS AND ACQUISITIONS IN INDIA

Mergers and acquisitions are regulated under various laws in India. The objective of the laws is to make these deals transparent and protect the interest of all shareholders. They are regulated through the provisions of:

The Companies Act, 1956

The Act lays down the legal procedures for mergers or acquisitions:

(i) Permission for merger: Two or more companies can amalgamate only when the amalgamation is permitted under their memorandum of association. Also, the acquiring company should have the permission in its object clause to carry on the business of the acquired company. In the absence of these provisions in the memorandum of association, it is necessary to seek the permission of the shareholders, board of directors and the Company Law Board before affecting the merger.

(ii) Information to the stock exchange: The acquiring and the acquired companies should inform the stock exchanges (where they are listed) about the merger.

(iii) Approval of board of directors: The board of directors of the individual companies should approve the draft proposal for amalgamation and authorize the managements of the companies to further pursue the proposal.

(iv) Application in the High Court: An application for approving the draft amalgamation proposal duly approved by the board of directors of the individual companies should be made to the High Court.

(v) Shareholders' and creators' meetings: The individual companies should hold separate meetings of their shareholders and creditors for approving the amalgamation scheme. At least, 75 per cent of shareholders and creditors in separate meeting, voting in person or by proxy, must accord their approval to the scheme.

(vi) Sanction by the High Court: After the approval of the shareholders and creditors, on the petitions of the companies, the High Court will pass an order, sanctioning the amalgamation scheme after it is satisfied that the scheme is fair and reasonable. The date of the Court's hearing will be published in two newspapers, and also, the regional director of the Company Law Board will be intimated.

(vii) Filing of the Court order: After the Court order, its certified true copies will be filed with the Registrar of Companies.

(viii) Transfer of assets and liabilities: The assets and liabilities of the acquired company will be transferred to the acquiring company in accordance with the approved scheme, with effect from the specified date.

(ix) Payment by cash or securities: As per the proposal, the acquiring company will exchange shares and debentures and/or cash for the shares and debentures of the acquired company. These securities will be listed on the stock exchange.

The Competition Act, 2002

The Act regulates the various forms of business combinations through Competition Commission of India. Under the Act, no person or enterprise shall enter into a combination, in the form of an acquisition, merger or amalgamation, which causes or is likely to cause an appreciable adverse effect on competition in the relevant market and such a combination shall be void. Enterprises intending to enter into a combination may give notice to the Commission, but this notification is voluntary. But, all combinations do not call for scrutiny unless the resulting combination exceeds the threshold limits in terms of assets or turnover as specified by the Competition Commission of India. The Commission while regulating a 'Combination' shall consider the following factors:

(i) Actual and potential competition through imports;

(ii) Extent of entry barriers into the market;

(iii) Level of combination in the market;

(iv) Degree of countervailing power in the market;

(v) Possibility of the combination to significantly and substantially increase prices or profits;

(vi) Extent of effective competition likely to sustain in a market;

(vii) Availability of substitutes before and after the combination;

(viii) Market share of the parties to the combination individually and as a combination;

(ix) Possibility of the combination to remove the vigorous and effective competitor or competition in the market;

(x) Nature and extent of vertical integration in the market;

(xi) Nature and extent of innovation;

(xii) Whether the benefits of the combinations outweigh the adverse impact of the combination.

Thus, the Competition Act does not seek to eliminate combinations and only aims to eliminate their harmful effects.

The other regulations are provided in the: The Foreign Exchange Management Act, 1999 and the Income Tax Act,1961. Besides, the Securities and Exchange Board of India (SEBI) has issued guidelines to regulate mergers and acquisitions. The SEBI (Substantial Acquisition of Shares and Take-overs) Regulations, 1997 and its subsequent amendments aim at making the take-over process transparent, and also protect the interests of minority shareholders.

28.5 TOP 10 MERGERS AND ACQUISITIONS IN INDIA FOR 2010

1. Tata Chemicals buys British Salt: Tata Chemicals bought British Salt; a UK based white salt producing company for about US $ 13 billion. The acquisition gives Tata access to very strong brine supplies and also access to British Salt's facilities as it produces about 800,000 tons of pure white salt every year

2. Reliance Power and Reliance Natural Resources Merger: This deal was valued at US $ 11 billion and turned out to be one of the biggest deals of the year. It eased out the path for Reliance power to get natural gas for its power projects

3. Airtel's acquisition of Zain in Africa: Airtel acquired Zain at about US $ 10.7 billion to become the third biggest telecom major in the world. Since Zain is one of the biggest players in Africa covering over 15 countries, Airtel's acquisition gave it the opportunity to establish its base in one of the most important markets in the coming decade

4. Abbott's acquisition of Piramal Healthcare Solutions: Abbott acquired Piramal healthcare solutions at US $ 3.72 billion which was 9 times its sales. Though the valuation of this deal made Piramal's take this move, Abbott benefited greatly by moving to leadership position in the Indian market

5. GTL Infrastructure Acquisition of Aircel Towers: This acquisition was worth about US $ 1.8 billion and brought GTL Infrastructure to the third position in terms of number of mobile towers – 33000. The money generated gave Aircel the funds for expansion throughout the country and also for rolling out its 3G services

6. ICICI Bank buys Bank of Rajasthan: This merger between the two for a price of ₹ 3000 crore would help ICICI improve its market share in northern as well as western India

7. JSW and Ispat Ki Kahani: Jindal Steel Works acquired 41% stake at ₹ 2,157 crore in Ispat Industries to make it the largest steel producer in the country. This move would also help Ispat return to profitability with time

8. Reckitt Benckiser goes shopping: Reckitt acquired Paras Pharma at a price of US $ 726 million to basically strengthen its healthcare business in the country. This was Reckitt's move to establish itself as a strong consumer health care player in the fast growing Indian market.

9. Mahindra goes International: Mahindra acquired a 70% controlling stake in troubled South Korea auto major Ssang Yong at US $ 463 million. Along with the edge it would give Mahindra in terms of the R&D capabilities, this deal would also help them utilize the 98 country strong dealer network of Sang Yong

10. Fortis Healthcare Acquisitions: Fortis Healthcare, the unlisted company owned by Malvinder and Shivinder Singh looks set to make it two in two in terms of acquisitions. After acquiring Hong Kong's Quality Healthcare Asia Ltd for around ₹ 882 crore last month, they are planning on acquiring Dental Corp, the largest dental services provider in Australia at ₹ 450 crore.

As you see in the list, the M&A's have happened across industries and sectors like banking, automotive, healthcare, FMCG, telecom etc. This shows that this really has been the dream year of Indian industry.

28.6 MERGERS AND ACQUISITIONS IN INDIA: THE LATEST TRENDS

Till recent past, the incidence of Indian entrepreneurs acquiring foreign enterprises was not so common. The situation has undergone a sea change in the last couple of years. Acquisition of foreign companies by the Indian businesses has been the latest trend in the Indian corporate sector.

There are different factors that played their parts in facilitating the mergers and acquisitions in India. Favourable government policies, buoyancy in economy, additional liquidity in the corporate sector, and dynamic attitudes of the Indian entrepreneurs are the key factors behind the changing trends of mergers and acquisitions in India.

The Indian IT and ITES sectors have already proved their potential in the global market. The other Indian sectors are also following the same trend. The increased participation of the Indian companies in the global corporate sector has further facilitated the merger and acquisition activities in India.

Recently the Indian companies have undertaken some important acquisitions. Some of those are as follows:

Hindalco acquired Canada based Novelis. The deal involved transaction of $5,982 million. Tata Steel Acquired Corus Group plc. The acquisition deal amounted to $12,000 million. Dr. Reddy's Labs acquired Betapharm through a deal worth of $597 million. Ranbaxy Labs acquired Terapia SA. The deal amounted to $324 million. Suzlon Energy acquired Hansen Group through a deal of $565 million. The acquisition of Daewoo Electronics Corp. by Videocon involved transaction of $729 million. HPCL acquired Kenya Petroleum Refinery Ltd. The deal amounted to $500 million. VSNL acquired Teleglobe through a deal of $239 million.

When it comes to mergers and acquisitions deals in India, the total number was 287 from the month of January to May in 2007. It has involved monetary transaction of US $47.37 billion. Out of these 287 merger and acquisition deals, there have been 102 cross country deals with a total valuation of US $28.19 billion.

Top 10 billion dollar mergers and acquisitions India has seen

1. **Tata Steel's** mega ta eover of European steel major Corus for $12.2 billion. The biggest ever for an Indian company. This is the first big thing which marked the arrival of India Inc on the global stage. The next big thing everyone is talking about is Tata Nano.
2. **Vodafone's** purchase of 52% stake in Hutch Essar for about **$10 billion**. Essar group still holds 32% in the Joint venture.
3. Hindalco of Aditya Birla group's acquisition of Novellis for **$6 billion.**
4. **Ranbaxy's** sale to Japan's Daiichi for **$4.5 billion.** Sing brothers sold the company to Daiichi and since then there is no real good news coming out of Ranbaxy.
5. **ONGC** acquisition of Russia based **Imperial Energy** for $2.8 billion. This marked the turnaround of India's hunt for natural reserves to compete with China.
6. **NTT DoCoMo** Tata Tele services deal for **$2.7 billion**. The second biggest telecom deal after the Vodafone. Reliance MTN deal if went through would have been a good addition to the list.
7. **HDFC Bank** acquisition of Centurion Bank of Punjab for **$2.4 billion.**
8. **Tata Motors** acquisition of luxury car maker **Jaguar Land Rover** for **$2.3 billion.** This could probably the most ambitious deal after the Ranbaxy one. It certainly landed Tata Motors into lot of trouble.
9. Wind Energy premier **Suzlon Energy's** acquisition of **RePower** for **$1.7 billion.**
10. **Reliance Industries** taking over Reliance Petroleum Limited (RPL) for 8500 crores or **$1.6 billion.**

❑❑❑

29 International Financial Management

29.1 INTRODUCTION

International Financial Management came into being when the countries of the world started opening their doors for each other. This phenomenon is well known with the name of "liberalization". Due to the open environment and freedom to conduct business in any corner of the world, entrepreneurs started looking for opportunities even outside their country-boundaries. The spark of liberalization was further aired by swift progression in telecommunications and transportation technologics that too with increased accessibility and daily dropping prices. Apart from everything else, we cannot forget the contribution of financial innovations such as currency derivatives; cross border stock listings, multi-currency bonds and international mutual funds.

The resultant of liberalization and technology advancement is today's dynamic international business environment. Financial management for a domestic business and an international business is as dramatically different as the opportunities in the two. The meaning and objective of financial management does not change in international financial management but the dimensions and dynamics changes drastically.

International financial management, essentially an extension of corporate finance to a global context has undergone an extraordinary metamorphosis since the mid-1960. From a relatively stable and predictable economic environment at that time, the forces of inflation, technological innovation, and deregulation led to new and volatile markets and a plethora of financial instruments. Many of these developments would not have been possible without the academic research in this subject which went from mainly descriptive and anecdotal to analytical. Arguably the most important theoretical developments in finance took place since then: the capital asset pricing model [CAPM], option pricing models, and the recognition of agency costs as a potential conflict of interest between management and shareholders of a firm. These are still areas of disagreement: the cost of capital for a company with global markets and investors needs more study; managing currency, interest rate, and other risks in a complex international organization is still a work in progress. On balance, the case can be made that the changes seen over more than three decades have been positive.

29.2 DEFINITION AND IMPORTANCE

IFM requires dealing with financial management on a global basis which requires knowledge of different currencies, foreign banking systems, foreign business and tax laws, as well as international investment opportunities. International financial management deals with the financial decisions taken in the area of international business.

The growth in international business is, first of all, evident in the form of highly inflated size of international trade. In the immediate post-war years, the general agreement on the Trade and Tariffs was set up in order to boost trade. It axed the trade barriers significantly over the years, as a result of which international trade grew manifold. Naturally, the financial involvement of the trader's exporters and importers and the quantum of the cross country transactions surged significantly. All this required proper management of international flow of funds for which the study of International Financial Management came to be indispensable.

Not unexpectedly, the second half of the twentieth century witnessed the emergence, and fast expansion, of multinational corporations. Normally, with the growth of international trade, the products of the exporter become mature in the importing countries. When the product becomes mature in the importing countries, the exporter starts manufacturing the product there so as to evade tariff and to supply it at the least cost. Thus it would not be wrong to say that the emergence of the multinational companies was the by-product of the expansion in world trade. There were some countries in the developing world too which were liberal in hosting the multinational companies. They imported technology on a big scale and built up their own manufacturing base. As a result, their own companies went international. Thus multinational company's emergent not only in developed countries but also in the developing world and because of their operation the cross country flow of funds increased substantially. The two way flow of funds, outward in the form of investment and inward in the form of repatriation divided, royalty, technical service fees, etc., required proper management and so the study of International Finance Management become a real necessity.

29.3 DIFFERENCE BETWEEN DOMESTIC FINANCIAL MANAGEMENT AND INTERNATIONAL FINANCIAL MANAGEMENT

Four major facts which differentiate international financial management from domestic financial management are introduction of foreign currency, political risk, market imperfections and enhanced opportunity set.

Foreign Exchange: It's an additional risk which a finance manager is required to cater to under an International Financial Management setting. Foreign exchange risk refers to the risk of fluctuating prices of currency which has the potential to convert a profitable deal into a loss making one.

Political Risks: Political risk may include any change in the economic environment of the country *viz.* Taxation Rules, Contract Act etc. It is pertaining to the government of a country which can anytime change the rules of the game in an unexpected manner.

Market Imperfection: Having done a lot of integration in the world economy, it has got a lot of differences across the countries in terms of transportation cost, different tax rates, etc. Imperfect markets force a finance manager to strive for best opportunities across the countries.

Enhanced Opportunity Set: By doing business in other than native countries, a business expands its chances of reaping fruits of different taste. Not only does it enhances the opportunity for the business but also diversifies the overall risk of a business.

Just like domestic financial management, the goal of International Financial Management is also to maximize the shareholder's wealth. The goal is not only is limited to the 'Shareholders' but extends to all 'Stakeholders' *viz.* employees, suppliers, customers etc. No goal can be achieved without achieving welfare of shareholders. In other words, maximizing shareholder's wealth would mean maximizing the price of the share. Here again comes a question, whether in which currency should the value of the share be maximized? This is an important decision to be taken by the management of the organization.

International level initiatives like General Agreement on Trade and Tariffs (GATT), The North American Free Trade Agreement (NAFTA), World Trade Organization (WHO) etc. has give promoted international trade and given it a shape. All because of liberalization and those international agreements, we have a buzz word called "MNC", *i.e.,* Multinational Corporations. MNCs enjoy an edge over other normal companies because of its international setting and best opportunities.

International Financial Management has become an important wing for all big MNCs. Without the expertise in International Financial Management, it can be difficult to sustain in the market because international financial markets have a total different shape and analytics compared to the domestic financial markets. A sound International Financial Management can help an organization achieve same efficiency and effectiveness in all markets.

29.4 COMPONENTS OF INTERNATIONAL FINANCIAL MANAGEMENT

IFM has four distinct parts:

1. Currencies and Asset Prices: What are the basic mechanics of exchange rates? What determines asset prices in global markets, and how do currencies influence stock prices?

2. Multinational Financial Decision Making: This part considers several of the central financial decisions multinational firms must make concerning capital structure, risk management, and tax optimization. How should firms capitalize subsidiaries around the world? When should firms partner with local firms? How are firms exposed to exchange rates, and how should firms hedge those exposures? How do tax considerations factor into internal financial decision-making?

3. Cross-border Valuation and Financing: This part covers how valuation techniques and financing decisions must be modified in a cross-border setting. How should firms think about the cost of capital around the world? How should investments in emerging markets be evaluated? How can firms capitalize on market imperfections in their financing and investment decisions?

4. Institutions and Finance: This part considers how differing institutional arrangements, both formal and informal, impact financial decision-making. The focus is on how differences in legal regimes, especially differences in the legal protection of creditors and shareholders, affect investment and restructuring decisions. The focus is also on investing in emerging markets using cases on M&A and PE transactions in developing economies, with an emphasis on the importance of informal institutional arrangements and relationship building.

29.5 BASIC MECHANICS OF EXCHANGE RATES

I. Introduction

(i) Money serves as a medium of exchange that simplifies transactions between millions of people interacting in a marketplace.

(ii) Transactions between people who live in different countries, however, is more complicated because of the existence of different mediums of exchange. Cross-border transactions therefore typically require a corresponding exchange of one currency for another.

(iii) An exchange rate describes the price of one currency in terms of another.

II. Exchange Rates

(i) The nominal exchange rate between two countries is the one country's currency in terms of the other country's currency.

(ii) Nonetheless, \$/foreign currency is the right way to think about exchange rates since we price goods that way as well, *i.e.,* we think of dollars per cabbage rather than cabbages per dollar.

(iii) We can multiply the price of a good denominated in foreign currency by the nominal exchange rate to convert it to domestic currency terms; we can divide the price of goods denominated in domestic currency by the nominal exchange rate to convert them to foreign currency terms. For example: if a BMW costs 40,000 Euros and the exchange rate between Germany and the U.S. was 1.25 \$/Euro then the dollar price of the BMW is 40,000 Euro * 1.25 \$/Euro = \$ 50,000. Similarly, if a Dell computer costs \$2400 then its price in Euros would be \$2400/(1.25 \$/Euro) = 1920 Euros.

(iv) An increase in 'e' is called a depreciation of the domestic currency, *i.e.,* in the United States, the dollar has decreased in value (more dollars are needed to by one unit of foreign currency). A decrease in 'e' is an appreciation of the domestic currency, *i.e.,* the dollar has increased in value (fewer dollars are needed to buy one unit of foreign currency.)

(v) Changes in the exchange rate change the relative price of goods in two countries. However, the nominal exchange rate is not the only variable that affects the relative price of goods in two countries, the price levels in each country matter as well. Economists use the real exchange rate to compare prices in two countries.

III. The Foreign Exchange Market

The Spot Market

(i) The spot market for foreign exchange is the market for currency delivered immediately or at the most within a couple of days. These exchange rates are typically for large blocs of currency, typically $1 million or more. Individuals who trade smaller amounts are likely to get much more unfavorable exchange rates.

(ii) Banks are typically willing to SELL foreign currency at a less advantageous rate than which they would be willing to BUY currency. The difference between the two prices is known as the "spread". The spread enables the bank to make money by dealing in currencies.

For example, at noon on Jan 8th 2004, my bank quoted a buying rate of 1.210 $/Euro and a selling rate of 1.315 $/Euro. This means that my bank would buy 1 Euro from me for 1.210 U.S. dollars but would charge 1.315 U.S. dollars to sell me 1 Euro. The difference between the two rates $0.105 is the "spread".

(iii) The spread is typically very small for large transactions and also for more commonly traded currencies. So the per-unit spread on buying and selling $10,000 worth of Nepali Rupees will be much higher than the per-unit spread on buying and selling $10,000,000 worth of Yen or Euros.

(iv) The information reported in the Wall Street Journal is for the mid-range rates, *i.e.* the average of the buying and the selling rates. For analytical ease, we will assume that spreads are pretty small and consider currencies being bought and sold for the same price for the purposes of this class. The key point is that for large transactions in major currencies, the buying rate, selling rate and by extension the mid-range rate are all pretty much identical, allowing us to proceed with the assumption of a single exchange rate.

What are the primary reasons that transactions occur in the spot market?

1. Clearing Transactions: When someone in the U.S. buys a car from Japan or buys a bond issued by the Turkish government that person has to exchange dollars for Yen or Turkish lira. This is usually done through the person's bank because the bank can take a large volume of clients' orders and do bulk trading of currencies.

2. Arbitrage: Arbitrage refers to actions that seek to take advantage of exchange rate discrepancies between different markets. Suppose that the $/Euro exchange rate is 0.95 in London and 0.949 in New York. Then banks can make a profit by exchanging dollars for Euros in New York and re-exchanging Euros for dollars in London.

Arbitrage is risk-free and therefore immensely profitable to those who can trade in bulk; correspondingly, the opportunities for arbitrage are fleeting unless there are restrictions on free currency trading set in place.

The existence of arbitrage ensures consistency between cross rates. So the dollar/yen rate should be equivalent to the dollar/euro multiplied by the euro/yen exchange rate, otherwise arbitragers can make money by trading through the euro.

Arbitrage also establishes exchange rates for rarely traded pairs of currency. The Nepali Rupee/Zambian Kwacha exchange rate will be equivalent to the Rupee/$ rate multiplied by the $/Kwacha rate.

3. Hedging: Firms that conduct transactions with international partners are exposed to currency risk.

Example: A specialty food store in the U.S. wants to import 5000 cans of mushy peas, each costing 1 pound sterling, from England. Payment is due in 30 days. If the exchange rate changes from 2 $/pound-sterling to 2.5 $/pound-sterling the cost increases from $10,000 to $12,500. (Alternatively, the dollar could appreciate to 1.75 dollars/pound sterling and the cost could fall to $8750.)

If the firm wants to avoid the risk of fluctuations in the amount of dollars it has to pay, *i.e.*, it wants to "lock-in" the dollar price of the goods, it can choose to buy 5000 Pounds-sterling on the spot market. This enables it to hedge against foreign exchange risk; the firm is said to have taken a closed position.

Hedging only protects against the downside: there are other instruments that allow you to take advantage of the upside as well: these are called options; we will discuss them later.

4. Speculation: Speculation is a transaction undertaken explicitly hoping to take advantage of exchange rate fluctuations. For example, someone who is certain that the dollar/pound exchange rate will go from 2 to 2.25 will exchange dollars for pounds now in the hope of exchanging them back later when the pound becomes more valuable.

IV. Players

Based on our analysis thus far, the major players in the foreign exchange market seem to be:

1. Banks: Performing transactions for corporations and individuals

2. Corporations: Large companies with sales in many countries in the world have to conduct transactions in many currencies, *e.g.*, Toyota build cars in Malaysia, Japan, the U.S. and Mexico and sells them in South Africa, England and Germany.

3. Non-bank Financial Institutions: mutual funds, pension funds that invest in stock markets and lend money to foreign companies.

4. Central Banks: occasionally central banks buy or sell currencies on the foreign exchange market.

Change Relative to Another Currency (Exchange Rate Quotes)

A "direct quote" measures how much of the domestic currency must be exchanged to receive one unit of the foreign currency (1 FC). Direct quotes allow the party using the quote to understand the price of the foreign currency in terms of its own "**base**" or "**domestic currency**". This method is frequently used in the United States, and direct quotes are published daily in financial papers such as The Wall Street Journal.

"**Indirect quotes**", also known as European terms, measure how many units of foreign currency will be received for one unit of the domestic currency. Thus, if the direct quote for a "**foreign currency (FC)**" is $0.25, then one FC would cost $0.25. The indirect quote would be the reciprocal of the direct quote, or 4 FC per dollar ($1.00 divided by $0.25).

Exchange Rate Quotes

Direct Quote : 1FC = $0.25

Indirect Quote: $1 = 4 FC

Foreign currency exchange rate quotes are reported in The Wall Street Journal and are also available on selected Web sites. Using Canada as an example, as of November 1, 2009, the direct quote is $0.6507, and the indirect quote is $1 = 1.5367 Canadian dollars.

The business news often reports that a currency has strengthened (gained) or weakened (lost) relative to another currency. Assuming a "**direct quote system**", such changes measure the difference between the new rate and the old rate, as a percentage of the old rate.

For example: if the dollar strengthened or gained 20% against a foreign currency (FC) from its previous rate of $0.25, the dollar would now command more FC (i.e., the FC would be cheaper to buy). To be exact, the new exchange rate would be $0.20 [$0.25 - (20% x 0.25)]. Therefore, the strengthening currency would be evidenced by a reduction in the directly quoted amount and an increase in the indirectly quoted amount.

The opposite would be true for a weakening of the domestic currency. The reaction to a strengthening or weakening of a currency depends on what type of transaction is contemplated.

For example: an American exporter would want a weaker dollar because the foreign importer would need fewer of its currency units to acquire a dollar's worth of U.S. goods. Thus, U.S. goods would cost less in terms of the foreign currency. If the dollar strengthened so that one could acquire more foreign currency units for a dollar, importers would benefit. Therefore, U.S. companies and citizens would have to spend fewer U.S. dollars to buy the imported goods.

Exchange rates often are quoted in terms of a "buying rate (the bid price)" and a "selling rate (the offered price)". The buying and selling rates represent what the currency broker (normally a large commercial bank) is willing to pay to acquire or sell a currency. The difference or spread between these two rates represents the broker's commission and is often referred to as the points. The spread is influenced by several factors, including the supply of and demand for the currency, the number of transactions taking place, currency risk, and the overall volatility of the market.

Example

Assume a currency broker agrees to pay $0.20 to a holder of a foreign currency and agrees to sell that currency to a buyer of foreign currency for $0.22. In this case, the broker will receive a commission of $0.02 ($0.22 - $0.20). In the United States, rates generally are quoted between the US dollar and a foreign currency. However, rates between two foreign currencies are also quoted and are referred to as cross rates.

29.6 TYPES OF EXCHANGE RATES

Exchange rates fall into two primary groups. A spot rate is the rate of exchange for a currency with delivery, selling, or buying of the currency normally occurring within two business days. In addition to exchange rates governing the immediate delivery of currency, forward rates apply to the exchange of different currencies at a future point in time, such as in 30 or 180 days. Although not all currencies are quoted in forward rates, virtually all major trading nations have forward rates.

An agreement to exchange currencies at a specified price with delivery at a specified future point in time is a forward contract. As more fully discussed in the derivatives module, a forward contract is a derivative instrument whose underlying is a foreign currency exchange rate. Forward exchange contracts may be held as an investment or held as part of a strategy to reduce or hedge against exchange rate risk associated with another transaction.

A "forward contract", used to hedge against the risk associated with changing exchange rates, specifies the future exchange date and the forward rate of exchange. Although future exchange dates typically are quoted in 30-day intervals, contracts can be written to cover any number of days. To illustrate a forward contract, assume the forward rate to buy a FC to be delivered in 90 days is $1.650. This means that, after the specified time from the inception of the contract date (90 days), one FC will be exchanged for $1.650, regardless of what the spot rate is at that time.

Several aspects of spot rates and forward rates are noteworthy

(i) First, typically both rates are constantly changing. Spot rates are revised daily; as they change, forward rates for the remaining time covered by a given forward contract also change even though the forward rate at inception is fixed. When there is no more remaining time, the current forward rate becomes the spot rate. Therefore, the value of a forward contract changes over the forward period. **For instance**: in the above example, if the forward rate is 1 FC = $1.652 with 30 days remaining, the right to buy FC at the original fixed forward rate of 1 FC = $1.650 suggests that the value of the forward contract has increased. Rather than paying a forward rate of $1.652 to acquire FC in 30 days, the holder of the original forward contract must only pay the fixed rate of $1.650.

(ii) Second, the ultimate value of the forward contract must be assessed by comparing the fixed forward rate against the spot rate at the settlement date. In the above example, at the settlement date, the holder of the contract will pay the fixed rate of 1 FC = $1.650 to buy an FC rather than the spot rate of 1 FC = $1.655. The total change in value is represented by the difference between the original fixed forward rate and the spot rate at settlement date.

(iii) Finally, the difference between a forward rate and a spot rate represents a premium or discount which is traceable to a number of factors. This difference between the spot and forward rate represents the time value of the forward contract. If the forward rate is greater than the spot rate at inception of the contract, the contract is said to be at a premium (as in the above example). The opposite situation results in a discount. Quoting premiums or discounts (known as forward differentials), rather than forward rates, is common industry practice.

Forward Rates Employ a Forward Exchange Contract:

At a Premium

Forward Rate > Spot Rate

(At inception of contract)

At a Discount

Forward Rate < Spot Rate

(At inception of contract)

At inception, the difference between the forward and spot rates represents a contract expense or income to the purchaser of the forward contract. A number of factors influence forward rates and, thus, account for the difference between a forward rate and a spot rate.

A primary factor is the interest rate differential between holding an investment in foreign currency and holding an investment in domestic currency over a period of time. It is for this reason that the difference between a forward rates is referred to as the time value of the forward contract. **For example**: if a broker sold a contract to deliver foreign currency in 30 days, **the interest differential would be the difference between**:

(a) The interest earned on investing foreign currency for the 30 days prior to delivery date and

(b) The 30 days of interest lost on the domestic currency that was not invested but was used to acquire the foreign currency needed for delivery.

Assume that the spot rate is 1 FC = \$0.60 and that you want to determine a 6-month forward rate. Further, assume that the dollar could be invested at 4.5% and the FC could be invested at 7.25%. The forward rate would be calculated as follows:

	U.S. Dollars	**Foreign Currency (FC)**
Value today	\$600.00	1,000 FC
Interest rate	4.5%	7.25%
Six months of interest	\$13.50	36.25 FC
Value in six months	\$613.50	1036.25 FC

6-month forward rate = \$613.50 / 1036.25 FC = 1 FC = \$0.592

The forward rate for a currency can also be derived by the following formula:

Forward rate = Direct spot rate at the beginning of period t × [1 – Interest rate for domestic investment during period t]/[1 – Interest rate for foreign country investment during period t]

$$.022 = \frac{13.50}{600}, \quad .03625 = \frac{36.25}{1000}$$

Using the formula to solve the previous example results in the following, based on 6-month interest rates:

Forward rate of $0.592 = $0.60 × [(1 + 0.0225)/(1 – 0.03625)]

If the interest yield on the FC is greater than the yield on the US dollar, the forward rate will be less than the spot rate (contract sells at a discount). The forward contract will sell at a premium if the opposite is true. The forward rate based on interest differentials will be slightly different than the quoted forward rate because the quoted rate includes a commission to the foreign currency broker.

Furthermore, other factors in addition to interest differentials could be incorporated into the forward rate. These other factors include the volatility of the spot rates, the time period covered by the contract, expectations of future exchange rate changes, and the political and economic environments of a given country.

Changes in exchange rates represent an additional business risk when transactions are denominated in a foreign currency. The accounting for foreign currency transactions measures this risk and demonstrates the use of both spot and forward rates. The current international monetary system is a floating system in which rates of exchange between currencies change in response to a variety of factors including trade balances, interest rates, money supply, and other economic factors. Spot rates represent the current rate of exchange between two currencies. A forward rate represents a future rate of exchange at a future point in time. If the forward rate exceeds the spot rate, the contract is at a premium rather than a discount.

29.7 CROSS BORDER VALUATION

- **Step 1:** Forecast foreign currency free cash flows

(a) Incorporate foreign currency inflation rates; (b) Use the appropriate marginal tax rate; and (c) Include the terminal value.

Method A

(Step 2) Determine foreign currency discount rates, using project-specific capital structure and the project specific ß;

(Step 3) Calculate the PV in the foreign currency;

(Step 4) Convert to home currency PV using the spot exchange rate.

Method B

(Step 2) Forecast exchange rates and convert FCF into home currency;

(Step 3) Determine home currency discount rates using project-specific capital structure and project specific ß;

(Step 4) Calculate the PV in home currency

Issues to Keep in Mind in Cross Border Valuation

Valuing a company across borders is similar, in principle, to valuing one at home.

But there are a few additional twists to keep in mind:

1. Choice of currency;
2. Earned vs. remitted income;
3. Tax rates;
4. Cost of capital; and
5. Treatment of country risk.

1. Choice of currency: You can choose either the home or the foreign currency in determining cash flows.

But foreign currency cash flows should be discounted at the foreign currency discount rate, and the home currency cash flows at the home currency discount rate.

If a project's value is likely to be particularly sensitive to exchange rates, it might be helpful to explicitly forecast the foreign currency cash flows and then convert them into home currency cash flows using a specific set of forecasted exchange rates.

2. Earned versus Remitted Income: It is preferable to use earned cash flows, whether or not those cash flows are actually remitted to the parent. The idea is that, the cash flow, even if retained in the subsidiary, ultimately belongs to the firm's shareholders. However, this assumes that the subsidiary earns a rate of return that is at least as high as its cost of capital.

3. Tax Rates: Different countries have different tax rates, requirements for timing of tax payments, and tax treaties with the home country. Other than to make the observation that one should: (a) have knowledge about the tax situation in the foreign country (*vis-a-vis* the home country), and (b) Always use the marginal tax rate applicable to the project.

4. The Appropriate Cost of Capital: It may be expedient (and probably accurate) to assume that the investors are indigenous to the home country in which the parent firm is headquartered. This means that you can use the home country-benchmarked cost of capital (adjusted, of course, for the risk characteristics of the project *vis-a-vis* the home country). The cost of equity will also depend on whether equity markets are integrated or segmented. If markets are segmented, one should use the home country market index; if integrated, a world index (*e.g.*, MSCI index).

If a non-US company has an ADR trading on the NYSE or NASDAQ, it is probably reasonable to assume that price moves in the US are affecting its expected returns in a much more substantial way than its home market. It is probably ok to derive the US\$ rE, and to then calculate a home currency rE (if needed) by using UIP.

5. Treatment of Country Risk: It really depends on two judgments that you must make: (i) Whether or not the country risk can be considered 'systematic'; (ii) Whether or not it is already captured in the project β. If the judgment is that country risk is unsystematic, you should ignore it.

In general, if country risk is a serious issue, it can be reflected in the cash flows or the discount rate. This is also a judgment call. For bonds it is necessary to add a country risk premium.

29.8 FOREIGN EXCHANGE RISK MANAGEMENT: PROCESS AND NECESSITY

Firms dealing in multiple currencies face a risk (an unanticipated gain/loss) on account of sudden/unanticipated changes in exchange rates, quantified in terms of exposures. Exposure is defined as a contracted, projected or contingent cash flow whose magnitude is not certain at the moment and depends on the value of the foreign exchange rates. The process of identifying risks faced by the firm and implementing the process of protection from these risks by financial or operational hedging is defined as foreign exchange risk management.

1. Kinds of Foreign Exchange Exposure: Risk management techniques vary with the type of exposure (accounting or economic) and term of exposure.

Accounting exposure, also called translation exposure, results from the need to restate foreign subsidiaries' financial statements into the parent's reporting currency and is the sensitivity of net income to the variation in the exchange rate between a foreign subsidiary and its parent.

Economic exposure is the extent to which a firm's market value, in any particular currency is sensitive to unexpected changes in foreign currency. Currency fluctuations affect the value of the firm's operating cash flows, income statement, and competitive position, hence market share and stock price. Currency fluctuations also affect a firm's balance sheet by changing the value of the firm's assets and liabilities, accounts payable, accounts receivables, inventory, loans in foreign currency, investments (CDs) in foreign banks; this type of economic exposure is called balance sheet exposure.

Transaction Exposure is a form of short term economic exposure due to fixed price contracting in an atmosphere of exchange-rate volatility. The most common definition of the measure of exchange-rate exposure is the sensitivity of the value of the firm, proxied by the firm's stock return, to an unanticipated change in an exchange rate. This is calculated by using the partial derivative function where the dependant variable is the firm's value and the independent variable is the exchange rate .

2. Necessity of managing foreign exchange risk: A key assumption in the concept of foreign exchange risk is that exchange rate changes are not predictable and that this is determined by how efficient the markets for foreign exchanges are. Research in the area of efficiency of foreign exchange markets has thus far been able to establish only a weak form of the efficient market hypothesis conclusively which implies that successive changes in exchange rates cannot be predicted by analysing the historical sequence of exchange rates. However, when the efficient markets theory is applied to the foreign exchange market under floating exchange rates there is some evidence to suggest that the present prices properly reflect all available information. This implies that exchange rates react to new information in an immediate and unbiased fashion, so that no one party can make a profit by this information and in any case, information on direction of the rates arrives randomly so exchange rates also fluctuate randomly. It implies that foreign exchange risk management cannot be done away with by employing resources to predict exchange rate changes.

Hedging as a tool to manage foreign exchange risk

A **hedge** is a financial term denoting an investment position intended to offset potential losses that may be incurred by a companion investment.

Possible vehicles for a hedge investment include stocks, ETFs, insurance, forward contracts, swaps, options, many types of over-the-counter and derivative products, futures contracts. Public futures markets were established in the 19th century to allow transparent, standardized, and efficient hedging of agricultural commodity prices; they have since expanded to include futures contracts for hedging the values of energy, precious metals, foreign currency, and interest rate fluctuations.

There is a spectrum of opinions regarding foreign exchange hedging. Some firms feel hedging techniques are speculative or do not fall in their area of expertise and hence do not venture into hedging practices. Other firms are unaware of being exposed to foreign exchange risks. There are a set of firms who only hedge some of their risks, while others are aware of the various risks they face, but are unaware of the methods to guard the firm against the risk. There is yet another set of companies who believe shareholder value cannot be increased by hedging the firm's foreign exchange risks as shareholders can themselves individually hedge themselves against the same using instruments like forward contracts available in the market or diversify such risks out by manipulating their portfolio.

There are some explanations backed by theory about the irrelevance of managing the risk of change in exchange rates. For example, the International Fisher effect states that exchange rates changes are balanced out by interest rate changes, the Purchasing Power Parity theory suggests that exchange rate changes will be offset by changes in relative price indices/inflation since the Law of One Price should hold. Both these theories suggest that exchange rate changes are evened out in some form or the other. Also, the Unbiased Forward Rate theory suggests that locking in the forward exchange rate offers the same expected return and is an unbiased indicator of the future spot rate. But these theories are perfectly played out in perfect markets under homogeneous tax regimes. Also, exchange rate-linked changes in factors like inflation and interest rates take time to adjust and in the meanwhile firms stand to lose out on adverse movements in the exchange rates. The existence of different kinds of market imperfections, such as incomplete financial markets, positive transaction and information costs, probability of financial distress, and agency costs and restrictions on free trade make foreign exchange management an appropriate concern for corporate management. It has also been argued that a hedged firm, being less risky can secure debt more easily and this enjoy a tax advantage (interest is excluded from tax while dividends are taxed). This would negate the *Modigliani-Miller proposition as shareholders cannot duplicate such tax advantages. The MM argument that shareholders can hedge on their own is also not valid on account of high transaction costs and lack of knowledge about financial manipulations on the part of shareholders.*

29.9 FOREIGN EXCHANGE RISK MANAGEMENT FRAMEWORK

Once a firm recognizes its exposure, it then has to deploy resources in managing it. A heuristic for firms to manage this risk effectively is presented below which can be modified to suit firm-specific needs *i.e.* some or all the following tools could be used.

1. Forecasts: After determining its exposure, the first step for a firm is to develop a forecast on the market trends and what the main direction/trend is going to be on the foreign exchange rates. The period for forecasts is typically 6 months. It is important to base the forecasts on valid assumptions. Along with identifying trends, a probability should be estimated for the forecast coming true as well as how much the change would be.

2. Risk Estimation: Based on the forecast, a measure of the *Value at Risk* (the actual profit or loss for a move in rates according to the forecast) and the *probability* of this risk should be ascertained. The risk that a transaction would fail due to *market-specific* should be taken into account. Finally, the Systems Risk that can arise due to inadequacies such as reporting gaps and implementation gaps in the firms' exposure management system should be estimated.

3. Benchmarking: Given the exposures and the risk estimates, the firm has to set its limits for handling foreign exchange exposure. The firm also has to decide whether to manage its exposures on a cost centre or profit centre basis. A cost centre approach is a defensive one and the main aim is ensure that cash flows of a firm are not adversely affected beyond a point. A profit centre approach on the other hand is a more aggressive approach where the firm decides to generate a net profit on its exposure over time.

4. Hedging: Based on the limits a firm set for itself to manage exposure, the firms then decides an appropriate hedging strategy. There are various financial instruments available for the firm to choose from: futures, forwards, options and swaps and issue of foreign debt.

5. Stop Loss: The firms risk management decisions are based on forecasts which are but estimates of reasonably unpredictable trends. It is imperative to have stop loss arrangements in order to rescue the firm if the forecasts turn out wrong. For this, there should be certain monitoring systems in place to detect critical levels in the foreign exchange rates for appropriate measure to be taken.

6. Reporting and Review: Risk management policies are typically subjected to review based on periodic reporting. The reports mainly include profit/loss status on open contracts after marking to market, the actual exchange/interest rate achieved on each exposure and profitability *vis-à-vis* the benchmark and the expected changes in overall exposure due to forecasted exchange/ interest rate movements. The review analyses whether the benchmarks set are valid and effective in controlling the exposures, what the market trends are and finally whether the overall strategy is working or needs change.

29.10 HEDGING STRATEGIES/INSTRUMENTS

A derivative is a financial contract whose value is derived from the value of some other financial asset, such as a stock price, a commodity price, an exchange rate, an interest rate, or even an index of prices. The main role of derivatives is that they reallocate risk among financial market participants, help to make financial markets more complete.

(i) Forwards: A forward is a made-to-measure agreement between two parties to buy/sell a specified amount of a currency at a specified rate on a particular date in the future. The depreciation of the receivable currency is hedged against by selling a currency forward. If the risk is that of a currency appreciation (if the firm has to buy that currency in future say for import), it can hedge by buying the currency forward. *E.g.*, if RIL wants to buy crude oil in US dollars six months hence, it can enter into a forward contract to pay INR and buy USD and lock in a fixed exchange rate for INR-USD to be paid after six months regardless of the actual INR Dollar rate at the time. In this example the downside is an appreciation of Dollar which is protected by a fixed forward contract. The main advantage of a forward is that it can be tailored to the specific needs of the firm and an exact hedge can be obtained. On the downside, these contracts are not marketable; they can't be sold to another party when they are no longer required and are binding.

(ii) Futures: A futures contract is similar to the forward contract but is more liquid because it is traded in an organized exchange, *i.e.*, the futures market. Depreciation of a currency can be hedged by selling futures and appreciation can be hedged by buying futures. Advantages of futures are that there is a central market for futures which eliminates the problem of double coincidence. Futures require a small initial outlay (a proportion of the value of the future) with which significant amounts of money can be gained or lost with the actual forwards price fluctuations. This provides a sort of leverage.

(iii) Options: A currency Option is a contract giving the right, not the obligation, to buy or sell a specific quantity of one foreign currency in exchange for another at a fixed price; called the Exercise Price or Strike Price. The fixed nature of the exercise price reduces the uncertainty of exchange rate changes and limits the losses of open currency positions. Options are particularly suited as a hedging tool for contingent cash flows, as is the case in bidding processes. Call Options are used if the risk is an upward trend in price (of the currency), while Put Options are used if the risk is a downward trend. Taking the example of RIL which needs to purchase crude oil in USD in six months, if RIL buys a Call option (as the risk is an upward trend in dollar rate), *i.e.*, the right to buy a specified amount of dollars at a fixed rate on a specified date, there are two scenarios. If the exchange rate movement is favourable, *i.e.*, the dollar depreciates, then RIL can buy them at the spot rate as they have become cheaper. In the other case, if the dollar appreciates compared to today's spot rate, RIL can exercise the option to purchase it at the agreed strike price. In either case RIL benefits by paying the lower price to purchase the dollar

(iv) Swaps: A swap is a foreign currency contract whereby the buyer and seller exchange equal initial principal amounts of two different currencies at the spot rate. The buyer and seller exchange fixed or floating rate interest payments in their respective swapped currencies over the term of the contract. At maturity, the principal amount is effectively re-swapped at a predetermined exchange rate so that the parties end up with their original currencies. The advantages of swaps are that firms with limited appetite for exchange rate risk may move to a partially or completely hedged position through the mechanism of foreign currency swaps, while leaving the underlying borrowing intact. Apart from covering the exchange rate risk, swaps also allow firms to hedge the floating interest rate risk. Consider an export oriented company that has entered into a swap for a notional principal of USD 1 mn at an exchange rate of 42/dollar. The company pays US six months LIBOR to the bank and receives 11.00% p.a. every six months on 1st January & 1st July, till 5 years. Such a company would have earnings in Dollars and can use the same to pay interest for this kind of borrowing (in dollars rather than in Rupee) thus hedging its exposures.

(v) Foreign Debt: Foreign debt can be used to hedge foreign exchange exposure by taking advantage of the International Fischer Effect relationship. This is demonstrated with the example of an exporter who has to receive a fixed amount of dollars in a few months from present. The exporter stands to lose if the domestic currency appreciates against that currency in the meanwhile so, to hedge this; he could take a loan in the foreign currency for the same time period and convert the same into domestic currency at the current exchange rate. The theory assures that the gain realised by investing the proceeds from the loan would match the interest rate payment (in the foreign currency) for the loan.

❑❑❑

30 Investment Banking

30.1 CONCEPT

An **investment bank** is a financial intermediary that performs a variety of services. This includes underwriting, acting as an intermediary between an issuer of securities and the investing public, facilitating mergers and other corporate reorganizations, and also acting as a broker for institutional clients.

An investment bank is a financial institution that assists individuals, corporations and governments in raising capital by underwriting and/or acting as the client's agent in the issuance of **securities**. An investment bank may also assist companies involved in **mergers and acquisitions**, and provide ancillary services such as market making, trading of derivatives, **fixed income** instruments, foreign exchange, **commodities**, and **equity securities**.

There are two main lines of business in investment banking. Trading securities for cash or for other securities (*i.e.*, facilitating transactions, market-making), or the promotion of securities (*i.e.*, **underwriting**, research, etc.) is the **"sell side"**. while dealing with **pension funds**, mutual funds, **hedge funds**, and the investing public (who consume the products and services of the sell-side in order to maximize their return on investment) constitutes the **"buy side"**. Many firms have buy and sell side components.

30.2 CASE EXAMPLE OF AN INVESTMENT BANK – KOTAK INVESTMENT BANKING

Kotak Investment Banking, a pioneer and leader in the equity capital markets, has worked on the development of some of the most path-breaking innovations in the Indian capital markets including the introduction of book building in public offers and the introduction of Qualified Institutional Placements (QIPs) in India. The firm has a strong track record of managing several industry-defining deals and has been the book runner for some landmark government disinvestments.

Key Recent Deals

In FY2011, Kotak Investment Banking was the lead manager to twelve out of the twenty six Initial /Follow on Public Equity Offerings (above ₹ 2.5 billion) accounting for ~ 62% of the total money raised in these offerings. They have helped companies raise over ₹ 350 billion in the domestic markets during FY2011. Some of their recent transactions include:

IPOs

(i) Muthoot Finance: In 2011, Book Running Lead Manager, ₹ 9 bn

(ii) Coal India: In 2010, Book Running Lead Manager, ₹ 152 bn

(iii) Jaypee Infratech: In 2010, Book Running Lead Manager, ₹ 22.3 bn

(iv) SKS Microfinance: In 2010, Book Running Lead Manager, ₹ 16.3 bn

(v) DB Realty: In 2010, Book Running Lead Manager, ₹ 15 bn

(vi) Prestige Estates Projects: In 2010, Book Running Lead Manager, ₹ 12 bn And many others.

(vii) Indian Depository Receipts (IDRs)

(viii) Standard Chartered: In 2010, Book Running Lead Manager – first-ever issuance of an IDR, ₹ 24.8 bn

FPOs

(i) Tata Steel: In 2011, Book Running Lead Manager, ₹ 34.8 bn

(ii) NMDC: In 2010, Book Running Lead Manager, ₹ 99.3 bn

(iii) NTPC: In 2010, Book Running Lead Manager, ₹ 84.8 bn

(iv) Rural Electrification Corporation: In 2010, Book Running Lead Manager, ₹ 35.3 bn

QIPs

(i) M&M Financial Services: In 2011, Book Running Lead Manager, ₹ 4.3 bn

(ii) Adani Enterprises: In 2010, Joint Global Coordinator and Book Running Lead Manager, ₹ 40 bn

(iii) Bharat Forge: In 2010, Joint Global Coordinator and Book Running Lead Manager - first-ever simultaneous yet unlinked issuance of Equity and Non-Convertible Debentures + Warrants in India, ₹ 6.2 bn

(iv) Godrej Consumer Products: In 2010, Book Running Lead Manager, ₹ 5.3 bn

(v) Strides Arcolab: In 2010, Book Running Lead Manager, ₹ 4.6 bn

(vi) Jubilant Organosys: In 2010, Book Running Lead Manager, ₹ 3.9 bn

(vii) Jyothy Laboratories: In 2010, Book Running Lead Manager, ₹ 2.3 bn

(viii) Mahindra Forgings: In 2010, Book Running Lead Manager, ₹ 1.8 bn

And many others.

Rights Issues

(i) Piramal Glass: In 2009, Lead Manager, ₹ 1.9 bn

(ii) State Bank of India: In 2008, Lead Manager, ₹ 167 bn

Landmark Transactions

(i) Coal India: Largest IPO in India till date, ₹ 152 bn

(ii) SKS Microfinance: First ever Initial Public Offer by a Microfinance Company in India

(iii) Bharat Forge: First ever simultaneous yet unlinked Issuance of Equity and NCD + Warrants through a Qualified Institutional Placement

(iv) NTPC: First FPO under alternate book building route

(v) Standard Chartered: First ever issuance of Indian Depository Receipts (IDRs)

(vi) HDFC: First ever QIP of NCD with detachable warrants

(vii) State Bank of India: Largest ever Equity Issuance in India, ₹ 167 bn

(viii) DLF: Largest Real Estate IPO in India till date, ₹ 91.9 bn etc.

30.3 ROLE OF INVESTMENT BANKS IN INDIA IN MERGER AND ACQUISITION

The following are important roles of investment bankers when executing mergers and acquisitions:

1. Once management knows the right transactions, investment bankers can keep deals from opening up to auctions.
2. Investment bankers can get the transaction done quickly and efficiently.
3. Investment bankers can help run auctions for pieces of the business that management doesn't want.
4. Investment bankers should be brought in only in the late stages to provide a fairness opinion or a valuation double check against what the internal staff has done. From the standpoint of the Board of Directors of the buyer company, this is a valuable check on management's enthusiasm for the deal. In that case, the investment banker serves a certification purpose.
5. If the company needs to finance the acquisition through an issue of debt or equity, having an investment banker involved is indispensable.
6. An investment banker can provide special skills in structuring a deal that has unusual features.

30.4 WHAT IS IPO?

IPO is the first **sale** of **stock** by a **company** to the **public**. The most **common** reason for a company to initiate an IPO is in **order** to **raise** more **capital**. One of the most difficult **parts** of an IPO is to **determine** the proper **price** to initially **offer** the new stock; too high and **investors** won't be interested, but too low and the company is sacrificing the **amount** of **money** that might have been made if they priced it higher. There is generally a **significant** amount of **risk** in an IPO, because the company going public is frequently small or relatively unknown, and hasn't had a **chance** to prove itself to the public; as such, they also have the **capacity** for significant **payoffs**.

30.5 IPO UNDERWRITING AND ROLE OF THE INVESTMENT BANKERS

Investment banks are essentially underwriters (or agent) that serves as the intermediary between an issuer of the securities and investing public. Think of it as a glorified version of real estate agents: instead of selling houses, the investment banker is facilitating the sale of companies in the form of shares.

IPO Underwriting (Some Basics)

As the underwriter of securities, investment banks can help clients raise capital in the form of stocks and bonds.

1. Identifying Clients: An IPO is a process in which a private company is turned into a public company. In other words, the company wants to sell its privately-held shares in a public market via the stock exchange platform in return for proceeds for the company's owners.

Everything starts when a client is interested in taking the company public and contact various investment banks for advice. Or it could be the other way round — investment banks identify companies with the potential of getting listed and contact these companies accordingly.

2. Pre-underwriting Counseling: During the first meeting, the investment bank gives advice to the client on the process of a stock offering, the pros and cons of becoming a public company, the indicative value of the company and the likelihood of a successful IPO.

It is highly likely that the clients are bank-shopping and so each investment bank will have to do a series of pitching work to get selected.

3. Signing the Engagement Letter: Once an investment bank is picked, the investment banking engagement letter is an important part of the process to outline the scope of the work, make sure the Bank is getting paid and most importantly to protect the Bank from legal liabilities as a result of this transaction.

4. Assembling the Team: By this time, the investment banking team will switch from the pitch mode to execution mode. At this point the work includes:

(a) Prepare a detailed outline of the IPO Underwriting timetable

(b) Recommend the legal counsel (lawyers) to participate in the deal

A typical "project team" includes:

(a) Core execution team

(b) Equity Capital Markets team

(c) In-house legal guys

(d) Outside legal counsel

(e) Client representatives

5. Drafting the SEC Registration Document: The investment banking team starts by drafting the Prospectus, the major document that needs to be submitted to the SEC (Securities and Exchange Commission) for approval. This document is an important source of information to make sure the investors are adequately informed before buying the shares of the company.

In most cases the prospectus contains hundreds of pages and a lot of energy and care is put into this document to make sure everything is correct and that it satisfies all the SEC requirements.

6. Constructing Financial Projection Models: At the same time, a financial projection will be made in order to determine the company's market value. This can be done based on client's own projection (with sanity checks based on industry parameters), or build from scratch if the client does not have a detailed projection model.

Once the projection is done, the investment bank can determine the value of the company using DCF and other relevant methodologies. Comparable company analysis is also done to determine the value based on how the clients' peers are evaluated in the public market.

7. Consulting On the Pricing of IPO: The capital market team works closely with the institutional sales (on the sales and trading side of investment bank) to "smell" the receptivity of the client from the public as well as the general market sentiment at that time. The equity capital market will then advise on the indicative price of the IPO.

The capital market team/core execution team will also prepare a one-page "sales page" for the institutional sales to market the deal to their clients (*i.e.* the hedge funds, pension funds and other institutional investors interested in IPOs)

8. Initiating the Research Report: For an IPO, a special situation occurs when the research analyst is brought over the "Chinese Wall" to help initiate the coverage of the company.

Normally, research analysts are barred from the dealings with investment banks to avoid confidential information (in the corporate finance department) being leaked to the public via the research analyst.

In this case, the research analyst will actually work closely with the bankers and the clients to prepare a report. This report is typically a positive one and is used as a way to "market" the client to the public.

As you can see, a #1 ranked research analyst will be a valuable asset to the investment bank as a whole as it attracts IPO business in the industry he/she is covering.

9. Forming and Managing the Syndicate: In many cases, the book-runner of the IPO (*i.e.*, the investment bank that helps to prepare the "book" for the client) cannot do all the work alone. In order to make sure all the new stocks can be sold on the launch date, the investment bankers will contact their competitors (*i.e.*, other investment bankers) to take part in this selling process.

This process is known as forming the "syndicate" — while the profit of being a syndicate is much less than that of a book-runner, investment banks are generally interested because it is a relatively easy job (provided the client is of good quality) and it is useful to brand building to get involved in the deal.

In the case of the "hot" IPOs, it is really a skill for the book-runner to allocate the shares appropriately for all the parties, so there is actually a lot of work involved.

10. Identifying Anchor Investors: Sometimes, it is a good strategic to consider having anchor investors to snap up a considerable portion of the new shares. They can be either institutional investors (*e.g.*, private equity funds and pension funds), a strategic investor (*e.g.*, a big player in similar industry as the client), or even rich families (this is more prevalent in Asia).

Anchor investors are great in shoring up confidence among the public and increase the "scarcity factor" on the IPO day.

11. Price Pegging: The pegging (stabilizing) the price of the issue is often done during the offering and distribution period. This after-marketing trading support is critical for the offering success and is arguably the part where investment banks can distinguish themselves from their lesser peers.

30.6 INVESTMENT BANKS IN INDIA — TOP 10

Investment Banks in India are particular type of organizations that sponsors capital needs of an enterprise. Executing private placement, submitting bond, functioning as a mediator and assisting mergers and acquisitions are some of the important features of Investment banking in India.

The top 10 Investment Banks in India offers large number of financial advisory services by tracking the economic trends, besides providing financial assistance to corporates and retail customers. Some of them are:

1. Avendus Capital: An investment bank providing mergers and acquisitions, fixed returns, controlled finance, calculated advisory facilities and Private Equity Syndication to its customers ranging from investors to corporates. The bank has a powerful research competence which it utilizes to close business deals in hostile circumstances. It presently concentrates on sectors where Indian firms have strategic expansion advantage namely Healthcare, Pharmaceuticals, IT Services, Consumer goods, manufacturing, etc.

2. Bajaj Capital: The Bajaj Capital Group is one of the renowned Investment consultant and Financial Planning firms in India. It is certified under the Category I of Merchant Bankers by SEBI. Bajaj Capital provides custom-made Fiscal Planning facilities and investment consultation to the investors, organizational investors, corporate, high income patrons and Non-Resident Indians (NRIs).

Being one of the biggest distributors of economic goods, Bajaj provides an extensive range of investment schemes such as general insurance, life insurance, mutual funds, etc to both public and private institutions.

3. Cholamandalam Investment and Finance Company: A combined fiscal service provider of three firms namely Cholamandalam DBS Finance Limited (CDFL), DBS Cholamandalam Distribution Limited and DBS Cholamandalam Securities Limited, Cholamandalam DBS operates in 16 international markets. DBS provides an extensive range of facilities to small and medium sized enterprise, corporate, customers and comprehensive banking activities across Middle East and Asia.

4. ICICI Securities Ltd: India's biggest equity house, ICICI Securities Ltd provide back-to-back banking solutions through its extensive distribution network to cater to the varied needs of its retail and corporate clients. The firm is listed under the Monetary Authority of Singapore (MAS) and Financial Services Authority, UK and has an authoritative place in the core divisions of its functional areas such as consultant services, fiscal good distribution, Equity Capital Markets Advisory Services, etc.

5. IDFC: Initiated in 1997 in Chennai, IDFC undertook the responsibility of providing financial support to 332 projects accruing a profit of up to ₹ 2,20,400 million. The sectors under IDFC's financial assistance are infrastructure, agri related business, transportation, healthcare, tourism and others.

6. Kotak Mahindra Capital Company: Initiator and leader in equity capital markets, Kotak Investment Banking has undertaken the developmental work of most ground breaking advances in the Indian capital markets comprising the launch of book building and Qualified Institutional Placements (QIPs) in India. The investment bank has an impressive track record of controlling various sectors and has played a major role in the government's milestone disinvestments.

7. SBI Capital Markets: SBICAPS is India's foremost investment bank and project consultant, aiding local firms in capital enlistment endeavors for last many years. The firm started it operations in 1986 and is an entirely owned subordinate of the State Bank of India. Asian Development Bank (ADB) possesses 13.84% stakes in equity segment of SBICAPS.

8. Tata Investment Corporation Limited (TICL): A non-banking financial company (NBFC), TICL is listed with the Reserve Bank of India under the group of 'Investment Company'. The firm's commercial activities constitute mainly of endowing in long-standing investments in equity of the firms in various sectors. The chief source of return for the firm entails income on investment trading and income accrued on dividend.

9. Yes Bank: This Investment Banking association is engaged in the classification, arrangement and implementation of deals for their clients in varied sectors and nations. Some of the archetypal transactions incorporate divestitures, private equity syndication, mergers and acquisitions and IPO consultation.

10. UTI Securities Ltd: Endorsed as a self-regulating professional body in 1994, UTI Securities Ltd., is one of the renowned investment bank of India. After the termination of Unit Trust of India (UTI) Act, the total share fund of UTISEL is now controlled by superintendent of particular enterprise of UTI. The firm has been offering all sorts of investment associated activities which incorporates investment banking and corporate consultation facilities.

30.7. ROLE AND CONTRIBUTION OF INVESTMENT BANKING IN INDIA

Investment Banking India has always been very crucial for the smooth flow of market transactions between various investors, companies, firms and the government. The economic downturn revealed that only the strong can swim against the tide and still remain afloat. Those skeptical must realize that the market has its own upheavals and downturns. When we look at the financial strength of these companies, we just cannot ignore them. No wonder, most of these firms bounced back once again. However, the future of Investment banking companies in India looks good, even though we may see new investment guidelines.

The banking scenario in India is itself huge, covering the different facets of the economy. By and large, investment banks in India are itseif an institution which generates funds in two different ways. The first manner in which it works is by drawing public funds via the capital market by way of selling stock in their company. The other way in which it operates is to seek for venture capital or private equity, as a substitute for a stake in their company.

The major work of investment banks includes a lot of consulting. For instance, they offer advices on mergers and acquisitions to companies. The other arena where they give advice are tracking the market and determining when should a company come out with a public offering and what is the best possible way to manage the public assets of businesses. The role that an investment bank plays sometimes gets overlapped with that of a private brokerage house. The usual advice of buying and selling is also given by investment banks.

There is no demarcating line between the investment banking and other forms of banking in India. This has been observed majorly of late. All banks nowadays want to provide their customers the best of services and create a niche for themselves and that is why apart from investment banks, all other banks too are aiming at making it big.

At the macro level, investment banking is related with the primary function of assisting the capital market in its function of capital intermediation, *i.e.*, the movement of financial resources from those who have them (the investors), to those who need to make use of them for producing GDP (the issuers). *Over the decades, investment banks have always suited the needs of the finance community and thus become one of the most vibrant and exciting segment of financial services.*

❑❑❑

31 Lease and Hire Purchasing

31.1 CONCEPT OF LEASE FINANCING

Lease financing denotes procurement of assets through lease. The subject of leasing falls in the category of finance. Leasing has grown as a big industry in the USA and UK and spread to other countries during the present century. In India, the concept was pioneered in 1973 when the First Leasing Company was set up in Madras and the eighties have seen a rapid growth of this business. *Lease as a concept involves a contract whereby the ownership, financing and risk taking of any equipment or asset are separated and shared by two or more parties.* Thus, the lessor may finance and lessee may accept the risk through the use of it while a third party may own it. Alternatively the lessor may finance and own it while the lessee enjoys the use of it and bears the risk. There are various combinations in which the above characteristics are shared by the lessor and lessee.

31.2 MEANING AND ADVANTAGES OF LEASE FINANCING

A lease transaction is a commercial arrangement whereby an equipment owner or Manufacturer conveys to the equipment user the right to use the equipment in return for a rental. In other words, lease is a contract between the owner of an asset (the lessor) and its user (the lessee) for the right to use the asset during a specified period in return for a mutually agreed periodic payment (the lease rentals). The important feature of a lease contract is separation of the ownership of the asset from its usage.

The lessee is the party leasing the property. The party receiving the payments from the lease (that is, the owner of the property) is the lessor.

Advantages of Lease Financing

(i) It offers fixed rate financing; you pay at the same rate monthly.

(ii) Leasing is inflation friendly. As the costs go up over five years, you still pay the same rate as when you began the lease, therefore making your dollar stretch farther. (In addition, the lease is not connected to the success of the business. Therefore, no matter how well the business does, the lease rate never changes.)

(iii) There is less upfront cash outlay; you do not need to make large cash payments for the purchase of needed equipment.

(iv) Leasing better utilizes equipment; you lease and pay for equipment only for the time you need it.

(v) There is typically an option to buy equipment at end of lease term.

(vi) You can keep upgrading; as new equipment becomes available you can upgrade to the latest models each time your lease ends.

(vii) Typically, it is easier to obtain lease financing than loans from commercial lenders.

(viii) It offers potential tax benefits depending on how the lease is structured.

31.3 TYPES OF LEASE AGREEMENTS

Lease agreements are basically of two types. They are (a) Financial lease and (b) Operating lease. The other variations in lease agreements are (c) Sale and lease back (d) Leveraged leasing and (e) Direct leasing.

Financial Lease

Long-term, non-cancellable lease contracts are known as financial leases. The essential point of financial lease agreement is that it contains a condition whereby the lessor agrees to transfer the title for the asset at the end of the lease period at a nominal cost. At lease it must give an option to the lessee to purchase the asset he has used at the expiry of the lease. Under this lease the lessor recovers 90% of the fair value of the asset as lease rentals and the lease period is 75% of the economic life of the asset. The lease agreement is irrevocable. Practically all the risks incidental to the asset ownership and all the benefits arising there from are transferred to the lessee who bears the cost of maintenance, insurance and repairs. Only title deeds remain with the lessor. Financial lease is also known as **'capital lease'**. In India, financial leases are very popular with high-cost and high technology equipment.

A financial lease does not provide for maintenance service, is not cancelable, and is fully amortized; that is, the lease covers the entire expected life of the equipment.

Advantages of Financial Leasing for the Client (Lessee)

(i) Up to 100% financing.

(ii) Leased asset can be used as the primary guarantee.

(iii) Medium to long-term financing periods according to the operational life cycle of the leased asset.

(iv) Payments are inclusive of insurance, maintenance and miscellaneous expenses.

(v) Proportion of the leasing installment with the client's (lessee) cash flow.

(vi) Financial leasing retains the credit limits appropriated for the lessee.

(vii) Promotes consistent development of productive assets.

(viii) Helps in financial planning.

(ix) Flexibility in payments.

(x) Provides new financing alternatives.

(xi) Possibility of fixed payments.

Who Benefits from Financial Leasing

(i) Individuals Sector (Retail)

(ii) Transportation Sector

(iii) Industrial Sector

(iv) Medical Sector

(v) Real estate

(vi) Educational Sector

(vii) Communication Sector and other services

Operating Lease

An operating lease, sometimes called a **service lease**, provides for both financing and maintenance. Generally, the operating lease contract is written for a period considerably shorter than the expected life of the leased equipment, and contains a cancellation clause.

An operating lease stands in contrast to the financial lease in almost all aspects. This lease agreement gives to the lessee only a limited right to use the asset. The lessor is responsible for the upkeep and maintenance of the asset. The lessee is not given any uplift to purchase the asset at the end of the lease period. Normally the lease is for a short period and even otherwise is revocable at a short notice. Mines, Computers hardware, trucks and automobiles are found suitable for operating lease because the rate of obsolescence is very high in this kind of assets.

Operating Leases have Four Disadvantages

1. A lease can place restrictions on the operations of the aircraft. A lease may restrict where you can base or how you can operate the aircraft. A lease may restrict geographic regions to which you can fly. A lease may prohibit commercial operations. These can arranged for as part of the initial lease agreement.

2. Leases have return conditions. When returning an aircraft from a lease, you must return it in some pre-agreed state of condition. The return conditions protect the lessor, not you as the lessee. You will likely pay a penalty for high utilization, or for engines that are not on a guaranteed maintenance program, and wear and tear beyond that accepted in the lease. When you own it, you can fly it as much as you need as you, the owner, accept the residual value risks.

3. Early returns from a lease can be costly. If you break a lease, you may be responsible for the remaining lease payments.

4. With a lease, you may loose tax advantages. An aircraft can be written off to a zero tax basis. Leases don't allow you that benefit as the lease payments can only be taken as expenses. This may result in higher short term taxes as the aircraft depreciation allowance can easily exceed the lease payment deduction.

Sale and Lease Back

It is a sub-part of finance lease. In a sale and leaseback arrangement, the firm owning the assets or properties sells it to another firm, often a financial institution, while simultaneously entering into an agreement to lease the property back from the firm in consideration of lease rentals. A sale and leaseback can be thought of as a type of financial lease.

However, under this arrangement, the assets are not physically exchanged but it all happens in records only. This is nothing but a paper transaction. Sale and lease back transaction is suitable for those assets, which are not subjected depreciation but appreciation, say land. The advantage of this method is that the lessee can satisfy himself completely regarding the quality of the asset and after possession of the asset convert the sale into a lease arrangement.

Under this transaction, the seller assumes the role of a lessee and the buyer assumes the role of a lessor. The seller gets the agreed selling price and the buyer gets the lease rentals. It is possible to structure the sale at agreed value (below or above the fair market price) and to adjust difference in the lease rentals. Thus the effect of profit/loss on sale of assets can be deferred.

Leveraged Leasing

Under leveraged leasing arrangement, a third party is involved beside lessor and lessee. The lessor borrows a part of the purchase cost (say 80%) of the asset from the third party *i.e.*, lender and the asset so purchased is held as security against the loan.

The lender is paid off from the lease rentals directly by the lessee and the surplus after meeting the claims of the lender goes to the lessor. The lessor, the owner of the asset is entitled to depreciation allowance associated with the asset.

Direct Leasing

Under direct leasing, a firm acquires the right to use an asset from the manufacturer directly. The ownership of the asset leased out remains with the manufacturer itself. The major types of direct lessor include manufacturers, finance companies, independent lease companies, special purpose leasing companies etc.

31.4 DIFFERENCE BETWEEN LASE AND LOAN

The difference between a lease and a loan:

A lease: Requires no down payment and finances only the value of the equipment expected to be depleted during the lease term. The lessee usually has an option to buy the equipment for its remaining value at the end of the lease.

The leased equipment itself is usually all that is needed to secure a lease transaction. A lease requires only a lease payment at the beginning of the first payment period which is usually much lower than the down payment.

The end user transfers all risk of obsolescence to the lessors as there is no obligation to own equipment at the end of the lease.

When leases are structured as true leases, the end user may claim the entire lease payment as a tax deduction. The equipment write-off is tied to the lease term, which can be shorter than IRS depreciation schedules, resulting in larger tax deductions each year. The deduction is also the same every year, which simplifies budgeting (equipment financed with a conditional sale lease is treated the same as owned equipment.)

More of the cash flow, especially the option to purchase the equipment, occurs later in the lease term when inflation makes dollars cheaper.

A loan: A loan requires the end user to invest a down payment in the equipment. The loan finances the remaining amount.

A loan usually requires the borrower to pledge other assets for collateral. A loan usually requires two expenditures during the first payment period; a down payment at the beginning and a loan payment at the end.

The end user bears all the risk of equipment devaluation because of new technology. End users may claim a tax deduction for a portion of the loan payment as interest and for depreciation, which is tied to depreciation schedules.

Financial Accounting Standards require owned equipment to appear as an asset with a corresponding liability on the balance sheet.

31.5 LEASING IN INDIA

Leasing has grown by leaps and bounds in the eighties but it is estimated that hardly 1% of the industrial investment in India is covered by the lease finance, as against 40% in USA and 30% in UK and 10% in Japan. The prospects of leasing in India are good due to growing investment needs and scarcity of funds with public financial institutions. This type of lease finances is particularly suitable in India where a large number of small companies have emerged more recently. Leasing in the sphere of land and building has been in existence in India for a long time, while equipment leasing has become very common in the recent times.

Evalution of Leasing in India

Leasing activity was initiated in India in 1973. The first leasing company of India, named First Leasing Company of India Ltd. was set up in that year by Farouk Irani, with industrialist A. C. Muthia. For several years, this company remained the only company in the country until 20th Century Finance Corporation was set up – this was around 1980.

By 1981, the trickle started and Shetty Investment and Finance, Jaybharat Credit and Investment, Motor and General Finance, and Sundaram Finance etc. joined the leasing game. The last three names, already involved with hire-purchase of commercial vehicles, were looking for a tax break and leasing seemed to be the ideal choice.

The industry entered the third stage in the growth phase in late 1982, when numerous financial institutions and commercial banks either started leasing or announced plans to do so. ICICI, prominent among financial institutions, entered the industry in 1983 giving a boost to the concept of leasing. Thereafter, the trickle soon developed into flood, and leasing became the new gold mine. This was also the time when the profit-performance of the two doyen companies, First Leasing and 20th Century had been made public, which contained all the fascination for many more companies to join the industry. In the meantime, International Finance Corporation announced its decision to open four leasing joint ventures in India. To add to the leasing boom, the Finance Ministry announced strict measures for enlistment of investment companies on stock-exchanges, which made many investment companies to turn overnight into leasing companies.

As per RBI's records by 31st March, 1986, there were 339 equipment leasing companies in India whose assets leased totaled ₹ 2395.5 million. One can notice the surge in number — from merely 2 in 1980 to 339 in 6 years.

Subsequent swings in the leasing cycle have always been associated with the capital market —whenever the capital markets were more permissive, leasing companies have flocked the market. Another significant phase in the development of Indian leasing was the Dahotre Committee's recommendations based on which the RBI formed guidelines on commercial bank funding to leasing companies. The growth of leasing in India has distinctively been assisted by funding from banks and financial institutions.

Banks themselves were allowed to offer leasing facilities much later - in 1994. However, even to date, commercial banking machinery has not been able to gear up to make any remarkable difference to the leasing scenario. The post-liberalization era has been witnessing the slow but sure increase in foreign investment into Indian leasing. Starting with GE Capital's entry, an increasing number of foreign-owned financial firms and banks are currently engaged or interested in leasing in India.

Leasing in India: Current Scenaio India at the 14th largest place in World leasing sounds incredible! But it is true, and true contrary to the internationally available statistics published by the London Financial Group. The Group's data, published every year in the World Leasing Yearbook would place India at some 36th place! When it comes to size, India has the obvious advantage of being such a vast nation.

Center for Monitoring of Indian Economy compiles data about Indian leasing volumes, which is carried as a part of India Leasing Yearbook published by the Association of Leasing and Financial Services Cos. The data compiled by the Center shows aggregate balance sheet value of leased and hired assets (though for balance sheet purposes, lease and hire-purchase transactions are distinguished, there is no material difference between the two - hence the volumes have been clubbed here) at about ₹ 261 billion (End March 1997). This is based on reporting by 226 companies, whereas the business, particularly hire-purchase, is spread amongst some 3000 large and small companies. Estimated outstanding business done by these firms is about ₹ 15 billion (at ₹ 5 million per such firm).

31.6 CONCEPT AND MEANING OF HIRE PURCHASE

Hire purchase is a type of instalment credit under which the hire purchaser, called the hirer, agrees to take the goods on hire at a stated rental, which is inclusive of the repayment of principal as well as interest, with an option to purchase. Under this transaction, the hire purchaser acquires the property (goods) immediately on signing the hire purchase agreement but the ownership or title of the same is transferred only when the last instalment is paid. The hire purchase system is regulated by the Hire Purchase Act., 1972. This Act defines a hire purchase as "an agreement under which goods are let on hire and under which the hirer has an option to purchase them in accordance with the terms of the agreement and includes an agreement under which:

1. The owner delivers possession of goods thereof to a person on condition that such person pays the agreed amount in periodic instalments;
2. The property in the goods is to pass to such person on the payment of the last of such instalments, and
3. Such person has a right to terminate the agreement at any time before the property so passes".

Hire purchase should be distinguished from instalment sale wherein property passes to the purchaser with the payment of the first instalment. But in case of HP (ownership remains with the seller until the last instalment is paid) buyer gets ownership after paying the last instalment.

A couple buys a three piece suite for ₹ 1,500. They have to pay a deposit of 10% and the amount outstanding is charged at 12% per annum. The amount owing is then paid off in 12 monthly instalments.

(a) How much will each instalment be?

Price of suite = ₹ 1,500

10% deposit = ₹ 1,500 × $\frac{10}{100}$

= ₹ 150

Outstanding balance = ₹ 1,500 – ₹ 150

= ₹ 1,350

$$\text{Interest at 12\%} = ₹\ 1{,}350 \times \frac{12}{100} = ₹\ 162$$

Total repayment = outstanding balance + interest

= ₹ 1,350 + ₹ 162

= ₹ 1,512

Monthly instalments = ₹ 1,512 ÷ 12

= ₹ 126

(b) What is the credit price and how much extra do you pay?

The credit price = deposit + monthly payments

= ₹ 150 + (₹ 126 × 12)

= ₹ 1,662

Extra amount paid = ₹ 1,662 – ₹ 1,500

= ₹ 162, which is the interest

31.7 DIFFERENCE BETWEEN LEASE FINANCING AND HIRE PURCHASE

Following are the points of distinction showing the differences between lease financing and hire purchase

1. Meaning: A lease transaction is a commercial arrangement, whereby an equipment owner or manufacturer conveys to the equipment user the right to use the equipment in return for a rental. Hire purchase is a type of instalment credit under which the hire purchaser agrees to take the goods on hire at a stated rental, which is inclusive of the repayment of principal as well as interest, with an option to purchase.

2. Option to user: No option is provided to the lessee (user) to purchase the goods.

Option is provided to the hirer (user).

3. Nature of expenditure: Lease rentals paid by the lessee are entirely revenue expenditure of the lessee. Only interest element included in the HP instalments is revenue

4. Expenditure by nature: Lease rentals comprise of 2 elements (1) finance charge and (2) capital recovery. HP instalments comprise of 3 elements (1) normal trading profit (2) finance charge and (3) recovery of cost of goods/assets.

31.8 FACTORING

Factoring is another type of financial service provided by the specialist organizations. When small scale firms sell on credit basis, collection of receivable poses a problem. In that case factoring organizations play an important role in collection of debtors. Factoring involves sale of receivables to specialized firm, called factors. Factors collect receivables and also advance cash against receivables to solve the client firm's liquidity problem. For providing their services, they charge interest on advance and commission for other services. In other words, factoring is an arrangement under which a financial institution (called factor) undertakes the task of collecting the book debts of its client in return for a service charge in the form of discount or rebate. The factoring institution eliminates the client's risk of bad debts by taking over the responsibility of book debts due to the client. The factoring institution advances a proportion of the value of book debts of the client immediately and the balance on maturity of book debts.

Factoring Procedure

The agreement between the supplier and the factor specifies the factoring procedure. Usually the firm sends the customer's order to the factor for evaluating the customer's creditworthiness and approval. Once the factor is satisfied about the customer's credit worthiness and agrees to buy receivables, the firm dispatches goods to the customer.

The customer will be informed that his account has been sold to the factor, and he is instructed to make payment directly to the factor. To perform his functions of credit evaluation and collection for a large number of clients, a factor may maintain a credit department with specialized staff. Once the factor has purchased a firm's receivables and if he agrees to own them, he will have to provide protection against any bad-debt losses to the firm.

Merits

1. As a result of factoring services, the enterprise can concentrate on manufacturing and selling.
2. The risk of bad debts is eliminated.
3. The factoring institution also provides advice on business trends and other related matters.

31.9 DIFFERENCE BETWEEN FINANCIAL LEASE AND OPERATING LEASE

A finance lease is a type of lease where the lessor has transferred the risks and rewards of ownership to the lessee. This includes maintenance of the asset and the risk of obsolescence. The lessee would have to bear these risks of ownership of the asset. In a finance lease, the lessee would pay an amount of lease payments which covers all or most of the cost of the asset to the lessor. The lessee would also have use of the asset for most of its useful life. A finance lease would usually give the lessee an option to purchase the asset after the lease term at a discounted price. A finance lease is not easily cancellable. Even if it was, there would be high penalties for cancellation. An example of a finance lease is the lease of a production machine by a company. The company would have to be responsible for the maintenance of the machine.

An operating lease on the other hand, is a lease where the lessor retains ownership of the asset. This means that the risk and rewards of ownership has not been transferred to the lessee. The lessor is liable for maintenance payments on the asset. After the lease period, the asset would still have a substantial residual value left. The lease period is also usually a minor part of the asset's useful life. An operating lease is also easily cancellable given a short notice. An example of an operating lease is the lease of computers by a company. The company does not need to pay for repairs of the computer and does not need to worry that the computers being obsolete as the lessor would be the one responsible for the computers.

SOLVED EXAMPLE BASED ON LEASE FINANCING

Problem 1.

XYZ Ltd is in the business of manufacturing steel utensils. The firm is planning to diversify and add a new product line. The firm can either buy the required machinery or get it on lease.

The machine can be purchased for ₹ 15,00,000. It is expected to have a useful life of 5 years with salvage value of ₹ 1,00,000 after the expiry of 5 years. The purchase can be financed by 20 per cent loan repayable in 5 equal annual instalments (inclusive of interest) becoming due at the end of each year. Alternatively, the machine can be taken on year-end lease rentals of ₹ 4,50,000 for 5 years. Advise the company on which option it should choose. For your exercise, you may assume the following:

(i) The machine will constitute a separate block for depreciation purposes. The company follows writtes down value method of depreciation, the rate of depreciation being 25 per cent.

(ii) Tax rate is 35 per cent and cost of capital is 18 per cent.

(iii) Lease rents are to be paid at the end of the year.

(iv) Maintenance expenses estimated at ₹ 30,000 per year are to be borne by the lessee.

Solution

PV of Cash Outflows Under Leasing Alternative:

Year-end	Lease rent after taxes [LR (1 — t)] [₹ 4,50,000 (1 – 0.35)]	PVIFA at 13%	Total PV
1–5	₹ 2,92,500	₹ 3.517	₹ 10,28,723

Borrowing/Buying Option

Equivalent annual loan instalment = ₹ 15,00,000/2.991 (PVIFA for 5 years at 20%) = ₹ 5,01,505.

PV of Cash Outflows Under Buying Alternative (after having loan)

Year -end	Loan instalment	Tax advantage on Interest (1 × 0.35)	Depreciation (D × 0.35)	Net cash outflows (col. 2 – col. 3 + 4)	PVIF @ 13%	Total PV
1	2	3	4	5	6	7
₹	₹	₹	₹	₹	₹	₹
1	5,01,505	1,05,000	1,31,250	2,65,255	0.885	2,34,751
2	5,01,505	90,895	98,437	3,12,173	0.783	2,44,431
3	5,01,505	73,968	73,828	3,53,709	0.693	2,45,120
4	5,01,505	53,656	55,371	3,92,478	0.613	2,40,589
5	5,01,505	29,114	41,528	4,30,863	0.543	2,33,959
					3.517	11,99,170
Less PV of salvage value (₹ 1,00,000 × 0.543)						(54,300)
Less PV of tax savings on short-term capital loss (₹3,55,958 – ₹1,00,00) × 0.35 = (89,585 × 0.543)						(48,645)
NPV of cash outflows						10,96,225

Recommendation: The company is advised to go for leasing as the PV of cash outflows (₹ 10,28,723) under leasing option is lower than under buy/borrow alternative (₹ 10,96,225).

Working Notes:

Schedule of Debt Payment

Year-end	Loan Instalment	Loan at the beginning of the year	Payments Interest (col.3 × 20%)	Principal Repayment	Loan outstanding at the end of the year (col.3 – col.5)
1	2	3	4	5	6
	₹	₹	₹	₹	₹
1	5,01,505	15,00,000	3,00,000	2,01,505	12,98,495
2	5,01,505	12,98,495	2,59,699	2,41,806	10,56,689
3	5,01,505	10,56,689	2,11,338	2,90,167	7,685,22
4	5,01,505	7,66,522	1,53,304	3,48,201	4,18,321
5	5,01,505	4,18,321	83,184	4,18,321	–

Schedule of Depreciation

Year	Depreciation (D) ₹	Balance at the end of the year ₹
1	15,00,000 × 0.25 = ₹ 3,75,000	11,25,000
2	11,25,000 × 0.25 = 2,81,250	8,43,750
3	8,43,750 × 0.25 = 2,10,937	6,32,813
4	6,32,813 × 0.25 = 1,58,203	4,74,610
5	4,74,610 × 0.25 = 1,18,652	3,55,958

31.10 LEASE VS. HIRE PURCHASE – PRACTICAL

A. Cost of Hire Purchase: (CHP)

		₹
	Down Payment	xxx
Add:	Service charges	xxx
		xxx
Add:	P.V. of hire purchase instalment – discounted by cost of debt (K_d)	xxx
		xxx
Less:	P.V. of depreciation tax shield – discounted by cost of capital (K)	(xxx)
Less:	P.V. of the net salvage value – discounted by cost of capital (K)	xxx
		xxx

B. Cost of Leasing:

	Lease Management fee	xxx
Add:	P.V. of lease payment – discounted by cost of debt (K_d)	xxx
		xxx
Less:	P.V. of tax shield on (lease payments + lease management fee) – discounted by cost of capital (K)	xxx
		xxx
Add:	P.V. of interest tax shield on H.P. – discounted by cost of capital (K)	xxx
		xxx

Decision: If the cost of Hire Purchase is less than cost of leasing, the hirer should prefer the H.P. alternative and vice versa.

Problem 2

A company has an investment plan amounting to ₹ 108 lakhs. The tax relevant rate of depreciation of the company is 25%, its marginal cost of capital and marginal cost of debt are 16% and 20% respectively and it is in 35% in tax bracket. It is examining financing alternatives for its capital expenditure. A proposal from a financing company, with the following salient features, is under its active consideration:

Hire Purchase Plan: The (flat) rate of interest per annum charged by the company is 16%. Repayment of the amount is to be made in advance, in 36 equated instalments. The hire purchaser is required to make down payment of 20%.

Leasing alternatives: Lease rentals are payable at ₹ 28 per thousand per month, in advance. The primary lease period can be assumed to be 5 years.

The net salvage valve of the equipment after 5 years can be assumed to be 33 lakhs. Which alternative – leasing or hire purchase should the company use ? why ?

Assume that SOYD method is used to allocate total charge.

Solution:

A: Calculation of Cost of Hire Purchase (CHP):

Cost of Hire Purchase (CHP)	₹ (in lakhs)
Down payment [108 × 20%]	21.60
Add: P.V. of H.P. Instalment [Note 1]	90.00
	111.60
Less: P.V. of depreciation tax shield [Note 2]	20.44
	91.16
Less: P.V. of the net salvage value — 33 × .476	15.71
Cost of Hire Purchase	75.45

Note 1: P.V. of H.P. Instalment (discounted by K_d)

	₹ (in lakhs)
Cash Price	108
Less: Down Payment [20% × 108]	21.60
Balance without H.P. Interest	86.40
Add: Interest @ 16% $\left[86.4 \times \frac{16}{100} \times 3\right]$	41.472
H.P. Price/ Total Instalment	127.872

Yearly Instalment = $\frac{127.872}{3}$

= 42.624 lakhs

Table : P.V. of instalments

Year	*Instalments (₹ in lakhs)*	*PVIF @ 20%*
1	42.624	0.8333
2	42.624	0.6944
3	42.624	0.5787
Total	PVIFA (20,3)	2.1064

$$P.V. = 2.1064 \times 42.624$$
$$= ₹\ 89.96 \text{ lakhs}$$
$$= 90 \text{ lakhs}$$

Note 2: P.V. of Depreciation tax shield – discounted by (K)

Cost/WDV	*₹ in lakhs*	*PVIF @ 16%*	*P.V.*
Cost	107		
Less: Depreciation (1st)	27 / 81	0.862	23.274
Less: Depreciation (2nd)	20.25 / 60.75	0.743	15.04
Less: Depreciation (3rd)	15.19 / 45.56	0.641	9.74
Less: Depreciatin (4th)	11.39 / 34.17	0.552	6.29
Less: Depreciation (5th)	8.54 / 25.63	0.476	4.06
Total	P.V. of Depreciation=		58.404

P.V. of Depreciation Tax Shield = P.V. of Depreciation × Tax rate

= 58.404 × 35% = ₹ 20.44 lakhs

B: Cost of Leasing (COL)

	Cost of Leasing (COL)	*₹ (in lakhs)*
	P.V. of lease payment (Note 1)	108.52
Less :	P.V. of Tax shield on lease payment (Note 2)	41.59
		66.93
Add :	P.V. of interest tax shield on hire purchase (Note 3)	11.56
	Cost of Leasing (COL)	78.49

Note 1: P.V. of lease payments (discounted by K_d):

Yearly lease payments or rentals

$$= 108 \times \frac{28}{1000} \times 12 = 36.288 = 36.29 \text{ lakhs}$$

Table: P.V. of lease rentals

Year	*Lease rentals (₹ in lakhs)*	*PVIF @ 20%*
1	36.29	0.8333
2	36.29	0.6944
3	36.29	0.5787
4	36.29	0.4822
5	36.29	0.4018
Total	PVIFA (20, 5)	2.9904

P.V. of lease rentals = 2.9904 × 36.29 = ₹ 108.52 lakhs

Note 2: P.V. of tax shield on lease payments (discounted by K):

Table: P.V. of lease

Year	*Lease rentals (₹ in lakhs)*	*PVIF @ 20%*
1	36.29	0.8621
2	36.29	0.7432
3	36.29	0.6406
4	36.29	0.5523
5	36.29	0.4761
Total	PVIFA (16, 5)	3.2743

P.V. of tax shield on lease payments

= P.V. of lease rentals × Tax rate

= (36.29 × 3.2743) × 0.35

= 118.82435 × 0.35

= ₹ 41.59 lakhs

Note 3: P.V. of interest tax shield on hire purchase: (discounted by K)

Total H.P. Interest = 41.472 lakhs

= 41.47 lakhs

Table 1: Allocation of Total Interest: SOYD Method

Year	*SOYD*	*Factor*	*Calculation*	*Interest (₹ in lakhs)*
1	$\frac{36+35+..........+25}{36+35+..........+1}$	$= \frac{366}{666}$	$\frac{366}{666} \times 41.47$	22.79
2	$\frac{24+23+..........+13}{36+35+..........+1}$	$= \frac{222}{666}$	$\frac{222}{666} \times 41.47$	13.82
3	$\frac{12+11+..........+1}{36+35+..........+1}$	$= \frac{78}{666}$	$\frac{78}{666} \times 41.47$	4.86
Total				41.47

P.V. of interest tax shild (discounted by 16%)

$$= [(22.79 \times 0.8621) + (13.82 \times 0.7432) + (4.86 \times 0.6406)] \times 0.35$$

$$= (19.65 + 10.27 + 3.11) \times 0.35 = ₹\ 11.56 \text{ lakhs}$$

Decision: Since the cost of leasing exceeds the cost of hire purchase, the company should acquire the equipment from the financing company under the hire purchase plan.

❑❑❑

32 Options and Futures in India

32.1 CONCEPT OF OPTION

In finance, an **option** is a derivative financial instrument that specifies a contract between two parties for a future transaction on an asset at a reference price. The buyer of the option gains the right, but not the obligation, to engage in that transaction, while the seller incurs the corresponding obligation to fulfill the transaction. The price of an option derives from the difference between the reference price and the value of the *underlying* asset (commonly a stock, a bond, a currency or a futures contract) plus a premium based on the time remaining until the expiration of the option. Other types of options exist, and options can in principle be created for any type of valuable asset.

An option which conveys the right to buy something is called a **call**; an option which conveys the right to sell is called a **put**. The reference price at which the underlying may be traded is called the strike price or exercise price. The process of activating an option and thereby trading the underlying at the agreed-upon price is referred to as *exercising* it. Most options have an expiration date. If the option is not exercised by the expiration date, it becomes void and worthless.

In return for granting the option, called *writing* the option, the originator of the option collects a payment, the *premium*, from the buyer. The writer of an option must make good on delivering (or receiving) the underlying asset or its cash equivalent, if the option is exercised.

An option can usually be sold by its original buyer to another party. Many options are created in standardized form and traded on an anonymous options exchange among the general public, while other over-the-counter options are customized ad hoc to the desires of the buyer, usually by an investment bank.

32.2 IMPORTANT TERMINOLOGY IN OPTIONS

Underlying: The specific security / asset on which an options contract is based.

Option Premium: This is the price paid by the buyer to the seller to acquire the right to buy or sell

Strike Price or Exercise Price: The strike or exercise price of an option is the specified/ pre-determined price of the underlying asset at which the same can be bought or sold if the option buyer exercises his right to buy/ sell on or before the expiration day.

Expiration date: The date on which the option expires is known as Expiration Date. On Expiration date, either the option is exercised or it expires worthless.

Exercise Date: is the date on which the option is actually exercised. In case of European Options the exercise date is same as the expiration date while in case of American Options, the options contract may be exercised any day between the purchase of the contract and its expiration date.

Open Interest: The total number of options contracts outstanding in the market at any given point of time.

Option Holder: is the one who buys an option which can be a call or a put option. He enjoys the right to buy or sell the underlying asset at a specified price on or before specified time. His upside potential is unlimited while losses are limited to the Premium paid by him to the option writer.

Option seller/writer: is the one who is obligated to buy (in case of Put option) or to sell (in case of call option), the underlying asset in case the buyer of the option decides to exercise his option. His profits are limited to the premium received from the buyer while his downside is unlimited.

Option Class: All listed options of a particular type (*i.e.*, call or put) on a particular underlying instrument, *e.g.*, all Sensex Call Options (or) all Sensex Put Options

Option Series: An option series consists of all the options of a given class with the same expiration date and strike price. *E.g.* BSXCMAY3600 is an options series which includes all Sensex Call options that are traded with Strike Price of 3600 & Expiry in May.

(BSX Stands for BSE Sensex (underlying index), C is for Call Option , May is expiry date and strike Price is 3600)

Assignment: When the holder of an option exercises his right to buy/ sell, a randomly selected option seller is assigned the obligation to honor the underlying contract, and this process is termed as Assignment.

32.3 CALL OPTIONS

A call option gives the holder (buyer/one who is long call), the right to buy specified quantity of the underlying asset at the strike price on or before expiration date.

The seller (one who is short call) however, has the obligation to sell the underlying asset if the buyer of the call option decides to exercise his option to buy.

Example: An investor buys One European call option on Infosys at the strike price of ₹ 3,500 at a premium of ₹ 100. If the market price of Infosys on the day of expiry is more than ₹ 3,500, the option will be exercised.

The investor will earn profits once the share price crosses ₹ 3,600 (Strike Price + Premium *i.e.* 3500+100).

Suppose stock price is ₹ 3,800, the option will be exercised and the investor will buy 1 share of Infosys from the seller of the option at ₹ 3,500 and sell it in the market at ₹ 3800 making a profit of ₹ 200 {(Spot price - Strike price) - Premium}.

In another scenario, if at the time of expiry stock price falls below ₹ 3,500 say suppose it touches ₹ 3,000, the buyer of the call option will choose not to exercise his option. In this case the investor loses the premium (₹ 100), paid which shall be the profit earned by the seller of the call option.

32.4 PUT OPTIONS

A Put option gives the holder (buyer/ one who is long Put), the right to sell specified quantity of the underlying asset at the strike price on or before a expiry date.

The seller of the put option (one who is short Put) however, has the obligation to buy the underlying asset at the strike price if the buyer decides to exercise his option to sell.

Example: An investor buys one European Put option on Reliance at the strike price of ₹ 300, at a premium of ₹ 25. If the market price of Reliance, on the day of expiry is less than ₹ 300, the option can be exercised as it is 'in the money'.

The investor's Breakeven point is ₹ 275 (Strike Price - premium paid), *i.e.*, investor will earn profits if the market falls below 275.

Suppose stock price is ₹ 260, the buyer of the Put option immediately buys Reliance share in the market @ ₹ 260 & exercises his option selling the Reliance share at ₹ 300 to the option writer thus making a net profit of ₹ 15 {(Strike price - Spot Price) - Premium paid}.

In another scenario, if at the time of expiry, market price of Reliance is ₹ 320, the buyer of the Put option will choose not to exercise his option to sell as he can sell in the market at a higher rate. In this case the investor loses the premium paid (*i.e.*, ₹ 25), which shall be the profit earned by the seller of the Put option.

32.5 HOW ARE OPTIONS DIFFERENT FROM FUTURES?

The significant differences in Futures and Options are as under:

1. Futures are agreements/contracts to buy or sell specified quantity of the underlying assets at a price agreed upon by the buyer and seller, on or before a specified time. Both the buyer and seller are obligated to buy/sell the underlying asset.

In case of options the buyer enjoys the right and not the obligation, to buy or sell the underlying asset.

2. Futures Contracts have symmetric risk profile for both buyers as well as sellers, whereas options have asymmetric risk profile.

3. In case of Options, for a buyer (or holder of the option), the downside is limited to the premium (option price) he has paid while the profits may be unlimited. For a seller or writer of an option, however, the downside is unlimited while profits are limited to the premium he has received from the buyer.

The futures contracts prices are affected mainly by the prices of the underlying asset. Prices of options are however, affected by prices of the underlying asset, time remaining for expiry of the contract and volatility of the underlying asset.

4. It costs nothing to enter into a futures contract whereas there is a cost of entering into an options contract, termed as Premium.

32.6 IN THE MONEY, AT THE MONEY AND OUT OF THE MONEY OPTIONS

An option is said to be 'at-the-money', when the option's strike price is equal to the underlying asset price. This is true for both puts and calls.

A call option is said to be in-the-money when the strike price of the option is less than the underlying asset price. For example, a Sensex call option with strike of 3900 is 'in-the-money', when the spot Sensex is at 4100 as the call option has value.

The call holder has the right to buy a Sensex at 3900, no matter how much the spot market price has risen. And with the current price at 4100, a profit can be made by selling Sensex at this higher price.

On the other hand, a call option is out-of-the-money when the strike price is greater than the underlying asset price. Using the earlier example of Sensex call option, if the Sensex falls to 3700, the call option no longer has positive exercise value. The call holder will not exercise the option to buy Sensex at 3900 when the current price is at 3700.

A put option is in-the-money when the strike price of the option is greater than the spot price of the underlying asset. For example, a Sensex put at strike of 4400 is in-the-money when the Sensex is at 4100. When this is the case, the put option has value because the put holder can sell the Sensex at 4400, an amount greater than the current Sensex of 4100.

Likewise, a put option is out-of-the-money when the strike price is less than the spot price of underlying asset. In the above example, the buyer of Sensex put option won't exercise the option when the spot is at 4800. The put no longer has positive exercise value.

Options are said to be deep in-the-money (or deep out-of-the-money) if the exercise price is at significant variance with the underlying asset price.

32.7 COVERED AND NAKED CALLS

A call option position that is covered by an opposite position in the underlying instrument (for example shares, commodities etc), is called a covered call.

Writing covered calls involves writing call options when the shares that might have to be delivered (if option holder exercises his right to buy), are already owned.

E.g. A writer writes a call on Reliance and at the same time holds shares of Reliance so that if the call is exercised by the buyer, he can deliver the stock.

Covered calls are far less risky than naked calls (where there is no opposite position in the underlying), since the worst that can happen is that the investor is required to sell shares already owned at below their market value.

When a physical delivery uncovered/ naked call is assigned an exercise, the writer will have to purchase the underlying asset to meet his call obligation and his loss will be the excess of the purchase price over the exercise price of the call reduced by the premium received for writing the call.

32.8 VALUE OF AN OPTION

In finance, the value of an option consists of two components, its **intrinsic value** and its **time value**. Time value is simply the difference on option value and intrinsic value. Time value is also known as extrinsic value, or instrumental value.

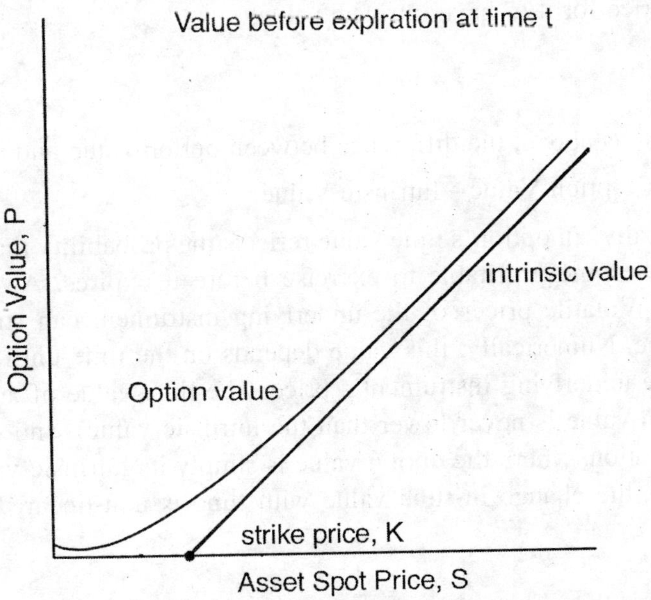

Option value (*i.e.* price) is found via a predictive formula such as Black-Scholes or using a numerical method such as the Binomial model. This price will reflect the "likelihood" of the option finishing "in-the-money". For an out-of-the-money option, the further in the future the expiration date - *i.e.* the longer the time to exercise - the higher the chance of this occurring, and thus the higher the option price; for an in-the-money option the chance of being in the money *decreases*; however the fact that the option cannot have negative value also works in the owner's favor. The sensitivity of the option value to the amount of time to expiry is known as the option's "theta"; see The Greeks. The option value will never be lower than its intrinsic value.

Intrinsic value

The **intrinsic value** of an option is the value of exercising it now. If the option has a positive monetary value, it is referred to as being in-the-money, otherwise it is referred to as being out-of-the-money. If an option is out-of-the-money at expiration, its holder will simply abandon the option and it will expire worthless. For this reason we assume that the owner of the option will never choose to lose money by exercising, thus an option can never have a negative value.

Value of a call option: max[(S " K),0], or (S " K) $^+$

Value of a put option: max[(K " S),0], or (K " S) $^+$

As seen on the graph, the intrinsic value of a call option is positive when the underlying asset's spot price S exceeds the option's strike price K.

The intrinsic value of an option must be a positive number or 0. It cannot be negative. For a call option, the strike price must be less than the price of the underlying asset for the call to have an intrinsic value greater than 0. For a put option, the strike price must be greater than the underlying asset price for it to have intrinsic value.

Time value

Time Value is, as above, the difference between option value and intrinsic value, *i.e.*

Time Value = Option Value - Intrinsic Value.

More specifically, an option's time value reflects the probability that the option will gain in intrinsic value or become profitable to exercise before it expires. An important factor is the option's volatility. Volatile prices of the underlying instrument can stimulate option demand, enhancing the value. Numerically, this value depends on the time until the expiration date and the volatility of the underlying instrument's price. The time value of an option is not negative (because the option value is never lower than the intrinsic value), and converges towards zero with time. At expiration, where the option value is simply its intrinsic value, time value is zero. Prior to expiration, the change in time value with time is non-linear, being a function of the option price.

32.9 DIFFERENT PRICING MODELS FOR OPTIONS

The theoretical option pricing models are used by option traders for calculating the fair value of an option on the basis of the earlier mentioned influencing factors.

An option pricing model assists the trader in keeping the prices of calls & puts in proper numerical relationship to each other & helping the trader make bids & offer quickly. The two most popular option pricing models are:

Black Scholes Model which assumes that percentage change in the price of underlying follows a normal distribution.

Binomial Model which assumes that percentage change in price of the underlying follows a binomial distribution.

32.10 WHO DECIDES ON THE PREMIUM PAID ON OPTIONS & HOW IS IT CALCULATED?

Options Premium is not fixed by the Exchange. The fair value/ theoretical price of an option can be known with the help of pricing models and then depending on market conditions the price is determined by competitive bids and offers in the trading environment.

An option's premium / price is the sum of Intrinsic value and time value (explained above). If the price of the underlying stock is held constant, the intrinsic value portion of an option premium will remain constant as well.

Therefore, any change in the price of the option will be entirely due to a change in the option's time value.

The time value component of the option premium can change in response to a change in the volatility of the underlying, the time to expiry, interest rate fluctuations, dividend payments and to the immediate effect of supply and demand for both the underlying and its option.

32.11 WHO ARE THE LIKELY PLAYERS IN THE OPTIONS MARKET?

Developmental institutions, Mutual Funds, FIs, FIIs, Brokers, Retail Participants are the likely players in the Options Market.

32.12 ADVANTAGES OF OPTIONS

Besides offering flexibility to the buyer in form of right to buy or sell, the major advantage of options is their versatility. They can be as conservative or as speculative as one's investment strategy dictates.

Some of the benefits of Options are as under:

1. High leverage as by investing small amount of capital (in form of premium), one can take exposure in the underlying asset of much greater value.
2. Pre-known maximum risk for an option buyer

3. Large profit potential and limited risk for option buyer

One can protect his equity portfolio from a decline in the market by way of buying a protective put wherein one buys puts against an existing stock position. This option position can supply the insurance needed to overcome the uncertainty of the marketplace. Hence, by paying a relatively small premium (compared to the market value of the stock), an investor knows that no matter how far the stock drops, it can be sold at the strike price of the Put any time until the Put expires.

E.g. An investor holding 1 share of Infosys at a market price of ₹ 3,800 thinks that the stock is over-valued and decides to buy a Put option' at a strike price of ₹ 3,800 by paying a premium of ₹ 200.

If the market price of Infosys comes down to ₹ 3,000, he can still sell it at ₹ 3,800 by exercising his put option. Thus, by paying premium of ₹ 200, his position is insured in the underlying stock.

32.13 CONCEPT OF FUTURES

Futures

A 'Future' is a contract to buy or sell the underlying asset for a specific price at a pre-determined time. If you buy a futures contract, it means that you promise to pay the price of the asset at a specified time. If you sell a future, you effectively make a promise to transfer the asset to the buyer of the future at a specified price at a particular time. Every futures contract has the following features:

- Buyer
- Seller
- Price
- Expiry

Some of the most popular assets on which futures contracts are available are equity stocks, indices, commodities and currency.

The difference between the price of the underlying asset in the spot market and the futures market is called 'Basis'. (As 'spot market' is a market for immediate delivery) The basis is usually negative, which means that the price of the asset in the futures market is more than the price in the spot market. This is because of the interest cost, storage cost, insurance premium etc., That is, if you buy the asset in the spot market, you will be incurring all these expenses, which are not needed if you buy a futures contract. This condition of basis being negative is called as 'Contango'.

Sometimes it is more profitable to hold the asset in physical form than in the form of futures. For *e.g.*, if you hold equity shares in your account you will receive dividends, whereas if you hold equity futures you will not be eligible for any dividend.

When these benefits overshadow the expenses associated with the holding of the asset, the basis becomes positive (*i.e.*, the price of the asset in the spot market is more than in the futures market). This condition is called 'Backwardation'. Backwardation generally happens if the price of the asset is expected to fall.

In finance, a **futures contract** is a standardized contract between two parties to exchange a specified asset of standardized quantity and quality for a price agreed today (the *futures price* or the strike price) but with delivery occurring at a specified future date, the *delivery date*. The contracts are traded on a futures exchange. The party agreeing to buy the underlying asset in the future, the "buyer" of the contract, is said to be "long", and the party agreeing to sell the asset in the future, the "seller" of the contract, is said to be "short". The terminology reflects the expectations of the parties — the buyer hopes the asset price is going to increase, while the seller hopes for a decrease. Note that the contract itself costs nothing to enter; the buy/sell terminology is a linguistic convenience reflecting the position each party is taking (long or short).

In many cases, the underlying asset to a futures contract may not be traditional "commodities" at all – that is, for financial futures, the underlying asset or item can be currencies, securities or financial instruments and intangible assets or referenced items such as stock indexes and interest rates.

While the futures contract specifies an exchange taking place in the future, the purpose of the futures exchange is to minimize the risk of default by either party. Thus the exchange requires both parties to put up an initial amount of cash, the margin. Additionally, since the futures price will generally change daily, the difference in the prior agreed-upon price and the daily futures price is settled daily also. The exchange will draw money out of one party's margin account and put it into the other's so that each party has the appropriate daily loss or profit. If the margin account goes below a certain value, then a margin call is made and the account owner must replenish the account. This process is known as *marking to market*. Thus on the delivery date, the amount exchanged is not the specified price on the contract but the spot value (since any gain or loss has already been previously settled by marking to market).

A closely related contract is a forward contract. A forward is like a futures in that it specifies the exchange of goods for a specified price at a specified future date. However, a forward is not traded on an exchange and thus does not have the interim partial payments due to marking to market. Nor is the contract standardized, as on the exchange.

Unlike an option, both parties of a futures contract must fulfill the contract on the delivery date. The seller delivers the underlying asset to the buyer, or, if it is a cash-settled futures contract, then cash is transferred from the futures trader who sustained a loss to the one who made a profit. To exit the commitment prior to the settlement date, the holder of a futures position can close out its contract obligations by taking the opposite position on another futures contract on the same asset and settlement date. The difference in futures prices is then a profit or loss.

32.14 FEATURES OF FUTURES

A futures contract is a standardized form of contract that is clearly recognizable by certain characteristics:

- A futures contract must always have an object or an underlying item.
- A futures contract must also stipulate the amount and units of the underlying item.
- The type of settlement is also always stipulated in the contract and it can be either physical or cash settlement. Physical settlement is a rarity; most futures contracts are settled in cash.
- The currency in which the settlement will be executed must be also always stipulated in a futures contract.
- The delivery month.
- The means of delivery.
- The last trading date must be also stipulated. It is obligatory to settle a futures contract by the last trading date stipulated in the contract.
- An additional item that is stipulated in a futures contract is the minimum permissible price fluctuation.

These characteristics help to ensure the liquidity of a futures contract. Futures contracts are a useful instrument in the hands of many investors but they are also a risky instrument: there are a number of variables that influence futures contracts. Hence originates the sometimes notorious volatility of futures contracts.

Futures contracts are volatile since the price of the commodities or financial instruments involved in these contracts can vary. As a result futures contracts entail a substantial risk to the investors involved in futures trading. *This is why the trading of futures is tightly regulated.* Futures contracts are traded through a futures exchange that acts as the counterparty in futures contracts. The exchange chooses randomly the party that will finally take delivery of the item stipulated in a contract.

32.15 MARGIN IN FUTURES TRADING

The fact that the exchange always acts as the counterparty in futures contracts and the fact that the price of futures contracts constantly fluctuates, create a substantial credit risk for the exchange. The contract owners, of course, are also liable to the effects of adverse developments in the price of a contract. To minimize the credit risk involved in each futures contract, the exchange demands collateral from the owners of the contract. This collateral is called initial margin. In the US this is called a performance bond. The initial margin can be lowered or waived for investors who have physical ownership of underlying items subject in a futures contract or for investors who have a balanced position.

Investors must also provide a maintenance margin which is lower than the initial margin and provides the minimum margin that must always be maintained in the investor's account. The maintenance margin is usually 80% of the initial margin.

Margin-to-equity ratio is a term used by investors and represents the ratio between the amount of an investor's capital that is tied to margins at any time and an investor's total capital. This is a key indicator of the health of an investor's portfolio that becomes all the more important because of the known volatility of futures contracts. A conservative trader will typically hold a margin-to-equity ratio in the order of 10 to 15% and an aggressive one will probably hold a margin-to-equity ratio in the order of 40%.

32.16 MARGIN IN OPTIONS TRADING

The treatment is slightly different for options. As options buyer have right to buy the stock/ index as per the details of contract, hence they have no obligation to pay anything. In other words there is no risk involved in option buying. Worst case is that whole of option premium is lost. As a buyer, you just pay the full premium price*contract lot size to buy the contract and that's it. No further margin requirements or daily mark to market adjustment.

32.17 INVESTORS WHO TRADE IN FUTURES CONTRACTS

There two types of investors who trade in futures contracts.

The hedgers who are defensive players and seek to protect themselves from price risk in the commodity or the financial instrument that they hold.

The speculators who seek to gain capital gain on price fluctuations on commodities or financial instruments.

32.18 TYPES OF FUTURES CONTRACTS

There are two types of futures contracts: the commodity futures and the financial futures.

Commodity futures are the futures contracts that have a given commodity as the underlying item of the contract. Table 1 below shows some examples of commodities futures.

Table 1: Commodities Futures

Grain & Oilseeds	*Livestock & Meat*	*Food, Fiber & Wood*	*Metals & Petroleum*
Corn	Beef	Potatoes	Gold
Oats	Cattle-Live	Rice	Silver
Soybean	Hogs-Lean	Sugar	Copper

Financial futures are the futures contracts that have a financial instrument as the underlying item of the contract. Table 2 below shows some examples of commodities futures.

Table 2: Financial futures

Currencies	*Interest rates*	*Securities*	*Indexes*
Canadian Dollar	Federal Funds - 30 Days	Bank CDs	Dow Jones Industrials
Japanese Yen	Treasury Bills	GNMA Pass through	Municipal Bond Index
Swiss Franc	Treasury Bonds - 30 Years	Stripped Treasuries	NYSE Composite

32.19 CALCULATION OF THE RETURN ON A FUTURES CONTRACT

The return on a futures contract comes from capital gain; high capital gain is possible due to the volatility of the prices of the commodities or financial instruments that from the underlying items of futures contracts.

One can calculate the return on a futures contract as follows:

$$\frac{\text{Selling Price} - \text{Purchase Price}}{\text{Margin Deposit}}$$

32.20 FUTURES AND OPTIONS MARKET IN INDIA

There are 3 National Exchanges for enabling the purchase and sale of commodities, futures and options. These are:

1. Multi-Commodity Exchange of India Ltd. (MCX)
2. National Commodities and Derivatives Exchange Ltd. (NCDEX)
3. National Multi-Commodity Exchange of India Ltd.

Under these 3 National Exchanges, there are a dozen active Bourses for trading, more than 2,000 brokers operating in 6,000 terminals and 10,000 active traders. All these are tracking the commodities prices round the clock. In the very First year of its commencement, *Commodities Trading in India clocked an annual turnover of ₹ 1400 Billion and is estimated to cross ₹ 10,000 Billion during this fiscal alone.*

The MCX has setup centers in Ahmadabad, Mumbai and Delhi for physical delivery of futures contracts in commodities. It plans to spread this network to Kolkata and Chennai. The NCDEX has recently launched in association with International Petroleum Exchange, London (IPE), the IPE Brent Crude Futures Contract, which is a landmark step towards integrating Indian Energy Markets with global Energy Markets. The MCX has tied up with Chicago Climate Exchange to trade in Carbon and Sulphur Financial Instruments for the global emissions marketplace. In near future, MCX will tie-up with, European Climate Exchange.

32.21 FUTURES AND OPTIONS IN INDIA

The Indian capital market has witness impressive growth and qualitative changes, especially over the last two decades. In the fifties, sixties and most of the seventies, it was in a dormant stage when the investors were generally not familiar with, or inclined towards, the corporate securities. During this time, only few companies accessed the capital market. As a consequence, trading volumes were low during these years. The process of liberalization of the Indian economy since the early nineties has contributed to changes in the capital market scenario. The entry of foreign investors in the market has resulted in a substantial change in the scale of operations. Now, we are on the threshold of introduction of trading in derivatives including futures and options, which is expected to bring a qualitative change in the capital market.

We will first consider analytically the Badla System which has been an integral part of the Indian markets for long and how does it compare with the futures and options. Along with it, a review is made of the form in which an option trading has been prevalent in the Indian capital market.

• The Badla System

The system of forward trading was prevalent in the Indian capital market for decades. It originated as fortnightly clearings, the clearings being meant as a contract for clearance and settlement through clearing house under the bye-laws and regulations of the stock exchanges. Such contracts for â˜clearing were prohibited in June 1969 by the government of India vide a notification under section 16(1) of the Securities Contract (Regulation) act 1956.This led to a reduction in the stock market activities.

A forward trading system was introduced by the government of India in July, 1983 in the Bombay, Calcutta, Delhi and Ahmadabad stock exchanges. Under the system, the listed shares were divided into two categories: specified and non-specified. The system permitted the carry-forward, or badla trading in specified shares. The underlying principle of the system was simply this that although, strictly, forward trading could not be undertaken, transactions were done on a spot basis, but the settlement was carried forward.

The system was stuffed with a strict schedule of regulatory measures like daily margins, carry over margins, automatic margins, limits on holdings of individuals, limits on price fluctuations-daily and fortnightly, etc. the system induced liquidity in the stock market, which was largely due to participation of the retail investors who otherwise had no access to fund the purchases. The badla system of trading worked well and led to a stupendous growth of the market in terms of various parameters like the number of investors, number of new issues, market capitalization and turnover.

The Badla system was banned in December 1993 by the market regulator, SEBI, presumably because it led to excessive speculation and/or its misuse. Based on the recommendations of the G S Patel committee that the SEBI had set up, a new carry forward trading system was introduced in January 1996. However, the system did not fond much favour with the broking and investing community. The revised carry forward system entails a number of restrictions which have made it unattractive.

• Limits on the Carry Forward Transactions

- Margins
- Limited Carry Forward
- Cumbersome Reporting Requirement

There were voices for relaxations in the stringent conditions laid down in the revised carry forward scheme from time to time and even demands for reviving the old badla system. The re-introduction of Badla trading was suggested in some quarters to be key to the revival of the capital market on account of their deep faith in the ingenuity of the system which simultaneously facilitates hare financing, share lending and carry forward.

• Badla: Operation and Rationale

We may look the modus operandi of badla, which has been prevalent I the Indian markets. Under the bye-laws of the stock exchanges, a contract in specified shares can be for

(a) Spot delivery

(b) For hand delivery

(c) For special delivery

(d) For the settlement

Unless otherwise stipulated, when entering into the contract, a contract is deemed to be for the current settlement.

At the end of a settlement, all the transactions for each broker are clubbed together and each broker's net position is worked out for that settlement. The brokers then decide in consultation with his clients whether they would accept/give delivery of the shares and pay/receive money in full for the same, would carry forward the sale/purchase. Thus, outstanding positions at the end of a settlement may be categorized as the seller, who want, and those who do not want, to give deliveries, and the buyers who want, and those who want do not want, to take deliveries.

Now the buyer does not want to take the delivery and desires to carry forward the transactions from the current settlement to next settlement period, he usually has to pay contango charge or the badla to the seller. It is a consideration for acquiring by the rights of the rights and the obligation in the shares. If some of the buyers do not want to take delivery in case the quantum of delivery sales exceeds the quantum of delivery purchase, the financiers know as uyaj badla wale emerge, who take the delivery in the current settlement from the seller giving the delivery and give the delivery I the next settlement to the buyers carrying forward the transactions, receiving the difference between the settlement rate and the sale rates for the next settlement as interest charges. This is termed as seedha badla and the transaction is known as uyaj badla or Mandi badla

The badla charges for carrying forward the transaction are determined by the inter-play of the market forces in a half-hour session at the end of the current settlement period and at the beginning of next settlement, known as Badla session. These charges, which vary in the half-hour badla session between scrips and also for the same scrip, depend upon various factors like prevailing interest rates, technical position of the market, etc.

The rationale for providing the badla facility to carry forward transactions from one settlement period of two weeks to another is that it imparts liquidity and breadth to the market. This allows the absorption of large purchases and sales in relatively narrow fluctuations in prices, leading to stability in the market. The carry forward system provided the investor an opportunity to enhance his position significantly towards liquidity, forecasting of the future market behaviour and reasonable level of speculation, which are essential ingredients for an efficient functioning of the secondary capital market.

In the absence of such a facility, all purchases would be required to be taken delivery of with the payments being in respect of the same and, similarly all sales outstanding at the end of the settlement have to result in delivery with respect to the consideration amount. Such a situation would lead to an ill-liquid and narrow market characterized by sharp oscillation in prices. This is reflected in the fact that the movement of prices in the specified group is relatively more orderly than in case of the non-specified shares.

• Badla versus futures and options

From our discussion about Badla, and the futures and options, it may be observed that;

1. In badla, all net position at the end of the settlement period can be carried forward and members pay or receive badla charges, while in futures and options, various combinations are available which in futures and options, various combinations are available which enable the operators to close or recluse the open position till the maturity period, and carry forward of open position to the next maturity period is neither necessary nor possible.
2. Badla is basically a financial mechanism. Badla financiers provide finance to the members with net bought positions. On the other hand, no such financing mechanism exists in futures and options.
3. Badla system encourages short sellers as they generally get badla charges. However, both bulls and bears have an opportunity to trade in case of options and futures.

• Options in India: Teji and Mandi

The operations in the Indian market have been confined to call options (known as teji), put options (known as mandi), their combination in the form of straddles (known as jhota or du-ranga) and bhav-bhav on stock only. While in options trading markets in the world, options with exercise price less than, equal to, greater than the stock price are available in the markets only out-of-the-money call options, *i.e.*, options with an exercise price higher than the current stock price, are traded. Hence the name is *teji*. The seller or the writer of such an option is called *teji* khaii-wal as he agrees to sell the share in case of a *teji* (the price arising out above the exercise price) for a value, the option premium. The buyer of the option is called teji lagaii-wal.

Similarly, the put options traded are also those which are out-of-the-money options *i.e.* options with an exercise price lower than the current stock price. The writers of such options agree to buy a share in the event of its price falling below the exercise price, *i.e.* mandi, in consideration for a premium. The writer of an option of this type is called the mandi khaii-wal while the buyer is a mandi lagaii-wal.

Both teji and mandi have an expiry time at the stroke of 15 minutes before the closing time of trading of the next business day. However, sometimes they are event-based, so that while they can originate any day the exercise date is fixed, like the day following the budget day or the day following the annual general meeting of the company whose share underlies the teji/mandi contract. The premium on teji/mandi options is fixed customarily, usually at 25 paise per share, and is not negotiable, although the strike price may be negotiated. On event-based options, the premium payable is double than that on the ordinary options.

The greater part of the derivative trading in India is in the form of jhota or fatak, which involves the buyer, known variously as lagaii-wal or lagane-wale or punter, the writer, known by various names like khaii-wal, khane-wala or bookie, and a broker, the mediator. A fatak involves a call option and put option available to the punter at exercise prices higher and lower than a certain value, which is generally the closing price of a share on a given day. The size of fatak, that is to say, the gap between the exercise prices of call and put options is generally higher before and after the market trading hours and it is smaller during these hours.

Another derivative traded in the market is known as bhav-bhav or nazrana. In this case, the closing price of the day is taken as the exercise price and the holder of nazrana can exercise a call or put option depending on the price of the stock. For instance, if the closing price of a stock is ₹ 66 on a given day, then the holder shall hold both options with him: buy the share from the bookie at a price of ₹ 66 or sell to him the share at the same price (₹ 66) at the time of exercise. It will obviously pay the option buyer to buy at ₹ 66 if the share price goes beyond this level and sell it to the writer at ₹ 66 if the share price decreases below ₹ 66.

In nazrana, then, the exercise price is fixed and so is the date of expiry. However, the premium is negotiable. The premium is roughly one-half of the amounts of gap in fatak. Thus, with the share price of ₹ 66 and a fatak with exercise prices of ₹ 63 and ₹ 69, the gap is equal to ₹ 3. In such case, the premium payable by a buyer shall be around ₹ 1.50 per share.

The nazrana apparently exposes the writer to greater risk by providing call and put options to the buyer at the same exercise price, in contrast to a fatak where the same options are given but with a gap in the exercise prices. However, a closer look at the two reveals that for a given amount of premium, one has to write option on a larger number of shares in case of a fatak than in case of nazrana. Accordingly, when there are significant fluctuations in the price of the underlying share, a fatak involves a far greater degree of risk than a nazrana.

The chronology of introduction of the futures and options in India is given below:

Although exchanges like Bombay Stock Exchanges and Vadodara Stock Exchange have for long shown their willingness for trading in futures and options, but a concerted effort in this direction was made by the National Stock Exchange (NSE) only in July 1995, when it considered the modalities of introducing derivative trading, mainly futures and options. Within a few months, NSE developed a system of future and option trading aiming at modifying the carry forward system to include future and options in its scope. By January 1996, the NSE started work on the scheme of such trading in March 1996; it made a presentation to SEBI on its plan to commence trading in futures and options. The exchange proposed to start with index based future and index base of options, which are seen as comparably safer forms of derivatives.

By May 1996, the NSE finalized the net worth requirement for the membership of the purposed future and options trading segments, which was set at 5 crore. These constitute NSE's first step towards initialing futures and options trading, which, the NSE visualized, would commence in the month of November, 1996.

The NSE decided for the future and options segment to have two type of membership (restrict to just corporate members): member trading only in futures products, and those who write options. The members were to further earmark cash deposits for the National securities Clearing Corporation Limited (NSCCOL). The deposits collected by the NSCCL were to form part of member's contribution to a separate settlement fund for the future and options segment, which was to commence operations along with trading in futures and options.

Around this time the Bombay Stock Exchange (BSE) also decided to form a committee to consider the introduction of trading in derivatives, government paper and debt market instruments. It proposed to be working on index- based future and submitted a proposal to SEBI.

THE SEBI, in the mean time, set up a special derivatives regulatory department which would coordinate and ensure the sharing the information between stock exchanges. It also set up the L.C. Gupta Committee to go into the question of derivatives trading and to suggest various policy and regulatory measures that need to be undertaken before trading is formally allowed.

Recently, the Union Law Ministry has asked SEBI to go ahead with the proposed introduction of futures and options trading without effecting changes in the Securities Contract Regulation Act (SCRA) 1956. In 1995, the Centre had passed an enabling legislation effecting changes in the SCRA which allowed the issuance and trading of options in securities.

The L.C.Gupta committee appointed by SEBI is likely to suggest the various policy and regulatory measures that need to be on place before derivatives trading may be formally allowed in India.

The trading of futures and options will see light of the day only after the SEBI gives its assent to it.

❑❑❑

33 Financial Forecasting

33.1 FINANCIAL FORECASTING-AN INTRODUCTION

Financial Forecasting describes the process by which firms think about and prepare for the future. The forecasting process provides the means for a firm to express its goals and priorities and to ensure that they are internally consistent. It also assists the firm in identifying the asset requirements and needs for external financing.

For example, the principal driver of the forecasting process is generally the sales forecast. Since most Balance Sheet and Income Statement accounts are related to sales, the forecasting process can help the firm assess the increase in Current and Fixed Assets which will be needed to support the forecasted sales level. Similarly, the external financing which will be needed to pay for the forecasted increase in assets can be determined.

Firms also have goals related to Capital Structure (the mix of debt and equity used to finance the firms assets), Dividend Policy, and Working Capital Management. Therefore, the forecasting process allows the firm to determine if its forecasted sales growth rate is consistent with its desired Capital Structure and Dividend Policy.

The forecasting approach presented in this section is the Percentage of Sales method. It forecasts the Balance Sheet and Income Statement by assuming that most accounts maintain a fixed proportion of Sales. This approach although fairly simple, illustrates many of the issues related to forecasting and can readily be extended to allow for a more flexible technique, such as forecasting items on an individual basis.

33.2 METHODS OF FINANCIAL FORECASTING

- Percentage of Sales Method
- External Financing Needed (EFN)
- Financial Forecasting Equations

A. Percentage of Sales Method

The Percentage of Sales Method is a Financial Forecasting approach which is based on the premise that most Balance Sheet and Income Statement Accounts vary with sales. Therefore, the key driver of this method is the Sales Forecast and based upon this, Pro-Forma Financial Statements (*i.e.*, forecasted) can be constructed and the firms needs for external financing can be identified. The calculations illustrated on this page will refer to the Balance Sheet and Income Statement which follow. The forecasted Sales growth rate in this example is 25%

Example: **Balance Sheet (₹ in Millions)**

Assets	**2000-2001**	**Liabilities and Owners' Equity**	**2000-2001**	**Income Statement (₹ in Millions)**	**2000-2001**
Current Assets					
Cash	200	**Current Liabilities**		Sales	1200
Accounts Receivable	400	Accounts Payable	400	Cost of Goods Sold	900
Inventory	600	Notes Payable	400	***Taxable Income***	300
Total Current Assets	1200	***Total Current Liabilities***	800	Taxes	90
Fixed Assets		**Long-Term Liabilities**		***Net Income***	210
Net Fixed Assets	800	Long-Term Debt	500	Dividends	70
Total Assets	2000	Total Long-Term Liabilities	500	Addition to Retained Earnings	140
		Owners' Equity			
		Common Stock (Re1 Par)	300		
		Retained Earnings	400		
		Total Owners' Equity	700		
		Total Liab. and Owners' Equity	2000		

Forecasted sales growth rate is 25%.

PERCENTAGES OF SALES

The first step is to express the Balance Sheet and Income Statement accounts which vary directly with Sales as percentages of Sales. This is done by dividing the balance for these accounts for the current year (2000-2001) by sales revenue for the current year.

The Balance Sheet accounts which generally vary closely with Sales are Cash, Accounts Receivable, Inventory, and Accounts Payable. Fixed Assets are also often tied closely to Sales, unless there is excess capacity. (The issue of excess capacity will be addressed in External Financing Needed section.) For this example, we will assume that Fixed Assets are currently at full capacity and, thus, will vary directly will sales.

Retained Earnings on the Balance Sheet represent the cumulative total of the firm's earnings which have been reinvested in the firm. Thus, the change in this account is linked to Sales; however, the link comes from relationship between Sales growth and Earnings.

The Notes Payable, Long-Term Debt, and Common Stock accounts do not vary automatically with Sales. The changes in these accounts depend upon how the firm chooses to raise the funds needed to support the forecasted growth in Sales.

On the Income Statement, Costs are expressed as a percentage of Sales. Since we are assuming that all costs remain at a fixed percentage of Sales, Net Income can be expressed as a percentage of Sales. This indicates the Profit Margin.

Taxes are expressed as a percentage of Taxable Income (to determine the tax rate). Dividends and Addition to Retained Earnings are expressed as a percentage of Net Income to determine the Payout and Retention Ratios respectively.

Percentage of Sales Calculations

The examples in this box illustrate the calculations which were used to determine the percentages provided in the following Balance Sheet and Income Statement.

Cash	Cash/Sales = 200/1200 = .1667 = 16.67%
Inventory	Inventory/Sales = 600/1200 = .5 = 50%
Accounts Payable	(Accounts Payable)/Sales = 400/1200 = .3333 = 33.33%
Costs	Costs/Sales = 900/1200 = .75 = 75%
Taxes	Taxes/(Taxable Income) = 90/300 = .3 = 30%
Net Income	(Net Income)/Sales = 210/1200 = .175 = 17.5%
Dividends	Dividends/(Net Income) = 70/210 = .3333 = 33.33%

Balance Sheet (₹ in Millions)

Assets	*2000-2001*	%	*Liabilities and Owners' Equity*	*2000-2001*	%
Current Assets			**Current Liabilities**		
Cash	200	16.67%	Accounts Payable	400	33.33%
Accounts Receivable	400	33.33%	Notes Payable	400	N/A
Inventory	600	50.00%	***Total Current Liabilities***	800	
Total Current Assets	1200		**Long-Term Liabilities**		
Fixed Assets			Long-Term Debt	500	N/A
Net Fixed Assests	800	66.67%	Total Long-Term Liabilities	500	
			Owners' Equity		
Total Assets	2000		Common Stock ($1 Par)	300	N/A
			Retained Earnings	400	N/A
			Total Owners' Equity	700	
			Total Liab. and Owners' Equity	2000	

Income Statement (₹ in Millions)

	2000-2001	%
Sales	1200	
Cost of Goods Sold	900	75%
Taxable Income	300	25%
Taxes	90	30%
Net Income	210	17.5%
Dividends	70	33.33%
Addition to Retained Earnings	140	66.67%

Partial Pro-Forma

The next step is to construct the Partial Pro-forma Financial Statements. First, determine the forecasted Sales level. This is done my multiplying Sales for the current year (2000-2001) by one plus the forecasted growth rate in Sales. (Forecasted growth in sale is 25%)

$S_1 = S_0 (1 + g) = 1200(1 + .25) = 1500$

Where

- S_1 = the forecasted Sales level,
- S_0 = the current Sales level, and
- g = the forecasted growth rate in Sales.

Once the forecasts Sales level has been determined, the Balance Sheet and Income Statement accounts which vary directly with Sales can be determined by multiplying the percentages by the Sales forecast. The accounts which do not vary directly with Sales are simply transferred to the Partial Pro-Forma Financial Statements at their current levels.

Retained Earnings on the Balance Sheet are the one item whose amount is determined using a slightly different procedure. The Partial Pro-Forma balance for Retained Earnings equals Retained Earnings in the current year plus the forecasted Addition to Retained Earnings from the Partial Pro-Forma Income Statement. The balances for summary accounts, such as Total Current Assets and Total Current Liabilities, are determined by summing their constituent accounts.

Partial Pro-Forma Calculations

The examples in this box illustrate the calculations which were used to derive the following Partial Pro-Forma Balance Sheet and Income Statement.

Cash	(Cash%)(Sales Forecast) = (16.67%)(1500) = 250
Inventory	(Inventory%)(Sales Forecast) = 50%(1500) = 750
Costs	(Costs%)(Sales Forecast) = 75%(1500) = 1200
Addition to Retained Earnings	(Addition to Retained Earnings%)(Net Income Forecast) = 66.67%(262.5) = 175
Retained Earnings (Balance Sheet)	=Retained Earnings + Addition to Retained Earnings = 400 + 175

Balance Sheet (₹ in Millions)

Assets	*2000-2001*	*2001-2002*	*Liabilities and Owners' Equity*	*2000-2001*	*2001-2002*
Current Assets			**Current Liabilities**		
Cash	200	250	Accounts Payable	400	500
Accounts Receivable	400	500	Notes Payable	400	400
Inventory	600	750	***Total Current Liabilities***	800	900
Total Current Assets	1200	1500	**Long-Term Liabilities**		
			Long-Term Debt	500	500
			Total Long-Term Liabilities	500	500
Fixed Assets			**Owners' Equity**		
Net Fixed Assests	800	1000	Common Stock (Re 1 Par)	300	300
			Retained Earnings	400	575
Total Assets	2000	2500	***Total Owners' Equity***	700	875
			Total Liab. and Owners' Equity	2000	2275

Income Statement (₹ in Millions)

	2000-2001	*2001-2002*
Sales	1200	1500
Cost of Goods Sold	900	1125
Taxable Income	300	375
Taxes	90	112.5
Net Income	210	262.5
Dividends	70	87.5
Addition to Retained Earnings	140	175

B. External Financing Needed (EFN)

The External Financing Needed (EFN) can be determined from the Partial Pro-Forma Balance Sheet. It is simply equal to the difference between Partial Pro-Forma Total Assets and Partial Pro-Forma Total Liabilities and Owners' Equity.

EFN = 2500 - 2275 = 225 (From the earlier example).

Pro-Forma Financial Statements

The final step is to determine how the EFN is to be raised. Firms can choose to raise the EFN by borrowing on short-term basis (Notes Payable), borrowing on a long-term basis (Long-Term Debt), issuing equity (Common Stock), or some combination of the above. The chosen method is called the **Plug**.

In this example we shall assume that the EFN is to be raised through long-term borrowing. Thus the plug is Long-Term Debt. To determine the Pro-Forma Financial Statements simply increase Long-Term Debt by the EFN of ₹ 225 determined in the previous step.

Balance Sheet (₹ in Millions)

Assets	*2000-2001*	*2001-2002*	*Liabilities and Owners' Equity*	*2000-2001*	*2001-2002*
Current Assets			**Current Liabilities**		
Cash	200	250	Accounts Payable	400	500
Accounts Receivable	400	500	Notes Payable	400	400
Inventory	600	750	***Total Current Liabilities***	800	900
Total Current Assets	1200	1500	**Long-Term Liabilities**		
			Long-Term Debt	500	500
Fixed Assets			Total Long-Term Liabilities	725	725
Net Fixed Assets	800	1000	**Owners' Equity**		
			Common Stock (Re 1 Par)	300	300
Total Assets	2000	2500	Retained Earnings	400	575
			Total Owners' Equity	700	875
			Total Liab. and Owners' Equity	2000	2500

Income Statement (₹ in Millions)

	2000-2001	*2001-2002*
Sales	1200	1500
Cost of Goods Sold	900	1125
Taxable Income	300	375
Taxes	90	112.5
Net Income	210	262.5
Dividends	70	87.5
Addition to Retained Earnings	140	175

725 = 500 + 225

C. Financial Forecasting Equations

Forecasted Sales $S_1 = S_0(1 + g)$

$$\text{Full Capacity Sales} = \frac{S_0}{\%\text{ of Capacity}}$$

External Financing Needed$(S_1 < S_{FC})$ $$EFN = \frac{A_0}{S_0}(S_1 - S_0)\frac{L_0^*}{S_0}(S_1 - S_0) - (PM)(S_1)(b)$$

$$EFN_1 = \frac{TCA_0}{S_0}(S_{FC} - S_0)\frac{L_0^*}{S_0}(S_{FC} - S_0) - (PM)(S_{FC})(b)$$

External Financing Needed$(S_1 > S_{FC})$

$$EFN_1\left(\frac{TCA_0}{S_0} + \frac{FA_0}{S_{FC}}\right)(S_1 - S_{FC}) - \frac{L_0^*}{S_0}(S_1 - S_{FC}) - (PM)(S_1 - S_{FC})(b)$$

$$EFN = EFN_1 + EFN_2$$

33.3 UNDERSTANDING FINANCIAL FORECASTING IN FIVE EASY STEPS!

Step One: Discover the Needs of Your Business a financial forecast is vital to the success of any organization as it will influence the planning stages and decision making within your business. In order to understand the needs of your business, there are some questions you need to ask of yourself such as, what future decisions might your forecast change or impact? Who will be affected by these decisions? How much detail should you provide in your forecast and what tools will help others understand the data? What time frame should your financial forecast report cover: weeks, months, quarters or even years? What methods will be used to ensure accuracy, and what margin of error will be acceptable? Finally, and probably the most important, what would be the impact upon your business due to under or overcastting in your report.

Step Two: Getting Key Data for the Forecast Knowing what data you need to gather and how many years you should go back is essential to creating a clear and accurate picture of your business's financial history. If you are only going to estimate a short distance in the future, less data can be used, however the general rule is to have at least two to five years of historical data for a proper forecast. You should enlist the assistance of all data sources at your disposal in order to create the most in-depth data sets, including spreadsheets, databases from various departments, multiple healthcare data systems and enterprise data warehouse, if available, should be used. The more areas you gather your resources from, the more variations in behavior within the organization can be used to help you paint a full picture of the data at hand.

Step Three: Design a Forecast Model to Suit Your Needs You will now need to decide what type of forecasting model to use based upon the unique contributing factors of historical data, business need and other influencing factors that you have established up to this point. The model you choose is essential to your final presentation because the technique or algorithm that you ultimately use will help to support and determine your projections. The three major forecasting categories that you should focus on and deliver are cause-and-effect, judgment and time series. In order to choose the best model for your particular organization, it may be a good idea to consult with an expert for advice on which type to use.

Step Four: Assess Your Results. You should utilize the most recent time period from your gathered historical data to create the model of your financial forecast. The accuracy of your overall forecast model should be measured using the gathered statistical functions.

Step Five: Assign the Data to the Model By the time you plug in all the data and create a forecast, you should have a complete picture to share with everyone concerned in a way that they will be able to use effectively. Ideally, you should be able to tailor your financial forecast for each business area within your organization and re-package it appropriately for each user's needs.

33.4 FINANCIAL PLANNING

Financial planning is the process of determining future action on the formation and use of financial resources. The purpose of financial planning is ensuring the reproduction process as appropriate in terms of volume and structure of financial resources. The type of plans are as follows:

(1) Strategic plans, *i.e.*, plans for general business development. In the financial aspect of these plans one defines the most important financial ratios and proportions of reproduction, characterized by investment strategies and opportunities for reinvestment and savings. Strategic plans define the scope and structure of the financial resources necessary for the functioning of the enterprise. Current plans are developed on the base of the strategic ones by means of their specification. If the strategic plan provides an indicative list of financial resources, their extent and direction, then the mutual agreement of each type of attachment with their sources of funding is carried out in the network of the ongoing planning, the effectiveness of each possible source of funding is studied, and financial evaluation of the major activities of the enterprise and the ways of obtaining income is carried out.

(2) Operational plans, *i.e.* short-term tactical plans that are directly related to the achievement of the company (production plan, plan of purchasing raw materials, etc.).

Any action plan should be accompanied by an estimate of expenditures – budget formulation, which is a quantitative embodiment of the plan, describing the income and expenses for a specific time and resource requirements to achieve a given plan targets. The budget is created to perform the proposed action that defines its role as a basis for monitoring and evaluating the performance of the company.

❑❑❑

34 Asset Liability Management

34.1 CONCEPT AND DEFINITION

In banking, **asset and liability management** is the practice of managing risks that arise due to mismatches between the assets and liabilities (debts and assets) of the bank. This can also be seen in insurance.

Banks face several risks such as the liquidity risk, interest rate risk, credit risk and operational risk. Asset Liability management (ALM) is a strategic management tool to manage interest rate risk and liquidity risk faced by banks, other financial services companies and corporations.

Banks manage the risks of Asset liability mismatch by matching the assets and liabilities according to the maturity pattern or the matching the duration, by hedging and by securitization. Much of the techniques for hedging stem from the delta hedging concepts introduced in the Black-Scholes model and in the work of Robert C. Merton and Robert A. Jarrow.

Asset-liability management (ALM) is a term whose meaning has evolved. It is used in slightly different ways in different contexts. ALM was pioneered by financial institutions, but corporations now also apply ALM techniques.

Traditionally, banks and insurance companies used accrual accounting for essentially all their assets and liabilities. They would take on liabilities, such as deposits, life insurance policies or annuities. They would invest the proceeds from these liabilities in assets such as loans, bonds or real estate. All assets and liabilities were held at book value. Doing so disguised possible risks arising from how the assets and liabilities were structured.

> Consider a bank that borrows USD 100MM at 3.00% for a year and lends the same money at 3.20% to a highly-rated borrower for 5 years. For simplicity, assume interest rates are annually compounded and all interest accumulates to the maturity of the respective obligations. The net transaction appears profitable—the bank is earning a 20 basis point spread—but it entails considerable risk. At the end of a year, the bank will have to find new financing for the loan, which will have 4 more years before it matures. If interest rates have risen, the bank may have to pay a higher rate of interest on the new financing than the fixed 3.20 it is earning on its loan.

Suppose, at the end of a year, an applicable 4-year interest rate is 6.00%. The bank is in serious trouble. It is going to be earning 3.20% on its loan and paying 6.00% on its financing. Accrual accounting does not recognize the problem. The book value of the loan (the bank's asset) is:

$$100MM\ (1.032) = 103.2MM \qquad ...(1)$$

The book value of the financing (the bank's liability) is:

$$100MM\ (1.030) = 103.0MM. \qquad ...(2)$$

Based upon accrual accounting, the bank earned USD 200,000 in the first year.

Market value accounting recognizes the bank's predicament. The respective market values of the bank's asset and liability are:

$$\frac{100MM(1.032)^5}{(1.060)^4}$$

$$100MM\ (1.030) = 103.0MM.$$

From a market-value accounting standpoint, the bank has lost USD 10.28MM.

So which result offers a better portrayal of the bank' situation, the accrual accounting profit or the market-value accounting loss? The bank is in trouble, and the market-value loss reflects this. Ultimately, accrual accounting will recognize a similar loss. The bank will have to secure financing for the loan at the new higher rate, so it will accrue the as-yet unrecognized loss over the 4 remaining years of the position.

The problem in this example was caused by a mismatch between assets and liabilities. Prior to the 1970's, such mismatches tended not to be a significant problem. Interest rates in developed countries experienced only modest fluctuations, so losses due to asset-liability mismatches were small or trivial. Many firms intentionally mismatched their balance sheets. Because yield curves were generally upward sloping, banks could earn a spread by borrowing short and lending long.

Things started to change in the 1970s, which ushered in a period of volatile interest rates that continued into the early 1980s. US regulation Q, which had capped the interest rates that banks could pay depositors, was abandoned to stem a migration overseas of the market for USD deposits. Managers of many firms, who were accustomed to thinking in terms of accrual accounting, were slow to recognize the emerging risk. Some firms suffered staggering losses. Because the firms used accrual accounting, the result was not so much bankruptcies as crippled balance sheets.

34.2 ASSET-LIABILITY RISK

Increasingly, managers of financial firms focused on **asset-liability risk**. The problem was not that the value of assets might fall or that the value of liabilities might rise. It was that capital might be depleted by narrowing of the difference between assets and liabilities—that the values of assets and liabilities might fail to move in tandem. Asset-liability risk is a leveraged form of risk. The capital of most financial institutions is small relative to the firm's assets or liabilities, so small percentage changes in assets or liabilities can translate into large percentage changes in capital.

Exhibit 1 illustrates the evolution over time of a hypothetical company's assets and liabilities. Over the period shown, the assets and liabilities change only slightly, but those slight changes dramatically reduce the company's capital (which, for the purpose of this example, is defined as the difference between assets and liabilities). In Exhibit 1, the capital falls by over 50%, a development that would threaten almost any institution.

Example: Asset-Liability Risk

Exhibit 1

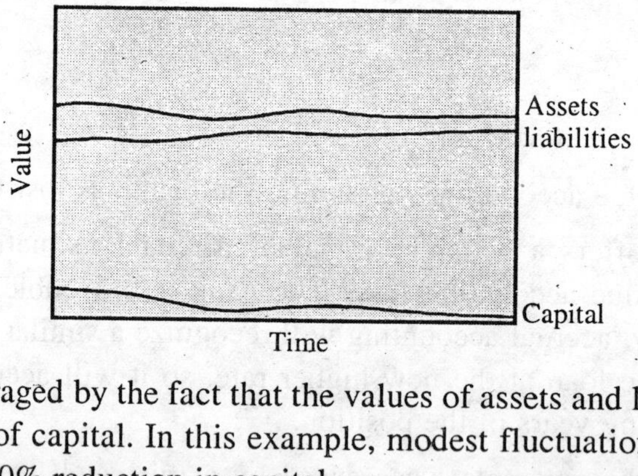

Asset-liability risk is leveraged by the fact that the values of assets and liabilities each tend to be greater than the value of capital. In this example, modest fluctuations in values of assets and liabilities result in a 50% reduction in capital.

Accrual accounting could disguise the problem by deferring losses into the future, but it could not solve the problem. Firms responded by forming asset-liability management (ALM) departments to assess asset-liability risk. They established ALM committees comprised of senior managers to address the risk.

34.3 TECHNIQUES FOR ASSESSING ASSET-LIABILITY RISK

Techniques for assessing asset-liability risk came to include gap analysis *and* duration analysis. These facilitated techniques of gap management and duration matching of assets and liabilities. Both approaches worked well if assets and liabilities comprised fixed cash flows. Options, such as those embedded in mortgages or callable debt, posed problems that gap analysis could not address. Duration analysis could address these in theory, but implementing sufficiently sophisticated duration measures was problematic. *Accordingly, banks and insurance companies also performed scenario analysis.*

With scenario analysis, several interest rate scenarios would be specified for the next 5 or 10 years. These might assume declining rates, rising rates, a gradual decrease in rates followed by a sudden rise, etc. Scenarios might specify the behavior of the entire yield curve, so there could be scenarios with flattening yield curves, inverted yield curves, etc. Ten or twenty scenarios might be specified in all. Next, assumptions would be made about the performance of assets and liabilities under each scenario. Assumptions might include prepayment rates on mortgages or surrender rates on insurance products. Assumptions might also be made about the firm's performance—the rates at which new business would be acquired for various products. Based upon these assumptions, the performance of the firm's balance sheet could be projected under each scenario. If projected performance was poor under specific scenarios, the ALM committee might adjust assets or liabilities to address the indicated exposure. A shortcoming of scenario analysis is the fact that it is highly dependent on the choice of scenarios. It also requires that many assumptions be made about how specific assets or liabilities will perform under specific scenarios.

In a sense, ALM was a substitute for market-value accounting in a context of accrual accounting. It was a necessary substitute because many of the assets and liabilities of financial institutions could not—and still cannot be marked to market. This spirit of market-value accounting was not a complete solution. A firm can earn significant mark-to-market profits but go bankrupt due to inadequate cash flow. Some techniques of ALM—such as duration analysis—do not address liquidity issues at all. Others are compatible with cash-flow analysis. With minimal modification, a gap analysis can be used for cash flow analysis. Scenario analysis can easily be used to assess liquidity risk.

Firms recognized a potential for liquidity risks to be overlooked in ALM analyses. They also recognized that many of the tools used by ALM departments could easily be applied to assess liquidity risk. Accordingly, the assessment and management of liquidity risk became a second function of ALM departments and ALM committees. ***Today, liquidity risk management is generally considered a part of ALM.***

ALM has evolved since the early 1980's. *Today, financial firms are increasingly using market-value accounting for certain business lines.* This is true of universal banks that have trading operations. For trading books, techniques of market risk management—value-at-risk ,market risk limits, etc.—are more appropriate than techniques of ALM. In financial firms, ALM is associated with those assets and liabilities—those business lines—that are accounted for on an accrual basis. This includes bank lending and deposit taking. It includes essentially all traditional insurance activities.

34.4 THE SCOPE OF ALM ACTIVITIES

The scope of ALM activities has widened. Today, ALM departments are addressing (non-trading) foreign exchange risks and other risks. Also, ALM has extended to non-financial firms. Corporations have adopted techniques of ALM to address interest-rate exposures, liquidity risk and foreign exchange risk. They are using related techniques to address commodities risks. For example, airlines' hedging of fuel prices or manufacturers' hedging of steel prices are often presented as ALM.

34.5 LIQUIDITY RISK MANAGEMENT

Liquidity is the ability of a bank to fund increases in assets and meet obligations as they come due, without incurring unacceptable losses. The fundamental role of banks in the maturity transformation of short-term deposits into long-term loans makes banks inherently vulnerable to liquidity risk, both of an institution-specific nature and that which affects markets as a whole. Virtually every financial transaction or commitment has implications for a bank's liquidity.. **Effective liquidity risk management** helps ensure a bank's ability to meet cash flow obligations, which are uncertain as they are affected by external events and other agents' behaviour. Liquidity risk management is of paramount importance because a liquidity shortfall at a single institution can have system-wide repercussions. Financial market developments in the past decade have increased the complexity of liquidity risk and its management. *Effective LRM* is *the management of liquidity by raising sufficient funds either by increasing liabilities or by converting assets promptly and at a reasonable cost.*

34.6 BENEFITS OF EFFECTIVE LIQUIDITY MANAGEMENT

Potential benefits

If an appropriate liquidity management solution is effectively implemented, the corporation stands to enjoy a range of benefits (these otherwise representing opportunity costs):

Balance consolidation: This is realized by eliminating the cost of maintaining cash deficits and surpluses in the same currency that could otherwise have been offset. In financial terms, it is determined by the differential between the interest rates applicable to the credit and debit balances that are offset.

Balance aggregation: Increasing the size of the aggregate cash position attracts better interest terms than those achievable on individual balances left idle or invested separately. It is a function of the interest-rate differential between the rates achieved with and without aggregation.

Balance stability: Connecting multiple accounts into a larger liquidity structure has the portfolio effect of reducing overall net balance volatility. As a result, it becomes easier to identify and isolate a stable liquidity "core" within this net balance. This confers two primary advantages:

- The structure is better able to absorb unexpected cash flow events and mitigate their impact, thereby also minimizing the effect of any inaccuracies in the cash forecasting process.
- Determining accurate "time slicing" of available cash is easier, thereby facilitating more efficient distribution of investments across the maturity spectrum.

(An accurate assessment of this type of benefit is more complex and requires the utilization of statistical concepts.)

Net balance utilization: This is the minimization of the opportunity cost of being unable to extract the maximum value from the aggregate net cash flow. The scale of this benefit depends upon various factors, including:

- The size and stability of the core element;
- Medium-term cash forecasting accuracy; and
- The corporate's financial position (*i.e.* whether typically a net depositor or borrower).

In financial terms, the net balance utilization benefit results from the interest-rate differential between the current and the alternative usage of the net liquidity (*i.e.* reduced funding cost or enhanced investment yield).

Other benefits: Other potential benefits derived from effective liquidity management include:

- Management cost/time savings, particularly when using passive and fully automated techniques;
- Increased visibility and control of cash flows;
- More rigorous counterparty risk management, such as on idle balances or balances invested locally with institutions not validated/approved by treasury;
- Reduced dependency on local credit facilities;
- Improved enterprise-wide liquidity risk management; and
- Greater strategic financial flexibility.

34.7 TECHNIQUES OF LIQUIDITY MANAGEMENT

Liquidity management techniques broadly fall into two main groups, depending upon the method used to consolidate balances:

Physical balance consolidation:

- Cash concentration, also referred to as zero balancing, sweeping or physical cash pooling.

Notional balance consolidation:

- Notional pooling.
- Interest enhancement.

(a) Cash concentration

Cash concentration works by making transfers between master and subordinate accounts to aggregate balances physically. These transfers can be subject to various criteria specified by the client, which can include a number of options:

- The balance to be left on the subordinate account (*e.g.*, zero or pegged/target account balancing).
- Whether flows are single or bi-directional (*i.e.*, whether flows are always moving in a predetermined direction - such as from subordinate to master account in a one-way sweep transaction, or both).
- The frequency and timing of concentration (*e.g.*, intra-day and/or end-of-day; single or multiple events at predetermined times).
- The layering and sequencing of the concentration activity, *i.e.*, single or multiple accounts concentration levels (single tier: many to one, or multi-level: many to few to one).
- The control of transaction execution by applying additional discretionary configurations, including (among others) a balance threshold, minimum transaction size, credit or inter-company lending limits.

Cash concentration achieves the mobilization and consolidation of the available balances to a master account from where the net position can be invested or funded. One unique characteristic of this technique is that it does not automatically compensate a participant entity for its contribution. Instead, this is accomplished via a separate mechanism, which can be offered as a supplementary service or independently administered by the user.

Advantages

Cash concentration combines simplicity and clarity of how funds move through a complex liquidity structure and is an accepted technique in many jurisdictions; even more regulated ones (as regards onshore transactions).

It can operate on a single or cross-entity basis. Since it establishes clear bilateral relationships across participating accounts and their respective holders, this facilitates inter-company lending arrangements if different entities are involved. If that is the case, the basic service can be supplemented with inter-company lending portfolio administration.

It is important to note that cross-entity concentration does not automatically imply the initiation of an inter-company loan; this is ultimately determined by the business relationship among these parties. For example, if an agency arrangement is in place, whereby the subordinate account entity is a collection agent for the master account entity, then the relationship has a different nature and it will be covered by the agency agreement rather than an inter-company loan document. The underlying arrangement determines how the contribution of a participant is compensated. In the case of an inter-company loan transaction, the loan terms between the two parties (*e.g.* interest rate, interest period and frequency of settlement) regulate such compensation.

This process can be administered by the user, with the assistance of a treasury management system or similar tools, or outsourced to the banking provider who offers it as an on-demand service.

Two other important features are specific to this technique. First, by making use of inter-company transactions for multiple entity structures, the financial reporting of any cash holding is improved. Typically, a reduction in the size of the balance sheet is possible; by netting off opposite positions held by the master account holder, as well as reporting related party holdings instead of cash or short-term financing with banks. Second, a properly engineered cash concentration structure leads to a reduction in both overall and participant-level credit requirements. This is because the group of accounts shares intra-day credit facilities with a much more limited overnight credit line at the top of the structure.

At its simplest level, cash concentration offers simplicity and improved control, in addition to the generic liquidity management benefits outlined above. Depending upon the jurisdictions involved, these benefits may also apply in the case of cross-border cash concentration.

In our experience, cash concentration techniques are more suitable for corporations that have some of the following characteristics:

- A functionally centralized (or centralizing) management culture;
- A preference for fully automated or passive management tools;
- An existing (or intended) inter-company lending framework;
- A focus on balance sheet reduction and/or tax planning;
- Aversion to complex legal documentation and cross-indemnity provisions;
- The ability to support an inter-company due diligence process, but not more complex operations;
- A desire to establish a regionally or globally consistent liquidity management model with no or few variations; and
- A desire to reduce dependency on credit.

(b) Notional pooling

Notional pooling differs from cash concentration in that it operates by performing an interest calculation across a group of designated accounts on a purely notional basis. There is no physical movement or commingling of funds and therefore the original beneficial ownership structure of balances is maintained.

The other main differentiating feature of this technique relates to how it generates what is commonly referred to as the "pool net advantage", or net benefit. In the more standard version of notional pooling, an algorithm is used to determine the impact of two factors:

1. The degree of balance offsetting in any given day (*i.e.* the matching proportion of debit and credit balances); and

2. Any interest differential between the pool-level and account-level conditions applied (different interest rate settings can be applied to each level).

These two factors determine the pool net advantage, which is then applied according to the client's preferred allocation method (subject to any regulatory restrictions). The resulting allocation of compensation among pool participants is more flexible than in the case of cash concentration.

One final but important consideration relates to credit requirements. A notional pooling structure is typically more credit intensive as credit lines will be required for any participating accounts that are expected to have material swings in balances or structural deficits.

Advantages

For some corporations, with concerns relating to inter-company lending documentation and administration, the fact that notional pooling does not involve any commingling of funds represents an important advantage over cash concentration. A further unique characteristic is that establishing a multi-currency notional pool is relatively straightforward and much more effective; in significant contrast with the difficulties associated with multi-currency cash concentration.

Apart from the above, notional pooling can be very convenient when dealing with issues relating to corporate culture. If local finance directors have traditionally enjoyed considerable autonomy, there may be significant internal resistance to physical movement of "their" funds via cash concentration. The fact that notional pooling leaves balances in the original entity's control, fully segregated from other funds, allays these concerns. In situations like this, notional pooling can be a useful tactical mechanism to improve liquidity management performance immediately, with a view to moving to cash concentration in the longer term (if appropriate/advantageous).

(c) Interest enhancement

Interest enhancement is conceptually similar to notional pooling in that no physical movement of funds is involved. However, it works by applying preferential pricing across a group of accounts on the basis of pre-determined criteria that are typically based on a net aggregate balance threshold. For example, a company with multiple credit balances distributed across its various operating centers may find that individually these balances only qualify for the lowest interest-rate tier payable on credit balances. By contrast, under an interest-enhancement arrangement, the total of these balances is used to enhance the qualifying tier of the individual balances. Nevertheless, the technique must comply with any applicable banking or local regulations regarding the retribution of an account, in the form of an interest amount.

Advantages

Interest enhancement is an extremely flexible mechanism and can operate on a single or multiple currencies, as well as a single- or multiple-location basis. Unlike other liquidity techniques it has far fewer regulatory implications and is therefore well suited to both deregulated markets as well as jurisdictions with capital movement restrictions. The main reason for this is that the mechanism works on the basis of relationship-based preferential pricing, rather than net balance treatment.

Interest enhancement is also not static in that it takes into account the dynamic profile of the relationship between bank and corporation as it changes from one day to the next. As such, the interest computation is adjusted on a daily basis to take into account all balances held with the institution and their contribution to the overall relationship to determine the appropriate pricing.

In contrast with notional pooling or cash concentration, an interest-enhancement structure involves considerably less cost and effort on a corporate's part to implement. As such, in addition to being a convenient remedy for balances in more regulated jurisdictions, it can be invaluable as a stepping stone to more sophisticated liquidity management techniques. To that end, interest enhancement also increases the degree of control and automation, as well as improving the net liquidity position of an organization.

34.8 WEALTH MANAGEMENT –CONCEPT, SERVICES, IMPORTANCE, RANGE

The term wealth management formed with two words wealth & Management. The meaning of wealth is – Funds, Assets, investments and cash it means the term wealth management deft with funds Asset, instrument, cash and any other item of similar nature. While defining wealth Management we have to think in planned manner. "Wealth Management is an all inclusive set of strategies that aims to grow, manage, protect and distribute assets in a much planned systematic and integrated manner. "

Broadly speaking, wealth management is an investment advisory discipline that incorporates financial planning, investment portfolio management and a number of aggregated financial services. High Net Worth Individuals (HNWIs), small business owners and families who desire the assistance of a credentialed financial advisory specialist call upon wealth managers to coordinate retail banking, estate planning, legal resources, tax professionals and investment management. Wealth managers can be an independent Certified Financial Planner, MBAs, Chartered Strategic Wealth Professional, CFA Charter holders or any credentialed professional money manager who works to enhance the income, growth and tax favored treatment of long-term investors. Wealth management is often referred to as a high-level form of private banking for the especially affluent. One must already have accumulated a significant amount of wealth for wealth management strategies to be effective.

Wealth management services may include:

- Portfolio Management Services
- Multi Manager Investment Solutions
- Portfolio Advisory
- Trading in Equity, Currency, Interest Rate Futures
- Depository Services
- Mutual Funds & IPOs

- Fixed Income Products
- Near Risk-free Arbitrage Products
- Structured Products
- Real Estate Funds
- Private Equity Funds
- Financial Planning
- Pay-roll services to Corporates
- Providing Financial advises etc.

The term wealth management also now a days having very importance. So many Banking companies are engaged in the business of wealth management. The premier insurance industry is now booming because so many bankers are also adopting and playing safe in the business of insurance the term called is Bancassurance. Now a day's wealth Management has very craze in the business world.

WEALTH MANAGEMENT RANGE: - The range of wealth management can be expressed by the following chart.

34.9 ADVANTAGES AND LIMITATIONS IF WEALTH MANAGEMENT

The following are the advantages of wealth management concept.

(1) Helpful in Tax Planning: The wealth management professional always shows the good path to the customers and provide the service of tax planning. How to minimize the tax and save more money?

(2) Helpful in Selection of Investment Strategy: Another advantage from the customer point of view is with the help of WM Professional the customer can easily know the investment strategy and analyze risk and return.

(3) Helpful in Estate Management: With the help of wealth management professional we can also manage our estate. Estate management is a task to provide objective administration of our funds tailored to aim in responsible distribution and protection of our overall estate.

(4) Helpful in forward looking: We can say planning, that recognizes as our estate grows and changes occurs we require some team of professionals who help us in future planning.

(5) Helpful for Indian Economy: Banks which are engaged in business of WM earning revenues from the foreign countries *i.e.*, outsourcing for economy.

Limitations

1. WM Reduces the Scope of Management: Though we all know that management has existence at all levels of life and society but the term wealth management only related with the higher level means rich people, and is not having any plans and provisions for poor and lower and middle level of society.

2. Chances of Fraud: Another demerit or limitation of the WM concept is it is not showing the actual position. The customer doesn't know about the things going on with using his wealth and there may be chances of forgery and fraud with customers.

3. Actual Picture VS Inflation: What is the actual position of market we don't know because every thing is done by some WM professionals. So we can not assume our position in the market that also results in inflation because economy is unknown about the actual state. There may be chance that the customers are in risk but they are showing the false return and vice-versa.

34.10 WEALTH MANAGEMENT: INDIAN CONCERN, CASE EXAMPLES

Some times people confuse asset management or financial management with the wealth management. But wealth management has very broad area.

Position of India in Wealth Management

In the annual survey done by Cap Gemini, SA and Merrill Lynch it was found that ranks of millionaires grew 6% in the previous year, because the number of richer people grew in India & China where India is competing China. India & China posted the biggest gain in millionaires advancing by 23% & 20% respectively.

When we are watching the world wide increase in number of millionaires the facts collected by Cap Gemini, S.A. and Merrill Lynch survey report. India has 23% growth in the last year. The biggest Asian economy China stands on second position with 20%, west Asia 16%, United States 4% and United Kingdom (UK) 2%.

So we can understand that there are more opportunities in the wealth management business in Asia especially in India.

CASE EXAMPLE 1: ICICI BANK & WEALTH MANAGEMENT:

In India ICICI bank and Axis-Bank are very well known banks in the field of wealth management. ICICI Bank will float subsidiary for the purpose of WM activities in Canada & other market even as ICICI has rolled out ICICI Group Global Private Clients for those with net worth of $ 1 million or more. ICICI GCPC launched their business in Dubai very recently in the month of April-08 and caught 2500 clients. They are going to add another 1000 high network clients this year.

ICICI Bank is using the services of global players like Merrill Lynch, City group, and UBS for catching the clients for Wealth Management business. ICICI Bank and its subsidiaries are engaged in the development of various attractive products (services) for the clients with net worth of $ 1 million.

The eyes of ICICI Group Global Pvt. Clients on the rising number of dollar millionaires at present they are 100,000 in number in few year the number will definitely increase. India's No. 2 lender banker ICICI expects to sustain the 70% growth in its private wealth management business. ICICI has 150,000 customers with investible surplus of at least ₹ 10 lakhs equity, real estate and private equity is driving the private banking business in India. *India has market of wealth management about $ 600 billion.*

CASE EXAMPLE 2: AXIS BANK & WEALTH MANAGEMENT

One of India's leading private sector bankers Axis bank also combined with Banque Privee Edmond de Rothschild Europe based wealth management expertise institution & is going to make new standard for the NRI's wealth management.

The LCF Rothschild group has based its reputation in the area of wealth management on its big banking experience. Actually the institution is engaged in the task of providing financial advise to the Europe's leading families, Government and various corporations for the last '7' generations.

The Axis Bank 5th largest bank by market capitalization in India provides payroll services to over 12000 corporates across 2.8 million salary accounts. The market capitalization of Axis Bank was 235 million in the last year 2007 is engaged in the business of wealth management, with its international presence in Dubai, Singapore, Hong Kong, Shanghai and so on.

❑❑❑

35 Current Scenerio of Indian Banking Industry with Retail Banking

35.1 INTRODUCTION

The banking system in India is significantly different from that of the other Asian nations, because of the country's unique geographic, social, and economic characteristics. Though the sector opened up quite late in India compared to other developed nations, like the US and the UK, the profitability of Indian banking sector is at par with that of the developed countries and at times even better on some parameters. For instance, return on equity and assets of the Indian banks are on par with Asian banks, and higher when compared to that of the US and the UK.

35.2 EVOLUTION

Banking in India has had an early origin, where the indigenous bankers played a very important role in lending money and financing foreign trade and commerce. The General Bank of India was the first Joint Stock Bank to be established in the year 1786. In the first half of the nineteenth century, the East India Company established three banks: the Bank of Bengal in 1809, the Bank of Bombay in 1840 and the Bank of Madras in 1843. These three banks, also known as Presidency banks were amalgamated in 1920, and became the Imperial Bank of India in 1921. With the passing of the State Bank of India Act in 1955, the undertaking of the Imperial Bank of India was taken by the newly constituted State Bank of India. The Reserve Bank of India, which is the Central Bank, was created in 1935 by passing Reserve Bank of India Act, 1934, commands wide ranging powers for licensing, supervision and control of banks.

Banks in India are mainly classified into Scheduled Banks and Non-Scheduled Banks. Scheduled Banks are the ones, which are included in the second schedule of the RBI Act 1934 and they comply with the minimum statutory requirements. Non-Scheduled Banks are joint stock banks, which are not included in the second Schedule of the RBI Act 134, on account of the failure to comply with the minimum requirements for being scheduled.

35.3 REFORMS GALORE

Financial Sector reforms set in motion, in 1991, have greatly changed the face of Indian banking industry. The industry has moved gradually from a regulated environment to a deregulated market economy. The market developments kindled by liberalisation and globalisation have resulted in changes in the intermediation role of banks. The pace of transformation has been more significant in recent times with technology acting as a catalyst. While the banking system has done fairly well in adjusting to the new market dynamics, greater challenges lie ahead. Financial sector would be opened up for greater international competition under WTO agreement by 2009. Basel-II norms specify banks to assess credit, market and operations risks and make higher provisioning for covering them. Banks will have to gear up to meet stringent prudential capital adequacy norms under Basel II. In the mid-term review of Annual Policy for year 2007, RBI has extended the earlier intended Basel II compliance deadline of March 31, 2007 which is now being implemented by the banks in India. RBI set the deadline of March 31, 2008, for foreign banks in India and Indian banks operating abroad, for meeting Basel-II norms. All other scheduled commercial banks will have to adhere to the guidelines by March 31, 2009. RBI extended the time in order to help banks to install appropriate system for complete adherence to Basel-II. In addition to WTO and Basel II, the Free Trade Agreements (FTAs) with Singapore, may have an impact on the shape of things to come. Banks will also have to cope with challenges posed by technological innovations and the need to prepare for changes.

Indian banking sector reform has been unique in the world in that it combines a comprehensive reorientation of competition, regulation and ownership in a non-disruptive and cost-effective manner. Indeed, banking reform is a good illustration of the dynamism of the public sector in managing the overhang problems and the pragmatism of public policy in enabling the domestic and foreign private sectors to compete and expand.

Looking at the present status of the banking sector, admittedly, there is scope for considerable improvement. Yet, its strength and resilience in ensuring growth and stability have been recognised universally. In the major emerging economies, India compares favourably in the services sector and is seeking to compete in the manufacturing sector, while it tries to catch up on the fiscal and infrastructural fronts. However, it is in the financial and banking sectors that India is unarguably ahead than most of the emerging economies.

35.4 CURRENT STATUS

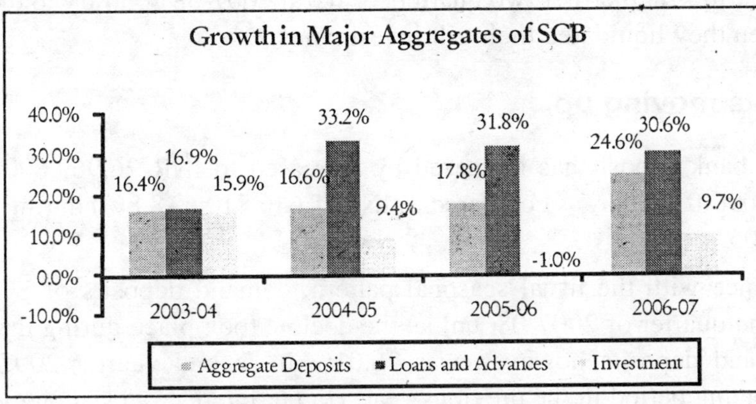

Source: RBI, Cygnus Research

The performance of Indian banking sector has been phenomenal during 2006-07. Extremely encouraging macro-economic environment provided bank credit growth further boost in the second successive year. The demand for credit was mostly driven by housing and retail sectors. In spite of higher bank deposits, the credit growth surpassed bank deposit growth rate during 2006-07. Most of the banks were compelled to liquidate a portion of Government security holdings. Consequently, investments in bonds/debentures/shares of the corporate sector also went down. However, presently in fiscal 2006-07, the bank deposit rate is also accelerating and has been able to accommodate consistent growth rate of bank credits.

35.5 MONETARY AND LIQUIDITY POSITION: RELATIVELY STABLE

Monetary and liquidity position of the country have been comforting during fiscal 2006-07, which has impacted on the performance of the scheduled commercial banks (SCB) till date. The growth rate of time deposits has complemented the high demand for credits. The non-food credit

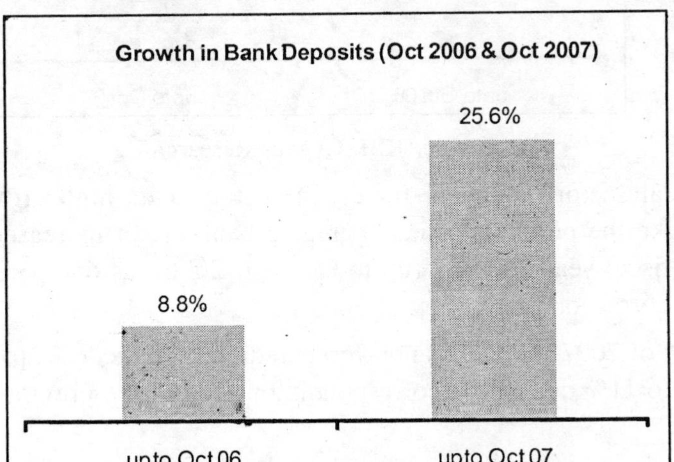

Source: RBI, Cygnus Research

has grown by more than 23% for past one year and more. Banks also increased their reserves in Government securities in the first two quarters of fiscal 2007-08 contrary to the last two quarters of 2006-07, when they liquidated their gilt investments.

Bank deposits moving up

Aggregate bank deposit has increased by increased to INR 26,969,800m (25.6%) during the fiscal year 2006-07 so far, as compared to INR21,646,810m (8.8%) during the corresponding period of 2005-06.

In accordance with the usual seasonal pattern, demand deposits of SCBs have gone up during the second quarter of 2007-08, unlike the decline took place during the previous quarter. Growth in demand deposits however, was 26.01% in second quarter 2007-08, compared to 22.1% corresponding period in the previous year. Higher interest rates, along with availability of tax benefits under Section 80C have also attracted more time deposits. It has grown by 11.9% during the first half (April- Sept) 2007-08 period, as compared to 11.6% during corresponding period of previous fiscal.

Buoyant credit demand

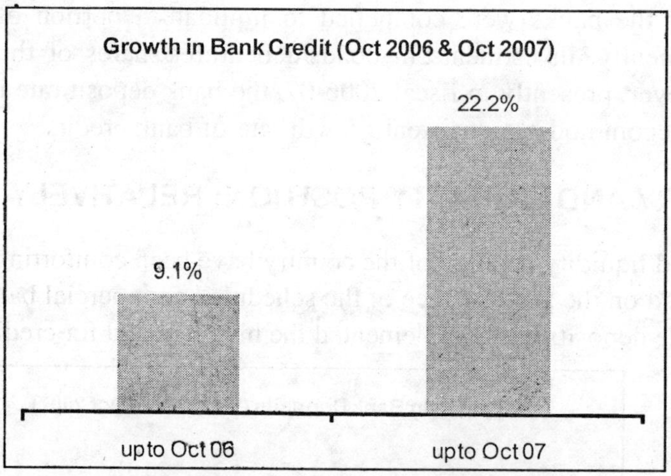

Source: RBI, Cygnus Research

The commercial sector's demand for credit sustained its high growth during the fiscal 2006-07 also just like the previous year. Aggregate bank credit increased by INR1,366,430m (9.1%), during the fiscal year 2006-07 (up to October, 2006), as compared to INR1,191,680m (10.3%) during the corresponding period of 2005-06.

In the first half of 2007-08, SCB's non-food credit has come down to 5.6% during October 2007, as compared to 11% during the corresponding period of the previous year.

35.6 INFLATIONARY PRESSURE DECREASES

High levels of capacity utilisation in a number of industries, along with supply shocks from primary articles, were reflected in a rise in the inflation rate during 2006-07. which however alleviated to some extent during January 2007 with declining of oil prices. But the overall core inflation remained stiff only.

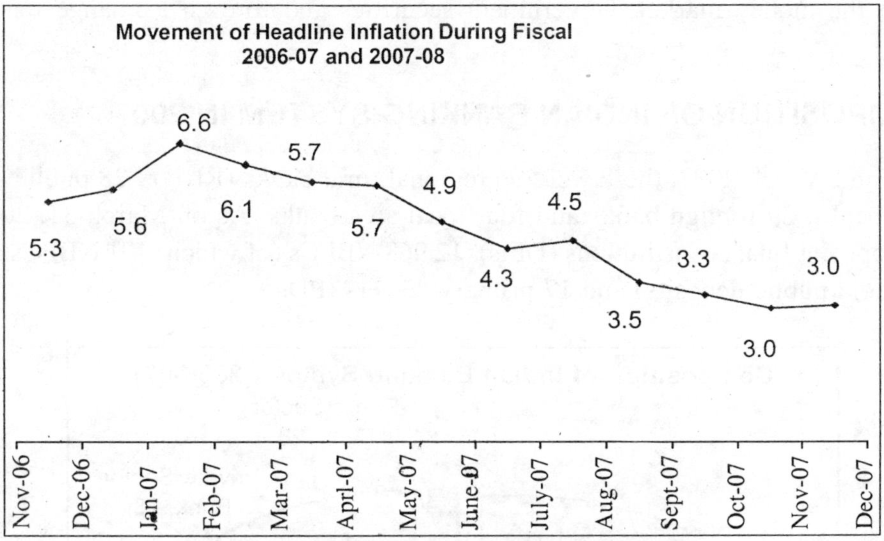

Source: RBI, Cygnus Research

In India, the head line inflation has so far remained within controllable limit. The average WPI inflation moved up to 5.4 per cent during 2006-07 from 4.4 per cent a year ago. Prices of primary articles exerted upward pressure on inflation during 2006-07, reflecting shortfalls in domestic supply of major agricultural crops. Fuel group inflation, which had dominated the inflation outcome during the preceding two years, eased significantly during the second half of the fiscal year 2006-07 to reach its lowest rate in over a decade. According to RBI, containing inflationary expectations would continue to pose a challenge to monetary management in the coming years. All the policy would take into account a year-on-year inflation rate in the range of 5-5.5% for 2006-07.

Inflation, measured by variations in the WPI, on a year-on-year basis, eased from 5.9% at end of March 2007 to 3.0% by October 2007. The annual inflation rate for all major groups, primary articles, fuel group and manufactured products was lower at 5.1%, (-)1.5% and 3.9%, respectively, as of October 2007 compared with 10.7 %, 1.0% and 6.1%, respectively, at end-March 2007.

35.7 CREDIT MARKET

A major development engaging attention all over the globe in the recent period has been the turmoil in financial markets in the United States and Europe and the sudden plunge in credit market confidence triggered by the US sub-prime mortgage crisis. India has been one of the largest recipients of portfolio inflows during 2006-07. Insofar as India is concerned, the recent developments in the international financial market have not had any significant impact on the Indian Financial Markets.

The Indian financial markets have maintained its organized state during 2006-07 in spite of firming up of interest rate in the second half of the fiscal. RBI's policy for increasing depth and liquidity in the money market, Government securities and foreign exchange market is being continued.

35.8 COMPOSITION OF INDIAN BANKING SYSTEM IN 2007

As in end-March 2007, there were 96 regional rural banks (RRB), 28 public sector banks, 25 private banks, 29 foreign banks and four local area banks. As on March 31, 2007, there are eight development finance institutions (DFIs), 12,968 NBFCs (of which, 401 NBFCs are permitted to accept/ hold public deposits) and 17 primary dealers (PDs.)

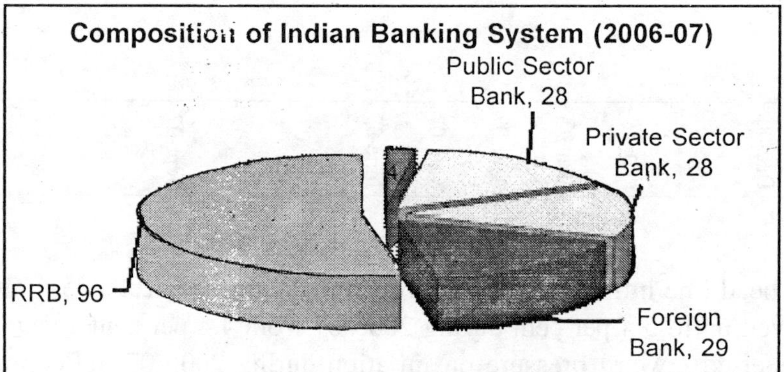

Source: RBI; Cygnus Research

Among the 25 private sector banks, 20 are old and 5 are new. Currently, there are 29 Foreign Banks in India, registered with the RBI. Banks like Standard Charted Bank, HSBC Bank, ABN AMRO Bank, Citibank are doing some major business here. BNP Paribas, Bank of America and Deutsche Bank have established themselves as wholesale corporate banks.

35.9 GEOGRAPHIC SPREAD

As per the current data published by RBI, urban and metropolitan areas account for 34.6% of the total bank branches, while a major portion of total deposits, as well as credit are contributed these branches. Nearly 49.4% of total bank deposits and 65% of credit came from these metropolitan branches in fiscal 2006-07. As the competition is increasing in the metropolitans, urban and semi-urban centres shall present huge opportunities for growth of retail credit. Currently, scheduled commercial banks are serving 57,042 centres, of which 29,460 were single office centres and 39 centres had 100 or more bank branches.

35.10 KEY BUSINESS SEGMENTS

Key business segments in SCBs

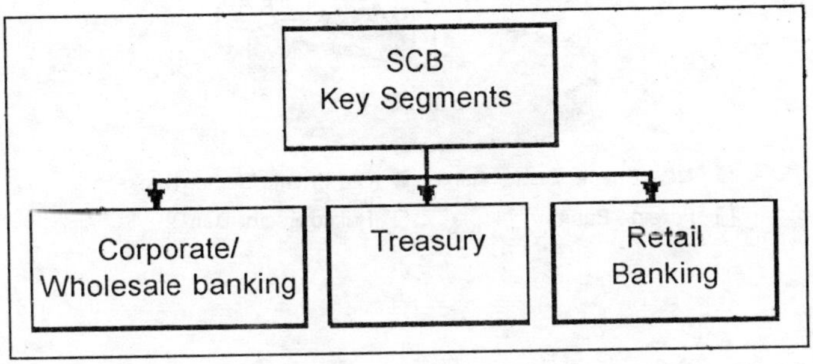

Source: Cygnus Reseh

Scheduled commercial banks, (SCB), operate in three segments: Retail, Corporate and Treasury. Traditionally they operated predominantly in corporate and treasury segment only. The emergence of the third segment can be attributed, to a large extent, to the entry of new private sector banks in the industry.

New Private sector banks like ICICI, HDFC, UTI and IDBI have changed the whole banking landscape. These banks have given tough competition to the public sector banks with innovative product introductions, aggressive marketing and pricing, and by using state of the art technology. The massive growth in retail portfolio and sharp decline in interest rates have been the key drivers in increasing the profitability of Indian banks.

35.11 PUBLIC SECTOR BANKS ARE STILL LEADING

Despite increasing competition, public sector banks continue to dominate the Indian banking landscape, with more than 72.3% of all the assets for the financial year 2006-07. This scale of operations bestows upon them a higher bargaining power, enabling them to play a dominant role in the liquidity and interest rate levels in the system. However, the scenario is undergoing a change with the growth of the new private sector banks, which are in a more advantageous position, because of their superior technology based operations, higher employer efficiency and a lower Non-Performing Assets (NPA) level.

4.7.1: Assets held by different banking group - 1996-97

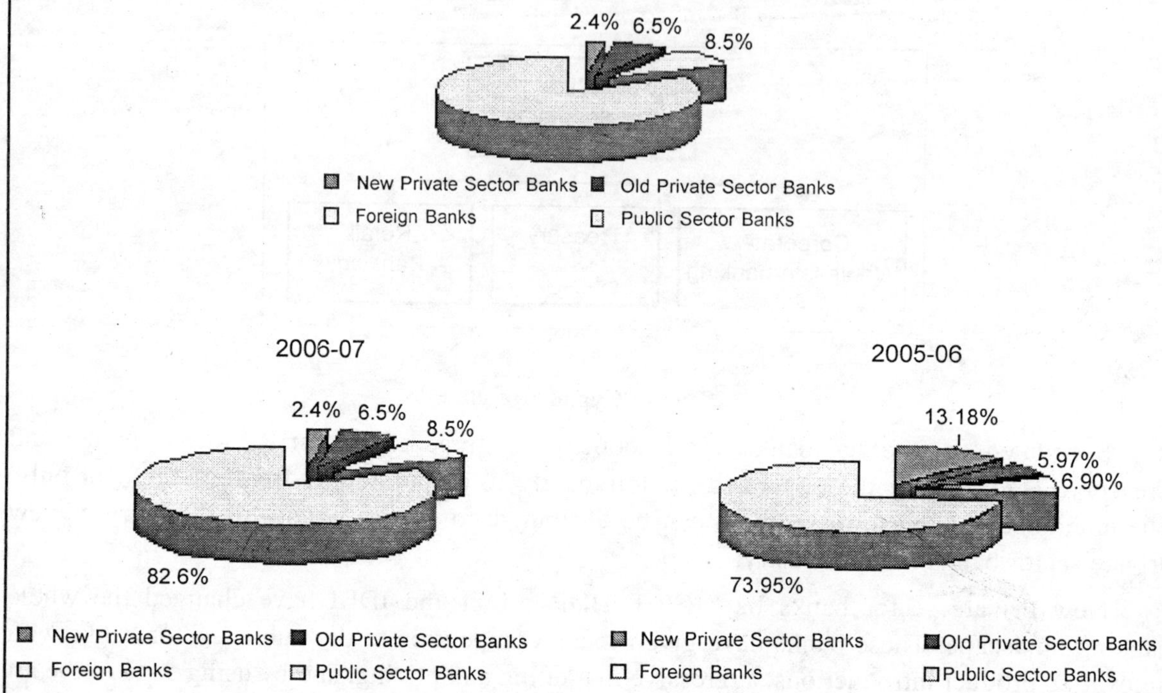

Source: RBI, Cygnus Research

35.12 RETAIL BANKING — AN INDIAN SCENARIO

Introduction

Riding on the ongoing boom in the Indian economy, the banking industry is growing at faster rate like never before. A larger option for the consumer is getting translated into a larger demand for financial products and customisation of services is fast becoming the norm than competitive advantage. Retail banking has become one of the happening segments in the banking industry.

Retail banking broadly refers to the products and services of commercial banks for individual customers, both on liabilities and assets sides. Fixed, current/savings accounts are on the liabilities side; and loans *e.g.* personal, housing, auto and educational on the assets side. Ubiquitous retail banking products are capable of meeting the new generation customers with "anywhere, anytime, any-type banking" having come to stay. Retail deposit banking products include flexi/saving/ recurring accounts, short-term deposits and deferred pension-linked deposit accounts which have played pivotal role in mobilising deposit resources. And among the important retail lending products are loans for housing, white goods, education, vehicles, gold and festivals, apart from insurance products, and domestic and global debit/credit cards. The new generation bank's retail banking sector consists of multiple products delivering through multiple channels of distribution to multiple customer groups.

Credit growth zooms

Sectoral deployment of credit indicates that demand for retail credit is emerging as a major component of bank credit. During 2006-07, almost 28% the incremental bank credit was absorbed by the retail sector (mainly on account of loans for housing). Industry accounted for another 26% of the incremental credit while agricultural sector absorbed 13.6% of the incremental credit.

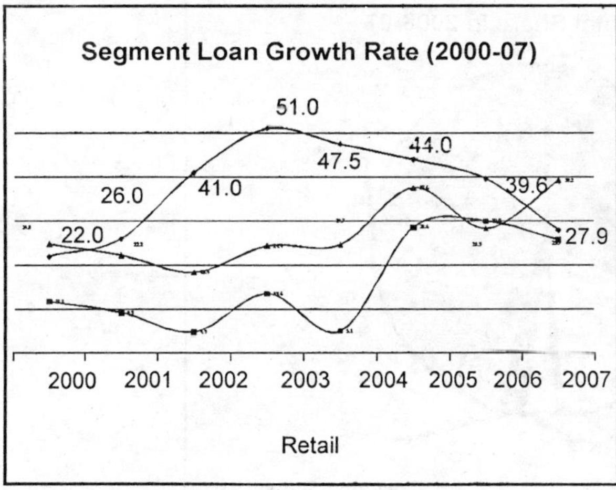

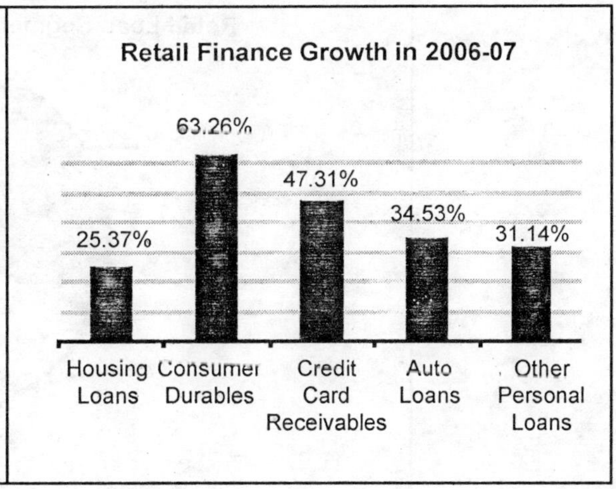

Source: Cygnus Estimates

Although the growth of retail portfolio of banks decelerated to 29.9 % during 2006-07 from 40.9 % in 2005-06, it still grew faster than the overall credit portfolio of the banking sector (28.5%) There is still shortage of housing units in urban and in the metropolis. The surge in home is the one of the growth drivers in bank credit. The retail loan market has decisively got transformed from a sellers' market to a buyers' market. Gone are the days where getting a retail loan was somewhat cumbersome. Now-a-days retail banking is driven by innovative and tailored products, multi-packed financial benefits and technology.

Segments of Retail Lending

Mortgage lending leads

In India total asset size of the retail banking industry grew at a CAGR of 36% to reach a value of USD125 billion in 2007. In future the retail banking industry is likely to reach a value of USD300 billion by 2010. Housing loans constituted a lion's share of 46% of the total retail portfolio which declined by 14.56% Y-o-Y from previous year. The second major component of retail finance is auto. It constitutes around 17% of total retail landing and has a promising future due to the rising income level among Indian households and increasing appetite of consumers for possessing vehicle. The other major retail finance products are consumer durables, personal finance and credit card receivables.

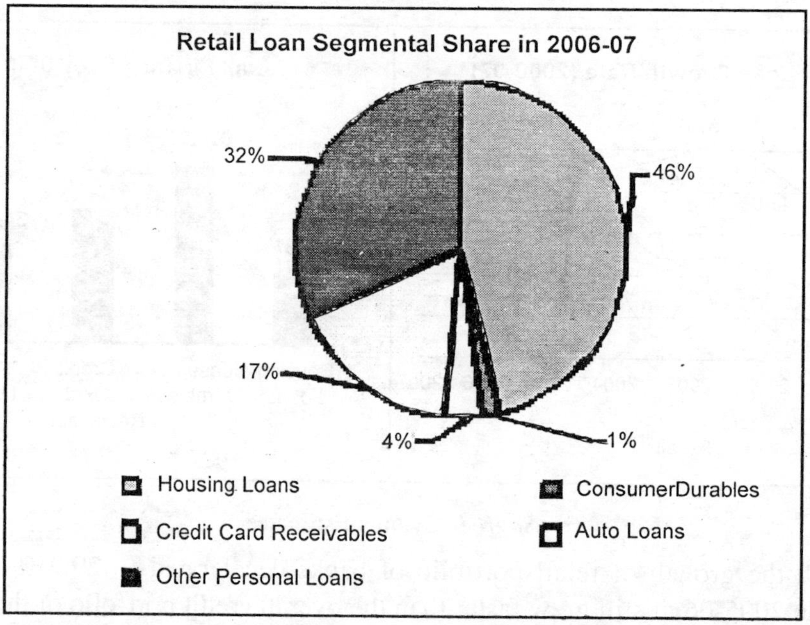

Source: RBI; Cygnus Research

Retail Credit: Geographical Spread (2005-06)

With the more number of the high income group, metro dominates with 44% of retail credit disbursements during 2006-07, followed by 27% in the urban areas and the balance being in the semi urban and rural areas.

In terms of retail credit distribution to the total credit distribution region-wise, in Semi Urban, Urban, retail credit form 18% of the total credit distributed in the same region, whereas for rural and metropolitan cities this figure stood at 25% and 21% of the total credit distributed in the same region.

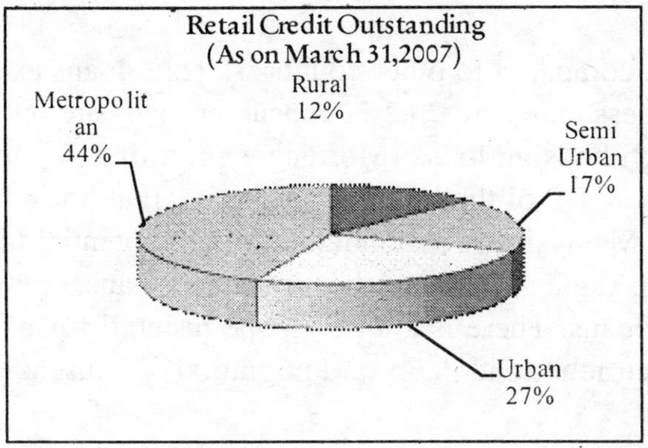

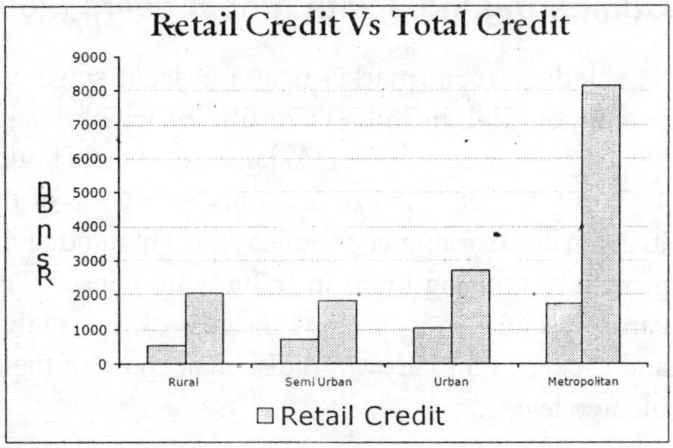

Source: RBI, Cygnus Estimates

Category wise Distribution (2006-07)

Category wise analysis of retail credit reveals the long term loan has about 68%, housing loans contribute most of it, over the years, and loan disbursals to women has gone down in period 2005-06, reaching about 11% as compared to 12% in 2004-05. However, the size of loan is normally small. Over 97% of the loans number wise and 57% value wise are in the range of INR. 25,000 to INR. 5, 00,000.

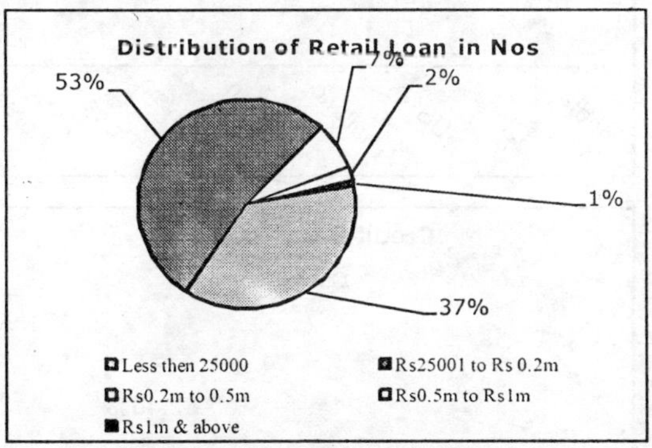

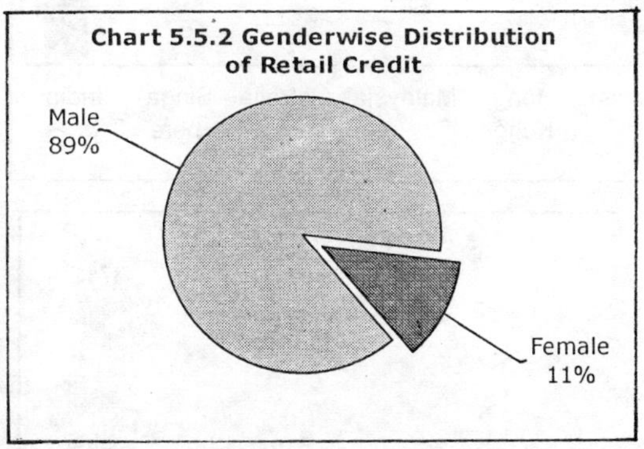

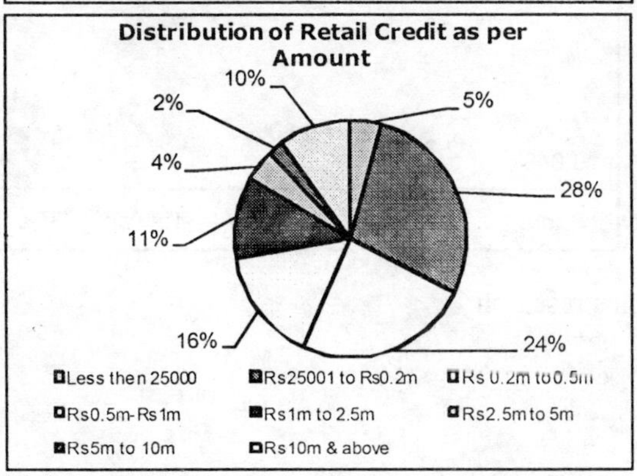

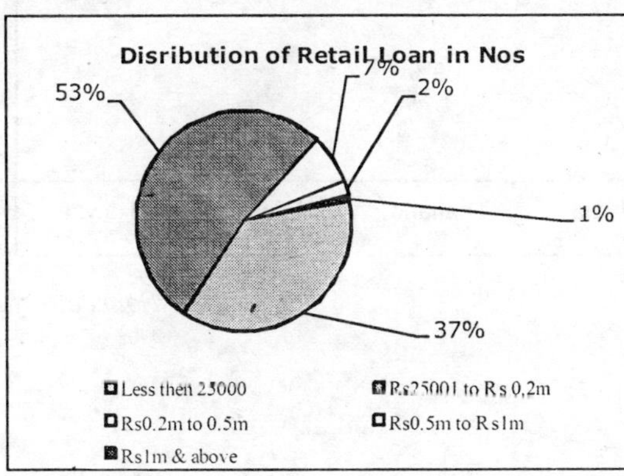

Source: Cygnus Estimates

Comparing India with global peers (2005)

India's retail market is at a nascent stage as compared to other countries. Total loans as a percent of GDP in India is 28.6%, of which business loans are 23.2%, consumer loans are only 8% as compared to other Asian countries. Though housing loans (Mortgages) constitute about 49% of total retail loans, it is only about 1% of the GDP of the India. Considering that housing loans in comparable economies like Thailand and Malaysia are much higher, future potential for growth of housing loans in India is immense. The same applies to other consumer loans, credit card presentation as well as the rest of the retail loans. There is a lot of scope in retail finance and is expected to grow rapidly on account of the current trend in upward migration of household income levels.

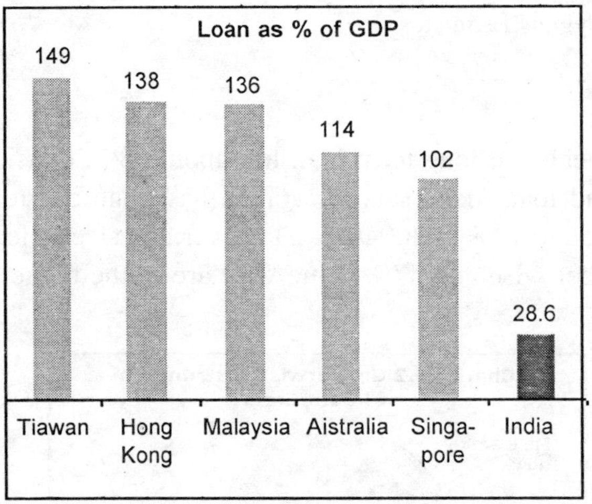

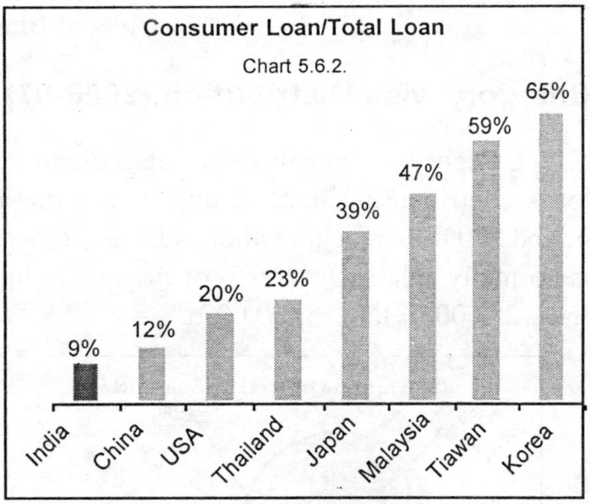

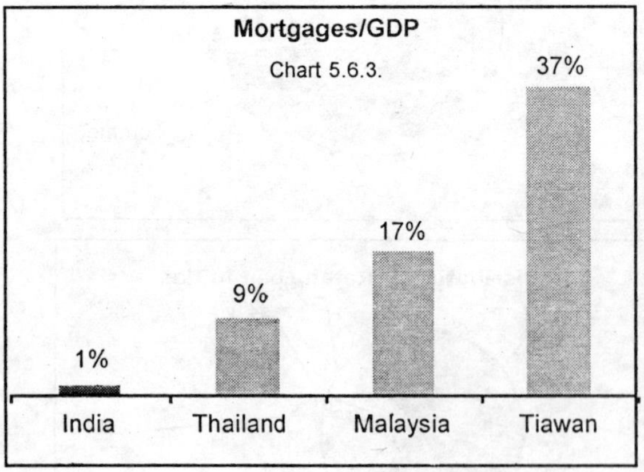

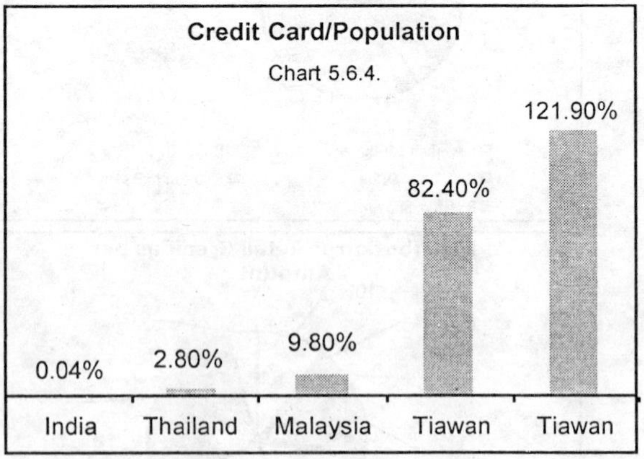

Source: Cygnus research

Major players and their market share

The market share of the major players is calculated based on total retail loan outstanding given by RBI as on 31st March, 2007 and that of banks also.

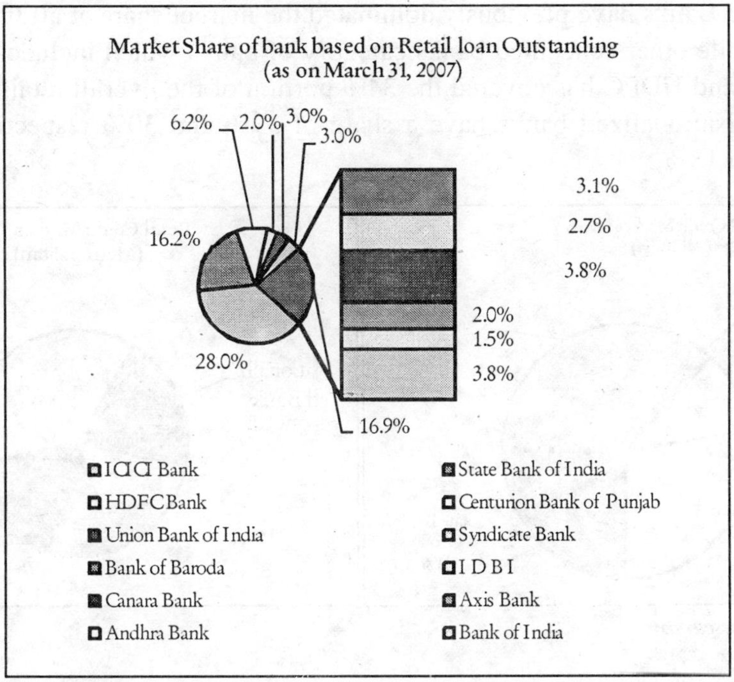

Source: Cygnus Research

ICICI a leader among private banks with 28% market share

ICICI is the leader in retail loan disbursement among private banks. It has the largest retail loan portfolio, with 28% market share, among the banks in the country. Its retail portfolio has increased from INR 921.98 billion as on March 31 2006 to INR 1,277 billion on March 31 2007. Also, ICICI Bank share of retail loans as a percentage of total advances is the highest at 68% in FY07. .

SBI does the catching up

SBI is rapidly growing in the retail space. The retail portfolio has grown at a robust rate of almost 21% during 2006-07 and retail loans outstanding reached INR735.96 billion. Presently the retail loan portfolio possesses a market share of 16.2%. Housing loans is contributing the biggest proportion at 49% of total retail loans. Aggressive marketing drive has brought the segment just a percentage behind the bank's biggest segment of mid-corporate loans which constitute 24% of total loan book position. The bank is leveraging its vast branch network and highest number of ATMs to have more pie in the retail credit.

Geographic dominance (2006-07)

Nationalized banks losing hold and new generation private sector banks dominate at all India as well metropolitan area

Nationalized Banks have previously dominated the market share at all India level has come down to 30%, while other scheduled banks category of banks which include aggressive private players as ICICI and HDFC has covered the 34% portion of the overall retail credit. In metros, other SCBs and Nationalized banks have a share of 39% and 30% respectively, followed by foreign bank with 18%.

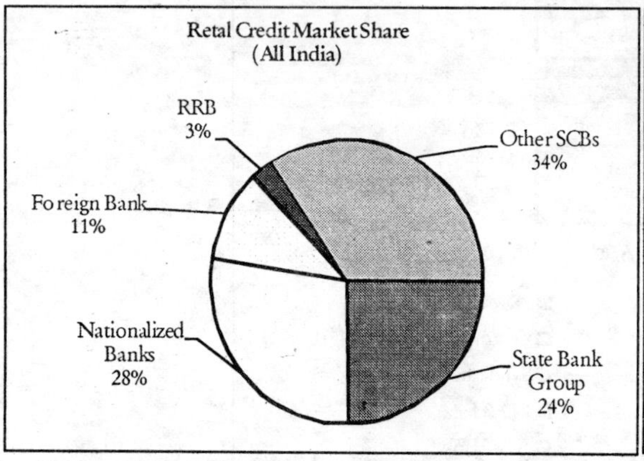

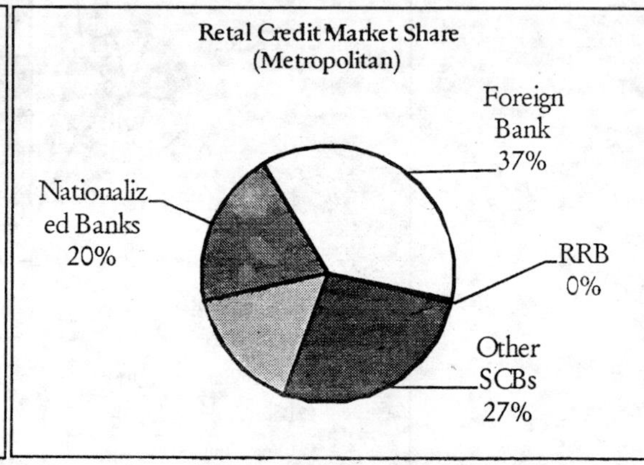

Source: Cygnus Research

Public sector banks still ahead in other areas

As we move down from metros to the urban, semi urban and rural areas, the share of private banks comes down steeply and PSU banks dominate the market. Market share of state bank of India group increases from 29% from Urban to 51% in Semi-urban market. This can be attributed to the vast branch network of public sector banks in semi-urban area. The other reason could be the local flavour. The share of foreign banks is 1% in Urban and nil in Semi-Urban area.

Retail Credit Market Share (Region-wise)

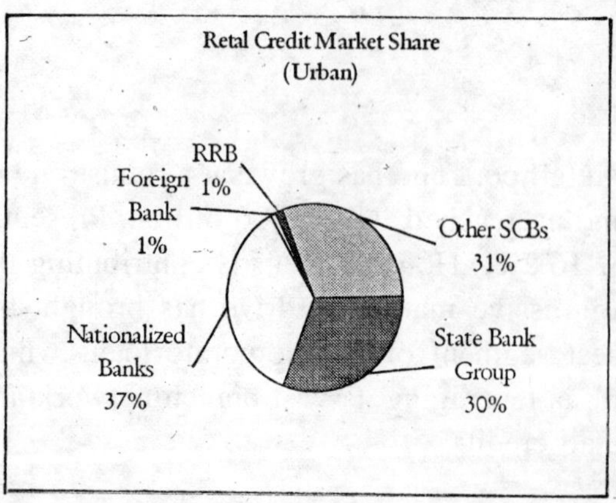

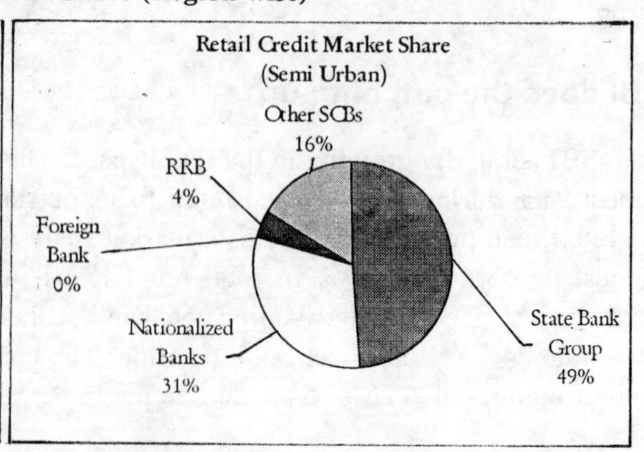

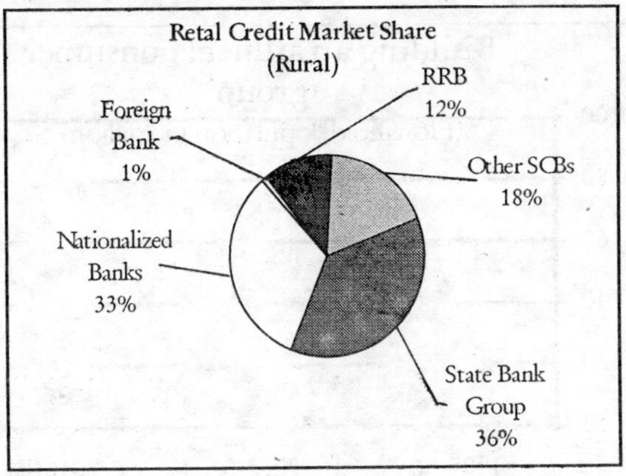

Source: RBI, Cygnus Estimates

Recent Trends

Changing Demographic profile drives the growth

India is a young nation today. At present more than 70 % of the population is less than 35 years old. At this prime age there needs are galloping due to changing lifestyle. What is heartening that their increasing personal income raises the loan repayment ability thereby loan entitlement. These all are making our banking honchos go gaga about the explosive retail growth which was not thought of even 4-5 years ago.

TABLE : Changing consumer demographics
• Increasingly wealthy and growing middle-class disposable incomes
• The youngest population in the world
• Increasing literacy levels
• Higher adaptability to technology
• Urbanization is a long lasting trend
• Growing consumerism
• Fiscal incentives for housing loan
• Fastest economics growth over the decade
• Higher growth in service sector
• Growing competition among the banks

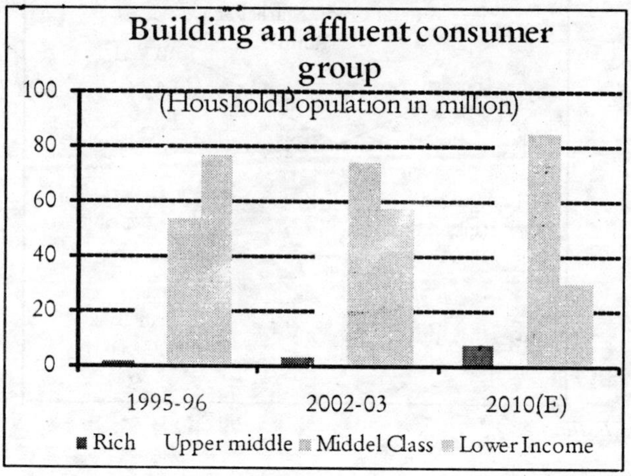

Source: Cygnus Research

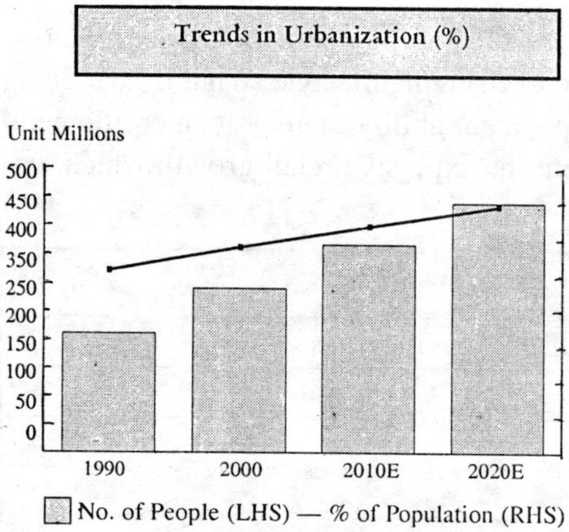

(Source: Cygnus Research)

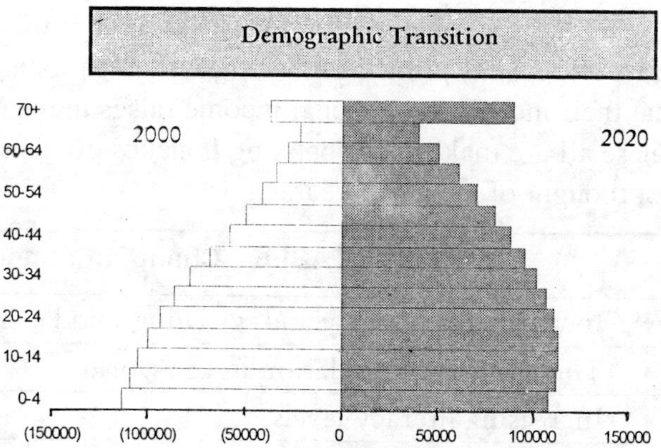

(Source: RBI, Cygnus Research)

Players' Response aggressively to the changing environment

❑❑❑

CONCEPTS ON EMERGING FINANCIAL ISSUES WITH EXERCISES

A Forwards and Futures

A1. FUTURE PRICES: COST OF CARRY

'Cost of carry' refers to the costs associated with purchasing and carrying/holding a commodity for a specified period of time. The following formula describes a general cost of carry price relationships between the cash (or spot) price and the future price of the commodity.

Future Price = Cash Price + Interest Costs p.u. + Storage Cost p.u.

Or, $$FP_{t,T} = CP_t + (CP_t \times R_{t,T} \times \frac{T-t}{365 or, 12}) + CS_{t,T}$$

Where, FP = The future price at time t for a futures contract requiring delivery at time T = $FP_{t,T}$

CP_t = The cash (or spot) price at time t

$R_{t,T}$ = Risk–free interest p.a.

$CS_{t,T}$ = The costs of storing the physical commodity p.u. for the time period (T–t)

Interest Costs p.u. = $CP_t \times R_{t,T} \times \frac{T-t}{365 or, 12}$

Future Prices is higher than Cash (or spot) Prices, due to 'Cost of Carry'.

Problem 1. On Aug 10, 2009 the cash (on spot) price of gold was ₹ 8000. At the close of trading on August 10, the settlement price of the October 2009 gold futures contract was ₹ 8800. The annualized borrowing rate was about 10%. Finally the cost of storing gold is significantly high at ₹ 500. Calculate the futures price.

Solution: The time from August 10, 2009 to October 2009 = 2 months

Future Price = Cash Price + Interest Costs p.u. + Storage Cost p.u.

$$= CP_t + (CP_t \times R_{t,T} \times \frac{T-t}{12}) + CS_{t,T}$$

$$= 8000 + (8000 \times 0.10 \times \frac{2}{12}) + 500$$

= 8000+133+500 = ₹ 8633

A2. BASIS, CONTANGO AND BACKWARDATION

Basis – It is difference between cash (on spot) price and future price.

$Basis_{t,T} = (CashPrice)_t - (FuturePrice)_{t,T}$; Here, Basis is negative

Contango Market: The condition of "Future Price>Cash Price" is commonly referred to as contango market, meaning that the relationship (shown in **A1.**) between future prices and cash prices is determined solely by the 'cost of carry' as a result of which basis is negative.

Backwardation: Backwardation refers to a market in which "Future Price<Cash (or spot) Price" and hence basis is positive. This condition occurs if future prices are determined by consideration other than (or in addition to) cost–of–carry factors.

A3. FORWARD PRICE FOR AN ASSET PROVIDING NO INCOME

$$F_0 = S_0 \times e^{rt}$$

Where, F_0 = Forward Price Today,

r = Risk–free rate of interest p.a. with continuous compounding, for an investment maturing a time T.

S_0 = Price of asset underlying the forward contract today

t = Time when the future contract matures

e = 2.718

Problem 2. Consider a three month–forward contract to buy a zero–coupon bond that will mature one year from today. The current price of the bond is ₹ 850. 3 month risk–free rate of interest, being continuously compounded is 8% p.a. Calculate the forward–price of the bond.

Solution: $F_0 = 850 \times e^{0.8 \times \frac{3}{12}} = 850 \times e^{0.02}$ = ₹ 885.23

A4. VALUE OF A FORWARD CONTRACT

$$f = (F_o - K)e^{-rt}$$

Where, r = Risk–free rate for a maturity time t.

F_o = Current forward price for the contract

f = Value today of a long forward contract,

t = Time to maturity of the contract,

K = Delivery Price/Strike Price

Problem 3. A 6 month forward contract of a non-dividend–paying stock is currently selling at ₹ 25. The strike price is ₹ 24. The risk–free rate of interest (with continuous compounding) is 10% p.a. Find the forward price and the value of forward contract. [$e^{.05} = 2.718^{.05} = 1.051265646$]

Solution: Forward Price, $= F_0 = S_0 \times e^{rt} = 25 \times e^{0.1 \times \frac{6}{12}} = 25 \times e^{0.1 \times 0.5} = 26.28$

Value of Forward contract,

$$f = (F_0 - K)e^{-rt}$$
$$= (26.28 - 24)e^{-0.1 \times 0.5}$$
$$= 2.17$$

A5. HEDGING, BASIS RISK

Concept of Hedging: In ordinary parlance, hedging simply refers to an activity that reduces risk. It is basically concerned with the reduction of market exposure risk. The market exposure cannot be avoidable, but can be hedged or offset by trading in futures, options, and other derivative instruments.

Short Hedges: A short hedge is a hedge that involves a short position in future contracts. It is appropriate when the hedger already owns an asset and expects to sell it at the same time in future and also when a hedger does not own an asset right now, but knows that the asset will be owned at some time in the future.

Long Hedges: A long hedge is a hedge that involves a long position in future contracts. It is appropriate when a company knows it will have to purchase a certain asset in the future and wants to lock in a price now.

The Basis: The basis in a hedging situation is:

Spot price of asset to be hedged – Future price of contract used

When the future contract is on a financial asset, basis is:

Future Price – Spot Price

- **Strengthening of the Basis:** When the basis increases due to, increase in spot price > increase in future price.
- **Weakening of the Basis:** When the basis decreases due to, increase in future price > increase in spot price.

Basis Risk & Hedging Strategies using Futures: The basis risk arises from the hedgers' uncertainty as to the difference between the spot price and future price.

Basis at the time of $t_1 = b_1 = S_1 - F_1$

Where, S_1 = Spot price at time t_1

F_1 = Future Price at time t_1

Consider first a situation where a company/hedger knows, it will sell the asset at time t_2 and initiates a short hedge at time t_1. The price related for the asset is S_2 and the profit on the future position = $F_1 - F_2$

The effective price obtained for the asset with hedging is

$$= S_2 + (F_1 - F_2)$$

$$= F_1 + (S_2 - F_2)$$

$$= F_1 + b_2 \text{ [Since, Basis at the time of } t_2 = b_2 = (S_2 - F_2)]$$

The value of F_1 is known at the time of t_1. If b_2 is known at this time, a perfect hedge would result. Now consider next a situation where a company knows, it will buy the asset at time t_2 and initiates a long hedge at time t_1. The price paid for the asset is S_2 and the loss on the hedge is $(F_1 - F_2)$. The effective price that is paid with hedging is:

$$S_2 + (F_1 - F_2) = F_1 + (S_2 - F_2) = F_1 + b_2$$

The value of F_1 is known at time t_1 and the term b_2 represents basis risk.

Problem 4. Spot and future prices, at the time of hedge is initiated, are ₹ 1,150 and ₹ 1,120, respectively and that at the time hedge is closed out, they are ₹ 1,100 and ₹ 1,090 respectively.

(a) Calculate the effective price obtained for the asset with hedging when hedger knows that the asset will be sold at the time hedge is closed out and taken a short future position (short hedge) at the time the hedge is initiated.

(b) Calculate the effective price paid for the asset with hedging when hedger knows that the asset will be purchased at the time hedge is closed and initiates a long hedge at the time the hedge is initiated.

Solution: $S_1 = 1150$; $S_2 = 1100$; $F_1 = 1120$; and $F_2 = 1090$

From the definition of the basis we get, $b_1 = (S_1 - F_1) = (1150 - 1120) = 30$

$$b_2 = (S_2 - F_2) = (1100 - 1090) = 10$$

(a) Effective Price = $S_2 + (F_1 - F_2) = S_2$ + Gain = 1100 + (1120 – 1090) = 1130.

Or, $F_1 + b_2 = 1120 + 10 = 1130$

(b) Effective Price = $S_2 + (F_1 - F_2)$ = 1100 + (1120 – 1090) = 1130.

The value of F_1 is known at time t_1 and the term b_2 represents basis risk.

A6 HEDGE RATIO (HR), POSITION TO BE HEDGED, NIFTY INDEX VALUE, NO. OF FUTURE CONTRACTS

- The optimal hedge ratio is the product of coefficient of correlation between ΔCP (change in spot price) and ΔFP (change in futures price) and the ratio of standard deviation of ΔCP to the standard deviation of ΔFP. Hedge ratio is also equivalent of beta (b) which is a measure of market risk.

$$\therefore \qquad HR = r \, . \, \frac{\sigma \Delta CP}{\sigma \Delta FP}$$

Where, = S.D. of change in spot price = $\sigma\Delta CP$

= S.D. of change in futures price = $\sigma\Delta FP$

r = coefficient of correlation between the change in spot price and change in futures price

- The position to be hedged = Stock value × Beta of stock
- NIFTY Index Value = Market lot × NIFTY future Index Value
- No. of future contracts = $\frac{\text{Position to be hedged}}{\text{Nifty Index Value}}$

Problem 5. An investor has investment of 1000 shares of a Public Ltd, Co. The spot market price each share is ₹ 1,195. He wants to keep the investment for another one month but expects a fall in its price. The investor chooses to hedge by buying future contracts on NIFTY available at 1992 at this moment. The standard deviation of the change in the price of stock over a one–month period is ₹ 38. The standard deviation of the changes in futures price of NIFTY Index over a one–month period is ₹ 41 and the coefficient of correlation between the one–month change in price of the company and one–month change in the NIFTY futures price is 0.72. Determine hedge ratio (HR) and the number of NIFTY Contracts required. (Market lot = 200)

Solution:

$$HR = r \, . \, \frac{\sigma \Delta CP}{\sigma \Delta FP}$$

$$= 0.72 \times \frac{38}{41} = 0.67$$

Hedge ratio (HR) 0.67 is also equivalent of beta which is a measure of market risk.

Position to be hedged = Stock value × Beta of stock = (1195 × 1000) × 0.67 = 800650

NIFTY Index Value = Market lot × NIFTY future Index Value = 200 × 1992 = 384000

$$\text{No. of future contracts} = \frac{\text{Position to be hedged}}{\text{Nifty Index Value}} = \frac{800650}{398400} = 2.0096637 = 2$$

Thus, to fully hedge the purchase of 1000 stock investments, the investor needs to sell 2 NIFTY future contracts.

Problem 6. It is February 2, 2010 today. An Indian company expects to receive Euros at the end of April on its sales to French Company. The May future price for the Euro is currently 0.0146. Devise a strategy to lock in a price if Euro 0.0146 plus the bases. Show the result if the spot price of Euro in April may happen to be 0.0140 and the future price to be 0.0142.

Solution:

Strategy

1. Short May Euro Futures Contracts on February 2, 2010.

2. Close out the contract when Euro arrives at the end of May.

Basis Risk : It arises from the hedger company's uncertainty as to the difference between the spot price and May futures price of the Euro at the end of May.

Outcome : Given, $S_2 = 0.0140$; $F_2 = 0.0142$;

$$b_2 = S_2 - F_2 = \text{Basis} = 0.0140 - 0.0142 = -0.0002$$

Gain on future $= F_1 - F_2 = 0.0146 - 0.0142 = +\ 0.0004$

The effective price in rupees per Euro received by the hedger is the end of April spot price plus the gain :

$$S_2 + (F_1 - F_2) = S_2 + \text{Gain} = 0.0140 + 0.0004 = 0.0144$$

Alternatively, $F_1 + b_2 = 0.0146 + -(-0.0002) = 0.0144$

B Financial Evaluation of Merger

B1. COSTS AND BENEFITS OF A MERGER

When firm A acquires firm B, firm A is making capital investment decision and firm B is making a capital divestment decision; the assumption is firm A pays cash compensation to firm B.

Benefit of the merger = PV of the combined entity (PV_{AB}) – PV of the two entities if they remain separate ($PV_A + PV_B$) = $PV_{AB} - (PV_A + PV_B)$

Cost of the merger (from the point of view of firm A) = Cash – PV_B (assuming that compensation to firm B is paid in cash)

Cash = Cash payment made for acquiring firm B by firm A

NPV to A = Benefit of the merger – cost of the merger

$= \{PV_{AB} - (PV_A + PV_B)\} - (\text{Cash} - PV_B)$

$= PV_{AB} - \text{Cash} - PV_A$

NPV to B = Cost of the merger from the point of view of firm A = Cash – PV_B = Cost

Problem 7. Re: Company A pays cash compensation to company B for acquiring it

	Company A	*Company B*
Market value of the companies	4 crores	1 crore

If the two firms merge, cost savings with a present value of ₹ 1 crore would occur. Company A proposes to offer ₹ 1.20 crores cash compensation to acquire company B. Calculate the NPV of the merger of the two companies.

Solution PV_A = 4 crores; = PV_B = 1 crore

PV_{AB} = PV of the combined entity

Benefit $= PV_{AB} - (PV_A + PV_B)$

Or, 1 crore $= PV_{AB} - (4 + 1)$

Or, $PV_{AB} = 6$ crores

Cost of the merger (from the point of view of Company A)

$= \text{Cash} - PV_B = 1.20$ crores – 1 crore = 0.20 crore = 20 lakhs

NPV to A = Benefit of the merger – cost of the merger

$= \{PV_{AB} - (PV_A + PV_B)\} - (\text{Cash} - PV_B)$

= 1 crore – 0.20 crore

= 0.80 crore = 80 lakhs

Alternatively NPV to A $= PV_{AB} - \text{Cash} - PV_A$

= 6 crores – 1.20 crores – 4 crores

= 0.80 crore = 80 lakhs

NPV to B $= \text{Cash} - PV_B$

= 1.20 crores – 1 crore

= 0.20 crore = 20 lakhs = Cost

B2. COMPENSATION IN STOCK

In practice, however, compensation is usually paid, not in cash, but in the form of stock. When this happens, the cost component in the present value calculation needs to be calculated with care, if firm A acquires firm B (say).

- Aparent cost of acquiring firm B = No. of shares offered by firm A in exchange for all shares of firm B X Market price/share of firm A
- But true cost is greater than this apparent cost as follows:

While calculating true cost, one must recognize that B's shareholders end up owning a fraction of the share capital of the combined firm.

Therefore, True Cost $= \alpha \times PV_{AB} - PV_B$ (in stead of, Cost $= \text{Cash} - PV_B$)

Where α = share of B in the combined entity

$$= \frac{\text{No. of shares offered by firm A in exchage}}{\text{No. of shares holding byA + No. of shares offered by firm A in exchange}}$$

Problem 8. Company A plans to acquire Company B, the relevant financial details of the two companies, prior to the merger announcement, are:

	Company A	*Company B*
Market price per share (₹)	100	40
No. of shares	20,00,000	10,00,000
Market Value of the firm (₹)	10 crores	2 crores

The merger is expected to bring gains which have a present value of ₹ 2 crores. Company A offered 5,00,000 shares in exchange of 10,00,000 shares to the shareholders of Company B. Calculate true cost and NPV of the merger of two companies.

Solution: True Cost $= \alpha \times PV_{AB} - PV_B$

$$\alpha = \frac{5,00,000}{20,00,000 + 5,00,000} = \frac{5,00,000}{25,00,000} = 0.2$$

We have, Benefit $= PV_{AB} - (PV_A + PV_B)$

Or, PV_{AB} $= PV_A + PV_B + \text{Benefit}$

= 10 crores + 2 crores + 2 crores

= 14 crores

True Cost $= \alpha \times PV_{AB} - PV_B$

= (0.2 X 14 crores) – 2 crores

= Re. 0.80 crore

= ₹ 80 lakhs

NPV to A = Benefit of the merger – cost of the merger

= 2 crores – 0.80 crore

= ₹ 1.20 crores

NPV to B = Cost = ₹ 80 lakhs

Alternatively,

NPV to A = Benefit of the merger – cost of the merger

$= \{PV_{AB} - (PV_A + PV_B)\} - (\alpha \times PV_{AB} - PV_B)$

= {14 crores – (10 crores + 2 crores)} – {(0.2 × 14 crores) – 2 crores}

= (14 crores – 12 crores) – (2.8 crores – 2 crores)

= 2 crores – 0.80 crore

= ₹ 1.2 crores

NPV to B $= \alpha \times PV_{AB} - PV_B$

= 0.2 X 14 crores – 2 crores

= 2.8 crores – 2 crores

= 0.80 crores

= ₹ 80 lakhs

C Financial Evaluation of Leasing (Lease vs. Borrowing)

C1. PROCESS OF FINANCIAL EVALUATION OF LEASING

The process of financial evaluation in a lease transaction generally involves 3 steps:

1. Appraisal of the client in terms of his financial strength and credit worthiness
2. Evaluation of the security/collateral security offered , and
3. Financial evaluation of the proposal

The most critical part of a leading transaction both to the lessor and the lessee is the financial evaluation of the proposal. The objective of this is to identify the cheaper source of finance to a lessee and better investment alternative to the lessor.

C2. LESSEE'S PERSPECTIVE (CHOICE BETWEEN DEBT FINANCING VERSUS LEASE FINANCING)

The lease evaluation from the lessee's point of view involves a choice between debt financing versus lease financing. The decision criteria used is the Net Present Value of Leasing [NPV (L)] or Net advantage of Leasing (NAL). *The discount rate used is the marginal cost of capital for all cash flows other than lease payments and the pre-tax cost of debt for lease payments.* Calculation of Net Present Value of Leasing [NPV (L)] or Net advantage of Leasing (NAL) can be presented in general format as follows: **(if only one discount rate is given in the problem)**

Years *Particulars*	*0*	*1*	*2*	*3*	......	.....
1. Cost of investment	+xxx					
2. Depreciation		xxx	xxx	xxx	xxx	xxx
3. Loss of depreciation tax Shield		–xxx	– xxx	–xxx	–xxx	–xxx
4. Lease Payment		–xxx	– xxx	–xxx	–xxx	–xxx
5. Tax shield on lease Payment (4 X tax rate)		+xxx	+xxx	+xxx	+xxx	+xxx
6. Salvage value						–xxx
7. Tax shield on Interest (Interest p.a. X tax rate)		–xxx	– xxx	–xxx	–xxx	–xxx
8. Cash flow of lease (1)+(3)+(4)+(5)+(6)+(7)	+xxx	–xxx	– xxx	–xxx	–xxx	–xxx
9. Present Value Interest Factor (PVIF)	1.00	xxx	xxx	xxx	xxx	xxx
10. Present Value of Cash Inflow (8×9)	+xxx	–xxx	– xxx	–xxx	–xxx	–xxx

Net Present Value of Leasing [NPV (L)] or Net advantage of Leasing (NAL) :

Present Value of Cash Flow of Year 0 + Present values of Cash flow during the life time of asset or Project

If NPV is positive, the leasing alternative should be used, otherwise the borrowing alternative may be preferable.

Calculation of Net Present Value of Leasing [NPV (L)] or Net advantage of Leasing (NAL) can be presented in general format as follows: **(if both discount rates– post-tax marginal cost of capital and pre-tax cost of long-term debt are given in the problem)**

Years *Particulars*	*0*	*1*	*2*	*3*	......	.....
1. Cost of investment	+xxx					
2. Depreciation		xxx	xxx	xxx	xxx	xxx
3. Loss of depreciation tax Shield		–xxx	– xxx	–xxx	–xxx	–xxx
4. Lease Payment		–xxx	– xxx	–xxx	–xxx	–xxx
5. Tax shield on lease Payment (4 × tax rate)		+xxx	+xxx	+xxx	+xxx	+xxx
6. Salvage value						–xxx
7. Tax shield on Interest (Interest p.a. × tax rate)		–xxx	– xxx	–xxx	–xxx	–xxx

(Contd...)

8. Cash flow excluding lease payment (1)+(3)+(5)+(6)+(7)	+xxx	–xxx	– xxx	–xxx	–xxx	–xxx
9. Present Value Interest Factor (PVIF)–*using **post–tax marginal cost of capital***	xxx	xxx	xxx	xxx	xxx	xxx
10. Present Value of Cash Flow excluding lease payment (8 × 9)	+xxx	–xxx	– xxx	–xxx	–xxx	–xxx
11. Present Value Interest Factor (PVIF)–*using **Pre–tax cost of long–term debt***		xxx	xxx	xxx	xxx	xxx
12. Present Value of lease Payment (4 × 11)		–xxx	– xxx	–xxx	–xxx	–xxx
13. Total Present Value of Cash flow (10+12)	+xxx	–xxx	– xxx	–xxx	–xxx	–xxx

Net Present Value of Leasing [NPV (L)] or Net advantage of Leasing (NAL):

Present Value of Cash Flow of Year 0 + Present values of Cash flow during the life time of asset or Project

If NPV is positive, the leasing alternative should be used, otherwise the borrowing alternative may be preferable.

C3. LESSOR'S PERSPECTIVE

The lease evaluation from the point of view of the lessor aims at ascertaining whether to accept a lessee proposal or to choose from alternative proposals. As in the case of an evaluation by a lessee, the appraisal method used is the discounted cash flow technique based on the lessor's cash flow. The lease related cash flow from his angle consists of the followings:

(a) outflows in terms of the initial investment /acquisition cost of the asset at the inception of the lease; income tax on lease payments, VAT on lease transactions, if any; lease administration expenses, such as rental collection charges, expenses on suits for recovery, other direct costs and so on;

(b) inflows such as lease rentals, management fee tax shield on depreciation, residual/ salvage value etc.

Problem 9. Excel Industries Ltd. has decided to go for an air conditioning plant costing ₹ 30 million. The company is considering 2 alternatives as follows:

1. leasing the plant, and

2. borrowing and purchasing the plant. Sharp leasing is willing to lease the plant to Excel Industries Ltd. at an annual lease rental of ₹ 8.1 million for 5 years, the lease rental being payable in arrears.

The tax relevant depreciation rate on the plant is 25% as per the WDV method. The net salvage value of the plant after 5 years is expected to be 6.4 million. The company has an effective tax rate of 35% and rate of interest on debt is 7% p.a. (pre-tax cost of debt). What is the Net Present Value of Leasing [NPV (L)] or Net advantage of Leasing (NAL) ?

Solution: (₹ in million)

Years / *Particulars*	*0*	*1*	*2*	*3*	*4*	*5*
1. Cost of investment	+30.000					
2. Depreciation		7.500	5.625	4.219	3.164	2.373
3. Loss of depreciation tax Shield (2 × 35%)		–2.625	–1.969	–1.477	–1.107	0.831
4. Lease Payment		–8.100	–8.100	–8.100	–8.100	–8.100
5. Tax shield on lease Payment (8.1 × 35%)		+2.835	+2.835	+2.835	+2.835	+2.835
6. Salvage value						–6.400
7. Tax shield on Interest (7%of 30 × 35%)		–0.735	–0.735	–0.735	–0.735	–0.735
8. Cash flow of lease (1)+(3)+(4)+(5)+(6)+(7)	+30.000	–8.625	–7.969	–7.477	–7.107	–13.231
9. Present Value Interest Factor (PVIF) @ 7%	1.00	0.935	0.873	0.816	0.763	0.713
10. Present Value of Cash Flow (8 × 9)	+30.000	–8.064	–6.957	–6.101	–5.422	–9.434

Net Present Value of Leasing [NPV (L)] or Net advantage of Leasing (NAL) :

Present Value of Cash Flow of Year 0 + Present values of Cash flow during the life time of asset or Project = +30.000 + (–8.064 –6.957 –6.101 –5.422 –9.434) = – 5.978 millions.

Since NPV is negative, borrowing alternative may be preferable.

D Calculation of NAV of Mutual Funds

D1. NAV (NET ASSET VALUE)

Whenever we buy open ended mutual fund units, the number of units we get for our investment, is calculated based on Net Asset Value (NAV) of the fund. Similarly when we sell our units the amount to be returned to us is calculated based on NAV. NAV is the fund's share price. NAV is actually NAV per unit but every one use the term NAV as a short form. NAV is the Net Assets of the fund per number of units outstanding. It is calculated by the below formula:

$$\frac{\text{M.V. of the investments + Receivables + Other Accrued Income + Other assets – Accrued Expenses –Other Payables – Other liabilities } \textbf{(Current value of the fund portfolio)}}{\text{No. of units outstanding as on the NAV date}}$$

M.V. of investment is closing price of the securities/debentures as per last trading

Accrued Income = Dividends and Interests to be received

Other Assets = Cash, Cash equivalents

If NAV value of a scheme is high it does not mean that the unit is over priced. In case of open ended mutual funds, they actually reflect the market price of the fund's assets at premium not at discount.

Problem 10. Suppose there are 3 investors in a mutual fund – X, Y and Z

X had invested ₹ 25,000

Y had invested ₹ 35,000

Z had invested ₹ 40,000

The mutual fund company had decided to initially issue shares (units) at ₹ 100 each. Now, suppose the fund manager had invested ₹ 30,000 in Company 1, ₹ 30,000 in Company 2 and ₹ 40,000 in Company 3. After 1 year, the value of investment in Company 1 has become ₹ 50,000, in Company 2 ₹ 20,000 and in Company 3 ₹ 50,000.

Calculate (a) NAV per share (NAV)

(b) Value of each investor's portfolio

(c) Rate of return on investment after 1 year

Solution: Workings: Initial corpus of the mutual fund

= ₹ (25,000 + 35,000 + 40,000)

= ₹ 1,00,000

X has got MF units	= 25,000 ÷ 100 =	250
Y has got MF units	= 35,000 ÷ 100 =	350
Z has got MF units	= 40,000 ÷ 100 =	400
		1,000 units at ₹ 100 each

Total value of the mutual fund portfolio = ₹ (50,000 + 20,000 + 50,000) = ₹ 1,20,000

$$\text{(a) NAV per share} = \frac{\text{Current value of the fund portfolio}}{\text{No. of funds units}} = \frac{₹\ 1{,}20{,}000}{1{,}000} = ₹\ 120$$

(b) Value of Investment's portfolio: NAV of each unit X No. of units held by that investor

Value of X's portfolio = ₹ 120 × 250 = ₹ 30,000

Value of Y's portfolio = ₹ 120 × 350 = ₹ 42,000

Value of Z's portfolio = ₹ 120 × 400 = ₹ 48,000

$$\text{(c) Rate of return on investment after 1 year} = \frac{1{,}20{,}000 - 1{,}00{,}000}{1{,}00{,}000} \times 100$$

$$= \frac{20{,}000}{1{,}00{,}000} \times 100$$

$$= 20\%$$

Problem 11. A mutual fund owns 400 shares of an MNC1 Company, **cur**rently trading at ₹ 450 and 400 shares of MNC2, currently trading at ₹ 4,250. The fund has 500 shares outstanding.

(a) What is the NAV of the fund?

(b) If investors expect the price of MNC1 company's shares to increase to ₹ 650 and the price of MNC2 shares to decrease to ₹ 4,000 by the end of the year, what is the expected NAV at the end of the year? Is there any decline in the expected NAV price? If so, what is the percentage of decline?

(c) Assume that expected price of the MNC1 shares is realized at ₹ 650, what is the maximum price decrease that one can occur to the MNC2 shares to realize an end-of-year NAV equal to the NAV estimated in (a)?

Solution:

(a) NAV of the fund $= \dfrac{(400 \times ₹\ 450 + 400 \times ₹\ 4{,}250)}{500} = \dfrac{1{,}80{,}000 + 17{,}00{,}000}{500}$

$= \dfrac{₹\ 18{,}80{,}000}{500} = ₹\ 3760/\text{share}$

(b) Expected NAV $= \dfrac{(400 \times ₹\ 650 + 400 \times ₹\ 4{,}000)}{500} = \dfrac{2{,}60{,}000 + 16{,}00{,}000}{500}$

$= \dfrac{18{,}60{,}000}{500} = ₹\ 3{,}720/\text{share}$, *i.e.*, decline of 1.064%

$\left(\dfrac{3{,}760 - 3{,}720}{3{,}760} \times 100\right)$

(c) $\dfrac{400 \times 650}{500} + \dfrac{400 \times Pm}{500} = 3760$

Or, Pm = ₹ 4050/share, a decline of ₹ 200 – in compare to ₹ 4250/share

D2. OPEN-ENDED AND CLOSE-ENDED FUNDS

Open-ended funds allow shares to be purchased and redeemed according to investor's demand. The NAV of open–ended funds is determined only by changes in the value of the assets owned. In close-ended funds, the number of shares of the fund is fixed. If investors need to redeem their shares, they sell them to another investor. Thus the demand for the fund shares can provide another source of return for the investors as the market price of the fund may exceed the NAV of the fund. Close-ended funds, such as real estate investment trusts, tend to be more specialized.

Problem 12. Open-ended fund A owns 100 shares of Company1 valued at ₹ 100 each and 50 shares of Company 2 valued at ₹ 50 each. Close-ended fund B owns 75 shares of Company 1 and 100 shares of Company 2. Each fund has 100 shares of stock outstanding.

(a) What are the NAVs of both funds using these prices?

(b) Assume that in one month the price of Company 1 stock has increased to ₹ 105 and the price of Company 2 stock has decreased to ₹ 45. How do these changes impact the NAV of both funds? If the funds purchased at the NAV prices in (a) and sold at month-end, what would be the realized returns on the investments?

(c) Assume that another 100 shares of Company 1 are added to Fund A, what is the effect on fund A's NAV if the stock prices remain unchanged from the original prices?

Solution

(a) $$\text{NAV (open–ended)} = \frac{100 \times ₹\,100 + 50 \times ₹\,50}{100} = ₹\,125$$

$$\text{NAV (close–ended)} = \frac{75 \times ₹\,100 + 100 \times ₹\,50}{100} = ₹\,125$$

(b) $$\text{NAV (open–ended)} = \frac{100 \times ₹\,105 + 50 \times ₹\,45}{100} = ₹\,127.50$$

$$\%\text{ Change in NAV} = \frac{₹\,127.50 - 125.00}{125.00} \times 100 = 2\%$$

$$\text{NAV (close–ended)} = \frac{75 \times ₹\,105 + 100 \times ₹\,45}{100} = ₹\,123.75\%$$

$$\%\text{ Change in NAV} = \frac{₹\,123.75 - 125.00}{125.00} \times 100 = -\,1\%$$

(c) $$\text{NAV (open–ended)} = \frac{200 \times ₹\,100 + 50 \times ₹\,50}{100} = ₹\,225.00$$

❑❑❑

Case Studies on Financial Issues

Case Studies

Case 1 Re: Cost of Capital and optimal capital structure of SAP AG

You have the opportunity to visit SAP AG, the business software company. Based in Walldorf, Germany, SAP offers software development and implementation in application areas such as accounting, logistics and human–resource management to large businesses in Europe, North America and around the world. In 2000 the company had sales of over EUR 6.2 billion.

In recent months the company's stock price has been depressed, and management is concerned about re–examining the financial structure. Management is also concerned with the financing of forthcoming acquisitions: should SAP continue to take advantage of its strong cash flow, or should it begin to use debt financing? If it does raise additional debt, the proceeds will be used for a stock buyback.

You have been asked to evaluate whether the company has an appropriate amount of debt. In 2001 the following information about SAP's current position was collected:

Current share price:	117 EUR
Shares outstanding:	316 million
Beta of the stock based on the German DAX index: 1.3	
Debt outstanding:	200 EUR million
Debt rating:	AAA
Market rate on bonds with rating	AAA 5.65%
Government-10 year bond rate:	4.80%

DAX long-run expected return 9.80% or 5.00% over governments

Company's marginal tax rate: 38%

2001 estimated pre tax profit: 1568

2001 estimated book value of equity: 3734

Based on the company's business, its interest coverage and other factors, the following table shows what an increase in long term debt would do to the company's ratings and its cost of borrowing as well as several key ratios:

Additional debt	New Rating	Interest rate	Interest expense	Interest coverage ratio	Debt/ capitalization	Debt/ book equity
0	AAA	5.65%	11	139.76	1%	0.1
2500	AAA	5.65%	153	11.28	7%	0.7
5000	A+	6.22%	323	5.85	14%	1.4
7500	A–	6.56%	669	3.34	27%	2.7
10000	BB–	9.40%	1,429	2.10	41%	4.1

Questions:

1. Should SAP take on additional debt? If so, how much?
2. What is the weighted average cost of capital before and after the additional debt?
3. How much does SAP's value increase as a result of the lower cost of capital? What will be the estimated price per share after the company takes on new debt?

Notes:

1. To answer these questions, you will have to obtain updated data about the company, its share price, etc.
2. To assess the impact on SAP's value, you may assume that the additional value comes from the savings from a lower cost of capital each year, and that the savings will continue indefinitely.

Case 2 Re: Financial Analysis of HLL

Balance Sheet of Hindustan Lever Limited

Hindustan Lever Ltd. ₹ Crore	Dec–96 12mths	Dec–97 12mths	Dec–98 12mths	Dec–99 12mths	Dec–00 12mths	Dec–01 12mths
Gross fixed assets	1047.9	1122.8	1364.4	1454.1	1669.6	1889.45
Land & building	223.7	278.3	347.91	385.6	425.3	504.97
Plant & machinery	628	636.5	762.28	779.6	877.6	1013.71
Other fixed assets	102.4	120.9	163.84	185	237.1	260.24
Capital WIP	93.8	87.1	90.37	103.9	129.6	110.53
Less: cumulative depreciation	326.4	328.8	400.1	447.1	511.5	586.9
Net fixed assets	721.5	794	964.3	1007.1	1158.2	**1302.55**
Revalued assets	0.6	0.6	0.6	0.6	0.6	0.6
Investments	328.6	544.5	729.51	1068	1832.1	1668.93
In group/associate cos.	191.8	253.6	296.46	299.1	440.3	352.6
In mutual funds	2.7	77.7	77.67	80.8	104.8	504.42
Other investments	134.1	213.2	355.38	688.1	1287	811.91
Marketable investment	76.3	183.5	370.5	523.8	935.6	586.83
Market value of quoted investment	215.3	573.7	645.14	863.2	969.9	593.85
Deferred tax assets	0	0	0	0	0	349.61
Inventories	903.4	1044.6	1145.68	1309.8	1181.8	1240.05
Raw materials and stores	389.8	484.2	560.06	593.4	539.2	597.12
Raw materials	366.3	455.6	534.78	565.1	514.6	568.31
Stores and spares	23.5	28.6	25.28	28.3	24.6	28.81
Finished and semi–finished goods	514.1	560.4	585.62	716.4	638.9	635.71
Finished goods	470	521.2	548.63	673.8	589.7	587.99
Semi–finished goods	44.1	39.2	36.99	42.6	49.2	47.72
Other stock	0	0	0	0	3.78	7.22
Receivables	720.8	582.11	803.16	860.4	1054.8	1268.7
Sundry debtors	143.5	145.4	192.94	233.7	264.5	424.79
Debtors exceeding six months	30.3	22.8	14.63	10.7	7.6	7.82
Accrued income	9.3	8.3	13.68	27.4	46.4	45.75
Advances/loans to corporate bodies	30.6	56.1	144.07	51.7	291.6	214.85
Group/associate cos.	30.6	56.1	144.07	51.7	76.8	74.85
Other cos.	0	0	0	0	0	0
Deposits with govt./agencies	16.8	33.5	35.62	42.2	37.7	45.73
Advance payment of tax	0	0.01	0	0	0	0
Other receivables	520.6	338.8	416.85	505.4	414.6	537.58
Cash & bank balance	203.3	574.5	659.88	810.3	522	913.15
Cash in hand	1.3	2.5	1.59	5.47	1.47	1.41
Bank balance	202.8	572	658.29	804.9	520.6	911.74
Intangible assets (not written off)	0	0	89.47	80	47.3	22.38
Intangible assets (goodwill, etc.)	0	0	89.47	80	47.3	22.38
Total Assets	**2878.1**	**3539.71**	**4392**	**5135.6**	**5796.2**	**6765.37**

Hindustan Lever Ltd. ₹ Crore	Dec–96 12mths	Dec–97 12mths	Dec–98 12mths	Dec–99 12mths	Dec–00 12mths	Dec-01 12mths
Net worth	938.1	1261.2	1713.03	2102.5	2488	3043.69
Authorized capital	225	225	225	225	225	225
Issued capital	145.8	199.1	219.57	219.5	220	220.12
Paid-up equity capital	145.8	199.1	219.57	219.5	220	220.12
Preference capital	0	0	0	0	0	0
Reserves & surplus	792.37	1062.1	1493.46	1883	2268	2823.57
Free Reserves	761.8	1030.5	1459.4	1861.7	2249.4	2802.64
Share premium reserves	46	121.2	178	194.9	194.9	263.26
Other free reserves	715.8	909.3	1281.4	1666.8	2054.5	2539.38
Specific reserves	29.9	31	33.39	20.7	18	20.26
Revaluation reserves	0.6	0.6	0.6	0.6	0.6	0.67
Accumulated losses	0	0	0	0	0	0
Borrowings	260	186.4	264.31	177.2	111.5	83.73
Bank borrowing	35.1	3.2	90.57	110.9	55.5	24.7
Short-term bank borrowings	31.2	3.2	90.57	110.9	55.5	24.7
Long-term bank borrowings	3.9	0	0	0	0	0
Financial institutional borrowings	12.2	8	4.11	0.2	0	0
Govt./sales tax deferral borrowings	0	0	0	0	0	0
Debentures/bonds	18.6	18.5	17.78	0	0	0
Fixed deposits	91.3	87.3	86.72	5.2	0	0
Borrowings from corporate bodies	1.5	0	0	0	0	0
Commercial paper	15	0	0	0	0	0
Other borrowings	86.3	69.4	65.13	60.9	56	59.03
Secured borrowings	96.4	65.7	146.75	141.3	69.2	43.04
Unsecured borrowings	163.6	120.7	117.56	35.9	42.3	40.69
Current portion of long-term debt	22.6	4.1	2.79	2.3	11	3.33
Total foreign currency borrowings	0	0	0	0	0	0
Deferred tax liabilities	0	0	0	0	0	103.13
Current liabilities & provisions	1680	2092.11	2414.66	2855.9	3196.7	3534.82
Current liabilities	1438	1673.61	1858.02	2143.4	2233.9	2410.42
Sundry creditors	1142.3	1596.01	1787.36	2081.4	2163.3	2347.19
Interest accrued/due	15.4	17.8	16.5	7.5	5.3	2.63
Creditors for capital goods	0	0	0	0	0	0
Other current liabilities	280.3	59.8	54.16	54.5	65.3	60.6
Share application money	230.9	0	0	0	0	0
Advance against WIP	0	0	0	0	3	7.09
Provisions	242	418.5	556.64	712.5	962.8	1124.4
Tax provision	26.4	71.8	40.2	49	172.2	51.89
Dividend provision	129.4	189.2	272.27	374.6	440.1	550.31
Dividend tax provision	0	0	0	0	0	0
Other provisions	86.2	157.5	244.17	288	350.5	522.2
Total liabilities	**2878.1**	**3539.71**	**4392**	**5135.6**	**5796.2**	**6765.37**
Contingent liabilities						
Bills discounted	30.4	41.4	30.83	31.9	99.5	74.65
Disputed taxesLetters of credit	0.000.00	0.000.00	0.000.00	0.000.00	0.000.00	0.000.00
Total guaranteesFuture lease rent payable	59.30.00	55.30.00	57.370.00	12.000.00	49.60.00	0.000.00
Liabilities on capital account	39.2	49.0	39.09	0.00	0.00	0.00

INCOME STATEMENT OF HINDUSTAN LEVER LIMITED

Hindustan Lever Ltd. ₹ Crore	**Dec–96 12mths**	**Dec–97 12mths**	**Dec–98 12mths**	**Dec–99 12mths**	**Dec–00 12mths**	**Dec–01 12mths**
Income	7137.8	8363.3	10261.57	10978.3	11458.3	11861.77
Other income	106.7	165.2	183.93	269.3	305.9	283.14
Change in stocks	15.2	46.4	–7.9	128.52	–83.85	–4.63
Non-recurring income	137.8	50.4	47.15	14.4	47.8	310.93
Expenditure						
Raw materials, stores, etc.	4533.4	5201.9	6158.31	6548.4	6388.8	6381.54
Wages & salaries	385	448.7	527.23	584.1	614.3	591.7
Energy (power & fuel)	105.8	110.8	118.43	123.1	139.9	152.77
Indirect taxes (excise, etc.)	577.1	626.5	835.44	861.8	870.1	920.66
Advertising & marketing expenses	283	490.6	676.86	746.5	709.2	835.75
Distribution expenses	279.2	289.1	345.77	366.2	446	465.86
Others	386.6	474.9	544.02	596.9	712.4	761.8
Non-recurring expenses	139.9	54	49.43	20.4	20.7	146.01
Profits/losses						
PBDIT	707.5	928.8	1229.4	1543.1	1826.8	2195.13
Financial charges (incl. Lease rent)	57	33.8	29.28	22.3	13.1	7.74
PBDT	650.5	895	1200.2	1520.8	1813.7	2187.39
Depreciation	55.2	57.9	101.05	128.7	130.9	144.66
PBT	595.3	837.1	1099.2	1392.1	1682.8	2042.73
Tax provision	192.55	270	293	318	355	402.42
PAT	402.8	567.1	806.2	1074.1	1327..8	1640.31
Appropriation of profits						
Dividends	261.9	372.44	531.35	711.09	942.3	1158.31
Equity dividend	249	338.5	463.46	638.1	770.2	1100.62
Dividend tax	12.9	33.9	67.9	72.9	172.1	57.69
Retained earnings	140.9	194.7	274.9	363.1	385.5	482

Questions:

1. How the financial ratios are calculated by using the balance sheet and income statement of HLL, the largest fast moving consumer goods company in India? Offer necessary interpretations from the ratios.
2. Also prepare the common size financial statements of HLL.
3. Show the complete financial analysis of HLL.

Hints:

Current Ratio

Calculation of current ratio for HLL

	1997	**1998**	**1999**	**2000**	**2001**
Current assets	2240.99	2753.33	3295.08	3321.35	3712.06

Current liabilities	2093.01	2503.92	2966.85	3252.71	3559.52
Current ratio	1.071	1.1	1.111	1.021	1.043

The norm for the current ratio in FMCG industry is 2:1. The current ratio of HLL is almost equal to 1:1, which is less than the norm. On an average, for every rupee of current liability, HLL has ₹ 1.069 of current assets. The current ratio can be better judged if it is studied along with ratios such as inventory turnover and receivables turnover.

The higher the receivables and inventory turnover, greater the firm's ability to pay its current liabilities. Generally, a low current ratio indicates the firm's inability to meet its current obligations. But a high current ratio may represent unnecessary blocking of liquid assets such as cash and cash equivalents.

Quick Ratio : Calculation of quick ratio for HLL

	1997	**1998**	**1999**	**2000**	**2001**
Quick assets	792.53	1126.87	1399.13	1632.7	1835.23
Current liabilities	2093.01	2503.92	2966.85	3252.71	3559.52
Quick ratio	0.38	0.45	0.47	0.5	0.52

A quick ratio of 1:1 is usually considered satisfactory. In the case of HLL, a low quick ratio as well as a low current ratio may indicate poor working capital management.

Debtors Turnover Ratio: Calculation of debtors' turnover ratio for HLL

	1997	**1998**	**1999**	**2000**	**2001**
Net credit sales	8363.3	10261.57	10978.31	11458.3	11861.77
Average debtors	144.49	169.19	213.34	249.13	344.65
Debtors' turnover ratio	57.88	60.65	51.45	45.99	34.41

The debtors' turnover ratio of HLL shows a downward trend. In this case, the average collection period of HLL must also be calculated and analyzed.

Average Collection Period: Calculation of average collection period

	1997	**1998**	**1999**	**2000**	**2001**
Days in a year	365	365	365	365	365
Debtors' turnover	57.88	60.65	51.46	45.99	34.41
ACP	6.3	6	7	7.9	10.6

Here, the average collection period is gradually increasing, indicating that an extended line of credit has been allowed. There was a sharp decline in the debtors' turnover ratio in 1999, and the decline continued till 2001. The fall in debtors' turnover ratio can be attributed to any of the following reasons:

- There might be an increase in the volume of sales relative to the increase in debtors.
- The firm might have extended the credit period for debtors.
- The firm's debt collection team is not performing well, as a result rate of which the realization has come down.

Interest Coverage Ratio: Calculation of interest coverage ratio for HLL

	1997	1998	1999	2000	2001
PBIT/interest	870.9/33.8	1128.4/29.2	1414.4/22.3	1695.9/13.1	2050.47/7.74
Interest coverage	25.76	38.64	63.43	129.46	264.92

This ratio shows the number of times the interest charges on long-term liabilities have been collected before the deduction of interest and tax. A high interest coverage ratio implies that the company can easily meet its interest burden even if profit before interest and taxes suffers a sharp decline. The interest coverage ratio for HLL is going up every year, implying that it can meet its interest obligations even if there is a decline in profits. From the creditors' point of view, the larger the coverage; the greater the firm's capacity to handle fixed-charge liabilities and the more assured the payment of interest to the creditors. A low ratio is a warning signal which indicates that the firm is using excessive debt and does not have the ability to pay interest to creditors. However, a very high ratio implies an unused debt capacity.

Net Profit Margin: Calculation of net profit margin for HLL

	1997	1998	1999	2000	2001
Net Profit/Net Sales × 100	567.1 / 7736.75	806.2 / 9426.13	1074.1/ 10116.45	1327.8/ 10588.18	1640.31/ 10941.11
Net Margin	7.32	8.55	10.61	12.54	14.99

The net profit margin of HLL has increased significantly. The high net profit margin implies higher returns to shareholders in the form of dividends and stock price appreciation.

Return on Assets (ROA): Calculation of ROA for HLL

	1997	1998	1999	2000	2001
PAT/Average total assets * 100	567.1/ 3208.9	806.2/ 3965.85	1074.1/ 4763.8	1327.8/ 5465.9	1640.31/ 6280.78
ROA	17.67	20.32	22.55	24.29	26.12

The above calculations show an upward trend in the return on total assets. However, these calculations do not include the interest payable to the creditors of the firm in the net profits. To calculate the actual returns on total assets, interest should be included in net profits, because assets are financed by owners as well as creditors.

Over Trading Ratio: Calculation of over trading ratio

A company intending to increase its sales should ensure that it has sufficient net working capital to fall back on in the event of creditors becoming due for payment or else the company may have to face a severe liquidity crisis. An increase in the net working capital along with an increase in sales will help the company avoid a liquidity crisis.

	1997	1998	1999	2000	2001
Net working capital	147.98	249.41	328.23	68.64	152.54
Credit sales	8363.3	10261.57	10978.31	11458.3	11861.77
Over trading ratio	0.017	0.024	0.029	0.006	0.013

The over trading ratio for HLL shows an upward trend till 1999, which indicates an increase in the net working capital, along with an increase in sales. But in 2000 and 2001, the company's net working capital did not increase in proportion to the increase in sales.

Working Capital Performance Ratio: Calculation of working capital performance ratio

This ratio refers to the sources through which the debtors of a firm are financed. A company can finance its debtors through its trade creditors or its advance payments from customers.

	1997	1998	1999	2000	2001
Trade debtors	582.11	803.16	860.4	1054.8	1268.7
Trade creditors	1596.02	1787.36	2081.4	2164.3	2347.19
Working capital performance ratio	0.364	0.449	0.413	0.487	0.54

A working capital ratio of 2:1 is desirable. The ratio more than 2 indicates a better ability to meet ongoing and unexpected bill payments. The ratio less than 2 indicates that the company may have difficulties meeting its short–term commitments and that additional working capital support is required. In HLL's case, though this ratio is well below the desirable 2:1 ratio, it is increasing every year.

COMMON SIZE INCOME STATEMENT OF HLL (% of income)

	1997	1998	1999	2000	2001
Raw materials & Stores etc.	62.19	60.01	59.64	55.75	53.79
Wages & Salaries	5.36	5.14	5.32	5.36	4.98
Energy (Power & Fuel)	1.32	1.15	1.12	1.22	1.29
Indirect Taxes (Excise etc.)	7.49	8.14	7.85	7.59	7.76
Advertising & Marketing Expenses	5.86	6.59	6.79	6.18	7.04
Distribution Expenses	3.45	3.36	3.34	3.89	3.92
Others	5.67	5.3	5.43	6.22	6.42
Tax Provision	3.23	2.86	2.89	3.098	3.39
PAT	6.78	7.85	9.78	11.58	13.82
Gross Sales	100	100	100	100	100

COMMON SIZE BALANCE SHEET OF HLL (% of asset)

Liabilities	1997	1998	1999	2000	2001
Equity Share Capital	5.62	5	4.27	3.79	3.25
Reserves & Surplus	30	34	36.66	39.13	41.73
Borrowings	5.26	6.02	3.45	1.92	1.23
Current liabilities & Provisions	59	55	55.61	55	52.24
Total Liabilities	100	100	100	100	100
Assets					
Fixed Assets	22.43	21.96	19.61	19.97	19.25
Investments	15.38	16.6	20.8	31.06	24.67
Inventories	29.51	26.09	25.5	20.4	18.33
Receivables	16.45	18.31	16.76	18.21	18.75
Cash & Bank Balances	16.23	15.02	15.78	9	13.51
Total assets	100	100	100	100	100

Case 3 Re: Indian Financial System

Globalization: The Role of Institution Building in the Financial Sector: The Indian Case

This case study traces the evolution of the Indian financial system. India has had a long tradition of financial institution building. At Independence, India inherited a fairly diversified set up, both in respect of institutions and market. There was gradual increase in State control over the financial system until the initiation of the financial sector reform process. Under State control there was a tremendous increase in the spread of financial services across the economy.

Financial sector reforms, introduced in the backdrop of a serious balance of payments crisis in 1991, have been aimed at increasing stability and efficiency of the system. Towards this end, the regulatory and supervisory framework has also moved from micro-governance towards macro-management; imparting greater freedom to both institutions and markets in resource allocation, pricing and risk management. A salient feature of the reforms has been that of 'gradualism', which is credited with the advantage of enhancing macro stability, while fostering appropriate microeconomic linkages. The salutary effect of the institution building process in the post–reform period has been evident across both institutions and markets. The effect, however, has been uneven across sectors, reflecting largely the differential phasing in of sector specific reforms, keeping in view their overall systemic importance. The Indian experience also suggests that the sequencing of policies across institutions needs to be tempered with individual country–specific characteristics and circumstances, drawing upon international best practices.

The Institutional Building Process

Early Days of Institution Building: Post-Independence Up to 1968

India has a long history of financial intermediation. The first bank in India to be set up on modern lines was in 1770 by an agency house. The earliest but short-lived attempt to establish a central bank was in 1773. India was also a forerunner in terms of development of financial markets. The Bombay Stock Exchange was functional as early as 1870. The first life insurance company in the country, Oriental Life Insurance Company, had been established as far back in 1818 and the first general (non-life) insurance company was set up in 1850. By independence, India had a fairly well developed commercial banking system in existence. In 1951, there were 566 private commercial banks in India with 4,151 branches, the overwhelming majority of which were confined to larger towns and cities. Savings in the form of bank deposits accounted for less that 1 per cent of national income, forming around 12 per cent of the estimated saving of the household sector. The Reserve Bank of India (RBI) was originally established in 1935 by an Act promulgated by the then Government of India, but as a shareholders institution like the Bank of England. After India's independence, in the context of the need for close integration between its policies and those of the Government the Reserve Bank became a state owned institution from January 1, 1949. It was only in this year that the Banking Regulation Act was enacted to provide a framework for regulation and supervision of commercial banking activity. However, despite the widespread development of the banking system, the Indian financial system was characterized by lack of depth at the time of independence. Organized credit institutions had a negligible presence in rural India. The entire process of institution building in the post–

independence period revolved around the country's need to mobilize savings in order to raise the investment rate and to channel resources to identified sectors of the economy, notably agriculture and industry. The objective of economic development had assumed a sense of urgency in the 1950s with the launching of the Five Year Plans. At the beginning of planning in 1951, the Indian economy operated at relatively low levels of saving and investment. The Plan observed that the desirable rate of growth in output could be achieved only if investment could be stepped up substantially. The planning strategy was based on the concept of a mixed economy where both public and private sectors had a role to play with regard to investment activity and in mobilization of resources. The First Five Year Plan stated, "Central banking in a planned economy can hardly be confined to the regulation of the overall supply of credit or to a somewhat negative regulation of the flow of bank credit. It would have to take on a direct active role, firstly, in creating or helping to create the machinery needed for financing developmental activities all over the country and secondly, ensuring that the finance available flows in the directions intended". Thus, the experience during this period suggested that institution building and development of the financial system was propelled by the vision of the country's central planners after Independence. The vision was to ensure that sectoral needs of credit to agriculture and industry were met in an organized manner. The RBI was vested with the major responsibility of developing the institutional infrastructure in the financial system. The commercial banking system was expanded to take care of the general banking needs of accepting deposits and extend short-term working capital to industry. In order to accelerate the pace of extension of banking facilities in the country and to provide a greater response to the credit needs of the cooperative sector, the biggest commercial bank State Bank of India was brought under the majority ownership of the RBI. To cater to the long-term financing needs of industry at the national level, and in the absence of a well-developed capital market, Development Finance Institutions (DFIs) were established under the majority ownership of the RBI. The RBI also set up a mechanism to provide concessional finance to these institutions. State Finance Corporations (SFCs) were set up to cater to long-term needs of industry at the State level. The financing needs of the rural agriculture sector was sought to be fulfilled by a three-tier cooperative banking structure which was complemented by UCBs at the urban sector level. The accelerated pace of public investment and industrialization during the end of 1950s and the early 1960s created conditions for stepping up private investment in industry. The Unit Trust of India came into existence in 1964 also initially sponsored by RBI to provide a channel for retail investors for participating in the capital market. Recognizing that exports did not receive much attention from the country's planners in the early years, an Export Risks Insurance Corporation was set up in July 1957, which was later converted into the Export Credit and Guarantee Corporation in January 1964. The RBI concentrated on regulation, mechanisms and organizations in its role of institution building. For instance, following serious financial difficulties and the failure of several banks, including two relatively large scheduled banks, a deposit insurance scheme was set up in 1962 with the establishment of the Deposit Insurance Corporation,

Bank Nationalization and After: 1969-1990 (The Pre-Reform Years)

Even though the Indian banking system made considerable progress both functionally and in terms of geographical coverage during the above period, there were still many rural and semi-urban areas, which were not served by banks. Moreover, the large industries and big and established houses tended to enjoy a major portion of the credit facilities, to the detriment of the priority sectors such as agriculture, small-scale industries and exports. Thus, to bring about a wider diffusion of banking facilities and changes in the pattern of bank lending, the scheme of social control over banks that envisaged organizational and legislative changes was initiated by the Government. The systems of credit planning which identified priorities for loans and advances and Lead Bank Scheme that sought to make the banking system an instrument of development were instruments of social control over banks. This transitory phase was followed by the nationalization of banks. In July 1969, these 14 largest commercial banks were nationalized as a major step to ensure adequate credit flow into genuine productive areas in conformity with Plan priorities. Bank nationalization served to intensify the social objective of ensuring that financial intermediaries fully met the credit demands for productive purposes. Two significant aspects of nationalization were (i) rapid branch expansion and (ii) channeling of credit according to plan priorities. To meet the broad objectives, banking facilities were made available in hitherto uncovered areas, so as to enable them to not only mop up potential savings and meet the credit gaps in agriculture and small-scale industries, thereby helping to bring large areas of economic activities within the organized banking system. As a consequence, the perceived need of the borrower gained primacy over commercial considerations in the banking sector. In April 1980, six more private sector banks were nationalized, thus extending the domain of public control over the banking system.

By the middle of the 1970s, it was felt that the task of providing agricultural credit on the requisite scale could not be met by commercial banks, unless they acquire specialized knowledge of rural setting. Against this background, Regional Rural Banks (RRBs) were set up in 1975 to fill this gap in financing. Consequently, by the end of 1975, three separate institutional arrangements – commercial banks, cooperative banks and RRBs – known as the *multi-agency approach* for providing credit in the rural areas emerged. Establishment of National Bank for Agriculture and Rural Development (NABARD) in 1982 was an important landmark in the history of cooperative credit. The objective of NABARD was to create institutional arrangements at national level for financing, coordinating, guiding, and controlling cooperative credit system. To facilitate this, NABARD was given certain regulatory control over rural credit cooperatives. In order to give specialized and focused attention to different segments of industry, certain other specialized financial institutions have come into existence since the 1980s that, in a broad sense, could be included in the genre of DFIs. Apart from NABARD (catering to the agricultural sector), Export–Import (EXIM) Bank of India (catering to export finance), Small Industries Development Bank of India (SIDBI) (catering to credit needs of small industries), and National Housing Bank (NHB) (catering to housing finance). Most recently, the Infrastructure Development Finance Company (IDFC) came into being in 1997 to promote investment of the private sector in infrastructure. In addition to their roles as DFIs, NABARD and NHB have also been entrusted with certain supervisory responsibilities.

There were attempts to develop the capital markets during the 1980s by increasing participants and instruments, improving transparency, reducing transaction costs and ensuring safety in settlement procedures. Companies were facing severe constraints in raising money through equity as they faced tight regulation. Issuance of capital through the equity route, debentures and public sector bonds emerged as new instruments for raising resources in the primary market. The secondary market also witnessed an increase in number of stock exchanges, listed companies and market capitalization. As the stock markets developed, efforts were diverted towards greater transparency and investor protection. Several specialized institutions such as credit rating agencies (*e.g.*, CRISIL, CARE and ICRA) and custodial service provider companies (*e.g.*, Stock Holding Corporation of India Limited (SHCIL)) also took shape during this period. An important development was the establishment of the Over the Counter Exchange of India (OTCEI). The most important development during this period was the setting up of the Securities and Exchange Board of India (SEBI) in 1988.The government securities market was mainly a captive market dictated by the borrowing needs of the Government. Banks were required to hold a certain proportion of their liabilities in the form of government securities. This statutory liquidity ratio (SLR) was increased gradually as the borrowing needs of the Government increased. In order to facilitate the large borrowing requirements of the Government, interest rates on Government securities were artificially pegged at low levels, unrelated to market conditions. The provision of fiscal accommodation through *ad hoc* treasury bills (issued by RBI on tap at a fixed interest rate of 4.6 per cent) led to high levels of monetization of fiscal deficit during the major part of the 1980s. In order to check the effects of such large-scale monetization, the CRR was frequently increased to control liquidity. The money market, which was intended as a market for equilibrating the demand and supply of funds in the inter-bank market was narrow and relatively illiquid with control on interest rates. It was only in the late 1980s that the interest rate in the inter-bank call money market was deregulated and new instruments like the Commercial Paper and Certificates of Deposits were introduced to make the market more liquid.

The dominance of the public sector and state ownership persisted during the 1980s. The financial system was shaped and architectured to meet the objectives of the Government enunciated through the Plans. Hence, both the liabilities and asset sides of the balance sheets of the financial institutions were controlled. The authorities believed that the main objectives of these institutions were to mobilize savings at low cost and deploy them into identified priority sectors at subsidized rates. Markets did not exist in the true sense. Capital markets were controlled and hence transaction costs were high. The government securities market was just a captive market for raising debt for the Government and the money market was restricted to the inter-bank call money market where interest rates were controlled for most part of the 1980s. Such control resulted in several inefficiencies creeping into the banking system. Repression assumed the form of a high and administered interest rate structure with a large measure of built-in cross-subsidization (in the form of minimum lending rates for commercial sector), high levels of pre-emption of primary and secondary reserve requirements, in the form of cash reserve ratio (CRR) and statutory liquidity ratio (SLR).

On the eve of the reforms in 1991, the SLR and cash reserve ratio (CRR) together pre-empted as much as 63.5 per cent of the bank's deployable resources. Retail lending to riskier areas of business with the 'free' portion of bank's resources engendered 'adverse selection' of borrowers. With limited prospects of recovery, this raised costs and affected the quality of bank assets. Quantitative restrictions (branch licensing and restrictions on new lines of business) and inflexible management structures severely constrained the operational independence and functional autonomy of banks. Inflationary expectations and the inequitable tax structures exacerbated the strains on the exchequer, since resources for developmental purposes were not readily forthcoming. As the quality of asset portfolio of banks rapidly deteriorated, it was evident that the profitability of the banking system was severely compromised. In addition, the widespread market segmentation and the constraints on competition exacerbated the already fragile situation. The market for short term funds was reserved for banks and the market for long-term funds was the exclusive domain of Development Financial Institutions (DFIs)5. Direct access of corporate borrowers to lenders (disintermediation) was strictly controlled and non-bank financial companies (NBFCs) were allowed to collect funds only for corporates.

1991 and After: The Reform Years

Major Policy Stance of Reform

The reform in the financial sector was attuned to the reform of the economy, which now signified opening up. Greater opening up underscores the importance of moving to international best practices quickly since investors tend to benchmark against such best practices and standards.

Since 1991, the Indian financial system has undergone radical transformation. Reforms have altered the organizational structure, ownership pattern and domain of operation of banks, DFIs and NBFCs. The main thrust of reforms in the financial sector was the creation of efficient and stable financial institutions and markets. Reforms in the banking and non banking sectors focused on creating a deregulated environment, strengthening the prudential norms and the supervisory system, changing the ownership pattern, and increasing competition.

The policy environment was stanched to enable greater flexibility in the use of resources by banks through reduced statutory pre-emption. Interest rate deregulation rendered greater freedom to banks to price their deposits and loans and the Reserve Bank moved away from micromanaging the banks on both the asset and liability-side. The idea was to impart operational flexibility and functional autonomy with a view to enhancing efficiency, productivity and profitability. The objective was also to create an enabling environment where existing banks could respond to changing circumstances and compete with new domestic private and foreign institutions that were permitted to operate. Instead, the Reserve Bank focused on tighter prudential norms in the form of capital adequacy ratio, asset recognition norms, provisioning requirements, exposure norms and improved level of transparency and disclosure standards. As the market opens up, the need for monitoring and supervising becomes even more important systemically. The greater flexibility and the prudential regulation were fortified by 'on-site inspections' and 'off-site surveillance'. Furthermore, moving away from the closed economy objectives of ensuring appropriate credit planning and credit allocation, the inspection objectives and procedures, have been redefined to evaluate the bank's safety and soundness; to appraise the quality of the Board and management; to ensure compliance with banking laws and regulation; to provide an appraisal of soundness of the bank's assets; to analyze the financial factors which determine bank's solvency and to identify areas where corrective action is needed to strengthen the institution and improve its performance.

Lessons From The Indian Experience

The process of globalization has important implications for the financial sector and the institutions comprising it. In an increasingly globalized environment, the role of the policy maker in the domestic institutional building process can be envisaged in the form of providing a stable macroeconomic environment, increasing competition, establishing a strong regulatory and supervisory framework, evolving an enabling legal system and strengthening the technological infrastructure. A well-knitted institutional set up facilitates the growth and development process of an economy. Effective institutions can make the difference in the success of market reforms. If the financial system is well diversified and the markets are liquid and deep, effective mobilization and allocation of resources will be ensured. Many broad generalizations can be discerned from the Indian experience.

Development of the Indian financial system is premised on the conviction that financial development makes fundamental contributions to economic growth. At the time of Independence, the financial system was fairly liberal. By the 1960s, controls over the financial system were tightened and priority was to set up institutions to mobilize saving and allocate the saving to specified priority sectors. The RBI was vested with the responsibility of developing the institutional infrastructure in the country. Towards this end, controls on lending and deposit rates were introduced and specialized development banks, catering to varied segments of the economy were established. This institutional design did not achieve the desired results.

The process culminated with the two-stage nationalization process of banks, first in 1969 and thereafter in 1980. Around the same time, insurance business was also brought under the domain of Government control in phases. The process of nationalization expanded the reach of financial services to remote parts of the country. However, the basic principle of mobilizing the saving and channeling the resources to certain sectors at a price not related to the market remained. Notwithstanding the numerous achievements of 'social banking', such as branch expansion and diversion of credit to rural sectors, the high degree of controls on the financial system also manifested itself in several inefficiencies, most notably financial repression. In order to address these shortcomings, gradual liberalization of the financial system was initiated in the late 1980s, which received greater momentum in the 1990s. The closed-economy framework gradually gave way to greater externally oriented and liberal financial (open) system. The 1990s witnessed the advent of economic reforms in the country encompassing trade, industry and the real sectors. The external sector was liberalized. The country adopted a flexible exchange rate regime early in the reform period and encouraged non-debt creating flows in the form of foreign direct investment and foreign institutional investment. Liberalization of the external current account was also undertaken early in the reform cycle. The macroeconomic environment would then influence institutional building. As the economy opens up, the financial system can no longer afford to remain repressed. The financial system will also have to undertake reforms in the form of interest rate deregulation, prudential regulation, good supervisory standards, legal changes and technological up gradation. New institutions operating on market principles would emerge and old institutions would either have to change to cope with the emerging changes or close. Thus, macroeconomic reform and reform in the financial system will have to progress concomitantly. In the early 1990s, a wide-ranging set of reforms, encompassing both financial institutions and markets were undertaken, that paved the way for a more market-driven allocation and pricing of resources. The basic dimensions of the process of globalization have tended to exhibit itself, both domestically; in terms of greater integration of domestic financial markets with global ones and internationally, in terms of the adoption of a process of gradual convergence with international best practices.

Questions:

1. Describe the Indian Financial System before reforms had taken place in 1991.
2. State the institutional building process in India; also state the effects of the institution building process in the post-reform period.
3. What is meant by the 'process of globalization'? What are the implications of this process on the financial sector and the institutions?
4. Explain the radical transformation of Indian financial system since 1991. What are the reasons for that transformation?
5. Explain 'Financial sector reform'. How did it affect the development of capital and money market in India after 1991?

Case 4 Re: Fund Flow and Cash Flow of Mahindra Satyam

Mahindra Satyam (BSE: 500376) is a Brand identity of **Satyam Computer Services Limited.** Satyam Computer Services Limited was founded in 1987 by B Ramalinga Raju. Mahindra Satyam is a part of the Mahindra Group which is one of the top 10 industrial firms based in India. The company offers consulting and information technology (IT) services spanning various sectors and is listed on the New York Stock Exchange, the National Stock Exchange (India) and Bombay Stock Exchange (India). In June 2009, the company unveiled its new brand identity "Mahindra Satyam" subsequent to its takeover by the Mahindra Group's IT arm, Tech Mahindra. Mahindra Satyam has offices in 32 countries. Mahindra Satyam is ranked 17 in the list of IT services providers in India according to a study by Cyber Media's Dataquest Research in 2011.

Services Provided by Mahindra Satyam

Mahindra Satyam provides services in the following areas:

- Aerospace and Defense
- Banking, Financial Services and Insurance
- Energy and Utilities
- Life Sciences and Healthcare
- Manufacturing, Chemicals and Automotive
- Public Services and Education
- Retail
- Consumer Packaged Goods
- Travel, Transport, Logistics
- Telecom, Infrastructure, Media and Entertainment and Semiconductors

Apart from those services company offers the following horizontal services.

- Extended Enterprise Solutions
- Web Commerce Solutions
- Business Intelligence Services
- Quality Consulting
- Strategic Outsourcing Services
- Industry Native Solutions
- Business Services Group – BSG (BPO)
- Engineering Services
- Product management

Partnership & Merger

Feb 11, 2010, Mahindra Satyam, has entered into a partnership with the Integr8 Group, Africa's largest privately owned ICT service and solutions provider.

In case of Inorganic growth, Mahindra Satyam's proposed merger with Tech Mahindra may be delayed all because of legal issues, and ambiguity over jurisdiction between investigating agencies and the government. The merger has been delayed due to two tax cases pending with the Income Tax claiming over ₹ 2,700 crore for both.

Big turnaround of the company

The company had reported a consolidated net loss of ₹ 233.3 crore for the July–September quarter of 2010. Even though the company got 245 crores profit in Q4 for 2010–2011, but due to outside payments nearly 570 crores for SEK,UNIPAID and Class Action Suit in Q4 (Total 641 crores for the year 2010–2011), the company had reported a consolidated net loss of ₹ 327 crore for the Jan–Mar quarter of 2010–2011. IT firm Mahindra Satyam today posted a consolidated net profit of ₹ 225.2 crore for the quarter ended June 30, 2011. During the quarter, the company added 2,172 people (net), taking total headcount to 31,438 as of June 30, 2011.

Capital Structure of Mahindra Satyam

Share Capital

The paid up share capital stands at ₹ 2,353 Million as on March 31, 2011 compared to ₹ 2,352 Million as on March 31, 2010. The increase of ₹ 1 Million during the year is due to conversion of options into shares by employees under various Associate Stock Option Schemes (ASOPs). Here is the year wise capital structure of the company from 2000.

Table 1: Capital Structure of Mahindra Satyam

Period		Instrument	Authorized Capital (₹ cr)	Issued Capital (₹ cr)	PAID UP		
From	To				Shares (nos)	Face Value ₹	Capital (₹ cr)
2010	2011	Equity Share	280	235.3		2	235.3
2009	2010	Equity Share	280	235.24	1176185762	2	235.24
2008	2009	Equity Share	280	134.78	673894792	2	134.78
2007	2008	Equity Share	160	134.1	670479293	2	134.1
2006	2007	Equity Share	160	133.44	667196009	2	133.44
2005	2006	Equity Share	75	64.89	324449539	2	64.89
2004	2005	Equity Share	75	63.85	319265291	2	63.85
2003	2004	Equity Share	75	63.25	316251710	2	63.25
2002	2003	Equity Share	75	62.91	314542800	2	62.91
2001	2002	Equity Share	75	62.91	314540000	2	62.91
2000	2001	Equity Share	75	56.24	281190000	2	56.24

Total Income

Total income decreased to ₹ 50,660 Million in the current year from ₹ 51,134 Million in the previous year thereby leading to a decrease of ₹ 474 Million.

IT Services Revenues

Revenues from IT services of ₹ 47,414 Million (₹ 50,904 Million for FY 2009–10) comprises of revenue from Overseas / Exports market ₹ 45,294 Million (₹ 48,558 Million for FY 2009–10) and from domestic market of ₹ 2,120 Million (₹ 2,346 Million for FY 2009–10). The software revenue mix based on various parameters is as follows.

Table 2: Segmental Revenue

₹ in Million

	31.03.2011		31.03.2010	
Offshore	21761	45.90%	24,491	48.11%
Onsite/offsite	25653	54.10%	26,413	51.89%
Total	47414	100%	50904	100%

Profit and loss account

The debit balance in profit and loss account of ₹ 23,346 Million at the beginning of the year was further increased to ₹ 24,622 Million for the year ending March 31, 2011 due to the loss of ₹ 1,276 Million for the year ending March 31, 2011.

Table 3: Profit & Loss Account as on 31.03.2011

₹ in Million

	31.03.2011	31.03.2010
Income		
Income from Operations	47,761	51,005
Other Income	2,899	129
	50,660	**51,134**
Expenditure		
Personnel Expenses	32,920	36,648
Operating and Administration Expenses	10,084	8,705
Provision for Diminution in the value of Long-Term Investments	393	
	43,397	**45,353**
PBDIT	7,263	5,781
Interest and Financing Charges	92	254
Depreciation/Amortization	1,499	1,908
	1591	2162
PBEI&T	5,672	3,619
Less: Exceptional item	6,411	4,169
Loss before tax	–739	–550
Less: Income Tax –	537	143
Fringe Benefit Tax		19
Net (Loss) for the Year	**–1,276**	**–712**

Table 4: Balance Sheet as on 31.03.2011

₹ in Million

Source of Fund	31.03.2011	31.03.2010
Shareholders' Funds		
Share Capital	2,353	2,352
Share Application Money Pending Allotment		1
Reserves and Surplus	43,881	43,963
	46,234	**46,316**
Loan Funds		
Secured Loans	315	420
SUB TOTAL	46,549	46,736
Amounts Pending Investigation Suspense Account	12,304	12,304
TOTAL	58,853	59,040
Application of Fund		
Fixed Assets		
Gross Block	20,204	18,189
Less: Accumulated Depreciation/Amortization	14,067	12,859
Net Block	6,137	5,330
Capital Work-in-Progress	2,683	3,730
	8,820	**9,060**
Investments	5,321	7,266
Current Asset		
Inventories	592	
Sundry Debtors	11,127	8,505
Cash and Bank Balances	26,498	20,920
Other Current Assets	3,655	4,717
Loans and Advances	3,319	3791
	45191	**37933**
Current Liability		
Current Liabilities	14,686	7,890
Provisions	10,415	10,675
	25,101	**18,565**
Net Current Assets	20,090	19,368
Debit Balance in Profit and Loss Account	24,622	23,346
SUB TOTAL	58,853	59,040
Difference	0	0

Note: Secured Loans:

The secured loan balance as at March 31, 2011 is ₹ 315 Million as compared to ₹ 420 Million as at March 31, 2010. The decrease of ₹ 105 Million over the previous period is primarily due to repayment of the finance lease obligations during the year. This decrease is partially offset by increase on account of new car leases entered into by the Company during the current year. No other loans were taken during the current year.

Questions:

Prepare

(*i*) Cash from Operation

(*ii*) Cash Flow Statement for the year ended 31.03.2011

(*iii*) Fund Flow Statement for the year ended 31.03.2011

Case 5 Re: Cash Management System

Traditionally having a paper-based clearing system involving not only high processing cost but security risk, cash management in India has certainly undergone a paradigm change. From a product-centric approach, the focus for almost all banks today has shifted emphatically to the customer. And success is all about bringing the maximum possible delivery channels to the prospect's doorstep.

In the rapidly transforming world of business, banking faces its biggest challenge yet – constant change. With every bank seeming to offer service possible, efficiency coupled with innovative value added solutions have emerged as the key business differentiators that affect a bank's bottom line. Confronted with shrinking deposits/margins, rising customer expectations and intensifying competition, banks must at all times strive to be a step ahead of industry standards. At the same time, they cannot lose sight of credit risk, a natural byproduct of the increasingly complex relationships in today's dynamic markets.

For some time now, technology has been the key driving force behind every successful bank. In such an environment, the ability to recognize and capture market share depends entirely on the bank's competence to evolve technically and offer the customer a seamless process flow. The objective of a cash management system is to improve revenue, maximize profits, minimize costs and establish efficient management systems to assist and accelerate growth.

Today a corporate treasurer's dilemma is multifaceted. With more movement towards the regional/central liquidity management in the complex structure of rules and regulations, further complication is caused by taxation issues. What a corporate treasurer needs as VOC – Visibility of funds, optimized returns on funds, and Control over receivables and payables. Treasury can face a number of issues related to the slow movement of funds, locked working capital, loss of float income, high cost of funds, time consuming reconciliation and manual processes. In India the cash management business primarily involves collections and payments services.

Cash Management in India

Products offered by banks under collections (paper and electronic):

Local cheque collections.

High value (0 Day clearing).

Magnetic ink character recognition (MICR) (three day clearing of cheques).

Outstation cheque collections

Cheques drawn on branch locations.

Cheques drawn on correspondent bank locations.

Cheques drawn on coordinator locations.

House cheque collections.

Outside network cheque collections.

Cash collections.

ECS–Debit.

Post dated cheque collections.

Invoice collections.

Capital market collections.

Products offered by banks under payments (paper and electronic):

Demand drafts/bankers cheques.

Customer cheques.

Locally payable.

Payable at par.

RTGS/NEFT/ECS.

Cash disbursement.

Payments within bank.

Capital market payments.

The Reserve Bank of India (RBI) has placed an emphasis on upgrading technological infrastructure. Electronic banking, cheque imaging, enterprise resource planning (ERP), real time gross settlement (RTGS) is just few of the new initiatives.

The evolution of payment systems such as RTGS has posed some tough challenges for cash management providers. It is important that banks now look towards a shift to fees from float although all those cash management providers who have factored in float money in their product pricing might take a hit. But of course there are opportunities also attached like collection and disbursal of payments on-line across the banks.

There are a number of regulatory and policy changes that have facilitated an efficient cash management system (CMS). Fox example, the Enactment of Information Technology Act gives legal recognition to electronic records and digital signatures. The establishment of the Clearing Corporation of India in order to establish a safe institutional structure for the clearing and settlement of trades in foreign exchange (FX), money and debt markets has indeed helped the development of financial infrastructure in terms of clearing and settlement. Other innovations that have supported in streamlining the process are:

- Introduction of the Centralized Funds Management Service to facilitate better management of fund flows.
- Structured Financial Messaging Solution, a communication protocol for intra-bank and interbank messages.

Evolution of Services

One of the emerging cash management services in India is payment outsourcing. Though cheques and drafts are a popular mode of payment in India, it is obviously a time consuming procedure because of the manual processing required. This is an area where payment outsourcing can help. It allows corporates to reduce their overheads and focus on their core competencies and, as a result, benefit from speed and accuracy. The enhanced security it offers also allows for tighter fraud control. For the Indian payment system to become completely seamless there are many variables that need to be tackled, such as regulatory and legal issues, customer behaviour and infrastructure. As more corporates and banks have added technology to their processes, the issues surrounding connectivity security have become much important.

Today, treasurers need to ensure that they are equipped to make the best decisions. For this, it is imperative that the information they require to monitor risk and exposure is accurate, reliable and fast. A strong cash management solution can give corporates a business advantage and it is very important in executing the financial strategy of a company. The requirement of an efficient cash management solution in India is to execute payments, collect receivables and managing liquidity. Traditional or e-business objectives, in India there are different cash management solutions.

Cash Management Solutions Offered in India

Account reconciliation services: Balancing a cheque book for a very large business can be quite a difficult process. Banks have developed a system to overcome this issue. They allow companies to upload a list of all the cheques whereby at the end of the month, the bank statement will show not only the cleared cheques but also uncleared ones.

Positive pay: An effective anti-fraud measure for cheque disbursements. Using the cheque issuance data, updated regularly with cheque issuance and payment, the bank balances all cheques offered for payment. In the case of any discrepancies, the cheque is reported as an exception and is returned.

Balance reporting services: Balance reporting provides help in procuring a company's current banking information from its accounts. With this service the banks can offer almost all types of transaction-specific details on activities related to payment like deposits, cheques, wire transfers etc. It also helps in an effective and efficient management of regular cash flow.

Lockbox: Facilitates the cash improvement where, instead of being delivered to business address, customer payments are delivered to a special post office (PO) box. It is only the customers' payments that are delivered in the PO box and the company's own bank collects the amount and delivers them to the banks of the customers. The bank of the customers opens and processes the payments for direct deposit to the bank account. Lockbox contents regularly removed and processed.

Questions

1. Explain the trend of cash management system in India.
2. 'In India the cash management business primarily involves collections and payments services'. Explain.
3. State the products offered by banks under collections (paper and electronic) and also state the products offered by banks under payments (paper and electronic).
4. State the difference between traditional system and modern system of cash management apart from focus and techniques.
5. Explain briefly the cash management solutions offered in India. What was the role of RBI in relation thereto?

Case 6 Re: Inventory Management System of Wal-Mart

Wal-Mart Increases its Supplier's Inventory Levels

Most notably, Wal-Mart's JIT efforts are leaving their suppliers with more inventories. At the same time, they do not want backorders. The only way to do this is to be able to replenish their stock at a moment's notice. So what does this do to their suppliers? According to Logistics Management, it shoots supplier's inventories straight up. The demands that Wal-Mart places on its suppliers are incredible because of the power Wal-Mart places on its suppliers. Suppliers are forced to hold incredible safety stocks to make sure they can satisfy Wal-Mart's demands.

Basically, the suppliers don't have a choice in the matter. Wal-Mart's business, even with the demands on service, is too good to pass up. But, Wal-Mart is not about to have a stock out due to some supplier's inability to provide a 99% service level. Wal-Mart, like many huge companies, will not wait. Many companies are requiring shorter lead times even as more companies implement 'zero tolerance' policies for late shipments. Zero tolerance is a hell of a statement from a company that knows service level. To provide even a 97% service level compared to a 95% service can result in a huge increase in inventory. Zero-tolerance is wild. In fact it is actually impossible. No matter what a company holds in inventory, there is always the possibility that Wal-Mart could order one more than that. Couple this with a shorter lead time to Wal-Mart and inventories are staggering.

Wal-Mart is ordering fewer cases more frequently. For a company, this means that they can either produce smaller batches, or hold onto more inventories. Because if a company cannot produce less and faster, than they have to produce a large amount and then, instead of producing a large amount and getting rid of it all at once, they have to get rid of it slowly over time, which increases average inventory. While Wal-Mart may be getting the good end of the deal, one thing is for sure, there's a reason suppliers put up with these demands, and it's not because the business with Wal-Mart is bad.

Questions

1. Explain Wal-Mart's JIT efforts.
2. How does Wal-Mart increase average inventory?
3. Illustrate the concept of 'Zero tolerance'.
4. 'Wal-Mart is ordering fewer cases more frequently' Explain.

Case 7 Re: Debtors Management System – Debt recovery procedure

A. EDF Energy, one of the largest energy companies in the UK EDF Energy is one of the largest energy companies in the UK, generating around seven per cent of the UK's electricity, and employing nearly 13,000 people. Over a quarter of the UK population depends on EDF Energy for their electricity. One of the less glamorous but nevertheless vital tenets of this huge business is debt collection.

The telephone has proven to be an effective method for collecting this debt, as it offers immediacy and implicitly demands a response in a way that a written reminder cannot hope to do. By linking the psychology of the phone call into the efficiencies offered by a quality dialler, EDF Energy saw the potential benefits available.

The Challenge

EDF Energy had historically used outbound agents to manually call customers by sifting through paperwork so the dialler was seen as a way of cutting down the processing time and enabling greater management control over the calls being made.

The Solution:

Thanks to an existing relationship with Rostrvm Solutions and proof that its dialler could cope with the volume, it was installed in 2003 at EDF Energy's site in Exeter. "We ran it for a year and it quickly proved its worth," explains Kevin McKay, outbound dialing team manager at EDF Energy. "Since then we have significantly increased the volumes of customers we are contacting through the dialer and the results have been very encouraging. **Rostrvm Solutions Limited** is an innovative UK–based company that designs, develops and supports software applications for the call centre and back office process management and reporting. When you ring a customer just after they have received their traditional reminder, there's up to a 40 per cent success rate of making contact and conducting a debt collection transaction and implicitly demands a response in a way that a written reminder cannot hope to do Proactive contact.

The Results

Kevin says the goal here is to increase cash flow, secure customer future usage and avoid the need for any further debt collection activity. The signs are good. "Agents are collecting substantial values per month in hard cash via debit card or completing a direct debit over the phone. If we waited for a response from a paper based reminder, we could wait a week, 14 days, or longer." With a greater understanding of the times when these calls are most effective, EDF Energy have been able to recruit additional staff to further improve performance and fully utilize desk space at traditionally quieter times in the office. There are plans within EDF Energy to further develop the scope of the outbound dialer within its collections function and as Kevin describes "the quality of the **rostrvm** product and support given by the **rostrvm** team fully fits EDF Energy's needs".

B. Citibank Code for collection of dues & Repossession of Security

The GCB India Collections Code outlines minimum requirements that need to be adhered by the Citibank N.A./authorized representative when contacting a customer for due payments. These requirements are also aligned to the minimum standards of banking practices for banks set by BCSBI (The Banking Code and Standards Board of India).

TCS Ltd is the authorized entity responsible for contacting customers on behalf of Citibank N.A. Besides TCS Ltd other Third Party Vendors may also contact Customers on behalf of Citibank N.A. The code is a mandatory requirement for all individuals/persons/vendors/entities who contact the Customer(s) on behalf of Citibank N.A. This document contains material proprietary to Citibank NA. Duplication and dissemination either in part or in full, without authorization is prohibited.

Citibank's policy of treating debtors and managing debt collection

All Customers (including Customers who are late in paying or in default) must be treated with respect, dignity, courtesy and fairness in debt collection efforts. Citibank believes this is not only the right thing to do, but also the most effective.

It is imperative that all persons involved in collection related activities follow this policy. All Customer Assistance Specialists (CAS) must strictly agree to abide by this policy described below prior to beginning collection activities with respect to the Customers. This policy applies to all employees of Citigroup including TCS Ltd and/or other affiliates and employees/agents of companies that may be retained to collect on consumer debts on behalf of Citibank NA in India.

YOU MUST READ, UNDERSTAND AND AGREE TO ABIDE BY THESE GUIDELINES PRIOR TO BEGINNING COLLECTIONS ON DEBTS OWED BY THE CUSTOMERS.

Failure to comply will result in disciplinary action and may result in permanent termination of employment and or business with TCS Ltd/Citibank NA.

The following are the core underpinnings of the collection process. These are an extract of the Citibank collection values.

1. **Customers deserve to be treated with dignity.** Customer Assistance Specialists should always remain professional during telephone conversations and visits. No written or verbal threats, abuse or rudeness is permitted. Customer Assistance Specialists should use only acceptable business language, even if the other party does not.

2. **Customer Assistance Specialists deserve to be treated with dignity.** They may refer the customer to management, or end calls when a customer becomes abusive or threatening. Customers should be informed prior to termination of such calls. All calls where the customer becomes abusive or threatening should be appropriately documented.

3. All calls being made to the Customer(s) must be recorded as per requirements of the Code of Conduct stipulated by the Reserve Bank of India. No calls may be made by any of the Agents unless there is recording facility for the same, especially by Customer Assistance Specialists

from their individual mobile phones unless they said call is absolutely necessitated for checking on the availability of the Customers or for directions to the location of the Customers . Customer Assistance Specialists should always identify themselves and the company/entity that they represent at the very beginning of every interaction with customers and the Customers must be informed that the call is being recorded.

4. Customers are entitled to privacy. Privacy policies apply to all conversations with third parties, as stipulated in this document. The Customers must be informed that their call is being recorded. Unrecorded calls to Customers are to be avoided.

5. All collection activities should be consistent with the guidelines provided in this document and in compliance with the Code for collections of dues stipulated (from time to time) by the Reserve Bank of India. All letters, telegrams and other communication must be in the format approved by compliance and/or Citibank legal counsel.

6. Customers should be called only between **0700 Hrs and 1900 Hrs** unless exceptional circumstances described in this Code warrant deviation from this timeframe. Under no circumstances, customer can be called beyond 2100hrs.

7. Customers should be called no more often than is reasonable in the context of the debt, and the conversations logged on the system and the convenience of the Customer(s) to talk, should be enquired at the beginning of each call.

8. Customer requests that calls/visits to place of work be stopped are to be honored if he/she provides a suitable alternate where he/she may be reached during collection working hours. Such customers should be asked to provide an alternate address/phone number where they may be reached.

9. Customer's questions should be answered in full. They should be provided with information requested, given assistance and issues resolved. Accounts with unresolved issues are to be escalated to management.

10. Customer or third party requests for supervisor names or requests to speak with supervisor should always be honoured.

11. Customer Assistance Specialist notes on the collection system should be clear, concise, accurate and free of editorial comments. All attempts, contacts, conversation and actions are to be noted on the collection system.

Why you may contact a customer

A customer is to be contacted for debt collection only under the following circumstances:

- When not contacting the Customer may lead to the imposition of an additional cost on the customer or may impact the customer's credit history/rating, *e.g.*, customer spending pattern indicates that the customer may be about to breach his/her credit line;
- When the customer has not paid on payment date (including grace days) and this is likely to impact the customer's credit history and/or is likely to cause a financial loss to Citibank.

When you may contact a customer

It has been Citibank's experience in India that individuals with full-time employment routinely are awake by 06:00 Hrs in order to be at their jobs at the time required. Accordingly calls must normally be limited from 0700 hrs to 1900 hrs. A customer may be contacted beyond 1900 hrs till 2100 hrs on:

1. Phone, if customer has not been contactable within last 48 hrs.
2. On personal visit, if the customer has been non contactable during last two visits.

Questions:

1. Explain Rostrvm Solutions.
2. Explain the debt collection procedure of EDF Energy.
3. How EDF Energy did get their success in debt collection?
4. Explain the possible best policy for treating the debtors.
5. Illustrate Citibank's policy of treating debtors and managing debt collection.
6. What may be the core programmes of the collection process if the debt cannot be collected even after the reminders?
7. What is the justification of using outbound agents to manually call customers?

Case 8 Re: Risk and Return – When risk is not bad!

A case study of Financial Planning

Ms Anita Modi was a 24-Yr old single lady, *i.e.,* she had no dependents. She was a salaried individual earning ₹ 45,000 per month (pm). Her investment portfolio comprised only of assured return schemes, *i.e.*, fixed deposits, bonds and small savings schemes.

Observations of Fund Manager

Prima facie, the client seemed to be a risk-averse individual, hence the 'equity-free' investment portfolio. In turn, she had lost out on the benefits of asset allocation. Her portfolio sorely lacked the presence of an equity component, among other asset classes.

Finally, Ms. Modi had fallen prey to a common malady. She would invest in a random and directionless manner, *i.e.,* she was yet to set any concrete investment objectives like buying a house property or retirement planning.

The course of action

A series of discussions had taken place between the Fund manager and Ms. Modi to better understand her risk appetite and the reasons for the 'equity-free' portfolio. The Fund manager was surprised to learn that she wasn't a risk-averse investor at all. How did he ascertain that? Well, he asked her one simple question – If she was investing in the stock markets for the long-term, and the stock markets were to fall 20.0% the next day, would she panic? Her answers (and should be for any investor who has monies committed for the long-term to the stock markets) was an emphatic "No".

The reason Ms Modi had steered clear of equity/mutual fund investments was because she didn't quite understand what they were and how they functioned. On the other hand, investments in fixed deposits and small savings schemes were something she was conversant with and had traditionally invested in. Hence, she chose to stick to the same time-tested investment avenues. This adds a new aspect to the earlier discussion on risk – wherein one fails to invest in line with his risk appetite (in this case take on an adequate degree of risk), on account of lack of awareness. So here the fund manager had a client who had a high risk appetite, but was not taking on any risk at all! The result – a sub-optimal asset allocation, which delivered meager tax–adjusted returns.

The Fund manager's first task was to impress upon her the importance of asset allocation. Simply put, asset allocation entails investing in various asset classes in different proportions, depending on the investor's risk appetite and investment objectives. The underlying intention is to offset a downside in one asset class, by the presence of another. In Ms. Modi's case, there was a need to incorporate equities in the portfolio. Also other assets like gold and real estate needed to enter the portfolio in suitable proportions over time. The aim being to convert the portfolio from an assured return–dominated one to one that was aptly diversified across asset classes.

An example will help us better understand the importance and benefits of holding a portfolio that is well–diversified across various asset classes. Let's assume that we are dealing with a risk–taking investor who has failed to invest in line with his risk profile. As a result instead of holding a portfolio dominated by equities, he holds one that is debt–heavy. Case 1 shows the investor's present asset allocation wherein debt and gold account for 70.0% of the portfolio; this asset allocation results in a weighted return of 8.2%.

Now, let's consider Case 2, wherein the same investor realigns his portfolio to match his risk profile. As a result of the realignment, equities emerge as the dominant asset class. The investor's new portfolio yields a weighted return of 12.625%, *i.e.*, an uptick of more than 54% approximate over Case 1.

Get the right allocation

	Expected Rate of Return	Case 1		Case 2	
		Asset Allocation	**Weighted Return**	**Asset Allocation**	**Weighted Return**
Real estate	12.0%	25.0%	3.0%	25.0%	3.0%
Equities	16.0%	5.0%	0.8%	50.0%	8.0%
Debt	8.0%	30.0%	2.4%	12.5%	1.0%
Govt. debt & gold	5.0%	40.0%	2.0%	12.5%	0.625%
		100.0%	8.2%	100.0%	12.625%

The noteworthy feature of this example is that, it isn't a case of taking on more risk to clock better returns. Instead, it's a case of realigning the portfolio to match the investor's risk profile and benefiting in the process.

Now let's get back to Ms. Modi's case and her second problem area, *i.e.*, not setting investment objectives. Ms. Modi's investment activity was carried out in an "off the cuff" manner. She wasn't aware of the importance of setting objectives before commencing any investment activity. As a result, she was yet to decide on any concrete investment objectives. It transpired that Ms. Modi planned to get married in about 3 years. So there was an investment objective that merited immediate attention – accumulating monies for the wedding. As per Ms. Modi's estimate, she would need (at present cost levels) a corpus of ₹ 5,00,000 to meet the wedding expenses.

The Fund manager created an investment plan that would help the client meet the aforementioned investment objective. His recommendation to Ms. Modi was that investments be made only in equities. The reason being she already had enough exposure to debt instruments; so to get the overall asset allocation right, incremental monies needed to flow into equities. Fund Manager's view to utilize equities was also based on the fact that he had an adequate time frame to achieve the target, *i.e.*, 5 years. Equities as an asset class are best equipped to deliver over longer time frames. Finally, Ms. Modi's appetite for taking on risk also contributed to the decision of the Fund manager who found out that Ms. Modi could meet her objective by investing approximately ₹ 8,123 per month at 15.0% p.a.

The next step, which was very critical, was to educate Mr. Modi about what equity mutual funds were all about and how she could benefit by investing in the same. The Fund manager had chosen the mutual funds route (diversified equity funds in particular) over direct equity investing. The reason being investing directly in equities is akin to a full-time activity. The same would entail researching various stocks, tracking them closely and making changes in the portfolio, in line with changing market conditions.

Ms Modi's wedding corpus

Particulars		
Amount to be accumulated	₹	500,000
Tenure to meet the target	Yrs	5
Expected inflation	%	7.0
Future value of money to be accumulated	₹	701,276
Solution:		
Money to be accumulated...	₹	701,276
Assumed return (Post–tax)	%	15.0
Annual saving required	₹	104,010
Or simply, a monthly investment of	₹	8,123

A retail investor like Ms Modi had neither the time nor the competence to do so. Instead, by opting for the mutual fund route, she could access the equity markets and also benefit from the services of a qualified and competent fund manager. Our recommendation for Ms. Modi was to start off a systematic investment plan in a few diversified equity funds, which were selected based on a research process.

Conclusion

The striking feature of this case study was the degree of risk that the client was taking on, without being aware of the same. Her investments in assured return schemes (which on the surface seem like "safe" investments) meant that she was deprived of a proper asset allocation and ended up with a portfolio yielding sub–par returns.

Her *ad-hoc* investment style meant that she was not equipped to provide for any of the future needs/obligations. Clearly in Ms. Modi's case, playing safe was a rather risky proposition. This case only underscores the need for professional and expert advice while investing, lest one errs on the side of caution!

Finally, while it may appear very simple at the end, we recommend that investors who find themselves in a similar situation should not simply replicate Ms. Modi's plan. Rather they must discuss the situation with their financial planner and let him come up with a tailor-made investment solution.

Questions:

1. What is the investment portfolio of Ms. Modi, being a retail investor?
2. What is the striking feature of this case study?
3. What are the observations of Fund Manager about Ms. Modi's portfolio?
4. What was the problem with the current investment portfolio of Ms. Modi?
5. What are the recommendations of Fund manager to resolve the problem of investment portfolio of the client?
6. State the investment objectives of Ms. Modi and how the objective can be fulfilled by the Fund manager?
7. Does Fund manager's plan follow the 'risk-return trade off' principle, while Ms. Modi is a retail investor?
8. What is meant by 'tailor-made investment solution'?
9. Why the Fund manager had chosen the mutual funds route (diversified equity funds in particular) over direct equity investing.

Case 9 Re: Dividend policy FPL Group Inc

Why do firms pay dividend?

- Firms pay dividends to balance their asset and capital structures when their earnings outstrip their investment opportunities.
- Firms pay dividends to mitigate agency problems when they have excess earnings.

Cons of cash dividend payment

- A dividend policy is irrelevant or has no impact on the firm's value because investors have the ability to create "homemade" dividends.
- Little to no dividend payout is more favorable for investors. This is because taxation on a dividend is higher than tax on capital gains.
- Dividends are taxed as ordinary incomes
- Dividends can reduce internal source of financing
- Once established, dividends cuts are hard to make without adversely affecting a firm's stock price

Pros of cash dividend payment

- Cash dividends can underscore good results and provide support to stock price
- Dividends may attract institutional investors who preferred some returns from dividends
- Stock price usually increases with the announcement of a new or increased dividends
- Dividends absorb cash flow so they may help reduce agency problems

About FPL

FPL Group, Inc. is a holding company that provides electricity to 7.3 million people in Miami, southern Florida, and 14 other states through its subsidiaries Florida Power & Light and FPL Energy. Its oil, natural gas, and nuclear power plants provide energy for residential, industrial, and commercial customers. The company is also the largest wind power owner in the nation.

Major issues of FPL in 1994

- Negotiation between FPL and FERC (Federal Energy·Regulatory Commission) to settle the lawsuit against FPL for changing excessive rates and denying fair access to its transmission system;
- Lower investment rate due to the fact that FPL probably does not raise dividends;
- Suggestion of dividend cuts by FPL's managers;
- FPL's stock price has fallen by 19.6% while the S&P index has decreased by 22.1%;

- Rising interest rate and increasing competition in electric industry;

From investors' perspective, the current payout ratio is appropriate to some extent.

- FPL's current payout ratio = 0, Cash dividend/net income = 107.7%.
- For institutional investors who hold 36.9% of FPL's total common stocks, this payout ratio may be appropriate because they likely prefers high payout ratio in seeking for high earnings from their investment. If FPL tries to maintain this ratio, it can satisfy those small investors but it has to increase this ration over time to satisfy these investors' expectation.
- For individual investors who hold 51.9% of FPL's total common stocks, the payout ratio has little meaning because they can use homemade dividend strategy to obtain capital gains rather than receive cash dividends due to higher taxes imposed on dividends. Furthermore, they do not need dividends to convert shares to cash. FPL's decision to cut payout ration does not really affect the value of these individual investors.
- In expert's opinion, FPL currently maintains an inappropriate payout ratio. Given the situation that the new regulation will be soon implemented, FPL will face strong competition not only from Florida but also from all other possible states. FPL can not protect itself by restricting access to its transmission system since it was sued for doing so. To prepare for competition and sustainable growth in near future, the best way FPL can do is to use its excess cash to invest in new positive NPV projects. Therefore, FPL should not maintain the high pay-out ratio at 107.7%. Instead, it should lower this ratio to or below the average ratio of the industry (82.9%) since the dividend cut does not lower the firm's value.

Recommendations on FPL's stocks

- First, FPL should declare to cut dividends. The company should not worry about a lawsuit against its lower dividend policy as the dividend cut does not affect the majority of its investors (individual investors). Upon the announcement of dividend cut, the stock price can decrease so FPL should use its excess cash to buy back its stock to increase the stock price whenever it falls down.
- Then, FPL should use Buy and Hold strategy to repurchase its stocks and hold them regardless of market fluctuations. This solution as a long term investment can help FPL increase its stock price which has fallen in early 1994. By doing so, FPL can get rid of its excess cash of $150 million per year. FPL also can use this strategy to increase incentive compensation by granting stock options to employees and thus, increase employment commitment and recruiting attractiveness to have competent personnel for future growth.
- FPL should use its excess cash to invest more in new profitable projects, acquire new companies and profitable assets, and reinvest in financial assets.

Questions:

1. Why do firms pay dividend?
2. What are the advantages and disadvantages of paying cash dividends?
3. When does dividend policy become irrelevant in increasing the firm's value?
4. Illustrate the circumstances where a company can suggest for dividend cuts.
5. Why the payout ratio has little meaning to the individual investors, who hold more than 51% of FPL's total common stocks?
6. When institutional investors do prefer high payout ratio?
7. Why FPL should not maintain the high payout ratio at 107.7%?
8. When a company use Buy and Hold strategy to repurchase its stocks and hold them regardless of market fluctuations?
9. Illustrate the concept of 'granting stock options to employees'.

Case 10 Re: Capital Expenditure Decisions

A developing country is situated on the coast of Africa. Its government, now democratically elected, has produced a programme of economic reforms aimed at promoting investment in the country and reducing its dependence on foreign aid.

A major feature of this programme is the privatization of companies and corporations which are currently 100% owned by the government, *e.g.*, hotels, breweries and coffee production. For the time being, the government is not considering privatizing services such as post, railways or the provision of basic telecommunications (this is mainly the fixed-line, voice telephony service).

It does, however, wish to attract private capital to provide new services such as cellular (mobile) telephones and data communication.

Global Telecommunications Inc (GTI) is a company registered in the USA but with global business interests. Its shares are not listed on a stock exchange, but industry sources estimate that it could command a market capitalization of around US$ 200m. It has established itself as a specialist in the provision of mobile telephone (cellular) services. It is currently negotiating with the government of that developing country mentioned above for a license to provide such services in the country and has already spent US$ O.5m in surveys and miscellaneous expenses. If GTI were successful in the negotiations, it would be the company's first experience of working in a developing country.

Forecast cash flows

Based on a recent World Bank report, GTI estimates that there is a market for between 10,000 and 15,000 customers in a rectangular geographical area bounded by the capital city and three other main towns. The proposed cellular service will operate in this relatively prosperous 'urban rectangle' but the poorer, rural areas outside the rectangle will not be covered.

The market for 10,000 lines is, apart from potential disasters, virtually guaranteed. GTI estimates that the initial investment for this number of lines will be US$ 25m. The company has asked the Govt. of that country for a five-year exclusivity period (a period when no other company will be allowed to enter the market to compete). Net operating cash flows, based on a network of 10,000 lines, are forecast to be:

Year:	1	2	3	4	5
Net operating cash flows (US$ m):	3.5	4.8	5.6	6.8	7.2

In year 6, competitors are likely to enter the market and cash flows are expected to fall to around US$ 6m per annum. For the purposes of evaluation, GTI assumes this annual net cash flow will be maintained indefinitely from year 6 onwards on a network of 10,000 lines. The figures are, of course, an extreme simplification of what would be a complex appraisal.

Discount rate

There is some dispute about the discount rate to be used for the evaluation of this project. The company's cost of capital is 15% per annum constant, and this is the rate which is being suggested. However, the managing director thinks this is a particularly risky project. Although all calculations and negotiations with the Govt. of that country are in US$, much of the cash inflow will be in local currency. The technical director says that, as the project increases international diversification, it actually reduces the company's risk, so a lower rate should be used. The finance director notes that the cash flows for each year are highly correlated with those of the previous and subsequent years and this also will affect risk.

In theory, projects should be evaluated using a specific risk-adjusted discount rate which reflects the risk of that project. In order to determine a discount rate for a project we should use a 'proxy' company's beta and include this in the capital asset pricing model. In practice this is almost impossible to do, particularly in a developing country. Even if we assume that: (i) the government of that developing country has agreed to allow GTI to increase prices in line with depreciation of the local currency; (ii) it can be trusted not to prevent expropriation of profits and dividends; and (iii) GTI accepts there will be no political interference in its operations, three risks remain.

Risk 1: Demand is at the level forecast by the World Bank.

Risk 2: Installation of the network does not meet geographical problems which were not foreseen.

Risk 3: Civil disturbances.

The specific risk-adjusted discount rate is suggested as 20%.

Questions

1. Calculate Undiscounted and discounted pay-back period.
2. Calculate Net Present Value and offer necessary comments.
3. Caculate Internal Rate of Return.
4. Which one is superior among NPV and IRR while evaluating the project?
5. Why this project should be evaluated by a specific risk–adjusted discount rate?
6. What is the difference between the opinions of Managing Director, Finance Director and Technical Director?
7. What is the key to the acceptability of this project? Explain.

Hints:

Project cash flows 0, 1, 2, 3, 4, 5 (Year)

Initial investment 25.0

Net operating cash flows 3.5, 4.8, 5.6, 6.8, 7.2

Terminal value (6m/0.2) * 30.0

Discount factor (at 20%) 1, 0.83, 0.69, 0.58, 0.48, 0.40

Discounted cash flows – 25.0, 2.9, 3.3, 3.2, 3.3, 14.9

Cumulative DCFs – 25.0, –22.1, –18.8, –15.5, –12.2, 2.7

[*] The terminal value is calculated as perpetuity, *i.e.*, we assume year 5's cash flows will continue indefinitely and the discount rate of 20% also remains constant

This proposal suggests that the project is just about viable using a discount rate for 20%, the internal rate of return being around 23.5%. The undiscounted payback period is just under five years. It is not possible to work out the discounted payback period without doing calculations on cash flows beyond year 6. This has not been provided at this stage. However, if this proposal is unacceptable to the Govt. of that developing country it can only be used as a benchmark against which alternative options may be compared.

The key to the acceptability of the project is GTI's attitude to risk. Telecommunications is a high-technology industry and accustomed to certain levels of risk, but developing a new network in a developing country, and in a country, in which the company has no previous knowledge, is compounding the risk factors. As noted earlier, the main risks may be summarized as follows:

Currency risk: Unless GTI has built into its license a Tight to increase tariffs when the currency of Govt. depreciates.

Political risk: That the government will honour its agreement in the license and will allow the company to remit profits and dividends as promised.

Case 11 Re: Merger and Acquisition — Planning

Few organizations have expertise integrating business after mergers and acquisitions activity, yet business success is dependent upon successful integration of its People, Process, Technology and a well planned M&A strategy. Without a well thought and effectively managed plan, the merger or acquisition risks an incomplete integration, business frustration, loss of critical staff, higher costs and an unnecessary complex environment. Successful integration starts before the merger or acquisition. Due diligence must be used to develop an integration strategy, plan and team that will give confidence to all stakeholders. Identifying key decisions around which applications, infrastructure and IT processes can go forward and key actions to create the new organization after the merger or acquisition is also a necessity. Global merger and acquisitions in the insurance sector has reached all time record of 148.7 billion dollars in 2008, up 34 per cent from the previous year. Strategic activity accounted for 97 per cent of total activity in the industry, as compared to 83 per cent in 2007. Insurance companies in the United States made the maximum number of acquisitions. US–based insurers made acquisitions worth $71.6 billion, up by 102 per cent from the deals in 2007. Deals worth over $10 billion each accounted for nearly 36 per cent of 2008 volume, which stood $53.4 billion, up from just 10 per cent in 2007 whereas deals in the range of $1 billion to $5 billion range made up 25 per cent of the total with an announced value of $36.7 billion.

About Cognizant

Cognizant (NASDAQ: CTSH) is a leading provider of information technology, consulting and business process outsourcing services. Cognizant's single-minded passion is to dedicate our global technology and innovation know-how, our industry expertise and worldwide resources to working together with clients to make their businesses stronger. A member of the NASDAQ–100 Index and S&P 500 Index, Cognizant is a Forbes Global 2000 company and a member of the Fortune 1000 and is ranked among the top information technology companies in Business Week's Hot Growth and Top 50 Performers listings.

Key Challenges in Mergers & Acquisitions

The post-merger integration phase covers the operational part of any merger project. Often this phase determines if the merger becomes a success or failure. The four key aspects of any business organization are typically Strategy, People, Process and Technology. Many of the critical success factors of the post-merger integration is "soft" factors, which involve people and their interactions with technology and process. Value is created by focus and adherence to strategy.

Therefore, Cognizant feels it is necessary to focus attention on issues such as:

a. Development of a new management structure for the new, larger organization; especially overcoming leadership problems in very large units

b. Bringing together formerly separate units from both former organizations

c. Allocation of clear roles and responsibilities in the emergent merged entity

d. Communication of the new strategic objectives and the new vision of the merged organization

e. Implementation of a new shared corporate culture and management culture

f. Integration of the multiple IT organizations

g. Reduction in redundancy and duplication of IT systems

h. Harmonization of management compensation and management incentive systems

i. Overcoming of language barriers and country specific cultural differences

j. Overcoming of staff's suspiciousness of the other organization

k. Knowledge transfer among units that are to be integrated

l. Maintenance of customer and intermediary relationships during integration

m. Employees who fear being earmarked redundant

n. Impact on the existing corporate culture

Pre-merger Planning

a. Undertake Due diligence and Assessment of integration effort

b. Finalize the Insurance portfolio for re-alignment based on the list from 'Target Assessment' phase

c. Identify possible change in company rating and anticipate the rating agency reaction

d. Structure the deal to best monetize the assets

e. Plan for Day One and conduct internal dry runs

Planning for M&A

a. Pair IT and business across merged entity to form cross functional teams to develop detailed area wise integration plan and prepare for joint IT governance

b. Conduct joint dry runs and perfect execution plans

c. Enable communication to all stakeholders

d. Provide BAU services (Helpdesks, Production support, System availability, Scalability, etc)

e. Implement execution plans and programs covering functional areas, applications, data and infrastructure elements

f. Enable fulfillment of regulatory and legal requirements

g. Complete Phase 1 of consolidation of book of business, migration of data and customers, product rationalization, infrastructure consolidation

h. Enable cross-selling and up-selling

i. Refine and detail IT governance plans

j. Fine tune the execution plans

Execution

Effective senior management team for execution

a. Common Vision and Strategy Workshops

b. Experiential Learning Workshops

c. Creating effective governance groups

New culture supporting new enterprise strategy

a. Planning Participation

b. Team Launch Workshops

c. Coaching

d. Interactive simulations

Cognizant's IT Integration Approach during M&A

Cognizant's roadmap to support clients during Merger and Acquisition transaction has structured mile stones and processes to continuously raise the bar in order to execute effectively.

Target Assessment

a. Identify and assess sources of synergy (cost and revenue), costs for synergy extraction and accrual of long term benefits

b. Analyze the existing system architecture to decide if it is ready to accommodate the systems of the target organization. In an insurance industry merger, this would also include analysis of the fitment of various products in the portfolio of the merging companies

c. Assess existing staff skills and carry out adequate resource planning, a product realignment exercise might also be carried out

d. At the end of this phase, the IT organization articulates the principles that would guide the integration decisions, system integration strategy and approximate timelines for achieving each milestone of integration

Meet integration and business operation goals

a. Implement the new organization design & IT governance plans

b. Execute HR policies, procedures and processes that support the Guiding Principles

c. Implement business processes that match customer, cost, quality and employee satisfaction goals

d. Complete phase 2 of consolidation of book of business, product rationalization, application ,integration and rationalization, Infrastructure consolidation

Deliver on Targets

a. Implement the post 'Execution phase' plans

b. Complete Phase 3 of Application integration and rationalization, and Infrastructure consolidation

c. Enable automatic consolidation of Book of Business based on Straight–Through–Processing

d. Comprehensively implement IT Governance plans

Questions:

1. 'Successful integration starts before the merger or acquisition' – Explain.
2. 'Due diligence must be used to develop an integration strategy, plan and team that will give confidence to all stakeholders' – Explain how due diligence can be used.
3. How global merger and acquisitions in the insurance sector has reached all time record in 2008?
4. What are the critical success factors of the post-merger integration of Cognizant?
5. Explain Cognizant's IT Integration Approach during M&A.
6. Illustrate the pre-merger planning of Cognizant.
7. How senior management team is involved for execution of M&A?
8. Illustrate the concept of 'Due diligence'.

Case 12 Re: Current Investment Banking scenario in India

Unlike Goldman Sachs, Merrill Lynch and Morgan Stanley, Citigroup and JPMorgan do not have joint ventures with local partners in India's booming investment banking market. But they have climbed to the top of league tables for mergers and acquisitions as well as stock deals on the back of strong corporate ties.

"The strength of the Citigroup platform is the 1,000 plus corporate relationships in India that we have," said Pramit Jhaveri, head of investment banking in India for Citigroup.

Both groups are competing intensely for investment banking fees that are expected to grow by up to 40 per cent this year, fueled by an economy growing at about 7 per cent and foreign institutions flocking to invest.

After a relatively late launch of investment banking in India since 2000, Citigroup has grown to be the top M&A adviser for the last two years. JPMorgan, meanwhile, jumped to third in 2004 after not even reaching the top 10 in 2003.

The story is similar for securities underwriting. Citigroup has become the world's largest securities underwriter, with JPMorgan and Switzerland's UBS using their own relationships to build business.

To be sure, Goldman, Merrill and Morgan Stanley remain strong in India. They were the top three underwriters of stock offerings last year as equity issuance rose to $9.95 billion from $1.90 billion, according to data firm Dealogic.

One key advantage of their joint venture structure is retail distribution.

Morgan Stanley has teamed up with JM Financial Group, Goldman is aligned with Kotak Mahindra Bank Ltd. and Merrill works with DSP Financial Consultants Ltd.

"A year ago, the conventional wisdom in our industry was if a company wanted to raise $200 million, they had to leave the country," said Rajeev Gupta, joint managing director for DSP Merrill. "The threshold for going overseas today is $2 billion, not $200 million."

The local network enjoyed by the joint ventures becomes more important as the domestic market gets bigger.

"We can give (companies) a choice of which market fits their needs," said Gupta. "They know you are not giving them a recommendation linked to their limitations."

But the stand–alone banks are gaining momentum with deliberate expansions. In the 1990s, JPMorgan ended a joint venture with ICICI Bank Ltd. in 1998 and set out on its own, taking many of the venture's bankers with it.

By beefing up its investment banking staff, the bank has been able to win high-profile deals such as the $1.17 billion IPO of Tata Consultancy Services Ltd.

"Basically the (India) story's a great one, and it's getting better," said JPMorgan senior country officer Dominic Price. "You can't ignore 7 per cent plus growth."

Investment bankers identify joint venture partners, define acquisition strategy, structure and enter into joint venture agreements and successfully execute mergers and acquisitions (M&A). They also help to raise private equity capital.

The major work of investment banks includes a lot of consulting. For instance, they offer advices on mergers and acquisitions to companies. The other arena where they give advice are tracking the market and determining when should a company come out with a public offering and what is the best possible way to manage the public assets of businesses. The role that an investment bank plays sometimes gets overlapped with that of a private brokerage house. The usual advice of buying and selling is also given by investment banks.

There is no demarcating line between the investment banking and other forms of banking in India. This has been observed majorly of late. All banks nowadays want to provide their customers the best of services and create a niche for themselves and that is why apart from investment banks, all other banks too are aiming at making it big.

At the macro level, investment banking is related with the primary function of assisting the capital market in its function of capital intermediation, *i.e.*, the movement of financial resources from those who have them (the investors), to those who need to make use of them for producing GDP (the issuers). Over the decades, investment banks have always suited the needs of the finance community and thus become one of the most vibrant and exciting segment of financial services.

Questions:

1. Explain the concept of 'Investment Banking'.
2. State the scenario of Investment Banking in India.
3. Explain the reasons for growth of Investment Banking in India.
4. Explain the roles of Investment Banks at the macro level.
5. 'Investment bankers identify joint venture partners' Explain with examples.

❑❑❑

A Appendix A — Tables

I. FUTURE VALUE INTEREST FACTOR (FVIF)

Period, n	1%	2%	3%	4%	5%	6%	7%	8%	9%	10%	11%	12%	13%	14%
1	1.010	1.020	1.030	1.040	1.050	1.060	1.070	1.080	1.090	1.100	1.110	1.120	1.130	1.140
2	1.020	1.040	1.061	1.082	1.102	1.124	1.145	1.166	1.188	1.210	1.232	1.245	1.277	1.300
3	1.030	1.061	1.093	1.125	1.158	1.191	1.225	1.260	1.295	1.331	1.368	1.405	1.443	1.482
4	1.041	1.082	1.126	1.170	1.216	1.262	1.311	1.360	1.412	1.464	1.518	1.574	1.630	1.689
5	1.051	1.104	1.159	1.217	1.276	1.338	1.403	1.469	1.539	1.611	1.685	1.762	1.842	1.925
6	1.062	1.126	1.194	1.265	1.340	1.419	1.501	1.587	1.677	1.772	1.870	1.974	2.082	2.195
7	1.072	1.149	1.230	1.316	1.407	1.504	1.606	1.714	1.828	1.949	2.076	2.211	2.353	2.502
8	1.083	1.172	1.267	1.369	1.477	1.594	1.718	1.851	1.993	2.144	2.305	2.476	2.658	2.853
9	1.094	1.195	1.305	1.423	1.551	1.689	1.838	1.999	2.172	2.358	2.558	2.773	3.004	3.252
10	1.105	1.219	1.344	1.480	1.629	1.791	1.967	2.159	2.367	2.594	2.839	3.106	3.395	3.707
11	1.116	1.243	1.384	1.539	1.710	1.898	2.105	2.332	2.580	2.853	3.152	3.479	3.836	4.226
12	1.127	1.268	1.426	1.601	1.796	2.012	2.252	2.518	2.813	3.138	3.498	3.896	4.335	4.818
13	1.138	1.294	1.469	1.665	1.886	2.133	2.410	2.720	3.066	3.452	3.883	4.363	4.898	5.492
14	1.149	1.319	1.513	1.732	1.980	2.261	2.579	2.937	3.342	3.797	4.310	4.887	5.535	6.261
15	1.161	1.346	1.558	1.801	2.079	2.397	2.759	3.172	3.642	4.177	4.785	5.474	6.254	7.138
16	1.173	1.373	1.605	1.873	2.183	2.540	2.952	3.426	3.970	4.595	5.311	6.130	7.067	8.137
17	1.184	1.400	1.653	1.948	2.292	2.693	3.159	3.700	4.328	5.054	5.895	6.866	7.986	9.276
18	1.196	1.428	1.702	2.026	2.407	2.854	3.380	3.996	4.717	5.560	6.544	7.690	9.024	10.575
19	1.208	1.457	1.754	2.107	2.527	3.026	3.617	4.316	5.142	6.116	7.263	8.613	10.197	12.056
20	1.220	1.486	1.806	2.191	2.653	3.207	3.870	4.661	5.604	6.728	8.062	9.646	11.523	13.743
24	1.270	1.608	2.033	2.563	3.225	4.049	5.072	6.341	7.911	9.850	12.239	15.179	18.790	23.212
25	1.282	1.641	2.094	2.666	3.386	4.292	5.427	6.848	8.623	10.835	13.585	17.000	21.231	26.462
30	1.348	1.811	2.427	3.243	4.322	5.743	7.612	10.063	13.268	17.449	22.892	29.960	39.116	50.950
40	1.489	2.208	3.262	4.801	7.040	10.286	14.974	21.725	31.409	45.259	65.001	93.051	132.782	188.884

II. PRESENT VALUE INTEREST FACTOR (PVIF)

Period, *n*	1%	2%	3%	4%	5%	6%	7%	8%	9%	10%	11%	12%	13%	14%
1	0.990	0.980	0.971	0.962	0.952	0.943	0.935	0.926	0.917	0.909	0.901	0.893	0.885	0.877
2	0.980	0.961	0.943	0.925	0.907	0.890	0.873	0.857	0.842	0.826	0.812	0.797	0.783	0.769
3	0.971	0.942	0.915	0.889	0.864	0.840	0.816	0.794	0.772	0.751	0.731	0.712	0.693	0.675
4	0.961	0.924	0.889	0.855	0.823	0.792	0.763	0.735	0.708	0.683	0.659	0.636	0.613	0.592
5	0.951	0.906	0.863	0.822	0.784	0.747	0.713	0.681	0.650	0.621	0.593	0.567	0.543	0.519
6	0.942	0.888	0.838	0.790	0.746	0.705	0.666	0.630	0.596	0.564	0.535	0.507	0.480	0.456
7	0.933	0.871	0.813	0.760	0.711	0.665	0.623	0.583	0.547	0.513	0.482	0.452	0.425	0.400
8	0.923	0.853	0.789	0.731	0.677	0.627	0.582	0.540	0.502	0.467	0.434	0.404	0.376	0.351
9	0.914	0.837	0.766	0.703	0.645	0.592	0.544	0.500	0.460	0.424	0.391	0.361	0.333	0.308
10	0.905	0.820	0.744	0.676	0.614	0.558	0.508	0.463	0.422	0.386	0.352	0.322	0.295	0.270
11	0.896	0.804	0.722	0.650	0.585	0.527	0.475	0.429	0.388	0.350	0.317	0.287	0.261	0.237
12	0.887	0.788	0.701	0.625	0.557	0.497	0.444	0.397	0.356	0.319	0.286	0.257	0.231	0.208
13	0.879	0.773	0.681	0.601	0.530	0.469	0.415	0.368	0.326	0.290	0.258	0.229	0.204	0.182
14	0.870	0.758	0.661	0.577	0.505	0.442	0.388	0.340	0.299	0.263	0.232	0.205	0.181	0.160
15	0.861	0.743	0.642	0.555	0.481	0.417	0.362	0.315	0.275	0.239	0.209	0.183	0.160	0.140
16	0.853	0.728	0.623	0.534	0.458	0.394	0.339	0.292	0.252	0.218	0.188	0.163	0.141	0.123
17	0.844	0.714	0.605	0.513	0.436	0.371	0.317	0.270	0.231	0.198	0.170	0.146	0.125	0.108
18	0.836	0.700	0.587	0.494	0.416	0.350	0.296	0.250	0.212	0.180	0.153	0.130	0.111	0.095
19	0.828	0.686	0.570	0.475	0.396	0.331	0.276	0.232	0.194	0.164	0.138	0.116	0.098	0.083
20	0.820	0.673	0.554	0.456	0.377	0.312	0.258	0.215	0.178	0.149	0.124	0.104	0.087	0.073
24	0.788	0.622	0.492	0.390	0.310	0.247	0.197	0.158	0.126	0.102	0.082	0.066	0.053	0.043
25	0.780	0.610	0.478	0.375	0.295	0.233	0.184	0.146	0.116	0.092	0.074	0.059	0.047	0.038
30	0.742	0.552	0.412	0.308	0.231	0.174	0.131	0.099	0.075	0.057	0.044	0.033	0.026	0.020
40	0.672	0.453	0.307	0.208	0.142	0.097	0.067	0.046	0.032	0.022	0.015	0.011	0.008	0.005

III. FUTURE VALUE OF AN ANNUITY INTEREST FACTOR (FVIFA)

Period, n	1%	2%	3%	4%	5%	6%	7%	8%	9%	10%	11%	12%	13%	14%
1	1.000	1.000	1.000	1.000	1.000	1.000	1.000	1.000	1.000	1.000	1.000	1.000	1.000	1.000
2	2.010	2.020	2.030	2.040	2.050	2.060	2.070	2.080	2.090	2.100	2.110	2.120	2.130	2.140
3	3.030	3.060	3.091	3.122	3.152	3.184	3.215	3.246	3.278	3.310	3.342	3.374	3.407	3.440
4	4.060	4.122	4.184	4.246	4.310	4.375	4.440	4.506	4.573	4.641	4.710	4.779	4.850	4.921
5	5.101	5.204	5.309	5.416	5.526	5.637	5.751	5.867	5.985	6.105	6.228	6.353	6.480	6.610
6	6.152	6.308	6.468	6.633	6.802	6.975	7.153	7.336	7.523	7.716	7.913	8.115	8.323	8.536
7	7.214	7.434	7.662	7.898	8.142	8.394	8.654	8.923	9.200	9.487	9.783	10.089	10.405	10.730
8	8.286	8.583	8.892	9.214	9.549	9.897	10.260	10.637	11.028	11.436	11.859	12.300	12.757	13.233
9	9.369	9.755	10.159	10.583	11.027	11.491	11.978	12.488	13.021	13.579	14.164	14.776	15.416	16.085
10	10.462	10.950	11.464	12.006	12.578	13.181	13.816	14.487	15.193	15.973	16.722	17.549	18.420	19.337
11	11.567	12.169	12.808	13.486	14.207	14.972	15.784	16.645	17.560	18.531	19.561	20.655	21.814	23.044
12	12.683	13.412	14.192	15.026	15.917	16.870	17.888	18.977	20.141	21.384	22.713	24.133	25.650	27.271
13	13.809	14.680	15.618	16.627	17.713	18.882	20.141	21.495	22.953	24.523	26.212	28.029	29.985	32.089
14	14.947	15.974	17.086	18.292	19.599	21.051	22.550	24.215	26.019	27.975	30.095	32.393	34.883	37.581
15	16.097	17.293	18.599	20.024	21.579	23.276	25.129	27.152	29.361	31.772	34.405	37.280	40.417	43.842
16	17.258	18.639	20.157	21.825	23.657	25.673	27.880	30.324	33.003	35.950	39.190	42.753	46.672	50.980
17	18.430	20.012	21.762	23.698	25.840	28.213	30.840	33.750	36.974	40.545	44.501	48.884	53.739	59.118
18	19.615	21.412	23.414	25.645	28.132	30.906	33.999	37.450	41.301	45.599	50.396	55.750	61.725	68.394
19	20.811	22.841	25.117	27.671	30.539	33.760	37.739	41.446	46.018	51.159	56.939	63.440	70.749	78.969
20	22.019	24.297	26.870	29.778	33.066	36.786	40.995	45.762	51.160	57.275	64.203	72.052	80.947	91.025
24	26.973	30.422	34.426	39.083	44.502	50.816	58.177	66.765	76.790	88.497	102.174	118.155	136.831	158.659
25	28.243	32.030	36.450	41.646	47.727	54.865	63.249	73.106	84.701	98.347	114.413	133.334	155.620	181.871
30	34.785	40.568	47.575	56.085	66.439	79.058	94.461	113.283	136.308	164.494	199.021	241.333	293.199	356.787
40	48.886	60.402	75.401	95.026	120.080	154.762	199.635	259.057	337.882	442.593	581.826	767.091	#####	#####

IV. PRESENT VALUE OF AN ANNUITY INTEREST FACTOR (PVIFA)

Period, n	1%	2%	3%	4%	5%	6%	7%	8%	9%	10%	11%	12%	13%	14%
1	0.990	0.980	0.971	0.962	0.952	0.943	0.935	0.926	0.917	0.909	0.901	0.893	0.885	0.877
2	1.970	1.942	1.913	1.886	1.859	1.833	1.808	1.783	1.759	1.736	1.713	1.690	1.668	1.647
3	2.941	2.884	2.829	2.775	2.723	2.673	2.624	2.577	2.531	2.487	2.444	2.402	2.361	2.322
4	3.902	3.808	3.717	3.630	3.546	3.465	3.387	3.312	3.240	3.170	3.102	3.037	2.974	2.914
5	4.853	4.713	4.580	4.452	4.329	4.212	4.100	3.993	3.890	3.791	3.696	3.605	3.517	3.433
6	5.795	5.601	5.417	5.242	5.076	4.917	4.766	4.623	4.486	4.355	4.231	4.111	3.998	3.889
7	6.728	6.472	6.230	6.002	5.786	5.582	5.389	5.206	5.033	4.868	4.712	4.564	4.423	4.288
8	7.652	7.325	7.020	6.733	6.463	6.210	5.971	5.747	5.535	5.335	5.146	4.968	4.799	4.639
9	8.566	8.162	7.786	7.435	7.108	6.802	6.515	6.247	5.995	5.759	5.537	5.328	5.132	4.946
10	9.471	8.983	8.530	8.111	7.722	7.360	7.024	6.710	6.418	6.145	5.889	5.650	5.426	5.216
11	10.368	9.787	9.253	8.760	8.306	7.887	7.499	7.139	6.805	6.495	6.207	5.938	5.687	5.453
12	11.255	10.575	9.954	9.385	8.863	8.384	7.943	7.536	7.161	6.814	6.492	6.194	5.918	5.660
13	12.134	11.348	10.635	9.986	9.394	8.853	8.358	7.904	7.487	7.103	6.750	6.424	6.122	5.842
14	13.004	12.106	11.296	10.563	9.899	9.295	8.745	8.244	7.786	7.367	6.982	6.628	6.302	6.002
15	13.865	12.849	11.938	11.118	10.380	9.712	9.108	8.559	8.061	7.606	7.191	6.811	6.462	6.142
16	14.718	13.578	12.561	11.652	10.838	10.106	9.447	8.851	8.312	7.824	7.379	6.974	6.604	6.265
17	15.562	14.292	13.166	12.166	11.274	10.477	9.763	9.122	8.544	8.022	7.549	7.120	6.729	6.373
18	16.398	14.992	13.754	12.659	11.690	10.828	10.059	9.372	8.756	8.201	7.702	7.250	6.840	6.467
19	17.226	15.678	14.324	13.134	12.085	11.158	10.336	9.604	8.950	8.365	7.839	7.366	6.938	6.550
20	18.046	16.351	14.877	13.590	12.462	11.470	10.594	9.818	9.128	8.514	7.963	7.469	7.025	6.623
24	21.243	18.914	16.936	15.247	13.799	12.550	11.469	10.529	9.707	8.985	8.348	7.784	7.283	6.835
25	22.023	19.523	17.413	15.622	14.094	12.783	11.654	10.675	9.823	9.077	8.422	7.843	7.330	6.873
30	25.808	22.397	19.600	17.292	15.373	13.765	12.409	11.258	10.274	9.427	8.694	8.055	7.496	7.003
40	32.835	27.355	23.115	19.793	17.159	15.046	13.332	11.925	10.757	9.779	8.951	8.244	7.634	7.105

Appendix B — Glossary of Financial Terms

Accrued interest – The interest due on a bond since the last interest payment was made. The buyer of the bond pays the market price plus accrued interest.

Acquisition – The acquiring of control of one corporation by another. In "unfriendly" takeover attempts, the potential buying company may offer a price well above current market values, new securities and other inducements to stockholders. The management of the said company might ask for a better price or try to join up with a third company.

American Depositary Receipt (ADR) – A security issued by a U.S. bank in place of the foreign shares held in trust by that bank, thereby facilitating the trading of foreign shares in U.S. markets.

Amortization – Accounting for expenses or charges as applicable rather than as paid.

It includes such practices as depreciation, depletion, write-off of intangibles, prepaid expenses and deferred charges.

Annual report – The formal financial statements issued yearly by a corporation. The annual report shows assets, liabilities, revenues, expenses and earnings — how the company stood at the close of the business year, how it fared profit-wise during the year, as well as other information of interest to shareowners.

Arbitrage – A technique employed to take advantage of differences in price. If, for example, ABC stock can be bought in New York for $10 a share and sold in London at $10.50, an arbitrageur may simultaneously purchase ABC stock here and sell the same amount in London, making a profit of $.50 a share, less expenses. Arbitrage may also involve the purchase of rights to subscribe to a security, or the purchase of a convertible security – and the sale at or about the same time of the security obtainable through exercise of the rights or of the security obtainable through conversion.

Assets – Everything a corporation owns or that is due to it: cash, investments, money due it, materials and inventories, which are called current assets; buildings and machinery, which are known as fixed assets; and patents and goodwill, called intangible fixed assets.

Balance sheet – A condensed financial statement showing the nature and amount of a company's assets, liabilities and capital on a given date. In amounts, the balance sheet shows what the company owned, what it owed and the ownership interest in the company of its stockholders.

Bear -- Someone who believes the market will decline.

Bear market – A declining market, is called Bear market.

Bearer bond – A bond that does not have the owner's name registered on the books of the issuer. Interest and principal, when due, are payable to the holder.

Bid and Asked – Often referred to as a quotation or quote. The bid is the highest price anyone wants to pay for a security at a given time, the asked is the lowest price anyone will take at the same time.

Block – A large holding or transaction of stock – popularly considered to be 10,000 shares or more.

Blue chip – A company known nationally for the quality and wide acceptance of its products or services, and for its ability to make money and pay dividends.

Bond – A bond is evidence of a debt on which the issuing company usually promises to pay the bondholders a specified amount of interest for a specified length of time, and to repay the loan on the expiration date. In every case a bond represents debt - its holder is a creditor of the corporation and not a part owner, as is the shareholder.

Book value – An accounting term. Book value of a stock is determined from a company's records, by adding all assets then deducting all debts and other liabilities, plus the liquidation price of any preferred issues. The sum arrived at is divided by the number of common shares outstanding and the result is book value per common share. Book value of the assets of a company or a security may have little relationship to market value.

Broker – An agent who handles the public's orders to buy and sell securities, commodities or other property. A commission is charged for this service.

Bull – One who believes the market will rise.

Bull market – An advancing market, is called Bull market.

Buy side – The portion of the securities business in which institutional orders originate.

Callable – A bond issue, all or part of which may be redeemed by the issuing corporation under specified conditions before maturity. The term also applies to preferred shares that may be redeemed by the issuing corporation.

Capital gain or capital loss – Profit or loss from the sale of a capital asset.

Capital stock – All shares representing ownership of a business, including preferred and common.

Capitalization – Total amount of the various securities issued by a corporation. Capitalization may include bonds, debentures, preferred and common stock, and surplus. Bonds and debentures are usually carried on the books of the issuing company in terms of their par or face value. Preferred and common shares may be carried in terms of par or stated value. Stated value may be an arbitrary figure decided upon by the director or may represent the amount received by the company from the sale of the securities at the time of issuance.

Cash flow – Reported net income of a corporation plus amounts charged off for depreciation, depletion, amortization, and extraordinary charges to reserves, which are bookkeeping deductions and not paid out in rupees.

Certificate of deposit (CD) – A money market instrument characterized by its set date of maturity and interest rate. There are two basic types of CDs: traditional and negotiable. Traditional bank CDs typically incur an early-withdrawal penalty, while negotiable CDs have secondary market liquidity with investors receiving more or less than the original amount depending on market conditions.

Collateral – Securities or other property pledged by a borrower to secure repayment of a loan.

Commission – The broker's basic fee for purchasing or selling securities or property as an agent.

Commission broker – An agent who executes the public's orders for the purchase or sale of securities or commodities.

Common stock – Securities that represent an ownership interest in a corporation. If the company has also issued preferred stock; both common and preferred have ownership rights. Common stockholders assume the greater risk, but generally exercise the greater control and may gain the greater award in the form of dividends and capital appreciation. The terms common stock and capital stock are often used interchangeably when the company has no preferred stock.

Consolidated balance sheet – A balance sheet showing the financial condition of a corporation and its subsidiaries.

Convertible – A bond, debenture or preferred share that may be exchanged by the owner for common stock or another security, usually of the same company, in accordance with the terms of the issue.

Coupon bond – Bond with interest coupons attached. The coupons are clipped as they come due and presented by the holder for payment of interest.

Current assets – Those assets of a company that are reasonably expected to be realized in cash, sold or consumed during one year. These include cash, receivables and money due usually within one year, as well as inventories.

Current liabilities – Money owed and payable by a company, usually within one year. Example: Creditors.

Dealer – An individual or firm in the securities business who buys and sells stocks and bonds as a principal rather than as an agent. The dealer's profit or loss is the difference between the price paid and the price received for the same security. The dealer's confirmation must disclose to the customer that the principal has been acted upon. The same individual or firm may function, at different times, either as a broker or dealer.

Debenture – A promissory note backed by the general credit of a company and usually not secured by a mortgage or lien on any specific property.

Debit balance – In a customer's margin account, that portion of the purchase price of stock, bonds or commodities that is covered by credit extended by the broker to the margin customer.

Delayed opening – The postponement of trading of an issue on a stock exchange beyond the normal opening of a day's trading because of market conditions that have been judged by exchange officials to warrant such a delay. Reasons for the delay might be an influx of either buy or sell orders, an imbalance of buyers and sellers, or pending corporate news that requires time for dissemination.

Depletion accounting – Natural resources, such as metals, oil, gas and timber, that conceivably can be reduced to zero over the years, present a special problem in capital management. Depletion is an accounting practice consisting of charges against earnings based upon the amount of the asset taken out of the total reserves in the period for which accounting is made. It does not represent any cash outlay nor are any funds earmarked for the purpose.

Depreciation – Normally, charges against earnings to write off the cost less salvage value, of an asset over its estimated useful life. It is a bookkeeping entry and does not represent any cash outlay nor are any funds earmarked for the purpose.

Discount – The amount by which a preferred stock or bond may sell below its par value. Also used as a verb to mean "takes into account" as the price of the stock has discounted the expected dividend cut.

Diversification – Spreading investments among different types of securities and various companies in different fields.

Dividend – The payment designated by the board of directors to be distributed pro rata among the shares outstanding. On preferred shares, it is generally a fixed amount. On common shares, the dividend varies with the fortunes of the company and the amount of cash on hand, and may be omitted if business is poor or the directors determine to withhold earnings to invest in plant and equipment. Sometimes a company will pay a dividend out of past earnings even if it is not currently operating at a profit. Basically dividend is that portion of profit available to shareholders which is distributed.

Dollar-cost-averaging – A system of buying securities at regular intervals with a fixed dollar amount. Under this system investors buy by the dollars' worth rather than by the number of shares. If each investment is of the same number of dollars, payments buy more shares when the price is low and fewer when it rises. Thus temporary downswings in price benefit investors if they continue periodic purchases in both good and bad times, and the price at which the shares are sold is more than their average cost. Dollar-cost-averaging does not assure a profit and does not protect against loss in declining markets. Since dollar-cost averaging involves continuous investment in securities regardless of fluctuating price levels of such securities, investors should consider their financial ability to continue purchases through periods of low price levels.

Dow theory – A theory of market analysis based upon the performance of the Dow Jones Industrial Average and transportation stock price averages. The theory says that the market is in a basic upward trend if one of these averages advances above a previous important high, accompanied or followed by a similar advance in the other. When both averages dip below previous important lows, this is regarded as confirmation of a downward trend. The Dow Jones is one type of market index.

Earnings report – A statement, also called an income statement, issued by a company showing its earnings or losses over a given period. The earnings report lists the income earned, expenses and the net result.

Equity – The ownership interest of common and preferred stockholders in a company. It also refers to excess of value of securities over the debit balance in a margin account.

Ex-dividend – A synonym for "without dividend." The buyer of a stock selling ex-dividend does not receive the recently declared dividend. When stocks go ex-dividend, the stock tables include the symbol "x" following the name.

Ex-rights – Without the rights. Corporations raising additional money may do so by offering their stockholders the right to subscribe to new or additional stock, usually at a discount from the prevailing market price. The buyer of a stock selling ex-right is not entitled to the rights.

Face value – The value of a bond that appears on the face of the bond, unless the value is otherwise specified by the issuing company. Face value is ordinarily the amount the issuing company promises to pay at maturity. Face value is not an indication of market value. Sometimes it is referred to as par value, when shares are issued neither at a premium, nor at a discounts.

Fixed charges – A company's fixed expenses, such as bond interest, which it has agreed to pay whether or not earned, and which are deducted from income before earnings on equity capital are computed.

Floor – The huge trading area - about the size of a trading field - where stocks, bonds and options are bought and sold on the Stock Exchanges.

Floor broker – A member of the stock exchange who executes orders on the floor of the Exchange to buy or sell any listed securities.

Free and open market – A market in which supply and demand are freely expressed in terms of price. Contrasts with a controlled market in which supply, demand and price may all be regulated.

Funded debt – Usually interest-bearing bonds or debentures of a company. Could include long-term bank loans. Does not include short-term loans, preferred or common stock.

Gilt-edged – High-grade bond issued by a company that has demonstrated its ability to earn a comfortable profit over a period of years and pay its bondholders their interest without interruption.

Growth stock – Stock of a company with a record of growth in earnings at a relatively rapid rate.

Holding company – A corporation that owns the securities of another, in cases with minimum 51% voting control.

Hypothecation – The pledging of securities as collateral - for example, to secure the debit balance in a margin account.

Income bond – Generally income bonds promise to repay principal but to pay interest only when earned. In some cases unpaid interest on an income bond may accumulate as a claim against the corporation when the bond becomes due. An income bond may also be issued in lieu of preferred stock.

Index – A statistical yardstick expressed in terms of percentages of a base year or years. An index is not an average. Example: BSE Index, Cost of Lividing Index.

Institutional investor – An organization whose primary purpose is to invest its own assets or financial resources or those held in trust by it for others. Includes pension funds, investment companies, insurance companies, universities and banks.

Investment – The use of money for the purpose of making more money, to gain income, increase capital, or both.

Investment banker – Also known as an underwriter. The middleman between the corporation issuing new securities and the public. The usual practice is for one or more investment bankers to buy outright from a corporation a new issue of stocks or bonds. The group forms a syndicate to sell the securities to individuals and institutions. Investment bankers also distribute very large blocks of stocks or bonds - perhaps held by an estate.

Liabilities – All the claims against a corporation. Liabilities include accounts, wages and salaries payable; dividends declared payable; accrued taxes payable; and fixed or long-term liabilities, such as mortgage bonds, debentures and bank loans.

Liquidation – The process of converting securities or other property into cash. The dissolution of a company, with cash remaining after sale of its assets and payment of all indebtedness being distributed to the shareholders.

Liquidity – The ability of the market in a particular security to absorb a reasonable amount of buying or selling at reasonable price changes. Liquidity is one of the most important characteristics of a good market. In another sense it means ability of a firm to pay short-term obligation within a year.

Listed stock – The stock of a company that is traded on a securities exchange (NSE, BSE).

Load – The portion of the offering price of shares of open-end investment companies in excess of the value of the underlying assets. Covers sales commissions and all other costs of distribution. The load is usually incurred only on purchase, there being, in most cases, no charge when the shares are sold (redeemed).

Yield to maturity – The yield of a bond to maturity takes into account the price discount from or premium over the face amount. It is greater than the current yield when the bond is selling at a discount and less than the current yield when the bond is selling at a premium.

Zero coupon bond – A bond that pays no interest but is priced, at issue, at a discount from its redemption price.

C Appendix C — Few Issues–with Cases and Examples

1. NET ASSET VALUE (NAV) — Concept, its' impact on the returns, case examples on NAV calculation and of a leading MF

Concept:

Net asset value (NAV) is a term used to describe the value of an entity's assets less the value of its liabilities. The term is most commonly used in relation to open-ended or mutual funds because shares of such funds are redeemed at their net asset value. NAV is a mutual fund's price per share or exchange-traded fund's (ETF) per-share value. In both cases, the per-share amount of the fund is calculated by dividing the total value of all the securities in its portfolio, less any liabilities, by the number of fund shares outstanding.

In the context of mutual funds, NAV per share is computed once a day based on the closing market prices of the securities in the fund's portfolio. All mutual funds' buy and sell orders are processed at the NAV of the trade date. However, investors must wait until the following day to get the trade price. However, the term NAV may also be used as a synonym for book value or the equity value of a business. Net asset value may represent the value of the total equity, or it may be divided by the number of shares outstanding held by investors and, thereby, represent the net asset value *per share*.

Net asset values and other accounting and recordkeeping activities are the result of the process of Fund Accounting, sometimes called securities accounting, investment accounting and/or portfolio accounting. Fund Accounting systems are sophisticated computerized systems used to account for investor capital flows in and out of a fund, purchases and sales of investments and related investment income, gains, losses and operating expenses of the fund. The fund's investments and other assets are valued on a regular schedule such as daily, weekly or monthly, depending on the fund and associated regulatory or sponsor requirements. There is no universal method or basis of valuing assets and liabilities for the purposes of calculating net asset value used throughout the world, and the criteria used for the valuation will depend upon the circumstances, the purposes of the valuation and any regulatory and/or accounting principles that may apply.

Net Asset Value is the market value of the assets of the scheme minus its liabilities. The per unit NAV is the net asset value of the scheme divided by the number of units outstanding on the Valuation Date. Thus, NAV of a mutual fund unit is nothing but the 'book value.'

NAV = Market value of the assets minus its liabilities

A fund's *NAV* fluctuates along with the value of its underlying investments. The formula for NAV of a fund is:

NAV = Market Value of all securities held by fund + Receivables + Other accrued incomes + Cash and equivalent holdings – Fund liabilities/Total fund shares outstanding as on the NAV date.

OR

$$NAV = \frac{\text{Fund Assets} - \text{Fund Liabilities}}{\text{Outstanding Shares}}$$

Example: Let's assume at the close of trading yesterday that a particular mutual fund held ₹ 10,500,000 worth of securities, ₹ 2,000,000 of cash, and ₹ 500,000 of liabilities. If the fund had 1,000,000 shares outstanding, then yesterday's NAV would be:

NAV = (₹10,500,000 + ₹2,000,000 – ₹500,000) / 1,000,000 = ₹12.00

A fund's NAV will change daily as the value of a fund's securities, cash held, liabilities, and the number of shares outstanding fluctuates.

NAV and its impact on the returns

It is often felt that MF with lower NAV will give better returns. This again is due to the wrong perception about NAV. An example will make it clear that returns are independent of the NAV.

Say, you have ₹ 10,000 to invest. Say one Fund A has an NAV of ₹ 10 and another Fund B has NAV of ₹ 50. You will get 1000 units of Fund A or 200 units of Fund B. After one year, both funds would have grown equally as their portfolio is same, say by 25%. Then NAV after one year would be ₹ 12.50 for Fund A and ₹ 62.50 for Fund B. The value of your investment would be 1000*12.50 = ₹ 12,500 for Fund A and 200*62.5 = ₹ 12,500 for Fund B. Thus your returns would be same irrespective of the NAV.

An FMCG company share at, say, ₹ 1,000 may give a better return than say a jute company share at ₹ 50, since IT sector would show a much higher growth rate than jute industry (₹ 1000 may basically be over or under priced, which will not be the case with MF NAV).

Case example of NAV calculation — HDFC SL Crest

HDFC has launched a new scheme, SL Crest which is an invest cum insurance plan but for the first time a plan guarantees Highest NAV with a minimum NAV assured. Here are few basic facts:

1. Offer price is ₹ 10 on date of launch.
2. Highest NAV Guarantee option is ₹ 15 or the Highest NAV during the **first seven years** of the plan.
3. The plan matures in 10 years.
4. Minimum Premium paying term is 5 years which is paid annually.
5. Minimum premium amount is 50 thousand INR.
6. You can withdraw your investment minimum after five years but you get it at current NAV and not the highest. That means if current rate is 13 which is less than 15, you get 13 and not 15. However this also means that if the rate is 18 you get 18 not 15.
7. To get the Maximum NAV benefit, you should withdraw only at the end of seventh year,.
8. Sum Assured is 10 times the annual premium. This means if your premium is 10K your insurance is 1 lakh.
9. Below some sample conditions have been taken to understand how CREST will perform and what percentage of profit you will get. Also it has been compared with NSC which gives 8% interest yearly.

Assumptions to make calculation simpler:

- Sample NAV values have been taken to calculate for first five years.
- A period of Five Years for profit calculation has been considered..
- 10 thousand as minimum premium

Assuming that maximum NAV went to ₹ 17 in Five years which is more than guaranteed NAV of 15, one can make a profit of 25%.

NSC Calculations : Investing same amount of premium to buy NSC every year gives you a guaranteed income of 17200 on same investment amount. Here you have a profit of 34.4%.

Year	Investment	NAV	Unit
1st	10000	10	1000
2nd	10000	13	769
3rd	10000	15	667
4th	10000	17	588
5TH	10000	15	667
Total	**50000**	**17**	**3691**

Total Unit	3691
Highest NAV	17
Investment	50000
Return Value	62747
Profit Percentage	25%

HDFC SL Crest

NSC		
Year	Investment	Return
1st	10000	16000
2nd	10000	14000
3rd	10000	13200
4th	10000	12400
5TH	10000	11600
Total	**50000**	**67200**

Investment	50000
Return Value	67200
Profit Percentage	34%

NSC

Now for HDFC SL Crest to beat the NSC income in this scenario, the NAV should reach 67200/3691 = 18.2

2. MUTUAL FUNDS IN INDIA, TYPES, HISTORY, SEBI REGULATIONS, CASE EXAMPLE OF A LEADING MF

Introduction of Mutual Fund in India / Mutual Fund History

The origin of mutual fund industry in India is with the introduction of the concept of mutual fund by UTI in the year 1963. Though the growth was slow, but it accelerated from the year 1987 when non-UTI players entered the industry.

In the past decade, Indian mutual fund industry had seen dramatic improvements, both quality wise as well as quantity wise. Before, the monopoly of the market had seen an ending phase, the Assets Under Management (AUM) was ₹ 67bn. The private sector entry,to the fund family raised the AUM to ₹ 470 bn in March 1993 and till April 2004, it reached the height of 1,540 bn.

Putting the AUM of the Indian Mutual Funds Industry into comparison, the total of it is less than the deposits of SBI alone, constitute less than 11% of the total deposits held by the Indian banking industry.

The main reason of its poor growth is that the mutual fund industry in India is new in the country. Large sections of Indian investors are yet to be intellectuated with the concept. Hence, it is the prime responsibility of all mutual fund companies, to market the product correctly abreast of selling.

The mutual fund industry can be broadly put into four phases according to the development of the sector. Each phase is briefly described as under.

First Phase - 1964-87

Unit Trust of India (UTI) was established on 1963 by an Act of Parliament. It was set up by the Reserve Bank of India and functioned under the Regulatory and administrative control of the Reserve Bank of India. In 1978 UTI was de-linked from the RBI and the Industrial Development Bank of India (IDBI) took over the regulatory and administrative control in place of RBI. The first scheme launched by UTI was Unit Scheme 1964. At the end of 1988 UTI had ₹6,700 crores of assets under management.

Second Phase - 1987-1993 (Entry of Public Sector Funds)

Entry of non-UTI mutual funds. SBI Mutual Fund was the first followed by Canbank Mutual Fund (Dec 87), Punjab National Bank Mutual Fund (Aug 89), Indian Bank Mutual Fund (Nov 89), Bank of India (Jun 90), Bank of Baroda Mutual Fund (Oct 92). LIC in 1989 and GIC in 1990. The end of 1993 marked ₹47,004 as assets under management.

Third Phase - 1993-2003 (Entry of Private Sector Funds)

With the entry of private sector funds in 1993, a new era started in the Indian mutual fund industry, giving the Indian investors a wider choice of fund families. Also, 1993 was the year in which the first Mutual Fund Regulations came into being, under which all mutual funds, except UTI were to be registered and governed. The erstwhile Kothari Pioneer (now merged with Franklin Templeton) was the first private sector mutual fund registered in July 1993.

The 1993 SEBI (Mutual Fund) Regulations were substituted by a more comprehensive and revised Mutual Fund Regulations in 1996. The industry now functions under the SEBI (Mutual Fund) Regulations 1996.

The number of mutual fund houses went on increasing, with many foreign mutual funds setting up funds in India and also the industry has witnessed several mergers and acquisitions. As at the end of January 2003, there were 33 mutual funds with total assets of ₹ 1,21,805 crores.

The Unit Trust of India with ₹44,541 crores of assets under management was way ahead of other mutual funds.

Fourth Phase - since February 2003

This phase had bitter experience for UTI. It was bifurcated into two separate entities. One is the Specified Undertaking of the Unit Trust of India with AUM of ₹29,835 crores (as on January 2003). The Specified Undertaking of Unit Trust of India, functioning under an administrator and under the rules framed by Government of India and does not come under the purview of the Mutual Fund Regulations.

The second is the UTI Mutual Fund Ltd, sponsored by SBI, PNB, BOB and LIC. It is registered with SEBI and functions under the Mutual Fund Regulations. With the bifurcation of the erstwhile UTI which had in March 2000 more than ₹76,000 crores of AUM and with the setting up of a UTI Mutual Fund, conforming to the SEBI Mutual Fund Regulations, and with recent mergers taking place among different private sector funds, the mutual fund industry has entered its current phase of consolidation and growth. As at the end of September, 2004, there were 29 funds, which manage assets of ₹153108 crores under 421 schemes.

Definition

The SEBI regulations, 1993 defines a mutual fund as "a fund in the form of a trust by a sponsor, to raise money by the trustees trough the sale of units to the public, under one or more schemes, for investing in securities in accordance with these regulations"

A mutual fund is a professionally-managed firm of collective investments that pools money from many investors and invests it in stocks bonds, short-term money market instruments, and/ or other securities. In a mutual fund, the fund who is also known as the portfolio manager, trades the fund's underlying securities, realizing capital or losses, and collects the dividend or interest income. The investment proceeds are then passed along to the individual investors. *The value of a share of the mutual fund, known as the net asset value per share (NAV), is calculated daily based on the total value of the fund divided by the number of shares currently issued and outstanding.*

Advantages of mutual funds

Mutual funds have advantages compared to direct investing in individual securities.[3] These include:

- Increased diversification
- Daily liquidity
- Professional investment management
- Ability to participate in investments that may be available only to larger investors
- Service and convenience

- Government oversight
- Ease of comparison

Disadvantages of mutual funds

Mutual funds have disadvantages as well, which include[1]:

- Fees
- Less control over timing of recognition of gains
- Less predictable income
- No opportunity to customize

SEBI REGULATION ON THE INVESTMENT OF A MUTUAL FUND:

The investments of a mutual fund are subjected to a set of regulations prescribed by SEBI. Presently following restrictions apply.

- No term loan shall be granted by a mutual fund scheme.
- A mutual fund, under all its schemes taken together, will not own more than 10% of any company's paid up capital carrying voting rights.
- A scheme may invest in another scheme under the same asset management company or any other mutual fund without charging any fees, provided that the aggregate inter – scheme investment is made by all the schemes under the same management.
- Transfers of investment from one scheme to another scheme of mutual fund is permitted provided that —
  - (a) Such transfers are done at the prevailing market price for quoted instruments on spot basis.
  - (b) The securities so transferred shall be in conformity with the investment objectives of the schemes to which such transfer has been made.
  - (c) The registration and accounting of the transactions is completed and ratified in the next meeting of the board of trustees.
- A mutual fund may borrow to meet liquidity needs, for the purpose of repurchase, redemption of units, or repayment of interest or dividend to the unit holders. Such borrowings shall not exceed 20% of the net asset of the scheme and the duration of the borrowing shall not exceed 6 months. The fund may borrow from permissible entities at prevailing market rates and may offer the assets of the schemes as collateral for such borrowings.
- A scheme shall not invest more than 15% of its NAV in debt instruments issued by a single issuer which are rated not below investment grade by an authorized credit rating agency. Such investment limit may be extended to 20% of the NAVof the scheme with the prior approval of Board of Trustees and the Board of Asset Management Company.

This limit, however, is not applicable for investment in government's securities and money market instruments.

- A scheme shall not invest more than 10% of its NAV in unrated debt instruments issued by a single issuer and the total investment in such instruments shall not exceed 25% of the NAV of the scheme.
- A mutual fund will buy and sell securities on the basis of deliveries. It can no tmake short sales or engage in carry forward transactions.
- A scheme shall not make any investment in—
  - (a) Any unlisted security of an associates or group company of the sponsor.
  - (b) Any security issued by way of private placement by an associate or group company of the sponsor.
  - (c) The listed securities of group companies of the sponsor in excess of 25% of the net assets.
- The investment manager may invest in a scheme from time to time. The percentage of such investments to the total net assets may vary from time to time and can be upto100% of the net assets of the schemes.
- A scheme shall not invest more than 10% of its NAV in the equity shares or equity related instruments of any one company.
- A scheme may invest in ADRs/GD₹ of Indian companies listed on overseas stock exchanges to the extent and in a manner approved by RBI .A scheme shall not invest more than 5% of its NAV in unlisted equity shares or equity related instruments in case of an open ended schemes and 10% of its NAV in case a of closed ended scheme.

TAX SAVING ON MUTUAL FUND:

A. There are two types of tax-saving funds, equity-linked savings schemes (ELSS) and pension funds. ELSS schemes are basically diversified equity schemes, which have a three-year lock-in. Investments here — subject to a maximum of ₹ 10,000 — receive a tax rebate of 0 to 20 per cent depending on the income slab. As these are equity instruments they have the maximum risk-return potential among all asset classes. What this means is that return has a propensity to vary with great intensity. Although an average tax-saving mutual fund delivered 16.36 per cent in 2002, the range of returns was extreme. Thus, in that year, the best tax-saving fund delivered 42.61 per cent and the worst was down 3.16 per cent. The best ways to overcome the vagaries of stock markets is to diversify. Diversification can be across funds and, more importantly, across time periods. By investing regularly every year in these funds one can set up a long-term systematic investment plan. The other route for saving taxes is pension funds, even though there are currently only two such funds in operation, Franklin Templeton's Templeton India Pension Fund and UTI's Retirement Benefit Plan. Introduced for the first time in 1997, pension funds are hybrid schemes, which have a debt orientation; and carry the same tax benefit as ELSS. From the tax point of view, bonus units are conceptually similar to dividend stripping, but somewhat more complex. Bonus units that a fund issue is deemed to have been acquired at zero cost. Thus, whenever they are sold, the entire sale price is treated as capital gains. However, at the time of issue of bonus, the NAV of the fund drops in a proportion that is identical to the ratio at which bonus funds are issued. This fall in the NAV is a capital loss as far as the original units are concerned and it is here that tax benefits can be realized. The original units can be sold off with a capital loss, which can be used to set off other capital gains. The bonus units carry a high tax liability though since you will pay taxes on the entire sale price.

Example: Suppose you hold 10,000 units of a fund whose NAV is ₹ 15. You made the purchase less than a year ago at an NAV of ₹ 12. If today you decide to sell these units, you will fetch ₹ 1.5 lakhs, out of which ₹ 30,000 will be short-term capital gain. On this, you are likely to pay a tax of ₹ 9,000 –30 per cent of gains

Types of Mutual Funds in India

By Structure	By Nature	By Investment Objective
Closed Ended Funds	Equity	Growth Schemes
Open Ended Funds	Debt	Income Schemes
Interval funds	Balance	Balanced Schemes
		Index Funds

Let us discuss each of these types in detail:

A. TYPES OF MUTUAL FUNDS BY STRUCTURE

Close Ended Fund/ Scheme: A close-ended fund or scheme has a stipulated maturity period For *e.g.*, 5-7 years. The fund is open for subscription only during a specified period at the time of launch of the scheme. Investors can invest in the scheme at the time of the initial public issue and thereafter they can buy or sell the units of the scheme on the stock exchanges where the units are listed. In order to provide an exit route to the investors, some close-ended funds give an option of selling back the units to the mutual fund through periodic repurchase at NAV related prices or they are listed in secondary market.

Open Ended Fund/ Scheme: An open-ended mutual fund is the most common type of mutual fund available for investment. An investor can choose to invest or transact in these schemes when ever he likes to. In an open-ended mutual fund, there is no limit to the number of investors, shares, or overall size of the fund, unless the fund manager decides to close the fund to new investors in order to keep it manageable. The value or share price of an open-ended mutual fund is determined at the market close every day and is called the Net Asset Value (NAV).

Interval Schemes: Interval Schemes are that scheme, which combines the features of open-ended and close-ended schemes. The units may be traded on the stock exchange or may be open for sale or redemption during pre-determined intervals at NAV related prices. FMP or the Fixed Maturity Plans are the example for these types of schemes.

B. TYPES OF MUTUAL FUNDS BY NATURE

Equity mutual funds: These funds invest a maximum part of their corpus into equities holdings. The structure of the fund may vary different for different schemes and the fund manager's outlook on different stocks. The Equity Funds are sub-classified depending upon their investment objective, as follows:

- Diversified Equity Funds
- Mid-Cap Funds
- Small Cap Funds
- Sector Specific Funds
- Tax Savings Funds (ELSS)

Equity investments are meant for a longer time horizon, thus Equity funds rank high on the risk-return matrix.

Debt mutual funds: The objective of these Funds is to invest in debt papers. Government authorities, private companies, banks and financial institutions are some of the major issuers of debt papers. By investing in debt instruments, these funds ensure low risk and provide stable income to the investors. Debt funds are further classified as:

- Gilt Funds
- Income Funds
- MIPs
- Short Term Plans
- Liquid Funds

Balanced funds: As the name suggest they, are a mix of both equity and debt funds. They invest in both equities and fixed income securities, which are in line with pre-defined investment objective of the scheme. These schemes aim to provide investors with the best of both the worlds. Equity part provides growth and the debt part provides stability in returns.

C. TYPES OF MUTUAL FUNDS BY INVESTMENT OBJECTIVE

Growth Schemes

Growth Schemes are also known as equity schemes. The aim of these schemes is to provide capital appreciation over medium to long-term. These schemes normally invest a major part of their fund in equities and are willing to bear short-term decline in value for possible future appreciation.

Income Schemes

Income Schemes are also known as debt schemes. The aim of these schemes is to provide regular and steady income to investors. These schemes generally invest in fixed income securities such as bonds and corporate debentures. Capital appreciation in such schemes may be limited.

Index Schemes

Index schemes attempt to replicate the performance of a particular index such as the BSE Sensex or the NSE 50. The portfolio of these schemes will consist of only those stocks that constitute the index. The percentage of each stock to the total holding will be identical to the stocks index weight age. And hence, the returns from such schemes would be more or less equivalent to those of the Index

Mutual Fund Houses (AMCs) in India

AIG Global Investment
Baroda Pioneer Mutual Fund
Birla Sun Life Mutual Fund
Canara Robeco Mutual Fund
DBS Chola Mutual Fund
DSP Blackcock Mutual Fund
Escorts Mutual Fund
Goldman Sachs Mutual Fund
HSBC Mutual Fund
IDBI Mutual Fund
IIFL Mutual Fund
ING Mutual Fund
JPMorgan Mutual Fund
L&T Mutual Fund
Mirae Asset Mutual Fund
Motilal Oswal Mutual Fund
Pramerica Mutual Fund
Quantum Mutual Fund
Religare Mutual Fund
SBI Mutual Fund
Sundaram Mutual Fund
Taurus Mutual Fund
UTI Mutual Fund

Axis Mutual Fund
Bharti AXA Mutual Fund
BNP Paribas Mutual Fund
Daiwa Mutual Fund
Deutsche Mutual Fund
Edelweiss Mutual Fund
Franklin Templeton Mutual Fund
HDFC Mutual Fund
ICICI Prudential Mutual Fund
IDFC Mutual Fund
India Bulls Mutual Fund
JM Financial Mutual Fund
Kotak Mahindra Mutual Fund
LIC Nomura Mutual Fund
Morgan Stanley Mutual Fund
Peerless Mutual Fund
Principal Mutual Fund
Reliance Mutual Fund
Sahara Mutual Fund
Shinsei Mutual Fund
Tata Mutual Fund
Union KBC Mutual Fund

Case example of a leading mutual fund in India – SBI MF

SBI Mutual Fund was set up on 29 June 1987; SBI Mutual Fund is a joint venture between the State Bank of India, India's largest bank and Societe Generale Asset Management of France, one of the world's leading fund management companies. SBI Funds Management Private Limited was incorporated on 7th February 1992 to manage assets of the mutual fund.

SBI Mutual Fund is one of the premier fund houses in India with an enviable track record in judicious investments and consistent wealth creation. Today, the fund house manages over ₹ 20000 crores of assets across more than 40 schemes. The fund serves its vast family of over 3.5 million investors by reaching out to them through a network of over 100 points of acceptance, 26 investor service centres, 33 investor service desks, 52 district organizers and 2 Overseas Official Points of Acceptance located in Doha and Dubai. SBI MF has been delivering value to its customers over the years. SBI MF has an outstanding record of judicious investments and consistent wealth creation. In its twenty years of operation SBI mutual fund has been the proud recipient of the ICRA online awards- 8 times, CNBC TV 18 Crisil award 2006 and most recently with CNBC TV 18 Mutual Fund of the year 2007. Since the market has been becoming complex over the years there are requirements for clear understanding of innumerable parameters regarding the market movements and performance of mutual funds. At SBI MF, considerable resources are invested to gain, maintain and sustain profitable insights into market movements. At SBI MF it is made sure that the investors get maximum benefits year after year. The expert team at SBI MF consisting of experienced and market savvy researchers prepare comprehensive analytical and informative report on diverse sectors and identify stocks that promise high performance in the future.

Much of the credit for sustained performance of SBI Mutual Fund goes to the fund management team. They are the real performers whose expertise, skills and capabilities reward the investors. The risk management team also contributes enormously in protecting the interest of the investors, headed by the chief risk officer (CRO). The CRO is responsible for managing risk within the organization including investments, marketing, operations etc.

Mentioned below are the schemes offered by SBI Mutual Fund for investment in India:

All Schemes | Balanced | Equity Diversified | ETF | FMP | Gilt | Debt | Index | Liquid | Sector | Tax Saving

All Schemes	1mth	3mth	6mth	1yr	3yr	5yr	NAV	Size*
SBI Gold Exchange Traded Scheme (Exchange traded funds)	-3.58	16.52	25.48	33.77	NA	NA	2626.22	0.00
SBI Dynamic Bond Fund-Growth (Debt)	0.20	2.06	4.89	9.15	5.34	3.20	12.35	0.00
SBI Magnum Income Fund-FRP-Savings Plus Bond - Growth (Debt)	0.73	2.29	4.61	8.98	7.86	7.20	15.94	0.00
SBI Short Horizon Debt Fund-Ultra Short Term - Institutional-Growth (Debt)	0.73	2.26	4.51	8.68	6.72	NA	13.42	0.00
SBI Magnum Income Fund-Floating Rate Plan-Long Term-Growth (Debt)	0.76	2.34	4.59	8.67	7.18	6.79	15.52	0.00

SBI Arbitrage Opportunities Fund-Growth (Debt)	0.52	1.74	4.29	8.67	6.26	NA	14.11	0.00
SBI Short Horizon Debt Fund-Ultra Short-term - Retail - Growth (Debt)	0.72	2.24	4.46	8.59	6.40	NA	13.22	0.00
SBI Magnum Insta Cash Fund-Liquid Floater - Growth (Liquid)	0.70	2.14	4.35	8.53	6.64	7.19	17.72	0.00
SBI Premier Liquid Fund-Super Institutional-Growth (Liquid)	0.73	2.24	4.43	8.49	6.38	NA	16.15	0.00
SBI Premier Liquid Fund– Institutional-Growth (Liquid)	0.72	2.22	4.40	8.44	6.33	6.96	16.32	0.00
SBI Magnum Insta Cash–Cash Plan (Liquid)	0.71	2.18	4.32	8.32	6.33	6.99	22.78	0.00
SBI Short Horizon Debt Fund– Short-term-Institutional-Growth (Debt)	0.34	1.64	3.78	7.55	NA	NA	11.72	0.00
SBI Short Horizon Debt Fund– Short-term-Retail - Growth (Debt)	0.34	1.62	3.74	7.37	7.02	NA	13.30	0.00
SBI Magnum Debt Fund Series-24 Months-2-Growth (Debt)	0.60	2.28	4.47	6.84	NA	NA	10.71	27.73
SBI Magnum Gilt Short-term Plan-Growth (Gilt)	0.49	1.78	3.52	6.80	6.42	7.02	20.24	0.00
SBI Magnum Income Fund– Growth (Debt)	-0.08	1.44	3.45	6.44	6.17	4.55	24.38	0.00
SBI Magnum Income Plus Fund-Savings Plan - Growth (Debt)	0.32	1.37	3.62	5.80	3.75	2.25	11.67	0.00
SBI Magnum Gilt Long-term Plan PF - Regular - Growth (Gilt)	-0.68	0.38	1.37	4.73	2.64	3.67	12.90	0.00
SBI Magnum Gilt Long-term Plan-Growth (Gilt)	-0.69	0.37	1.34	4.67	2.57	3.60	20.11	0.00
SBI Magnum Debt Fund Series-60 Months - 1 - Growth (FMP)	0.03	1.51	2.89	4.54	NA	NA	10.48	10.47
SBI Magnum Gilt Long-term Plan-PF-Fixed Period – 1 year - Growth (Gilt)	-0.72	0.25	1.10	4.20	2.12	3.33	12.55	0.00
SBI Magnum Monthly Income Plan-Floater - Growth (Debt)	0.14	0.62	1.30	4.08	8.11	5.17	13.65	0.00
SBI Magnum Gilt Long-term Plan-PF-Fixed Period - 2 year - Growth (Gilt)	-0.73	0.22	1.04	4.05	1.97	2.99	12.39	0.00
SBI Capital Protection Oriented Fund-Series I-Growth (Debt)	NA	0.75	1.62	3.91	7.12	NA	11.20	219.10
SBI Magnum Gilt Long-term Plan-PF - Fixed Period - 3 year - Growth (Gilt)	-0.75	0.18	0.96	3.89	1.82	2.84	12.17	0.00
SBI Magnum Children Benefit Plan (Debt)	-0.70	-0.28	1.05	2.32	9.24	6.72	23.04	0.00
SBI Magnum Income Plus Fund-Investment Plan - Growth (Debt)	0.78	0.60	1.52	1.77	7.61	5.40	16.50	0.00
SBI Magnum Monthly Income Plan-Growth (Debt)	-0.10	0.14	0.52	1.17	5.56	4.37	20.37	0.00

SBI Magnum Debt Fund Series- 18 Months - 4 - Growth	0.69	2.26	4.52	NA	NA	NA	10.70	193.35
SBI Magnum Debt Fund Series - 367 Days - 3 - Growth	0.65	NA	NA	NA	NA	NA	10.23	90.01
SBI Magnum Debt Fund Series - 13 Months - 11 - Retail - Growth (Debt)	0.76	2.25	4.59	NA	NA	NA	10.57	327.45
SBI Magnum Debt Fund Series - 367 Days - 1 - Growth (FMP)	0.69	2.35	NA	NA	NA	NA	10.35	102.93
SBI Capital Protection Oriented Fund-Series II - Growth (Capital Protection)	0.19	1.49	1.90	NA	NA	NA	10.29	109.01
SBI Magnum Debt Fund Series - 370 Days - 8 - Growth	0.73	2.17	4.53	NA	NA	NA	10.74	663.21
SBI Magnum Debt Fund Series - 180 Days - 19 - Growth	0.74	2.17	NA	NA	NA	NA	10.35	146.15
SBI Magnum Debt Fund Series - 367 Days - 6 - Growth (Debt)	NA	NA	NA	NA	NA	NA	10.06	0.00
SBI Magnum Debt Fund Series - 370 Days - 10 - Growth	0.71	2.31	4.70	NA	NA	NA	10.63	960.35
SBI Magnum Debt Fund Series - 370 Days - 7 - Growth (FMP)	0.72	2.16	4.48	NA	NA	NA	10.78	416.73
SBI Magnum Debt Fund Series - 36 Months - 1 - Growth (Debt)	0.37	2.12	NA	NA	NA	NA	10.39	44.31
SBI Magnum Debt Fund Series - 370 Days - 9 - Growth	0.71	2.30	4.69	NA	NA	NA	10.66	635.10
SBI Magnum Debt Fund Series - 180 Days - 20 - Growth (Short-term debt)	0.74	2.19	NA	NA	NA	NA	10.28	208.62
SBI Magnum Debt Fund Series – 367 Days - 2 - Growth (FMP)	0.74	2.27	NA	NA	NA	NA	10.30	144.84
SBI Magnum Debt Fund Series – 370 Days - 15 - Growth	0.67	2.34	NA	NA	NA	NA	10.39	433.04
SBI Magnum Debt Fund Series - 15 Months - 6 - Growth	0.71	2.36	4.88	NA	NA	NA	10.68	125.29
SBI Gold Fund - Growth	NA	NA	NA	NA	NA	NA	9.50	0.00
SBI Magnum Debt Fund Series – 180 Days - 21 - Growth	0.72	NA	NA	NA	NA	NA	10.15	163.07
SBI Magnum Debt Fund Series – 180 Days - 17 - Growth (Short-term debt)	0.70	2.21	NA	NA	NA	NA	10.44	252.65
SBI Magnum Debt Fund Series – 370 Days - 11 - Growth (FMP)	0.77	2.29	4.67	NA	NA	NA	10.56	1155.77
SBI Magnum Debt Fund Series – 367 Days - 5 - Growth (FMP)	0.63	NA	NA	NA	NA	NA	10.15	169.85
SBI Magnum Debt Fund Series - 18 Months - 6 - Growth (FMP)	0.68	2.24	4.44	NA	NA	NA	10.65	29.12
SBI Magnum Debt Fund Series– 90 Days - 48 - Growth	0.74	NA	NA	NA	NA	NA	10.18	411.07

SBI Magnum Debt Fund Series– 370 Days - 13 - Growth	0.76	2.28	NA	NA	NA	NA	10.47	190.85
SBI Magnum Debt Fund Series– 18 Months - 5 - Growth	0.68	2.29	4.54	NA	NA	NA	10.66	70.36
SBI Magnum Debt Fund Series– 367 Days - 4 - Growth (Debt)	0.66	NA	NA	NA	NA	NA	10.19	63.71
SBI Magnum Debt Fund Series – 180 Days - 18 - Growth (Short term debt)	0.73	2.22	NA	NA	NA	NA	10.41	501.75
SBI Magnum Debt Fund Series – 370 Days - 12 - Growth (FMP)	0.75	2.22	NA	NA	NA	NA	10.48	738.81
SBI Magnum Debt Fund Series - 90 Days - 47 - Growth	0.69	NA	NA	NA	NA	NA	10.20	45.27
SBI Magnum Debt Fund Series - 370 Days - 14 - Growth (FMP)	0.66	2.27	NA	NA	NA	NA	10.43	157.93
SBI Magnum Sector Funds Umbrella- Emerg Buss Fund - Growth (Equity Diversified)	-0.85	-1.23	4.40	-2.05	33.74	10.04	43.39	0.00
SBI Magnum Sector Funds Umbrella- Pharma - Growth (Sector)	-3.04	-9.64	-3.31	-2.67	23.62	4.34	43.00	0.00
SBI Magnum Global Fund 94 - Growth (Equity Diversified)	-1.92	-5.73	-1.20	-9.29	26.29	7.78	55.25	0.00
SBI Magnum NRI Investment Fund - Flexi Asset Plan - Growth (Debt)	-0.34	-5.08	-6.06	-12.06	15.12	4.00	27.75	0.00
SBI Magnum Equity Fund - Growth (Equity Diversified)	1.16	-8.06	-9.76	-15.37	20.32	10.12	40.15	0.00
SBI Magnum Balanced Fund - Growth (Balanced)	0.82	-9.03	-11.24	-17.38	13.34	6.73	45.41	0.00
SBI Magnum Index Fund - Growth (Index)	2.73	-9.09	-13.59	-18.48	13.12	5.03	43.35	0.00
SBI Magnum Tax Gain Scheme 93- Growth (Tax Saving)	0.79	-8.43	-11.53	-18.53	15.72	6.79	54.62	0.00
SBI Magnum COMMA Fund - Growth (Equity Diversified)	-1.20	-6.78	-10.87	-19.37	16.89	7.99	22.15	0.00
SBI Magnum Mid cap Fund - Growth (Equity Diversified)	-3.82	-8.66	-8.58	-20.61	17.23	1.32	20.88	0.00
SBI Magnum Blue-chip Fund - Growth (Equity Diversified)	0.31	-9.78	-13.11	-21.08	14.80	2.84	12.92	0.00
SBI Magnum Multiplier Plus 93 - Growth (Equity Diversified)	-0.78	-10.20	-11.85	-21.37	17.13	8.86	72.82	0.00
SBI PSU Fund - Growth	-1.13	-9.89	-12.41	-22.08	NA	NA	8.75	0.00
SBI One India Fund - Growth (Equity Diversified)	NA	-9.18	-12.30	-22.15	12.96	NA	9.70	0.00
SBI Magnum Sector Funds Umbrella - Contra - Growth (Equity Diversified)	0.94	-10.31	-13.35	-23.74	14.81	7.28	49.34	0.00
SBI Magnum Multi Cap Fund - Growth (Equity Diversified)	0.46	-12.64	-15.59	-24.78	10.74	0.90	15.21	0.00
SBI Tax Advantage Fund - Series 1 - Growth (Tax Saving)	-2.17	-13.09	-13.38	-24.82	13.69	NA	10.36	0.00
SBI Infrastructure Fund - Series I - Growth (Sector)	-1.56	-9.80	-14.06	-28.66	6.03	NA	8.19	0.00

*Size of the scheme (*i.e.* corpus) is in Rupees crores

3. FACTORING – AN INTRODUCTION AND FINANCIAL EVALUATION, EXAMPLE

Introduction

A financing method in which a business owner sells accounts receivable at a discount to a third-party funding source to raise capital

One of the oldest forms of business financing, factoring is the cash-management tool of choice for many companies. Factoring is very common in certain industries, such as the clothing industry, where long receivables are part of the business cycle.

In a typical factoring arrangement, the client makes a sale, delivers the product or service and generates an invoice. The factor (the funding source) buys the right to collect on that invoice by agreeing to pay client, the invoice's face value less a discount—typically 2 to 6 per cent. The factor pays 75 per cent to 80 per cent of the face value immediately and forwards the remainder (less the discount) when client's customer pays. Because factors extend credit not to their clients but to their clients' customers, they are more concerned about the customers' ability to pay than the client's financial status. That means a company with creditworthy customers may be able to factor even if it can't qualify for a loan.

Once used mostly by large corporations, factoring is becoming more widespread. Still, plenty of misperceptions about factoring remain. Factoring is not a loan; it does not create a liability on the balance sheet or encumber assets. It is the sale of an asset—in this case, the invoice. And while factoring is considered one of the most expensive forms of financing, that's not always true. Yes, when you compare the discount rate factors charge against the interest rate banks charge, factoring costs more. But if you can't qualify for a loan, it doesn't matter what the interest rate is. Factors also provide services banks do not: They typically take over a significant portion of the accounting work for their clients, help with credit checks, and generate financial reports to let you know where you stand.

Definition

Factoring is a financial option for the management of receivables. In simple definition, it is the conversion of credit sales into cash. In factoring, a financial institution (factor) buys the accounts receivable of a company (Client) and pays up to 80%(rarely up to 90%) of the amount immediately on agreement. Factoring company pays the remaining amount (Balance 20%-finance cost-operating cost) to the client when the customer pays the debt. Collection of debt from the customer is done either by the factor or the client depending upon the type of factoring. The account receivable in factoring can either be for a product or service. Examples are factoring against goods purchased, factoring for construction services (usually for government contracts where the government body is capable of paying back the debt in the stipulated period of factoring. Contractors submit invoices to get cash instantly), factoring against medical insurance etc. Let us see how factoring is done against an invoice of goods purchased.

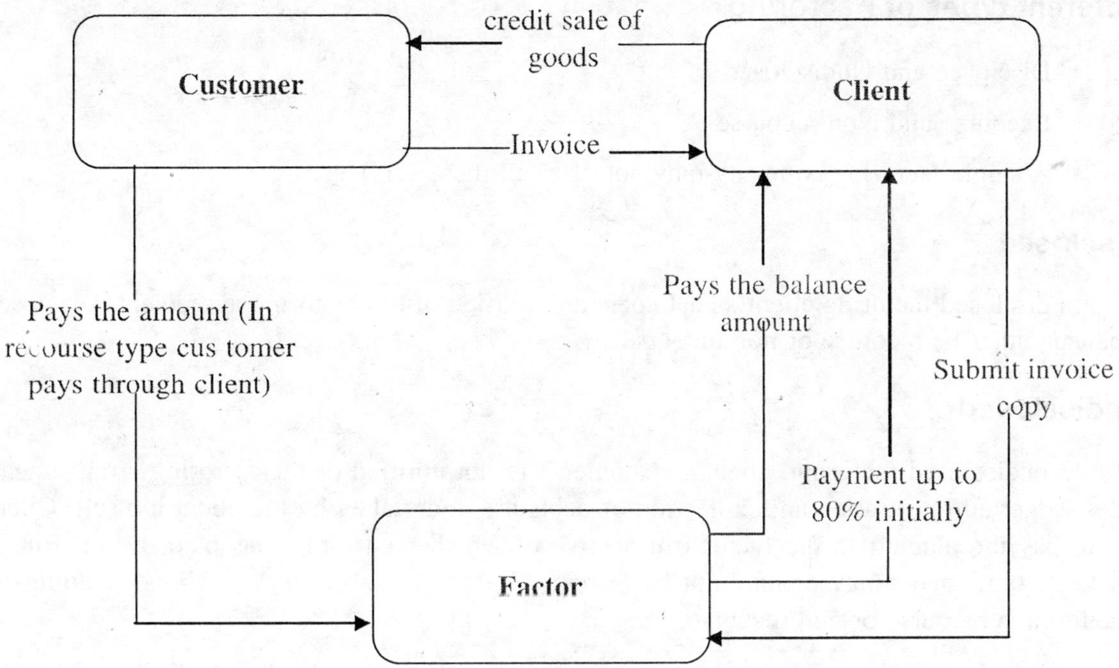

Characteristics of factoring

Usually the period for factoring is 90 to 150 days. Some factoring companies allow even more than 150 days.

Factoring is considered to be a costly source of finance compared to other sources of short term borrowings.

Factoring receivables is an ideal financial solution for new and emerging firms without strong financials. This is because credit worthiness is evaluated based on the financial strength of the customer (debtor). Hence these companies can leverage on the financial strength of their customers.

Bad debts will not be considered for factoring.

Credit rating is not mandatory. But the factoring companies usually carry out credit risk analysis before entering into the agreement.

Factoring is a method of off balance sheet financing.

Cost of factoring=finance cost + operating cost. Factoring cost vary according to the transaction size, financial strength of the customer etc. The cost of factoring vary from 1.5% to 3% per month depending upon the financial strength of the client's customer.

Indian firms offer factoring for invoices as low as 1000 ₹.

For delayed payments beyond the approved credit period, penal charge of around 1-2% per month over and above the normal cost is charged (it varies like 1% for the first month and 2% afterwards).

Different types of Factoring

- Disclosed and Undisclosed
- Recourse and Non recourse
- A single factoring company may not offer all these services.

Disclosed

In disclosed factoring client's customers are notified of the factoring agreement. Disclosed type can either be recourse or non recourse.

Undisclosed

In undisclosed factoring, client's customers are not notified of the factoring arrangement. Sales ledger administration and collection of debts are undertaken by the client himself. Client has to pay the amount to the factor irrespective of whether customer has paid or not. But in disclosed type factor may or may not be responsible for the collection of debts depending on whether it is recourse or non recourse.

Recourse factoring

In recourse factoring, client undertakes to collect the debts from the customer. If the customer don't pay the amount on maturity, factor will recover the amount from the client. This is the most common type of factoring. Recourse factoring is offered at a lower interest rate since the risk by the factor is low. Balance amount is paid to client when the customer pays the factor.

Non recourse factoring

In non recourse factoring, factor undertakes to collect the debts from the customer. Balance amount is paid to client at the end of the credit period or when the customer pays the factor whichever comes first. The advantage of non recourse factoring is that continuous factoring will eliminate the need for credit and collection departments in the organization.

Factoring companies in India

Canbank Factors Limited

SBI Factors and Commercial Services Pvt. Ltd

The Hongkong and Shanghai Banking Corporation Ltd

Foremost Factors Limited

Global Trade Finance Limited

Export Credit Guarantee Corporation of India Ltd

Citibank NA, India

Small Industries Development Bank of India (SIDBI)

Standard Chartered Bank

Cost-benefit Analysis of Factoring (Financial Evaluation)

The cost-benefit analysis of factoring is concerned with comparing of costs and benefits associated with factoring. A firm would prefer to have factoring arrangements if the risk of default or non-payment is high and the cost involved by way of fees and service charges of the factor are less than the benefits associated with the same. The following examples illustrate the financial evaluation of factoring.

Example: Bharat Ltd. decides to liberalize credit to increase its sales. The liberalized credit policy will bring additional sales of ₹ 3,00,000. The variable costs will be 60 % of sales and. There will be 10% risk for non-payment and 5 % collection costs. Will the company benefit from the new credit policy?

Solution

Additional Sales Revenue	₹ 3,00,000
Less: Variables Cost (60%) Incremental Revenue	1,80,000
Incremental Revenue	1,20,000
Less: 10% for non-payment risk	30,000
	90,000
Less 5% for costs of collection	15,000
Additional Revenue from increased sales due to liberal credit policy	75,000

D Model Questions and Guidelines to Answers

A SAMPLE OF A MODEL QUESTION BANK

SECTION - A

Answer the following. Each carries 2 marks.

1. (a) How do you calculate operating leverage?
   (b) What do you mean by cash flow?
   (c) What do you mean by Trading on equity?
   (d) What do you mean by wealth maximization?
   (e) How do you arrive at the combined leverage?
   (f) Mention the steps involved in the capital budgeting process.
   (g) What is Net Present Value Method?
   (h) What do you mean by scrip dividend?
   (i) What is Inventory management?
   (j) What do you mean by Dividend Policy?
   (k) What do you mean by Receivable Management?
   (l) What are the objects of cash management?

SECTION - B

Answer the following. Each carries 5 marks.

2. Examine the need for financial planning.
3. What are the importances of adequate working capital?
4. A company has ₹ 10,00,000 variable cost of ₹ 7,00,000 and fixed cost of ₹ 2,00,000 and debt of ₹ 5,00,000 at 10% rate of interest. What are the operating and financial leverages?
5. Mention the salient features of Net Present Value Method.
6. Brief the different forms of Dividend.

7. A industry is considering investment in a project which cost ₹ 6, 00,000. The cash flows are ₹ 1,20,000, ₹ 1,40,000, ₹ 1,80,000, ₹ 2,00,000, ₹ 2,50,000. Calculate pay back.
8. What are the consequences of holding excess inventory?
9. Mention the significance of cash management.

SECTION – C

Answer the following. Each carries 15 to 20 marks.

10. (a) What is financial management?
    (b) Explain the basic functions of financial management. How does risk return trade off take place?
11. (a) Discuss the concepts of 'risk' and 'return
    (b) Explain with suitable illustration the Capital Asset pricing model.
12. (a) What is the difference between mutually exclusive and independent projects?
    (b) A company is considering the following investments projects:

	Cash Flows			
Projects	Co	C1	C2	C3
	₹	₹	₹	₹
A	(10,000)	10,000	-	-
B	(10,000)	7,500	7,500	
C	(10,000)	2,000	4,000	12,000
D	(10,000)	8,000	3,000	3,000

Evaluate them on the basis of Payback and ARR.

13. (a) Explain and illustrate financial lease and operating lease, and differentiate between the two.
    (b) Enumerate the recent developments in Indian capital market.
14. (a) Given below is the data of two companies:

Particulars	X Ltd.	Y Ltd
Sales	₹ 4,00,000	₹ 3,50,000
Variable cost	40% sales	40% of sales
Fixed cost	₹ 25,000	₹ 30,000
Interest	₹ 1,40,000	₹ 80,000

Calculate operating leverage, financial leverage and total leverage.

    (b) Briefly explain the factors that influence the capital structure of a firm.

15. (a) Why do the firms pay dividend? Explain.
    (b) Explain the rationale for share buy-back.
16. (a) Explain the concepts of ABC analysis and 'Just in time' relating to inventory control.
    (b) What is Economic order Quantity? Explain the process of its determination with an example.
17. (a) Explain and illustrate Net operating income approach and Net Income Approach to the theory of capital structure; and state the assumptions there of.
    (b) Write explanatory notes on ***any*** *two* of the following:
    Project financing
    Time value of money
    Factoring
    Venture capital

QUESTION BANK: FINANCIAL MANAGEMENT

SAMPLE PAPER 1

General Instructions as guideline to answers

1. *Answers to questions carrying 1 mark may be from one word to one sentence.*
2. *Answers to questions carrying 3 marks may be from 50-75 words.*
3. *Answers to questions carrying 4-5 marks may be about 150 words.*
4. *Answers to questions carrying 6 marks may be about 200 words.*
5. *Attempt all parts of a question together.*

1. What is business finance? 1
2. What is financial management? 1
3. What are the three decisions of finance function? 1
4. What is another name of short term investment decisions? 1
5. What is floatation cost? 1
6. What do you mean by financial leverage? 1
7. When is said to be capital structure optimum? 1
8. What are fixed assets? 1
9. How is working capital calculated? 1
10. What is the capital structure of a company? 1

11. "Sound financial management is the key to the prosperity of the business." Explain. 3
12. Explain in brief any three decisions involved in the financial management. 3
13. State the objectives of the financial management? 3
14. Explain the importance of financial planning? 3
15. "Share capital is better than debt capital" In the favour of this statement explain one factor which affects the capital structure? 3
16. Explain briefly any four points of the role of financial management. 4
17. Explain any four factors affecting the dividend policy of the company. 4
18. To avoid the problem of shortage and surplus of funds what is required in the financial management? Name the concept and explain its any three points of importance. 4
19. How does cost of equity affect the capital structure of the company? Explain with example. 4
20. Name the process which helps in determining the objectives, policies, procedures, programmes and budgets to deal with the financial activities of an enterprise. Explain its three points of importance. 4
21. Explain briefly the factors affecting investment decisions. 5
22. Explain in brief any five factors that should be taken into consideration while determining the long term dividend policy. 5
23. Explain the factors affecting the capital budgeting decisions. 5
24. Explain the term "Trading on equity." Why, When and How it can be used by a business organization? 5
25. Explain the role of financial planning. 5
26. Explain briefly the factors determining the working capital of an organization? 6
27. Every manager has to take three major decisions while performing the finance function. Explain them. 6
28. Are the shareholders of a company likely to gain with the debt component in the capital employed? Explain with the help of an example. 6
29. Describe the factors that determine the capital structure of a company. 6
30. What is meant by financial management? Explain its role. 6

SAMPLE PAPER 2

General Instructions

1. Answers to questions carrying 1 mark may be from one word to one sentence.
2. Answers to questions carrying 3 marks may be from 50-75 words.
3. Answers to questions carrying 4-5 marks may be about 150 words.
4. Answers to questions carrying 6 marks may be about 200 words.
5. Attempt all parts of a question together.

1. A company wants to establish a new unit in which a machinery of worth ₹ 1,00,000 is involve. Identify the decision involved in financial management? 1
2. What is meant by capital structure? 1
3. Clarify EBIT-EPS analysis? 1
4. Which is the most costly capital of a company? 1
5. Name the concept which increases the return on equity shares with a charge in the capital structure of a company. 1
6. What is meant by capital budgeting decisions? 1
7. Identify the decision taken in financial management which affects the liquidity as well as profitability of a business. 1
8. What are the main sources of the funds? 1
9. What is a dividend decision? 1
10. What are the factors affecting the dividend decisions? 1
11. What is financial risk? Why does it arise? 3
12. Explain the "Earnings before interest and taxes- EBIT." 3
13. What do you mean by business finance? 3
14. How capital budgeting decisions are taken? 3
15. What do you mean by financial planning? 3
16. Discuss the role of floatation cost on capital structure. 4
17. What is meant by financial management? Explain any three decisions involved in the financial management. 4
18. How the control of existing shareholders affects? How this situation can be avoided? 4
19. Explain the concept of wealth maximization as an objective of financial management. 4
20. What is required to tackle the uncertainty in respect of availability and timings of funds? Name the concept involved and explain any three points of its importance. 4
21. Explain the five factors affecting financing decisions. 5

22. Explain the factors affecting the capital budgeting decisions. 5
23. What do you mean by the term Trading on equity? How it can be used by an organization? 5
24. Explain briefly the factors determining the working capital of an organization? 5
25. Explain the role of financial planning. 5
26. Explain briefly the factors affecting the fixed capital of an organization? 6
27. Explain any six factors affecting the dividend decisions of a company. 6
28. "Wealth maximization is an important objective of financial management." Explain briefly. 6
29. Explain the role of financial planning in financial management? 6
30. Describe the factors that determine the capital structure of a company. 6

SAMPLE PAPER 3

General Instructions

1. Answers to questions carrying 1 mark may be from one word to one sentence.

2. Answers to questions carrying 3 marks may be from 50-75 words.

3. Answers to questions carrying 4-5 marks may be about 150 words.

4. Answers to questions carrying 6 marks may be about 200 words.

5. Attempt all parts of a question together.

1 Give the name of two types of funds. 1

2 What is the formula for calculating interest coverage ratio? 1

3 What are the objectives of the financial management? 1

4 What is another name of the long term investment decisions? 1

5 Why capital structure decision is important? 1

6 What is the cheapest source of finance? 1

7 What are financial risks? 1

8 What is the effect of higher use of debt in the business? 1

9 What does debt service coverage ratio indicate? 1

10 Give two components of borrowed funds? 1

11 What is meant by capital structure? Explain. 3

12 How stock exchange market conditions affect the capital structure of the company? 3

13 How capital structure of other company affects the capital structure decisions? 3

14 What do you understand by the working capital? 3

15 What is the importance of the financial planning? 3

16 How regulatory framework does affect the capital structure of the company? 4

17 Explain briefly the importance and scope of capital budgeting? 4

18 Explain briefly the factors affecting the investments decisions? 4

19 How working capital does affect the liquidity and profitability of a business? 4

20 "Financial planning does not serve any useful purpose." Comment. 4

21 Explain the factors affect the amount of fixed capital. 5

22 Explain the factors that determine the capital structure of a company. 5

23 Explain by giving any four reasons, why capital budgeting decisions are important? 5

24 Explain briefly the factors determining the working capital of an organization? 5

25 How does trading on equity increase the return on equity shares? Explain with an example. 5

26 Explain the factors affecting the financing decisions. 6

27 Explain objectives of financial management? 6

28 Explain the role of financial planning. 6

29 Write a short note on finance function. 6

30 What is meant by financial management? Explain its role. 6

QUESTION BANK (ONE MARK QUESTIONS ONLY)

1. What is business finance?
2. What is financial management?
3. What are the three decisions of finance function?
4. What is another name of short term investment decisions?
5. What is floatation cost?
6. What do you mean by financial leverage?
7. When is said to be capital structure optimum?
8. What are fixed assets?
9. How is working capital calculated?
10. What is the capital structure of a company?
11. A company wants to establish a new unit in which a machinery of worth ₹ 10,00,000 is involved. Identify the decision involved in financial management?
12. What is meant by capital structure?

13. Clarify EBIT-EPS analysis?
14. Which is the most costly capital of a company?
15. Name the concept which increases the return on equity shares with a charge in the capital structure of a company.
16. What is meant by capital budgeting decisions?
17. Identify the decision taken in financial management which affects the liquidity as well as profitability of a business.
18. What are the main sources of the funds?
19. What is a dividend decision?
20. What are the factors affecting the dividend decisions?
21. Give the name two types of funds.
22. What is the formula for calculating interest coverage ratio?
23. What are the objectives of the financial management?
24. What is another name of the long term investment decisions?
25. Why capital structure decision is important?
26. What is the cheapest source of finance?
27. What are financial risks?
28. What is the effect of higher use of debt in the business?
29. What does debt service coverage ratio indicate?
30. Give two components of borrowed funds?

QUESTION BANK (THREE AND FOUR MARKS QUESTIONS)

THREE AND FOUR MARKS QUESTIONS

1. "Sound financial management is the key to the prosperity of the business." Explain.
2. Explain in brief any three decisions involved in the financial management.
3. State the objectives of the financial management?
4. Explain the importance of financial planning?
5. "Share capital is better than debt capital" In the favor of this statement explain one factor which affects the capital structure?
6. Explain briefly any four points of the role of financial management.
7. Explain any four factors affecting the dividend policy of the company.
8. To avoid the problem of shortage and surplus of funds what is required in the financial management? Name the concept and explain its any three points of importance.
9. How does cost of equity affect the capital structure of the company? Explain with example.

10. Name the process which helps in determining the objectives, policies, procedures, programmes and budgets to deal with the financial activities of an enterprise. Explain its three points of importance.
11. What is financial risk? Why does it arise?
12. Explain the "Earnings before interest and taxes- EBIT."
13. What do you mean by business finance?
14. How capital budgeting decisions are taken?
15. What do you mean by financial planning?
16. Discuss the role of floatation cost on capital structure.
17. What is meant by financial management? Explain any three decisions involved in the financial management.
18. How the control of existing shareholders affects? How this situation can be avoided?
19. Explain the concept of wealth maximization as an objective of financial management.
20. What is required to tackle the uncertainty in respect of availability and timings of funds? Name the concept involved and explain any three points of its importance.
21. What is meant by capital structure? Explain.
22. How stock exchange market conditions affect the capital structure of the company?
23. How capital structure of other company affects the capital structure decisions?
24. What do you understand by the working capital?
25. What is the importance of the financial planning?
26. How regulatory framework does affect the capital structure of the company?
27. Explain briefly the importance and scope of capital budgeting?
28. Explain briefly the factors affecting the investments decisions?
29. How working capital does affect the liquidity and profitability of a business?
30. "Financial planning does not serve any useful purpose." Comment.

QUESTION BANK (FIVE AND SIX MARKS QUESTIONS)

1 Explain the factors affect the amount of fixed capital.

2 Explain the factors that determine the capital structure of a company.

3 Explain by giving any four reasons, why capital budgeting decisions are important?

4 Explain briefly the factors determining the working capital of an organization?

5 How does trading on equity increase the return on equity shares? Explain with an example.

6 Explain the factors affecting the financing decisions.

7 Explain objectives of financial management?

8 Explain the concept of financial planning.

9 Write a short note on finance function.

10 What is meant by financial management? Explain its role.

11 Explain the five factors affecting financing decisions.

12 Explain the factors affecting the capital budgeting decisions.

13 What do you mean by the term "Trading on equity?" How it can be used by an organization?

14 Explain briefly the factors determining the working capital of an organization.

15 Explain the role of financial planning.

16 Explain briefly the factors affecting the fixed capital of an organization.

17 Explain any six factors affecting the dividend decisions of a company.

18 "Wealth maximization is an important objective of financial management." Explain briefly.

19 Explain the role of financial planning in financial management.

20 How should the capital structure of a company formed?

21 Explain the factors affect the amount of fixed capital.

22 Explain the factors that determine the capital structure of a company.

23 Explain by giving any four reasons, why capital budgeting decisions are important?

24 Explain briefly the factors determining the working capital of an organization.

25 How does trading on equity increase the return on equity shares? Explain with an example.

26 Explain the factors affecting the financing decisions.

27 Write a short note on finance function.

E Understanding Basic Accounting and Role of Computer for Non-Financial Managers

Basic Finance for Non-Financial Managers in corporates and role of computer in accounting

It's not just accountancy specialists who deal with spreadsheets, and figures, and the financial side of business. It's highly likely that, as a line manager or department head, you're going to have to analyze a spreadsheet at some point, or have some form of financial recording to do as part of your job description.

Financial management is a crucial aspect of any thriving business. Profit maximization, or stockholder wealth maximization, are two real concerns for any organization – and they depend on solid financial decisions. To make good decisions, management needs good information. And that information comes from the accounting system.

From the accounting system come the financial statements. These statements contain important information about the organization's operating results. This information is important for effective management, and financial control. As a manager, or any other person with financial responsibility, you have to be able to interpret this information yourself.

Financial statements contain important information about your company's operating results and financial position. The relationship between certain items of financial data can be used to identify areas where your firm excels and, more importantly, where there are opportunities for improvement. Using, understanding, and interpreting these statements will help you make much better business decisions.

The Basic Financial Statements

Businesses record their performance in standard formats called financial statements. The most common of these are:

- Balance Sheet (also known as a Statement of Financial Position, or a Statement of Financial Condition).
- Income Statement (Statement of Profit and Loss, Statement of Earnings, Statement of Operations).
- Cash Flow Statement.

While these statements look at different aspects of the company, they are interrelated and dependent on each other, as information from one is needed to prepare the others. The key to understanding accounts is to have a good grasp of what the basic statements are there to do: how they are prepared, what they tell you, and what they don't.

The Bookkeeping Process

Every time your organization conducts a business transaction, the status of the accounts changes. In a retail company, for example, when a sale is made, the cash account increases, and the inventory decreases. The bookkeeping process keeps track of these changes in various ledgers and journals. The financial statements are then prepared using this information.

Accounting is based on the fundamental accounting equation:

Total Assets = Total Liabilities + Equity

This essentially means that the difference between what the business owns and what it owes represents the equity the company's owners have.

To keep this equation in balance means that, with each transaction, at least two accounts and the balances in those accounts – will change. Accounting is the process of keeping track of those changes, and recording and then reporting them.

To keep track of transactions efficiently, a General Journal (Original Book of Entry) is used. The journal records what happened, the accounts affected, and the amounts.

Once you've identified the accounts that are involved, you need to apply the rules. This involves the following (Golden Rules):

- Asset and Expense accounts are increased by a debit, and decreased by a credit.
- Liabilities, Equity, and Revenue accounts are increased by a credit, and decreased by a debit.
- Debit is the receiver, credit is the giver.

Having a chronological record of the business' transactions is very useful, should you need to go back and review a particular transaction at a later date. The problem with keeping information in this format, though, is that there is no way to determine what the actual balance in each account is after each transaction. For example, you may need to know how much cash is actually in the cash account, and thus in the bank account, at any given time. To keep track of account balances, accountants use what is called a General Ledger.

The General Ledger consists of ledger accounts, one for each account set up in the Chart of Accounts. Debits and credits to each account are posted to the ledger from the journal, and the balance is kept current. Posting is the process of transferring amounts from the general journal to specific general ledger accounts. Because entries are recorded in the ledger after the journal, the general ledger is often called the Book of Final Entry.

JOURNAL

In accounting, a **"journal"** refers to a financial record kept in the form of a book, spreadsheet, or accounting software that contains all the recorded financial transaction information about a business. The entry made is known as journal entry and the process of writing the journal entry is called journalising. Entries are made datewise and they reflect what account is debited and what account is credited.

Characteristics of Journal

Journal has the following features:

1. Journal is the first successful step of the double entry system. A transaction is recorded first of all in the journal. So the journal is called the book of original entry.
2. A transaction is recorded on the same day it takes place. So, journal is called Day Book.
3. Transactions are recorded chronologically, So, journal is called chronological book
4. For each transaction the names of the two concerned accounts indicating which is debited and which is credited, are clearly written in two consecutive lines. This makes ledger-posting easy. That is why journal is called "Assistant to Ledger" or "subsidiary book"
5. Narration is written below each entry.
6. The amount is written in the last two columns – debit amount in debit column and credit amount in credit column.

Advantages of Journal:

The following are the advantages of journal:

1. Each transaction is recorded as soon as it takes place. So there is no possibility of any transaction being omitted from the books of account.
2. Since the transactions are kept recorded in journal, chronologically with narration, it can be easily ascertained when and why a transaction has taken place.
3. For each and every transaction which of the two concerned accounts will be debited and which account credited, are clearly written in journal. So, there is no possibility of committing any mistake in writing the ledger.
4. Journal shows the complete story of a transaction in one entry.
5. Any mistake in ledger can be easily detected with the help of journal.

Objective of an Entry:

While recording transactions in journal the following two objects must be aimed at:

1. That each entry in the journal should be so clear that at any future time we may, without the aid of memory, perceive the exact nature of the transactions.
2. That each transaction should be so classified that we may easily obtain the aggregate effect of such transactions at the end of a certain period.

Narration of an Entry:

It is the remark or explanation put below each entry in the journal. The journal is a book of original entry and all possible details have to recorded in connection with each and every transaction entered there. The details are laid out in the form of a remark at the end of each journal entry, which is called **narration.**

Form of Journal:

Date (1)	Particulars (2)	L.F. (3)	Dr. Amount (4)	Cr. Amount (5)

Column (1) is meant for writing the date of the transaction.

Column (2) is used for recording the names of the two accounts affected by transactions.

Column (3) is meant for noting the number of the page of the ledger on on which the particular account appears in that book.

Column (4) shows the amount to be debited to the account named.

Column (5) shows the amount to be credited to the account stated.

Golden Rules are:

1. Rule for Personal accounts:

Debit the receiver and credit the giver.

2. Rule for Real accounts:

Debit what comes in and credit what goes out, (for assets). Opposite is for liabilities.

3. Rule for Nominal accounts:

Debit all expenses/losses and credit all income/gains.

Rules of Journalizing:

The act of recording transactions in journal is called journalizing. The rules may be summarized as follows:

1. Use two separate lines for writing the names of the two accounts concerned in each transaction.
2. write the name of the debtor or account to be debited in the first line and the name of the creditor or the account to be credited in the next line
3. Write the name of the account to be debited close to the line starting the particulars column and that of the account to be credited at a short distance from this line.
4. Use "Dr" after each debit item and "To" before each credit. The term "Cr." after a credit item is unnecessary, as if one account is debtor, the other must be creditor.
5. To separate one entry from another a line is drawn below every entry to cover particulars column only. The line does not extend to amount column.

Example 1: On first January, 2010 A started business with capital of ₹ 20,000 and his transactions of the month were as follows:

Jan.2	Purchased building for cash	8,000
Jan.8	Purchased goods from C	1,000
Jan.15	Sold goods for cash	500
Jan.20	Goods returned to C	100
Jan.22	Sold goods to R	400
Jan.25	R returned goods	25
Jan.31	Salaries paid for the month	200
Jan.31	Rent paid for the month	150

Solution:

Journal of A

Date	*Particulars*		*L.F*	*Debit*	*Credit*
Jan. 1	Cash Account	...Dr.		20,000	
	To Capital Account				20,000
	(Capital introduced)				
Jan 2.	Building Account	...Dr.		8,000	
	To Cash Account				8,000
	(Building purchased for cash)				
Jan. 8	Purchases Account	...Dr.		1,000	
	To C Account				1,000
	(Goods purchased on credit form C)				

Jan. 15	Cash Account	...Dr.	500	
	To Sales Account			500
	(Goods sold for cash)			
Jan. 20	C Account	...Dr.	100	
	To purchases Returns Account			100
	(Goods returned to C)			
Jan. 22	R Account	...Dr.	400	
	To Sales Account			400
	(Goods sold on credit)			
Jan. 25	Sales returns Account	...Dr.	25	
	To R Account			25
	(Goods returned by him)			
Jan. 31	Salaries Account	...Dr.	200	
	To Cash Account			200
	(Salaries paid)			
Jan. 31	Rent Account	...Dr.	150	
	To Cash Account			150
	(Rent paid in cash)			
	Total		**30,375**	**30,375**

Capital Account: The proprietor's account in the business books is called "capital account". Whenever the proprietor invests money in the business, instead of giving credit to his name, capital account should be credited.

Drawings Account: Any cash or goods taken away by the proprietor for his personal use are called his drawings and are debited to "Drawings Account". Drawings account like the capital account is personal account of the proprietor.

Casts and Carry Forwards: In bookkeeping casting means totaling. The first page of the journal will be cast by drawing a line across the money column. The total of this page will be carried forward to the to the top of second page. The total of the second page will be carried forward to the third page and so on until the last page gives the final total.

When carrying forward the total of the one page to another, the words "carried forward" or "carried over" should be written at the bottom of the first page and words "brought forward" the top of the next page. The abbreviations c/f or c/o and b/f can also be used.

Compound Journal Entries: When two or more transactions of the same nature take place on the same date, a compound journal entry may be made instead of making separate entries for each transaction.

Trade Discount: No entry is passed for trade discount. The purchases or sales should be recorded at net price *i.e.*, after deducting the trade discount from the list price.

Goods Given Away: Sometimes goods are (a) given away as charity (b) taken by the proprietor for his private use (c) distributed free as samples. Such goods are not sales. Therefore they are not credited to sales account but are credited to purchases account because they reduce the amount of goods purchased.

Example 2: On first April 2010 a merchant started business with a capital of ₹ 15,000 and his transactions of the month were as follows:

April 2	Purchased machinery for ₹ 7,000, in cash.
April 3	Bought furniture from S ₹ 300, in cash.
April 7	Purchased goods for cash ₹ 2,500
April 8	Sold goods to R & Sons ₹ 1,500
April 10	Bought goods from B, ₹ 1,000 and from C ₹ 2,000
April 12	Received cash from R & Sons ₹ 1,450, allowed him discount of ₹ 50.
April 15	Paid B cash ₹ 975, discount received ₹ 25.
April 16	Returned goods to C ₹ 500
April 17	Sold goods to Din Mohammad ₹ 800
April 20	Goods returned by Din Mohammad ₹ 200
April 21	Purchased from K goods of the list price of ₹ 600 subject to a 10 per cent trade discount.
April 22	Paid C cash ₹ 1,500
April 25	Gave away charity cash ₹ 50 and goods worth ₹ 30.
April 27	Distributed goods worth ₹ 200 as free samples and goods taken away by the proprietor for personal use ₹ 100
April 28	Amount withdrawn by the proprietor for private use ₹ 200
April 31	Salaries paid for the month ₹ 500

Record these transactions in the journal.

Solution:

Journal

Date	*Particulars*		*L.F*	*Debit*	*Credit*
April 1	Cash Account	...Dr.		15,000	
	To Capital Account				15,000
	(Capital introduced)				
April 2	Machinery Account	...Dr.		7,000	
	To Cash Account				7,000
	(Machinery purchased)				
April 3	Furniture Account	...Dr.		2,500	
	To Cash Account				2,500
	(Goods purchased for cash C)				
April 7	Purchases Account	...Dr.		3,000	
	To Cash Account				3,000
	(Goods purchased for cash)				
April 8	R & Sons	...Dr.		1,500	
	To Sales Account				1,500
	(Goods sold on credit)				
April 10	Purchases Account	...Dr.		3,000	
	To B Account				1,000
	To C Account				2,00
	(Goods purchased on credit)				
April 12	Cash Account	...Dr.		1,450	
	Discount Allowed Account			50	
	To R & Sons				1,500
	(Cash received and discount allowed)				
April 15	B Account	...Dr.		1,000	
	To Cash Account				975
	To Discount Received Account				25
	(Salaries paid)				
April 16	C Account	...Dr.		500	
	To Purchases Return Account				500
	(Goods returned to C)				

Date	Particulars		Dr.	Cr.
April 17	Din Mohammad	...Dr.	800	
	To Sales Account			800
	(Goods sold on credit)			
April 20	Sales Returns Account	...Dr.	200	
	To Din Mohammad			200
	(Goods returned by him)			
April 21	Purchases Account	...Dr.	540	
	To K Account			540
	(Goods purchased on credit)			
April 22	C Account	...Dr.	1,500	
	To Cash Account			1,500
	(Cash paid to C)			
April 25	Charity Account	...Dr.	80	
	To Cash Account			50
	To Purchases Account			30
	(Cash and goods given in charity)			
April 27	Free samples Account	...Dr.	200	
	Drawings Account	...Dr.	100	
	To Purchases Account			300
	(Goods distributed free and taken by the proprietor for private use)			
April 28	Drawings Account	...Dr.	200	
	To Cash			200
	(Cash drawn by the proprietor)			
April 31	Salaries Account	...Dr.	500	
	To Cash Account			500
	(Salaries paid in cash)			

Notes:

(a) In actual practice even the word "Dr." is not written after the name of the account to be debited, because it is also implied.

(b) When writing the name of a personal account, it is not considered necessary to add the word "account" after the name of the person.

The journalizing and posting process are the first two steps of the entire accounting cycle. From there, the Financial Statements are prepared.

What is a ledger?

A ledger can be visualized as a book containing a page for each of the accounts a firm maintains. Accounts are maintained to reflect assets, liabilities, owners' equity, revenues and expenses of the firm. All business transactions in the Journal are posted in the respective accounts in the ledger so that the necessary information connected with individual accounts is obtained as and when required.

The ledger helps to achieve the following results in respect of various categories of accounts.

1. Personal accounts would show how much money the firm needs to receive from its customers and how much it has to pay to its suppliers.
2. The real accounts would reflect the values of the properties and stocks.
3. The nominal accounts would reflect the revenues earned from various sources of income and the amount spent on various expense items.

Standard Form of Ledger Account

Account Title (Name of the Account)

Dr. Cr.

Date	Particulars	Journal Folio (Account Credited)	Amount (₹)	Particulars Date	Journal Folio (Account Debited)	Amount (₹)
	To			By		

The ledger account is divided into two equal sides. The left hand side is called the Debit side and the right hand side is called the Credit side. The abbreviations Dr. and Cr. are placed at the top to indicate debit and credit sides. In the exhibit debit side and credit side are written in expanded form for clarity.

The Procedure of Posting in the Ledger Account

The journal entry normally specifies one account to be debited and one account to be credited. The page in the ledger corresponding to one of the accounts (let us say the account to be debited) is opened and the entry is made in the following manner :

Making the debit entry

The date column on the debit side is filled with the transaction date as in the journal entry.As the account in the ledger is to be debited; the transaction is entered on the debit side.

The name of the other account included in the journal entry of the transaction (the account to be credited in the transaction) is entered in the particulars column. The account name is preceded with "To". The Journal folio column is used to record the page number of the journal in which the transaction (posted to the ledger now) is written. In the amount column, the amount involved in the transaction as written in the journal entry is posted.

Making the credit entry

The page (in the ledger) corresponding to the account to be credited is opened. The date column on the credit side is filled with the transaction date as in the journal entry on the credit side. The transaction is entered on the credit side. The name of the other account included in the journal entry of the transaction (the account to be debited in the transaction) is entered in the particulars column. The account name is preceded by "By". The journal page number is written in the journal folio column. The amount of the transaction is entered in the amount column.

Balancing of Accounts at the end of the Period

At the end of each period, month or year, personal and real accounts are balanced. In balancing, the difference between the total debits amounts and credit amounts is determined.

Credit balance

If the total of credit side is bigger than the total of debit side, the difference is credit balance (the account has a credit balance). This credit balance is written on the debit side of ledger account and in the particulars column the words "To Balance c/d" are written.

Debit balance

If the total of debit side is bigger than the total of credit side, the difference is debit balance (the account has a debit balance). This debit balance is written on the credit side of ledger account and in the particulars column the words "By Balance c/d" are written. After inserting "To Balance c/d" or "By Balance c/d" on the short side of the account, the totals of both sides will be same. The totals of both sides are placed in the same line at the same level in the account. Then the balance is brought down or entered on the opposite side (heavier side) below the closing line (the line where both totals are written. The first day of the new period is entered in the date column. The words "Balance b/d" are written in the particulars column. The balance is written in the amount column.

Balance Sheet

A Balance Sheet indicates the financial position of a business at one point in time; it shows what the business owns and owes. The general journal captures day-to-day account balances. At the end of an accounting period, a Balance Sheet is prepared.

The Balance Sheet has three sections:

Assets – the things of value that the company owns.

Liabilities – obligations to pay or provide goods or services at some later date.

Equity – the amount of net assets (assets - liabilities) owing to the owners of the business.

The Balance Sheet is named as such because the total of the assets must equal the total of the liabilities and equity. What a company owns equals what it owes to its creditors and owners.

Income Statement

At certain points during the year, each business wants to know how well it is doing. Is it earning a profit? Is it losing money? Just how well is it doing compared to other firms? Is it likely to be able to earn a profit in the future? To answer these questions, it uses an Income Statement.

The Income Statement communicates the inflow of **revenue**, and the outflow of **expenses**, over a given period of time. Revenue is the inflow of assets (*i.e.*, cash or accounts receivable) to a company in return for services performed, or goods sold. Expenses are the outflow or consumption of assets (*i.e.*, cash, inventory, supplies), or obligations incurred (*i.e.*, accounts payable, taxes payable) while generating revenue. The difference between these two is the **Net Profit.**

An Income Statement therefore shows the operating profit (or loss) of a business.

Cash Flow Statement

The Cash Flow Statement records inflows and outflows of cash during a period of time, and is divided into cash flow from operations, financing, and investing activities. To prepare a statement of cash flow you must convert net income from accrual-based accounting to cash. You therefore have to add and subtract changes in non-cash accounts that have accrued during the period.

For instance, you need to add back depreciation amounts, because although depreciation expense decreases net income, it has no bearing on actual cash. Likewise, you have to deduct any decreases in accounts payable because that is a use of cash that was not accounted for on the Income Statement. The following table outlines the major sources and uses of cash:

Sources of Cash	**Uses of Cash**
Operations	Cash Dividends
New loans	Repayment of loans
New stock issues or owner investment	Repurchase of stock
Sale of property, plant, or equipment	Purchase of property, plant, or equipment
Sale of other non-current asset	Purchase of other non-current asset

By analyzing the differences between the balance sheets for the beginning of the period and the end of the period, and accounting for the net income for the period, you can prepare a Cash Flow Statement:

Financial Statement Interpretation

Armed with some knowledge of accounts, it's important to understand what the statements actually tell you.

What an Income Statement says:

- The Income Statement reports the main and any secondary sources of income. For example, Fees Earned would be the primary revenue in a dental office. If they had bonds, a secondary source of revenue would be Interest Earned from Bond Investment.
- The terms used to describe the revenue will provide a clue about the nature of the organization. For example, Fees Earned implies a service company; Commissions Earned implies a brokerage; while Sales Revenue implies a retail or wholesale firm.
- The items listed as expenses are expired, meaning they have no useful value left.
- The result of matching the revenues and expenses yields the Net Income or Net Earnings if the statement is called the Earnings Statement. The term 'net' implies that the revenues and expenses have been matched, and therefore there is not an over or under statement of the income (loss).

What an Income Statement does not say:

- An Income Statement does not predict the future net income for any accounting period. Since the future is full of uncertainty, a reader of a historical Income Statement can't rely on the reported results of any single period for an indication of future results.
- An Income Statement, no matter how well prepared, does not provide an exact measurement of net income for the accounting period. No matter how hard you try, it is impossible to get an exact match. Consider, for example, an advertising expense. If management spent $1,000 in December on advertising, and achieved $5,000 sales revenue for December, that does not mean that the advertising brought in exactly $5,000 revenue. There may also be revenue generated in January that can be attributed to the December advertising. When it is difficult to measure, the expense is accounted for in the period it was incurred.
- An Income Statement does not report True Profit, which is the difference between total funds invested over the life of the company and funds realized from the sale of the company. To calculate this, you would have to calculate the difference between assets invested during the lifetime of the business, and the amount finally received from remaining assets after winding up the business. You would also have to deduct any personal withdrawals because these were actually paid out of the 'profits.'
- Net Income does not mean cash! Always keep in mind that net income is the excess revenue over related expenses for a specific accounting period. Cash has very little to do with determining net income. True, revenue refers to an inflow of cash and expense to an outflow, but often the inflow of cash is used for further investment. Additionally, revenues and expenses are recorded at the time of occurrence, not when cash changes

hands. What about the case of depreciation expense which does not represent an outflow of cash at all?

What a Balance Sheet says:

- A Balance Sheet gives readers a detailed summary of the assets and claims against those assets, as at a particular date.
- A Balance Sheet provides the reader with information about the financial position of the firm with regard to its ability to pay current debts. By comparing the current assets to the current liabilities, the reader can assess whether the company is in a position to meet to meet its short-term financial obligations.
- A Balance Sheet gives the reader a view of the firm's financial position to carry on its business operations. The fixed-asset section indicates how many resources the company has working for it to assist in revenue generation.
- Finally, a Balance Sheet reveals the strength of the owner's claim against the assets. Remember, however, that this claim is residual or the remaining claim after the creditors'.

What a Balance Sheet does not say:

- A Balance Sheet does not report the details of how the profits were made. That information comes from the Income Statement.
- A Balance Sheet does not show the claims of the creditors and the owner(s) against a specific asset. The claims are against the assets in general.
- The word 'Capital' under owner's equity must not be interpreted as cash. The investment can come in many forms – cash being just one of them. The owner's original cash investment may have gone primarily to purchase fixed assets in order to assist revenue generation. Capital means investment not cash.
- A Balance Sheet does not report the market value, current value, or worth of a business. Many readers believe the total assets represent a bundle of future cash reserves. This is not true because fixed assets are reported at historical cost, and their purpose is to assist revenue generation. They are not intended for sale to enhance cash flow.

Role of computer in accounting – an introduction

Earlier the accountant was required to prepare summary of transactions and financial statements manually. When a system contains only human resources it is called manual system; when it uses only computer resources, it is called computerized system and when it uses both human and computer resources, it is called computer-based system. The advanced technology involves various machines capable of performing different accounting functions, for example, a billing machine. This machine is capable of computing discount, adding net total and posting the requisite data to the relevant accounts. With substantial increase in the number of transactions, a machine was developed which could store and process accounting data in no time. Such advancement leads to number of growing successful organizations. A newer version of machine is evolved with increased speed, storage, and processing capacity. A computer to which they were connected operated these machines. As a result, the maintenance of accounting data on a real-time basis became almost essential. Now maintaining accounting records become more convenient with the computerized accounting.

The computerized accounting uses the concept of databases. For this purpose an accounting software is used to implement a computerized accounting system. It does away the necessity to create and maintain journals, ledgers, etc., which are essential part of manual accounting. Some of the commonly used accounting softwares are **Tally, Cash Manager etc.** Accounting software is used to implement a computerized accounting. The computerized accounting is based on the concept of database. It is basic software which allows access to the data contained in the data base. It is a system to manage collection of data insuring at the same time that it remains reliable and confidential.

Following are the components of Computerized accounting software:

1. Preparation of accounting documents: Computer helps in preparing accounting documents like Cash Memo, Bills and invoices etc., and preparing accounting vouchers.

2. Recording of transactions: Every day business transactions are recorded with the help of computer software. Logical scheme is implied for codification of account and transaction. Every account and transaction is assigned a unique code. *The grouping of accounts is done from the first stage*. This process simplifies the work of recording the transactions.

3. Preparation of Trial Balance and Financial Statements: After recording of transaction, the data is transferred into Ledger account automatically by the computer. Trial Balance is prepared by the computer to check accuracy of the records. With the help of trial balance the computer can be programmed to prepare Trading, Profit and Loss account and Balance Sheet.

Transaction processing system (TPS) is the first stage of computerized accounting system. The purpose of any TPS is to record, process, validate and store transactions that occur in various functional areas of a business for subsequent retrieval and usage. TPS involves following steps in processing a transaction: Data Entry, Data Validation, Processing and Revalidation, Storage, Information and Reporting.

A comprehensive accounting software Financial Accounting, Billing including Excise , Inventory (batch wise / location wise), Sales Tax Reports , Excise reports / Registers , Job work management, consignment sales , customized billing formats and other documents.

SAP Accounting Products

SAP Business One is affordable, easy-to-use business management software designed specifically for small and midsize businesses. It enables you to manage your critical business functions across sales, distribution, and financials, all in a single integrated system. With SAP Business One, you can instantaneously access a complete and up-to-the-minute view of your business, so you can respond to customers faster and grow your business more profitably.

The SAP Business One application offers a comprehensive and integrated set of tools to effectively manage all financial processes in your organization. As the core functionality of SAP

Business One, financials management incorporates all key accounting processes, such as journal entries, accounts receivable, and accounts payable. Real-time accounting functions trigger accounting postings automatically when relevant business events occur.

SAP Business One supports automatic tax calculations as well as multi-currency transactions. Posting templates and recurring postings further streamline and simplify your accounting processes.

Controlling software in SAP Business One allows you to define and manage budgets and compare actual and planned figures at any time to get an accurate and up-to-date picture of your business. Profit or cost centers are easily created and let you allocate revenue and expenses according to distribution rules – which are customizable and specific to your business.

The banking software in SAP Business One provides all the tools and functionality necessary to manage all your payment processing, including checks, cash, credit cards, and bank transfers. The reconciliation tool allows you to easily reconcile incoming and outgoing payments with vendor and customer invoices.

SAP Business One offers powerful financial reporting tools such as balance sheets, profit and loss statements, cash flow statements, and aging reports. The XL Reporter tool in SAP Business One enables the seamless integration of financial reports into Microsoft Excel templates.

SAP Key Strengths

- The SAP Business One application offers a comprehensive and integrated set of tools to effectively manage all financial processes in your organization.
- As the core functionality of SAP Business One, financials and accounting management incorporates all key accounting processes, such as journal entries, accounts receivable, and accounts payable.
- Real-time accounting functions trigger accounting postings automatically when relevant business events occur. SAP Business One supports automatic tax calculations as well as multi-currency transactions. Posting templates and recurring postings further streamline and simplify your accounting processes.
- SAP Business One offers powerful financial reporting tools such as balance sheets, profit and loss statements, cash flow statements, and aging reports. The XL Reporter tool in SAP Business One enables the seamless integration of financial reports into Microsoft Excel templates.
- The banking software in SAP Business One provides all the tools and functionality necessary to manage all your payment processing, including checks, cash, credit cards, and bank transfers. The reconciliation tool allows you to easily reconcile incoming and outgoing payments with vendor and customer invoices.
- Profit or cost centers are easily created and let you allocate revenue and expenses according to distribution rules – which are customizable and specific to your business.

F Technical Analysis of Stock

What Is Technical Analysis?

Technical analysis is a method of evaluating securities by analyzing the statistics generated by market activity, such as past prices and volume. Technical analysis is the study of market action (price, volume and open interest) through use of charts to determine current market / price trend and anticipate future market / price trend. Technical analysts do not attempt to measure a security's intrinsic value, but instead use charts and other tools to identify patterns that can suggest future activity.

Unlike fundamental analysts, technical analysts don't care whether a stock is undervalued - the only thing that matters is a security's past trading data and what information this data can provide about where the security might move in the future.

The field of technical analysis is based on three assumptions:

1. The market discounts everything.
2. Price moves in trends.
3. History tends to repeat itself.

1. The Market Discounts Everything

A major criticism of technical analysis is that it only considers price movement, ignoring the fundamental factors of the company. However, technical analysis assumes that, at any given time, a stock's price reflects everything that has or could affect the company - including fundamental factors. Technical analysts believe that the company's fundamentals, along with broader economic factors and market psychology, are all priced into the stock, removing the need to actually consider these factors separately. This only leaves the analysis of price movement, which technical theory views as a product of the supply and demand for a particular stock in the market.

2. Price Moves in Trends

In technical analysis, price movements are believed to follow trends. This means that after a trend has been established, the future price movement is more likely to be in the same direction as the trend than to be against it. Most technical trading strategies are based on this assumption.

3. History Tends To Repeat Itself

Another important idea in technical analysis is that history tends to repeat itself, mainly in terms of price movement. The repetitive nature of price movements is attributed to market psychology; in other words, market participants tend to provide a consistent reaction to similar market stimuli over time. Technical analysis uses chart patterns to analyze market movements and understand trends. Although many of these charts have been used for more than 100 years, they are still believed to be relevant because they illustrate patterns in price movements that often repeat themselves.

Technical Analysis: Fundamental Vs. Technical Analysis

Technical analysis and fundamental analysis are the two main schools of thought in the financial markets. As we've mentioned, technical analysis looks at the price movement of a security and uses this data to predict its future price movements. Fundamental analysis, on the other hand, looks at economic factors, known as fundamentals. Let's get into the details of how these two approaches differ and how technical and fundamental analysis can be used together to analyze securities.

The Differences

(a) Charts vs. Financial Statements

At the most basic level, a technical analyst approaches a security from the charts, while a fundamental analyst starts with the financial statements.

By looking at the balance sheet, cash flow statement and income statement, a fundamental analyst tries to determine a company's value. In financial terms, an analyst attempts to measure a company's intrinsic value. In this approach, investment decisions are fairly easy to make - if the price of a stock trades below its intrinsic value, it's a good investment. Although this is an oversimplification (fundamental analysis goes beyond just the financial statements) for the purposes of this tutorial, this simple tenet holds true.

Technical traders, on the other hand, believe there is no reason to analyze a company's fundamentals because these are all accounted for in the stock's price. Technicians believe that all the information they need about a stock can be found in its charts.

(b) Time Horizon

Fundamental analysis takes a relatively long-term approach to analyzing the market compared to technical analysis. While technical analysis can be used on a timeframe of weeks, days or even minutes, fundamental analysis often looks at data over a number of years.

The different timeframes that these two approaches use is a result of the nature of the investing style to which they each adhere. It can take a long time for a company's value to be reflected in the market, so when a fundamental analyst estimates intrinsic value, a gain is not realized until the stock's market price rises to its "correct" value. This type of investing is called 'value investing' and assumes that the short-term market is wrong, but that the price of a particular stock will correct itself over the long run. This "long-run" can represent a timeframe of as long as several years, in some cases.

Furthermore, the numbers that a fundamentalist analyzes are only released over long periods of time. Financial statements are filed quarterly and changes in earnings per share don't emerge on a daily basis like price and volume information. Also remember that fundamentals are the actual characteristics of a business. New management can't implement sweeping changes overnight and it takes time to create new products, marketing campaigns, supply chains, etc. Part of the reason that fundamental analysts use a long-term timeframe, therefore, is because the data they use to analyze a stock is generated much more slowly than the price and volume data used by technical analysts.

(c) Trading Versus Investing

Not only is technical analysis more short term in nature than fundamental analysis, but the goals of a purchase (or sale) of a stock are usually different for each approach. In general, technical analysis is used for a trade, whereas fundamental analysis is used to make an investment. Investors buy assets they believe can increase in value, while traders buy assets they believe they can sell to somebody else at a greater price. The line between a trade and an investment can be blurry, but it does characterize a difference between the two schools.

Can They Co-Exist?

Although technical analysis and fundamental analysis are seen by many as polar opposites - the oil and water of investing - many market participants have experienced great success by combining the two. For example, some fundamental analysts use technical analysis techniques to figure out the best time to enter into an undervalued security. Oftentimes, this situation occurs when the security is severely oversold. By timing entry into a security, the gains on the investment can be greatly improved.

Alternatively, some technical traders might look at fundamentals to add strength to a technical signal. For example, if a sell signal is given through technical patterns and indicators, a technical trader might look to reaffirm his or her decision by looking at some key fundamental data. Oftentimes, having both the fundamentals and technicals on your side can provide the best-case scenario for a trade.

While mixing some of the components of technical and fundamental analysis is not well received by the most devoted groups in each school, there are certainly benefits to at least understanding both schools of thought.

Technical Analysis: The Use of Trend line

Technical analysis is built on the assumption that prices trend. Trend Lines are an important tool in technical analysis for both trend identification and confirmation. A trend line is a straight line that connects two or more price points and then extends into the future to act as a line of support or resistance. Many of the principles applicable to support and resistance levels can be applied to trend lines as well.

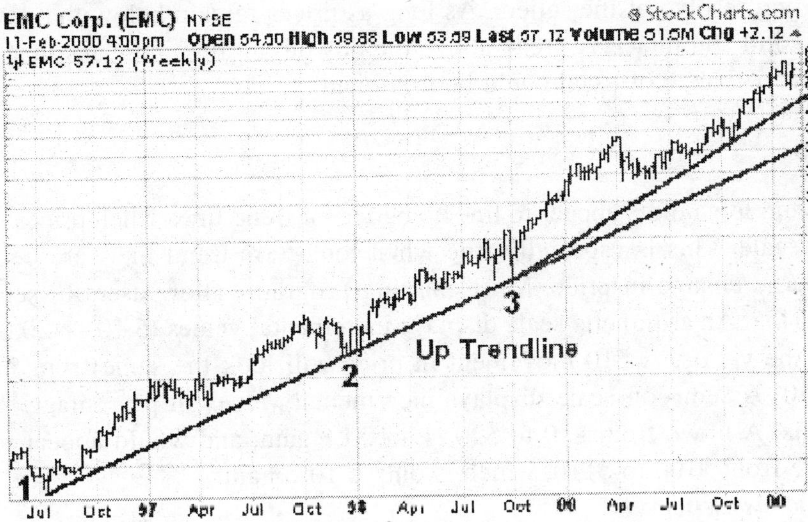

Uptrend Line

An uptrend line has a positive slope and is formed by connecting two or more low points. The second low must be higher than the first for the line to have a positive slope. Uptrend lines act as support and indicate that net-demand (demand less supply) is increasing even as the price rises. A rising price combined with increasing demand is very bullish, and shows a strong determination on the part of the buyers. As long as prices remain above the trend line, the uptrend is considered solid and intact. A break below the uptrend line indicates that net-demand has weakened and a change in trend could be imminent.

Downtrend Line

A downtrend line has a negative slope and is formed by connecting two or more high points. The second high must be lower than the first for the line to have a negative slope.

Downtrend lines act as resistance, and indicate that net-supply (supply less demand) is increasing even as the price declines. A declining price combined with increasing supply is very bearish, and shows the strong resolve of the sellers. As long as prices remain below the downtrend line, the downtrend is solid and intact. A break above the downtrend line indicates that net-supply is decreasing and that a change of trend could be imminent.

Scale Settings

High points and low points appear to line up better for trend lines when prices are displayed using a semi-log scale. This is especially true when long-term trend lines are being drawn or when there is a large change in price. Most charting programs allow users to set the scale as arithmetic or semi-log. An arithmetic scale displays incremental values (5,10,15,20,25,30) evenly as they move up the y-axis. A $10 movement in price will look the same from $10 to $20 or from $100 to $110. A semi-log scale displays incremental values in percentage terms as they move up the y-axis. A move from $10 to $20 is a 100% gain, and would appear to be a much larger than a move from $100 to $110, which is only a 10% gain.

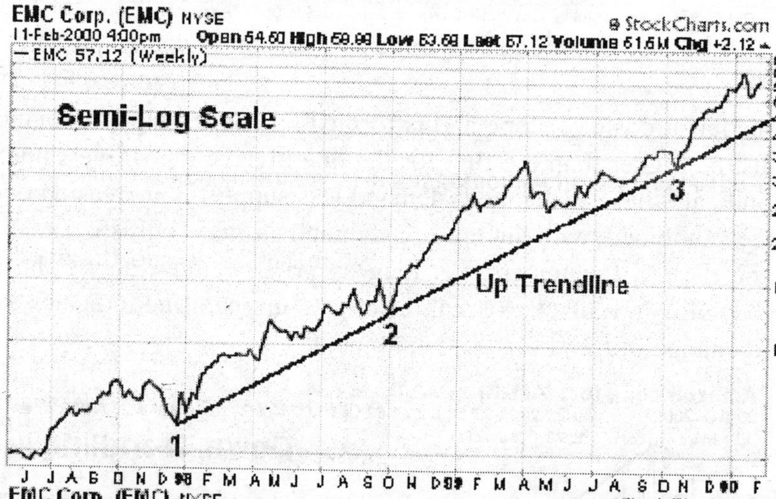

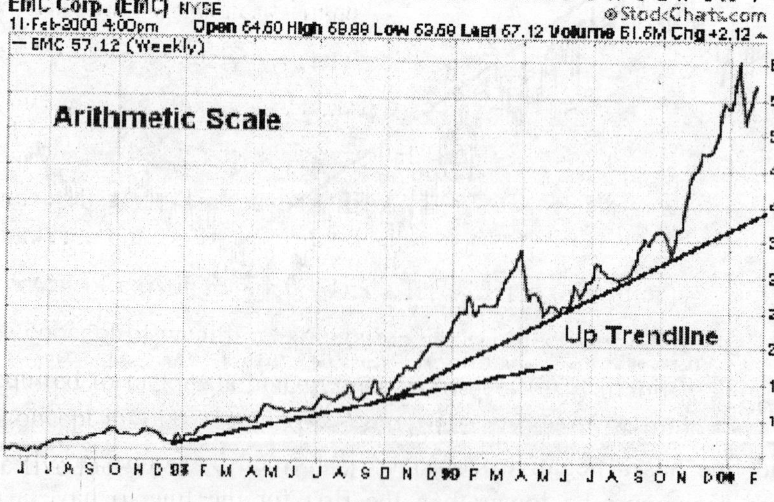

In the case of EMC there was a large price change over a long period of time. While there were not any false breaks below the uptrend line on the arithmetic scale, the rate of ascent appears smoother on the semi-log scale. EMC doubled three times in less than two years. On the semi-log scale, the trend line fits all the way up. On the arithmetic scale, three different trend lines were required to keep pace with the advance.

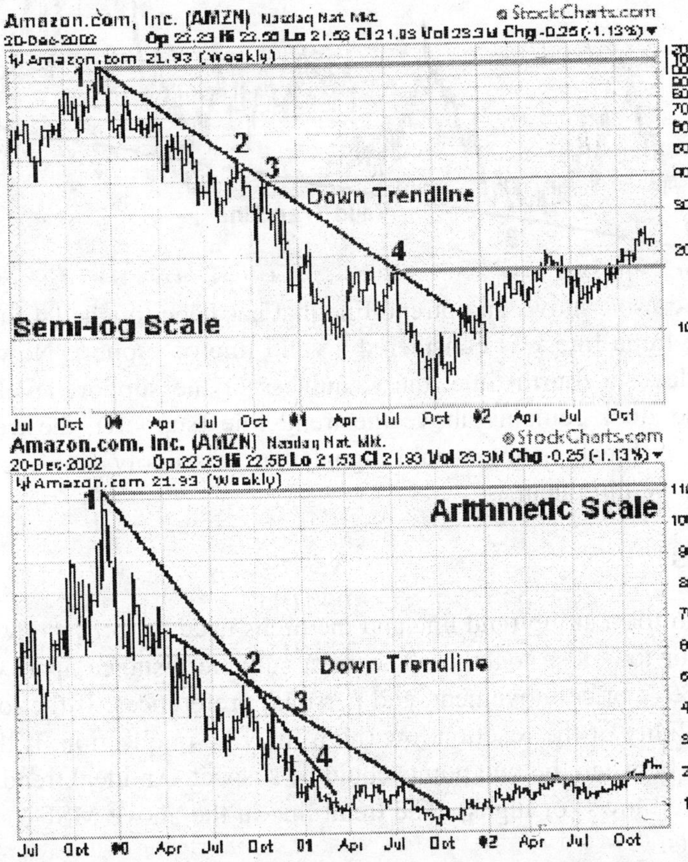

In the case of Amazon.com there were two false breaks above the downtrend line as the stock declined during 2000 and 2001. These false break outs could have led to premature buying as the stock continued to decline after each one. The stock lost 60% of its value three times over a two year period. The semi-log scale reflects the percentage loss evenly, and the downtrend line was never broken.

Validation

It takes two or more points to draw a trend line The more points are used to draw the trend line, the more validity attached to the support or resistance level represented by the trend line. It can sometimes be difficult to find more than 2 points from which to construct a trend line Even though trend lines are an important aspect of technical analysis, it is not always possible to draw trend lines on every price chart. Sometimes the lows or highs just don't match up, and it is best not to force the issue. The general rule in technical analysis is that it takes two points to draw a trend line and the third point confirms the validity.

The chart of Microsoft shows an uptrend line that has been touched 4 times. After the third touch in Nov-99, the trend line was considered a valid line of support. Now that the stock has bounced off of this level a fourth time, the soundness of the support level is enhanced even more. As long as the stock remains above the trend line (support), the trend will remain in control of the bulls. A break below would signal that net-supply was increasing and that a change in trend could be imminent.

Spacing of Points

The lows used to form an uptrend line and the highs used to form a downtrend line should not be too far apart, or too close together. The most suitable distance apart will depend on the time frame, the degree of price movement, and personal preferences. If the lows (highs) are too close together, the validity of the reaction low (high) may be in question. If the lows are too far apart, the relationship between the two points could be suspect. An ideal trend line is made up of relatively evenly spaced lows (or highs). The trend line in the above MSFT example represents well-spaced low points.

On the Wal-Mart example, the second high point appears to be too close to the first high point for a valid trend line; however, it would be feasible to draw a trend line beginning at point 2 and extending down to the February reaction high.

Angles

As the steepness of a trend line increases, the validity of the support or resistance level decreases. A steep trend line results from a sharp advance (or decline) over a brief period of time. The angle of a trend line created from such sharp moves is unlikely to offer a meaningful support or resistance level. Even if the trend line is formed with three seemingly valid points, attempting to play a trend line break or to use the support and resistance level established it will often prove difficult.

The trend line for Yahoo! was touched four times over a 5-month period. The spacing between the points appears OK, but the steepness of the trend line is unsustainable, and the price is more likely than not to drop below the trend line. However, trying to time this drop or make a play after the trend line is broken is a difficult task. The amount of data displayed and the size of the chart can also affect the angle of a trend line. Short and wide charts are less likely to have steep trend lines than long and narrow charts. Keep that in mind when assessing the validity and sustainability of a trend line.

Internal Trend Lines

Sometimes there appears to be the possibility for drawing a trend line, but the exact points do not match up cleanly. The highs or lows might be out of whack, the angle might be too steep or the points might be too close together. If one or two points could be ignored, then a fitted trend line could be formed. With the volatility present in the market, prices can over-react, and produce spikes that distort the highs and lows. One method for dealing with over-reactions is to draw internal trend lines. Even though an internal trend line ignores price spikes, the ignoring should be within reason.

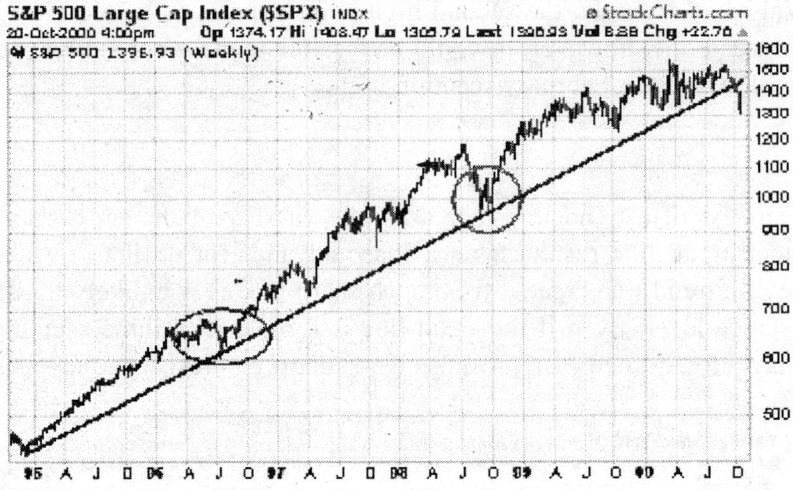

The long-term trend line for the S&P 500 extends up from the end of 1994, and passes through low points in Jul-96, Sept-98 and Oct-98. These lows were formed with selling climaxes, and represented extreme price movements that protrude beneath the trend line. By drawing the trend line through the lows, the line appears to be at a reasonable angle, and the other lows match up extremely well.

Sometimes, there is a price cluster with a high or low spike sticking out. A price cluster is an area where prices are grouped within a tight range over a period of time. The price cluster can be used to draw the trend line, and the spike can be ignored. The Coca-Cola chart shows an internal trend line that is formed by ignoring price spikes and using the price clusters, instead. In October and November 1998, Coke formed a peak, with the November peak just higher than the October peak (1). If the November peak had been used to draw a trend line, then the slope would have been more negative, and there would have appeared to be a breakout in Dec-98 (gray line). However, this would have only been a two-point trend line, because the May-June highs are too close together (black arrows). Once the Dec-99 peak formed (green arrow), it would have been possible to draw an internal trend line based on the price clusters around the Oct/Nov-98 and the

Dec-99 peaks (blue line). This trend line is based on three solid touches, and it accurately forecasts resistance in Jan-00 (blue arrow).

Conclusion

Trend lines can offer great insight, but if used improperly, they can also produce false signals. Other items - such as horizontal support and resistance levels or peak-and-trough analysis - should be employed to validate trend line breaks. While trend lines have become a very popular aspect of technical analysis, they are merely one tool for establishing, analyzing, and confirming a trend. Trend lines should not be the final arbiter, but should serve merely as a warning that a change in trend may be imminent. By using trend line breaks for warnings, investors and traders can pay closer attention to other confirming signals for a potential change in trend.

Dow Theory

The ideas of Charles Dow, the first editor of the Wall Street Journal, form the basis of technical analysis today. In a nutshell, this theory seeks to study the major movements in the market with a view to establish trendss.

Dow created the Industrial Average, of top blue chip stocks, and a second average of top railroad stocks (now the Transport Average). He believed that the behavior of the averages reflected the hopes and fears of the entire market. The behavior patterns that he observed apply to markets throughout the world.

The Dow Theory classifies the movements in stock prices into: (a) Primary movements; (b) Secondary reactions; (c) Minor movements.

Markets fluctuate in more than one time frame at the same time:

Nothing is more certain than that the market has three well defined movements which fit into each other.

- The first is the daily variation due to local causes and the balance of buying and selling at that particular time (Ripple).
- The secondary movement covers a period ranging from days to weeks, averaging probably between six to eight weeks (Wave).
- The third move is the great swing covering anything from months to years, averaging between 6 to 48 months. (Tide).

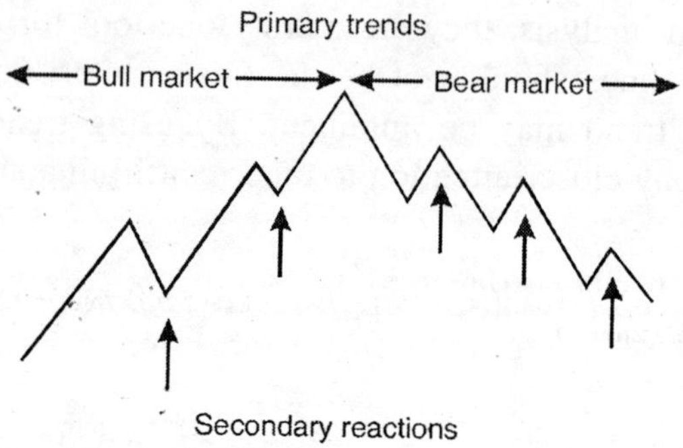

- Bull markets are broad upward movements of the market that may last several years, interrupted by secondary reactions. Bear markets are long declines interrupted by secondary rallies. These movements are referred to as the primary trend.
- Secondary movements normally retrace from one third to two thirds of the primary trend since the previous secondary movement.
- Daily fluctuations are important for short-term trading, but are unimportant in analysis of broad market movements.
- Various cycles have subsequently been identified within these broad categories.

Bull markets

- Bull markets commence with reviving confidence as business conditions improve.
- Prices rise as the market responds to improved earnings
- Rampant speculation dominates the market and price advances are based on hopes and expectations rather than actual results.

Bear markets

- Bear markets start with abandonment of the hopes and expectations that sustained inflated prices.
- Prices decline in response to disappointing earnings.
- Distress selling follows as speculators attempt to close out their positions and securities are sold without regard to their true value.

Ranging Markets

- A secondary reaction may take the form of a 'line' which may endure for several weeks.
- Price fluctuates within a narrow range of about five per cent.

Lines

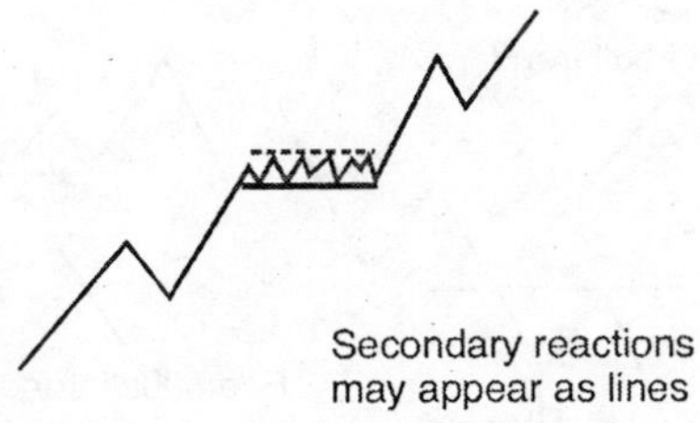

Breakouts from a range can occur in either direction.

- Advances above the upper limit of the line signal accumulation and higher prices;
- Declines below the lower limit indicate distribution and lower prices;
- Volume is used to confirm price breakouts.

Trends

Bull Trends

A bull trend is identified by a series of rallies where each rally exceeds the highest point of the previous rally. The decline, between rallies, ends above the lowest point of the previous decline.

Successive higher highs and higher lows.

Bull Trend

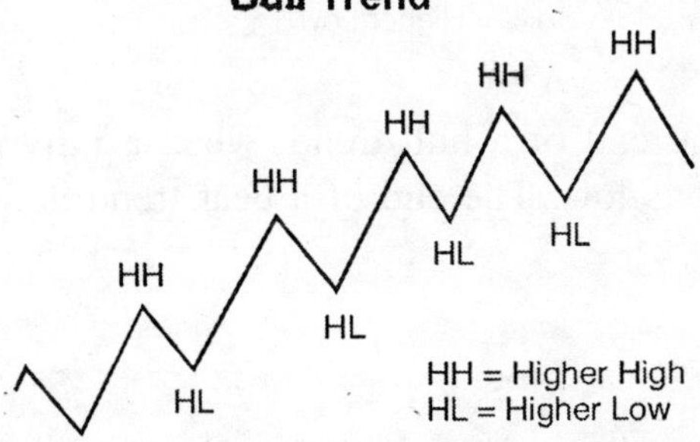

The start of an up trend is signaled when price makes a higher low (trough), followed by a rally above the previous high (peak):

Start = higher Low + break above previous High.

The end is signaled by a lower high (peak), followed by a decline below the previous low (trough):

End = lower High + break below previous Low.

Bull Trend: Start and End

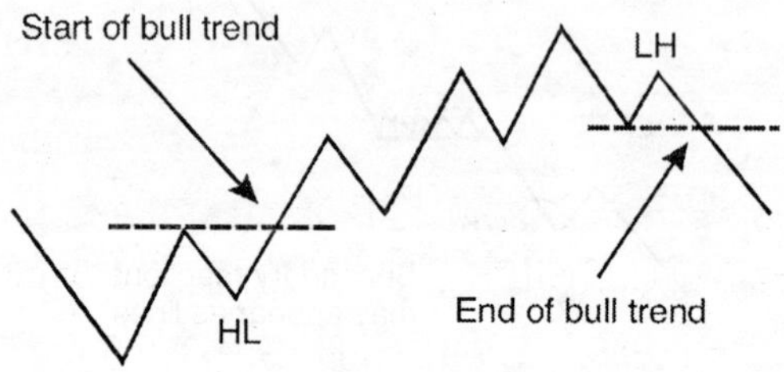

Bear Trends

Each successive rally fails to penetrate the high point of the previous rally. Each decline terminates at a lower point than the preceding decline.

Successive lower highs and lower lows.

Bear Trend

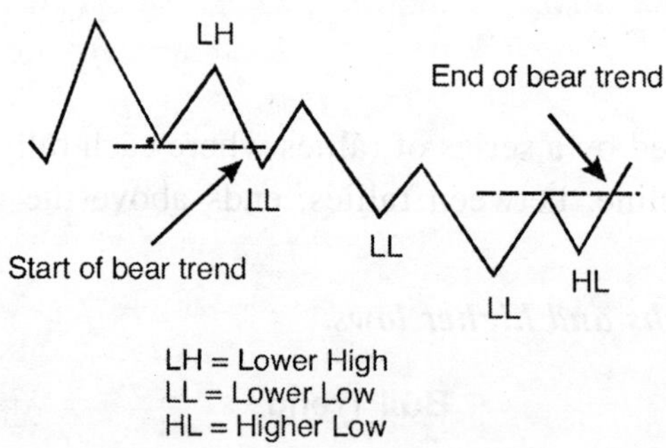

A bear trend starts at the end of a bull trend: when a rally ends with a lower peak and then retreats below the previous low. The end of a bear trend is identical to the start of a bull trend.

Large Corrections

A large correction occurs when price falls below the previous low (during a bull trend) or where price rises above the previous high (in a bear trend).

Large Corrections: Start and End of Trends

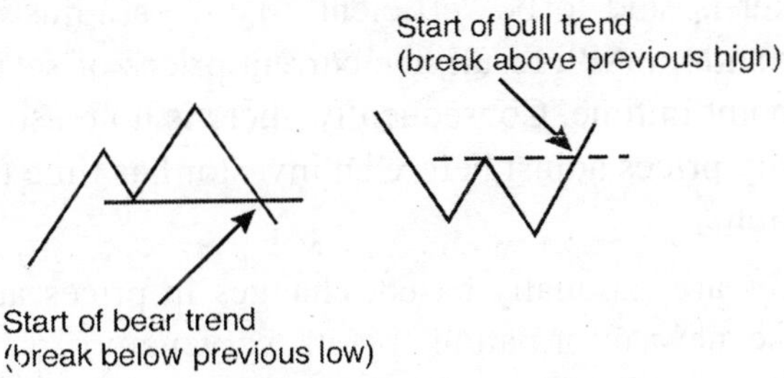

Some purists argue that a trend ends if the sequence of higher highs and higher lows is broken. Others argue that a bear trend has not started until there is a lower High and Low nor has a bull trend started until there is a higher Low and High.

For practical purposes: **Only accept large corrections as trend changes in the primary trend:**

- A bull trend starts when price rallies above the previous high,
- A bull trend ends when price declines below the previous low,
- A bear trend starts at the end of a bull trend (and vice versa)

The Efficient Markets Hypothesis

What Does *Efficient Market Hypothesis - EMH* Mean?

An investment theory that states it is impossible to "beat the market" because stock market efficiency causes existing share prices to always incorporate and reflect all relevant information. According to the EMH, stocks always trade at their fair value on stock exchanges, making it impossible for investors to either purchase undervalued stocks or sell stocks for inflated prices. As such, it should be impossible to outperform the overall market through expert stock selection or market timing, and that the only way an investor can possibly obtain higher returns is by purchasing riskier investments.

The efficient markets hypothesis (EMH), popularly known as the **Random Walk Theory**, is the proposition that current stock prices fully reflect available information about the value of the firm, and there is no way to earn excess profits, (more than the market over all), by using this information. It deals with one of the most fundamental and exciting issues in finance – why prices change in security markets and how those changes take place. It has very important implications for investors as well as for financial managers.

Many investors try to identify securities that are undervalued, and are expected to increase in value in the future, and particularly those that will increase more than others. Many investors, including investment managers, believe that they **can** select securities that will outperform the market. They use a variety of forecasting and valuation techniques to aid them in their investment decisions. Obviously, any edge that an investor possesses can be translated into substantial profits.

The efficient markets hypothesis (EMH) suggests that profiting from predicting price movements is very difficult and unlikely. The main engine behind price changes is the arrival of new information. A market is said to be "efficient" if prices adjust quickly and, on average, without bias, to new information. As a result, the current prices of securities reflect all available information at any given point in time. Consequently, there is no reason to believe that prices are too high or too low. Security prices adjust before an investor has time to trade on and profit from a new a piece of information.

However, while prices are rationally based, changes in prices are expected to be random and unpredictable, because new information, by its very nature, is unpredictable. Therefore stock prices are said to follow a **random walk**.

THREE VERSIONS OF THE EFFICIENT MARKETS HYPOTHESIS

The efficient markets hypothesis predicts that market prices should incorporate all available information at any point in time. There are, however, different *kinds* of information that influence security values. Consequently, financial researchers distinguish among three versions of the Efficient Markets Hypothesis, depending on what is meant by the term "all available information".

Weak Form Efficiency

The weak form of the efficient markets hypothesis asserts that the current price fully incorporates information contained in the past history of prices *only*. That is, nobody can detect mis-priced securities and "beat" the market by analyzing past prices. The weak form of the hypothesis got its name for a reason – security prices are arguably the most public as well as the most easily available pieces of information. Thus, one should not be able to profit from using something that "everybody else knows". On the other hand, many financial analysts attempt to generate profits by studying exactly what this hypothesis asserts is of no value - past stock price series and trading volume data. This technique is called **technical analysis**.

The empirical evidence for this form of market efficiency, and therefore against the value of technical analysis, is pretty strong and quite consistent. After taking into account transaction, costs of analyzing and of trading securities it is very difficult to make money on publicly available information such as the past sequence of stock prices.

Semi-strong Form Efficiency

The semi-strong-form of market efficiency hypothesis suggests that the current price fully incorporates *all publicly available* information. Public information includes not only past prices, but also data reported in a company's financial statements (annual reports, income statements, filings for the Security and Exchange Commission, etc.), earnings and dividend announcements, announced merger plans, the financial situation of company's competitors, expectations regarding macroeconomic factors (such as inflation, unemployment), etc. In fact, the public information does not even have to be of a strictly financial nature. For example, for the analysis of pharmaceutical companies, the relevant public information may include the current (published) state of research in pain-relieving drugs.

The assertion behind semi-strong market efficiency is still that one should not be able to profit using something that "everybody else knows" (the information *is* public). Nevertheless, this assumption is far stronger than that of weak-form efficiency. Semi strong efficiency of markets requires the existence of market analysts who are not only financial economists able to comprehend implications of vast financial information, but also macroeconomists, experts adept at understanding processes in product and input markets. Arguably, acquisition of such skills must take a lot of time and effort. In addition, the "public" information may be relatively difficult to gather and costly to process. It may not be sufficient to gain the information from, say, major newspapers and company-produced publications. One may have to follow wire reports, professional publications and databases, local papers, research journals etc. in order to gather all information necessary to effectively analyze securities.

Strong Form Efficiency

The strong form of market efficiency hypothesis states that the current price fully incorporates *all* existing information, both public and private (sometimes called inside information). The main difference between the semi-strong and strong efficiency hypotheses is that in the latter case, nobody should be able to systematically generate profits even if trading on information *not* publicly known at the time. In other words, the strong form of EMH states that a company's management (insiders) are not be able to systematically gain from inside information by buying company's shares ten minutes after they decided (but did not publicly announce) to pursue what they perceive to be a very profitable acquisition. Similarly, the members of the company's research department are not able to profit from the information about the new revolutionary discovery they completed half an hour ago. The rationale for strong-form market efficiency is that the market anticipates, in an unbiased manner, future developments and therefore the stock price may have incorporated the information and evaluated in a much more objective and informative way than the insiders. Not surprisingly, though, empirical research in finance has found evidence that is inconsistent with the strong form of the EMH.

BASIC TOOL IN TECHNICAL ANALYSIS

The basic tool in technical analysis is movement in prices measured by charts. These types of charts that are commonly used are:

(a) Line Chart

(b) Bar Chart

(c) Point and Figure Chart.

Bibliography

A. REFERENCE BOOKS

1. Khan & Jain : Financial Management
2. J.J. Clark & T.J. Hindelang: Capital Budgeting; Planning and Control of Expenditure
3. D.R. Mehta : Working Capital Management
4. Prof. A.P. Rao : Management Accounting
5. James C Van Horne : Financial Management and Policy
6. P.V. Kulkarni : Financial Management
7. I.M. Pandey : Financial Management
8. Prof. A.P. Rao : Cases and Problems on Financial Management
9. Bhabatash Banerjee : Financial Policy and Management Accounting
10. Prasanna Chandra : Financial Management (Theory & Practice)
11. P.G. Apte : International Financial Management
12. M. Grinblatt and S. Titman : Financial Markets and Corporate Strategy
13. The ICFAI University : Financial Management
14. Prasanna Chandra : Investment Analysis and Portfolio Management
15. Samir K. Barua, J. R. Verma & V. Raghonathan : Portfolio Management
16. L.M. Bhole : Financial Institutions and Markets
17. B.K. Chatterjee : Cost and Management Accounting
18. V.K. Kapoor : Operation Research
19. The ICFAI University : Investment Banking and Financial Services (Volume I and Volume II)
20. P. Saravanavel : Management Control System (Principles and Practice)
21. H. Markowitch : Portfolio Selection : Efficient Diversification of Investment
22. Gaither and Frazier : Operations Management

23. Dr. Manju Gupta : Contemporary Issues in Mergers and Acquisitions
24. The ICFAI University : Security Analysis
25. J.C. Cox & M. Rubinstein : Options Markets
26. A. Auerbach : Corporate Takeover, Causes and Consequences
27. M. Stigum : The Money Market, Myth, Reality and Practice
28. The ICFAI University Press : Portfolio Organiser
29. Prasanna Chandra : Valuation of Equity Shares in India
30. The ICFAI University : Equity Markets
31. T.R.Venkatesh : Indian Financial Markets
32. Dr. G. Kotreshwar : Risk Management (Insurance & Derivatives)
33. H.R. Machiraju : Indian Financial System
34. M.N. Arora : Cost Accounting (Principles and Practice)
35. Dr. Sakshi Vasudeva : Accounting for Business Managers
36. Kevin : Commodity and Financial Derivatives
37. Welsch, Hilton & Gordon : Budgeting; Profit Planning and Control
38. Fabozzi & Modigliani : Capital Markets; Institutions and Instruments
39. Shashi Gupta and Neeti Gupta : Financial Management
40. G. Foster : Financial Statement Analysis
41. O.M. Joy : Introduction to Financial Management
42. G.A. Wolsch : Budgeting, Profit Planning and Control

B. JOURNALS AND REVIEWS

1. Harvard Business Review
2. Indian Journal of Finance
3. Financial Analyst
4. V Share
5. Indian Management, Journal of AIMA, New Delhi
6. Dalal Street Investment Journal
7. Report of the Finance Commission
8. Report of the Currency and Finance, Reserve Bank of India
9. Journal of Emerging Market Finance
10. ICFAI Journal of Applied Finance

[illegible]

[illegible]

[illegible]

[illegible]

[illegible] Money Market Mutual Funds and [illegible]

[illegible]

[illegible]

[illegible]

[illegible]

[illegible]

[illegible]

[illegible]

[illegible]

[illegible]

[illegible]

[illegible]

[illegible]

[illegible]

[illegible]

[illegible]

JOURNALS AND REVIEWS

3. [illegible]
4. [illegible]

7. Report of the [illegible]

9. [illegible]
